THE LEGAL ENVIRONMENT OF BUSINESS AND ONLINE COMMERCE

SEVENTH EDITION

Business Ethics, E-Commerce, Regulatory, and International Issues

Henry R. Cheeseman

Clinical Professor of Business Law
Director of the Legal Studies Program, Marshall School of Business
University of Southern California

PEARSON

Boston   Columbus   Indianapolis   New York   San Francisco   Upper Saddle River
Amsterdam   Cape Town   Dubai   London   Madrid   Milan   Munich   Paris   Montréal   Toronto
Delhi   Mexico City   São Paulo   Sydney   Hong Kong   Seoul   Singapore   Taipei   Tokyo

Editorial Director: Sally Yagan
Editor in Chief: Donna Battista
Associate Vice President, Executive Editor: Stephanie Wall
Senior Editorial Project Manager: Karen Kirincich
Director of Marketing: Patrice Jones
Director of Editorial Services: Ashley Santora
Editorial Assistant: Jane Avery
Editorial Assistant: Lauren Zanedis
Senior Managing Editor: Nancy Fenton
Senior Production Project Manager: Nancy Freihofer
Senior Manufacturing Buyer: Megan Cochran
Art Director: Steven Frim
AV Manager, Rights and Permissions: Rachel Youdelman
Full-Service Project Management/Composition: PreMediaGlobal
Printer/Binder: Courier/Kendallville
Cover Printer: Lehigh-Phoenix
Text Font: ITC Caslon 224 Std

Credits and acknowledgments borrowed from other sources and reproduced, with permission, in this textbook appear on the appropriate page within text.

Photo Credits: All photos courtesy of the author, Henry Cheeseman, except for the following. Part Opener pages: Gary Blakeley/Fotolia; International icon: Alessandroiryna/iStockphoto; Contemporary Environment Icon: Iofoto/Shutterstock; U.S. Supreme Court icon: Gary Blakeley/Shutterstock; Landmark Law icon: Ambient Ideas/Shutterstock; Ethics Cases icon: Brian A. Jackson/Shutterstock; Ethics icon: Montego/Shutterstock; Digital Law icon: Pagadesign/iStockphoto; Internet Exercises icon: Laurent Davoust/iStockphoto; Marble background: Reyhan/Shutterstock; page 6: UPI/New York World-Telegram and The Sun Newspaper Photograph Collection/Library of Congress Prints and Photographs Division [LC-USZ62-127042]/Bettmann/Corbis; page 213: Sascha Burkard/Shutterstock; page 402: World History Archive/Newscom; page 542: Courtesy of the World Trade Organization.

Many of the designations by manufacturers and sellers to distinguish their products are claimed as trademarks. Where those designations appear in this book, and the publisher was aware of a trademark claim, the designations have been printed in initial caps or all caps.

Library of Congress Cataloging-in-Publication Data
Cheeseman, Henry R.
  The legal environment of business and online commerce : business ethics, e-commerce, regulatory, and international issues / Henry R. Cheeseman. —7th ed.
    p. cm.
  Includes index.
  ISBN-13: 978-0-13-287088-7
  ISBN-10: 0-13-287088-6
  1. Business law—United States.   I. Title.

KF889.C4336 2013
346.7307—dc23

                                    2011042172

10 9 8 7 6 5 4 3

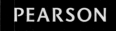

ISBN 10:   0-13-287088-6
ISBN 13: 978-0-13-287088-7

BRIEF CONTENTS

CONTENTS

x **Contents**

Dedication

"You can never go home again,
but the truth is you can never leave home,
so it's all right."

Maya Angelou

Mackinac Bridge, St. Ignace, Michigan

The places of one's life help shape our values, give us families and friends, and provide opportunities for work and play. I thank the following places where I have had the opportunity to call home: St. Ignace, Michigan; Miami, Florida; Milwaukee, Wisconsin; Colorado Springs, Colorado; Los Angeles, California; Sun Valley, Idaho; Chicago, Illinois; Mackinac Island, Michigan; Boston, Massachusetts; Westwood and Brentwood, Los Angeles, California; Santa Monica, California; Ladera Ranch, California; and now, St. Ignace, Michigan.

PREFACE

NEW TO THE SEVENTH EDITION

This edition of *The Legal Environment of Business and Online Commerce* is a significant revision of Professor Cheeseman's legal environment textbook that includes many new cases, statutes, and features.

New U.S. Supreme Court Cases

More than fifteen new U.S. Supreme Court cases, including:

- *Walmart Stores, Inc. v. Dukes* (certification of a class denied)
- *AT&T Mobility LLC v. Concepcion* (class action waivers in arbitration agreements are enforceable)
- *Brown, Governor of California v. Entertainment Merchants Association* (content of violent video games is protected speech)
- *Kentucky v. King* (exigent circumstances support police warrantless search of a home)
- *Thompson v. North American Stainless, LP* (Title VII permits third-party retaliation claims to be brought against an employer)
- *Citizens United v. Federal Election Commission* (Federal restrictions on campaign financing violated the U.S. Constitution)

New State and Federal Court Cases

More than fifteen new state and federal court cases, including:

- *The Facebook, Inc. v. Winklevoss* (settlement agreement enforced concerning the founding of Facebook)
- *Does I-XI, Workers in China, Bangladesh, Indonesia, Swaziland, and Nicaragua v. Walmart Stores, Inc.* (foreign workers not intended beneficiaries of Walmart's contracts with foreign suppliers)
- *Chanel, Inc. v. Banks* (personal jurisdiction over an Internet seller found)
- *V Secret Catalogue, Inc. and Victoria's Secret Stores, Inc. v. Moseley* (tarnishment of a senior mark by a junior mark)
- *Yarde Metals, Inc. v. New England Patriots Limited Partnership* (parol evidence not admitted to change terms of a ticketholder's contract)
- *Rainey v. Domino's Pizza, LLC* (franchisor not liable for an accident caused by franchisee's delivery person)

New Statutes

Coverage of many new federal statutes, including:

- Consumer Financial Protection Act of 2010
- Dodd-Frank Wall Street Reform and Consumer Protection Act of 2010
- Americans with Disabilities Act Amendments Act of 2008 (ADAAA)
- Health Care Reform Act of 2010
- Genetic Information Nondiscrimination Act (GINA) of 2009
- Lilly Ledbetter Fair Pay Act of 2009
- Credit CARD Act of 2009

New Special Features on Ethics, Contemporary Environment, Digital Law, and International Law

More than twenty new special features, including:

- *Bernie Madoff Steals Billions of Dollars in Pyramid Scheme*
- *BP Oil Spill*
- *Bankruptcy of General Motors Corporation*
- *New Top-Level Domain Names*
- *English-Only Requirement in the Workplace*
- *New Warnings Required on Cigarette Packages and Advertisements*

New Text Material

New text and chapter materials, including:

- More than thirty new examples
- More than fifty new Critical Legal Thinking Cases
- More than fifteen new Ethics Cases

To the Students

Each semester, as I stand up in front of a new group of students in my business law and legal environment classes, I am struck by the thought that, cases and statutes aside, I know two very important things that the students have yet to learn. The first is that I draw as much from them as they do from me. Their youth, enthusiasm, and questions—and even the doubts a few of them hold about the relevance of law to their futures—fuel my teaching. They don't know that every time they open their minds to look at an issue from a new perspective or critically question something, I have gotten a wonderful reward for the work I do.

The other thing I know is that both teaching and learning the legal environment are all about stories. These stories come from the legal cases in this book, as well as the important cases and stories that each professor personally brings to the classroom. These stories provide the framework on which students will hang everything they learn about the law in class. It is my hope that long after the specific language of cases or statutes have faded, students will retain that framework. Several years from now, "unintentional torts" may draw only a glimmer of recognition with business managers who learn about them as students in my class this year. However, they will likely recall the story of the woman who sued McDonald's for damages for serving her coffee that was too hot and caused her injuries.

I remind myself of these two facts every time I sit down to work on writing and revising *The Legal Environment of Business and Online Commerce*, as well. My goal is to present business law, ethics, and the legal environment in a way that will spur students to ask questions, to go beyond rote memorization.

Business law is an evolving outgrowth of its environment, and the legal environment keeps changing. This seventh edition of *The Legal Environment of Business and Online Commerce* emphasizes coverage of online law and e-commerce as key parts of the legal environment. In addition, this book covers social, ethical, and international issues that are important to the study of business law.

It is my wish that my commitment to these goals shines through in this labor of love, and I hope you have as much pleasure in using this book as I have had in creating it for you.

Henry Cheeseman

AN INTEGRATED SUPPLEMENTS PACKAGE

For Instructors

We offer a variety of electronic supplements to meet the unique teaching needs of each instructor. Supplements that accompany this text are available for download by instructors only at our Instructor Resource Center, at **www.pearsonhighered.com/irc**.

- **Video Cases**   The Instructor's DVD includes brief video cases, taken from the ABC News Video Library, for use in class.

- **Instructors' Manual**   Designed to facilitate teaching the material.

- **Test Item File**   To aid in the preparation of tailor made tests.

- **TestGen**   TestGen allows instructors to customize tests.

ABOUT THE AUTHOR

Henry R. Cheeseman is clinical professor of Business Law, director of the Legal Studies Program, and co-director of the Minor in Business Law Program at the Marshall School of Business of the University of Southern California (USC), Los Angeles, California.

Professor Cheeseman earned a bachelor's degree in finance from Marquette University, both a master's in business administration (MBA) and a master's in business taxation (MBT) from the University of Southern California, a juris doctor (JD) degree from the University of California at Los Angeles (UCLA) School of Law, a master's degree with an emphasis on law and economics from the University of Chicago, and a master's in law (LLM) degree in financial institutions law from Boston University.

Professor Cheeseman currently teaches business law and legal environment courses in both the Master of Business Administration (MBA) and undergraduate programs of the Marshall School of Business of the University of Southern California. At the MBA level, he teaches courses on corporate law, securities regulation, mergers and acquisitions, and bankruptcy law. At the undergraduate level, he teaches courses on the legal environment of business and law and finance.

Professor Cheeseman has earned the "Golden Apple" Teaching Award on many occasions by having been voted by the students as the best professor at the Marshall School of Business of the University of Southern California. He was named a fellow of the Center for Excellence in Teaching at the University of Southern California by the dean of the Marshall School of Business. The USC's Torch and Tassel Chapter of the Mortar Board, a national senior honor society, tapped Professor Cheeseman for recognition of his leadership, commitment, and excellence in teaching.

Professor Cheeseman writes leading business law and legal environment textbooks that are published by Pearson. These include *Business Law: Legal Environment, Online Commerce, Business Ethics, and International Issues*; *Contemporary Business and Online Commerce Law*; *The Legal Environment of Business and Online Commerce*; *Essentials of Contemporary Business Law*; and *Introduction to Law: Its Dynamic Nature*. Professor Cheeseman has also co-authored a textbook entitled *Contemporary Employment Law*.

Professor Cheeseman is an avid traveler and amateur photographer. Many of the interior photographs for this book were taken by Professor Cheeseman.

ACKNOWLEDGMENTS

When I first began writing this book, I was a solitary figure, researching cases and statutes, writing text, and editing cases. As time passed, others entered upon the scene—copy editors, developmental editors, research assistants, reviewers, and production personnel—and touched the project and made it better. Although my name appears on the cover of this book, it is no longer mine alone. I humbly thank the following persons for their contributions to this project.

THE EXCEPTIONAL PEARSON PROFESSIONALS

I appreciate the ideas, encouragement, effort, and decisions of the management team at Pearson, including Stephanie Wall, Associate Vice President/Executive Editor; Donna Battista, Editor in Chief; and Nancy Fenton, Senior Managing Editor. Many thanks to Nancy Freihofer and Karen Kirincich for shepherding this seventh edition of *The Legal Environment of Business and Online Commerce* through many phases of editing and production at Prentice Hall.

A special thank you to Andrea Stefanowicz of PreMediaGlobal.

PERSONAL ACKNOWLEDGMENTS

My Family

I thank my wife, Jin Du. I thank my parents—Henry B. and Florence L. Cheeseman, deceased—who had a profound effect on me and my ability to be a professor and writer. I also thank my brother Gregory, with the special bond that exists between us as twins, and the rest of my family: my sister, Marcia, deceased; Gregory's wife, Lana; my nephew, Gregory, and his wife Karen; my niece, Nicky, and her husband, Jerry; and my great-nieces Lauren, Addison, and Shelby.

Students

I'd like to acknowledge the students at the University of Southern California (USC) and the students at other colleges and universities in the United States and around the world. Their spirit, energy, and joy are contagious. I love teaching my students (and, as importantly, their teaching me). At the end of each semester, I am sad that the students I have come to know are moving on. But each new semester brings another group of students who will be a joy to teach. And the cycle continues.

Colleagues

Certain people and colleagues are enjoyable to work with and have made my life easier as I have endeavored to write this new edition of *Business Law*. I would like to thank Kerry Fields, my colleague in teaching business law courses at USC, who is an excellent professor and a wonderful friend. I would also like to thank Helen Pitts, Debra Jacobs, Terry Lichvar, and Jean Collins at the Marshall School of Business, who are always a joy to work with. I especially thank the professors who teach business law and legal environment courses for their dedication to the discipline and to their students.

Reviewers

I would like to personally thank the following reviewers, who have spent considerable time and effort reviewing the manuscripts for previous and current editions of *The Legal Environment of Business and Online Commerce* and whose comments, suggestions, and criticisms have been vital to the final project.

David Austill, *Union University*
William N. Bockanic, *John Carroll University*
Eli C. Bortman, *Babson College*
Thomas D. Cavenagh, *North Central College*
Gregory P. Cermignano, *Widener University*
Carole A. Cummings, *Wilmington University*
Carol Docan, *Cal State University, Northridge*
Howard Ellis, *Millersville University*
Lynda Fuller, *Wilmington University*
Ed Gac, *University of Colorado*
Gary S. Gaffney, *Florida Atlantic University*
Gamewell Gantt, *Idaho State University*
Troy E. Grandel, *Wilmington University*
Lori K. Harris-Ransom, *Caldwell College*
Frederick G. Hoffman, *Oakland University*
Duane R. Lambett, *California State University, Hayward*
William Maakestad, *Western Illinois University*
Marian Matthews, *Central New Mexico Community College*
Gregory McCann, *Stetson University*
Susan J. Mitchell, *Des Moines Area Community College*
Amelia P. Nelson, *Anderson School of Management/University of New Mexico*
Barton Pachino, *Cal State University, Northridge*
Jeffrey D. Penley, J.D., *Gardner-Webb University*
Neal A. Phillips, *University of Delaware*
Darka Powers, *Northeastern Illinois University*
James Rittenbaum, *St. Louis University*
Scott Sandstrom, *College of the Holy Cross*
Allen Simonson, *Montclair State University*
Elisabeth Shapiro, *Southwestern College*
Cherie Sherman, *Ramapo College of New Jersey*
S. Jay Sklar, *Temple University*
Joanie Sompayrac, *University of Tennessee–Chattanooga*
Dennis A. Wallace, *University of New Mexico*
Stuart Waterstone, *Valley College/Pierce College*
Kim Wong, *Central New Mexico Community College*
John A. Wrieden, *Florida International University*

AUTHOR'S PERSONAL STATEMENT

While writing this Preface and Acknowledgment, I have thought about the thousands of hours I have spent researching, writing, and preparing this manuscript. I've loved every minute, and the knowledge gained has been sufficient reward for the endeavor.

I hope this book and its supplementary materials will serve you as well as they have served me.

With joy and sadness,
emptiness and fullness,
honor and humility,
I surrender the fruits of this labor

Henry R. Cheeseman

Legal and Ethical Environment

CHAPTER

1

Legal Heritage and the Digital Age

STATUE OF LIBERTY, NEW YORK HARBOR
The Statue of Liberty stands majestically in New York Harbor. During the American Revolution, France gave the colonial patriots substantial support in the form of money for equipment and supplies, officers and soldiers who fought in the war, and ships and sailors who fought on the seas. Without the assistance of France, it is unlikely that the American colonists would have won their independence from Britain. In 1886, the people of France gave the Statue of Liberty to the people of the United States in recognition of their friendship that was established during the American Revolution. Since then, the Statue of Liberty has become a symbol of liberty and democracy throughout the world.

Learning Objectives

After studying this chapter, you should be able to:

1. Define *law*.
2. Describe the functions of law.
3. Explain the development of the U.S. legal system.
4. List and describe the sources of law in the United States.
5. Discuss the importance of the U.S. Supreme Court's decision in *Brown v. Board of Education*.

Chapter Outline

Introduction to Legal Heritage and the Digital Age

What Is Law?
    LANDMARK U.S. SUPREME COURT CASE • *Brown v. Board of Education*

Schools of Jurisprudential Thought
    INTERNATIONAL LAW • *Command School of Jurisprudence of North Korea*

History of American Law
    INTERNATIONAL LAW • *Adoption of English Common Law in America*
    INTERNATIONAL LAW • *Civil Law System of France and Germany*

Sources of Law in the United States
    CONTEMPORARY ENVIRONMENT • *How a Bill Becomes Law*

Digital Law

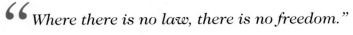

Where there is no law, there is no freedom."

—John Locke
Second Treatise of Government, Sec. 57

Introduction to Legal Heritage and the Digital Age

Every society makes and enforces laws that govern the conduct of the individuals, businesses, and other organizations that function within it. In the words of Judge Learned Hand, "Without law we cannot live; only with it can we insure the future which by right is ours. The best of men's hopes are enmeshed in its success."[1]

Although the law of the United States is primarily based on English common law, other legal systems, such as Spanish and French civil law, also influence it. The sources of law in this country are the U.S. Constitution, state constitutions, federal and state statutes, ordinances, administrative agency rules and regulations, executive orders, and judicial decisions by federal and state courts.

Businesses that are organized in the United States are subject to its laws. They are also subject to the laws of other countries in which they operate. Businesses organized in other countries must obey the laws of the United States when doing business here. In addition, businesspeople owe a duty to act ethically in the conduct of their affairs, and businesses owe a responsibility not to harm society.

This chapter discusses the nature and definition of law, theories about the development of law, and the history and sources of law in the United States.

Human beings do not ever make laws; it is the accidents and catastrophes of all kinds happening in every conceivable way that make law for us.

Plato, Laws IV, 709

What Is Law?

The law consists of rules that regulate the conduct of individuals, businesses, and other organizations in society. It is intended to protect persons and their property against unwanted interference from others. In other words, the law forbids persons from engaging in certain undesirable activities. Consider the following passage:

> *Hardly anyone living in a civilized society has not at some time been told to do something or to refrain from doing something, because there is a law requiring it, or because it is against the law. What do we mean when we say such things? Most generally, how are we to understand statements of the form "x is law"? This is an ancient question. In his Memorabilia (I, ii), Xenophon reports a statement of the young Alcibiades, companion of Socrates, who in conversation with the great Pericles remarked that "no one can really deserve praise unless he knows what a law is."*
>
> *At the end of the 18th century, Immanuel Kant wrote of the question "What is law?" that it "may be said to be about as embarrassing to the jurist as the well-known question 'What is truth?' is to the logician."[2]*

Where law ends, there tyranny begins.

William Pitt, first Earl of Chatham
Case of Wilkes (speech)

Definition of *Law*

The concept of **law** is broad. Although it is difficult to state a precise definition, *Black's Law Dictionary* gives one that is sufficient for this text:

> *Law, in its generic sense, is a body of rules of action or conduct prescribed by controlling authority, and having binding legal force. That which must be obeyed and followed by citizens subject to sanctions or legal consequences is a law.[3]*

law
That which must be obeyed and followed by citizens, subject to sanctions or legal consequences; a body of rules of action or conduct prescribed by controlling authority and having binding legal force.

Functions of the Law

Commercial law lies within a narrow compass, and is far purer and freer from defects than any other part of the system.

Henry Peter Brougham
*House of Commons,
February 7, 1828*

The law is often described by the function it serves in a society. The primary *functions* served by the law in this country are:

1. Keeping the peace

   Example Some laws make certain activities crimes.

2. Shaping moral standards

   Example Some laws discourage drug and alcohol abuse.

3. Promoting social justice

   Example Some laws prohibit discrimination in employment.

4. Maintaining the status quo

   Example Some laws prevent the forceful overthrow of the government.

5. Facilitating orderly change

   Example Laws are enacted only after considerable study, debate, and public input.

6. Facilitating planning

   Example Well-designed commercial laws allow businesses to plan their activities, allocate their productive resources, and assess the risks they take.

7. Providing a basis for compromise

   Example Laws allow for the settlement of cases prior to trial. Approximately 90 percent of all lawsuits are settled in this manner.

8. Maximizing individual freedom

   Example The rights of freedom of speech, religion, and association are granted by the First Amendment to the U.S. Constitution.

CONCEPT SUMMARY
FUNCTIONS OF THE LAW

1. Keep the peace	5. Facilitate orderly change
2. Shape moral standards	6. Facilitate planning
3. Promote social justice	7. Provide a basis for compromise
4. Maintain the status quo	8. Maximize individual freedom

Fairness of the Law

The law, in its majestic equality, forbids the rich as well as the poor to sleep under bridges.

Anatole France

On the whole, the U.S. legal system is one of the most comprehensive, fair, and democratic systems of law ever developed and enforced. Nevertheless, some misuses and oversights of our legal system—including abuses of discretion and mistakes by judges and juries, unequal applications of the law, and procedural mishaps—allow some guilty parties to go unpunished.

Example In *Standefer v. United States*,[4] the Supreme Court of the United States *affirmed* (let stand) the criminal conviction of a Gulf Oil Corporation executive for aiding and abetting the bribery of an Internal Revenue Service agent. The agent had been acquitted in a separate trial. In writing the opinion of the

Court, Chief Justice Warren Burger stated, "This case does no more than manifest the simple, if discomforting, reality that different juries may reach different results under any criminal statute. That is one of the consequences we accept under our jury system."

Flexibility of the Law

U.S. law evolves and changes along with the norms of society, technology, and the growth and expansion of commerce in the United States and the world. The following quote by Judge Jerome Frank discusses the value of the adaptability of law:

Law must be stable and yet it cannot stand still.

Roscoe Pound
Interpretations of Legal History (1923)

> The law always has been, is now, and will ever continue to be, largely vague and variable. And how could this be otherwise? The law deals with human relations in their most complicated aspects. The whole confused, shifting helter-skelter of life parades before it—more confused than ever, in our kaleidoscopic age.
>
> Men have never been able to construct a comprehensive, eternalized set of rules anticipating all possible legal disputes and formulating in advance the rules which would apply to them. Situations are bound to occur which were never contemplated when the original rules were made. How much less is such a frozen legal system possible in modern times?
>
> The constant development of unprecedented problems requires a legal system capable of fluidity and pliancy. Our society would be straightjacketed were not the courts, with the able assistance of the lawyers, constantly overhauling the law and adapting it to the realities of ever-changing social, industrial, and political conditions; although changes cannot be made lightly, yet rules of law must be more or less impermanent, experimental and therefore not nicely calculable.
>
> Much of the uncertainty of law is not an unfortunate accident; it is of immense social value.[5]

One of the most important cases ever decided by the U.S. Supreme Court—*Brown v. Board of Education*—is discussed in the following feature. This case shows the flexibility of the law in that the U.S. Supreme Court overturned a past decision of the U.S. Supreme Court.

WEB EXERCISE
To view court documents related to *Brown v. Board of Education,* go to **www.loc.gov/exhibits/brown/brown-brown.html**.

LANDMARK U.S. SUPREME COURT CASE

Brown v. Board of Education

"We conclude that in the field of public education the doctrine of 'separate but equal' has no place."
—Warren, Justice

When the original 13 states ratified the Constitution of the United States of America in 1788, they created a democratic form of government and granted certain rights to the people. But all persons were not treated equally, as many people, including many drafters of the Constitution, owned African American slaves. It was more than 75 years before the Civil War was fought between the Union states and the Confederate states over the preservation of the union and slavery. Slavery was abolished by the Thirteenth Amendment to the Constitution in 1865. The Fourteenth Amendment, added to the Constitution in 1868, contains the Equal Protection Clause, which provides that no state shall "deny to any person within its jurisdiction the equal protection of the laws." The original intent of this amendment was to guarantee equality to freed African Americans. But equality was denied to African Americans for years. This included discrimination in housing, transportation, education, jobs, service at restaurants, and other activities.

(continued)

In 1896, the U.S. Supreme Court decided the case *Plessy v. Ferguson.*[6] In that case, the state of Louisiana had a law that provided for separate but equal accommodations for African American and white railway passengers. An African American passenger challenged the state law. The Supreme Court held that the "separate but equal" state law did not violate the Equal Protection Clause of the Fourteenth Amendment. The "separate but equal" doctrine was then applied to all areas of life, including public education. Thus, African American and white children attended separate schools, often with unequal facilities.

It was not until 1954 that the U.S. Supreme Court decided a case that challenged the separate but equal doctrine as it applied to public elementary and high schools. In **Brown v. Board of Education,**[7] a consolidated case that challenged the separate school systems of four states—Kansas, South Carolina, Virginia, and Delaware—the Supreme Court decided to revisit the separate but equal doctrine announced by its forbearers in another century. This time, a unanimous Supreme Court, in an opinion written by Chief Justice Earl Warren, reversed prior precedent and held that the separate but equal doctrine violated the Equal

Protection Clause of the Fourteenth Amendment to the Constitution. In its opinion, the Court stated:

> *We cannot turn the clock back to 1868 when the Amendment was adopted, or even to 1896 when* Plessy v. Ferguson *was written. Today, education is perhaps the most important function of state and local governments.*
>
> *We conclude that in the field of public education the doctrine of "separate but equal" has no place. Separate educational facilities are inherently unequal. Therefore, we hold that the plaintiffs and others similarly situated for whom actions have been brought are, by reason of the segregation complained of, deprived of the equal protection of the laws guaranteed by the Fourteenth Amendment.*

After *Brown v. Board of Education* was decided, it took court orders as well as U.S. Army enforcement to integrate many of the public schools in this country. The *Brown v. Board of Education* case demonstrates that one Supreme Court case can overrule prior Supreme Court cases

Mrs. Nettie Hunt, sitting on steps of Supreme Court, holding newspaper, explaining to her daughter Nikie the meaning of the Supreme Court's decision banning school segregation.

to promote justice. *Brown v. Board of Education*, 347 U.S. 483, 74 S.Ct. 686, 98 L.Ed. 873, **Web** 1954 U.S. Lexis 2094 (Supreme Court of the United States, 1954)

Case Questions

Critical Legal Thinking
What does the Equal Protection Clause of the Fourteenth Amendment to the U.S. Constitution provide?

Ethics
Was the Equal Protection Clause properly applied in the early U.S. Supreme Court decision *Plessy v. Ferguson?* Explain.

Contemporary Business
It has been said that the U.S. Constitution is a "living document"—that is, one that can adapt to changing times. Do you think this is a good policy? Or should the U.S. Constitution be interpreted narrowly and literally, as originally written?

Schools of Jurisprudential Thought

The philosophy or science of the law is referred to as **jurisprudence**. There are several different philosophies about how the law developed, ranging from the classical natural theory to modern theories of law and economics and critical legal studies. Classical legal philosophies are discussed in the following paragraphs.

jurisprudence
The philosophy or science of law.

Natural Law School

The **Natural Law School** of jurisprudence postulates that the law is based on what is "correct." Natural law philosophers emphasize a **moral theory of law**— that is, law should be based on morality and ethics. Natural law is "discovered" by humans through the use of reason and choosing between good and evil.

Examples Documents such as the U.S. Constitution, the Magna Carta, and the United Nations Charter reflect this theory.

The law is not a series of calculating machines where definitions and answers come tumbling out when the right levers are pushed.

William O. Douglas
The Dissent, A Safeguard of Democracy (1948)

Historical School

The **Historical School** of jurisprudence believes that the law is an aggregate of social traditions and customs that have developed over the centuries. It believes that changes in the norms of society will gradually be reflected in the law. To these legal philosophers, the law is an evolutionary process.

Example Historical legal scholars look to past legal decisions (precedent) to solve contemporary problems.

Analytical School

The **Analytical School** of jurisprudence maintains that the law is shaped by logic. Analytical philosophers believe that results are reached by applying principles of logic to the specific facts of a case. The emphasis is on the logic of the result rather than on how the result is reached.

Example If the U.S. Constitution would have freed the slaves or granted females the right to vote, it would not have been ratified by the states in 1788.

Sociological School

The **Sociological School** of jurisprudence asserts that the law is a means of achieving and advancing certain sociological goals. The followers of this philosophy, known as *realists*, believe that the purpose of law is to shape social behavior. Sociological philosophers are unlikely to adhere to past law as precedent.

Example Laws that impose penalties for drunk driving reflect this theory.

Command School

The philosophers of the **Command School** of jurisprudence believe that the law is a set of rules developed, communicated, and enforced by the ruling party rather than a reflection of the society's morality, history, logic, or sociology. This school maintains that the law changes when the ruling class changes.

Example During certain military conflicts, such as World War II and the Vietnam Conflict, the federal government has enacted draft laws that require men of a certain age to serve in the military if they meet certain physical and other requirements.

Critical Legal Studies School

The **Critical Legal Studies School** proposes that legal rules are unnecessary and are used as an obstacle by the powerful to maintain the status quo. Critical legal theorists argue that legal disputes should be solved by applying arbitrary rules that are based on broad notions of what is "fair" in each circumstance. Under this theory, subjective decision making by judges would be permitted.

Example This school postulates that often rape laws make it difficult for women to prove legally that they have been raped because these laws have mostly been drafted from a male's perspective. Therefore, says this school, these laws should be ignored and the judge should be free to decide whether rape has occurred in his or her subjective decision-making.

Law and Economics School

The **Law and Economics School** believes that promoting market efficiency should be the central goal of legal decision making. This school is also called the **Chicago School**, named after the University of Chicago, where it was first developed.

Example Proponents of law and economics theory suggest that the practice of appointing counsel, free of charge, to prisoners who bring civil rights cases should be abolished. They believe that if a prisoner cannot find a lawyer who will take the case on a contingency-fee basis or *pro bono* (free of charge), the case is probably not worth bringing.

CONCEPT SUMMARY

SCHOOLS OF JURISPRUDENTIAL THOUGHT

School	Philosophy
Natural Law	Postulates that law is based on what is "correct." It emphasizes a moral theory of law—that is, law should be based on morality and ethics.
Historical	Believes that law is an aggregate of social traditions and customs.
Analytical	Maintains that law is shaped by logic.
Sociological	Asserts that the law is a means of achieving and advancing certain sociological goals.
Command	Believes that the law is a set of rules developed, communicated, and enforced by the ruling party.
Critical Legal Studies	Maintains that legal rules are unnecessary and that legal disputes should be solved by applying arbitrary rules based on fairness.
Law and Economics	Believes that promoting market efficiency should be the central concern of legal decision making.

The following feature discusses the Command School of jurisprudence in North Korea.

International Law

Command School of Jurisprudence of North Korea

PYONGYANG, NORTH KOREA

This is the Kim Il Sung statue and Mount Paekto–Mansudae Grand Monument in Pyongyang, the capital of North Korea. North Korea—the Democratic People's Republic of Korea (or DPRK)—is a one-party communist dictatorship that has been ruled by one family since 1948. The country was first commanded by the late Kim Il Sung ("Great Leader") and then by his son Kim Jong–Il ("Dear Leader"). His son, Kim Jong–un, is expected to continue the family dynasty. North Korea's legal system is based on communist theory and the Command School of jurisprudence. There is no judicial review of government-enacted laws or activities. The United States and North Korea do not have formal diplomatic relations. In this photograph, North Koreans pay homage to the Great Leader's statue.

History of American Law

When the American colonies were first settled, the English system of law was generally adopted as the system of jurisprudence. This was the foundation from which American judges developed a common law in America.

English Common Law

English common law was law developed by judges who issued their opinions when deciding cases. The principles announced in these cases became *precedent*

English common law
Law developed by judges who issued their opinions when deciding a case. The principles announced in these cases became precedent for later judges deciding similar cases.

for later judges deciding similar cases. The English common law can be divided into cases decided by the *law courts*, *equity courts*, and *merchant courts*.

Law Courts   Prior to the Norman Conquest of England in 1066, each locality in England was subject to local laws, as established by the lord or chieftain in control of the local area. There was no countrywide system of law. After 1066, William the Conqueror and his successors to the throne of England began to replace the various local laws with one uniform system of law. To accomplish this, the king or queen appointed loyal followers as judges in all local areas. These judges were charged with administering the law in a uniform manner, in courts that were called **law courts**. Law at that time tended to emphasize the form (legal procedure) over the substance (merit) of a case. The only relief available at law courts was a monetary award for damages.

Two things most people should never see made: sausages and laws.

An old saying

Chancery (Equity) Courts   Because of some unfair results and limited remedies available in the law courts, a second set of courts—the **Court of Chancery** (or **equity court**)—was established. These courts were under the authority of the Lord Chancellor. Persons who believed that the decision of a law court was unfair or believed that the law court could not grant an appropriate remedy could seek relief in the Court of Chancery. Rather than emphasize legal procedure, the chancery court inquired into the merits of the case. The chancellor's remedies were called *equitable remedies* because they were shaped to fit each situation. Equitable orders and remedies of the Court of Chancery took precedence over the legal decisions and remedies of the law courts.

Merchant Courts   As trade developed during the Middle Ages, the merchants who traveled about England and Europe developed certain rules to solve their commercial disputes. These rules, known as the "law of merchants," or the **Law Merchant**, were based on common trade practices and usage. Eventually, a separate set of courts was established to administer these rules. This court was called the **Merchant Court**. In the early 1900s, the Merchant Court was absorbed into the regular law court system of England.

The following feature discusses the adoption of English common law in the United States.

International Law

Adoption of English Common Law in America

All the states of the United States of America except Louisiana base their legal systems primarily on the English common law. In the United States, the law, equity, and merchant courts have been merged. Thus, most U.S. courts permit the aggrieved party to seek both legal and equitable orders and remedies.

The importance of common law to the American legal system is described in the following excerpt from Justice Douglas's opinion in the 1841 case *Penny v. Little*:

The common law is a beautiful system, containing the wisdom and experiences of ages. Like the people it ruled and protected, it was simple and crude in its infancy and became enlarged, improved, and polished as the nation advanced in civilization, virtue, and intelligence. Adapting itself to the conditions and circumstances of the people and relying upon them for its administration, it necessarily improved as the condition of the people was elevated. The inhabitants of this country always claimed the common law as their birthright, and at an early period established it as the basis of their jurisprudence.[8]

Currently, the law of the United States is a combination of law created by the judicial system and by congressional legislation.

The following feature discusses the development of the civil law system in Europe.

International Law

Civil Law System of France and Germany

One of the major legal systems that has developed in the world in addition to the Anglo-American common law system is the **Romano-Germanic civil law system**. This legal system, which is commonly called the **civil law**, dates to 450 BCE, when Rome adopted the Twelve Tables, a code of laws applicable to the Romans. A compilation of Roman law, called the *Corpus Juris Civilis* ("Body of Civil Law"),

was completed in CE 534. Later, two national codes—the **French Civil Code of 1804** (the **Napoleonic Code**) and the **German Civil Code of 1896**—became models for countries that adopted civil codes.

In contrast to the Anglo-American law, in which laws are created by the judicial system as well as by congressional legislation, the civil code and parliamentary statutes that expand and interpret it are the sole sources of the law in most civil law countries. Thus, the adjudication of a case is simply the application of the code or the statutes to a particular set of facts. In some civil law countries, court decisions do not have the force of law.

Many countries in Europe still follow the civil law system.

Sources of Law in the United States

In the more than 200 years since the founding of the United States and adoption of the English common law, the lawmakers of this country have developed a substantial body of law. The *sources of modern law* in the United States are discussed in the paragraphs that follow.

Constitutions

The **Constitution of the United States of America** is the *supreme law of the land*. This means that any law—whether federal, state, or local—that conflicts with the U.S. Constitution is unconstitutional and, therefore, unenforceable.

The principles enumerated in the U.S. Constitution are extremely broad because the founding fathers intended them to be applied to evolving social, technological, and economic conditions. The U.S. Constitution is often referred to as a "living document" because it is so adaptable.

The U.S. Constitution established the structure of the federal government. It created three branches of government and gave them the following powers:

- The **legislative branch (Congress)** has the power to make (enact) the law.
- The **executive branch (president)** has the power to enforce the law.
- The **judicial branch (courts)** has the power to interpret and determine the validity of the law.

Powers not given to the federal government by the Constitution are reserved for the states. States also have their own constitutions. **State constitutions** are often patterned after the U.S. Constitution, although many are more detailed. State constitutions establish the legislative, executive, and judicial branches of state government and establish the powers of each branch. Provisions of state constitutions are valid unless they conflict with the U.S. Constitution or any valid federal law.

Constitution of the United States of America
The supreme law of the United States.

The Constitution of the United States is not a mere lawyers' document: it is a vehicle of life, and its spirit is always the spirit of age.

Woodrow Wilson
Constitutional Government in the United States (1927)

Treaties

treaty
A compact made between two or more nations.

The U.S. Constitution provides that the president, with the advice and consent of two-thirds of the Senate, may enter into **treaties** with foreign governments. Treaties become part of the supreme law of the land. With increasing international economic relations among nations, treaties will become an even more important source of law that will affect business in the future.

U.S. CONGRESS, WASHINGTON, DC
The U.S. Congress, which is a bicameral system made up of the U.S. Senate and the U.S. House of Representatives, creates federal law by enacting statutes. Each state has two senators and is allocated a certain number of representatives based on population.

Federal Statutes

statute
Written law enacted by the legislative branch of the federal and state governments that establishes certain courses of conduct that covered parties must adhere to.

Statutes are written laws that establish certain courses of conduct that covered parties must adhere to. The **U.S. Congress** is empowered by the Commerce Clause and other provisions of the U.S. Constitution to enact **federal statutes** to regulate foreign and interstate commerce.

Examples The federal Clean Water Act regulates the quality of water and restricts water pollution. The federal Securities Act of 1933 regulates the issuance of securities. The federal National Labor Relations Act establishes the right of employees to form and join labor organizations.

Federal statutes are organized by topic into **code books**. This is often referred to as **codified law**. Federal statutes can be found in these hardcopy books and online.

The following feature describes how a bill becomes law.

Contemporary Environment

How a Bill Becomes Law

The U.S. Congress is composed of two chambers, the **U.S. House of Representatives** and the **U.S. Senate**. Thousands of **bills** are introduced in the U.S. Congress each year, but only a small percentage of them become law. The process of legislation at the federal level is as follows:

1. A member of the U.S. House of Representatives or U.S. Senate introduces a bill in his or her **chamber**. The

member who introduces the bill is its "sponsor." Often there are cosponsors. The bill is assigned a number: "H.R. #" for House bills and "S #" for Senate bills. The bill is printed in the public *Congressional Record*. The bill is available in hard copy and on the Internet.

2. The bill is referred to the appropriate **committee** for review and study. The committee can do the following: (1) reject the bill, (2) report it to the full chamber for

vote, (3) simply not act on it, in which case the bill is said to have "died in committee"—many bills meet this fate, or (4) send the bill to a **subcommittee** for further study. A subcommittee can let the bill die or report it back to the full committee.

3. Bills that receive the vote of a committee are reported to the full chamber, where they are debated and voted on. If the bill receives a majority vote of the chamber, it is sent to the other chamber, where the previously outlined process is followed. Bills originated in one chamber often die in the other chamber. If the second chamber makes no changes in the original bill, the bill is reported for vote by that chamber. If the second chamber makes significant changes to the bill, a **conference committee** that is made up of members of both chambers will try to reconcile the differences. If a comprised version is agreed to by the conference committee, the bill is reported for vote.

4. A bill that is reported to a full chamber must receive the majority vote of the chamber, and if it receives this vote, it is forwarded to the other chamber. If a majority of the second chamber approves the bill, it is then sent to the president's desk.

5. If the president signs a bill, it becomes law. If the president takes no action for ten days, the bill automatically becomes law. If the president vetoes the bill, the bill can be passed into law if two-thirds of the members of the House and two-thirds of the members of the Senate vote to override the veto and approve the bill. Many bills that are vetoed by the president do not obtain the necessary two-thirds vote to override the veto.

If both chambers are controlled by the same political party—Democratic Party or Republican Party—and the president is also a member of the controlling party, a bill has a more likely chance of becoming law. If the chambers are more equally divided between members of the different parties or the president is of a different party than the majority in the chambers, a bill, if it does survive and becomes law, is more likely to be a compromise bill.

Because of this detailed and political legislative process, few of the many bills that are submitted by members of the U.S. House of Representatives or U.S. Senate become law.

State Statutes

State legislatures enact **state statutes**. Such statutes are placed in code books. State statutes can be assessed in these hardcopy code books or online.

Examples The state of Florida has enacted the Lake Okeechobee Protection Act to protect Lake Okeechobee and the northern Everglades ecosystem. The Nevada Corporations Code outlines how to form and operate a Nevada corporation. The Texas Natural Resources Code regulates oil, gas, mining, geothermal, and other natural resources in the state.

Ordinances

State legislatures often delegate lawmaking authority to local government bodies, including cities and municipalities, counties, school districts, water districts, and such. These governmental units are empowered to adopt **ordinances**. Ordinances are also codified.

Examples The city of Mackinac Island, Michigan, a city of 1800s Victorian houses and buildings, has enacted ordinances that keep the island car free, keep out fast-food chains, and require buildings to adhere to era-specific aesthetic standards. Other examples of city ordinances include zoning laws, building codes, sign restrictions, and such.

ordinance
Law enacted by local government bodies, such as cities and municipalities, counties, school districts, and water districts.

Executive Orders

The executive branch of government, which includes the president of the United States and state governors, is empowered to issue **executive orders**. This power is derived from express delegation from the legislative branch and is implied from the U.S. Constitution and state constitutions.

Example When the United States is at war with another country, the president of the United States usually issues executive orders prohibiting U.S. companies from selling goods or services to that country.

executive order
An order issued by a member of the executive branch of the government.

Regulations and Orders of Administrative Agencies

The legislative and executive branches of federal and state governments are empowered to establish **administrative agencies** to enforce and interpret statutes enacted by Congress and state legislatures. Many of these agencies regulate business.

Examples Congress has created the Securities and Exchange Commission (SEC) to enforce federal securities laws and the Federal Trade Commission (FTC) to enforce consumer protection statutes.

Congress or the state legislatures usually empower these agencies to adopt **administrative rules and regulations** to interpret the statutes that the agency is authorized to enforce. These rules and regulations have the force of law. Administrative agencies usually have the power to hear and decide disputes. Their decisions are called **orders**. Because of their power, administrative agencies are often informally referred to as the "fourth branch of government."

Judicial Decisions

When deciding individual lawsuits, federal and state courts issue **judicial decisions**. In these written opinions, a judge or justice usually explains the legal reasoning used to decide the case. These opinions often include interpretations of statutes, ordinances, and administrative regulations and the announcement of legal principles used to decide the case. Many court decisions are reported in books that are available in law libraries.

Doctrine of Stare Decisis   Based on the common law tradition, past court decisions become **precedent** for deciding future cases. Lower courts must follow the precedent established by higher courts. That is why all federal and state courts in the United States must follow the precedents established by U.S. Supreme Court decisions.

The courts of one jurisdiction are not bound by the precedent established by the courts of another jurisdiction, although they may look to each other for guidance.

Example State courts of one state are not required to follow the legal precedent established by the courts of another state.

Adherence to precedent is called the doctrine of ***stare decisis*** ("to stand by the decision"). The doctrine of *stare decisis* promotes uniformity of law within a jurisdiction, makes the court system more efficient, and makes the law more predictable for individuals and businesses. A court may later change or reverse its legal reasoning if a new case is presented to it and change is warranted. The doctrine of *stare decisis* is discussed in the following excerpt from Justice Musmanno's decision in *Flagiello v. Pennsylvania*:

> *Without* stare decisis, *there would be no stability in our system of jurisprudence.* Stare decisis *channels the law. It erects lighthouses and flies the signal of safety. The ships of jurisprudence must follow that well-defined channel which, over the years, has been proved to be secure and worthy.*[9]

administrative agencies
Agencies (such as the Securities and Exchange Commission and the Federal Trade Commission) that the legislative and executive branches of federal and state governments are empowered to establish.

judicial decision
A decision about an individual lawsuit issued by a federal or state court.

precedent
A rule of law established in a court decision. Lower courts must follow the precedent established by higher courts.

stare decisis
Latin for "to stand by the decision." Adherence to precedent.

CONCEPT SUMMARY

SOURCES OF LAW IN THE UNITED STATES

Source of Law	Description
Constitutions	The U.S. Constitution establishes the federal government and enumerates its powers. Powers not given to the federal government are reserved to the states. State constitutions establish state governments and enumerate their powers.

Source of Law	Description
Treaties	The president, with the advice and consent of two-thirds of the Senate, may enter into treaties with foreign countries.
Codified law: statutes and ordinances	Statutes are enacted by Congress and state legislatures. Ordinances are enacted by municipalities and local government bodies. They establish courses of conduct that covered parties must follow.
Executive orders	Issued by the president and governors of states. Executive orders regulate the conduct of covered parties.
Regulations and orders of administrative agencies	Administrative agencies are created by the legislative and executive branches of government. They may adopt rules and regulations that regulate the conduct of covered parties as well as issue orders.
Judicial decisions	Courts decide controversies. In doing so, a court issues an opinion that states the decision of the court and the rationale used in reaching that decision.

Priority of Law in the United States

As mentioned previously, the U.S. Constitution and treaties take precedence over all other laws in the United States. Federal statutes take precedence over federal regulations. Valid federal law takes precedence over any conflicting state or local law. State constitutions rank as the highest state law. State statutes take precedence over state regulations. Valid state law takes precedence over local laws.

Where law ends, there tyranny begins.

William Pitt, first
Earl of Chatham

Digital Law

In a span of about three decades, computers have revolutionized society. Computers, once primarily used by businesses, have permeated the lives of most families as well. In addition to computers, many other digital devices are commonly in use, such as smartphones, tablet computers, televisions, digital cameras, electronic game devices, and others. In addition to the digital devices, technology has brought new ways of communicating, such as e-mail and texting, as well as the use of social networks.

The electronic age arrived before new laws were written that were unique and specific for this environment. Courts have applied existing laws to the new digital environment by requiring interpretations and applications. In addition, new laws have been written that apply specifically to this new environment. The U.S. Congress has led the way, enacting many new federal statutes to regulate the digital environment.

Key Terms and Concepts

Administrative agency (14)
Administrative rules and regulations (14)
Analytical School (7)
Bill (12)
Brown v. Board of Education (6)
Chamber (12)
Civil law (11)
Code book (12)
Codified law (12)
Command School (8)
Committee (12)
Conference committee (13)
Constitution of the United States of America (11)
Court of Chancery (equity court) (10)
Critical Legal Studies School (8)
English common law (9)
Executive branch (president) (11)
Executive order (13)
Federal statute (12)
French Civil Code of 1804 (Napoleonic Code) (11)
German Civil Code of 1896 (11)
Historical School (7)
Judicial branch (courts) (11)
Judicial decision (14)

Jurisprudence (7)
Law (4)
Law courts (10)
Law and Economics
   School (Chicago
   School) (8)
Law Merchant (10)

Legislative branch
   (Congress) (11)
Merchant Court (10)
Moral theory of law (7)
Natural Law School (7)
Order (14)
Ordinance (13)

Precedent (14)
Romano-Germanic civil
   law system (11)
Sociological School (7)
Stare decisis (14)
State constitution (11)
State statute (13)

Statute (12)
Subcommittee (13)
Treaty (12)
U.S. Congress (12)
U.S. House of
   Representatives (12)
U.S. Senate (12)

Law Case with Answer
Minnesota v. Mille Lacs Band of Chippewa Indians

Facts   When the Constitution was ratified by the original colonies in 1788, it delegated to the federal government the exclusive power to regulate commerce with Native American tribes. During the next one hundred years, as the colonists migrated westward, the federal government entered into many treaties with Native American nations. One such treaty was with the Ojibwe Indians in 1837, whereby the tribe sold land located in the Minnesota territory to the United States. The treaty provided: "The privilege of hunting, fishing, and gathering wild rice, upon the lands, the rivers and the lakes included in the territory ceded, is guaranteed to the Indians."

The state of Minnesota was admitted into the Union in 1858. In the late 1900s, the state of Minnesota began interfering with the Native American treaty rights, particularly concerning hunting and fishing rights. Minnesota wanted to restrict the hunting and fishing rights granted in the federal treaty. In 1990, the Mille Lacs Band of the Ojibwe Indians sued the state of Minnesota, seeking declaratory judgment that they retained the hunting, fishing, and gathering rights provided in the 1837 treaty and an injunction to prevent Minnesota from interfering with those rights. The state of Minnesota argued that when Minnesota entered the Union in 1858, those rights were extinguished. Were the treaty rights granted to the Mille Lacs Band of the Ojibwe Indians by the federal government in 1837 extinguished when the state of Minnesota was admitted as a state in 1858?

Answer   No, the treaty rights granted to the Mille Lacs Band of the Ojibwe Indians by the federal government in 1837 were not extinguished when the state of Minnesota was admitted as a state in 1858. The state of Minnesota argued that the Ojibwe's rights under the treaty were extinguished when Minnesota was admitted to the Union. But in making this legal argument, the state of Minnesota was wrong. There is no clear evidence of federal congressional intent to extinguish the treaty rights of the Ojibwe Indians when Minnesota was admitted as a state in 1858. The language admitting Minnesota as a state made no mention of Indian treaty rights. Therefore, the Ojibwe Indians still possess those treaty rights. It was unfair of the state of Minnesota to try to extinguish clearly delineated legal rights granted to the Ojibwe Native Americans more than 150 years before. The state of Minnesota was obviously unfairly trying to take away rights granted to Native Americans so that others in society—namely non–Native American hunters and fishers—would benefit. The hunting, fishing, and gathering rights guaranteed to the Ojibwe Native Americans in the 1837 treaty are still valid and enforceable. *Minnesota v. Mille Lacs Band of Chippewa Indians*, 526 U.S. 172, 119 S.Ct. 1187, 143 L.Ed.2d 270, **Web** 1999 U.S. Lexis 2190 (Supreme Court of the United States)

Critical Legal Thinking Cases

1.1 Fairness of the Law   In 1909, the state legislature of Illinois enacted a statute called the "Woman's 10-Hour Law." The law prohibited women who were employed in factories and other manufacturing facilities from working more than 10 hours per day. The law did not apply to men. W. C. Ritchie & Co., an employer, brought a lawsuit that challenged the statute as being unconstitutional, in violation of the Equal Protection Clause of the Illinois constitution. In upholding the statute, the Illinois Supreme Court stated:

It is known to all men (and what we know as men we cannot profess to be ignorant of as judges) that woman's physical structure and the performance of maternal functions place her at a great disadvantage in the battle of life; that while a man can work for more than 10 hours a day without injury to himself, a woman, especially when the burdens of motherhood are upon her, cannot; that while a man can work standing upon his feet for more than 10 hours a day, day after day, without injury to himself, a woman cannot; and that to require a woman to stand upon her feet for more than 10 hours in any one day and perform severe manual labor while thus standing, day after day, has the effect to impair her health, and that as weakly and sickly women cannot be mothers of vigorous children.

We think the general consensus of opinion, not only in this country but in the civilized countries of Europe, is, that a working day of not more than 10 hours for women is justified for the following reasons: (1) the physical organization of women, (2) her maternal function, (3) the rearing and education of children, (4) the maintenance of the home; and these conditions are, so far, matters of general knowledge that the courts will take judicial cognizance of their existence.

Surrounded as women are by changing conditions of society, and the evolution of employment which environs them, we agree fully with what is said by the Supreme Court of Washington in the Buchanan Case; "law is, or ought to be, a progressive science."

Is the statute fair? Would the statute be lawful today? Should the law be a "progressive science"? *W. C. Ritchie & Co. v. Wayman, Attorney for Cook County, Illinois*, 244 Ill. 509, 91 N.E. 695, **Web** 1910 Ill. Lexis 1958 (Supreme Court of Illinois)

1.2 Fairness of the Law Eminem is a famous hip-hop and rap artist who won a Grammy Award for his music in the movie *8 Mile*, in which he starred. Eminem's lyrics often contain references to his personal experiences. In "Brain Damage," a song from his 1999 CD *The Slim Shady LP*, Eminem sang lyrics he had written about his childhood experiences with DeAngelo Bailey. The lyrics read in part:

I was harassed daily by this fat kid named D'Angelo Bailey

He banged my head against the urinal til he broke my nose …
Soaked my clothes in blood,
Grabbed me and choked my throat.
This is for every time you took my orange juice, or stole my seat in the lunchroom and drank my chocolate milk.
Every time you tipped my tray and it dropped and spilt.
I'm getting you back bully! Now once and for good.

DeAngelo Bailey sued Eminem for $1 million, alleging that the lyrics were untrue and slanderous. Eminem's mother publicly defended her son's account of the bullying by Bailey. Under questioning, Bailey admitted that when he was in fourth grade, he was part of a group at school that did "bully type things," such as pushing Eminem down. Bailey described what was done to Eminem as "jokes, play games, you know, like we probably like—I mean this is kid stuff, so I'm saying." Bailey also testified that he was present when his friends pushed Eminem and that he would personally bump into Eminem by throwing a "little shove." Bailey offered no evidence to refute Eminem's claims in his deposition that Bailey was bigger than him, shoved him into walls, called him names, took his orange juice, and knocked over his books.

After hearing all the evidence, Judge Deborah Servitto granted summary disposition in favor of Eminem. She wrote her opinion:

Mr. Bailey complains that his rap is trash
So he's seeking compensation in the form of cash.
Bailey thinks he's entitled to some money gain
Because Eminem used his name in vain.
The lyrics are stories no one would take as fact
They're an exaggeration of a childish act.
It is therefore this court's ultimate position
That Eminem is entitled to summary disposition.

On appeal, the Court of Appeals of Michigan upheld the trial court's decision in favor of Eminem. Was the lawsuit warranted? Do you agree with the court's decision? *DeAngelo Bailey v. Marshall Bruce Mathers, III, a/k/a Eminem*, 2005 Mich.App. Lexis 930 (Court of Appeals of Michigan)

Ethics Cases

1.3 Ethics In 1975, after the war in Vietnam, the U.S. government discontinued draft registration for men in this country. In 1980, after the Soviet Union invaded Afghanistan, President Jimmy Carter asked Congress for funds to reactivate draft registration. President Carter suggested that both males and females be required to register. Congress allocated funds only for the registration of males. Several men who were subject to draft registration brought a lawsuit that challenged the law as being unconstitutional, in violation of the Equal Protection Clause of the U.S. Constitution. The U.S. Supreme Court upheld the constitutionality of the draft registration law, reasoning as follows:

The question of registering women for the draft not only received considerable national attention and was the subject of wide-ranging public debate, but also was extensively considered by Congress in hearings, floor debate, and in committee. The foregoing clearly establishes that the decision to exempt women from registration was not the "accidental by-product of a traditional way of thinking about women."

This is not a case of Congress arbitrarily choosing to burden one of two similarly situated groups, such as would be the case with an all-black or all-white, or an all-Catholic or all-Lutheran, or an all-Republican or all-Democratic registration. Men and women are simply not similarly situated for purposes of a draft or registration for a draft.

Justice Marshall dissented, stating:

The Court today places its imprimatur on one of the most potent remaining public expressions of "ancient canards about the proper role of women." It upholds a statute that requires males but not females to register for the draft, and which thereby categorically excludes women from a fundamental civil obligation. I dissent.

Rostker, Director of Selective Service v. Goldberg, 453 U.S. 57, 101 S.Ct. 2646, 69 L.Ed.2d 478, **Web** 1981 U.S. Lexis 126 (Supreme Court of the United States)

1. What arguments did the U.S. Supreme Court assert to justify requiring males, but not females, to register for the draft?
2. Is the law, as determined by the U.S. Supreme Court, fair?
3. Do you agree with the dissent?

1.4 Ethics In "techie" circles, Kevin D. Mitnick became the underground icon of computer hackers. During a decade's reign, Mitnick terrorized the federal government, universities, and high-tech companies such as Sun Microsystems, Novell Corporation, MCI Communications, and Digital Equipment Corporation by breaking into their computer systems. Mitnick used his computer skills to penetrate his victims' computer systems to steal secret information and wreak havoc with their software and data.

Mitnick, a self-taught computer user, has a history of computer-related crime. As a 17-year-old, he was placed on probation for stealing computer manuals from a Pacific Bell Telephone switching center in Los Angeles. Mitnick was next accused of breaking into federal government and military computers. He has also been accused of breaking into the nation's telephone and cellular telephone networks, stealing thousands of data files and trade secrets from corporate targets, obtaining at least 20,000 credit card numbers of some of the country's richest persons, and sabotaging government, university, and private computer systems around the nation. Mitnick was arrested and convicted of computer crimes and served time in prison.

Upon release from prison, he was put on probation and placed in a medical program to treat his compulsive addiction to computers, which included a court order to not touch a computer or modem. Mitnick dropped out of sight and evaded federal law enforcement officials for several years, as he continued a life of computer crime.

Mitnick's next undoing came when he broke into the computer of Tsutomu Shimomura, a researcher at the San Diego Supercomputer Center. Shimomura, a cybersleuth who advises the FBI and major companies on computer and Internet security, made it his crusade to catch the hacker who broke into his computer. Shimomura watched electronically as Mitnick invaded other computers across the country, but he could not physically locate Mitnick because he disguised his whereabouts by breaking into telephone company computers and rerouting all his computer calls. Eventually, Shimomura's patient watching paid off, as he traced the electronic burglar to Raleigh, North Carolina. Shimomura flew to Raleigh, where he used a cellular-frequency-direction-finding antenna to locate Mitnick's apartment. The FBI was notified, and an arrest warrant was obtained from a judge at his home. The FBI arrested Mitnick at his apartment. Mitnick was placed in jail without bail, pending the investigation of his case.

Mitnick's computer crimes spree has been estimated to have cost his victims several hundreds of millions of dollars in losses, but Mitnick was not accused of benefiting financially from his deeds. Mitnick entered into a plea agreement with federal prosecutors. The U.S. District Court judge sentenced Kevin Mitnick to 46 months in prison, including time served, and ordered him to pay $4,125 in restitution to the companies he victimized. The judge called this a token amount but did not order a larger restitution because she believed Mitnick would not be able to pay more. After serving his time in prison, Mitnick was released. As part of the sentencing, Mitnick cannot use electronic devices, from PCs to cellular telephones, during an additional probationary period following his release from prison. Mitnick is now acting as a consultant to businesses, advising them how to protect themselves from computer hackers.

1. Was Mitnick guilty of a crime?
2. Did Mitnick act unethically? Do you think hackers cause much economic loss?
3. Should Mitnick have been given a greater sentence in this case? Why or why not?

Internet Exercises

1. Visit the website of Ellis Island, at **www .nps.gov/elis.**

2. Visit the website of the U.S. Capitol building, at **www.nps.gov/nr/travel/wash/dc76.htm.**

3. Go to **www.uscis.gov/portal/site/uscis**. Find information on this website about becoming a citizen of the United States.

4. Visit the website **www.whitehouse.gov**. What information do you find there?

Endnotes

1. *The Spirit of Liberty*, 3rd ed. (New York: Alfred A. Knopf, 1960).
2. "Introduction," *The Nature of Law: Readings in Legal Philosophy*, ed. M. P. Golding (New York: Random House, 1966).
3. *Black's Law Dictionary*, 5th ed. (St. Paul, Minnesota: West).
4. 447 U.S. 10, 100 S.Ct. 1999, 64 L.Ed.2d 689, **Web** 1980 U.S. Lexis 127 (Supreme Court of the United States).

5. *Law and the Modern Mind* (New York: Brentano's, 1930).
6. 163 U.S. 537, 16 S.C. 1138, 141 L.Ed 256, **Web** 1896 U.S. Lexis 3390 (Supreme Court of the United States, 1896).
7. 347 U.S. 483, 74 S.Ct. 686, 98 L.Ed. 873, **Web** 1954 U.S. Lexis 2094 (Supreme Court of the United States, 1954).
8. 4 Ill. 301, 1841 Ill. Lexis 98 (Ill.).
9. 417 Pa. 486, 208 A.2d 193, **Web** 1965 Pa. Lexis 442 (Supreme Court of Pennsylvania).

2

Ethics and Social Responsibility of Business

HUE, VIETNAM

"Outsourcing" is one of the most despised words to workers in the United States who have lost their jobs to workers in foreign countries. As is well known, American companies typically "outsource" the production of many of the goods that are eventually sold in America (e.g., clothing, athletic shoes, toys). The reason they do so is because they can get the goods produced at a lower cost in foreign countries and then make higher profits when they sell the goods in the United States. By having their goods made in foreign countries, U.S. companies avoid the expenses of occupational safety laws that require workplaces to be safe to work in, the cost of workers' compensation laws that pay workers if they are injured on the job, fair labor standards laws that prevent child labor and require the payment of minimum wages and overtime wages, the payment of health care and pension benefits for employees, the payment of Social Security taxes, and so on. Is it ethical for U.S. companies to "export" the production of their goods to foreign workers who have none of these protections?

Learning Objectives

After studying this chapter, you should be able to:

1. Describe how law and ethics intertwine.
2. Describe the moral theories of business ethics.
3. Describe the theories of the social responsibility of business.
4. Examine the provisions of the Sarbanes-Oxley Act.
5. Describe corporate social audits.

Chapter Outline

Introduction to Ethics and Social Responsibility of Business

Ethics and the Law
   ETHICS • *Bernie Madoff Steals Billions of Dollars in Pyramid Scheme*

Business Ethics
   ETHICS • *Corporation Ratted Out Under the Whistleblower Statute*

Social Responsibility of Business
   CASE 2.1 • U.S. SUPREME COURT • *Walmart Stores, Inc. v. Samara Brothers, Inc.*
   LANDMARK LAW • *Sarbanes-Oxley Act Requires Public Companies to Adopt Codes of Ethics*
   CASE 2.2 • U.S. SUPREME COURT • *Citizens United v. Federal Election Commission*
   INTERNATIONAL LAW • *Conducting Business in Russia*

" *Ethical considerations can no more be excluded from the administration of justice, which is the end and purpose of all civil laws, than one can exclude the vital air from his room and live."*

—John F. Dillon
  Laws and Jurisprudence of England and America Lecture I (1894)

Introduction to Ethics and Social Responsibility of Business

Businesses organized in the United States are subject to its laws. They are also subject to the laws of other countries in which they operate. In addition, businesspersons owe a duty to act ethically in the conduct of their affairs, and businesses owe a social responsibility not to harm society.

Although much of the law is based on ethical standards, not all ethical standards have been enacted as law. The law establishes a minimum degree of conduct expected by persons and businesses in society. Ethics demands more. This chapter discusses business ethics and the social responsibility of business.

Ethics precede laws as man precedes society.

Jason Alexander
Philosophy for Investors (1979)

Ethics and the Law

Ethics and the law are intertwined. Sometimes the rule of **law** and the rule of **ethics** demand the same response by a person confronted with a problem.

Example Federal and state laws make bribery unlawful. A person violates the law if he or she bribes a judge for a favorable decision in a case. Ethics would also prohibit this conduct.

However, in some situations, the law may permit an act that is ethically wrong.

Example Occupational safety laws set minimum standards for emissions of dust from toxic chemicals in the workplace. Suppose a company can reduce the emission below the legal standard by spending additional money. The only benefit from the expenditure would be better employee health. Ethics would require the extra expenditure; the law would not.

Another situation occurs where the law demands certain conduct but a person's ethical standards are contrary.

Example Federal law prohibits employers from hiring certain illegal alien workers. Suppose an employer advertises the availability of a job and receives no response except from a person who cannot prove he or she is a citizen of this country or does not possess a required visa. The worker and his or her family are destitute. Should the employer violate the law and hire him or her? The law says no, but ethics may say yes (see **Exhibit 2.1**).

The following case is a classic example of greed, fraud, and a breach of ethics.

ethics
A set of moral principles or values that governs the conduct of an individual or a group.

He who seeks equality must do equity.

Joseph Story
Equity Jurisprudence (1836)

Law   Ethics

Exhibit 2.1 LAW AND ETHICS

Ethics

Bernie Madoff Steals Billions of Dollars in Pyramid Scheme

"Here the message must be sent that Mr. Madoff's crimes were extraordinarily evil."

—Chin, District Judge

One of the oldest and still most often used frauds is the **pyramid scheme**, also referred to as a **Ponzi scheme**. It works like this: A promoter offers investors an unusually

(continued)

high rate of return on their investment. The promoter usually claims to have figured out a way to beat the system. Investors, enticed by the promised high return, give the promoter their money to invest. The promoter keeps soliciting more investors. The promoter then offers to pay the original investors back their money with the promised high return, and he has the money to do so with the money raised from the new investors. Then human psychology takes over: The investors who are offered their investment back often "reinvest" this money, maybe add some more money to their investment, and bring friends and family members into the scheme. The pyramid is built as layer after layer of new investors are added to the fraud.

The promoter usually does not invest the money but instead uses it to support a lavish lifestyle. Even if the promoter invests some of the money, it is highly unlikely that he can match the investment returns he has promised. There is one true caveat about a pyramid scheme: It will eventually collapse as the promoter runs out of people to dupe or too many investors want their money back at the same time, or both.

One of the largest pyramid schemes was run by Bernie Madoff over a twenty-year period beginning in the 1980s. Over the years, Madoff enticed investors to invest billions of dollars with him, with the classic promise of extraordinary returns. Madoff joined country clubs, served on boards of directors of charitable organizations and universities, and traveled in high and wealthy circles, trolling for his victims.

Madoff did not invest his clients' money. When investors requested their money back, he paid them out of new money that he had raised from other investors. Madoff used much of the money to pay for his and his family's lavish lifestyle. Madoff and his wife, Ruth, had a Manhattan penthouse, a beachfront mansion in the Hamptons on Long Island, and a villa on the French Riviera. He owned three yachts, and Ruth had jewelry worth millions of dollars.

Madoff was able to run his pyramid scheme for two decades without getting caught. However, in 2008, after a recession hit the United States and the stock market plummeted, investors tried to recover billions of dollars of their investments from Madoff. Madoff could no longer keep his fraud afloat. Madoff was arrested by the Federal Bureau of Investigation (FBI).

In 2009, Madoff appeared in federal court and pleaded guilty to securities fraud, wire fraud, mail fraud, money laundering, perjury, and filing false documents with the Securities and Exchange Commission (SEC). Many investors lost their life savings.

The U.S. District Court judge called Madoff's fraud "unprecedented" and "staggering" and sentenced Madoff to 150 years in prison, without the possibility of parole. The judge stated, "Here the message must be sent that Mr. Madoff's crimes were extraordinarily evil." Madoff, age 71, was committed to the federal prison in Butner, North Carolina. As part of his sentencing, Madoff was also ordered to pay $170 billion in restitution, but only a small amount will be recovered. The government agreed to let Madoff's wife Ruth keep $2.5 million. *United States v. Madoff* (United States District Court for the Southern District of New York)

Ethics Questions Did Bernie Madoff act ethically in this case? Did he act illegally? Are the investors to blame for their misfortune? Explain. Why do pyramid schemes keep working?

Business Ethics

The ultimate justification of the law is to be found, and can only be found, in moral considerations.

Lord MacMillan
Law and Other Things (1937)

How can ethics be measured? The answer is very personal: What one person considers ethical another may consider unethical. However, there do seem to be some universal rules about what conduct is ethical and what conduct is not. The following material discusses five major theories of ethics: (1) *ethical fundamentalism*, (2) *utilitarianism*, (3) *Kantian ethics*, (4) *Rawls's social justice theory*, and (5) *ethical relativism*.

Ethical Fundamentalism

ethical fundamentalism
A theory of ethics which says that a person looks to an outside source for ethical rules or commands.

False Claims Act (Whistleblower Statute)
A federal statute that permits private parties to sue companies for fraud on behalf of the government and share in any monetary recovery.

Under **ethical fundamentalism**, a person looks to an *outside source* for ethical rules or commands. This may be a book (e.g., the Bible, the Koran) or a person (e.g., Karl Marx). Critics argue that ethical fundamentalism does not permit people to determine right and wrong for themselves. Taken to an extreme, the result could be considered unethical under most other moral theories. For example, a literal interpretation of the maxim "an eye for an eye" would permit retaliation.

The following ethics feature discusses the incentives that employees have to report illegal activities of their employers in certain circumstances.

Ethics

Corporation Ratted Out Under the Whistleblower Statute

"Bayer employees were to obey not only 'the letter of the law but the spirit of the law as well.'"

—Bayer Corporation's Ethics Video

The Bayer Corporation (Bayer) is a U.S. subsidiary corporation of the giant German-based Bayer A.G. Bayer is a large pharmaceutical company that produces prescription drugs, including its patented antibiotic Cipro. Bayer sold Cipro to private health providers and hospitals, including Kaiser Permanente Medical Care Program, the largest health maintenance organization in the United States. Bayer also sold Cipro to the federal government's Medicaid program, which provides medical insurance to the poor. Federal law contains a "best price" rule that prohibits a company that sells a drug to Medicaid from charging Medicaid a price higher than the lowest price for which it sells the drug to private purchasers.

Kaiser told Bayer that it would not purchase Cipro from Bayer—and would switch to a competitor's antibiotics—unless Bayer reduced the price of Cipro. Bayer's executives came up with a plan whereby Bayer would put a private label on its Cipro and not call it Cipro and sell the antibiotic to Kaiser at a 40 percent discount. Thus, Bayer continued to charge Medicaid the full price for Cipro while giving Kaiser a 40 percent discount through the private labeling program. One of Bayer's executives who negotiated this deal with Kaiser was George Couto, a corporate account manager.

Everything went well for Bayer until Couto attended a mandatory ethics training class at Bayer at which a video of Helge Wehmeier, then company chief executive, was shown. When the video stated that Bayer employees were to obey not only "the letter of the law but the spirit of the law as well," some of the Bayer executives laughed. Later that day, Couto attended a staff meeting at which it was disclosed that Bayer kept $97 million from Medicaid by using the discounted private labeling program for Kaiser and other health care companies. Two days later, Couto wrote a memorandum to his boss, questioning the legality

Office of the Whistleblower Protection Program

of the private labeling program in light of Medicaid's "best price" law.

When he received no response to his memo, Couto contacted a lawyer. Couto filed a *qui tam* **lawsuit** under the federal **False Claims Act**[2]—also known as the **Whistleblower Statute**—which permits private parties to sue companies for fraud on behalf of the government. The whistleblower can be awarded up to 25 percent of the amount recovered on behalf of the federal government, even if the informer has been a co-conspirator in perpetrating the fraud.

After the case was filed, the U.S. Department of Justice took over the case, as allowed by law, and filed criminal and civil charges against Bayer. After discovery was taken, Bayer pleaded guilty to one criminal felony and agreed to pay federal and state governments $257 million to settle the civil and criminal cases. Couto, age 39, died of pancreatic cancer three months prior to the settlement. He was awarded $34 million, which went to his three children. *United States ex. rel. Estate of George Couto v. Bayer Corporation* (United States District Court for the District of Massachusetts)

Ethics Questions   Did managers at Bayer obey the letter of the law? Did the managers at Bayer obey the spirit of the law? Why did the managers of the corporation do what they did? Did Bayer act ethically in this case? Did Couto act ethically in this case? Should Couto have benefitted from his own alleged illegal conduct?

Utilitarianism

Utilitarianism is a moral theory with origins in the works of Jeremy Bentham (1748–1832) and John Stuart (1806–1873). This moral theory dictates that people must choose the action or follow the rule that provides the *greatest good to society*. This does not mean the greatest good for the greatest number of people.

Example If an action would increase the good of twenty-five people by one unit each and an alternative action would increase the good of one person by twenty-six units, then, according to utilitarianism, the latter action should be taken.

utilitarianism
A moral theory which dictates that people must choose the action or follow the rule that provides the greatest good to society.

WEB EXERCISE
Visit the website of the Walmart Watch, at **www.walmartwatch.com**. What is one of the current issued discussed at this site?

Utilitarianism has been criticized because it is difficult to estimate the "good" that will result from different actions, it is difficult to apply in an imperfect world, and it treats morality as if it were an impersonal mathematical calculation.

Example A company is trying to determine whether it should close an unprofitable plant located in a small community. Utilitarianism would require that the benefits to shareholders from closing the plant be compared with the benefits to employees, their families, and others in the community in keeping it open.

Kantian Ethics

Kantian ethics (duty ethics)
A moral theory which says that people owe moral duties that are based on universal rules, such as the categorical imperative "Do unto others as you would have them do unto you."

Immanuel Kant (1724–1804) is the best-known proponent of **duty ethics**, also called **Kantian ethics**. Kant believed that people owe moral duties that are based on *universal rules*. Kant's philosophy is based on the premise that people can use reasoning to reach ethical decisions. His ethical theory would have people behave according to the *categorical imperative* "Do unto others as you would have them do unto you."

Example According to Kantian ethics, keeping a promise to abide by a contract is a moral duty even if that contract turns out to be detrimental to the obligated party.

The universal rules of Kantian ethics are based on two important principles: (1) consistency—that is, all cases are treated alike, with no exceptions—and (2) reversibility—that is, the actor must abide by the rule he or she uses to judge the morality of someone else's conduct. Thus, if you are going to make an exception for yourself, that exception becomes a universal rule that applies to all others.

Whatever the human law may be, neither an individual nor a nation can commit the least act of injustice against the obscurest individual without having to pay the penalty for it.

Henry David Thoreau

Example If you rationalize that it is acceptable for you to engage in deceptive practices, it is acceptable for competitors to do so also.

A criticism of Kantian ethics is that it is difficult to reach consensus as to what the universal rules should be.

Rawls's Social Justice Theory

John Locke (1632–1704) and Jean-Jacques Rousseau (1712–1778) proposed a *social contract* theory of morality. Under this theory, each person is presumed to have entered into a social contract with all others in society to obey moral rules that are necessary for people to live in peace and harmony. This implied contract states, "I will keep the rules if everyone else does." These moral rules are then used to solve conflicting interests in society.

The leading proponent of the modern justice theory was John Rawls (1921–2002), a philosopher at Harvard University. Under **Rawls's social justice theory**, fairness is considered the essence of justice. The principles of justice should be chosen by persons who do not yet know their station in society—thus, their "veil of ignorance" would permit the fairest possible principles to be selected.

Example Under Rawls's social justice theory, the principle of equal opportunity in employment would be promulgated by people who would not yet know if they were in a favored class.

As a caveat, Rawls also proposed that the least advantaged in society must receive special assistance in order to realize their potential. Rawls's theory of social justice is criticized for two reasons. First, establishing the blind "original position" for choosing moral principles is impossible in the real world. Second, many persons in society would choose not to maximize the benefit to the least advantaged persons in society.

Ethical Relativism

Ethical relativism holds that individuals must decide what is ethical based on their own feelings about what is right and wrong. Under this moral theory, if a person meets his or her own moral standard in making a decision, no one can criticize him or her for it. Thus, there are no universal ethical rules to guide a person's conduct. This theory has been criticized because action that is usually thought to be unethical (e.g., committing fraud) would not be unethical if the perpetrator thought it was in fact ethical. Few philosophers advocate ethical relativism as an acceptable moral theory.

Rawls's social justice theory
A moral theory which asserts that fairness is the essence of justice. The theory proffers that says each person is presumed to have entered into a social contract with all others in society to obey moral rules that are necessary for people to live in peace and harmony.

The notion that a business is clothed with a public interest and has been devoted to the public use is little more than a fiction intended to beautify what is disagreeable to the sufferers.

Justice Holmes
Tyson & Bro-United Theatre Ticket Officers v. Banton (1927)

ethical relativism
A moral theory which holds that individuals must decide what is ethical based on their own feelings about what is right and wrong.

CONCEPT SUMMARY

THEORIES OF ETHICS

Theory	Description
Ethical fundamentalism	Persons look to an outside source (e.g., the Bible, the Koran) or a central figure for ethical guidelines.
Utilitarianism	Persons choose the alternative that would provide the greatest good to society.
Kantian ethics	A set of universal rules that establish ethical duties. The rules are based on reasoning and require (1) consistency in application and (2) reversibility.
Rawls's social justice theory	Moral duties are based on an implied social contract. Fairness is justice. The rules are established from an original position of a "veil of ignorance."
Ethical relativism	Individuals decide what is ethical, based on their own feelings as to what is right or wrong.

Social Responsibility of Business

Businesses do not operate in a vacuum. Decisions made by businesses have far-reaching effects on society. In the past, many business decisions were based solely on a cost–benefit analysis and how they affected the "bottom line." Such decisions, however, may cause negative externalities for others.

Example The dumping of hazardous wastes from a manufacturing plant into a river affects the homeowners, farmers, and others who use the river's waters.

social responsibility
A theory that requires corporations and businesses to act with awareness of the consequences and impact that their decisions will have on others.

Social responsibility requires corporations and businesses to act with awareness of the consequences and impact that their decisions will have on others. Thus, corporations and businesses are considered to owe some degree of responsibility for their actions.

Four theories of the social responsibility of business are discussed in the following paragraphs: (1) *maximize profits*, (2) *moral minimum*, (3) *stakeholder interest*, and (4) *corporate citizenship*.

Maximize Profits

maximizing profits
A theory of social responsibility which says that a corporation owes a duty to take actions that maximize profits for shareholders.

The traditional view of the social responsibility of business is that business should **maximize profits** for shareholders. This view, which dominated business and the law during the 19th century, holds that the interests of other constituencies (e.g., employees, suppliers, residents of the communities in which businesses are located) are not important in and of themselves.

Example In the famous case *Dodge v. Ford Motor Company*,[3] a shareholder sued Ford Motor Company when its founder, Henry Ford, introduced a plan to reduce the prices of cars so that more people would be put to work and more people could own cars. The shareholders alleged that such a plan would not increase dividends. Mr. Ford testified, "My ambition is to employ still more men, to spread the benefits of this industrial system to the greatest number, to help them build up their lives and their homes." The court sided with the shareholders and stated the following:

> *[Mr. Ford's] testimony creates the impression that he thinks the Ford Motor company has made too much money, has had too large profits and that, although large profits might still be earned, a sharing of them with the public, by reducing the price of the output of the company, ought to be undertaken.*
>
> *There should be no confusion of the duties which Mr. Ford conceives that he and the stockholders owe to the general public and the duties which in law he and his codirectors owe to protesting, minority stockholders. A business corporation is organized and carried on primarily for the profit of the stockholders. The powers of the directors are to be employed for that end. The discretion of directors is to be exercised in the choice of means to attain that end and does not extend to a change in the end itself, to the reduction of profits, or to the nondistribution of profits among stockholders in order to devote them to other purposes.*

Public policy: That principle of the law which holds that no subject can lawfully do that which has a tendency to be injurious to the public or against the public good.

Lord Truro
Egerton v. Brownlow (1853)

Milton Friedman, who won the Nobel Prize in economics when he taught at the University of Chicago, advocated the theory of maximizing profits for shareholders. Friedman asserted that in a free society, "there is one and only one social responsibility of business—to use its resources and engage in activities designed to increase its profits as long as it stays within the rules of the game, which is to say, engages in open and free competition without deception and fraud."[4]

The following case examined the lawfulness of Walmart knocking off another company's product design.

CASE 2.1   *U.S. SUPREME COURT Business Ethics*

Walmart Stores, Inc. v. Samara Brothers, Inc.

529 U.S. 205, 120 S.Ct. 1339, 146 L.Ed.2d 182, Web 2000 U.S. Lexis 2197
Supreme Court of the United States

"Their suspicions aroused, however, Samara officials launched an investigation, which disclosed that Walmart [was] selling the knockoffs of Samara's outfits."

—Justice Scalia

Facts

Samara Brothers, Inc. (Samara), is a designer and manufacturer of children's clothing. The core of Samara's business is its annual new line of spring and summer children's garments. Samara sold its clothing to retailers, which in turn sold the clothes to consumers. Walmart Stores, Inc. (Walmart), operates a large chain of budget warehouse stores that sell thousands of items at very low prices. Walmart contacted one of its suppliers, Judy-Philippine, Inc. (JPI), about the possibility of making a line of children's clothes just like Samara's successful line. Walmart sent photographs of Samara's children's clothes to JPI (with the name "Samara" readily discernible on the labels of the garments) and directed JPI to produce children's clothes exactly like those in the photographs. JPI produced a line of children's clothes for Walmart that copied the designs, colors, and patterns of Samara's clothing. Walmart then sold this line of children's clothing in its stores, making a gross profit of over $1.15 million on these clothes in one selling season.

Samara discovered that Walmart was selling the knockoff clothes at a price that was lower than Samara's retailers were paying Samara for its clothes. After sending unsuccessful cease-and-desist letters to Walmart, Samara sued Walmart, alleging that Walmart stole Samara's trade dress (i.e., look and feel) in violation of Section 43(a) of the Lanham Act. Although not finding that Samara's clothes had acquired a secondary meaning in the minds of the public, the U.S. District Court held in favor of Samara and awarded damages. The U.S. Court of Appeals affirmed the award to Samara. Walmart appealed to the U.S. Supreme Court.

Issue

Must a product's design have acquired a secondary meaning before it is protected as trade dress?

Language of the U.S. Supreme Court

The Lanham Act, in Section 43(a), gives a producer a cause of action for the use by any person of "any word, term, name, symbol, or device, or any combination thereof which is likely to cause confusion as to the origin, sponsorship, or approval of his or her goods." The text of Section 43(a) provides little guidance as to the circumstances under which unregistered trade dress may be protected. It does require that a producer show that the allegedly infringing feature is likely to cause confusion with the product for which protection is sought. In an action for infringement of unregistered trade dress a product's design is protectable only upon a showing of secondary meaning.

Decision

The U.S. Supreme Court held that a product's design has to have acquired a secondary meaning in the public's eye before it is protected as trade dress under Section 43(a) of the Lanham Act. The Supreme Court reversed the decision of the U.S. Court of Appeals and remanded the case for further proceedings, consistent with its opinion.

Case Questions

Critical Legal Thinking
What is trade dress? Should it have been protected in this case?

Ethics
Even if Walmart's conduct was ruled legal, was it ethical?

Contemporary Business
What can companies like Samara do to protect themselves from similar conduct by Walmart or other larger companies? Explain.

Moral Minimum

moral minimum
A theory of social responsibility which says that a corporation's duty is to make a profit while avoiding causing harm to others.

Some proponents of corporate social responsibility argue that a corporation's duty is to *make a profit while avoiding causing harm to others*. This theory of social responsibility is called the **moral minimum**. Under this theory, as long as business avoids or corrects the social injury it causes, it has met its duty of social responsibility.

Example A corporation that pollutes a body of water and then compensates those whom the pollution has injured has met its moral minimum duty of social responsibility.

The legislative and judicial branches of government have established laws that enforce the moral minimum of social responsibility on corporations.

Examples Occupational safety laws establish minimum safety standards for protecting employees from injuries in the workplace. Consumer protection laws establish safety requirements for products and make manufacturers and sellers liable for injuries caused by defective products.

The following feature discusses how the landmark Sarbanes-Oxley Act promotes ethics in business.

Landmark Law

Sarbanes-Oxley Act Requires Public Companies to Adopt Codes of Ethics

In the late 1990s and early 2000s, many large corporations in the United States were found to have engaged in massive financial frauds. Many of these frauds were perpetrated by the chief executive officers and other senior officers of the companies. Financial officers, such as chief financial officers and controllers, were also found to have been instrumental in committing these frauds. In response, Congress enacted the **Sarbanes-Oxley Act of 2002 (SOX)**, which makes certain conduct illegal and establishes criminal penalties for violations. In addition, the Sarbanes-Oxley Act prompts companies to encourage senior officers of public companies to act ethically in their dealings with shareholders, employees, and other constituents.

Section 406 of the Sarbanes-Oxley Act requires a public company to disclose whether it has adopted a **code of ethics** for senior financial officers, including its principal financial officer and principal accounting officer. In response, public companies have adopted codes of ethics for their senior financial officers. Many public companies have included all officers and employees in the coverage of their codes of ethics.

Section 406 of the Sarbanes-Oxley Act
A section that requires a public company to disclose whether it has adopted a code of ethics for senior financial officers.

stakeholder interest
A theory of social responsibility which says that a corporation must consider the effects its actions have on persons other than its shareholders.

Stakeholder Interest

Businesses have relationships with all sorts of people besides their shareholders, including employees, suppliers, customers, creditors, and the local community. Under the **stakeholder interest** theory of social responsibility, a corporation must consider the effects its actions have on these *other stakeholders*. For example, a corporation would violate the stakeholder interest theory if it viewed employees solely as a means of maximizing shareholder wealth.

The stakeholder interest theory is criticized because it is difficult to harmonize the conflicting interests of stakeholders.

Example In deciding to close an unprofitable manufacturing plant, certain stakeholders would benefit (e.g., shareholders and creditors), whereas other stakeholders would not (e.g., current employees and the local community).

In the following case, the U.S. Supreme Court decided an important political speech and ethics issue.

CASE 2.2   *U.S. SUPREME COURT Corporate Political Speech and Ethics*

Citizens United v. Federal Election Commission

130 S.Ct. 876, 175 L.Ed.2d 753, Web 2010 U.S. Lexis 766 (2010)
Supreme Court of the United States

"The First Amendment has its fullest and most urgent application to speech uttered during a campaign for political office. For these reasons, political speech must prevail against laws that would suppress it, whether by design or inadvertence."

—Kennedy, Justice

Facts

Section 441b of the Federal Election Campaign Act prohibits corporations and labor unions from using general treasury funds to make direct campaign contributions to political candidates, to make independent expenditures that expressly advocate the election or defeat of a political candidate through any form of media, or to make independent expenses for speech defined as "electioneering communications." Federal campaign financing laws are administered by the Federal Election Commission (FEC), a federal government agency. Violations of the laws provide for civil and criminal penalties.

In January 2008, Citizens United released a film entitled *Hillary: The Movie* (*Hillary*). The film was a feature-length 90-minute documentary about then Senator Hillary Clinton, who was a candidate in the Democratic Party's 2008 presidential primary election. *Hillary* was a negative advertisement that mentions Senator Clinton by name and depicts interviews with politcal commentators and other persons, most of them quite critical of Senator Clinton. The film informed the electorate that Senator Clinton was unfit for office and that viewers should vote against her in the Democratic Party's primary election.

Citizens United wanted to promote a planned video-on-demand offering of *Hillary* by running advertisements on broadcast and cable television. In December 2007, Citizens United sued the FEC, alleging that the federal restrictions on campaign financing violated the corporation's free speech rights as guaranteed by the First Amendment. The U.S. District Court denied Citizens United's motion

for an injunction. The U.S. Supreme Court agreed to hear the case.

Issue

Do the challenged federal restrictions on campaign financing and electioneering violate the free speech rights of Citizens United?

Language of the U.S. Supreme Court

The First Amendment provides that "Congress shall make no law … abridging the freedom of speech." The law before us is an outright ban, backed by criminal sanctions. Thus, the following acts would all be felonies: The Sierra Club runs an ad that exhorts the public to disapprove of a Congressman who favors logging in national forests; the National Rifle Association publishes a book urging the public to vote for the challenger because the incumbent U. S. Senator supports a handgun ban; and the American Civil Liberties Union creates a Web site telling the public to vote for a Presidential candidate in light of that candidate's defense of free speech. These prohibitions are classic examples of censorship.

The First Amendment has its fullest and most urgent application to speech uttered during a campaign for political office. For these reasons, political speech must prevail against laws that would suppress it, whether by design or inadvertence.

The Court has recognized that First Amendment protection extends to corporations. Corporations and other associations, like individuals, contribute to the discussion, debate, and the dissemination of information and ideas that the First Amendment seeks to foster. Political speech is indispensable to decisionmaking in a democracy, and this is

(continued)

no less true because the speech comes from a corporation rather than an individual.

Decision

In a 5 to 4 decision, the U.S. Supreme Court held that the government may not limit corporate expenditures for political speech and that the challenged campaign financing restrictions were unconstitutional. The Supreme Court held that the First Amendment free speech rights of Citizens United had been violated.

Case Questions

Critical Legal Thinking

Should corporations have the same First Amendment free speech rights as individuals?

Ethics

Do you think that special interest groups have too much influence on the election of politicians? After this decision, will corporations, labor unions, and other organizations have an unfair advantage over ordinary citizens in political elections? The U.S. Supreme Court's decision has been critized because it allows foreign corporations and entities to give money to political candidates running for office in the United States. Should this be a concern?

Contemporary Business

This case has been hailed as one of the most important business decisions made by the U.S. Supreme Court in years. How important is this decision to business, labor unions, and other organizations?

Corporate Citizenship

corporate citizenship
A theory of social responsibility which says that a business has a responsibility to do good.

In civilized life, law floats in a sea of ethics.

Earl Warren

The **corporate citizenship** theory of social responsibility argues that business has a responsibility to do well. That is, business is responsible for helping to solve social problems that it did little, if anything, to cause.

Example Under the corporate citizenship theory of social responsibility, corporations owe a duty to subsidize schools and help educate children.

This theory contends that corporations owe a duty to promote the same social goals as individual members of society. Proponents of this "do good" theory argue that corporations owe a debt to society to make it a better place and that this duty arises because of the social power bestowed on them. That is, this social power is a gift from society and should be used to good ends.

A major criticism of this theory is that the duty of a corporation to do good cannot be expanded beyond certain limits. There is always some social problem that needs to be addressed, and corporate funds are limited. Further, if this theory were taken to its maximum limit, potential shareholders might be reluctant to invest in corporations.

CONCEPT SUMMARY

THEORIES OF SOCIAL RESPONSIBILITY

Theory	Social Responsibility
Maximizing profits	To maximize profits for stockholders
Moral minimum	To avoid causing harm and to compensate for harm caused
Stakeholder interest	To consider the interests of all stakeholders, including stockholders, employees, customers, suppliers, creditors, and the local community
Corporate citizenship	To do well and solve social problems

International Law

Conducting Business in Russia

ST. PETERSBURG, RUSSIA
Russia was once the leading country of the Union of Soviet Socialist Republics (USSR), also known as the Soviet Union. Russia was a socialist communist state until the collapse of the Soviet Union in 1989. Since then, it has followed a course of capitalism. However, Russian capitalism is fraught with corruption by government officials and business persons. Russia is ranked as one of the worst countries for corruption and bribery in the world. Therefore, foreign companies sometimes find it difficult to do business in Russia without violating ethical principles.

Key Terms and Concepts

Code of ethics (28)

Corporate citizenship (30)

Ethical fundamentalism (22)

Ethical relativism (25)

Ethics (21)

Ethics and the law (21)

False Claims Act (Whistleblower Statute) (23)

Kantian ethics (duty ethics) (24)

Law (21)

Maximize profits (26)

Moral minimum (28)

Pyramid scheme (Ponzi scheme) (21)

Qui tam lawsuit (23)

Rawls's social justice theory (25)

Sarbanes-Oxley Act of 2002 (SOX) (28)

Section 406 of the Sarbanes-Oxley Act (28)

Social responsibility (26)

Stakeholder interest (28)

Utilitarianism (23)

Law Case with Answer
United States v. Sun-Diamond Growers of California

Facts The Sun-Diamond Growers of California is a trade association that engages in marketing and lobbying activities on behalf of its 5,000 member-growers of raisins, figs, walnuts, prunes, and hazelnuts. Sun-Diamond gave Michael Epsy, U.S. secretary of agriculture, tickets to sporting events (worth $2,295), luggage ($2,427), meals ($665), and a crystal bowl ($524) while two matters in which Sun-Diamond members had an interest in were pending before the secretary of agriculture. The two matters were decided in Sun-Diamond's favor. The United States sued Sun-Diamond criminally for making illegal gifts to a public official, in violation of the federal antibribery and gratuity statute [18 U.S.C. Sections 201(b) and 201(c)]. The United States sought to recover a monetary fine against Sun-Diamond. Did Sun-Diamond violate the federal antibribery and gratuity statute by giving these items to the U.S. secretary of agriculture?

Answer No, Sun-Diamond did not violate the federal antibribery and gratuity statute by giving these items to the U.S. Secretary of Agriculture. A criminal conviction under the federal antibribery and gratuity statute requires a showing of a direct nexus between the value conferred on the public official and the official act performed by the public official in favor of the giver. The antibribery and gratuity statute requires more than a showing that a gift was motivated, at least in part, by the recipient's capacity to exercise governmental power or influence in the donor's favor without necessarily showing that it was connected to a particular official act. This meaning of the statute is incorrect because of the peculiar results that it would produce: It would criminalize, for example, token gifts to the president based on his official position and not linked to any identifiable act—such as the replica jerseys given by championship sports teams each year during ceremonial White House visits. There must be proof of a direct nexus between the gratuity given and the public official's act before the federal antibribery and gratuity statute is violated. Because no such direct nexus was shown in this case, there is no violation of the federal antibribery and gratuity statute. *United States v. Sun-Diamond Growers of California*, 526 U.S. 398, 119 S.Ct. 1402, 143 L.Ed.2d 576, **Web** 1999 U.S. Lexis 3001 (Supreme Court of the United States)

1. Did Sun-Diamond act ethically in this case?
2. Did the U.S. secretary of agriculture act ethically in accepting the gifts from Sun-Diamond?
3. Why do you think Sun-Diamond gave the gifts to U.S. secretary of agriculture?

Ethics Cases

2.1 Ethics Papa John's International, Inc., is the third-largest pizza chain in the United States, with more than 2,050 locations. Papa John's adopted a new slogan—"Better Ingredients. Better Pizza."—and applied for and received a federal trademark for this slogan. Papa John's spent over $300 million building customer recognition and goodwill for this slogan. This slogan has appeared on millions of signs, shirts, menus, pizza boxes, napkins, and other items, and it has regularly appeared as the tag line at the end of Papa John's radio and television advertisements.

Pizza Hut, Inc., is the largest pizza chain in the United States, with more than 7,000 restaurants. Pizza Hut launched a new advertising campaign in which it declared "war" on poor-quality pizza. The advertisements touted the "better taste" of Pizza Hut's pizza and "dared" anyone to find a better pizza. Pizza Hut also filed a civil action in federal court, charging Papa John's with false advertising, in violation of Section 43(a) of the federal Lanham Act. *Pizza Hut, Inc. v. Papa John's International, Inc.*, 227 F.3d 489, **Web** 2000 U.S. App. Lexis 23444 (United States Court of Appeals for the Fifth Circuit)

1. What is the difference between false advertising and puffery? Are consumers smart enough to see through companies' puffery?
2. Is the Papa John's advertising slogan "Better Ingredients. Better Pizza." false advertising?
3. Did Papa John's act ethically in making the claims it made?

2.2 Ethics McDonald's Corporation operates the largest fast-food restaurant chain in the United States and the world. It produces such famous foods as the Big Mac hamburger, Chicken McNuggets, the Egg McMuffin, French fries, shakes, and other foods. A McDonald's survey showed that 22 percent of its customers are "Super Heavy Users," meaning that they eat at McDonald's ten times or more a month. Super Heavy Users make up approximately 75 percent of McDonald's sales. The survey also found that 72 percent of McDonald's customers were "Heavy Users," meaning they ate at McDonald's at least once a week.

Jazlyn Bradley consumed McDonald's foods her entire life during school lunch breaks and before and after school, approximately five times per week, ordering two meals per day. When Bradley was 19 years old, she sued McDonald's Corporation for causing her obesity and health problems associated with obesity.

Plaintiff Bradley sued McDonald's in U.S. District Court for violating the New York Consumer Protection Act, which prohibits deceptive and unfair acts and practices. She alleged that McDonald's misled her, through its advertising campaigns and other publicity, that its food products were nutritious, of a beneficial nutritional nature, and easily part of a healthy lifestyle if consumed on a daily basis. The plaintiff sued on behalf of herself and a class of minors residing in the state of New York who purchased and consumed McDonald's products. McDonald's filed a motion with the U.S. District Court to dismiss the plaintiff's complaint. Did the plaintiff state a valid case against McDonald's for deceptive and unfair acts and practices in violation of the New York Consumer Protection Act? *Bradley v. McDonald's Corporation*, **Web** 2003 U.S. Dist. Lexis 15202 (United States District Court for the Southern District of New York)

1. Is McDonald's liable to Bradley for deceptive and unfair acts and practices?
2. Does McDonald's act ethically is selling products that it knows causes obesity? Should McDonald's have disclosed the information it knew about Heavy Users?
3. Congress enacted a federal statute that requires restaurant chains with 20 or more outlets to disclose calorie counts on their food items. The law took effect in 2011. Do you think that many McDonald's customers will consider this information before purchasing their food items?

2.3 Ethics The Warner-Lambert Company has manufactured and distributed Listerine antiseptic mouth wash since 1879. Its formula has never changed. Ever since Listerine's introduction, the company has represented the product as being beneficial in preventing and curing colds and sore throats. Direct advertising of these claims to consumers began in 1921. Warner-Lambert spent millions of dollars annually advertising these claims in print media and in television commercials.

After one hundred years of Warner-Lambert's making such claims, the Federal Trade Commission (FTC) filed a complaint against the company, alleging that it had engaged in false advertising, in violation of federal law. Four months of hearings were held before an administrative law judge that produced an evidentiary record of more than four thousand pages of documents from forty-six witnesses. After examining the evidence, the FTC issued an opinion which held that the company's representations that Listerine prevented and cured colds and sore throats were false. The U.S. Court of Appeals affirmed. *Warner-Lambert Company v. Federal Trade Commission*, 183 U.S. App. D.C. 230, 562 F.2d 749, **Web** 1977 U.S. App. Lexis 11599 (United States Court of Appeals for the District of Columbia Circuit)

1. Is Warner-Lambert guilty of fraud? If so, what remedies should the court have imposed on the company?
2. Why did Warner-Lambert make claims that Listerine cured colds?
3. Did Warner-Lambert act ethically in making its claims for Listerine?

2.4 Ethics The Johns Manville Corporation was a profitable company that made a variety of building and other products. It was a major producer of asbestos, which was used for insulation in buildings and for a variety of other uses. It has been medically proven that excessive exposure to asbestos causes asbestosis, a fatal lung disease. Thousands of employees of the company and consumers who were exposed to asbestos and contracted this fatal disease sued the company for damages. Eventually, the lawsuits were being filed at a rate of more than 400 per week.

In response to the claims, Johns Manville Corporation filed for reorganization bankruptcy. It argued that if it did not, an otherwise viable company that provided thousands of jobs and served a useful purpose in this country would be destroyed and that without the declaration of bankruptcy, a few of the plaintiffs who first filed their lawsuits would win awards of hundreds of millions of dollars, leaving nothing for the remainder of the plaintiffs. Under the bankruptcy court's protection, the company was restructured to survive. As part of the release from bankruptcy, the company contributed money to a fund to pay current and future claimants. The fund was not large enough to pay all injured persons the full amounts of their claims. *In re Johns-Mansville Corporation*, 36 B.R. 727, **Web** 1984 Bankr. Lexis 6384 (United States Bankruptcy Court for the Southern District of New York)

1. Is Johns Manville liable for negligence?
2. Was it ethical for Johns Manville to declare bankruptcy?
3. Did Johns Manville meet its duty of social responsibility in this case?

2.5 Ethics The Reverend Leon H. Sullivan, a Baptist minister from Philadelphia who was also a member of the board of directors of General Motors Corporation, proposed a set of rules to guide American-owned companies doing business in the Republic of South Africa. The *Sullivan Principles*, as they became known, call for the nonsegregation of races in South Africa. They call for employers to (a) provide equal and fair employment practices for all employees and (b) improve the quality of employees' lives outside the work environment in such areas as housing, schooling, transportation, recreation, and health facilities. The principles also require signatory companies to report regularly and to be graded on their conduct in South Africa. Eventually, several hundred U.S. corporations with affiliates doing business in South Africa subscribed to the Sullivan Principles.

To put additional pressure on the government of the Republic of South Africa to end apartheid, Reverend Sullivan called for the complete withdrawal of all U.S. companies from doing business in or with South Africa. Very few companies agreed to do so.

1. Which of the following theories of social responsibility were the companies that subscribed to the Sullivan Principles following?
   a. Maximizing profits
   b. Moral minimum
   c. Stakeholder interest
   d. Corporate citizenship
2. Do companies owe a social duty to withdraw from doing business in countries that engage in discrimination or other human rights violations? Why or why not?
3. Should universities divest themselves of investments in companies that conduct business in countries that engage in human rights violations? Why or why not?

2.6 Ethics Kaiser Aluminum & Chemical Corporation entered into a collective bargaining agreement with the United Steelworkers of America, a union that represented employees at Kaiser's plants. The agreement contained an affirmative-action program to increase the representation of minorities in craft jobs. To enable plants to meet these goals, on-the-job training programs were established to teach unskilled production workers the skills necessary to become craft workers. Assignment to the training program was based on seniority, except that the plan reserved 50 percent of the openings for black employees.

Thirteen craft trainees were selected from Kaiser's Gramercy plant for the training program. Of these, seven were black and six were white. The most senior black trainee selected had less seniority than several white production workers who had applied for the

positions but were rejected. Brian Weber, one of the white rejected employees, instituted a class action lawsuit, alleging that the affirmative-action plan violated Title VII of the Civil Rights Act of 1964, which made it "unlawful to discriminate because of race" in hiring and selecting apprentices for training programs. The U.S. Supreme Court upheld the affirmative-action plan in this case. The decision stated:

> We therefore hold that Title VII's prohibition against racial discrimination does not condemn all private, voluntary, race-conscious affirmative action plans. At the same time, the plant does not unnecessarily trammel the interests of the white employees. Moreover, the plan is a temporary measure; it is not intended to maintain racial balance, but simply to eliminate a manifest racial imbalance.

Steelworkers v. Weber, 443 U.S. 193, 99 S.Ct. 2721, 61 L.Ed.2d 480, **Web** 1979 U.S. Lexis 40 (Supreme Court of the United States)

1. Why did the federal government enact Title VII of the Civil Rights Act of 1964? Explain.
2. Do companies owe a duty of social responsibility to provide affirmative-action programs?
3. Does anyone suffer economic loss because of affirmative action programs?

2.7 Ethics Iroquois Brands, Ltd., a Delaware corporation, had $78 million in assets, $141 million in sales, and $6 million in profits. As part of its business, Iroquois imported pâté de foie gras (goose pâté) from France and sold it in the United States. Iroquois derived only $79,000 in revenues from sales of such pâté. The French company force-fed the geese from which the pâté was made. Peter C. Lovenheim, who owned 200 shares of Iroquois common stock, wanted to include a shareholder proposal in Iroquois's annual proxy materials to be sent to shareholders. His proposal criticized the company because the force-feeding caused "undue stress, pain and suffering" to the geese and requested that shareholders vote to have Iroquois discontinue importing and selling pâté produced by this method.

Iroquois refused to allow the information to be included in its proxy materials. Iroquois asserted that its refusal was based on the fact that Lovenheim's proposal was "not economically significant" and had only "ethical and social" significance. The company reasoned that because corporations are economic entities, only an economic test applied to its activities, and it was not subject to an ethical or a social responsibility test. *Lovenheim v. Iroquois Brands, Ltd.*, 618 F.Supp. 554, **Web** 1985 U.S. Dist. Lexis 21259 (United States District Court for the District of Columbia)

1. Is the company correct? Should only an economic test be applied in judging the activities of a corporation?

2. Should a corporation also be subject to a social responsibility test other than profit making when conducting business? Explain.

3. Should shareholders be allowed to challenge the decisions of corporate directors?

Internet Exercises

1. Use an Internet search engine to find the advertising slogans for the following restaurants or products: Burger King, Domino's, Pepsi, and Coca-Cola. Do they create a factual impression? Or are they mere "puffing"?

2. Visit the website of Walmart Watch, at **www.walmartwatch.com**. What is the purpose of this group? Go to McDonald's website **www.mcdonalds.ca/NutritionCalculator/index_en.html**. Say that you are planning to eat a BigMac, large French fries, and a large chocolate shake at McDonald's. How many calories are in this meal? How many grams of fat? If you have been to a McDonald's restaurant, have you seen this information? If you are ever at a McDonald's restaurant, ask to see the information.

3. Visit the website **http://media.corporate-ir.net/media_files/IROL/11/112761/corpgov/Ethics%20_Current.pdf**. This is the "Statement of Ethics" of the Wal-Mart Corporation. Read "A Message from Our Chairman and President & CEO" on page 2. Also read "Guiding Ethical Principles" on page 3.

Endnotes

1. **Web** 2004 Cal. Lexis 3284 (Supreme Court of California).
2. 31 U.S.C. Sections 3729–3733.
3. 204 Mich. 459, 170 N.W. 668, **Web** 1919 Mich. Lexis 720 (Supreme Court of Michigan).
4. Milton Friedman, "The Social Responsibility of Business Is to Increase Its Profits," *New York Times Magazine*, September 13, 1970.

CHAPTER

3

Courts, Jurisdiction, and Administrative Agencies

U.S. DISTRICT COURT, LAS VEGAS, NEVADA
This is the Lloyd D. George United States District Court for the District of Nevada, which is located in Las Vegas, Nevada. This is a federal trial court. This court, along with the other U.S. district courts located throughout the country, hears and decides lawsuits concerning matters over which it has jurisdiction. State, Washington, DC, and U.S. territory courts hear and decide matters over which they have jurisdiction. The process of bringing and defending lawsuits, preparing for court, and the trial itself is complicated, time-consuming, and expensive.

Learning Objectives

After studying this chapter, you should be able to:

1. Describe state court systems.
2. Describe the federal court system.
3. Compare the jurisdiction of state courts with that of federal courts.
4. List and describe the types of decisions that are issued by the U.S. Supreme Court.
5. Describe administrative agencies and the main features of administrative law.

Chapter Outline

Introduction to Courts, Jurisdiction, and Administrative Agencies

State Court Systems
  CONTEMPORARY ENVIRONMENT • *Delaware Courts Specialize in Hearing Business Disputes*

Federal Court System

Supreme Court of the United States
  CONTEMPORARY ENVIRONMENT • *The Process of Choosing a U.S. Supreme Court Justice*
  CONTEMPORARY ENVIRONMENT • *"I'll Take You to the U.S. Supreme Court!"*

Jurisdiction of Federal Courts
  CASE 3.1 • **U.S. SUPREME COURT** • *Hertz Corporation v. Friend*

Standing to Sue, Jurisdiction, and Venue
  LANDMARK U.S. SUPREME COURT CASE •
  International Shoe Company v. State of Washington

Chapter Outline (continued)

> " *I was never ruined but twice; once when I lost a lawsuit, and once when I won one.*"
>
> —Voltaire

Introduction to Courts, Jurisdiction, and Administrative Agencies

There are two major court systems in the United States: (1) the federal court system and (2) the court systems of the 50 states, Washington, DC (District of Columbia), and territories of the United States. Each of these systems has jurisdiction to hear different types of lawsuits.

Federal and state governments have created administrative agencies to assist in implementing and enforcing laws. The operation of these administrative agencies is governed by a body of administrative law.

This chapter discusses the federal court system, state court systems, jurisdiction of courts, and administrative agencies.

The glorious uncertainty of law.

Thomas Wilbraham
A toast at a dinner of judges and counsel at Serjeants' Inn Hall

State Court Systems

Each state, Washington, DC, and each territory of the United States has its own separate court system (hereafter collectively referred to as **state courts**). Most state court systems include the following: *limited-jurisdiction trial courts, general-jurisdiction trial courts, intermediate appellate courts*, and a *supreme court*.

Limited-Jurisdiction Trial Courts

State **limited-jurisdiction trial courts**, which are sometimes referred to as **inferior trial courts**, hear matters of a specialized or limited nature.

Examples Traffic courts, juvenile courts, justice-of-the-peace courts, probate courts, family law courts, and courts that hear misdemeanor criminal law cases are limited-jurisdiction courts in many states.

Because limited-jurisdiction courts are trial courts, evidence can be introduced and testimony can be given. Most limited-jurisdiction courts keep records

limited-jurisdiction trial court (inferior trial court)
A court that hears matters of a specialized or limited nature.

of their proceedings. A decision of such a court can usually be appealed to a general-jurisdiction court or an appellate court.

Many states have also created **small claims courts** to hear civil cases involving small dollar amounts (e.g., $5,000 or less). Generally, the parties must appear individually and cannot have lawyers represent them. The decisions of small claims courts are often appealable to general-jurisdiction trial courts or appellate courts.

General-Jurisdiction Trial Courts

general-jurisdiction trial court (court of record)
A court that hears cases of a general nature that is not within the jurisdiction of limited-jurisdiction trial courts. Testimony and evidence at trial are recorded and stored for future reference.

Every state has a **general-jurisdiction trial court**. These courts are often referred to as **courts of record** because the testimony and evidence at trial are recorded and stored for future reference. These courts hear cases that are not within the jurisdiction of limited-jurisdiction trial courts, such as felonies, civil cases more than a certain dollar amount, and so on.

Some states divide their general-jurisdiction courts into two divisions, one for criminal cases and one for civil cases. Evidence and testimony are given at general-jurisdiction trial courts. The decisions handed down by these courts are appealable to an intermediate appellate court or the state supreme court, depending on the circumstances.

Intermediate Appellate Courts

intermediate appellate court (appellate court or court of appeal)
A court that hears appeals from trial courts.

In many states, **intermediate appellate courts** (also called **appellate courts** or **courts of appeal**) hear appeals from trial courts. They review the trial court record to determine whether there have been any errors at trial that would require reversal or modification of the trial court's decision. Thus, an appellate court reviews either pertinent parts or the whole trial court record from the lower court. No new evidence or testimony is permitted.

The parties usually file legal *briefs* with the appellate court stating the law and facts that support their positions. Appellate courts usually grant a brief oral hearing to the parties. Appellate court decisions are appealable to the state's highest court. In sparsely populated states that do not have an intermediate appellate court, trial court decisions can be appealed directly to the state's highest court.

Highest State Court

highest state court
The highest court in a state court system; it hears appeals from intermediate appellate state courts and certain trial courts.

There is a **highest state court** of each state's court system. Many states call this highest court the **state supreme court**. Some states use other names for their highest courts. The function of a state's highest court is to hear appeals from intermediate appellate state courts and certain trial courts. No new evidence or testimony is heard. The parties usually submit pertinent parts of or the entire lower court record for review. The parties also submit legal briefs to the court and are usually granted a brief oral hearing. Decisions of highest state courts are final unless a question of law is involved that is appealable to the U.S. Supreme Court.

Exhibit 3.1 portrays a typical state court system. **Exhibit 3.2** lists the websites for the court systems of 50 states, Washington, DC, and territories associated with the United States.

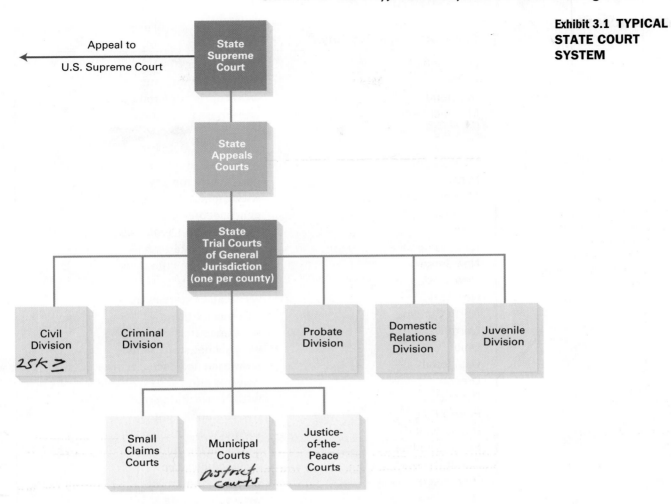

Exhibit 3.1 TYPICAL STATE COURT SYSTEM

Appeal to U.S. Supreme Court

State Supreme Court

State Appeals Courts

State Trial Courts of General Jurisdiction (one per county)

Civil Division

25K ≥

Criminal Division

Probate Division

Domestic Relations Division

Juvenile Division

Small Claims Courts

Municipal Courts

District Courts

Justice-of-the-Peace Courts

Exhibit 3.2 STATE, WASHINGTON, DC, AND TERRITORY COURT SYSTEMS

State, District, or Territory	Website
Alabama	www.judicial.state.al.us
Alaska	www.state.ak.us/courts
Arizona	www.supreme.state.az.us
Arkansas	www.courts.state.ar.us
California	www.courtinfo.ca.gov/courts
Colorado	www.courts.state.co.us
Connecticut	www.jud.state.ct.us
Delaware	www.courts.state.de.us
District of Columbia	www.dccourts.gov
Florida	www.flcourts.org
Georgia	georgiacourts.org
Guam	www.guamsupremecourt.com
Hawaii	www.courts.state.hi.us
Idaho	www.isc.idaho.gov
Illinois	www.state.il.us/court
Indiana	www.in.gov/judiciary
Iowa	www.judicial.state.ia.us
Kansas	www.kscourts.org
Kentucky	www.courts.ky.gov

Exhibit 3.2 (*CONTINUED*)

State, District, or Territory	Website
Louisiana	www.lasc.org
Maine	www.courts.state.me.us
Maryland	www.courts.state.md.us
Massachusetts	www.mass.gov/courts
Michigan	www.courts.michigan.gov
Minnesota	www.courts.state.mn.us
Mississippi	www.mssc.state.ms.us
Missouri	www.courts.mo.gov
Montana	www.montanacourts.org
Nebraska	court.nol.org
Nevada	www.nvsupremecourt.us
New Hampshire	www.courts.state.nh.us
New Jersey	www.judiciary.state.nj.us
New Mexico	www.nmcourts.com
New York	www.courts.state.ny.us
North Carolina	www.nccourts.org
North Dakota	www.ndcourts.com
Ohio	www.sconet.state.oh.us
Oklahoma	www.oscn.net/oscn/schome
Oregon	www.ojd.state.or.us
Pennsylvania	www.courts.state.pa.us
Puerto Rico	www.tribunalpr.org
Rhode Island	www.courts.state.ri.us
South Carolina	www.judicial.state.sc.us
South Dakota	www.sdjudicial.com
Tennessee	www.tsc.state.tn.us
Texas	www.courts.state.tx.us
Utah	www.utcourts.gov
Vermont	www.vermontjudiciary.org
Virginia	www.courts.state.va.us
Virgin Islands	www.visuperiorcourt.org
Washington	www.courts.wa.gov
Washington, DC	www.dccourts.org
West Virginia	www.wv.gov
Wisconsin	www.wicourts.gov
Wyoming	www.courts.state.wy.us

The following feature discusses special business courts.

Contemporary Environment

Delaware Courts Specialize in Hearing Business Disputes

In most states, business and commercial disputes are heard by the same courts that hear and decide criminal, landlord–tenant, matrimonial, medical malpractice, and other non-business-related cases. One major exception to this standard has been the state of Delaware, where a special chancery court hears and decides business litigation. The CC **Delaware Court of Chancery**, which decides cases involving corporate governance, fiduciary duties of corporate officers and directors, mergers and acquisitions, and other business issues, has earned a reputation for its expertise in handling and deciding corporate matters. Perhaps the existence of this special court and a corporation code that tends to favor corporate management are the primary reasons that more than 50 percent of the corporations listed on the New York Stock Exchange (NYSE) and the NASDAQ stock exchange are incorporated in Delaware.

Businesses tend to favor special commercial courts because the judges presiding over business cases have the expertise to handle complex commercial lawsuits. The courts are also expected to be more efficient in deciding

business-related cases, thus saving time and money for the parties. Other states are also establishing courts that specialize in commercial matters.

WEB EXERCISE
Go to the website of the Delaware Court of Chancery, at **www.courts .delaware.gov/Chancery**. Read the brief description of the court on this page.

STATE COURT
This is a county courthouse in the state of Michigan. Each state, the District of Columbia, and territories administered by the United States have their own court system. Most counties have a general-jurisdiction trial court. State courts resolve more than 95 percent of the lawsuits brought in this country.

Federal Court System

Article III of the U.S. Constitution provides that the federal government's judicial power is vested in one "Supreme Court." This court is the U.S. Supreme Court. Article III also authorizes Congress to establish "inferior" federal courts. Pursuant to its Article III power, Congress has established the U.S. district courts, the U.S. courts of appeals, and the U.S. bankruptcy courts. Pursuant to other authority in the Constitution, the U.S. Congress has established other federal courts. Federal judges of the U.S. Supreme Court, U.S. courts of appeals, and U.S. district courts are appointed for life by the president, with the advice and consent of the Senate. Judges of other courts are not appointed for life but are appointed for various periods of time (e.g., bankruptcy court judges are appointed for 14-year terms).

Special Federal Courts

The **special federal courts** established by Congress have limited jurisdiction. They include the following:

- **U.S. Tax Court.**   The **U.S. Tax Court** hears cases that involve federal tax laws. Website: **www.ustaxcourt.gov**.
- **U.S. Court of Federal Claims.**   The **U.S. Court of Federal Claims** hears cases brought against the United States. Website: **www.uscfc.uscourts.gov**.
- **U.S. Court of International Trade.**   The **U.S. Court of International Trade** handles cases that involve tariffs and international trade disputes. Website: **www.cit.uscourts.gov**.
- **U.S. Bankruptcy Court.**   The **U.S. Bankruptcy Court** hears cases that involve federal bankruptcy laws. Website: **www.uscourts.gov/bankruptcycourts.html**.
- **U.S. Court of Appeals for the Armed Forces.**   The **U.S. Court of Appeals for the Armed Forces** exercises appellate jurisdiction over members of the armed services. Website: **www.armfor.uscourts.gov**.
- **U.S. Court of Appeals for Veterans Claims.**   The **U.S. Court of Appeals for Veterans Claims** exercises jurisdiction over decisions of the Department of Veterans Affairs. Website: **www.uscourts.cavc.gov**.

U.S. District Courts

The **U.S. district courts** are the federal court system's trial courts of *general jurisdiction*. There are 94 U.S. district courts. There is at least one federal district court in each state and the District of Columbia, and heavily populated states have more than one district court. The geographical area served by each court is referred to as a **district**. The federal district courts are empowered to impanel juries, receive evidence, hear testimony, and decide cases. Most federal cases originate in federal district courts.

U.S. Courts of Appeals

The **U.S. courts of appeals** are the federal court system's intermediate appellate courts. There are 13 circuits in the federal court system. The first 12 are geographical. Eleven are designated by numbers, such as the "First Circuit," "Second Circuit," and so on. The geographical area served by each court is referred to as a **circuit**. The 12th circuit court, located in Washington, DC, is called the **District of Columbia Circuit**.

Congress created the 13th court of appeals in 1982. It is called the **Court of Appeals for the Federal Circuit** and is located in Washington, DC.[1] This court has special appellate jurisdiction to review the decisions of the Court of Federal Claims, the Patent and Trademark Office, and the Court of International Trade. This court was created to provide uniformity in the application of federal law in certain areas, particularly patent law.

As an appellate court, each of these courts hears appeals from the district courts located in its circuit as well as from certain special courts and federal administrative agencies. An appellate court reviews the record of the lower court or administrative agency proceedings to determine whether there has been any error that would warrant reversal or modification of the lower court decision. No new evidence or testimony is heard. The parties file legal briefs with the court and are given a short oral hearing. The judges of U.S. courts of appeals vary from approximately six to thirty. Appeals are usually heard by a three-judge panel. After a decision is rendered by the three-judge panel, a petitioner can request an *en banc* review by the full appeals court.

Exhibit 3.3 shows a map of the 13 federal circuit courts of appeals. Exhibit 3.4 lists the websites of the 13 U.S. courts of appeals.

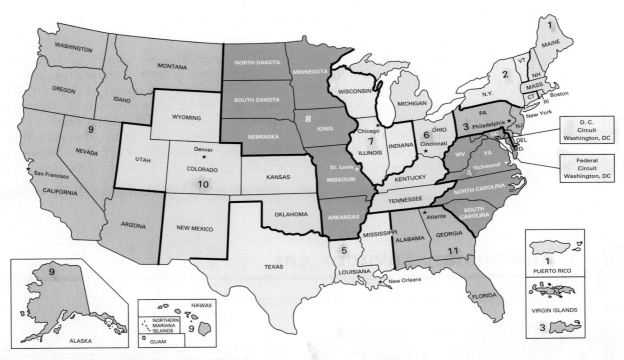

Exhibit 3.3 MAP OF THE FEDERAL CIRCUIT COURTS

Exhibit 3.4 FEDERAL COURTS OF APPEAL

United States Court of Appeals	Main Office	Website
First Circuit	Boston, Massachusetts	www.ca1.uscourts.gov
Second Circuit	New York, New York	www.ca2.uscourts.gov
Third Circuit	Philadelphia, Pennsylvania	www.ca3.uscourts.gov
Fourth Circuit	Richmond, Virginia	www.ca4.uscourts.gov
Fifth Circuit	Houston, Texas	www.ca5.uscourts.gov
Sixth Circuit	Cincinnati, Ohio	www.ca6.uscourts.gov
Seventh Circuit	Chicago, Illinois	www.ca7.uscourts.gov
Eighth Circuit	St. Paul, Minnesota	www.ca8.uscourts.gov
Ninth Circuit	San Francisco, California	www.ca9.uscourts.gov
Tenth Circuit	Denver, Colorado	www.ca10.uscourts.gov
Eleventh Circuit	Atlanta, Georgia	www.ca11.uscourts.gov
District of Columbia	Washington, DC	www.dcd.uscourts.gov
Court of Appeals for the Federal Circuit	Washington, DC	www.cafc.uscourts.gov

Supreme Court of the United States

The highest court in the land is the **Supreme Court of the United States**, also called the **U.S. Supreme Court**, which is located in Washington, DC. The Court is composed of nine justices who are nominated by the president and confirmed by the Senate. The president appoints one justice as **chief justice**. The **Chief Justice of the U.S. Supreme Court** is responsible for the administration of the Supreme Court. The other eight justices are **Associate Justices of the U.S. Supreme Court**.

Supreme Court of the United States (U.S. Supreme Court)
The highest court in the United States, located in Washington, DC. The Supreme Court was created by Article III of the U.S. Constitution.

Following is Alexis de Tocqueville's description of the Supreme Court's role in U.S. society:

> *The peace, the prosperity, and the very existence of the Union are vested in the hands of the justices of the Supreme Court. Without them, the Constitution would be a dead letter: the executive appeals to them for assistance against the encroachments of the legislative power; the legislature demands their protection against the assaults of the executive; they defend the Union from the disobedience of the states, the states from the exaggerated claims of the Union; the public interest against private interests, and the conservative spirit of stability against the fickleness of the democracy.*

The following feature discusses the process of choosing a U.S. Supreme Court justice.

Contemporary Environment

The Process of Choosing a U.S. Supreme Court Justice

In an effort to strike a balance of power between the executive and legislative branches of government, Article II, Section 2, of the U.S. Constitution gives the president the power to appoint Supreme Court justices "with the advice and consent of the Senate." This means that the majority of the one hundred senators must approve the president's nominee in order for that nominee to become a justice of the U.S. Supreme Court.

In 1993, President Bill Clinton, a Democrat, with the consent of the Senate, placed Ruth Bader Ginsburg, a moderate liberal, on the Court. She was the second female to serve on the U.S. Supreme Court.

President George W. Bush, a Republican, placed two justices on the Supreme Court. In 2005, when presiding Chief Justice Rehnquist died, President Bush nominated John G. Roberts, Jr., to be the next chief justice of the Supreme Court. Justice Roberts, a conservative, was easily confirmed by the Senate. In the same year, Justice Sandra Day O'Connor, the centrist vote on the Court, resigned from the Supreme Court. President Bush nominated Samuel A. Alito, Jr., a conservative, to fill the vacancy. Justice Alito was confirmed by a majority vote of the Senate.

President Barack Obama was inaugurated as president in January 2009. Within months after taking office, he had the opportunity to nominate a justice for the U.S. Supreme when

Justice Souter retired from the Court. President Obama nominated Sonia Sotomayor, a liberal, for the seat. Sotomayor was born in the Bronx, New York City, and is of Puerto Rican descent. As a child, she was raised in public housing projects. Sotomayor graduated from Princeton and then Yale Law School, attending both schools on scholarships. After practicing law, she served as a U.S. District Court judge and a U.S. Court of Appeals justice of the federal court system. Sotomayor was confirmed to the Supreme Court by a majority vote of the U.S. Senate, becoming the first Hispanic person to be a justice of the U.S. Supreme Court and the third female appointed to the Court.

In 2010, President Obama had a second opportunity to nominate another justice, when 90-year-old Justice Stevens retired. The president nominated Elena Kagan, the U.S. solicitor general. Kagan clerked for Justice Thurgood Marshall when he was a justice of the Supreme Court. Kagan, although not a judge, was a constitutional law professor at the University of Chicago and Harvard University law schools and served as dean of Harvard Law School. Kagan was confirmed by a majority vote of the U.S. Senate.

A president who is elected to one or two four-year terms in office may have the opportunity to nominate justices to the U.S. Supreme Court who, if confirmed, may serve many years after the president leaves office.

WEB EXERCISE
Go to **www.supremecourt.gov/about/members.aspx**. Click on the names of the current members of the U.S. Supreme Court and read their short biographies.

Jurisdiction of the U.S. Supreme Court

The Supreme Court, which is an appellate court, hears appeals from federal circuit courts of appeals and, under certain circumstances, from federal district courts, special federal courts, and the highest state courts. No new evidence or testimony is heard. As with other appellate courts, the lower court record is reviewed to determine whether there has been an error that warrants a reversal or modification of the decision. Legal briefs are filed, and the parties are granted a brief oral hearing. The Supreme Court's decision is final.

The federal court system is illustrated in **Exhibit 3.5**.

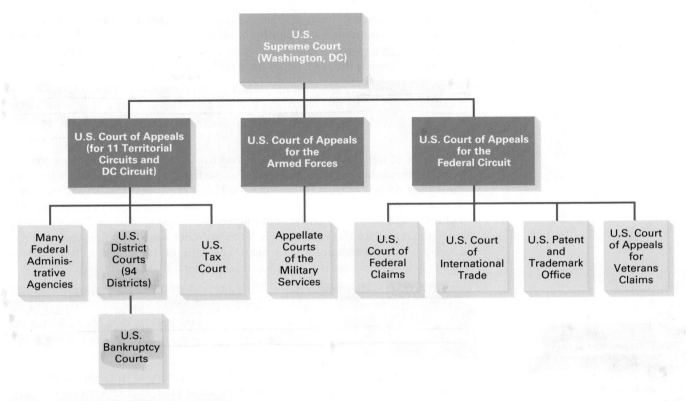

Exhibit 3.5 FEDERAL COURTS OF APPEAL

Decisions of the U.S. Supreme Court

The U.S. Constitution gives Congress the authority to establish rules for the appellate review of cases by the Supreme Court, except in the rare case in which mandatory review is required. Congress has given the Supreme Court discretion to decide what cases it will hear.[2]

A petitioner must file a **petition for certiorari**, asking the Supreme Court to hear the case. If the Court decides to review a case, it issues a **writ of certiorari**. Because the Court issues only about one hundred opinions each year, writs are usually granted only in cases involving constitutional and other important issues.

Each justice of the Supreme Court, including the chief justice, has an equal vote. The Supreme Court can issue several types of decisions:

1. **Unanimous decision.**   If all the justices voting agree as to the outcome and reasoning used to decide a case, it is a **unanimous decision**. Unanimous decisions are precedent for later cases.

   Example Suppose all nine justices hear a case, and all nine agree to the outcome (e.g., the petitioner wins) and the reason why (e.g., the Equal Protection Clause of the U.S. Constitution had been violated); this is a unanimous decision. This unanimous decision becomes precedent for later cases.

2. **Majority decision.**   If a majority of the justices agree as to the outcome and reasoning used to decide a case, it is a **majority decision**. Majority decisions are precedent for later cases. A majority decision occurs if five, six, seven, or eight justices vote for the same outcome for the same reason.

   Example If all nine justices hear a case, and five of them agree as to the outcome (e.g., the petitioner wins) and all of these five justices agree to the same reason

petition for certiorari
A petition asking the Supreme Court to hear a case.

writ of certiorari
An official notice that the Supreme Court will review a case.

Sancho: But if this is hell, why do we see no lawyers?

Clarindo: They won't receive them, lest they bring lawsuits here.

Sancho: If there are no lawsuits here, hell's not so bad.

Lope de Vega
The Star of Seville,
Act 3, Scene 2

why (e.g., the Equal Protection Clause of the U.S. Constitution has been violated), it is a majority opinion. The majority opinion becomes precedent for later cases and has the same force of law as a unanimous decision. The votes of the remaining four justices for the respondent have no legal effect whatsoever.

3. **Plurality decision.** If a majority of the justices agree as to the outcome of a case but not as to the reasoning for reaching the outcome, it is a **plurality decision**. A plurality decision settles the case but is not precedent for later cases.

Example If all nine justices hear a case, and five of them agree as to the outcome (e.g., the petitioner wins), but not all of these five agree to the reason why (e.g., three base their vote on a violation of the Equal Protection Clause and two base their vote on a violation of the Due Process Clause of the U.S. Constitution), it is a plurality decision. Five justices have agreed to the same outcome, but those five have not agreed for the same reason. The petitioner wins his or her case, but the decision is not precedent for later cases. The votes of the remaining four justices for the respondent have no legal effect whatsoever.

4. **Tie decision.** Sometimes the Supreme Court sits without all nine justices being present. This could happen because of illness, conflict of interest, or a justice not having been confirmed to fill a vacant seat on the Court. If there is a **tie decision**, the lower court decision is affirmed. Such votes are not precedent for later cases.

Example A petitioner wins her case at the U.S. Court of Appeals. At the U.S. Supreme Court, only eight justices hear the case. Four justices vote for the petitioner, and four justices vote for the respondent. This is a tie vote. The petitioner remains the winner because she won at the Court of Appeals. This decision of the Supreme Court sets no precedent for later cases.

A justice who agrees with the outcome of a case but not the reason proffered by other justices can issue a **concurring opinion** that sets forth his or her reasons for deciding the case. A justice who does not agree with a decision can file a **dissenting opinion** that sets forth the reasons for his or her dissent.

The following feature discusses the process for having a case heard by the U.S. Supreme Court.

WEB EXERCISE
Go to the website of the U.S. Supreme Court, at **www.supremecourtus.gov**. Who are the nine justices of the U.S. Supreme Court? Who is the Chief Justice? Who was the last Supreme Court justice appointed to the Court?

Contemporary Environment

"I'll Take You to the U.S. Supreme Court!"

In reality, the chance of ever having a case heard by the highest court is slim to none. Each year, approximately ten thousand petitioners ask the Supreme Court to hear their cases. In recent years, the Supreme Court has accepted only fewer than one hundred of these cases for full review each term.

Each of the nine Supreme Court justices has law clerks—recent law school graduates usually chosen from elite law schools across the country—who assist them. The justices rarely read the appellate petitions but instead delegate this task to their law clerks. A clerk writes a short memorandum, discussing the key issues raised by the appeal, and recommends to the justices whether they should grant or deny a review. The justices meet once a week to discuss what cases merit review. The votes of four justices are necessary to grant an appeal and schedule

an oral argument before the Court; this is called the **rule of four**. Written opinions by the justices are usually issued many months later.

So what does it take to win a review by the Supreme Court? The U.S. Supreme Court usually decides to hear cases involving major constitutional questions, such as freedom of speech, freedom of religion, equal protection, and due process. The Supreme Court also hears many cases involving the interpretation of statutes enacted by Congress. The Court rarely decides day-to-day legal issues such as breach of contract, tort liability, or corporations law unless they involve more important constitutional or federal law questions.

So the next time you hear someone say, "I'll take you to the U.S. Supreme Court!" just say, "Probably not!"

Jurisdiction of Federal Courts

Article III, Section 2, of the U.S. Constitution sets forth the jurisdiction of federal courts. Federal courts have *limited jurisdiction* to hear cases involving a *federal question* or *diversity of citizenship*. These are each discussed in the following paragraphs.

Federal Question

The federal courts have subject matter jurisdiction to hear cases involving "federal questions." **Federal question cases** are cases arising under the U.S. Constitution, treaties, and federal statutes and regulations. There is no dollar-amount limit on federal question cases that can be brought in federal court.[3]

federal question case
A case arising under the U.S. Constitution, treaties, or federal statutes and regulations.

Example A defendant is sued by a plaintiff for engaging in insider trading, in violation of the Securities Exchange Act of 1934, which is a federal statute. This lawsuit involves a federal question, a federal statute, and therefore qualifies to be brought in federal court.

Diversity of Citizenship

A case may be brought in federal court even though it involves a nonfederal subject matter question, which would usually be heard by state, Washington, DC, or territory courts, if there is diversity of citizenship. **Diversity of citizenship** occurs if a lawsuit involves (1) citizens of different states or (2) a citizen of a state and a citizen or subject of a foreign country. A corporation is considered to be a citizen of the state in which it is incorporated and in which it has its principal place of business.

diversity of citizenship
A means for bringing a lawsuit in federal court that involves a nonfederal question if the parties are (1) citizens of different states or (2) a citizen of a state and a citizen or subject of a foreign country.

If there is diversity of citizenship, the plaintiff may bring the case in either state or federal court. If a plaintiff brings a diversity of citizenship case in federal court, it remains there. If the plaintiff brings a diversity of citizenship case in state court, it remains there unless the defendant removes the case to federal court. Federal courts must apply the relevant state law to diversity of citizenship cases.

The original reason for providing diversity of citizenship jurisdiction to federal courts was to prevent state court bias against nonresidents, although this reason has been questioned as irrelevant in modern times. The federal court must apply the appropriate state's law in deciding the case. The dollar amount of the controversy must exceed the sum or value of $75,000.[4] If this requirement is not met, action must be brought in the appropriate state, Washington, DC, or territory court.

Example Henry, a resident of the state of Idaho, is driving his automobile in the state of Idaho when he negligently hits an automobile driven by Mary, a resident of the state of New York. Mary is injured in the accident. There is no federal question involved in this case; it is an automobile accident that involves state negligence law. However, there is diversity of citizenship in this case because the parties are residents of different states. Therefore, Mary can sue Henry and bring her case in federal court in Idaho, and if she does, the case will remain in federal court. If she brings the case in Idaho state court, the case will remain in Idaho state court unless Henry has the case removed to federal court. If this case is heard by a federal court, the court must apply Idaho law to the case.

Federal courts have **exclusive jurisdiction** to hear cases involving federal crimes, antitrust, bankruptcy, patent and copyright cases, suits against the United States, and to most admiralty cases. State courts cannot hear these cases.

CONCEPT SUMMARY

JURISDICTION OF FEDERAL COURTS

Type of Jurisdiction	Description
Federal question	Cases arising under the U.S. Constitution, treaties, and federal statutes and regulations. There is no dollar-amount limit for federal question cases that can be brought in federal court.
Diversity of citizenship	Cases between citizens of different states or between a citizen of a state and a citizen or subject of a foreign country. Federal courts must apply the appropriate state law in such cases. The controversy must exceed $75,000 for the federal court to hear the case.

The following U.S. Supreme Court case involves diversity of citizenship jurisdiction when a corporation is a party to a lawsuit.

CASE 3.1   *U.S. SUPREME COURT Diversity of Citizenship*

Hertz Corporation v. Friend

130 S.Ct. 43, 174 L.Ed.2d 627, Web 2009 U.S. Lexis 5114 (2009)
Supreme Court of the United States

"A corporation shall be deemed to be a citizen of any State by which it has been incorporated and of the State where it has its principal place of business."

—Breyer, Justice

Facts

Melinda Friend, a California citizen, sued the Hertz Corporation in California state court, seeking damages for Hertz's alleged violation of California's wage and hour laws. Hertz filed notice to remove the case to federal court, asserting diversity of citizenship of the parties. Friend argued that because Hertz operated more than 270 rental car locations and had more than 2,000 employees in California, it was a citizen of California, and diversity of citizenship did not apply and the case could not be moved to federal court. Hertz alleged that because it was incorporated in the state of Delaware and its headquarters office was in the state of New Jersey, it was a citizen of those states and not a citizen of California. Hertz concluded that because it was not a citizen of California but plaintiff Friend was, there was diversity of citizenship, and Friend's California state court action could be moved to federal court. The U.S. District Court held that Hertz was a citizen of California and that the case could not be moved to federal court. The U.S. Court of Appeals affirmed this decision. Hertz appealed to the U.S. Supreme Court.

Issue

Is Hertz Corporation a citizen of California?

Language of the U.S. Supreme Court

The federal diversity jurisdiction statute provides that "a corporation shall be deemed to be a citizen of any State by which it has been incorporated and of the State where it has its principal place of business" 28 U. S. C. §1332(c)(1). And we conclude that the phrase "principal place of business" refers to the place where the corporation's high level officers direct, control, and coordinate the corporation's activities. Lower federal courts have often metaphorically called that place the corporation's "nerve center." We believe that the "nerve center" will typically be found at a corporation's headquarters. The metaphor of a corporate "brain," while not precise, suggests a single location.

Decision of the U.S. Supreme Court

The U.S. Supreme Court held that Hertz's corporate headquarters—its nerve center—is located in New Jersey, not California. As such, there is diversity of citizenship with Friend, a California citizen, and the case could be moved to federal court. The plaintiff will get her day in court, but it will be in federal court and not California state court.

Case Questions

Critical Legal Thinking

What is diversity of citizenship? What is the public policy for recognizing diversity of citizenship jurisdiction of federal courts?

Ethics

Was it ethical for Hertz to try to avoid trial in California state court? Why would Hertz want the case tried in federal court rather than in state court?

Contemporary Business

What are the consequences of this decision for corporations and for plaintiffs who are suing corporations?

Note   Hertz has sufficient "minimum contacts" with California to be subject to suit in California. However, because of diversity of citizenship, the case will be heard by a federal court located in California and not in California state court. The federal court will apply California law in deciding the case. Hertz is a citizen of Delaware, where its articles of incorporation are filed, and of New Jersey, where its headquarters is located. If Hertz was sued in the state court in either of these two states, there is no diversity of citizenship, and Hertz could not remove the case to federal court.

Jurisdiction of State Courts

State courts and the courts of Washington, DC, and territories of the United States have jurisdiction to hear cases that federal courts do not have jurisdiction to hear. These usually involve laws of states, Washington, DC, territories, and local governments (e.g., cities, counties).

Examples Cases involving real estate, corporations, partnerships, limited liability companies, contracts, sales and lease contracts, and negotiable instruments are usually state law subject matters. (Remember that state law cases that involve diversity of citizenship can be heard by federal courts.)

State courts have **concurrent jurisdiction** with federal courts to hear cases involving diversity of citizenship and federal questions over which federal courts do not have exclusive jurisdiction. If a case involving concurrent jurisdiction is brought by a plaintiff in federal court, the case remains in federal court. If the plaintiff brings a case involving concurrent jurisdiction in state court, the defendant can either let the case be decided by the state court or remove the case to federal court. If a case does not qualify to be brought in federal court, it must be brought in the appropriate state court.

Exhibit 3.6 illustrates the jurisdiction of federal and state courts.

Exhibit 3.6 JURISDICTION OF FEDERAL AND STATE COURTS

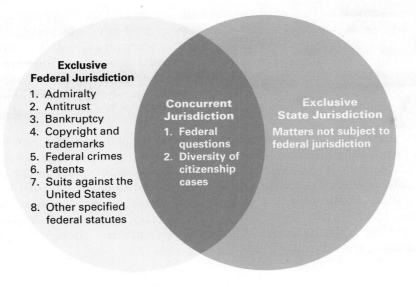

Exclusive Federal Jurisdiction

1. Admiralty
2. Antitrust
3. Bankruptcy
4. Copyright and trademarks
5. Federal crimes
6. Patents
7. Suits against the United States
8. Other specified federal statutes

Concurrent Jurisdiction

1. Federal questions
2. Diversity of citizenship cases

Exclusive State Jurisdiction

Matters not subject to federal jurisdiction

Standing to Sue, Jurisdiction, and Venue

Not every court has the authority to hear all types of cases. First, to bring a lawsuit in a court, the plaintiff must have *standing to sue*. In addition, the court must have *personal jurisdiction* or other jurisdiction to hear the case, and the case must be brought in the proper *venue*. These topics are discussed in the following paragraphs.

Standing to Sue

standing to sue
Some stake in the outcome of a lawsuit.

To bring a lawsuit, a plaintiff must have **standing to sue**. This means the plaintiff must have some stake in the outcome of the lawsuit.

Example Linda's friend Jon is injured in an accident caused by Emily. Jon refuses to sue. Linda cannot sue Emily on Jon's behalf because she does not have an interest in the result of the case.

A few states now permit investors to invest money in a lawsuit for a percentage return of any award of judgment. Courts hear and decide actual disputes involving specific controversies. Hypothetical questions will not be heard, and trivial lawsuits will be dismissed.

In Personam Jurisdiction

***in personam* jurisdiction (personal jurisdiction)**
Jurisdiction over the parties to a lawsuit.

service of process
A summons being served on a defendant to obtain personal jurisdiction over him or her.

A court's jurisdiction over a person is called ***in personam* jurisdiction**, or **personal jurisdiction**. A *plaintiff*, by filing a lawsuit with a court, gives the court *in personam* jurisdiction over himself or herself. The court must also have *in personam* jurisdiction over the *defendant*, which is usually obtained by having a summons served to that person within the territorial boundaries of the state (i.e., **service of process**). Service of process is usually accomplished by personal service of the summons and complaint on the defendant.

If personal service is not possible, alternative forms of notice, such as mailing of the summons or publication of a notice in a newspaper, may be permitted. A corporation is subject to personal jurisdiction in the state in which it is incorporated, has its principal office, or is doing business.

A party who disputes the jurisdiction of a court can make a *special appearance* in that court to argue against imposition of jurisdiction. Service of process is not permitted during such an appearance.

long-arm statute
A statute that extends a state's jurisdiction to nonresidents who were not served a summons within the state.

Long-Arm Statute In most states, a state court can obtain jurisdiction in a civil lawsuit over persons and businesses located in another state or country through the state's **long-arm statute**. These statutes extend a state's jurisdiction to nonresidents who were not served a summons within the state. The nonresident defendant in the civil lawsuit must have had some **minimum contact** with the state such that the maintenance of that lawsuit in that state does not offend traditional notions of fair play and substantial justice.[5]

The exercise of long-arm jurisdiction is generally permitted over nonresidents who have (1) committed torts within the state (e.g., caused an automobile accident in the state), (2) entered into a contract either in the state or that affects the state (and allegedly breached the contract), or (3) transacted other business in the state that allegedly caused injury to another person.

Following is the landmark U.S. Supreme Court case that established the minimum contacts standard.

LANDMARK U.S. SUPREME COURT CASE

International Shoe Company v. State of Washington

How far can a state go to require a person or business to defend himself, herself, or itself in a court of law in that state? That question was presented to the Supreme Court of the United States in the landmark case *International Shoe Company v. State of Washington*.[6]

The International Shoe Company was a Delaware corporation that had its principal place of business in St. Louis, Missouri. The company manufactured and distributed shoes throughout the United States. The company maintained a sales force throughout the United States. In the state of Washington, its sales representative did not have a specific office but sold shoes door-to-door and sometimes at temporary locations. The sales representatives were paid commissions based on the number of shoes they sold.

The state of Washington assessed an unemployment tax on International Shoe for the sales representative it had in the state. When International Shoe failed to pay, Washington served personal service on a sales representative of the company in Washington and mailed the service of process to the company's headquarters in St. Louis. International Shoe appeared specially to argue that it did not do sufficient business in Washington to warrant having to pay unemployment taxes in that state. The office of unemployment ruled against International Shoe, and the Appeals Tribunal, the Superior Court, and the Supreme Court of Washington agreed. International Shoe appealed to the U.S. Supreme Court. In its decision, the U.S. Supreme Court stated:

Due process requires only that in order to subject a defendant to a judgment in personam, if he be not present within the territory of the forum, he have certain minimum contacts with it such that the maintenance of that suit does not offend traditional notions of fair play and substantial justice.

Applying these standards, the activities carried on in behalf of International Shoe in the state of Washington were neither irregular nor casual. They were systematic and continuous throughout the years in question. They resulted in a large volume of interstate business, in the course of which International Shoe received the benefits and protection of the laws of the state, including the right to resort to the courts for the enforcement of its rights. The obligation which is here sued upon arose out of those very activities. It is evident that these operations establish sufficient contacts or ties with the state of the forum to make it reasonable and just, according to our traditional conception of fair play and substantial justice, to permit the state to enforce the obligations which International Shoe has incurred there.

Thus, the famous "minimum contacts" test and "traditional notions of fair play and substantial justice" establish when a state may subject a person or business to the walls of its courtrooms. Obviously, this is not a bright-line test, so battles of in personam jurisdiction abound to this day.

In Rem Jurisdiction

A court may have jurisdiction to hear and decide a case because it has jurisdiction over the property of the lawsuit. This is called *in rem* jurisdiction ("jurisdiction over the thing").

Example A state court would have jurisdiction to hear a dispute over the ownership of a piece of real estate located within the state. This is so even if one or more of the disputing parties live in another state or states.

in rem jurisdiction
Jurisdiction to hear a case because of jurisdiction over the property of the lawsuit.

Quasi In Rem Jurisdiction

Sometimes a plaintiff who obtains a judgment against a defendant in one state will try to collect the judgment by attaching property of the defendant that is located in another state. This is permitted under *quasi in rem* jurisdiction, or **attachment jurisdiction**. Under the **Full Faith and Credit Clause** of the U.S. Constitution

quasi in rem jurisdiction (attachment jurisdiction)
Jurisdiction that allows a plaintiff who obtains a judgment in one state to try to collect the judgment by attaching property of the defendant located in another state.

(Article IV, Section 1), a judgment of a court of one state must be given "full faith and credit" by the courts of another state.

Example A plaintiff wins a dollar judgment against a defendant in California court. The defendant owns property in Ohio. If the defendant refuses to pay the judgment, the plaintiff can file a lawsuit in Ohio to enforce the California judgment and collect against the defendant's property in Ohio.

CONCEPT SUMMARY

IN PERSONAM, IN REM, AND QUASI IN REM JURISDICTION

Type of Jurisdiction	Description
In personam jurisdiction	With *in personam* jurisdiction, a court has jurisdiction over the parties to the lawsuit. The plaintiff submits to the jurisdiction of the court by filing the lawsuit there. Personal jurisdiction is obtained over the defendant through *service of process* to that person.
In rem jurisdiction	With *in rem* jurisdiction, a court has jurisdiction to hear and decide a case because it has jurisdiction over the property at issue in the lawsuit (e.g., real property located in the state).
Quasi in rem jurisdiction	A plaintiff who obtains a judgment against a defendant in one state may utilize the court system of another state to attach property of the defendant that is located in the second state.

Venue

venue
A concept that requires lawsuits to be heard by the court with jurisdiction that is nearest the location in which the incident occurred or where the parties reside.

Venue requires lawsuits to be heard by the court of the court system that has jurisdiction to hear the case that is located nearest to where the incident occurred, where witnesses and evidence are available, and such other relevant factors.

Example Harry, a resident of the state of Georgia, commits a felony crime in Los Angeles County, California. The California Superior Court system has jurisdiction to hear the case. The superior court located in the county of Los Angeles is the proper venue because the crime was committed in Los Angeles, the witnesses are probably from the area, and so on. Although Harry lives in Georgia, the state of Georgia is not the proper venue for this case.

Occasionally, pretrial publicity may prejudice jurors located in the proper venue. In such cases, a **change of venue** may be requested so that a more impartial jury can be found. The courts generally frown upon **forum shopping** (i.e., looking for a favorable court without a valid reason).

Forum-Selection and Choice-of-Law Clauses

One issue that often comes up when parties from different states or countries have a legal dispute is which jurisdiction's court will be used. Also, sometimes there is a dispute as to which jurisdiction's laws apply to a case. When the parties have not agreed in advance, courts must make the decision about which court has jurisdiction and what law applies. This situation causes ambiguity, and resolving it will cost the parties time and money.

forum-selection clause
A contract provision that designates a certain court to hear disputes concerning the nonperformance of a contract.

Therefore, parties sometimes agree in their contract as to what state's courts, or what federal court, or what country's court will have jurisdiction to hear a legal dispute should one arise. Such clauses in contracts are called **forum-selection clauses** or **choice of forum clauses**. Of course, the selected court must have jurisdiction to hear the case.

In addition to agreeing to a forum, the parties also often agree in contracts as to what state's law or country's law will apply in resolving a dispute. These clauses are called **choice-of-law clauses**. The selected law may be of a jurisdiction that does not have jurisdiction to hear the case.

Example Export Company, located in Shanghai, China, enters into a contract with Import Company, located in San Francisco, California, United States, whereby Export Company agrees to deliver designated goods to Import Company. In their contract, the parties agree that if there is a dispute, the Superior Court of California, located in San Francisco, will hear the case and that the United Nations Convention on Contracts for the International Sale of Goods (CISG) will be the contract law that will be applied in resolving the dispute.

choice-of-law clause
A contract provision that designates a certain state's law or country's law to be applied to disputes concerning the nonperformance of a contract.

Jurisdiction in Cyberspace

Obtaining personal jurisdiction over a defendant in another state has always been difficult for courts. Today, with the advent of the Internet and the ability of persons and businesses to reach millions of people in other states electronically, particularly through websites, modern issues arise as to whether courts have jurisdiction in cyberspace. For example, if a person in one state uses the website of an Internet seller located in another state, can the user sue the Internet seller in his or her state under that state's long-arm statute?

One seminal case that addressed jurisdiction in cyberspace was *Zippo Manufacturing Company v. Zippo Dot Com, Inc.*[7] Zippo Manufacturing Company (Zippo) manufacturers its well-known line of tobacco lighters in Bradford, Pennsylvania, and sells them worldwide. Zippo Dot Com, Inc. (Dot Com), which was a California corporation with its principal place of business and its servers located in Sunnyvale, California, operated an Internet website that transmitted information and sexually explicit material to its subscribers.

Zippo Manufacturing Company v. Zippo Dot Com, Inc.
An important case that established a test for determining when a court has jurisdiction over the owner or operator of an interactive, semi-interactive, or passive website.

Three thousand of Dot Com's 140,000 paying subscribers worldwide were located in Pennsylvania. Zippo sued Dot Com in U.S. District Court in Pennsylvania for trademark infringement. Dot Com defended, alleging that it was not subject to personal jurisdiction in Pennsylvania because the "minimum contacts" and "traditional notions of fair play and substantial justice" standards were not met and therefore did not permit Pennsylvania to assert jurisdiction over it. In addressing jurisdiction, the court created a "sliding scale" in order to measure the nature and quality of the commercial activity effectuated in a forum state through a website:

> At one end of the spectrum are situations where a defendant clearly does business over the Internet. If the defendant enters into contracts with residents of a foreign jurisdiction that involve the knowing and repeated transmission of computer files over the Internet, personal jurisdiction is proper. At the opposite end are situations where a defendant has simply posted information on an Internet Web site which is accessible to users in foreign jurisdictions. A passive Web site that does little more than make information available to those who are interested in it is not grounds for the exercise of personal jurisdiction. The middle ground is occupied by interactive Web sites where a user can exchange information with the host computer. In these cases, the exercise of jurisdiction is determined by examining the level of interactivity and commercial nature of the exchange of information that occurs on the Web site.

In applying this standard, the court found that the case involved doing business over the Internet. The court held that Dot Com was subject to personal jurisdiction under the Pennsylvania long-arm statute and ordered Dot Com to defend itself in Pennsylvania.

In the following case, a court had to decide whether it had jurisdiction over an Internet seller.

CASE 3.2   *Jurisdiction over an Internet Seller*

Chanel, Inc. v. Banks

Web 2010 U.S. Dist. Lexis 135374 (2010)
United States District Court for Maryland

"The *Zippo* court distinction between interactive, semi-interactive, and passive websites is also particularly relevant."

—Gauvey, Magistrate Judge

Facts

Chanel, Inc., is a corporate entity duly organized under the laws of the state of New York, with its principal place of business in New York City. Chanel is engaged in the business of manufacturing and distributing throughout the world various luxury goods, including handbags, wallets, and numerous other products under the federally registered trademark "Chanel" and monogram marks.

Chanel filed suit in U.S. District Court in Maryland against defendant Ladawn Banks, a resident of Florida. Chanel alleges that Banks owned and operated the fully interactive website **www.lovenamebrands.com**, through which she sold handbags and wallets bearing counterfeit trademarks identical to the registered Chanel marks. Chanel claimed that the counterfeit goods were substantially inferior in quality to Chanel's genuine goods and that the defendant's actions confused consumers as to the origin of the counterfeit goods. The goods at issue in this case were sold to a resident of Maryland. Chanel sought a default judgment against the defendant, an award of damages, and a permanent injunction against the defendant's further violation of its trademarks. The court first had to address the issue of whether it had personal jurisdiction over the defendant.

Issue

Does the court have personal jurisdiction over the defendant?

Language of the Court

According to Chanel, although defendant Banks is a resident of Florida, she conducted business in this jurisdiction via several interactive websites. The domain name "lovenamebrands.com" was registered anonymously, but shows Banks' Florida address. That defendant allegedly sold counterfeit Chanel goods via her website to a Maryland customer demonstrates that she directed electronic activity into the state and gives rise to a potential cause of action cognizable in the state's courts.

The Zippo court distinction between interactive, semi-interactive, and passive websites is also particularly relevant. Semi-interactive sites, such as defendant's website "lovenamebrands.com," are websites through which there have not occurred a high volume of transactions between the defendant and residents of the foreign jurisdiction, yet which do enable residents to exchange information with the host computer. Defendant's website at issue in this case was highly interactive and provided a platform for the commercial exchange of information, goods, and funds. Thus, this Court has personal jurisdiction over defendant in this matter.

Decision

The U.S. Court of Appeals for Maryland held that defendant Banks was subject to personal jurisdiction of the court. The Court granted default judgment to Chanel, assessed damages of $133,712 against Banks, and issued a permanent injunction prohibiting Banks from infringing on Chanel's trademarks.

Case Questions

Critical Legal Thinking
What is the Zippo test for finding jurisdiction over a website owner?

Ethics
Do you think Banks acted unethically in this case?

Contemporary Business
Has the Internet created special problems for trademark and copyright holders?

Administrative Agencies

Federal and state governments enact laws that regulate business. The legislative and executive branches of government have created numerous **administrative agencies** to assist in implementing and enforcing these laws. The operation of these administrative agencies is governed by a body of administrative law. Because of their importance, administrative agencies are informally referred to as the "fourth branch of government."

Administrative law is a combination of *substantive law* and *procedural law*. **Substantive administrative law** is the law that has been created that the administrative agency enforces—that is, the federal statute enacted by Congress or the state statute enacted by a state legislature. **Procedural administrative law** establishes the procedures that an administrative agency must follow while enforcing substantive administrative laws.

Examples Congress created the federal Environmental Protection Agency (EPA) to enforce substantive environmental laws (e.g., Clean Air Act, Clean Water Act) that protect the environment. In enforcing these laws, the EPA must follow certain established procedural rules (e.g., notice, hearing).

administrative agencies
Agencies that governments create to enforce regulatory statutes.

administrative law
Law that governments enact to regulate industries, businesses, and professionals.

Administrative Agencies

Federal and state governments create administrative agencies. **Federal administrative agencies** include the Department of Homeland Security, the federal Food and Drug Administration (FDA), the National Labor Relations Board (NLRB), and the Equal Employment Opportunity Commission (EEOC), to name a few. **State administrative agencies** include corporations departments, departments of real estate, state environmental protection agencies, and health departments. State law authorizes the creation of **local administrative agencies** such as city zoning boards, school districts, sewage districts, and such.

Some administrative agencies regulate businesses and industries collectively.

Example The federal Occupational Health and Safety Administration (OSHA) enforces safety and health standards for the workplaces of most industries and businesses in the country.

Some administrative agencies are created to regulate specific industries.

Example The Federal Communications Commission (FCC) regulates the operation of television and radio stations.

federal administrative agencies
Federal administrative agencies that are created by the U.S. Congress.

state administrative agencies
Agencies created by legislative branches of states to administer state regulatory laws.

local administrative agencies
Agencies created by cities, municipalities, and counties to administer local regulatory law.

Powers of Administrative Agencies

Administrative agencies usually have the following powers:

- **Rule making.** Many federal statutes expressly authorize an administrative agency to issue **substantive rules**. A substantive regulation is much like a statute: It has the force of law, and covered persons and businesses must adhere to it. Violators may be held civilly or criminally liable, depending on the rule.

  Example The federal Securities and Exchange Commission (SEC) has adopted rules that enforce federal securities law.

- **Judicial authority.** Administrative agencies usually have the **judicial authority** to adjudicate cases through an administrative proceeding.

  Example The federal Occupational Safety and Health Administration (OSHA) can bring agency proceedings against an employer for violating worker safety rules.

substantive rule
A rule issued by an administrative agency that has the force of law and to which covered persons and businesses must adhere.

> *Good government is an empire of laws.*
>
> John Adams
> *Thoughts on Government (1776)*

Administrative Procedure Act (APA)
A federal statute that establishes procedures for federal administrative agencies to follow while conducting their affairs.

- **Executive power.** Administrative agencies are usually granted **executive powers**, such as the power to investigate and prosecute possible violations of statutes and rules. This often includes the power to issue an **administrative subpoena** to a business or person to obtain information.

  Example The U.S. Department of Justice has the power to investigate whether companies have engaged in price fixing, in violation of federal antitrust law.

- **Licensing.** Many administrative agencies are empowered to issue a **license** before a person can engage in certain professions or businesses.

  Example The Federal Office of the Comptroller of the Currency (OCC), a federal government agency, issues charters for national banks.

The following feature discusses the federal Administrative Procedure Act.

Landmark Law

Administrative Procedure Act

In 1946, Congress enacted the **Administrative Procedure Act (APA)**.[8] This act is very important because it establishes procedures that federal administrative agencies must follow in conducting their affairs. The APA establishes notice requirements of actions that the federal agency plans to take. It requires hearings to be held in most cases, and it requires certain procedural safeguards and protocols to be followed at these proceedings. The APA also establishes how federal administrative agencies can adopt **rules and regulations**. This includes providing notice of proposed **rule making**, granting a time period for

receiving comments from the public regarding proposed rule making, and holding hearings to take evidence. The APA provides a procedure for receiving evidence and hearing requests for the granting of federal licenses (e.g., to operate a national bank). The APA also establishes notice and hearing requirements and rules for conducting agency adjudicative actions, such as actions to take away certain parties' licenses (e.g., a securities broker's licenses).

Most states have enacted administrative procedural acts that govern state administrative procedures.

Administrative Law Judge

administrative law judge (ALJ)
An employee of an administrative agency who presides over an administrative proceeding and decides questions of law and fact concerning a case.

Administrative law judges (ALJs) preside over administrative proceedings. They decide questions of law and fact concerning a case. There is no jury. An ALJ is an employee of the administrative agency. Both the administrative agency and the respondent may be represented by counsel. Witnesses may be examined and cross-examined, evidence may be introduced, objections may be made, and such. An ALJ's decision is issued in the form of an **administrative order**. The order must state the reasons for the ALJ's decision. The order becomes final if it is not appealed. An appeal consists of a review by the agency. Further appeal can be made to the appropriate federal court (in federal agency actions) or state court (in state agency actions).

Decisions of administrative law judges are subject to **judicial review**. Statutes often designate the federal or state court that has the power to review an administrative agency decision or rule.

The following feature compares the legal systems of Japan and the United States.

International Law

Judicial System of Japan

GOLDEN PAVILION, KYOTO, JAPAN

Key Terms and Concepts

Administrative agencies (55)
Administrative law (55)
Administrative law judge (ALJ) (56)
Administrative order (56)
Administrative Procedure Act (APA) (56)
Administrative subpoena (56)
Article III of the U.S. Constitution (41)
Associate Justice of the U.S. Supreme Court (43)
Change of venue (52)
Chief Justice (43)
Chief Justice of the U.S. Supreme Court (43)
Choice of forum clause (52)
Choice-of-law clause (53)
Circuit (42)
Concurrent jurisdiction (49)
Concurring opinion (46)

Court of Appeals for the Federal Circuit (42)
Delaware Court of Chancery (40)
Dissenting opinion (46)
District (42)
District of Columbia circuit (42)
Diversity of citizenship (47)
En banc review (42)
Exclusive jurisdiction (47)
Executive power (56)
Federal administrative agency (55)
Federal question case (47)
Forum shopping (52)
Forum-selection clause (52)
Full Faith and Credit Clause (51)
General-jurisdiction trial court (court of record) (38)
Highest state court (38)

In personam jurisdiction (personal jurisdiction) (50)
In rem jurisdiction (51)
Intermediate appellate court (appellate court or courts of appeal) (38)
International Shoe Company v. State of Washington (51)
Judicial authority (55)
Judicial review (56)
Licensing (56)
Limited-jurisdiction trial court (inferior trial court) (37)
Local administrative agency (55)
Long-arm statute (50)
Majority decision (45)
Minimum contact (50)
Petition for certiorari (45)
Plurality decision (46)
Procedural administrative law (55)

Quasi in rem jurisdiction (attachment jurisdiction) (51)
Rules and regulations (56)
Rule of four (46)
Rule making (56)
Service of process (50)
Small claims court (38)
Special federal court (42)
Standing to sue (50)
State administrative agency (55)
State courts (37)
State supreme court (38)
Substantive administrative law (55)
Substantive rule (55)
Supreme Court of the United States (U.S. Supreme Court) (43)
Tie decision (46)
Unanimous decision (45)
U.S. Bankruptcy Court (42)

Law Case with Answer
Carnival Cruise Lines, Inc. v. Shute

Facts   Mr. and Mrs. Shute, residents of the state of Washington, purchased passage for a seven-day cruise on the *Tropicale*, a cruise ship operated by Carnival Cruise Lines. Inc. (Carnival). They paid the fare to the travel agent, who forwarded the payment to Carnival's headquarters in Miami, Florida. Carnival prepared the tickets and sent them to the Shutes. Each ticket consisted of five pages, including contract terms. The ticket contained a forum-selection clause that designated the state of Florida as the forum for any lawsuits arising under or in connection with the ticket and cruise. The Shutes boarded the *Tropicale* in Los Angeles, which set sail for Puerto Vallarta, Mexico. While the ship was on its return voyage and in international waters off the coast of Mexico, Mrs. Shute was injured when she slipped on a deck mat during a guided tour of the ship's galley. Upon return to the state of Washington, she filed a negligence lawsuit against Carnival in U.S. District Court in Washington, seeking damages. Carnival defended, arguing that the lawsuit could only be brought in a court located in the state of Florida, pursuant to the forum-selection clause contained in its ticket. Is the forum-selection clause enforceable?

Answer   Yes, the forum-selection clause contained in the Carnival Cruise Lines ticket is enforceable against Mrs. Shute. Including a reasonable forum clause in a form contract is permissible for several reasons. First, a cruise line has a special interest in limiting the number of jurisdictions in which it could potentially be subject to a lawsuit. Because a cruise ship typically carries passengers from many locales, it is likely that a mishap on a cruise could subject the cruise line to litigation in several different jurisdictions. Second, a clause establishing the forum for dispute resolution dispels any confusion as to where lawsuits arising from the contract must be brought and defended, sparing litigants the time and expense of pretrial motions to determine the correct forum and conserving judicial resources needed to decide such issues. Finally, passengers who purchase tickets containing a forum-selection clause benefit in reduced fares that reflect the savings that the cruise line enjoys by limiting where it may be sued. The forum-selection clause in the Carnival Cruise Lines ticket was fair and reasonable and therefore enforceable against Mrs. Shute. If Mrs. Shute wishes to sue Carnival Cruise Lines, she must do so in a court in the state of Florida, not in a court in the state of Washington. *Carnival Cruise Lines, Inc. v. Shute*, 499 U.S. 585, 111 S.Ct. 1522, 113 L.Ed.2d 622, **Web** 1991 U.S. Lexis 2221 (Supreme Court of the United States).

Critical Legal Thinking Cases

3.1 Standing to Sue   McDonald's Corporation owns, operates, and franchises fast food restaurants. Over the course of years, McDonald's ran promotional games such as "Monopoly Game at McDonald's," "Who Wants to be a Millionaire," and other games where high-value prizes, including vehicles and cash up to $1 million, could be won. A person could win by collecting certain games pieces distributed by McDonald's. McDonald's employed Simon Marketing, Inc. (Simon) to operate the promotional games. An investigation by the Federal Bureau of Investigation (FBI) uncovered a criminal ring led by Jerome Jacobson, Director of Security at Simon, whereby he embezzled games pieces and diverted them to "winners" who collected more than $20 million in high-value prizes. After being caught, Jacobson and other members of the ring entered guilty pleas in connection with the conspiracy.

The Burger King Corporation, a competitor of McDonald's, owns, operates, and franchises fast food restaurants. One franchisee is Phoenix of Broward, Inc. (Phoenix), which operates a Burger King restaurant in Ft. Lauderdale, Florida. Phoenix brought a class action lawsuit in U.S. District Court on behalf of Burger King franchises against McDonald's, alleging that McDonald's engaged in false advertising in violation of the federal Lanham Act when it advertised that players had an equal chance of winning high-value prizes when in fact they did not because of the Jacobson's criminal conspiracy. Phoenix alleged that it suffered injuries of lost sales because of McDonald's false advertising claims.

McDonald's filed a Motion to Dismiss Phoenix's lawsuit, asserting that Phoenix had no standing to sue. Did plaintiff Phoenix have standing to sue McDonald's? *Phoenix of Broward, Inc. v. McDonald's Corporation*, 441 F.Supp2d 1241, **Web** 2006 U.S. Dist. Lexis 55112 (United States District Court for the Northern District of Georgia)

3.2 Jurisdiction Four friends, John Bertram, Matt Norden, Scott Olson, and Tony Harvey, all residents of Ohio, traveled to the Upper Peninsula of Michigan to go snowmobiling. On their first day of snowmobiling, after going about 135 miles, the lead snowmobiler, Olson, came to a stop sign on the snowmobile trail where it intersected a private driveway. As Olson approached the sign, he gave the customary hand signal and stopped his snowmobile. Harvey, second in line, was going too fast to stop, so Olson pulled his snowmobile to the right side of the private driveway. Harvey, to avoid hitting Olson, pulled his snowmobile to the left and went over a 5- or 6-foot snow embankment. Bertram, third in line, going about 30 miles per hour, slammed on his brake, turned 45 degrees, and slammed into Olson's snowmobile. Bertram was thrown from his snowmobile. Norden, fourth in line, could not stop, and his snowmobile hit Bertram's leg. Bertram's tibia and fibula were both fractured and protruded through his skin. Bertram underwent surgery to repair the broken bones.

Bertram filed a lawsuit against Olson, Harvey, and Norden in a trial court in Ohio, claiming that each of his friends was liable to him for their negligent snowmobile operation. A Michigan statute specifically stated that snowmobilers assumed the risks associated with snowmobiling. Ohio law did not contain an assumption of the risk rule regarding snowmobiling. The three defendants made a motion for summary judgment. Does Michigan or Ohio law apply to this case? *Bertram v. Norden, et al.*, 159 Ohio App.3d 171, 823 N.E.2d 478, **Web** 2004 Ohio App. Lexis 550 (Court of Appeals of Ohio)

3.3 Federal Question Nutrilab, Inc., manufactures and markets a product known as Starch Blockers. The purpose of the product is to block the human body's digestion of starch as an aid in controlling weight. The U.S. FDA classified Starch Blockers as a drug and requested that it be removed from the market until the FDA approved its use. The FDA claimed that it had the right to classify new products as drugs and prevent their

distribution until their safety is determined. Nutrilab disputed the FDA's decision and wanted to bring suit to halt the FDA's actions. Do the federal courts have jurisdiction to hear this case? *Nutrilab, Inc. v. Schweiker*, 713 F.2d 335, **Web** 1983 U.S. App. Lexis 25121 (United States Court of Appeals for the Seventh Circuit)

3.4 Jurisdiction James Clayton Allison, a resident of the state of Mississippi, was employed by the Tru-Amp Corporation as a circuit breaker tester. As part of his employment, Allison was sent to inspect, clean, and test a switch gear located at the South Central Bell Telephone Facility in Brentwood, Tennessee. One day, when he attempted to remove a circuit breaker manufactured by ITE Corporation (ITE) from a bank of breakers, a portion of the breaker fell off. The broken piece fell behind a switching bank and, according to Allison, caused an electrical fire and explosion. Allison was severely burned in the accident. Allison brought suit against ITE in a Mississippi state court, claiming more than $50,000 in damages. Can this suit be removed to federal court? *Allison v. ITE Imperial Corp.*, 729 F.Supp. 45, **Web** 1990 U.S. Dist. Lexis 607 (United States District Court for the Southern District of Mississippi)

3.5 Administrative Regulation George Carlin, a satiric humorist, recorded a 12-minute monologue called "Filthy Words." He began by referring to his thoughts about "the words you couldn't say on the public airwaves" and then proceeded to list those words, repeating them over and over again in a variety of colloquialisms. At about 2 o'clock in the afternoon a New York radio station, owned by Pacifica Foundation (Pacifica), broadcast Carlin's "Filthy Words" monologue. A father who heard the broadcast while driving with his young son filed a complaint with the Federal Communications Commission (FCC), a federal administrative agency charged with regulating broadcasting. The Federal Communications Act forbids the use of "any obscene, indecent, or profane language by means of radio communications." Therefore, the FCC issued an order granting the complaint and informing Pacifica that the order would be considered in future licensing decisions involving Pacifica. Is the FCC regulation legal? *Federal Communications Commission v. Pacifica Foundation*, 438 U.S. 726, 98 S.Ct. 3026, 57 L.Ed.2d 1073, **Web** 1978 U.S. Lexis 135 (Supreme Court of the United States)

Ethics Cases

3.6 Ethics One day Joshua Gnaizda, a 3-year-old, received what he (or his mother) thought was a tantalizing offer in the mail from Time, Inc. The front of the envelope contained a

see-through window that revealed the following statement: "Joshua Gnaizda, I'll give you this versatile new calculator watch free just for opening this envelope." Beneath the offer was a picture of the calculator watch itself. When Joshua's mother opened the envelope, she realized that the see-through window had not revealed the full text of Time's offer. Not viewable through the see-through window were the following words: "And mailing this Certificate today." The certificate required Joshua to purchase a subscription to *Fortune* magazine in order to receive the free calculator watch. Joshua (through his father, a lawyer) sued Time in a class action lawsuit, seeking compensatory damages in an amount equal to the value of the calculator watch and $15 million in punitive damages. The trial court dismissed the lawsuit as being too trivial for the court to hear. Joshua appealed. *Harris v. Time, Inc.*, 191 Cal.App.3d 449, 237 Cal.Rptr. 584, **Web** 1987 Cal.App. Lexis 1619 (Court of Appeal of California)

1. Did Time act ethically?
2. What is a frivolous lawsuit? Was Joshua's lawsuit against Time, Inc., a frivolous lawsuit?
3. Was the claimed damages of $15 million excessive?

3.7 Ethics   The National Enquirer, Inc., is a Florida corporation with its principal place of business in Florida. It publishes the *National Enquirer*, a national weekly newspaper with a total circulation of more than five million copies. About six hundred thousand copies, almost twice the level in the next highest state, are sold in California. The *Enquirer* published an article about Shirley Jones, an entertainer. Jones, a California resident, filed a lawsuit in California state court against the *Enquirer* and its president, who was a resident of Florida. The California lawsuit sought damages for alleged defamation, invasion of privacy, and intentional infliction of emotional distress. *Calder v. Jones*, 465 U.S. 783, 104 S.Ct. 1482, 79 L.Ed.2d 804, **Web** 1984 U.S. Lexis 4 (Supreme Court of the United States)

1. What kind of paper is the *National Enquirer*?
2. Was it ethical for The National Enquirer, Inc., to try to avoid suit in California?
3. Are the defendants subject to suit in California? Why or why not?

Internet Exercises

1. Go to Exhibit 3.2 in the chapter. Find the website that represents your state or district or territory and go to that website. What is the name of the highest court? In what city is the highest state court located?

2. Use an Internet search engine to find whether your state has a small claims court. If so, what is the dollar amount limit for cases to qualify for small claims court?

3. Go to the map that appears in Exhibit 3.3 in this chapter. Find the federal court of appeals that serves your geographical area. What states are represented by that circuit court? Visit the website of that court that is listed in Exhibit 3.4. What city is the primary court located in? How many judges does the circuit court have?

4. Go to the website of the U.S. Supreme Court, at **www.supremecourtus.gov**. Who are the nine justice of the U.S. Supreme Court? What president appointed each justice, and what political party (e.g., Democrat, Republican) did that president belong to?

5. Visit the website of the U.S. Department of Homeland Security, at **www.dhs.gov**. What does this federal government agency regulate?

6. Visit the website of the federal Food and Drug Administration (FDA), at **www.fda.gov**. What does this federal government agency regulate?

Endnotes

1. Federal Courts Improvement Act of 1982, Public Law 97-164, 96 Stat. 25, 28 U.S.C. Sections 1292 and 1295.
2. Effective September 25, 1988, mandatory appeals were all but eliminated, except for reapportionment cases and cases brought under the Civil Rights Act and Voting Rights Act, antitrust laws, and the Presidential Election Campaign Fund Act.
3. Prior to 1980, there was a minimum dollar amount controversy requirement of $10,000 to bring a federal question action in federal court. This minimum amount was eliminated by the Federal Question Jurisdictional Amendment Act of 1980, Public Law 96-486.
4. The amount was raised to $75,000 by the 1996 Federal Courts Improvement Act, Title 28 U.S.C. Section 1332(a).
5. *International Shoe Co. v. Washington*, 326 U.S. 310, 66 S.Ct. 154, 90 L.Ed. 95, **Web** 1945 U.S. Lexis 1447 (Supreme Court of the United States).
6. 326 U.S. 310, 66 S.Ct. 154, 90 L.Ed 95, **Web** 1945 U.S. Lexis 1447 (Supreme Court of the United States).
7. 952 F.Supp. 1119, Web 1997 U.S. Dist. Lexis 1701 (United States District Court for the Western District of Pennsylvania).
8. 5 U.S.C. Sections 551–706.

CHAPTER 4

Judicial, Alternative, and E-Dispute Resolution

OLD COURTHOUSE, ST. LOUIS, MISSOURI
This is the old state courthouse located in St. Louis, Missouri. It is now part of the national monument.

Learning Objectives

After studying this chapter, you should be able to:

1. Describe the pretrial litigation process.
2. Describe how a case proceeds through trial.
3. Describe how a trial court decision is appealed.
4. Explain the use of arbitration and other nonjudicial methods of alternative dispute resolution.
5. Describe e-courts and e-dispute resolution.

Chapter Outline

Introduction to Judicial, Alternative, and E-Dispute Resolution

Pretrial Litigation Process

Pleadings
    CASE 4.1 • U.S. SUPREME COURT • *Walmart Stores, Inc. v. Dukes*

Discovery

Pretrial Motions

Settlement Conference
    CONTEMPORARY ENVIRONMENT • *Cost–Benefit Analysis of a Lawsuit*

Trial

Appeal
    ETHICS • *Frivolous Lawsuit*
    INTERNATIONAL LAW • *British Legal System*

Chapter Outline (continued)

Alternative Dispute Resolution
  LANDMARK LAW • *Federal Arbitration Act*
  CASE 4.2 • **U.S. SUPREME COURT** • *AT&T Mobility LLC v. Concepcion*

E-Courts and E-Dispute Resolution
  DIGITAL LAW • *E-Dispute Resolution*
  INTERNATIONAL LAW • *Solving Tribal Disputes, Mali, West Africa*

> ❝ *We're the jury, dread our fury!"*
>
> —William S. Gilbert
> *Trial by Jury*

Introduction to Judicial, Alternative, and E-Dispute Resolution

Pieces of evidence, each by itself insufficient, may together constitute a significant whole and justify by their combined effect a conclusion.

Lord Wright
Grant v. Australian Knitting Mills, Ltd. (1936)

The process of bringing, maintaining, and defending a lawsuit is called *litigation*. It is also called *judicial dispute resolution* because courts are used to decide the case. Litigation is a difficult, time-consuming, and costly process that must comply with complex procedural rules. Although it is not required, most parties employ a lawyer to represent them when they are involved in a lawsuit.

Several forms of *nonjudicial dispute resolution* have developed in response to the expense and difficulty of bringing a lawsuit. These methods, collectively called *alternative dispute resolution*, are being used more and more often to resolve contract and commercial disputes.

The computer, e-mail, and the Internet are now heavily used in resolving legal disputes. Many courts either allow or mandate that documents be submitted to the court electronically. Lawyers often correspond with each other, hold depositions, and do various other tasks using electronic means. In addition, electronic arbitration and mediation is often used to resolve legal disputes. The resolution of legal disputes using electronically are often referred to as *e-dispute resolution*.

This chapter discusses the judicial litigation process, alternative dispute resolution, and e-dispute resolution.

Pretrial Litigation Process

litigation
The process of bringing, maintaining, and defending a lawsuit.

The bringing, maintaining, and defense of a lawsuit are generally referred to as the *litigation process*, or **litigation**. The pretrial litigation process can be divided into the following major phases: *pleadings*, *discovery*, *pretrial motions*, and *settlement conference*. Each of these phases is discussed in the paragraphs that follow.

Pleadings

pleadings
The paperwork that is filed with the court to initiate and respond to a lawsuit.

The paperwork that is filed with the court to initiate and respond to a lawsuit is referred to as the **pleadings**. The major pleadings are the *complaint*, the *answer*, the *cross-complaint*, and the *reply*.

Complaint and Summons

To initiate a lawsuit, the party who is suing (the **plaintiff**) must file a **complaint** in the proper court. The complaint names the parties to the lawsuit, alleges the ultimate facts and law violated, and contains a "prayer for relief" for a remedy to be awarded by the court. The complaint can be as long as necessary, depending on the case's complexity. A sample complaint appears in **Exhibit 4.1**.

plaintiff
The party who files a complaint.

complaint
The document a plaintiff files with the court and serves on the defendant to initiate a lawsuit.

Exhibit 4.1 SAMPLE COMPLAINT

In the United States District Court for the District of Idaho

John Doe
    Plaintiff

Civil No. 2-1001

    v.

COMPLAINT

Jane Roe

    Defendant

The plaintiff, by and through his attorney, alleges:

1. The plaintiff is a resident of the State of Idaho, the defendant is a resident of the State of Washington, and there is diversity of citizenship between the parties.
2. The amount in controversy exceeds the sum of $75,000, exclusive of interest and costs.
3. On January 10, 2013, plaintiff was exercising reasonable care while walking across the intersection of Sun Valley Road and Main Street, Ketchum, Idaho when defendant negligently drove her car through a red light at the intersection and struck plaintiff.
4. As a result of the defendant's negligence, plaintiff has incurred medical expenses of $104,000 and suffered severe physical injury and mental distress.

WHEREFORE, plaintiff claims judgment in the amount of $1,000,000 interest at the maximum legal rate, and costs of this action.

By _____
Edward Lawson
Attorney for Plaintiff
100 Main Street
Ketchum, Idaho

Once a complaint has been filed with the court, the court will issue a summons. A **summons** is a court order directing the defendant to appear in court and answer the complaint. The complaint and summons are served on the defendant. This is called **service of process**. Usually this is accomplished by a sheriff, another government official, or a private process server personally serving the complaint and summons on the defendant. If personal service has been tried and is unsuccessful, the court may permit alternative forms of service, such as by mail, fixing the complaint on the last known address of the defendant, or by e-mail.

summons
A court order that directs the defendant to appear in court and answer the complaint.

Answer

The **defendant**, the party who is being sued, must file an **answer** to the plaintiff's complaint. The defendant's answer is filed with the court and served on the plaintiff. In the answer, the defendant admits or denies the allegations contained in the plaintiff's complaint. A judgment is entered against a defendant who admits all of the allegations in the complaint. The case proceeds if the defendant denies all or some of the allegations.

If the defendant does not answer the complaint, a **default judgment** is entered against him or her. A default judgment establishes the defendant's liability. The plaintiff then has only to prove damages.

answer
The defendant's written response to a plaintiff's complaint that is filed with the court and served on the plaintiff.

Third Party Summons

In addition to answering the complaint, a defendant's answer can assert **affirmative defenses**.

Examples If a complaint alleges that the plaintiff was personally injured by the defendant, the defendant's answer could state that he or she acted in self-defense. Another affirmative defense would be an assertion that the plaintiff's lawsuit is barred because the *statute of limitations* (time within which to bring the lawsuit) has expired.

Cross-Complaint and Reply

cross-complaint
A document filed by the defendant against the plaintiff to seek damages or some other remedy.

reply
A document filed by the original plaintiff to answer the defendant's cross-complaint.

A defendant who believes that he or she has been injured by the plaintiff can file a **cross-complaint** against the plaintiff in addition to an answer. In the cross-complaint, the defendant (now the **cross-complainant**) sues the plaintiff (now the **cross-defendant**) for damages or some other remedy. The original plaintiff must file a **reply** (answer) to the cross-complaint. The reply, which can include affirmative defenses, must be filed with the court and served on the original defendant.

CONCEPT SUMMARY	

PLEADINGS

Type of Pleading	Description
Complaint	A document filed by a plaintiff with a court and served with a *summons* on the defendant. It sets forth the basis of the lawsuit.
Answer	A document filed by a defendant with a court and served on the plaintiff. It usually denies most allegations of the complaint.
Cross-complaint and reply	A document filed and served by a defendant if he or she countersues the plaintiff. The defendant is the *cross-complainant*, and the plaintiff is the *cross-defendant*. The cross-defendant must file and serve a *reply* (answer).

Intervention and Consolidation

intervention
The act of others to join as parties to an existing lawsuit.

If other persons have an interest in a lawsuit, they may *intervene* and become parties to the lawsuit. This is called **intervention**.

Example A bank that has made a secured loan on a piece of real estate can intervene in a lawsuit between parties who are litigating ownership of the property.

consolidation
The act of a court to combine two or more separate lawsuits into one lawsuit.

If several plaintiffs have filed separate lawsuits stemming from the same fact situation against the same defendant, the court can *consolidate* the cases into one case if doing so would not cause undue prejudice to the parties. This is called **consolidation**.

Example If a commercial airplane crashes, killing and injuring many people, the court could consolidate all the lawsuits against the defendant airplane company. This is because the deaths and injuries all relate to the same fact situation.

Class Action

class action
A lawsuit where a group of plaintiffs with common claims collectively bring a lawsuit against a defendant.

If certain requirements are met, a lawsuit can be brought as a **class action**. A class action occurs when a group of plaintiffs collectively bring a lawsuit against a defendant. Usually, one or several named plaintiffs file a lawsuit against a defendant on behalf of herself, himself, or themselves and other similarly situated alleged aggrieved parties.

In order to maintain a class action lawsuit, a class must be *certified* by the appropriate federal or state court. A class can be certified if the legal and factual claims of all of the parties are common, it is impracticable for individual claimants to bring multiple lawsuits against the defendant, the claims and defenses are typical for the plaintiffs and the defendant, and the representative parties will adequately protect the interests of the class. A class will not be certified if there is not sufficient commonality among the plaintiffs' claims or if the court otherwise finds that a class action is not suitable to the facts of the case.

If a court certifies a class, notice of the class action must be sent, published, or broadcast to class members. Class members have the right to opt out of the class action and pursue their own legal process against the defendant. If a class action lawsuit is won or a settlement is obtained from the defendant, the members of the class share the proceeds as determined by the court.

Attorneys are often more likely to representative a class of plaintiffs, with aggregate monetary claims, than an individual plaintiff with a small claim. Where appropriate, class action lawsuits increases court efficiency and lowers the costs of litigation. Class actions are usually disfavored by defendants.

In the following case, the U.S. Supreme Court decided whether a lawsuit could proceed as a class action.

CASE 4.1   *U.S. SUPREME COURT Class Action Lawsuit*

Walmart Stores, Inc. v. Dukes

131 S.Ct. 2541, 180 L.Ed.2d 374, Web 2011 U.S. Lexis 4567 (2011)
Supreme Court of the United States

"The crux of this case is commonality—the rule requiring a plaintiff to show that there are questions of law or fact common to the class."

—Scalia, Justice

Facts

Walmart is the nation's largest private employer. The company operates more than 3,500 stores and employs more than one million people. Pay and promotion decisions at Walmart are generally delegated to local mangers' broad discretion. Walmart has a policy against discrimination in making employment decisions.

Three individual plaintiffs, who were employees of Walmart, joined together and brought a class action lawsuit against Walmart. The lawsuit alleged that Walmart systematically engaged in sex discrimination, in violation of Title VII of the Civil Rights Act of 1964. The class would consist of about one and a half million plaintiffs, current and former female employees of Walmart. The plaintiffs sought an injunction and declaratory relief and the award of back pay from Walmart.

The U.S. District Court certified the class to permit the class action lawsuit to proceed. The U.S. Court of Appeals affirmed the certification of the class. Walmart appealed to the U.S. Supreme Court, challenging the certification of the class.

Issue

Is the certification of the class justified by law?

Language of the U.S. Supreme Court

Class certification is governed by Federal Rule of Civil Procedure 23. The party seeking certification must demonstrate that there are questions of law or fact common to the class, the claims or defenses of the representative parties are typical of the claims or defenses of the class, and the representative parties will fairly and adequately protect the interests of the class.

The crux of this case is commonality—the rule requiring a plaintiff to show that there are questions of law or fact common to the class. Commonality requires the plaintiff to demonstrate that the class members have suffered the same injury. Because respondents provide no convincing proof of a companywide discriminatory pay and promotion policy, we have concluded that they have not established the existence of any common question. In sum, we agree with Chief Judge Kozinski that the members of the class:

"held a multitude of different jobs, at different levels of Walmart's hierarchy, for variable lengths of time, in 3,400 stores, sprinkled across 50 states, with a kaleidoscope of

(continued)

supervisors (male and female), subject to a variety of regional policies that all differed.... They have little in common but their sex and this lawsuit."

Federal Rule of Civil Procedure 23 does not authorize class certification when each individual class member would be entitled to a different injunction or declaratory judgment against the defendant. Similarly, it does not authorize class certification when each class member would be entitled to an individualized award of monetary damages. Walmart is entitled to individualized determinations of each employee's eligibility for back pay.

Decision

The U.S. Supreme Court held that the case did not qualify for class certification. The U.S. Supreme Court reversed the decision of the U.S. Court of Appeals that had held otherwise.

Case Questions

Critical Legal Thinking
What is the purpose of a class action lawsuit? What are the requirements to have a class certified?

Ethics
Do you think that Wamart will face many individual sex discrimination lawsuits now that the class has been decertified?

Contemporary Business
What are the possible costs and consequences to a business that faces a class action lawsuit?

Statute of Limitations

statute of limitations
A statute that establishes the period during which a plaintiff must bring a lawsuit against a defendant.

A **statute of limitations** establishes the period during which a plaintiff must bring a lawsuit against a defendant. If a lawsuit is not filed within this time period, the plaintiff loses his or her right to sue. A statute of limitations begins to "run" at the time the plaintiff first has the right to sue the defendant (e.g., when the accident happens or when the breach of contract occurs).

Federal and state governments have established statutes of limitations for each type of lawsuit. Most are from one to four years, depending on the type of lawsuit.

Example The state of Idaho has a two-year statute of limitations for personal injury actions. On July 1, 2013, Otis negligently causes an automobile accident in Sun Valley, Idaho, in which Cha-Yen is injured. Cha-Yen has until July 1, 2015, to bring a negligence lawsuit against Otis. If she waits longer than that, she loses her right to sue him.

Discovery (Request to admit)

discovery
A legal process during which each party engages in various activities to discover facts of the case from the other party and witnesses prior to trial.

The legal process provides for a detailed pretrial procedure called **discovery**. During discovery, each party engages in various activities to discover facts of the case from the other party and witnesses prior to trial. Discovery serves several functions, including preventing surprises, allowing parties to thoroughly prepare for trial, preserving evidence, saving court time, and promoting the settlement of cases. The major forms of discovery are discussed in the following paragraphs.

Deposition

deposition
Oral testimony given by a party or witness prior to trial. The testimony is given under oath and is transcribed.

deponent
A party who gives his or her deposition.

A **deposition** is oral testimony given by a party or witness prior to trial. The person giving a deposition is called the **deponent**. A *party* to the lawsuit must give a deposition if called upon by the other party to do so. The deposition of a *witness* can be given voluntarily or pursuant to a subpoena (court order). The deponent can be required to bring documents to the deposition. Most depositions are taken at the office of one of the attorneys. The deponent is placed under oath and then asked questions orally by one or both of the attorneys. The questions and answers are recorded in written form by a court reporter. Depositions can also be videotaped. The deponent is given an opportunity to correct his or her answers prior to signing the deposition. Depositions are used to preserve evidence (e.g., if the deponent is deceased, ill, or not otherwise available at trial) and impeach testimony given by witnesses at trial.

Interrogatories

Interrogatories are written questions submitted by one party to a lawsuit to another party. The questions can be very detailed. In addition, certain documents might be attached to the answers. A party is required to answer interrogatories in writing within a specified time period (e.g., 60 to 90 days). An attorney usually helps with the preparation of the answers. The answers are signed under oath.

interrogatories
Written questions submitted by one party to another party. The questions must be answered in writing within a stipulated time.

Production of Documents

Often, particularly in complex business cases, a substantial portion of a lawsuit may be based on information contained in documents (e.g., memorandums, correspondence, company records). One party to a lawsuit may request that the other party produce all documents that are relevant to the case prior to trial. This is called **production of documents**. If the documents sought are too voluminous to be moved or are in permanent storage, or if their movement would disrupt the ongoing business of the party that is to produce them, the requesting party may be required to examine the documents at the other party's premises.

production of documents
A request by one party to another party to produce all documents relevant to the case prior to the trial.

Physical or Mental Examination

In cases that concern the physical or mental condition of a party, a court can order the party to submit to certain **physical or mental examinations** to determine the extent of the alleged injuries. This would occur, for example, where the plaintiff has been injured in an accident and is seeking damages for physical injury and mental distress.

physical or mental examination
A court-ordered examination of a party to a lawsuit before trial to determine the extent of the alleged injuries.

CONCEPT SUMMARY
DISCOVERY

Type	Description
Deposition	Oral testimony given by a *deponent*, either a party or witness. Depositions are transcribed.
Interrogatories	Written questions submitted by one party to the other party of a lawsuit. They must be answered within a specified period of time.
Production of documents	Copies of all relevant documents obtained by a party to a lawsuit from another party upon order of the court.
Physical or mental examination	Court-ordered examination of a party where injuries are alleged that could be verified or disputed by such examination.

Pretrial Motions

There are several **pretrial motions** that parties to a lawsuit can make to try to resolve or dispose of all or part of a lawsuit prior to trial. The two pretrial motions are *motion for judgment on the pleadings* and *motion for summary judgment*.

pretrial motion
A motion a party can make to try to dispose of all or part of a lawsuit prior to trial.

Motion for Judgment on the Pleadings

motion for judgment on the pleadings
A motion that alleges that if all the facts presented in the pleadings are taken as true, the party making the motion would win the lawsuit when the proper law is applied to these asserted facts.

A **motion for judgment on the pleadings** can be made by either party once the pleadings are complete. This motion alleges that if all the facts presented in the pleadings are true, the party making the motion would win the lawsuit when the proper law is applied to these facts. In deciding this motion, the judge cannot consider any facts outside the pleadings.

Motion for Summary Judgment

motion for summary judgment
A motion which asserts that there are no factual disputes to be decided by the jury and that the judge can apply the proper law to the undisputed facts and decide the case without a jury. These motions are supported by affidavits, documents, and deposition testimony.

The trier of fact (i.e., the jury or, if there is no jury, the judge) determines factual issues. A **motion for summary judgment** asserts that there are no factual disputes to be decided by the jury and that the judge should apply the relevant law to the undisputed facts and decide the case. Thus, the case can be decided before trial by a judge who comes to a conclusion and issues a summary judgment in the moving party's favor. Motions for summary judgment, which can be made by either party, are supported by evidence outside the pleadings. Affidavits from the parties and witnesses, documents (e.g., a written contract between the parties), depositions, and such are common forms of evidence.

If, after examining the evidence, the court finds no factual dispute, it can decide the issue or issues raised in the summary judgment motion. It may then dispense with the entire case or with part of the case. If the judge finds that a factual dispute exists, the motion will be denied, and the case will go to trial.

Settlement Conference

settlement conference (pretrial hearing)
A hearing before a trial in order to facilitate the settlement of a case.

Federal court rules and most state court rules permit the court to direct the attorneys or parties to appear before the court for a **settlement conference**, or **pretrial hearing**. One of the major purposes of such hearings is to facilitate the settlement of a case. Pretrial conferences are often held informally in the judge's chambers. If no settlement is reached, the pretrial hearing is used to identify the major trial issues and other relevant factors. More than 95 percent of all cases are settled before they go to trial.

The following feature discusses the cost–benefit analysis of a lawsuit.

Contemporary Environment

Cost–Benefit Analysis of a Lawsuit

The choice of whether to bring or defend a lawsuit should be analyzed like any other business decision. This includes performing a **cost–benefit analysis** of the lawsuit. For the plaintiff, it may be wise not to sue. For the defendant and the plaintiff, it may be wise to settle the case. The following factors should be considered in deciding whether to bring or settle a lawsuit:

- The probability of winning or losing
- The amount of money to be won or lost
- Lawyers' fees and other costs of litigation

- Loss of time by managers and other personnel
- The long-term effects on the relationship and reputation of the parties
- The amount of prejudgment interest provided by law
- The aggravation and psychological costs associated with a lawsuit
- The unpredictability of the legal system and the possibility of error
- Other factors peculiar to the parties and lawsuit

Trial

Pursuant to the Seventh Amendment to the U.S. Constitution, a party to a civil action at law is guaranteed the right to a **jury trial** in a case in federal court.[1] Most state constitutions contain a similar guarantee for state court actions. If either party requests a jury, the trial will be by jury. If both parties waive their right to a jury, the trial will occur without a jury. The judge sits as the **trier of fact** in nonjury trials. At the time of trial, each party usually submits to the judge a **trial brief** that contains legal support for its side of the case.

A trial can last less than one day to many months, depending on the type and complexity of the case. A typical trial is divided into stages. The stages of a trial are discussed in the following paragraphs.

trier of fact
The jury in a jury trial; the judge where there is not a jury trial.

Jury Selection

The pool of potential jurors is usually selected from voter or automobile registration lists. Individuals are selected to hear specific cases through a process called *voir dire* ("to speak the truth"). Lawyers for each party and the judge can ask prospective jurors questions to determine whether they would be biased in their decisions. Biased jurors can be prevented from sitting on a particular case. Once the appropriate number of jurors is selected (usually six to twelve jurors, depending on the jurisdiction), they are **impaneled** to hear the case and are sworn in. Several *alternative jurors* are usually also selected to replace jurors who cannot complete the trial because of sickness or other reason. The trial is ready to begin. A jury can be **sequestered** (i.e., separated from family, etc.) in important cases. Jurors are paid fees for their service.

voir dire
The process whereby the judge and attorneys ask prospective jurors questions to determine whether they would be biased in their decisions.

Courts of appeals should be constantly alert to the trial judge's firsthand knowledge of witnesses, testimony, and issues; in other words, appellate courts should give due consideration to the first-instance decision maker's "feel" for the overall case.

Justice Ginsburg
Weisgram v. Marley Company,
528 U.S. 440, 120 S.Ct. (2000)

Opening Statements

Each party's attorney is allowed to make an **opening statement** to the jury at the beginning of a trial. During an opening statement, an attorney usually summarizes the main factual and legal issues of the case and describes why he or she believes the client's position is valid. The information given in this statement is not considered as evidence.

The Plaintiff's Case

A plaintiff bears the **burden of proof** to persuade the trier of fact of the merits of his or her case. This is called the **plaintiff's case**. The plaintiff's attorney calls witnesses to give testimony. After a witness has been sworn in, the plaintiff's attorney examines (i.e., questions) the witness. This is called **direct examination**. Documents and other evidence can be introduced through each witness. After the plaintiff's attorney has completed his or her questions, the defendant's attorney can question the witness. This is called **cross-examination**. The defendant's attorney can ask questions only about the subjects that were brought up during the direct examination. After the defendant's attorney completes his or her questions, the plaintiff's attorney can ask questions of the witness. This is called **re-direct examination**.

The Defendant's Case

The **defendant's case** proceeds after the plaintiff has concluded his or her case. The defendant's case must (1) rebut the plaintiff's evidence, (2) prove any affirmative defenses asserted by the defendant, and (3) prove any allegations contained in the defendant's cross-complaint. The defendant's witnesses are examined on direct examination by the defendant's attorney. The plaintiff's attorney can cross-examine each witness. This is followed by re-direct examination by the defendant and re-cross-examination by the plaintiff.

Rebuttal and Rejoinder

WEB EXERCISE
Go to **www.eff.org/IP/digitalradio/ XM_complaint.pdf** to view a copy of a complaint filed in U.S. District Court.

After the defendant's attorney has finished calling witnesses, the plaintiff's attorney can call witnesses and put forth evidence to rebut the defendant's case. This is called a **rebuttal**. The defendant's attorney can call additional witnesses and introduce other evidence to counter the rebuttal. This is called the **rejoinder**.

Closing Arguments

At the conclusion of the presentation of the evidence, each party's attorney is allowed to make a **closing argument** to the jury. Each attorney tries to convince the jury to render a verdict for his or her client by pointing out the strengths in the client's case and the weaknesses in the other side's case. Information given by the attorneys in their closing statements is not evidence.

Jury Instructions, Deliberation, and Verdict

jury instructions (charges)
Instructions that the judge gives to the jury that inform jurors of the law to be applied in the case.

Once the closing arguments are completed, the judge reads **jury instructions** (or **charges**) to the jury. These instructions inform the jury about what law to apply when they decide the case.

Examples In a criminal trial, the judge reads the jury the statutory definition of the crime charged. In an accident case, the judge reads the jury the legal definition of *negligence*.

After the judge reads the jury instructions, the jury retires to the jury room to consider the evidence and reach a conclusion. This is called **jury deliberation**.

This process can take from a few minutes to many weeks. After deliberation, the jury reaches a **verdict**. In civil cases, the jury will assess damages against the defendant if they have held in favor of the plaintiff. The jury often assesses penalties in criminal cases.

Entry of Judgment

After the jury has returned its verdict, in most cases the judge will enter a **judgment** to the successful party, based on the verdict. This is the official decision of the court.

The court may, however, overturn the verdict if it finds bias or jury misconduct. This is called a **judgment notwithstanding the verdict** (or **judgment n.o.v.** or **j.n.o.v.**)

In a civil case, the judge may reduce the amount of monetary damages awarded by the jury if he or she finds the jury to have been biased, emotional, or inflamed. This is called **remittitur**.

The trial court usually issues a **written memorandum** that sets forth the reasons for the judgment. This memorandum, together with the trial transcript and evidence introduced at trial, constitutes the permanent **record** of the trial court proceeding.

Appeal

In a civil case, either party can **appeal** the trial court's decision once a **final judgment** is entered. Only the defendant can appeal in a criminal case. The appeal is made to the appropriate appellate court. A **notice of appeal** must be filed by a party within a prescribed time after judgment is entered (usually within sixty or ninety days).

The appealing party is called the **appellant**, or **petitioner**. The responding party is called the **appellee**, or **respondent**. The appellant is often required to post bond (e.g., one-and-one-half times the judgment) on appeal.

The parties may designate all or relevant portions of the trial record to be submitted to the appellate court for review. The appellant's attorney usually must file an **opening brief** with the court that sets forth legal research and other information to support his or her contentions on appeal. The appellee can file a **responding brief** that answers the appellant's contentions. Appellate courts usually permit a brief oral argument at which each party's attorney is heard.

An appellate court will reverse a lower court decision if it finds an **error of law** in the record.

Examples Errors of law occur if prejudicial evidence was admitted at trial when it should have been excluded, prejudicial evidence was admitted that was obtained through an unconstitutional search and seizure, the jury was improperly instructed by the judge, and the like.

An appellate court will not reverse a **finding of fact** made by a jury, or if there is no jury then made by a judge, unless such finding is unsupported by the evidence or is contradicted by the evidence. Very few trial court decisions are reversed because most findings of fact are supported by the evidence. In rare occasions, an appellate court will overturn a jury verdict if the appellate court cannot, from the record of the trial court, find sufficient evidence to support the trier of fact's findings.

The ethics of bringing a frivolous lawsuit is discussed in the following feature.

appeal
The act of asking an appellate court to overturn a decision after the trial court's final judgment has been entered.

appellant (petitioner)
The appealing party in an appeal.

appellee (respondent)
The responding party in an appeal.

Ethics

Frivolous Lawsuit

Although most lawsuits that are filed have some merit, some lawsuits do not. These are called *frivolous lawsuits*. Consider the following case. The Chungs are Korean U.S. residents who came to this country more than ten years ago. The Chungs opened a dry-cleaning store and eventually owned three dry-cleaning stores in the Washington, DC (DC), area. Roy L. Pearson was a DC administrative judge who was a customer at one of the Chungs' dry-cleaning stores. Pearson walked to the Chungs' store because he did not have a car.

The Chungs had signs in the window of their store that stated "Satisfaction Guaranteed" and "Same Day Service." Pearson claimed that the Chungs lost a pair of his pants. He sued the Chungs for $67 million in damages, alleging that they violated the DC Consumer Protection Act. Pearson later reduced his demand to $54 million. Pearson demanded $3 million for violation of the "Satisfaction Guaranteed" sign, $2 million for mental suffering and inconvenience, $500,000 in legal fees for representing himself, $6 million for 10 years of rental car fees to drive to another dry-cleaning shop, and $51 million to help similarly dissatisfied DC customers. Pearson stated that he had no choice but to take on "the awesome responsibility" for suing the Chungs on behalf of every DC resident.

The court, in denying class action status, stated, "The court has significant concerns that the plaintiff is acting in bad faith." After hearing testimony of witnesses, the trial court judge ruled in favor of the Chungs. Pearson made a motion to reconsider to the trial court, which was denied. A website was set up to accept donations for the Chungs' legal fees of $83,000, which were eventually paid by donations.

A DC commission voted against reappointing Pearson for a 10-year term as an administrative law judge in part because his lawsuit against the Chungs demonstrated a lack of "judicial temperament." Pearson lost a $100,000-per-year salary. The Chungs sold the dry-cleaning store involved in the dispute. Pearson filed an appeal with the DC Court of Appeals, but the court rejected his appeal. *Pearson v. Chung*, No. 07-CV-872, District of Columbia Court of Appeals, 2008

Ethics Questions   What is a frivolous lawsuit? Do you think Pearson's lawsuit had any merit? Do you think Pearson acted in "bad faith" in this case? How much emotional distress do you think the Chungs suffered because of this lawsuit?

The following feature discusses the British legal system.

International Law

British Legal System

LONDON, ENGLAND
London is the capital of the country of England. English law is based on common law, that is, law made by judges who decide cases by applying legal precedent established in prior cases (stare decisis) and their common sense. The court system of England consists of

trial courts that hear criminal and civil cases and appellate courts. The House of Lords, in London, is the supreme court of appeal. The legal profession of England is divided into two groups, solicitors and barristers. Solicitors are lawyers who have direct contact with clients and handle legal matters for clients other than appearing in court. Barristers are engaged to appear in court on behalf of a client. The United Kingdom of Great Britain consists of four countries, England, Wales, Scotland, and Northern Ireland. England and Wales are part of the same judicial district, while Scotland and Northern Ireland have their own court systems.

Alternative Dispute Resolution

The use of the court system to resolve business and other disputes can take years and cost thousands, or even millions, of dollars in legal fees and expenses. In commercial litigation, the normal business operations of the parties are often disrupted. To avoid or reduce these problems, businesses are increasingly turning to methods of **alternative dispute resolution (ADR)** and other aids to resolving disputes. The most common forms of ADR are *negotiation, arbitration, mediation, mini-trial, fact-finding*, and *judicial referee*.

alternative dispute resolution (ADR)
Methods of resolving disputes other than litigation.

Negotiation

The simplest form of alternative dispute resolution is engaging in negotiations between the parties to try to settle a dispute. **Negotiation** is a procedure whereby the parties to a legal dispute engage in discussions to try to reach a voluntary settlement of their dispute. Negotiation may take place either before a lawsuit is filed, after a lawsuit is filed, or before other forms of alternative dispute resolution are used.

In a negotiation, the parties, who are often represented by attorneys, negotiate with each other to try to reach an agreeable solution to their dispute. During negotiation proceedings, the parties usually make offers and counteroffers to one another. The parties or their attorneys also may provide information to the other side in order to assist the other side in reaching an amicable settlement.

Many courts require that the parties to a lawsuit engage in settlement discussions prior to trial to try to negotiate a settlement of the case. In such a case, the judge must be assured that a settlement of the case is not possible before he or she permits the case to go to trial. A judge may convince the parties to engage in further negotiations if he or she determines that the parties are not too far apart in the negotiations of a settlement.

If a settlement of a dispute is reached through negotiation, a settlement agreement is drafted that contains the terms of the agreement. A **settlement agreement** is an agreement that is voluntarily entered into by the parties to a dispute that settles the dispute. Each side must sign the settlement agreement for it to be effective. The settlement agreement is usually submitted to the court, and the case will be dismissed based on the execution of the settlement agreement.

negotiation
A procedure whereby the parties to a dispute engage in discussions and bargaining to try to reach a voluntary settlement of their dispute.

Arbitration

A common form of ADR is **arbitration**. In arbitration, the parties choose an impartial third party to hear and decide the dispute. This neutral party is called the **arbitrator**. Arbitrators are usually members of the American Arbitration Association (AAA) or another arbitration association. Labor union agreements, franchise agreements, leases, employment contracts, and other commercial

arbitration
A form of alternative dispute resolution in which the parties choose an impartial third party to hear and decide the dispute.

arbitration clause
A clause in a contract that requires disputes arising out of the contract to be submitted to arbitration.

contracts often contain **arbitration clauses** that require disputes arising out of the contract to be submitted to arbitration. If there is no arbitration clause, the parties can enter into a **submission agreement** whereby they agree to submit a dispute to arbitration after the dispute arises.

Congress enacted the *Federal Arbitration Act* to promote the arbitration of disputes.[2] Many states have adopted the **Uniform Arbitration Act**, which promotes the arbitration of disputes at the state level. Many federal and state courts have instituted programs to refer legal disputes to arbitration or another form of ADR.

ADR services are usually provided by private organizations or individuals who qualify to hear and decide certain disputes. A landmark federal arbitration statute is discussed in the following feature.

Landmark Law

Federal Arbitration Act

"By agreeing to arbitrate a statutory claim, a party does not forgo the substantive rights afforded by the statute, it only submits to their resolution in an arbitral, rather than a judicial, forum."

—White, Justice

The **Federal Arbitration Act (FAA)** was originally enacted in 1925 to reverse long-standing judicial hostility to arbitration agreements that had existed at English common law and had been adopted by U.S. courts. The FAA provides that arbitration agreements involving commerce are valid, irrevocable, and enforceable contracts, unless some grounds exist at law or equity (e.g., fraud, duress) to revoke them. The FAA permits one party to obtain a court order to compel arbitration if the other party has failed or refused to comply with an arbitration agreement.

The U.S. Supreme Court has held that the FAA does not allow federal courts to decide issues of law that have been decided by an arbitrator. The court can either confirm the arbitration ward or vacate it, or it can correct and modify it if the there has been an egregious departure from the parties' agreed-upon arbitration.[3]

Since the FAA's enactment, the courts have wrestled with the problem of which types of disputes should be arbitrated. Breach of contract cases, tort claims, and such are clearly candidates for arbitration if there is a valid arbitration agreement. In addition, the U.S. Supreme Court has enforced arbitration agreements that call for the resolution of disputes arising under federal statutes. The Supreme Court has stated, "By agreeing to arbitrate a statutory claim, a party does not forgo the substantive rights afforded by the statute, it only submits to their resolution in an arbitral, rather than a judicial, forum."[4]

Federal Arbitration Act (FAA)
A federal statute that provides for the enforcement of most arbitration agreements.

Arbitration Procedure   An arbitration agreement often describes the specific procedures that must be followed for a case to proceed to and through arbitration. If one party seeks to enforce an arbitration clause, that party must give notice to the other party. The parties then select an arbitration association or arbitrator, as provided in the agreement. The parties usually agree on the date, time, and place of the arbitration (e.g., at the arbitrator's office, at a law office, at some other agreed-upon location).

At the arbitration, the parties can call witnesses to give testimony and introduce evidence to support their case and refute the other side's case. Rules similar to those followed by federal courts are usually followed at an arbitration hearing. Often, each party pays a filing fee and other fees for the arbitration. Sometimes the agreement provides that one party will pay all the costs of the arbitration. Arbitrators are paid by the hour, day, or other agreed-upon method of compensation.

After an arbitration hearing is complete, the arbitrator reaches a decision and issues an award. The parties often agree in advance to be bound by the arbitrator's decision and remedy. This is called **binding arbitration**. In this situation, the decision and award of the arbitrator cannot be appealed to the courts.

If the arbitration is not binding, the decision and award of the arbitrator can be appealed to the courts. This is called **nonbinding arbitration**. Courts usually give great deference to an arbitrator's decision and award.

If an arbitrator has rendered a decision and an award but a party refuses to abide by the arbitrator's decision, the other party may file an action in court to have the arbitrator's decision enforced.

WEB EXERCISE
Go to the website of the American Arbitration Association (AAA), at **http://www.adr.org/sp.asp?id=28749** and read the information on arbitration.

Mediation

Mediation is a form of negotiation in which a neutral third party assists the disputing parties in reaching a settlement of their dispute. The neutral third party is called a **mediator**. The mediator is usually a person who is an expert in the area of the dispute or a lawyer or retired judge. The mediator is selected by the parties as provided in their agreement or as otherwise agreed by the parties. Unlike an arbitrator, however, a mediator does not make a decision or an award.

mediation
A form of alternative dispute resolution in which the parties use a mediator to propose a settlement of their dispute.

Examples Parties to a divorce action often use mediation to try to help resolve the issues involved in the divorce, including property settlement, payment of alimony and child support, custody of children, visitation rights, and other issues.

A mediator's role is to assist the parties in reaching a settlement. The mediator usually acts as an intermediary between the parties. In many cases, the mediator will meet with the two parties at an agreed-upon location, often the mediator's office or one of the offices of the parties. The mediator will then meet with both parties, usually separately, to discuss each side of the case.

After discussing the facts of the case with both sides, the mediator will encourage settlement of the dispute and will transmit settlement offers from one side to the other. In doing so, the mediator points out the strengths and weaknesses of each party's case and gives his or her opinion to each side about why they should decrease or increase their settlement offers.

If the parties agree to a settlement, a settlement agreement is drafted that expresses their agreement. Execution of the settlement agreement ends the dispute. The parties, of course, must perform their duties under the settlement agreement. If an agreement is not reached, the parties may proceed to a judicial resolution of their case.

Mini-Trial

A **mini-trial** is a voluntary private proceeding in which lawyers for each side present a shortened version of their case to the representatives of both sides. The representatives of each side who attend the mini-trial have the authority to settle the dispute. In many cases, the parties also hire a neutral third party—often someone who is an expert in the field concerning the disputed matter or a legal expert—who presides over the mini-trial. After hearing the case, the neutral third party often is called upon to render an opinion as to how the court would most likely decide the case.

During a mini-trial, the parties get to see the strengths and weaknesses of their own position and that of the opposing side. Once the strengths and weaknesses of both sides are exposed, the parties to a mini-trial often settle the case. The parties also often settle a mini-trial based on the opinion rendered by the neutral third party. If the parties settle their dispute after a mini-trial, they enter into a settlement agreement that sets forth their agreement.

Mini-trials serve a useful purpose in that they act as a substitute for a real trial, but they are much briefer and not as complex and expensive to prepare for. Because the strengths and weaknesses of both sides' cases are exposed, the parties are usually more realistic regarding their own positions and the merits of settling the case prior to an expensive, and often risky, trial.

How many a dispute could have been deflated into a single paragraph if the disputants had dared to define their terms.

Aristotle

Fact-Finding

In some situations, called **fact-finding**, the parties to a dispute employ a neutral third party to act as a fact-finder to investigate the dispute. The fact-finder is authorized to investigate the dispute, gather evidence, prepare demonstrative evidence, and prepare reports of his or her findings.

A fact-finder is not authorized to make a decision or an award. In some cases, a fact-finder will recommend settlement of the case. The fact-finder presents the evidence and findings to the parties, who may then use the information in negotiating a settlement if they wish.

Judicial Referee

If the parties agree, the court may appoint a **judicial referee** to conduct a private trial and render a judgment. Referees, who are often retired judges, have most of the same powers as trial judges, and their decisions stand as judgments of the court. The parties usually reserve their right to appeal.

The following case discusses the lawfulness of class action waivers in arbitration agreements.

CASE 4.2   *U.S. SUPREME COURT Class Action Waiver*

AT&T Mobility LLC v. Concepcion

131 S.Ct. 1740, 179 L.Ed.2d 742, Web 2011 U.S. Lexis 3367 (2011)
Supreme Court of the United States

"Requiring the availability of classwide arbitration interferes with fundamental attributes of arbitration and thus creates a scheme inconsistent with the FAA."

—Scalia, Justice

Facts

AT&T Mobility LLC (AT&T) advertised that a consumer who purchased AT&T phone service would receive a free phone. When the Concepcions purchased AT&T service in California, they were not charged for the phone, but they were charged $30.22 in sales tax based on the phone's retail value. The Concepcions filed a complaint against AT&T in U.S. District Court, alleging that AT&T had engaged in false advertising and fraud because the phones were not free. Their complaint was consolidated into a class action against AT&T. The AT&T contract contained an arbitration agreement that requires consumers to submit any claims they may have against AT&T to arbitration. In addition, the arbitration agreement provided that a claimant waived his or her right to bring or join a class action arbitration proceeding.

AT&T made a motion to compel arbitration, as provided under the terms of the arbitration agreement. The Concepcions contested the motion, alleging that

the class action waiver was unconscionable under California law. California law provided that class action waivers are unconscionable because they require consumers to bring many individual small claims rather than being able to bring their claims jointly against the same defendant. AT&T alleged that the Federal Arbitration Act (FAA) preempted the California state law. The U.S. District Court and the U.S. Court of Appeals agreed with the Conceptions, finding AT&T's class action waiver unconscionable. AT&T appealed to the U.S. Supreme Court.

Issue

Does the Federal Arbitration Act (FAA) preempt California's law that outlaws class action waivers?

Language of the U.S. Supreme Court

Requiring the availability of classwide arbitration interferes with fundamental attributes of arbitration and thus creates a scheme inconsistent with the FAA. California's rule interferes with arbitration. The switch from bilateral to class arbitration sacrifices the principal advantage of arbitration—its informality—and makes the process slower, more costly, and more likely to generate procedural morass than final judgment. In bilateral arbitration, parties forgo the procedural rigor and appellate review of the courts in order to realize the benefits of private dispute resolution: lower costs, greater efficiency and speed, and the ability to choose expert adjudicators to resolve specialized disputes. Other courts have noted the risk of "in terrorem" settlements that class actions entail, and class arbitration would be no different. Arbitration is poorly suited to the higher stakes of class litigation.

Decision

The U.S. Supreme Court held that California's law prohibiting class action waivers was preempted by the Federal Arbitration Act (FAA) and therefore the Concepcions must arbitrate their claim against AT&T individually and not within a class of consumers.

Case Questions

Critical Legal Thinking
What is a class action waiver?

Ethics
Is it ethical for employers to include arbitration clauses in employment contracts that waive the right of claimants to bring class action arbitration proceedings?

Contemporary Business
Who do you think benefits most from class action waiver clauses in arbitration agreements: employers or employees?

E-Courts and E-Dispute Resolution

The Internet, e-mail, and websites have radically changed how lawyers and courts operate. They have enabled many normal communications between lawyers and courts to be conducted electronically. Also, these technologies have made it possible to settle disputes online. The following paragraphs discuss these issues.

E-Courts

When litigation takes place, the clients, lawyers, and judges involved in the case are usually buried in papers. These papers include pleadings, interrogatories, documents, motions to the court, briefs, and memorandums, among many other papers. By the time a case is over, reams of paper are stored in dozens, if not hundreds, of boxes. In addition, court appearances, for even a very small matter, must be made in person.

Example Lawyers often wait hours for a 10-minute scheduling conference or another conference with a judge. The time it takes to drive to and from court also has to be taken into account, which in some areas may amount to hours.

Today, because of the Internet and other technologies, **electronic courts**, or **e-courts**, also referred to as **virtual courthouses**, are substantially being used by courts. Technology allows for the **electronic filing—e-filing**—of pleadings, briefs, and other documents related to a lawsuit. In addition, technology allows for the scanning of evidence and documents into a computer for storage and retrieval and for e-mailing correspondence and documents to the court, the opposing counsel, and clients. Scheduling and other conferences with the judge or opposing counsel are held via telephone conferences and e-mail.

Many courts have instituted electronic document filing and tracking. In some courts, e-filing of pleadings and other documents is now mandatory. Companies such as Microsoft and LexisNexis have developed systems to manage e-filings of court documents.

The following feature discusses e-dispute resolution.

electronic court (e-court) (virtual courthouse)
A court that either mandates or permits the electronic filing of pleadings, briefs, and other documents related to a lawsuit.

e-dispute resolution
The use of online alternative dispute resolution services to resolve a dispute.

electronic arbitration (e-arbitration)
The arbitration of a dispute using online arbitration services.

electronic mediation (e-mediation)
The mediation of a dispute using online mediation services.

Digital Law

E-Dispute Resolution

Legal disputes are now often resolved using **electronic dispute resolution**, or **e-dispute resolution**. Many ADR service providers offer **electronic arbitration**, or **e-arbitration**. Most of these services allow a party to a legal dispute to register the dispute with the service and then notify the other party by e-mail of the registration of the dispute. The parties may be represented by attorneys if they so choose.

Most online arbitration requires the registering party to submit an amount that the party is willing to accept or pay to the other party in the online arbitration. The other party is afforded the opportunity to accept the offer. If that party accepts the offer, a settlement has been reached. The other party, however, may return a counteroffer. The process continues until a settlement is reached or one or both of the parties remove themselves from the online ADR process.

Several websites offer **electronic mediation**, or **e-mediation** services. In an online mediation, the parties sit before their computers and sign onto the website. A chat room is assigned to each party and the mediator, and another is set aside for both parties and the mediator. The individual chat rooms are used for private conversations with the online mediator, and the other chat room is for conversations between both parties and the mediator.

Online arbitration and online mediation services charge fees, but the fees are reasonable. In an online arbitration or online mediation, a settlement can be reached rather quickly, without paying substantial lawyers' fees and court costs. The parties also act through a more objective online process rather than meet face-to-face or negotiate over the telephone, either of which could involve verbal arguments.

If a legal dispute is not settled using e-arbitration or e-mediation, the parties may pursue their case in the courts.

International Law

Solving Tribal Disputes, Mali, West Africa

MALI, WEST AFRICA
These are mask dancers of the Dogon tribe who primarily live in Mali, West Africa. The Dogon are organized in villages. In resolving disputes, the Dogan usually do not go to government courts. Instead, a council of elders from the village hears and decides disputes between members of the village and administers justice in the local area.

Key Terms and Concepts

Affirmative defense (64)
Alternative dispute resolution (ADR) (73)
Answer (63)
Appeal (71)
Appellant (petitioner) (71)
Appellee (respondent) (71)
Arbitration (73)
Arbitration clause (74)
Arbitrator (73)
Binding arbitration (74)
Burden of proof (70)
Class action (64)
Closing argument (70)
Complaint (63)
Consolidation (64)
Cost–benefit analysis (68)
Cross-complainant (64)
Cross-complaint (64)
Cross-defendant (64)
Cross-examination (70)
Defendant (63)
Defendant's case (70)
Default judgment (63)
Deponent (66)
Deposition (66)

Direct examination (70)
Discovery (66)
Electronic court (e-court) (virtual courthouse) (77)
Electronic arbitration (e-arbitration) (78)
Electronic dispute resolution (e-dispute resolution) (78)
Electronic filing (e-filing) (77)
Electronic mediation (e-mediation) (78)
Error of law (71)
Fact-finding (76)
Federal Arbitration Act (FAA) (74)
Final judgment (71)
Finding of fact (71)
Impanel (69)
Interrogatory (67)
Intervention (64)
Judgment (71)
Judgment notwithstanding the verdict (judgment n.o.v. or j.n.o.v.) (71)

Judicial referee (76)
Jury deliberation (70)
Jury instructions (charges) (70)
Jury trial (69)
Litigation (62)
Mediation (75)
Mediator (75)
Mini-trial (75)
Motion for judgment on the pleadings (68)
Motion for summary judgment (68)
Negotiation (73)
Nonbinding arbitration (75)
Notice of appeal (71)
Opening brief (71)
Opening statement (69)
Physical or mental examination (67)
Plaintiff (63)
Plaintiff's case (70)
Pleadings (62)
Pretrial motion (67)
Production of documents (67)

Rebuttal (70)
Record (71)
Re-direct examination (70)
Rejoinder (70)
Remittitur (71)
Reply (64)
Responding brief (71)
Sequestered (69)
Service of process (63)
Settlement agreement (73)
Settlement conference (pretrial hearing) (68)
Statute of limitations (66)
Submission agreement (74)
Summons (63)
Trial brief (69)
Trier of fact (69)
Uniform Arbitration Act (74)
Verdict (71)
Voir dire (69)
Written memorandum (71)

Law Case with Answer

Norgart v. Upjohn Company

Facts Kristi Norgart McBride lived with her husband in Santa Rosa, California. Kristi suffered from manic-depressive mental illness (now called bipolar disorder). In this disease, a person cycles between manic episodes (ultra-happy, expansive, and extroverted) and depressive episodes. The disease is often treated with prescription drugs. Kristi attempted suicide. A psychiatrist prescribed an anti-anxiety drug. One year later, Kristi attempted suicide again by overdosing on drugs. The doctor prescribed Halcion, a hypnotic drug, and added Darvocet-N, a mild narcotic analgesic. Five months later, after descending into a severe depression, Kristi committed suicide by overdosing on Halcion and Darvocet-N. Exactly six years after Kristi's death Leo and Phyllis Norgart, Kristi's parents, filed a lawsuit against the Upjohn Company, the maker of Halcion, to recover monetary damages for the wrongful death of their daughter, based on Upjohn's alleged failure to warn of the unreasonable dangers of taking Halcion. Upjohn argued that the one-year statute of limitations for wrongful death actions had run and that the case against it should be dismissed. Was the Norgarts' action for wrongful death barred by the one-year statute of limitations?

Answer Yes, the Norgarts' action for wrongful death against Upjohn was barred by the one-year statute of limitations. The purpose of the statute of limitations is to protect defendants from the stale claims of dilatory plaintiffs. It has as a related purpose to stimulate plaintiffs to assert fresh claims against defendants in a diligent fashion. Under the one-year statute of limitations relevant to this case, the plaintiffs must have brought their cause of action for wrongful death within one year of accrual—that is, one year from their daughter's death. The Norgarts were too late—exactly five years too late—in bringing their wrongful death action against Upjohn. The Upjohn Company was entitled to judgment as a matter of law, based on the fact that the one-year statute of limitations for a wrongful death action had run out, thus barring the plaintiff's lawsuit. *Norgart v. The Upjohn Company*, 21 Cal.4th 383, 87 Cal.Rptr.2d 453, **Web** 1999 Cal. Lexis 5308 (Supreme Court of California)

Critical Legal Thinking Cases

4.1 Summary Judgment Plaintiff Phyllis Toote filed a lawsuit against Pathmark Stores, Inc., a grocery store, and Canada Dry Bottling Company of New York, a bottler and distributor of soda. In her complaint, the plaintiff alleged that the defendants were liable for negligence for injuries she suffered when she fell over cases of soda that were stacked on the floor of the supermarket when she was shopping at the supermarket.

Defendant Pathmark took plaintiff Toote's deposition, in which she stated that she had entered the supermarket, and upon entering the store, she immediately walked to the soda aisle. Toote stated that she did not see the soda stacked on the floor before she fell over the soda. In the deposition, Toote stated that she did not know how long the soda had been on the floor before she tripped and fell. Pathmark made a motion for summary judgment, alleging that plaintiff Toote could not establish how long the soda had been on the floor before she fell. The Motion Court denied Pathmark's motion for summary judgment, finding that there were questions of fact to be decided by the jury. Pathmark appealed. Should the court grant Pathmark's motion for summary judgment? *Toote v. Canada Dry Bottling Company of New York, Inc. and Pathmark Stores, Inc.*, 7 A.D.3d 251, 776 N.Y.S.2d 42, **Web** 2004 N.Y. App.Div. Lexis 6470 (Supreme Court of New York, Appellate Division)

4.2 Long-Arm Statute Sean O'Grady, a professional boxer, was managed by his father, Pat. Sean was a contender for the world featherweight title. Pat entered into a contract with Magna Verde Corporation, a Los Angeles–based business, to co-promote a fight between Sean and the then-current featherweight champion. The fight was scheduled to take place in Oklahoma City, Oklahoma. To promote the fight, Pat O'Grady scheduled a press conference. At the conference, Pat was involved in a confrontation with a sportswriter named Brooks. He allegedly struck Brooks in the face. Brooks brought suit against Pat O'Grady and Magna Verde Corporation in an Oklahoma state court. Court records showed that the only contact that Magna Verde had with Oklahoma was that a few of its employees had taken several trips to Oklahoma to plan the title fight. The fight was never held. Oklahoma has a long-arm statute. Magna Verde was served by mail and made a special appearance in Oklahoma state court to argue that Oklahoma does not have personal jurisdiction over it. Does Oklahoma have jurisdiction over Magna Verde Corporation? *Brooks v. Magna Verde Corp.*, 1980 Ok.Civ.App. 40, 619 P.2d 1271, **Web** 1980 Okla. Civ.App. Lexis 118 (Court of Appeals of Oklahoma)

4.3 Physical Examination Robert Schlagenhauf worked as a bus driver for the Greyhound Corporation. One night, the bus he was driving rear-ended a tractor-trailer. Seven passengers on the bus were injured and sued Schlagenhauf and Greyhound Corporation for damages. The complaint alleged that Greyhound was negligent for allowing Schlagenhauf to drive a bus when it knew that his eyes and vision "were impaired and deficient." The plaintiffs petitioned the court to order Schlagenhauf to be medically examined concerning these allegations. Schlagenhauf objected to the examination. Who wins? *Schlagenhauf v. Holder*, 379 U.S. 104, 85 S.Ct. 234, 13 L.Ed.2d 152, **Web** 1964 U.S. Lexis 152 (Supreme Court of the United States)

4.4 Interrogatories Cine Forty-Second Street Theatre Corporation operated a movie theater in New York City's Times Square area. Cine filed a lawsuit against Allied Artists Pictures Corporation, alleging that Allied Artists and local theater owners illegally attempted to prevent Cine from opening its theater, in violation of federal antitrust law. The suit also alleged that once Cine opened the theater, the defendants conspired with motion picture distributors to prevent Cine from exhibiting first-run, quality films. Attorneys for Allied Artists served a set of written questions concerning the lawsuit on Cine. Does Cine have to answer these questions? *Cine Forty-Second Street Theatre Corp. v. Allied Artists Pictures Corp.*, 602 F.2d 1062, **Web** 1979 U.S. App. Lexis 13586 (United States Court of Appeals for the Second Circuit)

Ethics Cases

4.5 Ethics Dennis and Francis Burnham were married in West Virginia. One year later, the couple moved to New Jersey, where their two children were born. After eleven years of marriage, the Burnhams decided to separate. Mrs. Burnham, who intended to move to California, was to have custody of the children. Mr. Burnham agreed to file for divorce on grounds of irreconcilable differences. Mr. Burnham threatened to file for divorce in New Jersey on grounds of desertion. After unsuccessfully demanding that Mr. Burnham adhere to the prior agreement, Mrs. Burnham brought suit for divorce in California state court. One month later, Mr. Burnham visited California on a business trip. He then visited his children in the San Francisco Bay area, where his wife resided. He took the older child to San Francisco for the weekend. Upon returning the child to Mrs. Burnham's home, he was served with a California court summons and a copy of Mrs. Burnham's divorce petition. He then returned to New Jersey. Mr. Burnham made a special appearance in the California court and moved to quash the service of process. *Burnham v. Superior Court of California*, 495 U.S. 604, 110 S.Ct. 2105, 109 L.Ed.2d 631, **Web** 1990 U.S. Lexis 2700 (Supreme Court of the United States)

1. Did Mrs. Burnham act ethically in having Mr. Burnham served on his visit to California?
2. Did Mr. Burnham act ethically in trying to quash the service of process?
3. Is the service of process good? Why or why not?

4.6 Ethics   AMF Incorporated and Brunswick Corporation both manufacture electric and automatic bowling center equipment. The two companies became involved in a dispute over whether Brunswick had advertised certain automatic scoring devices in a false and deceptive manner. The two parties settled the dispute by signing an agreement that any future problems between them involving advertising claims would be submitted to the National Advertising Council for arbitration. Brunswick advertised a new product, Armor Plate 3000, a synthetic laminated material used to make bowling lanes. Armor Plate 3000 competed with wooden lanes produced by AMF. Brunswick's advertisements claimed that bowling centers could save up to $500 per lane per year in maintenance and repair costs if they switched to Armor Plate 3000 from wooden lanes. AMF disputed this claim and requested arbitration. *AMF Incorporated v. Brunswick Corp.*, 621 F.Supp. 456, **Web** 1985 U.S. Dist. Lexis 14205 (United States District Court for the Eastern District of New York)

1. What is arbitration? Why do parties enter into arbitration agreements?
2. Is it ethical for a party to try to avoid arbitration if they have agreed to arbitrate their claims?
3. Is the arbitration agreement in this case enforceable?

Internet Exercises

1. Visit **www.abanet.org/tech/ltrc/research/efiling/** for a discussion of e-filings and the use of electronic documents in federal courts.

2. Visit **www.abanet.org/tech/ltrc/research/efiling/** to find out if your state's court system allows for the electronic filing of complaints, answers, and other documents filed with the court.

3. Go to **www.statutes-of-limitations.com/state/**. Click on your state to find out what the statute of limitations is for filing a negligence action in your state.

4. Visit the website of the Jams, a provider of alternative dispute resolution services, at **www.jamsadr.com/arbitration/defined.asp** and read about the various types of arbitration.

5. Go to the website of the American Arbitration Association (AAA), at **www.adr.org**. Does the AAA provide online dispute resolution?

Endnotes

1. There is no right to a jury trial for actions in equity (e.g., injunctions, specific performance).
2. 9 U.S.C. Section 1 et seq.
3. *Hall Street Associates, L.L.C. v. Mattel, Inc.*, 552 U.S. 576, 128 S.Ct. 1396, 170 L.Ed.2d 254, **Web** 2008 U.S. Lexis 2911 (Supreme Court of the United States).
4. *Gilmer v. Interstate/Johnson Lane Corporation*, 500 U.S. 20, 111 S.Ct. 1647, 114 L.Ed.2d 26, **Web** 1991 U.S. Lexis 2529 (Supreme Court of the United States).

Constitution and Public Law

Constitutional Law for Business and E-Commerce

CONSTITUTION OF THE UNITED STATES OF AMERICA

The U.S. Constitution was adopted in 1787 and was ratified by each state in the name of "the people." Ratification by the required number of states was completed on June 21, 1788. The U.S. Constitution establishes the federal government and delegates certain powers to the federal government.

Learning Objectives

After studying this chapter, you should be able to:

1. Describe the concept of federalism and the doctrine of separation of powers.
2. Define and apply the Supremacy Clause of the U.S. Constitution.
3. Explain the federal government's authority to regulate interstate commerce and foreign commerce.
4. Explain how the freedoms of speech, assembly, religion, and the press are protected by the First Amendment and how commercial speech may be limited.
5. Explain the doctrines of equal protection and due process.

Chapter Outline

Chapter Outline *(continued)*

> " *We the People of the United States, in Order to form a more perfect Union, establish Justice, insure domestic Tranquility, provide for the common defense, promote the general Welfare, and secure the Blessings of Liberty to ourselves and our Posterity, do ordain and establish this Constitution for the United States of America.*"

—*Preamble to the Constitution of the United States of America*

Introduction to Constitutional Law for Business and E-Commerce

Prior to the American Revolution, each of the thirteen original colonies operated as a separate sovereignty under the rule of England. In September 1774, representatives of the colonies met as a Continental Congress. In 1776, the colonies declared independence from England, and the American Revolution ensued. The **Declaration of Independence** was the document that declared independence from England.

This chapter examines the major provisions of the U.S. Constitution and the amendments that have been added to the Constitution. Of particular importance, this chapter discusses how these provisions affect the operations of business in this country. The Constitution, with amendments, is set forth as Appendix A to this book.

Constitution of the United States of America

In 1778, the Continental Congress formed a **federal government** and adopted the **Articles of Confederation**. The Articles of Confederation created a federal Congress composed of representatives of the thirteen new states. The Articles of Confederation was a particularly weak document that gave limited power to the newly created federal government. It did not provide Congress with the power to levy and collect taxes, to regulate commerce with foreign countries, or to regulate interstate commerce.

The **Constitutional Convention** was convened in Philadelphia in May 1787. The primary purpose of the convention was to strengthen the federal government. After substantial debate, the delegates agreed to a new **U.S. Constitution**. The Constitution was reported to Congress in September 1787. State ratification of the Constitution was completed in 1788. Many amendments, including the Bill of Rights, have been added to the Constitution since that time.

The nation's armour of defence against the passions of men is the Constitution. Take that away, and the nation goes down into the field of its conflicts like a warrior without armour.

Henry Ward Beecher
Proverbs from Plymouth Pulpit, 1887

WEB EXERCISE
Go to **www.ushistory.org/ declaration/document/index.htm** for the text of the Declaration of Independence. Read the first two paragraphs of the Declaration of Independence.

U.S. Constitution
The fundamental law of the United States of America. It was ratified by the states in 1788.

The U.S. Constitution, as amended, serves three major functions: (1) It creates the three branches of the federal government (i.e., the legislative, executive, and judicial branches), (2) it allocates powers to these branches, and (3) it protects individual rights by limiting the government's ability to restrict those rights.

The Constitution provides that it may itself be amended to address social and economic changes. Some important constitutional concepts are discussed in the following paragraphs.

Federalism and Delegated Powers

federalism
The U.S. form of government in which the federal government and the fifty state governments share powers.

Our country's form of government is referred to as **federalism**. This means that the federal government and the fifty state governments share powers.

When the states ratified the Constitution, they **delegated** certain powers—called **enumerated powers**—to the federal government.

enumerated powers
Certain powers delegated to the federal government by the states.

Example The federal government is authorized to regulate interstate commerce and foreign affairs.

Any powers that are not specifically delegated to the federal government by the Constitution are *reserved* to the state governments. These are called **reserved powers**. State governments are empowered to deal with local affairs.

Examples States enact laws that provide for the formation and regulation of partnerships and corporations. Cities adopt zoning laws that designate certain portions of a city as residential areas and other portions as business and commercial areas.

Doctrine of Separation of Powers

As mentioned previously, the federal government is divided into three branches:

legislative branch
The part of the U.S. government that makes federal laws. It is known as Congress (the Senate and the House of Representatives).

1. **Article I: Legislative branch.** *Article I* of the Constitution establishes the **legislative branch** of the federal government. The legislative branch is responsible for making federal law. This branch is **bicameral**; that is, it consists of the Senate and the House of Representatives. Collectively, they are referred to as **U.S. Congress**, or simply **Congress**.[1] Each state has two senators in the **U.S. Senate**. The number of representatives to the **U.S. House of Representatives** is based on the population of each state. The current number of representatives is determined by the most recent census.

executive branch
The part of the U.S. government that enforces the federal law; it consists of the president and vice president.

2. **Article II: Executive branch.** *Article II* of the Constitution establishes the **executive branch** of the federal government by providing for the election of the president and vice president. The president is not elected by popular vote but instead is selected by the **Electoral College**, whose representatives are appointed by state delegations.[2] The executive branch of government is responsible for enforcing federal law.

judicial branch
The part of the U.S. government that interprets the law. It consists of the Supreme Court and other federal courts.

3. **Article III: Judicial branch.** *Article III* of the Constitution establishes the **judicial branch** of the federal government by establishing the U.S. Supreme Court and providing for the creation of other federal courts by Congress.[3] The judicial branch is responsible for interpreting the U.S. Constitution and federal law.

Checks and Balances

checks and balances
A system built into the U.S. Constitution to prevent any one of the three branches of the government from becoming too powerful.

Certain **checks and balances** are built into the Constitution to ensure that no one branch of the federal government becomes too powerful. Examples of some of the checks and balances in our system of government are as follows:

- The judicial branch has authority to examine the acts of the other two branches of government and determine whether those acts are constitutional.[4]
- The executive branch can enter into treaties with foreign governments only with the advice and consent of the Senate.

- The legislative branch is authorized to create federal courts and determine their jurisdiction and to enact statutes that change judicially made law.
- The president has veto power over bills passed by Congress. The bill goes back to Congress, where a vote of two-thirds of each the U.S. Senate and the U.S. House of Representatives is required to override the president's veto.
- The House of Representatives has the power to impeach the president for certain activities, such as treason, bribery, and other crimes. The Senate has the power to try an impeachment case. A two-thirds vote of the Senate is required to impeach the president.

CONCEPT SUMMARY
BASIC CONSTITUTIONAL CONCEPTS

Concept	Description
Federalism	The Constitution created the federal government. The federal government, the 50 state governments, and Washington, DC, share powers in this country.
Delegated powers	When the states ratified the Constitution, they delegated certain powers to the federal government. These are called *enumerated powers*.
Reserved powers	Those powers not granted to the federal government by the Constitution are reserved to the state governments.
Separation of powers	Each branch of the federal government has separate powers. These powers are: a. Legislative branch—power to make the law. b. Executive branch—power to enforce the law. c. Judicial branch—power to interpret the law.
Checks and balances	Certain checks and balances are built into the Constitution to ensure that no one branch of the federal government becomes too powerful.

Supremacy Clause

The **Supremacy Clause** establishes that the U.S. Constitution and federal treaties, laws, and regulations are the supreme law of the land.[5] State and local laws that conflict with valid federal law are unconstitutional. The concept of

Supremacy Clause
A clause of the U.S. Constitution that establishes the U.S. Constitution and federal treaties, laws, and regulations as the supreme law of the land.

SUPREME COURT OF THE UNITED STATES, WASHINGTON, DC
The highest court in the land is the Supreme Court of the United States, located in Washington, DC. The U.S. Supreme Court decides the most important constitutional law cases and other important issues it deems ripe for review and decision. The Supreme Court's unanimous and majority decisions are precedent for all the other courts in the country.

preemption doctrine

A doctrine which provides that federal law takes precedence over state or local law.

federal law taking precedence over state or local law is commonly called the **preemption doctrine**.

Congress may expressly provide that a particular federal statute *exclusively* regulates a specific area or activity. No state or local law regulating the area or activity is valid if there is such a statute. More often, though, federal statutes do not expressly provide for exclusive jurisdiction. In these instances, state and local governments have *concurrent jurisdiction* to regulate the area or activity. However, any state or local law that "directly and substantially" conflicts with valid federal law is preempted under the Supremacy Clause.

In the following case, the U.S. Supreme Court held that a federal law preempted state law claims.

CASE 5.1   *U.S. SUPREME COURT Supremacy Clause*

Bruesewitz v. Wyeth LLC

131 S.Ct. 1068, 179 L.Ed.2d 1, Web 2011 U.S. Lexis 1085 (2011)
Supreme Court of the United States

"The Act reflects a sensible choice to leave complex epidemiological judgments about vaccine design to the FDA and the National Vaccine Program rather than juries."

—Scalia, Justice

Facts

Vaccines are biological preparations administered (usually by needle) to improve immunity to a particular disease. They usually contain an agent that resembles a disease-causing microorganism. Vaccines are subject to federal premarket approval of the federal Food and Drug Administration (FDA). The elimination of communicable diseases through vaccination became one of the greatest achievements of public health in the 20th century. By the 1970s and 1980s, vaccines had been so effective in preventing infectious diseases that the public became more concerned with the risk of injury from vaccinations themselves. This led to a massive increase in vaccine-related tort litigation against the manufacturers of vaccines. One group of manufacturers that were subject to such lawsuits was the manufacturers who made vaccines against diphtheria, tetanus, and pertussis (DTP). This destabilized the vaccine market, causing two of the tree domestic manufacturers of DTP to withdraw from the market.

In response, the U.S. Congress enacted the National Childhood Vaccine Injury Act of 1986 (NCVIA). One of the provisions of the NCVIA stated:

No vaccine manufacturer shall be liable in a civil action for damages arising from a vaccine-related injury or death associated with the

administration of a vaccine after October 1, 1988, if the injury or death resulted from side effects that were unavoidable even though the vaccine was properly prepared and was accompanied by proper directions and warnings.

Hanna Bruesewitz was born in 1991. In 1992, her pediatrician administered doses of DTP vaccine manufactured by Lederle Laboratories (later purchased by Wyeth LLC). Hanna immediately started to experience seizures, and she has suffered seizures since being vaccinated. Hanna's parents filed a lawsuit against Lederle, alleging that the company was liable for strict liability and negligent design of the vaccine. The U.S. District Court granted Wyeth summary judgment, holding that Bruesewitz's causes of action were preempted by the NCVIA. The U.S. Court of Appeals affirmed the judgment. Bruesewitz appealed to the U.S. Supreme Court.

Issue

Does the preemption provision in the federal NCVIA bar state law design-defect product liability claims against vaccine manufacturers?

Language of the U.S. Supreme Court

Provided that there was proper manufacture and warning, any remaining side effects, including those resulting from design defects, are deemed to have been unavoidable. State-law design-defect claims are therefore preempted. Drug manufacturers often could trade a little less efficacy for a little more safety, but the safest design is not always the best one. Striking the right balance between safety and efficacy is especially difficult with respect to vaccines, which affect public as well as individual health. The Act reflects a sensible choice to leave complex epidemiological judgments about vaccine design to the FDA and the National Vaccine Program rather than juries. We hold that the National Childhood Vaccine Injury Act preempts all design-defect claims against vaccine manufacturers brought by plaintiffs who seek compensation for injury or death caused by vaccine side effects.

Decision

The U.S. Supreme Court held that the federal NCVIA preempted state law design-defect product liability claims. The Supreme Court affirmed the decision of the U.S. Court of Appeals.

Case Questions

Critical Legal Thinking
What would be the consequence if there were not a Supremacy Clause in the U.S. Constitution?

Ethics
Did Wyeth act ethically in denying liability in this case?

Contemporary Business
What are the positive consequences of the enactment of the NCVIA? Are there any negative consequences?

Commerce Clause

The **Commerce Clause** of the U.S. Constitution grants Congress the power "to regulate commerce with foreign nations, and among the several states, and with Indian tribes."[6] Because this clause authorizes the federal government to regulate commerce, it has a greater impact on business than any other provision in the Constitution. Among other things, this clause is intended to foster the development of a national market and free trade among the states.

The U.S. Constitution grants the federal government the power to regulate three types of commerce:

1. Commerce with Native American tribes
2. Foreign commerce
3. Interstate commerce

Each of these is discussed in the following paragraphs.

> **Commerce Clause**
> A clause of the U.S. Constitution that grants Congress the power "to regulate commerce with foreign nations, and among the several states, and with Indian tribes."

Commerce with Native Americans

Before Europeans arrived in the "New World," the land had been occupied for thousands of years by people we now refer to as Native Americans. There were many different Native American tribes, each having its own independent and self-governing system of laws.

When the United States was first founded over two hundred years ago, it consisted of the original thirteen colonies, all located in the east, primarily on the Atlantic Ocean. At that time, the U.S. Constitution gave the federal government the authority to regulate commerce with the Native American tribes—in both the original thirteen states and the territory that was to eventually become the United States of America.

Under its Commerce Clause powers, the federal government entered into treaties with many Native American nations. Most tribes, in the face of white settlers' encroachment on their land and federal government pressure, were forced to sell their lands to the federal government. The Native Americans received money and goods for land. The federal government obtained many treaties through unscrupulous means, cheating the Native Americans of their land. These tribes were then relocated to other, smaller, pieces of land called *reservations*, often outside their typical tribal lands. The federal government eventually broke many of the treaties.

Once Native Americans came under U.S. authority, they lost much of their political power. Most tribes were allowed to keep their own governments but were placed under the "protection" of the U.S. government. In general, the United States treats Native Americans as belonging to separate nations, similarly to the way it treats Spain or France; however, it still considers Native Americans "domestic dependent" nations with limited sovereignty.

Today, many Native Americans live on reservations set aside for various tribes. Others live and work outside reservations.

Let our last sleep be in the graves of our native land!

Osceola

Indian Gaming Regulatory Act   In the late 1980s, the federal government authorized Native American tribes to operate gaming facilities. Congress passed the **Indian Gaming Regulatory Act,**[7] which sets the terms of casino gambling and other gaming activities on tribal land. This act allows Native Americans to negotiate with the states for gaming compacts and ensures that the states do so in good faith. If a state fails to do so, the tribe can bring suit in federal court to force the state to comply. Today, casinos operated by Native Americans can be found in many states. Profits from the casinos have become an important source of income for members of certain tribes.

Foreign Commerce

foreign commerce
Commerce with foreign nations. The Commerce Clause grants the federal government the authority to regulate foreign commerce.

The Commerce Clause of the U.S. Constitution gives the federal government the *exclusive power* to regulate commerce with foreign nations. This is often referred to as the **Foreign Commerce Clause**. Direct and indirect regulation of *foreign commerce* by state or local governments that unduly burdens foreign commerce violates the Commerce Clause and is therefore unconstitutional.

The federal government could enact a law that forbids another country from doing business in the United States if that country engages in activities that are not condoned by the United States. A state, however, could not enact a law that forbids a foreign country from doing business in that state if that country engages in activities that are not condoned by that state.

Examples The state of Michigan is the home of General Motors Corporation, Ford Motor Company, and Chrysler Corporation, the three largest automobile manufacturers in the United States. Suppose the Michigan state legislature enacts a law that imposes a 100 percent tax on any automobile imported from a foreign country that is sold in Michigan but does not impose the same tax on domestic automobiles sold in Michigan. The Michigan tax violates the Foreign Commerce Clause and is therefore unconstitutional and void. However, the federal government could enact a 100 percent tax on all foreign automobiles but not domestic automobiles sold in the United States, and that law would be valid.

Interstate Commerce

interstate commerce
Commerce that moves between states or that affects commerce between states.

The Commerce Clause gives the federal government the authority to regulate **interstate commerce**. Originally, the courts interpreted this clause to mean that the federal government could only regulate commerce that moved *in* interstate commerce. The modern rule, however, allows the federal government to regulate activities that *affect* interstate commerce.

Under the **effects on interstate commerce test**, the regulated activity does not itself have to be in interstate commerce. Thus, any local (*intrastate*) activity that has an effect on interstate commerce is subject to federal regulation. Theoretically, this test subjects a substantial amount of business activity in the United States to federal regulation.

The American Constitution is, so far as I can see, the most wonderful work ever struck off at a given time by the brain and purpose of man.

W. E. Gladstone
Kin Beyond Sea (1878)

Example In the famous case ***Wickard, Secretary of Agriculture v. Filburn,***[8] a federal statute limited the amount of wheat that a farmer could plant and harvest for home consumption. Filburn, a farmer, violated the law. The U.S. Supreme Court upheld the federal statute on the grounds that it involved interstate commerce because the statute was designed to prevent nationwide surpluses and shortages of wheat. The Court reasoned that wheat grown for home consumption would affect the supply of wheat available in interstate commerce.

The following landmark U.S. Supreme Court case concerns interstate commerce.

LANDMARK U.S. SUPREME COURT CASE

Heart of Atlanta Motel v. United States

"One need only examine the evidence which we have discussed . . . to see that Congress may . . . prohibit racial discrimination by motels serving travelers, however 'local' their operations may appear."

—Clark, Justice

The Heart of Atlanta Motel, which was located in the state of Georgia, had 216 rooms available to guests. The motel was readily accessible to motorists using U.S. interstate highways 75 and 85 and Georgia state highways 23 and 41. The motel solicited patronage from outside the state of Georgia through various national advertising media, including magazines of national circulation. The motel maintained more than 50 billboards and highway signs within the state of Georgia. Approximately 75 percent of the motel's registered guests were from out of state. The Heart of Atlanta Motel refused to rent rooms to blacks. Congress enacted the **Civil Rights Act of 1964**, which made it illegal for motels, hotels, and other public accommodations to discriminate against guests based on their race. After the act was passed, the Heart of Atlanta Motel continued to refuse to rent rooms to blacks. The owner-operator of the motel brought a declaratory relief action in U.S. District Court, *Heart of Atlanta Motel v. United States*, to have the Civil Rights Act of 1964 declared unconstitutional. The plaintiff argued that Congress, in passing the act, had exceeded its powers to regulate interstate commerce under the Commerce Clause of the U.S. Constitution. The U.S. District Court upheld the Civil Rights Act and enjoined the owner-operator of the Heart of Atlanta Motel from discriminating against blacks. The owner-operator of the motel appealed to the U.S. Supreme Court.

The U.S. Supreme Court held that the provisions of the Civil Rights Act of 1964 that prohibited discrimination in accommodations properly regulated interstate commerce. In reaching its decision, the U.S. Supreme Court stated:

The power of Congress over interstate commerce is not confined to the regulation of commerce among the states. It extends to those activities intrastate which so affect interstate commerce or the exercise of the power of Congress over it as to make regulation of them appropriate means to the attainment of a legitimate end, the exercise of the granted power of Congress to regulate interstate commerce.

Thus the power of Congress to promote interstate commerce also includes the power to regulate the local incidents thereof, including local activities in both the States of origin and destination, which might have a substantial and harmful effect upon that commerce. One need only examine the evidence which we have discussed above to see that Congress may—as it has—prohibit racial discrimination by motels serving travelers, however "local" their operations may appear.

The U.S. Supreme Court held that the challenged provisions of the Civil Rights Act of 1964 were constitutional, as a proper exercise of the commerce power of the federal government. *Heart of Atlanta Motel v. United States*, 379 U.S. 241, 85 S.Ct. 348, 13 L.Ed.2d 258, *Web* 1964 U.S. Lexis 2187 (Supreme Court of the United States)

State Police Power

The states did not delegate all power to regulate business to the federal government. They retain the power to regulate **intrastate commerce** and much interstate commerce that occurs within their borders. This is commonly referred to as states' **police power**.

police power
Power that permits states and local governments to enact laws to protect or promote the public health, safety, morals, and general welfare.

Police power permits states (and, by delegation, local governments) to enact laws to protect or promote the *public health, safety, morals, and general welfare*. This includes the authority to enact laws that regulate the conduct of business.

Examples State real property laws, personal property laws, and state environmental laws are enacted under state police power.

Dormant Commerce Clause

Dormant Commerce Clause
A situation in which the federal government has the Commerce Clause power to regulate an area of commerce but has chosen not to regulate that area of commerce.

unduly burden interstate commerce
A concept which says that states may enact laws that protect or promote the public health, safety, morals, and general welfare, as long as the laws do not unduly burden interstate commerce.

If the federal government has chosen not to regulate an area of interstate commerce that it has the power to regulate under its Commerce Clause powers, this area of commerce is subject to what is referred to as the **Dormant Commerce Clause**. A state, under its police power, can enact laws to regulate that area of commerce. However, if a state enacts laws to regulate commerce that the federal government has the power to regulate but has chosen not to regulate, the Dormant Commerce Clause prohibits the state's regulation from **unduly burdening interstate commerce**.

Example Under its interstate commerce powers, the federal government, could, if it wanted to, regulate corporations. However, the federal government has chosen not to. Thus states regulate corporations. Assume that one state's corporations code permits only corporations from that state but from no other state to conduct business in that state. That state's law would unduly burden interstate commerce and would be unconstitutional.

E-Commerce and the Constitution

The advent of the Internet has caused a revolution in how commerce is conducted. The Internet and other computer networks permit parties to obtain website domain names and conduct business electronically. This is usually referred to as **electronic commerce**, or **e-commerce**. Some businesses that conduct e-commerce over the Internet do not have any physical location, and many "brick-and-mortar" businesses augment their traditional sales with e-commerce sales as well. Currently, a significant portion of the sales of goods, licensing of intellectual property, and sales of services are accomplished through e-commerce. Because e-commerce is commerce, it is subject to the Commerce Clause of the U.S. Constitution.

In the following case, the U.S. Supreme Court had to decide whether a state law caused an undue burden on interstate commerce.

Digital Law

E-Commerce and the Commerce Clause

"State bans on interstate direct shipping represent the single largest regulatory barrier to expanded e-commerce in wine."

—Kennedy, Justice

In this Information Age, federal and state governments have had to grapple with how to regulate the Internet and e-commerce. The federal government seems to be taking the upper hand in passing laws that regulate business conducted in cyberspace, thus creating laws

that apply uniformly across the country. However, states have also enacted laws that regulate the Internet and e-commerce. State laws that unduly burden interstate e-commerce are unconstitutional, however. Consider the following case.

The state of Michigan regulates the sale of wine within its boundaries. Michigan law permits in-state wineries to sell wine directly to consumers, including by mail, Internet, and other means of sale. Michigan law prohibits out-of-state wineries from selling wine directly to Michigan consumers, including over the Internet. Michigan instead requires out-of-state wineries to sell their wine to Michigan wholesalers, who then sell the wine to Michigan retailers, who then sell the wine to Michigan consumers. Many small wineries across the country rely on the Internet to sell wine to residents in other states. Out-of-state wineries that are required by law to sell wine to Michigan wholesalers would incur a cost that in-state-wineries would not incur, thus making it more costly and often unprofitable for out-of-state wineries to sell to Michigan consumers.

Domaine Alfred, a small winery located in San Luis Obispo, California, and several other out-of-state wineries that were prohibited from selling wine directly to Michigan consumers sued Michigan. The plaintiff wineries alleged that the Michigan law caused an undue burden on interstate e-commerce, in violation of the Commerce Clause of the U.S. Constitution. The U.S. District Court ruled in favor of Michigan. The U.S. Court of Appeals reversed

and ruled in favor of the out-of-state wineries, finding that the Michigan law caused an undue burden on interstate e-commerce. The state of Michigan appealed to the U.S. Supreme Court.

The U.S. Supreme Court held that the Michigan state law that discriminated against out-of-state wineries in favor of in-state wineries caused an undue burden on interstate e-commerce, in violation of the Commerce Clause of the U.S. Constitution. The U.S. Supreme Court stated, "Technological improvements, in particular the ability of wineries to sell wine over the Internet, have helped make direct shipments an attractive sales channel. State bans on interstate direct shipping represent the single largest regulatory barrier to expanded e-commerce in wine." In this case, the U.S. Supreme Court saved e-commerce from a discriminatory state law. *Granholm, Governor of Michigan v. Heald*, 544 U.S. 460, 125 S.Ct. 1885, 161 L.Ed.2d 796, **Web** 2005 U.S. Lexis 4174 (Supreme Court of the United States, 2005)

Bill of Rights and Other Amendments to the U.S. Constitution

The U.S. Constitution provides that it may be amended. Currently, there are twenty-seven **amendments to the U.S. Constitution**.

In 1791, the ten amendments that are commonly referred to as the **Bill of Rights** were approved by the states and became part of the U.S. Constitution. The Bill of Rights guarantees certain fundamental rights to natural persons and protects those rights from intrusive government action.

> **Bill of Rights**
> The first ten amendments to the Constitution that were added to the U.S. Constitution in 1791.

Examples Fundamental rights guaranteed in the **First Amendment** include *freedom of speech*, *freedom to assemble*, *freedom of the press*, and *freedom of religion*. Most of these rights have also been found applicable to so-called artificial persons (i.e., corporations).

In addition to the Bill of Rights, seventeen other amendments have been added to the Constitution. These amendments cover a variety of issues.

Examples The additional seventeen amendments to the Constitution have abolished slavery, prohibited discrimination, authorized the federal income tax, given women the right to vote, specifically recognized that persons 18 years of age and older have the right to vote, and taken other actions.

Originally, the Bill of Rights limited intrusive action by the *federal government* only. Intrusive actions by state and local governments were not limited until the *Due Process Clause of the Fourteenth Amendment* was added to the Constitution in 1868. The Supreme Court has applied the **incorporation doctrine** and held that most of the fundamental guarantees contained in the Bill of Rights are applicable to *state and local government* action. The amendments to the Constitution that are most applicable to business are discussed in the sections that follow.

Freedom of Speech

One of the most honored freedoms guaranteed by the Bill of Rights is the **freedom of speech** of the First Amendment. Many other constitutional freedoms would be meaningless without it. The First Amendment's Freedom of Speech Clause protects speech only, not conduct. The U.S. Supreme Court places speech into three

> **freedom of speech**
> The right to engage in oral, written, and symbolic speech protected by the First Amendment.

PROTEST, LOS ANGELES, CALIFORNIA
The Freedom of Speech Clause of the First Amendment to the U.S. Constitution protects the right to engage in political speech. Freedom of speech is one of Americans' most highly prized rights.

> *I disapprove of what you say, but I will defend to the death your right to say it.*
>
> Voltaire

fully protected speech
Speech that cannot be prohibited or regulated by the government.

categories: (1) *fully protected*, (2) *limited protected*, and (3) *unprotected speech*. These types of speech are discussed in the following paragraphs.

Fully Protected Speech

Fully protected speech is speech that the government cannot prohibit or regulate. The government cannot prohibit or regulate the content of fully protected speech.

Example Political speech is an example of fully protected speech. Thus, the government could not enact a law that forbids citizens from criticizing the current president.

The First Amendment protects oral, written, and symbolic speech.

Example Burning the American flag in protest to a federal government military action is protected symbolic speech.

In the following case, the U.S. Supreme Court decided an important First Amendment issue.

CASE 5.2   *U.S. SUPREME COURT Free Speech and Violent Video Games*

Brown, Governor of California v. Entertainment Merchants Association

131 S.Ct. 2729, 180 L.Ed.2d 708, 2011 U.S. Lexis 4802 (2011)
Supreme Court of the United States

"And whatever the challenges of applying the Constitution to ever-advancing technology, the basic principles of freedom of speech and the press, like the First Amendment's command, do not vary when a new and different medium for communication appears."

—Scalia, Justice

Facts

Video games are played by millions of youth and adults. In terms of dollars, sales of video games exceed receipts in the movie industry. Some video games contain violent content. The Entertainment

Software Rating Board, an industry-sponsored self-regulatory organization, assigns age-specific ratings to each video game. The Video Software Dealers Association encourages retailers not to sell or rent games marked AO (adult only; for those 18 and older) to minors and not to sell or rent video games marked M (mature; for those 17 and older) to minors without parental consent.

[California enacted a state statute that prohibits the sale or rental of "violent video games" to minors. The act covers games] in which the range of options available to a player includes

killing, maiming, dismembering, or sexually assaulting an image of a human being, if those acts are depicted" in a manner that "a reasonable person, considering the game as a whole, would find appeals to a deviant or morbid interest of minors," that is "patently offensive to prevailing standards in the community as to what is suitable for minors," and that "causes the game, as a whole, to lack serious literary, artistic, political, or scientific value for minors. [Violation of the act is punishable by a civil fine of up to $1,000.]

Members of the video game and software industries challenged the enforcement of the act. The U.S. District Court concluded that the act violated the First Amendment and permanently enjoined its enforcement. The U.S. Court of Appeals affirmed the decision. California appealed to the U.S. Supreme Court.

Issue

Does the California act that restricts violent video games violate the First Amendment?

Language of the U.S. Supreme Court

Like the protected books, plays, and movies that preceded them, video games communicate ideas—and even social messages—through many familiar literary devices (such as characters, dialogue, plot, and music) and through features distinctive to the medium (such as the player's interaction with the virtual world). That suffices to confer First Amendment protection. And whatever the challenges of applying the Constitution to ever-advancing technology, the basic principles of freedom of speech and the press, like the First Amendment's command, do not vary when a new and different medium for communication appears.

California wishes to create a wholly new category of content-based regulation that is permissible only for speech directed at children. That is unprecedented and mistaken. Minors are entitled to a significant measure of First Amendment protection, and only in relatively narrow and well-defined circumstances may government bar public dissemination of protected materials to them.

California's argument would fare better if there were a longstanding tradition in this country of specially restricting children's access to depictions of violence, but there is none. Certainly the books we give children to read—or read to them when they are younger—contain no shortage of gore. Grimm's Fairy Tales, for example, are grim indeed. As her just deserts for trying to poison Snow White, the wicked queen is made to dance in red hot slippers "till she fell dead on the floor, a sad example of envy and jealousy." Cinderella's evil stepsisters have their eyes pecked out by doves. And Hansel and Gretel (children!) kill their captor by baking her in an oven.

High-school reading lists are full of similar fare. Homer's Odysseus blinds Polyphemus the Cyclops by grinding out his eye with a heated stake. In the Inferno, Dante and Virgil watch corrupt politicians struggle to stay submerged beneath a lake of boiling pitch, lest they be skewered by devils above the surface. And Golding's Lord of the Flies recounts how a schoolboy called Piggy is savagely murdered by other children while marooned on an island.

Here, California has singled out the purveyors of video games for disfavored treatment—at least when compared to booksellers, cartoonists, and movie producers—and has given no persuasive reason why. Even where the protection of children is the object, the constitutional limits on governmental action apply. And as a means of assisting concerned parents the Act is seriously overinclusive because it abridges the First Amendment rights of young people whose parents think violent video games are a harmless pastime. Legislation such as this, which is neither fish nor fowl, cannot survive strict scrutiny.

Decision

The U.S. Supreme Court held that the California act violated the First Amendment to the U.S. Constitution.

Case Questions

Critical Legal Thinking
Should First Amendment rights extend to violent video games? Or do they fall in a special dangerous class of medium that should not be accorded the same First Amendment protections as books and movies?

Ethics
Does the majority have the right to legislate what the minority should see and hear? Do video game producers act ethically in producing violent video games?

Contemporary Business
Was the California law clear and easy to obey?

Limited Protected Speech

The Supreme Court has held that certain types of speech have only *limited protection* under the First Amendment. The government cannot forbid this type of speech, but it can subject this speech to *time, place, and manner restrictions*. Two major forms of **limited protected speech** are *offensive speech* and *commercial speech*:

limited protected speech
Speech that the government may not prohibit but that is subject to time, place, and manner restrictions.

- **Offensive Speech.** **Offensive speech** is speech that offends many members of society. (It is not the same as obscene speech, however.) The Supreme Court has held that the content of offensive speech may not be forbidden but that it may be restricted by the government under time, place, and manner restrictions.

offensive speech
Speech that is offensive to many members of society. It is subject to time, place, and manner restrictions.

  Example The Federal Communications Commission (FCC) is a federal administrative agency that regulates radio, television, and cable stations. Under its powers, the FCC has regulated the use of offensive language on television by limiting such language to time periods when children would be unlikely to be watching (e.g., late at night).

commercial speech
Speech used by businesses, such as advertising. It is subject to time, place, and manner restrictions.

- **Commercial Speech.** **Commercial speech**, such as advertising, was once considered unprotected by the First Amendment. However, today, because of U.S. Supreme Court decisions, the content of commercial speech is protected but is also subject to time, place, and manner restrictions.

  Example In *Virginia State Board of Pharmacy v. Virginia Citizens Consumer Council, Inc.*,[9] the U.S. Supreme Court held that a state statute that prohibited a pharmacist from advertising the price of prescription drugs was unconstitutional because it violated the Freedom of Speech Clause. The U.S. Supreme Court held that this was commercial speech that was protected by the First Amendment.

  Example A city can prohibit billboards along its highways for safety and aesthetic reasons if other forms of advertising (e.g., print media) are available. This is a lawful place restriction.

Unprotected Speech

unprotected speech
Speech that is not protected by the First Amendment and may be forbidden by the government.

The U.S. Supreme Court has held that certain speech is **unprotected speech** that is not protected by the First Amendment and may be totally forbidden by the government. The Supreme Court has held that the following types of speech are unprotected speech:

1. **Dangerous speech**

   Example Yelling "fire" in a crowded theater when there is no fire is not protected speech.

2. **Fighting words that are likely to provoke a hostile or violent response from an average person**[10]

   Example Walking up to a person and intentionally calling that person names because of race or ethnicity would not be protected speech if it would likely cause the person being called the names to respond in a hostile manner.

3. **Speech that incites the violent or revolutionary overthrow of the government.** However, the mere abstract teaching of the morality and consequences of such action is protected.[11]

4. **Defamatory language**[12]

   Examples Committing libel or slander by writing or telling untrue statements about another person or committing product disparagement or trade libel by writing or telling untrue statements about a company's products or services is not protected speech, and the injured party may bring a civil lawsuit to recover damages.

5. Child pornography[13]

   Example Selling material depicting children engaged in sexual activity is unprotected speech.

6. **Obscene speech.**[14]   If speech is considered **obscene speech**, it has no protection under the Freedom of Speech Clause of the First Amendment and can be banned by the government.

   Examples Movies, videos, music, and other forms of speech that are obscene are unprotected speech.

The definition of *obscenity* has plagued the courts. The definition of *obscene speech* is quite subjective. One Supreme Court justice stated, "I know it when I see it."[15] In ***Miller v. California***, the U.S. Supreme Court determined that speech is obscene when:

1. The average person, applying contemporary community standards, would find that the work, taken as a whole, appeals to the *prurient interest*.
2. The work depicts or describes, in a patently offensive way, sexual conduct specifically defined by the applicable state law.
3. The work, taken as a whole, lacks serious literary, artistic, political, or scientific value.[16]

States are free to define what constitutes obscene speech. Movie theaters, magazine publishers, and so on are often subject to challenges that the materials they display or sell are obscene and therefore not protected by the First Amendment. Over the years, the content of material that has been found to be obscene has shifted to a more liberal view as the general norms of society have become more liberal. Today, fewer obscenity cases are brought than have been in the past.

In the following case, the U.S. Supreme Court had to decide if certain contemptuous speech was protected by the First Amendment.

> **obscene speech**
> Speech that (1) appeals to the prurient interest, (2) depicts sexual conduct in a patently offensive way, and (3) lacks serious literary, artistic, political, or scientific value.

> *The Constitution of the United States is not a mere lawyers' document: It is a vehicle of life, and its spirit is always the spirit of the age.*
>
> Woodrow Wilson
> *Constitutional Government in the United States (1927)*

CASE 5.3   *U.S. SUPREME COURT Free Speech*

Snyder v. Phelps

131 S.Ct. 1207, 179 L.Ed.2d 172, Web 2011 U.S. Lexis 1903 (2011)
Supreme Court of the United States

"Speech is powerful. It can stir people to action, move them to tears of both joy and sorrow, and—as it did here—inflict great pain. On the facts before us, we cannot react to that pain by punishing the speaker."

—Roberts, Chief Justice

Facts

Fred Phelps founded the Westboro Baptist Church in Topeka, Kansas. The church's congregation believes that God hates and punishes the United States for its tolerance of homosexuality, particularly in the U.S. military. The church frequently communicates its views by picketing at military funerals. In more than twenty years, the members of Westboro Baptist have picketed nearly six hundred funerals.

Lance Corporal Matthew Snyder, a member of the U.S. Marines, was killed in Iraq in the line of duty. Lance Corporal Snyder's father, Albert Snyder, selected the Catholic Church in the Snyders' hometown of Westminster, Maryland, as the site for his son's funeral.

Phelps decided to travel to Maryland with six other Westboro Baptist parishioners—two of his daughters and four of his grandchildren—to picket at Lance Corporal Snyder's funeral service. The Westboro congregation members picketed while standing on public land adjacent to a public street approximately 1,000 feet from the church. They carried placards that read "God Hates the USA/Thank God for 9/11," "America is Doomed," "Don't Pray for the USA," "Thank God for Dead Soldiers," and "You're Going

(continued)

to Hell." The picketers sang hymns and recited Bible verses. The funeral procession passed within 200 to 300 feet of the picket site.

Snyder filed a lawsuit against Phelps, Phelps's daughters, and the Westboro Baptist Church (collective "Westboro") in U.S. District Court. Snyder alleged intentional infliction of emotional distress and other state law tort claims. Westboro argued that their speech was protected by the First Amendment. The jury found for Snyder and held Westboro liable for $2.9 million in compensatory damages and $8 million in punitive damages. The U.S. District Court remitted the punitive damages to $2.1 million. The U.S. Court of Appeals held that the First Amendment protected Westboro's speech and reversed the judgment. Snyder appealed to the U.S. Supreme Court.

Issue

Does the Free Speech Clause of the First Amendment shield church members from tort liability for their funeral picketing speech?

Language of the U.S. Supreme Court

Whether the First Amendment prohibits holding Westboro liable for its speech in this case turns largely on whether that speech is of public or private concern, as determined by all the circumstances of the case. The "content" of Westboro's signs plainly relates to broad issues of interest to society at large, rather than matters of "purely private concern." We have repeatedly referred to public streets as the archetype of a traditional public forum, noting that "time out of mind" public streets and sidewalks have been used for public assembly and debate. Simply put, the church members had the right to be where they were.

Given that Westboro's speech was at a public place on a matter of public concern, that speech is entitled to "special protection" under the First Amendment. Such speech cannot be restricted simply because it is upsetting or arouses contempt. Indeed, the point of all speech protection is to shield just those choices of content that in someone's eyes are misguided, or even hurtful.

Speech is powerful. It can stir people to action, move them to tears of both joy and sorrow, and—as it did here—inflict great pain. On the facts before us, we cannot react to that pain by punishing the speaker. As a Nation we have chosen a different course—to protect even hurtful speech on public issues to ensure that we do not stifle public debate. That choice

requires that we shield Westboro from tort liability for its picketing in this case.

Decision

The U.S. Supreme Court held that the First Amendment protected Westboro's speech in this case. The U.S. Supreme Court held that Mr. Snyder could not recover tort damages for the emotional distress he suffered because of Westboro's speech.

Dissenting Opinion, Justice Alito

Our profound national commitment to free and open debate is not a license for the vicious verbal assault that occurred in this case. Mr. Snyder wanted what is surely the right of any parent who experiences such an incalculable loss: to bury his son in peace. But respondents, members of the Westboro Baptist Church, deprived him of that elementary right. As a result, Albert Snyder suffered severe and lasting emotional injury. The Court now holds that the First Amendment protected respondents' right to brutalize Mr. Snyder. I cannot agree.

Case Questions

Critical Legal Thinking

Is the distinction between "public" and "private" concerns the proper test to determine whether the First Amendment shields specific speech? Can private concerns be turned into public concerns by carrying signs that profess a public issue?

Ethics

Did the Westboro picketers know that they were causing personal grief to Mr. Snyder, who had lost his son? Should they have let Mr. Snyder bury his son in peace?

Contemporary Business

Was this a difficult case to decide? How would you have decided this case?

Note Most states have enacted funeral protection laws that set distance and time limitations on picketing at funerals. Most of these laws make it unlawful to engage in picketing before (e.g., one hour), during, and after (e.g., one hour) of a funeral, and set a minimum number of feet (e.g., 300 feet) that picketers must remain away from funeral services at churches, synagogues, temples, and cemeteries. The federal government has enacted a statute that prohibits funeral protests at Arlington National Cemetery and other national cemeteries where military funerals occur. Many of these laws have been challenged on free speech grounds. The governments argue that the time and distance restrictions are reasonable time, place, and manner restrictions on speech.

In the following case, the U.S. Supreme Court examined free speech rights on the Internet.

Digital Law

Free Speech in Cyberspace

"As the most participatory form of mass speech yet developed, the Internet deserves the highest protection from government intrusion."

—Stevens, Justice

Once or twice a century, a new medium comes along that presents new problems for applying freedom of speech rights. This time it is the Internet. Congress enacted the **Computer Decency Act**, which made it a felony to knowingly make "indecent" or "patently offensive" materials available on computer systems, including the Internet, to persons under 18 years of age. Immediately, more than fifty cyberspace providers and users filed a lawsuit, challenging the act as a violation of their free speech rights granted under the First Amendment to the Constitution. The U.S. District Court agreed with the plaintiffs and declared the act an unconstitutional violation of the Freedom of Speech Clause.

On appeal, the U.S. Supreme Court agreed and held that the act was an unconstitutional violation of free speech rights. The Supreme Court concluded that the Internet allows an individual to reach an audience of millions at almost no cost, setting it apart from TV, radio, and print media, which are prohibitively expensive to use.

The Court stated, "As the most participatory form of mass speech yet developed, the Internet deserves the highest protection from government intrusion." The Court declared emphatically that the Internet must be given the highest possible level of First Amendment free speech protection.

Proponents of the Computer Decency Act argued that the act was necessary to protect children from indecent materials. The Supreme Court reasoned that limiting the content on the Internet to what is suitable for a child resulted in unconstitutionally limiting adult speech. The Court noted that children are far less likely to trip over indecent material on the Internet than on TV or radio because the information must be actively sought out on the Internet. The Court noted that less obtrusive means for protecting children are available, such as requiring parents to regulate their children's access to materials on the Internet and placing filtering and blocking software on computers to control what their children see on the Internet. It still remains a crime under existing laws to transmit *obscene* materials over the Internet. *Reno v. American Civil Liberties Union*, 521 U.S. 844, 117 S.Ct. 2329, 138 L.Ed.2d 874, **Web** 1997 U.S. Lexis 4037 (Supreme Court of the United States)

THOMAS JEFFERSON MEMORIAL, WASHINGTON, DC
The United States has had many blemishes on its citizen's constitutional rights. For example, during World War II, Japanese Americans were involuntarily placed in camps. During the McCarthy hearings of the 1950s, citizens who were communists or associated with communists were "blackballed" from their occupations, most notably in the film industry. Women did not get the right to vote until the nineteenth Amendment was added to the U.S. Constitution in 1920. It was not until the mid-1960s that equal opportunity laws outlawed discrimination in the workplace based on race and sex.

Freedom of Religion

Freedom of religion is a key concept addressed by the First Amendment. The First Amendment contains two separate religion clauses: the *Establishment Clause* and the *Free Exercise Clause*. These two clauses are discussed in the following paragraphs.

Establishment Clause

Establishment Clause
A clause of the First Amendment that prohibits the government from either establishing a state religion or promoting one religion over another.

The U.S. Constitution requires federal, state, and local governments to be neutral toward religion. The **Establishment Clause** prohibits the government from either establishing a government-sponsored religion or promoting one religion over another. Thus, it guarantees that there will be no state-sponsored religion.

Example The U.S. Supreme Court ruled that an Alabama statute that authorized a one-minute period of silence in school for "meditation or voluntary prayer" was invalid.[17] The Court held that the statute endorsed religion.

Free Exercise Clause

Free Exercise Clause
A clause of the First Amendment that prohibits the government from interfering with the free exercise of religion in the United States.

The **Free Exercise Clause** prohibits the government from interfering with the free exercise of religion in the United States. Generally, this clause prevents the government from enacting laws that either prohibit or inhibit individuals from participating in or practicing their chosen religions.

Examples Federal, state, or local governments could not enact a law that prohibits all religions. The government could not enact a law that prohibits churches, synagogues, mosques, or temples. The government could not prohibit religious practitioners from celebrating their major holidays and high holy days.

Example In *Church of Lukumi Babalu Aye, Inc. v. City of Hialeah, Florida*[18] the U.S. Supreme Court held that a city ordinance that prohibited ritual sacrifices of chickens during church service violated the Free Exercise Clause and that such sacrifices should be allowed.

Of course, the right to be free from government intervention in the practice of religion is not absolute.

Example Human sacrifices are unlawful and are not protected by the First Amendment.

CONCEPT SUMMARY
FREEDOM OF RELIGION

Clause	Description
Establishment Clause	Prohibits the government from establishing a government-sponsored religion and from promoting one religion over other religions.
Free Exercise Clause	Prohibits the government from enacting laws that either prohibit or inhibit individuals from participating in or practicing their chosen religions.

Equal Protection Clause

Fourteenth Amendment
An amendment added to the U.S. Constitution in 1868 that contains the Due Process, Equal Protection, and Privileges and Immunities Clauses.

Equal Protection Clause
A clause which provides that a state cannot "deny to any person within its jurisdiction the equal protection of the laws."

The **Fourteenth Amendment** was added to the U.S. Constitution in 1868. Its original purpose was to guarantee equal rights to all persons after the Civil War. The **Equal Protection Clause** of the Fourteenth Amendment provides that a state cannot "deny to any person within its jurisdiction the equal protection of the laws."

Although this clause expressly applies to state and local government action, the Supreme Court has held that it also applies to federal government action.

This clause prohibits state, local, and federal governments from enacting laws that classify and treat "similarly situated" persons differently. Artificial persons, such as corporations, are also protected. Note that this clause is designed to prohibit invidious discrimination: It does not make the classification of individuals unlawful per se.

Standards of Review

The Supreme Court, over years of making decisions involving the Equal Protection Clause, has held that the government can treat people or businesses differently from one another if the government has sufficient justification for doing so. The Supreme Court has adopted three different standards of review for deciding whether the government's different treatment of people or businesses violates or does not violate the Equal Protection Clause:

1. **Strict scrutiny test.**   Any government activity or regulation that classifies persons based on a *suspect class* (e.g., race, national origin, citizenship) or involves *fundamental rights* (e.g., voting) is reviewed for lawfulness using a **strict scrutiny test**. This means that the government must have an exceptionally important reason for treating persons differently because of their race in order for such unequal treatment to be lawful. Under this standard, many government classifications of persons based on race are found to be unconstitutional. Others are found lawful.

    Race origin religion

    strict scrutiny test
    A test that is applied to classifications based on a suspect class (e.g., race, national origin, citizenship) or involves fundamental rights (e.g., voting).

    Example A government rule that permits persons of one race but not of another race to receive government benefits such as Medicaid would violate this test.

2. **Intermediate scrutiny test.**   The lawfulness of government classifications based on a *protected classes* (e.g., gender) is examined using an **intermediate scrutiny test**. This means that the government must have an important reason for treating persons differently because of their sex in order for such unequal treatment to be lawful. Applying this standard, many government classifications of persons based on sex are found to be unconstitutional. Under this standard, the courts must determine whether the government classification is "reasonably related" to a legitimate government purpose.

    intermediate scrutiny test
    A test that is applied to classifications based on a protected class other than race (e.g., gender).

    Example The federal government's requirement that males (upon reaching the age of 18) must register for a military draft but that females do not have to register for the draft has been found constitutional by the U.S. Supreme Court.[19]

3. **Rational basis test.**   The lawfulness of all government classifications that do not involve suspect or protected classes is examined using a **rational basis test**. Under this test, the courts will uphold government regulation as long as there is a justifiable reason for the law. This standard permits much of the government regulation of business.

    rational basis test
    A test that is applied to classifications not involving a suspect or protected class.

    Example Providing government subsidies to farmers but not to those in other occupations is permissible.

    Example The federal government's Social Security program, which pays benefits to older members of society but not to younger members of society, is lawful. The reason is that older members of society have earned this right during the course of their lifetimes.

Due Process Clauses

The Fifth and Fourteenth Amendments to the U.S. Constitution both contain **Due Process Clauses**. These clauses provide that no person shall be deprived of "life, liberty, or property" without due process of the law. The Due Process

Due Process Clause
A clause which provides that no person shall be deprived of "life, liberty, or property" without due process of the law.

Clause of the <u>Fifth Amendment applies to federal government action;</u> that of the <u>Fourteenth Amendment applies to state and local government action.</u> It is important to understand that the government is not prohibited from taking a person's life, liberty, or property. However, the government must follow due process to do so. There are two categories of due process: *substantive* and *procedural*.

Substantive Due Process

The **substantive due process** category of due process requires that government statutes, ordinances, regulations, and other laws be clear on their face and not overly broad in scope. The test of whether substantive due process is met is whether a "reasonable person" could understand the law to be able to comply with it. Laws that do not meet this test are declared *void for vagueness*.

Example A city ordinance making it illegal for persons to wear "clothes of the opposite sex" would be held unconstitutional as void for vagueness because a reasonable person could not clearly determine whether his or her conduct violates the law.

Most government laws, although often written in "legalese," are considered not to violate substantive due process.

Procedural Due Process

The **procedural due process** form of due process requires that the government give a person proper *notice* and *hearing* of legal action before that person is deprived of his or her life, liberty, or property.

Example If the federal government or a state government brings a criminal lawsuit against a defendant for the alleged commission of a crime, the government must notify the person of its intent (by charging the defendant with a crime) and provide the defendant with a proper hearing (a trial).

Privileges and Immunities Clauses

The purpose of the U.S. Constitution is to promote nationalism. If the states were permitted to enact laws that favored their residents over out-of-state residents, the concept of nationalism would be defeated. Both Article IV of the Constitution and the Fourteenth Amendment contain **Privileges and Immunities Clauses** that prohibit states from enacting laws that unduly discriminate in favor of their residents. Note that the Privileges and Immunities Clause applies only to citizens; it does not protect corporations.

Example A state cannot enact a law that prevents residents of other states from owning property or businesses in that state.

Courts have held that certain types of discrimination that favor state residents over nonresidents do not violate the Privileges and Immunities Clause.

Examples State universities are permitted to charge out-of-state residents higher tuition than they charge in-state residents. States are also permitted to charge higher fees to nonresidents for hunting and fishing licenses.

International Law

Human Rights Violations in Myanmar

MYANMAR
The country of Myanmar (also called Burma) is ruled by a junta composed of its military generals. The country has been accused of human rights violations, including using child labor and forced labor, eliminating political dissidents, and strict censorship. The country, once a democracy, has been run by the military since 1962.

Key Terms and Concepts

Amendments to the U.S. Constitution (93)
Articles of Confederation (85)
Bicameral (86)
Bill of Rights (93)
Checks and balances (86)
Civil Rights Act of 1964 (91)
Commerce Clause (89)
Commercial speech (96)
Computer Decency Act (99)
Constitutional Convention (85)
Declaration of Independence (85)

Delegated (86)
Dormant Commerce Clause (92)
Due Process Clause (101)
Effects on interstate commerce test (90)
Electoral College (86)
Electronic commerce (e-commerce) (92)
Enumerated powers (86)
Equal Protection Clause (100)
Establishment Clause (100)
Executive branch (86)
Federal government (85)
Federalism (86)

First Amendment (93)
Foreign Commerce Clause (90)
Fourteenth Amendment (100)
Free Exercise Clause (100)
Freedom of religion (100)
Freedom of speech (93)
Fully protected speech (94)
Heart of Atlanta Motel v. United States (91)
Incorporation doctrine (93)
Indian Gaming Regulatory Act (90)

Intermediate scrutiny test (101)
Interstate commerce (90)
Intrastate commerce (91)
Judicial branch (86)
Legislative branch (86)
Limited protected speech (96)
Miller v. California (97)
Obscene speech (97)
Offensive speech (96)
Police power (91)
Preemption doctrine (88)
Privileges and Immunities Clause (102)

Procedural due process (102)	Substantive due process (102)	Unprotected speech (96)	U.S. Constitution (85)
Rational basis test (101)	Supremacy Clause (87)	*Wickard, Secretary of Agriculture v. Filburn* (90)	U.S. House of Representatives (86)
Reserved powers (86)	Unduly burden interstate commerce (92)	U.S. Congress (Congress) (86)	U.S. Senate (86)
Strict scrutiny test (101)			

Law Case with Answer
Reno, Attorney General of the United States v. Condon, Attorney General of South Carolina

Facts   State departments of motor vehicles (DMVs) register automobiles and issue driver's licenses. State DMVs require automobile owners and drivers to provide personal information such as name, address, telephone number, vehicle description, Social Security number, medical information, and a photograph, as a condition for registering an automobile or obtaining a driver's license. Many states' DMVs sold this personal information to individuals, advertisers, and businesses, which then used this information to solicit business from the registered automobile owners and drivers. Sales of automobile owners' and drivers' personal information generated significant revenues for the states.

After receiving thousands of complaints from individuals whose personal information had been sold, the Congress of the United States enacted the Driver's Privacy Protection Act of 1994 (DPPA).[20] This federal statute prohibits a state from selling the personal information of a person unless the state obtains that person's affirmative consent to do so. South Carolina sued the United States, alleging that the federal government did not have power under the Commerce Clause of the U.S. Constitution to adopt the federal DPPA that prohibits the state from selling personal information of its registered automobile owners and drivers. Was the federal DPPA properly enacted by the U.S. Congress pursuant to the Commerce Clause power granted to the federal government by the U.S. Constitution?

Answer   Yes, the federal Driver's Privacy Protection Act (DPPA) was properly enacted by the U.S. Congress pursuant to the Commerce Clause power granted to the federal government by the U.S. Constitution. The DPPA is a proper exercise of Congress's authority to regulate interstate commerce under the Commerce Clause. The personal, identifying information that the DPPA regulates is a thing in interstate commerce, and that the sale or release of that information in interstate commerce is therefore a proper subject of congressional regulation.

The motor vehicle information that the states have historically sold is used by insurers, manufacturers, direct marketers, and others engaged in interstate commerce to contact automobile owners and drivers via customized solicitations. The information is also used in the stream of interstate commerce by various public and private entities for matters related to interstate motoring. Because automobile owners' and drivers' information is an article of commerce, its sale or release into the interstate stream of business is sufficient to support federal regulation. Congress had the authority under the Commerce Clause of the U.S. Constitution to enact the federal Driver's Privacy Protection Act. Therefore, a state cannot sell or otherwise distribute the personal information of registered drivers unless the state obtains that person's affirmative consent to do so. *Reno, Attorney General of the United States v. Condon, Attorney General of South Carolina*, 528 U.S. 141, 120 S.Ct. 666, 145 L.Ed.2d 587, **Web** 2000 U.S. Lexis 503 (Supreme Court of the United States)

Critical Legal Thinking Cases

5.1 Supremacy Clause   The U.S. Congress enacted the federal Motor Carrier Act of 1980. This act deregulated the trucking industry to make it competitively market oriented. In addition, Congress enacted two other federal statutes that preempted the regulation of trucking by the states. Subsequently, the state of

Maine adopted a state statute that regulated the trucking industry. One provision of the state statute forbids anyone other than a Maine-licensed tobacco retailer to accept an order for delivery of tobacco. Another provision forbids anyone knowingly to transport a tobacco product to a person in Maine unless either the sender or the receiver has a Maine license. Several trucking associations brought a lawsuit in federal court, claiming that federal law preempted Maine's statute. Does federal law preempt the two provisions of the Maine state statute at issue in this case? *Rowe, Attorney General of Maine v.New Hampshire Motor Transport Association*, 128 S.Ct. 989, 169 L.Ed.2d 933, **Web** 2008 U.S. Lexis 2010 (Supreme Court of the United States)

5.2 Establishment Clause McCreary County and Pulaski County (the Counties), Kentucky, placed in their courthouses large, gold-framed copies of the Ten Commandments. In both courthouses, the Ten Commandments were prominently displayed so that visitors could see them. The Ten Commandments hung alone, not with other paintings and such. The American Civil Liberties Union of Kentucky (ACLU) sued the Counties in U.S. District Court, alleging that the placement of the Ten Commandments in the courthouses violated the Establishment Clause of the U.S. Constitution. The U.S. District Court granted a preliminary injunction ordering the removal of the Ten Commandments from both courthouses. The Counties added copies of the Magna Carta, the Declaration of Independence, the Bill of Rights, and other nonreligious items to the display of the Ten Commandments. The U.S. District Court reissued the injunction against this display, and the U.S. Court of Appeals affirmed. The Counties appealed to the U.S. Supreme Court. Does the display of the Ten Commandments in the Counties' courthouses violate the Establishment Clause? *McCreary County, Kentucky v. American Civil Liberties Union of Kentucky*, 545 U.S. 844, 125 S.Ct. 2722, 162 L.Ed.2d 729, **Web** 2005 U.S. Lexis 5211 (Supreme Court of the United States)

5.3 Supremacy Clause The military regime of the country of Myanmar (previously called Burma) has been accused of major civil rights violations, including using forced and child labor, imprisoning and torturing political opponents, and harshly repressing ethnic minorities. These inhumane actions have been condemned by human rights organizations around the world. The state legislators of the state of Massachusetts were so appalled at these actions that they enacted a state statute banning the state government from purchasing goods and services from any company that did business with Myanmar.

The U.S. Congress enacted a federal statute that delegated power to the president of the United States to regulate U.S. dealings with Myanmar. The federal statute (1) banned all aid to the government of Myanmar except for humanitarian assistance, (2) authorized the president to impose economic sanctions against Myanmar, and (3) authorized the president to develop a comprehensive multilateral strategy to bring democracy to Myanmar.

The National Foreign Trade Council—a powerful Washington, DC–based trade association with more than 500 member companies—filed a lawsuit against Massachusetts to have the state law declared unconstitutional. The council argued that the Massachusetts "anti-Myanmar" statute conflicted with the federal statute and that, under the Supremacy Clause, the state statute was preempted by the federal statute. Does the Massachusetts anti-Myanmar state statute violate the Supremacy Clause of the U.S. Constitution? *Crosby, Secretary of Administration and Finance of Massachusetts v. National Foreign Trade Council*, 530 U.S. 363, 120 S.Ct. 2288, 147 L.Ed.2d 352, **Web** 2000 U.S. Lexis 4153 (Supreme Court of the United States)

5.4 Separation of Powers In 1951, a dispute arose between steel companies and their employees about the terms and conditions that should be included in a new labor contract. At the time, the United States was engaged in a military conflict in Korea that required substantial steel resources from which to make weapons and other military goods. On April 4, 1952, the steelworkers' union gave notice of a nationwide strike called to begin at 12:01 A.M. April 9. The indispensability of steel as a component in weapons and other war materials led President Dwight D. Eisenhower to believe that the proposed strike would jeopardize the national defense and that governmental seizure of the steel mills was necessary in order to ensure the continued availability of steel. Therefore, a few hours before the strike was to begin, the president issued Executive Order 10340, which directed the secretary of commerce to take possession of most of the steel mills and keep operating. The steel companies obeyed the order under protest and brought proceedings against the president. Is this seizure of the steel mills constitutional? *Youngstown Co. v. Sawyer, Secretary of Commerce*, 343 U.S. 579, 72 S.Ct. 863, 96 L.Ed.2d 1153, **Web** 1952 U.S. Lexis 2625 (Supreme Court of the United States)

5.5 Privileges and Immunities Clause During a period of a booming economy in Alaska, many residents of other states moved there in search of work. Construction work on the Trans-Alaska Pipeline was a major source of employment. The Alaska legislature enacted an act called the Local Hire Statute. This act required employers to hire Alaska residents in preference to nonresidents. Is this statute constitutional? *Hicklin v. Orbeck, Commissioner of the Department of Labor of Alaska*, 437 U.S. 518, 98 S.Ct. 2482, 57 L.Ed.2d 397, **Web** 1978 U.S. Lexis 36 (Supreme Court of the United States)

5.6 Commercial Speech The city of San Diego, California, enacted a city zoning ordinance that prohibited outdoor advertising display signs, including billboards. On-site signs at a business location were exempted from this rule. The city based the restriction on traffic safety and aesthetics. Metromedia, Inc., a company in the business of leasing commercial billboards to advertisers, sued the city of San Diego, alleging that the zoning ordinance was unconstitutional. Is it? *Metromedia, Inc. v. City of San Diego*, 453 U.S. 490, 101 S.Ct. 2882, 69 L.Ed.2d 800, **Web** 1981 U.S. Lexis 50 (Supreme Court of the United States)

5.7 Equal Protection Clause The state of Alabama enacted a statute that imposed a tax on premiums earned by insurance companies. The statute imposed a 1 percent tax on domestic insurance companies (i.e., insurance companies that were incorporated in Alabama and had their principal office in the state). The statute imposed a 4 percent tax on the premiums earned by out-of-state insurance companies that sold insurance in Alabama. Out-of-state insurance companies could reduce the premium tax by 1 percent by investing at least 10 percent of their assets in Alabama. Domestic insurance companies did not have to invest any of their assets in Alabama. Metropolitan Life Insurance Company, an out-of-state insurance company, sued the state of Alabama, alleging that the Alabama statute violated the Equal Protection Clause of the U.S. Constitution. Who wins and why?

Metropolitan Life Insurance Co. v. Ward, Commissioner of Insurance of Alabama, 470 U.S. 869, 105 S.Ct. 1676, 84 L.Ed.2d 751, **Web** 1985 U.S. Lexis 80 (Supreme Court of the United States)

5.8 Supremacy Clause The Clean Air Act, a federal statute, establishes national air pollution standards for fleet vehicles such as buses, taxicabs, and trucks. The South Coast Air Quality Management District (South Coast) is a political entity of the state of California. South Coast establishes air pollution standards for the Los Angeles, California, metropolitan area. South Coast enacted fleet rules that prohibited the purchase or lease by public and private fleet operators of vehicles that do not meet stringent air pollution standards set by South Coast. South Coast's fleet emission standards are more stringent than those set by the federal Clean Air Act. The Engine Manufacturers Association (Association), a trade association that represents manufacturers and sellers of vehicles, sued South Coast, claiming that South Coast's fleet rules are preempted by the federal Clean Air Act. The U.S. District Court and the U.S. Court of Appeals upheld South Coast's fleet rules. The Association appealed to the U.S. Supreme Court. Are South Coast's fleet rules preempted by the federal Clean Air Act? *Engine Manufacturers Association v. South Coast Air Quality Management District*, 541 U.S. 246, 124 S.Ct. 1756, 158 L.Ed.2d 529, **Web** 2004 U.S. Lexis 3232 (Supreme Court of the United States)

Ethics Cases

5.9 Ethics The Raiders are a professional football team and a National Football League (NFL) franchisee. Each NFL franchise is independently owned. Al Davis was an owner and the managing general partner of the Raiders. The NFL establishes schedules, negotiates television contracts, and otherwise promotes NFL football, including conducting the Super Bowl each year. The Raiders play home and away games against other NFL teams.

For years, the Raiders played their home games in Oakland, California. The owners of the Raiders decided to move the team from Oakland to Los Angeles, California, to take advantage of the greater seating capacity of the Los Angeles Coliseum, the larger television market of Los Angeles, and other economic factors. The team was to be renamed the Los Angeles Raiders. The city of Oakland brought an eminent domain proceeding in court to acquire the Raiders as a city-owned team. *City of Oakland, California v. Oakland Raiders*, 174 Cal.App.3d 414, 220 Cal.Rptr. 153, **Web** 1985 Cal.App. Lexis 2751 (Court of Appeal of California)

1. What is eminent domain?
2. Is it socially responsible for a professional sports team to move from one city to another city? What are the economic and other consequences of such a move?
3. Can the city of Oakland acquire the Raiders through eminent domain? Why or why not?

5.10 Ethics Congress enacted the Flag Protection Act, which made it a crime to knowingly mutilate, deface, physically defile, burn, or trample the U.S. flag. The law provided for fines and up to one year in prison upon conviction.[21] Certain individuals set fire to several U.S. flags on the steps of the U.S. Capitol in Washington, DC, to protest various aspects of the federal government's foreign and domestic policy. In a separate incident, other individuals set fire to a U.S. flag to protest the act's passage. All these individuals were prosecuted for violating the act. The district courts held the federal act unconstitutional, in violation of the defendants' First Amendment free speech rights, and dismissed the charges. The U.S. government appealed to the U.S. Supreme Court, which consolidated the two cases. Who wins? *United States v. Eichman*, 496 U.S. 310, 110 S.Ct. 2404, 110 L.Ed.2d 287, **Web** 1990 U.S. Lexis 3087 (Supreme Court of the United States)

1. What is symbolic speech? Can it be protected speech under the First Amendment?
2. What are the arguments in favor of enforcing the Flag Protection Act? What are the arguments in favor of dismissing the act?
3. Who wins and why?

Internet Exercises

1. To view a map of the original thirteen colonies, go to **http://en.wikipedia.org/wiki/13_colonies**.

2. Visit the website of the U.S. Senate, **www.senate.gov**. Click on "Senators." Go to "Choose a State" and select your state. Who are the U.S. Senators that represent you state?

3. Go to **https://forms.house.gov/wyr/welcome.shtml**. Select your state or territory. Type in your zip code. Click "Contact My Representative." What is the name of your representative?

4. Go to **http://ap.grolier.com/staticbp?page=/static/hist_links.html&templatename=/static/ap.html**.

Scroll down to the current president's name. Click on "Biography at the White House" and read the first news item under "Latest Headlines." What is the topic of this news item?

5. Visit the website of the Supreme Court of the United States, at **www.supremecourtus.gov**. Click on "About the Supreme Court." Click on "Biographies of Current Justices." Read the biography of the current chief justice of the Supreme Court. What is name of the chief justice? What president nominated the chief justice?

6. Go to **www.youtube.com/watch?v=Gve7avdld78&feature=related** and view the video about the "Trail of Tears." When did this occur?

Endnotes

1. To be elected to Congress, an individual must be a U.S. citizen, either naturally born or granted citizenship. To serve in the Senate, a person must be 30 years of age or older. To serve in the House of Representatives, a person must be 25 years of age or older.
2. To be president, a person must be 35 years of age or older and a natural citizen of the United States. According to the Twenty-Second Amendment to the Constitution, a person can serve only two full terms as president.
3. Federal court judges and justices are appointed by the president, with the consent of the Senate.
4. The principle that the U.S. Supreme Court is the final arbiter of the U.S. Constitution evolved from *Marbury v. Madison*, 1 Cranch 137, 5 U.S. 137, 2 L.Ed. 60, **Web** 1803 U.S. Lexis 352 (Supreme Court of the United States, 1803). In that case, the Supreme Court held that a judiciary statute enacted by Congress was unconstitutional.
5. Article VI, Section 2.
6. Article I, Section 8, Clause 3.
7. 25 U.S.C. Sections 2701–2721.
8. 317 U.S. 111, 63 S.Ct. 82, 87 L.Ed.122, **Web** 1942 U.S. Lexis 1046 (Supreme Court of the United States).
9. 425 U.S. 748, 96 S.Ct. 1817, 48 L.Ed.2d 346, **Web** 1976 U.S. Lexis 55 (Supreme Court of the United States).
10. *Chaplinsky v. New Hampshire*, 315 U.S. 568, 62 S.Ct. 766, 86 L.Ed. 1031, **Web** 1942 U.S. Lexis 851 (Supreme Court of the United States).
11. *Brandenburg v. Ohio*, 395 U.S. 444, 89 S.Ct. 1827, 23 L.Ed.2d 430, **Web** 1969 U.S. Lexis 1367 (Supreme Court of the United States).
12. *Beauharnais v. Illinois*, 343 U.S. 250, 72 S.Ct. 725, 96 L.Ed. 919, **Web** 1952 U.S. Lexis 2799 (Supreme Court of the United States).
13. *New York v. Ferber*, 458 U.S. 747, 102 S.Ct. 334, 73 L.Ed.2d 1113, **Web** 1982 U.S. Lexis 12 (Supreme Court of the United States).
14. *Roth v. United States*, 354 U.S. 476, 77 S.Ct. 1304, 1 L.Ed.2d 1498, **Web** 1957 U.S. Lexis 587 (Supreme Court of the United States).
15. Justice Stewart in *Jacobellis v. Ohio*, 378 U.S. 184, 84 S.Ct. 1676, 12 L.Ed.2d 793, **Web** 1964 U.S. Lexis 822 (Supreme Court of the United States).
16. 413 U.S. 15, 93 S.Ct. 2607, 37 L.Ed.2d 419, **Web** 1973 U.S. Lexis 149 (Supreme Court of the United States).
17. *Wallace v. Jaffree*, 472 U.S. 38, 105 S.Ct. 2479, 86 L.Ed.2d 29, **Web** 1985 U.S. Lexis 91 (Supreme Court of the United States).
18. 508 U.S. 520, 113 S.Ct. 2217, 124 L.Ed.2d 472, **Web** 1993 U.S. Lexis 4022 (Supreme Court of the United States).
19. *Rostker v. Goldberg*, 453 U.S. 57, 101 S.Ct. 2646, 69 L.Ed.2d 478, **Web** 1981 U.S. Lexis 126 (Supreme Court of the United States).
20. 18 U.S.C. Sections 2721–2775.
21. 18 U.S.C. Section 700.

6

Torts and Strict Liability

FOOTBALL FIELD
Football helmets and other sports equipment are usually designed to be as safe as possible. However, many manufacturers have discontinued making football helmets because of the exposure to product liability lawsuits.

Learning Objectives

After studying this chapter, you should be able to:

1. List and describe intentional torts against persons.
2. List and explain the elements necessary to prove negligence.
3. Describe the business torts of disparagement, false imprisonment, and fraud.
4. Define the doctrine of *strict liability*.
5. Apply the doctrine of strict liability to product defects.

Chapter Outline

Introduction to Torts and Strict Liability

Intentional Torts
 CASE 6.1 • *Walmart Stores, Inc. v. Cockrell*

Unintentional Torts (Negligence)
 ETHICS • *Ouch! McDonald's Coffee Is Too Hot!*
 LANDMARK LAW • *Palsgraf v. The Long Island Railroad Company*

Special Negligence Doctrines
 CASE 6.2 • *Lilya v. The Greater Gulf State Fair, Inc.*

Strict Liability and Product Liability
 CASE 6.3 • *Domingue v. Cameco Industries, Inc.*

" Negligence is not actionable unless it involves the invasion of a legally protected interest, the violation of a right. Proof of negligence in the air, so to speak, will not do."

—Chief Judge Cardozo
  Palsgraf v. Long Island Railroad Co. (1928)

Introduction to Torts and Strict Liability

Tort is the French word for a "wrong." The law provides remedies to persons and businesses that are injured by the tortious actions of others. Most torts are either intentional torts or unintentional torts, such as negligence. The distinction between the two types is based on the concept of *fault*. Under tort law, an injured party can bring a *civil lawsuit* to seek compensation for a wrong done to the party or to the party's property. Many torts have their origin in common law. The courts and legislatures have extended tort law to reflect changes in modern society.

Tort damages are monetary damages that are sought from the offending party. They are intended to compensate the injured party for the injury suffered. Such injury may consist of past and future medical expenses, loss of wages, pain and suffering, mental distress, and other damages caused by the defendant's tortious conduct. If the victim of a tort dies, his or her beneficiaries can bring a *wrongful death action* to recover damages from the defendant.

If a product defect causes injury or death to purchasers, lessees, users, or bystanders, the injured party or the heirs of a deceased person may bring legal actions and recover damages under certain tort doctrines. These tort doctrines include negligence, misrepresentation, and the modern theory of *strict liability*. Under the doctrine of strict liability, defendants may be held liable without fault. The liability of manufacturers, sellers, lessors, and others for injuries caused by defective products is commonly referred to as *product liability*. If a violation of strict liability has been found, the plaintiff may also recover *punitive damages* if the defendant's conduct has been reckless or intentional.

This chapter discusses intentional torts, negligence, strict liability, and product liability.

Intentional Torts

The law protects a person from unauthorized touching, restraint, or other contact. In addition, the law protects a person's reputation and privacy. Violations of these rights are actionable as torts. **Intentional torts** against persons are discussed in the paragraphs that follow.

Assault

Assault is (1) the threat of <u>immediate harm or offensive contact</u> or (2) any action that arouses <u>reasonable apprehension of imminent harm</u>. Actual physical contact is unnecessary. Threats of future harm are not actionable.

Examples Suppose a 6-foot-5-inch, 250-pound person makes a fist and threatens to punch a 5-foot, 100-pound person. If the threatened person is afraid that he or she will be physically harmed, that person can sue the threatening person to recover damages for the assault.

Battery

Battery is unauthorized and harmful or offensive physical contact with another person that causes injury. Basically, the interest protected here is each person's reasonable sense of dignity and safety. Direct physical contact, such as intentionally

---

tort
A wrong. There are three categories of torts: (1) intentional torts, (2) unintentional torts (negligence), and (3) strict liability.

Thoughts much too deep for tears subdue the Court When I assumpsit bring, and godlike waive a tort.

J. L. Adolphus
The Circuiteers (1885)

intentional tort
A category of torts that requires that the defendant possessed the intent to do the act that caused the plaintiff's injuries.

assault *Threat*
(1) The threat of immediate harm or offensive contact or (2) any action that arouses reasonable apprehension of imminent harm. Actual physical contact is unnecessary for an action to be assault.

battery *—Action*
Unauthorized and harmful or offensive direct or indirect physical contact with another person that causes injury.

hitting someone with a fist, is battery. Indirect physical contact between the victim and the perpetrator is also battery if injury results.

Examples Throwing a rock, shooting an arrow or a bullet, knocking off a hat, pulling a chair out from under someone, and poisoning a drink are all instances of actionable battery. The victim need not be aware of the harmful or offensive contact (e.g., it may take place while the victim is asleep).

Assault and battery often occur together, although they do not have to (e.g., the perpetrator hits the victim on the back of the head without any warning).

False Imprisonment

false imprisonment
The intentional confinement or restraint of another person without authority or justification and without that person's consent.

The intentional confinement or restraint of another person without authority or justification and without that person's consent constitutes **false imprisonment**. The victim may be restrained or confined by physical force, barriers, threats of physical harm, or the perpetrator's false assertion of legal authority (i.e., false arrest). A threat of future harm or moral pressure is not considered false imprisonment. The false imprisonment must be complete.

Examples A person who locks the doors in a house or an automobile and does not let another person leave is liable for false imprisonment.

Shoplifting and Merchant Protection Statutes

merchant protection statutes (shopkeeper's privilege)
Statutes that allow merchants to stop, detain, and investigate suspected shoplifters without being held liable for false imprisonment if (1) there are reasonable grounds for the suspicion, (2) suspects are detained for only a reasonable time, and (3) investigations are conducted in a reasonable manner.

Shoplifting causes substantial losses to retail and other merchants each year. Oftentimes, suspected shoplifters are stopped by store employees, and their suspected shoplifting is investigated. These stops sometimes lead to the merchant being sued for false imprisonment because the merchant detained the suspect.

Almost all states have enacted **merchant protection statutes**, also known as the **shopkeeper's privilege**. These statutes allow merchants to stop, detain, and investigate suspected shoplifters without being held liable for false imprisonment if:

1. There are *reasonable grounds* for the suspicion.
2. Suspects are detained for only a *reasonable time*.
3. Investigations are conducted in a *reasonable manner*.

Proving these elements is sometimes difficult. The following case applies the merchant's protection statute.

CASE 6.1   *False Imprisonment*

Walmart Stores, Inc. v. Cockrell

61 S.W.3d 774, Web 2001 Tex.App. Lexis 7992
Court of Appeals of Texas

"He made me feel like I was scum. That I had no say-so in the matter, that just made me feel like a little kid on the block, like the bully beating the kid up...."

—Karl Cockrell

Facts

Karl Cockrell and his parents went to the layaway department at a Walmart store. Cockrell stayed for about five minutes and decided to leave. As he was going out the front door, Raymond Navarro, a Walmart loss-prevention officer, stopped him and requested that Cockrell follow him to the manager's office. Once in the office, Navarro told him to pull his pants down. Cockrell put his hands between his shorts and underwear, pulled them out, and shook them. Nothing fell out. Next, Navarro told him to take off his shirt. Cockrell raised his shirt, revealing a large bandage that covered a surgical wound on the right side of his abdomen. Cockrell had recently had a liver transplant. Navarro asked him to take off the bandage, despite Cockrell's explanation that the bandage maintained a sterile environment around his surgical wound. On Navarro's insistence, Cockrell took down the bandage, revealing the wound. Afterward, Navarro apologized and let Cockrell go. Cockrell sued Walmart to recover damages for false imprisonment. Walmart defended, alleging that the shopkeeper's privilege protected it from liability. The trial court found in favor of Cockrell and awarded Cockrell $300,000 for his mental anguish. Walmart appealed.

Issue

Does the shopkeeper's privilege protect Walmart from liability under the circumstances of the case?

Language of the Court

Neither Raymond Navarro nor any other store employee saw Cockrell steal merchandise. However Navarro claimed he had reasons to suspect Cockrell of shoplifting. He said that Cockrell was acting suspiciously, because he saw him in the women's department standing very close to a rack of clothes and looking around. We conclude that a rational jury could have found that Navarro did not "reasonably believe" a theft had occurred and therefore lacked authority to detain Cockrell. Navarro's search was unreasonable in scope, because he had no probable cause to believe that Cockrell had hidden any merchandise

under the bandage. Removal of the bandage compromised the sterile environment surrounding the wound.

Cockrell testified that after Navarro let him go he was shaking, crying, nervous, scared, and looking around to make sure no one else was trying to stop him. When he arrived at home he was crying, nervous, and still "pretty well shook up." His mother said that he stayed upset for a "long time" and would not go out of the house.

Decision

The court of appeals upheld the trial court's finding that Walmart had falsely imprisoned Cockrell and had not proved the shopkeeper's privilege. The court of appeals upheld the trial court's judgment that awarded Cockrell $300,000 for mental anguish.

Case Questions

Critical Legal Thinking
What is the tort of false imprisonment? Explain.

Ethics
Did Navarro, the Walmart employee, act responsibly in this case? Did Walmart act ethically in denying liability in this case?

Contemporary Business
What does the shopkeeper's privilege provide? What are the elements necessary to prove the shopkeeper's privilege? Do you think Walmart had a good chance of proving the shopkeeper's privilege in this case?

Misappropriation of the Right to Publicity

Each person has the exclusive legal right to control and profit from the commercial use of his or her name and identity during his or her lifetime. This is a valuable right, particularly to well-known persons such as sports figures and movie stars. Any attempt by another person to appropriate a living person's name or identity for commercial purposes is actionable. The wrongdoer is liable for the tort of **misappropriation of the right to publicity** (also called the **tort of appropriation**).

Example A company that uses a likeness of a famous actress in its advertising without the actress's permission is liable for this tort.

Invasion of the Right to Privacy

The law recognizes each person's right to live his or her life without being subjected to unwarranted and undesired publicity. A violation of this right constitutes the tort of **invasion of the right to privacy**. If a fact is public information, there is no claim to privacy.

misappropriation of the right to publicity (tort of appropriation)
An attempt by another person to appropriate a living person's name or identity for commercial purposes.

invasion of the right to privacy
The unwarranted and undesired publicity of a private fact about a person. The fact does not have to be untrue.

Every # is Recoverable

Examples Secretly taking photos of another person with a cell phone camera in a men's or women's locker room would constitute invasion of the right to privacy. Reading someone else's mail, wiretapping someone's telephone, and reading someone else's e-mail without authorization to do so are also examples of invasion of the right to privacy.

Defamation of Character

A person's reputation is a valuable asset. Therefore, every person is protected from false statements made by others during his or her lifetime. This protection ends upon a person's death. The tort of **defamation of character** requires a plaintiff to prove that:

1. The defendant made an *untrue statement of fact* about the plaintiff.
2. The statement was intentionally or accidentally *published* to a third party. In this context, *publication* simply means that a third person heard or saw the untrue statement. It does not require appearance in newspapers, magazines, or books.

A false statement that appears in writing or other fixed medium is **libel**. An oral defamatory statement is **slander**.

Examples False statements that appear in a letter, newspaper, magazine, book, photograph, movie, video, and the like would be libel. If a person makes an untrue statement of fact about another person to a third person, it would be slander.

The publication of an untrue statement of fact is not the same as the publication of an *opinion*. The publication of opinions is usually not actionable. Because defamation is defined as an untrue statement of fact, truth is an absolute defense to a charge of defamation.

Examples The statement "My lawyer is lousy" is an opinion and is not defamation. The statement "My lawyer has been disbarred from the practice of law," when she has not been disbarred, is an untrue statement of fact and is actionable as defamation.

Public Figures as Plaintiffs   In ***New York Times Co. v. Sullivan***,[1] the U.S. Supreme Court held that *public officials* cannot recover for defamation unless they can prove that the defendant acted with "actual malice." *Actual malice* means that the defendant made the false statement knowingly or with reckless disregard of its falsity. This requirement has since been extended to **public figure** plaintiffs such as movie stars, sports personalities, and other celebrities.

Disparagement   Business firms rely on their reputation and the quality of their products and services to attract and keep customers. That is why state unfair-competition laws protect businesses from disparaging statements made by competitors or others. **Disparagement**, also called **trade libel**, **product disparagement**, and **slander of title**, depending on the circumstances, is an untrue statement made by one person or business about the products, services, property, or reputation of another business.

Example If a competitor of John Deere tractors told a prospective customer that "John Deere tractors often break down," when in fact they rarely do, that would be product disparagement.

Intentional Misrepresentation (Fraud)

One of the most pervasive business torts is **intentional misrepresentation**. This tort is also known as **fraud** or **deceit**. It occurs when a wrongdoer deceives another person out of money, property, or something else of value. A person who

---

defamation of character
A false statement made by one person about another. In court, the plaintiff must prove that (1) the defendant made an untrue statement of fact about the plaintiff and (2) the statement was intentionally or accidentally published to a third party.

libel
A false statement that appears in a letter, newspaper, magazine, book, photograph, movie, video, and so on.

slander
Oral defamation of character.

Hard cases make bad law.
Legal maxim

fact vs. opinions

disparagement (trade libel, product disparagement, or slander of title)
False statements about a competitor's products, services, property, or business reputation.

intentional misrepresentation (fraud or deceit)
The intentional defrauding of a person out of money, property, or something else of value.

has been injured by intentional misrepresentation can recover damages from the wrongdoer. Four elements are required to find fraud:

1. The wrongdoer made a false representation of material fact.
2. The wrongdoer had knowledge that the representation was false and intended to deceive the innocent party.
3. The innocent party justifiably relied on the misrepresentation.
4. The innocent party was injured.

Item 2, which is called **scienter**, refers to intentional conduct. It also includes situations in which the wrongdoer recklessly disregards the truth in making a representation that is false. Intent or recklessness can be inferred from the circumstances.

Example Matt, a person claiming to be a minerals expert, convinces one hundred people to invest $10,000 each with him so that he can purchase, on their behalf, a gold mine he claims is located in the state of North Dakota. Matt shows the prospective investors photographs of a gold mine to substantiate his story. The investors give Matt their money. There is no gold mine. Instead, Matt runs off with the investors' money. Matt intended to steal the money from the investors. This is an example of fraud: (1) Matt made a false representation of fact (there was no gold mine and he did not intend to invest their money to purchase the gold mine); (2) Matt knew that his statements were false and intended to steal the investors money; (3) the investors relied on Matt's statements; and (4) the investors were injured by losing their money.

Intentional Infliction of Emotional Distress

In some situations, a victim may suffer mental or emotional distress without first being physically harmed. The *Restatement (Second) of Torts* provides that a person whose *extreme and outrageous* conduct intentionally or recklessly causes severe emotional distress to another is liable for that emotional distress.[2] This is called the tort of **intentional infliction of emotional distress**, or the **tort of outrage**.

The plaintiff must prove that the defendant's conduct was "so outrageous in character and so extreme in degree as to go beyond all possible bounds of decency, and to be regarded as atrocious and utterly intolerable in a civilized society."[3] The tort does not require any publication to a third party or physical contact between the plaintiff and defendant.

Example A credit collection agency intrusively berating a debtor for being a "deadbeat debtor" in front of his family as he is exiting religious services is outrageous conduct that constitutes intentional infliction of emotional distress.

Malicious Prosecution

Businesses and individuals often believe they have a reason to sue someone to recover damages or other remedies. If the plaintiff has a legitimate reason to bring a lawsuit and does so, but the plaintiff does not win the lawsuit, he or she does not have to worry about being sued by the person whom he or she sued. But a losing plaintiff does have to worry about being sued by the defendant in a second lawsuit for **malicious prosecution** if certain elements are met. In a lawsuit for malicious prosecution, the original defendant sues the original plaintiff. In this second lawsuit, which is a *civil* action for damages, the original defendant is the plaintiff and the original plaintiff is the defendant. To succeed in a malicious prosecution lawsuit, the courts require the plaintiff to prove all of the following:

1. The plaintiff in the original lawsuit (now the defendant) instituted or was responsible for instituting the original lawsuit.

He that's cheated twice by the same man, is an accomplice with the Cheater.

Thomas Fuller
Gnomologia (1732)

intentional infliction of emotional distress (tort of outrage)
A tort that says a person whose extreme and outrageous conduct intentionally or recklessly causes severe emotional distress to another person is liable for that emotional distress.

malicious prosecution
A lawsuit in which the original defendant sues the original plaintiff. In the second lawsuit, the defendant becomes the plaintiff and vice versa.

2. There was no *probable cause* for the first lawsuit (i.e., it was a frivolous lawsuit).
3. The plaintiff in the original action brought it with *malice*. (Caution: This is a very difficult element to prove.)
4. The original lawsuit was terminated in favor of the original defendant (now the plaintiff).
5. The current plaintiff suffered injury as a result of the original lawsuit.

The courts do not look favorably on malicious prosecution lawsuits because they feel such lawsuits inhibit the original plaintiff's incentive to sue.

Example One student actor wins a part in a play over another student actor. To get back at the winning student, the rejected student files a lawsuit against the winning student, alleging intentional infliction of emotional distress, defamation, and negligence. The lawsuit is unfounded, but the winning student must defend the lawsuit. The jury returns a verdict exonerating the defendant. The defendant now can sue the plaintiff for malicious prosecution and has a very good chance of winning the lawsuit.

Unintentional Torts (Negligence)

unintentional tort (negligence)
A doctrine that says a person is liable for harm that is the foreseeable consequence of his or her actions.

Under the doctrine of **unintentional tort**, commonly referred to as **negligence**, a person is liable for harm that is a *foreseeable consequence* of his or her actions. *Negligence* is defined as "the omission to do something which a reasonable man would do, or doing something which a prudent and reasonable man would not do."[4]

To be successful in a negligence lawsuit, the plaintiff must prove that (1) the defendant owed a *duty of care* to the plaintiff, (2) the defendant *breached* this duty of care, (3) the plaintiff suffered *injury*, (4) the defendant's negligent act *caused* the plaintiff's injury, and (5) the defendant's negligent act was the *proximate cause* of the plaintiff's injuries. Each of these elements is discussed in the paragraphs that follow.

Duty of Care

duty of care
The obligation people owe each other not to cause any unreasonable harm or risk of harm.

To determine whether a defendant is liable for negligence, it must first be ascertained whether the defendant owed a *duty of care* to the plaintiff. **Duty of care** refers to the obligation people owe each other—that is, the duty not to cause any unreasonable harm or risk of harm.

Examples Each person owes a duty to drive his or her car carefully, not to push or shove on escalators, not to leave skateboards on the sidewalk, and the like. Businesses owe a duty to make safe products, not to cause accidents, and so on.

No court has ever given, nor do we think ever can give, a definition of what constitutes a reasonable or an average man.

Lord Goddard C.J.R.
Regina v. McCarthy (1954)

The courts decide whether a duty of care is owed in specific cases by applying a **reasonable person standard**. Under this test, the courts attempt to determine how an *objective, careful, and conscientious person would have acted in the same circumstances* and then measure the defendant's conduct against that standard. The defendant's subjective intent ("I did not mean to do it") is immaterial in assessing liability.

Defendants with a particular expertise or competence are measured against a **reasonable professional standard**. Applying this test, the courts attempt to determine how an objective, careful, and conscientious equivalent professional would have acted in the same circumstances and then measure the defendant professional's conduct against that standard.

Examples A brain surgeon is measured against a reasonable brain surgeon standard. A general practitioner doctor who is the only doctor who serves a small community is measured against a reasonable small town general practitioner standard.

Breach of the Duty of Care

Once a court finds that the defendant actually owed the plaintiff a duty of care, it must determine whether the defendant breached that duty. A **breach of the duty of care** is the failure to exercise care. In other words, it is the failure to act as a reasonable person would act. A breach of this duty may consist of an action.

breach of the duty of care A failure to exercise care or to act as a reasonable person would act.

Example Throwing a lit match on the ground in the forest and causing a fire is a breach of a duty of care.

Injury to Plaintiff

Even though a defendant's negligent act may have breached a duty of care owed to the plaintiff, this breach is not actionable unless the plaintiff suffers **injury** to himself or herself or injury to his or her property. That is, the plaintiff must have suffered some injury before he or she can recover any damages. The damages recoverable depend on the effect of the injury on the plaintiff's life or profession.

injury A plaintiff's personal injury or damage to his or her property that enables him or her to recover monetary damages for the defendant's negligence.

Examples Suppose that a man injures his hand when a train door malfunctions. The train company is found negligent. If the injured man is a star professional basketball player who makes $5 million per year, with an expected seven years of good playing time left, this plaintiff can recover multiple millions of dollars because he can no longer play professional basketball. If the injured man is a college professor with fifteen years until retirement who is making only one-fortieth per year what the basketball player makes, he can recover some money for his injuries. However, because he makes a lot less per year than the professional basketball player and because he can continue working, albeit with more difficulty, the professor can recover much less for the same injury.

Negligence is the omission to do something which a reasonable man would do, or doing something which a prudent and reasonable man would not do.

B. Alderson
Blyth v. Birmingham Waterworks Co. (1856)

The following is a classic case involving the issue of negligence.

Ethics

Ouch! McDonald's Coffee Is Too Hot!

McDonald's Corporation found itself embroiled in one of the most famous negligence cases of modern times. Stella Liebeck, a 79-year-old resident of Albuquerque, New Mexico, visited a drive-through window of a McDonald's restaurant with her grandson Chris. Her grandson, the driver of the vehicle, placed the order for breakfast. When breakfast came at the drive-through window, Chris handed a hot cup of coffee to Stella. Chris pulled over so that Stella could put cream and sugar in her coffee. Stella took the lid off the coffee cup she held in her lap, and the hot coffee spilled in her lap. As a result of the spill, Stella suffered third-degree burns on her legs, thighs, groin, and buttocks. Stella was driven to the emergency room and was hospitalized for seven days. She required medical treatment and later returned to the hospital to have skin grafts. She suffered permanent scars from the incident.

Stella's medical costs were $11,000. Stella asked McDonald's to pay her $20,000 to settle the case, but McDonald's offered only $800. Stella refused this settlement and sued McDonald's in court for negligence for selling coffee that was too hot and for failing to warn her of the danger of the hot coffee it served. At trial,

McDonald's denied that it had been negligent and asserted that Stella's own negligence—opening a hot coffee cup on her lap—had caused her injuries. The jury heard the following evidence:

- McDonald's enforces a quality-control rule that requires its restaurants and franchises to serve coffee at 180 to 190 degrees Fahrenheit.
- Third-degree burns occur on skin in just two to five seconds when coffee is served at 185 degrees.
- McDonald's coffee temperature was 20 degrees hotter than coffee served by competing restaurant chains.
- The temperature of McDonald's coffee was approximately 40 to 50 degrees hotter than normal house-brewed coffee.
- McDonald's had received more than 700 prior complaints of people who had been scalded by McDonald's coffee.
- McDonald's did not place a warning on its coffee cups to alert patrons that the coffee it served was exceptionally hot.

(continued)

Based on this evidence, the jury concluded that McDonald's had acted recklessly and awarded Stella $200,000 in compensatory damages, which was then reduced by $40,000 because of her own negligence, and $2.7 million in punitive damages. The trial court judge reduced the amount of punitive damages to $480,000, which was three times the amount of compensatory damages. McDonald's now places a warning on its coffee cups that its coffee is hot. *Liebeck v. McDonald's Restaurants, P.T.S., Inc.* (New Mexico District Court, Bernalillo County, New Mexico, 1994)

Ethics Questions   Do you think that McDonald's properly warned Stella Liebeck of the dangers of drinking McDonald's hot coffee? Do you think McDonald's acted ethically in offering Stella an $800 settlement? Was the award of punitive damages justified in this case? Why or why not?

Actual Cause

actual cause (causation in fact)
The actual cause of negligence. A person who commits a negligent act is not liable unless actual cause can be proven.

A defendant's negligent act must be the **actual cause** (also called **causation in fact**) of the plaintiff's injuries. The test is this: "But for" the defendant's conduct, would the accident have happened? If the defendant's act caused the plaintiff's injuries, there is causation in fact.

Examples Suppose a corporation negligently pollutes the plaintiff's drinking water. The plaintiff dies of a heart attack unrelated to the polluted water. Although the corporation has acted negligently, it is not liable for the plaintiff's death. There were a negligent act and an injury, but there was no cause-and-effect relationship between them. If, instead, the plaintiff had died because of the polluted drinking water, there would have been causation in fact, and the polluting corporation would have been liable.

Proximate Cause

proximate cause (legal cause)
A point along a chain of events caused by a negligent party after which that party is no longer legally responsible for the consequences of his or her actions.

Under the law, a negligent party is not necessarily liable for all damages set in motion by his or her negligent act. Based on public policy, the law establishes a point along the damage chain after which the negligent party is no longer responsible for the consequences of his or her actions. This limitation on liability is referred to as **proximate cause** (also called **legal cause**). The general test of proximate cause is *foreseeability*. A negligent party who is found to be the actual cause—but not the proximate cause—of the plaintiff's injuries is not liable to the plaintiff. Situations are examined on a case-by-case basis.

The classic law case that defined proximate cause, *Palsgraf v. The Long Island Railroad Company*, is discussed in the following feature.

Landmark Law

Palsgraf v. The Long Island Railroad Company

"Proof of negligence in the air, so to speak, will not do."
—Cardozo, Justice

The landmark case establishing the doctrine of proximate cause is *Palsgraf v. The Long Island Railroad Company*,[5] a New York case decided in 1928. Helen Palsgraf was standing on a platform, waiting for a passenger train. The Long Island Railroad Company owned and operated the trains and employed the station guards. As a man carrying a package wrapped in a newspaper tried to board the moving train, railroad guards tried to help him. In doing so, the package was dislodged from the man's arm, fell to the railroad tracks, and exploded. The package contained hidden fireworks. The explosion shook the railroad platform, causing a scale located on the platform to fall on Helen Palsgraf, injuring her. Palsgraf sued the railroad for negligence.

Justice Benjamin Cardozo denied Palsgraf's recovery, finding that the railroad was not the proximate cause of her injuries and was therefore not liable to Palsgraf for negligence. In his decision, Justice Cardozo eloquently addressed the issue of proximate cause:

The conduct of the defendant's guard, if a wrong in its relation to the holder of the package, was not a wrong in its relation to the plaintiff, standing far away. Relatively to her it was not negligence at all. Nothing in the situation gave notice that the falling package had in it the potency of peril to persons thus removed. Negligence is not actionable unless it involves the invasion of a legally protected interest, the violation of a right. Proof of negligence in the air, so to speak, will not do.

CONCEPT SUMMARY

ELEMENTS OF NEGLIGENCE

1. The defendant owed a *duty of care* to the plaintiff.
2. The defendant *breached this duty*.
3. The plaintiff suffered *injury*.
4. The defendant's negligent act was the *actual cause* (or *causation in fact*) of the plaintiff's injuries.
5. The defendant's negligent act was the *proximate cause* (or *legal cause*) of the plaintiff's injuries. The defendant is liable only for the *foreseeable* consequences of his or her negligent act. Damage

Special Negligence Doctrines

The courts have developed many *special negligence doctrines*. The most important of these are discussed in the paragraphs that follow.

Professional Malpractice

Professionals, such as doctors, lawyers, architects, accountants, and others, owe a duty of ordinary care in providing their services. This duty is known as the *reasonable professional standard*. A professional who breaches this duty of care is liable for the injury his or her negligence causes. This liability is commonly referred to as **professional malpractice**.

Examples A surgeon who amputates the wrong leg of a patient is liable for *medical malpractice*. A lawyer who fails to file a document with the court on time, causing a client's case to be dismissed, is liable for *legal malpractice*.

professional malpractice
The liability of a professional who breaches his or her duty of ordinary care.

Negligent Infliction of Emotional Distress

Some jurisdictions have extended the tort of emotional distress to include the **negligent infliction of emotional distress**. Here, a person who is not physically injured by the defendant's negligence but suffers emotional distress because of the defendant's action can recover damages from the defendant for emotional distress.

The most common example of negligent infliction of emotional distress involves bystanders who witness the injury or death of a relative that is caused by another's negligent conduct. Under this tort, the bystander, even though not personally physically injured, may be able to recover damages against the negligent party for his or her own mental suffering. Many states require that the following elements be proved in bystander cases:

negligent infliction of emotional distress
A tort that permits a person to recover for emotional distress caused by the defendant's negligent conduct.

1. A close relative was killed or injured by the defendant.
2. The plaintiff suffered severe emotional distress.
3. The plaintiff's mental distress resulted from a sensory and contemporaneous observance of the accident.

Some states require that the plaintiff's mental distress be manifested by some physical injury; other states have eliminated this requirement.

Example A father is walking his young daughter to school when a driver of an automobile negligently runs off the road and onto the sidewalk, hitting the girl but not her father. Suppose that the young daughter dies from her injuries. The father suffers severe emotional distress by seeing his daughter die and manifests his distress by suffering physically. The father can recover damages for negligent infliction of emotional distress for the severe distress he suffered by seeing his daughter die.

Negligence *Per Se*

Statutes often establish duties owed by one person to another. The violation of a statute that proximately causes an injury is **negligence *per se***.

Example Some cities have an ordinance that places the responsibility for fixing public sidewalks in residential areas on the homeowners whose homes front the sidewalks. A homeowner is liable if he or she fails to repair a damaged sidewalk in front of his or her home if a pedestrian trips and is injured because of the unrepaired sidewalk. The injured party does not have to prove that the homeowner owed the duty because the statute establishes that.

Res Ipsa Loquitur

If a defendant is in control of a situation in which a plaintiff has been injured and has superior knowledge of the circumstances surrounding the injury, the plaintiff might have difficulty proving the defendant's negligence. In such a situation, the law applies the doctrine of ***res ipsa loquitur*** (Latin for "the thing speaks for itself"). This doctrine raises a presumption of negligence and switches the burden to the defendant to prove that he or she was not negligent. *Res ipsa loquitur* applies in cases where the following elements are met:

1. The defendant had exclusive control of the instrumentality or situation that caused the plaintiff's injury.
2. The injury would not have ordinarily occurred but for someone's negligence.

Examples Haeran goes in for major surgery and is given anesthesia to put her to sleep during the operation. Sometime after the operation, it is discovered that a surgical instrument was left in Haeran during the operation. She suffers severe injury because of the left-in instrument. Haeran has no way to identify which doctor or nurse carelessly left the instrument in her body. In this case, the court can apply the doctrine of *res ipsa loquitur* and place the presumption of negligence on the defendants. Any defendant who can prove that he or she did not leave the instrument in Haeran escapes liability; any defendant who does not disprove his or her negligence is liable. Other typical *res ipsa loquitur* cases involve commercial airplane crashes, falling elevators, and the like.

Good Samaritan Laws

In the past, liability exposure made many doctors, nurses, and other medical professionals reluctant to stop and render aid to victims in emergency situations, such as highway accidents. Almost all states have enacted **Good Samaritan laws** that relieve medical professionals from liability for injury caused by their ordinary negligence in such circumstances. Good Samaritan laws protect medical professionals only from liability for their *ordinary negligence*, not for injuries caused by their gross negligence or reckless or intentional conduct. Most Good Samaritan laws protect licensed doctors, nurses, and laypersons certified in cardiopulmonary resuscitation (CPR). Laypersons not trained in CPR are not generally protected by Good Samaritan statutes—that is, they are liable for injuries caused by their ordinary negligence in rendering aid.

Assumption of the Risk

If a plaintiff knows of and voluntarily enters into or participates in a risky activity that results in injury, the law recognizes that the plaintiff assumed, or took on, the risk involved. Thus, the defendant can raise the defense of **assumption of the risk** against the plaintiff. This defense assumes that the plaintiff (1) had knowledge of the specific risk and (2) voluntarily assumed that risk.

Example Under assumption of the risk, a race-car driver assumes the risk of being injured or killed in a crash.

In the following case, the court had to decide whether the plaintiff had assumed the risk.

CASE 6.2   *Assumption of the Risk*

Lilya v. The Greater Gulf State Fair, Inc.

855 So.2d 1049, Web 2003 Ala. Lexis 57
Supreme Court of Alabama

"Here, the only evidence of danger stemming from the mechanical bull ride is the most open and obvious characteristic of the ride: the possibility of falling off the mechanical bull."

—Houston, Justice

Facts

The Greater Gulf State Fair, Inc., operated the Gulf State Fair in Mobile County, Alabama. One of the events at the fair was a mechanical bull ride for which participants paid money to ride the mechanical bull. A mechanical bull is a ride where the rider sits on a motorized device shaped like a real bull, and the ride simulates a real bull ride as the mechanical bull turns, twists, and bucks. The challenge is to stay on the bull and not be thrown off. A large banner above the ride read "Rolling Thunder."

John Lilya and a friend watched as a rider was thrown from the mechanical bull. Lilya also watched as his friend paid and rode the bull and also was thrown off. Lilya then paid the $5 admission charge and signed a release agreement that stated:

> I acknowledge that riding a mechanical bull entails known and unanticipated risks which could result in physical or emotional injury, paralysis, death, or damage to myself, to property, or to third parties. I expressly agree and promise to accept and assume all of the risks existing in this activity. My participation in this activity is purely voluntary, and I elect to participate in spite of the risks.

Lilya boarded the mechanical bull and was immediately thrown off onto a soft pad underneath the bull. Lilya reboarded the bull for a second ride. The bull ride began again and became progressively faster, spinning and bucking to the left and right until Lilya fell off the bull. On the fall, Lilya landed on his head and shoulders, and he suffered a fractured neck. Lilya sued Gulf State Fair to recover damages for his severe injuries. The trial court granted summary judgment to Gulf State Fair, finding that Lilya had voluntarily assumed an open and obvious danger. Lilya appealed.

Issue

Was riding a mechanical bull an open and obvious danger for which Lilya had voluntarily assumed the risk when he rode the mechanical bull?

Language of the Court

Here, the only evidence of danger stemming from the mechanical bull ride is the most open and obvious characteristic of the ride: the possibility of falling off the mechanical bull. Lilya was aware that the two riders who had ridden the mechanical bull immediately before he rode it had fallen off. He noticed the thick floor mat, and he knew that the mat was there to protect riders when they fell. Also, he signed a release that explicitly stated that riding the mechanical bull involved inherent risks and that the risks included falling off or being thrown from the bull which could result in head, neck, and back injuries. Additionally, the very name of the ride—"Rolling Thunder"—hanging on a banner above the ride, gives a somewhat graphic indication of what is the very nature of bull riding: an extremely turbulent, ride the challenge of which is to hang on and not fall off. "Volenti non fit injuria" (a person who knowingly and voluntarily risks danger cannot recover for any resulting injury).

Decision

The Supreme Court of Alabama held that riding a mechanical bull and being thrown and injured by the bull is an open and obvious danger and that Lilya had voluntarily assumed the risk when he rode the bull and was thrown and injured. The state supreme

(continued)

court affirmed the trial court's grant of summary judgment in favor of Gulf State Fair.

Case Questions

Critical Legal Thinking
What does the doctrine of assumption of the risk provide? Do you think the doctrine of assumption of the risk should be recognized by the law? Explain.

Ethics
Did Gulf State Fair act ethically by making money from such a dangerous activity as mechanical bull riding? Did Lilya act ethically in suing for damages?

Contemporary Business
What public purpose does the defense of assumption of the risk serve? What would be the consequences if this defense were not available? Explain.

Contributory and Comparative Negligence

Sometimes a plaintiff is partially liable for causing his own injuries. In such cases, the law usually penalizes the plaintiff for his negligence. States apply one of the two following standards:

contributory negligence
A doctrine that says a plaintiff who is partially at fault for his or her own injury cannot recover against the negligent defendant.

- **Contributory negligence.**   Some states apply the doctrine of **contributory negligence**, which holds that a plaintiff who is partially at fault for his own injury cannot recover against the negligent defendant.

  Example Suppose a driver who is driving over the speed limit negligently hits and injures a pedestrian who is jaywalking against a red "Don't Walk" sign. Suppose the jury finds that the driver is 80 percent responsible for the accident and the jaywalker is 20 percent responsible. The pedestrian suffered $100,000 in injuries. Under the doctrine of contributory negligence, the pedestrian cannot recover any damages from the driver.

comparative negligence (comparative fault)
A doctrine under which damages are apportioned according to fault.

- **Comparative negligence.**   Many states have replaced the doctrine of contributory negligence with the doctrine of **comparative negligence**, also called **comparative fault**. Under this doctrine, damages are apportioned according to fault.

  Example When the comparative negligence rule is applied to the previous example, in which the pedestrian suffered $100,000 of injuries, the result is much

AUTOMOBILES AT NIGHT
Motor vehicle accidents are a primary cause of injury and death in the United States. Most accidents are a result of negligence. Each year, over six million motor vehicle accidents occur that result in over three million injuries and approximately 40,000 fatalities of passenger car and truck occupants, pedestrians, motorcyclists, and bicyclists. Thus, approximately 110 people die every day in motor vehicle accidents in this country.

fairer. The plaintiff-pedestrian, who was 20 percent at fault for causing his own injuries, can recover 80 percent of his damages (or $80,000) from the negligent defendant-driver.

Several states have adopted **partial comparative negligence**, which provides that a plaintiff must be less than 50 percent responsible for causing his or her own injuries to recover under comparative negligence; otherwise, contributory negligence applies.

Strict Liability and Product Liability

Defective products often cause a person's injuries. The injured party can sue a product manufacturer or seller for **product liability**. A plaintiff can sue a party—usually the manufacturer—for being *negligent* in producing a defective product that caused the victim's injuries.

Another tort doctrine, the *doctrine of strict liability*, has been developed that applies to product defect cases. **Strict liability** removes many of the difficulties for the plaintiff associated with negligence lawsuits. Most states have now adopted this doctrine as a basis for product liability actions.

strict liability
A tort doctrine that makes manufacturers, distributors, wholesalers, retailers, and others in the chain of distribution of a defective product liable for the damages caused by the defect, *irrespective of fault*.

Liability Without Fault

Unlike negligence, strict liability does not require the injured person to prove that the defendant breached a duty of care. Strict liability is **liability without fault**. A seller can be found strictly liable even though he or she has exercised all possible care in the preparation and sale of his or her product.

The doctrine of strict liability applies to sellers and lessors of products who are engaged in the business of selling and leasing products. Casual sales and transactions by nonmerchants are not covered.

Example If a person sells a defective product to a neighbor in a casual sale, he is not strictly liable if the product causes injury.

Strict liability applies only to products, not to services.

All in the Chain of Distribution Are Liable

All parties in the **chain of distribution** of a defective product are strictly liable for the injuries caused by that product. Thus, all manufacturers, distributors, wholesalers, retailers, lessors, and subcomponent manufacturers may be sued and assessed liability under the doctrine of strict liability. This view is based on public policy: Lawmakers presume that sellers and lessors will insure against the risk of a strict liability lawsuit and spread the cost to their consumers by raising the price of products.

chain of distribution
All manufacturers, distributors, wholesalers, retailers, lessors, and subcomponent manufacturers involved in a transaction.

A defendant who has not been negligent but who is made to pay a strict liability judgment can bring a separate action against the negligent party in the chain of distribution to recover its losses.

Example Suppose a subcomponent manufacturer produces a defective tire and sells it to a truck manufacturer. The truck manufacturer places the defective tire on one of its new-model trucks. The truck is sold to a retail car dealership. Ultimately, the car dealership sells the truck to a buyer. The defective tire causes an accident in which the buyer is injured. All the parties in the tire's chain of distribution can be sued by the injured party; in this case, the liable parties are the subcomponent manufacturer, the truck manufacturer, and the car dealership.

Exhibit 6.1 compares the doctrines of negligence and strict liability.

Exhibit 6.1 NEGLIGENCE AND STRICT LIABILITY COMPARED

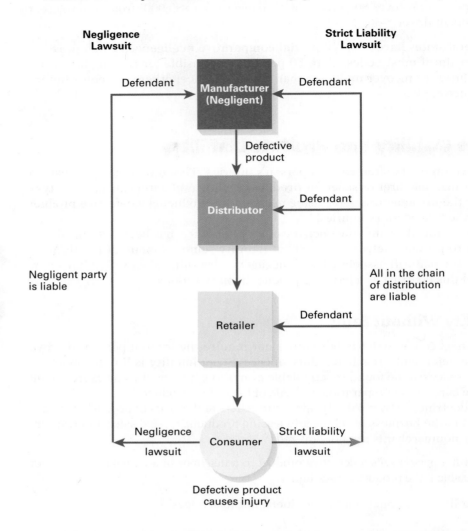

Nobody has a more sacred obligation to obey the law than those who make the law.

Sophocles

punitive damages
Monetary damages that are awarded to punish a defendant who either intentionally or recklessly injured the plaintiff.

Under strict liability, manufacturers, distributors, sellers, and lessors of a defective product are liable to the consumer who purchased the product and any user of the product. Users include the purchaser or lessee, family members, guests, employees, customers, and persons who passively enjoy the benefits of the product (e.g., passengers in automobiles). Bystanders (e.g., pedestrians on a sidewalk) are also protected by the doctrine.

Damages for personal injuries are recoverable in all jurisdictions that have adopted the doctrine of strict liability. Property damage is recoverable in most jurisdictions. In product liability cases, a court can award **punitive damages** if it finds that the defendant's conduct was committed with intent or with reckless disregard for human life. Punitive damages are meant to punish the defendant and to send a message to the defendant (and other companies) that such behavior will not be tolerated.

To recover for strict liability, the injured party must first show that the product that caused the injury was somehow *defective*. The most common types of **defects** are (1) *defect in manufacture*, (2) *defect in design*, (3) *failure to warn*, and (4) *defect in packaging*. These defects are discussed in the following paragraphs.

Defect in Manufacture

defect in manufacture
A defect that occurs when a manufacturer fails to (1) properly assemble a product, (2) properly test a product, or (3) adequately check the quality of the product.

A **defect in manufacture** occurs when the manufacturer fails to properly *assemble* a product, properly *test* a product, or adequately *check* the quality of a product.

Example A manufacturer produces a ladder that has a loose screw holding one of the ladder rungs to the side of the ladder. When a user climbs up the ladder, the step breaks because of the loose screw, and the user falls and is injured. Here there is a defect in manufacture: The other ladders produced by the manufacturer are properly made, whereas this particular ladder has been assembled improperly. The injured victim can sue under strict liability and recover damages for her injuries.

Defect in Design

A **defect in design** occurs when a product is designed incorrectly. In this case, not just one item has a defect but all of the products are defectively designed and can cause injury.

defect in design
A defect that occurs when a product is improperly designed.

Examples Design defects that have supported strict liability awards include toys designed with removable parts that could be swallowed by children, machines and appliances designed without proper safeguards, and trucks and other vehicles designed with defective parts.

In the following case, the court had to decide whether there was a design defect.

CASE 6.3   *Design Defect*

Domingue v. Cameco Industries, Inc.

936 So.2d 282, Web 2006 La.App. Lexis 1593 (2006)
Court of Appeal of Louisiana

"Evidence of the blind spot was clear and showed that a person of the decedent's height could not be seen by the driver until he was more than sixteen feet in front of the truck."

—Decuir, Judge

Facts

Russel Domingue, Charles Judice, and Brent Gonsoulin, who were employed by M. Matt Durand, Inc. (MMD), were stockpiling barite ore at a mine site. Judice and Gonsoulin were operating Cameco 405-B articulating dump trucks (ADTs) that were manufactured by Cameco Industries, Inc. Each of the trucks weighed over 25 tons and could carry a load of more than 20 metric tons. Judice and Gonsoulin were offloading ore from a barge and transporting and dumping it at a site where Domingue was using a bulldozer to push the barite onto a growing pile of ore. The two ADTs would make trips, passing each other on the way to and from the barge.

Gonsoulin, who was new to the job, had trouble dumping a large load of barite. Domingue, who was an experienced ADT operator, got off the bulldozer and walked to Gonsoulin's ADT to give his coworker advice on how to dump a heavy load. Meanwhile, Judice made another trip to dump ore and turned his ADT around to return to the barge. At the same time, Domingue was walking back to his bulldozer.

Judice testified that he then saw "a pair of sunglasses and cigarettes fly." Judice immediately stopped his ADT and discovered Domingue's body, which he had run over. Domingue's widow, on behalf of herself and her children, filed suit against Cameco, alleging that there was design defect in the ADT that caused a forward "blind spot" for anyone operating an ADT. The trial court found a design defect and held Cameco 30 percent responsible for causing Domingue's death. Damages were set at $1,101,050. Cameco appealed.

Issue

Is the forward blind spot on Cameco's 405-B dump truck a design defect?

Language of the Court

Evidence of the blind spot was clear and showed that a person of the decedent's height could not be seen by the driver until he was more than sixteen feet in front of the truck. He could not be seen from head to toe until he was standing over fifty-two feet in front of the truck. The configuration of the truck which created the blind spot was not necessary for the proper functioning of the truck, and, in fact, design modifications costing about $5,000.00 could have eliminated or

(continued)

greatly reduced the blind spot. The trial court considered this evidence and determined Cameco was 30% at fault in causing the accident which resulted in Mr. Domingue's death. We find no manifest error in this conclusion.

Decision

The court of appeal held that the blind spot on Cameco's 405-B dump truck was a design defect and upheld the trial court's judgment in favor of Domingue's family.

Case Questions

Critical Legal Thinking
Could the design of the dump truck have been made safer?

Ethics
Should Cameco have spent the extra $5,000 to greatly reduce or eliminate the blind spot?

Contemporary Business
What are the positive results of holding businesses liable for design defects?

Failure to Warn

Certain products are inherently dangerous and cannot be made any safer and still accomplish the purpose for which they are designed. Many such products have risks and side effects caused by their use. Manufacturers and sellers owe a duty to warn consumers and users about the dangers of using these products. A proper and conspicuous warning placed on the product insulates the manufacturer and others in the chain of distribution from strict liability. **Failure to warn** of these dangerous propensities is a defect that will support a strict liability action.

failure to warn
A defect that occurs when a manufacturer does not place a warning on the packaging of products that could cause injury if the danger is unknown.

Example Prescription medicine must contain warnings of its side effects. That way, a person can make an informed decision about whether to use the medicine. If a manufacturer produces a prescription medicine but fails to warn about its known side effects, any person who uses the medicine and suffers from the unwarned-against side effects can sue and recover damages based on failure to warn.

Defect in Packaging

Manufacturers owe a duty to design and provide safe packages for their products. This duty requires manufacturers to provide packages and containers that are tamperproof or that clearly indicate whether they have been tampered with. Certain manufacturers, such as drug manufacturers, owe a duty to place their products in containers that cannot be opened by children. A manufacturer's failure to meet this duty—a **defect in packaging**—subjects the manufacturer and others in the chain of distribution of the product to strict liability.

defect in packaging
A defect that occurs when a product has been placed in packaging that is insufficiently tamperproof.

A manufacturer is strictly liable in tort when an article he places on the market, knowing that it is to be used without inspection for defects, proves to have a defect that causes injury to a human being.

Traynor, Justice
Greenman v. Yuba Power Products, Inc. (1963)

Example A manufacturer of salad dressing fails to put a tamperproof seals on its salad dressings (i.e., caps that have a seal that shows whether or not they have been opened). A person purchases several bottles of the salad dressing from a grocery store, opens the caps, places the poison cyanide in the dressings, replaces the caps, and places the bottles back on the grocery store shelves. Consumers who purchase and use the salad dressing suffer injuries and death. Here, the salad dressing manufacturer would be strictly liable for failing to place a tamperproof seal on its products.

Defenses to Product Liability

Defendant manufacturers and sellers in negligence and strict liability actions may raise certain defenses to the imposition of liability: Some of the most common defenses are:

- **Generally known danger.**   Certain products are inherently dangerous and are known to the general population to be so. Manufacturers and sellers are not strictly liable for failing to warn of **generally known dangers**.

Example Because it is a known fact that guns shoot bullets, manufacturers and sellers of guns do not have to place a warning on the barrel of a gun warning of this generally known danger.

- **Government contractor defense.**   Defense and other contractors that manufacture products to government specifications are not usually liable if such a product causes injury.

    Example A manufacturer that produces a weapon to U.S. Army specifications is not liable if the weapon is defective and causes injury.

- **Abnormal misuse of a product.**   A manufacturer or seller is relieved of product liability if the plaintiff has abnormally misused the product.

    Example A manufacturer or seller of a power lawn mower is not liable if a consumer lifts a power lawn mower on its side to cut a hedge and is injured when the lawn mower falls and cuts him.

- **Supervening event.**   The manufacturer or seller is not liable if a product is materially altered or modified after it leaves the seller's possession and the alteration or modification causes an injury.

    Example A seller is not liable if a consumer purchases a truck and then replaces the tires with large off-road tires that cause the truck to roll over, injuring the driver or another person.

- **Assumption of the risk.**   The doctrine of assumption of the risk can be asserted as a defense to a product liability action. For this defense to apply, the defendant must prove that (1) the plaintiff knew and appreciated the risk and (2) the plaintiff voluntarily assumed the risk.

    Example A prescription drug manufacturer warns of the dangerous side effects of taking a prescription drug. A user is injured by a disclosed side effect. The user assumed the disclosed risk and therefore the manufacturer is not liable for product liability.

- **Statute of repose.**   Some states have enacted **statutes of repose**, which limit a manufacturer's and seller's liability to a certain number of years from the date when the product was first sold. The period of repose varies from state to state.

    statute of repose
    A statute that limits a seller's liability to a certain number of years from the date when a product was first sold.

    Example Assume that a state statute of repose for strict liability is seven years. If a purchaser purchases a product on May 1, 2013, the statute of repose expires May 1, 2020. If the product is defective but does not cause injury until after that date, the manufacturer and sellers are relieved of liability.

Key Terms and Concepts

Abnormal misuse (125)
Actual cause (causation in fact) (116)
Assault (109)
Assumption of the risk (118)
Battery (109)
Breach of the duty of care (115)
Chain of distribution (121)
Comparative negligence (comparative fault) (120)

Contributory negligence (120)
Defamation of character (112)
Defect (122)
Defect in design (123)
Defect in manufacture (122)
Defect in packaging (124)
Disparagement (trade libel, product disparagement, or slander of title) (112)

Duty of care (114)
Failure to warn (124)
False imprisonment (110)
Generally known danger (124)
Good Samaritan law (118)
Government contractor defense (125)
Injury (115)
Intentional infliction of emotional distress (tort of outrage) (113)

Intentional misrepresentation (fraud or deceit) (112)
Intentional tort (109)
Invasion of the right to privacy (111)
Liability without fault (121)
Libel (112)
Malicious prosecution (113)
Merchant protection statute (shopkeeper's privilege) (110)

Misappropriation of the right to publicity (tort of appropriation) (111)

Negligence *per se* (118)

Negligent infliction of emotional distress (117)

New York Times Co. v. Sullivan (112)

Palsgraf v. The Long Island Railroad Company (116)

Partial comparative negligence (121)

Product liability (121)

Professional malpractice (117)

Proximate cause (legal cause) (116)

Public figure (112)

Punitive damages (122)

Reasonable person standard (114)

Reasonable professional standard (114)

Res ipsa loquitur (118)

Scienter (113)

Slander (112)

Statute of repose (125)

Strict liability (121)

Supervening event (125)

Tort (109)

Unintentional tort (negligence) (114)

Law Case with Answer
Themed Restaurants, Inc., d.b.a Lucky Cheng's v. Zagat Survey, Inc.

Facts   Zagat Survey, LLC, publishes the famous Zagat series of dining, travel, and leisure guides for different cities and locations. The Zagat restaurant guides list and rank each reviewed restaurant from 0 to 30 for such categories as food, décor, and service. These ratings are calculated from surveys of customers of the restaurants, and the Zagat guides often quote anonymous consumer comments. Lucky Cheng's is a restaurant owned by Themed Restaurants, Inc., that is located in Manhattan, New York City. The *Zagat Survey of New York City Restaurants* rated the food at Lucky Cheng's as 9 and rated the décor and service as 15. The Zagat guide then stated: "God knows you don't go for the food at this East Village Asian-Eclectic." Themed Restaurants sued Zagat for disparagement (trade libel). Is Zagat liable for trade libel?

Answer   No, Zagat is not liable for trade libel. Trade libel is an untrue statement of fact made by one person or business about the products, services, property, or reputation of another business.

To prove trade libel, the plaintiff must show that the defendant (1) made an untrue statement of fact about the plaintiff's products, services, property, or business reputation; (2) published that untrue statement to a third party; (3) knew the statement was not true; and (4) made the statement maliciously (i.e., with intent to injure the plaintiff).

Restaurant ratings and reviews almost invariably constitute expressions of opinion. In this case, Zagat's ratings and comments about Lucky Cheng's restaurant that appeared in the Zagat guide were not statements of fact. Instead, they were mere opinions and were therefore not actionable as trade libel. Therefore, trade libel did not occur. *Themed Restaurants, Inc., d.b.a. Lucky Cheng's v. Zagat Survey*, LLC, 801 N.Y.S.2d 38, **Web** 2005 N.Y. App.Div. Lexis 9275 (Supreme Court of New York, Appellate Division)

Critical Legal Thinking Cases

6.1 Negligence   One morning, after working at night, Tim Clancy was driving a Chevrolet S-10 pickup truck on State Road 231. Clancy fell asleep at the wheel of the truck. Robert and Dianna Goad, husband and wife, were riding separate motorcycles on the other side of the road. Clancy's truck crossed the center line of the road and collided with Dianna's motorcycle. The collision immediately severed Dianna's leg above the knee, and she was thrown from her motorcycle into a water-filled ditch at the side of the road. Clancy was awakened by the sound of the impact, and the truck veered into the ditch as well. Robert stopped his motorcycle, ran back to the scene of the accident, and held Dianna's head out of the water-filled ditch.

Clancy called 911, and when the paramedics arrived, Dianna was taken to the hospital. Dianna remained in a coma for two weeks. Her leg had to be amputated. In addition, Dianna suffered from a fractured pelvic bone, a fractured left elbow, and a lacerated spleen, which had to be removed. Dianna endured multiple skin graft procedures. At the time of the trial, Dianna had undergone seven surgeries, she had taken more than 6,800 pills, and her medical expenses totaled more than $368,000. Furthermore, Dianna's medical expenses and challenges continue and are expected to continue indefinitely. In addition, Dianna has been fitted with a "C-leg," a computerized prosthetic leg. A C-leg needs to be replaced every three to five years, at full cost. Dianna sued Clancy to recover damages based on his negligence. Has Clancy been negligent? If so, what amount of damages should be awarded to Dianna? *Clancy v. Goad*, 858 N.E.2d 653, **Web** 2006 Ind. App. Lexis 2576 (Court of Appeals of Indiana)

6.2 Duty and Causation Michael Carneal was a 14-year-old freshman student at Heath High School in Paducah, Kentucky. Carneal regularly played the violent interactive video and computer games "Doom," "Quake," "Castle Wolfenstein," "Rampage," "Nightmare Creatures," "Mech Warrior," "Resident Evil," and "Final Fantasy." These games involved the player shooting virtual opponents with computer guns and other weapons. Carneal also watched videotaped movies, including one called *The Basketball Diaries*, in which a high-school-student protagonist dreams of killing his teacher and several of his fellow classmates. Carneal took a .22-caliber pistol and five shotguns into the lobby of Heath High School and shot several of his fellow students, killing three and wounding many others. The three students killed were Jessica James, Kayce Steger, and Nicole Hadley.

The parents of the three dead children sued the producers and distributors of the violent video games and movies that Carneal had watched previous to the shooting. The parents sued to recover damages for wrongful death, alleging that the defendants were negligent in producing and distributing such games and movies to Carneal. Are the video and movie producers liable to the plaintiffs for selling and licensing violent video games and movies to Carneal, who killed the plaintiffs' three children? *James v. Meow Media, Inc.*, 300 F.3d 683, **Web** 2002 U.S. App. Lexis 16185 (United States Court of Appeals for the Sixth Circuit)

6.3 Strict Liability Leo Dolinski purchased a bottle of Squirt, a soft drink, from a vending machine at a Sea and Ski plant, his place of employment. Dolinski opened the bottle and consumed part of its contents. He immediately became ill. Upon examination, it was found that the bottle contained the decomposed body of a mouse, mouse hair, and mouse feces. Dolinski visited a doctor and was given medicine to counteract nausea. Dolinski suffered physical and mental distress from consuming the decomposed mouse and thereafter possessed an aversion to soft drinks. The Shoshone Coca-Cola Bottling Company (Shoshone) had manufactured and distributed the Squirt bottle. Dolinski sued Shoshone, basing his lawsuit on the doctrine of strict liability. Does the doctrine of strict liability apply to this case? If so, is there a defect on which to base a case for strict liability? *Shoshone Coca-Cola Bottling Company v. Dolinski*, 420 P.2d 855, **Web** 1966 Nev. Lexis 260 (Supreme Court of Nevada)

6.4 Design Defect Intex Recreation Corporation designed and sold the Extreme Sno-Tube II. This snow tube is ridden by a user down snow-covered hills and can reach speeds of 30 miles per hour. The snow tube has no steering device, and therefore a rider may end up spinning and going down a hill backward. Dan Falkner bought an Extreme Sno-Tube II and used it for sledding the same day. During Falkner's second run, the tube rotated him backward about one-quarter to one-third of the way down the hill. A group of parents, including Tom Higgins, stood near the bottom of the hill. Higgins saw 7-year-old Kyle Potter walking in the path of Falkner's speeding Sno-Tube. Higgins ran and grabbed Potter to save him from harm, but while he was doing so, the Sno-Tube hit Higgins and threw him into the air. Higgins landed on his forehead, which snapped his head back. The impact severed Higgins's spinal cord and left him quadriplegic. Higgins sued Intex for damages based on strict liability. Is the snow tube defective? *Higgins v. Intex Recreation Corporation*, 199 P.3d 421, **Web** 2004 Wash.App. Lexis 2424 (Court of Appeals of Washington)

6.5 Merchant Protection Statute LaShawna Goodman went to a local Walmart store in Opelika, Alabama, to do some last-minute holiday shopping. She brought along her two young daughters and a telephone she had purchased earlier at Walmart to exchange. She presented the telephone and receipt to a Walmart employee, who took the telephone. Unable to find another telephone she wanted, Goodman retrieved the previously purchased telephone from the employee, bought another item, and left. Outside, Goodman was stopped by Walmart security personnel and was accused of stealing the phone. Goodman offered to show the Walmart employees the original receipt, but the Walmart employees detained her and called the police. Goodman was handcuffed in front of her children. Walmart filed criminal charges against Goodman.

At the criminal trial, Goodman was acquitted of all charges. Goodman then filed a civil lawsuit against Walmart Stores, Inc., to recover damages for falsely accusing her of stealing the telephone and false imprisonment. Walmart asserted the defense that it was within its rights to have detained Goodman as it did and to have prosecuted her based on its investigation. Walmart asserted that the merchant protection statute protected its actions in this case. Was Walmart's conduct ethical? Did Walmart act responsibly by bringing criminal charges against Goodman? Did Walmart present sufficient evidence to prove that it should be protected by the merchant protection statute? *Walmart Stores, Inc. v. Goodman*, 789 So.2d 166, **Web** 2000 Ala. Lexis 548 (Supreme Court of Alabama)

6.6 Negligence Seventeen-year-olds Adam C. Jacobs and David Messer made the acquaintance of 17-year-old waitress Sarah Mitchell at a pizza restaurant in Indianapolis, Indiana. Jacobs and Messer returned to the restaurant when Mitchell's shift ended at midnight, and the trio went to Messer's home. At approximately 2:30 A.M., Mitchell drove her Honda Accord with Jacobs in the front seat and Messer in the back seat. Jacobs suggested that they "jump the hills" on Edgewood Avenue, which he had done at least twenty times before. The speed limit for Edgewood Avenue, a two-lane road, was 40 miles per hour. Mitchell accelerated to approximately 80 miles per hour to jump the "big hill" on Edgewood Avenue near its crossroad at Emerson Avenue. The car crested the hill at 80 miles per hour, went airborne for a considerable distance, and landed in the middle of the road. Mitchell lost control of the car and over-steered to the right. The car sideswiped an Indiana Bell Telephone Company, Inc., utility pole (pole 65) and spun clockwise several times. The car then slammed broadside into an Indianapolis Power & Light Company utility pole (pole 66) and caught on fire. The two utility poles were located approximately 25 feet from Edgewood Avenue, at the edge of the utility companies' right of way. Messer escaped from the burning wreckage but was unable to rescue the unconscious Mitchell and Jacobs, both of whom died.

Susan J. Carter, the personal representative of the estate of Adam C. Jacobs, sued Indiana Bell and Indianapolis Power, alleging that the companies were negligent in the placement of their utility poles along Edgewood Avenue. Has Indiana Bell or Indianapolis Power breached its duty of care to Jacobs and proximately caused his death? *Carter v. Indianapolis Power & Light Company and Indiana Bell Telephone Company, Inc.*, 837 N.E.2d 509, **Web** 2005 Ind.App. Lexis 2129 (Court of Appeals of Indiana)

6.7 Strict Liability Senco Products, Inc. (Senco), manufactures and markets a variety of pneumatic nail guns, including the SN325 nail gun, which discharges 3.25-inch nails. The SN325 uses special nails designed and sold by Senco. The SN325 will discharge a nail only if two trigger mechanisms are activated; that is, the user must both squeeze the nail gun's finger trigger and press the nail gun's muzzle against a surface, activating the bottom trigger, or safety. The SN325 can fire up to nine nails per second if the trigger is continuously depressed and the gun is bounced along the work surface, constantly reactivating the muzzle safety/trigger.

The evidence disclosed that the SN325 double-fired once in every 15 firings. Senco rushed the SN325's production in order to maintain its position in the market, modifying an existing nail gun model so that the SN325 could shoot longer nails, without engaging in additional testing to determine whether the use of longer nails in that model would increase the prevalence of double-fire.

John Lakin was using a Senco SN325 nail gun to help build a new home. When attempting to nail two-by-fours under the eaves of the garage, Lakin stood on tiptoe and raised a two-by-four over his head. As he held the board in position with his left hand and the nail gun in his right hand, he pressed the nose of the SN325 up against the board, depressed the safety, and pulled the finger trigger to fire the nail into the board. The gun fired the first nail and then double fired, immediately discharging an unintended second nail that struck the first nail. The gun recoiled violently backward toward Lakin and, with Lakin's finger still on the trigger, came into contact with his cheek. That contact activated the safety/trigger, causing the nail gun to fire a third nail. This third nail went through Lakin's cheekbone and into his brain. The nail penetrated the frontal lobe of the right hemisphere of Lakin's brain, blocked a major artery, and caused extensive tissue damage.

Lakin was unconscious for several days and ultimately underwent multiple surgeries. He suffers permanent brain damage and is unable to perceive information from the left hemisphere of the brain. He also suffers partial paralysis of the left side of his body. Lakin has undergone a radical personality change and is prone to violent outbursts. He is unable to obtain employment. Lakin's previously warm and loving relationship with his wife and four children has been permanently altered. He can no longer live with his family and instead resides in a supervised group home for brain-injured persons. Lakin and his wife sued Senco for strict liability based on design defect. Is Senco liable to Lakin for strict liability based on a design defect in the SN325 that allowed it to double-fire? *Lakin v. Senco Products, Inc.*, 144 Ore.App. 52, 925 P.2d 107, **Web** 1996 Ore.App. Lexis 1466 (Court of Appeals of Oregon)

6.8 Design Defect Lorenzo Peterson was swimming in a swimming pool with a friend at an apartment complex. Lorenzo watched his friend swim to the bottom of the pool, slide an unattached drain cover away, and then slide it back. Lorenzo thought his friend had hidden something inside the drain, so he swam to the bottom of the pool. Lorenzo slid the drain cover aside and stuck his arm inside the drain. The 300 to 400 pounds of pull of the drain pump held Lorenzo trapped underwater. At least seven people tried to free Lorenzo to no avail. When the police arrived, they broke down the door to the pool equipment room and turned off the drain pump.

Lorenzo was trapped underwater for twelve minutes, which left him irreversibly brain damaged. Evidence at trial showed that Sta-Rite's drain covers are designed to screw down, but often a drain cover becomes loose. Further evidence showed that there had been more than twenty prior suction-entrapment accidents involving Sta-Rite's drain covers and pumps. Evidence showed that others had designed a pool drain pump with a mechanism that would automatically shut off a pool drain pump when it detected that it was pulling more than it should. Sta-Rite did not install such safety features on its drain pumps, however.

Lorenzo, through his relatives, sued Sta-Rite Industries, Inc., the manufacturer of the drain, under the doctrine of strict liability to recover damages for Lorenzo's injuries. The plaintiff alleged that the underwater pool drain was defectively designed because it did not contain a shut-off mechanism. Is there a design defect? *Sta-Rite Industries, Inc. v. Peterson*, 837 So.2d 988, **Web** 2003 Fla.App. Lexis 1673 (Court of Appeal of Florida, 2003)

6.9 Negligence Curtis R. Wilhelm owned beehives and kept the hives on property he owned. John Black, who operated a honeybee business, contracted to purchase some beehives from Wilhelm. Black employed Santos Flores, Sr., to help him pick up the beehives from Wilhelm. Black provided Flores with a protective suit to wear while picking up the beehives. Neither Wilhelm nor Black informed Flores of the danger of working with bees. After picking up beehives from Wilhelm's home, Black and Flores drove to remote property owned by Wilhelm to pick up other beehives. Flores opened the veil on his protective suit. After loading one beehive onto the truck, Flores started staggering and yelling for help. Flores sustained several bee stings, suffered anaphylactic shock reaction, and died before an ambulance could reach him. Flores's wife and children sued Wilhelm and Black for negligence for failing to warn Flores of the dangers of working with beehives and the possibility of dying of anaphylactic shock if stung by a bee. Has Wilhelm acted negligently by failing to warn Flores of the dangers of working with beehives? *Wilhelm v. Flores*, 133 S.W.3d 726, **Web** 2003 Tex.App. Lexis 9335 (Court of Appeals of Texas)

Ethics Cases

6.10 Ethics Radio station KHJ was a successful Los Angeles broadcaster of rock music that commanded a 48 percent market share of the teenage audience in the Los Angeles area. KHJ was owned and operated by RKO General, Inc. KHJ inaugurated a promotion titled "The Super Summer Spectacular." As part of this promotion, KHJ had a disc jockey known as "The Real Don Steele" ride around the Los Angeles area in a conspicuous red automobile. Periodically KHJ would announce to its radio audience Steele's location. The first listener to thereafter locate Steele and answer a question received a cash prize and participated in a brief interview on the air with Steele. One KHJ broadcast identified Steele's next destination as Canoga Park. Robert Sentner, 17 years old, heard the broadcast and immediately drove to Canoga Park. Marsha Baime, 19 years old, also heard the broadcast and drove to Canoga Park. By the time Sentner and Baime located Steele, someone else had already claimed the prize. Without the knowledge of the other, Sentner and Baime each decided to follow Steele to the next destination and to be first to "find" him.

Steele proceeded onto the freeway. For the next few miles, Sentner and Baime tried to jockey for position closest to the Steele vehicle, reaching speeds of up to 80 miles per hour. There is no evidence that the Steele vehicle exceeded the speed limit. When Steele left the freeway at the Westlake off ramp, Sentner and Baime tried to follow. In their attempts to do so, they knocked another vehicle, driven by Mr. Weirum, into the center divider of the freeway, where it overturned. Mr. Weirum died in the accident. Baime stopped to report the accident. Sentner, after pausing momentarily to relate the tragedy to a passing police officer, got back into his car, pursued and successfully located Steele, and collected the cash prize. The wife and children of Mr. Weirum brought a wrongful death negligence action against Sentner, Baime, and RKO General. *Weirum v. RKO General, Inc.*, 15 Cal.3d 40, 539 P.2d 36, 123 Cal. Rptr. 468, **Web** 1975 Cal. Lexis 220 (Supreme Court of California)

1. What are the elements to prove negligence?
2. Did RKO General, Inc., act responsibly in this case? Why or why not?
3. Who wins and why?

6.11 Ethics Guy Portee, a 7-year-old, resided with his mother in an apartment building in Newark, New Jersey. Edith and Nathan Jaffee owned and operated the building. One day, Guy became trapped in the building's elevator, between its outer door and the wall of the elevator shaft. When someone activated the elevator, the boy was dragged up to the third floor. Another child who saw the accident ran to seek help. Soon afterward, Renee Portee, the boy's mother, and officers from the Newark Police Department arrived. The officers worked for hours, trying to release the boy, during which time the mother watched as her son moaned, cried out, and flailed his arms. The police contacted the Atlantic Elevator Company, which was responsible for the installation and maintenance of the elevator, and requested that the company send a mechanic to assist in the effort to free the boy. Apparently, no one came. The boy suffered multiple bone fractures and massive internal hemorrhaging. He died while still trapped, his mother a helpless observer.

After her son's death, Renee became severely distressed and seriously self-destructive. Subsequently she attempted to take her own life. She survived, and the wound she gave herself was repaired by surgery, but thereafter she required considerable physical therapy.

She had received extensive counseling and psychotherapy to help overcome the mental and emotional problems associated with her son's death. Renee sued the Jaffees and Atlantic to recover damages for her emotional distress. *Portee v. Jaffee*, 84 N.J. 88, 417 A.2d 521, **Web** 1980 N.J. Lexis 1387 (Supreme Court of New Jersey)

1. What are the elements to prove negligent infliction of emotional distress?
2. Did any of the defendants act unethically in this case?
3. Are the Jaffees liable? Is the Atlantic Elevator Company liable?

Internet Exercises

1. Go to **www.supreme.courts.state.tx.us/historical/1998/feb/970558.pdf** and read the case *Walmart Stores v. Resendez*. What issue was involved in this case? Was Walmart found liable in this case? Why or why not?

2. Go to **www.people.com/people** to find headlines about current movie stars. Are these articles and photographs a violation of the stars' right to privacy?

3. Go to **www.people.com/people/article/0,,20189329,00.html?xid=rss-fullcontentcnn** to read an article about the paparazzi and the death of Princess Diana of England. To view a video of the funeral highlights for Princess Diana, go to **www.youtube.com/watch?v=86MQSbZo28Y**.

4. Go to **www.consumeraffairs.com/news04/2006/04/ca_pepsi.html** and read the article about Pepsi.

5. The National Highway Traffic Safety Administration (NHTSA) is a federal administrative agency empowered with the authority to test the safety of products and to recall unsafe products. Go to the NHTSA's website, at **www.nhtsa.dot.gov**. Find a product that has recently been recalled by the NHTSA.

6. Go to **www.productliabilitylawblog.com/2008/03/general_motors_settles_defecti.html** and read the article about General Motors settling a product liability lawsuit.

7. Go to **www.patentstorm.us/patents/6736280.html** to view the abstract for a patent for a tamperproof cap for bottles.

Endnotes

1. 376 U.S. 254, 84 S.Ct. 710, 11 L.Ed.2d 686, **Web** 1964 U.S. Lexis 1655 (Supreme Court of the United States).
2. *Restatement (Second) of Torts*, Section 46.
3. *Restatement (Second) of Torts*, Section 46, Comment d.
4. Justice B. Anderson, *Blyth v. Birmingham Waterworks Co.*, 11 Exch. 781, 784 (1856).
5. 248 N.Y. 339, 162 N.E. 99, **Web** 1928 N.Y. Lexis 1269 (Court of Appeals of New York)

CHAPTER 7

Criminal Law and Cyber Crimes

NEW YORK POLICE DEPARTMENT, TIMES SQUARE, NEW YORK CITY
Criminal cases make up a large portion of cases tried in courts of this country. Criminal cases are bought against persons for violating federal, state, and local laws. Suspected criminals are provided many rights by the U.S. Constitution and state constitutions. Parties in this country are free from unreasonable searches and seizures of evidence, and any evidence obtained illegally is considered "tainted" evidence and cannot be used in court. People who are suspected of a criminal act may assert their right of privilege against self-incrimination and may choose not to testify at any pretrial proceedings or at trial. Parties have a right to a public trial by a jury of their peers. In addition, if convicted of a crime, the criminal is free from cruel and unusual punishment.

Learning Objectives

After studying this chapter, you should be able to:

1. List and describe the essential elements of a crime.
2. Describe criminal procedure, including arrest, indictment, arraignment, and the criminal trial.
3. Identify and define business and white-collar crimes.
4. List and describe cyber crimes.
5. Explain the constitutional safeguards provided by the Fourth, Fifth, Sixth, and Eighth Amendments to the U.S. Constitution.

Chapter Outline

> *" It is better that ten guilty persons escape, than that one innocent suffer."*
>
> —Sir William Blackstone

Introduction to Criminal Law and Cyber Crimes

For members of society to peacefully coexist and commerce to flourish, people and their property must be protected from injury by other members of society. Federal, state, and local governments' **criminal laws** are intended to afford this protection by providing an incentive for persons to act reasonably in society and imposing penalties on persons who violate them.

The United States has one of the most advanced and humane criminal law systems in the world. It differs from other criminal law systems in several respects. Under many other countries' legal systems, a person accused of a crime is presumed guilty unless the person can prove he or she is not. A person charged with a crime in the United States is **presumed innocent until proven guilty**. The **burden of proof** in a criminal trial is on the government to prove that the accused is guilty of the crime charged. Further, the accused must be found guilty **beyond a reasonable doubt**. Conviction requires unanimous jury vote. A person charged with a crime in the United States is also provided with substantial constitutional safeguards during the criminal justice process.

Many crimes are referred to as *white-collar crimes* because they are most often committed by business managers and employees. These crimes include fraud, bribery, and other such crimes. In addition, in the Information Age, many *cyber crimes* are committed using computers and the Internet. This chapter discusses criminal procedure, crimes, business and white-collar crimes, cyber crimes, and the constitutional safeguards afforded criminal defendants.

Definition of a Crime

crime
A violation of a statute for which the government imposes a punishment.

A **crime** is defined as any act done by an individual in violation of those duties that he or she owes to society and for the breach of which the law provides that the wrongdoer shall make amends to the public. Many activities have been considered crimes through the ages, whereas other crimes are of recent origin.

Penal Codes and Regulatory Statutes

penal code
A collection of criminal statutes.

Statutes are the primary source of criminal law. Most states have adopted comprehensive **penal codes** that define in detail the activities considered to be crimes within their jurisdictions and the penalties that will be imposed for their commission. A comprehensive federal criminal code defines federal crimes.[1]

Examples Each state has a criminal penal code that lists and defines the activities that are illegal in that state. These crimes include first-degree murder, burglary, robbery, arson, rape, and other crimes.

regulatory statutes
Statutes such as environmental laws, securities laws, and antitrust laws that provide for criminal violations and penalties.

In addition, state and federal **regulatory statutes** often provide for criminal violations and penalties. The state and federal legislatures are continually adding to the list of crimes.

Example Federal securities statutes are regulatory statutes that establish rules for disclosure of information before securities can be sold to the public. These federal statutes also make it a crime for an issuer of securities to defraud investors.

The penalty for committing a crime may consist of the imposition of a fine, imprisonment, both, or some other form of punishment (e.g., probation). Generally, imprisonment is imposed to (1) incapacitate the criminal so he or she will not harm others in society, (2) provide a means to rehabilitate the criminal, (3) deter others from similar conduct, and (4) inhibit personal retribution by the victim.

Parties to a Criminal Action

In a criminal lawsuit, the government (not a private party) is the **plaintiff**. The government is represented by a lawyer called the **prosecutor**, or prosecuting attorney. The accused, which is usually an individual or a business, is the **defendant**. The accused is represented by a **defense attorney**. Sometimes the accused will hire a private attorney to represent him if he can afford to do so. If the accused cannot afford a private defense lawyer, the government will provide one free of charge. This government defense attorney is often called a **public defender**.

Law cannot persuade, where it cannot punish.

Thomas Fuller
Gnomologia (1732)

Classification of Crimes

Crimes are classified from serious to minor. A crime is usually classified as one of the following:

- **Felony.** Felonies are the most serious kinds of crimes. Felonies include crimes that are *mala in se*—that is, inherently evil. Felonies are usually punishable by imprisonment. In some jurisdictions, certain felonies (e.g., first-degree murder) are punishable by death. Federal law[2] and some state laws require mandatory sentencing for specified crimes. Many statutes define different degrees of crimes (e.g., first-, second-, and third-degree murder). Each degree earns different penalties. Serious violations of regulatory statutes are also felonies.

  Examples Most crimes against persons (e.g., murder, rape) and certain business-related crimes (e.g., embezzlement, bribery) are felonies in most jurisdictions.

felony
The most serious type of crime; inherently evil crime. Most crimes against persons and some business-related crimes are felonies.

- **Misdemeanor.** Misdemeanors are less serious than felonies. They are crimes *mala prohibita*; that is, they are not inherently evil but are prohibited by society. Misdemeanors carry lesser penalties than felonies. They are usually punishable by fines and/or imprisonment for one year or less.

  Examples Many crimes committed against property, such as robbery, burglary, and less serious violations of regulatory statutes, are classified as misdemeanors in most jurisdictions.

misdemeanor
A crime that is less serious than a felony; not inherently evil but prohibited by society. Many crimes against property are misdemeanors.

- **Violation.** Violations are the least serious of crimes. These crimes are generally punishable by fines. Occasionally, one day or a few days of imprisonment are imposed.

  Examples Crimes such as traffic violations, jaywalking, and such are usually classified as violations.

violation
A crime that is neither a felony nor a misdemeanor that is usually punishable by a fine.

CONCEPT SUMMARY

CLASSIFICATION OF CRIMES

Classification	Description
Felony	The most serious kinds of crimes. They are *mala in se* (inherently evil) and are usually punishable by imprisonment.
Misdemeanor	Crimes that are less serious than felonies. They are *mala prohibita* (prohibited by society) and are usually punishable by fine and/or imprisonment for less than 1 year.
Violation	Crimes that are neither felonies nor misdemeanors. Violations are generally punishable by a fine.

Intent Crimes

Most crimes require **criminal intent** to be proven before the accused can be found guilty of the defined crime. Two elements must be proven for a person to be found guilty of an **intent crime**, (1) criminal act (*actus reus*) and (2) criminal intent (*mens rea*):

intent crime
A crime that requires the defendant to be found guilty of committing a criminal act (*actus reus*) with criminal intent (*mens rea*).

1. **Criminal act (*actus reus*).** The defendant must have actually performed the prohibited act. The actual performance of the criminal act is called the ***actus reus*** (guilty act). Sometimes, the omission of an act can constitute the requisite *actus reus*.

Examples Killing of someone without legal justification constitutes a criminal act (*actus reus*). This is because the law forbids persons from killing one another. If a taxpayer who is under a legal duty to file income tax returns and pay income taxes that are due the government fails to do so, there is the requisite criminal act (*actus reus*). A person who commits auto theft has engaged in a criminal act.

actus reus
"Guilty act"—the actual performance of a criminal act.

mens rea
"Evil intent"—the possession of the requisite state of mind to commit a prohibited act.

2. **Criminal intent (*mens rea*).** To be found guilty of an intent crime, the accused must be found to have possessed the requisite state of mind when the act was performed. This is called ***mens rea*** (evil intent). Juries may infer a defendant's intent from the facts and circumstances of the case. Many jurisdictions have defined intent crimes as either *general intent* crimes or *specific intent* crimes:

   a. **Specific intent crime.** Specific intent crimes require that the perpetrator intended to achieve a specific result from his illegal act.

specific intent crime
A crime that requires that the perpetrator intended to achieve a specific result from his or her illegal act.

Examples Premeditated murder is a specific intent crime because the perpetrator intends a specific result, the death of the victim. Arson, forgery, and fraud are other examples of specific intent crimes.

   b. **General intent crime.** General intent crimes require that the perpetrator either knew or should have known that her actions would lead to harmful results. The government does not have to prove that the accused intended the precise harm that resulted from her actions.

general intent crime
A crime that requires that the perpetrator either knew or should have known that his or her actions would lead to harmful results.

Examples Assault and battery are usually considered general intent crimes because the perpetrator intends to commit the crime but does not know the actual result of the crime in advance.

Individual criminal statutes state whether the crime requires a showing of specific or general intent. Some jurisdictions have eliminated the distinction between specific and general crimes.

Merely thinking about committing a crime is not a crime because no action has been taken. Thus, merely thinking about killing someone or evading taxes and not actually doing so is not a crime.

CONCEPT SUMMARY

ELEMENTS OF AN INTENT CRIME

Element	Description
Actus reus	Guilty act
Mens rea	Evil intent

nonintent crime
A crime that imposes criminal liability without a finding of *mens rea* (intent).

Nonintent Crimes

Most states have enacted laws that define certain unintended conduct as a crime. These are called **nonintent crimes**. Nonintent crimes are often imposed for reckless or grossly negligent conduct that causes injury to another person. The crime of involuntary manslaughter is a non-intent crime.

Example A person drives his automobile 55 miles per hour while in a 35-miles-per-hour traffic zone. While doing so, the driver cannot stop his car at a red traffic light, enters the pedestrian crossing, and kills a pedestrian. Here the driver's conduct is reckless. He is guilty of the nonintent crime of involuntary manslaughter.

The following feature discusses how criminal acts may also be the basis for civil tort actions by an injured victim or a deceased victim's relatives.

Contemporary Environment

Criminal Acts as the Basis for Tort Actions

An injured victim of a crime, or the relatives of a deceased victim of a crime, may bring a *civil tort action* against a wrongdoer who has caused the injury or death during the commission of a criminal act. Civil lawsuits are separate from the government's criminal action against the wrongdoer. In a civil lawsuit, the plaintiff usually wants to recover monetary damages from the wrongdoer.

Example A person commits the crime of battery and physically injures the victim. In this case, the government can prosecute the perpetrator for the crime of battery. In addition, the victim may sue the perpetrator in a civil lawsuit to recover monetary damages for the injuries the victim suffers because of the attack.

In many cases, a person injured by a criminal act will not sue the criminal to recover civil damages because the criminal is often **judgment proof**—that is, the criminal does not have the money to pay a civil judgment.

Criminal and civil law differ in the following ways:

Issue	Civil Law	Criminal Law
Party who brings the action	The plaintiff	The government
Trial by jury	Yes, except actions for equity	Yes
Burden of proof	Preponderance of the evidence	Beyond a reasonable doubt
Jury vote	Judgment for plaintiff requires specific jury vote (e.g., 9 of 12 jurors)	Conviction requires unanimous jury vote
Sanctions and penalties	Monetary damages and equitable remedies (e.g., injunction, specific performance)	Imprisonment, capital punishment, fine, probation

Criminal Procedure

The procedure for initiating and maintaining a criminal action is quite detailed. It includes both pretrial procedures and the actual trial.

Arrest

Before the police can **arrest** a person for the commission of a crime, they usually must obtain an **arrest warrant** based on a showing of probable cause. The police go before a judge and present the evidence they have for arresting the suspect. If the judge finds that there is *probable cause* to issue the warrant, she will do so. The police will then use the arrest warrant to arrest the suspect. **Probable cause** is defined as the substantial likelihood that a person either committed or is about to commit a crime.

Example The police have obtained information from a reliable informant about the criminal activity of an individual and further investigate the situation and arrive at the

arrest warrant
A document for a person's detainment based on a showing of probable cause that the person committed a crime.

probable cause
Evidence of the substantial likelihood that a person either committed or is about to commit a crime.

conclusion that the individual who is the target of their investigation is involved in the illegal selling of drugs. The police can take this evidence, place it before a judge, and request that the judge issue an arrest warrant. If the judge believes there is probable cause, the judge will issue an arrest warrant. The police can then arrest the suspect pursuant to the arrest warrant.

An arrest can be made without obtaining an arrest warrant if there is no time to obtain one or it is otherwise not feasible to obtain a warrant prior to the arrest. **Warrantless arrests** must be based on probable cause.

Examples The police can make a warrantless arrest if they arrive during the commission of a crime, when a person is fleeing from the scene of a crime, or when it is likely that evidence will be destroyed.

Example In *Atwater v. Lago Vista, Texas*,[3] the U.S. Supreme Court held that a police officer may make a warrantless arrest pursuant to a minor criminal offense. Gail Atwater was driving her pickup truck in Lago Vista, Texas, with her 3-year-old son and 5-year-old daughter in the front seat. None of them were wearing seat belts. Bart Turek, a Lago Vista police officer, observed the seat belt violation and pulled Atwater over. A friend of Atwater's arrived at the scene and took charge of the children. Turek handcuffed Atwater, placed her in his squad car, and drove her to the police station. Atwater was booked, her mug shot was taken, and she was placed in a jail cell for about one hour, until she was released on $310 bond. Atwater ultimately pleaded no contest to the misdemeanor seat belt offenses and paid a $50 fine. Atwater sued the City of Lago Vista and the police officer for compensatory and punitive damages for allegedly violating her Fourth Amendment right to be free from unreasonable seizure. The U.S. Supreme Court ruled against Atwater, finding that the Fourth Amendment permits police officers to make a warrantless arrest pursuant to a minor criminal offense.

After a person is arrested, he or she is taken to the police station to be booked. **Booking** is the administrative procedure for recording an arrest, fingerprinting the suspect, taking a photograph of the suspect (often called a "mug shot"), and so on.

Indictment or Information

An accused person must be formally charged with a crime before he or she can be brought to trial. This is usually done through the issuance of a **grand jury indictment** or a **magistrate's information statement**.

Evidence of serious crimes, such as murder, is usually presented to a **grand jury**. Most grand juries comprise between six and twenty-four citizens who are charged with evaluating the evidence presented by the government. Grand jurors sit for a fixed period of time, such as one year. If the grand jury determines that there is sufficient evidence to hold the accused for trial, it issues an **indictment**. Note that the grand jury does not determine guilt. If an indictment is issued, the accused will be held for later trial.

For lesser crimes (e.g., burglary, shoplifting), the accused will be brought before a **magistrate** (judge). A magistrate who finds that there is enough evidence to hold the accused for trial will issue an **information** statement.

The case against the accused is dismissed if neither an indictment nor information statement is issued.

Arraignment

If an indictment or information is issued, the accused is brought before a court for an **arraignment** proceeding, during which the accused is (1) informed of the charges against him and (2) asked to enter a **plea**. The accused may plead **guilty** or **not guilty**.

---

warrantless arrest
An arrest that is made without obtaining an arrest warrant. The arrest must be based on probable cause and a showing that it was not feasible to obtain an arrest warrant.

WEB EXERCISE
Go to **www.fbi.gov** and click on "Most Wanted" and then "Ten Most Wanted Fugitives." Who is the number-one fugitive listed, and what crime is he or she wanted for?

indictment
The charge of having committed a crime (usually a felony), based on the judgment of a grand jury.

information
The charge of having committed a crime (usually a misdemeanor), based on the judgment of a judge (magistrate).

arraignment
A hearing during which the accused is brought before a court and is (1) informed of the charges against him or her and (2) asked to enter a plea.

Example Peter has been arrested for the crime of automobile theft. At the arraignment, Peter is asked how he pleads. Peter replies, "Not guilty." Peter has pleaded "not guilty" rather than "guilty." The majority of accused persons plead not guilty at their arraignments.

Nolo Contendere   A party may enter a plea of *nolo contendere* whereby the accused agrees to the imposition of a penalty but does not admit guilt. The government has the option of accepting a *nolo contendere* plea or requiring the defendant to plead guilty or not guilty. If the government agrees to accept the *nolo contendere* plea, the accused and the government usually enter into a plea bargain in which the accused agrees to the imposition of a penalty but does not admit guilt. A *nolo contendere* plea cannot be used as evidence of liability against the accused at a subsequent civil trial. Corporate defendants often enter this plea.

Example The government brings charges against a corporation for criminally violating environmental pollution laws. The government and the corporation enter into an agreement whereby the corporation pleas *nolo contendere* and agrees to pay a fine of $5 million but does not plead guilty to the violation.

Plea Bargain

Sometimes the accused and the government enter into **plea bargain** negotiations prior to trial with the intent of avoiding a trial. If an agreement is reached, the government and the accused will execute a **plea bargaining agreement** that sets forth the terms of their agreement.

> **plea bargain agreement**
> An agreement in which the accused admits to a lesser crime than charged. In return, the government agrees to impose a lesser sentence than might have been obtained had the case gone to trial.

Example An accused is charged with first-degree murder, which if proven carries a penalty of life imprisonment. The government and the accused engage in plea bargaining, and an agreement is reached whereby the accused agrees to plead guilty to the crime of second-degree murder, which carries a maximum penalty of twenty years in jail. Therefore, a trial is avoided.

The government engages in plea bargaining to save costs, avoid the risks of a trial, and prevent further overcrowding of prisons. In return, the government agrees to impose a lesser penalty or sentence on the accused than might have been obtained had the case gone to trial and the accused found guilty. The accused often agrees to a plea bargain to avoid the risks of trial where if he was found guilty he would be subject to a greater penalty than the penalty imposed by the plea bargain he has agreed to with the government. Approximately 95 percent of criminal cases are plea bargained and do not go to trial. Of those that go to trial, the government wins a conviction in approximately 75 percent of these cases.

Criminal Trial

At a criminal trial, all jurors must *unanimously* agree before the accused is found *guilty* of the crime charged. If even one juror disagrees (i.e., has reasonable doubt) about the guilt of the accused, the accused cannot be found guilty of the crime charged. If all the jurors agree that the accused did not commit the crime, the accused is found *not guilty* of the crime charged. After trial, the following rules apply:

- If the defendant is found guilty, he or she may appeal.
- If the defendant is found not guilty, the government cannot appeal.
- If the jury cannot come to a **unanimous decision** about the defendant's guilt one way or the other, the jury is considered a **hung jury**. In this situation, the government may choose to retry the case before a new judge and jury.

> **hung jury**
> A jury that cannot come to a unanimous decision about the defendant's guilt. In the case of a hung jury, the government may choose to retry the case.

Example A defendant is tried for the crime of murder. A twelve-person jury hears the case. If ten jurors find the defendant guilty but two jurors find the defendant not guilty, then there is a hung jury. The government may retry the defendant and often does so with such a vote. However, if the vote had been four jurors voting guilty and eight jurors voting not guilty, it is highly unlikely the government would retry the case.

Common Crimes

Many **common crimes** are committed against persons and property. Some of the most important common crimes against persons and property are discussed in the following paragraphs.

Murder

murder
The unlawful killing of a human being by another with *malice aforethought*—the element of *mens rea* (guilty mind).

Murder is defined as the unlawful killing of a human being by another with *malice aforethought*—the element of *mens rea* (guilty mind). In most states, there are several degrees of murder—such as *first-degree murder*, *second-degree murder*, and *third-degree murder*—depending on the circumstances of the case.

Felony Murder Rule   Sometimes a murder is committed during the commission of another crime even though the perpetrator did not originally intend to commit murder. Most states hold the perpetrator liable for the crime of murder in addition to the other crime. This is called the **felony murder rule**. The intent to commit the murder is inferred from the intent to commit the other crime. Many states also hold accomplices liable under this doctrine.

Robbery

robbery
The taking of personal property from another person by the use of fear or force.

In common law, **robbery** is defined as the taking of personal property from another person or business by the use of fear or force. Robbery with a deadly weapon is generally considered aggravated robbery (or armed robbery) and carries a harsher penalty.

Examples If a person threatens another person with a gun unless the victim gives her purse to that person, this constitutes the crime of robbery. If a person pick pockets somebody's wallet, it is not robbery because there has been no use of force or fear. This is a theft.

Burglary

burglary
The taking of personal property from another's home, office, or commercial or other type of building.

In common law, **burglary** is defined as "breaking and entering a dwelling at night" with the intent to commit a felony. Modern penal codes have broadened this definition to include daytime thefts from homes, offices, commercial buildings, and other buildings. In addition, the "breaking in" element has been abandoned by most modern definitions of burglary. Thus, unauthorized entering of a building through an unlocked door is sufficient. Aggravated burglary (or armed burglary) carries stiffer penalties.

Example Harold breaks into Sibel's home and steals jewelry and other items. Harold is guilty of the crime of burglary because he entered a dwelling without permission to do so and committed theft.

Larceny

larceny
The taking of another's personal property other than from his or her person or building.

In common law, **larceny** is defined as the wrongful and fraudulent taking of another person's personal property that is not robbery or burglary. Most personal property—including tangible property, trade secrets, computer programs, and other business property—is subject to larceny. Neither the use of force nor the entry of a building is required.

Examples Stealing automobiles and stealing XM satellite radios from automobiles are considered larcenies.

Some states distinguish between grand larceny and petit larceny. This distinction depends on the value of the property taken.

Theft

Some states have dropped the distinction among the crimes of robbery, burglary, and larceny. Instead, these states group these crimes under the general crime of **theft**. Most of these states distinguish between grand theft and petit theft. The distinction depends on the value of the property taken.

Receiving Stolen Property

It is a crime for a person to (1) knowingly **receive stolen property** and (2) intend to deprive the rightful owner of that property. Knowledge and intent can be inferred from the circumstances. The stolen property can be any tangible property (e.g., personal property, money, negotiable instruments, stock certificates).

Example David is walking down the street and is approached by a man who offers to sell David a Rolex watch "at a cheap price." David looks at the twenty Rolex watches that the man has, chooses one that would normally sell in a retail store for $1,000, and pays $200 for it. It is an actual Rolex. David is guilty of the crime of receiving stolen property because it could easily be proven by circumstantial evidence that he had knowledge that the watch was stolen property.

receiving stolen property
A crime that involves (1) knowingly receiving stolen property and (2) intending to deprive the rightful owner of that property.

Arson

In common law, **arson** is defined as the malicious or willful burning of the dwelling of another person. Modern penal codes have expanded this definition to include the burning of all types of private, commercial, and public buildings.

Examples An owner of a motel burns down the motel to collect fire insurance proceeds. The owner is guilty of the crime of arson. In this case, the insurance company does not have to pay the proceeds of any insurance policy on the burned property to the arsonist-owner. On the other hand, if a third-party arsonist burned down the motel without the knowledge or assistance of the owner, the third party is the arsonist, and the owner is entitled to recover the proceeds of any fire insurance he had on the property.

arson
The willful or malicious burning of a building.

Business and White-Collar Crimes

Certain types of crimes are prone to being committed by businesspersons. These crimes are often referred to as **white-collar crimes**. Such crimes usually involve cunning and deceit rather than physical force. Many of the most important white-collar crimes are discussed in the paragraphs that follow.

white-collar crime
A type of crime that is prone to being committed by businesspersons.

Forgery

The crime of **forgery** occurs if a written document is fraudulently made or altered and that change affects the legal liability of another person. Counterfeiting, falsifying public records, and materially altering legal documents are examples of forgery.

forgery
The fraudulent making or alteration of a written document that affects the legal liability of another person.

Example Signing another person's signature to a check or changing the amount of a check without the owner's permission is forgery.

Note that signing another person's signature without intent to defraud is not forgery.

Example Forgery has not been committed if one spouse signs the other spouse's payroll check for deposit in a joint checking or savings account at the bank.

Embezzlement

embezzlement
The fraudulent conversion of property by a person to whom that property was entrusted.

The crime of **embezzlement** is the fraudulent conversion of property by a person to whom that property was entrusted. Typically, embezzlement is committed by an employer's employees, agents, or representatives (e.g., accountants, lawyers, trust officers, treasurers). Embezzlers often try to cover their tracks by preparing false books, records, or entries.

The key element here is that the stolen property was *entrusted* to the embezzler. This differs from robbery, burglary, and larceny, where property is taken by someone not entrusted with the property.

Examples A bank entrusts a teller to take deposits from its customers and deposit them into the customers' accounts at the bank. Instead, the bank teller absconds with the money. This is embezzlement. A lawyer who steals money from a trust fund that has been entrusted to him to administer commits the crime of embezzlement.

Bribery

bribery
A crime in which one person gives another person money, property, favors, or anything else of value for a favor in return. A bribe is often referred to as a *payoff* or *kickback*.

Bribery is one of the most prevalent forms of white-collar crime. A bribe can be money, property, favors, or anything else of value. The crime of commercial bribery entails the payment of bribes to private persons and businesses. This type of bribe is often referred to as a **kickback**, or **payoff**. Intent is a necessary element of this crime. The offeror of a bribe commits the crime of bribery when the bribe is tendered. The offeree is guilty of the crime of bribery when he or she accepts the bribe. The offeror can be found liable for the crime of bribery even if the person to whom the bribe is offered rejects the bribe.

Example Harriet Landers is the purchasing agent for the ABC Corporation and is in charge of purchasing equipment to be used by the corporation. Neal Brown, the sales representative of a company that makes equipment that can be used by the ABC Corporation, offers to pay her a 10 percent kickback if she buys equipment from him. She accepts the bribe and orders the equipment. Both parties are guilty of bribery.

Modern penal codes also make it a crime to bribe public officials.

Example If a real estate developer who is constructing an apartment building offers to pay the building inspector to overlook a building code violation, this is bribery.

Extortion

extortion (blackmail)
A threat to expose something about another person unless that other person gives money or property.

The crime of **extortion** involves the obtaining of property from another, with his or her consent, induced by wrongful use of actual or threatened force, violence, or fear. Extortion occurs when a person threatens to expose something about another person unless that other person gives money or property. The truth or falsity of the information is immaterial. Extortion of private persons is commonly referred to as **blackmail**. Extortion of public officials is called **extortion under color of official right**.

Example A person knows that an executive who works for a company has been engaged in a physical altercation with another person. The person who knows this information threatens the executive that he will disclose this fact to the company unless the executive pays him money. The person who makes the threat of exposure has committed the crime of extortion even though the fact he threatens to divulge is true.

Criminal Fraud

Obtaining title to property through deception or trickery constitutes the crime of **false pretenses**. This crime is commonly referred to as **criminal fraud** or **deceit**.

Example Bob, a stockbroker, promises Mary, a prospective investor, that he will use any money she invests with him to purchase interests in oil wells. Based on this promise, Mary decides to make the investment. Bob never intended to invest the money. Instead, he used the money for his personal needs. This is criminal fraud.

criminal fraud (false pretenses or deceit)
A crime that involves obtaining title to property through deception or trickery.

Mail Fraud and Wire Fraud

Federal law prohibits the use of mail or wires (e.g., telephone, television, radio, computer) to defraud another person. These crimes are called **mail fraud**[4] and **wire fraud**,[5] respectively. The government often includes these crimes in a criminal charge against a defendant who is charged with committing another crime but who also used the mail or wires to further her crime. Sometimes the government prosecutes a suspect under these statutes if there is insufficient evidence to prove the real crime that the criminal was attempting to commit or did commit. Persons convicted of mail or wire fraud are subject to imprisonment and the imposition of monetary fines.

There are some frauds so well conducted that it would be stupidity not to be deceived by them.

C. C. Colton
Lacon, Volume 1 (1820)

Money Laundering

When criminals make money from illegal activities, they are often faced with the problem of having large sums of money and no record of how this money was earned. This could easily tip off the government to their illegal activities. In order to "wash" the money and make it look as though it was earned legitimately, many criminals purchase legitimate businesses and run the money through those businesses to "clean" it before they receive the money. The legitimate business has "cooked" books, showing faked expenditures and receipts, in which the illegal money is buried. Restaurants, motels, and other cash businesses make excellent money laundries.

To address the problem of **money laundering**, the federal government enacted the **Money Laundering Control Act**.[6] This act makes it a crime to:

- Knowingly engage in a *monetary transaction* through a financial institution involving property from an unlawful activity worth more than $10,000.

    Examples Monetary transactions through a financial institution include making deposits, making withdrawals, conducting transactions between accounts, or obtaining monetary instruments such as cashiers' checks, money orders, and travelers' checks from a bank or another financial institution for more than $10,000.

- Knowingly engage in a *financial transaction* involving the proceeds of an unlawful activity.

    Examples Financial transactions involving the proceeds of an illegal activity include buying real estate, automobiles, personal property, intangible assets, or anything else of value with money obtained from illegal activities.

Money Laundering Control Act
A federal statute that makes it a crime to (1) knowingly engage in a *money transaction* through a financial institution involving property from an unlawful activity worth more than $10,000 and (2) knowingly engage in a *financial transaction* involving the proceeds of an unlawful activity.

Thus, money laundering itself is now a federal crime. The money that is washed could have been made from illegal gambling operations, drug dealing, fraud, or other crimes, including white-collar crimes. Persons convicted of money laundering can be fined up to $500,000 or twice the value of the property involved, whichever is greater, and sentenced to up to twenty years in federal prison. In addition, violation of the act subjects any property involved in or traceable to the offense to forfeiture to the government.

Racketeer Influenced and Corrupt Organizations Act (RICO)

Racketeer Influenced and Corrupt Organizations Act (RICO)
A federal act that provides for both criminal and civil penalties for racketeering.

Organized crime has a pervasive influence on many parts of the U.S. economy. To combat this activity, Congress enacted the Organized Crime Control Act. The **Racketeer Influenced and Corrupt Organizations Act (RICO)** is part of this act.[7] Originally, RICO was intended to apply only to organized crime. However, the broad language of the RICO statute has been used against non–organized crime defendants as well. RICO, which provides for both criminal and civil penalties, is one of the most important laws affecting business today.

Criminal RICO   RICO makes it a federal crime to acquire or maintain an interest in, use income from, or conduct or participate in the affairs of an enterprise through a pattern of racketeering activity. An *enterprise* is defined as a corporation, a partnership, a sole proprietorship, another business or organization, or the government.

    Racketeering activity consists of a number of specifically enumerated federal and state crimes, including such activities as gambling, arson, robbery, counterfeiting, and dealing in narcotics. Business-related crimes, such as bribery, embezzlement, mail fraud, and wire fraud, are also considered racketeering. To prove a *pattern of racketeering*, at least two of these acts must be committed by the defendant within a ten-year period. Commission of the same crime twice within this ten-year period constitutes **criminal RICO** as well.

    Individual defendants found criminally liable for RICO violations can be fined, imprisoned for up to twenty years, or both. In addition, RICO provides for the *forfeiture* of any property or business interests (even interests in a legitimate business) that were gained because of RICO violations. This provision allows the government to recover investments made with monies derived from racketeering activities. The government may also seek civil penalties for RICO violations. These include injunctions, orders of dissolution, reorganization of business, and divestiture of the defendant's interest in an enterprise.

Civil RICO   Persons injured by a RICO violation can bring a private **civil RICO** action against the violator to recover for injury to business or property. A successful plaintiff may recover *treble damages* (three times the actual loss) plus attorneys' fees.

Criminal Conspiracy

criminal conspiracy
A crime in which two or more persons enter into an agreement to commit a crime and an overt act is taken to further the crime.

A **criminal conspiracy** occurs when two or more persons enter into an *agreement* to commit a crime. To be liable for a criminal conspiracy, a person must commit an *overt act* to further the crime. The crime itself does not have to be committed, however. The government usually brings criminal conspiracy charges if (1) the defendants have been thwarted in their efforts to commit the substantive crime or (2) there is insufficient evidence to prove the substantive crime.

Example Two securities brokers agree over the telephone to commit a securities fraud. They obtain a list of potential victims and prepare false financial statements necessary for the fraud. Because they entered into an agreement to commit a crime and took an overt act, the brokers are guilty of the crime of criminal conspiracy, even if they never carry out the securities fraud.

The following feature discusses the criminal liability of corporations for the acts of its officers, directors, and employees.

Ethics

Corporate Criminal Liability

A *corporation* is a fictitious legal person that is granted legal existence by the state when certain requirements are met. A corporation cannot act on its own behalf. Instead, it must act through *agents*, such as board of directors, officers, and employees.

Originally, under the common law, it was generally held that corporations lacked the criminal mind (*mens rea*) to be held criminally liable. Modern courts, however, impose **corporate criminal liability**. These courts have held that corporations are criminally liable for the acts of their directors, officers, and employees. Because corporations cannot be put in prison, they are usually sanctioned with fines, loss of a license or franchise, and the like.

Corporate directors, officers, and employees are individually liable for crimes that they commit on behalf of or to further the interests of the corporation. In addition, under certain circumstances, a corporate manager can be held criminally liable for the criminal activities of his or her subordinates. To be held criminally liable, the manager must have failed to supervise the subordinates appropriately. This is an evolving area of the law.

Ethics Questions   Why is criminal liability imposed on a corporation? Do you think that the penalties (e.g., jail time) that are imposed on corporate executives for white-collar crimes are sufficient?

Cyber Crimes

The development of computers, e-mail, and the Internet has made it easier for criminals to perpetrate many existing crimes and has created the ability for them to commit crimes that did not exist before the digital age. These are commonly referred to as **cyber crimes**. The government has had to apply existing laws to these new mediums and develop new laws to attack digital crimes.

One of the most pervasive monetary crimes today is Internet fraud. The following feature discusses the crime of cyber identity theft.

cyber crime
A crime that is committed using computers, e-mail, the Internet, or other electronic means.

Digital Law

Internet Fraud: Identity Theft

The advent of the computer and the Internet has made one type of crime—identity theft—easier to commit. Identity theft was around long before the computer was invented, but computers and the Internet have made it much easier for criminals to obtain the information they need to commit identity theft. In **identity theft**—or **ID theft**—one person steals information about another person to pose as that person and take the innocent person's money or property or to purchase goods and services using the victim's credit information.

To commit ID theft, thieves must first obtain certain information about the victim. This could be the victim's name, Social Security number, credit card numbers, bank account information, and other personal information. With the use of computers, criminals can more easily obtain the information they need to commit ID theft. Credit card fraud is one of the crimes most commonly committed by ID thieves. An ID thief may use a victim's existing credit

card or open new credit card accounts in the victim's name and purchase goods and services with these credit cards, often using the Internet.

To address the growing problem of ID theft, Congress enacted the **Identity Theft and Assumption Deterrence Act**.[8] This statute makes it a federal crime to knowingly transfer or use, without authority, the identity of another person with the

DETER·DETECT·DEFEND

intent to commit any unlawful activity as defined by federal law and state and local felony laws. Violators can be sentenced to prison for up to fifteen years and have any property used in the commission of ID theft forfeited to the government.

The following feature discusses a federal criminal law designed specifically to apply to computers.

Digital Law

Crime of Intentionally Accessing and Acquiring Information from a Computer

The Internet and Information Age ushered in a whole new world for education, business and consumer transactions. It also made possible cyber crimes. Prosecutors and courts have wrestled over how to apply existing laws written in a nondigital age to new Internet-related abuses.

Congress responded by enacting the **Information Infrastructure Protection Act (IIP Act)**.[9] In this federal law, Congress addressed computer-related crimes as distinct offenses. The IIP Act provides protection for any computer attached to the Internet.

The IIP Act makes it a federal crime for anyone to intentionally access and acquires information from a protected computer without authorization. The IIP Act does not require that the defendant accessed a protected computer for commercial benefit. Thus, persons who transmit a computer virus over the Internet or hackers who trespass into Internet-connected computers may be criminally prosecuted under the IIP Act. Even merely observing data on a protected computer without authorization is sufficient to meet the requirement that the defendant has accessed a protected computer. Criminal penalties for violating the IIP Act include imprisonment and fines.

The IIP Act gives the federal government a much-needed weapon for directly prosecuting cyber-crooks, hackers, and others who enter, steal, destroy, or look at others' computer data without authorization.

Protection Against Unreasonable Search and Seizure

unreasonable search and seizure
Protection granted by the Fourth Amendment for people to be free from unreasonable search and seizure by the government.

search warrant
A warrant issued by a court that authorizes the police to search a designated place for specified contraband, articles, items, or documents. A search warrant must be based on probable cause.

exclusionary rule
A rule that says evidence obtained from an unreasonable search and seizure can generally be prohibited from introduction at a trial or an administrative proceeding against the person searched.

The criminal is to go free because the constable has blundered.

Chief Judge Cardozo
People v. Defore (1926)

In many criminal cases, the government relies on information obtained from searches of individuals and businesses. The **Fourth Amendment** to the U.S. Constitution protects persons and corporations from overzealous investigative activities by the government. It protects the rights of the people from **unreasonable search and seizure** by the government. It permits people to be secure in their persons, houses, papers, and effects.

Reasonable search and seizure by the government is lawful. **Search warrants** based on probable cause are necessary in most cases. Such a warrant specifically states the place and scope of the authorized search. General searches beyond the specified area are forbidden. **Warrantless searches** are permitted only (1) *incident to arrest*, (2) where evidence is in "plain view," or (3) where it is likely that evidence will be destroyed. Warrantless searches are judged by the probable cause standard.

Exclusionary Rule

Evidence obtained from an unreasonable search and seizure is considered tainted evidence ("fruit of a tainted tree"). Under the **exclusionary rule**, such evidence can generally be prohibited from introduction at a trial or an administrative proceeding against the person searched. However, this evidence is freely admissible against other persons. The U.S. Supreme Court created a *good faith exception* to the exclusionary rule.[10] This exception allows evidence otherwise obtained illegally to be introduced as evidence against the accused if the police officers who conducted the unreasonable search reasonably believed that they were acting pursuant to a lawful search warrant.

In the following case, the U.S. Supreme Court addressed the issue of the lawfulness of a warrantless search of a living space.

CASE 7.1   *U.S. SUPREME COURT Exigent Circumstances*

Kentucky v. King

131 S.Ct. 1849, 179 L.Ed.2d 865, Web 2011 U.S. Lexis 3541 (2011)
Supreme Court of the United States

> "And—what is relevant here—the need to prevent the imminent destruction of evidence has long been recognized as a sufficient justification for a warrantless search."
>
> —Alito, Justice

Facts

Kentucky undercover police officers set up a controlled buy of cocaine outside an apartment complex. After the deal took place, uniformed police moved in on the suspect. The suspect ran to a breezeway of an apartment building. As the officers arrived to the area they heard a door shut. At the end of the breezeway there were two apartments, one on the left and one on the right. The officers smelled marijuana smoke emanating from the apartment on the left.

The officers banged on the door as loudly as they could, while yelling "Police!" As soon as the officers started banging on the door they heard people moving inside and things being moved inside the apartment. These noises led the officers to believe that drug-related evidence was about to be destroyed. At that point, the officers kicked in the door and entered the apartment, where they found three people, including Hollis King, his girlfriend, and a guest who was smoking marijuana. The officers saw marijuana and powder cocaine in plain view. A further search turned up crack cocaine, cash, and drug paraphernalia. Police eventually entered the apartment on the right side of the breezeway and found the suspect who was the initial target of their investigation.

King was indicted for criminal violations, including trafficking in marijuana, trafficking in controlled substances, and persistent felony offender status. King filed a motion to have the evidence suppressed as the fruits of an illegal warrantless search. The Kentucky trial court denied the motion, finding that exigent circumstances justified the warrantless entry. King was sentenced to 11 years imprisonment.

The Kentucky Court of Appeals affirmed the judgment, but the Kentucky Supreme Court reversed, finding that the warrantless search was not lawful. The state of Kentucky appealed to the U.S. Supreme Court.

Issue

Did exigent circumstances exist that supported the police's warrantless search of the apartment?

Language of the U.S. Supreme Court

The warrant requirement is subject to certain reasonable exceptions. One well-recognized exception applies when the exigencies of the situation make the needs of law enforcement so compelling that a warrantless search is objectively reasonable under the Fourth Amendment. This Court has identified several exigencies that may justify a warrantless search of a home. Police officers may enter premises without a warrant when they are in hot pursuit of a fleeing suspect. And—what is relevant here—the need to prevent the imminent destruction of evidence has long been recognized as a sufficient justification for a warrantless search.

Destruction of evidence issues probably occur most frequently in drug cases because drugs may be easily destroyed by flushing them down a toilet or rinsing them down a drain. Occupants who elect to attempt to destroy evidence have only themselves to blame for the warrantless exigent-circumstances search that may ensue.

Decision

The U.S. Supreme Court held that exigent circumstances existed that justified the warrantless search and seizure of the evidence used against King.

(continued)

Case Questions

Critical Legal Thinking

Is it difficult to determine when exigent circumstances exist that would justify warrantless search?

Ethics

Is it ethical for a defendant to try to keep damaging evidence out at trial? Does the Fourth Amendment protection against unreasonable search and seizure trump any ethical considerations?

Contemporary Business

Are businesses subject to warrantless search and seizure?

In the following case, the U.S. Supreme Court addressed the lawfulness of a warrantless search.

CASE 7.2   *U.S. SUPREME COURT Search and Seizure*

Arizona v. Gant

129 S.Ct. 1710, 173 L.Ed.2d 485, Web 2009 U.S. Lexis 3120 (2009)
Supreme Court of the United States

"Because police could not reasonably have believed either that Gant could have accessed his car at the time of the search or that evidence of the offense for which he was arrested might have been found therein, the search in this case was unreasonable."

—Stevens, Justice

Facts

Acting on an anonymous tip that a residence was being used to sell drugs, Tucson, Arizona, police officers knocked on the front door of the residence. Rodney Gant opened the door, and the police asked to speak to the owner. Gant identified himself and stated that the owner was expected to return later. The police officers left the residence. Later, the police conducted a records search that revealed that there was an outstanding warrant for Gant's arrest for driving with a suspended license.

When the police officers returned to the house that evening, Gant drove up in an automobile, parked in the driveway, got out of his car, and shut the door. One of the police officers called to Gant and he walked toward the officer. When Gant was about 10 to 12 feet from the car, the officer arrested Gant, handcuffed him, and locked him in the backseat of a patrol car.

The police officers searched Gant's car and found a gun and a bag of cocaine. Gant was charged with possession of a narcotic drug for sale. At the criminal trial, Gant moved to suppress the evidence seized from the car on the ground that the warrantless search violated the Fourth Amendment. The Arizona trial court held that the search was permissible as a search incident to an arrest. The jury found Gant guilty, and he was sentenced to a three-year term in prison. The Arizona Supreme Court held that the search of Gant's car was unreasonable and violated the Fourth Amendment and that the evidence was inadmissible at trial. The case was appealed to the U.S. Supreme Court.

Issue

Is the warrantless search of Gant's automobile justified as a search incident to an arrest?

Language of the U.S. Supreme Court

Our analysis begins, as it should in every case addressing the reasonableness of a warrantless search, with the basic rule that searches conducted outside the judicial process, without prior approval by judge or magistrate, are per se unreasonable under the Fourth Amendment—subject only to a few specifically established and well-delineated exceptions. Among the exceptions to the warrant requirement is a search incident to a lawful arrest. The exception derives from interests in officer safety and evidence preservation that are typically implicated in arrest situations.

In Chimel v. California[11] *we held that a search incident to arrest may only include the arrestee's person and the area "within his immediate control"—construing that phrase to mean the area from within which he might gain possession of a weapon or destructible evidence.*

Neither the possibility of access nor the likelihood of discovering offense-related evidence authorized the search in this case. Gant clearly was not within reaching distance of his car at the time of the search. Gant was arrested for driving with a suspended license—an offense for which police could not expect to find evidence in the passenger compartment of Gant's car. Because police could not reasonably have believed either that Gant could have accessed his car at the time of the search or that evidence of the offense for which he was arrested might have been found therein, the search in this case was unreasonable.

Decision

The U.S. Supreme Court held that the warrantless search in this case did not qualify for the incident to arrest exception to obtaining a search warrant. It also held that the search violated the Fourth Amendment, and that the evidence found in Gant's automobile must be suppressed. The U.S. Supreme Court affirmed the judgment of the Arizona Supreme Court.

Case Questions

Critical Legal Thinking

What requirements must be met for police officers to conduct a warrantless search of an automobile under the incident to arrest exception to obtaining a search warrant?

Ethics

Should a person who is guilty of a crime be exonerated because the evidence of the crime has been obtained through an illegal search? What is the purpose of the Fourth Amendment?

Contemporary Business

Are businesses subject to police search? Are businesses accorded the same protection from unreasonable searches as individuals?

Searches of Business Premises

Generally, the government does not have the right to search business premises without a search warrant.[12] However, certain hazardous and regulated industries are subject to warrantless searches if proper statutory procedures are met.

Examples Sellers of firearms, liquor stores and bars that sell alcohol, coal mines, and the like are businesses subject to warrantless searches.

Privilege Against Self-Incrimination

The **Fifth Amendment** to the U.S. Constitution provides that no person "shall be compelled in any criminal case to be a witness against himself." Thus, a person cannot be compelled to give testimony against himself. A person who asserts this right is described as having "taken the Fifth." This protection applies to federal cases and is extended to state and local criminal cases through the Due Process Clause of the Fourteenth Amendment. The right established by the Fifth Amendment is referred to as the **privilege against self incrimination**.

Nontestimonial evidence (e.g., fingerprints, body fluids) may be obtained without violating the Fifth Amendment.

The protection against **self-incrimination** applies only to natural persons who are accused of crimes. Therefore, artificial persons (e.g., corporations, partnerships) cannot raise this protection against incriminating testimony.[13] Thus, business records of corporations and partnerships are not generally protected from disclosure, even if they incriminate individuals who work for the business. However, certain "private papers" of businesspersons (e.g., personal diaries) are protected from disclosure.

privilege against self-incrimination
The Fifth Amendment provision that a person may not be required to be a witness against himself or herself in a criminal case.

Miranda Rights

Many people have not read and memorized the provisions of the U.S. Constitution. The U.S. Supreme Court recognized this fact when it decided the landmark case *Miranda v. Arizona* in 1966.[14] In that case, the Supreme Court held that the Fifth Amendment privilege against self-incrimination is not useful unless a criminal suspect has knowledge of this right. Therefore, the Supreme Court required that the following warning—colloquially called the ***Miranda* rights**—be read to a criminal suspect before he or she is interrogated by the police or other government officials:

* You have the right to remain silent.
* Anything you say can and will be used against you.
* You have the right to consult a lawyer and to have a lawyer present with you during interrogation.
* If you cannot afford a lawyer, a lawyer will be appointed free of charge to represent you.

Many police departments read an accused a more detailed version of the *Miranda* rights (see **Exhibit 7.1**). This is designed to cover all issues that a detainee might encounter while in police custody. A detainee may be asked to sign a statement acknowledging that the *Miranda* rights have been read to him or her.

Any statements or confessions obtained from a suspect before he or she has been read the *Miranda* rights can be excluded from evidence at trial. In 2000, the U.S. Supreme Court upheld *Miranda* in *Dickerson v. United States*.[15] In that opinion, Chief Justice Rehnquist stated, "We do not think there is justification for overruling *Miranda*. *Miranda* has become embedded in routine police practice to the point where the warnings have become part of our national culture."

Exhibit 7.1 *MIRANDA RIGHTS*

* You have the right to remain silent and refuse to answer questions. Do you understand?
* Anything you say may be used against you in a court of law. Do you understand?
* You have the right to consult an attorney before speaking to the police and to have an attorney present during questioning now or in the future. Do you understand?
* If you cannot afford an attorney, one will be appointed for you before any questioning if you wish. Do you understand?
* If you decide to answer questions now without an attorney present, you will still have the right to stop answering at any time until you talk to an attorney. Do you understand?
* Knowing and understanding your rights as I have explained them to you, are you willing to answer my questions without an attorney present?

Attorney–Client Privilege and Other Privileges

To obtain a proper defense, an accused should tell his lawyer the truth so that the lawyer can prepare the best defense she can for him. However, the accused must be able tell his attorney facts about his case without fear that the attorney will be called as a witness against him. This information is protected from disclosure by the **attorney–client privilege** recognized by the Fifth Amendment. Either the client or the attorney can raise this privilege. For the privilege to apply, the information must be told to the attorney in his or her capacity as an attorney and not as a friend or neighbor or such.

Example Cedric is accused of murder and employs Gloria, a renowned criminal attorney, to represent him. During the course of their discussions, Cedric confesses to the murder. Gloria cannot be a witness against Cedric at his criminal trial.

Miranda **rights**

Rights that a suspect must be informed of before being interrogated, so that the suspect will not unwittingly give up his or her Fifth Amendment right.

attorney–client privilege

A rule that says a client can tell his or her lawyer anything about the case without fear that the attorney will be called as a witness against the client.

The Fifth Amendment has also recognized the following privileges under which an accused may keep the following individuals from being witnesses against him:

- **Psychiatrist/psychologist–patient privilege** so that the accused may tell the truth in order to seek help for his condition
- **Priest/rabbi/minister/imam–penitent privilege** so that the accused may tell the truth in order to repent, be given help, and seek forgiveness for his deed
- **Spouse–spouse privilege** so that the family will remain together
- **Parent–child privilege** so that the family will remain together

A spouse or child who is injured by a spouse or parent (e.g., domestic abuse) may testify against the accused. In addition, if the accused discloses that he is planning to commit a crime in the future (e.g., murder), the accused's lawyer; psychiatrist or psychologist; or priest, rabbi, minister, or imam is required to report this to the police or other relevant authorities.

The U.S. Supreme Court has held that there is no accountant–client privilege under federal law.[16] Thus, an accountant could be called as a witness in cases involving federal securities laws, federal mail or wire fraud, or other federal crimes. Nevertheless, approximately twenty states have enacted special statutes that create an **accountant–client privilege**. An accountant cannot be called as a witness against a client in a court action in a state where these statutes are in effect. However, federal courts do not recognize this privilege.

At the present time in this country there is more danger that criminals will escape justice than that they will be subjected to tyranny.

Justice Holmes,
Dissenting Opinion
Kepner v. United States (1904)

Immunity from Prosecution

On occasion, the government may want to obtain information from a suspect who has asserted his or her Fifth Amendment privilege against self-incrimination. The government can often achieve this by offering the suspect **immunity from prosecution**. Immunity from prosecution means that the government agrees not to use against a person granted immunity any evidence given by that person. Once immunity is granted, the suspect loses the right to assert his or her Fifth Amendment privilege.

immunity from prosecution
The government's agreement not to use against a person granted immunity any evidence given by that person.

Example Grants of immunity are often given when the government wants a suspect to give information that will lead to the prosecution of other, more important, criminal suspects.

Partial grants of immunity are also available. A suspect must agree to a partial grant of immunity in order for it to occur.

In serious cases, the government can place a witness in a government protective program whereby, after the trial, the witness and her family are permanently moved to an undisclosed location, given a new identity, and provided monetary assistance. Such a witness is also usually protected prior to trial.

Other Constitutional Protections

Besides those already discussed in this chapter, there are many other provisions in the U.S. Constitution and its amendments that guarantee and protect certain other rights in the criminal process. Several of these additional rights are described in the paragraphs that follow.

Fifth Amendment Protection Against Double Jeopardy

The **Double Jeopardy Clause** of the Fifth Amendment protects persons from being tried twice for the same crime.

Double Jeopardy Clause
A clause of the Fifth Amendment that protects persons from being tried twice for the same crime.

Example If a state tries a suspect for the crime of murder and the suspect is found not guilty, the state cannot bring another trial against the accused for the same crime.

This is so even if more evidence later surfaces that would lead to conviction. The government is given the opportunity to bring its case against an accused once and cannot keep retrying the same case.

If the same act violates the laws of two or more jurisdictions, each jurisdiction may try the accused.

Example If an accused kidnaps a person in one state and brings the victim across a state border into another state, the act violates the laws of two states and the federal government. Thus, three jurisdictions can prosecute the accused without violating the Double Jeopardy Clause.

If an accused is tried once and the jury reaches a *hung jury*—that is, the verdict is not unanimously either guilty or not guilty—the government can retry the case against the accused without violating the Double Jeopardy Clause.

Sixth Amendment Right to a Public Jury Trial

WEB EXERCISE
Go to **http://usdoj.gov/usao/** and read the mission statement of U.S. attorneys of the U.S. Department of Justice.

The **Sixth Amendment** guarantees that a criminal defendant has the **right to a public jury trial**. This includes the rights (1) to be tried by an impartial jury of the state or district in which the alleged crime was committed, (2) to confront (cross-examine) the witnesses against the accused, (3) to have the assistance of a lawyer, and (4) to have a speedy trial.[17]

Eighth Amendment Protection Against Cruel and Unusual Punishment

The **Eighth Amendment** protects criminal defendants from **cruel and unusual punishment**. For example, it prohibits the torture of criminals. However, this clause does not prohibit capital punishment.[18] The U.S. Supreme Court has held that in capital punishment cases, death by lethal injection is not cruel and unusual punishment.[19]

Key Terms and Concepts

Accountant–client privilege (149)
Actus reus (134)
Arraignment (136)
Arrest (135)
Arrest warrant (135)
Arson (139)
Attorney–client privilege (148)
Beyond a reasonable doubt (132)
Booking (136)
Bribery (140)
Burden of proof (132)
Burglary (138)
Civil RICO (142)
Common crime (138)
Corporate criminal liability (143)

Crime (132)
Criminal act (134)
Criminal conspiracy (142)
Criminal fraud (false pretenses or deceit) (141)
Criminal intent (134)
Criminal law (132)
Criminal RICO (142)
Cruel and unusual punishment (150)
Cyber crime (143)
Defendant (133)
Defense attorney (133)
Double Jeopardy Clause (149)
Eighth Amendment (150)
Embezzlement (140)

Exclusionary rule (144)
Extortion (blackmail) (140)
Extortion under color of official right (140)
Felony (133)
Felony murder rule (138)
Fifth Amendment (147)
Forgery (139)
Fourth Amendment (144)
General intent crime (134)
Grand jury (136)
Grand jury indictment (136)
Guilty (136)
Hung jury (137)
Identity theft (ID theft) (143)

Identity Theft and Assumption Deterrence Act (143)
Immunity from prosecution (149)
Indictment (136)
Information (136)
Information Infrastructure Protection Act (IIP Act) (144)
Intent crime (134)
Involuntary manslaughter (135)
Judgment proof (135)
Kickback (payoff) (140)
Larceny (138)
Magistrate (136)
Magistrate's information statement (136)

Mail fraud (141)
Mala in se (133)
Mala prohibita (133)
Mens rea (134)
Miranda rights (148)
Misdemeanor (133)
Money laundering (141)
Money Laundering
  Control Act (141)
Murder (138)
Nolo contendere (137)
Nonintent crime (134)
Not guilty (136)
Parent–child privilege
  (149)
Penal code (132)

Plaintiff (133)
Plea (136)
Plea bargain (137)
Plea bargaining
  agreement (137)
Presumed innocent
  until proven guilty
  (132)
Priest/rabbi/minister/
  imam–penitent
  privilege (149)
Privilege against
  self-incrimination
  (147)
Probable cause (135)
Prosecutor (133)

Psychiatrist/
  psychologist–patient
  privilege (149)
Public defender (133)
Racketeer Influenced and
  Corrupt Organizations
  Act (RICO) (142)
Reasonable search and
  seizure (144)
Receiving stolen property
  (139)
Regulatory statutes (132)
Right to a public jury
  trial (150)
Robbery (138)
Search warrant (144)

Self-incrimination (147)
Specific intent crime
  (134)
Sixth Amendment (150)
Spouse–spouse privilege
  (149)
Theft (139)
Unanimous decision
  (137)
Unreasonable search and
  seizure (144)
Violation (133)
Warrantless arrest (136)
Warrantless search (144)
White-collar crime (139)
Wire fraud (141)

Law Case with Answer
City of Indianapolis, Indiana v. Edmond

Facts   The police of the city of Indianapolis, Indiana, began to operate vehicle roadblock checkpoints on Indianapolis roads in an effort to interdict unlawful drugs. Once a car had been stopped, police questioned the driver and passengers and conducted an open-view examination of the vehicle from the outside. A narcotics-detection dog walked around outside each vehicle. The police conducted a search and seizure of the occupants and vehicle only if particular suspicion developed from the initial investigation. The overall "hit rate" of the program was approximately 9 percent.

James Edmond and Joel Palmer, both of whom were attorneys who had been stopped at one of the Indianapolis checkpoints, filed a lawsuit on behalf of themselves and the class of all motorists who had been stopped or were subject to being stopped at such checkpoints. They claimed that the roadblocks violated the Fourth Amendment's prohibition against unreasonable search and seizure. Does the Indianapolis highway checkpoint program, whereby police, without individualized suspicion, stop vehicles for the primary purpose of discovering and interdicting illegal narcotics violate the Fourth Amendment to the U.S. Constitution?

Answer   Yes, the Indianapolis highway checkpoint program whereby police, without individualized suspicion, stop vehicles for the primary purpose of discovering and interdicting illegal narcotics, does

violate the Fourth Amendment to the U.S. Constitution. The Fourth Amendment requires that searches and seizures be reasonable. A search or seizure is ordinarily unreasonable in the absence of individualized suspicion of wrongdoing. In only limited circumstances does this rule not apply. The Fourth Amendment would not approve a checkpoint program whose primary purpose is to detect evidence of ordinary criminal wrongdoing. Because the primary purpose of the Indianapolis narcotics checkpoint program is to uncover evidence of ordinary criminal wrongdoing, the program contravenes the Fourth Amendment.

Of course, certain circumstances might justify a law enforcement checkpoint where the primary purpose would be necessary for some emergency. For example, the Fourth Amendment would permit an appropriately tailored roadblock set up to thwart an imminent terrorist attack or to catch a dangerous criminal who is likely to flee by way of a particular route. But barring such emergencies—which did not exist in this case—the police cannot use a checkpoint program whose primary purpose is to detect evidence of ordinary criminal wrongdoing of possessing or uses illegal narcotics. The vehicle roadblock checkpoint used in this case violates the Fourth Amendment. *City of Indianapolis, Indiana v. Edmond*, 531 U.S. 32, 121 S.Ct. 447, 148 L.Ed.2d 333, **Web** 2000 U.S. Lexis 8084 (Supreme Court of the United States, 2000)

Critical Legal Thinking Cases

7.1 Search and Seizure Government agents suspected that marijuana was being grown in the home of Danny Kyllo, which was part of a triplex building in Florence, Oregon. Indoor marijuana growth typically requires high-intensity lamps. In order to determine whether an amount of heat was emanating from Kyllo's home consistent with the use of such lamps, federal agents used a thermal imager to scan the triplex. Thermal imagers detect infrared radiation and produce images of the radiation. The scan of Kyllo's home, which was performed from an automobile on the street, showed that the roof over the garage and a side wall of Kyllo's home were "hot." The agents used this scanning evidence to obtain a search warrant authorizing a search of Kyllo's home. During the search, the agents found an indoor growing operation involving more than one hundred marijuana plants.

Kyllo was indicted for manufacturing marijuana, a violation of federal criminal law. Kyllo moved to suppress the imaging evidence and the evidence it led to, arguing that it was an unreasonable search that violated the Fourth Amendment to the U.S. Constitution. Is the use of a thermal-imaging device aimed at a private home from a public street to detect relative amounts of heat within the home a "search" within the meaning of the Fourth Amendment? *Kyllo v. United States*, 533 U.S. 27, 121 S.Ct. 2038, 150 L.Ed.2d 94, **Web** 2001 U.S. Lexis 4487 (Supreme Court of the United States)

7.2 Search and Seizure Bernardo Garcia had served time in jail for methamphetamine (meth) offenses. Upon release from prison, a person reported to the police that Garcia had brought meth to her and used it with her. Another person told police that Garcia bragged that he could manufacture meth in front of a police station without being caught. A store's security video system recorded Garcia buying ingredients used in making meth. From someone else, the police learned that Garcia was driving a Ford Tempo.

The police found the car parked on the street near where Garcia was staying. The police placed a global positioning system (GPS) tracking device underneath the rear bumper of the car so the device could receive and store satellite signals that indicate the device's location. Using the device, the police learned that Garcia had been visiting a large tract of land. With permission of the owner of the land, the police conducted a search and discovered equipment and materials to manufacture meth. While the police were there, Garcia arrived in his car. The police had not obtained a search warrant authorizing them to place the GPS tracker on Garcia's car.

The government brought criminal charges against Garcia. At Garcia's criminal trial in U.S. District Court, the evidence the police obtained using the GPS system was introduced. Based on this evidence, Garcia was found guilty of crimes related to the manufacture of meth. Garcia appealed to the U.S. Court of Appeals, arguing that the use of the GPS tracking system by the police was an unreasonable search in violation of the Fourth Amendment to the Constitution. Does the police officers' use of the GPS system without first obtaining a search warrant constitute an unreasonable search in violation of the Fourth Amendment? *United States of America v. Garcia*, **Web** 2007 U.S. App. Lexis 2272 (United States Court of Appeals for the Seventh Circuit)

7.3 Criminal Liability of Corporations Representatives of hotels, restaurants, hotel and restaurant supply companies, and other businesses located in Portland, Oregon, organized an association to attract conventions to their city. Members were asked to make contributions equal to 1 percent of their sales to finance the association. To aid collections, hotel members, including Hilton Hotels Corporation, agreed to give preferential treatment to suppliers who paid their assessments and to curtail purchases from those who did not. This agreement violated federal antitrust laws. The United States sued the members of the association, including Hilton Hotels, for the crime of violating federal antitrust laws. Can a corporation be held criminally liable for the acts of its representatives? If so, what criminal penalties can be assessed against the corporation? *United States v. Hilton Hotels Corp.*, 467 F.2d 1000, **Web** 1972 U.S. App. Lexis 7414 (United States Court of Appeals for the Ninth Circuit)

7.4 Criminal Fraud Miriam Marlowe's husband purchased a life insurance policy on his own life, naming his wife as the beneficiary. Three years later, after Marlowe's husband died in a swimming accident, Marlowe received payment on the life insurance policy. Marlowe later met John Walton, a friend of a friend. He convinced Marlowe and her representative that he had a friend who worked for the State Department and had access to gold in Brazil and that the gold could be purchased in Brazil for $100 an ounce and sold in the United States for $300 an ounce. Walton convinced Miriam to invest $25,000. Instead of investing the money in gold in Brazil, Walton opened an account at Tracy Collins Bank in the name of Jeffrey McIntyre Roberts and deposited Miriam's money in the account. He later withdrew the money in cash. What crime has Walton committed? *State of Utah v. Roberts*, 711 P.2d 235, **Web** 1985 Utah Lexis 872 (Supreme Court of Utah)

7.5 Bribery The city of Peoria, Illinois, received federal funds from the Department of Housing and

Urban Development (HUD) to be used for housing rehabilitation assistance. The city of Peoria designated United Neighborhoods, Inc. (UNI), a corporation, to administer the funds. Arthur Dixon was UNI's executive director, and James Lee Hinton was its housing rehabilitation coordinator. In these capacities, they were responsible for contracting with suppliers and trades people to provide the necessary goods and services to rehabilitate the houses. Evidence showed that Dixon and Hinton used their positions to extract 10 percent payments back on all contracts they awarded. What crimes have Dixon and Hinton committed? *Dixon and Hinton v. United States*, 465 U.S. 482, 104 S.Ct. 1172, 79 L.Ed.2d 458, **Web** 1984 U.S. Lexis 35 (Supreme Court of the United States)

7.6 Administrative Search Lee Stuart Paulson owned a liquor license for My House, a bar in San Francisco. The California Department of Alcoholic Beverage Control is the administrative agency that regulates bars in that state. The California Business and Professions Code, which is administered by the department, prohibits "any kind of illegal activity on licensed premises." An anonymous informer tipped the department that narcotics were being sold on the premises of My House, an establishment that sold liquor, and that the narcotics were kept in a safe behind the bar on the premises. A special department investigator entered the bar during its hours of operation, identified himself, and informed Paulson that he was conducting an inspection. The investigator, who did not have a search warrant, opened the safe without seeking Paulson's consent. Twenty-two bundles of cocaine, totaling 5.5 grams, were found in the safe. Paulson was arrested. At his criminal trial, Paulson challenged the lawfulness of the search. Is the warrantless search of the safe a lawful search? *People v. Paulson*, 216 Cal.App.3d 1480, 265 Cal.Rptr. 579, **Web** 1990 Cal.App. Lexis 10 (Court of Appeal of California)

7.7 Privilege Against Self-Incrimination John Doe was the owner of several sole proprietorship businesses. During the course of an investigation of corruption in awarding county and municipal contracts, a federal grand jury served several subpoenas on John Doe, demanding the production of certain business records. The subpoenas demanded the production of the following records: (1) general ledgers and journals, (2) invoices, (3) bank statements and canceled checks, (4) financial statements, (5) telephone company records, (6) safe deposit box records, and (7) copies of tax returns. John Doe filed a motion in federal court, seeking to quash the subpoenas, alleging that producing these business records would violate his Fifth Amendment privilege of not testifying against himself. Must John Doe disclose the records? *United States v. John Doe*, 465 U.S. 605, 104 S.Ct. 1237, 79 L.Ed.2d 552, **Web** 1984 U.S. Lexis 169 (Supreme Court of the United States)

7.8 Search and Seizure Joseph Burger was the owner of a junkyard in Brooklyn, New York. His business consisted, in part, of dismantling automobiles and selling their parts. The state of New York enacted a statute that requires automobile junkyards to keep certain records. The statute authorizes warrantless searches of vehicle dismantlers and automobile junkyards without prior notice. One day, five plain-clothes officers of the Auto Crimes Division of the New York City Police Department entered Burger's junkyard to conduct a surprise inspection. Burger did not have either a license to conduct the business or records of the automobiles and vehicle parts on his premises, as required by state law. After conducting an inspection of the premises, the officers determined that Burger was in possession of stolen vehicles and parts. He was arrested and charged with criminal possession of stolen property. Burger moved to suppress the evidence. Did Burger act ethically in trying to suppress the evidence? Does the warrantless search of an automobile junkyard pursuant to a state statute that authorizes such a search constitute an unreasonable search and seizure in violation of the Fourth Amendment to the U.S. Constitution? *New York v. Burger*, 482 U.S. 691, 107 S.Ct. 2636, 96 L.Ed.2d 601, **Web** 1987 U.S. Lexis 2725 (Supreme Court of the United States)

Ethics Cases

7.9 Ethics Leo Shaw, an attorney, entered into a partnership agreement with three other persons to build and operate an office building. From the outset, it was agreed that Shaw's role was to manage the operation of the building. Management of the property was Shaw's contribution to the partnership; the other three partners contributed the necessary capital. Ten years later, the other partners discovered that the loan on the building was in default and that foreclosure proceedings were imminent. Upon investigation, they discovered that Shaw had taken approximately $80,000 from the partnership's checking account. After heated discussions, Shaw repaid $13,000. When no further payment was forthcoming, a partner filed a civil suit against Shaw and notified the police. The state filed a criminal complaint against

Shaw. Subsequently, Shaw repaid the remaining funds as part of a civil settlement. At his criminal trial Shaw argued that the repayment of the money was a defense to the crime of embezzlement. *People v. Shaw*, 10 Cal. App. 4th 969, 12 Cal.Rptr.2d 665, **Web** 1992 Cal.App. Lexis 1256 (Court of Appeal of California)

1. What is necessary to prove the crime of embezzlement?
2. Did Shaw act ethically in this case? Would your answer be different if he had really only "borrowed" the money and had intended to return it?
3. Is Shaw guilty of the crime of embezzlement? Why or why not?

7.10 Ethics   Ronald V. Cloud purchased the Cal-Neva Lodge, a hotel and casino complex located in the Lake Tahoe area on the California–Nevada border, for $10 million. Cloud was a sophisticated 68-year-old entrepreneur who was experienced in buying and selling real estate and had real estate holdings valued at more than $65 million. He also had experience in banking and finance, having been the founder and chairman of Continental National Bank of Fresno. After two years of mounting operation losses, Cloud closed the Cal-Neva Lodge and actively began seeking a new buyer. Cloud met with Jon Perroton and orally agreed to transfer the lodge to Perroton for approximately $17 million. Perroton met with an executive of Hibernia Bank (Hibernia) to discuss a possible loan to finance the purchase of the lodge. Perroton made multiple false representations and presented false documents to obtain a $20 million

loan from Hibernia. In particular, Perroton misrepresented the sale price for the lodge to be $27.5 million and stated that $7.5 million had already been paid to Cloud. An escrow account was opened with Transamerica Title Company (Transamerica).

Cloud and his attorney and Perroton met at Transamerica to sign mutual escrow instructions. Cloud reviewed the instructions and noticed that the sale price and down payment figures were incorrectly stated at $27.5 million and $7.5 million, respectively, and that the Hibernia loan was for $20 million, almost $3 million above what he knew to be the true sale price. Cloud signed the escrow instructions. Later, Cloud signed a settlement statement containing the same false figures and signed a grant deed to the property. The sale closed with Hibernia making the $20 million loan to Perroton. Subsequently, when the loan went into default, Continental Insurance Company (Continental) paid Hibernia its loss of $7.5 million on the bank's blanket bond insurance policy. The United States sued Cloud for aiding and abetting a bank fraud in violation of federal law (18 U.S.C. Sections 2 and 1344). The jury convicted Cloud of the crime and ordered him to make restitution of $7.5 million to Continental. Cloud appealed his conviction. *United States v. Cloud*, 872 F.2d 846, **Web** 1989 U.S. App. Lexis 4534 (United States Court of Appeals for the Ninth Circuit)

1. What is the crime of aiding and abetting?
2. Did cloud act ethically in this case?
3. Is Cloud guilty of aiding and abetting a bank fraud?

Internet Exercises

1. Go to **http://wings.buffalo.edu/law/bclc/web/website/allcodes2.htm** and find the penal code of the state in which your college or university is located. Find and read your state's definition of murder.

2. Go to **www.thelaborers.net/indictments/bellomo/indictment_criminal_genovese_family-2006-2-23.htm** and read a grand jury indictment of the Genovese organized crime family.

3. Go to the Florida penal code at **www.leg.state.fl.us/** statutes. Read the statutory definition of first-degree murder in the Florida penal code.

4. Go to **http://newsinfo.inquirer.net/breakingnews/world/view/20080211-118178/UPDATE** and read about the theft of $168 million of paintings from a museum. Use **www.google.com** to find out whether any of these paintings have been recovered yet.

5. To test your knowledge about ID theft, go to the FTC's website, at **http://onguardonline.gov/quiz/idtheft_quiz.html**, and take the online quiz.

6. Go to **https://complaint.ic3.gov** to view the complaint referral form of the Internet Crime Complaint Center.

Endnotes

1. Title 18 of the U.S. Code contains the federal criminal code.
2. Sentencing Reform Act of 1984, 18 U.S.C. Section 3551 et seq.
3. 532 U.S. 318, 121 S.Ct. 1536, 149 L.Ed.2d 549, **Web** 2001 U.S. Lexis 3366 (Supreme Court of the United States).
4. 18 U.S.C. Section 1341.

5. 18 U.S.C. Section 1343.

6. 18 U.S.C. Section 1957.

7. 18 U.S.C. Sections 1961–1968.

8. 18 U.S.C. Section 1028.

9. 18 U.S.C. Section 1030.

10. *United States v. Leon*, 468 U.S. 897, 104 S.Ct. 3405, 82 L.Ed.2d 677, **Web** 1984 U.S. Lexis 153 (Supreme Court of the United States).

11. 395 U.S. 752, 89 S.Ct. 2034, 23 L.Ed.2d 685, **Web** 1969 U.S. Lexis 1166 (Supreme Court of the United States).

12. *Marshall v. Barlow's Inc.*, 436 U.S. 307, 98 S.Ct. 1816, 56 L.Ed.2d 305, **Web** 1978 U.S. Lexis 26 (Supreme Court of the United States).

13. *Bellis v. United States*, 417 U.S. 85, 94 S.Ct. 2.179, 40 L.Ed.2d 678, **Web** 1974 U.S. Lexis 58 (Supreme Court of the United States)

14. 384 U.S. 436, 86 S.Ct. 1602, 16 L.Ed.2d 694, **Web** 1966 U.S. Lexis 2817 (Supreme Court of the United States).

15. 530 U.S. 428, 120 S.Ct. 2326, 147 L.Ed.2d 405, **Web** 2000 U.S. Lexis 4305 (Supreme Court of the United States).

16. 409 U.S. 322, 93 S.Ct. 611, 34 L.Ed.2d 548, **Web** 1973 U.S. Lexis 23 (Supreme Court of the United States).

17. The Speedy Trial Act requires that a criminal defendant be brought to trial within seventy days after indictment [18 U.S.C. Section 316(c) (1)]. Continuances may be granted by the court to serve the "ends of justice."

18. *Baldwin v. Alabama*, 472 U.S. 372, 105 S.Ct. 2727, 86 L.Ed.2d 300, **Web** 1985 U.S. Lexis 106 (Supreme Court of the United States).

19. *Baze v. Rees*, 128 S.Ct. 1520, 170 L.Ed.2d 420, **Web** 2008 U.S. Lexis 3476 (Supreme Court of the United States).

8 Intellectual Property and Cyber Piracy

COPYRIGHT OF BOOKS
The owners of copyright material such as books, movies, CDs, DVDs, and video games; the owners of trademarks such as McDonald's Corporation and Starbucks Corporation; the creators of patents such as Microsoft Corporation and Intel Corporation; the owners of trade secrets such as the Coca-Cola Corporation; and the owners of other intellectual property lose substantial revenues caused by the sale of knockoffs of their intellectual property. Computers and software programs have helped increase cyber piracy of intellectual property. Intellectual property is protected by a variety of civil and criminal laws.

Learning Objectives

After studying this chapter, you should be able to:

1. Describe the business tort of misappropriating a trade secret.
2. Describe how an invention can be patented under federal patent laws and the penalties for patent infringement.
3. List the items that can be copyrighted and describe the penalties of copyright infringement.
4. Define *trademark* and *service mark* and describe the penalties for trademark infringement.
5. Define *cyber piracy* and describe the penalties for engaging in cyber infringement of intellectual property rights.

Chapter Outline

Introduction to Intellectual Property and Cyber Piracy

Intellectual Property

Trade Secret
 ETHICS • *Coca-Cola Employee Tries to Sell Trade Secrets to Pepsi-Cola*

Patent
 CASE 8.1 • U.S. SUPREME COURT • *Bilski v. Kappos, Director, Patent and Trademark Office*

Copyright
 DIGITAL LAW • *Digital Millennium Copyright Act Makes It a Crime to Circumvent Encryption Technology*

Trademark
 CASE 8.2 • *Intel Corporation v. Intelsys Software, LLC*
 CASE 8.3 • *V Secret Catalogue, Inc. and Victoria's Secret Stores, Inc. v. Moseley*

" *The Congress shall have the power ... to promote the Progress of Science and useful Arts, by securing for limited Times to Authors and Inventors the exclusive Right to their respective Writings and Discoveries.*"

—*Article 1, Section 8, Clause 8 of the U.S. Constitution*

Introduction to Intellectual Property and Cyber Piracy

The U.S. economy is based on the freedom of ownership of property. In addition to real estate and personal property, *intellectual property rights* have value to both businesses and individuals. This is particularly the case in the modern era of the Information Age, computers, and the Internet.

Federal law provides protections for intellectual property rights, such as patents, copyrights, and trademarks. Certain federal statutes provide for either civil damages or criminal penalties, or both, to be assessed against infringers of patents, copyrights, and trademarks. Trade secrets form the basis of many successful businesses, and they are protected from misappropriation. State law imposes civil damages and criminal penalties against persons who misappropriate trade secrets.

This chapter discusses trade secrets, patents, copyrights, and trademarks and protecting them from infringement, misappropriation, and cyber piracy.

And he that invents a machine augments the power of a man and the well-being of mankind.

Henry Ward Beecher
Proverbs from Plymouth Pulpit—Business

Intellectual Property

Intellectual property is a term that describes property that is developed through an intellectual and creative process. Intellectual property falls into a category of property known as *intangible rights*, which are not tangible physical objects.

Most persons are familiar with the fact that intellectual property includes patents, copyrights, and trademarks. It also includes trade secrets. For patents, think of Microsoft's patents on its Windows operating system. Microsoft has obtained more than ten thousand patents. For copyrights, think of music, movies, books, and video games. For trademarks, think of Nike's recognizable "*Just do it*" and Swoosh logo and McDonald's *Big Mac* and "*I'm lovin' it.*" For trade secrets, think of Coca-Cola Company's secret recipe for making Coca-Cola. Patents, trademarks, and copyrights give their owners or holders monopoly rights for specified periods of time. Trade secrets remain valuable as long as they are not easily discovered.

Intellectual property is of significant value to companies in the United States and globally as well. Over one-half of the value of large companies in the United States is related to their intangible property rights. Some industries are intellectual property intensive, such as the music and movie industries. Other industries that are not intellectual property intensive, such as the automobile and food industries, are still highly dependent on their intellectual property rights.

Because of their intangible nature, intellectual property rights are more subject to misappropriation than is tangible property. It is almost impossible to steal real estate, and it is often difficult to steal tangible property such as equipment, furniture, and other personal property. However, intellectual property rights are much easier to misappropriate. Think of counterfeit compact discs (CDs) and DVDs and fake designer purses. In addition, computers and cyber piracy make it easier to steal many forms of intellectual property. The misappropriation of intellectual property rights is one of the major threats to companies today.

intellectual property
Patents, copyrights, trademarks, and trade secrets. Federal and state laws protect intellectual property rights from misappropriation and infringement.

Where a new invention promises to be useful, it ought to be tried.

Thomas Jefferson

Trade Secret

trade secret
A product formula, pattern, design, compilation of data, customer list, or other business secret.

Many businesses are successful because their **trade secrets** set them apart from their competitors. Trade secrets may be product formulas, patterns, designs, compilations of data, customer lists, or other business secrets. Many trade secrets do not qualify to be—or simply are not—patented, copyrighted, or trademarked. Many states have adopted the **Uniform Trade Secrets Act** to give statutory protection to trade secrets.

State unfair competition laws allow the owner of a trade secret to bring a lawsuit for *misappropriation* against anyone who steals a trade secret. For the lawsuit to be actionable, the defendant (often an employee of the owner or a competitor) must have obtained the trade secret through unlawful means, such as theft, bribery, or industrial espionage. No tort has occurred if there is no misappropriation.

The owner of a trade secret is obliged to take all reasonable precautions to prevent that secret from being discovered by others. If the owner fails to take such actions, the secret is no longer subject to protection under state unfair competition laws. Precautions to protect a trade secret may include fencing in buildings, placing locks on doors, hiring security guards, and the like.

Examples The most famous trade secret is the formula for Coca-Cola. This secret recipe, which is referred to by the code name "Merchandise 7X," is kept in a bank vault in Atlanta, Georgia. The formula is supposedly known by only two executives who have signed non-disclosure agreements. Another secret recipe that is protected as a trade secret is KFC's secret recipe of eleven herbs and spices for the batter used on the Colonel's Original Recipe Kentucky Fried Chicken.

Reverse Engineering

WEB EXERCISE
Go to **www.usatoday.com/money/ industries/food/2005-07-22-kfc- secret-recipe_x.htm** and read about how KFC protects its secret recipe.

A competitor can lawfully discover a trade secret by performing **reverse engineering** (i.e., taking apart and examining a rival's product or re-creating a secret recipe). A competitor who has reverse engineered a trade secret can use the trade secret but not the trademarked name used by the original creator of the trade secret.

Example An inventor invents a new formula for a perfume. The inventor decides to not get a patent for her new formula (because patent protection is good only for twenty years). Instead, the inventor chooses to try to protect it as a trade secret, which gives her protection for as long a period of time as she can successfully keep it a secret. Another party purchases the perfume, chemically analyzes the perfume, and discovers the formula. The trade secret has been reverse engineered and the second party may begin producing a perfume using the inventor's formula.

Misappropriation of a Trade Secret

The owner of a trade secret can bring a **civil lawsuit** under state law against anyone who has **misappropriated a trade secret** through unlawful means, such as theft, bribery, or industrial espionage. Generally, a successful plaintiff in a trade secret action can (1) recover the *profits* made by the offender from the use of the trade secret, (2) recover for *damages*, and (3) obtain an *injunction* prohibiting the offender from divulging or using the trade secret.

Economic Espionage Act

Economic Espionage Act (EEA)
A federal statute that makes it a crime for any person to convert a trade secret for his or her own or another's benefit, knowing or intending to cause injury to the owners of the trade secret.

Congress enacted the federal **Economic Espionage Act (EEA)**,[1] which makes it a federal *crime* to steal another's trade secrets. Under the EEA, it is a federal crime for any person to convert a trade secret to his or her benefit or for the benefit of others, knowing or intending that the act would cause injury to the owner of the trade secret. The definition of *trade secret* under the EEA is very broad and parallels the definition used under the civil laws of misappropriating a trade secret.

One of the major reasons for the passage of the EEA was to address the ease of stealing trade secrets through computer espionage and using the Internet. Confidential information can be downloaded onto a CD or Flash drive, placed in a pocket, and taken from the legal owner. Computer hackers can crack into a company's computers and steal customer lists, databases, formulas, and other trade secrets. The EEA is a very important weapon in addressing computer and Internet espionage and penalizing those who commit it.

The EEA provides for severe criminal penalties. The act imposes prison terms on individuals of up to fifteen years per criminal violation. An organization can be fined up to $10 million per criminal act. The criminal prison term for individuals and the criminal fine for organizations can be increased if the theft of a trade secret was made to benefit a foreign government.

The following case involves the misappropriation of a trade secret.

Ethics

Coca-Cola Employee Tries to Sell Trade Secrets to Pepsi-Cola

"What if you knew the markets they [Coca-Cola] were going to move into and out of ... and beat them to the punch."

—Letter to PepsiCo

In February 2007, former Coca-Cola secretary Joya Williams was convicted by a federal jury of conspiring to steal trade secrets and attempting to sell them to archrival PepsiCo for $1.5 million. Along with Williams, two other co-conspirators were arrested and pled guilty.

The conspiracy was initially foiled when rival PepsiCo produced a letter sent to the company by one of the co-conspirators that offered Coca-Cola trade secrets to the highest bidder. "What if you knew the markets they [Coca-Cola] were going to move into and out of ... and beat them to the punch," the letter stated. PepsiCo notified Coca-Cola officials and federal authorities, who initiated an investigation into the matter by the Federal Bureau of Investigation (FBI). Williams was fired as a secretary in Coca-Cola's global branding department when the initial allegations came to light.

The federal government brought criminal charges against Williams. During trial, prosecutors produced the letter as well as a videotape of Williams putting confidential documents and samples of Coke products that were still in development into her bag. According to court records, the stolen materials included details of an upcoming Coke product code-named Project Lancelot. Coke's 120-year-old "secret formula" recipe was not involved.

The jury returned a guilty verdict, and the trial court judge sentenced Williams to eight years in jail. The U.S. Court of Appeals upheld the decision. The Court stated that the sentence was justified based on the harm that Coca-Cola could have suffered if Williams and her co-conspirators had succeeded in selling its trade secrets to a rival and the danger to the U.S. economy these crimes pose. *United States v. Williams*, **Web** 2008 U.S. App. Lexis 6073 (United States Court of Appeals for the Eleventh Circuit, 2008)

Ethics Questions Did Williams act loyally in this case? Did PepsiCo do what it was supposed to do in this case? How likely is it that PepsiCo would have paid Williams and her co-conspirators the money they demanded?

Patent

When drafting the Constitution of the United States of America, the founders of the United States provided for protection of the work of inventors and writers. Article I, Section 8 of the Constitution provides, "The Congress shall have Power ... To promote the Progress of Science and useful Arts, by securing for limited Times to Authors and Inventors the exclusive Right to their respective Writings and Discoveries." Pursuant to the express authority granted in the U.S.

Federal Patent Statute
A federal statute that establishes the requirements for obtaining a patent and protects patented inventions from infringement.

patent
A grant by the federal government upon the inventor of an invention for the exclusive right to use, sell, or license the invention for a limited amount of time.

U.S. Court of Appeals for the Federal Circuit
A special federal appeals court that hears appeals from the Board of Patent Appeals and Interferences and federal court concerning patent issues.

The patent system added the fuel of interest to the fire of genius.

Abraham Lincoln

Exhibit 8.1 PATENT APPLICATION FOR THE FACEBOOK SOCIAL NETWORKING SYSTEM

Constitution, Congress enacted the **Federal Patent Statute** of 1952[2] to provide for obtaining and protecting patents.

A **patent** is a grant by the federal government upon the inventor of an invention for the exclusive right to use, sell, or license the invention for a limited amount of time.

Patent law is intended to provide an incentive for inventors to invent and make their inventions public and to protect patented inventions from infringement. Federal patent law is exclusive; there are no state patent laws. Applications for patents must be filed with the **U.S. Patent and Trademark Office (PTO)** in Washington, DC.

U.S. Court of Appeals for the Federal Circuit

The **U.S. Court of Appeals for the Federal Circuit** in Washington, DC, was created in 1982. This is a special federal appeals court that hears appeals from the Board of Patent Appeals and Interferences of the U.S. Patent and Trademark Office and federal courts concerning patent issues. This Court was created to promote uniformity in patent law.

Patent Application

To obtain a patent, a **patent application** must be filed with the PTO in Washington, DC. The PTO provides for the online submission of patent applications and supporting documents through its EFS-Web system. A patent application must contain a written description of the invention. Patent applications are complicated. Therefore, an inventor should hire a patent attorney to assist in obtaining a patent for an invention.

If a patent is granted, the invention is assigned a **patent number**. Patent holders usually affix the word *patent* or *pat.* and the patent number on the patented article. If a patent application is filed but a patent has not yet been issued, the applicant usually places the words **patent pending** on the article. Any party can challenge either the issuance of a patent or the validity of an existing patent.

Exhibit 8.1 shows excerpts from the patent application for the Facebook social networking system (US Patent 20070192299).

Systems and Methods for Social Mapping

Abstract

A system, method, and computer program for social mapping is provided. Data about a plurality of social network members is received. A first member of the plurality of social network members is allowed to identify a second member of the plurality of social network members with whom the first member wishes to establish a relationship. The data is then sent to the second member about the first member based on the identification. Input from the second member is received in response to the data. The relationship between the first member and the second member is confirmed based on the input in order to map the first member to the second member.

Subject Matter That Can Be Patented

utility patent
A patent that protects the functionality of an invention.

Most patents are **utility patents**, that is, they protect the functionality of the item. The term *patent* is commonly used in place of the words *utility patent*.

Only certain subject matter can be patented. Federal patent law recognizes categories of innovation that can be patented. These include:

- Machines
- Processes
- Compositions of matter
- Improvements to existing machines, processes, or compositions of matter
- Designs for an article of manufacture
- Asexually reproduced plants
- Living material invented by a person.

Abstractions and scientific principles cannot be patented unless they are part of the tangible environment.

Example Einstein's Theory of Relativity ($E = mc^2$) cannot be patented.

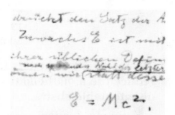

For centuries, most patents involved tangible inventions and machines, such as the telephone and the light bulb. Next, chemical and polymer inventions were patented. Then biotechnology patents were granted. More recently, subject matter involving the computer, Internet, and e-commerce has been added to what can be patented.

Requirements for Obtaining a Patent

To be patented, an invention must be (1) *novel, (2) useful,* and (3) *nonobvious.* An invention must meet all three of these requirements. If an invention is found to not meet any one of these requirements, it cannot be patented:

1. **Novel.** An invention is **novel** if it is new and has not been invented and used in the past. If an invention has been used in "prior art," it is not novel and cannot be patented.

   Example College and professional football games are often shown on television. It is often difficult, however, for a viewer to tell how far the offensive team must go to get a first down and keep possession of the football. Inventors invented a system whereby a yellow line is digitally drawn across the football field at the distance that a team has to go to obtain a first down. This "yellow line" invention qualified for a patent because it was novel.

2. **Useful.** An invention is **useful** if it has some practical purpose. If an invention has only theoretical benefit and no useful purpose, it cannot be patented.

   Example A cardboard or heavy paper sleeve that can be placed over the outside of a paper coffee cup so that the cup will not be too hot to hold serves a useful purpose. Many coffee shops use these sleeves. The sleeve serves a useful purpose and therefore qualifies to be patented.

3. **Nonobvious.** If an invention is **nonobvious**, it qualifies for a patent; if it is obvious, then it does not qualify for a patent.

   Example An invention called "Forkchops" was found to be nonobvious and was granted a patent. Forkchops consist of chopsticks with a spoon on one end of one of the chopsticks and a fork on one end of the other chopstick. Thus, when eating, a user can either use the chopstick ends or the spoon and fork ends.

   Example An inventor filed for a patent for a "waffle fry," which is a fried slice of potato with a waffle shape that is not as thick as a typical French fry but is thicker than a potato chip. Thus, the thickness of a waffle fry is somewhere in between the thickness of a French fry and a potato chip. The court rejected a patent for the waffle fry because it was obvious that a potato could be sliced into different sizes.

The following case involves a patent application.

CASE 8.1   *U.S. SUPREME COURT Patent*

Bilski v. Kappos, Director, Patent and Trademark Office

130 S.Ct. 3218, 177 L.Ed.2d 792, Web 2010 U.S. Lexis 5521 (2010)
Supreme Court of the United States

"The concept of hedging, described in claim 1 and reduced to a mathematical formula in claim 4, is an unpatentable abstract idea."

—Kennedy, Justice

Facts

Bernard Bilski and Rand Warsaw filed a patent application with the U.S. Patent and Trademark Office (PTO). The application sought patent protection for a claimed invention that explains how buyers and sellers of commodities in the energy market can hedge against the risk of price changes. The key claims are claims 1 and 4. Claim 1 describes a series of steps instructing how to hedge risk. Claim 4 puts the concept articulated in claim 1 into a simple mathematical formula. The remaining claims describe how claims 1 and 4 can be applied to allow energy suppliers and consumers to minimize the risks resulting from fluctuations in market demand for energy. The PTO rejected the patent application, holding that it merely manipulates an abstract idea and solves a purely mathematical problem. The U.S. Court of Appeals affirmed. Petitioners Bilski and Warsaw appealed to the U.S. Supreme Court.

Issue

Is the petitioners' claimed invention patentable?

Language of the U.S. Supreme Court

Section 101 specifies four independent categories of inventions or discoveries that are eligible for protection: processes, machines, manufactures, and compositions of matter. The Court's precedents provide three specific exceptions to Section 101's broad patent-eligibility principles: laws of nature, physical phenomena, and abstract ideas. The concepts covered by these exceptions are part of the
storehouse of knowledge of all men free to all men and reserved exclusively to none.

Petitioners seek to patent both the concept of hedging risk and the application of that concept to energy markets. It is clear that petitioners' application is not a patentable process. Claims 1 and 4 in petitioners' application explain the basic concept of hedging, or protecting against risk. Hedging is a fundamental economic practice long prevalent in our system of commerce and taught in any introductory finance class. The concept of hedging, described in claim 1 and reduced to a mathematical formula in claim 4, is an unpatentable abstract idea. Allowing petitioners to patent risk hedging would preempt use of this approach in all fields, and would effectively grant a monopoly over an abstract idea. The patent application here can be rejected under our precedents on the unpatentability of abstract ideas.

Decision of the U.S. Supreme Court

The U.S. Supreme Court held that the concept of hedging is an abstract idea that cannot be patented.

Case Questions

Critical Legal Thinking
Is it often difficult for the U.S. Patent and Trademark Office to determine the patentability of claims in patent applications?

Ethics
Do you think that it was obvious that hedging is an abstract concept that cannot be patented?

Contemporary Business
Does the patent system promote or detract from business innovation?

Patent Period

In 1995, in order to bring the U.S. patent system into harmony with the patent systems of the majority of other developed nations, Congress made the following important changes in U.S. patent law:

- Utility patents for inventions are valid for *twenty years* (instead of the previous term of seventeen years).
- The patent term begins to run from the date the patent application is *filed* (instead of when the patent is issued, as was previously the case).

The United States still follows the **first-to-invent rule** rather than the *first-to-file rule* followed by some other countries. Thus, in the United States, the first person to invent an item or a process is given patent protection over a later inventor who was first to file a patent application.

Example On January 31, 2013, an inventor invents a chemical formula for a product that can be released into the air and eliminate air pollution. The inventor keeps her discovery secret, however. Two years later, another inventor invents exactly the same chemical formula. The next day, the second inventor files a patent application with the PTO and is issued a patent. The first inventor later discovers this fact and challenges the patent. The first inventor will win her patent challenge because she was the first to invent the invention. The second inventor, although the first to file for the patent, loses the patent.

After the patent period runs out, the invention or design enters the **public domain**, which means that anyone can produce and sell the invention without paying the prior patent holder.

Example On January 3, 2013, an inventor invents a formula for a new prescription drug. The inventor files for and is granted a twenty-year patent for this invention. Twenty years after the filing of the patent application, on February 1, 2033, the patent expires. At that time, the patent enters the public domain, and anyone can use the formula to produce exactly the same prescription drug.

WEB EXERCISE
Go to **www.uspto.gov**. Go to the left column entitled "Patents". Click on number 2 "Search." Towards the middle of the page that appears, find the term "Patent Number Search." Click on this term. In the open line under the term "Query", type in the patent number 3741662. Click on "Search." Read the information about this patent.

One-Year "On Sale" Doctrine

Under the **one-year "on sale" doctrine**, also called the **public use doctrine**, a patent may not be granted if the invention was used by the public for more than one year prior to the filing of a patent application. This doctrine forces inventors to file their patent applications at the proper time.

Example Suppose Cindy invents a new invention on January 10, 2013. She allows the public to use this invention and does not file a patent application until February 10, 2014. As a result, Cindy loses the right to patent her invention because she has waited over one year after her product has been used by the public before filing to patent her invention.

one-year "on sale" doctrine (public use doctrine)
A doctrine that says a patent may not be granted if the invention was used by the public for more than one year prior to the filing of the patent application.

Provisional Patent Application

Congress enacted the **American Inventors Protection Act**, which permits an inventor to file a **provisional application** with the PTO so that the inventor has time to prepare and file a final and complete patent application with the PTO. This "provisional right" gives an inventor three months to prepare a final patent application.

In addition, the act requires the PTO to issue a patent within three years from the date of filing a patent application. The act provides that non–patent holders may challenge a patent as being overly broad by requesting a contested reexamination of the patent application by the PTO. This provides that the reexamination will be within the confines of the PTO; the decision of the PTO can be appealed to the U.S. Court of Appeals for the Federal Circuit in Washington, DC.

provisional application
An application that an inventor may file with the PTO to obtain three months to prepare a final patent application.

Patent Infringement

Patent holders own exclusive rights to use and exploit their patents. **Patent infringement** occurs when someone makes unauthorized use of another's patent.

patent infringement
Unauthorized use of another's patent. A patent holder may recover damages and other remedies against a patent infringer.

STATUE OF LIBERTY
The Statue of Liberty is one of the most famous design patents. It was patented in the United States by Auguste Bartholdi on February 18, 1879. Patent No. 11,023.

In a suit for patent infringement, a successful plaintiff can recover (1) money damages equal to a reasonable royalty rate on the sale of the infringed articles, (2) other damages caused by the infringement (e.g., loss of customers), (3) an order requiring the destruction of the infringing article, and (4) an injunction preventing the infringer from such action in the future. The court has the discretion to award up to treble damages if the infringement was intentional.

Design Patent

design patent
A patent that may be obtained for the ornamental nonfunctional design of an item.

In addition to utility patents, a party can obtain a design patent. A **design patent** is a patent that may be obtained for the ornamental nonfunctional design of an item. A design patents is valid for fourteen years.

Examples The design of a chair, a door knob, a perfume bottle, and the outside of a computer are examples of design patents.

Copyright

copyright
A legal right that gives the author of qualifying subject matter, and who meets other requirements established by copyright law, the exclusive right to publish, produce, sell, license, and distribute the work.

Copyright Revision Act
A federal statute that (1) establishes the requirements for obtaining a copyright and (2) protects copyrighted works from infringement.

Article I, Section 8 of the Constitution of the United States of America authorizes Congress to enact statutes to protect the works of writers for limited times.

Pursuant to this authority, Congress has enacted copyright statutes that establish the requirement for obtaining a copyright. **Copyright** is a legal right that gives the author of qualifying subject matter, and who meets other requirements established by copyright law, the exclusive right to publish, produce, sell, license, and distribute the work.

The **Copyright Revision Act** of 1976[3] currently governs copyright law. The act establishes the requirements for obtaining a copyright and protects copyrighted works from infringement. Federal copyright law is exclusive; there are no state copyright laws. Federal copyright law protects the work of authors and other creative persons from the unauthorized use of their copyrighted materials and provides a financial incentive for authors to write, thereby increasing the number of creative works available in society. Copyrights can be sold or licensed to others, whose rights are then protected by copyright law.

Tangible Writing

Only **tangible writings**—writings that can be physically seen—are subject to copyright registration and protection. The term *writing* has been broadly defined.

Examples Books, periodicals, and newspapers; lectures, sermons, addresses, and poems; musical compositions; plays, motion pictures, and radio and television productions; maps; works of art, including paintings, drawings, jewelry, glassware, tapestry, and lithographs; architectural drawings and models; photographs, including prints, slides, and filmstrips, greeting cards, and picture postcards; photoplays, including feature films, cartoons, newsreels, travelogues, and training films; and sound recordings published in the form of tapes, cassettes, CDs, and MP3 files qualify for copyright protection.

Registration of Copyrights

To be protected under federal copyright law, a work must be the original work of the author. A copyright is automatically granted when an author produces his or her work.

Example When a student writes a term paper for his class, he owns a copyright to his work.

In 1989, the United States signed the **Berne Convention**, an international copyright treaty. This law eliminated the need to place the symbol © or the word *copyright* or *copr.* on a copyrighted work. However, it is still advisable to place the copyright notice © and the year of publication and the author's name on many copyrighted works because it notifies the world that the work is protected by a copyright, identifies the owner of the copyright, and shows the year of its publication. This will help eliminate a defendant's claim of innocent copyright.

Example Copyright © 2012 Henry Richard Cheeseman.

Published and unpublished works may be registered with the **U.S. Copyright Office** in Washington, DC. **Registration of a copyright** is permissive and voluntary and can be effectuated at any time during the term of the copyright. Copyright registration creates a public record of the copyrighted work. A **copyright registration certificate** is issued to the copyright holder. Registration permits a holder to obtain statutory damages for copyright infringement, which may be greater than actual damages, and attorney's fees.

The **Copyright Term Extension Act**[4] of 1998 extended copyright protection to the following:

1. Individuals are granted copyright protection for their lifetime plus seventy years.
2. Copyrights owned by businesses are protected for the shorter of either:
   a. 120 years from the year of creation
   b. 95 years from the year of first publication

The law in respect to literature ought to remain upon the same footing as that which regards the profits of mechanical inventions and chemical discoveries.

William Wordsworth
Letter (1838)

After the copyright period runs out, the work enters the **public domain**, which means that anyone can publish the work without paying the prior copyright holder.

Example If an author publishes a novel on April 1, 2003, and lives until August 1, 2037, his heirs will own the copyright until August 1, 3007.

CONCEPT SUMMARY
COPYRIGHT PERIOD

Type of Holder	Copyright Period
Individual	Life of the author plus 70 years beyond the author's life
Business	The shorter of either 95 years from the year of first publication or 120 years from the year of creation

Copyright Infringement

Copyright infringement occurs when a party copies a substantial and material part of the plaintiff's copyrighted work without permission. The copying does not have to be either word for word or the entire work. A plaintiff can bring a civil action against the alleged infringer and, if successful, recover (1) the profit made by the defendant from the copyright infringement, (2) damages suffered by the plaintiff, (3) an order requiring the impoundment and destruction of the infringing works, and (4) an injunction preventing the defendant from infringing in the future. The court, in its discretion, can award statutory damages for willful infringement in lieu of actual damages.

The federal government can bring criminal charges against a person who commits copyright infringement. Criminal copyright infringement, including infringement committed without monetary gain, is punishable by up to five years in federal prison.

Fair Use Doctrine

A copyright holder's right in a work is not absolute. The law permits certain limited unauthorized use of copyrighted materials under the **fair use doctrine**. The following uses are protected under this doctrine: (1) quotation of the copyrighted work for review or criticism or in a scholarly or technical work, (2) use in a parody or satire, (3) brief quotation in a news report, (4) reproduction by a teacher or student of a small part of the work to illustrate a lesson, (5) incidental reproduction of a work in a newsreel or broadcast of an event being reported, and (6) reproduction of a work in a legislative or judicial proceeding. The copyright holder cannot recover for copyright infringement where fair use is found.

Examples A student is assigned to write a paper in class about a certain subject matter. The student conducts research and writes her paper. In her paper, the student uses two paragraphs from a copyrighted book and places these paragraphs in quotation marks and properly cites the source and author in a footnote. This is fair use for academic purposes. However, if the student copies and uses three pages from the book, this would not be fair use and would constitute copyright infringement whether she footnotes the author or not.

Example *Saturday Night Live* is a comedy television show that is on television on Saturday nights. *Saturday Night Live* often does parodies and satires on famous musicians. This is an example of parody fair use.

No Electronic Theft (NET) Act

In 1997, Congress enacted the **No Electronic Theft Act**[5], or **NET Act**, a federal statute that *criminalizes* certain copyright infringement. The NET Act prohibits any person from willfully infringing a copyright for the purpose of either commercial advantage or financial gain, or by reproduction or distribution even without commercial advantage or financial gain, including by electronic means. Thus, the NET Act makes it a federal crime to reproduce, share, or distribute copyrighted electronic works including movies, songs, software programs, video games, and the like.

Examples Violations include distributing copyrighted works without permission of the copyright holder over the Internet, uploading such works to a website, and posting information about the availability of such uploaded electronic works.

Criminal penalties for violating the act include imprisonment for up to five years and fines of up to $250,000. Subsequent violators may be fined and imprisoned for up to ten years. The creation of the NET Act adds a new law that the federal government can use to criminally attack copyright infringement and curb digital piracy.

The NET Act also permits copyright holders to sue violators in a civil lawsuit and recover monetary damages of up to $150,000 per work infringed.

The following feature discusses a federal law designed to protect digital copyright material.

Digital Millennium Copyright Act (DMCA)
A federal statute that prohibits unauthorized access to copyrighted digital works by circumventing encryption technology or the manufacture and distribution of technologies designed for the purpose of circumventing encryption protection of digital works.

Digital Law

Digital Millennium Copyright Act Makes It a Crime to Circumvent Encryption Technology

The Internet makes it easier than ever before for people to illegally copy and distribute copyrighted works. To combat this, software and entertainment companies have developed "wrappers" and **encryption technology** to protect their copyrighted works from unauthorized access. Not to be outdone, software pirates have devised ways to crack these wrappers and protection devices.

Software and entertainment companies lobbied Congress to enact federal legislation to make the cracking of their wrappers and selling of technology to do so illegal. In response, Congress enacted the **Digital Millennium Copyright Act (DMCA)**,[6] a federal statute that does the following:

- Prohibits unauthorized access to copyrighted *digital works* by circumventing the wrapper or encryption technology that protects the intellectual property
- Prohibits the manufacture and distribution of technologies, products, or services primarily designed for the purpose of circumventing wrappers or encryption technology protecting digital works

Examples Microsoft releases a new software program that it will license to users for a monetary fee. Microsoft has placed electronic encryption technology in the software to prevent illegal piracy of the program. A hacker develops software that cracks encryption technology. This is a violation

of the DMCA. The hacker then sells and distributes his software program to others. This is also a violation of the DMCA. One of these parties uses the software to break through Microsoft's antipiracy technology and obtains a copy of the Microsoft software program. This is a violation of the DMCA whether this party uses the Microsoft program or not. If this person uses the Microsoft program, he will be liable for copyright infringement.

Congress granted exceptions to DMCA liability to (1) software developers to achieve compatibility of their software with the protected work; (2) federal, state, and local law enforcement agencies conducting criminal investigations; (3) parents who are protecting children from pornography or other harmful materials available on the Internet; (4) Internet users who are identifying and disabling cookies and other identification devices that invade their personal privacy rights; and (5) nonprofit libraries, educational institutions and archives that access a protected work to determine whether to acquire the work.

The DMCA imposes civil and criminal penalties. A successful plaintiff in a civil action can recover actual damages from first-time offenders and treble damages from repeat offenders, costs and attorneys' fees, an order for the destruction of illegal products and devices, and an injunction against future violations by the offender.

Trademark

Businesses often develop company names, as well as advertising slogans, symbols, and commercial logos, to promote the sale of their goods and services. Companies such as Nike, Microsoft, Louis Vuitton, and McDonald's spend millions of dollars annually promoting their names, slogans, symbols, and logos to gain market recognition from consumers. The U.S. Congress has enacted trademark laws to provide legal protection for these names, slogans, and logos.

A **mark** is a is any trade name, symbol, word, logo, design, or device used to identify and distinguish goods of a manufacturer or seller or services of a provider from those of other manufacturers, sellers, or providers.

In 1946, Congress enacted the **Lanham (Trademark) Act**,[7] commonly referred to as the **Lanham Act**, to provide federal protection to trademarks, service marks, and other marks. This act, as amended, is intended to (1) protect the owner's

mark
Any trade name, symbol, word, logo, design, or device used to identify and distinguish goods of a manufacturer or seller or services of a provider from those of other manufacturers, sellers, or providers.

investment and goodwill in a mark and (2) prevent consumers from being confused as to the origin of goods and services.

Registration of a Mark

Marks can be registered with the U.S. Patent and Trademark Office (PTO) in Washington, DC. A registrant must file an application with the PTO wherein the registrant designates the name, symbol, slogan, or logo that he is requesting to be registered. A registrant must prove either that he has used the intended mark in commerce (e.g., actually used in the sale of goods or services) or states that he intends to use the mark in commerce within six months from the filing of the application. In the latter case, if the proposed mark is not used in commerce within this six-month period, the applicant loses the right to register the mark. However, the applicant may file for a six-month extension to use the mark in commerce, which is often granted by the PTO.

The PTO provides for the paper filing of the application or for the electronic filing of the application through its **Trademark Electronic Application System (TEAS)**. A party other than the registrant can submit an *opposition* to a proposed registration of a mark.

The PTO will register a mark if it determines that the mark does not infringe any existing marks, the applicant has paid the registration fee (approximately $375), and other requirements for registering the mark have been met.

Once the PTO has issued a registration of the mark, the owner is entitled to use the registered mark symbol ® in connection with a registered trademark or service mark. The symbol ® is used to designate marks that have been registered with the PTO. The use of the symbol ® is not mandatory, although it is wise to use the ® symbol to put others on notice that the trademark or service mark is registered with the PTO. Once a mark is registered, it is given nationwide effect, serves as constructive notice that the mark is the registrant's personal property, and provides that federal lawsuits may be brought to protect the mark. The original registration of a mark is valid for ten years, and it can be renewed for an unlimited number of ten-year periods.

While the application is pending with the PTO, the registrant cannot use the symbol ®. However, during the application period, a registrant can use the symbol **TM** for goods or **SM** for services to alert the public to his or her legal claim. TM and SM may also be used by parties who claim a mark for goods or services but have not filed an application with the PTO to register the mark. In summary, TM and SM are used to designate unregistered trademarks and service marks, respectively.

A party who sell goods and services using brand names and product or service names is not required to register these names with the PTO. The party who does not register a name with the PTO still has legal rights in the name and can sue to prevent others from using the name. The lawsuit will be in state court, however. A party can use the symbols TM and SM with his goods or services, respectively, even if there is no application pending at the PTO.

A party may file for the **cancelation** of a previously registered mark if the party believes that the registrant did not meet the requirements for being issued the mark or if a mark has been abandoned.

Lanham (Trademark) Act (Lanham Act)
A federal statute that (1) establishes the requirements for obtaining a federal mark and (2) protects marks from infringement.

®
A symbol that is used to designate marks that have been registered with the U.S. Patent and Trademark Office.

WEB EXERCISE
Go to **www.coca-cola.com** to see trademarks of the Coca-Cola Corporation.

TM
A symbol that designates an owner's legal claim to an unregistered mark that is associated with a product.

SM
A symbol that designates an owner's legal claim to an unregistered mark that is associated with a service.

CONCEPT SUMMARY

MEANING OF SYMBOLS USED IN ASSOCIATION WITH MARKS

Symbol	Meaning
TM	Unregistered mark used with goods
SM	Unregistered mark used with services
®	Registered mark

Types of Marks

The word *mark* collectively refers to *trademarks, service marks, certification marks,* and *collective membership marks*:

- **Trademark.** A **trademark** is a distinctive mark, symbol, name, word, motto, or device that identifies the *goods* of a particular business.

  Examples *Coca-Cola* (The Coca-Cola Company), *Big Mac* (McDonald's Corporation), *Mac* (Apple Computer), *Intel Inside* (Intel Corporation), *Better Ingredients. Better Pizza.* (Papa John's Pizza), and *Harley* (Harley-Davidson Motor Company) are trademarks.

- **Service mark.** A **service mark** is used to distinguish the *services* of the holder from those of its competitors.

  Examples *FedEx* (FedEx Corporation), *The Friendly Skies* (United Airlines, Inc.), *Big Brown* (UPS Corporation), *Weight Watchers* (Weight Watchers International, Inc.), and *Citi* (Citigroup, Inc.) are service marks.

- **Certification mark.** A **certification mark** is a mark usually owned by a non-profit cooperative or association. The owner of the mark establishes certain geographical location requirements, quality standards, material standards, or mode of manufacturing standards that must be met by a seller of products or services in order to use the certification mark. If a seller meets these requirements, the seller applies to the cooperative or association to use the mark on its products or in connection with the sale of services. The owner of the certification mark usually licenses sellers who meet the requirements to use the mark. A party does not have to be a member of the organization to use the mark.

  Examples A *UL* mark certifies that products meet safety standards set by Underwriters Laboratories, Inc. The *Good Housekeeping Seal of Approval* certifies that products meet certain quality specifications set by *Good Housekeeping* magazine (Good Housekeeping Research Institute). Other certification marks are *Certified Maine Lobster*, which indicates lobster or lobster products originating in the coastal waters of the state of Maine (Maine Lobster Promotion Council); *100% Napa Valley*, which is associated with grape wine from the Napa Valley, California (Napa Valley Vintners Association); and *Grown in Idaho*, which indicates potatoes grown in the state of Idaho (State of Idaho Potato Commission).

- **Collective membership mark.** A **collective membership mark** is owned by an organization (such as an association) whose members use it to identify themselves with a level of quality or accuracy or other characteristics set by the organization. Only members of the association or organization can use the mark. A collective membership mark identifies membership in an organization but does not identify goods or services.

  Examples *CPA* is used to indicate that someone is a member of the Society of Certified Public Accountants, *Teamster* is used to indicate that a person is a member of The International Brotherhood of Teamsters (IBT) labor union, and *Realtor* is used to indicate that a person is a member of the National Association of Realtors. Other collective marks are *Boy Scouts of America*, *League of Women Voters*, and *National Honor Society*.

Certain marks cannot be registered. They include (1) the flag or coat of arms of the United States, any state, municipality, or foreign nation; (2) marks that are immoral or scandalous; (3) geographical names standing alone (e.g., "South"); (4) surnames standing alone (note that a surname can be registered if it is accompanied by a picture or fanciful name, such as *Smith Brothers cough drops*); and (5) any mark that resembles a mark already registered with the federal PTO.

trademark
A distinctive mark, symbol, name, word, motto, or device that identifies the goods of a particular business.

service mark
A mark that distinguishes the services of the holder from those of its competitors.

certification mark
A mark that certifies that a seller of a product or service has met certain geographical location requirements, quality standards, material standards, or mode of manufacturing standards established by the owner of the mark.

collective membership mark
A mark that indicates that a person has met the standards set by an organization and is a member of that organization.

Distinctiveness or Secondary Meaning

To qualify for federal protection, a mark must be either (1) *distinctive* or (2) have acquired a *secondary meaning*.

distinctive mark
Being unique and fabricated.

- **Distinctive.** A **distinctive mark** would be a word or design that is unique. It therefore qualifies as a mark. The words of the mark must not be ordinary words or symbols.

    Examples Words such as *Xerox* (Xerox Corporation), *Acura* (Honda Motor Corporation), *Google* (Google Inc.), *Exxon* (Exxon Mobil Corporation), and *Pinkberry* (Pinkberry, Inc.) are distinctive words and therefore qualify as marks.

secondary meaning
A brand name that has evolved from an ordinary term.

- **Secondary meaning.** Ordinary words or symbols that have taken on a secondary meaning can qualify as marks. These are words or symbols that have an established meaning but have acquired a **secondary meaning** that is attached to a product or service.

    Examples *Just Do It* (Nike Corporation), *I'm lovin' it* (McDonald's Corporation), *Windows* (Microsoft Corporation), and *Ben & Jerry's Ice Cream* (Unilever) are ordinary words that have taken on a secondary meaning when used to designate the products or services of the owners of the marks.

Words that are descriptive but have no secondary meaning cannot be trademarked.

Trademark Infringement

trademark infringement
Unauthorized use of another's mark. The holder may recover damages and other remedies from the infringer.

The owner of a mark can sue a third party for the unauthorized use of the mark. To succeed in a **trademark infringement** case, the owner must prove that (1) the defendant infringed the plaintiff's mark by using it in an unauthorized manner and (2) such use is likely to cause confusion, mistake, or deception of the public as to the origin of the goods or services.

A successful plaintiff can recover (1) the profits made by the infringer through the unauthorized use of the mark, (2) damages caused to the plaintiff's business and reputation, (3) an order requiring the defendant to destroy all goods containing the unauthorized mark, and (4) an injunction preventing the defendant from such infringement in the future. The court has discretion to award up to *treble* damages where intentional infringement is found.

WEB EXERCISE
Go to **www.videojug.com/film/ how-to-spot-a-fake-louis-vuitton- bag** and watch the video "How to Spot a Fake Louis Vuitton Bag."

In the following case, the court found trademark infringement.

CASE 8.2   *Trademark Infringement*

Intel Corporation v. Intelsys Software, LLC

Web 2009 U.S. Dist. Lexis 14761 (2009)
United States District Court for the Northern District of California

"Defendant's conduct has, and will continue to have, an adverse effect on the value of and distinctive quality of the INTEL mark."

—Wieking, District Judge

Facts

Intel Corporation is a large company that distributes its entire line of products and services under the registered trademark and service mark "INTEL." The company also owns numerous marks that incorporate its INTEL marks as a permanent component, such as the marks "INTEL INSIDE," INTEL SPEEDSTEP," INTEL XEON," and "INTEL NETMERGE." Intelsys Software, LLC, which is owned by another party, develops software applications for network utilities and wireless applications. Intelsys uses the mark "Intelsys Software" and maintains a website at **www.intelsys.com**. Intel Corporation brought an action in U.S. District Court against Intelsys

Software, LLC, alleging that Intelsys infringed on Intel's trademarks and service marks in violation of the Lanham Act. Intel filed a motion for judgment and a permanent injunction against Intelsys's use of the mark "INTEL" in any of its company, product, or service names.

Issue

Is there trademark infringement that warrants the issuance of a permanent injunction against Intelsys?

Language of the Court

Defendant uses the mark "Intelsys Software," which incorporates Plaintiff's INTEL trademark and adds the generic term "sys"—a common abbreviation for "systems"—and the generic term "software." Defendant markets its products and services through similar channels of trade and to similar customers as Plaintiff. Defendant's unauthorized use of the Intelsys Software name and trademark falsely indicates to consumers that Defendant's products and services are in some manner connected with, or related to, Plaintiff. Defendant's use of the mark allows it to benefit from the goodwill established by Plaintiff. Defendant also has caused, and will

likely continue to cause, consumers to be confused regarding the source, nature and quality of the products and services it is promoting or selling. Defendant's conduct has, and will continue to have, an adverse effect on the value of and distinctive quality of the INTEL mark.

Decision

The U.S. District Court granted judgment to Intel and issued a permanent injunction prohibiting Defendant from using the name Intelsys as a trade name or name of any products or services.

Case Questions

Critical Legal Thinking
What is the test for finding trademark infringement?

Ethics
Do you think that defendant Intelsys intended to take advantage of Intel's strong trademarks and service marks?

Contemporary Business
Do you think that trademark infringement happens very often? Be honest: Have you ever purchased any good or service knowing that the seller had engaged in trademark infringement?

Generic Names

When filing for a trademark, if a word, name, or slogan is too generic, it cannot be registered as a trademark. If a word is not generic, it can be trademarked.

Examples The word *apple* cannot be trademarked because it is a generic name. However, the brand name *Apple Computer* is permitted to be trademarked because it is not a generic name. The word *secret* cannot be trademarked because it is a generic name. However, the brand name *Victoria's Secret* is permitted to be trademarked because it is not a generic name.

Once a company has been granted a trademark or service mark, the company usually uses the mark as a brand name to promote its goods or services. Obviously the owner of the mark wants to promote its brand so that consumers and users will easily recognize the brand name.

However, sometimes a company may be *too* successful in promoting a mark, and at some point in time, the public begins to use the brand name as a common name to denote the type of product or service being sold rather than as the trademark or service mark of the individual seller. A trademark that becomes a common term for a product line or type of service is called a **generic name**. Once a trademark becomes a generic name, the term loses its protection under federal trademark law.

generic name
A term for a mark that has become a common term for a product line or type of service and therefore has lost its trademark protection.

Example Sailboards are boards that have sails mounted on them that people use to ride on water such as oceans and lakes. There were many manufacturers and sellers of sailboards. However, the most successful manufacturer of these sailboards used the trademarked brand name Windsurfer. However, the word *windsurfer* was used so often by the public for all brands of sailboards that the trademarked name "Windsurfer" was found to be a generic name and its trademark was canceled.

Exhibit 8.2 lists names that at one time were trademarked but lost trademark protection because the trademarked name became overused and generic. Exhibit 8.3 lists trademarked names that are at some risk of becoming generic names.

Exhibit 8.2 GENERIC NAMES

The following once-trademarked names have been so overused to designate an entire class of products that they have been found to be generic and have lost their trademark status.

Windsurfer	Frisbee
Laser	Trampoline
Escalator	Cornflakes
Kerosene	Yo-yo
Formica	Raisin brand
Thermos	Tollhouse cookies
Linoleum	Nylon

Exhibit 8.3 NAMES AT RISK OF BECOMING GENERIC NAMES

Certain trademark and service marks are often used improperly and have some risk in the future of becoming generic names. Several of these marks are listed below, with their proper use and typical misuse also noted:

Mark	Proper Use	Misuse
Xerox	"Copy this document on a Xerox brand copier."	"Go xerox this."
Google	"Use the Google search engine to find information about him.	"Just google him."
FedEx	"Use FedEx overnight delivery service to send this package."	"Please fedex this."
Rollerblade	"Let's go inline skating on our Rollerblade inline skates."	"Let's go rollerblading."

CONCEPT SUMMARY

TYPES OF INTELLECTUAL PROPERTY PROTECTED BY FEDERAL LAW

Type	Subject Matter	Term
Patent	Inventions (e.g., machines; processes; compositions of matter; designs for articles of manufacture; and improvements to existing machines and processes). Invention must be novel, useful, and nonobvious. *Public use doctrine:* Patent will not be granted if the invention was used in public for more than 1 year prior to the filing of the patent application.	Patents on articles of manufacture and processes: 20 years; design patents: 14 years.

Type	Subject Matter	Term
Copyright	Tangible writing (e.g., books, magazines, newspapers, lectures, operas, plays, screenplays, musical compositions, maps, works of art, lithographs, photographs, postcards, greeting cards, motion pictures, newsreels, sound recordings, computer programs, and mask works fixed to semiconductor chips). Writing must be the original work of the author. The *fair use doctrine* permits the use of copyrighted material without consent for limited uses (e.g., scholarly work, parody or satire, and brief quotation in news reports).	Individual holder: life of author plus 70 years. Corporate holder: the shorter of either 120 years from the year of creation or 95 years from the year of first publication
Trademark	Marks (e.g., name, symbol, word, logo, or device). Marks include trademarks, service marks, certification marks, and collective marks. Mark must be distinctive or have acquired a secondary meaning. *Generic name:* A mark that becomes a common term for a product line or type of service and, therefore, loses its protection under federal trademark law.	Original registration: 10 years. Renewal registration: unlimited number of renewals for 10-year terms.

Diluting, Blurring, or Tarnishing Trademarks

Many companies that own trademarks spend millions of dollars each year advertising and promoting the quality of the goods and services sold under their names. Many of these become household names that are recognized by millions of consumers, such as Coca-Cola, McDonald's, Microsoft, and Nike.

Traditional trademark law protected these marks where an infringer used the mark and confused consumers as to the source of the goods or services. For example, if a knockoff company sold athletic shoes and apparel under the name "Nike," there would be trademark infringement because there would be confusion as to the source of the goods.

Often, however, a party would use a name similar to, or close to but not exactly identical to, a holder's trademark name and sell other goods or services or misuse the name. Because there was no direct competition, the trademark owner often could not win a trademark infringement case.

To address this problem, Congress enacted the **Federal Trademark Dilution Act (FTDA)**[8] of 1995 to protect famous marks from **dilution**. The FTDA provides that owners of marks have a valuable property right in their marks that should not be *diluted*, *blurred*, *tarnished*, or *eroded* in any way by another.

Dilution is broadly defined as the lessening of the capacity of a famous mark to identify and distinguish its holder's goods and services, regardless of the presence or absence of competition between the owner of the mark and

Federal Trademark Dilution Act (FTDA)
A federal statute that protects famous marks from dilution, erosion, blurring, or tarnishing.

the other party. The two most common forms of dilution are blurring and tarnishment:

- **Blurring** occurs where a party uses another party's famous mark to designate a product or service in another market so that the unique significance of the famous mark is weakened.

  Examples Examples of blurring include Rolex skateboards or eBay toiletries.

- **Tarnishment** occurs where a famous mark is linked to products of inferior quality or is portrayed in an unflattering, immoral, or reprehensible context likely to evoke negative beliefs about the mark's owner.

  Example An example of tarnishment is using the mark Microsoft on a deck of unsavory playing cards.

Congress revised the FTDA when it enacted the **Trademark Dilution Revision Act of 2006**[9]. This act provides that a dilution plaintiff does not need to show that it has suffered actual harm to prevail in its dilution lawsuit, but instead only show that there would be the *likelihood of dilution*. The FTDA, as amended, has three fundamental requirements that the holder of the senior mark must prove:

1. Its mark is famous.
2. The use by the other party is commercial.
3. The use by the other party causes *a likelihood of dilution* of the distinctive quality of the mark.

The following case involves the dilution of a famous mark.

CASE 8.3   *Dilution of a Trademark*

V Secret Catalogue, Inc. and Victoria's Secret Stores, Inc. v. Moseley

605 F.3d 382, Web 2010 U.S. App. Lexis 10150 (2010)
United States Court of Appeals for the Sixth Circuit

"The phrase 'likely to cause dilution' used in the new statute significantly changes the meaning of the law from 'causes actual harm' under the preexisting law."

—Merritt, Circuit Judge

Facts

Victoria's Secret is a successful worldwide retailer of women's lingerie, clothing, and beauty products that owns the famous trademark "Victoria's Secret." A small store in Elizabethtown, Kentucky, owned and operated by Victor and Cathy Moseley, used the business names "Victor's Secret" and "Victor's Little Secret." The store sold adult videos, novelties, sex toys, and racy lingerie. Victoria's Secret sued the Moseleys alleging a violation of the Federal Trademark Dilution Act of 1995. The case eventually was decided by the U.S. Supreme Court in favor of the Moseleys when the Court found that there was no showing of *actual dilution* by the junior marks as required by the statute. Congress overturned the Supreme Court's decision by enacting the Trademark Dilution Revision Act of 2006, which requires the easier showing of a *likelihood of dilution* by the senior mark. On remand, the U.S. District Court applied the new likelihood of confusion test, found a presumption of tarnishment of the Victoria's Secret mark that the Moseley's failed to rebut, and held against the Moseleys. The Moseleys appealed to the U.S. Court of Appeals.

Issue

Is there tarnishment of the Victoria's Secret senior mark by the Moseleys' use of the junior marks Victor's Secret and Victor's Little Secret?

Language of the Court

The phrase "likely to cause dilution" used in the new statute significantly changes the meaning of the law from "causes actual harm" under the preexisting law. The burden of proof problem should now be interpreted to create a kind of rebuttable presumption, or at least a very strong inference, that a new mark used to sell sex-related products is likely to tarnish a famous mark if there is a clear semantic association between the two.

In the present case, the Moseleys have had two opportunities in the District Court to offer evidence that there is no real probability of tarnishment and have not done so. Without evidence to the contrary or a persuasive defensive theory that rebuts the presumption, the defendants have given us no basis to reverse the judgment of the District Court.

Decision

The U.S. Court of Appeals affirmed the U.S. District Court's judgment in favor of Victoria's Secret.

Case Questions

Critical Legal Thinking

Do you think that Congress often uses its "veto power" over the U.S. Supreme Court's interpretation of a federal statute by enacting another statute to change the result of a Supreme Court's decision?

Ethics

Do you think the Moseleys were trading off of Victoria's Secret famous name? Do you think that the Moseleys had a legitimate claim to their business names because the husband's name was Victor?

Contemporary Business

Did the change in the Trademark Dilution Revision Act of 2006 favor famous trademark holders?

Key Terms and Concepts

American Inventors Protection Act (163)
Berne Convention (165)
Blurring (174)
© (165)
Cancelation (168)
Certification mark (169)
Civil lawsuit (158)
Collective membership mark (169)
Copyright (164)
Copyright infringement (166)
Copyright registration certificate (165)
Copyright Revision Act (164)
Copyright Term Extension Act (165)
Design patent (164)
Digital Millennium Copyright Act (DMCA) (167)
Dilution (173)
Distinctive mark (170)

Economic Espionage Act (EEA) (158)
Encryption technology (167)
Fair use doctrine (166)
Federal Patent Statute (160)
Federal Trademark Dilution Act (FTDA) (173)
First-to-invent rule (163)
Generic name (171)
Intellectual property (157)
Lanham (Trademark) Act (Lanham Act) (167)
Mark (167)
Misappropriation of a trade secret (158)
No Electronic Theft Act (NET Act) (166)
Nonobvious (161)
Novel (161)
One-year "on sale" doctrine (public use doctrine) (163)

Patent (160)
Patent application (160)
Patent infringement (163)
Patent number (160)
Patent pending (160)
Provisional application (163)
Public domain (for copyright) (165)
Public domain (for patent) (163)
® (168)
Registration of a copyright (165)
Reverse engineering (158)
Secondary meaning (170)
Service mark (169)
SM (168)
Tangible writings (164)
Tarnishment (174)

TM (168)
Trademark (169)
Trademark Dilution Revision Act of 2006 (174)
Trademark Electronic Application System (TEAS) (168)
Trademark infringement (170)
Trade secret (158)
Uniform Trade Secrets Act (158)
U.S. Copyright Office (165)
U.S. Court of Appeals for the Federal Circuit (160)
U.S. Patent and Trademark Office (PTO) (160)
Useful (161)
Utility patent (160)

Law Case with Answer
Retail Services Inc. v. Freebies Publishing

Facts   Eugene F. Zannon and Gail Zannon filed an application on behalf of Freebies Publishing with the U.S. Patent and Trademark Office (PTO) to register the word "Freebies" as a trademark. The PTO granted applicant Freebies Publishing the registration of the word "Freebies." Thereafter, Freebies Publishing registered the Internet domain name freebies.com. Freebies Publishing operated its business from the website free bies.com.

Two years after Freebies Publishing was granted the trademark to "Freebies," Retail Services Inc. (RSI) registered the Internet domain name freebie.com and began operating a website that promoted free offerings of goods and services for clients. RSI filed an action in federal court, seeking an order that RSI's use of the domain and website name freebie.com did not infringe Freebies Publishing's trademark "Freebies" and that this trademark was generic and should be canceled. Is the word *freebies* a generic word that does not qualify as a trademark and whose trademark status should be canceled?

Answer   Yes, the word *freebies* is generic and does not qualify to be registered as a federal trademark.

As a slang term, "freebie" means something given or received without charge or an article or service given for free. For a long time, "freebie" has been understood to mean something that is provided free. Freebies Publishing's site is but one of hundreds of websites that incorporate the word "freebie" of "freebies" into their domain names. These websites are so common that the term "freebie site" is often used to refer to other sites that, like Freebies Publishing's, offer information about free products or services. In addition, advertisements in newspapers and elsewhere often use the phrase "freebie" to designate something that will be given to a consumer for free.

Thus, in the public's mind, "freebies" indicates free or almost free products and is not solely identified with the Zannons or their website. The word *freebies* is a generic name, and a generic word cannot function as a trademark. Therefore, the trademark granted to Freebies Publishing for the word "Freebies" must be canceled. RSI is permitted to operate its website www .freebie.com. *Retail Services Inc. v. Freebies Publishing*, 364 F.3d 535, **Web** 2004 U.S. App. Lexis 7130 (United States Court of Appeals for the Fourth Circuit)

Critical Legal Thinking Cases

8.1 Fair Use   James W. Newton, Jr., is an accomplished avant-garde jazz composer and flutist. Newton wrote a composition for the song "Choir," a piece for flute and voice that incorporated elements of African American gospel music. Newton owns the copyright to the composition "Choir." The Beastie Boys, a rap and hip-hop group, used six seconds of Newton's "Choir" composition in their song "Pass the Mic" without obtaining a license from Newton to do so. Newton sued the Beastie Boys for copyright infringement. The Beastie Boys defended, arguing that their use of six seconds of Newton's song was *de minimis* and therefore fair use. Does the incorporation of a short segment of a copyrighted musical composition into a new musical recording constitute fair use, or is it copyright infringement? *Newton v. Beastie Boys*, 349 F.3d 591, **Web** 2003 U.S. App. Lexis 22635 (United States Court of Appeals for the Ninth Circuit)

8.2 Patent   Pioneer Hi-Bred International, Inc. (Pioneer) holds patents that cover the company's inbred and hybrid corn and corn seed products. A hybrid plant patent protects the plant, its seeds, variants, mutants, and modifications of the hybrid. Pioneer sells its patented

hybrid seeds under a limited label license that provides: "License is granted solely to produce grain and/or forage." The license states that it "does not extend to the use of seed from such crop or the progeny thereof for propagation or seed multiplication."

J.E.M. Ag Supply, Inc., doing business as Farm Advantage, Inc. (Farm Advantage), purchased patented hybrid seeds from Pioneer in bags bearing this license agreement. Farm Advantage created seed from the hybrid corn products it grew from Pioneer's patented hybrid seed. Pioneer sued Farm Advantage, alleging that Farm Advantage had infringed its patent. Farm Advantage filed a counterclaim of patent invalidity, arguing that Pioneer hybrid plant seed patents are not patentable subject matter. Farm Advantage appealed to the U.S. Supreme Court. Are sexually reproducing hybrid plants patentable subject matter? *J.E.M. Ag Supply, Inc., d.b.a. Farm Advantage, Inc. v. Pioneer Hi-Bred International, Inc.*, 534 U.S. 124, 122 S.Ct. 593, 151 L.Ed. 2d 508, **Web** 2001 U.S. Lexis 10949 (Supreme Court of the United States)

8.3 Patent   Amazon.com has become one of the biggest online retailers. Amazon.com, Inc., enables customers to find and purchase books, music, videos, consumer electronics, games, toys, gifts, and other items over the Internet by using its website **www.amazon.com**. As an early entrant into this market, Amazon.com became a leader in e-commerce. Other e-commerce retailers began offering goods and services for sale over the web.

One problem that Amazon.com and other e-commerce retailers faced was that more than 50 percent of potential customers who went shopping online and selected items for purchase abandoned their transactions before checkout. To address this problem, Amazon.com devised and implemented a method that enabled online customers to purchase selected items with a single click of a computer mouse button. A customer who had previously registered his or her name, address, and credit card number with Amazon.com could complete purchases by clicking an instant "buy" button. Amazon.com applied for a software patent for its one-click ordering system, and the U.S. Patent and Trademark Office (PTO) granted patent no. 5,960,411 ('411 patent) to Amazon.com. Amazon.com designated this as the "1-click®" ordering system.

While Amazon.com's patent application was pending, other online retailers began offering similar one-click ordering systems. One was Barnesandnoble.com, which operates a website through which it sells books, software, music, movies, and other items. Amazon.com sued Barnesandnoble.com, alleging patent infringement, and sought an injunction against Barnesandnoble.com from using its one-click ordering system. Barnesandnoble.com defended, asserting that a one-click ordering system is clearly obvious and, therefore, did not meet the required "nonobvious" test of federal patent law for an invention to qualify for a patent. Is Amazon's 1-click ordering system nonobvious and therefore qualified for a patent? *Amazon.com, Inc. v. Barnesandnoble.com, Inc.*, 239 F.3d 1343, **Web** 2001 U.S. App. Lexis 2163 (United States Circuit Court of Appeals for the Federal Circuit)

8.4 Copyright   When Spiro Agnew resigned as vice president of the United States, President Richard M. Nixon appointed Gerald R. Ford as vice president. Amid growing controversy surrounding the Watergate scandal, President Nixon resigned, and Vice President Ford acceded to the presidency. As president, Ford pardoned Nixon for any wrongdoing regarding the Watergate affair and related matters. Ford served as president until he was defeated by Jimmy Carter in the presidential election. Ford entered into a contract with Harper & Row Publishers, Inc., to publish his memoirs in book form. The memoirs were to contain significant unpublished materials concerning the Watergate affair and Ford's personal reflections on that time in history. The publisher instituted security measures to protect the confidentiality of the manuscript. Several weeks before the book was

to be released, an unidentified person secretly brought a copy of the manuscript to Victor Navasky, editor of *The Nation*, a weekly political commentary magazine. Navasky, knowing that his possession of the purloined manuscript was not authorized, produced a 2,250-word piece titled "The Ford Memoirs" and published it in an issue of *The Nation*. Verbatim quotes of between three hundred and four hundred words from Ford's manuscript, including some of the most important parts, appeared in the article. Harper & Row sued the publishers of *The Nation* for copyright infringement. Who wins? *Harper & Row, Publishers, Inc. v. Nation Enterprises*, 471 U.S. 539, 105 S.Ct. 2218, 85 L.Ed.2d 588, **Web** 1985 U.S. Lexis 17 (Supreme Court of the United States)

8.5 Fair Use Doctrine   Once in the past, when the city of New York teetered on the brink of bankruptcy, on the television screens of America there appeared an image of a top-hatted Broadway showgirl, backed by an advancing phalanx of dancers, chanting: "I-I-I-I-I-I Love New Yo-o-o-o-o-o-o-rk." As an ad campaign for an ailing city, it was an unparalleled success. Crucial to the campaign was a brief but exhilarating musical theme written by Steve Karmin called "I Love New York." Elsmere Music, Inc. owned the copyright to the music. The success of the campaign did not go unnoticed. The popular weekly variety program *Saturday Night Live* (*SNL*) performed a comedy sketch over National Broadcasting Company's network (NBC). In the sketch, the cast of *SNL*, portraying the mayor and members of the chamber of commerce of the biblical city of Sodom, were seen discussing Sodom's poor public image with out-of-towners and its effect on the tourist trade. In an attempt to recast Sodom's image in a more positive light, a new advertising campaign was revealed, with the highlight of the campaign being a song "I Love Sodom" sung a cappella by a chorus line of *SNL* regulars to the tune of "I Love New York." Elsmere Music did not see the humor of the sketch and sued NBC for copyright infringement. Who wins? *Elsmere Music, Inc. v. National Broadcasting Co., Inc.*, 623 F.2d 252, **Web** 1980 U.S. App. Lexis 16820 (United States Court of Appeals for the Second Circuit)

8.6 Trademark   Clairol Incorporated manufactures and distributes hair tinting, dyeing, and coloring preparations. Clairol embarked on an extensive advertising campaign to promote the sale of its "Miss Clairol" hair-color preparations that included advertisements in national magazines, on outdoor billboards, on radio and television, in mailing pieces, and on point-of-sale display materials to be used by retailers and beauty salons. The advertisements prominently displayed the slogans "Hair Color So Natural Only Her Hairdresser Knows for Sure" and "Does She or Doesn't She?" Clairol registered these slogans as trademarks. During the next decade, Clairol spent more than $22 million on advertising materials, resulting in more than a billion separate audio and visual impressions using the slogans. Roux Laboratories, Inc., a manufacturer of hair-coloring products and a competitor of Clairol's, filed an opposition to Clairol's registration of the slogans as trademarks. Do the slogans qualify for trademark protection? *Roux Laboratories, Inc. v. Clairol Inc.*, 427 F.2d 823, **Web** 1970 CCPA Lexis 344 (United States Court of Customs and Patent Appeals)

8.7 Generic Name   The Miller Brewing Company, a national brewer, produces a reduced-calorie beer called "Miller Lite." Miller began selling beer under this name and spent millions of dollars promoting the Miller Lite brand name on television, in print, and via other forms of advertising. Falstaff Brewing Corporation had brewed and distributed a reduced-calorie beer called "Falstaff Lite." Miller brought suit under the Lanham Act, seeking an injunction to prevent Falstaff from using the term *Lite*. Is the term *Lite* a generic name that does not qualify for trademark protection? *Miller Brewing Co. v. Falstaff Brewing Corp.*, 655 F.2d 5, **Web** 1981 U.S. App. Lexis 11345 (United States Court of Appeals for the First Circuit)

8.8 Copyright Infringement   Elvis Presley, a rock-and-roll singer, became a musical icon during a career that spanned more than twenty years, until he died at the age of 42. Many companies and individuals own copyrights to Presley's songs, lyrics, photographs, movies, and appearances on TV shows. Millions of dollars of Elvis Presley-related copyrighted materials are sold or licensed annually.

Passport Video produced a video documentary titled *The Definitive Elvis*, comprising sixteen one-hour episodes. The producers interviewed more than two hundred people regarding virtually all aspects of Elvis's life. Passport sold the videos commercially for a profit. Approximately 5 to 10 percent of the videos were composed of copyrighted music and appearances of Presley on television and in movies owned by copyright holders other than Passport. Passport did not obtain permission to use those copyrighted works. Elvis Presley Enterprises, Inc., and other companies and individuals that owned copyrights to the Presley works used by Passport sued Passport for copyright infringement. Passport defended, arguing that its use of the copyrighted materials was fair use. The U.S. District Court held in favor of the plaintiff copyright holders and enjoined Passport from further distribution of its documentary videos. Passport appealed.

Did Passport act ethically in including the Elvis Presley copyrighted material in its video? Why do you think Passport Video did so? Has there been fair use in this case, or has there been copyright infringement? *Elvis Presley Enterprises, Inc. v. Passport Video*, 349 F.3d 622, **Web** 2003 U.S. App. Lexis 22775 (United States Court of Appeals for the Ninth Circuit)

Ethics Cases

8.9 Ethics   Cecilia Gonzalez downloaded 1,370 copyrighted songs on her computer, using the Kazaa file-sharing network over a period of a few weeks, and she kept them on her computer until she was caught. BMG Music, a producer of music CDs, sued Gonzalez for copyright infringement for downloading thirty songs to which BMG owned the copyrights. Gonzalez defended, arguing that her downloading of these copyrighted songs was lawful. Gonzalez's position is that she was just sampling music to determine what she liked enough to buy at retail. Instead of erasing songs that she decided not to buy, she retained them. As she tells the tale, downloading on a try-before-you-buy basis is good advertising for copyright proprietors, expanding the value of their inventory. Gonzalez also proffered the defense that "everyone was doing it" and that there greater offenders then her. *BMG Music v. Gonzalez*, 430 F.3d 888, **Web** 2005 U.S. App. Lexis 26903 (United States Court of Appeals for the Seventh Circuit)

1. What is copyright infringement? Did Gonzalez engage in copyright infringement?

2. Do you think that Gonzalez knew that she was stealing someone's copyrighted work when she copied the music onto her computer?

3. Have you ever downloaded music by using a peer-to-peer file-sharing program without paying the musician or the music company? Have you ever violated copyright law in any other way?

8.10 Ethics   Integrated Cash Management Services, Inc. (ICM) designs and develops computer software programs and systems for banks and corporate financial departments. ICM's computer programs and systems are not copyrighted, but they are secret. After Alfred Sims Newlin and Behrouz Vafa completed graduate school, they were employed by ICM as computer programmers. They worked at ICM for several years, writing computer programs. They left ICM to work for Digital Transactions, Inc. (DTI). Before leaving ICM, however, they copied certain ICM files onto computer disks. Within two weeks of starting to work at DTI, they created prototype computer programs that operated in substantially the same manner as comparable

ICM programs and were designed to compete directly with ICM's programs. ICM sued Newlin, Vafa, and DTI for misappropriation of trade secrets. *Integrated Cash Management Services, Inc. v. Digital Transactions, Inc.*, 920 F.2d 171, **Web** 1990 U.S. App. Lexis 20985 (United States Court of Appeals for the Second Circuit)

1. What is a trade secret?
2. Did defendants Newlin and Vafa act ethically in this case?
3. Are the defendants liable?

Internet Exercises

1. Use **www.google.com** and see if you can find the purported secret recipe for original Coca-Cola posted on someone's website.

2. Go to the website of the U.S. Patent and Trademark Office (PTO) at **www.uspto.gov**. Read the basic facts about patents. What is the approximate cost for filing a patent application with the PTO?

3. Go to the website of the U.S. Court of Appeals for the Federal Circuit in Washington, DC, at **http://www.cafc.uscourts.gov/**. Click on "About the Court." Read about the authority of this court.

4. The PTO provides for the online submission of patent applications and documents through its EFS-Web system. Read about this system at **www.uspto.gov/ebc/efs_help.html**.

5. Go to the website of the U.S. Copyright Office, at **www.copyright.gov**. Click on "Frequently Asked Questions (FAQ)" and then click on "Do I have to register with your office to be protected?" Then click on "Copyright Registration." What are the advantages of registering a copyright with the U.S. Copyright Office?

6. Go to **www.youtube.com**. Search for a movie that is currently showing in movie theaters. Can you find any video clips of the movie that appear on YouTube that you think violate copyright law?

7. Go to **www.microsoft.com/library/toolbar/3.0/trademarks/en-us.mspx** to view a list of the trademarks owned by Microsoft Corporation.

Endnotes

1. 18 U.S.C. Sections 1831–1839.
2. 35 U.S.C. Section 10 et seq.
3. 17 U.S.C. Section 101 et seq.
4. Public Law No. 105-298 (1998).
5. Public Law No. 105-147 (1997).
6. 17 U.S.C. 1201.
7. 15 U.S.C. Section 1114 et seq.
8. 15 U.S.C. Section 1125.
9. Public Law No. 109-312 (2006).

Contracts, Commercial Law, and E-Commerce

CHAPTER

9

Formation of Traditional and E-Contracts

HOUSE FOR SALE
The owner of this house has offered the house for sale. The owner's offer contains the offering price and other terms that the owner wishes to be met before he will sell the house. An interested buyer can purchase the house by agreeing to those terms. Most likely, however, the interested buyer will make a counteroffer whereby she offers a lower price and possibly other terms that she wants met before she is obligated to purchase the house. If the parties eventually mutually agree to a price and other terms, a contract has been formed. There has been an offer and an acceptance, therefore creating an enforceable contract. Consideration has been paid by both parties: the seller has sold his property—the house—and the buyer paid money.

Learning Objectives

After studying this chapter, you should be able to:

1. Define *contract* and list the elements necessary to form valid traditional and e-contracts.
2. Describe and distinguish among valid, void, voidable, and unenforceable contracts.
3. Describe offer, acceptance, and consideration.
4. Identify illegal contracts that are contrary to statutes and that violate public policy.
5. Describe e-commerce and define *e-contract*.

Chapter Outline

Introduction to Formation of Traditional and E-Contracts

Definition of a Contract

Classifications of Contracts
    CASE 9.1 • *Wrench LLC v. Taco Bell Corporation*

Agreement
    CASE 9.2 • *The Facebook, Inc. v. Winklevoss*
    CONTEMPORARY ENVIRONMENT • *Option Contract*

Consideration

Capacity to Contract

Legality
    ETHICS • *Illegal Gambling Contract*

Unconscionable Contracts

E-Commerce
    DIGITAL LAW • *E-Contracts and E-Licenses*
    INTERNATIONAL LAW • *International Contract Law in China*

> **"** *The movement of the progressive societies has hitherto been a movement from status to contract."*
>
> —Sir Henry Maine
>   *Ancient Law, Chapter 5*

Introduction to Formation of Traditional and E-Contracts

Contracts are voluntarily entered into by parties. The terms of a contract become *private law* between the parties. One court has stated that "the contract between parties is the law between them and the courts are obliged to give legal effect to such contracts according to the true interests of the parties."[1]

Most contracts are performed without the aid of the court system. This is usually because the parties feel a moral duty to perform as promised. Although some contracts, such as illegal contracts, are not enforceable, most are **legally enforceable**.[2] This means that if a party fails to perform a contract, the other party may call upon the courts to enforce the contract.

E-commerce has become a large part of commerce and trade. Goods are sold over the Internet through commercial and other websites, using *e-contracts*, and parties agree to *e-licenses* over the Internet. In addition, e-contracts can be formed by use of *e-mail*. Contract law has had to develop to handle issues involving e-commerce, e-contracts, and e-licenses.

This chapter introduces the study of contract law. Such topics as the definition of *contract*, offer and acceptance, consideration, capacity to contract, lawfulness of contracts, and e-commerce and e-contracts are discussed in this chapter.

Definition of a Contract

A **contract** is an agreement that is enforceable by a court of law or equity. A simple and widely recognized definition of *contract* is provided by the *Restatement (Second) of Contracts*: "A contract is a promise or a set of promises for the breach of which the law gives a remedy or the performance of which the law in some way recognizes a duty."[3]

Parties to a Contract

Every traditional contract and e-contract involves at least two parties. The **offeror** is the party who makes an offer to enter into a contract. The **offeree** is the party to whom the offer is made (see **Exhibit 9.1**). In making an offer, the offeror promises to do—or to refrain from doing—something. The offeree then has the power to create a contract by accepting the offeror's offer. A contract is created if the offer is accepted. No contract is created if the offer is not accepted.

Example Ross makes an offer to Elizabeth to sell his automobile to her for $10,000. In this case, Ross is the offeror and Elizabeth is the offeree.

"When I use a word," Humpty Dumpty said, in rather a scornful tone, "it means just what I choose it to mean—neither more nor less."

"The question is," said Alice, "whether you can make words mean so many different things."

"The question is," said Humpty Dumpty, "which is to be master—that's all."

Lewis Carroll
Alice's Adventures in Wonderland (1865)

legally enforceable contract
A contract in which if one party fails to perform as promised, the other party can use the court system to enforce the contract and recover damages or another remedy.

contract
According to the *Restatement (Second) of Contracts*, "A promise or a set of promises for the breach of which the law gives a remedy or the performance of which the law in some way recognizes a duty."

offeror
The party who makes an offer to enter into a contract.

offeree
The party to whom an offer to enter into a contract is made.

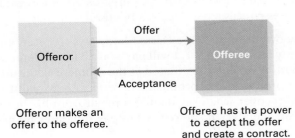

Offeror makes an offer to the offeree.

Offeree has the power to accept the offer and create a contract.

Exhibit 9.1 PARTIES TO A CONTRACT

Elements of a Contract

For a contract to be enforceable, the following four basic requirements must be met:

1. **Agreement.**   For a contract to be enforceable, there must be an *agreement* between the parties. This requires an *offer* by the offeror and an *acceptance* of the offer by the offeree. There must be mutual assent by the parties.
2. **Consideration.**   A promise must be supported by a bargained-for *consideration* that is legally sufficient. Money, personal property, real property, provision of services, and such qualify as consideration.
3. **Contractual capacity.**   The parties to a contract must have *contractual capacity* for the contract to be enforceable against them. Contracts cannot be enforced against parties who lacked contractual capacity when they entered into the contracts.
4. **Lawful object.**   The object of a contract must be lawful. Most contracts have a **lawful object**. However, contracts that have an illegal object are void and will not be enforced.

Defenses to the Enforcement of a Contract

Two *defenses* may be raised to the enforcement of contracts:

1. **Genuineness of assent.**   The consent of the parties to create a contract must be genuine. If the consent is obtained by duress, undue influence, or fraud, there is no real consent.
2. **Writing and form.**   The law requires that certain contracts be in writing or in a certain form. Failure of such a contract to be in writing or to be in proper form may be raised against the enforcement of the contract.

The requirements to form an enforceable contract and the defenses to the enforcement of contracts are discussed in this chapter and the following chapter.

Classifications of Contracts

There are several types of contracts. Each differs somewhat in formation, enforcement, performance, and discharge. The different types of contracts are discussed in the following paragraphs.

Bilateral and Unilateral Contracts

Contracts are either *bilateral* or *unilateral*, depending on what the offeree must do to accept the offeror's offer. The language of the offeror's promise must be carefully scrutinized to determine whether it is an offer to create a bilateral contract or a unilateral contract. If there is any ambiguity as to which it is, it is presumed to be a bilateral contract.

A contract is a **bilateral contract** if the offeror's promise is answered with the offeree's promise of acceptance. In other words, a bilateral contract is a "promise for a promise." This exchange of promises creates an enforceable contract. No act of performance is necessary to create a bilateral contract.

Example Mary, the owner of the Chic Dress Shop, says to Peter, a painter, "If you promise to paint my store by July 1, I will pay you $3,000." Peter says, "I promise to do so." A *bilateral contract* was created at the moment Peter promised to paint the dress shop (a promise for a promise). If Peter fails to paint the shop, Mary can sue Peter and recover whatever damages result from his breach of contract. Similarly, Peter can sue Mary if she refuses to pay him after he has performed as promised.

The law has outgrown its primitive stage of formalism when the precise word was the sovereign talisman, and every slip was fatal. It takes a broader view today. A promise may be lacking, and yet the whole writing may be "instinct with an obligation," imperfectly expressed.

Cardozo, Justice
Wood v. Duff-Gordon (1917)

bilateral contract
A contract entered into by way of exchange of promises of the parties; "a promise for a promise."

A contract is a **unilateral contract** if the offeror's offer can be accepted only by the performance of an act by the offeree. There is no contract until the offeree performs the requested act. An offer to create a unilateral contract cannot be accepted by a promise to perform. It is a "promise for an act."

Example Mary, the owner of the Chic Dress Shop, says to Peter, a painter, "If you paint my shop by July 1, I will pay you $3,000." This offer creates a *unilateral contract*. The offer can be accepted only by the painter's performance of the requested act. If Peter does not paint the shop by July 1, there has been no acceptance, and Mary cannot sue Peter for damages. If Peter paints the shop by July 1, Mary owes Peter $3,000. If Mary refuses to pay, Peter can sue Mary to collect payment.

Problems can arise if the offeror in a unilateral contract attempts to revoke an offer after the offeree has begun performance. Generally, an offer to create a unilateral contract can be revoked by the offeror any time prior to the offeree's performance of the requested act. However, the offer cannot be revoked if the offeree has begun or has substantially completed performance.

Example Suppose Alan Matthews tells Sherry Levine that he will pay her $5,000 if she finishes the Boston Marathon. Alan cannot revoke the offer once Sherry starts running the marathon.

> **unilateral contract**
> A contract in which the offeror's offer can be accepted only by the performance of an act by the offeree; a "promise for an act."

> *Contracts must not be the sports of an idle hour, mere matters of pleasantry and badinage, never intended by the parties to have any serious effect whatever.*
>
> Lord Stowell
> *Dalrymple v. Dalrymple (1811)*

Formal and Informal Contracts

Contracts may be classified as either *formal* or *informal*. **Formal contracts** are contracts that require a special form or method of creation. Many informal contracts require *specific words*. The most common forms of formal contracts are the **negotiable instrument** (e.g., a check needs the words "Pay to the order of"), **letter of credit** (e.g., a bank guarantees the payment by a buyer who purchases goods on credit from a seller if the buyer does not pay for the goods), a **recognizance** where someone agrees to pay a sum of money if another person does not pay it (e.g., a bail bond), and **contract under seal** (e.g., a wax seal is placed on the contract).

All contracts that do not qualify as formal contracts are called **informal contracts** (or **simple contracts**). The term is a misnomer. Valid informal contracts (e.g., leases, sales contracts, service contracts) are fully enforceable and may be sued upon if breached. They are called *informal contracts* only because no special form or method is required for their creation. Thus, the parties to an informal contract can use any words they choose to express their contract. The majority of the contracts entered into by individuals and businesses are informal contracts.

> **formal contract**
> A contract that requires a special form or method of creation.

> **informal contract (simple contract)**
> A contract that is not formal. Valid informal contracts are fully enforceable and may be sued upon if breached.

Valid, Void, Voidable, and Unenforceable Contracts

Contract law places contracts in the following categories:

1. **Valid contract.** A **valid contract** meets all the essential elements to establish a contract. In other words, it (1) consists of an agreement between the parties, (2) is supported by legally sufficient consideration, (3) is between parties with contractual capacity, and (4) accomplishes a lawful object. A valid contract is enforceable by at least one of the parties.

   Example Helen enters into a written contract to purchase a house from Marilyn for $1 million. There is legal consideration—a house in exchange for $1 million—and the object of the contract is lawful. Both Helen and Marilyn have contractual capacity. In this case, there is a valid contract. If either party fails to perform the contract when due, the other party can sue to enforce the contract against the breaching party.

2. **Void contract.** A **void contract** has no legal effect. It is as if no contract had ever been created. A contract to commit a crime is void. If a contract is void,

> **valid contract**
> A contract that meets all the essential elements to establish a contract; a contract that is enforceable by at least one of the parties.

> **void contract**
> A contract that has no legal effect; a nullity.

then neither party is obligated to perform the contract and neither party can enforce the contract.

Example Harold and Melville enter into a contract to burglarize University Bank and steal the money on deposit at the bank. If Harold refuses to perform the contract—that is, he refuses to participate in the burglary—Melville cannot sue Harold to perform the contract.

voidable contract
A contract in which one or both parties have the option to void their contractual obligations. If a contract is voided, both parties are released from their contractual obligations.

3. **Voidable contract.** A **voidable contract** is a contract in which at least one party has the *option* to void his or her contractual obligations. If the contract is voided, both parties are released from their obligations under the contract. If the party with the option chooses to ratify the contract, both parties must fully perform their obligations.

With certain exceptions, contracts may be voided by minors; insane persons; intoxicated persons; persons acting under duress, undue influence, or fraud; and in cases involving mutual mistake.

Example Ida, an adult, enters into a contract with Spencer, who is 16 years old and a minor, to purchase an automobile owned by Spencer. This is a voidable contract because Spencer, the minor, can get out of the contract, but Ida, the adult, cannot get out of the contract.

unenforceable contract
A contract in which the essential elements to create a valid contract are met but there is some legal defense to the enforcement of the contract.

4. **Unenforceable contract.** With an **unenforceable contract**, there is some legal defense to the enforcement of the contract. If a contract is required to be in writing under the Statute of Frauds but is not in writing, the contract is unenforceable. The parties may voluntarily perform a contract that is unenforceable.

Example Elliot and Sarah enter into an oral contract whereby Elliot will sell his house to Sarah for $1 million. Because this is a contract for the sale of real estate, it is required to be in writing. However, because it is an oral contract, neither Elliot nor Sarah can sue the other for not performing the contract. However, if Elliot and Sarah complete the contract—that is, Elliot signs over the deed to his house to Sarah, and Sarah pays Elliot $1 million—the contract is performed, and neither party can undo the contract.

Executory and Executed Contracts

A contract that has not been performed by both sides is called an **executory contract**. Contracts that have been fully performed by one side but not by the other are classified as executory contracts.

executory contract
A contract that has not been fully performed by either or both sides.

Examples Suppose Elizabeth signs a contract to purchase a new BMW automobile from Ace Motors. She has not yet paid for the car, and Ace Motors has not yet delivered the car to Elizabeth. This is an executory contract because the contract has not yet been performed. If Elizabeth has paid for the car but Ace Motors has not yet delivered the car to Elizabeth, there is an executory contract because Ace Motors has not performed the contract.

A completed contract—that is, one that has been fully performed on both sides—is called an **executed contract**.

executed contract
A contract that has been fully performed by both sides; a completed contract.

Example If in the prior example Elizabeth has paid for the car and Ace Motors has delivered the car to Elizabeth, the contract has been fully performed by both parties and is an executed contract.

Express and Implied-in-Fact Contracts

express contract
An agreement that is expressed in written or oral words.

An **actual contract** may be either *express* or *implied-in-fact*. These are described in the following material. An **express contract** is stated in oral or written words.

Most personal and business contracts are express contracts. A contract that is oral or written is an express contract.

Examples A written agreement to buy an automobile from a dealership is an express contract because it is in written words. An oral agreement to purchase a neighbor's bicycle is an express contract because it is in oral words.

An **implied-in-fact contract** is implied from the conduct of the parties. The following elements must be established to create an implied-in-fact contract: (1) The plaintiff provided property or services to the defendant, (2) the plaintiff expected to be paid by the defendant for the property or services and did not provide the property or services gratuitously, and (3) the defendant was given an opportunity to reject the property or services provided by the plaintiff but failed to do so.

In the following case, the court had to decide whether there was an implied-in-fact contract.

implied-in-fact contract
A contract in which agreement between parties has been inferred from their conduct.

CASE 9.1 *Implied-in-Fact Contract*

Wrench LLC v. Taco Bell Corporation
256 F.3d 446, Web 2001 U.S. App. Lexis 15097 (2001)
United States Court of Appeals for the Sixth Circuit

"The district court found that appellants produced sufficient evidence to create a genuine issue of material fact regarding whether an implied-in-fact contract existed between the parties."

—Graham, Circuit Judge

Facts
Thomas Rinks and Joseph Shields created the Psycho Chihuahua cartoon character, which they promote, market, and license through their company, Wrench LLC. Psycho Chihuahua is a clever, feisty, cartoon character dog with an attitude, a self-confident, edgy, cool dog who knows what he wants and will not back down. Rinks and Shields attended a licensing trade show in New York City, where they were approached by two Taco Bell employees, Rudy Pollak, a vice president, and Ed Alfaro, a creative services manager. Taco Bell owns and operates a nationwide chain of fast-food Mexican restaurants. Pollak and Alfaro expressed interest in the Psycho Chihuahua character for Taco Bell advertisements because they thought his character would appeal to Taco Bell's core consumers, males aged 18 to 24. Pollak and Alfaro obtained some Psycho Chihuahua materials to take back with them to Taco Bell's headquarters.

Later, Alfaro contacted Rinks and asked him to create art boards combining Psycho Chihuahua with the Taco Bell name and image. Rinks and Shields prepared art boards and sent them to Alfaro, along with

Psycho Chihuahua t-shirts, hats, and stickers. Alfaro showed these materials to Taco Bell's vice president of brand management as well as to Taco Bell's outside advertising agency. Alfaro tested the Psycho Chihuahua marketing concept with focus groups. Rinks suggested to Alfaro that instead of using the cartoon version of Psycho Chihuahua in its advertisements, Taco Bell should use a live Chihuahua dog manipulated by computer graphic imaging that had the personality of Psycho Chihuahua and a love for Taco Bell food. Rinks and Shields gave a formal presentation of this concept to Taco Bell's marketing department. One idea presented by Rinks and Shields was a commercial in which a male Chihuahua dog passed by a female Chihuahua dog in order to get to Taco Bell food. Taco Bell did not enter into an express contract with Wrench LLC, Rinks, or Shields.

Just after Rinks and Shields's presentation, Taco Bell hired a new outside advertising agency, Chiat/Day. Taco Bell gave Chiat/Day materials received from Rinks and Shields regarding Psycho Chihuahua. Three months later, Chiat/Day proposed using a Chihuahua in Taco Bell commercials. One commercial had a male Chihuahua passing up a female Chihuahua to get to a person seated on a bench eating Taco Bell food. Chiat/Day says that it conceived these ideas by itself. Taco Bell aired its Chihuahua commercials in the United States, and they became an instant success and the basis of its advertising. Taco Bell paid nothing to Wrench LLC or to Rinks

(continued)

and Shields. Plaintiffs Wrench LLC, Rinks, and Shields sued defendant Taco Bell to recover damages for breach of an implied-in-fact contract. On this issue, the District Court agreed with the plaintiffs. The decision was appealed.

Issue

Have the plaintiffs Wrench LLC, Rinks, and Shields stated a cause of action for the breach of an implied-in-fact contract?

Language of the Court

The district court found that appellants produced sufficient evidence to create a genuine issue of material fact regarding whether an implied-in-fact contract existed between the parties. On appeal, Taco Bell argues that this conclusion was erroneous, and asserts that the record contains no evidence of an enforceable contract. We agree with the district court's finding that appellants presented sufficient evidence to survive summary judgment on the question of whether an implied-in-fact contract existed under Michigan law.

Decision

The U.S. Court of Appeals held that the plaintiffs had stated a proper cause of action against defendant

Taco Bell for breach of an implied-in-fact contract. The Court of Appeals remanded the case for trial.

Note　The U.S. Supreme Court denied review of the decision in this case. In 2003, a federal court jury ordered Taco Bell to pay $30 million to plaintiffs Thomas Rinks and Joseph Shields for stealing their idea for the Psycho Chihuahua commercials. Later, the court awarded an additional $11.8 million in prejudgment interest, bringing the total award to almost 42 million.

Case Questions

Critical Legal Thinking
What does the doctrine of implied-in-fact contract provide? Explain.

Ethics
Did Taco Bell act ethically in this case? Did Chiat/Day act ethically in this case?

Contemporary Business
What is the purpose of recognizing implied-in-fact contracts? Do you think there was an implied-in-fact contract in this case? If so, what damages should have been awarded to the plaintiffs?

Web Exercise
Go to **www.youtube.com/watch?v=B0oEw0IMLXI** for a video clip of Taco Bell's Chihuahua commercial.

Quasi-Contract (Implied-in-Law Contract)

quasi-contract (implied-in-law contract)
An equitable doctrine whereby a court may award monetary damages to a plaintiff for providing work or services to a defendant even though no actual contract existed. The doctrine is intended to prevent unjust enrichment and unjust detriment.

The equitable doctrine of **quasi-contract**, also called **implied-in-law contract**, allows a court to award monetary damages to a plaintiff for providing work or services to a defendant even though no actual contract existed between the parties. Recovery is generally based on the reasonable value of the services received by the defendant.

The doctrine of quasi-contract is intended to prevent *unjust enrichment* and *unjust detriment*. It does not apply where there is an enforceable contract between the parties. A quasi-contract is imposed where (1) one person confers a benefit on another, who retains the benefit, and (2) it would be unjust not to require that person to pay for the benefit received.

Example　Heather is driving her automobile when she is involved in a serious automobile accident in which she is knocked unconscious. She is rushed to Metropolitan Hospital, where the doctors and other staff perform the necessary medical procedures to save her life. Heather comes out of her coma, and after recovering is released from the hospital. Subsequently, Metropolitan Hospital sends Heather a bill for its services. The charges are reasonable. Under the doctrine of quasi-contract, Heather is responsible for any charges that are not covered by her insurance coverage.

CONCEPT SUMMARY
CLASSIFICATIONS OF CONTRACTS

Formation
1. **Bilateral contract.** A promise for a promise.
2. **Unilateral contract.** A promise for an act.
3. **Express contract.** A contract expressed in oral or written words.
4. **Implied-in-fact contract.** A contract inferred from the conduct of the parties.
5. **Implied-in-law contract (quasi-contract).** A contract implied by law to prevent unjust enrichment.
6. **Formal contract.** A contract that requires a special form or method of creation.
7. **Informal contract.** A contract that requires no special form or method of creation.

Enforceability
1. **Valid contract.** A contract that meets all the essential elements of establishing a contract.
2. **Void contract.** No contract exists.
3. **Voidable contract.** A contract in which at least one party has the option of voiding the contract.
4. **Unenforceable contract.** A contract that cannot be enforced because of a legal defense.

Performance
1. **Executed contract.** A contract that is fully performed on both
2. **Executory contract.** A contract that is not fully performed by one or both parties.

Agreement

Agreement is the manifestation by two or more persons of the substance of a traditional or e-contract. It requires an *offer* and an *acceptance*. Often, prior to entering into a contract, the parties engage in preliminary negotiations about price, time of performance, and such. At some point, one party makes an offer to the other party. The person who makes the offer is called the *offeror*, and the person to whom the offer is made is called the *offeree*. The offer sets forth the terms under which the offeror is willing to enter into the contract. The offeree has the power to create an agreement by accepting the offer.

agreement
The manifestation by two or more persons of the substance of a contract.

Requirements of an Offer

Section 24 of the *Restatement (Second) of Contracts* defines an **offer** as "the manifestation of willingness to enter into a bargain, so made as to justify another person in understanding that his assent to that bargain is invited and will conclude it." Three elements are required for an offer to be effective: (1) The offeror must *objectively intend* to be bound by the offer, (2) the terms of the offer must be *definite or reasonably certain*, and (3) the offer must be *communicated* to the offeree.

The terms of an offer must be clear enough for the offeree to be able to decide whether to accept or reject the terms of the offer. If the terms are indefinite, the courts usually cannot enforce the contract or determine an appropriate remedy for its breach. Generally, an offer (and contract) must contain the following terms: (1) identification of the parties, (2) identification of the subject matter and quantity, (3) consideration to be paid, and (4) time of performance. Complex contracts usually state additional terms. The making of an offer is shown in **Exhibit 9.2**.

offer
According to the *Restatement (Second) of Contracts*, "The manifestation of willingness to enter into a bargain, so made as to justify another person in understanding that his assent to that bargain is invited and will conclude it."

Exhibit 9.2 OFFER

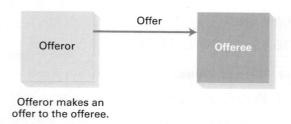

Offeror makes an
offer to the offeree.

Objective Intent

objective theory of contracts
A theory that says the intent to contract is judged by the reasonable person standard and not by the subjective intent of the parties.

A contract is a mutual promise.

William Paley
The Principles of Moral and Political Philosophy (1784)

The intent to enter into a contract is determined using the **objective theory of contracts**—that is, whether a reasonable person viewing the circumstances would conclude that the parties intended to be legally bound.

Examples The statement "I will buy your building for $2 million" is a valid offer because it indicates the offeror's present intent to contract. A statement such as "Are you interested in selling your building for $2 million?" is not an offer. It is an invitation to make an offer or an invitation to negotiate.

Offers that are made in jest, anger, or undue excitement do not include the necessary objective intent.

Example The owner of Company A has lunch with the owner of Company B. In the course of their conversation, Company A's owner exclaims in frustration, "For $200, I'd sell the whole computer division!" An offer such as that cannot result in a valid contract.

In the following case, the court enforced a contract.

CASE 9.2 *Contract*

The Facebook, Inc. v. Winklevoss

Web 2011 U.S. App. Lexis 7430 (2011)
United States Court of Appeals for the Ninth Circuit

"At some point, litigation must come to an end. That point has now been reached."

—Kozinski, Circuit Judge

Facts

Mark Zuckerberg, Cameron Winklevoss, Tyler Winklevoss, and Divya Narendra were schoolmates at Harvard University. The Winklevoss twins, along with Narendra, started a company called ConnectU. They alleged that Zuckerberg stole their idea and created Facebook, and in a lawsuit they filed claims against Facebook and Zuckerberg. The court ordered the parties to mediate their dispute. After a day of negotiations, the parties signed a handwritten, one-and-one-third-page "Term Sheet & Settlement Agreement." In the agreement, the Winklevosses agreed to give up their claims in exchange for cash and Facebook stock. The Winklevosses were to receive $20 million in cash and $45 million of Facebook stock valued at $36 per share.

The parties stipulated that the settlement agreement was "confidential," "binding," and "may be submitted into evidence to enforce it." The agreement granted all parties mutual releases. The agreement stated that the Winkelvosses represented and warranted that "they have no further right to assert against Facebook" and have "no further claims against Facebook and its related parties." Facebook became an extremely successful social networking site, with its value exceeding over $30 billion at the time the next legal dispute arose.

Subsequently, in a lawsuit, the Winklevosses brought claims against Facebook and Zuckerberg, alleging that Facebook and Zuckerberg had engaged in fraud at the time of forming the settlement agreement. The Winklevosses alleged that Facebook and Zuckerberg had misled them into believing that Facebook shares were worth $36 per share at the time of settlement, when in fact an internal Facebook document valued the stock at $8.88 per share for tax code purposes. The Winklevosses sought to rescind the settlement agreement. The U.S. District Court enforced the settlement agreement. The Winklevosses appealed.

Issue

Is the settlement agreement enforceable?

Language of the Court

The Winklevosses are sophisticated parties who were locked in a contentious struggle over ownership rights in one of the world's fastest-growing companies. They engaged in discovery, which gave them access to a good deal of information about their opponents. They brought half-a-dozen lawyers to the mediation. When adversaries in a roughly equivalent bargaining position and with ready access to counsel sign an agreement to "establish a general peace," we enforce the clear terms of the agreement. Parties involved in litigation know that they are locked in combat with an adversary and thus have every reason to be skeptical of each other's claims and representations. They can use discovery to ferret out a great deal of information before even commencing settlement negotiations. They can further protect themselves by requiring that the adverse party supply the needed information, or provide specific representations and warranties as a condition of signing the settlement agreement.

There are also very important policies that favor giving effect to agreements that put an end to the expensive and disruptive process

of litigation. The Winklevosses are not the first parties bested by a competitor who then seek to gain through litigation what they were unable to achieve in the marketplace. And the courts might have obliged, had the Winklevosses not settled their dispute and signed a release of all claims against Facebook. With the help of a team of lawyers and a financial advisor, they made a deal that appears quite favorable in light of recent market activity. For whatever reason, they now want to back out. Like the district court, we see no basis for allowing them to do so. At some point, litigation must come to an end. That point has now been reached.

Decision

The U.S. Court of Appeals upheld the decision of the U.S. District Court that enforced the settlement agreement.

Case Questions

Critical Legal Thinking
What is the purpose of settlement agreements?

Ethics
Did anyone act unethically in this case?

Contemporary Business
How important are settlement agreements to businesses that are involved in contract and legal disputes? What percentage of civil lawsuits are settled?

Auctions

In an **auction**, the seller offers goods for sale through an auctioneer. Unless otherwise expressly stated, an auction is considered an **auction with reserve**—that is, it is an invitation to make an offer. The seller retains the right to refuse the highest bid and withdraw the goods from sale. A contract is formed only when the auctioneer strikes the gavel down or indicates acceptance by some other means. The bidder may withdraw his or her bid prior to that time.

Example If an auction is an auction with reserve and an item is offered at $100,000 but the highest bid is $75,000, the auctioneer does not have to sell the item.

If an auction is expressly announced to be an **auction without reserve**, the participants reverse the roles: The seller is the offeror, and the bidders are the offerees. The seller must accept the highest bid and cannot withdraw the goods from sale. However, if the auctioneer has set a minimum bid that it will accept, the auctioneer has to sell the item only if the highest bid is equal to or greater than the minimum bid.

auction with reserve
An auction in which the seller retains the right to refuse the highest bid and withdraw the goods from sale. Unless expressly stated otherwise, an auction is an auction with reserve.

auction without reserve
An auction in which the seller expressly gives up his or her right to withdraw the goods from sale and must accept the highest bid.

Termination of an Offer

An offer may be terminated by certain *acts of the parties*. The acts of the parties that terminate an offer are:

revocation of an offer
Withdrawal of an offer by the offeror that terminates the offer.

- **Revocation of an offer by the offeror.**   Under the common law, an offeror may revoke (i.e., withdraw) an offer any time prior to its acceptance by the offeree. Generally, an offer can be so revoked even if the offeror promised to keep the offer open for a longer time. The **revocation** may be communicated to the offeree by the offeror or by a third party and made by (1) the offeror's express statement (e.g., "I hereby withdraw my offer") or (2) an act of the offeror that is inconsistent with the offer (e.g., selling the goods to another party). Generally, a revocation of an offer is not effective until it is actually received by the offeree.

rejection of an offer
Express words or conduct by the offeree that rejects an offer. Rejection terminates the offer.

- **Rejection of an offer by the offeree.**   An offer is terminated if the offeree *rejects* it. Any subsequent attempt by the offeree to accept the offer is ineffective and is construed as a new offer that the original offeror (now the offeree) is free to accept or reject. A **rejection** may be evidenced by the offeree's express words (oral or written) or conduct. Generally, a rejection of an offer is not effective until it is actually received by the offeror.

counteroffer
A response by an offeree that contains terms and conditions different from or in addition to those of the offer. A counteroffer terminates the previous offer.

- **Counteroffer by the offeree.**   A **counteroffer** by the offeree simultaneously terminates the offeror's offer and creates a new offer. Offerees' making of counteroffers is the norm in many transactions. A counteroffer terminates the existing offer and puts a new offer into play. The previous offeree becomes the new offeror, and the previous offeror becomes the new offeree. Generally, a counteroffer is not effective until it is actually received by the offeror.

Example Fei says to Harold, "I will sell you my house for $700,000." Harold says, "I think $700,000 is too high; I will pay you $600,000." Harold has made a counteroffer. Fei's original offer is terminated, and Harold's counteroffer is a new offer that Fei is free to accept or reject.

lapse of time
A stated time period after which an offer terminates. If no time is stated, an offer terminates after a reasonable time.

An offer expires at the **lapse of time** of an offer. An offer may state that it is effective only until a certain date. Unless otherwise stated, the time period begins to run when the offer is actually received by the offeree and terminates when the stated time period expires.

Examples If an offer states "This offer is good for ten days," the offer expires at midnight of the tenth day after the offer was made. If an offer states "This offer must be accepted by January 1, 2014," the offer expires at 11:59 p.m. on January 1, 2014.

If no time is stated in an offer, the offer terminates after a "reasonable time," dictated by the circumstances.

The following feature discusses the use of an option contract to require that an offer be kept open for a specified period of time.

Contemporary Environment

Option Contract

An offeree can prevent the offeror from revoking his or her offer by paying the offeror compensation to keep the offer open for an agreed-upon period of time. This creates what is called an **option contract**. In other words, the offeror agrees not to sell the property to anyone except the offeree during the option period. An option contract is a contract in which the original offeree pays consideration (usually money) in return for the original offeror giving consideration (time of the option period). The death or incompetency of either party does not terminate an option contract unless the contract is for the performance of a personal service.

Example Anne offers to sell a piece of real estate to Hal for $1 million. Hal wants time to investigate the property for possible environmental problems and to arrange financing if he decides to purchase the property, so he pays Anne $20,000 to keep her offer open to him for six months. At any time during the option period, Hal may exercise his option and pay Anne the $1 million purchase price. If Hal lets the option expire, however, Anne may keep the $20,000 and sell the property to someone else. Often option contracts are written so that if the original offeree purchases the property, the option amount is applied to the sale price.

An offer can be *terminated by operation of law*. An offer is terminated by operation of law if, prior to the acceptance of the offer, one of the following events occur: (1) The subject matter of the offer is destroyed through no fault of either party, (2) either the offeror or the offeree dies or becomes incompetent, or (3) the object of the offer is made illegal by law.

Acceptance

Acceptance is "a manifestation of assent by the offeree to the terms of the offer in a manner invited or required by the offer as measured by the objective theory of contracts."[4] Recall that, generally, (1) unilateral contracts can be accepted only by the offeree's performance of the required act and (2) a bilateral contract can be accepted by an offeree who promises to perform (or, where permitted, by performance of) the requested act. The acceptance of an offer is illustrated in **Exhibit 9.3**.

acceptance
According to the *Restatement (Second) of Contracts*, "A manifestation of assent by the offeree to the terms of the offer in a manner invited or required by the offer as measured by the objective theory of contracts."

Exhibit 9.3 ACCEPTANCE OF AN OFFER

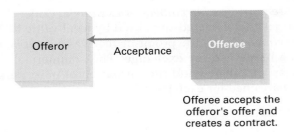

Offeree accepts the offeror's offer and creates a contract.

An offeree's acceptance must be **unequivocal**. For an acceptance to exist, the offeree must accept the terms as stated in the offer. This is called the **mirror image rule**.

mirror image rule
A rule which states that for an acceptance to exist, the offeree must accept the terms as stated in the offer.

Example Abraham says to Caitlin, "I will sell you my iPhone for $300." Caitlin says, "Yes, I will buy your iPhone at that price." This is an unequivocal acceptance that creates a contract.

Mailbox Rule

Under the common law of contracts, acceptance of a bilateral contract occurs when the offeree *dispatches* the acceptance by an authorized means of communication. This rule is called the **acceptance-upon-dispatch rule** or, more commonly, the **mailbox rule**. An acceptance must be properly addressed, packaged in an appropriate envelope or container, and have prepaid postage or delivery charges. Under common law, if an acceptance is not properly dispatched, it is not effective until it is actually received by the offeror.

Generally, an offeree must accept an offer by an **authorized means of communication**. Most offers do not expressly specify the means of communication required for acceptance. The common law recognizes certain implied means of communication. **Implied authorization** may be inferred from what is customary

acceptance-upon-dispatch rule (mailbox rule)
A rule which states that an acceptance is effective when it is dispatched, even if it is lost in transmission.

in similar transactions, usage of trade, or prior dealings between the parties. Section 30 of the *Restatement (Second) of Contracts* permits *implied authorization* "by any medium reasonable in the circumstances." Thus, in most circumstances, a party may send an acceptance by mail, overnight delivery service, fax, or e-mail.

An offer can stipulate that acceptance must be by a specified means of communication (e.g., registered mail, telegram). Such stipulation is called **express authorization**. If the offeree uses an unauthorized means of communication to transmit the acceptance, the acceptance is not effective, even if it is received by the offeror within the allowed time period, because the means of communication was a condition of acceptance.

Consideration

consideration
Something of legal value given in exchange for a promise.

Consideration must be given before a contract can exist. **Consideration** is defined as something of legal value given in exchange for a promise. Consideration can come in many forms. The most common types consist of either a tangible payment (e.g., money, property) or the performance of an act (e.g., providing legal services). Less usual forms of consideration include the forbearance of a legal right (e.g., accepting an out-of-court settlement in exchange for dropping a lawsuit) and noneconomic forms of consideration (e.g., refraining from "drinking, using tobacco, swearing, or playing cards or billiards for money"[5] for a specified time period). Written contracts are presumed to be supported by consideration. This rebuttable presumption, however, may be overcome by sufficient evidence.

legal value
Support for a contract when either (1) the promisee suffers a legal detriment or (2) the promisor receives a legal benefit.

Consideration consists of two elements: (1) Something of *legal value* must be given (e.g., either a legal benefit must be received or legal detriment must be suffered) and (2) there must be a *bargained-for exchange*. Under the modern law of contracts, a contract is considered supported by **legal value** if (1) the promisee suffers a *legal detriment* or (2) the promisor receives a *legal benefit*. A contract must arise from a **bargained-for exchange**. The commercial setting in which business contracts are formed and the formation of most personal contracts usually involve a bargained-for exchange.

bargained-for exchange
Exchange that parties engage in that leads to an enforceable contract.

Gift Promise

gift promise (gratuitous promise)
A promise that is unenforceable because it lacks consideration.

Gift promises, also called **gratuitous promises**, are unenforceable because they lack consideration. To change a gift promise into an enforceable promise, the promisee must offer to do something in exchange—that is, in consideration—for the promise. Gift promises cause considerable trouble for persons who do not understand the importance of consideration.

Example On May 1, Mrs. Colby promises to give her son $10,000 on June 1. When June 1 arrives, Mrs. Colby refuses to pay the $10,000. The son cannot recover the $10,000 because it was a gift promise that lacked consideration. If, however, Mrs. Colby promises to pay her son $10,000 if he earns an "A" in his business law course and the son earns the "A," the contract is enforceable, and the son can recover the $10,000.

A completed gift promise cannot be rescinded for lack of consideration.

Example On May 1, Mr. Smith promises to give his granddaughter $10,000 on June 1. If on or before June 1 Mr. Smith actually gives the $10,000 to his granddaughter, it is a completed gift promise. Mr. Smith cannot thereafter recover the money from his granddaughter, even if the original promise lacked consideration.

Contracts That Lack Consideration

Some contracts seem as though they are supported by consideration even though they are not. These contracts *lack consideration* and are therefore unenforceable. Several types of contracts that fall into this category are contracts based on:

- **Illegal consideration.** A contract cannot be supported by a promise to refrain from doing an illegal act because that is **illegal consideration**. Contracts based on illegal consideration are void.

  Example A person threatens a business owner "I will burn your business down unless you agree to pay me $10,000." Out of fear, the business owner promises to pay the money. This agreement is not an enforceable contract because the consideration given—not to burn a business—is illegal consideration. Thus, the extortionist cannot enforce the contract against the business owner.

- **Illusory promise.** If parties enter into a contract but one or both of the parties can choose not to perform their contractual obligations, the contract lacks consideration. Such promises, which are known as **illusory promises** (or **illusory contracts**), are unenforceable.

  Example A contract which provides that one of the parties has to perform only if he or she chooses to do so is an illusory promise.

- **Preexisting duty.** A promise lacks consideration if a person promises to perform an act or do something he is already under an obligation to do. This is called a **preexisting duty**. The promise is unenforceable because no new consideration has been given.

  Example Statutes prohibit police officers from demanding money for investigating and apprehending criminals and prohibit fire fighters from demanding payment for fighting fires. If a person agrees to such a demand, she does not have to pay it because public servants are under a preexisting duty to perform their functions.

- **Past consideration.** Problems of **past consideration** often arise when a party promises to pay someone money or other compensation for work done in the past. Past consideration is not consideration for a new promise; therefore, a promise based on past consideration is not enforceable.

  Example Felipe, who has worked in management for the Acme Corporation for thirty years, is retiring. The president of Acme says, "Because you were such a loyal employee, Acme will pay you a bonus of $100,000." Subsequently, the corporation refuses to pay the $100,000. Unfortunately for Felipe, he has already done the work for which he has been promised to be paid. The contract is unenforceable against Acme because it is based on past consideration.

illegal consideration
A promise to refrain from doing an illegal act. Such a promise does not support a contract.

illusory promise (illusory contract)
A contract into which both parties enter but one or both of the parties can choose not to perform their contractual obligations. Thus, the contract lacks consideration.

preexisting duty
Something a person is already under an obligation to do. A promise lacks consideration if a person promises to perform a preexisting duty.

past consideration
A prior act or performance. Past consideration (e.g., prior acts) will not support a new contract. New consideration must be given.

Capacity to Contract

Generally, the law presumes that the parties to a contract have the requisite **contractual capacity** to enter into the contract. Certain persons do not have this capacity, however, including minors, insane persons, and intoxicated persons. The common law of contracts and many state statutes protect persons who lack contractual capacity from having contracts enforced against them. The party asserting incapacity or his or her guardian, conservator, or other legal representative bears the burden of proof.

There is grim irony in speaking of freedom of contract of those who, because of their economic necessities, give their service for less than is needful to keep body and soul together.

Harlan Fiske Stone
Morehead v. N.Y. ex rel. Tipaldo (1936)

Minors: The Infancy Doctrine

Minors do not always have the maturity, experience, or sophistication needed to enter into contracts with adults. Common law defines minors as females under the age of 18 and males under the age of 21. In addition, many states have enacted statutes that specify the **age of majority**. The most prevalent age of

minor
A person who has not reached the age of majority.

majority is 18 years of age for both males and females. Any age below the statutory age of majority is called the **period of minority**.

To protect minors, the law recognizes the **infancy doctrine**, which gives minors the right to **disaffirm** (or *cancel*) most contracts they have entered into with adults. This right is based on public policy, which reasons that minors should be protected from the unscrupulous behavior of adults. Under the infancy doctrine, a minor has the option of choosing whether to enforce a contract (i.e., the contract is *voidable* by a minor). The adult party is bound to the minor's decision. If both parties to a contract are minors, both parties have the right to disaffirm the contract.

If a minor has transferred consideration—money, property, or other valuables—to a competent party before disaffirming the contract, that party must place the minor in status quo. That is, the minor must be restored to the same position he or she was in before the minor entered into the contract. This restoration is usually done by returning the consideration to the minor. If the consideration has been sold or has depreciated in value, the competent party must pay the minor the cash equivalent. Generally, a minor is obligated only to return the goods or property he or she has received from the adult in the condition it is in at the time of disaffirmance.

Example When Sherry is 17 years old (a minor), she enters into a contract to purchase an automobile costing $10,000 from Bruce, a competent adult. Bruce, who believes that Sherry is an adult and does not ask for verification of her age, delivers ownership of the automobile to Sherry after he receives her payment of $10,000. Subsequently, before Sherry reaches the age of 18 (the age of majority), she is involved in an automobile accident caused by her own negligence. The automobile sustains $7,000 worth of damage in the accident (the automobile is now worth only $3,000). Sherry can disaffirm the contract, return the damaged automobile to Bruce, and recover $10,000 from Bruce. In this result, Sherry recovers her entire $10,000 purchase price from Bruce, and Bruce has only a damaged automobile worth $3,000.

Minors are obligated to pay for the **necessaries of life** that they contract for. Otherwise, many adults would refuse to sell these items to them. There is no standard definition of what is a necessary of life. The minor's age, lifestyle, and status in life influence what is considered necessary.

Examples Items such as food, clothing, shelter, and medical services are generally understood to be necessities of life. Goods and services such as automobiles, tools of trade, education, and vocational training have also been found to be necessaries of life in some situations.

Mentally Incompetent Persons

Mental incapacity may arise because of mental illness, brain damage, mental retardation, senility, and the like. The law protects people suffering from substantial mental incapacity from enforcement of contracts against them because such persons may not understand the consequences of their actions in entering into a contract. The law has developed two standards concerning contracts of mentally incompetent persons: (1) adjudged insane and (2) insane but not adjudged insane.

In certain cases, a relative, a loved one, or another interested party may institute a legal action to have someone declared legally (i.e., adjudged) insane. If after hearing the evidence at a formal judicial or administrative hearing the person is **adjudged insane**, the court will make that person a ward of the court and appoint a guardian to act on that person's behalf. Any contract entered into by a person who has been adjudged insane is *void*. That is,

---

infancy doctrine
A doctrine that allows minors to disaffirm (cancel) most contracts they have entered into with adults.

The right of a minor to disaffirm his contract is based upon sound public policy to protect the minor from his own improvidence and the overreaching of adults.

Justice Sullivan
Star Chevrolet v. Green (1985)

Insanity vitiates all acts.

Sir John Nicholl
Countess of Portsmouth v. Earl of Portsmouth (1828)

adjudged insane
Declared legally insane by a proper court or administrative agency. A contract entered into by a person adjudged insane is *void*.

no contract exists. The court-appointed guardian is the only one who has the legal authority to enter into contracts on behalf of the person who has been adjudged insane.

If no formal ruling has been made about a person's sanity but the person suffers from a mental impairment that makes him or her legally insane—that is, the person is **insane but not adjudged insane**—any contract entered into by this person is *voidable* by the insane person. Unless the other party does not have contractual capacity, he or she does not have the option to void the contract. A person who has dealt with an insane person must place that insane person in status quo if the contract is either void or voided by the insane person.

Intoxicated Persons

Most states provide that contracts entered into by certain **intoxicated persons** are voidable by those persons. The intoxication may occur because of alcohol or drugs. The contract is not voidable by the other party if that party had contractual capacity at the time the contract was formed.

Under the majority rule, a contract is voidable only if the person was so intoxicated when the contract was entered into that he or she was incapable of understanding or comprehending the nature of the transaction. In most states, this rule holds even if the intoxication was self-induced. The amount of alcohol or drugs that must be consumed for a person to be considered legally intoxicated to disaffirm contracts varies from case to case. The factors that are considered include the user's physical characteristics and his or her ability to "hold" intoxicants.

A person who disaffirms a contract based on intoxication generally must be returned to the status quo. In turn, the intoxicated person generally must return the consideration received under the contract to the other party and make restitution that returns the other party to status quo. After becoming sober, an intoxicated person can ratify the contracts he or she entered into while intoxicated.

Legality

One requirement to have an enforceable contract is that the object of the contract must be lawful. Most contracts that individuals and businesses enter into are **lawful contracts** that are enforceable. These include contracts for the sale of goods, services, real property, and intangible rights; the lease of goods; property leases; licenses; and other contracts.

Some contracts have illegal objects. A contract with an illegal object is *void* and therefore unenforceable. These contracts are called **illegal contracts**. Because illegal contracts are void, the parties cannot sue for nonperformance. Further, if an illegal contract is executed, the court will generally leave the parties where it finds them. The burden of proving that a contract is unlawful rests on the party who asserts its illegality.

Contracts Contrary to Statutes

Both federal and state legislatures have enacted statutes that prohibit certain types of conduct. Contracts to perform activities that are prohibited by statute are illegal contracts. **Contracts contrary to statutes** include gambling contracts, contracts that provide for usurious rates of interest, and contracts that violate licensing statutes.

In the following case, the court analyzes whether there was an illegal gambling contract.

insane but not adjudged insane
Being insane but not having been adjudged insane by a court or an administrative agency. A contract entered into by such person is generally *voidable*. Some states hold that such a contract is void.

intoxicated person
A person who is under contractual incapacity because of ingestion of alcohol or drugs to the point of incompetence.

Men intoxicated are sometimes stunned into sobriety.

Lord Mansfield
R. v. Wilkes (1770)

illegal contract
A contract that has an illegal object. Such contracts are *void*.

Ethics

Illegal Gambling Contract

"The trial court could not have compelled Ryno to honor his wager by delivering the BMW to Tyra. However, Ryno did deliver the BMW to Tyra and the facts incident to that delivery are sufficient to establish a transfer by gift of the BMW from Ryno to Tyra."

—Farris, Judge

R. D. Ryno, Jr., owned Bavarian Motors, an automobile dealership in Fort Worth, Texas. One day, Lee Tyra discussed purchasing a BMW M-1 from Ryno for $125,000. Ryno then suggested a double-or-nothing coin flip, to which Tyra agreed. If the Ryno won the coin flip, Tyra would have to pay $250,000 for the car; if Tyra won the coin flip, he would get the car for free. The coin was flipped, and Tyra won the coin flip. Ryno said, "It's yours," and handed Tyra the keys, title, and possession to the car. Tyra drove away in the BMW. A lawsuit ensued as to the ownership of the car.

The court held that when Tyra won the coin toss and Ryno voluntarily gave the keys, title, and possession of the BMW to Tyra, this was a performed illegal gambling contract. There was sufficient evidence to find that Ryno intended to transfer to Tyra his ownership interest in the BMW at the time he delivered the documents, keys, and possession of the automobile to Tyra. The court left the parties where it found them: Tyra had the keys, title, and possession of the BMW; Ryno did not have either the car or payment for the car.

Note   If, when Tyra won the coin toss, Ryno had refused to give the BMW to Tyra, the result of this case would have been different. Tyra could not have compelled Ryno to honor his wager. This is because courts will not enforce an executory illegal gambling contract. The court would again have left the parties where it found them: Ryno would have had ownership and possession of the car and refused to honor the wager; Tyra would have won the coin toss but could not obtain the car from Ryno. *Ryno v. Tyra*, 752 S.W.2d 148, **Web** 1988 Tex.App. Lexis 1646 (Court of Appeals of Texas)

Ethics Questions   Did Ryno act ethically in this case? Did Tyra act ethically in this case? Should the court have helped Ryno to recover the BMW from Tyra? Why or why not?

---

contract contrary to public policy
A contract that has a negative impact on society or that interferes with the public's safety and welfare.

Certain contracts are illegal because they are **contrary to public policy**. Such contracts are void. Although *public policy* eludes precise definition, the courts have held contracts to be contrary to public policy if they have a negative impact on society or interfere with the public's safety and welfare.

Exculpatory Clause

exculpatory clause (release of liability clause)
A contractual provision that relieves one (or both) of the parties to a contract from tort liability for ordinary negligence.

An **exculpatory clause** (also called a **release of liability clause**) is a contractual provision that relieves one (or both) of the parties to a contract from tort liability. An exculpatory clause can relieve a party of liability for ordinary negligence. It cannot be used in a situation involving willful conduct, intentional torts, fraud, recklessness, or gross negligence. Exculpatory clauses are often found in leases, sales contracts, sporting event ticket stubs, parking lot tickets, service contracts, and the like. Such clauses do not have to be reciprocal (i.e., one party may be relieved of tort liability, whereas the other party is not).

Example A person voluntarily enrolls in a parachute jump course and signs a contract containing an exculpatory clause that relieves the parachute center of liability for ordinary negligence. If that person is injured in a jump because of the ordinary negligence of the jump center, the exculpatory clause would be enforced against him.

Example If a department store has a sign above the entrance stating "The store is not liable for the ordinary negligence of its employees," this would be an illegal exculpatory clause and would not be enforced.

Unconscionable Contracts

The general rule of freedom of contract holds that if the object of a contract is lawful and the other elements for the formation of a contract are met, the courts will enforce the contract according to its terms. However, when a contract is so oppressive or manifestly unfair as to be unjust, the law has developed the equity doctrine of unconscionability to prevent the enforcement of such contracts. The doctrine of unconscionability is based on public policy. A contract found to be unconscionable under this doctrine is called an **unconscionable contract**.

The courts are given substantial discretion in determining whether a contract or contract clause is unconscionable. There is no single definition of *unconscionability*. This doctrine may not be used merely to save a contracting party from a bad bargain. Unconscionable contracts are sometimes found where there is a consumer contract that takes advantage of uneducated, poor, or elderly people who have been persuaded to enter into unfair contracts.

The following elements must be shown to prove that a contract or a clause in a contract is unconscionable: (1) The parties possessed severely unequal bargaining power, (2) the dominant party unreasonably used its unequal bargaining power to obtain oppressive or manifestly unfair contract terms, and (3) the adhering party had no reasonable alternative.

If the court finds that a contract or a contract clause is unconscionable, it may (1) refuse to enforce the contract, (2) refuse to enforce the unconscionable clause but enforce the remainder of the contract, or (3) limit the applicability of any unconscionable clause so as to avoid any unconscionable result. The appropriate remedy depends on the facts and circumstances of each case. Note that because unconscionability is a matter of law, the judge may opt to decide the case without a jury trial.

Example Suppose a door-to-door salesperson sells a poor family a freezer full of meat and other foods for $3,000, with monthly payments for sixty months at 20 percent interest. If the actual cost of the freezer and the food is $1,000, this contract could be found to be unconscionable. The court could either find the entire contract unenforceable or rewrite the contract so that it has reasonable terms.

E-Commerce

As we entered the 21st century, a new economic shift brought the United States and the rest of the world into the Information Age. Computer technology and the use of the Internet increased dramatically. A new form of commerce—**electronic commerce, or e-commerce**—is flourishing. All sorts of goods and services are now sold over the Internet. You can purchase automobiles and children's toys, participate in auctions, purchase airline tickets, make hotel reservations, and purchase other goods and services over the Internet. Companies such as Microsoft Corporation, Google Inc., Facebook, Inc., and other technology companies license the use of their software over the Internet.

Much of the new cyberspace economy is based on **electronic contracts (e-contracts)** and **electronic licenses (e-licenses)**. Electronic licensing is usually of computer and software information. E-commerce has created problems for forming e-contracts and e-licenses over the Internet, enforcing e-contracts and e-licenses, and providing consumer protection. In many situations, traditional contract rules apply to e-contracts and e-licenses. Many states have adopted rules that specifically regulate e-commerce transactions. The federal government has also enacted several laws that regulate e-contracts and e-licenses.

The following feature discusses a uniform law that provides rules for the formation and performance of computer information contracts and licenses.

---

unconscionable contract
A contract that courts refuse to enforce in part or at all because it is so oppressive or manifestly unfair as to be unjust.

An unconscionable contract is one which no man in his senses, not under delusion, would make, on the one hand, and which no fair and honest man would accept on the other.

Fuller, Chief Justice
Hume v. United States (1889)

electronic commerce (e-commerce)
The sale and lease of goods and services and other property and the licensing of software over the Internet or by other electronic means.

electronic contract (e-contract)
A contract that is formed electronically.

electronic license (e-license)
An electronic contract that licenses the use of computer and software information.

Uniform Computer Information Transactions Act (UCITA)
A model act that establishes uniform legal rules for the formation and enforcement of electronic contracts and licenses.

Digital Law

E-Contracts and E-Licenses

The National Conference of Commissioners on Uniform State Laws (a group of lawyers, judges, and legal scholars) drafted the **Uniform Computer Information Transactions Act (UCITA)**.

The UCITA establishes uniform legal rules for the formation and enforcement of electronic contracts and licenses. The UCITA addresses most of the legal issues that are encountered while conducting e-commerce over the Internet.

The UCITA is a model act that does not become law until a state legislature adopts it as a statute for the state. Although most states have not adopted the UCITA, the UCITA has served as a model for states that have enacted their own statutes that govern e-commerce. Because of the need for uniformity of e-commerce rules, states are attempting to adopt uniform laws to govern the creation and enforcement of cyberspace contracts and licenses.

International Law

International Contract Law in China

BEIJING, CHINA

This is a photograph of the Forbidden City, Beijing, China. In 1999, China dramatically overhauled its contract laws by enacting the **Unified Contract Law (UCL)**. *This new set of laws changed many outdated business and commercial contract laws. The UCL was designed to provide users with a consistent and easy-to-understand set of statutes that more closely resembled international business contracting principles. It also provides for the resolution of contract disputes by the application of the rule of law.*

The UCL covers all the parts of contract law that should be familiar to Western businesses, including the definitions of contract, acceptance, consideration, performance, breach of contract, and remedies. Even so, there are many aspects of the UCL that differ from U.S. contract law, and anyone doing business in China or with a Chinese company should study it carefully.

Key Terms and Concepts

Acceptance (193)
Acceptance-upon-dispatch rule (mailbox rule) (193)
Actual contract (186)
Adjudged insane (196)
Age of majority (195)
Agreement (189)
Auction (191)
Auction with reserve (191)
Auction without reserve (191)
Authorized means of communication (193)
Bargained-for exchange (194)
Bilateral contract (184)
Consideration (194)
Contract (183)
Contract contrary to public policy (198)
Contract contrary to statutes (197)
Contract under seal (185)
Contractual capacity (195)

Counteroffer (192)
Disaffirm (196)
Electronic commerce (e-commerce) (199)
Electronic contract (e-contract) (199)
Electronic license (e-license) (199)
Exculpatory clause (release of liability clause) (198)
Executed contract (186)
Executory contract (186)
Express authorization (194)
Express contract (186)
Formal contract (185)
Genuineness of assent (184)
Gift promise (gratuitous promise) (194)
Illegal consideration (195)
Illegal contract (197)
Illusory promise (illusory contract) (195)
Implied authorization (193)

Implied-in-fact contract (187)
Infancy doctrine (196)
Informal contract (simple contract) (185)
Insane but not adjudged insane (197)
Intoxicated person (197)
Lapse of time (192)
Lawful contract (197)
Lawful object (184)
Legal value (194)
Legally enforceable contract (183)
Letter of credit (185)
Minor (195)
Mirror image rule (193)
Negotiable instrument (185)
Objective theory of contracts (190)
Offer (189)
Offeree (183)
Offeror (183)
Option contract (192)
Past consideration (195)

Period of minority (196)
Preexisting duty (195)
Quasi-contract (implied-in-law contract) (188)
Recognizance (185)
Rejection of an offer (192)
Restatement (Second) of Contracts (189)
Revocation of an offer (192)
Unconscionable contract (199)
Unenforceable contract (186)
Unequivocal acceptance (193)
Unified Contract Law (UCL) (200)
Uniform Computer Information Transactions Act (UCITA) (200)
Unilateral contract (185)
Valid contract (185)
Void contract (185)
Voidable contract (186)
Writing and form (184)

Law Case with Answer
City of Everett, Washington v. Mitchell

Facts Al and Rosemary Mitchell owned a small secondhand store. The Mitchells attended Alexander's Auction, where they frequently shopped to obtain merchandise for their business. While at the auction, they purchased a used safe for $50. They were told by the auctioneer that the inside compartment of the safe was locked and that no key could be found to unlock it. The safe was part of the Sumstad estate. Several days after the auction, the Mitchells took the safe to a locksmith to have the locked compartment opened. When the locksmith opened the compartment, he found $32,207 in cash. The locksmith called the city of Everett police, who impounded the money. The city of Everett commenced an action against the Sumstad estate and the Mitchells to determine the owner of the cash that was found in the safe. Who owns the money found in the safe?

Answer The Mitchells, who purchased the locked safe at the auction, own the money found in the safe. Under the objective theory of contracts, the outward manifestation of assent made by each party to the other is conclusive of the contract. The subjective intention of the parties is irrelevant. A contract is an obligation attached by the mere force of law to certain acts of the parties, usually words, which ordinarily accompany and represent a known intent. The Mitchells were aware of the rule of the auction that all sales were final. Furthermore, the auctioneer made no statement reserving rights to any contents of the safe to the Sumstad estate. Under these circumstances, reasonable persons would conclude that the auctioneer manifested an objective intent to sell the safe and its contents and that the parties mutually assented to enter into that sale of the safe and the contents of the locked compartment. Under the objective theory of contracts, a contract was formed between the seller and the buyer of the safe. Judgment should be rendered in favor of the Mitchells. *City of Everett, Washington v. Mitchell*, 631 P.2d 366, **Web** 1981 Wash. Lexis 1139 (Supreme Court of Washington)

Critical Legal Thinking Cases

9.1 Quasi-Contract Samuel E. Powell, Jr., and Susan Thompson-Powell, husband and wife, borrowed $37,700 from Delaware Farm Credit and gave a mortgage to Delaware Farm Credit that pledged two pieces of real property as collateral for the loan. The first piece of property was 2.7 acres of land owned as marital property. Susan had inherited the other piece of property and owned it. Eight years later, Samuel Jr. and Susan defaulted on the mortgage. Samuel Jr. went to his father, Samuel E. Powell, Sr., and orally agreed that if his father would pay the mortgage and the back taxes, he would pay his father back. Samuel Sr. paid off the mortgage and the back taxes owed on the properties. Susan was not a party to this agreement.

Two years later, Samuel Jr. and Susan divorced. The divorce court ordered that the 2.7 acres of marital real property be sold and the sale proceeds to be divided 50 percent to each party. When the property was sold, Samuel Jr. paid Samuel Sr. one-half of the monies he had previously borrowed from his father. Samuel Sr. sued Susan to recover the other half of the money. Susan defended, alleging that she was not a party to the contract between Samuel Jr. and Samuel Sr. and therefore was not bound by it. Samuel Sr. argued that Susan was liable to him for one-half of the money based on the doctrine of quasi-contract. Who wins? *Powell v. Thompson-Powell*, **Web** 2006 Del.C.P. Lexis 10 (Court of Common Pleas of Delaware)

9.2 Agreement The movie *Flashdance* tells a story of a female construction worker who performs at night as an exotic dancer. She performs an innovative form of dancing that includes a chair dance. Her goal is to obtain formal dance training at a university. The movie is based on the life of Maureen Marder, a nightclub dancer. Paramount Pictures Corporation used information from Marder to create the screenplay for the movie. Paramount paid Marder $2,300, and Marder signed a general release contract, which provided that Marder "releases and discharges Paramount Picture Corporation of and from each and every claim, demand, debt, liability, cost and expense of any kind or character which have risen or are based in whole or in part on any matters occurring at any time prior to the date of this Release." Marder also released Paramount from claims "arising out of or in any way connected with either directly or indirectly, any and all arrangements in connection with the preparation of screenplay material and the production, filming and exploitation of *Flashdance*."

Paramount released the movie *Flashdance*, which grossed more than $150 million in domestic box office receipts and is still shown on television and distributed through DVD rentals. Subsequently, Sony Music

Entertainment paid Paramount for release of copyright and produced a music video for the Jennifer Lopez song "I'm Glad." The video featured Lopez's performance as a dancer and singer. Marder believes that the video contains re-creations of many well-known scenes from *Flashdance*. Marder brought a lawsuit in U.S. District Court against Paramount, Sony, and Lopez. Marder sought a declaration that she had rights as a co-author of *Flashdance* and a co-owner with Paramount of the copyright to *Flashdance*. She sued Sony and Lopez for allegedly violating her copyright in *Flashdance*. Is the general release Marder signed an enforceable contract? *Marder v. Lopez*, 450 F.3d 445, **Web** 2006 U.S. App. Lexis 14330 (United States Court of Appeals for the Ninth Circuit)

9.3 Mirror Image Rule Norma English made an offer to purchase a house owned by Michael and Laurie Montgomery (Montgomery) for $272,000. In her offer, English also proposed to purchase certain personal property—paving stones and a fireplace screen worth a total of $100—from Montgomery. When Montgomery received English's offer, Montgomery made many changes to English's offer, including deleting the paving stones and fireplace screen from the personal property that English wanted. When English received the Montgomery counteroffer, English accepted and initialed all of Montgomery's changes except that English did not initial the change that deleted the paving stones and fireplace screen from the deal.

Subsequently, Montgomery notified English that because English had not completely accepted the terms of Montgomery's counteroffer, Montgomery was therefore withdrawing from the deal. That same day, Montgomery signed a contract to sell the house to another buyer for $285,000. English sued Montgomery for specific performance of the contract. Montgomery defended, arguing that the mirror image rule was not satisfied because English had not initialed the provision that deleted the paving stones and fireplace screen. Is there an enforceable contract between English and Montgomery? *Montgomery v. English*, 902 So.2d 836, **Web** 2005 Fla.App. Lexis 4704 (Court of Appeal of Florida)

9.4 Consideration Raymond P. Wirth signed a pledge agreement which stated that in consideration of his interest in education and "intending to be legally bound," he irrevocably pledged and promised to pay Drexel University the sum of $150,000. The pledge agreement provided that an endowed scholarship would be created in Wirth's name. The pledge agreement stated: "I acknowledge that Drexel's promise to use the amount pledged by me shall constitute full and adequate consideration for this pledge." Wirth died two months after signing the pledge but before any money had been paid to Drexel. When the estate of Wirth refused to honor the pledge, Drexel sued the estate to collect the $150,000. The estate alleged that the pledge was unenforceable because of lack of consideration. Is the pledge agreement supported by consideration and therefore enforceable against the estate of Wirth? *In the Matter of Wirth*, 14 A.D.3d 572, 789 N.Y.S.2d 69, **Web** 2005 N.Y. App. Div. Lexis 424 (Supreme Court of New York, Appellate Division)

9.5 Gifts   Lester Cooper suffered serious injuries that caused him to be hospitalized for an extended time period. While he was hospitalized, Julie Smith, whom Cooper had met the year before, and Janet Smith, Julie's mother, made numerous trips to visit him. A romantic relationship developed between Cooper and Julie. While in the hospital, Cooper proposed marriage to Julie, and she accepted. Cooper ultimately received an $180,000 settlement for his injuries.

After being released from the hospital, Cooper moved into Janet's house and lived with Janet and Julie. Over the next couple months, Cooper purchased a number of items for Julie, including a diamond engagement ring, a car, a computer, a tanning bed, and horses. On Julie's request, Cooper paid off Janet's car. Cooper also paid for various improvements to Janet's house, such as having a new furnace installed and having wood flooring laid in the kitchen. Several months later, the settlement money had run out, and Julie had not yet married Cooper. About six months later, Julie and Cooper had a disagreement, and Cooper moved out of the house. Julie returned the engagement ring to Cooper. Cooper sued Julie and Janet to recover the gifts or the value of the gifts he had given them. Can Cooper recover the gifts or the value of the gifts he gave to Julie and Janet Smith? *Cooper v. Smith*, 800 N.E.2d 372, **Web** 2003 Ohio App. Lexis 5446 (Court of Appeals of Ohio)

9.6 Mental Incapacity   Martha M. Carr suffered from schizophrenia and depression. Schizophrenia is a psychotic disorder that is characterized by disturbances in perception, inferential thinking, delusions, hallucinations, and grossly disorganized behavior. Depression is characterized by altered moods and diminished ability to think or concentrate. Carr was taking two prescription drugs for her mental diseases, Haldol and Cogentin. Carr, a resident of New York, inherited from her mother a 108-acre tract of unimproved land in South Carolina. Carr contacted Raymond C. and Betty Campbell (Campbell), who had leased the property for 30 years, about selling the property to them. Carr asked Campbell how much the property was worth, and Campbell told Carr $54,000. Carr and Campbell entered into a written contract for $54,000, which averaged $500 an

acre. Campbell paid Carr earnest money. Carr subsequently missed the closing day for the sale of the property, returned the earnest money, and refused to sell the property to Campbell. Campbell sued Carr to obtain a court judgment ordering Carr to specifically perform the contract. At trial, evidence and expert witness testimony placed the value of the property at $162,000, or $1,500 an acre. Testimony showed that Campbell knew that the value of the property exceeded $54,000. Does Carr, because of her mental diseases of schizophrenia and depression, lack the mental capacity to enter into the contract with Campbell? *Campbell v. Carr*, 603 S.E.2d 625, **Web** 2004 S.C.App. Lexis 276 (Court of Appeals of South Carolina)

9.7 Illegal Contract   Andrew Parente had a criminal record. He and Mario Pirozzoli, Jr., formed a partnership to open and operate the Speak Easy Café in Berlin, Connecticut, which was a bar that would serve alcohol. The owners were required to obtain a liquor license from the state of Connecticut before operating the bar. Because the state of Connecticut usually would not issue a liquor license to anyone with a criminal record, it was agreed that Pirozzoli would form a corporation called Centerfolds, Inc., to own the bar, sign the real estate lease for the bar in his name, and file for the liquor license in his name only. Pirozzoli did all of these things. Parente and Pirozzoli signed a partnership agreement which acknowledged that Parente was an equal partner in the business. The state of Connecticut granted the liquor license, and the bar opened for business. Parente and Pirozzoli shared the profits of the bar. Six years later, Pirozzoli terminated the partnership and kept the business. Parente sued Pirozzoli for breach of the partnership agreement to recover the value of his alleged share of the business. Parente's share would have been $138,000. Pirozzoli defended, arguing that the partnership agreement was an illegal contract that should not be enforced against him. Is the partnership agreement an illegal contract that is void and unenforceable by the court? *Parente v. Pirozzoli*, 866 A.2d 629, **Web** 2005 Conn.App. Lexis 25 (Appellate Court of Connecticut)

9.8 Counteroffer   Wilbert Heikkila listed eight parcels of real property for sale. David McLaughlin submitted written offers to purchase three of the parcels. Three printed purchase agreements were prepared and submitted to Heikkila with three earnest-money checks from McLaughlin. Writing on the purchase agreements, Heikkila changed the price of one parcel from $145,000 to $150,000, changed the price of another parcel from $32,000 to $45,000, and changed the price of the third parcel from $175,000 to $179,000. Heikkila also changed the closing dates on all three of the properties, added a reservation of mineral rights to all three, and signed the purchase agreements.

McLaughlin did not sign the purchase agreements to accept the changes before Heikkila withdrew his offer to sell. McLaughlin sued to compel specific performance of the purchase agreements under the terms of the agreements before Heikkila withdrew his offer. The district court granted Heikkila's motion to dismiss McLaughlin's claim. McLaughlin appealed. Does a contract to convey real property exist between Heikkila and McLaughlin? *McLaughlin v. Heikkila*, 697 N.W.2d 231, **Web** 2005 Minn.App. Lexis 591 (Court of Appeals of Minnesota)

9.9 Contract Contrary to Public Policy   Ellen and Richard Alvin Flood, who were married, lived in a mobile home in Louisiana. Richard worked as a maintenance man, and Ellen was employed at an insurance agency. Evidence at trial showed that Ellen was unhappy with her marriage. Ellen took out an insurance policy on the life of her husband and named herself as beneficiary. The policy was issued by Fidelity & Guaranty Life Insurance Company (Fidelity). Seven years after the marriage, Richard became unexpectedly ill. He was taken to the hospital, where his condition improved. After a visit at the hospital from his wife, however, Richard died. Ellen was criminally charged with the murder of her husband by poisoning. Evidence showed that six medicine bottles at the couple's home, including Tylenol and paregoric bottles, contained arsenic. The court found that Ellen had fed Richard ice cubes laced with arsenic at the hospital. Ellen was tried and convicted of the murder of her husband. Ellen, as beneficiary of Richard's life insurance policy, requested Fidelity to pay her the benefits. Fidelity refused to pay the benefits and returned all premiums paid on the policy. This suit followed. The district court held in favor of Ellen Flood and awarded her the benefits of the life insurance policy. Fidelity appealed. Is the life insurance policy an illegal contract that is void? *Flood v. Fidelity & Guaranty Life Insurance Company*, 394 So.2d 1311, **Web** 1981 La.App. Lexis 3538 (Court of Appeal of Louisiana)

9.10 Equity   *Mighty Morphin' Power Rangers* was a phenomenal success as a television series. The Power Rangers battled to save the universe from all sorts of diabolical plots and bad guys. They were also featured in a profitable line of toys and garments bearing the Power Rangers logo. The name and logo of the Power Rangers are known to millions of children and their parents worldwide. The claim of ownership of the logo for the Power Rangers ended up in a battle in a courtroom.

David Dees is a designer who works as d.b.a. David Dees Illustration. Saban Entertainment, Inc. (Saban), which owns the copyright and trademark to Power Rangers figures and the name "Power Ranger," hired Dees as an independent contractor to design a logo for the Power Rangers. The contract signed by the parties was titled "Work-for-Hire/Independent Contractor Agreement." The contract was drafted by Saban with the help of its attorneys; Dees signed the agreement without the representation of legal counsel.

Dees designed the logo currently used for the Power Rangers and was paid $250 to transfer his copyright ownership in the logo. Subsequently, Dees sued Saban to recover damages for copyright and trademark infringement. Saban defended, arguing that Dees was bound by the agreement he had signed. What is the concept "A contract is a contract is a contract"? Does the doctrine of equity save Dees from his contract? Is Dees bound by the contract? *Dees, d/b/a David Dees Illustration v. Saban Entertainment, Inc.*, 131 F.3d 146, **Web** 1997 U.S. App. Lexis 39173 (United States Court of Appeals for the Ninth Circuit)

Ethics Cases

9.11 Ethics   A landlord leased a motel he owned to lessees for a ten-year period. The lessees had an option to extend the lease for an additional ten years. To do so, they had to give written notice to the landlord three months before the first ten-year lease expired. The lease provided for forfeiture of all furniture, fixtures, and equipment installed by the lessees, free of any liens, upon termination of the lease. For almost ten years, the lessees devoted most of their assets and a great deal of their energy to building up the business. During this time, they transformed a disheveled, unrated motel into a AAA three-star operation. With the landlord's knowledge, the lessees made extensive long-term improvements that greatly increased the value of both the property and the business. The landlord knew that the lessees had obtained long-term financing for the improvements that would extend well beyond the first 10-year term of the lease. The landlord also knew that the only source of income the lessees had to pay for these improvements was the income generated from the motel business.

The lessees told the landlord orally in a conversation that they intended to extend the lease. The lessees had instructed their accountant to exercise the option on time. Despite reminders from the lessees, the accountant failed to give the written notice within three months of the expiration of the lease. As soon as they discovered the mistake, the lessees personally delivered written notice of renewal of the option to the landlord, thirteen days too late. The landlord rejected it as late and instituted a lawsuit for unlawful detainer to evict the lessees. The lessees asked the court to invoke the doctrine of equity and save them from their error. *Romasanta v. Mitton*, 189 Cal.App.3d 1026, 234 Cal.Rptr. 729, **Web** 1987 Cal.App. Lexis 1428 (Court of Appeal of California)

1. What does the doctrine of equity provide?
2. Did the landlord act unethically in this case?
3. Should the doctrine of equity be applied to save the lessees from their contractual error?

9.12 Ethics The United Arab Emirates (UAE), a country in the Middle East, held a competition for the architectural design of a new embassy it intended to build in Washington, DC. Elena Sturdza, an architect licensed in Maryland and Texas, entered the competition and submitted a design. After reviewing all of the submitted designs, UAE notified Sturdza that she had won the competition. UAE and Sturdza entered into

contract negotiations, and over the next two years, they exchanged multiple contract proposals. During that time, at UAE's request, Sturdza modified her design. She agreed to defer billing UAE for her work until the execution of their contract. At last, UAE sent Sturdza a final agreement. Sturdza informed UAE that she assented to the contract. Without explanation, however, UAE stopped communicating with Sturdza. UAE hired another architect to design the embassy. Sturdza filed suit against UAE to recover damages for breach of contract or, alternatively, under the equity doctrine of quantum meruit, to prevent unjust enrichment to UAE. UAE defended, alleging that because Sturdza did not have an architectural license issued by Washington, DC, that she could not recover damages. *Sturdza v. United Arab Emirates*, 11 A.3d 251, **Web** 2011 D.C. App. Lexis 2 (District of Columbia Court of Appeals)

1. What is an illegal contract?
2. Was it ethical for UAE not to pay Sturdza? Could UAE have paid Sturdza without violating the law?
3. Who wins this case and why?

Internet Exercises

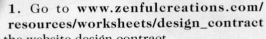

1. Go to www.zenfulcreations.com/resources/worksheets/design_contract.htm. Read the website design contract.

2. For information about auctions, visit the websites of two premiere auction houses: Sotheby's, at www.sothebys.com, and Christie's, at www.christies.com.

3. Go to www.oscn.net/applications/oscn/DeliverDocument.asp?CiteID=74212 and read the jury instruction on the issue of quasi-contract.

4. Go to www.nytimes.com/2006/03/05/business/05goodie.html and read about gifts to movie stars.

5. Go to www.npr.org/templates/story/story.php?storyId=12819904 and read the article about illegal gambling.

6. Go to "Petitioner's Jurisdictional Brief" at www.floridasupremecourt.org/clerk/briefs/2005/1001-1200/05-1186_JurisIni.pdf. Scroll to the bottom of page 9 and read "II Strict Application of the 'Mirror Image Rule' Produces Harsh and Inequitable Results" on pages 9 and 10 and read the "Conclusion" on page 10.

Endnotes

1. *Rebstock v. Birthright Oil & Gas Co.*, 406 So.2d 636, **Web** 1981 La.App. Lexis 5242 (Court of Appeal of Louisiana).
2. *Restatement (Second) of Contracts*, Section 1.
3. *Restatement (Second) of Contracts*, Section 1.
4. *Restatement (Second) of Contracts*, Section 50(1).
5. *Hamer v. Sidwa*, 124 N.Y. 538, 27 N.E. 256, **Web** 1891 N.Y. Lexis 1396 (Court of Appeal of New York).

Performance and Breach of Traditional and E-Contracts

CARS FOR SALE
The history of car sales has generated many cases of contracts tainted by mistake and fraud.

Learning Objectives

After studying this chapter, you should be able to:

1. Explain genuineness of assent.
2. List and describe the contracts that must be in writing, according to the Statute of Frauds.
3. Describe the performance of traditional contracts and e-contracts.
4. Describe compensatory, consequential, and liquidated damages.
5. Define the equitable remedies of specific performance, reformation, and injunction.

Chapter Outline

" *Freedom of contract begins where equality of bargaining power begins.* "

—Oliver Wendell Holmes, Jr.
June 4, 1928

Introduction to Performance and Breach of Traditional and E-Contracts

Once a contract is formed, the parties owe a duty to perform it, whether it is a traditional contract or an e-contract. Certain defenses or events may discharge a party's duty to perform. If a party has an enforceable duty to perform but fails to do so, there is a breach of the traditional contract or e-contract. The nonbreaching party can sue to recover certain remedies, including monetary damages or nonmonetary remedies, depending on the circumstances of the case.

This chapter covers the topics of genuineness of assent, the writing requirements of the Statute of Frauds, contract performance, discharge of performance, breach of contract, and remedies for breach of contract.

The meaning of words varies according to the circumstances of and concerning which they are used.

Justice Blackburn
Allgood v. Blake (1873)

Genuineness of Assent

Voluntary assent by the parties is necessary to create an enforceable contract. One of the primary defenses to the enforcement of a contract is that the assent of one or both of the parties to the contract was not genuine or real. A contract may not be enforced if the assent of one or both of the parties to the contract was not genuine or real.

Genuineness assent may be missing because a party entered into a contract based on *mistake*, *fraudulent misrepresentation*, *duress*, or *undue influence*. Problems concerning **genuineness of assent** are discussed in this chapter.

genuineness of assent
The requirement that a party's assent to a contract be genuine.

Unilateral Mistake

In a **unilateral mistake**, only one party is mistaken about a material fact regarding the subject matter of the contract. In most cases of unilateral mistake, the mistaken party will not be permitted to rescind the contract. The contract will be enforced on its terms.

Example If a buyer contracts to purchase a new automobile while thinking that there is a V-8 engine in the automobile when in fact there is a V-6 engine in the automobile, this unilateral mistake does not excuse the buyer from the contract.

unilateral mistake
A mistake in which only one party is mistaken about a material fact regarding the subject matter of a contract.

Mutual Mistake of a Material Fact

A party may rescind a contract if there has been a **mutual mistake of a material fact**.[1] A **material fact** is a fact that is important to the subject matter of a contract. An ambiguity in a contract may constitute a mutual mistake of a material fact. An ambiguity occurs where a word or term in the contract is susceptible to more than one logical interpretation. If there has been a mutual mistake, the contract may be rescinded on the grounds that no contract has been formed because there has been no "meeting of the minds" between the parties.

Example In the celebrated case *Raffles v. Wichelhaus*,[2] which has become better known as the case of the good ship *Peerless*, the parties agreed on a sale of cotton that was to be delivered from Bombay by the ship. There were two ships named *Peerless*, however, and each party, in agreeing to the sale, was referring to a different ship. Because the sailing times of the two ships were materially different, neither party was willing to agree to shipment by the other *Peerless*. The court ruled that there was no binding contract because each party had a different ship in mind when the contract was formed.

mutual mistake of a material fact
A mistake made by both parties concerning a material fact that is important to the subject matter of a contract.

Words are chameleons, which reflect the color of their environment.

Justice L. Hand
Commissioner v. National Carbide Co. (1948)

Mutual Mistake of Value

mutual mistake of value
A mistake that occurs if both parties know the object of the contract but are mistaken as to its value.

A **mutual mistake of value** exists if both parties know the object of the contract but are mistaken as to its value. Here, the contract remains enforceable by either party because the identity of the subject matter of the contract is not at issue. If the rule were different, almost all contracts could later be rescinded by the party who got the "worst" of the deal.

Example Helen cleans her attic and finds a red and green silkscreen painting of a tomato soup can. She has no use for the painting, so she offers to sell it to Qian for $100. Qian, who thinks that the painting is "cute," accepts the offer and pays Helen $100. It is latter discovered that the painting is worth $2 million because it was painted by the famous American pop artist Andy Warhol. Neither party knew this at the time of contracting. It is a mistake of value. Helen cannot recover the painting.

Fraud

A misrepresentation occurs when an assertion is made that is not in accord with the facts.[3] An intentional misrepresentation occurs when one person consciously decides to induce another person to rely and act on a misrepresentation. **Intentional misrepresentation** is commonly referred to as **fraudulent misrepresentation**, or **fraud**. When fraudulent misrepresentation is used to induce another to enter into a contract, the innocent party's assent to the contract is not genuine, and the contract is voidable by the innocent party.[4] The innocent party can either rescind the contract and obtain restitution or enforce the contract and sue for contract damages.

intentional misrepresentation (fraudulent misrepresentation or fraud)
An event that occurs when one person consciously decides to induce another person to rely and act on a misrepresentation.

To prove fraud, the following elements must be shown.

1. **Misrepresentation of a material fact.**   To prove fraud, the wrongdoer must have made a false representation of material fact. A **misrepresentation of a material fact** by the wrongdoer may occur by words (oral or written) or by the conduct of a party. To be actionable as fraud, the misrepresentation must be of a past or existing *material fact*. This means that the misrepresentation must have been a significant factor in inducing the innocent party to enter into the contract. It need not have been the sole factor. Statements of opinion or predictions about the future generally do not form the basis for fraud.

2. **Intent to deceive.**   To prove fraud, the wrongdoer must have intended to deceive the innocent party. To prove that a person intended to deceive an innocent party, the person making the misrepresentation must have either had knowledge that the representation was false or made it without sufficient knowledge of the truth. This is called **scienter ("guilty mind")**. The misrepresentation must have been made with the **intent to deceive** the innocent party. Intent can be inferred from the circumstances.

scienter ("guilty mind")
Knowledge that a representation is false or that it was made without sufficient knowledge of the truth.

3. **Reliance on the misrepresentation.**   To prove fraud, the innocent party must have justifiably relied on the misrepresentation. A misrepresentation is not actionable unless the innocent party to whom the misrepresentation was made relied on the misrepresentation and acted on it. An innocent party who acts in **reliance on a misrepresentation** must justify his or her reliance. Justifiable reliance is generally found unless the innocent party knew that the misrepresentation was false or was so extravagant as to be obviously false.

4. **Injury to the innocent party.**   To prove fraud, the innocent party must have been injured. To recover damages, the innocent party must prove that the fraud caused him or her **economic injury**. The measure of damages is the difference between the value of the property as represented and the actual value of the property. This measure of damages gives the innocent party the "benefit of the bargain." In the alternative, the buyer can rescind the contract and recover the purchase price.

A charge of fraud is such a terrible thing to bring against a man that it cannot be maintained in any court unless it is shown that he had a wicked mind.

M. R. Lord Esher
Le Lievre v. Gould (1732)

Example Lyle tells Candice that he is forming a partnership to invest in drilling for oil in an oil field and invites her to invest in this venture. In reality, there is no oil field, and Lyle intends to use whatever money he receives from Candice for his personal expenses. Candice relies on Lyle's statements and invests $30,000 with Lyle. Lyle absconds with Candice's $30,000 investment. Here, there has been fraud in the inducement. Candice has been induced to give Lyle $30,000 based on Lyle's misrepresentation of fact. Candice can rescind the contract and recover the money from Lyle, if she can find him and locate his money or property.

Individuals must be on guard in their commercial and personal dealings so as not to be defrauded. Basically, something sounding "too good to be true" is a signal that the situation might be fraudulent. Although the law permits a victim of fraud to rescind the contract and recover damages from the wrongdoer, often the wrongdoer cannot be found or the money has been spent.

In the following case, the court found fraud and awarded punitive damages.

CASE 10.1   *Fraud*

Krysa v. Payne
176 S.W.3d 150, Web 2005 Mo.App. Lexis 1680 (2005)
Court of Appeals of Missouri

"Punitive damages differ from compensatory damages in that compensatory damages are intended to redress the concrete loss that the plaintiff has suffered by reason of the defendant's wrongful conduct, while the well-established purpose of punitive damages is to inflict punishment and to serve as an example and a deterrent to similar conduct."

—Ellis, Judge

Facts

Frank and Shelly Krysa were shopping for a truck to pull their 18-foot trailer. During the course of their search, they visited Payne's Car Company, a used car dealership owned by Emmett Payne. Kemp Crane, a used car salesman, showed the Krysas around the car lot. The Krysas saw an F-350 truck that they were interested in purchasing. Crane told the Krysas that the truck would tow their trailer and that the truck would make it to 400,000 miles, and that it was "a one-owner trade-in." The Krysas took the truck for a test drive and decided to purchase the truck. The Krysas, who had to borrow some of the money from Mrs. Krysa's mother, paid for the truck and took possession.

Later that day, the Krysas noticed that the power locks did not work on the truck. A few days later, the truck took three hours to start. The heater was not working. Mr. Krysa tried to fix some problems and noticed that the radiator was smashed up, the radiator cap did not have a seal, and the thermostat was missing. Mr. Krysa noticed broken glass on the floor underneath the front seats and that the driver's side window had been replaced. Shortly thereafter, Mr. Krysa attempted to tow his trailer, but within 2 miles, he had his foot to the floor trying to get the truck to pull the trailer. A large amount of smoke was pouring out of the back of the truck. Mr. Krysa also noticed that the truck was consuming a lot of oil. Mr. Krysa obtained a CARFAX report for the truck, which showed that the truck had had thirteen prior owners. Evidence proved that the truck was actually two halves of different trucks that had been welded together. An automobile expert told the Krysas not to drive the truck because it was unsafe.

Mr. Krysa went back to the dealership to return the truck and get his money back. Payne told Krysa that he would credit the purchase price of the truck toward the purchase of one of the other vehicles on the lot but that he would not give Krysa his money back. Krysa could not find another vehicle on Payne's used car lot that would suit his needs. The Krysas sued Payne for fraudulent nondisclosure and fraudulent misrepresentation, and they sought to recover compensatory and punitive damages. The jury returned a verdict for the Krysas and awarded them $18,449 in compensatory damages and $500,000 in punitive damages. Payne appealed the award of punitive damages.

(continued)

Issue

Has Payne engaged in fraudulent nondisclosure, fraudulent misrepresentation, and reckless disregard for the safety of the Krysas and the public to support the award of $500,000 in punitive damages?

Language of the Court

Punitive damages differ from compensatory damages in that compensatory damages are intended to redress the concrete loss that the plaintiff has suffered by reason of the defendant's wrongful conduct, while the well-established purpose of punitive damages is to inflict punishment and to serve as an example and a deterrent to similar conduct. While the damage actually sustained by the Krysas was relatively small and was economic in nature, the record clearly supports a finding that Payne acted indifferently to or in reckless disregard of the safety of the Krysas in selling them a vehicle that he knew or should have known was not safe to drive and that the potential harm to the Krysas was much greater than the harm that was actually incurred.

The evidence also supported a finding that the harm sustained by Krysas was the result of intentional malice, trickery, or deceit, and was not merely an accident. Payne had a significant amount of work done to the vehicle to make it appear to be in good shape. Thus, in society's eyes, viewing the totality of the circumstances, Payne's conduct can only be seen as exhibiting a very high degree of reprehensibility.

Decision

The court of appeals found that Payne's fraudulent concealment, fraudulent misrepresentation, and reckless disregard for the safety of the Krysas and the public justified the award of $500,000 in punitive damages to the Krysas.

Case Questions

Critical Legal Thinking

What is fraudulent concealment? What is fraudulent misrepresentation?

Ethics

Did Payne, the used car dealer, act ethically in this case? Should punitive damages have been awarded in this case? Why or why not?

Contemporary Business

Do you have any apprehension about purchasing a car from a used car dealership? Why or why not?

Duress

duress
A situation in which a party threatens to do a wrongful act unless another party enters into a contract.

Duress occurs when one party threatens to do some wrongful act unless another party enters into a contract. If a party to a contract has been forced into making the contract, the assent is not voluntary. Such a contract is not enforceable against the innocent party. The threat to commit physical harm or extortion unless someone enters into a contract constitutes duress.

Undue Influence

undue influence
A situation in which one person takes advantage of another person's mental, emotional, or physical weakness and unduly persuades that person to enter into a contract; the persuasion by the wrongdoer must overcome the free will of the innocent party.

The courts may permit the rescission of a contract based on the equitable doctrine of **undue influence**. Undue influence occurs when one person (the **dominant party**) takes advantage of another person's mental, emotional, or physical weakness and unduly persuades that person (the **servient party**) to enter into a contract. The persuasion by the wrongdoer must overcome the free will of the innocent party. A contract that is entered into because of undue influence is voidable by the innocent party.[5]

Example Mr. Johnson, who is 70 years old, has a stroke and is partially paralyzed. He is required to use a wheelchair, and he needs constant nursing care. Prior to his stroke, Mr. Johnson had executed a will, leaving his property upon his death equally to his four grandchildren. Edward, a licensed nurse, is hired to care for Mr. Johnson on a daily basis, and Mr. Johnson relies on Edward's care. Edward works for Mr. Johnson for two years before Mr. Johnson passes away. It is later discovered that Mr. Johnson had executed a written contract with Edward three months before he died, deeding a valuable piece of real estate to Edward. If it is shown that Edward has used his dominant

GOLDEN PAVILION, KYOTO, JAPAN
In some countries of the world, such as Japan, China, Korea, Vietnam, and other countries of Asia, individuals often follow the tradition of using a seal as their signature. The seal is a character or set of characters carved onto one end of a cylinder-shaped stamp—made out of ivory, stone, metal, wood, plastic, or other material. A party places the end bearing the characters in ink and then applies this end to the document to be signed, leaving an ink imprint that serves as the party's signature. Government agencies and corporations often use seals on contracts. Seals are usually registered with the government. Today, however, such seals are being replaced by hand-applied signatures in many commercial transactions.

and fiduciary position to unduly influence Mr. Johnson to enter into this contract, then the contract is invalid. If no undue influence is shown, the contract with Edward is valid, and Edward will receive the property deeded to him by Mr. Johnson.

A verbal contract isn't worth the paper it's written on.
Samuel Goldwyn

Statute of Frauds

Today, every U.S. state has enacted a **Statute of Frauds** that requires certain types of contracts to be in *writing*. This statute is intended to ensure that the terms of important contracts are not forgotten, misunderstood, or fabricated. One court stated about the Statute of Frauds, "It is the purpose of the Statute of Frauds to suppress fraud, i.e., cooked-up claims of agreement, sometimes fathered by wish, sometimes imagined in the light of subsequent events, and sometimes simply conjured up."[6]

Generally, an **executory contract** that is not in writing even though the Statute of Frauds requires it to be in writing is unenforceable by either party. (If the contract is valid in all other respects, however, it may be voluntarily performed by the parties.) The Statute of Frauds is usually raised by one party as a defense to the enforcement of the contract by the other party.

If an oral contract that should have been in writing under the Statute of Frauds is already executed, neither party can seek to **rescind** the contract on the grounds of noncompliance with the Statute of Frauds. Contracts that are required to be in writing under the Statute of Frauds are discussed in the following paragraphs.

Statute of Frauds
A state statute that requires certain types of contracts to be in writing.

Statute of Frauds: That unfortunate statute, the misguided application of which has been the cause of so many frauds.

Bacon, Viscount
Morgan v. Worthington (1878)

Contracts Involving Interests in Real Property

Under the Statute of Frauds, any contract that transfers an ownership interest in **real property** must be in writing to be enforceable. Real property includes the land itself, buildings, trees, soil, minerals, timber, plants, crops, fixtures, and things permanently affixed to the land or buildings. Certain items of personal property that are permanently affixed to the real property are fixtures that become part of the real property.

real property
Land itself, as well as buildings, trees, soil, minerals, timber, plants, crops, fixtures and other things permanently affixed to the land or buildings.

Example Built-in cabinets in a house are *fixtures* that become part of the real property.

Other contracts that transfer an ownership interest in land must be in writing under the Statute of Frauds. These interests include mortgages, leases for a term over one year, and express easements.

Doctrine of Part Performance   The courts have developed the equitable doctrine of **part performance**. This doctrine allows the court to order such an oral contract to be specifically performed if performance is necessary to avoid injustice. For this performance exception to apply, most courts require that the purchaser either pay part of the purchase price and take possession of the property or make valuable improvements on the property.

Example Mr. Smith owns a farm. Mr. Smith has two children, Mary and Joe. Joe has moved to the city, become a lawyer, and practices law. When Mary is about to leave home and move to the city, Mr. Smith says to her "Mary, if you stay here and work the farm with me, I will give you the farm when I die." Mary relies on this promise and helps work the farm for five years before Mr. Smith dies. When Mr. Smith's will is read, he leaves the farm to Joe. In this situation, even though Mr. Smith's promise to Mary was oral, and normally not enforceable under the Statute of Frauds, the court will apply the equitable doctrine of part performance and award the farm to Mary.

Agents' Contracts

Many state Statutes of Frauds require that **agents' contracts** to sell real property covered by the Statute of Frauds be in writing to be enforceable. The requirement is often referred to as the **equal dignity rule**. Some state Statutes of Frauds expressly state that the real estate broker and agents' contracts must be in writing.

Example Under this rule, real estate broker contracts must be in writing.

One-Year Rule

According to the Statute of Frauds, an executory contract that cannot be performed by its own terms within one year of its formation must be in writing.[7] This **one-year rule** is intended to prevent disputes about contract terms that may otherwise occur toward the end of a long-term contract. If the performance of the contract is possible within the one-year period, the contract may be oral. The extension of an oral contract might cause the contract to violate the Statute of Frauds if the original term and the extension period exceed one year.

Guaranty Contract

A **guaranty contract** occurs when one person agrees to answer for the debts or duties of another person. Guaranty contracts are required to be in writing under the Statute of Frauds.[8] In a guaranty situation, there are at least three parties and two contracts. The *first contract*, which is known as the **original contract**, or **primary contract**, is between the debtor and the creditor. It does not have to be in writing (unless another provision of the Statute of Frauds requires it to be). The *second contract*, called the *guaranty contract*, is between the person who agrees to pay the debt if the primary debtor does not (i.e., the **guarantor**) and the original creditor. The guarantor's liability is secondary because it does not arise unless the party primarily liable fails to perform.

UCC Contract for the Sale or Lease of Goods

Section 2-201(1) of the Uniform Commercial Code (UCC) is the basic Statute of Frauds provision for **sales contracts**. It states that contracts for the sale of goods

Don't get it right, just get it written.

James Thurber

part performance
An equitable doctrine that allows the court to order an oral contract for the sale of land or transfer of another interest in real property to be specifically performed if it has been partially performed and performance is necessary to avoid injustice.

Most of the disputes in the world arise from words.

Lord Mansfield, C. J.
Morgan v. Jones (1773)

equal dignity rule
A rule which says that agents' contracts to sell property covered by the Statute of Frauds must be in writing to be enforceable.

one-year rule
A rule which states that an executory contract that cannot be performed by its own terms within one year of its formation must be in writing.

guaranty contract
A promise in which one person agrees to answer for the debts or duties of another person. It is a contract between the guarantor and the original creditor.

guarantor
A person who agrees to pay a debt if the primary debtor does not.

Section 2-201(1) of the Uniform Commercial Code (UCC)
A section of the Uniform Commercial Code (UCC) which states that sales contracts for the sale of goods costing $500 or more must be in writing.

costing *$500 or more* must be in writing to be enforceable. (Revised Article 2 raises this amount to $5,000.) If the contract price of an original sales contract is below $500, it does not have to be in writing under the **UCC Statute of Frauds**. However, if a *modification* of the sales contract increases the sales price to $500 or more, the modification has to be in writing to be enforceable.

Section 2A-201(1) of the UCC is the Statute of Frauds provision that applies to the lease of goods. It states that **lease contracts** involving payments of *$1,000 or more* must be in writing. (Revised Article 2A raises this amount to $20,000.) If a lease payment of an original lease contract is less than $1,000, it does not have to be in writing under the UCC Statute of Frauds. However, if a *modification* of the lease contract increases the lease payment to $1,000 or more, the modification has to be in writing to be enforceable.

Formality of the Writing

Some written commercial contracts are long, detailed documents that have been negotiated by the parties and drafted and reviewed by their lawyers. Others are preprinted forms with blanks that can be filled in to fit the facts of a particular situation.

A written contract does not, however, have to be either drafted by a lawyer or formally typed to be legally binding. Generally, the law only requires a writing containing the essential terms of the parties' agreement. Thus, any writing—including letters, telegrams, invoices, sales receipts, checks, and handwritten agreements written on scraps of paper—can be an enforceable contract under this rule.

Required Signature

The Statute of Frauds and the UCC require a written contract, whatever its form, to be signed *by the party against whom enforcement is sought*. The signature of the person who is enforcing the contract is not necessary. Thus, a written contract may be enforceable against one party but not the other party. Generally, the signature may appear anywhere on the writing. In addition, it does not have to be a person's full legal name. The signature may be affixed by an authorized agent.

Examples The person's last name, first name, nickname, initials, seal, stamp, engraving, or other symbol or mark (e.g., an *X*) that indicates the person's intent can be binding.

Parol Evidence Rule

By the time a contract is reduced to writing, the parties usually have engaged in prior or contemporaneous discussions and negotiations or exchanged prior writings. Any oral or written words outside the *four corners* of the written contract are called **parol evidence**. *Parol* means "word."

The **parol evidence rule** states that if a written contract is a complete and final statement of the parties' agreement (i.e., a **complete integration**), any prior or contemporaneous oral or written statements that alter, contradict, or are in addition to the terms of the written contract are inadmissible in any court proceeding concerning the contract.[9]

The parties to a written contract may include a clause stipulating that the contract is a complete integration and the exclusive expression of their agreement and that parol evidence may not be introduced to explain, alter, contradict, or add to the terms of the contract. This type of clause, called a **merger clause**, or an **integration clause**, expressly reiterates the parol evidence rule.

Section 2A-201(1) of the UCC
A section of the Uniform Commercial Code (UCC), which states that lease contracts involving payments of $1,000 or more must be in writing.

To break an oral agreement which is not legally binding is morally wrong.

Bava Metzi'a
The Talmud

John Hancock's bold signature on the U.S. Declaration of Independence is one of the most famous signatures in history.

Counsel Randle Jackson: In the book of nature, my lords, it is written— Lord Ellenborough: Will you have the goodness to mention the page, sir, if you please?

Lord Campbell
Lives of the Chief Justices (1857)

parol evidence
Any oral or written words outside the four corners of a written contract.

parol evidence rule
A rule that says if a written contract is a complete and final statement of the parties' agreement, any prior or contemporaneous oral or written statements that alter, contradict, or are in addition to the terms of the written contract are inadmissible in court regarding a dispute over the contract. There are several exceptions to this rule.

merger clause (integration clause)
A clause in a contract which stipulates that it is a complete integration and the exclusive expression of the parties' agreement.

In the following case, the court refused to admit parol evidence and enforced the express terms of a written contract.

CASE 10.2 *Parol Evidence Rule*

Yarde Metals, Inc. v. New England Patriots Limited Partnership

834 N.E.2d 1233, Web 2005 Mass. App. Lexis 904 (2005)
Appeals Court of Massachusetts

"The purchase of a ticket to a sports or entertainment event typically creates nothing more than a revocable license."

—Greenberg, Judge

Facts

Yarde Metals, Inc. (Yarde), was a season ticket holder to New England Patriots professional home football games. The football team is owned by the New England Patriots Limited Partnership (Patriots). Yarde permitted a business associate to attend a Patriots game. However, the associate was ejected from the game for disorderly conduct. Subsequently, the Patriots sent Yarde a letter terminating his season ticket privileges in the future. Yarde sued the Patriots, claiming that the Patriots had breached his implied contractual right to purchase season tickets. The Patriots countered that the Patriots's written contract with season ticket holders expressly provided that the "purchase of season tickets does not entitle purchaser to renewal in a subsequent year." The Patriots asserted that because the contract with Yarde was an express written contract, Yarde's claim of an implied right to purchase season tickets in the future was parol evidence and was inadmissible to change the express terms of the contract. The trial court dismissed Yarde's case. Yarde appealed.

Issue

Does Yarde have an implied right to purchase Patriots' season tickets?

Language of the Court

The purchase of a ticket to a sports or entertainment event typically creates nothing more
than a revocable license. Where there is a seemingly clear transaction—Yarde purchased tickets to ten games—we cannot infer an annual renewal right. More importantly, such a theory would disregard the Patriots' express disclaimers of any right of the purchaser to renew in subsequent years printed on game tickets and informational material provided to season ticket holders. The ticket specifically stated that "purchase of season tickets does not entitle purchaser to renewal in a subsequent year." Parol evidence is not generally admissible to vary the unambiguous terms of the contract. Yarde has articulated no basis on which we can ignore the language on the ticket.

Decision

The appeals court held that there was an express written contract between Yarde and the Patriots, and that the parol evidence rule prevented Yarde's alleged implied right to purchase season tickets from becoming part of that contract. The appeals court affirmed the trial court's dismissal of Yarde's case.

Case Questions

Critical Legal Thinking
What is the parol evidence rule?

Ethics
Was it ethical for the Patriots to terminate Yarde's season ticket privileges? Was there good cause to do so?

Contemporary Business
What would be the consequences if there were no parol evidence rule?

Third-Party Rights

An honest man's word is as good as his bond.

Don Quixote

Third parties acquire rights under other people's contracts in two situations: (1) as *assignees* to whom rights are subsequently transferred and (2) as *intended third-party beneficiaries* to whom the contracting parties intended to give rights under the contract at the time of contracting.

Assignment

In many cases, the parties to a contract can transfer their rights under the contract to other parties. The transfer of contractual rights is called an **assignment of rights** or just an **assignment**.

A party who owes a duty of performance pursuant to a contract is called the **obligor**. A party who is owed a right under a contract is called the **obligee**. An obligee who transfers the right to receive performance is called an **assignor**. The party to whom the right has been transferred is called the **assignee**. The assignee can assign the right to yet another person (called a **subsequent assignee**, or **subassignee**).

Generally, no formalities are required for a valid assignment of rights. Although the assignor often uses the word *assign*, other words or terms, such as *sell*, *transfer*, *convey*, and *give*, are sufficient to indicate intent to transfer a contract right.

Example A person who is owed money by a debtor has a *right*—the right to be paid. The person who is owed the money can assign this right to another party.

assignment of rights (assignment)
The transfer of contractual rights by an obligee to another party.

assignor
An obligee who transfers a right.

assignee
A party to whom a right has been transferred.

Make fair agreements and stick to them.

Confucius

Intended Third-Party Beneficiary

When parties enter into a contract, they can agree that the performance of one of the parties should be rendered to or should directly benefit a third party. Under such circumstances, the third party is called an **intended third-party beneficiary**. An intended third-party beneficiary can enforce the contract against the party who promised to render performance.[10]

Example The person named as the beneficiary in another's life insurance policy is an intended beneficiary. If the insured dies and the life insurance company refuses to pay the beneficiary, the beneficiary can sue the life insurance company to recover the death benefits.

In many instances, the parties to a contract unintentionally benefit a third party when a contract is performed. In such situations, the third party is referred to as an **incidental beneficiary**. An incidental beneficiary has no rights to enforce or sue under other people's contracts.

Often, the courts are asked to decide whether a third party is an intended or an incidental beneficiary, as in the following case.

intended third-party beneficiary
A third party who is not in privity of contract but who has rights under the contract and can enforce the contract against the promisor.

That what is agreed to be done, must be considered as done.

Lord Chancellor
Lord Hardwicke
Guidot v. Guidot (1745)

incidental beneficiary
A party who is unintentionally benefited by other people's contracts.

CASE 10.3 *Third-Party Beneficiary*

Does I–XI, Workers in China, Bangladesh, Indonesia, Swaziland, and Nicaragua v. Walmart Stores, Inc.

572 F.3d. 677, Web 2009 U.S. App. Lexis 15279 (2009)
United States Court of Appeals for the Ninth Circuit

"Because, as we view the supply contracts, Walmart made no promise to monitor the suppliers, no such promise flows to plaintiffs as third-party beneficiaries."

—Gould, Circuit Judge

Facts

Walmart Stores, Inc., owns and operates a chain of large "big box" discount department and warehouse stores; it is the largest company in the United States. Walmart is also the largest importer in the United States of foreign-produced goods. Walmart developed a code of conduct for its foreign suppliers entitled "Standards for Suppliers" (Standards). These Standards require foreign suppliers to adhere to local law and local industry working conditions, such as those related to pay, hiring forced labor, child labor, and discrimination. These Standards

(continued)

are incorporated into Walmart's supply contracts with foreign suppliers. The Standards provide that Walmart may make onsite inspections of production facilities and permit Walmart to cancel orders with, or terminate, any foreign supplier that fails to comply with the Standards.

Workers at foreign suppliers in China, Bangladesh, Indonesia, Swaziland, and Nicaragua who produced and sold goods to Walmart sued Walmart in U.S. District Court. The foreign workers alleged that they were third-party beneficiaries to Walmart's contract with its foreign suppliers and that they were due damages for Walmart's breach of the Standards. They alleged that their employers regularly violated the Standards and that Walmart failed to investigate working conditions at foreign suppliers, knew that the Standards were being violated, and failed to enforce the Standards contained in these contracts. The U.S. District Court held that the plaintiffs were not intended third-party beneficiaries to Walmart's contracts with its foreign suppliers and dismissed their lawsuit. The plaintiffs appealed.

Issue
Are the foreign workers intended third-party beneficiaries under Walmart's contracts with its foreign suppliers?

Language of the Court
> Plaintiffs rely on this language in the Standards: "Walmart will undertake affirmative measures, such as on-site inspection of production facilities, to implement and monitor said standards." We agree with the district court that this language does not create a duty on the part of Walmart to monitor

the suppliers, and does not provide plaintiffs a right of action against Walmart as third-party beneficiaries. The language and structure of the agreement show that Walmart reserved the right to inspect the suppliers, but did not adopt a duty to inspect them. Because, as we view the supply contracts, Walmart made no promise to monitor the suppliers, no such promise flows to plaintiffs as third-party beneficiaries. Plaintiffs' allegations are insufficient to support the conclusion that Walmart and the suppliers intended for plaintiffs to have a right of performance against Walmart under the supply contracts.

Decision
The U.S. Court of Appeals held that the plaintiff foreign workers were not intended third-party beneficiaries to Walmart's contracts with its foreign suppliers. The U.S. Court of Appeals affirmed the dismissal of the plaintiff's case.

Case Questions

Critical Legal Thinking
Did Walmart's Standards provide much protection to foreign workers? Why or why not?

Ethics
Should Walmart require that its foreign suppliers provide the same protections to their workers as are required in the United States?

Contemporary Business
Why do Walmart and other U.S. companies purchase goods they sell from foreign suppliers? Are such purchases likely to slow down or accelerate in the future?

Covenants and Conditions

In contracts, parties make certain promises to each other. These promises may be classified as *covenants* or *conditions*. The difference between them is discussed in the following paragraphs.

Covenant

covenant
An unconditional promise to perform.

A **covenant** is an *unconditional* promise to perform. Nonperformance of a covenant is a breach of contract that gives the other party the right to sue. The majority of provisions in contracts are covenants.

Example Seed Company borrows $400,000 from Rural Bank and signs a promissory note to repay the $400,000 plus 10 percent interest in one year. This promise is a covenant. That is, it is an unconditional promise to perform.

Conditions of Performance

A **conditional promise** (or **qualified promise**) is not as definite as a covenant. The promisor's duty to perform or not perform arises only if the **condition** does or does not occur.[11] A conditional promise becomes a covenant if the condition is met, however.

Generally, contract language such as *if, on condition that, provided that, when, after,* and *as soon as* indicate a condition. A single contract may contain numerous conditions that trigger or excuse performance. Two types of conditions are:

- **Condition precedent.** If a contract requires the occurrence (or nonoc-currence) of an event *before* a party is obligated to perform a contractual duty, this is a **condition precedent**. The happening (or nonhappening) of the event triggers the contract or duty of performance. If the event does not occur, no duty to perform the contract arises because there is a failure of condition.

  Example A company offers a college senior a job but makes it a condition of employ-ment that the college student graduate; otherwise, the company will not hire her. The student must graduate, or the company does not have to hire her.

- **Condition subsequent.** A **condition subsequent** exists when there is a con-dition in a contract that provides that the occurrence or nonoccurrence of a specific event automatically excuses the performance of an existing duty to perform. That is, failure to meet the condition subsequent relieves the other party from obligation under the contract.

  Example An employee's contract stipulates that he can be fired if he fails a drug test. If the employee fails a drug test, the employer can fire him.

condition
A qualification of a promise that becomes a covenant if it is met. There are three types of conditions: conditions precedent, conditions subsequent, and concurrent conditions.

condition precedent
A condition that requires the occur-rence of an event before a party is obligated to perform a duty under a contract.

condition subsequent
A condition whose occurrence or nonoccurrence of a specific event automatically excuses the perfor-mance of an existing contractual duty to perform.

Discharge of Performance

A party's duty to perform under a contract may be discharged by *mutual agree-ment* of the parties or by *impossibility of performance*. These methods of discharge are discussed in the paragraphs that follow.

Discharge by Agreement

The parties to a contract may mutually agree to **discharge** their contractual du-ties under a contract. The different methods for discharging a contract by mutual agreement are:

- **Mutual rescission.** If a contract is wholly or partially executory on both sides, the parties can agree to rescind (i.e., cancel) the contract. **Mutual rescission** requires parties to enter into a second agreement that expressly terminates the first one.
- **Novation.** A **novation agreement** (commonly called **novation**) substitutes a third party for one of the original contracting parties. The new substituted party is obligated to perform a contract. All three parties must agree to the substitution. In a novation, the exiting party is relieved of liability on the contract.
- **Accord and satisfaction.** The parties to a contract may agree to settle a contract dispute by an **accord and satisfaction**. The agreement whereby the parties agree to accept something different in satisfaction of the original contract is called an *accord*.[12] The performance of an accord is called a *satisfaction*. An accord does not discharge the original contract. It only sus-pends it until the accord is performed. Satisfaction of the accord discharges

It is a vain thing to imagine a right without a remedy: for want of right and want of remedy are reciprocal.

Lord Chief Justice Holt
Ashby v. White (1703)

both the original contract and the accord. If an accord is not satisfied when it is due, the aggrieved party may enforce either the accord or the original contract.

Discharge by Impossibility of Performance

impossibility of performance (objective impossibility)
Nonperformance that is excused if a contract becomes impossible to perform. It must be objective impossibility, not subjective.

Under certain circumstances, the nonperformance of contractual duties is excused—that is, discharged—because of *impossibility of performance*. **Impossibility of performance** (or **objective impossibility**) occurs if a contract becomes impossible to perform.[13] The impossibility must be objective impossibility ("it cannot be done") rather than subjective impossibility ("I cannot do it").

The following types of objective impossibility excuse nonperformance: the death or incapacity of the promisor prior to the performance of a personal service contract, the destruction of the subject matter of a contract prior to performance, and a supervening illegality that makes performance of the contract illegal.

Force Majeure Clause

force majeure clause
A clause in a contract in which the parties specify certain events that will excuse nonperformance.

The parties may agree in a contract that certain events will excuse nonperformance of the contract. These clauses are called ***force majeure* clauses**.

Example A *force majeure* clause usually excuses nonperformance caused by natural disasters such as floods, tornadoes, earthquakes, and such. Modern clauses also often excuse performance due to labor strikes, shortages of raw materials, and the like.

Men keep their agreements when it is an advantage to both parties not to break them.

Solon (c. 600 B.C.)

Breach of Contract

breach of contract
A contracting party's failure to perform an absolute duty owed under a contract.

There are three types of performance of a contract: (1) *complete performance*, (2) *substantial performance (or minor breach)*, and (3) *inferior performance (or material breach)*. A **breach of contract** occurs if one or both of the parties do not perform their duties as specified in the contract. These concepts are discussed in the following paragraphs.

Complete Performance

complete performance (strict performance)
A situation in which a party to a contract renders performance exactly as required by the contract. Complete performance discharges that party's obligations under the contract.

Most contracts are discharged by the **complete performance**, or **strict performance**, of the contracting parties. Complete performance occurs when a party to a contract renders performance exactly as required by the contract. A fully performed contract is called an **executed contract**. **Tender of performance** (or **tender**) also discharges a party's contractual obligations. Tender is an unconditional and absolute offer by a contracting party to perform his or her obligations under the contract.

tender of performance (tender)
An unconditional and absolute offer by a contracting party to perform his or her obligations under a contract.

Example Ashley, who owns a women's retail store, contracts to purchase high-fashion blue jeans from a manufacturer for $75,000. At the time of performance, Ashley tenders the $75,000. Ashley has performed her obligation under the contract once she tenders the $75,000 to the manufacturer. Assume that the manufacturer tenders the jeans to Ashley when required to do so, and Ashley accepts the jeans. There is complete performance of the contract.

Substantial Performance (Minor Breach)

substantial performance
Performance by a contracting party that deviates only slightly from complete performance.

Substantial performance occurs when there has been a **minor breach** of contract. In other words, it occurs when a party to a contract renders performance that deviates slightly from complete performance. The nonbreaching party may try to convince the breaching party to elevate his or her performance to complete performance. If the breaching party does not correct the breach, the nonbreach-

minor breach
A breach that occurs when a party renders substantial performance of his or her contractual duties.

ing party can sue to recover *damages* by (1) deducting the cost to repair the defect from the contract price and remitting the balance to the breaching party or (2) suing the breaching party to recover the cost to repair the defect if the breaching party has already been paid.

Examples Donald Trump contracts with Big Apple Construction Co. to have Big Apple construct an office building for $100 million. The architectural plans call for installation of three-ply windows in the building. Big Apple constructs the building exactly to plan except that it installs two-ply windows. There has been substantial performance. It would cost $5 million to install the correct windows. If Big Apple agrees to replace the windows and does so, its performance is elevated to complete performance, and Trump must pay the entire contract price. However, if Trump has to hire someone else to replace the windows, he may deduct this cost of repair of $5 million from the contract price of $100 million and remit the difference of $95 million to Big Apple. If Trump has already paid the $100 million, and Big Apple refuses to install the proper windows, he can sue and recover the $5 million.

No cause of action arises from a bare promise.

Legal maxim

Inferior Performance (Material Breach)

A **material breach** of a contract occurs when a party renders **inferior performance** of his or her contractual obligations that impairs or destroys the essence of the contract. There is no clear line between a minor breach and a material breach. A determination must be made in each case.

Where there has been a material breach of contract, the nonbreaching party may *rescind* the contract and seek restitution of any compensation paid under the contract to the breaching party. **Rescission** is an action to undo a contract. The nonbreaching party is discharged from any further performance under the contract. Alternatively, the nonbreaching party may treat the contract as being in effect and sue the breaching party to recover *damages*.

material breach
A breach that occurs when a party renders inferior performance of his or her contractual duties.

inferior performance
A situation in which a party fails to perform express or implied contractual obligations and impairs or destroys the essence of a contract.

rescission
An action to rescind (undo) a contract.

Monetary Damages

Where there has been a breach of a contract, the nonbreaching party may recover **monetary damages** from a breaching party. Monetary damages are available whether the breach was minor or material. Monetary damages are sometimes referred to as **dollar damages**. Several types of monetary damages may be awarded. These include *compensatory, consequential,* and *liquidated nominal damages*, as discussed in the following paragraphs.

monetary damages (dollar damages)
An award of money.

The very definition of a good award is that it gives dissatisfaction to both parties.

Sir Thomas Plumer,
Master of the Rolls
Goodman v. Sayers (1820)

Compensatory Damages

Compensatory damages are intended to compensate a nonbreaching party for the loss of the bargain. In other words, they place the nonbreaching party in the same position as if the contract had been fully performed by restoring the "benefit of the bargain."

Example If a company hires an employee for three years at $100,000 per year but breaches the contract after one year, the employee can sue to recover two years' salary—$200,000—if she cannot find a comparable job.

Example Harriet contracts with a developer to build a house for her for $1 million. The developer has built in a $200,000 profit for himself in the contract—that is, it will cost him $800,000 to build the house. After the contractor has spent $100,000 in construction costs, Harriet breaches the contract and tells the builder to quit. Here, the builder can recover $300,000 from Harriet—the $100,000 construction costs plus the $200,000 profit he would have made. This result will make the contractor "whole."

compensatory damages
An award of money intended to compensate a nonbreaching party for the loss of the bargain. Compensatory damages place the nonbreaching party in the same position as if the contract had been fully performed by restoring the "benefit of the bargain."

Consequential Damages

consequential damages (special damages or foreseeable damages)
Foreseeable damages that arise from circumstances outside a contract. To be liable for these damages, the breaching party must know or have reason to know that the breach will cause special damages to the other party.

A nonbreaching party can sometimes recover **consequential damages**, or **special damages**, from the breaching party. Consequential damages are **foreseeable damages** that arise from circumstances outside a contract. To be liable for consequential damages, the breaching party must know or have reason to know that the breach will cause special damages to the other party. However, consequential damages are often disclaimed in a sales or license agreement. This means that the breaching party is not responsible to pay consequential damages.

Example A student installs a new software program on his computer that is licensed from a software company. The license price was $100. The software was installed, but it was defective. The software causes files in the computer, including the student's class notes, Ph.D. dissertation, and other valuable information, to be deleted. These were the only copies of the files. The student suffers a loss by having his only copies of these important materials deleted because of the newly installed software. These losses are consequential damages. However, the software license contains a disclaimer stating that the licensor is not liable for consequential damages. Therefore, the student cannot recover monetary damages for his consequential damages. The student can, however, recover $100 in compensatory damages for the license price he paid for the defective software.

Liquidated Damages

liquidated damages
Damages that parties to a contract agree in advance should be paid if the contract is breached.

Under certain circumstances, the parties to a contract may agree in advance to the amount of damages payable upon a breach of contract. These damages are called **liquidated damages**. To be lawful, the actual damages must be difficult or impracticable to determine, and the liquidated amount must be reasonable in the circumstances. An enforceable **liquidated damages clause** is an exclusive remedy, even if actual damages are later determined to be different.

Example Alaska Oil Company discovers a new rich oil field in the northernmost part of Alaska. Alaska Oil contracts to purchase special oil-drilling equipment from Tundra Equipment Corporation that is necessary to drill holes in the hard ground in the Alaska tundra. The contract states that the equipment is to be delivered by July 1, 2014. The parties know that Alaska Oil cannot start digging the oil holes until it receives this equipment. It is uncertain how great the oil flow will be from the drilled oil holes. The parties place in their contract a liquidated damages clause which states that Tundra Equipment will pay $20,000 per day in liquidated damages for each day after July 1, 2014, that the equipment is not delivered. This is an enforceable liquidated damages clause because actual damages are difficult to determine, and the liquidated amount is reasonable in the circumstances. Thus, if Tundra Equipment does not deliver the equipment until July 1, 2015, it owes Alaska Oil $7,300,000 (365 days × $20,000 per day).

A liquidated damages clause is considered a **penalty** if actual damages can be clearly determined in advance or if the liquidated damages are excessive or unconscionable. If a liquidated damages clause is found to be a penalty, it is unenforceable. The nonbreaching party may then recover actual damages.

Mitigation of Damages

mitigate
A nonbreaching party's legal duty to avoid or reduce damages caused by a breach of contract.

If a contract has been breached, the law places a duty on the innocent nonbreaching party to make reasonable efforts to **mitigate** (i.e., avoid or reduce) the resulting damages. The extent of mitigation required depends on the type of contract involved. If an employer breaches an employment contract, the employee owes a duty to mitigate damages by trying to find substitute employment. The employee is only required to accept *comparable employment*. The courts consider such factors as compensation, rank, status, job description, and geographical location in determining the comparability of jobs.

Example An actress is hired to play the leading female role in a romantic comedy to be filmed in New York City and is to be paid $10 million. The film company cancels the contract. The actress tries to find another role but is only offered a leading female role in a Western movie to be filmed in Death Valley, for which she is to be paid $10 million. Although the pay is the same, the actress does not have to accept this other job because it is not a comparable role. She can recover $10 million from the film company.

Equitable Remedies

Equitable remedies are available if there has been a breach of contract that cannot be adequately compensated through a legal remedy. These remedies are also available to prevent unjust enrichment. The most common equitable remedies are *specific performance*, *reformation*, and *injunction*, discussed in the following paragraphs.

equitable remedy
A remedy that is available if there has been a breach of contract that cannot be adequately compensated through a legal remedy or to prevent unjust enrichment.

Specific Performance

An award of **specific performance** orders the breaching party to perform the acts promised in a contract. The courts have the discretion to award this remedy if the subject matter of the contract is *unique*.

Examples Specific performance is available to enforce land contracts because every piece of real property is considered to be unique. Works of art, antiques, items of sentimental value, rare coins, stamps, heirlooms, and such also fit the requirement for uniqueness. Most other personal property does not.

Specific performance of personal service contracts is not granted because the courts would find it difficult or impracticable to supervise or monitor performance of such a contract.

Example A famous singer contracts to perform a concert but then refuses to appear. The promoters of the concert cannot obtain an order of specific performance to force the singer to perform.

specific performance
A remedy that orders the breaching party to perform the acts promised in the contract. Specific performance is usually awarded in cases in which the subject matter is unique, such as in contracts involving land, heirlooms, and paintings.

Reformation

Reformation is an equitable doctrine that permits the court to rewrite a contract to express the parties' true intentions. Reformation is usually available to correct clerical errors in contracts.

Example A clerical error is made during the typing of a contract, and both parties sign the contract without discovering the error. If a dispute later arises, the court can reform the contract to correct the clerical error so the contract reads as the parties originally intended.

reformation
An equitable doctrine that permits the court to rewrite a contract to express the parties' true intentions.

Injunction

An **injunction** is a court order that prohibits a person from doing a certain act. To obtain an injunction, the requesting party must show that he or she will suffer irreparable injury if the injunction is not issued.

Example A professional basketball team enters into a five-year employment contract with a basketball player. The basketball player breaches the contract and enters into a contract to play for a competing professional basketball team. Here, the first team can obtain an injunction to prevent the basketball player from playing for the other team during the remaining term of the original contract.

injunction
A court order that prohibits a person from doing a certain act.

CONCEPT SUMMARY

TYPES OF EQUITABLE REMEDIES

Type of Equitable Remedy	Description
Specific performance	A court orders the breaching party to perform the acts promised in the contract. The subject matter of the contract must be unique.
Reformation	A court rewrites a contract to express the parties' true intentions. This remedy is usually used to correct clerical errors.
Injunction	A court prohibits a party from doing a certain act. Injunctions are available in contract actions only in limited circumstances.

Key Terms and Concepts

Accord and satisfaction (217)
Agents' contract (212)
Assignment of rights (assignment) (215)
Assignee (215)
Assignor (215)
Breach of contract (218)
Compensatory damages (219)
Complete integration (213)
Complete performance (strict performance) (218)
Condition (217)
Condition precedent (217)
Condition subsequent (217)
Conditional promise (qualified promise) (217)
Consequential damages (special damages or foreseeable damages) (220)
Covenant (216)

Discharge by agreement (217)
Dominant party (210)
Duress (210)
Economic injury (208)
Equal dignity rule (212)
Equitable remedies (221)
Executed contract (218)
Executory contract (211)
Force majeure clause (218)
Genuineness of assent (207)
Guarantor (212)
Guaranty contract (212)
Inferior performance (219)
Impossibility of performance (objective impossibility) (218)
Incidental beneficiary (215)
Injunction (221)
Intended third-party beneficiary (215)
Intent to deceive (208)
Intentional misrepresentation (fraudulent misrepresentation or fraud) (208)
Lease contract (213)

Liquidated damages (220)
Liquidated damages clause (220)
Material breach (219)
Material fact (207)
Merger clause (integration clause) (213)
Minor breach (218)
Misrepresentation of a material fact (208)
Mitigate (220)
Monetary damages (dollar damages) (219)
Mutual mistake of a material fact (207)
Mutual mistake of value (208)
Mutual rescission (217)
Novation agreement (novation) (217)
Obligee (215)
Obligor (215)
One-year rule (212)
Original contract (primary contract) (212)
Parol evidence (213)
Parol evidence rule (213)
Part performance (212)
Penalty (220)

Real property (211)
Reformation (221)
Reliance on a misrepresentation (208)
Rescind (211)
Rescission (219)
Sales contract (212)
Scienter ("guilty mind") (208)
Section 2-201(1) of the Uniform Commercial Code (UCC) (212)
Section 2A-201(1) of the UCC (213)
Servient party (210)
Specific performance (221)
Statute of Frauds (211)
Subsequent assignee (subassignee) (215)
Substantial performance (218)
Tender of performance (tender) (218)
UCC Statute of Frauds (213)
Undue influence (210)
Unilateral mistake (207)

Law Case with Answer

California and Hawaiian Sugar Company v. Sun Ship, Inc.

Facts   The California and Hawaiian Sugar Company (C&H), a California corporation, is an agricultural cooperative owned by 14 sugar plantations in Hawaii. It transports raw sugar to its refinery in Crockett, California. Sugar is a seasonal crop, with about 70 percent of the harvest occurring between April and October. C&H requires reliable seasonal shipping of the raw sugar from Hawaii to California. Sugar stored on the ground or left unharvested suffers a loss of sucrose and goes to waste.

After C&H was notified by its normal shipper that it would be withdrawing its services at a specified date in the future, C&H commissioned the design of a large hybrid vessel—a tug of a catamaran design consisting of a barge attached to the tug. After substantial negotiation, C&H contracted with Sun Ship, Inc. (Sun Ship), a Pennsylvania corporation, to build the vessel for $25,405,000. The contract gave Sun Ship nearly two years to build and deliver the ship to C&H. The contract also contained a liquidated damages clause calling for a payment of $17,000 per day for each day that the vessel was not delivered to C&H after the agreed-upon delivery date. Sun Ship did not complete the vessel until eight and one-half months after the agreed-upon delivery date. Upon delivery, the vessel was commissioned and christened the *Moku Pahu*.

During the season that the boat had not been delivered, C&H was able to find other means of shipping the crop from Hawaii to its California refinery. Evidence established that actual damages suffered by C&H because of the nonavailability of the vessel from Sun Ship were $368,000. When Sun Ship refused to pay the liquidated damages, C&H filed suit to require payment of $4,413,000 in liquidated damages under the contract. Can C&H recover the liquidated damages from Sun Ship?

Answer Yes, C&H can recover the liquidated damages from Sun Ship. Contracts are contracts because they contain enforceable promises, and absent some overriding public policy, those promises are to be enforced.

Here there was a liquidated damages clause entered into by two experienced businesses. They could have each assessed the value of the risk in this case. C&H faced an uncertain loss if Sun Ship did not deliver the boat at the agreed-upon time. C&H's loss, should the boat not be delivered in time, could have been the loss of an entire season's crop. Therefore, the parties placed in their contract a liquidated damages clause that would protect C&H from reasonably estimated economic loss should Sun Ship fail to perform the contract on time. Proof of this loss is difficult. Whatever the loss, the parties had promised each other that $17,000 per day was a reasonable measure. Where each of the parties is content to take the risk of the contract turning out in a particular way, a contracting party should not be released from the contract in the face of no misrepresentations or other want of fair dealing. Here, Sun Ship agreed to pay liquidated damages of a fixed amount after assessing its risks. Merely because the other party, C&H, figured out a way to have its sugar transferred from Hawaii to the processing plants in California while incurring slight actual damages does not relieve Sun Ship from its bargain. In this case, there is no evidence that the liquidated damages clause is a penalty. On the contrary, it was agreed upon by two experienced parties. Therefore, the liquidated damages clause should be enforced against Sun Ship. Therefore, C&H should be awarded the $4,413,000 in liquidated damages plus interest. *California and Hawaiian Sugar Company v. Sun Ship, Inc.*, 794 F.2d 1433, **Web** 1986 U.S. App. Lexis 27376 (United States Court of Appeals for the Ninth Circuit)

Critical Legal Thinking Cases

10.1 Intended or Incidental Beneficiary The Phillies, L.P., the owner of the Philadelphia Phillies professional baseball team (Phillies), decided to build a new baseball stadium called Citizens Bank Park (the Project). The Phillies entered into a contract (Agreement) with Driscoll/Hunt Joint Venture (DH) whereby DH would act as the construction manager of the Project. In that capacity, DH entered into multiple contracts with subcontractors to provide material and services in constructing the Project. One such subcontractor was Ramos/Carson/DePaul, Joint Venture (RCD), which was hired to install concrete foundations for the Project. The Project was beset with numerous delays and disruptions, for which RCD claimed it was owed additional compensation from DH and the Phillies. Subcontractor RCD sued the Phillies to recover the compensation, alleging it was an intended beneficiary to the Phillies–DH Agreement, thus giving it rights to recover compensation from the Phillies. The Phillies argued that RCD was merely an incidental beneficiary to the Phillies–DH

Agreement and could not recover compensation from the Phillies. Is RCD an intended or an incidental beneficiary of the Phillies–DH Agreement? *Ramos/Carson/DePaul, a Joint Venture v. The Phillies, L.P.*, **Web** 2006 Phil.Ct.Com. PL Lexis 397 (Common Pleas Court of Philadelphia County, Pennsylvania)

10.2 Specific Performance Jean-Claude Kaufmann owned approximately 37 acres of real property located in the town of Stephentown, Rensselaer County, New York. The property is located in a wooded area and is improved with a 19th-century farmhouse. Kaufmann and his spouse, Christine Cacace, resided in New York City and used the property as a weekend or vacation home. After Kaufmann and Cacace lost their jobs, their financial situation prompted Kaufmann to list the property for sale for $350,000.

Richard Alba and his spouse (Albas) looked at the property and offered Kaufmann the full asking price. The parties executed a contract for sale, and the

Albas paid a deposit, obtained a mortgage commitment, and procured a satisfactory home inspection and title insurance. A date for closing the transaction was set. Prior to closing, Cacace sent the Albas an e-mail, indicating that she and Kaufmann had "a change of heart" and no longer wished to go forward with the sale. Albas sent a reply e-mail, stating their intent to go forward with the scheduled closing. Cacace responded with another e-mail, informing the Albas that she had multiple sclerosis and alleging that the "remorse and dread" over the impending sale was making her ill. When Kaufmann refused to close, the Albas sued, seeking specific performance, and moved for summary judgment. Is order of specific performance of the real estate contract warranted in this case? *Alba v. Kaufmann*, 810 N.Y.S.2d 539, **Web** 2006 N.Y.App. Div. Lexis 2321 (Supreme Court of New York, Appellate Division)

10.3 *Force Majeure* **Clause** Leo and Elizabeth Facto contracted with Snuffy Pantagis Entertainment, Inc., doing business as Pantagis Renaissance, a banquet hall, for a wedding reception for 150 people, to be held in the evening between 6:00 P.M. and 11:00 P.M. The total contract price was $10,578, all of which was paid in advance. The contract contained a *force majeure* clause, which stated, "Snuffy's will be excused from performance under this contract if it is prevented from doing so by an act of God (e.g., flood, power failure, etc.), or other unforeseen events or circumstances."

Less than forty-five minutes after the wedding reception began, there was an area-wide power failure where the Pantagis Renaissance was located. At that time, the guests were being served alcohol and hors d'oeuvres. The power failure caused all of the lights, except emergency lights, to go out and the air conditioning system to shut off. In addition, the band that was hired to play at the reception was unable to play because electricity was required to operate their instruments. The lack of lighting impeded the wedding photographer and videographer from taking pictures and videos. On the day of the reception, the temperature was in the upper 80s and low 90s, and the humidity was high. As a result, the Factos and their guests became extremely uncomfortable. Some guests resorted to pouring water over their heads to keep cool. Evidence was introduced that showed that Pantagis Renaissance served alcoholic beverages until approximately 7:30 P.M. and served the salad portion of the meal. After the emergency lights, which were operated by battery power, went out, the only illumination was provided by candelabras on the tables. Shortly after 9:00 P.M., the police evacuated the facility.

The Factos sued Pantagis Renaissance for breach of contract, seeking recovery of the $10,578 they prepaid for the wedding reception, plus $6,000 paid to

the band, $3,810 paid to the wedding photographer, and $3,242 paid to the videographer. Does the *force majeure* clause bar the plaintiff's breach of contract claim? *Facto v. Snuffy Pantagis Entertainment, Inc.*, 915 A.2d 59 (Superior Court of New Jersey)

10.4 Unilateral Mistake Wells Fargo Credit Corporation (Wells Fargo) obtained a judgment of foreclosure on a house owned by Mr. and Mrs. Clevenger. The total indebtedness stated in the judgment was $207,141. The foreclosure sale was scheduled for 11:00 A.M. on a specified day at the west front door of the Hillsborough County Courthouse. Wells Fargo was represented by a paralegal, who had attended more than 1,000 similar sales. Wells Fargo's handwritten instruction sheet informed the paralegal to make one bid at $115,000, the tax-appraised value of the property. Because the first "1" in the number was close to the "$," the paralegal misread the bid instruction as $15,000 and opened the bidding at that amount.

Harley Martin, who was attending his first judicial sale, bid $20,000. The county clerk gave ample time for another bid and then announced, "$20,000 going once, $20,000 going twice, sold to Harley... ." The paralegal screamed, "Stop, I'm sorry. I made a mistake!" The certificate of sale was issued to Martin. Wells Fargo filed suit to set aside the judicial sale based on its unilateral mistake. Does Wells Fargo's unilateral mistake constitute grounds for setting aside the judicial sale? *Wells Fargo Credit Corporation v. Martin*, 650 So.2d 531, **Web** 1992 Fla.App. Lexis 9927 (Court of Appeal of Florida)

10.5 Guaranty Contract Glenn A. Page (Glenn) had a long-term friendship with Jerry Sellers, an owner of Gulf Coast Motors. Glenn began borrowing money from Gulf Coast Motors on a recurring basis during a two-year period. The loan process was informal: Gulf Coast Motors set up a ledger account and recorded each loan made to Glenn, and Glenn would sign the ledger "I agree to pay Jerry Sellers as above." At various times, Glenn would make small payments toward his account, but he would thereafter borrow more money. At the times the loans were made, Glenn was not working and had no assets in his own name. There was no evidence as to what Glenn used the loan proceeds for, but evidence showed that he had a gambling problem.

Sellers testified that toward the end of the two-year period of making loans to Glenn, he telephoned Mary R. Page, Glenn's wife, and Mary orally guaranteed to repay Glenn's loans. Mary had significant assets of her own. Mary denied that she had promised to pay any of Glenn's debt, and she denied that Sellers had asked her to pay Glenn's debt. Gulf Coast Motors sued Glenn and Mary to recover payment for the unpaid loans. Is Mary's alleged oral promise to guarantee her husband's debts an enforceable guaranty contract? *Page v. Gulf Coast Motors*, 903 So.2d 148, **Web** 2004 Ala.Civ.App. Lexis 982 (Court of Civil Appeal of Alabama)

10.6 Rescission of a Contract Patricia Dianne Hickman inherited one-half interests to two pieces of real property when her mother died. One of the properties, in Bienville Parish, Louisiana, contained 45 acres of woodland. The second property, in Madison Parish, Louisiana, contained approximately 236 acres of land and a house. Patricia was 20 years old and had a mental condition that required medication. Patricia, who lived separately from her parents, received a telephone call from her father, Joe Hickman, to come and visit him. Joe was ill with cancer and lived with his sister Christine Bates and her husband, who are parents of Keith Bates, Patricia's first cousin.

The day after Patricia arrived, Joe informed Patricia that an important concern of his was for her to sell her interests in the two pieces of property to Keith Bates and his wife Sheila (the Bates). Joe expressed his doubts that Patricia would be able to maintain the properties and his interest in keeping the property in the family. Patricia agreed to sell the properties to the Bates for $500. Patricia signed legal documents that had been drawn by an attorney prior to her arrival. Subsequently, through a friend, Patricia sued the Bates to rescind the contracts that sold her interest in the two pieces of property to them, alleging fraud. Expert testimony at trial valued the Madison Parish property at $259,000 and the Bienville Parish property at $20,700. Should the sales contracts be rescinded because of fraud, and if so, should Patricia be awarded attorneys' fees? *Hickman v. Bates*, 889 So.2d 1249, **Web** 2004 La.App. Lexis 3076 (Court of Appeal of Louisiana)

10.7 Liquidated Damages The Trump World Tower is a seventy-two-story luxury condominium building that was being constructed at 845 United Nations Plaza in Manhattan, New York. Donald Trump was managing general partner of the building. 845 UN Limited Partnership (845 UN) began selling condominiums at the building before the building was constructed. The condominium offering plan required a nonrefundable down payment of 25 percent of the purchase price. The purchase contract provided that if a purchaser defaulted and did not complete the purchase, 845 UN could keep the 25 percent down payment as liquidated damages.

Cem Uzan and Hakan Uzan, brothers and Turkish billionaires, each contracted to purchase two condominium units on the top floors of the building. Cem and Hakan were both represented by attorneys. Over the course of two years, while the building was being constructed, the brothers paid the 25 percent nonrefundable down payment of $8 million. On September 11, 2001, before the building was complete, terrorists attacked New York City by flying two planes into the World Trade Center, the city's two tallest buildings, murdering thousands of people.

Cem and Hakan sent letters to 845 UN, rescinding their purchase agreements because of the terrorist attack that occurred on September 11. They alleged that it would be dangerous to live in a high-rise building in New York City. 845 UN terminated the four purchase agreements and kept the 25 percent down payments on the four condominiums as liquidated damages. Cem and Hakan sued 845 UN, alleging that the money should be returned to them. 845 UN defended, arguing that the 25 percent nonrefundable down payment was an enforceable liquidated damages clause. Is the liquidated damages clause enforceable? *Uzan v. 845 UN Limited Partnership*, 10 A.D.3d 230, 778 N.Y.S.2d 171, **Web** 2004 N.Y.App. Div. Lexis 8362 (Supreme Court of New York, Appellate Division)

Ethics Cases

10.8 Ethics Arlene and Donald Warner inherited a home at 101 Molimo Street in San Francisco. The Warners obtained a $170,000 loan on the property. Donald Warner and Kenneth Sutton were friends. Donald Warner proposed that Sutton and his wife purchase the residence. His proposal included a $15,000 down payment toward the purchase price of $185,000. The Suttons were to pay all the mortgage payments and real estate taxes on the property for five years and at any time during the five-year period, they could purchase the house. All this was agreed to orally.

The Suttons paid the down payment and cash payments equal to the monthly mortgage to the Warners. The Suttons paid the annual property taxes on the house. The Suttons also made improvements to the property. Four and one-half years later, the Warners reneged on the oral sales/option agreement. At that time, the house had risen in value to between $250,000 and $320,000. The Suttons sued for specific performance of the sales agreement. The Warners defended, alleging that the oral promise to sell real estate had to be in writing under the Statute of Frauds and was therefore unenforceable. *Sutton v. Warner*, 12 Cal.App.4th 415, 15 Cal.Rptr.2d 632, **Web** 1993 Cal.App. Lexis 22 (Court of Appeal of California)

1. What is the Statute of Frauds? Who would win if the Statute of Frauds were applied to this case?
2. Did the Warners act ethically in this case?
3. What does the doctrine of part performance provide? Does it apply in this case?

10.9 Ethics   Rafael Chodos is a California attorney who specializes in the law of fiduciary duty, which includes a party's obligation to act honestly and with loyalty when performing his or her legal duties to another. Chodos sent a detailed proposal and table of contents to Bancroft-Whitney, the leading publisher of legal texts, to write a treatise on fiduciary duties. The editors at Bancroft-Whitney were enthusiastic about the proposal and sent Chodos a standard-form "author agreement" that set forth the terms of the publishing contract. Chodos was to be paid 15 percent of the gross revenues from the sales of the treatise. Chodos and Bancroft-Whitney signed the agreement.

For three years Chodos wrote the manuscript. He significantly limited the time spent on his law practice and spent over 3,600 hours writing the manuscript. During this time, Chodos worked with editors of Bancroft-Whitney in developing and editing the manuscript. Midway through this period, West Publishing Group purchased Bancroft-Whitney, and the two companies merged. The Bancroft-Whitney editors, now employed by West, continued to work with Chodos on editing and developing the manuscript. Three years after beginning, Chodos submitted the final manuscript to West. West editors suggested changes to the manuscript, which Chodos completed. West sent Chodos a letter, apologizing for delays in publication and assuring him that publication would take place within three months.

However, one month after the promised publication date, Chodos received a letter from West's marketing department, stating that West had decided not to publish Chodos's manuscript because it did not "fit with [West's] current product mix" and because of concerns about its "market potential." West admitted, however, that the manuscript was of "high quality" and that its decision was not due to any literary shortcomings of Chodos's work. Chodos filed a lawsuit against West, alleging breach of contract. *Chodos v. West Publishing Company, Inc.*, **Web** 2004 U.S. App. Lexis 4109 (United States Court of Appeals for the Ninth Circuit)

1. Do an author and a publisher have a special relationship that differs from a normal commercial arrangement? Explain.
2. Did West act unethically in this case?
3. Did West Publishing breach the author agreement it had with Chodos? If so, what damages would you award him?

Internet Exercises

1. Go to www.sba.gov/smallbusinessplanner/plan/getready/serv_sguide_sbaass.html and read about the Small Business Association's program that guarantees loans made to small businesses by lending institutions.

2. Go to **www.mactech.com/articles/mactech/Vol.09/09.10/TimeBomb/index.html** and read the article titled "Time Bombs, Stop Devices and Other Stuff," which discusses contract and other rights of software developers.

Endnotes

1. *Restatement (Second) of Contracts*, Section 152.
2. 59 Eng.Rep. 375 (1864).
3. *Restatement (Second) of Contracts*, Section 159.
4. *Restatement (Second) of Contracts*, Sections 163 and 164.
5. *Restatement (Second) of Contracts*, Section 176.
6. *Elias v. George Sahely & Co.*, 1983 App.Cas. (P.C.) 646, 655.
7. *Restatement (Second) of Contracts*, Section 130.
8. *Restatement (Second) of Contracts*, Section 112.
9. *Restatement (Second) of Contracts*, Section 213.
10. *Restatement (Second) of Contracts*, Section 302.
11. The *Restatement (Second) of Contracts*, Section 224, defines *condition* as "an event, not certain to occur, which must occur, unless its nonperformance is excused, before performance under a contract is due."
12. *Restatement (Second) of Contracts*, Section 281.
13. *Restatement (Second) of Contracts*, Section 261.

CHAPTER 11

E-Commerce and Digital Law

DIGITAL LAW AND E-COMMERCE
The development of the Internet and electronic commerce has required courts to apply existing law to online commerce transactions and e-contracts and spurred the federal Congress and state legislatures to enact new laws that govern the formation and enforcement of e-contracts.

Learning Objectives

After studying this chapter, you should be able to:

1. Describe the laws that apply to e-mail contracts, e-commerce, and web contracts.
2. Describe e-licensing and the provisions of the Uniform Computer Information Transactions Act (UCITA).
3. Describe the provisions of the federal Electronic Signatures in Global and National Commerce Act (E-SIGN Act)
4. Describe laws that protect privacy in cyberspace.
5. Define *Internet domain names* and describe how domain names are registered and protected.

Chapter Outline

> " *Through the use of chat rooms, any person with a phone line can become a town crier with a voice that resonates farther than it could from any soapbox. Through the use of Web pages, mail exploders, and newsgroups, the same individual can become a pamphleteer.* "

—Stevens, Justice
Reno v. American Civil Liberties Union, 521 U.S. 844 (1997)

Introduction to E-Commerce and Digital Law

**electronic commerce
(e-commerce)**
The sale of goods and services by computer over the Internet.

The use of the Internet and the World Wide Web to sell, lease, or license goods, services, and intellectual property through **electronic commerce**, or **e-commerce**, have exploded. Large and small businesses sell goods and services over the Internet through **websites** and registered *domain names*. Consumers and businesses can purchase almost any good or service they want over the Internet, using sites such as Amazon.com, eBay, and others. Businesses and individuals may register domain names to use on the Internet. Anyone who infringes on these rights may be stopped from doing so and is liable for damages.

In addition, software and information may be licensed either by physically purchasing the software or information and installing it on a computer or by merely downloading the software or information directly into a computer.

The 'Net is a waste of time, and that's exactly what's right about it.

William Gibson

Many legal scholars and lawyers argued that traditional rules of contract law do not adequately meet the needs of Internet transactions and software and information licensing. These concerns led to an effort to create new contract law for electronic transactions. After much debate, the National Conference of Commissioners on Uniform State Laws developed the *Uniform Computer Information Transactions Act (UCITA)*. This model act provides uniform and comprehensive rules for contracts involving computer information transactions and software and information licenses.

The federal government has also enacted many federal statutes that regulate the Internet and e-commerce. Federal law has been passed that regulates the Internet and protects personal rights while using the Internet.

This chapter covers Internet law, domain names, e-commerce, e-contracts, licensing of software, and other laws that regulate the Internet and e-commerce.

Internet

Internet (Net)
A collection of millions of computers that provide a network of electronic connections between the computers.

The **Internet**, or **Net**, is a collection of millions of computers that provide a network of electronic connections between the computers. Hundreds of millions of computers are connected to the Internet. The Internet's evolution helped usher in the Information Age. Individuals and businesses use the Internet for communication of information and data.

World Wide Web

World Wide Web
An electronic connection of millions of computers that support a standard set of rules for the exchange of information.

The **World Wide Web** consists of millions of computers that support a standard set of rules for the exchange of information called Hypertext Transfer Protocol (HTTP). Web-based documents are formatted using common coding languages. Businesses and individuals can access the web by registering with a service such as America Online (AOL).

Individuals and businesses can have their own websites. A website is composed of electronic documents known as webpages. Websites and webpages are stored on servers throughout the world, and these servers are operated by *Internet service providers (ISPs)*. Individuals view websites by using web-browsing software such as Microsoft Internet Explorer and Mozilla Firefox Each website has a unique online address.

The web has made it extremely attractive to conduct commercial activities online. Companies such as Amazon.com and eBay are e-commerce powerhouses that sell all sorts of goods and services. Existing brick-and-mortar companies, such as Walmart, Merrill Lynch, and Dell Computer, sell their goods and services online as well. E-commerce over the web will continue to grow dramatically each year.

E-Mail Contracts

Electronic mail, or **e-mail**, is one of the most widely used applications for communication over the Internet. Using e-mail, individuals around the world can instantaneously communicate in electronic writing with one another. Each person can have an e-mail address that identifies him or her by a unique address. E-mail is replacing telephone and paper communication between individuals and businesses.

Many contracts are now completed by using e-mail. These are referred to as **electronic mail contracts**, or **e-mail contracts**. E-mail contracts are enforceable as long as they meet the requirements necessary to form a traditional contract. This includes agreement, consideration, capacity, and lawful object. Traditional challenges to the enforcement of a contract, such as fraud, duress, intoxication, insanity, and other defenses may be asserted against the enforcement of an e-mail contract. E-mail contracts usually meet the requirements of the Statute of Frauds, which requires certain contracts to be in writing, such as contracts for the sale of real estate, contracts for the sale of goods that cost $500 or more, and other contracts listed in the relevant Statute of Frauds.

Often, the use of e-mail communication is somewhat informal. In addition, an e-mail contract may not have the formality of a paper contract that includes the final terms and conditions of the parties' agreement. The terms of the parties' agreement may have to be gleaned from several e-mails that have been communicated between the parties. In such case, the court can integrate several e-mails in order to determine the terms of the parties' agreement.

The following feature discusses a federal law that regulates spam e-mail.

electronic mail (e-mail)
Electronic written communication between individuals using computers connected to the Internet.

electronic mail contract (e-mail contract)
A contract that is entered into by the parties by use of e-mail.

Controlling the Assault of Non-Solicited Pornography and Marketing Act (CAN-SPAM Act)
A federal statute that places certain restrictions on persons and businesses that send unsolicited commercial advertising (spam) to e-mail accounts, prohibits falsified headers, prohibits deceptive subject lines, and requires spammers to label sexually oriented e-mail as such.

Digital Law

Regulation of E-Mail Spam

Americans are being bombarded in their e-mail accounts by **spam**—unsolicited commercial advertising. Spammers try to sell people literally anything. Spam accounts for approximately three-quarters of all business e-mail traffic. In addition, many spam messages are fraudulent and deceptive, including misleading subject lines. It takes time and money to sort through, review, and discard unwanted spam.

In 2003, Congress enacted the federal **Controlling the Assault of Non-Solicited Pornography and Marketing Act (CAN-SPAM Act)**.[1] The act (1) prohibits spammers from using falsified headers in e-mail messages, including the originating domain name and e-mail address; (2) prohibits deceptive subject lines that mislead a recipient of the contents or subject matter of the message; (3) requires that recipients of spam be given the opportunity to opt out and not have the spammer send e-mail to the recipient's address; and (4) requires spammers who send sexually oriented e-mail to properly label it as such. The Federal Trade Commission (FTC), a federal administrative agency, is empowered to enforce the CAN-SPAM Act.

In effect, the CAN-SPAM Act does not can spam but instead approves businesses to use spam as long as they do not lie. The act provides a civil right of action to Internet access services that have suffered losses because of spam. The act does not, however, provide a civil right of action to individuals who have received unsolicited spam. The CAN-SPAM Act does not regulate spam sent internationally to Americans from other countries. In essence, the CAN-SPAM Act is very weak in helping consumers ward off the spam that deluges them daily.

In 2004, the FTC adopted a rule that requires that sexually explicit spam e-mail contain a warning on the subject line reading "SEXUALLY EXPLICIT." The FTC rule also prohibits the messages themselves from containing graphic material. The graphic material can appear only after the recipient has opened the e-mail message.

In the following case, the court was presented with an issue involving spam.

CASE 11.1   *E-Mail Spam*

Facebook, Inc. v. Porembski

Web 2011 U.S. Dist. Lexis 9668 (2011)
United States District Court for the Northern District of California

"The record demonstrates that defendants willfully and knowingly violated the statutes in question by engaging in the circumvention of Facebook's security measures."

—Fogel, District Judge

Facts

Facebook, Inc., owns and operates the social networking website located at **www.facebook.com**. Facebook users can admit friends to view the information they post on their Facebook site, and then others can ask to also be added as friends and so on. Facebook users must register with the website and agree to Facebook's Statement of Rights and Responsibilities (SRR). Facebook maintains strict policies against spam or any other form of unsolicited advertising by users. Facebook filed a lawsuit in U.S. District Court against Philip Porembski and PP Web Services, LLC, which was controlled by Porembski. Facebook alleged that Porembski registered as a Facebook user and was bound by the SSR. Porembski created PP Web Services LLC and was the sole person to act on its behalf. Through fraudulent misrepresentations, Porembski obtained over 116,000 Facebook users' account information. PP Web Services then sent more than 7.2 million spam messages to these Facebook users. Facebook alleged that the defendants' spamming activities violated the federal Controlling the Assault of Non-Solicited Pornography and Marketing Act (CAN-SPAM Act). Facebook sought damages and a permanent injunction against the defendants.

Issue

Have the defendants violated the CAN-SPAM Act?

Language of the Court

The record demonstrates that defendants willfully and knowingly violated the statutes
in question by engaging in the circumvention of Facebook's security measures. The court will award statutory damages of $50.00 per violation of the CAN-SPAM Act, for a total award of $360,000,000 under that Act. As a result of defendants' spam campaign, Facebook has received more than 8,000 user complaints, and more than 4,500 Facebook users have deactivated their accounts. Defendants have demonstrated a willingness to continue their activities without regard for Facebook's security measures or cease and desist requests. Thus, it is appropriate that defendants be permanently enjoined from accessing and abusing Facebook services. Facebook's request for permanent injunctive relief is granted.

Decision

The U.S. District Court held that the defendants had violated the CAN-SPAM Act, awarded Facebook $360,000,000 in damages, and issued a permanent injunction against the defendants.

Case Questions

Critical Legal Thinking
What is spam? Do you think that enactment of the CAN-SPAM Act was warranted?

Ethics
Did Porembski act ethically in this case? Will Facebook recover its awarded damages?

Contemporary Business
What would be the consequences if Facebook users were subjected to spam?

Internet Service Provider (ISP)

Internet service providers (ISPs) are companies that provide consumers and businesses with access to the Internet. ISPs provide e-mail accounts to users, Internet access, and storage on the Internet. ISPs offer a variety of access devices and services, including dial-up, cable, DSL, broadband wireless, Ethernet, satellite Internet access, and other services to connect users to the Internet. There are also web-hosting services that allow users to create their own websites and provide storage space for website users.

A provision in the federal **Communications Decency Act** of 1996 provides: "No provider or user of an interactive computer service shall be treated as the publisher or speaker of any information provided by another information content provider."[2] Thus, ISPs are not liable for the content transmitted over their networks by e-mail users and websites.

> **Communications Decency Act**
> A federal statute which provides that Internet service providers (ISPs) are not liable for the content transmitted over their networks by e-mail users and websites.

E-Commerce and Web Contracts

The Internet and **web contracts**, also called **e-contracts**, have increased as means of conducting personal and commercial business. Internet sellers, lessors, and licensors use web addresses to sell and lease goods and services and license software and other intellectual property over the Internet. Internet sellers, leasors, and licensors use web addresses to list the goods and services and intellectual property available and to provide the means for purchasing, leasing, or licensing these goods, services, and intellectual property. Internet sellers, lessors, and licensors, such as **www.amazon.com**, **www.dell.com**, **www.microsoft.com**, and others, use the Internet extensively to sell, lease, or license goods, services, and intellectual property. Assuming that all the elements to establish a traditional contract are present, a web contract is valid and enforceable.

In the following case, the court considered whether a web contract was enforceable.

> **Web contract (e-contract)**
> A contract that is entered into by purchasing, leasing, or licensing goods, services, software, or other intellectual property from websites operated by sellers, lessors, and licensors.

CASE 11.2 *Web Contract*

Hubbert v. Dell Corporation
835 N.E.2d 113 (2005)
Appellate Court of Illinois

"The blue hyperlinks on the defendant's Web pages, constituting the five-step process for ordering the computers, should be treated the same as a multi-page written paper contract."

—Hopkins, Justice

Facts
Plaintiffs Dewayne Hubbert, Elden Craft, Chris Grout, and Rhonda Byington purchased computers from Dell Computer online through Dell's website. Before purchasing their computers, each of the plaintiffs configured the model and type of computer he or she wished to order from Dell's webpages. To make their purchase, each of the plaintiffs completed online order forms on five pages on Dell's website. On each of the five pages, Dell's "Terms and Conditions of Sale" were accessible by clicking on a blue hyperlink. In order to find the terms and conditions, the plaintiffs would have had to click on the blue hyperlink and read the terms and conditions of sale. On the last page of the five page order form the following statement appeared: "All sales are subject to Dell's Terms and Conditions of Sale."

The plaintiffs filed a lawsuit against Dell, alleging that Dell misrepresented the speed of the microprocessors included in the computers they purchased. Dell made a demand for arbitration, asserting that the plaintiffs were bound by the arbitration agreement that was contained in the Terms and Conditions of Sale. The plaintiffs countered that the arbitration clause was not part of their web contract because the Terms and Conditions of Sale were not conspicuously displayed as part of their web contract. The trial court sided with the plaintiffs, finding that the arbitration clause was unenforceable because the terms and conditions of sale were not adequately communicated to the plaintiffs. Dell appealed.

Issue
Are Dell's Terms and Conditions of Sale adequately communicated to the plaintiffs?

(continued)

Language of the Court

We find that the online contract included the "Terms and Conditions of Sale." The blue hyperlink entitled "Terms and Conditions of Sale" appeared on numerous Web pages the plaintiffs completed in the ordering process. The blue hyperlinks on the defendant's Web pages, constituting the five-step process for ordering the computers, should be treated the same as a multipage written paper contract. The blue hyperlink simply takes a person to another page of the contract, similar to turning the page of a written paper contract. Although there is no conspicuousness requirement, the hyperlink's contrasting blue type makes it conspicuous.

The statement that the sales were subject to the defendant's "Terms and Conditions of Sale," combined with making the "Terms and Conditions of Sale" accessible online by blue hyperlinks, was sufficient notice to the plaintiffs that purchasing the computers online would make the "Terms and Conditions of Sale" binding on them. Because the "Terms and Conditions of Sale" were a part of the online contract, they were bound by the "Terms and Conditions of Sale," including the arbitration clause.

Decision

The appellate court held that the Terms and Conditions of Sale, which included the arbitration clause, was part of the web contract between the plaintiffs and Dell. The appellate court reversed the decision of the trial court.

Case Questions

Critical Legal Thinking
Should web contracts be treated any differently from traditional contracts?

Ethics
Did the plaintiffs act ethically in claiming that the Terms and Conditions of Sale were not included in their web contract with Dell? Do you read the terms and conditions of sale when you purchase goods over the Internet?

Contemporary Business
Do Internet sellers expect consumers to read the detailed terms and conditions of sale contained in web contracts?

The following feature discusses a federal statute that established rules for electronic contracts and electronic signatures.

Digital Law

Electronic Signatures in Global and National Commerce Act (E-SIGN Act)

In 2000, the federal government enacted the **Electronic Signatures in Global and National Commerce Act (E-SIGN Act)**.[3] This act is a federal statute enacted by Congress and therefore has national reach. The act is designed to place the world of electronic commerce on a par with the world of paper contracts in the United States.

Writing Requirement of the Statute of Frauds Met
One of the main features of the E-SIGN Act is that it recognizes electronic contracts as meeting the writing requirement of the Statute of Frauds for most contracts. Statutes of Frauds are state laws that require certain types of contracts to be in writing. The 2000 federal act provides that electronically signed contracts cannot be denied effect because they are in electronic form or delivered electronically. The act also provides that record retention requirements are satisfied if the records are stored electronically.

The federal law was passed with several provisions to protect consumers. First, consumers must consent to receiving electronic records and contracts. Second, to receive electronic records, consumers must be able to demonstrate that they have access to the electronic records. Third, businesses must tell consumers that they have the right to receive hard-copy documents of their transactions.

E-Signatures Recognized as Valid
In the past, signatures have been hand-applied by the person signing a document. However, in the electronic

commerce world, individuals provide verification in different ways: "What is your mother's maiden name?" "Slide your smart card in the sensor," or "Look into the iris scanner." But are electronic signatures sufficient to form an enforceable contract? The federal E-SIGN Act made the answer clear.

The E-SIGN Act recognizes **electronic signatures**, or **e-signatures**. The act gives an e-signature the same force and effect as a pen-inscribed signature on paper. The act is technology neutral, however, in that the law does not define or decide which technologies should be used to create a legally binding signature in cyberspace. Loosely defined, a **digital signature** is some electronic method that identifies an individual. The challenge is to make sure that someone who uses a digital signature is the person he or she claims

to be. The act provides that a digital signature can basically be verified in one of three ways:

1. By something the signatory knows, such as a secret password, pet's name, and so forth
2. By something a person has, such as a smart card, which looks like a credit card and stores personal information
3. By biometrics, which uses a device that digitally recognizes part of the individual, such as fingerprints or the retina or iris of the eye

The verification of electronic signatures is creating a need for the use of scanners and methods for verifying personal information.

Counteroffers Ineffectual Against Electronic Agent

Many Internet sellers have websites that use electronic agents to sell goods and services. An **electronic agent** is any computer system that has been established by a seller to accept orders. Webpage order systems are examples of electronic agents.

Traditionally, when humans deal with each other face to face, by telephone, or in writing, their negotiations might consist of an exchange of several offers and counteroffers until agreed-upon terms are reached and a contract is formed. Each new counteroffer extinguishes the previous offer and becomes a new viable offer.

Most webpages use electronic ordering systems that do not have the ability to evaluate and accept counteroffers or to make counteroffers. Most state laws recognize this limitation and provide that an e-contract is formed if an individual takes action that causes the electronic agent to cause performance or promise benefits to the individual. Thus, counteroffers are not effective against electronic agents.

Example Green Company has a website that uses an electronic ordering system for placing orders for products sold by the company. Freddie accesses the Green Company's website and orders a product costing $1,000. Freddie enters the product code and description, his mailing address and credit card information, and other data needed to complete the transaction. The Green Company's web ordering system does not provide a method for a party to submit a counteroffer. After ordering the goods on the website, Freddie sends an e-mail to the Green Company, stating, "I will accept the product I ordered if, after two weeks of use, I am satisfied with the product." However, because Freddie has placed the order with an electronic agent, Freddie has ordered the product, and his counteroffer is ineffectual.

E-Licensing

Much of the new cyberspace economy is based on electronic contracts and the licensing of computer software and information. E-commerce created problems for forming contracts over the Internet, enforcing e-commerce contracts, and providing consumer protection. To address these problems, in 1999, the National Conference of Commissioners on Uniform State Laws (a group of lawyers, judges, and legal scholars) drafted the **Uniform Computer Information Transactions Act (UCITA)**. This act is discussed in the following feature.

> **Electronic Signatures in Global and National Commerce Act (E-SIGN Act)**
> A federal statute that (1) recognizes electronic contracts as meeting the writing requirement of the Statute of Frauds and (2) recognizes and gives electronic signatures (e-signatures) the same force and effect as pen-inscribed signatures on paper.

> **Uniform Computer Information Transactions Act (UCITA)**
> A model state law that creates contract law for the licensing of information technology rights.

Digital Law

Uniform Computer Information Transactions Act (UCITA)

The Uniform Computer Information Transactions Act (UCITA) is a model act that establishes a uniform and comprehensive set of rules that govern the creation, performance, and enforcement of computer information transactions. A computer information transaction is an agreement to create, transfer, or license computer information or information rights [UCITA 102(a)(11)].

The UCITA does not become law until a state's legislature enacts it as a state statute. Most states have adopted e-commerce and licensing statutes that are similar to many of the provisions of the UCITA as their law for computer transactions and the licensing of software and informational rights. The UCITA will be used here as the basis for discussing state laws that affect computer, software, and licensing contracts.

Unless displaced by the UCITA, state law and equity principles, including principal and agent law, fraud, duress, mistake, trade secret law, and other state laws, supplement the UCITA [UCITA § 114]. Any provisions of the UCITA that are preempted by federal law are unenforceable to the extent of the preemption [UCITA § 105(a)].

License

Intellectual property and information rights are extremely important assets of many individuals and companies. Patents, trademarks, copyrights, trade secrets, data, software programs, and such constitute valuable intellectual property and information rights.

The owners of intellectual property and information rights often wish to transfer limited rights in the property or information to parties for specified purposes and limited duration. The agreement that is used to transfer such limited rights is called a **license**, which is defined as follows [UCITA 102(a)(40)]:

License means a contract that authorizes access to, or use, distribution, performance, modification, or reproduction of, information or information rights, but expressly limits the access or uses authorized or expressly grants fewer than all rights in the information, whether or not the transferee has title to a licensed copy. The term includes an access contract, a lease of a computer program, and a consignment of a copy.

The parties to a license of intellectual property are the licensor and the licensee. The **licensor** is the party who owns the intellectual property or information rights and obligates him- or herself to transfer rights in the property or information to the licensee. The **licensee** is the party who is granted limited rights in or access to the intellectual property or information [UCITA 102(a)(41) and 102(a)(42)]. A **licensing** arrangement is illustrated in **Exhibit 11.1**.

A license grants the contractual rights expressly described in the license and the right to use information rights within the licensor's control that are necessary to exercise the expressly described rights [UCITA § 307(a)]. A license can grant the licensee the exclusive rights to use the information. With an **exclusive license**, for the specified duration of the license, the licensor will not grant to any other person rights in the same information [UCITA § 307(f)(2)].

E-License

Most software programs and digital applications are electronically licensed by the owner of the program or application to a user of a computer or digital device. An **electronic license**, or **e-license**, is contract whereby the owner of

license
A contract that transfers limited rights in intellectual property and informational rights.

licensor
An owner of intellectual property or informational rights who transfers rights in the property or information to the licensee.

licensee
A party who is granted limited rights in or access to intellectual property or informational rights owned by a licensor.

exclusive license
A license that grants the licensee exclusive rights to use informational rights for a specified duration.

electronic license (e-license)
A contract whereby the owner of software or a digital application grants limited rights to the owner of a computer or digital device to use the software or digital application for a limited period and under specified conditions.

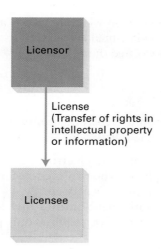

Exhibit 11.1 LICENSING
ARRANGEMENT

software or a digital application grants limited rights to the owner of a computer or digital device to use the software or a digital application for a limited period and under specified conditions. The owner of the program or application is the **electronic licensor**, or **e-licensor**, and the owner of the computer or digital device to whom the license is granted is the **electronic licensee**, or **e-licensee**.

Example Dorothy owns a computer and licenses a computer software program from SoftWare Company to use on her computer. Dorothy downloads the software onto her computer from SoftWare Company's website. There is an e-license between the two parties. SoftWare Company is the e-licensor, and Dorothy is the e-licensee.

Licensing Agreement

A licensor and a licensee usually enter into a written **licensing agreement** that expressly states the terms of their agreement. Licensing agreements tend to be very detailed and comprehensive contracts. This is primarily because of the nature of the subject matter and the limited uses granted in the intellectual property or informational rights.

   The parties to a contract for the licensing of information owe a duty to perform the obligations stated in the contract. If a party fails to perform as required, there is a breach of the contract. Breach of contract by one party to a licensing agreement gives the nonbreaching party certain rights, including the right to recover damages or other remedies [UCITA 701].

licensing agreement
A detailed and comprehensive written agreement between a licensor and a licensee that sets forth the express terms of their agreement.

Privacy in Cyberspace

E-mail, computer data, and other electronic communications are sent daily by millions of people, using computers and the Internet. Recognizing that the use of computer and other electronic communications raises special issues of privacy, the federal government enacted the *Electronic Communications Privacy Act (ECPA)*.[4]

Electronic Communications Privacy Act

The **Electronic Communications Privacy Act (ECPA)** makes it a crime to intercept an electronic communication at the point of transmission, while in transit, when stored by a router or on a server, or after receipt by the intended recipient. An electronic communication includes any transfer of signals, writings, images, sounds, data, or intelligence of any nature. The ECPA makes it illegal to access stored e-mail as well as e-mail in transmission.

Electronic Communications Privacy Act (ECPA)
A federal statute that makes it a crime to intercept an electronic communication at the point of transmission, while in transit, when stored by a router or server, or after receipt by intended recipient. There are some exceptions to this law.

Example Henry owns a computer on which he sends and receives e-mail. Harriet learns Henry's access code to his e-mail account. Harriet opens Henry's e-mail and reads his e-mails. Harriet has violated the ECPA.

Exceptions to the ECPA

The ECPA provides that stored electronic communications may be accessed without violating the law by the following:

1. The party or entity providing the electronic communication service. A primary example is an employer who can access stored e-mail communications of employees using the employer's service.
2. Government and law enforcement entities that are investigating suspected illegal activity. Disclosure would be required only pursuant to a validly issued warrant.

Example John works for the National Paper Corporation. In his job, he has access to a computer on which to conduct work for his employer. John receives and sends e-mail that is work related. John also has access on his computer to the Internet. The National Paper Corporation investigates what John has been viewing on his computer and what is stored on his computer. During its investigation, the National Paper Corporation discovers that John has been viewing and storing child pornography images. The National Paper Corporation fires John for his conduct because it violates company policy, of which John is aware. Here, the National Paper Company did not violate the ECPA.

The ECPA provides for criminal penalties. In addition, the ECPA provides that an injured party may sue for civil damages for violations of the ECPA.

Domain Names

Most businesses conduct e-commerce by using websites on the Internet. Each website is identified by a unique Internet **domain name**.

domain name
A unique name that identifies an individual's or company's website.

Examples The domain name for the publisher of this book—Pearson Education—is **www.pearsonhighered.com**. The domain name for Microsoft Corporation is **www.microsoft.com**. The domain name for McDonald's Corporation is **www.mcdonalds.com**.

Registration of Domain Names

Domain names need to be registered. The first step in registering a domain name is to determine whether any other party already owns the name. For this purpose, InterNIC maintains a "Whois" database that contains the domain names that have been registered. The InterNIC website is located online at **www.internic.net**.

Domain names can also be registered at Network Solutions, Inc.'s, website, which is located at **www.networksolutions.com**, as well as at other sites. An applicant must complete a registration form, which can be done online. It usually costs less than $50 to register a domain name for one year, and the fee may be paid by credit card online. Some country-specific domain names are more expensive to register.

Domain Name Extensions

The most commonly used top-level extensions for domain names are set forth in **Exhibit 11.2**.

.com	This extension represents the word *commercial* and is the most widely used extension in the world. Most businesses prefer a .com domain name because it is a highly recognized business symbol.
.net	This extension represents the word *network*, and it is most commonly used by ISPs, Web-hosting companies, and other businesses that are directly involved in the infrastructure of the Internet. Some businesses also choose domain names with a .net extension.
.org	This extension represents the word *organization* and is primarily used by nonprofit groups and trade associations.
.info	This extension signifies a resource website. It is an unrestricted global name that may be used by businesses, individuals, and organizations.
.biz	This extension is used for small-business websites.
.us	This extension is for U.S. websites. Many businesses choose this extension, which is a relatively new extension.
.mobi	This extension is reserved for websites that are viewable on mobile devices.
.bz	This extension was originally the country code for Belize, but it is now unrestricted and may be registered by anyone from anycountry. It is commonly used by small businesses.
.name	This extension is for individuals, who can use it to register personalized domain names.
.museum	This extension enables museums, museum associations, and museum professionals to register websites.
.coop	This extension represents the word *cooperative* and may be used by cooperative associations around the world.
.aero	This extension is exclusively reserved for the aviation community. It enables organizations and individuals in that community to reserve websites.
.pro	This extension is available to professionals, such as doctors, lawyers, and consultants.
.edu	This extension is for educational institutions.

There are other domain name extensions available. Countries have country-specific extensions assigned to the country. Many countries make these domain name extensions available for private purchase for commercial use.

Exhibit 11.2 COMMONLY USED TOP-LEVEL EXTENSIONS FOR DOMAIN NAMES

WEB EXERCISE
Think up an Internet domain name you would like to use for a business. Go to the Network Solutions website, at **www.networksolutions.com**, and see if that name is available with the top-level domain extension .com.

WEB EXERCISE
Go to **www.networksolutions.com**. See if your name is available in the .name extension.

The following feature discusses the creation of new top-level domain names.

Digital Law

New Top-Level Domain Names

Prior to 2011, there were twenty-two **top-level domain names (TLDs)**, including .com, .net, .org, and .biz. However, it was often difficult to obtain a new domain name using these suffixes because many names had already been taken. In 2011, the **Internet Corporation for Assigned Names and Numbers (ICANN)**, the organization that oversees the registration and regulation of domain names, issued new rules that permit a party to register a domain name with new TLD suffixes that are personalized.

The new rules permit companies to have their own company name TLD, such as .canon, .google, .cocacola, and such. In addition, companies can obtain TLDs for specific products, such as .ipad or .prius. Such TLDs will help companies with the branding of their company names and products. New TLDs can also be registered for

(continued)

industries and professions, such as .bank, .food, .basketball, and .dentist.

Under the new rules, cities and other governmental agencies can register their names, such as .nyc (New York City), .paris (Paris, France), and .quebec (Quebec, Canada). Even persons sharing a cultural identity could have their own TLD, such as .kurd (for Kurds living in Iraq and elsewhere) or .ven (Venetian community, Italy). Another important change is that the new rules permit TLDs to be registered in languages other than English, including Arabic, Chinese, French, Russian, Spanish, and other languages.

Obtaining a new TLD does not come cheap. The cost to apply for a new TLD is about $200,000, and there is an annual maintenance fee of about $75,000. The cost should keep away many squatters, but it may also be

prohibitive for small businesses. To obtain a new TLD, a party must file a detailed 200-page application with ICANN, which will then process and investigate the application. The application process can take nine months or longer.

If there are multiple applicants for the same TLD, ICANN will determine the winner by applying specified criteria. Parties holding trademarks of the TLD are given preference over other applicants. A party who obtains a new TLD can license the use of the name to other parties and establish qualifications that must be met to obtain such a license.

The new rules are the biggest change in domain names in over four decades. The new rules substantially expand the number of TLDs available, permits companies and others to personalize their TLDs, and will change the way people find information on the Internet.

Cybersquatting on Domain Names

Anticybersquatting Consumer Protection Act (ACPA)
A federal statute that permits trademark owners and famous persons to recover domain names that use their names where the domain name has been registered by another person or business in bad faith.

Sometimes a party will register a domain name of another party's trademarked name or famous person's name. This is called **cybersquatting**. Often the domain name owner will have registered the domain name in order to obtain payment for the name from the trademark holder or the famous person whose name has been registered as a domain name.

Trademark law was of little help in this area, either because the famous person's name was not trademarked or because, even if the name was trademarked, trademark laws required distribution of goods or services to find infringement, and most cybersquatters did not distribute goods or services but merely sat on the Internet domain names.

The following feature discusses an important federal law that restricts cybersquatting.

Digital Law

Federal Law Prohibits Cybersquatting on Domain Names

In 1999, the U.S. Congress enacted the **Anticybersquatting Consumer Protection Act (ACPA)**.[5] The act was specifically aimed at cybersquatters who register Internet domain names of famous companies and people and hold them hostage by demanding ransom payments from the famous company or person.

The act has two fundamental requirements: (1) The name must be famous and (2) the domain name must have been registered in bad faith. Thus, the law prohibits the act of cybersquatting itself if it is done in **bad faith**.

The first issue in applying the statute is whether the domain name is someone else's famous name. Trademarked names qualify; nontrademarked names—such as those of famous actors, actresses, singers, sports stars, politicians, and such—are also protected. The second issue is whether the domain name was registered in bad faith. In determining bad faith, a court may consider the

extent to which the domain name resembles the trademark owner's name or the famous person's name, whether goods or services are sold under the name, the holder's offer to sell or transfer the name, whether the holder has acquired multiple Internet domain names of famous companies and persons, and other factors.

The act provides for the issuance of cease-and-desist orders and injunctions against the domain name registrant. The court may order the domain name registrant to turn over the domain name to the trademark owner or famous person. The law also provides for monetary penalties. The ACPA gives owners of trademarks and persons with famous names rights to prevent the kidnapping of Internet domain names by cyberpirates.

Examples The Academy Award–winning actress Julia Roberts was awarded the domain name **http://juliaroberts.com**

from a male registrant who had no legitimate claim to the domain name and was found to have registered the domain name in bad faith. The singer nicknamed Sting was not so fortunate because the word *sting* is generic, allowing someone else to originally register and keep the domain name **http://sting.com**.

The following case involves a domain name dispute.

CASE 11.3   *Domain Name*

New York Yankees Partnership d/b/a The New York Yankees Baseball Club

Claim Number FA0609000803277 (2006)
National Arbitration Forum

"Such use by Moniker is indicative of an intent to disrupt the business of the Yankees, and constitutes registration and use of the disputed domain name in bad faith."

—Kalina, Judge

Facts

The New York Yankees Partnership d/b/a/ The New York Yankees Baseball Club (Yankees) is among the world's most recognized and followed sports teams, having won more than twenty World Series Championships and more than thirty American League pennants. The Yankees own the trademark for the NEW YORK YANKEES (Reg. No. 1,073,346), which was issued to the Yankees by the U. S. Patent and Trademark Office (USPTO) on September 13, 1977. Moniker Online Services, Inc. (Moniker), registered the domain name **www.nyyankees.com**. Moniker operated a commercial website under this domain name, where it offered links to third-party commercial websites that sold tickets to Yankees baseball games and where it sold merchandise bearing the NEW YORK YANKEES trademark without the permission of the Yankees. The Yankees filed a complaint with the National Arbitration Forum, alleging that Moniker had registered the domain in bad faith, in violation of the Internet Corporation for Assigned Names and Numbers (ICANN) Uniform Domain Dispute Resolution Policy and seeking to obtain the domain name from Moniker.

Issue

Has Moniker violated the Uniform Domain Dispute Resolution Policy?

Language of the Arbitrator

The complaint has sufficiently demonstrated that Moniker's <nyyankees.com> domain name is confusingly similar to complainant's NEW YORK YANKEES mark. Moniker uses the <nyyankees.com> domain name to operate a website providing links to third-party commercial websites offering tickets to professional sporting events of the Yankees and merchandise bearing the Yankees NEW YORK YANKEES mark. There is no evidence in the record to suggest that Moniker is commonly known by the disputed domain name. Such use by Moniker is indicative of an intent to disrupt the business of the Yankees, and constitutes registration and use of the disputed domain name in bad faith.

Decision

The arbitrator held that Moniker had violated the Uniform Domain Dispute Resolution Policy and ordered that the **www.nyyankees.com** domain name be transferred from Moniker to the Yankees.

Case Questions

Critical Legal Thinking
Do you think that the element of bad faith was shown in this case? Why or why not?

Ethics
Did Moniker act ethically in obtaining and using the **www.nyyankees.com** domain name and website?

Contemporary Business
Do you think that many parties register domain names similar to existing famous trademarks? Why would they do this?

Web Exercise
Go to **http://www.nyyankees.com** to see the trademarks used by the New York Yankees professional baseball team.

Key Terms and Concepts

Anticybersquatting
  Consumer Protection
  Act (ACPA) (238)
Bad faith (238)
Communications
  Decency Act (231)
Controlling the Assault
  of Non-Solicited
  Pornography and
  Marketing Act
  (CAN-SPAM Act)
  (229)
Cybersquatting (238)
Digital signature (233)
Domain name (236)
Electronic agent (233)

Electronic Communi-
  cations Privacy Act
  (ECPA) (235)
Electronic commerce
  (e-commerce) (228)
Electronic license
  (e-license) (234)
Electronic licensee
  (e-licensee) (235)
Electronic licensor
  (e-licensor) (235)
Electronic mail (e-mail)
  (229)
Electronic mail contract
  (e-mail contract)
  (229)

Electronic signature
  (e-signature) (233)
Electronic Signatures in
  Global and National
  Commerce Act
  (E-SIGN Act) (232)
Exclusive license
  (234)
Internet (Net) (228)
Internet Corporation for
  Assigned Names and
  Numbers (ICANN)
  (237)
Internet service provider
  (ISP) (230)
License (234)

Licensee (234)
Licensing (234)
Licensing agreement
  (235)
Licensor (234)
Spam (229)
Top-level domain name
  (TLD) (237)
Uniform Computer
  Information
  Transactions Act
  (UCITA) (233)
Web contract
  (e-contract) (231)
Website (228)
World Wide Web (228)

Law Case with Answer

John Doe v. GTE Corporation

Facts   Someone secretly took video cameras into the locker room and showers of the Illinois State University football team. Videotapes showing these undressed players were displayed at the website http://univ .youngstuds.com, operated by Franco Productions. The Internet name concealed the name of the person responsible. GTE Corporation, an ISP, provided a high-speed connection and storage space on its server so that the content of the website could be accessed. The nude images passed over GTE's network between Franco Productions and its customers. The football players sued Franco Productions and GTE for monetary damages. Franco Productions defaulted when it could not be located. Is GTE Corporation, the ISP, liable for damages to the plaintiff football players?

Answer   No, GTE Corporation, the ISP, is not liable for damages to the plaintiff football players. A part of the federal Communications Decency Act of 1996 provides: "No provider or user of an interactive computer service shall be treated as the publisher or speaker of any information provided by another information content provider." Just as the telephone company is not liable as an aider and abettor for tapes or narcotics sold by phone, and the Postal Service is not liable for tapes sold and delivered by mail, so a web host cannot be classified as an aider and abettor of criminal activities conducted through access to the Internet. GTE is not a "publisher or speaker." Therefore, GTE cannot be liable under any state law theory to the persons harmed by Franco's material. Thus, GTE Corporation, the ISP, is not liable for the nude videos of the football players transmitted over its system by Franco Productions. *John Doe v. GTE Corporation*, 347 F.3d 655, **Web** 2003 U.S. App. Lexis 21345 (United States Court of Appeals for the Seventh Circuit)

Critical Legal Thinking Cases

11.1 Cybersquatting   Ernest & Julio Gallo Winery (Gallo) is a famous maker of wines that is located in California. The company registered the trademark "Ernest & Julio Gallo" in 1964 with the U. S. Patent and Trademark Office. The company has spent over $500 million promoting its brand name and has sold more than four billion bottles of wine. Its name has taken on a secondary meaning as a famous trademark name. Steve, Pierce, and Fred Thumann created Spider Webs Ltd., a limited partnership, to register Internet domain names. Spider Webs registered more than two thousand Internet domain names, including http:// ernestandjuliogallo.com. Spider Webs is in the business of selling domain names. Gallo filed suit against Spider Webs Ltd. and the Thumanns, alleging violation of the federal Anticybersquatting Consumer Protection Act (ACPA). The U.S. District Court held in favor of Gallo and ordered Spider Webs to transfer the domain name http://ernestandjuliogallo.com to Gallo. Spider Webs Ltd. appealed. Who wins? *E. & J. Gallo Winery v. Spider Webs Ltd.*, 286 F.3d 270, **Web** 2002 U.S. App. Lexis 5928 (United States Court of Appeals for the Fifth Circuit)

11.2 Domain Name   Francis Net, a freshman in college and a computer expert, browses websites for hours each day. One day, she thinks to herself, "I can make money registering domain names and selling them for a fortune." She has recently seen an advertisement for Classic Coke, a cola drink produced and marketed by Coca-Cola Company. Coca-Cola Company has a famous trademark on the term *Classic Coke* and has spent millions of dollars advertising this brand and making the term famous throughout the United States and the rest of the world. Francis goes to the website www.networksolutions.com, an Internet domain name registration service, to see if the Internet domain name classiccoke.com has been taken. She discovers that it is available, so she immediately registers the Internet domain name classiccoke.com for herself and pays the $70 registration fee with her credit card. Coca-Cola Company decides to register the Internet domain name classiccoke.com, but when it checks at Network Solutions, Inc.'s, website, it discovers that Francis Net has already registered the Internet domain name. Coca-Cola Company contacts Francis, who demands $500,000 for the name. Coca-Cola Company sues Francis to prevent Francis from using the Internet domain name classiccoke.com and to recover it from her under the federal Anticybersquatting Consumer Protection Act (ACPA). Who wins?

11.3 E-Mail Contract   The Little Steel Company is a small steel fabricator that makes steel parts for various metal machine shop clients. When Little Steel Company receives an order from a client, it must locate and purchase 10 tons of a certain grade of steel to complete the order. The Little Steel Company sends an e-mail message to West Coast Steel Company, a large steel company, inquiring about the availability of 10 tons of the described grade of steel. The West Coast Steel Company replies by e-mail that it has available the required 10 tons of steel and quotes $450 per ton. The Little Steel Company's purchasing agent replies by e-mail that the Little Steel Company will purchase the 10 tons of described steel at the quoted price of $450 per ton. The e-mails are signed electronically by the Little Steel Company's purchasing agent and the selling agent of the West Coast Steel Company. When the steel arrives at the Little Steel Company's plant, the Little Steel Company rejects the shipment, claiming the defense of the Statute of Frauds. The West Coast Steel Company sues the Little Steel Company for damages. Who wins?

11.4 Electronic Signature   David Abacus uses the Internet to place an order to license software for his computer from Inet.License, Inc. (Inet), through Inet's electronic website ordering system. Inet's webpage order form asks David to type in his name, mailing address, telephone number, e-mail address, credit card information, computer location information, and personal identification number. Inet's electronic agent requests that David verify the information a second time before it accepts the order, which David does. The license duration is two years, at a license fee of $300 per month. Only after receiving the verification of information does Inet's electronic agent place the order and send an electronic copy of the software program to David's computer, where he installs the new software program. David later refuses to pay the license fee due Inet because he claims his electronic signature and information were not authentic. Inet sues David to recover the license fee. Is David's electronic signature enforceable against him?

11.5 License   Tiffany Pan, a consumer, intends to order three copies of a financial software program from iSoftware, Inc. Tiffany, using her computer, enters iSoftware's website, http://isoftware.com, and places an order with the electronic agent taking orders for the website. The license is for three years at $300 per month for each copy of the software program. Tiffany enters the necessary product code and description; her name, mailing address, and credit card information; and other data necessary to place the order. When the electronic order form prompts Tiffany to enter the number of copies of the software program she is ordering, Tiffany mistakenly types in "30." iSoftware's electronic agent places the order and ships thirty copies of the software program to Tiffany. When Tiffany receives the thirty copies of the software program, she ships them back to iSoftware with a note stating, "Sorry, there has been a mistake. I only meant to order 3 copies of the software, not 30." When iSoftware bills Tiffany for the license fees for the thirty copies, Tiffany refuses to pay. iSoftware sues Tiffany to recover the license fees for thirty copies. Who wins?

11.6 License   Metatag, Inc., is a developer and distributor of software and electronic information rights over the Internet. Metatag produces a software program called Virtual 4-D Link. A user of the Virtual 4-D Link program merely types in the name of a city and address anywhere in the world, and the computer transports the user there and creates a four-dimensional space and a sixth sense unknown to the world before. The software license is nonexclusive, and Metatag licenses its Virtual 4-D Link to millions of users worldwide. Nolan Bates, who has lived alone with his mother for too long, licenses the Virtual 4-D Link program for five years, for a license fee of $350 per month. Bates uses the program for two months before his mother discovers why he has had a smile on his face lately. Bates, upon his mother's urging, returns the Virtual 4-D Link software program to Metatag, stating that he is canceling the license. Metatag sues Bates to recover the unpaid license fees. Who wins?

11.7 E-Contract Einstein Financial Analysts, Inc. (EFA), has developed an electronic database that has recorded the number of plastic pails manufactured and sold in the United States since plastic was first invented. Using this data and a complicated patented software mathematical formula developed by EFA, a user can predict with 100 percent accuracy (historically) how the stock of each of the companies of the Dow Jones Industrial Average will perform on any given day of the year. William Buffet, an astute billionaire investor, wants to increase his wealth, so he enters into an agreement with EFA, whereby he is granted the sole right to use the EFA data (updated daily) and its financial model for the next five years. Buffet pays EFA $100 million for the right to the data and mathematical formula. After using the data and software formula for one week, Buffet discovers that EFA has also transferred the right to use the EFA plastic pail database and software formula to his competitor. Buffet sues EFA. What type of arrangement have EFA and Buffet entered into? Who wins?

11.8 E-License An Internet firm called Info.com, Inc., licenses computer software and electronic information over the Internet. Info.com has a website, http://info.com, where users can license Info.com software and electronic information. The website is operated by an electronic agent; a potential user enters Info.com's website and looks at available software and electronic information that is available from Info.com. Mildred Hayward pulls up the Info.com website on her computer and decides to order a certain type of Info.com software. Hayward enters the appropriate product code and description; her name, mailing address, and credit card information; and other data needed to complete the order for a three-year license at $300 per month; the electronic agent has Hayward verify all the information a second time. When Hayward has completed verifying the information, she types at the end of her order, "I accept this electronic software only if after I have used it for two months I still personally like it." Info.com's electronic agent delivers a copy of the software to Hayward, who downloads the copy of the software onto her computer. Two weeks later, Hayward sends the copy of the software back to Info.com, stating, "Read our contract: I personally don't like this software; cancel my license." Info.com sues Hayward to recover the license payments for three years. Who wins?

Ethics Cases

11.9 Ethics BluePeace.org is a new environmental group that has decided that expounding its environmental causes over the Internet is the best and most efficient way to spend its time and money to advance its environmental causes. To draw attention to its websites, BluePeace.org comes up with catchy Internet domain names. One is http://macyswearus.org, another is http://exxonvaldezesseals.org, and another is http://generalmotorscrashesdummies.org. The http://macyswearus.org website first shows beautiful women dressed in mink fur coats sold by Macy's Department Stores and then goes into graphic photos of minks being slaughtered and skinned and made into the coats. The http://exxonvaldezesseals.org website first shows a beautiful, pristine bay in Alaska, with the *Exxon Valdez* oil tanker quietly sailing through the waters, and then it shows photos of the ship breaking open and spewing forth oil and then seals who are gooed with oil, suffocating and dying on the shoreline. The website http://generalmotorscrashesdummies.org shows a General Motors automobile involved in normal crash tests with dummies followed by photographs of automobile accident scenes where people and children lay bleeding and dying after an accident involving General Motors automobiles. Macy's Department Stores,

the Exxon Oil Company, and the General Motors Corporation sue BluePeace.org for violating the federal Anticybersquatting Consumer Protection Act (ACPA).

1. What does the ACPA prohibit? What must be shown to find a violation of the ACPA?
2. Did BluePeace.org acted unethically in this case?
3. Who wins this case and why?

11.10 Ethics Apricot.com is a major software developer that licenses software to be used over the Internet. One of its programs, called Match, is a search engine that searches personal ads on the Internet and provides a match for users for potential dates and possible marriage partners. Nolan Bates subscribes to the Match software program from Apricot.com. The license duration is five years, with a license fee of $200 per month. For each subscriber, Apricot.com produces a separate webpage that shows photos of the subscriber and personal data. Bates places a photo of himself with his mother, with the caption, "Male, 30 years old, lives with mother, likes quiet nights at home." Bates licenses the Apricot.com Match software and uses it twelve hours each day, searching for his Internet match. Bates does not pay

Apricot.com the required monthly licensing fee for any of the three months he uses the software. After using the Match software but refusing to pay Apricot .com its licensing fee, Apricot.com activates the disabling bug in the software and disables the Match software on Bates's computer. Apricot.com does this with no warning to Bates. It then sends a letter to Bates stating, "Loser, the license is canceled!" Bates sues Apricot.com for disabling the Match software program.

1. What requirements must be met before Apricot. com can disable the Match software program?
2. Did Bates act ethically? Did Apricot.com act ethically?
3. Who wins this case and why?

Internet Exercises

1. Pick out a country. Use **www.google .com** or another Internet search engine and find the domain suffix is for this country.

2. Go to **www.rwgusa.net/bt.htm** to find out how to register a Bhutan .bt domain name. Go to **www.rwgusa .net/com_bt.htm** to find out how to register a Bhutan com.bt domain name.

3. The first step in registering a domain name is to determine whether any other party already owns the name. For this purpose, InterNIC maintains a "Whois" database that contains the domain names that have been registered. The InterNIC website is located at **www.internic.net**. Choose a domain name using the .com suffix and use **www.interic.net** to find out whether that name has been registered.

4. Domain names can be registered at Network Solutions, Inc.'s website, which is located at **www .networksolutions.com**. Choose a domain name using the .net suffix and use **www.networksolutions.com** to find out whether that name has been registered.

5. Use **www.google.com** or another Internet search engine and find an article that discusses the sale of a domain name. What was the domain name, and what price was it sold for?

6. Go to **http://msdnaa.oit.umass.edu/Neula.asp** and read the agreement. To what product does this license agreement apply?

Endnotes

1. 15 U.S.C. Sections 7701–7713.
2. 47 U.S.C. Section 230(c)(1).
3. 15 U.S.C. Chapter 96.

4. 18 U.S.C. Section 2510.
5. 15 U.S.C. Section 1125(d).

CHAPTER

12 UCC Sales and Lease Contracts and Warranties

FREIGHTER

Common carriers, such as freighters and other ships, carry goods for buyers and sellers on the Great Lakes and other waterways in the United States and on oceans and other bodies of water worldwide. Risk of loss of the goods while in transit depends on the shipping terms used in the shipping or destination contract.

Learning Objectives

After studying this chapter, you should be able to:

1. Define sales contracts governed by Article 2 of the UCC.
2. Define lease contracts governed by Article 2A of the UCC.
3. Describe the formation, performance, and remedies for breach of sales and lease contracts.
4. List and describe express and implied warranties.
5. Describe e-sales contracts and e-license contracts.

Chapter Outline

Introduction to UCC Sales and Lease Contracts and Warranties

Uniform Commercial Code (UCC)
  LANDMARK LAW • *Uniform Commercial Code (UCC)*

Article 2 (Sales)

Article 2A (Leases)
  CONTEMPORARY ENVIRONMENT • *Revised Article 2 (Sales) and Revised Article 2A (Leases)*

Formation of Sales and Lease Contracts
  CONTEMPORARY ENVIRONMENT • *UCC Firm Offer Rule*
  CONTEMPORARY ENVIRONMENT • *UCC Permits Additional Terms*
  CONTEMPORARY ENVIRONMENT • *"Battle of the Forms"*
  CONTEMPORARY ENVIRONMENT • *UCC Written Confirmation Rule*

E-Sales and E-Lease Contracts

Risk of Loss
  CONTEMPORARY ENVIRONMENT • *Commonly Used Shipping Terms*

Chapter Outline (continued)

" *Commercial law lies within a narrow compass, and is far purer and freer from defects than any other part of the system.*"

—Henry Peter Brougham
 House of Commons, February 7, 1828

Introduction to UCC Sales and Lease Contracts and Warranties

Most tangible items—such as books, clothing, tools, automobiles, and equipment—are considered *goods*. Toward the end of the 1800s, England enacted a statute (the Sales of Goods Act) that codified the common law rules of commercial transactions. In the United States, laws governing the sale of goods also developed. In 1906, the **Uniform Sales Act** was promulgated in the United States. This act was enacted in many states. In 1949, the National Conference of Commissioners on Uniform State Laws promulgated a comprehensive statutory scheme called the Uniform Commercial Code (UCC). The UCC covers most aspects of commercial transactions.

Article 2 (Sales) of the UCC governs the sale of goods, and *Article 2A (Leases)* of the UCC governs personal property leases. These articles are intended to provide clear, easy-to-apply rules that place the risk of loss of the goods on the party most able to either bear the risk or insure against it. The common law of contracts governs if either Article 2 or Article 2A is silent on an issue. Article 2 (Sales) and Article 2A (Leases) have been revised. *Revised Article 2 (Sales)* and *Revised Article 2A (Leases)* recognize the importance of electronic contracting and have established rules for the creation and enforcement of e-sales and e-lease contracts.

This chapter discusses the formation, performance, enforcement, breach, and the remedies available for the breach of sales and lease contracts and e-sales and e-lease contracts. This chapter also covers the creation and enforcement of sales and lease contract warranties.

When a manufacturer engages in advertising in order to bring his goods and their quality to the attention of the public and thus to create consumer demand, the representations made constitute an express warranty running directly to a buyer who purchases in reliance thereon. The fact that the sale is consummated with an independent dealer does not obviate the warranty.

Francis, Justice
*Henningsen v. Bloomfield
Motors, Inc. (1960)*

Uniform Commercial Code (UCC)

One of the major frustrations of businesspersons conducting interstate business is that they are subject to the laws of each state in which they operate. To address this problem, in 1949, the National Conference of Commissioners on Uniform State Laws promulgated the **Uniform Commercial Code (UCC)**. The following feature discusses the UCC.

Uniform Commercial Code (UCC)
A model act that includes comprehensive laws that cover most aspects of commercial transactions. All the states have enacted all or part of the UCC as statutes.

Landmark Law

Uniform Commercial Code (UCC)

The UCC is a **model act** drafted by the American Law Institute and the National Conference of Commissioners on Uniform State Laws. This model act contains uniform rules that govern commercial transactions. For the UCC or any part of the UCC to become law in a state, that state needs to enact the UCC as its commercial law statute. All states except Louisiana have adopted some version of the UCC.

The UCC is divided into articles, with each article establishing uniform rules for a particular facet of commerce in this country. The articles of the UCC are:

Article 1	General Provisions
Article 2	Sales
Revised Article 2	Sales
Article 2A	Leases
Revised Article 2A	Leases
Article 3	Negotiable Instruments
Article 4	Bank Deposits
Article 4A	Funds Transfers

Article 5	Letters of Credit
Article 6	Bulk Transfers and Bulk Sales
Article 7	Warehouse Receipts, Bills of Lading and Other Documents of Title
Article 8	Investment Securities
Article 9	Secured Transactions
Revised Article 9	Secured Transactions

The UCC is continually being revised to reflect changes in modern commercial practices and technology. Article 2, which establishes rules that govern the sale of goods, was revised. Article 2A, which governs leases of personal property, was also revised. Article 4A was added to regulate the use of wire transfers in the banking system. Articles 3 and 4, which cover the creation and transfer of negotiable instruments and the clearing of checks through the banking system, were substantially amended. Article 9, which covers secured transactions in personal property, was also revised.

Article 2 (Sales)

Article 2 (Sales)
An article of the UCC that governs sales of goods.

All states except Louisiana have adopted some version of **Article 2 (Sales)** of the UCC. Article 2 is also applied by federal courts to sales contracts governed by federal law. Article 2 has recently been revised. This article, referred to as *Revised Article 2 (Sales)*, has been adopted by some states.

What Is a Sale?

sale
The passing of title of goods from a seller to a buyer for a price.

Article 2 of the UCC applies to transactions in goods [UCC 2-102]. All states have held that Article 2 applies to **sales contracts** for the sale of goods. A **sale** consists of the passing of title of goods from a seller to a buyer for a price [UCC 2-106(1)].

Example The purchase of a large piece of equipment by a business is a sale subject to Article 2, whether the equipment was paid for using cash, credit card, or another form of consideration (see **Exhibit 12.1**).

Exhibit 12.1 SALES TRANSACTION

What Are Goods?

goods
Tangible things that are movable at the time of their identification to a contract.

Goods are defined as tangible things that are movable at the time of their identification to a contract [UCC 2-105(1)]. Specially manufactured goods and the unborn young of animals are examples of goods. Certain items are not considered goods and are not subject to Article 2. Money and intangible items are not tangible goods.

Examples Stocks, bonds, and patents are not tangible goods.

Real estate is not a tangible good because it is not movable [UCC 2-105(1)]. However, minerals, structures, growing crops, and other things that are severable from real estate may be classified as goods, subject to Article 2.

Examples The sale and removal of a chandelier in a house is a sale of goods subject to Article 2 because its removal would not materially harm the real estate. The sale and removal of the furnace, however, would be a sale of real property because its removal would cause material harm [UCC 2-107(2)].

A lean agreement is better than a fat judgment.

Proverb

Goods Versus Services

Contracts for the provision of services—including legal services, medical services, and dental services—are not covered by Article 2. Sometimes, however, a sale involves both the provision of a service and a good in the same transaction. Such a sale is referred to as a **mixed sale**. Article 2 applies to mixed sales only if the goods are the predominant part of the transaction. Whether the sale of goods is the predominant part of a mixed sale is decided by courts on a case-by-case basis.

Example A dentist places a denture in a patient. Here, although the denture is a good, the predominant part of the transaction is the provision of services by the dentist. Therefore, the UCC would not apply to the transaction.

mixed sale
A sale that involves the provision of a service and a good in the same transaction.

Article 2A (Leases)

Personal property leases are a billion-dollar industry. Consumer leases of automobiles or equipment and commercial leases of such items as aircraft and industrial machinery fall into this category. **Article 2A (Leases)** of the UCC directly addresses personal property leases [UCC 2A-101]. It establishes a comprehensive, uniform law covering the formation, performance, and default of leases in goods [UCC 2A-102, 2A-103(h)].

Article 2A is similar to Article 2. In fact, many Article 2 provisions were simply adapted to reflect leasing terminology and practices that carried over to Article 2A.

Article 2A (Leases)
An article of the UCC that governs leases of goods.

Definition of *Lease*

A **lease** of goods is a transfer of the right to the possession and use of named goods for a set term in return for certain consideration [UCC 2A-103(1)(i)(x)]. Leased goods can be anything from a rental car leased to an individual for a few days to a complex line of industrial equipment leased to a multinational corporation for a number of years.

In a **lease contract**, the **lessor** is the person who transfers the right of possession and use of goods under the lease [UCC 2A-103(1)(p)]. The **lessee** is the person who acquires the right to possession and use of goods under a lease [UCC 2A-103(1)(n)].

Example Ingersoll-Rand Corporation, which manufactures robotic equipment, enters into a lease to lease robotic equipment to Dow Chemical. Ingersoll-Rand is the lessor, and Dow Chemical is the lessee (see **Exhibit 12.2**).

lease
A transfer of the right to the possession and use of named goods for a set term in return for certain consideration.

lessor
A person who transfers the right of possession and use of goods under a lease.

lessee
A person who acquires the right to possession and use of goods under a lease.

Exhibit 12.2 LEASE

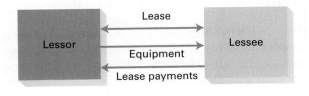

The following feature discusses the revision of UCC Article 2 and Article 2A.

Contemporary Environment

Revised Article 2 (Sales) and Revised Article 2A (Leases)

After years of study and debate, in 2003 **Revised Article 2 (Sales)** and **Revised Article 2A (Leases)** were promulgated by the National Conference of Commissioners on Uniform State Laws and the American Law Institute.

The modifications to Article 2 and Article 2A include changes to provisions that were controversial in the past, as well as the addition of new provisions to recognize changes in the commercial environment. Revised Articles 2 and 2A are considered to be the most modern and efficient rules governing the sales and leases of goods. In addition,

Revised Articles 2 and 2A contain many new provisions and rules that recognize the importance of electronic contracting for the sale and lease of goods. The revised articles provide rules for the creation and enforcement of electronic contracts for the sale and lease of goods. It is expected that after sufficient study some states will adopt the revised articles.

This chapter notes he changes and differences that Revised Articles 2 and 2A have made to current UCC sales and lease laws.

Formation of Sales and Lease Contracts

As with general contracts, the formation of sales and lease contracts requires an offer and an acceptance. The UCC-established rules for each of these elements often differ considerably from common law.

A contract for the sale or lease of goods may be made in any manner sufficient to show agreement, including conduct by both parties that recognizes the existence of a contract [UCC 2-204(1), 2A-204(1)]. Under the UCC, an agreement sufficient to constitute a contract for the sale or lease of goods may be found even though the moment of its making is undetermined [UCC 2-204(2), 2A-204(2)].

Open Terms

Sometimes the parties to a sales or lease contract leave open a major term in the contract. The UCC is tolerant of open terms. According to UCC 2-204(3) and 2A-204(3), a contract does not fail because of indefiniteness if (1) the parties intended to make a contract and (2) there is a reasonably certain basis for giving an appropriate remedy. In effect, certain **open terms** are permitted to be "read into" a sales or lease contract. This rule is commonly referred to as the **gap-filling rule**. Some examples of terms that are commonly left open are discussed in the following list.

- **Open price term.**   If a sales contract does not contain a specific price (**open price term**), a "reasonable price" is implied at the time of delivery. For example, a contract may provide that a price is to be fixed by a market rate, such as a commodities market rate.
- **Open payment term.**   If the parties to a sales contract do not agree on payment terms, payment is due at the time and place at which the buyer is to receive the goods. If delivery is authorized and made by way of document of title, payment is due at the time and place at which the buyer is to receive the document of title, regardless of where the goods are to be received [UCC 2-310].
- **Open delivery term.**   If the parties to a sales contract do not agree to the time, place, and manner of delivery of the goods, the place for delivery is the seller's place of business. If the seller does not have a place of business, delivery is to be made at the seller's residence. If identified goods are located at some other

place, and both parties know of this fact at the time of contracting, that place is the place of delivery [UCC 2-308].

- **Open time term.**   If the parties to a sales contract do not set a specific time of performance for any obligation under the contract, the contract must be performed within a reasonable time.
- **Open assortment term.**   If the assortment of goods to a sales contract is left open, the buyer is given the option of choosing those goods. The buyer must make the selection in good faith and within limits set by commercial reasonableness [UCC 2-311(2)].

The following feature discusses a unique UCC rule.

firm offer rule
A UCC rule which says that a merchant who makes an offer to buy, sell, or lease goods and assures the other party in a separate writing that the offer will be held open cannot revoke the offer for the time stated or, if no time is stated, for a reasonable time.

Contemporary Environment

UCC Firm Offer Rule

Recall that the common law of contracts allows the offeror to revoke an offer any time prior to its acceptance. The UCC recognizes an exception to this rule, which is called the **firm offer rule**. This rule states that a *merchant* who (1) offers to buy, sell, or lease goods and (2) gives a written and signed assurance on a separate form that the offer will be held open cannot revoke the offer for the time stated or, if no time is stated, for a reasonable time. The maximum amount of time permitted under this rule is three months [UCC 2-205, 2A-205].

Example On June 1, Sophisticated LLC, a BMW automobile dealer, offers to sell a BMW M3 coupe to Mandy for $60,000. Sophisticated LLC signs a written assurance to keep that offer open to Mandy until July 15. On July 5, Sophisticated LLC sells the car to another buyer. On July 15, Mandy tenders $60,000 for the car. Sophisticated LLC is a merchant subject to the firm offer rule. Sophisticated LLC is liable to Mandy for breach of contract. Thus, if Mandy has to pay $70,000 for the car at another dealership, she can recover $10,000 from Sophisticated LLC.

Acceptance

Both common law and the UCC provide that a contract is created when the offeree (i.e., the buyer or lessee) sends an acceptance to the offeror (i.e., the seller or lessor), not when the offeror receives the acceptance.

Examples A sales or lease contract is made when the acceptance letter is delivered to the post office. The contract remains valid even if the post office loses the letter. An e-contract is made when the offeree sends an e-mail or another electronic document to the offeror.

Unless otherwise unambiguously indicated by language or circumstance, an offer to make a sales or lease contract may be accepted in any manner and by any reasonable medium of acceptance [UCC 2-206(1)(a), 2A-206(1)].

The following feature discusses an area of the law where the UCC differs from the common law of contracts.

Law must be stable and yet it cannot stand still.

Roscoe Pound
Interpretations of Legal History (1923)

additional terms
A UCC rule that permits an acceptance of a sales contract to contain additional terms and still act as an acceptance rather than a counteroffer in certain circumstances.

Contemporary Environment

UCC Permits Additional Terms

Under common law's **mirror image rule**, an offeree's acceptance must be on the same terms as the offer. The inclusion of **additional terms** in the acceptance is considered a **counteroffer** rather than an acceptance. Thus, a counteroffer extinguishes the offeror's original offer.

UCC 2-207(1) is more liberal than the mirror image rule. It permits definite and timely expression of acceptance or written confirmation to operate as an acceptance even though the contract contains terms that are additional to or different from the offered terms, unless the acceptance

(continued)

is expressly conditional on assent to such terms. This rule differs for *merchants* and *nonmerchants*.

If one or both parties to a sales contract are nonmerchants, any additional terms are considered **proposed additions** to the contract. The proposed additions do not constitute a counteroffer or extinguish the original offer. If the offeree's proposed additions are accepted by the original offeror, they become part of the contract. If they are not accepted, the sales contract is formed on the basis of the terms of the original offer [UCC 2-207(2)].

Example A salesperson at a Lexus dealership offers to sell a coupe to a buyer for $60,000. The buyer replies, "I accept your offer, but I would like to have a satellite radio in the car." The satellite radio is a proposed addition to the contract. If the salesperson agrees, the contract between the parties consists of the terms of the original offer plus the additional term regarding the satellite radio. If the salesperson rejects the proposed addition, the sales contract consists of the terms of the original offer because the buyer made a definite expression of acceptance.

The following feature discusses how the UCC resolves a problem that commonly occurs between merchants.

Contemporary Environment

UCC "Battle of the Forms"

When merchants negotiate sales contracts, they often exchange preprinted forms. These "boilerplate" forms usually contain terms that favor the drafter. Thus, an offeror who sends a standard form contract as an offer to the offeree may receive an acceptance drafted on the offeree's own form contract. This scenario—commonly called the **battle of the forms**—raises important questions: Is there a contract? If so, what are its terms? The UCC provides guidance in answering these questions.

Under UCC 2-207(2), if both parties are merchants, any additional terms contained in an acceptance become part of the sales contract unless (1) the offer expressly limits acceptance to the terms of the offer, (2) the additional terms materially alter the terms of the original contract, or (3) the offeror notifies the offeree that he or she objects to the additional terms within a reasonable time after receiving the offeree's modified acceptance.

In the battle of the forms, there is no contract if the additional terms so materially alter the terms of the original offer that the parties cannot agree on the contract. This fact-specific determination is made by the courts on a case-by-case basis.

UCC Statute of Frauds

Statute of Frauds
A rule in the UCC that requires all contracts for the sale of goods costing $500 or more and lease contracts involving payments of $1,000 or more to be in writing.

The UCC includes **Statute of Frauds** provisions that apply to sales and lease contracts. Article 2 provides that contracts for the *sale of goods* costing *$500 or more* must be in writing [UCC 2-201(1)]. Revised Article 2 raises this amount to $5,000. Article 2A provides that *lease* contracts involving payments of *$1,000 or more* must be in writing [UCC 2A-201(1)]. Revised Article 2A raises this amount to $20,000.

The following feature discusses a unique UCC rule that applies to contracts between merchants.

Contemporary Environment

UCC Written Confirmation Rule

Pursuant the **written confirmation rule**, if both parties to an oral sales or lease contract are merchants, the Statute of Frauds writing requirement can be satisfied if (1) one of the parties to an oral agreement sends a written confirmation of the sale or lease within a reasonable time after contracting and (2) the other merchant does not give written notice of an objection to the contract within ten days after receiving the confirmation. This situation is true even though the party receiving the written confirmation has not signed it. The only stipulations are that the confirmation is sufficient and that the party to whom it was sent has reason to know its contents [UCC 2-201(2)].

Example A merchant-seller in Chicago orally contracts by telephone to sell goods to a merchant-buyer in Phoenix for $100,000. Within a reasonable time after contracting, the seller sends sufficient written confirmation to the buyer of the agreed-upon transaction. The buyer, who has reason to know the contents of the written confirmation, fails to object to the contents of the confirmation in writing within ten days after receiving it. Under the UCC, the Statute of Frauds has been met, and the buyer cannot thereafter raise it against enforcement of the contract.

Identification of Goods

The **identification of goods** is rather simple. It means distinguishing the goods named in a contract from the seller's or lessor's other goods. The seller or lessor retains the risk of loss of the goods until he or she identifies them to a sales or lease contract. Further, UCC 2-401(1) and 2-501 prevent title to goods from passing from the seller to the buyer unless the goods are identified to the sales contract. In a lease transaction, title to the leased goods remains with the lessor or a third party. It does not pass to the lessee.

Passage of Title

Once the goods that are the subject of a contract exist and have been identified, title to the goods may be transferred from the seller to the buyer. Under UCC 2-401(1), **title** to goods passes from the seller to the buyer in any manner and on any conditions explicitly agreed upon by the parties. If the parties do not agree to a specific time, title passes to the buyer when and where the seller's performance with reference to the physical delivery is completed.

In a **shipment contract** that requires the seller to ship the goods to the buyer via a common carrier and the seller is required to make proper shipping arrangements and deliver the goods into the carrier's hands, title passes to the buyer at the time and place of shipment [UCC 2-401(2)(a)]. In a **destination contract** that requires the seller to deliver the goods either to the buyer's place of business or to another destination specified in the sales contract, title passes to the buyer when the seller tenders delivery of the goods at the specified destination [UCC 2-401(2)(b)].

E-Sales and E-Lease Contracts

Revised Article 2 (Sales) and Revised Article 2A (Leases) contain provisions that recognize the importance of electronic contracting in sales and lease transactions. The revised articles contain new definitions that apply to **electronic sales contracts (e-sales contracts)** and **electronic lease contracts (e-lease contracts)**. The following are some of the new definitions for electronic commerce and their implications:

- *Electronic* means relating to technology having electrical, digital, magnetic, wireless, optical, electromagnetic, or similar capabilities [Revised UCC 2-103(1)(f), Revised UCC 2A-103(1)(h)]. This term, as used throughout Revised Articles 2 and 2A, extends many of the provisions and rules of the UCC to cover electronic contracting of sales and lease contracts.
- *Electronic agent* means a computer program or an electronic or other automated means used independently to initiate an action or respond to electronic records or performances in whole or in part, without review or action by an individual [Revised UCC 2-103(1)(g), Revised UCC 2A-103(1)(i)]. This definition, as used in many of the provisions of UCC Articles 2 and 2A, allows for the contracting for the sale and lease of goods over the Internet, using websites to order or lease goods.
- *Electronic record* means a record created, generated, sent, communicated, received, or stored by electronic means [Revised UCC 2-103(1)(h), Revised UCC 2A-103(1)(j)]. This term is often used in Revised Articles 2 and 2A to replace

battle of the forms
A UCC rule which states that if both parties are merchants, additional terms contained in the acceptance become part of the sales contract *unless* (1) the offer expressly limits the acceptance to the terms of the offer, (2) the additional terms materially alter the original contract, or (3) the offeror notifies the offeree that he or she objects to the additional terms within a reasonable time after receiving the offeree's modified acceptance. There is no contract if the additional terms so materially alter the terms of the original offer that the parties cannot agree on the contract.

written confirmation rule
A rule which provides that if both parties to an oral sales or lease contract are merchants, the Statute of Frauds writing requirement can be satisfied if (1) one of the parties to the oral agreement sends a written confirmation of the sale or lease within a reasonable time after contracting and (2) the other merchant does not give written notice of an objection to the contract within ten days after receiving the confirmation.

identification of goods
Distinguishing of the goods named in a contract from the seller's or lessor's other goods.

title
Legal, tangible evidence of ownership of goods.

the word *writing* and thus recognizes that UCC contracts and other information may be sent or stored by electronic means rather than in tangible writings.

- *Record* means information that is inscribed on a tangible medium or that is stored in an electronic or other medium and is retrievable in perceivable form [Revised UCC 2-103(1)(m), Revised UCC 2A-103(1)(cc)]. The term *record* is now used in many of the provisions of Revised Articles 2 and 2A in place of the term *writing* and thus further recognizes the importance of electronic contracting.

These terms are used throughout the provisions of Revised Article 2 (Sales) and Revised Article 2A (Leases). These definitions expand the coverage of the provisions of UCC Article 2 and Article 2A to electronic contracting of sales and lease contracts.

Risk of Loss

Article 2 of the UCC allows the parties to a sales contract to agree among them who will bear the **risk of loss** if the goods subject to the contract are lost or destroyed. If the parties do not have a specific agreement concerning the assessment of the risk of loss, the UCC mandates who will bear the risk of loss. In a *shipment contract* the risk of loss passes to the buyer when the seller delivers the conforming goods to the carrier; the buyer bears the risk of loss of the goods during transportation [UCC 2-509(1) (a)]. In a *destination contract* the seller bears the risk of loss of the goods during their transportation; the risk of loss does not pass until the goods are tendered to the buyer at the specified destination [UCC 2-509(1)(b)].

The following feature discusses commonly used shipping terms.

Contemporary Environment

Commonly Used Shipping Terms

Often, goods subject to a sales contract are shipped by a common carrier such as a trucking company, a ship, or a railroad. Many sales contracts contain **shipping terms** that have different legal meanings and consequences. The following are commonly used shipping terms:

- **F.O.B. (free on board)** *point of shipment* requires the seller to arrange to ship the goods and put the goods in the carrier's possession. The buyer bears the shipping expense and risk of loss while the goods are in transit [UCC 2-319(1)(a)].

   Example If a shipment contract specifies "F.O.B. Anchorage, Alaska," and the goods are shipped from New Orleans, Louisiana, the buyer bears the shipping expense and risk of loss while the goods are in transit to Anchorage, Alaska.

- **F.A.S. (free alongside ship)** *port of shipment* or **F.A.S. (vessel)** *port of shipment* requires the seller to deliver and tender the goods alongside the named vessel or on the dock designated and provided by the buyer. The seller bears the expense and risk of loss until this is done [UCC 2-319(2)(a)]. The buyer bears shipping costs and the risk of loss during transport.

   Example If a contract specifies "F.A.S. *The Gargoyle*, New Orleans," and the goods are to be shipped to

Anchorage, Alaska, the seller bears the expense and risk of loss until it delivers the goods into the hands of the vessel *The Gargoyle* in New Orleans. Once this is done, the buyer pays the shipping costs, and the risk of loss passes to the buyer during transport to Anchorage, Alaska.

- **C.I.F. (cost, insurance, and freight)** is a pricing term that means that the price includes the cost of the goods and the costs of insurance and freight. **C.& F. (cost and freight)** is a pricing term that means that the price includes the cost of the goods and the cost of freight. In both cases, the seller must, at his or her own expense and risk, put the goods into the possession of a carrier. The buyer bears the risk of loss during transportation [UCC 2-320(1)(3)].

   Example If a contract specifies "C.I.F. *The Gargoyle*, New Orleans, Louisiana" or "C.&F. *The Gargoyle*, New Orleans, Louisiana," and the goods are to be shipped to Anchorage, Alaska, the seller bears the expense and risk of loss until it delivers the goods into the hands of the vessel *The Gargoyle* in New Orleans. Once this is done, the risk of loss passes to the buyer during transport from New Orleans to Anchorage, Alaska.

- **F.O.B. (free on board)** *place of destination* requires the seller to bear the expense and risk of loss until the goods are tendered to the buyer at the place of destination [UCC 2-319(1)(b)].

  Example If a destination contract specifies "F.O.B. Anchorage, Alaska," and the goods are shipped from New Orleans, Louisiana, the seller bears the expense and risk of loss before and while the goods are in transit until the goods are tendered to the buyer at the port of Anchorage, Alaska.

- **Ex-ship (from the carrying vessel)** requires the seller to bear the expense and risk of loss until the goods are unloaded from the ship at its port of destination [UCC 2-322(1)(b)].

Example If a contract specifies "Ex-ship, *The Gargoyle*, Anchorage, Alaska," and the goods are shipped from New Orleans, Louisiana, the seller bears the expense and risk of loss before and until the goods are unloaded from *The Gargoyle* at the port in Anchorage, Alaska.

- **No-arrival, no-sale contract** requires the seller to bear the expense and risk of loss of the goods during transportation. However, the seller is under no duty to deliver replacement goods to the buyer because there is no contractual stipulation that the goods will arrive at the appointed destination [UCC 2-324(a),(b)].

The parties to a lease contract may agree as to who will bear the risk of loss of the goods if they are lost or destroyed. If the parties do not so agree in the case of an **ordinary lease**, if the lessor is a merchant, the risk of loss passes to the lessee on the receipt of the goods [UCC 2A-219].

To protect against financial loss that would occur if goods were damaged, destroyed, lost, or stolen, the parties to sales and lease contracts should purchase insurance against such loss. If the goods are then lost or damaged, the insured party receives reimbursement from the insurance company for the loss. Both the buyer and seller, or the lessee and lessor, can have an insurable interest in the goods at the same time [UCC 2-501, 2A-218].

Sales of Goods by Nonowners

Sometimes people sell goods even though they do not hold valid title to them. The UCC anticipated many of the problems this situation could cause and established rules concerning the title, if any, that could be transferred to purchasers.

Stolen Goods

In a case in which a buyer purchases goods or a lessee leases goods from a thief who has stolen them, the purchaser does not acquire title to the goods, and the lessee does not acquire any leasehold interest in the goods. The real owner can reclaim the goods from the purchaser or lessee [UCC 2-403(1)]. This is called **void title** or **void leasehold interest**.

Example Jack steals a truckload of Sony high-definition television sets that are owned by Electronics Store. The thief resells the televisions to City-Mart, which does not know that the goods were stolen. If Electronics Store finds out where the televisions are, it can reclaim them. This is because the thief had no title in the goods, so title was not transferred to City-Mart. There is void title. City-Mart's only recourse is against the thief, if he or she can be found.

Fraudulently Obtained Goods

A seller or lessor has **voidable title** or **voidable leasehold interest** to goods if he obtained the goods through fraud, if his check for the payment of the goods or lease is dishonored, or if he impersonated another person.

A person with voidable title to goods can transfer good title to a **good faith purchaser for value** or a good leasehold interest to a **good faith subsequent lessee**. A good faith purchaser or lessee for value is someone who pays sufficient

void title
A situation in which a thief acquires no title to goods he or she steals.

voidable title
A title that a purchaser has if goods were obtained by (1) fraud, (2) a check that is later dishonored, or (3) impersonation of another person.

good faith purchaser for value
A person to whom good title can be transferred from a person with voidable title. The real owner cannot reclaim goods from a good faith purchaser for value.

good faith subsequent lessee
A person to whom a lease interest can be transferred from a person with voidable title. The real owner cannot reclaim the goods from the subsequent lessee until the lease expires.

consideration or rent for the goods to the person he or she honestly believes has good title to or leasehold interest in those goods [UCC 2-201(1), 1-201(44) (d)]. The real owner cannot reclaim goods from such a purchaser or lessee [UCC 2-403(1)].

Example Max buys a Rolex watch from his neighbor Dorothy for nearly fair market value. It is later discovered that Dorothy obtained the watch from Jewelry Store with a "bounced check"—that is, a check for which there were insufficient funds to pay for the Rolex watch. Jewelry Store cannot reclaim the watch from Max because Max, the second purchaser, purchased the watch in good faith and for value.

Entrustment Rule

buyer in the ordinary course of business
A person who, in good faith and without knowledge that the sale violates the ownership or security interests of a third party, buys goods in the ordinary course of business from a person in the business of selling goods of that kind. A buyer in the ordinary course of business takes the goods free of any third-party security interest in the goods.

If an owner *entrusts* the possession of his or her goods to a merchant who deals in goods of that kind, the merchant has the power to transfer all rights (including title) in the goods to a **buyer in the ordinary course of business** [UCC 2-403(2)]. The real owner cannot reclaim the goods from this buyer. This is called the **entrustment rule**.

Example Kim brings her diamond ring to Ring Store to be repaired. Ring Store both sells and repairs jewelry. Kim leaves (entrusts) her ring at the store until it is repaired. Ring Store sells Kim's ring to Harold, who is going to propose marriage to Gretchen. Harold, a buyer in the ordinary course of business, acquires title to the ring. Kim cannot reclaim her ring from Harold (or Gretchen). Her only recourse is to sue Ring Store.

The entrustment rule also applies to leases. If a lessor entrusts the possession of his or her goods to a lessee who is a merchant who deals in goods of that kind, the merchant-lessee has the power to transfer all the lessor's and lessee's rights in the goods to a buyer or sublessee in the ordinary course of business [UCC 2A-305(2)].

CONCEPT SUMMARY
PASSAGE OF TITLE BY NONOWNER THIRD PARTIES

Type of Transaction	Title Possessed by Seller	Innocent Purchaser	Purchaser Acquires Title to Goods
Goods acquired by theft are resold.	Void title	Good faith purchaser for value	No. Original owner may reclaim the goods.
Goods acquired by fraud or dishonored check are resold.	Voidable title	Good faith purchaser for value	Yes. Purchaser takes goods, free of claim of original owner.
Goods entrusted by owner to merchant who deals in that type of goods are resold.	No title	Buyer in the ordinary course of business	Yes. Purchaser takes goods, free of claim of original owner.

electronic record
A record that is created, generated, sent, communicated, received, or stored by electronic means.

electronic agent
A computer program or an electronic or other automated means used independently to initiate an action or respond to electronic records or performances in whole or in part, without review or action by an individual.

E-Communications and E-Signatures

Written contracts and written signatures are given effect by Article 2 (Sales) and Article 2A (Leases) of the UCC. Revised Article 2 (Sales) and Revised Article 2A (Leases) establish the following rules for electronic sales and lease contracts:

- A record or signature may not be denied legal effect or enforcement solely because it is in electronic form [Revised UCC 2-211(1), Revised UCC 2A-222(1)]. This provision states that electronic contracts and electronic signatures are to be given legal effect and can be enforced against contracting parties.
- An **electronic record** or **electronic signature (e-signature)** is attributable to a person if it was the act of the person or the person's **electronic agent** [Revised UCC 2-212, Revised UCC 2A-223]. This provision permits a person to conduct

business himself or through electronic agents, using electronic records and electronic signatures.

- If the receipt of an **electronic communication** has a legal effect, it has that effect even if no individual is aware of its receipt [Revised UCC 2-213(1), Revised UCC 2A-224(1)]. This rule acknowledges the legal effect of electronic communications that are received by electronic agents such as Internet websites.
- Receipt of an **electronic acknowledgment** of an electronic communication establishes that the communication was received but, in itself, does not establish that the content sent corresponds to the content received [Revised UCC 2-213(2), Revised UCC 2A-224(2)]. Thus, an electronic acknowledgement of the receipt of an electronic communication proves that the electronic communication was received. This acknowledgment does not, in itself, establish what the content of the electronic communication was, however. That must come from other evidence.

These rules place electronic signatures on par with written signatures. They also establish special conditions regarding the receipt of electronic communications.

The buyer needs a hundred eyes, the seller not one.

George Herbert
Jacula Prudentum (1651)

Remedies for Breach of Sales and Lease Contracts

Goods that are accepted must be paid for [UCC 2-607(1)]. Unless the parties to a contract agree otherwise, payment is due from a buyer when and where the goods are delivered, even if the place of delivery is the same as the place of shipment. Buyers often purchase goods on credit extended by the seller. Unless the parties agree to other terms, the credit period begins to run from the time the goods are shipped [UCC 2-310]. A lessee must pay lease payments in accordance with the lease contract [UCC 2A-516(1)].

Convenience is the basis of mercantile law.

Lord Mansfield
Medcalf v. Hall (1782)

Seller's and Lessor's Remedies

Various remedies are available to sellers and lessors if a buyer or lessee breaches a sales or lease contract. These remedies are set forth in **Exhibit 12.3**.

Exhibit 12.3 SELLER'S AND LESSOR'S REMEDIES

Possession of Goods at the Time of the Buyer's or Lessee's Breach	Seller's or Lessor's Remedies
Goods in the possession of the seller or lessor	1. Withhold delivery of the goods [UCC 2-703(a), 2A-523(1)(c)]. 2. Demand payment in cash if the buyer is insolvent [UCC 2-702(1), 2A-525(1)]. 3. Resell or release the goods and recover the difference between the contract or lease price and the resale or release price [UCC 2-706, 2A-527]. 4. Sue for breach of contract and recover as damages either of the following: a. The difference between the market price and the contract price [UCC 2-708(1), 2A-528(1)] b. Lost profits [UCC 2-708(2), 2A-528(2)] 5. Cancel the contract [UCC 2-703(f), 2A-523(1)(a)].
Goods in the possession of a carrier or bailee	1. Stop goods in transit [UCC 2-705(1), 2A-526(1)]. a. Carload, truckload, planeload, or larger shipment if the buyer is solvent. b. Any size shipment if the buyer is insolvent.

(continued)

Possession of Goods at the Time of the Buyer's or Lessee's Breach	Seller's or Lessor's Remedies

Goods in the possession of the buyer or lessee	1. Sue to recover the purchase price or rent [UCC 2- 709(1), 2A-525(1)].
	2. Reclaim the goods [UCC 2-507(2), 2A-529(1)].
	  a. The seller delivers goods in cash sale, and the buyer's check is dishonored.
	  b. The seller delivers goods in a credit sale, and the goods are received by an insolvent buyer.

Buyer's and Lessee's Remedies

The UCC provides a variety of remedies to a buyer or lessee upon the seller's or lessor's breach of a sales or lease contract. These remedies are set forth in **Exhibit 12.4**.

Exhibit 12.4 BUYER'S AND LESSEE'S REMEDIES

Situation	Buyer's or Lessee's Remedy
Seller or lessor refuses to deliver the goods or delivers nonconforming goods that the buyer or lessee does not want.	1. Reject nonconforming goods [UCC 2-601, 2A-509]. 2. Revoke acceptance of nonconforming goods [UCC 2-608, 2A-517(1)]. 3. Cover [UCC 2-712, 2A-518]. 4. Sue for breach of contract and recover damages [UCC 2-713, 2A-519]. 5. Cancel the contract [UCC 2-711(1), 2A-508(1)(a)].
Seller or lessor tenders nonconforming goods and the buyer or lessee accepts them.	1. Sue for ordinary damages [UCC 2-714(1), 2A-516(1)]. 2. Deduct damages from the unpaid purchase or rent price [UCC 2-714(1), 2A-516(1)].
Seller or lessor refuses to deliver the goods and the buyer or lessee wants them.	1. Sue for specific performance [UCC 2-716(1), 2A-521(1)]. 2. Replevy the goods [UCC 2-716(3), 2A-521(3)]. 3. Recover the goods from an insolvent seller or lessor [UCC 2-502, 2A-522].

Agreements Affecting Remedies

The UCC permits parties to a sales or lease contract to establish in advance in their contract the damages that will be paid upon a breach of the contract. Such preestablished damages, called **liquidated damages**, substitute for actual damages. In a sales or lease contract, liquidated damages are valid if they are reasonable in light of the anticipated or actual harm caused by the breach, the difficulties of proof of loss, and the inconvenience or nonfeasibility of otherwise obtaining an adequate remedy [UCC 2-718(1), 2A-504].

liquidated damages
Damages that will be paid upon a breach of contract that are established in advance.

Warranties

The doctrine of **caveat emptor**—"let the buyer beware"—governed the law of sales and leases for centuries. Finally, the law recognized that consumers and other purchasers and lessees of goods needed greater protection. Article 2 of the Uniform Commercial Code (UCC), adopted in whole or in part by all 50 states, establishes

Warranties are favored in law, being a part of a man's assurance.

Coke First Institute

certain warranties that apply to the sale of goods. Article 2A of the UCC, adopted in almost all states, establishes warranties that apply to lease transactions.

Warranties are the buyer's or lessee's assurance that the goods meet certain standards. Warranties, which are based on contract law, may be either *expressly* stated or *implied* by law. If the seller or lessor fails to meet a warranty, the buyer or lessee can sue for breach of warranty.

Express Warranties

Express warranties are created when a seller or lessor affirms that the goods he or she is selling or leasing meet certain standards of quality, description, performance, or condition [UCC 2-313(1), 2A-210(1)]. Express warranties can be either written, oral, or inferred from the seller's conduct. It is not necessary to use formal words such as *warrant* or *guarantee* to create an express warranty.

Example A statement such as "This car has been driven only 20,000 miles" is an express warranty because it is a statement of fact.

A seller's or lessor's **statement of opinion** (i.e., **puffing**) or commendation of goods does not create an express warranty. It is often difficult to determine whether a seller's statement is an affirmation of fact (which creates an express warranty) or a statement of opinion (which does not create a warranty). An affirmation of the *value* of goods does not create an express warranty [UCC 2-313(2), 2A-210(2)].

Example A used car salesperson's saying "This is the best used car available in town" does not create an express warranty because it is an opinion and mere puffing.

Implied Warranty of Merchantability

If a seller or lessor of a good is a *merchant* with respect to goods of that kind, the sales contract or lease contract contains an **implied warranty of merchantability** of the good unless this implied warranty is properly disclaimed [UCC 2-314(1),

warranty
A seller's or lessor's express or implied assurance to a buyer or lessee that the goods sold or leased meet certain quality standards.

express warranty
A warranty that is created when a seller or lessor makes an affirmation that the goods he or she is selling or leasing meet certain standards of quality, description, performance, or condition.

Nobody has a more sacred obligation to obey the law than those who make the law.

Sophocles

implied warranty of merchantability
Unless properly disclosed, a warranty that is implied that sold or leased goods are fit for the ordinary purpose for which they are sold or leased, as well as other assurances.

RESTAURANT
*The **implied warranty of fitness for human consumption** is an implied warranty that food and drink served by restaurants, bars, fast-food outlets, coffee shops, vending machines, and other purveyors of food and drink be safe for human consumption.*

implied warranty of fitness for human consumption
A warranty that applies to food or drink consumed on or off the premises of restaurants, grocery stores, fast-food outlets, and vending machines.

2A-212(1)]. The implied warranty of merchantability does not apply to sales or leases by nonmerchants or casual sales.

An implied warranty requires that the following standards be met: (1) The goods must be fit for the ordinary purposes for which they are used; (2) the goods must be adequately contained, packaged, and labeled; (3) the goods must be of an even kind, quality, and quantity within each unit; (4) the goods must conform to any promise or affirmation of fact made on the container or label; (5) the quality of the goods must pass without objection in the trade; or (6) fungible goods must meet a fair average or middle range of quality.

Example A consumer purchases a lawn chair. When he sits on the chair, it collapses, causing him injury. Here the implied warranty of merchantability has been breached because the chair was not fit for the ordinary purpose for which it is to be used. If, however, the same person is injured because he or she uses the chair as a ladder and it tips over, there is no breach of implied warranty because serving as a ladder is not the ordinary purpose of a chair.

Implied Warranty of Fitness for a Particular Purpose

implied warranty of fitness for a particular purpose
A warranty that arises where a seller or lessor warrants that the goods will meet the buyer's or lessee's expressed needs.

The UCC contains an **implied warranty of fitness for a particular purpose**. This implied warranty is breached if the goods do not meet the buyer's or lessee's expressed needs. The warranty applies to both merchant and nonmerchant sellers and lessors [UCC 2-315, 2A-213]

Example Susan wants to buy lumber to build a small deck in her backyard. She goes to Joe's Lumber Yard to purchase the lumber and describes to Joe, the owner of the lumber yard, the size of the deck she intends to build. Susan also tells Joe that she is relying on him to select the right lumber for the project. Joe selects the lumber and states that the lumber will serve Susan's purpose. Susan buys the lumber and builds the deck. Unfortunately, the deck collapses because the lumber was not strong enough to support it. Susan can sue Joe for breach of the implied warranty of fitness for a particular purpose.

Warranty Disclaimers

warranty disclaimer
A statement that negates express and implied warranties.

Warranties can be *disclaimed*, or limited. If an *express warranty* is made, it can be limited only if the **warranty disclaimer** and the warranty can be reasonably construed with each other. All implied warranties of quality may be disclaimed. The rules for disclaiming implied warranties are:

- **"As is" disclaimer.** Expressions such as *as is*, *with all faults*, or other language that makes it clear to the buyer that there are no implied warranties disclaims all implied warranties. An **"as is" disclaimer** is often included in sales contracts for used vehicles and other used products.
- **Disclaimer of the implied warranty of merchantability.** If the "as is" type of disclaimer is not used, disclaimers of the *implied warranty of merchantability* must specifically mention the term *merchantability* for the implied warranty of merchantability to be disclaimed. These disclaimers may be oral or written.
- **Disclaimer of the implied warranty of fitness for a particular purpose.** If the "as is" type of disclaimer is not used, the *implied warranty of fitness for a particular purpose* may be disclaimed in general language, without specific use of the term *fitness*. The disclaimer has to be in writing.

WEB EXERCISE
Go to **www.cptech.org/ecom/ ucita/licenses/liability.html** and read Microsoft's "Warranty and Liability Disclaimer Clauses in Current Shrinkwrap and Clickwrap Contracts."

Magnuson-Moss Warranty Act
A federal statute that regulates written warranties on consumer products.

Conspicuous Disclaimer. Written disclaimers must be conspicuously displayed to be valid. The courts construe **conspicuous** to mean noticeable to a reasonable person [UCC 2-316, 2A-214]. A heading printed in uppercase letters or a typeface that is larger or in a different style than the rest of the body of a sales or lease contract is considered to be conspicuous. Different-color type is also considered conspicuous.

Landmark Law

Magnuson-Moss Warranty Act

In 1975, Congress enacted the **Magnuson-Moss Warranty Act**,[1] which covers written warranties related to *consumer products*. This federal act is administered by the Federal Trade Commission (FTC). Consumer transactions, but not commercial and industrial transactions, are governed by the act.

The Magnuson-Moss Warranty Act does not require a seller or lessor to make an *express* written warranty. However, sellers or lessors who do make express warranties are subject to the provisions of the act. If a warrantor chooses to make an express warranty, the Magnuson-Moss Warranty Act requires that the warranty be labeled as either "full" or "limited." The fact that a warranty is full or limited must be conspicuously displayed. The disclosures must be in "understandable language":

- **Full warranty.** For a warranty to qualify as a **full warranty**, the warrantor must guarantee that a defective product will be repaired or replaced free during the warranty period. The warrantor must indicate whether there is a time limit on the full warranty (e.g., "full 36-month warranty").

- **Limited warranty.** In a **limited warranty**, the warrantor limits the scope of the warranty in some way. A warranty that covers the cost of parts, but not the cost of labor, to fix a defective product is a limited warranty. So too is an automobile warranty that covers the cost to replace or repair the powertrain, but no other parts, of an automobile.

The act stipulates that sellers or lessors who make express written warranties related to **consumer products** are forbidden from disclaiming or modifying the implied warranties of merchantability and fitness for a particular purpose.

A consumer may bring a *civil action* against a defendant for violating the provisions of the Magnuson-Moss Warranty Act. A successful plaintiff can recover damages, attorneys' fees, and other costs incurred in bringing the action. The act authorizes warrantors to establish an informal dispute resolution procedure. Aggrieved consumers must assert their claims through this procedure before they can take legal action.

The following feature discusses a source of international contract law.

International Law

United Nations Convention on Contracts for the International Sale of Goods (CISG)

International contracts of companies located in Singapore and around the world are often governed by the **United Nations Convention on Contracts for the International Sale of Goods (CISG)**. The CISG is a model act for international sales contracts. The CISG is the work of many countries and several international organizations. Singapore and more than 70 other countries are signatories to the CISG.

The CISG provides legal rules that govern the formation, performance, and enforcement of international sales contracts entered into between international businesses. Many of its provisions are remarkably similar to those of the U.S. Uniform Commercial Code (UCC). The CISG incorporates rules from all the major legal systems. It has, accordingly, received widespread support from developed, developing, and Communist countries.

The CISG applies to contracts for the international sale of goods. The buyer and seller must have their places of business in different countries. In order for the CISG to apply to an international sales contract, either (1) both of

the nations must be parties to the convention or (2) the contract specifies that the CISG controls. The contracting parties may agree to exclude (i.e., opt out of) or modify the application of the CISG.

Key Terms and Concepts

Additional terms (249)
Article 2 (Sales) (246)
Article 2A (Leases) (247)
"As is" disclaimer (258)
Battle of the forms (250)
Buyer in the ordinary course of business (254)
Caveat emptor (256)
C.&F. (cost and freight) (252)
C.I.F. (cost, insurance, and freight) (252)
Conspicuous (258)
Consumer products (259)
Counteroffer (249)
Destination contract (251)
Electronic acknowledgment (255)
Electronic agent (254)
Electronic communication (255)
Electronic lease contract (e-lease contract) (251)
Electronic record (254)
Electronic sales contract (e-sales contract) (251)

Electronic signature (e-signature) (254)
Entrustment rule (254)
Ex-ship (from the carrying vessel) (253)
Express warranty (257)
F.A.S. (free alongside ship) *port of shipment* (252)
F.A.S. (*vessel*) *port of shipment* (252)
Firm offer rule (249)
F.O.B. (free on board) *point of shipment* (252)
F.O.B. (free on board) *place of destination* (253)
Full warranty (259)
Gap-filling rule (248)
Good faith purchaser for value (253)
Good faith subsequent lessee (253)
Goods (246)
Identification of goods (251)
Implied warranty of fitness for a particular purpose (258)

Implied warranty of fitness for human consumption (257)
Implied warranty of merchantability (257)
Lease (247)
Lease contract (247)
Lessee (247)
Lessor (247)
Limited warranty (259)
Liquidated damages (256)
Magnuson-Moss Warranty Act (259)
Mirror image rule (249)
Mixed sale (247)
Model act (246)
No-arrival, no-sale contract (253)
Open price term (248)
Open term (248)
Ordinary lease (253)
Proposed additions (250)
Revised Article 2 (Sales) (248)
Revised Article 2A (Leases) (248)
Risk of loss (252)
Sale (246)

Sales contract (246)
Shipment contract (251)
Shipping terms (252)
Statement of opinion (puffing) (257)
Statute of Frauds (250)
Title (251)
Uniform Commercial Code (UCC) (245)
Uniform Sales Act (245)
United Nations Convention on Contracts for the International Sale of Goods (CISG) (259)
Void leasehold interest (253)
Void title (253)
Voidable leasehold interest (253)
Voidable title (253)
Warranty (257)
Warranty disclaimer (258)
Written confirmation rule (250)

Law Case with Answer
Mitsch v. Rockenbach Chevrolet

Facts   Joseph Mitsch purchased a used Chevrolet Yukon sport-utility vehicle (SUV) from Rockenbach Chevrolet. The Yukon was manufactured by General Motors Corporation (GMC). The Yukon had been driven over 36,000 miles. The purchase contract with Rockenbach Chevrolet contained the following disclaimer:

AS IS
THIS USED MOTOR VEHICLE IS SOLD AS IS. THE PURCHASER WILL BEAR THE ENTIRE EXPENSE OF REPAIRING OR CORRECTING ANY DEFECTS THAT PRESENTLY EXIST OR THAT MAY OCCUR IN THE VEHICLE.

Mitsch purchased GMC's extended service plan for the Yukon. During a period of approximately 18 months Mitsch experienced problems with the Yukon's transmission, engine, suspension, and climate control. All of the repairs were made by GMC dealerships and paid for by the GMC extended service plan. Mitsch sued Rockenbach Chevrolet for breach of the implied warranty of merchantability and sought to rescind his acceptance of the Yukon. Rockenbach Chevrolet argued that the "as is" disclaimer barred Mitsch's claim. Mitsch alleged that the "as is" disclaimer was not conspicuous and should be voided. Is the "as is" disclaimer conspicuous, and does it therefore properly disclaim the implied warranty of merchantability?

Answer   Yes, the "as is" disclaimer was conspicuous and therefore properly disclaimed the implied warranty of merchantability. An "as is" disclaimer properly disclaims all express and implied warranties.

Therefore, an "as is" disclaimer properly disclaims an implied warranty of merchantability if the disclaimer is conspicuous. A disclaimer is conspicuous if it is so written that a reasonable person against whom it is to operate ought to have noticed it. A printed heading in capital letters is conspicuous. Here, the heading "AS IS" was in capital letters. Language in the body of a form purchase contract is conspicuous if it is larger than the rest of the contract. Here, the words "**THIS USED MOTOR VEHICLE IS SOLD AS IS. THE PURCHASER WILL BEAR THE ENTIRE**

EXPENSE OF REPAIRING OR CORRECTING ANY DEFECTS THAT PRESENTLY EXIST OR THAT MAY OCCUR IN THE VEHICLE" were all in capital letters in the purchase contract that Mitsch signed. The "as is" disclaimer in the purchase contract was conspicuous and therefore disclaimed the implied warranty of merchantability. Therefore, Rockenbach Chevrolet was granted summary judgment, and Mitsch's lawsuit was dismissed. *Mitsch v. Rockenbach Chevrolet*, 359 Ill. App.3d 99, 833 N.E.2d 936, **Web** 2005 Ill.App. Lexis 699 (Appellate Court of Illinois)

Critical Legal Thinking Cases

12.1 Good or Service? Brenda Brandt was admitted to Sarah Bush Lincoln Health Center (Health Center) to receive treatment for urinary incontinence. During the course of an operation, the doctor surgically implanted a ProteGen Sling (sling) in Brandt. Subsequently, the manufacturer of the sling, Boston Scientific Corporation, issued a recall of the sling because it was causing medical complications in some patients. Brandt suffered serious complications and had the sling surgically removed.

Brandt sued Boston Scientific Corporation and Health Center for breach of the implied warranty of merchantability included in Article 2 (Sales) of the Uniform Commercial Code (UCC). Health Center filed a motion with the court to have the case against it dismissed. Health Center argued that it was a provider of services and not a merchant that sold goods, and because the UCC (Sales) applies to the sale of goods, Health Center was not subject to the UCC. Health Center proved that Brandt's bill was $11,174.50 total charge for her surgery, with a charge of $1,659.50, or 14.9%, for the sling and its surgical kit. Is the transaction between Brandt and Health Center predominantly the provision of services or the sale of goods? *Brandt v. Boston Scientific Corporation and Sarah Bush Lincoln Health Center*, 792 N.E.2d 296, **Web** 2003 Ill. Lexis 785 (Supreme Court of Illinois)

12.2 Entrustment Rule In 1962, Andy Warhol, a famous artist, created a silkscreen on canvas titled *Red Elvis*. *Red Elvis* consists of thirty-six identical faces of Elvis Presley on a red background, and it is approximately 5.75 feet in height and 4.35 feet in width. Kerstin Lindholm was an art collector who, for thirty years, had been represented by Anders Malmberg, an art dealer. In 1987, with the assistance and advice of Malmberg, Lindholm purchased *Red Elvis* for $300,000.

In 1996, the Guggenheim Museum in New York City decided to sponsor an Andy Warhol exhibition.

The staff of the Guggenheim contacted Malmberg to see if Lindholm was willing to lend *Red Elvis* to the exhibition. Lindholm agreed, and *Red Elvis* was placed in the Guggenheim's exhibition. When the Guggenheim exhibition was completed in 2000, Malmberg told Lindholm that he could place *Red Elvis* on loan to the Louisiana Museum in Denmark if Lindholm agreed. By letter dated March 20, 2000, Lindholm agreed and gave permission to Malmberg to obtain possession of *Red Elvis* from the Guggenheim Museum and place it on loan to the Louisiana Museum. Instead of placing *Red Elvis* on loan to the Louisiana Museum, Malmberg, claiming ownership to *Red Elvis*, immediately contracted to sell *Red Elvis* to Peter M. Brant, an art collector, for $2.9 million. Brant had his lawyer do a UCC lien search and a search of the Art Loss Registry related to *Red Elvis*. These searches revealed no claims or liens against *Red Elvis*. Brant paid $2.9 million to Malmberg and received an invoice of sale and possession of *Red Elvis*.

Subsequently, Lindholm made arrangements to sell *Red Elvis* to a Japanese buyer for $4.6 million. Shortly thereafter, Lindholm discovered the fraud. Lindholm brought a civil lawsuit in the state of Connecticut against Brant to recover *Red Elvis*. Brant argued that he was a buyer in the ordinary course of business because he purchased *Red Elvis* from an art dealer to whom Lindholm had entrusted *Red Elvis*, and he had a claim that was superior to Lindholm's claim of ownership. Is Brant a buyer in the ordinary course of business who has a claim of ownership to *Red Elvis* that is superior to that of the owner Lindholm? *Lindholm v. Brant*, 925 A.2d 1048, **Web** 2007 Conn. Lexis 264 (Supreme Court of Connecticut)

12.3 Implied Warranty of Merchantability Nancy Denny purchased a Bronco II, a small sport-utility vehicle (SUV) that was manufactured by Ford Motor Company. Denny testified that she purchased the Bronco for use on paved city and suburban streets and not for off-road use. When Denny was driving the vehicle on a paved road, she slammed on the brakes in an effort to avoid a deer that had walked directly into her SUV's path. The Bronco II rolled over, and Denny was severely injured. Denny sued Ford Motor Company to recover damages for breach of the implied warranty of merchantability.

Denny alleged that the Bronco II presented a significantly higher risk of occurrence of rollover accidents than did ordinary passenger vehicles. Denny introduced evidence at trial which showed that the Bronco II had a low stability index because of its high center of gravity, narrow tracks, and shorter wheelbase, as well as the design of its suspension system. Ford countered that the Bronco II was intended as an off-road vehicle and was not designed to be used as a conventional passenger automobile on paved streets. Has Ford Motor Company breached the implied warranty of merchantability? *Denny v. Ford Motor Company*, 87 N.Y.2d 248, 662 N.E.2d 730, 639 N.Y.S.2d 250, **Web** 1995 N.Y. Lexis 4445 (Court of Appeals of New York)

12.4 Implied Warranty of Fitness for a Particular Purpose   Felicitas Garnica sought to purchase a vehicle capable of towing a 23-foot Airstream trailer she had on order. She went to Mack Massey Motors, Inc. (Massey Motors), to inquire about purchasing a Jeep Cherokee that was manufactured by Jeep Eagle. After Garnica explained her requirements to the sales manager, he called the Airstream dealer concerning the specifications of the trailer Garnica was purchasing. The sales manager advised Garnica that the Jeep Cherokee could do the job of pulling the trailer. After purchasing the vehicle, Garnica claimed that it did not have sufficient power to pull the trailer. She brought the Jeep Cherokee back to Massey Motors several times for repairs for a slipping transmission. Eventually, she was told to go to another dealer. The drive shaft on the Jeep Cherokee twisted apart at 7,229 miles. Garnica sued Massey Motors and Jeep Eagle for damages, alleging breach of the implied warranty of fitness for a particular purpose. Have the defendants made and breached an implied warranty of fitness for a particular purpose? *Mack Massey Motors, Inc. v. Garnica*, 814 S.W.2d 167, **Web** 1991 Tex. Lexis 1814 (Court of Appeals of Texas)

12.5 Limited Warranty   Dean Solomon purchased a camera and lenses from a retailer that were manufactured by Canon USA, Inc. Both the camera and the lenses were accompanied by a one-year limited warranty issued by Canon that limited a purchaser's remedies to repair or replacement in the event of any defect in materials or workmanship. Approximately three months after Solomon purchased the items, he

notified Canon that he had encountered problems with the lenses when he was on an overseas vacation when an "error" message appeared on the camera when he changed lenses. In response, Canon repaired the camera. Several months later, Solomon notified Canon that the same problem reoccurred while he was on a subsequent vacation. Canon offered to repair the camera and lenses. Solomon refused the offer and sued Canon to revoke his acceptance and recover his purchase price. Is Canon's limited warranty enforceable? *Solomon v. Canon USA, Inc.*, **Web** 2010 N.Y.Misc. Lexis 6267 (Appellate Term of the Supreme Court of New York)

12.6 Firm Offer   Gordon Construction Company (Gordon) was a general contractor in the New York City area. Gordon planned on bidding for the job of constructing two buildings for the Port Authority of New York. In anticipation of its own bid, Gordon sought bids from subcontractors. E. A. Coronis Associates (Coronis), a fabricator of structured steel, sent a signed letter to Gordon. The letter quoted a price for work on the Port Authority project and stated that the price could change, based upon the amount of steel used. The letter contained no information other than the price Coronis would charge for the job. One month later, Gordon was awarded the Port Authority project. Four days later, Coronis sent Gordon a telegram, withdrawing its offer. Gordon replied that it expected Coronis to honor the price that it had previously quoted to Gordon. When Coronis refused, Gordon sued. Gordon claimed that Coronis was attempting to withdraw a firm offer. Who wins? *E. A. Coronis Associates v. Gordon Construction Co.*, 90 N.J. Super. 69, 216 A.2d 246, **Web** 1966 N.J.Super. Lexis 368 (Superior Court of New Jersey)

12.7 Battle of the Forms   Dan Miller was a commercial photographer who had taken a series of photographs that had appeared in the *New York Times*. *Newsweek* magazine wanted to use the photographs. When a *Newsweek* employee named Dwyer phoned Miller, he was told that 72 images were available. Dwyer said that he wanted to inspect the photographs and offered a certain sum of money for each photo *Newsweek* used. The photos were to remain Miller's property. Miller and Dwyer agreed to the price and the date for delivery. *Newsweek* sent a courier to pick up the photographs. Along with the photos, Miller gave the courier a delivery memo that set out various conditions for the use of the photographs. The memo included a clause that required *Newsweek* to pay $1,500 each if any of the photos were lost or destroyed. After *Newsweek* received the package, it decided it no longer needed Miller's work. When Miller called to have the photos returned, he was told that they had all been lost. Miller demanded that *Newsweek* pay him $1,500 for each of the 72 lost photos. Assuming that the court finds Miller and *Newsweek* to be merchants, are the clauses in the delivery memo part of the sales contract? *Miller v. Newsweek, Inc.*, 660 F.Supp. 852, **Web** 1987 U.S. Dist. Lexis 4338 (United States District Court for the District of Delaware)

12.8 Risk of Loss Martin Silver ordered two rooms of furniture from Wycombe, Meyer & Co., Inc. (Wycombe), a manufacturer and seller of custom-made furniture. On February 23, 1982, Wycombe sent invoices to Silver, advising him that the furniture was ready for shipment. Silver tendered payment in full for the goods and asked that one room of furniture be shipped immediately and that the other be held for shipment on a later date. Before any instructions were received as to the second room of furniture, it was destroyed in a fire. Silver and his insurance company attempted to recover the money he had paid for the destroyed furniture. Wycombe refused to return the payment, claiming that the risk of loss was on Silver. Who wins? *Silver v. Wycombe, Meyer & Co., Inc.*, 124 Misc.2d 717, 477 N.Y.S.2d 288, **Web** 1984 N.Y.Misc. Lexis 3319 (Civil Court of the City of New York)

Ethics Cases

12.9 Ethics Alex Abatti was the sole owner of A&M Produce Company (A&M), a small farming company located in California's Imperial Valley. Although Abatti had never grown tomatoes, he decided to do so. He sought the advice of FMC Corporation (FMC), a large diversified manufacturer of farming and other equipment, as to what kind of equipment he would need to process the tomatoes. An FMC representative recommended a certain type of machine, which A&M purchased from FMC pursuant to a form sales contract provided by FMC. Within the fine print, the contract contained one clause that disclaimed any warranty liability by FMC and a second clause which stated that FMC would not be liable for consequential damages if the machine malfunctioned.

A&M paid $10,680 down toward the $32,041 purchase price, and FMC delivered and installed the machine. A&M immediately began experiencing problems with the machine. It did not process the tomatoes quickly enough. Tomatoes began piling up in front of the belt that separated the tomatoes for weight-sizing. Overflow tomatoes had to be sent through the machine at least twice, causing damage to them. Fungus spread through the damaged crop. Because of these problems, the machine had to be continually started and stopped, which significantly reduced processing speed.

A&M tried on several occasions to get additional equipment from FMC, but on each occasion, its request was rejected. Because of the problems with the machine, A&M closed its tomato operation. A&M finally stated, "Let's call the whole thing off" and offered to return the machine if FMC would refund A&M's down payment. When FMC rejected this offer and demanded full payment of the balance due, A&M sued to recover its down payment and damages. It alleged breach of warranty caused by defect in the machine. In defense, FMC pointed to the fine print of the sales contract, stating that the buyer waived any rights to sue it for breach of warranty or to recover consequential damages from it. *A&M Produce Co. v. FMC Corp.*, 135 Cal.App.3d 473, 186 Cal.Rptr. 114, **Web** 1982 Cal.App. Lexis 1922 (Court of Appeal of California)

1. Did A&M act morally in signing the contract and then trying to get out from under its provisions?
2. Was it ethical for FMC to include waiver of liability and waiver of consequential damages clauses in its form contract?
3. Legally, are the waiver clauses unconscionable and therefore unenforceable?

12.10 Ethics Executive Financial Services, Inc. (EFS), purchased three tractors from Tri-County Farm Company (Tri-County), a John Deere dealership owned by Gene Mohr and James Loyd. The tractors cost $48,000, $19,000, and $38,000. EFS did not take possession of the tractors but instead left the tractors on Tri-County's lot. EFS leased the tractors to Mohr-Loyd Leasing (Mohr-Loyd), a partnership between Mohr and Loyd, with the understanding and representation by Mohr-Loyd that the tractors would be leased out to farmers. Instead of leasing the tractors, Tri-County sold them to three different farmers. EFS sued and obtained judgment against Tri-County, Mohr-Loyd, and Mohr and Loyd personally for breach of contract. Because that judgment remained unsatisfied, EFS sued the three farmers who bought the tractors to recover the tractors from them. *Executive Financial Services, Inc. v. Pagel*, 238 Kan. 809, 715 P.2d 381, **Web** 1986 Kan. Lexis 290 (Supreme Court of Kansas)

1. What does the entrustment rule provide? Explain.
2. Did Mohr and Loyd act ethically in this case?
3. Who owns the tractors, EFS or the farmers?

Internet Exercises

1. Go to website of the Chicago Board of Trade, at **www.cmegroup.com**. What is the current price of the next month's contract for soybean oil? Is the price up or down? Can this price be used to fill an open price term?

2. Go to **http://todiamonds.com/ buying%20diamonds%205%20c%27s.htm** and read "How to Choose and Buy a Diamond." What do these terms carat, color, clarity, and cut mean. Do the use of these terms create an express warranty?

3. Go to **www.technicolor.com.au/pages/Conditions .html#cat0_7**, a website of Technicolor. Read the section "8. Warranty, Disclaimer and Limitation of Liability."

Endnote

1. 15 U.S.C. Sections 2301–2312.

CHAPTER

13

Credit, Secured Transactions, and Bankruptcy

HOUSE

A house is often a person's most valuable asset. Often, homeowners borrow money to help provide the funds to purchase a house. Usually the lender takes back a mortgage that secures the house as collateral for the repayment of the loan. If the borrower defaults, the lender can bring a foreclosure proceeding to recover the collateral.

Learning Objectives

After studying this chapter, you should be able to:

1. Distinguish between unsecured and secured credit.
2. Describe security interests in real property and the foreclosure of mortgages.
3. Apply the provisions of Revised Article 9 (Secured Transactions) to secured transaction in personal property.
4. Compare surety and guaranty arrangements.
5. Describe the different forms of personal and business bankruptcy and the changes made by the Bankruptcy Abuse Prevention and Consumer Protection Act of 2005.

Chapter Outline

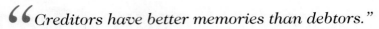

> " *Creditors have better memories than debtors.*"
>
> —Benjamin Franklin
> *Poor Richard's Almanack (1758)*

Introduction to Credit, Secured Transactions, and Bankruptcy

The U.S. economy is a credit economy. Consumers borrow money to make major purchases (e.g., homes, automobiles, appliances) and use credit cards (e.g., Visa, MasterCard) to purchase goods and services at clothing stores, restaurants, and other businesses. Businesses use credit to purchase equipment, supplies, and other goods and services. In a credit transaction, the borrower is the *debtor*, and the lender is the *creditor*.

Because lenders are sometimes reluctant to lend large sums of money simply on the borrower's promise to repay, many of them take a *security interest* in the property purchased or some other property of the debtor. The property in which the security interest is taken is called *collateral*. If the debtor does not pay the debt, the creditor can foreclose on and recover the collateral. If the collateral is personal property it is a *secured transaction* covered by Article 9 of the Uniform Commercial Code. If the collateral is real property, it is usually called a *mortgage*.

A lender who is unsure whether a debtor will have sufficient income or assets to repay a loan can require another person to guarantee payment. If the borrower fails to repay the loan, that person is responsible for paying it.

On occasion, borrowers become overextended and are unable to meet their debt obligations. Congress has enacted federal bankruptcy laws that provide methods for debtors to be relieved of some debt or enter into arrangements to pay debts in the future. Congress enacted the *Bankruptcy Abuse Prevention and Consumer Protection Act of 2005*, which makes it much more difficult for debtors to escape their debts under federal bankruptcy law. The 2005 act, which has been criticized by consumer groups for being too "creditor friendly," has been praised by many businesses, banks, and credit card issuers.

This chapter discusses unsecured credit, security interests in real property, secured transactions in personal property, and bankruptcy law.

Unsecured and Secured Credit

In a transaction involving the extension of **credit** (either unsecured or secured), there are two parties. The party extending the credit, the **lender**, is called the **creditor**. The party borrowing the money, the **borrower**, is called the **debtor** (see **Exhibit 13.1**).

If you think nobody cares if you're alive, try missing a couple of car payments.

Earl Wilson

Debtors are liars.

George Herbert
Jacula Prudentum (1651)

credit
Extension of a loan from one party to another.

creditor (lender)
The lender in a credit transaction.

debtor (borrower)
The borrower in a credit transaction.

Exhibit 13.1 DEBTOR AND CREDITOR

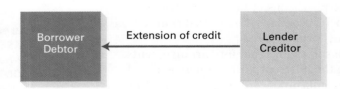

Example Prima Company goes to Urban Bank and borrows $100,000. In this case, Prima Company is the borrower-debtor, and Urban Bank is the lender-creditor.

Credit may be extended on either an *unsecured* or a *secured* basis.

Unsecured Credit

Unsecured credit does not require any security (collateral) to protect the payment of the debt. Instead, the creditor relies on the debtor's promise to

unsecured credit
Credit that does not require any security (collateral) to protect the payment of the debt.

repay the principal (plus any interest) when it is due. The creditor is called an **unsecured creditor**. In deciding whether to make the loan, the unsecured creditor considers the debtor's credit history, income, and other assets. If the debtor fails to make the payments, the creditor may bring legal action and obtain a judgment against him or her. If the debtor is **judgment-proof** (i.e., has little or no property or no income that can be garnished), the creditor may never collect.

Example A person borrows money from a bank, and the bank does not require any collateral for the loan. This is *unsecured credit*, and the bank is relying on the borrower's credit standing and income to pay back the loan. If the borrower fails to pay back the loan, the bank can sue the borrower to try to collect the unpaid loan.

Secured Credit

To minimize the risk associated with extending unsecured credit, a creditor may require a security interest in the debtor's property (**collateral**). The collateral secures payment of the loan. This type of credit is called **secured credit**. The creditor who has a security interest in collateral is called a **secured party**. Security interests may be taken in real, personal, intangible, and other property. If the debtor fails to make the payments when due, the collateral may be repossessed to recover the outstanding amount. Generally, if the sale of the collateral is insufficient to repay the loan plus interest, the creditor may bring a lawsuit against the debtor to recover a deficiency judgment for the difference.

Example A person obtains a loan from a lender to purchase an automobile, and the lender takes back a security interest in the automobile. This is an extension of *secured credit*, and the automobile is collateral for the loan. If the borrower fails to pay back the loan, the lender can foreclose and recover the automobile.

Security Interests in Real Property

Owners of real estate can create **security interests** in their property. This occurs if an owner borrows money from a lender and pledges real estate as security for repayment of the loan. A person who owns a piece of real property has an ownership interest in that property. A property owner who borrows money from a creditor may use his or her real estate as collateral for repayment of the loan. This type of collateral arrangement, known as a **mortgage**, is a *two-party instrument*. The **owner-debtor** is the **mortgagor**, and the **creditor** is the **mortgagee**. The parties to a mortgage are illustrated in **Exhibit 13.2**.

> **collateral**
> Personal property that is subject to a security agreement.

> **secured credit**
> Credit that requires security (collateral) that secures payment of the loan.

> **mortgage**
> An arrangement in which an owner of real property borrows money from a lender and pledges the real property as collateral to secure the repayment of the loan.

> **mortgagor (owner-debtor)**
> The owner-debtor in a mortgage transaction.

> **mortgagee (creditor)**
> The creditor in a mortgage transaction.

Exhibit 13.2 MORTGAGE ON REAL ESTATE

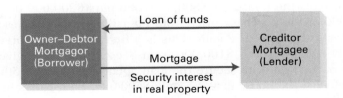

Example General Electric purchases a manufacturing plant for $10 million, pays $2 million cash as a down payment, and borrows the remaining $8 million from City Bank. General Electric is the debtor, and City Bank is the creditor. To secure the loan, General Electric gives a mortgage on the plant to City Bank. This is a secured loan, and the plant is collateral for the loan. General Electric is the mortgagor, and City Bank is the mortgagee. If General Electric defaults on the loan, the bank may take action under state law to foreclose and take the property.

Some states' laws provide for the use of a *deed of trust and note* in place of a mortgage. The **note** is the instrument that evidences the borrower's debt to the lender; the **deed of trust** is the instrument that gives the creditor a security interest in the debtor's property that is pledged as collateral.

Recording Statute

Most states have enacted **recording statutes** that require a mortgage or deed of trust to be recorded in the county recorder's office in the county in which the real property is located. These filings are public record and alert the world that a mortgage or deed of trust has been recorded against the real property. This record gives potential lenders or purchasers of real property the ability to determine whether there are any existing liens (mortgages) on the property.

The **nonrecordation of a mortgage** or deed of trust does not affect either the legality of the instrument between the mortgagor and the mortgagee or the rights and obligations of the parties. In other words, the mortgagor is obligated to pay the amount of the mortgage according to the terms of the mortgage, even if the document is not recorded. However, an improperly recorded document is not effective against either (1) subsequent purchasers of the real property or (2) other mortgagees or lienholders who have no notice of the prior mortgages.

Deficiency Judgment

Some states permit a mortgagee to bring a separate legal action to recover a deficiency from the mortgagor. If the mortgagee is successful, the court will award a **deficiency judgment** that entitles the mortgagee to recover the amount of the judgment from the mortgagor's other property.

Example Kaye buys a house for $800,000. She puts $200,000 down and borrows $600,000 from a bank, which takes a mortgage on the property to secure the loan. Kaye defaults, and when the bank forecloses on the property, it is worth only $500,000. There is a deficiency of $100,000 ($600,000 loan – $500,000 foreclosure sale price). The bank can recover the $100,000 deficiency from Kaye's other property. The bank has to bring a legal action against Kaye to do so.

Several states have enacted statutes that prohibit deficiency judgments regarding certain types of mortgages, such as loans for the original purchase of residential property. These statutes are called **antideficiency statutes**. Antideficiency statutes usually apply only to **first purchase money mortgages** (i.e., mortgages that are taken out to purchase houses). Second mortgages and other subsequent mortgages, even mortgages that refinance the first mortgage, usually are not protected by antideficiency statutes.

Example Assume that a house is located in a state that has an antideficiency statute. Qian buys the house for $800,000. She puts $200,000 down and borrows $600,000 of the purchase price from First Bank, which takes a mortgage on the property to secure the loan. This is a first purchase money mortgage. Subsequently, Qian borrows $100,000 from Second Bank and gives a second mortgage to Second Bank to secure the loan. Qian defaults on both loans, and when she defaults, the house is worth only $500,000. Both banks bring foreclosure proceedings to recover the house. First Bank can recover the house worth $500,000 at foreclosure. However, First Bank has a deficiency of $100,000 ($600,000 loan – $500,000 foreclosure sale price). Because of the state's antideficiency statute, First Bank cannot recover this deficiency from Qian; First Bank can only recover the house in foreclosure and must write off the $100,000 loss. Second Bank's loan, a second loan, is not covered by the antideficiency statute. Therefore, Second Bank can sue Qian to recover its $100,000 deficiency from Qian's other property.

The following feature discusses mechanic's liens on real property.

Contemporary Environment

Mechanic's Liens on Real Property

Owners of real property often hire contractors and laborers (e.g., painters, plumbers, roofers, bricklayers, furnace installers) to make improvements to that property. The contractors and laborers expend the time to provide their services as well as money to provide the materials for the improvements. Their investments are protected by state statutes that permit them to file a **mechanic's lien** against the improved real property.

When a lien is properly filed, the real property to which the improvements have been made becomes security for the payment of these services and materials. In essence, the lienholder has the equivalent of a mortgage on the property. If the owner defaults, the lienholder may foreclose on the lien, sell the property, and satisfy the debt plus interest and costs out of the proceeds of the sale. Any surplus must be paid to the owner-debtor. Generally, the lien must be foreclosed on during a specific period of time (commonly six months to two years) from the date the lien is filed.

Most state statutes permit an owner of real property to have contractors, subcontractors, laborers, and material persons who have provided services or materials to a real property project sign a written **release of lien** contract (also called a **lien release**), attesting to the receipt of payment and releasing any lien they might otherwise assert against the property. A lien release can be used by the property owner to defeat a statutory lienholder's attempt to obtain payment.

Secured Transactions in Personal Property

Many items of *personal property* are purchased with credit rather than cash. Because lenders are reluctant to lend large sums of money simply on the borrower's promise to repay, many of them take a *security interest* in either the item purchased or some other personal property of the debtor. The property in which a security interest is taken is called *collateral*.

Individuals and businesses purchase or lease various forms of tangible and intangible **personal property**. **Tangible personal property** includes equipment, vehicles, furniture, computers, clothing, jewelry, and such. **Intangible personal property** includes securities, patents, trademarks, and copyrights.

When a creditor extends credit to a debtor and takes a security interest in some personal property of the debtor, it is called a **secured transaction**. The secured party is the seller, lender, or other party in whose favor there is a security interest. If the debtor defaults and does not repay the loan, generally the secured party can foreclose and recover the collateral.

A **two-party secured transaction** occurs, for example, when a seller sells goods to a buyer on credit and retains a security interest in the goods. **Exhibit 13.3** illustrates a two-party secured transaction. A **three-party secured transaction** occurs when a seller sells goods to a buyer who has obtained financing from a third-party lender (e.g., bank) that takes a security interest in the goods sold.

mechanic's lien
A contractor's, laborer's, and material person's statutory lien that makes the real property to which services or materials have been provided security for the payment of the services and materials.

personal property
Tangible property such as equipment, vehicles, furniture, and jewelry, as well as intangible property such as securities, patents, trademarks, and copyrights.

secured transaction
A transaction that is created when a creditor makes a loan to a debtor in exchange for the debtor's pledge of personal property as security.

Exhibit 13.3 TWO-PARTY SECURED TRANSACTION

Revised Article 9—Secured Transactions

Article 9 (Secured Transactions) of the Uniform Commercial Code (UCC) governs secured transactions in personal property. Where personal property is used as collateral for a loan or the extension of credit, a resulting secured transaction is governed by Article 9 of the UCC.

After years of study and debate, **Revised Article 9 (Secured Transactions) of the UCC**, as promulgated by the National Conference of Commissioners on Uniform State Laws and the American Law Institute, became effective in 2001. Revised Article 9 includes modern and efficient rules that govern secured transactions in personal property. Revised Article 9 includes changes to provisions that have been controversial in the past, as well as new provisions that recognize changes in the commercial environment.

In addition, Revised Article 9 contains many new provisions and rules that recognize the importance of electronic commerce. Revised Article 9 provides rules for the creation, filing, and enforcement of electronic secured transactions.

Since its release in 2001, all states have enacted Revised Article 9 (Secured Transactions) as a UCC statute within their states. The following material in this chapter that covers secured transactions is based on the provisions of Revised Article 9.

Security Agreement

Unless a creditor has possession of the collateral, there must be a **security agreement**. A security agreement is an agreement that creates or provides for a security interest [Revised UCC 9-102(a)(73)]. To be valid, a security agreement must (1) clearly describe the collateral so that it can be readily identified, (2) contain the debtor's promise to repay the creditor, including terms of repayment (e.g., interest rate, time of payment), (3) set forth the creditor's rights upon the debtor's default, and (4) be signed by the debtor.

The debtor must have a current or future legal right in or the right to possession of the collateral. Thus, a debtor may give a creditor a security interest in goods currently owned or in the possession of the debtor or in goods to be later acquired by the debtor. At that time the rights of the secured party attach to the collateral. **Attachment** means that the creditor has an enforceable security interest against the debtor and can satisfy the debt out of the designated collateral [Revised UCC 9-203(a)].

The Floating Lien Concept

A security agreement may provide that the security interest attaches to property that was not originally in the possession of the debtor when the agreement was executed. This interest is usually referred to as a **floating lien**. A floating lien can attach to the following:

- **After-acquired property.**   Many security agreements contain a clause that gives the secured party a security interest in **after-acquired property** of the debtor. After-acquired property is property that the debtor acquires after the security agreement is executed [Revised UCC 9-204(a)].
- **Sale proceeds.**   Unless otherwise stated in a security agreement, if a debtor sells, exchanges, or disposes of collateral subject to such an agreement, the secured party automatically has the right to receive the **sale proceeds** of the sale, exchange, or disposition [Revised UCC 9-102(a)(64), 9-203(f), 9-315(a)].
- **Future advances.**   A debtor may establish a continuing or revolving line of credit at a bank. Certain personal property of the debtor is designated as collateral for future loans from the line of credit. A maximum limit that the debtor may borrow is set, but the debtor can draw against the line of credit at any time. Any **future advances** made against the line of credit are subject to the security interest in the collateral. A new security agreement does not have to be executed each time a future advance is taken against the line of credit [Revised UCC 9-204(c)].

Perfecting a Security Interest

The concept of **perfection of a security interest** establishes the right of a secured creditor against other creditors who claim an interest in the collateral. Perfection is a legal process. The three main methods of perfecting a security interest under the UCC are (1) perfection by filing a financing statement, (2) perfection by possession of collateral, and (3) perfection by a purchase money security interest in consumer goods. These three main methods of perfecting a security interest are discussed in the following paragraphs.

Perfection by Filing a Financing Statement

A creditor filing a **financing statement** in the appropriate government office is the most common method of perfecting a creditor's security interest in such collateral; this is known as **perfection by filing a financing statement** [Revised UCC 9-501]. The person who files the financing statement should request the filing officer to note on his or her copy of the document the file number, date, and hour of filing. A financing statement can be electronically filed [Revised UCC 9-102(a)(18)]. A uniform financing statement form, the **UCC Financing Statement (Form UCC-1)**, is used in all states [Revised UCC 9-521(a)].

State law specifies where a financing statement must be filed. A state may choose either the **secretary of state** or the **county recorder's office** in the county of the debtor's residence or, if the debtor is not a resident of the state, in the county where the goods are kept or in another county office or both. Most states require financing statements covering farm equipment, farm products, accounts, and consumer goods to be filed with the county clerk [Revised UCC 9-501].

Financing statements are available for review by the public. They serve as constructive notice to the world that a creditor claims an interest in a property. Financing statements are effective for five years from the date of filing [Revised UCC 9-515(a)]. A **continuation statement** may be filed up to six months prior to the expiration of a financing statement's five-year term. Such statements are effective for a new five-year term. Succeeding continuation statements may be filed [Revised UCC 9-515(d), 9-515(e)].

To be enforceable, a financing statement must contain the name of the debtor, the name and address of the secured party or a representative of the secured party, and the collateral covered by the financing statement [Revised UCC 9-502(a)]. The secured party can file the security agreement as a financing statement. A financing statement that provides only the debtor's trade name does not sufficiently provide the name of the debtor [Revised UCC 9-503(c)].

In the following case, the court had to determine whether the filing of a financing statement was effective.

financing statement
A document filed by a secured creditor with the appropriate government office that constructively notifies the world of his or her security interest in personal property.

perfection by possession of the collateral
A rule that says if a secured creditor has physical possession of the collateral, no financing statement has to be filed; the creditor's possession is sufficient to put other potential creditors on notice of the creditor's secured interest in the property.

UCC Financing Statement (Form UCC-1)
A uniform financing statement form that is used in all states.

Rather go to bed supperless than rise in debt.

Benjamin Franklin

CASE 13.1 *Filing a Financing Statement Under an Individual's Name*

Pankratz Implement Company v. Citizens National Bank

130 P.3d 57, Web 2006 Kan. Lexis 141 (2006)
Supreme Court of Kansas

"Thus, Pankratz' financing statement using the misspelled name of the debtor, while prior in time, was seriously misleading, ... "
—Davis, Justice

Facts

Rodger House purchased a tractor on credit from Pankratz Implement Company. House signed a note and security agreement that made the tractor collateral for the repayment of the debt. The creditor filed a financing statement with the Kansas secretary of state, using the misspelled name of the debtor, "Roger House." One year later, House obtained a loan from Citizens National Bank (CNB). House gave a security interest to CNB by pledging all equipment that he owned and that he may own in the future as collateral for the loan. CNB filed a financing

(continued)

statement with the Kansas secretary of state, using the correct name of the debtor, "Rodger House."

Several years later, while still owing money to Pankratz and CNB, House filed for bankruptcy. Pankratz filed a lawsuit in Kansas trial court to recover the tractor. CNB challenged the claim, alleging that it should be permitted to recover the tractor. The trial court found that Pankratz's misspelling of the debtor's first name on its financing statement was a minor error and granted summary judgment to Pankratz. The court of appeals held that Pankratz's misspelling of House's first name was seriously misleading and held in favor of CNB. Pankratz appealed.

Issue

Is Pankratz's filing of the financing statement under the wrong first name of the debtor seriously misleading?

Language of the Court

The undisputed facts in this case establish that a search under the debtor's correct name using the filing office's standard search logic did not disclose Pankratz' financing statement with the debtor's misspelled name. Thus, Pankratz' financing statement using the misspelled name of the debtor, while prior in time, was seriously misleading, causing the court of appeals to direct that judgment be entered for CNB.

Because the primary purpose of a financing statement is to provide notice to third parties that the creditor has an interest in the debtor's property and the financing statements are indexed under the debtor's name, it is particularly important to require exactness in the name used, the debtor's legal name. We conclude that Pankratz' filed financing statement was "seriously misleading."

Decision

The supreme court held that the misspelling of the debtor's name misled creditors and was therefore ineffectual in giving CNB notice of Pankratz's security interest in the tractor. The supreme court affirmed the judgment of the court of appeals in favor of CNB.

Case Questions

Critical Legal Thinking
Should Pankratz's error be excused? Why or why not?

Ethics
Did either party act unethically in this case? Was this a legitimate legal dispute?

Contemporary Business
Does the court's decision in this case provide additional certainty to secured creditors' claims? Did the decision signal that there would be fewer or more lawsuits in the future between competing secured creditors?

Perfection by Possession of Collateral

No financing statement has to be filed if the creditor has physical possession of the collateral; this is known as **perfection by possession of collateral**. The rationale behind this rule is that if someone other than the debtor is in possession of the property, a potential creditor is on notice that another may claim an interest in the debtor's property. A secured creditor who holds the debtor's property as collateral must use reasonable care in its custody and preservation [Revised UCC 9-310, 9-312(b), 9-313].

Perfection by a Purchase Money Security Interest in Consumer Goods

Sellers and lenders often extend credit to consumers to purchase consumer goods. **Consumer goods** include furniture, television sets, home appliances, and other goods used primarily for personal, family, or household purposes.

A creditor who extends credit to a consumer to purchase a consumer good under a written security agreement obtains a **purchase money security interest** in the consumer good. The agreement automatically perfects the creditor's security interest at the time of the sale. This is called **perfection by a purchase money**

purchase money security interest
An interest a creditor automatically obtains when he or she extends credit to a consumer to purchase consumer goods.

security interest in consumer goods. The creditor does not have to file a financing statement or take possession of the goods to perfect his or her security interest. This interest is called **perfection by attachment**, or the **automatic perfection rule** [Revised UCC 9-309(1)]. Exceptions require that a financing statement must be filed to perfect a security interest in motor vehicles, trailers, boats and fixtures.

Priority of Claims

Often, two or more creditors claim an interest in the same collateral or property. The UCC establishes the following rules for determining **priority of claims** of creditors:

1. **Secured versus unsecured claims.** A creditor who has the only secured interest in the debtor's collateral has priority over unsecured interests.
2. **Competing unperfected security interests.** If two or more secured parties claim an interest in the same collateral but neither has a perfected claim, the first to attach has priority [Revised UCC 9-322(a)(3)].
3. **Perfected versus unperfected claims.** If two or more secured parties claim an interest in the same collateral but only one has perfected his or her security interest, the perfected security interest has priority [Revised UCC 9-322(a)(2)].
4. **Competing perfected security interests.** If two or more secured parties have perfected security interests in the same collateral, the first to perfect (e.g., by filing a financing statement, by taking possession of the collateral) has priority [Revised UCC 9-322(a)(1)].

Buyer in the Ordinary Course of Business

A **buyer in the ordinary course of business** who purchases goods from a merchant takes the goods free of any perfected or unperfected security interest in the merchant's inventory, even if the buyer knows of the existence of the security interest. This rule is necessary because buyers would be reluctant to purchase goods if a merchant's creditors could recover the goods if the merchant defaulted on loans owed to secured creditors [Revised UCC 9-320(a), 1-201(9)].

A buyer in the ordinary course of business is a person who buys goods in good faith, without knowledge that the sale violates the rights of another person in the goods. The buyer purchases the goods in the ordinary course from a person in the business of selling goods of that kind.

Example Central Car Sales, Inc. (Central), a new car dealership, finances all its inventory of new automobiles at First Bank. First Bank takes a security interest in Central's inventory of cars and perfects this security interest. Kim, a buyer in the ordinary course of business, purchases a car from Central for cash. The car cannot be recovered from Kim even if Central defaults on its payments to the bank.

Default and Remedies

Article 9 of the UCC defines the rights, duties, and remedies of the secured party and the debtor in the event of **default**. The term *default* is not defined. Instead, the parties are free to define it in their security agreement. Events such as failing to make scheduled payments when due, bankruptcy of the debtor, breach of the warranty of ownership as to the collateral, and other such events are commonly defined in security agreements as default. Upon default by a debtor, the secured party may reduce his or her claim to judgment, foreclose, or otherwise enforce his or her security interest by any available judicial procedure [Revised UCC 9-601(a)].

Most secured parties seek to cure a default by **taking possession of the collateral**. This taking is usually done by **repossession** of the goods from the defaulting debtor. A secured party who chooses not to retain the collateral may sell, lease, or otherwise dispose of it in its current condition. Unless otherwise agreed, if the proceeds from the disposition of collateral are not sufficient to satisfy the debt to the secured party, the debtor is personally liable to the secured party for the payment of the deficiency. The secured party may bring an action to recover a *deficiency judgment* against the debtor [Revised UCC 9-608(a)(4)].

The proceeds from a sale, a lease, or another disposition are applied to pay reasonable costs and expenses, satisfy the balance of the indebtedness, and pay subordinate (junior) security interests. The debtor is entitled to receive any surplus that remains [Revised UCC 9-608].

The following feature discusses artisan's liens on personal property.

artisan's lien
A statutory lien given to workers on personal property to which they furnish services or materials in the ordinary course of business.

Contemporary Environment

Artisan's Liens on Personal Property

If a worker in the ordinary course of business furnishes services or materials to someone with respect to goods and receives a lien on the goods by statute, this **artisan's lien** prevails over all other security interests in the goods unless a statutory lien provides otherwise. Thus, such liens are often called **super-priority liens**. An artisan's lien is possessory; that is, the artisan must be in possession of the property in order to affect an artisan's lien.

Example Janice borrows money from First Bank to purchase an automobile. First Bank has a purchase money security interest in the car and files a financing statement. The automobile is involved in an accident, and Janice takes the car to Joe's Repair Shop (Joe's) to be repaired. Joe's retains an artisan's lien on the car for the amount of the repair work. When the repair work is completed, Janice refuses to pay. She also defaults on her payments to First Bank. If the car is sold to satisfy the liens, the artisan's lien is paid in full from the proceeds before First Bank is paid anything.

E-Secured Transactions

Revised Article 9 provides rules for the creation, filing, and enforcement of **electronic secured transactions**, or **e-secured transactions**. In Revised Article 9, the term **record** means information that is inscribed on a tangible medium or that is stored in an electronic or other medium and is retrievable in perceivable form [Revised UCC 9-102(a)(69)].

The term *record* is now used in many of the provisions of Revised Article 9 in place of the term *writing*. [Revised UCC 9-102(a)(39)]. Financing statements to perfect security interests in personal property may be in electronic form and filed and stored as electronic records. The filing of **electronic financing statements**, or **e-financing statements**, has increased substantially.

Surety and Guaranty Arrangements

Sometimes a creditor refuses to extend credit to a debtor unless a third person agrees to become liable on the debt. The third person's credit becomes the security for the credit extended to the debtor. This relationship may be either a *surety arrangement* or a *guaranty arrangement*. These arrangements are discussed in the following paragraphs.

surety arrangement
An arrangement in which a third party promises to be *primarily liable* with the borrower for the payment of the borrower's debt.

Surety Arrangement

In a strict **surety arrangement**, a third person—known as the **surety**, or **co-debtor**—promises to be liable for the payment of another person's debt. A person who acts as a surety is commonly called an **accommodation party**, or **cosigner**. Along with the principal debtor, the surety is **primarily liable** for paying the principal debtor's debt when it is due. The principal debtor does not have to be in default on the debt, and the creditor does not have to have exhausted all its remedies against the principal debtor before seeking payment from the surety.

Guaranty Arrangement

In a **guaranty arrangement**, a third person, the **guarantor**, agrees to pay the debt of the principal debtor if the debtor defaults and does not pay the debt when it is due. In this type of arrangement, the guarantor is **secondarily liable** on the debt. In other words, the guarantor is obligated to pay the debt only if the principal debtor defaults and the creditor has attempted unsuccessfully to collect the debt from the debtor.

guaranty arrangement
An arrangement in which a third party promises to be *secondarily liable* for the payment of another's debt.

CONCEPT SUMMARY
SURETY AND GUARANTY CONTRACTS

Type of Arrangement	Party	Liability
Surety contract	Surety	Primarily liable. The surety is a co-debtor who is liable to pay the debt when it is due.
Guaranty contract	Guarantor	Secondarily liable. The guarantor is liable to pay the debt if the debtor defaults and the creditor has attempted unsuccessfully to collect the debt from the debtor.

Bankruptcy

Article I, section 8, clause 4 of the U.S. Constitution provides that "The Congress shall have the power … to establish … uniform laws on the subject of bankruptcies throughout the United States." Bankruptcy law is exclusively federal law; there are no state bankruptcy laws. Congress enacted the original federal Bankruptcy Act in 1878.

The following feature discusses a landmark change in federal bankruptcy law.

Landmark Law

Bankruptcy Abuse Prevention and Consumer Protection Act of 2005

Over the years, Congress has adopted various bankruptcy laws. Federal **bankruptcy law** was completely revised by the **Bankruptcy Reform Act of 1978**.[1] The 1978 act substantially changed—and eased—the requirements for filing bankruptcy. The 1978 act made it easier for debtors to rid themselves of unsecured debt, primarily by filing for Chapter 7 liquidation bankruptcy.

For over a decade before 2005, credit card companies, commercial banks, and other businesses lobbied Congress to pass a new bankruptcy act that would reduce the ability of some debtors to relieve themselves of unwanted debt

through bankruptcy. In response, Congress enacted the **Bankruptcy Abuse Prevention and Consumer Protection Act of 2005**. The 2005 act substantially amended federal bankruptcy law, making it much more difficult for debtors to escape unwanted debt through bankruptcy.

The changes made by the 2005 act are integrated throughout this chapter. Federal bankruptcy law, as amended, is called the **Bankruptcy Code**, which is contained in Title 11 of the U.S. Code. The Bankruptcy Code establishes procedures for filing for bankruptcy, resolving creditors' claims, and protecting debtors' rights.

Bankruptcy Abuse Prevention and Consumer Protection Act of 2005
A federal act that substantially amended federal bankruptcy law. This act makes it more difficult for debtors to file for bankruptcy and have their unpaid debts discharged.

Bankruptcy Code
The name given to federal bankruptcy law, as amended.

bankruptcy courts
Special federal courts that hear and decide bankruptcy cases.

A trifling debt makes a man your debtor, a large one makes him your enemy.

Seneca
Epistulae Morales and Lucilium, Letters 63–65

voluntary petition
A petition filed by a debtor which states that the debtor has debts.

involuntary petition
A petition filed by creditors of a debtor which alleges that the debtor is not paying his or her debts as they become due.

proof of claim
A document required to be filed by a creditor that states the amount of his or her claim against the debtor.

proof of interest
A document required to be filed by an equity security holder that states the amount of his or her interest against the debtor.

automatic stay
The suspension of certain legal actions by creditors against a debtor or the debtor's property.

Types of Bankruptcy

The Bankruptcy Code is divided into chapters. Chapters 1, 3, and 5 set forth definitions and general provisions that govern case administration. The provisions of these chapters generally apply to all forms of bankruptcy.

Four special chapters of the Bankruptcy Code provide different types of bankruptcy under which individual and business debtors may be granted remedy. The four major types of bankruptcies are as follows:

Chapter	Type of Bankruptcy
Chapter 7	Liquidation
Chapter 11	Reorganization
Chapter 12	Adjustment of Debts of a Family Farmer or Fisherman with Regular Income

Bankruptcy Courts

Congress created a system of federal **bankruptcy courts**. These special courts are necessary because the number of bankruptcies would overwhelm the federal Districts Courts. The bankruptcy courts are part of the federal court system, and one bankruptcy court is attached to each of the ninety-four U.S. District Courts in the country. Bankruptcy judges, specialists who hear bankruptcy proceedings, are appointed for fourteen-year terms. The relevant District Court has jurisdiction to hear appeals from bankruptcy courts.

Federal law establishes the office of the **U.S. Trustee**. A U.S. Trustee is a federal government official who has responsibility for handling and supervising many of the administrative tasks associated with a bankruptcy case.[2] A U.S. Trustee is empowered to perform many of the tasks that the bankruptcy judge previously performed.

Bankruptcy Procedure

The Bankruptcy Code requires that certain procedures be followed for the commencement and prosecution of a bankruptcy case. A bankruptcy case is commenced when a **petition** is filed with the bankruptcy court. A **voluntary petition** can be filed by the debtor in Chapter 7 (liquidation), Chapter 11 (reorganization), Chapter 12 (family farmer or fisherman), and Chapter 13 (adjustment of debts) bankruptcy cases. An **involuntary petition**, which is a petition that is filed by a creditor or creditors and places the debtor into bankruptcy, can be filed in Chapter 7 and Chapter 11 cases.

A creditor must file a **proof of claim** stating the amount of his or her claim against the debtor. The document for filing a proof of claim is provided by the court. An equity security holder (e.g., a shareholder of a corporation) must file a **proof of interest**. Proofs of claim and proofs of interests are subject to verification by the court.

A **bankruptcy trustee** must be appointed in Chapter 7 (liquidation), Chapter 12 (family farmer or family fisherman), and Chapter 13 (adjustment of debts) bankruptcy cases. A trustee may be appointed in a Chapter 11 (reorganization) case upon a showing of fraud, dishonesty, incompetence, or gross mismanagement of the affairs of the debtor by current management. A trustee is the legal representative of the debtor's estate and has the power to sell and buy property, invest money, and such.

Automatic Stay

The filing of a bankruptcy petition automatically *stays*—that is, suspends—legal actions by creditors against the debtor or the debtor's property. This **automatic**

stay prevents creditors from instituting legal actions to collect prepetition debts, enforcing judgments obtained against the debtor, obtaining or enforcing liens against property of the debtor, or engaging in self-help activities (e.g., repossession of an automobile). The automatic stay prevents a "run" by the creditors to see who can first obtain the debtor's property. Actions to recover domestic support obligations (e.g., alimony, child support), the dissolution of a marriage, and child custody cases are not stayed in bankruptcy.

Bankruptcy Estate

The **bankruptcy estate** is created upon the commencement of a bankruptcy case. It includes all the debtor's legal and equitable interests in real, personal, tangible, and intangible property, wherever located, that exist when the petition is filed, and all interests of the debtor and the debtor's spouse in community property. Gifts, inheritances, life insurance proceeds, and property from divorce settlements that the debtor is entitled to receive within 180 days after the petition is filed are part of the bankruptcy estate.

Because the Bankruptcy Code is not designed to make the debtor a pauper, certain property is exempt from the bankruptcy estate. **Exempt property** is property of the debtor that he or she can keep and that does not become part of the bankruptcy estate. The creditors cannot claim this property.

The Bankruptcy Code establishes a list of property and assets that a debtor can claim as exempt property. The Bankruptcy Code permits states to enact their own exemptions. States that do so may give debtors the option of choosing between federal and state exemptions or require debtors to follow state law. The exemptions available under state law are often more liberal than those provided by federal law.

The federal Bankruptcy Code permits homeowners to claim a **homestead exemption** of $21,625 in their principal residence. Homestead exemptions provided by many state laws are significantly higher than the federal exemption. The 2005 act limits **abusive homestead exemptions** by preventing a debtor from exempting an amount greater than $136,875 if the property was acquired by the debtor within 1,215 days (approximately three years and four months) before the petition for bankruptcy is filed.

The 2005 act gives the bankruptcy court the power to void certain **fraudulent transfers** of a debtor's property made by the debtor within two years prior to filing a petition for bankruptcy. These are gifts or transfers of property to insiders (e.g., relatives) or to noninsiders with the intent to hinder, delay, or defraud a creditor.

Example If prior to filing for bankruptcy a debtor gives all of her jewelry to a relative, this is a fraudulent transfer that will be voided if the debtor is caught.

Chapter 7 Liquidation Bankruptcy

Chapter 7—Liquidation (also called **straight bankruptcy**) is a familiar form of bankruptcy.[3] In this type of bankruptcy proceeding, the debtor is permitted to keep a substantial portion of his or her assets (exempt assets), the debtor's nonexempt property is sold for cash and the cash is distributed to the creditors, and any of the debtor's unpaid debts are *discharged*. The debtor's future income, even if he or she becomes rich, cannot be reached to pay the discharged debt. Most Chapter 7 bankruptcy petitions are voluntarily filed by individuals.

Example Annabelle finds herself overburdened with debt, particularly credit card debt. Based on her income, Annabelle qualifies for Chapter 7 bankruptcy. At the time she files for Chapter 7 bankruptcy, her unsecured credit is $100,000. Annabelle has few assets, and most of those are exempt property (e.g., her clothes, some furniture). Her nonexempt property is $10,000, which will be sold to raise cash. The $10,000 in cash will be distributed to her debtors on a pro-rata basis—that is, each creditor will receive ten cents for every dollar of debt owed. The other $90,000 is

bankruptcy estate
A debtor's property and earnings that comprise the estate of a bankruptcy proceeding.

exempt property
Property that may be retained by a debtor pursuant to federal or state law that does not become part of the bankruptcy estate.

I will pay you some, and, as most debtors do, promise you indefinitely.

William Shakespeare
Henry IV, Part 11

Chapter 7—Liquidation (straight bankruptcy)
A form of bankruptcy in which the debtor's nonexempt property is sold for cash, the cash is distributed to the creditors, and any unpaid debts are discharged.

median income test
A bankruptcy rule which states that if a debtor's median family income is at or below the state's median family income for a family the same size as the debtor's family, the debtor can receive Chapter 7 relief.

Small debts are like small shot; they are rattling on every side, and can scarcely be escaped without a wound; great debts are like cannon; of loud noise, but little danger.

Samuel Johnson
Letters to Joseph Simpson
(1759)

Chapter 13—Adjustment of Debts of an Individual with Regular Income
A rehabilitation form of bankruptcy that permits bankruptcy courts to supervise the debtor's plan for the payment of unpaid debts in installments over the plan period.

Beggars can never be bankrupt.

Thomas Fuller
Gnomologia (1732)

Debt rolls a man over and over, binding him hand and foot, and letting him hang upon the fatal mesh until the long-legged interest devours him.

Henry Ward Beecher
Proverbs from Plymouth Pulpit
(1887)

Bankruptcy is a legal proceeding in which you put your money in your pants pocket and give your coat to your creditors.

Joey Adams

discharged—that is, the creditors have to absorb this loss. Annabelle is free from this debt forever. Annabelle is given a "fresh start," and her future earnings are hers.

The 2005 act substantially restricts the ability of debtors to obtain a Chapter 7 liquidation bankruptcy. The 2005 act added the *median income test* and the dollar-based *means test* that a debtor must pass before being permitted to obtain a discharge of debts under Chapter 7. Under the **median income test**, debtors who earn a median family income *equal to or below* the state's median family income for the size of the debtor's family qualifies for Chapter 7 bankruptcy. Debtors who earn higher than the family median income must meet a **means test** to qualify to file for Chapter 7. This complicated test determines the debtor's *disposable income*. If the debtor's disposable income exceeds a statutorily determined amount, he or she cannot file Chapter 7; if the debtor's disposable income does exceed a certain amount, he can still file Chapter 7. Debtors who do not qualify for Chapter 7 usually convert to Chapter 13 bankruptcy.

Chapter 13 Adjustment of Debts of an Individual with Regular Income

Chapter 13—Adjustment of Debts of an Individual with Regular Income is a rehabilitation form of bankruptcy for individuals.[4] Chapter 13 permits a qualified debtor to propose a plan to pay all or a portion of the debts he or she owes in installments over a specified period of time. The bankruptcy court supervises the debtor's plan for the payment.

Chapter 13 petitions are usually filed by individual debtors who do not qualify for Chapter 7 liquidation bankruptcy and by homeowners who want to protect nonexempt equity in their residence. Chapter 13 enables debtors to catch up on secured credit loans, such as home mortgages, and avoid repossession and foreclosure.

A debtor alone or with his or her spouse who owes less than $360,475 unsecured debt and less than $1,081,400 secured debt can file for Chapter 13 bankruptcy. If a debtor's debt exceeds one of these amounts, the debtor cannot file for Chapter 13 bankruptcy but could file for Chapter 11 bankruptcy.

Only individuals with regular income can file for Chapter 13, and the petition must be voluntary. An **individual with regular income** means an individual whose income is sufficiently stable and regular to enable such individual to make payments under a Chapter 13 plan. The petition must state that the debtor desires to affect an extension or a composition of debts, or both. An **extension** provides for a longer period of time for the debtor to pay his or her debts. A **composition** provides for the reduction of debts.

Chapter 13 Plan of Payment

The debtor must file a **plan of payment**. The debtor must include information about his or her finances, including a budget of estimated income and expenses during the period of the plan. The Chapter 13 plan may be either up to three years or up to five years, depending on the debtor's family income.

The plan must commit to payment of the debtor's disposable income during the plan period to pay prepetition creditors. **Disposable income** is defined as current monthly income less amounts reasonably necessary to be expended for the maintenance or support of the debtor and the dependants of the debtor. Expenses are not a person's actual expenses but expenses as determined by federal and state expenditure tables, which are usually much lower.

The debtor remains in possession of all of the property of the estate during the completion of the plan, except as otherwise provided by the plan. Under a Chapter 13 bankruptcy, a debtor's unpaid debts are not discharged until the plan period has expired, and then only if the debtor in good faith has paid his or her disposable income toward the reduction of the debt during the plan period.

Chapter 13 Discharge

There are two major differences between a Chapter 7 and Chapter 13 bankruptcy. First, in a Chapter 7 bankruptcy, the debtor is granted **discharge** of unpaid debts at the time of bankruptcy, whereas in a Chapter 13 bankruptcy, the debtor is not granted discharge until the three- or five-year plan period has expired. Second, in a Chapter 7 bankruptcy, the debtor can immediately keep the income he or she earns after discharge, whereas in a Chapter 13 bankruptcy, the debtor must pay his or her disposable income earned during the three- or five-year plan period to pay prepetition debts. A debtor must certify that all domestic support payments (e.g., child support, alimony) have been paid before a Chapter 13 discharge is granted.

discharge
A discharge in a Chapter 13 case that is granted to the debtor after the debtor's plan of payment is completed (which could be three years or up to five years).

Example Assume that Annabelle qualifies for Chapter 13 bankruptcy and that Annabelle owes unsecured credit of $100,000. The court accepts her plan of payment, whereby she will pay $700 disposable income each month for five years toward her prepetition debts. During the five-year period, Annabelle's lifestyle will be reduced considerably because she is paying her disposable income to pay off her prepetition debt. At the end of five years, she will have paid $42,000 (60 months × $700) toward her debt; at that time, her unpaid prepetition debt of $58,000 ($100,000 − $42,000) will be discharged.

As the following feature shows, special rules apply for the discharge of student loans in bankruptcy.

Contemporary Environment

Discharge of Student Loans in Bankruptcy

Upon graduation from college and professional schools, many students have borrowed money to pay tuition and living expenses. At this point in time, when a student might have large student loans and very few assets, he or she might be inclined to file for bankruptcy, in an attempt to have his or her student loans discharged.

To prevent such abuse of bankruptcy law, Congress amended the Bankruptcy Code to make it more difficult for students to have their student loans discharged in bankruptcy. Student loans are defined to include loans made by or guaranteed by government units, student loans made by nongovernment commercial institutions such as banks, and funds for scholarships, benefits, or stipends granted by educational institutions.

The Bankruptcy Code now states that student loans cannot be discharged in any form of bankruptcy unless their nondischarge would cause an **undue hardship** to the debtor and his or her dependants. Undue hardship is construed strictly and is difficult for a debtor to prove unless he or she can show severe physical or mental disability or that he or she is unable to pay for basic necessities such as food or shelter for his or her family.

Cosigners (e.g., parents who guarantee their child's student loan) must also meet the heightened undue hardship test to discharge their obligation.

Chapter 11—Reorganization Bankruptcy

Chapter 11—Reorganization of the Bankruptcy Code provides a method for reorganizing a debtor's financial affairs under the supervision of the bankruptcy court.[6] The goal of Chapter 11 is to reorganize the debtor with a new capital structure so that the debtor emerges from bankruptcy as a viable concern. This option, which is referred to as *reorganization bankruptcy*, is often in the best interests of the debtor and its creditors.

Chapter 11—Reorganization
A form of bankruptcy that allows the reorganization of the debtor's financial affairs under the supervision of the bankruptcy court.

CHAPTER 12 BANKRUPTCY

*This is a farm in the state of Idaho. **Chapter 12—Adjustment of Debts of a Family Farmer or Fisherman with Regular Income**[5] of the of the federal Bankruptcy Code contains special provisions for the reorganization bankruptcy of family farmers and family fisherman. Under Chapter 12, only the debtor may file a voluntary petition for bankruptcy. To qualify, a family farmer cannot have debt that exceeds $3,792,650, and a family fisherman cannot have debt that exceeds $1,757,475. The debtor files a plan of reorganization.*

The plan may modify secured and unsecured credit and assume or reject executory contracts and unexpired leases. The plan period is usually three years, although a court may increase the period to up to five years, based on showing of cause. To confirm a plan of reorganization, the bankruptcy court must find it to be feasible. During the plan period, the debtor makes the debt payments required by the plan. When the family farmer or family fisherman has completed making the payments required by the plan, the bankruptcy court will grant the debtor discharge of all the debts provided for by the plan.

Poor bankrupt.

William Shakespeare
Romeo and Juliet

plan of reorganization
A plan that sets forth a proposed new capital structure for a debtor to assume when it emerges from Chapter 11 reorganization bankruptcy.

The rich ruleth over the poor, and the borrower is servant to the lender.

Proverbs 22:7
The Bible

Chapter 11 is available to individuals, partnerships, corporations, and other business entities. The majority of Chapter 11 proceedings are filed by corporations that want to reorganize their capital structure by receiving discharge of a portion of their debts, obtaining relief from burdensome contracts, and emerge from bankruptcy as *going concerns*.

During a Chapter 11 proceeding, a debtor submits a **plan of reorganization** to the bankruptcy court and to the creditors and other interested parties. The plan of reorganization sets for the proposed changes in the debtor's financial structure that it believes necessary to emerge from Chapter 11 bankruptcy as a viable business entity that will then be able to pay its debts. Some important features of a Chapter 11 bankruptcy are described in the following paragraphs.

Automatic Stay

The filing of a Chapter 11 petition stays (suspends) actions by creditors to recover the debtor's property. This *automatic stay* suspends certain legal actions against the debtor or the debtor's property, including the ability of creditors to foreclose on assets given as collateral for their loans to the debtor. The automatic stay is extremely important to a business trying to reorganize under Chapter 11 because the debtor needs to keep its assets to stay in business.

Example Big Oil Company owns a manufacturing plant and has borrowed $50 million from a bank and used the plant as collateral for the loan. If Big Oil Company files for Chapter 11 bankruptcy, the automatic stay prevents the bank from foreclosing and taking the property. Once out of bankruptcy, Big Oil Company must pay the bank any unpaid arrearages and begin making the required loan payments again.

Executory Contracts and Unexpired Leases

A major benefit of Chapter 11 bankruptcy is that the debtor is given the opportunity to assume or reject executory contracts and unexpired leases. **Executory contracts** and **unexpired leases** are contracts or leases that have not been fully performed. In general, the debtor rejects unfavorable executory contracts and unexpired leases and assumes favorable executory contracts and unexpired leases.

Examples An Big Oil Company enters into a contract to sell oil to another company, and the contract has two years remaining when the oil company files for Chapter 11 bankruptcy. This is an *executory contract*. Big Oil Company has leased an office building for twenty years from a landlord to use as its headquarters building, and it has 15 years left on the lease when the oil company declares bankruptcy. This is an *unexpired lease*. In the Chapter 11 reorganization proceeding, Big Oil Company can reject (get out of) either the executory contract or the unexpired lease without any liability; it can keep either one if doing so is its best interests.

executory contract or unexpired lease
A contract or lease that has not been fully performed. With the bankruptcy court's approval, a debtor may reject executory contracts and unexpired leases in bankruptcy.

Discharge

In its plan of reorganization, the debtor will propose reducing its unsecured debt so that it can come out of bankruptcy with fewer debts to pay than when it filed for bankruptcy. If the plan is approved by the court, the court will confirm the plan of reorganization.

Example Big Oil Company has $100 million in secured debts (e.g., real estate mortgages, personal property secured transactions) and $100 million in unsecured credit when it files for Chapter 11 bankruptcy. In its plan of reorganization, Big Oil Company proposes to eliminate 60 percent—$60 million—of its unsecured credit. If the court approves, then Big Oil will emerge from bankruptcy owing only $40 million of prepetition unsecured debt. The other $60 million is discharged, and the creditors can never recover these debts in the future.

The bankruptcy court will **confirm** a plan of reorganization if the creditors agree to the plan. If unsecured creditors do not agree, the court can use its **cramdown** authority and make the dissenting class accept the plan. The creditors must receive at least what they would have received if the debtor had declared Chapter 7 liquidation bankruptcy.

The following feature involves the Chapter 11 bankruptcy of General Motors Corporation.

Ethics

Bankruptcy of General Motors Corporation

"Because for years I thought what was good for the country was good for General Motors and vice versa."

—Charles Erwin Wilson, President of General Motors Corporation *Comment before a committee of the U.S. Senate, 1953*

General Motors Corporation (GM) originally started in 1908 and grew to be the world's largest corporation. As of 2009, GM manufactured automobiles and other vehicles in 34 countries, sold vehicles in more than 140 countries, and employed more than 244,000 workers worldwide. Over the years, GM developed and acquired major brand names

of automobiles and vehicles such as Chevrolet, Pontiac, Cadillac, Buick, GMC trucks, Saturn, Hummer, Saab, and others.

The 1950s, 1960s, and 1970s were profitable times for GM, as it expanded operations in the United States and worldwide. However, beginning in the 1970s, foreign competition, primarily from automobile manufacturers in Japan and Germany, began to make inroads into the U.S. market. In subsequent years, GM was faulted for not developing better designs, for lack of quality, and for having an overly expensive labor and cost structure. By 2005, GM was posting losses of billions of dollars per year. During the recession of 2008, GM sales decreased

(continued)

by over 45 percent in one year. This led GM to consider a once inconceivable solution: to declare bankruptcy. Without help, GM would have to declare Chapter 7 liquidation.

Luckily for GM, the U.S. federal government decided that GM was "too big to fail." The federal government provided GM with an initial bailout of $20 billion of taxpayers' money. However, when this proved to be inadequate, the federal government decided to provide more than $30 billion of additional bailout money, but only if GM filed Chapter 11 bankruptcy and reorganized its financial structure and operations. So on June 1, 2009, GM filed for Chapter 11 bankruptcy. At the time of the filing, GM had liabilities of $172 billion and assets of $82 billion. The GM bankruptcy was the largest industrial bankruptcy in U.S. history.

The bankruptcy was a "prepackaged" bankruptcy, meaning that many agreements and compromises with interested parties were negotiated before the filing. Others claims were left to the discretion of the bankruptcy court to sort out. The old GM went into bankruptcy, and through complex legal arrangements, a leaner new GM emerged from bankruptcy. The results of GM's government-backed bankruptcy were as follows:

- The U.S. government provided more than $50 billion of taxpayer bailout money to GM. In exchange for the bailout, the federal government—the U.S. taxpayers—owned 60 percent of the new GM stock.
- The Canadian federal and provincial governments, which provided more than $8 billion of bailout money, owned 12 percent of GM stock.
- The United Auto Workers (UAW), a labor union that represents the majority of GM's nonmanagement workforce, agreed to concessions of lower wages and benefits in exchange for a 17.5 percent ownership interest in GM.
- GM bondholders who held over $27 billion of GM bonds were converted from bondholders to stockholders and given stock worth only a fraction of their original investment.
- GM shed over two-thirds of its debt, reducing its prebankruptcy debt of $54 billion to only $17 billion. In exchange, the unsecured creditors were given a 10 percent ownership of GM.
- GM's shareholders at the time of bankruptcy had the value of their investments wiped out.

- GM closed dozens of manufacturing and assembly plants, distribution centers, and other operations in the United States.
- GM shed more than 65,000 blue-collar jobs through buyouts, early-retirement offers, and layoffs. After the bankruptcy, GM employed approximately 40,000 hourly workers in the United States.
- GM canceled 2,000 of its 6,000 dealership licenses.
- GM eliminated its Pontiac, Saturn, Hummer, and Saab brand names. GM pared down to four vehicle brand names—Chevrolet, Cadillac, Buick, and GMC.
- GM was delisted from the New York Stock Exchange (NYSE) and was removed as one of the companies comprising the Dow Jones Industrial Average (DOW).
- GM emerged from bankruptcy with a new balance sheet, shed of much of its unwanted debt, almost $60 billion of cash in its pockets from the U.S. and Canadian governments, unwanted dealer and other contracts eliminated, fewer manufacturing and industrial plants, and a reduced workforce. The new GM is a much smaller company that will concentrate on the four brands of vehicles that it has kept. Much of GM's international operations were not affected by the bankruptcy, and a great deal of GM's future focus will be on international markets, such as China, Brazil, and other countries. GM has promised to become a "green" car company and to continue its research and eventual production of consumer electric vehicles. In April 2010, GM repaid the U.S. government $6.7 of the government's aid and paid the Canadian governments $1.4 of their loans to GM.

In 2010, GM issued an initial public offering of stock in which the U.S. government sold almost half of its stake in GM. The U.S. received almost $12 billion toward reducing its $50 billion bailout of GM. *In re General Motors Corporation*, Chapter 11 Case No. 09-50026 (REG) (United States Bankruptcy Court for the Southern District of New York)

Ethics Questions Is it ethical for a company to declare Chapter 11 bankruptcy? Is anyone hurt by a debtor declaring bankruptcy? If so, who is hurt? Was it ethical for General Motors to seek a taxpayer bailout? Is General Motors "too big to fail"?

Key Terms and Concepts

Abusive homestead
  exemption (277)
Accommodation party
  (cosigner) (275)
After-acquired property
  (270)

Antideficiency statute
  (268)
Article I, section 8,
  clause 4 of the U.S.
  Constitution
  (275)

Article 9 (Secured
  Transactions) of the
  Uniform Commercial
  Code (UCC) (269)
Artisan's lien (274)
Attachment (270)

Automatic stay (276)
Bankruptcy Abuse
  Prevention and
  Consumer Protection
  Act of 2005 (275)
Bankruptcy Code (275)

Bankruptcy court (276)
Bankruptcy estate (277)
Bankruptcy law (275)
Bankruptcy Reform Act of 1978 (275)
Bankruptcy trustee (276)
Buyer in the ordinary course of business (273)
Chapter 7—Liquidation (straight bankruptcy) (277)
Chapter 11—Reorganization (279)
Chapter 12—Adjustment of Debts of a Family Farmer or Fisherman with Regular Income (280)
Chapter 13—Adjustment of Debts of an Individual with Regular Income (278)
Collateral (267)
Composition (278)
Confirm (281)
Consumer goods (272)
Continuation statement (271)
County recorder's office (271)
Cram-down (281)
Credit (266)
Creditor (lender) (266)
Debtor (borrower) (266)
Deed of trust (268)
Default (273)

Deficiency judgment (268)
Discharge (279)
Disposable income (278)
Electronic financing statement (e-financing statement) (274)
Electronic secured transaction (e-secured transaction) (274)
Executory contract (281)
Exempt property (277)
Extension (278)
Financing statement (271)
First purchase money mortgage (268)
Floating lien (270)
Fraudulent transfer (277)
Future advances (270)
Guarantor (275)
Guaranty arrangement (275)
Homestead exemption (277)
Individual with regular income (278)
Intangible personal property (269)
Involuntary petition (276)
Judgment-proof (267)
Means test (278)
Mechanic's lien (269)
Median income test (278)
Mortgage (267)

Mortgagee (creditor) (267)
Mortgagor (debtor) (267)
Nonrecordation of a mortgage (268)
Note (268)
Perfection by attachment (automatic perfection rule) (273)
Perfection by filing a financing statement (271)
Perfection by possession of collateral (272)
Perfection by a purchase money security interest in consumer goods (272)
Perfection of a security interest (270)
Personal property (269)
Petition (276)
Plan of payment (278)
Plan of reorganization (280)
Primarily liable (275)
Priority of claims (273)
Proof of claim (276)
Proof of interest (276)
Purchase money security interest (272)
Record (274)
Recording statute (268)
Release of lien (lien release) (269)
Repossession (273)

Revised Article 9 (Secured Transactions) of the UCC (270)
Sale proceeds (270)
Secondarily liable (275)
Secretary of state (271)
Secured credit (267)
Secured party (267)
Secured transaction (269)
Security agreement (270)
Security interest (267)
Super-priority lien (274)
Surety (co-debtor) (274)
Surety arrangement (274)
Taking possession of the collateral (273)
Tangible personal property (269)
Three-party secured transaction (269)
Two-party secured transaction (269)
UCC Financing Statement (Form UCC-1) (271)
Undue hardship (279)
Unexpired lease (281)
Unsecured credit (266)
Unsecured creditor (267)
U.S. Trustee (276)
Voluntary petition (276)

Law Case with Answer

In re Lebovitz

Facts   Dr. Morris Lebovitz and Kerrye Hill Lebovitz, husband and wife, were residents of the state of Tennessee. Dr. Lebovitz filed for bankruptcy protection as a result of illness. Mrs. Lebovitz (Debtor) filed for bankruptcy because she had cosigned on a large loan with Dr. Lebovitz. Debtor is the owner of the following pieces of jewelry: a Tiffany 5-carat diamond engagement ring (purchase price $40,000–$50,000), a pair of diamond stud earrings of approximately 1 carat each, a diamond drop necklace of approximately 1 carat, and a Cartier watch. All these items were gifts from Dr. Lebovitz.

Tennessee opted out of the federal bankruptcy exemption provisions and adopted its own bankruptcy exemption provisions. Tennessee does not provide for an exemption for jewelry. Tennessee does provide for an exemption for "necessary and proper wearing apparel." Debtor claimed that her jewelry was necessary and proper wearing apparel and was therefore exempt property from the bankruptcy estate. The bankruptcy trustee filed an objection to the claim of exemption, arguing that Debtor's jewelry does not qualify for an exemption and should be part of the bankruptcy estate.

Does Debtor's jewelry qualify as necessary and proper wearing apparel and therefore is exempt property from the bankruptcy estate?

Answer   No, Debtor's jewelry does not qualify as necessary and proper wearing apparel and is therefore not exempt property from the bankruptcy estate. Mrs. Lebovitz's jewelry is part of the bankruptcy estate. Debtor argues that she should be able to exempt all of her jewelry as wearing apparel because the items are worn by Debtor regularly, have sentimental value to her because they were given to her by her husband, and were not purchased for investment. However, under Tennessee law, Debtor is not entitled to claim her jewelry as exempt because the items are neither necessary nor proper wearing apparel for a bankruptcy debtor. Thus, Debtor is not entitled to claim her jewelry as exempt from the bankruptcy estate. As difficult as this case is, given the unfortunate illness of Dr. Lebovitz that led to the bankruptcy filing, the law is clear: Whether Debtor's jewelry is valued at its wholesale value or retail value, the items constitute luxury items. The items constitute luxury items, not necessary or proper wearing apparel, and are not exempt property from Debtor's bankruptcy estate. Debtor's jewelry is property that must be included in the bankruptcy estate. *In re Lebovitz*, 344 B.R. 556, **Web** 2006 Bankr. Lexis 1044 (United States Bankruptcy Court for the Western District of Tennessee)

Critical Legal Thinking Cases

13.1 Financing Statement   PSC Metals, Inc. (PSC), entered into an agreement whereby it extended credit to Keystone Consolidated Industries, Inc., and took back a security interest in personal property owned by Keystone. PSC filed a financing statement with the state, listing the debtor's trade name, "Keystone Steel & Wire Co.," rather than its corporate name, "Keystone Consolidated Industries, Inc." When Keystone went into bankruptcy, PSC filed a motion with the bankruptcy court to obtain the personal property securing its loan. Keystone's other creditors and the bankruptcy trustee objected, arguing that because PSC's financing statement was defectively filed, PSC did not have a perfected security interest in the personal property. If this were true, then PSC would become an unsecured creditor in Keystone's bankruptcy proceeding. Is the financing statement filed in the debtor's trade name, rather than in its corporate name, effective? *In re FV Steel and Wire Company*, 310 B.R. 390, **Web** 2004 Bankr. Lexis 748 (United States Bankruptcy Court for the Eastern District of Wisconsin)

13.2 Buyer in the Ordinary Course of Business   Mike Thurmond operated Top Quality Auto Sales, a used car dealership. Top Quality financed its inventory of vehicles by obtaining credit under a financing arrangement with Indianapolis Car Exchange (ICE). ICE filed a financing statement that listed Top Quality's inventory of vehicles as collateral for the financing. Top Quality sold a Ford truck to Bonnie Chrisman, a used car dealer, who paid Top Quality for the truck. Chrisman in turn sold the truck to Randall and Christina Alderson, who paid Chrisman for the truck. When Chrisman filed to retrieve the title to the truck for the Aldersons, it was discovered that Top Quality had not paid ICE for the truck. ICE requested that the Indiana Bureau of Motor Vehicles (BMV) place a lien in its favor on the title of the truck. When ICE refused to release the lien on the truck, the Aldersons sued ICE to obtain title to the truck. The Aldersons asserted that Chrisman, and then they, were buyers in the ordinary course of business and therefore acquired the truck free of ICE's financing statement. ICE filed a counterclaim to recover the truck from the Aldersons. Are Chrisman and the Aldersons buyers in the ordinary course of business who took the truck free from ICE's security interest in the truck? *Indianapolis Car Exchange v. Alderson*, 910 N.E.2d 802, **Web** 2009 Ind.App. Lexis (Court of Appeals of Indiana)

13.3 Bankruptcy   Mark Ahmed and Ann Marie Jalajel (Debtors) filed a joint petition for Chapter 7 liquidation bankruptcy. On the schedule of personal property, Debtors listed two cars worth $58,395, a bank account with a balance of $1,156, household furnishing and clothing valued at $6,550, interests in twelve limited liability companies valued at $1.00 each, a dog valued at $1.00, and the following jewelry:

Item	Owner	Value
Necklaces earrings, bracelets, and watch	Wife	$1,500.00
Wedding ring	Wife	$7,000.00
Watch	Husband	$100.00
Wedding band	Husband	$300.00

Within two years prior to declaring bankruptcy, Debtors purchased twenty-eight pieces of jewelry for approximately $120,000. Prior to filing bankruptcy,

Debtors sold nine pieces of jewelry. Seven pieces of jewelry were reported as lost. After filing for bankruptcy, Debtors sold some jewelry and pawned a Rolex watch for $3,000. Two creditors objected to Debtors' claimed exemptions. A complaint was filed, alleging that Debtors knowingly and fraudulently made false oaths and material omissions and transferred and concealed property of the estate in an attempt to hinder, delay, and defraud creditors. The remedy sought was an order that Debtors be denied discharge. Based on the facts of the case, should Debtors be denied discharge? *In re Jalajel*, **Web** 2010 Bankr. Lexis ___ (United States Bankruptcy Court for the Eastern District of Virginia)

13.4 Discharge   Margaret Kawaauhau sought treatment from Dr. Paul Geiger for a foot injury. Dr. Geiger examined Kawaauhau and admitted her to the hospital to attend to the risks of infection. Although Dr. Geiger knew that intravenous penicillin would have been a more effective treatment, he prescribed oral penicillin, explaining that he thought that his patient wished to minimize the cost of her treatment. Dr. Geiger then departed on a business trip, leaving Kawaauhau in the care of other physicians. When Dr. Geiger returned, he discontinued all antibiotics because he believed that the infection had subsided. Kawaauhau's condition deteriorated over the next few days, requiring the amputation of her right leg below the knee. Kawaauhau and her husband sued Dr. Geiger for medical malpractice. The jury found Dr. Geiger liable and awarded the Kawaauhaus $355,000 in damages. Dr. Geiger, who carried no malpractice insurance, filed for bankruptcy in an attempt to discharge the judgment. Is a debt arising from a medical malpractice judgment that is attributable to negligent or reckless conduct dischargeable in bankruptcy? *Kawaauhau v. Geiger*, 523 U.S. 57, 118 S.Ct. 974, 140 L.Ed.2d 90, **Web** 1998 U.S. Lexis 1595 (Supreme Court of the United States)

13.5 Chapter 11 Reorganization   UAL Corporation was the parent company of United Airlines, which was the largest scheduled passenger commercial airline in the world. On a daily basis, the airline offered more than 1,500 flights to twenty-six countries. The airline also offered regional service to domestic hubs through United Express carriers. Eventually, low-cost airlines began taking business from United. In response, United lowered fares to compete with the low-cost airlines. However, United's cost structure could not support its new strategy, and the company began losing substantial money on its operations.

UAL filed for Chapter 11 reorganization bankruptcy. At the time of filing the petition, UAL owned or leased airplanes, equipment, trucks and other vehicles, docking space at airports, warehouses, office space, and other assets. In many cases, UAL had borrowed the money to purchase or lease these assets. Most of the lenders took back mortgages or security interests in the assets for which they had loaned money to UAL to purchase or lease. In addition, UAL owed unsecured creditors money that it could not repay, and it had executory contracts and unexpired leases that it also could not pay. What should UAL propose to do in its plan of reorganization that it files with the bankruptcy court? *In re UAL Corporation*

13.6 Priority of Security Interests   Paul High purchased various items of personal property and livestock from William and Marilyn McGowen. To secure the purchase price, High granted the McGowens a security interest in the personal property and livestock. Two and one-half months later, High borrowed $86,695 from Nebraska State Bank (Bank) and signed a promissory note, granting Bank a security interest in all his farm products, including but not limited to all his livestock. Bank immediately perfected its security agreement by filing a financing statement with the county clerk in Dakota County, Nebraska. The McGowens perfected their security interest by filing a financing statement and security agreement with the county clerk three months after Bank filed its financing statement. Three years later, High defaulted on the obligations owed to the McGowens and Bank. Whose security interest has priority? *McGowen v. Nebraska State Bank*, 229 Neb. 471, 427 N.W.2d 772, **Web** 1988 Neb. Lexis 290 (Supreme Court of Nebraska)

13.7 Fraudulent Transfer   Peter and Geraldine Tabala (Debtors), husband and wife, purchased a house in Clarkstown, New York. They purchased a Carvel ice cream business for $70,000 with a loan obtained from People's National Bank. In addition, the Carvel Corporation extended trade credit to Debtors. Two years after getting the bank loan, Debtors conveyed their residence to their three daughters, ages 9, 19, and 20, for no consideration. Debtors continued to reside in the house and to pay maintenance expenses and real estate taxes due on the property. On the date of transfer, Debtors owed obligations in excess of $100,000. Five months after conveying their residence to their daughters, Debtors filed a petition for Chapter 7 bankruptcy. The bankruptcy trustee moved to set aside Debtors' conveyance of their home to their daughters as a fraudulent transfer. Who wins? *In re Tabala*, 11 B.R. 405, **Web** 1981 Bankr. Lexis 3663 (United States Bankruptcy Court for the Southern District of New York)

13.8 Guaranty Contract   Murphy Oil USA, Inc. (Murphy Oil), entered into a contract to sell petroleum products to Price Oil, Inc. In order to do so, Murphy Oil required and obtained written guaranty contracts signed by Elmer Myers Armstrong and Frieda Armstrong (Armstrongs), guaranteeing that if Price Oil did not pay for oil delivered by Murphy Oil, they would pay the unpaid amount. Murphy Oil sold and delivered petroleum products to Price Oil for the price of $259,585.75. Price Oil did not thereafter make payment on this debt. Price Oil declared bankruptcy, and Murphy Oil received $66,246.28 from the bankruptcy proceeding. The Armstrongs did not make payment to Murphy Oil for the unpaid debt. Murphy Oil instituted a legal action against the Armstrongs to enforce the guaranty agreement against them to recover Price Oil's remaining debt owed to Murphy Oil, which at the time of the lawsuit was $193,339.47. Do the Armstrongs, as guarantors of Price Oil's debt to Murphy Oil, owe Murphy Oil the amount of the unpaid debt of Price Oil? *Murphy Oil USA, Inc. v. Armstrong*, **Web** 2006 U.S. Dist. Lexis 46289 (United States District Court for the Middle District of Alabama)

Ethics Cases

13.9 Ethics Jessie Lynch became seriously ill and needed medical attention. Her sister, Ethel Sales, took her to Forsyth Memorial Hospital in North Carolina for treatment. Lynch was admitted for hospitalization. Sales signed Lynch's admission form, which included the following section:

> *The undersigned, in consideration of hospital services being rendered or to be rendered by Forsyth County Memorial Hospital Authority, Inc., in Winston-Salem, N.C., to the above patient, does hereby guarantee payment to Forsyth County Hospital Authority, Inc., on demand all charges for said services and incidentals incurred on behalf of such patient.*

Lynch received the care and services rendered by the hospital until her discharge over 30 days later. The total bill during her hospitalization amounted to $7,977. When Lynch refused to pay the bill, the hospital instituted an action against Lynch and Sales to recover the unpaid amount. *Forsyth County Memorial Hospital Authority, Inc.*, 82 N.C.App. 265, 346 S.E.2d 212, **Web** 1986 N.C.App. Lexis 2432 (Court of Appeals of North Carolina)

1. What is a guaranty contract?
2. Did Lynch act ethically in denying liability?
3. Is Sales liable to Forsyth County Memorial Hospital Authority, Inc.?

13.10 Ethics Donald Wayne Doyle (Debtor) obtained a guaranteed student loan to enroll in a school for training truck drivers. Due to his impending divorce, Debtor never attended the program. The first monthly installment of approximately $50 to pay the student loan became due. Two weeks later, Debtor filed a voluntary petition for Chapter 7 bankruptcy.

Debtor was a 29-year-old man who earned approximately $1,000 per month at an hourly wage of $7.70 as a truck driver, a job that he had held for 10 years. Debtor resided on a farm, where he performed work in lieu of paying rent for his quarters. Debtor was paying monthly payments of $89 on a bank loan for his former wife's vehicle, $200 for his truck, $40 for health insurance, $28 for car insurance, $120 for gasoline and vehicular maintenance, $400 for groceries and meals, and $25 for telephone charges. In addition, a state court had ordered Debtor to pay $300 per month to support his children, ages 4 and 5. Debtor's parents were assisting him by buying him $130 of groceries per month. *In re Doyle*, 106 B.R. 272, **Web** 1989 Bankr. Lexis 1772 (United States Bankruptcy Court for the Northern District of Alabama)

1. What legal standard must be met to have a student loan discharged in bankruptcy?
2. Did Doyle act unethically in trying to have his student loan discharged in bankruptcy?
3. Should Doyle's student loan be discharged in bankruptcy?

Internet Exercises

1. There are three major credit reporting agencies from which you can obtain a copy of your credit report. Go to each of the following websites to see how to order a free credit report. If you want, order your credit report.

a. Equifax, at **www.equifax.com**
b. Experian, at **www.experian.com**
c. TransUnion, at **www.transunion.com**

2. Go to **www.sos.nh.gov/ucc/ucc1.pdf**. Scroll down past the form to the second page. Read "Instructions for National UCC Financing Statement (Form UCC1)."

3. Go to **www.ftc.gov/bcp/edu/pubs/consumer/credit/cre41.shtm** and read information from the Federal Trade Commission (FTC) about credit counseling before filing for bankruptcy.

Endnotes

1. 11 U.S.C. Sections 101–1330.
2. 28 U.S.C. Sections 586–589b.
3. 11 U.S.C. Sections 701–784.

4. 11 U.S.C. Sections 1301–1330.
5. 11 U.S.C. Sections 1201–1231.
6. 11 U.S.C. Sections 1101–1174.

Business Organizations and Investor Protection

CHAPTER
14

Small Business and General and Limited Partnerships

RESTAURANT, LOS ANGELES, CALIFORNIA
The Pantry Restaurant in downtown Los Angeles has been open "round the clock" 365 days a year since 1924.

Learning Objectives

After studying this chapter, you should be able to:

1. Define *entrepreneurship* and list the types of businesses that an entrepreneur can use to form and operate a business.
2. Define *sole proprietorship* and describe the liability of a sole proprietor.
3. Define *general partnership* and describe how general partnerships are formed.
4. Define *limited partnership* and describe how limited partnerships are formed.
5. Explain the tort and contract liability of general partners and limited partners.

Chapter Outline

Introduction to Small Business and General and Limited Partnerships

Entrepreneurship

Sole Proprietorship
   CONTEMPORARY ENVIRONMENT • *d.b.a.—"Doing Business As"*
   CASE 14.1 • *Bank of America, N.A. v. Barr*

General Partnership
   CONTEMPORARY ENVIRONMENT • *Uniform Partnership Act and Revised Uniform Partnership Act*
   CONTEMPORARY ENVIRONMENT • *Right of Survivorship of General Partners*

Limited Partnership
   CONTEMPORARY ENVIRONMENT • *Uniform Limited Partnership Act and Revised Uniform Limited Partnership Act*

" One of the most fruitful sources of ruin to a man of the world is the recklessness or want of principle of partners, and it is one of the perils to which every man exposes himself who enters into a partnership."

—Vice Chancellor Malins
   Mackay v. Douglas, 14 Eq. 106 at 118 (1872)

Introduction to Small Business and General and Limited Partnerships

An *entrepreneur* or *entrepreneurs* who want to start and operate a business must decide what type of business organization to form and whether he, she, or they qualify to do so. The major forms of business organization are *sole proprietorship, general partnership, limited partnership, limited liability partnership, limited liability company,* and *corporation.* The selection of business form depends on many factors, including the ease and cost of formation, the capital requirements of the business, the flexibility of making management decisions, government restrictions, personal liability, tax considerations, and the like.

   This chapter discusses small businesses, entrepreneurship, sole proprietorships, and general partnerships.

The partner of my partner is not my partner.

Legal maxim

Entrepreneurship

An **entrepreneur** is a person who forms and operates a business. An entrepreneur may start a business by himself or herself or may cofound a business with others. Most businesses started by entrepreneurs are small, although some grow into substantial organizations.

Examples Bill Gates and Paul Allen started Microsoft Corporation, which grew into a giant software company; Mark Zuckerberg founded Facebook, an extremely successful social networking service; Michael Dell started Dell Computer as a mail-order business that has become a leader in computer sales; and David Filo and Jerry Yang founded Yahoo!, which has become a global leader in providing Internet services.

   Every day, entrepreneurs in this country and elsewhere around the world create new businesses such as restaurants, clothing stores, insurance agencies, and many other forms of business. These businesses hire employees, provide new products and services, and contribute to the growth of economies of countries.

entrepreneur
A person who forms and operates a new business either by himself or herself or with others.

It is when merchants dispute about their own rules that they invoke the law.

Judge Brett
Robinson v. Mollett (1875)

Sole Proprietorship

A **sole proprietorship** is the simplest form of business organization. There is only one owner of the business, who is called the **sole proprietor.** There is no separate legal entity. Sole proprietorships are the most common form of business organization in the United States. Many small businesses—and a few large ones—operate in this way.

   There are several major advantages to operating a business as a sole proprietorship. They include the following:

- Forming a sole proprietorship is easy and does not cost a lot.
- The owner has the right to make all management decisions concerning the business, including those involving hiring and firing employees.

sole proprietorship
A form of business in which the owner is actually the business; the business is not a separate legal entity.

sole proprietor
The owner of a sole proprietorship.

- The sole proprietor owns all of the business and has the right to receive all of the business's profits.
- A sole proprietorship can be easily transferred or sold if and when the owner desires to do so; no other approval (e.g., from partners or shareholders) is necessary.

There are important disadvantages to this business form, too. For example, a sole proprietor's access to the capital is limited to personal funds plus any loans he or she can obtain, and a sole proprietor is legally responsible for the business's contracts and the torts he or she or any of his or her employees commit in the course of employment.

Creation of a Sole Proprietorship

Creating a sole proprietorship is easy. There are no formalities, and no federal or state government approval is required. Some local governments require all businesses, including sole proprietorships, to obtain licenses to do business within the city. If no other form of business organization is chosen, the business is by default a sole proprietorship.

The following feature discusses the requirement for businesses to file for a trade name under certain circumstances.

d.b.a. (doing business as)
A designation for a business that is operating under a trade name.

fictitious business name statement (certificate of trade name)
A document that is filed with the state that designates a trade name of a business, the name and address of the applicant, and the address of the business.

Contemporary Environment

d.b.a.—"Doing Business As"

A sole proprietorship can operate under the name of the sole proprietor or a **trade name**. For example, the author of this book can operate a sole proprietorship under the name "Henry R. Cheeseman" or under a trade name such as "The Big Cheese." Operating under a trade name is commonly designated as **d.b.a. (doing business as)** (e.g., Henry R. Cheeseman, doing business as "The Big Cheese").

Most states require all businesses—including sole proprietorships, general and limited partnerships, limited liability companies and limited liability partnerships, and corporations—that operate under a trade name to

file a **fictitious business name statement** (or **certificate of trade name**) with the appropriate government agency. The statement must contain the name and address of the applicant, the trade name, and the address of the business. Most states also require notice of the trade name to be published in a newspaper of general circulation serving the area in which the applicant does business.

These requirements are intended to disclose the real owner's name to the public. Noncompliance can result in a fine. Some states prohibit violators from maintaining lawsuits in the state's courts.

Personal Liability of a Sole Proprietor

A sole proprietor bears the risk of loss of the business; that is, the owner will lose his or her entire capital contribution if the business fails. In addition, the sole proprietor has **unlimited personal liability** (see **Exhibit 14.1**). Therefore, creditors may recover claims against the business from the sole proprietors' personal assets (e.g., home, automobile, bank accounts).

unlimited personal liability of a sole proprietor
The personal liability of a sole proprietor for the debts and obligations of a sole proprietorship.

Example Nathan opens a clothing store called "The Clothing Store" and operates it as a sole proprietorship. Nathan files the proper statement and publishes the necessary notice of the use of the trade name. Nathan contributes $25,000 of his personal funds to the business and borrows $100,000 from a bank in the name of the business.

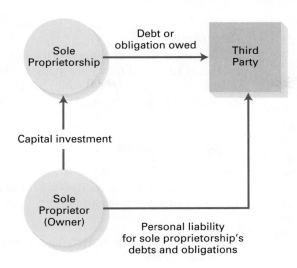

Exhibit 14.1 SOLE PROPRIETORSHIP

Assume that after several months, Nathan closes the business because it is unsuccessful. At the time it is closed, the business has no assets, owes the bank $100,000, and owes other debts of $25,000. Here, Nathan, the sole proprietor, is personally liable to pay the bank and all the debts of the sole proprietorship from his personal assets.

In the following case, the court had to decide the liability of a sole proprietor.

CASE 14.1 *Sole Proprietorship*

Bank of America, N.A. v. Barr

9 A.3d 816 (2010)
Supreme Judicial Court of Maine

"An individual doing business as a sole proprietor, even when business is done under a different name, remains personally liable for all of the obligations of the sole proprietorship."

—Alexander, Judge

Facts

Constance Barr was the sole owner of The Stone Scone, a business operated as a sole proprietorship. Based on documents signed by Barr on behalf of The Stone Scone, Fleet Bank approved a $100,000 unsecured small business line of credit for The Stone Scone. Fleet Bank sent a letter addressed to Barr and The Stone Scone, which stated, "Dear Constance H Barr: Congratulations! Your company has been approved for a $100000 Small Business Credit Express Line of Credit." The bank sent account statements addressed to both The Stone Scone and Barr. For four years, Fleet Bank provided funds to The Stone Scone. After that time, however, The Stone Scone did not make any further payments on the loan, leaving $91,444 unpaid principal. Pursuant to the loan agreement, interest on the unpaid principal balance continued to accrue at a rate of 6.5 percent per year. Bank of America, N.A., which had acquired Fleet Bank, sued The Stone Scone and Barr to recover the unpaid principal and interest. Barr stipulated to a judgment against The Stone Scone, which she had converted to an limited liability company, but denied personal responsibility for the unpaid debt. The trial court found Barr personally liable for the debt. Barr appealed.

Issue

Is Barr, the sole owner of The Stone Scone, personally liable for the unpaid debt?

(continued)

Language of the Court

The trial record contains sufficient evidence that Barr is personally liable for the debt owed to Bank of America. The evidence demonstrates that, at the time Barr acted on The Stone Scone's behalf to procure the small business line of credit, she was the owner of The Stone Scone and the sole proprietor of that business. An individual doing business as a sole proprietor, even when business is done under a different name, remains personally liable for all of the obligations of the sole proprietorship. As the sole proprietor of The Stone Scone when that sole proprietorship entered into the agreement for a line of credit with Fleet Bank, Barr became personally liable for the debts incurred on that line of credit account.

Decision

The supreme judicial court affirmed the trial court's judgment that held Barr personally liable, as the sole proprietor of The Stone Scone, for the sole proprietorship's unpaid debt owed to Bank of America.

Case Questions

Critical Legal Thinking
What is a sole proprietorship? What are the main attributes of sole proprietorship?

Ethics
Did Barr act ethically in denying responsibility for The Stone Scone's debts?

Contemporary Business
Why are sole proprietors held personally liable for the debts of their businesses?

Taxation of a Sole Proprietorship

A sole proprietorship is not a separate legal entity, so it does not pay taxes at the business level. Instead, the earnings and losses from a sole proprietorship are reported on each sole proprietor's personal income tax return. A sole proprietor has to file tax returns and pay taxes to state and federal governments.

General Partnership

general partnership (ordinary partnership)
An association of two or more persons to carry on as co-owners of a business for profit [UPA Section 6(1)].

General partnership, or **ordinary partnership**, has been recognized since ancient times. The English common law of partnerships governed early U.S. partnerships. The individual states expanded the body of partnership law.

A general partnership, commonly referred as a partnership, is a voluntary association of two or more persons for carrying on a business as co-owners for profit. The formation of a general partnership creates certain rights and duties among partners and with third parties. These rights and duties are established in the partnership agreement and by law. **General partners**, or **partners**, are personally liable for the debts and obligations of the partnership (see **Exhibit 14.2**).

general partners (partners)
Persons liable for the debts and obligations of a general partnership.

Formation of a General Partnership

Uniform Partnership Act (UPA)
A model act that codifies partnership law. Most states have adopted the UPA in whole or in part.

A business must meet four criteria to qualify as a general partnership under the UPA [UPA Section 6(1)]. It must be (1) an association of two or more persons (2) carrying on a business (3) as co-owners (4) for profit. A general partnership is a voluntary association of two or more persons. All partners must agree to the participation of each co-partner. A person cannot be forced to be a partner or to accept another person as a partner. The UPA's definition of *person* who may be a general partner includes natural persons, partnerships (including limited partnerships), corporations, and other associations. A business—a trade, an occupation, or a profession—must be carried on. The organization or venture must have a profit motive in order to qualify as a partnership, even though the business does not actually have to make a profit.

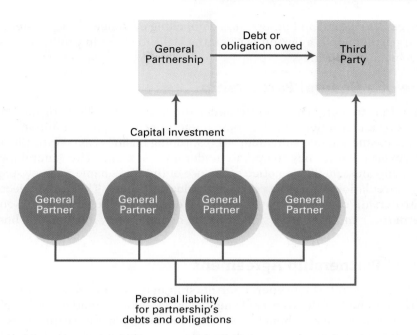

Exhibit 14.2 GENERAL PARTNERSHIP

Contemporary Environment

Uniform Partnership Act and Revised Uniform Partnership Act

In 1914, the National Conference of Commissioners on Uniform State Laws, which is a group of lawyers, judges, and legal scholars, promulgated the **Uniform Partnership Act (UPA)**. The UPA is a model act that codifies general partnership law. Its goal was to establish consistent partnership law that was uniform throughout the Unites States. The UPA has been adopted in whole or in part by most states, the District of Columbia, Guam, and the Virgin Islands. A **Revised Uniform Partnership Act (RUPA)** has been issued by the National Conference of Commissioners on Uniform State Laws, but it has not been adopted by many states.

The UPA covers most problems that arise in the formation, operation, and dissolution of general partnerships. Other rules of law or equity govern if there is no applicable provision of the UPA [UPA Section 5]. The UPA forms the basis of the study of general partnerships in this chapter.

A general partnership may be formed with little or no formality. Co-ownership of a business is essential to create a partnership. The most important factor in determining co-ownership is whether the parties share the business's profits and management responsibility.

Receipt of a share of business profits is *prima facie* evidence of a general partnership because nonpartners usually are not given the right to share in a business's profits. No inference of the existence of a general partnership is drawn if profits are received in payment of (1) a debt owed to a creditor in installments or otherwise; (2) wages owed to an employee; (3) rent owed to a landlord; (4) an annuity owed to a widow, widower, or representative of a deceased partner; (5) interest owed on a loan; or (6) consideration for the sale of goodwill of a business [UPA Section 7]. An agreement to share losses of a business is strong evidence of a general partnership.

The right to participate in the management of a business is important evidence for determining the existence of a general partnership, but it is not conclusive evidence because the right to participate in management is sometimes given to employees, creditors, and others. It is compelling evidence of the existence of a general partnership if a person is given the right to share in profits, losses, and management of a business.

Name of a General Partnership

A general partnership can operate under the names of any one or more of the partners or under a fictitious business name. A general partnership must file a fictitious business name statement—d.b.a. (doing business as)—with the appropriate government agency to operate under a trade name. The general partnership usually must publish a notice of the use of the trade name in a newspaper of general circulation where the partnership does business. The name selected by the partnership cannot indicate that it is a corporation (e.g., it cannot contain the term *Inc.*) and cannot be similar to the name used by any existing business entity.

General Partnership Agreement

The agreement to form a general partnership may be oral, written, or implied from the conduct of the parties. It may even be created inadvertently. No formalities are necessary, although a few states require general partnerships to file certificates of partnership with an appropriate government agency. General partnerships that exist for more than one year or are authorized to deal in real estate must be in writing under the Statute of Frauds.

It is good practice for partners to put their partnership agreement in writing. A written document is important evidence of the terms of the agreement, particularly if a dispute arises among the partners.

general partnership agreement (articles of general partnership or articles of partnership)
A written agreement that partners sign to form a general partnership.

A written agreement is called a **general partnership agreement**, or **articles of general partnership**, or **articles of partnership**. The parties can agree to almost any terms in their partnership agreement, except terms that are illegal. The articles of partnership can be short and simple or long and complex. If an agreement fails to provide for an essential term or contingency, the provisions of the UPA apply. Thus, the UPA acts as a gap-filling device to the partners' agreement.

Taxation of General Partnerships

General partnerships do not pay federal income taxes. Instead, the income and losses of partnership flow onto and have to be reported on the individual partners' personal income tax returns. This is called **flow-through taxation**. A general partnership has to file an information return with the government telling the government how much income was earned or the amount of losses incurred by the partnership. This way, the government tax authorities can trace whether partners are correctly reporting their income or losses.

Right to Participate in Management

right to participate in management
A situation in which, unless otherwise agreed, each partner has a right to participate in the management of a partnership and has an equal vote on partnership matters.

In the absence of an agreement to the contrary, all general partners have an equal **right to participate in the management** of the general partnership business. In other words, each partner has one vote, regardless of the proportional size of his or her capital contribution or share in the partnership's profits. Under the UPA, a simple majority decides most ordinary partnership matters [UPA Section 18]. If the vote is tied, the action being voted on is considered to be defeated.

Example Maude, George, Hillary, and Michael form a general partnership. $200,000 capital is contributed to the partnership, in the following amounts: Maude $60,000 (30 percent), George $10,000 (5 percent), Hillary $100,000 (50 percent), and Michael $30,000 (15 percent). Here, although the capital contributions of the partners differ significantly, each of the four partners has an equal say in the business. The partners can, by agreement, modify the UPA's majority rule by delegating management responsibility to a committee of partners or to a managing partner.

Right to Share in Profits

Unless otherwise agreed, the UPA mandates that a general partner has the right to an equal share in the partnership's profits and losses [UPA Section 18(a)]. The **right to share in the profits** of the partnership is considered to be the right to share in the earnings from the investment of capital.

Example Maude, George, Hillary, and Michael form a general partnership. Capital is contributed to the partnership in the following amounts: Maude 30 percent, George 5 percent, Hillary 50 percent, and Michael 15 percent. The partnership makes $100,000 profit for the year. Here, although the capital contributions of the partners differ significantly, each of the four partners will share equally in the profits of the business; each will receive $25,000.

Where a partnership agreement provides for the sharing of profits but is silent as to how losses are to be shared, losses are shared in the same proportion as profits. The reverse is not true, however. If a partnership agreement provides for the sharing of losses but is silent as to how profits are to be shared, profits are shared equally.

Partnership agreements can provide that profits and losses are to be allocated in proportion to the partners' capital contributions or in any other manner.

Example Partners with high incomes from other sources can benefit the most by having the losses generated by a partnership allocated in a greater portion to them.

It has been uniformly laid down in this Court, as far back as we can remember, that good faith is the basis of all mercantile transactions.

Justice Buller
Salomons v. Nissen (1788)

Right to an Accounting

General partners are not permitted to sue the partnership or other partners at law. Instead, they are given the right to bring an **action for an accounting** against other partners. An action for an accounting is a formal judicial proceeding in which the court is authorized to (1) review the partnership and the partners' transactions and (2) award each partner his or her share of the partnership assets [UPA Section 24]. An action results in a money judgment for or against partners, according to the balance struck.

Example If a partner suspects that another partner is committing fraud by stealing partnership assets, the partner can bring an action for an accounting.

action for an accounting
A formal judicial proceeding in which the court is authorized to (1) review the partnership and the partners' transactions and (2) award each partner his or her share of the partnership assets.

Tort Liability of General Partners

While acting on partnership business, a partner or an employee of the general partnership may commit a tort that causes injury to a third person. This tort could be caused by a negligent act, a breach of trust (e.g., embezzlement from a customer's account), breach of fiduciary duty, defamation, fraud, or another intentional tort. The general partnership is liable if the act is committed while the person is acting within the ordinary course of partnership business or with the authority of his or her co-partners. General partners have **unlimited personal liability** for the debts and obligations of the partnership.

Under the UPA, general partners have **joint and several liability** for torts and breaches of trust [UPA Section 15(a)]. This is so even if a partner did not participate in the commission of the act. This type of liability permits a third party to sue one or more of the general partners separately. Judgment can be collected only against the partners who are sued.

Example Nicole, Jim, and Maureen form a general partnership. Jim, while on partnership business, causes an automobile accident that injures Catherine, a pedestrian.

unlimited personal liability of a general partner
A general partner's personal liability for the debts and obligations of the general partnership.

joint and several liability
Tort liability of partners together and individually. A plaintiff can sue one or more partners separately. If successful, the plaintiff can recover the entire amount of the judgment from any or all of the defendant-partners who have been found liable.

Catherine suffers $100,000 in injuries. Catherine, at her option, can sue Nicole, Jim, or Maureen separately, or any two of them, or all of them.

The partnership and partners who are made to pay **tort liability** may seek indemnification from the partner who committed the wrongful act. A release of one partner does not discharge the liability of other partners.

Contract Liability of General Partners

As a legal entity, a general partnership must act through its agents—that is, its partners and employees. Contracts entered into with suppliers, customers, lenders, or others on the partnership's behalf are binding on the partnership. General partners have *unlimited personal liability* for contracts of the partnership.

joint liability
Liability of partners for contracts and debts of the partnership. A plaintiff must name the partnership and all of the partners as defendants in a lawsuit.

Under the UPA, general partners have **joint liability** for the contracts and debts of the partnership [UPA Section 15(b)]. This means that a third party who sues to recover on a partnership contract or debt must name all the general partners in the lawsuit. If such a lawsuit is successful, the plaintiff can collect the entire amount of the judgment against any or all of the partners. If the third party's suit does not name all the general partners, the judgment cannot be collected against any of the partners or the partnership assets. Similarly, releasing any general partner from the lawsuit releases them all. Some states provide that general partners are *jointly and severally liable* for the contracts of the general partnership.

A general partner who is made to pay more than his or her proportionate share of **contract liability** may seek indemnification from the partnership and from those partners who have not paid their share of the loss.

Liability of Incoming General Partners

A lawyer with his briefcase can steal more than a hundred men with guns.

Mario Puzo
The Godfather

A new partner who is admitted to a general partnership is liable for the existing debts and obligations (**antecedent debts**) of the partnership only to the extent of his or her capital contribution. The **incoming partner** is personally liable for debts and obligations incurred by the general partnership after becoming a partner.

Example Bubble.com is a general partnership with four partners. On May 1, Frederick is admitted as a new general partner by investing a $100,000 capital contribution. As of May 1, Bubble.com owes $800,000 of preexisting debt. After Frederick becomes a partner, the general partnership borrows $1 million of new debt. If the general partnership goes bankrupt and out of business still owing both debts, Frederick's capital contribution of $100,000 will go toward paying the $800,000 of existing debt owed by the partnership when he joined the partnership, but he is not personally liable for this debt. However, Frederick is personally liable for the $1 million of unpaid debt that the partnership borrowed after he became a partner.

Dissolution of a General Partnership

The duration of a partnership can be a fixed term (e.g., five years) or until a particular undertaking is accomplished (e.g., until a real estate development is completed), or it can be an unspecified term. A partnership with a fixed duration is called a **partnership for a term**. A partnership with no fixed duration is called a **partnership at will**.

dissolution of a general partnership
The change in the relationship of partners in a partnership caused by any partner ceasing to be associated in the carrying on of the business [UPA Section 29].

The **dissolution** of a partnership is "the change in the relation of the partners caused by any partner ceasing to be associated in the carrying on of the business" [UPA Section 29]. A partnership that is formed for a specific time (e.g., five years) or purpose (e.g., the completion of a real estate development) dissolves automatically upon the expiration of the time or the accomplishment of the objective. Any partner of a partnership at will (i.e., one without a stated time or purpose) may rightfully withdraw and dissolve the partnership at any time.

Unless a partnership is continued, the **winding up** of the partnership follows its dissolution. The process of winding up consists of the liquidation (sale) of partnership assets and the distribution of the proceeds to satisfy claims against the partnership. The surviving partners have the right to wind up the partnership. If a surviving partner performs the winding up, he or she is entitled to reasonable compensation for his or her services [UPA Section 18(f)].

winding up
The process of liquidating a partnership's assets and distributing the proceeds to satisfy claims against the partnership.

Wrongful Dissolution

A partner has the *power* to withdraw and dissolve the partnership at any time, whether it is a partnership at will or a partnership for a term. A partner who withdraws from a partnership at will has the *right* to do so and is therefore not liable for dissolving the partnership. A partner who withdraws from a partnership for a term prior to the expiration of the term does not have the right to dissolve the partnership. The partner's action causes a **wrongful dissolution** of the partnership. The partner is liable for damages caused by the wrongful dissolution of the partnership.

wrongful dissolution
A situation in which a partner withdraws from a partnership without having the right to do so at that time.

Example Ashley, Vivi, Qixia, and Tina form a general partnership called DownScale Partnership to operate an upscale men's clothing store. The partnership has a stated term of five years. After one year, Ashley decides to quit the partnership. Because Ashley has the *power* to quit the partnership, when she does so, the four-partner partnership dissolves. Ashley does not have the *right* to quit the partnership, and her action causes the wrongful dissolution of the partnership. She is liable for any damages caused by her wrongful dissolution of the partnership.

Distribution of Assets upon Dissolution

After partnership assets have been liquidated and reduced to cash, the proceeds are **distributed** to satisfy claims against the partnership. The debts are satisfied in the following order [UPA Section 40(b)]:

1. Creditors (except partners who are creditors)
2. Creditor-partners
3. Capital contributions
4. Profits

The partners can agree to change the priority of distributions among themselves. If the partnership cannot satisfy its creditors' claims, the partners are personally liable for the partnership's debts and obligations [UPA Sections 40(d), 40(f)]. After the proceeds are distributed, the partnership automatically terminates. Termination ends the legal existence of the partnership [UPA Section 30].

Fraud is infinite in variety: sometimes it is audacious and unblushing: sometimes it pays a sort of homage to virtue, and then it is modest and retiring: it would be honesty itself, if it could only afford it.

Lord MacNaghten
Reddaway v. Banham (1896)

Continuation of a General Partnership After Dissolution

The surviving, or remaining, partners have the right to continue a partnership after its dissolution. It is good practice for the partners of a partnership to enter into a **continuation agreement** that expressly sets forth the events that allow for continuation of the partnership, the amount to be paid outgoing partners, and other details.

When a partnership is continued, the old partnership is dissolved, and a new partnership is created. The new partnership is composed of the remaining partners

No nation was ever ruined by trade.

Benjamin Franklin

and any new partners admitted to the partnership. The creditors of the old partnership become creditors of the new partnership and have equal status with the creditors of the new partnership [UPA Section 41].

The following feature discusses an important partnership issue.

Contemporary Environment

Right of Survivorship of General Partners

A general partner is a co-owner with the other partners of the specific partnership property as a **tenant in partnership** [UPA Section 25(1)]. This is a special legal status that exists in a general partnership. Upon the death of a general partner, the deceased partner's right in specific partnership property vests in the remaining partner or partners; it does not pass to his or her heirs or next of kin. This is called the **right of survivorship**. The *value* of the deceased general partner's interest in the partnership passes to his or her beneficiaries or heirs upon his or her death, however. Upon the death of the last surviving partner, the rights in specific partnership property vest in the deceased partner's legal representative [UPA Section 25(2)(C)].

Example Jennifer, Harold, Shou-Ju, and Jesus form a general partnership to operate a new restaurant. After their first restaurant is successful, they expand until the partnership owns one hundred restaurants. At that time, Jennifer dies. None of the partnership assets transfer to Jennifer's heirs. For example, her heirs do not get twenty-five of the restaurants. Instead, under the right of survivorship, they inherit Jennifer's *ownership interest*, and her heirs now have the right to receive Jennifer's one-quarter of the partnership's profits each year.

---

right of survivorship
A rule which provides that upon the death of a general partner, the deceased partner's right in specific partnership property vests in the remaining partner or partners; the value of the deceased general partner's interest in the partnership passes to his or her beneficiaries or heirs.

limited partnership (special partnership)
A type of partnership that has two types of partners: general partners and limited partners.

general partners
Partners in a limited partnership who invest capital, manage the business, and are personally liable for partnership debts.

Liability of Outgoing Partners

The dissolution of a general partnership does not of itself discharge the liability of an **outgoing partner** for existing partnership debts and obligations. If a general partnership is dissolved, each general partner is personally liable for debts and obligations of the partnership that exist at the time of dissolution.

If a general partnership is dissolved because a general partner leaves the partnership and the partnership is continued by the remaining partners, the outgoing partner is personally liable for the debts and obligations of the partnership at the time of dissolution. The outgoing partner is not liable for any new debts and obligations incurred by the general partnership after the dissolution, as long as proper notification of his or her withdrawal from the partnership has been given to the creditor.

Limited Partnership

Today, all states have enacted statutes that provide for the creation of limited partnerships. In most states, these partnerships are called **limited partnerships**, or **special partnerships**. Limited partnerships are used for such business ventures as investing in real estate, drilling oil and gas wells, investing in movie productions, and the like.

Contemporary Environment

Uniform Limited Partnership Act and Revised Uniform Limited Partnership Act

In 1916, the National Conference of Commissioners on Uniform State Laws, a group composed of lawyers, judges, and legal scholars, promulgated the **Uniform Limited Partnership Act (ULPA)**. The ULPA contains a uniform set of provisions for the formation, operation, and dissolution of limited partnerships. Most states originally enacted this law.

In 1976, the National Conference of Commissioners on Uniform State Laws promulgated the **Revised Uniform Limited Partnership Act (RULPA)**, which provides a more modern, comprehensive law for the formation, operation, and dissolution of limited partnerships. This law supersedes the ULPA in the states that have adopted it. The RULPA provides the basic foundation for the discussion of limited partnership law in the following text. In 2001, certain amendments were made to the Uniform Limited Partnership Act. The changes made by these amendments are referenced in this chapter.

General and Limited Partners

A limited partnership has two types of partners: (1) **general partners**, who invest capital, manage the business, and are personally liable for partnership debts, and (2) **limited partners**, who invest capital but do not participate in management and are not personally liable for partnership debts beyond their capital contributions (see **Exhibit 14.3**).

limited partners
Partners in a limited partnership who invest capital but do not participate in management and are not personally liable for partnership debts beyond their capital contributions.

Exhibit 14.3 LIMITED PARTNERSHIP

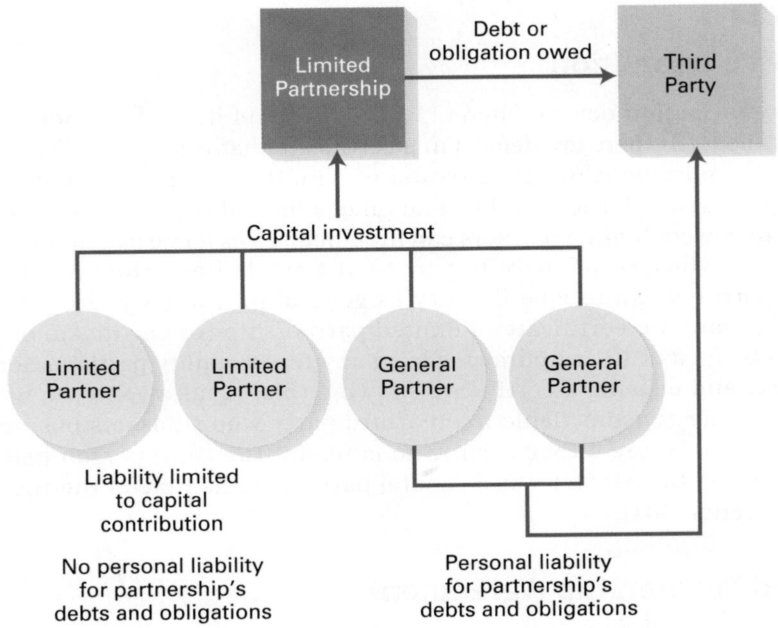

A limited partnership must have one or more general partners and one or more limited partners [RULPA Section 101(7)]. There are no upper limits on the number of general or limited partners allowed in a limited partnership. Any person—including natural persons, partnerships, limited partnerships, trusts, estates, associations, and corporations—may be a general or limited partner. A person may be both a general partner and a limited partner in the same limited partnership.

Revised Uniform Limited Partnership Act (RULPA)
A revision of the ULPA that provides a more modern, comprehensive law for the formation, operation, and dissolution of limited partnerships.

Formation of a Limited Partnership

The creation of a limited partnership is formal and requires public disclosure. The entity must comply with the statutory requirements of the RULPA or other state statutes. Under the RULPA, two or more persons must execute and sign a **certificate of limited partnership** [RULPA Sections 201, 206]. The certificate must contain the following information:

- Name of the limited partnership
- General character of the business

certificate of limited partnership
A document that two or more persons must execute and sign that makes a limited partnership legal and binding.

- Address of the principal place of business and name and address of the agent to receive service of legal process
- Name and business address of each general and limited partner
- Latest date on which the limited partnership is to dissolve
- Amount of cash, property, or services (and description of property or services) contributed by each partner and any contributions of cash, property, or services promised to be made in the future
- Any other matters that the general partners determine to include

The certificate of limited partnership must be filed with the secretary of state of the appropriate state and, if required by state law, with the county recorder in the county or counties in which the limited partnership carries on business. The limited partnership is formed when the certificate of limited partnership is filed. The certificate of limited partnership may be amended to reflect the addition or withdrawal of a partner and other matters [RULPA Section 202(a)].

Under the RULPA, the law of the state in which the limited partnership is organized governs the partnership, its internal affairs, and the liability of its limited partners [RULPA Section 901].

Defective Formation

defective formation
Incorrect creation of a limited partnership that occurs when (1) a certificate of limited partnership is not properly filed, (2) there are defects in a certificate that is filed, or (3) some other statutory requirement for the creation of a limited partnership is not met.

Defective formation occurs when (1) a certificate of limited partnership is not properly filed, (2) there are defects in a certificate that is filed, or (3) some other statutory requirement for the creation of a limited partnership is not met. If there is a substantial defect in the creation of a limited partnership, persons who thought they were limited partners can find themselves liable as general partners.

Partners who erroneously but in good faith believe they have become limited partners can escape liability as general partners by either (1) causing the appropriate certificate of limited partnership (or certificate of amendment) to be filed or (2) withdrawing from any future equity participation in the enterprise and causing a certificate showing this withdrawal to be filed. The limited partner remains liable to any third party who transacts business with the enterprise before either certificate is filed if the third person believed in good faith that the partner was a general partner at the time of the transaction [RULPA Section 304].

Limited Partnership Agreement

limited partnership agreement (articles of limited partnership)
A document that sets forth the rights and duties of general and limited partners; the terms and conditions regarding the operation, termination, and dissolution of a partnership; and so on.

Although not required by law, the partners of a limited partnership often draft and execute a **limited partnership agreement** (also called the **articles of limited partnership**) that sets forth the rights and duties of the general and limited partners; the terms and conditions regarding the operations, termination, and dissolution of the partnership; and so on. Where there is no such agreement, the certificate of limited partnership serves as the articles of limited partnership.

It is good practice to establish voting rights in a limited partnership agreement or certificate of limited partnership. The limited partnership agreement can provide which transactions must be approved by which partners (i.e., general, limited, or both). General and limited partners may be given unequal voting rights.

A limited partnership agreement may specify how profits and losses from the limited partnership are to be allocated among the general and limited partners. If there is no such agreement, the RULPA provides that profits and losses from a limited partnership are shared on the basis of the value of each partner's capital contribution [RULPA Section 503].

Example There are four general partners, each of whom contributes $50,000 in capital to the limited partnership, and four limited partners, each of whom contributes

$200,000 capital. The total amount of contributed capital is $1 million. The limited partnership agreement does not stipulate how profits and losses are to be allocated. Assume that the limited partnership makes $3 million in profits. Under the RULPA, each general partner would receive $150,000 in profit, and each limited partner would receive $600,000 in profit.

Liability of General and Limited Partners

The general partners of a limited partnership have **unlimited liability** for the debts and obligations of the limited partnerships. Thus, general partners have *unlimited personal liability* for the debts and obligations of the limited partnership. This liability extends to debts that cannot be satisfied with the existing capital of the limited partnership.

The RULPA permits a corporation or limited liability company to be a general partner or the sole general partner of a limited partnership. Where this is permissible, this type of general partner is liable for the debts and obligations of the limited partnership only to the extent of its capital contribution to the partnership.

Generally, limited partners have **limited liability** for the debts and obligations of the limited partnership. Limited partners are liable only for the debts and obligations of the limited partnership up to their capital contributions, and they are not personally liable for the debts and obligations of the limited partnership.

Example Gertrude and Gerald are the general partners of a limited partnership called Real Estate Development, Ltd. Lin, Leopold, Lonnie, and Lawrence are limited partners of the limited partnership and have each invested $100,000 in the limited partnership. Real Estate Development, Ltd., borrows $2 million from City Bank. After six months, the limited partnership goes bankrupt, still owing City Bank $2 million. The limited partnership has spent all of its capital and is broke. In this case, the four limited partners each lose their $100,000 capital investment but are not personally liable for the $2 million debt owed by the limited partnership to City Bank. The two general partners, however, are each personally liable to City Bank for the limited partnership's unpaid $2 million loan to City Bank.

Personal Guarantee

On some occasions, when limited partnerships apply for an extension of credit from a bank, a supplier, or another creditor, the creditor will not make the loan based on the limited partnership's credit history or ability to repay the credit. The creditor may require a limited partner to personally guarantee the repayment of the loan in order to extend credit to the limited partnership. If a limited partner personally guarantees a loan made by a creditor to the limited partnership and the limited partnership defaults on the loan, the creditor may enforce the **personal guarantee** and recover payment from the limited partner who personally guaranteed the repayment of the loan.

Management of a Limited Partnership

Under partnership law, general partners have the right to manage the affairs of the limited partnership. On the other hand, as a trade-off for limited liability, limited partners give up their right to participate in the control and management of the limited partnership. This means, in part, that limited partners have no right to bind the partnership to contracts or other obligations.

Under the RULPA, a limited partner is liable as a general partner if his or her participation in the control of the business is substantially the same as that of a general partner, but the limited partner is liable only to persons who reasonably believed him or her to be a general partner [RULPA Section 303(a)].

It is the spirit and not the form of law that keeps justice alive.

Earl Warren
The Law and the Future (1955)

unlimited liability of general partners
The unlimited personal liability of general partners of a limited partnership for the debts and obligations of the general partnership.

limited liability of limited partners
The limited liability of limited partners of a limited partnership only up to their capital contributions to the limited partnership; limited partners are not personally liable for the debts and obligations of the limited partnership.

Four things belong to a judge: to hear courteously, to answer wisely, to consider soberly, and to decide impartially.

Socrates

The RULPA clarifies the types of activities that a limited partner may engage in without losing his or her limited liability. These activities include [RULPA Sections 303(b), 303(c)]:

- Being an agent, an employee, or a contractor of the limited partnership
- Being a consultant or an advisor to a general partner regarding the limited partnership
- Acting as a surety for the limited partnership
- Approving or disapproving an amendment to the limited partnership agreement
- Voting on the following partnership matters:
    a. The dissolution and winding up of the limited partnership
    b. The sale, transfer, exchange, lease, or mortgage of substantially all of the assets of the limited partnership
    c. The incurrence of indebtedness by the limited partnership other than in the ordinary course of business
    d. A change in the nature of the business of the limited partnership
    e. The removal of a general partner

Let every nation know, whether it wishes us well or ill, that we shall pay any price, bear any burden, meet any hardship, support any friend, oppose any foe to assure the survival and the success of liberty.

John F. Kennedy
*Inaugural speech,
January 20, 1961*

Example Laura is an investor limited partner in a limited partnership. At some time after she becomes a limited partner, Laura thinks that the general partners are not doing a very good job managing the affairs of the limited partnership, so she participates in the management of the limited partnership. While she is doing so, a bank loans $1 million to the limited partnership, believing that Laura is a general partner because of her involvement in the management of the limited partnership. If the limited partnership defaults on the $1 million loan owed to the bank, Laura will be treated as a general partner and will be held personally liable for the loan, along with the general partners of the limited partnership.

Example Assume that in the previous example, the general partners of the limited partnership vote to make Laura, a limited partner, president of the limited partnership. Laura therefore has two distinct relationships with the limited partnership: first as an investor limited partner and second as a manager (president) of the limited partnership. In this case, Laura can lawfully participate in the management of the limited partnership without losing the limited liability shield granted by her limited partner status.

New **Section 303 of the RULPA** eliminates this restriction and permits limited partners to participate in the management of a limited partnership without losing their limited liability shield. The limited liability partnership agreement can permit certain or all limited partners a say in how the partnership's business should be run.

Dissolution of a Limited Partnership

Just like a general partnership, a limited partnership may be **dissolved** and its affairs wound up. The RULPA establishes rules for the dissolution and winding up of limited partnerships. Upon the dissolution and the commencement of the winding up of a limited partnership, a **certificate of cancellation** must be filed by the limited partnership with the secretary of state of the state in which the limited partnership is organized [RULPA Section 203].

After the assets of a limited partnership have been liquidated, the proceeds must be distributed. The RULPA provides the following order of **distribution of assets of a limited partnership** upon the winding up of a limited partnership [RULPA Section 804]:

1. *Creditors* of the limited partnership, including partners who are creditors (except for liabilities for distributions)

2. *Partners* with respect to:
   a. Unpaid distributions
   b. Capital contributions
   c. The remainder of the proceeds

The partners may provide in the limited partnership agreement for a different distribution among the partners, but the creditors must retain their first priority.

Key Terms and Concepts

Action for an accounting (297)
Antecedent debt (298)
Certificate of cancellation (304)
Certificate of limited partnership (301)
Continuation agreement (299)
Contract liability (298)
d.b.a. (doing business as) (292)
Defective formation (302)
Dissolution of a general partnership (298)
Dissolution of a limited partnership (304)
Distribution of assets of a general partnership (299)
Distribution of assets of a limited partnership (304)
Entrepreneur (291)

Fictitious business name statement (certificate of trade name) (292)
Flow-through taxation (296)
General partner of a general partnership (partner) (294)
General partner of a limited partnership (301)
General partnership (ordinary partnership) (294)
General partnership agreement (articles of general partnership or articles of partnership) (296)
Incoming partner (298)
Joint and several liability (297)
Joint liability (298)
Limited liability of limited partners (303)

Limited partner (300)
Limited partnership (special partnership) (300)
Limited partnership agreement (articles of limited partnership) (302)
Outgoing partner (300)
Partnership at will (298)
Partnership for a term (298)
Personal guarantee (303)
Revised Uniform Limited Partnership Act (RULPA) (301)
Revised Uniform Partnership Act (RUPA) (295)
Right of survivorship (300)
Right to participate in management (296)

Right to share in profits (297)
Section 303 of the RULPA (304)
Sole proprietor (291)
Sole proprietorship (291)
Tenant in partnership (300)
Tort liability (298)
Trade name (292)
Uniform Limited Partnership Act (ULPA) (300)
Unlimited liability of general partners (303)
Uniform Partnership Act (UPA) (295)
Unlimited personal liability of a general partner (297)
Unlimited personal liability of a sole proprietor (292)
Winding up (299)
Wrongful dissolution (299)

Law Case with Answer

Edward A. Kemmler Memorial Foundation v. Mitchell

Facts   Clifford W. Davis and Dr. William D. Mitchell formed a general partnership to purchase and operate rental properties for investment purposes. The general partnership purchased a parcel of real property from the Edward A. Kemmler Memorial Foundation (Foundation) on credit. Davis signed a $150,000 promissory note to the Foundation as "Cliff W. Davis, Partner." Prior to executing the note, Davis and Mitchell entered into an agreement between themselves that provided that only Davis, and not Mitchell, would be personally liable on the note to Foundation. They did not inform Foundation of this side agreement, however. When the partnership defaulted on the note, Foundation sued the partnership and both partners to recover on the note. Mitchell asserted in defense that the agreement with Davis relieved him of personal liability. Foundation argued that Mitchell, as a general partner, was personally liable on the note and that the Davis-Mitchell side agreement did not change Mitchell's personal liability to pay the note. Is Mitchell jointly liable on the note owed to Foundation?

Answer   Yes, Mitchell is jointly liable—personally liable—on the partnership note owed to Foundation.

Every general partner is an agent of a general partnership for the purpose of carrying on its business. The act of every partner, including the execution in the partnership name of any contract or instrument, binds the partnership, unless the partner so acting has in fact no authority to act for the partnership in the particular matter. Here, Davis had the authority as a general partner and bound the partnership when he signed a $150,000 promissory note to Foundation as "Cliff W. Davis, Partner."

If a promissory note is executed in the name of the partnership, the partnership is bound, unless a contradictory agreement between the partners is known to the parties with whom they are dealing. The side agreement between Davis and Mitchell, the two general partners, which relieved Mitchell of any personal liability for the promissory note, was not effective against Foundation, which had not agreed to such restriction on Mitchell's liability. Because Foundation had no knowledge of the agreement between Davis and Mitchell regarding Mitchell's liability for the note, Mitchell cannot avoid personal liability as a general partner on the promissory note owed to Foundation. The partnership is liable to Foundation for the unpaid note, and the two general partners, Davis and Mitchell, are jointly liable—personally liable—on the note owe to Foundation. *Edward A. Kemmler Memorial Foundation v. Mitchell*, 584 N.E.2d 695, **Web** 1992 Ohio Lexis 205 (Supreme Court of Ohio)

Critical Legal Thinking Cases

14.1 Sole Proprietorship James Schuster was a sole proprietor doing business as (d.b.a.) "Diversity Heating and Plumbing" (Diversity Heating). Diversity Heating was in the business of selling, installing, and servicing heating and plumbing systems. George Vernon and others (Vernon) owned a building that needed a new boiler. Vernon hired Diversity Heating to install a new boiler in the building. Diversity Heating installed the boiler and gave a warranty that the boiler would not crack for ten years. Four years later, James Schuster died. On that date, James's son, Jerry Schuster, inherited his father's business and thereafter ran the business as a sole proprietorship under the d.b.a. "Diversity Heating and Plumbing." One year later, the boiler installed in Vernon's building broke and could not be repaired. Vernon demanded that Jerry Schuster honor the warranty and replace the boiler. When Jerry Schuster refused to do so, Vernon had the boiler replaced at a cost of $8,203 and sued Jerry Schuster to recover this amount for breach of warranty. Jerry Schuster argued that he was a sole proprietor and as such he was not liable for the business obligations his father had incurred while operating his own sole proprietorship. Is Jerry Schuster liable for the warranty made by his father? *Vernon v. Schuster, d/b/a/ Diversity Heating and Plumbing*, 688 N.E.2d 1172, **Web** 1997 Ill. Lexis 482 (Supreme Court of Illinois)

14.2 Liability of General Partners Jose Pena and Joseph Antenucci were medical doctors who were partners in a medical practice. Both doctors treated Elaine Zuckerman during her pregnancy. Her son, Daniel Zuckerman, was born with severe physical problems. Elaine, as Daniel's mother and natural guardian, brought a medical malpractice suit against both doctors. The jury found that Pena was guilty of medical malpractice but that Antenucci was not. The amount of the verdict totaled $4 million. The trial court entered judgment against Pena but not against Antenucci. Plaintiff Zuckerman made a posttrial motion for judgment against both defendants. Is Antenucci jointly and severally liable for the medical malpractice of his partner, Pena? *Zuckerman v. Antenucci*, 478 N.Y.S.2d 578, **Web** 1984 N.Y.Misc. Lexis 3283 (Supreme Court of New York)

14.3 Right to an Accounting Charles Fial and Roger J. Steeby entered into a partnership called Audit Consultants to perform auditing services. Pursuant to the agreement, they shared equally the equity, income, and profits of the partnership. Originally, they performed the auditing services themselves, but as business increased, they engaged independent contractors to do some of the audit work. Fial's activities generated approximately 80 percent of the partnership's revenues. Unhappy with their agreement to divide the profits equally, Fial wrote a letter to Steeby seven years later, dissolving the partnership.

Fial asserted that the clients should be assigned based on who brought them into the business. Fial formed a new business called Audit Consultants of Colorado, Inc. He then terminated the original partnership's contracts with many clients and put them under contract with his new firm. Fial also terminated the partnership's contracts with the independent-contractor auditors and signed many of these auditors with his new firm. The partnership terminated about eleven months after Fial wrote the letter to Steeby. Steeby brought an action against Fial, alleging breach of fiduciary duty and seeking a final accounting. Who wins? *Steeby v. Fial*, 765 P.2d 1081, **Web** 1988 Colo.App. Lexis 409 (Court of Appeals of Colorado)

14.4 Tort Liability Thomas McGrath was a partner in the law firm Tarbenson, Thatcher, McGrath, Treadwell & Schoonmaker. One day, at approximately 4:30 P.M., McGrath went to a restaurant–cocktail establishment in Kirkland, Washington. From that time until about 11:00 P.M., he imbibed considerable alcohol while socializing and discussing personal and firm-related business. After 11:00 P.M., McGrath did not discuss firm business but continued to socialize and drink until approximately 1:45 A.M., when he and Fredrick Hayes, another bar patron, exchanged words. Shortly thereafter, the two encountered each other outside, and after another exchange, McGrath shot Hayes. Hayes sued McGrath and the law firm for damages. Who is liable? *Hayes v. Tarbenson, Thatcher, McGrath, Treadwell & Schoonmaker*, 50 Wash.App. 505, 749 P.2d 178, **Web** 1988 Wash.App. Lexis 27 (Court of Appeals of Washington)

14.5 Liability of General Partners Pat McGowan, Val Somers, and Brent Robertson were general partners of Vermont Place, a limited partnership formed for the purpose of constructing duplexes on an undeveloped tract of land in Fort Smith, Arkansas. The general partners appointed McGowan and his company, Advance Development Corporation, to develop the project, including contracting with materials people, mechanics, and other suppliers. None of the limited partners took part in the management or control of the partnership.

Eight months later, Somers and Robertson discovered that McGowan had not been paying the suppliers. They removed McGowan from the partnership and took over the project. The suppliers sued the partnership to recover the money owed them. The partnership assets were not sufficient to pay all their claims. Who is liable to the suppliers? *National Lumber Company v. Advance Development Corporation*, 293 Ark. 1, 732 S.W.2d 840, **Web** 1987 Ark. Lexis 2225 (Supreme Court of Arkansas)

14.6 Liability of Limited Partners Union Station Associates of New London (USANL) was a limited partnership formed under the laws of Connecticut. Allen M. Schultz, Anderson Nolter Associates, and the Lepton Trust were limited partners. The limited partners did not take part in the management of the partnership. The National Railroad Passenger Association (NRPA) entered into an agreement to lease part of a railroad facility from USANL. NRPA sued USANL for allegedly breaching the lease and also named the limited partners as defendants. Are the limited partners liable? *National Railroad Passenger Association v. Union Station Associates of New London*, 643 F.Supp. 192, **Web** 1986 U.S. Dist. Lexis 22190 (United States District Court for the District of Columbia)

14.7 Liability of Partners Raugust-Mathwig, Inc., a corporation, was the sole general partner of a limited partnership. Calvin Raugust was the major shareholder of this corporation. The three limited partners were Cal-Lee Trust, W.J. Mathwig, Inc., and W.J. Mathwig, Inc., and Associates. All three of the limited partners were valid corporate entities. Although the limited partnership agreement was never executed and a certificate of limited partnership was not filed with the state, the parties opened a bank account and began conducting business.

John Molander, an architect, entered into an agreement with the limited partnership to design a condominium complex and professional office building to be located in Spokane, Washington. The contract was signed on behalf of the limited partnership by its corporate general partner. Molander provided substantial architectural services to the partnership, but neither project was completed because of a lack of financing. Molander sued the limited partnership, its corporate general partner, the corporate limited partners, and Calvin Raugust individually to recover payments allegedly due him. Against whom can Molander recover? *Molander v. Raugust-Mathwig, Inc.*, 44 Wash.App. 53, 722 P.2d 103, **Web** 1986 Wash.App. Lexis 2992 (Court of Appeals of Washington)

Ethics Cases

14.8 Ethics When the Chrysler Credit Corporation (Chrysler Credit) extended credit to Metro Dodge, Inc. (Metro Dodge), Donald P. Peterson signed an agreement guaranteeing to pay the debt if Metro Dodge did not pay. When Metro Dodge failed to pay, Chrysler Credit sued Peterson on the guarantee and obtained a judgment of $350,000 against him. After beginning collection efforts, Chrysler Credit learned through discovery that Peterson owned four limited partnership units in Cedar Riverside Properties, a limited partnership. Chrysler Credit sued to obtain the money owed by Peterson from his interests in these other limited partnerships. *Chrysler Credit Corporation v. Peterson*, 342 N.W.2d 170, **Web** 1984 Minn.App. Lexis 2976 (Court of Appeals of Minnesota)

1. What is a personal guarantee?
2. Did Peterson act ethically in this case?
3. Can Chrysler Credit recover against Peterson's limited partnership interests?

14.9 Ethics   Robert K. Powers and Lee M. Solomon were among other limited partners of the Cosmopolitan Chinook Hotel (Cosmopolitan), a limited partnership. Cosmopolitan entered into a contract to lease and purchase neon signs from Dwinell's Central Neon (Dwinell's). The contract identified Cosmopolitan as a "partnership" and was signed on behalf of the partnership, "R. Powers, President." At the time the contract was entered into, Cosmopolitan had taken no steps to file its certificate of limited partnership with the state, as required by limited partnership law. The certificate was not filed with the state until several months after the contract was signed. When Cosmopolitan defaulted on payments due under the contract, Dwinell's sued Cosmopolitan and its general and limited partners to recover damages. *Dwinell's Central Neon v. Cosmopolitan Chinook Hotel*, 21 Wash.App. 929, 587 P.2d 191, **Web** 1978 Wash.App. Lexis 2735 (Court of Appeals of Washington)

1. What is a defective formation of a limited partnership?
2. Did the limited partners act ethically in denying liability on the contract?
3. Are the limited partners liable?

Internet Exercises

1. Go to www.sba.gov/smallbusinessplanner/plan/getready/SERV_SBPLANNER_ISENTFORU.html and read the discussion about entrepreneurship. Would entrepreneurship work for you?

2. Go to www.powerhomebiz.com/vol144/starbucks.htm and read the article "Learning from Starbucks: 10 Lessons for Small Businesses."

3. Go to www.nytimes.com/1990/08/21/sports/steinbrenner-says-he-has-signed-resignation.html and read about the former managing general partner of the New York Yankees professional baseball team.

4. Go to www.sfgate.com/cgi-bin/article.cgi?file=/chronicle/archive/2005/02/28/BUGJUBGR5D1.DTL&type=business and read the story of the founding of Yahoo, Inc. Go to http://docs.yahoo.com/info/values/ and read what Yahoo values and does not value.

15 Limited Liability Companies, Limited Liability Partnerships, and Special Forms of Business

CHICAGO, ILLINOIS
Many businesses operate as a limited liability company (LLC), and many professionals operate as a limited liability partnership (LLP). These forms of business provide limited liability to their owners.

Learning Objectives

After studying this chapter, you should be able to:

1. Define *limited liability company (LLC)* and describe the benefits of an LLC.
2. Define *limited liability partnership (LLP)* and describe the benefits of an LLP.
3. Define *franchise* and describe the various forms of franchises.
4. Define *licensing* and describe how intellectual property and software are licensed.
5. Describe special forms of business, such as joint ventures, strategic alliances, and international franchising.

Chapter Outline

" Justice is the end of government. It is the end of civil society. It ever has been, and ever will be pursued, until it be obtained, or until liberty be lost in the pursuit."

—James Madison
   The Federalist, No. 51 (1788)

Introduction to Limited Liability Companies, Limited Liability Partnerships, and Special Forms of Business

Morality cannot be legislated, but behavior can be regulated. Judicial decrees may not change the heart, but they can restrain the heartless.

Martin Luther King, Jr.
   Strength to Love (1963)

Owners may choose to operate a business as a *limited liability company (LLC)*. The use of LLCs as a form of conducting business in the United States is of rather recent origin. In 1977, Wyoming was the first state in the United States to enact legislation creating an LLC as a legal form for conducting business. All the states had enacted LLC statutes by 1998. Most LLC laws are quite similar, although some differences do exist between these state statutes.

Most states have enacted laws that permit certain types of professionals, such as accountants, lawyers, and doctors, to operate as *limited liability partnerships (LLPs)*. The owners of an LLP have limited liability for debts and obligations of the partnership.

Franchising is an important method for distributing goods and services to the public. Franchises—such as Coca-Cola, McDonald's, and KFC—operate domestically and around the world. *Licensing* permits one business to use another business's trademarks, service marks, trade names, and other intellectual property in selling goods, services, and software.

Several forms of business are used to conduct global business. In particular, these include *international franchising, joint ventures*, and *strategic alliances*. Multinational corporations—discussed in Chapter 16—conduct business worldwide.

This chapter discusses LLCs, LLPs, franchises, licensing, joint ventures, and strategic alliances that are used to conduct business domestically and globally.

Limited Liability Company (LLC)

An LLC is an unincorporated business entity that combines the most favorable attributes of general partnerships, limited partnerships, and corporations. An LLC may elect to be taxed as a partnership, the owners can manage the business, and the owners have limited liability for debts and obligations of the partnership. Many entrepreneurs who begin new businesses choose the LLC as their legal form for conducting business.

limited liability company (LLC)
An unincorporated business entity that combines the most favorable attributes of general partnerships, limited partnerships, and corporations.

Limited liability companies (LLCs) are creatures of state law, not federal law. An LLC can be created only pursuant to the laws of the state in which the LLC is being organized. These statutes, commonly referred to as **limited liability company codes**, regulate the formation, operation, and dissolution of LLCs. The owners of LLCs are usually called **members** (or, in some states, *shareholders*).

member
An owner of an LLC. Some states refer to members as *shareholders*.

An LLC is a separate *legal entity* (or legal person) distinct from its members [ULLCA Section 201]. LLCs are treated as artificial persons who can sue or be sued, enter into and enforce contracts, hold title to and transfer property, and be found civilly and criminally liable for violations of law.

The following feature discusses limited liability company law.

Contemporary Environment

Uniform Limited Liability Company Act and Revised Uniform Limited Liability Company Act

In 1996, the National Conference of Commissioners on Uniform State Laws (a group of lawyers, judges, and legal scholars) issued the **Uniform Limited Liability Company Act (ULLCA)**. The ULLCA codifies LLC law. Its goal is to establish comprehensive LLC law that is uniform throughout the United States. The ULLCA covers most problems that arise in the formation, operation, and termination of LLCs.

The ULLCA is not law unless a state adopts it as its LLC statute. The ULLCA was revised in 2006, and this revision is called the **Revised Uniform Limited Liability Company Act (RULLCA)**. Many states have adopted all or part of the ULLCA or the RULLCA as their LLC law. These acts form the basis of the study of limited liability companies in this chapter.

Taxation of LLCs

Under the Internal Revenue Code and regulations adopted by the Internal Revenue Service (IRS) for federal income tax purposes, an LLC is taxed as a partnership unless it elects to be taxed as a corporation. Thus, an LLC is not taxed at the entity level, but its income or losses **flow through** to the members' individual income tax returns. This avoids double taxation. Most LLCs accept the default status of being taxed as a partnership instead of electing to be taxed as a corporation.

Formation of an LLC

Under the ULLCA, an LLC may be organized by one or more persons. Some states require at least two members to organize an LLC. In states where an LLC may be organized by only one member, sole proprietors can obtain the benefit of the limited liability shield of an LLC.

An LLC can be organized in only one state, even though it can conduct business in all other states. When choosing a state for organization, the members should consider the LLC codes of the states under consideration. For the sake of convenience, most LLCs, particularly small ones, choose as the state of organization the state in which the LLC will be doing most of its business.

When starting a new LLC, the organizers must choose a name for the entity. The name must contain the words *limited liability company* or *limited company* or the abbreviation *L.L.C.*, *LLC*, *L.C.*, or *LC*. *Limited* may be abbreviated as *Ltd.*, and *company* may be abbreviated as *Co*. [ULLCA Section 105(a)].

Articles of Organization

Because LLCs are creatures of statute, certain formalities must be taken and statutory requirements must be met to form an LLC.

An LLC is formed by delivering **articles of organization** to the office of the secretary of state of the state of organization for filing. If the articles are in proper form, the secretary of state will file the articles. An LLC begins to exist when the articles of organization are filed. The filing of the articles of organization by the secretary of state is conclusive proof that the organizers have satisfied all the conditions necessary to create the LLC [ULLCA Section 202]. Under the ULLCA, the articles of organization of an LLC must set forth [ULLCA Section 203]:

- The name of the LLC
- The address of the LLC's initial office
- The name and address of the initial agent for service of process

Uniform Limited Liability Company Act (ULLCA)
A model act that provides comprehensive and uniform laws for the formation, operation, and dissolution of LLCs.

Revised Uniform Limited Liability Company Act (RULLCA)
A revision of the ULLCA that provides comprehensive and uniform laws for the formation, operation, and dissolution of LLCs.

articles of organization
The formal documents that must be filed at the secretary of state's office of the state of organization of an LLC in order to form the LLC.

WEB EXERCISE
Go to **http://form.sunbiz.org/ pdf/cr2e047.pdf** and read the information and forms necessary to form a Florida limited liability company.

- The name and address of each organizer
- Whether the LLC is a term LLC and, if so, the term specified
- Whether the LLC is to be a manager-managed LLC and, if so, the name and address of each manager
- Whether one or more of the members of the LLC are to be personally liable for the LLC's debts and obligations

The articles of organization may set forth provisions from the members' operating agreement and any other matter not inconsistent with law. An LLC can amend its articles of organization at any time by filing **articles of amendment** with the secretary of state [ULLCA Section 204].

The LLC is a **domestic LLC** in the state in which it is organized. The LLC law of the state governs the operation of the LLC. An LLC may do business in other states, however. To do so, the LLC must register as a **foreign LLC** in any state in which it wants to conduct business.

Operating Agreement

operating agreement
An agreement entered into among members that governs the affairs and business of the LLC and the relationships among members, managers, and the LLC.

Members of an LLC may enter into an **operating agreement** that regulates the affairs of the company and the conduct of its business and governs relations among the members, managers, and company [ULLCA Section 103(a)]. The operating agreement may be amended by the approval of all members unless otherwise provided in the agreement. The operating agreement and amendments may be oral but are usually written.

certificate of interest
A document that evidences a member's ownership interest in an LLC.

An LLC's operating agreement may provide that a member's ownership interest may be evidenced by a **certificate of interest** issued by the LLC [ULLCA Section 501(c)]. The certificate of interest acts the same as a stock certificate issued by a corporation.

There shall be one law for the native and for the stranger who sojourns among you.

Moses
Exodus 12:49

Unless otherwise agreed, the ULLCA mandates that a member has the right to an equal share in the LLC's profits [ULLCA Section 405(a)]. This is a default rule that the members can override by agreement and is usually a provision in their operating agreement. Losses from an LLC are shared equally unless otherwise agreed. Profits and losses from an LLC do not have to be distributed in the same proportion.

Distributional Interest

distributional interest
A member's ownership interest in an LLC that entitles the member to receive distributions of money and property from the LLC.

A member's ownership interest in an LLC is called a **distributional interest**. A member's distributional interest in an LLC is personal property and may be transferred in whole or in part [ULLCA Section 501(b)]. Unless otherwise provided in the operating agreement, a transfer of an interest in an LLC does not entitle the transferee to become a member of the LLC or to exercise any right of a member. A transfer entitles the transferee to receive only distributions from the LLC to which the transferor would have been entitled [ULLCA Section 502]. A transferee of a distributional interest becomes a member of the LLC if it is so provided in the operating agreement or if all the other members of the LLC consent [ULLCA Section 503(a)]. A transferor who transfers his or her distributional interest is not released from liability for the debts, obligations, and liabilities of the LLC [ULLCA Section 503(c)].

Liability LLC Members

The great can protect themselves, but the poor and humble require the arm and shield of the law.

Andrew Jackson

In the course of conducting business, the agents and employees of an LLC may entire into contracts on behalf of the LLC. Sometimes, however, the LLC may not perform these contracts. In addition, the agents or employees of an LLC may be engaged in accidents or otherwise cause harm to third parties when acting on LLC business. These third parties—whether in contract disputes or tort disputes—will look to be compensated for their loss or injuries.

An LLC is liable for any loss or injury caused to anyone as a result of a wrongful act or omission by a member, a manager, an agent, or an employee of the LLC who commits the wrongful act while acting within the ordinary course of business of the LLC or with authority of the LLC [ULLCA Section 302].

Example Sable, Silvia, and Samantha form SSS, LLC, to own and operate a business. Each member contributes $10,000 capital. While on LLC business, Sable drives her automobile and accidentally hits and injures Damon. Damon can recover damages for his injuries from Sable personally because she committed the negligent act. Damon can also recover damages from SSS, LLC, because Sable was acting within the scope of the ordinary business of the LLC when the accident occurred. Silvia and Samantha have limited liability only up to their capital contributions in SSS, LLC.

The general rule is that members are not personally liable to third parties for the debts, obligations, and liabilities of an LLC beyond their capital contribution. Members have **limited liability** (see **Exhibit 15.1**). The debts, obligations, and liabilities of an LLC, whether arising from contracts, torts, or otherwise, are solely those of the LLC [ULLCA Section 303(a)].

limited liability of members of LLCs
The liability of LLC members for the LLC's debts, obligations, and liabilities, which is limited to the extent of their capital contributions. Members of LLCs are not personally liable for the LLC's debts, obligations, and liabilities.

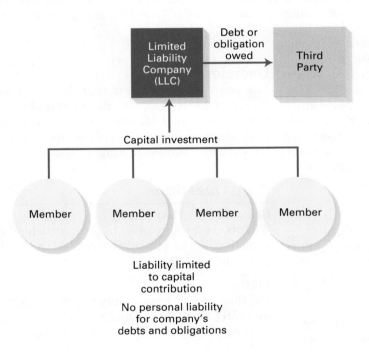

Exhibit 15.1 LIMITED LIABILITY COMPANY (LLC)

Example Jasmin, Shou-Yi, and Vanessa form an LLC, and each contributes $25,000 in capital. The LLC operates for a period of time, during which it borrows money from banks and purchases goods on credit from suppliers. After some time, the LLC experiences financial difficulty and goes out of business. If the LLC fails with $500,000 in debts, each of the members will lose her capital contribution of $25,000 but will not be personally liable for the rest of the unpaid debts of the LLC.

In the following case, the court addressed the issue of the limited liability of a member of an LLC.

CASE 15.1 *Limited Liability Company*

Siva v. 1138 LLC

2007 Ohio 4667, Web 2007 Ohio App. Lexis 4202 (2007)
Court of Appeals of Ohio

"Finally, the evidence did not show that Siva was misguided as to the fact he was dealing with a limited liability company."

—Brown, Judge

Facts

Five members—Richard Hess, Robert Haines, Lisa Hess, Nathan Hess, and Zack Shahin—formed a limited liability company called 1138 LLC. Ruthiran Siva owned a commercial building located at 1138 Bethel Road, Franklin County, Ohio. Siva entered into a written lease agreement with 1138 LLC whereby 1138 LLC leased premises in Siva's commercial building for a term of five years, at a monthly rental of $4,000. 1138 LLC began operating a bar on the premises. Six months later, 1138 LLC was in default and in breach of the lease agreement. Siva sued 1138 LLC and Richard Hess to recover damages. Siva received a default judgment against 1138 LLC, but there was no money in 1138 LLC to pay the judgment. Hess, who had been sued personally, defended, arguing that as a member-owner of the LLC, he was not personally liable for the debts of the LLC. The trial court found in favor of Hess and dismissed Siva's complaint against Hess. Siva appealed.

Issue

Is Richard Hess, a member-owner of 1138 LLC, personally liable for the debt owed by the LLC to Siva?

Language of the Court

Based upon the court's examination of the record, we find there was competent, credible evidence to support the trial court's determination. The evidence does not show that Hess purposely undercapitalized 1138 LLC, or that he formed the limited liability company in an effort to avoid paying creditors. According to Hess, the bar was never profitable. Based upon the evidence presented, a reasonable trier of fact could have concluded that 1138 LLC became insolvent due to unprofitable operations. Moreover, even if the record suggests poor business judgment by Hess, it does not demonstrate that he formed 1138 LLC to defraud creditors. Finally, the evidence did not show that Siva was misguided as to the fact he was dealing with a limited liability company. Siva's counsel drafted the lease agreement and Siva acknowledged at trial he did not ask any of the owners of 1138 LLC to sign the lease in an individual capacity.

Decision

The court of appeals held that Hess, as a member-owner of 1138 LLC, was not personally liable for the debt that the LLC owed to Siva. The court of appeals affirmed the decision of the trial court that dismissed Siva's complaint against Hess.

Case Questions

Critical Legal Thinking
What is the liability of an LLC for its debts? What is the liability of a member-owner of an LLC for the LLC's debts? Explain.

Ethics
Did Hess owe an ethical duty to pay the debt owed by 1138 LLC to Siva? Did Siva act ethically by suing Hess personally to recover the debt owed by the 1138 LLC?

Contemporary Business
What should Siva have done if he wanted Hess to be personally liable on the lease? Explain.

Liability of Managers

Managers of LLCs are not personally liable for the debts, obligations, and liabilities of the LLC they manage [ULLCA Section 303(a)].

Example An LLC that is engaged in real estate development hires Sarah Goldstein, a nonmember, to be its president. Sarah, while acting within the scope of her LLC authority, signs a loan agreement whereby the LLC borrows $1 million from a bank for the construction of an office building. If the LLC subsequently suffers financial difficulty and defaults on the bank loan, Sarah is not personally responsible for the loan. The LLC is liable for the loan, but Sarah is not because she was acting as the manager of the LLC.

Liability of a Member Tortfeasor

A person who intentionally or unintentionally (negligently) causes injury or death to another person is called a **tortfeasor**. A tortfeasor is personally liable to persons he or she injures and to the heirs of persons who die because of his or her conduct. This rule applies to members and managers of LLCs. Thus, if a member or a manager of an LLC negligently causes injury or death to another person, he or she is personally liable to the injured person or the heirs of the deceased person.

tortfeasor
A person who intentionally or unintentionally (negligently) causes injury or death to another person. A tortfeasor is liable to persons he or she injures and to the heirs of persons who die because of his or her conduct.

Management of an LLC

An LLC can be either a *member-managed LLC* or a *manager-managed LLC*. An LLC is a member-managed LLC unless it is designated as a manager-managed LLC in its articles of organization [ULLCA Section 203(a) (b)]. The distinctions between these two are as follows:

- **Member-managed LLC.** In this type of LLC, the members of the LLC have the right to manage the LLC.
- **Manager-managed LLC.** In this type of LLC, the members designate a manager or managers to manage the LLC, and by doing so, they delegate their management rights to the manager or managers, designated manager or managers have the authority to manage the LLC, and the members no longer have the right to manage the LLC. A manager may be a member of an LLC or a nonmember.

Whether an LLC is a member-managed or manager-managed LLC has important consequences on the right to bind the LLC to contracts and on determining the fiduciary duties owed by members to the LLC. These important distinctions are discussed in the paragraphs that follow.

Member-Managed LLC

In a **member-managed LLC**, each member has equal rights in the management of the business of the LLC, regardless of the size of his or her capital contribution. Any matter related to the business of the LLC is decided by a majority vote of the members [ULLCA Section 404(a)].

member-managed LLC
An LLC that has not designated that it is a manager-managed LLC in its articles of organization and that is managed by its members.

Example Allison, Jaeson, Stacy, Lan-Wei, and Ivy form NorthWest.com, LLC. Allison contributes $100,000 capital, and the other four members each contribute $25,000 capital. When deciding whether to add another line of products to the business, Stacy, Lan-Wei, and Ivy vote to add the line, and Allison and Jaeson vote against it. The line of new products is added to the LLC's business because three members voted yes, while two members voted no. It does not matter that the two members who voted no contributed $125,000 in capital collectively versus $75,000 in capital contributed by the three members who voted yes.

Manager-Managed LLC

In a **manager-managed LLC**, the members and nonmembers who are designated managers control the management of the LLC. The members who are not managers have no rights to manage the LLC unless otherwise provided in the operating agreement. In a manager-managed LLC, each manager has equal rights in the management and conduct of the company's business. Any matter related to

manager-managed LLC
An LLC that has designated in its articles of organization that it is a manager-managed LLC, and its nonmanager members give their management rights over to designated managers.

the business of the LLC may be exclusively decided by the managers by a majority vote of the managers [ULLCA Section 403(b)]. A manager must be appointed by a vote of a majority of the members; managers may also be removed by a vote of the majority of the members [ULLCA Section 404(b)(3)].

Certain actions cannot be delegated to managers but must be voted on by all members of the LLC. These include (1) amending the articles of organization, (2) amending the operating agreement, (3) admitting new members, (4) consenting to dissolve the LLC, (5) consenting to merge the LLC with another entity, and (6) selling, leasing, or disposing of all or substantially all of the LLC's property [ULLCA Section 404(c)].

CONCEPT SUMMARY

MANAGEMENT OF AN LLC

Type of LLC	Description
Member-managed LLC	The members do not designate managers to manage the LLC. The LLC is managed by its members.
Manager-managed LLC	The members designate certain members or nonmembers to manage the LLC. The LLC is managed by the designated managers; nonmanager members have no right to manage the LLC.

Agency Authority to Bind an LLC to Contracts

The designation of an LLC as member managed or manager managed is important in determining who has authority to bind the LLC to contracts. The following rules apply:

- **Member-managed LLC.** In a member-managed LLC, all members have agency authority to bind the LLC to contracts.

  Example If Theresa, Artis, and Yolanda form a member-managed LLC, each one of them can bind the LLC to a contract with a third party such as a supplier, purchaser, or landlord.

- **Manager-managed LLC.** In a manager-managed LLC, the managers have authority to bind the LLC to contracts, but nonmanager members cannot bind the LLC to contracts.

  Example Alexis, Derek, Ashley, and Sadia form an LLC. They designate the LLC as a manager-managed LLC and name Alexis and Ashley as the managers. Alexis, a manager, enters into a contract to purchase goods from a supplier for the LLC. Derek, a nonmanager member, enters into a contract to lease equipment on behalf of the LLC. The LLC is bound to the contract entered into by Alexis, a manager, but is not bound to the contract entered into by Derek, a nonmanager member.

An LLC is bound to contracts that members or managers have properly entered into on its behalf in the ordinary course of business [ULLCA Section 301].

CONCEPT SUMMARY

AGENCY AUTHORITY TO BIND AN LLC TO CONTRACTS

Type of LLC	Agency Authority
Member-managed LLC	All members have agency authority to bind the LLC to contracts.
Manager-managed LLC	The managers have authority to bind the LLC to contracts; the nonmanager members cannot bind the LLC to contracts.

Duty of Loyalty

A member of a member-managed LLC and a manager of a manager-managed LLC owe a *fiduciary* **duty of loyalty** to the LLC. This means that these parties must act honestly in their dealings with the LLC. The duty of loyalty includes the duty not to usurp the LLC's opportunities, make secret profits, secretly deal with the LLC, secretly compete with the LLC, or represent any interests adverse to those of the LLC [ULLCA Section 409(b)].

Example Ester, Yi, Maria, and Enrique form the member-managed LLC, Big.Business. com, LLC, which conducts online auctions over the Internet. Ester secretly starts a competing business to conduct online auctions over the Internet. Ester is liable for breaching her duty of loyalty to the LLC with Yi, Maria, and Enrique. Ester is liable for any secret profits she made, and her business will be shut down.

Example In the preceding example, suppose that Ester, Yi, Maria, and Enrique designated their LLC as a manager-managed LLC and named Ester and Yi managers. In this case, only the managers owe a duty of loyalty to the LLC, but nonmanager members do not. Therefore, Ester and Yi, the named managers, could not compete with the LLC; Maria and Enrique, nonmanager members, could compete with the LLC without any legal liability.

No Fiduciary Duty

A member of a manager-managed LLC who is not a manager owes no fiduciary duty of loyalty or care to the LLC or its other members [ULLCA Section 409(h)(1)]. Basically, a nonmanager member of a manager-managed LLC is treated equally to a shareholder in a corporation.

Example Felicia is a member of a thirty-person manager-managed LLC that is engaged in buying, developing, and selling real estate. Felicia is not a manager of the LLC but is just a member-owner. If a third party approaches Felicia with the opportunity to purchase a large and valuable piece of real estate that is ripe for development, and the price is below fair market value, Felicia owes no duty to offer the opportunity to the LLC. She may purchase the piece of real estate for herself without violating any duty to the LLC.

The following feature compares an LLC to other forms of business and highlights the advantages of an LLC over other forms of business.

> **duty of loyalty**
> A duty owed by a member of a member-managed LLC and a manager of a manager-managed LLC to be honest in his or her dealings with the LLC and to not act adversely to the interests of the LLC.

> *Business will be either better or worse.*
>
> Calvin Coolidge

Contemporary Environment

Advantages of Operating a Business as an LLC

What are the advantages of operating a business as an LLC rather than as a sole proprietorship, general partnership, limited partnership, C corporation, or S corporation? Some of the differences and advantages are as follows:

- An LLC can have any number of member-owners, whereas an S corporation can have only 100 shareholders.
- An LLC has flow-through taxation, just like general and limited partnerships and S corporations. Unlike an S corporation, an LLC does not have to file a form with the IRS to obtain flow-through taxation.
- S corporations cannot have shareholders other than estates, certain trusts, and individuals, whereas an LLC

can have these and other types of shareholders, such as general and limited partnerships, corporations, and other LLCs.

- An LLC can have nonresident alien member-owners, whereas an S corporation cannot have nonresident aliens as stockholders.
- An S corporation can have only one class of stock, whereas an LLC can have more than one class of interest, thereby permitting a more complex capital structure.
- An S corporation may not own more than 80 percent of another corporation, whereas an LLC may own all of other businesses.

(continued)

- An S corporation cannot be affiliated with other businesses, whereas an LLC can be part of an affiliated group of businesses.
- Members of LLCs can manage the LLC similarly to general partners who can manage a general partnership or a limited partnership, whereas shareholders of an S corporation do not have rights to manage the corporation.
- Members of LLCs can manage the business and still have limited liability, whereas the general partners of a general or limited partnership can manage the business of the partnership but do not have limited liability.
- Members of an LLC have limited liability like limited partners of a limited partnership, but unlike limited partners, member-owners of an LLC have a say in management without losing their limited liability.
- A limited partnership must have at least one general partner who is personally liable for the obligations of the partnership. An LLC provides limited liability to all members.
- Similar to corporations having professional management, an LLC can choose to be a manager-managed LLC whereby designated managers manage the affairs of the business. Nonmanager members thereby do not have rights to manage the LLC's business affairs.
- An LLC can be owned by one owner in most states. Therefore, an owner obtains limited liability that is not available to a sole proprietor of a sole proprietorship.
- Forming an LLC is no more complex than forming a corporation. Forming an LLC is more complex and costly than forming a sole proprietorship and usually more complex and costly than forming a general partnership or a limited partnership.

For these reasons, LLCs have become a preferred form of operating businesses in the United States.

Limited Liability Partnership (LLP)

limited liability partnership (LLP)
A special form of partnership in which all partners are limited partners, and there are no general partners.

Many states have enacted legislation to permit the creation of **limited liability partnerships (LLPs)**. In most states, the law restricts the use of LLPs to certain types of professionals, such as accountants, lawyers, and doctors. Nonprofessionals cannot use the LLP form of partnership. An LLP can be created only pursuant to the laws of the state in which the LLP is being organized. These statutes, commonly referred to as **limited liability partnership codes**, regulate the formation, operation, and dissolution of LLPs.

LLPs enjoy the *flow-through* tax benefit of other types of partnerships—that is, there is no tax paid at the partnership level, and all profits and losses are reported on the individual partners' income tax returns.

Articles of Limited Liability Partnership

articles of limited liability partnership
The formal documents that must be filed at the secretary of state's office of the state of organization of an LLP in order to form the LLP.

An LLP is created formally by filing **articles of limited liability partnership** with the secretary of state of the state in which the LLP is organized. This is a public document. The LLP is a **domestic LLP** in the state in which it is organized. The LLP law of the state governs the operation of the LLP. An LLP may do business in other states, however. To do so, the LLP must register as a **foreign LLP** in any state in which it wants to conduct business.

Many state laws require LLPs to carry a minimum of $1 million of liability insurance that covers negligence, wrongful acts, and misconduct by partners or employees of the LLP. This requirement guarantees that injured third parties will have compensation to recover for their injuries and is a quid pro quo for permitting partners to have limited liability.

Limited Liability of Partners

limited liability of partners of LLPs
The liability of LLP partners for the LLP's debts, obligations, and liabilities, which is limited to the extent of their capital contributions. Partners of LLPs are not personally liable for the LLP's debts, obligations, and liabilities.

In an LLP, there does not have to be a general partner who is personally liable for the debts and obligations of the partnership. Instead, *all* partners are **limited partners** who have **limited liability** and stand to lose only their capital contribution if the partnership fails. None of the partners is personally liable for the debts and obligations of the partnership beyond his or her capital contribution (see **Exhibit 15.2**).

Example Suppose Shou-Yi, Patricia, Ricardo, and Namira, all lawyers, form an LLP called Shou-Yi, Namira LLP to provide legal services. While providing legal services to

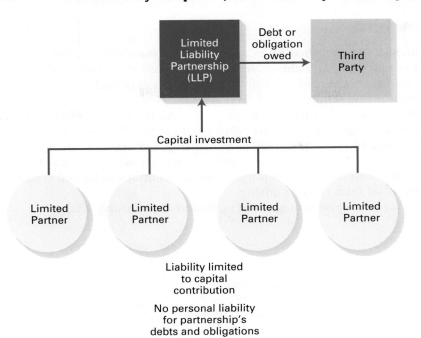

Exhibit 15.2 LIMITED LIABILITY PARTNERSHIP (LLP)

the LLP's client Multi Motors, Inc., Patricia commits legal malpractice (negligence). This malpractice causes Multi Motors, Inc., a huge financial loss. In this case, Multi Motors, Inc., can sue and recover against Patricia, the negligent party, and against Shou-Yi, Namira LLP. Shou-Yi, Ricardo, and Namira can lose their capital contribution in Shou-Yi, Namira LLP but are not personally liable for the damages caused to Multi Motors, Inc. Patricia is personally liable to Multi Motors, Inc., because she was the negligent party.

The following feature discusses how important the LLP form of business is to accounting firms.

Contemporary Environment

Accounting Firms Operate as LLPs

Prior to the advent of the limited liability partnership (LLP) form of doing business, accounting firms operated as general partnerships. The general partners were personally liable for the debts and obligations of the general partnership. In large accounting firms, this personal liability was rarely imposed because the partnership usually carried sufficient liability insurance to cover most awards to third-party plaintiffs in lawsuits.

When accounting firms formed as general partnerships were hit with large court judgments, the partners were personally liable. Many lawsuits were brought in conjunction with the failure of large commercial banks and other large firms that accountants had audited. Many of these firms failed because of fraud by their major owners and officers. The shareholders and creditors of these failed companies sued the auditors, alleging that the auditors had been negligent in not catching the fraud. Many juries agreed and awarded large awards against the accounting firms. Sometimes an accounting firm's liability insurance was not enough to cover a judgment, and personal liability was imposed on partners.

To address this issue, state legislatures created a new form of business, the LLP. This entity was particularly created for accountants, lawyers, and other professionals to offer their services under an umbrella of limited liability. The partners of an LLP have limited liability up to their capital contribution; the partners do not have personal liability for the debts and liabilities of the LLP, however.

Once LLPs were permitted by law, all of the "Big Four" accounting firms changed their status from general partnerships to LLPs. The signs and letterhead of each Big Four accounting firm prominently indicate that the firm is an LLP. Many other accounting firms have also changed over to LLP status, as have many law firms.

franchise
An arrangement that is established when one party (the *franchisor*) licenses another party (the *franchisee*) to use the franchisor's trade name, trademarks, commercial symbols, patents, copyrights, and other property in the distribution and selling of goods and services.

franchisor (licensor)
The party who grants a franchise and license to a franchisee in a franchise arrangement.

Franchise

A **franchise** is established when one party (the **franchisor**, or **licensor**) licenses another party (the **franchisee**, or **licensee**) to use the franchisor's trade name, trademarks, commercial symbols, patents, copyrights, and other property in the distribution and selling of goods and services. Generally, the franchisor and the franchisee are established as separate corporations. The term *franchise* refers to both the agreement between the parties and the franchise outlet.

There are several advantages to franchising. For example, the franchisor can reach lucrative new markets, the franchisee has access to the franchisor's knowledge and resources while running an independent business, and consumers are assured of uniform product quality.

A typical franchise arrangement is illustrated in **Exhibit 15.3**.

Exhibit 15.3 FRANCHISE

franchisee (licensee)
The party who is granted a franchise and license by a franchisor in a franchise arrangement.

distributorship franchise
A franchise in which the franchisor manufactures a product and licenses a franchisee to distribute the product to the public.

processing plant franchise
A franchise in which the franchisor provides a secret formula or process to the franchisee, and the franchisee manufactures the product and distributes it to retail dealers.

Types of Franchise

There are four basic forms of franchises: (1) *distributorship franchise*, (2) *processing plant franchise*, (3) *chain-style franchise*, and (4) *area franchise*. They are discussed in the following list:

- **Distributorship franchise.**   In a **distributorship franchise**, the franchisor manufactures a product and licenses a retail dealer to distribute a product to the public.

  Example Ford Motor Company manufactures automobiles and franchises independently owned automobile dealers (franchisees) to sell them to the public.

- **Processing plant franchise.**   In a **processing plant franchise**, the franchisor provides a secret formula or the like to the franchisee. The franchisee then manufactures the product at its own location and distributes it to retail dealers.

  Example The Coca-Cola Corporation, which owns the secret formulas for making Coca-Cola and other soft drinks, sells syrup concentrate to regional bottling companies who add water and sweeteners and produce and distribute soft drinks under the "Coca-Cola" name and other brand names.

- **Chain-style franchise.** In a **chain-style franchise**, the franchisor licenses the franchisee to make and sell its products or services to the public from a retail outlet serving an exclusive geographical territory. The product is made or the service provided by the franchise. Most fast-food franchises use this form.

Example The Pizza Hut Corporation franchises independently owned restaurant franchises to make and sell pizzas to the public under the "Pizza Hut" name.

- **Area franchise.** In an **area franchise**, the franchisor authorizes the franchisee to negotiate and sell franchises on behalf of the franchisor. The area franchisee is called a **subfranchisor**. An area franchise is granted for a certain designated geographical area, such as a state, a region, or another agreed-upon area. Area franchises are often used when a franchisor wants to enter a market in another country.

Example If Starbucks wanted to enter a foreign country to operate its coffee shops, it could grant an area franchise to a foreign company operating in the foreign country, which would then choose the individual franchisees in that country.

Franchise Agreement

A prospective franchisee must apply to the franchisor for a franchise. The **franchise application** often includes detailed information about the applicant's previous employment, financial and educational history, credit status, and so on. If an applicant is approved, the parties enter into a **franchise agreement** that sets forth the terms and conditions of the franchise. Most states require franchise agreements to be in writing.

A franchisor's ability to maintain the public's perception of the quality of the goods and services associated with its trade name, **trademarks**, and **service marks** is essential to its success. Most franchisors license the use of their trade names, trademarks, and service marks to their franchisees.

Franchisors are often owners of **trade secrets**, including product formulas, business plans and models, and other ideas. Franchisors license and disclose many of their trade secrets to franchisees.

Example The formula for the Coca-Cola soft drink is a highly protected trade secret.

Liability of Franchisors and Franchisees

If a franchise is properly organized and operated, the franchisor and franchisee are separate legal entities. Therefore, the franchisor deals with the franchisee as an *independent contractor*. Franchisees are liable on their own contracts and are liable for their own torts (e.g., negligence). Franchisors are liable for their own contracts and torts. Generally, neither party is liable for the contracts or torts of the other.

Example Suppose that McDonald's Corporation, a fast-food restaurant franchisor, grants a restaurant franchise to Tina Corporation. Tina Corporation opens the franchise restaurant. One day, a customer at the franchise spills a chocolate shake on the floor. The employees at the franchise fail to clean up the spilled shake, and one hour later, another customer slips on the spilled shake and suffers severe injuries. The injured customer can recover damages from the franchisee, Tina Corporation, because it was negligent. It cannot recover damages from the franchisor, McDonald's Corporation.

chain-style franchise
A franchise in which the franchisor licenses a franchisee to make and sell its products or distribute its services to the public from a retail outlet serving an exclusive territory.

area franchise
A franchise in which the franchisor authorizes a franchisee to negotiate and sell franchises on its behalf in designated areas. The area franchisee is called a *subfranchisor*.

franchise agreement
An agreement that a franchisor and franchisee enter into that sets forth the terms and conditions of a franchise.

The minute you read something that you can't understand, you can almost be sure that it was drawn up by a lawyer.

Will Rogers

WEB EXERCISE
Go to www.aboutmcdonalds.com/mcd/franchising/international_franchising_information.html and read about McDonald's international franchising opportunities. Select a country, click "Go," and find information about obtaining a McDonald's franchise in that country.

In the following case, the court had to decide whether a franchisor was liable for a franchisee's tort.

CASE 15.2 *Franchise Liability*

Rainey v. Domino's Pizza, LLC

998 A.2d 342, Web 2010 Me. Lexis 56 (2010)
Supreme Judicial Court of Maine

"In evaluating the requisite level of control, courts commonly distinguish between control over a franchisee's day-to-day operations and controls designed primarily to insure uniformity and the standardization of products and services."

—Jabar, Judge

Facts

Domino's Pizza, LLC, owns the Domino's Pizza trademark and other trademarks and service marks. Domino's is a franchisor that grants franchises to independent contractors who own and operate pizza restaurants under the Domino's Pizza name. Domino's granted a franchise to TDBO, Inc., to operate a franchise restaurant in Gorham, Maine. The relationship between Domino's Pizza and TDBO was governed by a franchise agreement. Under the agreement, Domino's established quality-control, marketing, and operational standards and had the right to receive royalty payments from TDBO. TDBO owned its own equipment, purchased supplies from sources licensed by Domino's, maintained its own records and bank accounts, hired and determined the wages of employees, and established the prices of its products. The agreement expressly stated that TDBO was an independent contractor and that Domino's was not liable for TDBO's debts and obligations.

Edward Langen was an employee of TDBO. Paul Rainey, while riding his motorcycle, was seriously injured in a collision with a car driven by Langen, who was delivering a pizza for his employer. Rainey sued Langen, TDBO, and Domino's, alleging negligence and vicarious liability. Domino's moved for summary judgment on the negligence and vicarious liability counts. The trial court granted a motion for summary judgment in favor of Domino's, finding that Domino's was not vicariously liable for its franchisee's negligence. Rainey appealed this judgment.

Issue

Under the facts of this case, can Domino's be held vicariously liable for the alleged negligence of its franchisee TDBO?

Language of the Court

In distinguishing between employees and independent contractors, we consider several factors, the most important of which is the "right to control." In evaluating the requisite level of control, courts commonly distinguish between control over a franchisee's day-to-day operations and controls designed primarily to insure uniformity and the standardization of products and services.

We now turn to the instant case. Based on our review of the agreement, we conclude that, although the quality control requirements and minimum operational standards are numerous, these controls fall short of reserving control over the performance of TDBO's day-to-day operations. In the end, the quality, marketing, and operational standards present in the agreement do not establish the supervisory control or right of control necessary to impose vicarious liability.

Decision

The court found that Domino's was not vicariously liable for the alleged negligence of its franchisee TDBO and affirmed the trial court's grant of summary judgment in favor of Domino's.

Case Questions

Critical Legal Thinking
What is vicarious liability?

Ethics
Did Domino's breach its duty of ethics by denying liability in this case?

Contemporary Business
What would be the consequences if all franchisors were held vicariously liable for the debts and obligations of their franchisees?

Licensing

Licensing is an important business arrangement in both domestic and international markets. **Licensing** occurs when one business or party that owns trademarks, service marks, trade names, and other intellectual property (the **licensor**) contracts to permit another business or party (the **licensee**) to use its trademarks, service marks, trade names, and other intellectual property in the distribution of goods, services, software, and digital information. This is called a **license**. A licensing arrangement is illustrated in **Exhibit 15.4**.

license
A business arrangement that occurs when the owner of intellectual property (the *licensor*) contracts to permit another party (the *licensee*) to use the intellectual property.

licensor
The party who grants a license.

Exhibit 15.4 LICENSE

Licensor

License
Grant of permission to use trademarks, service marks, trade names, and other intellectual property

Licensee

Example The Walt Disney Company owns the merchandising rights to Winnie the Pooh stories and all the characters associated with the Winnie the Pooh stories. The Walt Disney Company enters into an agreement whereby it permits the Beijing Merchandising Company, a business formed under Chinese law, to manufacture and distribute a line of clothing, children's toys, and other items bearing the likeness of the Winnie the Pooh characters. This is called a **license**. The Walt Disney Company is the licensor, and the Beijing Merchandising Company is the licensee.

licensee
The party to whom a license is granted.

Key Terms and Concepts

Area franchise (321)
Articles of amendment (312)
Articles of limited liability partnership (318)
Articles of organization (311)
Certificate of interest (312)
Chain-style franchise (321)
Distributorship franchise (320)
Distributional interest (312)
Domestic LLC (312)
Domestic LLP (318)
Duty of loyalty (317)

Flow-through taxation (311)
Foreign LLC (312)
Foreign LLP (318)
Franchise (320)
Franchise agreement (321)
Franchise application (321)
Franchisee (licensee) (320)
Franchisor (licensor) (320)
License (323)
Licensee (323)
Licensing (323)
Licensor (323)
Limited liability company (LLC) (310)

Limited liability company code (310)
Limited liability of members of LLCs (313)
Limited liability of partners of LLPs (318)
Limited liability partnership (LLP) (318)
Limited liability partnership code (318)
Limited partners (318)
Manager of LLCs (314)
Manager-managed LLC (315)

Member (310)
Member-managed LLC (315)
Operating agreement (312)
Processing plant franchise (320)
Revised Uniform Limited Liability Company Act (RULLCA) (311)
Service mark (321)
Subfranchisor (321)
Tortfeasor (315)
Trademark (321)
Trade secret (321)
Uniform Limited Liability Company Act (ULLCA) (311)

Law Case with Answer
Creative Resource Management, Inc. v. Soskin

Facts Nashville Pro Hockey, LLC, was a limited liability company organized under the laws of Tennessee. The LLC owned and operated the Nashville Nighthawks, a minor league professional hockey team. Nashville Pro Hockey, LLC, contracted with Creative Resource Management, Inc. (CRM), whereby CRM, for fees and other consideration, would provide employee leasing services to Nashville Pro Hockey, LLC. The contract was signed by Barry Soskin, the president of Nashville Pro Hockey, LLC. A paragraph in the contract provided: "By affixing my hand and seal to this agreement, I personally guarantee any and all payments payable as represented and outlined in this agreement." Nashville Pro Hockey, LLC, failed, owing CRM $29,626. CRM sued Nashville Pro Hockey, LLC, and Barry Soskin to recover the unpaid compensation. Soskin defended, alleging that his signature on the contract was in his representative capacity only and not in his individual capacity as a guarantor. Did Soskin's signature on the contract constitute a personal guarantee for the payment of the debt of Nashville Pro Hockey, LLC, to CRM and thereby make Soskin personally liable to CRM for the debt?

Answer Yes, Soskin's signature on the contract constituted a personal guarantee for the payment of the debts of Nashville Pro Hockey, LLC, to CRM, thereby making Soskin personally liable to CRM for the debt. The contract contained personal guarantee language in the body of the contract. The words "I personally guarantee any and all payments payable as represented and outlined in this agreement" reflect indisputably a guarantee by Soskin. Soskin insists that he signed only as a representative of the limited liability company. CRM insists that his signature imposes personal liability upon him. The stark fact is that the words "I personally guarantee" are meaningless if applied to Nashville Pro Hockey, LLC, and not to Barry Soskin individually. Since the words "I personally guarantee" cannot refer to Nashville Pro Hockey, LLC, and retain any meaning at all in the context of this agreement, they must of necessity reflect the personal guarantee of Barry Soskin. Thus, Soskin was a guarantor, and he is personally liable to repay the money owed to CRM by Nashville Pro Hockey, LLC. *Creative Resource Management, Inc. v. Soskin*, **Web** 1998 Tenn.App. Lexis 788 (Court of Appeals of Tennessee)

Critical Legal Thinking Cases

15.1 Liability of a Franchisor McDonald's Corporation (McDonald's) is a franchisor that licenses franchisees to operate fast-food restaurants and to use McDonald's trademarks and service marks. One such franchise, which was located in Oak Forest, Illinois, was owned and operated by McDonald's Restaurants of Illinois, the franchisee.

Recognizing the threat of armed robbery at its franchises, especially in the time period immediately after closing, McDonald's established a corporate division to deal with security problems at franchises. McDonald's prepared a manual for restaurant security operations and required its franchisees to adhere to these procedures.

A McDonald's regional security manager visited the Oak Forest franchise to inform the manager of security procedures. He specifically mentioned these rules: (1) No one should throw garbage out the backdoor after dark, and (2) trash and grease were to be taken out the side glass door at least one hour prior to closing. During his inspection, the security manager noted that the locks had to be changed at the restaurant and an alarm system needed to be installed for the backdoor. McDonald's security manager never followed up to

determine whether these security measures had been taken.

One month later, a six-woman crew, all teenagers, was working to clean up and close the Oak Forest restaurant. Laura Martin, Therese Dudek, and Maureen Kincaid were members of that crew. A person later identified as Peter Logan appeared at the back of the restaurant with a gun. He ordered the crew to open the safe and get him the money and then ordered them into the refrigerator. In the course of moving the crew into the refrigerator, Logan shot and killed Martin and assaulted Dudek and Kincaid. Dudek and Kincaid suffered severe emotional distress from the assault.

Evidence showed that Logan had entered the restaurant through the backdoor. Trial testimony proved that the work crew used the backdoor exclusively, both before and after dark, and emptied garbage and grease through the backdoor all day and all night. In addition, there was evidence that the latch on the backdoor did not work properly. Evidence also showed that the crew had not been instructed about the use of the backdoor after dark, the crew had never received copies of the McDonald's security manual, and the required warning about not using the backdoor after dark had not been posted at the restaurant.

Martin's parents and Dudek and Kincaid sued McDonald's to recover damages for negligence. Is McDonald's liable for negligence? *Martin v. McDonald's Corporation*, 572 N.E.2d 1073, **Web** 1991 Ill.App. Lexis 715 (Court of Appeals of Illinois)

15.2 Liability of Limited Partners In 2002, Damon Chargois and Cletus Ernster, both lawyers, formed a limited liability partnership known as Chargois & Ernster, L.L.P. (CELLP). CELLP prosecuted lawsuits against Dillard Department Stores, Inc. (Dillard's), alleging that Dillard's racially discriminated against customers. In June 2003, in an attempt to solicit business, CELLP developed a website that included a link using the "Dillard's" name and logo. Clicking on this link took visitors to dillardsalert.com, a separate website documenting acts of alleged racial profiling by the department store.

Dillard's sued CELLP in U.S. District Court for trademark infringement and cyberpiracy. On July 25, 2004, while the litigation continued, Chargois and Ernster dissolved their limited liability partnership, and CELLP's registration as a LLP expired. On November 2, 2004, the court entered a judgment ordering CELLP to pay Dillard's $143,500 in damages. When the judgment was not satisfied, Dillard's sued Chargois and Ernster in their individual capacities, alleging that the partners were personally responsible for the judgment. Are Chargois and Ernster personally liable for the unpaid judgment obtained against their law firm? *Evanston Insurance Company v. Dillard Department Stores, Inc.*, **Web** 2010 U.S. App. Lexis ___ (United States Court of Appeals for the Fifth Circuit)

15.3 Liability of a Franchisee The Southland Corporation (Southland) owns the 7-Eleven trademark and licenses franchisees to operate convenience stores using this trademark. Each franchise is independently owned and operated. The franchise agreement stipulates that the franchisee is an independent contractor who is authorized to make all inventory, employment, and operational decisions for the franchise.

Timothy Cislaw, 17 years old, died of respiratory failure. His parents filed a wrongful death action against the franchisee, a Costa Mesa, California, 7-Eleven franchise store, and Southland, alleging that Timothy's death resulted from his consumption of Djarum Specials (clove cigarettes) sold at the Costa Mesa, California, 7-Eleven franchise store. The Costa Mesa 7-Eleven was franchised to Charles Trujillo and Patricia Colwell-Trujillo. Southland defended, arguing that it was not liable for the alleged tortious conduct of its franchisee because the franchisee was an independent contractor. The plaintiffs alleged that the franchisee was Southland's agent and therefore Southland was liable for its agent's alleged negligence of selling the clove cigarettes to their son. Is the Costa Mesa franchisee an agent of Southland, thus making Southland liable for the alleged tortious conduct of its franchisee? Does the doctrine of apparent agency apply in this case? Who wins? *Cislaw v. Southland Corporation*, 4 Cal.App.4th 1284, 6 Cal.Rptr.2d 386, **Web** 1992 Cal.App. Lexis 375 (Court of Appeal of California)

15.4 Limited Liability Company Angela, Yoko, Cherise, and Serena want to start a new business that designs and manufactures toys for children. At a meeting in which the owners want to decide what type of legal form to use to operate the business, Cherise states:

We should use a limited liability company to operate our business because this form of business provides us, the owners, with a limited liability shield, which means that if the business gets sued and loses, we the owners are not personally liable to the injured party except up to our capital contribution in the business.

The others agree and form a limited liability company called Fuzzy Toys, LLC, to conduct the member-managed business. Each of the four owners contributes $50,000 as her capital contribution to the LLC. Fuzzy Toys, LLC, purchases $800,000 of liability insurance from Allied Insurance Company and starts business. Fuzzy Toys, LLC, designs and produces "Heidi," a new toy doll and female action figure. The new toy doll is an instant success, and Fuzzy Toys, LLC, produces and sells millions of these female action figures. After a few months, however, the LLC starts getting complaints that one of the parts of the female action figure is breaking off quite regularly, and some children are swallowing the part. The concerned member-managers of Fuzzy Toys, LLC, issue an immediate recall of the female action figure, but before all of the dolls are returned for a refund, Catherine, a 7-year-old child, swallows the toy's part and is severely injured. Catherine, through her mother, sues Fuzzy Toys, LLC, Allied Insurance Company, Angela, Yoko, Cherise, and Serena to recover damages for product liability. At the time of suit, Fuzzy Toys, LLC, has $200,000 of assets. The jury awards Catherine $10 million for her injuries. Who is liable to Catherine, and for how much? How much does Catherine recover?

15.5 Liability of Members Harold, Jasmine, Caesar, and Yuan form Microhard.com, LLC, a limited liability company, to sell computer hardware and software over the Internet. Microhard.com, LLC, hires Heather, a recent graduate of the University of Chicago and a brilliant software designer, as an employee. Heather's job is to design and develop software that will execute a computer command when the computer user thinks of the next command he or she wants to execute on the computer. Using Heather's research, Microhard.com, LLC, develops the Third Eye software program that does this. Microhard.com, LLC, sends Heather to the annual Comdex computer show in Las Vegas, Nevada, to unveil this revolutionary software. Heather goes to Las Vegas, and while there, she rents an automobile to get from the hotel to the computer show and to meet interested buyers at different locations in Las Vegas. While Heather is driving from her hotel to the site of the Comdex computer show, she negligently causes an accident in which she runs over Harold Singer, a pedestrian.

Singer, who suffers severe physical injuries, sues Microhard.com, LLC, Heather, Harold, Jasmine, Caesar, and Yuan to recover monetary damages for his injuries. Who is liable?

15.6 Liability of Members Isabel, Koshi, and Winchester each contribute $50,000 capital to form a limited liability company called Fusion Restaurant, LLC, which operates an upscale restaurant that serves "fusion" cuisine, combining foods from cultures around the world. Fusion Restaurant, LLC, as a business, borrows $1 million from Melon Bank for operating capital. Isabel, Koshi, and Winchester are so busy cooking, serving, and running the restaurant that they forget to hold members' meetings, keep minute books, or otherwise observe any usual company formalities for the entire first year of business. After this one year of hard work, Fusion Restaurant, LLC, suffers financial difficulties and defaults on the $1 million bank loan from Melon Bank. Melon Bank sues Fusion Restaurant, LLC, Isabel, Koshi, and Winchester to recover the unpaid bank loan. Who is liable?

15.7 Member-Managed LLC Jennifer, Martin, and Edsel form a limited liability company called Big Apple, LLC, to operate a bar in New York City. Jennifer, Martin, and Edsel are member-managers of the LLC. One of Jennifer's jobs as a member-manager is to drive the LLC's truck and pick up certain items of supply for the bar each Wednesday. On the way back to the bar one Wednesday after picking up the supplies for that week, Jennifer negligently runs over a pedestrian, Tilly Tourismo, on a street in Times Square. Tilly is severely injured and sues Big Apple, LLC, Jennifer, Martin, and Edsel to recover monetary damages for her injuries. Who is liable?

15.8 Duty of Loyalty Ally is a member and a manager of a manager-managed limited liability company called Movers & You, LLC, a moving company. The main business of Movers & You, LLC, is moving large corporations from old office space to new office space in other buildings. After Ally has been a member-manager of Movers & You, LLC, for several years, she decides to join her friend Lana and form another LLC, called Lana & Me, LLC. This new LLC provides moving services that move large corporations from old office space to new office space. Ally becomes a member-manager of Lana & Me, LLC, while retaining her member-manager position at Movers & You, LLC. Ally does not disclose her new position at Lana & Me, LLC, to the other members or managers of Movers & You, LLC. Several years later, the other members of Movers & You, LLC, discover Ally's other ownership and management position at Lana & Me, LLC. Movers & You, LLC, sues Ally to recover damages for her working for Lana & Me, LLC. Is Ally liable?

Ethics Cases

15.9 Ethics Christopher, Melony, Xie, and Ruth form iNet.com, LLC, a limited liability company. The four members are all Ph.D. scientists who have been working together in a backyard garage to develop a handheld wireless device that lets you receive and send e-mail, surf the Internet, use a word processing program that can print to any printer in the world, view cable television stations, and keep track of anyone you want anywhere in the world as well as zoom in on the person being tracked without that person knowing you are doing so. This new device, called Eros, costs only $29 but makes the owners $25 profit per unit sold. The owners agree that they will buy a manufacturing plant and start producing the unit in six months. Melony, who owns a one-quarter interest in iNet.com, LLC, decides she wants "more of the action" and soon, so she secretly sells the plans and drawings for the new Eros unit to a competitor for $100 million. The competitor comes out with exactly the same device, called Zeus, in one month and beats iNet.com, LLC, to market. The LLC, which later finds out about Melony's action, suffers damages of $100 million because of Melony's action. The LLC sues Melony to recover damages.

1. Is Melony liable to iNet.com, LLC? Explain.
2. Did Melony act ethically in this case? Explain
3. Is the duty of loyalty different for a member of an LLC if the member is not a manager of a manger-managed LLC?

15.10 Ethics Southland Corporation (Southland) owns the 7-Eleven trademark and licenses franchisees throughout the country to operate 7-Eleven stores. The franchise agreement provides for fees to be paid to Southland by each franchisee, based on a percentage of gross profits. In return, franchisees receive a lease of premises, a license to use the 7-Eleven trademark and trade secrets, advertising merchandise, and bookkeeping assistance. Vallerie Campbell purchased an existing 7-Eleven store in Fontana, California, and became a Southland franchisee. The franchise was designated #13974 by Southland. As part of the purchase, she applied to the state of California for transfer of the beer and wine license from the prior owner. Southland also executed the application. California approved the transfer and issued the license to "Campbell Vallerie Southland #13974."

An employee of Campbell's store sold beer to Jesse Lewis Cope, a minor who was allegedly intoxicated at the time. After drinking the beer, Cope drove his vehicle and struck another vehicle. Two occupants of the other vehicle, Denise Wickham and Tyrone Crosby, were severely injured, and a third occupant, Cedrick Johnson, was killed. Johnson (through his parents), Wickham, and Crosby sued Southland—but not Campbell—to recover damages. *Wickham v. The Southland Corporation*, 168 Cal.App.3d 49, 213 Cal.Rptr. 825, **Web** 1985 Cal.App. Lexis 2070 (Court of Appeal of California)

1. Is Southland legally liable for the negligent act of its franchisee Campbell?
2. Did Southland act ethically responsibly in denying liability in this case?
3. Would Campbell, the franchisee, have been held liable if the plaintiffs had sued her? Why do you think the plaintiffs sued Southland and not Campbell?

Internet Exercises

1. Go to www.dunkinfranchising.com/aboutus/franchise/franchise-overview.html to read about Dunkin' Donuts franchise opportunities.

2. Go to www.aboutmcdonalds.com/mcd/franchising/us_franchising.html and read information about domestic franchising in the United States. Can you find any information on becoming a McDonald's franchisee?

16 Corporations and the Sarbanes-Oxley Act

STOCK CERTIFICATE
Corporations have existed since medieval Europe when individual charters were granted by the ruler, usually a monarch—king or queen. Today, in the United States, corporations are created by meeting the requirements established by corporation codes. A corporation is owned by its shareholders, who elect board of director members to make policy decisions, who in turn employ corporate officers to run the day-to-day operations of the corporation.

Learning Objectives

After studying this chapter, you should be able to:

1. Define *corporation* and list the major characteristics of a corporation.
2. Describe the process of forming and financing a corporation.
3. Explain the rights, duties, and liability of directors, officers, and shareholders.
4. Describe how the Sarbanes-Oxley Act affects corporate governance.
5. Describe the operation of multinational corporations.

Chapter Outline

Introduction to Corporations and the Sarbanes-Oxley Act

Nature of the Corporation
  CASE 16.1 • *Menendez v. O'Niell*
  LANDMARK LAW • *Revised Model Business Corporation Act (RMBCA)*

Incorporation Procedure
  CONTEMPORARY ENVIRONMENT • *S Corporation Election for Federal Tax Purposes*

Financing the Corporation
  CONTEMPORARY ENVIRONMENT • *Delaware Attracts Corporate Formations*

Shareholders
  ETHICS • *Shareholder Resolutions*

Board of Directors
  DIGITAL LAW • *Corporation E-Communications*

Corporate Officers

Chapter Outline *(continued)*

❝*The biggest corporation, like the humblest private person, must be held to strict compliance with the will of the people.*❞

—Theodore Roosevelt
  Speech (1902)

Introduction to Corporations and the Sarbanes-Oxley Act

Corporations are the most dominant form of business organization in the United States, generating over 85 percent of the country's gross business receipts. Corporations range in size from one owner to thousands of owners. Corporations are formed pursuant to general corporation laws of the states. Owners of corporations are called shareholders. Shareholders are owners of a corporation who elect the board of directors and vote on fundamental changes in the corporation.

Shareholders, directors, and officers have different rights in managing a corporation. The shareholders elect the directors and vote on other important issues affecting the corporation. The directors are responsible for making policy decisions and employing officers. The officers are responsible for the corporation's day-to-day operations. As a legal entity, a corporation can be held liable for the acts of its directors and officers and for authorized contracts entered into on its behalf. Directors and officers can be held liable for breaches of their duties of loyalty and care.

After decades of many financial frauds and scandals involving directors and officers at some of the largest companies in the United States, in 2002 Congress enacted the *Sarbanes-Oxley Act (SOX)*.[1] This federal statute established rules to improve corporate governance, prevent fraud, and add transparency to corporate operations.

During the course of its existence, a corporation may go through certain fundamental changes. Corporations often engage in acquisitions of other corporations or businesses. This may occur by friendly merger or by hostile tender offer. Multinational corporations conduct international business around the world. This is usually done through a variety of business arrangements, including branch offices, subsidiary corporations, and such.

This chapter discusses the formation and financing of corporations, the rights, duties, and liability of corporate shareholders, directors, and officers, the rules established by Sarbanes-Oxley Act, mergers and hostile tender offers, and the use of multinational corporations to conduct international business.

A corporation is an artificial being, invisible, intangible, and existing only in the contemplation of law. Being the mere creature of the law, it possesses only those properties which the charter of its creation confers upon it, either expressly or as incidental to its very existence. These are such as supposed best calculated to effect the object for which it was created. Among the most important are immortality, and, if the expression may be allowed, individuality; properties by which a perpetual succession of many persons are considered as the same, and may act as a single individual.

John Marshall, Chief Justice
Dartmouth College v. Woodward, 4 Wheaton 518, 636 (1819)

Nature of the Corporation

corporation
A fictitious legal entity that is created according to statutory requirements.

corporation codes
State statutes that regulate the formation, operation, and dissolution of corporations.

[Corporations] cannot commit treason, nor be outlawed, nor excommunicated, for they have no souls.

Lord Edward Coke
Reports (vol. V, Case of Sutton's Hospital)

A **corporation** can be created only pursuant to the laws of the state of incorporation. These laws—commonly referred to as **corporation codes**—regulate the formation, operation, and dissolution of corporations. The state legislature may amend its corporate statutes at any time. Such changes may require a corporation's articles of incorporation to be amended.

The courts interpret state corporation statutes to decide individual corporate and shareholder disputes. As a result, a body of common law has evolved concerning corporate and shareholder rights and obligations.

A corporation is a separate **legal entity** (or **legal person**) for most purposes. Corporations are treated, in effect, as artificial persons created by the state that can sue or be sued in their own names, enter into and enforce contracts, hold title to and transfer property, and be found civilly and criminally liable for violations of law. Because corporations cannot be put in prison, the normal criminal penalty is the assessment of a fine, loss of a license, or another sanction. Corporations have unique characteristics, as discussed in the paragraphs that follow.

Characteristics of a Corporation

Corporations have the following unique characteristics:

- **Free transferability of shares.** Corporate shares are **freely transferable** by a shareholder by sale, assignment, pledge, or gift unless they are issued pursuant to certain exemptions from securities registration. Shareholders may agree among themselves as to restrictions on the transfer of shares. National securities markets, such as the New York Stock Exchange and NASDAQ, have been developed for the organized sale of securities.
- **Perpetual existence.** Corporations have **perpetual existence** unless a specific duration is stated in a corporation's articles of incorporation. The existence of a corporation can be voluntarily terminated by the shareholders. A corporation may be involuntarily terminated by the corporation's creditors if an involuntary petition for bankruptcy against the corporation is granted. The death, insanity, or bankruptcy of a shareholder, a director, or an officer of a corporation does not affect its existence.
- **Centralized management.** The *board of directors* makes policy decisions concerning the operation of a corporation. The members of the board of directors are elected by the shareholders. The directors, in turn, appoint *corporate officers* to run the corporation's day-to-day operations. Together, the directors and the officers form the **corporate management**.
- **Limited liability of shareholders.** As separate legal entities, corporations are liable for their own debts and obligations. Generally, the shareholders have only **limited liability**. That is, they are liable only to the extent of their capital contributions and do not have personal liability for the corporation's debts and obligations (see **Exhibit 16.1**).

limited liability of shareholders
A general rule of corporate law which provides that generally shareholders are liable only to the extent of their capital contributions for the debts and obligations of the corporation and are not personally liable for the debts and obligations of the corporation.

Example Tina, Vivi, and Qixia form IT.com, Inc., a corporation, and each contributes $100,000 capital. The corporation borrows $1 million from State Bank. One year later, IT.com, Inc., goes bankrupt and defaults on the $1 million loan owed to State Bank. At that time, IT.com, Inc.'s only asset is $50,000 cash, which State Bank recovers. Tina, Vivi, and Qixia each loses her $100,000 capital contribution, which IT.com, Inc., has spent. However, Tina, Vivi, and Qixia are not personally liable for the $950,000 still owed to State Bank. State Bank must absorb this loss.

In the following case, the court was asked to decide the liability of a shareholder for a corporation's debts.

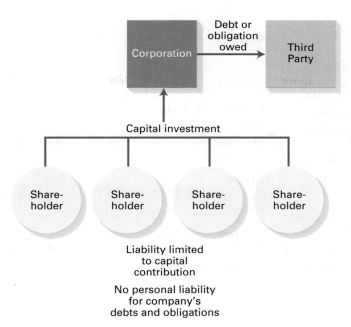

Exhibit 16.1 CORPORATION

CASE 16.1   *Shareholder's Limited Liability*

Menendez v. O'Niell

986 So.2d 255 (2008)
Court of Appeal of Louisiana

"As a general rule, a corporation is a distinct legal entity, separate from the individuals who comprise them, and individual shareholders are not liable for the debts of the corporation."

—Welch, Judge

Facts

A vehicle driven by Michael O'Niell crashed while traveling on Louisiana Highway 30. Vanessa Savoy, a 19-year-old guest passenger in the vehicle, sustained severe injuries as a result of the collision. O'Neill, who was under the legal drinking age, had been drinking at Fred's Bar and Grill prior to the accident. Fred's Bar is owned by Triumvirate of Baton Rouge, Inc., a corporation. Marc Fraioli is the sole shareholder and president of Triumvirate. Fraioli was not at Fred's Bar the night that O'Niell was served alcohol at the bar. Savoy, through a legal representative, brought a lawsuit against O'Niell, O'Niell's automobile insurance company, Triumvirate, and Fraioli, seeking damages for her injuries. Savoy alleged that O'Niell was intoxicated at the time of the accident and that his drinking caused the collision. Savoy alleged that Triumvirate was liable for serving O'Niell alcohol when he was underage and that Fraioli was liable as the owner of Triumvirate.

To prove that Triumvirate was a legally organized and operated corporation, at trial Fraioli introduced a copy of Triumvirate's articles of incorporation, its corporate charter issued by the state of Louisiana, and records that were kept by the corporation. Fraioli filed a motion for summary judgment asserting that as a shareholder of Triumvirate corporation he was not liable for the corporation's debts. The trial court granted summary judgment to Fraioli and dismissed him as a defendant in the case. Savoy appealed.

Issue

Is Fraioli personally liable for the debts of Triumvirate, a corporation in which he is the sole shareholder?

Language of the Court

The law on shareholder liability for the debts of a corporation is well-settled. As a general rule, a corporation is a distinct legal entity, separate from the individuals who comprise them, and individual shareholders are not liable for the debts of the corporation. Mr. Fraioli met his burden of proving Triumvirate's corporate existence. Plaintiff failed to offer any evidence

(continued)

identified by law as indicia that Mr. Fraioli and Triumvirate are not actually separate entities. Plaintiff instead relies on the fact that Triumvirate is solely owned, operated, and controlled by Mr. Fraioli. However, the involvement of a sole or majority share-holder in a corporation is not sufficient alone, as a matter of law, to establish a basis for disregarding the corporate entity.

Decision

The court of appeal held that Fraioli was not personally liable for the debts of the Triumvirate corporation, in which he was the sole shareholder. The court of appeal affirmed the trial court's

grant of summary judgment dismissing Fraioli from the case.

Case Questions

Critical Legal Thinking
Why does the law permit shareholders to avoid personal liability for the debts of the corporation they own?

Ethics
Was it ethical for Fraioli to assert the corporate shield to avoid liability in this case?

Contemporary Business
Did releasing Fraioli from liability also release Triumvirate from liability?

Publicly Held and Closely Held Corporations

publicly held corporation
A corporation that has many shareholders and whose securities are usually traded on national stock exchanges.

closely held corporation
A corporation owned by one or a few shareholders.

Revised Model Business Corporation Act (RMBCA)
A 1984 revision of the MBCA that arranges the provisions of the act more logically, revises the language to be more consistent, and makes substantial changes in the provisions.

Publicly held corporations have many shareholders. Often, they are large corporations with hundreds or thousands of shareholders, and their shares are usually traded on organized securities markets. The shareholders rarely participate in the management of such corporations.

Examples eBay, Inc., General Motors Corporation, Starbucks Corporation, Apple Computer, Inc., The Proctor & Gamble Company, Yahoo!, Inc., and Microsoft Corporation are examples of publicly held corporations.

A **closely held corporation**, on the other hand, is one whose shares are owned by a few shareholders who are often family members, relatives, or friends. Frequently, the shareholders are involved in the management of the corporation. The shareholders sometimes enter into buy-and-sell agreements that prevent outsiders from becoming shareholders.

The following feature discusses the Revised Model Business Corporation Act (RMBCA)

Landmark Law

Revised Model Business Corporation Act (RMBCA)

The Committee on Corporate Laws of the American Bar Association first drafted the **Model Business Corporation Act (MBCA)** in 1950. This model act was intended to provide a uniform law regulating the formation, operation, and termination of corporations.

In 1984, the committee completely revised the MBCA and issued the **Revised Model Business Corporation Act (RMBCA)**. Certain provisions of the RMBCA have been amended since 1984. The RMBCA arranges the provisions of the act more logically, revises the language of the act to be more consistent, and makes substantial changes in the

provisions of the model act. Many states have adopted all or part of the RMBCA. The RMBCA serves as the basis for the discussion of corporation law in this book.

There is no general federal corporation law governing the formation and operation of private corporations. Many federal laws regulate the operation of private corporations, however. These include federal securities laws, labor laws, antitrust laws, consumer protection laws, environmental protection laws, bankruptcy laws, and the like. These federal statutes are discussed in other chapters in this book.

Incorporation Procedure

Corporations are creatures of statute. Thus, the organizers of a corporation must comply with the state's corporation code to form a corporation. The procedure for *incorporating* a corporation varies somewhat from state to state. The procedure for incorporating a corporation is discussed in the following paragraphs.

Selecting a State for Incorporating a Corporation

A corporation can be incorporated in only one state, even though it can do business in all other states in which it qualifies to do business. In choosing a state for incorporation, the incorporators, directors, and/or shareholders must consider the corporation law of the states under consideration.

For the sake of convenience, most corporations (particularly small ones) choose the state in which the corporation will be doing most of its business as the state for incorporation. Large corporations generally opt to incorporate in the state with the laws that are most favorable to the corporation's internal operations (e.g., Delaware).

A corporation is a **domestic corporation** in the state in which it is incorporated. It is a **foreign corporation** in all other states and jurisdictions. An **alien corporation** is a corporation that is incorporated in another country.

When starting a new corporation, the organizers must choose a name for the entity. The name must contain the words *corporation*, *company*, *incorporated*, or *limited* or an abbreviation of one of these words (i.e., *Corp.*, *Co.*, *Inc.*, *Ltd.*). A trademark of the name can be obtained if available and desired. Also, a **domain name** for use by the corporation on the Internet should also be obtained.

Articles of Incorporation

The **articles of incorporation** (or **corporate charter**) is the basic governing document of a corporation. It must be drafted and filed with, and approved by, the state before the corporation can be officially incorporated. Under the RMBCA, the articles of incorporation must include [RMBCA Section 2.02(a)]:

- The name of the corporation
- The number of shares the corporation is authorized to issue
- The address of the corporation's initial registered office and the name of the initial registered agent
- The name and address of each incorporator

The articles of incorporation may also include provisions concerning (1) the period of duration (which may be perpetual), (2) the purpose or purposes for which the corporation is organized, (3) limitation or regulation of the powers of the corporation, (4) regulation of the affairs of the corporation, and (5) any provision that would otherwise be contained in the corporation's bylaws.

Exhibit 16.2 illustrates sample articles of incorporation.

Registered Agent The articles of incorporation must identify a *registered office* with a designated **registered agent** (either an individual or a corporation) in the state of incorporation [RMBCA Section 5.01]. Attorneys often act as the registered agents of corporations. The registered agent is empowered to accept service of process on behalf of the corporation. Service of summons, complaints, and other pleadings to start a lawsuit or legal proceeding against the corporation are served on the registered agent.

---

domestic corporation
A corporation in the state in which it was formed.

The corporation is, and must be, the creature of the state. Into its nostrils the state must breathe the breath of a fictitious life for otherwise it would be no animated body but individualistic dust.

Frederic William Maitland
Introduction to Gierke, Political Theories of the Middle Ages

articles of incorporation (corporate charter)
The basic governing documents of a corporation, which must be filed with the secretary of state of the state of incorporation.

WEB EXERCISE
To view the articles of incorporation of Microsoft Corporation, go to **www.microsoft.com/investor/ CorporateGovernance/Policies AndGuidelines/articlesincorp .aspx**.

registered agent
A person or corporation that is empowered to accept service of process on behalf of a corporation.

Exhibit 16.2 ARTICLES OF INCORPORATION

ARTICLES OF INCORPORATION
OF
THE BIG CHEESE CORPORATION

ONE: The name of this corporation is:

THE BIG CHEESE CORPORATION

TWO: The purpose of this corporation is to engage in any lawful act or activity for which a corporation may be organized under the General Corporation Law of California other than the banking business, the trust company business, or the practice of a profession permitted to be incorporated by the California Corporations Code.

THREE: The name and address in this state of the corporation's initial agent for service of process is:

Nikki Nguyen, Esq.
1000 Main Street
Suite 800
Los Angeles, California 90010

FOUR: This corporation is authorized to issue only one class of shares which shall be designated common stock. The total number of shares it is authorized to issue is 1,000,000 shares.

FIVE: The names and addresses of the persons who are appointed to act as the initial directors of this corporation are:

Shou-Yi Kang	100 Maple Street Los Angeles, California 90005
Frederick Richards	200 Spruce Road Los Angeles, California 90006
Jessie Quian	300 Palm Drive Los Angeles, California 90007
Richard Eastin	400 Willow Lane Los Angeles, California 90008

SIX: The liability of the directors of the corporation from monetary damages shall be eliminated to the fullest extent possible under California law.

SEVEN: The corporation is authorized to provide indemnification of agents (as defined in Section 317 of the Corporations Code) for breach of duty to the corporation and its stockholders through bylaw provisions or through agreements with the agents, or both, in excess of the indemnification otherwise permitted by Section 317 of the Corporations Code, subject to the limits on such excess indemnification set forth in Section 204 of the Corporations Code.

IN WITNESS WHEREOF, the undersigned, being all the persons named above as the initial directors, have executed these Articles of Incorporation.

Dated: January 1, 2014

Corporate Bylaws

In addition to the articles of incorporation, corporations are governed by their **bylaws**. Either the incorporators or the initial directors can adopt the bylaws of the corporation. The bylaws are much more detailed than are the articles of incorporation. They do not have to be filed with any government official. The bylaws govern the internal management structure of a corporation.

Examples Bylaws typically specify the time and place of the annual shareholders' meeting, how special meetings of shareholders are called, the time and place of annual and monthly meetings of the board of directors, how special meetings of the board of directors are called, the notice required for meetings, the quorum necessary to hold a shareholders' or board meeting, the required vote necessary to enact a corporate matter, the corporate officers and their duties, the committees of the board of directors and their duties, where the records of the corporation are kept, directors' and shareholders' rights to inspect corporate records, the procedure for transferring shares of the corporation, and such.

The shareholders of a corporation have the absolute right to amend the bylaws, and the board of directors may also usually amend the bylaws [RMBCA Section 10.20]. The bylaws are binding on the directors, officers, and shareholders of the corporation.

The board of directors has the authority to amend the bylaws unless the articles of incorporation reserve that right for the shareholders. The shareholders of the corporation have the absolute right to amend the bylaws even though the board of directors may also amend the bylaws [RMBCA Section 10.20].

bylaws
A detailed set of rules adopted by the board of directors after a corporation is incorporated that contains provisions for managing the business and the affairs of the corporation.

WEB EXERCISE
To view the bylaws of Microsoft Corporation, go to **www.microsoft .com/investor/Corporate Governance/PoliciesAnd Guidelines/bylaws.aspx**.

Organizational Meeting of the Board of Directors

An **organizational meeting** of the initial directors of a corporation must be held after the articles of incorporation are filed. At this meeting, the directors must adopt the bylaws, elect corporate officers, and transact such other business as may come before the meeting [RMBCA Section 2.05].

Examples An organizational meeting may address authorizing the issuance of shares, ratifying or adopting promoters' contracts, authorizing the reimbursement of promoters' expenses, selecting a bank, choosing an auditor, forming committees of the board of directors, fixing the salaries of officers, hiring employees, authorizing the filing of applications for government licenses to transact the business of the corporation, and empowering corporate officers to enter into contracts on behalf of the corporation.

The following feature discusses an election that can be made regarding federal tax obligations.

organizational meeting
A meeting that must be held by the initial directors of a corporation after the articles of incorporation are filed.

S corporation
A corporation that has met certain requirements and has elected to be taxed as an S corporation for federal income tax purposes. An S corporation pays no federal income tax at the corporate level. The S corporation's income or loss flows to the shareholders and must be reported on the shareholders' individual income tax returns.

Contemporary Environment

S Corporation Election for Federal Tax Purposes

A **C corporation** is a corporation that does not qualify to or does not elect to be federally taxed as an S corporation. Any corporation with more than one hundred shareholders is automatically a C corporation for federal income tax purposes. A C corporation must pay federal income tax at the corporate level. In addition, if a C corporation distributes its profits to shareholders in the form of dividends, the shareholders must pay personal income tax on the dividends. With a C corporation there is **double taxation**— that is, one tax paid at the corporate level and another paid at the shareholder level.

Congress enacted the **Subchapter S Revision Act**[2] to allow the shareholders of some corporations to avoid double taxation by electing **Subchapter S corporation** status. If a corporation elects to be taxed as an **S corporation**, it pays no federal income tax at the corporate level. As in a partnership, the corporation's income or loss flows to the shareholders' individual income tax returns.

Subchapter S election is particularly advantageous if (1) the corporation is expected to have losses that can be offset against other income of the shareholders or (2) the corporation is expected to make profits, and the shareholders' income tax brackets are lower than the corporation's. Profits are taxed to the shareholders even if the income is not distributed. Subchapter S election

only affects the *taxation* of a corporation; it does not affect attributes of the corporate form, including limited liability.

Corporations that meet the following criteria can elect to be taxed as S corporations:

- The corporation must be a domestic corporation.
- The corporation cannot be a member of an affiliated group of corporations.
- The corporation can have no more than 100 shareholders.
- Shareholders must be individuals, estates, or certain trusts. Corporations and partnerships cannot be shareholders.
- Shareholders must be citizens or residents of the United States. Nonresident aliens cannot be shareholders.
- The corporation cannot have more than one class of stock. Shareholders do not have to have equal voting rights.

An S corporation election is made by filing **Form 2553** with the Internal Revenue Service (IRS). The election can be rescinded by shareholders who collectively own at least a majority of the shares of the corporation. However, if the election is rescinded, another S corporation election cannot be made for five years.

Financing the Corporation

A corporation needs to finance the operation of its business. The most common way to do this is by selling *equity securities* and *debt securities*. **Equity securities** (or **stocks**) represent ownership rights in the corporation. Equity securities can be *common stock* and *preferred stock*. These are discussed in the following paragraphs.

equity securities (stocks)
Representation of ownership rights in a corporation.

Common Stock

Common stock is an equity security that represents the residual value of a corporation. Common stock has no preferences. That is, creditors and preferred shareholders must receive their required interest and dividend payments before common shareholders receive anything. Common stock does not have a fixed maturity date. If a corporation is liquidated, the creditors and preferred shareholders are paid the value of their interests first, and the common shareholders are paid the value of their interests (if any) last. Corporations may issue different classes of common stock [RMBCA Sections 6.01(a), 6.01(b)].

Persons who own common stock are called **common stockholders**. A common stockholder's investment in the corporation is represented by a **common stock certificate**. Common stockholders have the right to elect directors and to vote on mergers and other important matters. In return for their investment, common stockholders receive *dividends* declared by the board of directors.

Preferred Stock

Preferred stock is an equity security that is given certain *preferences and rights over common stock* [RMBCA Section 6.01(c)]. The owners of preferred stock are called **preferred stockholders**. Preferred stockholders are issued **preferred stock certificates** to evidence their ownership interest in the corporation.

Preferred stock can be issued in classes or series. One class of preferred stock can be given preference over another class of preferred stock. Like common stockholders, preferred stockholders have limited liability. Preferred stockholders generally are not given the right to vote for the election of directors or such. However, they are often given the right to vote if there is a merger or if the corporation has not made the required dividend payments for a certain period of time (e.g., three years).

Preferences of preferred stock must be set forth in the articles of incorporation. Preferred stock may have any or all of the following preferences, rights, or attributes:

- **Dividend preference.** A **dividend preference** is the right to receive a **fixed dividend** at set periods during the year (e.g., quarterly). The dividend rate is usually a set percentage of the initial offering price.
- **Liquidation preference.** The right to be paid before common stockholders if the corporation is dissolved and liquidated is called a **liquidation preference**. A liquidation preference is normally a stated dollar amount.
- **Cumulative dividend right.** A corporation must pay a preferred dividend if it has the earnings to do so. However, sometimes a corporation is not able to pay a preferred stock dividend when due. **Cumulative preferred stock** provides that any missed dividend payment must be paid in the future to the preferred shareholders before the common shareholders can receive any dividends.
- **Right to participate in profits.** **Participating preferred stock** allows a preferred stockholder to participate in the profits of the corporation along with the common stockholders. Participation is in addition to the fixed dividend paid on preferred stock. The terms of participation vary widely. Usually, the common stockholders must be paid a certain amount of dividends before participation is allowed.
- **Conversion right.** **Convertible preferred stock** permits the preferred stockholders to convert their shares into common stock. The terms and exchange rate of the conversion are established when the shares are issued. The holders of convertible preferred stock usually exercise this option if the corporation's common stock significantly increases in value.
- **Redeemable preferred stock.** **Redeemable preferred stock** (or **callable preferred stock**) permits a corporation to redeem (i.e., buy back) the preferred stock at some future date. The terms of the redemption are established when the shares are issued.

Authorized, Issued, and Outstanding Shares

The number of shares provided for in the articles of incorporation is called **authorized shares** [RMBCA Section 6.01]. The shareholders may vote to amend the articles of incorporation to increase this amount. Authorized shares that have been sold by the corporation are called **issued shares**. Not all authorized shares have to be issued at the same time. Authorized shares that have not been issued are called **unissued shares**. The board of directors can vote to issue unissued shares at any time without shareholder approval.

A corporation is permitted to repurchase its shares [RMBCA Section 6.31]. Repurchased shares are commonly called **treasury shares**. Treasury shares cannot be voted by the corporation, and dividends are not paid on these shares. Treasury shares can be reissued by the corporation. The shares that are in shareholder hands, whether originally issued or reissued treasury shares, are called **outstanding shares**. Only outstanding shares have the right to vote [RMBCA Section 6.03].

authorized shares
The number of shares provided for in a corporation's articles of incorporation.

issued shares
Authorized shares that have been sold by a corporation.

CONCEPT SUMMARY
TYPES OF SHARES

Type of Share	Description
Authorized	Shares authorized in the corporation's articles of incorporation.
Issued	Shares sold by the corporation.
Treasury	Shares repurchased by the corporation. These shares do not have the right to vote.
Outstanding	Issued shares minus treasury shares. These shares have the right to vote.

Debt Securities

A corporation often raises funds by issuing debt securities [RMBCA Section 3.02(7)]. **Debt securities** (also called **fixed income securities**) establish a debtor–creditor relationship in which the corporation borrows money from the investor to whom the debt security is issued. The corporation promises to pay interest on the amount borrowed and to repay the principal at some stated maturity date in the future. The corporation is the *debtor*, and the holder is the *creditor*. Three classifications of debt securities are as follows:

- **Debenture.** A debenture is a *long-term* (often thirty years or more), *unsecured* debt instrument that is based on a corporation's general credit standing. If the corporation encounters financial difficulty, unsecured debenture holders are treated as general creditors of the corporation (i.e., they are paid only after the secured creditors' claims are met).
- **Bond.** A bond is a *long-term* debt security that is *secured* by some form of *collateral* (e.g., real estate, personal property). Thus, bonds are the same as debentures except that they are secured. Secured bondholders can foreclose on the collateral in the event of nonpayment of interest, principal, or other specified events.
- **Note.** A note is a *short-term* debt security with a maturity of five years or less. Notes can be either *unsecured* or *secured*. They usually do not contain a conversion feature. They are sometimes made redeemable.

Indenture Agreement

The terms of a debt security are commonly contained in a contract between the corporation and the holder; this contract is known as an **indenture agreement**

debt securities (fixed income securities)
Securities that establish a debtor–creditor relationship in which the corporation borrows money from the investor to whom a debt security is issued.

debenture
A long-term unsecured debt instrument that is based on a corporation's general credit standing.

bond
A long-term debt security that is secured by some form of collateral.

note
A debt security with a maturity of five years or less.

indenture agreement (indenture)
A contract between a corporation and a holder that contains the terms of a debt security.

(or simply an **indenture**). The indenture generally contains the maturity date of the debt security, the required interest payment, the collateral (if any), rights to conversion into common or preferred stock, call provisions, any restrictions on the corporation's right to incur other indebtedness, the rights of holders upon default, and such. It also establishes the rights and duties of the indenture trustee. Generally, a trustee is appointed to represent the interest of the debt security holders. Bank trust departments often serve in this capacity.

The following feature discusses why the state of Delaware attracts corporate formations.

Contemporary Environment

Delaware Attracts Corporate Formations

The state of Delaware is the corporate haven of the United States. More than 50 percent of the publicly traded corporations in America, including 60 percent of the Fortune 500 companies, are incorporated in Delaware. In total, more than 500,000 business corporations are incorporated in Delaware. But why?

Remember that the state in which a corporation is incorporated determines the law that applies to the corporation: The corporation code of the state of incorporation applies to such things as election of directors, requirements for a merger to occur, laws for fending off corporate raiders, and such. So, even if a corporation does no business in Delaware, it can obtain the benefits of Delaware corporation law by incorporating in Delaware.

On the legislative side, Delaware has enacted the **Delaware General Corporation Law**. This law is the most advanced corporation law in the country, and the statute is particularly written to be of benefit to large corporations. For example, the Delaware corporation code provides for the ability of corporations incorporated in Delaware to adopt "poison pills" that make it difficult for another

company to take over a Delaware corporation unless the board of directors of the target corporation agrees and removes such poison pills. In addition, the legislature keeps amending the corporation code as the demands of big business warrant or need such changes. For instance, the legislature has enacted a state antitakeover statute that makes it difficult to take over a Delaware corporation unless the corporation's directors waive the state's antitakeover law and agree to be taken over.

On the judicial side, Delaware has a special court—the **court of chancery**—that hears and decides business cases. This court has been around for over two hundred years. In that time, it has interpreted Delaware corporation law favorably to large corporations in such matters as electing corporate boards of directors, eliminating negligence liability of outside directors, upholding the antitakeover provisions of the Delaware corporation code, and such. In addition, there are no emotional juries to worry about. The decisions of the chancery court are made by judges who are experts at deciding corporate law disputes. The court is known for issuing decisions favorable to large corporations as the court applies Delaware corporation law to decide disputes. Appeals from the court of chancery are brought directly to the supreme court of Delaware. Thus, Delaware courts have created a body of precedent of legal decisions that provides more assurance to Delaware corporations in trying to decide whether they will be sued and what the outcome will be if they do get sued.

The state of Delaware makes a substantial sum of money each year on fees charged to corporations incorporated within the state. Delaware is the "business state," providing advanced corporate laws and an expert judiciary for deciding corporate disputes.

Shareholders

shareholders
Owners of a corporation who elect the board of directors and vote on fundamental changes in the corporation.

A corporation's **shareholders** own the corporation (see **Exhibit 16.3**). Nevertheless, they are not agents of the corporation (i.e., they cannot bind the corporation to contracts), and the only management duty they have is the right to vote on matters such as the election of directors and the approval of fundamental changes in the corporation.

Exhibit 16.3
SHAREHOLDERS

Shareholders' Meetings

Annual shareholders' meetings are held to elect directors, choose independent auditors, and take other actions. These meetings must be held at the times fixed in the bylaws [RMBCA Section 7.01]. **Special shareholders' meetings** may be called by the board of directors, the holders of at least 10 percent of the voting shares of the corporation or any other person authorized to do so by the articles of incorporation or bylaws (e.g., the president) [RMBCA Section 7.02]. Special meetings may be held to consider important or emergency issues, such as a merger or consolidation of the corporation with one or more other corporations, the removal of directors, amendment of the articles of incorporation, or dissolution of the corporation. A corporation is required to give the shareholders written notice of the place, day, and time of annual and special meetings.

Shareholders do not have to attend a shareholders' meeting to vote. Shareholders may vote by *proxy*; that is, they can appoint another person (the proxy) as their agent to vote at a shareholders' meeting. The proxy may be directed exactly how to vote the shares or may be authorized to vote the shares at his or her discretion. Proxies may be in writing or posted online. The written document itself is called the **proxy** (or **proxy card**). Unless otherwise stated, a proxy is valid for eleven months [RMBCA Section 7.22].

Quorum and Vote Required

Unless otherwise provided in the articles of incorporation, if a majority of shares entitled to vote are represented at a meeting in person or by proxy, there is a **quorum** to hold the meeting. Once a quorum is present, the withdrawal of shares does not affect the quorum of the meeting [RMBCA Sections 7.25(a), 7.25(b)]. The affirmative *vote* of the majority of the *voting* shares represented at a shareholders' meeting constitutes an act of the shareholders for actions other than for the election of directors [RMBCA Section 7.25(c)].

Example A corporation has 20,000 shares outstanding. A shareholders' meeting is duly called to amend the articles of incorporation, and 10,001 shares are represented at the meeting. A quorum is present because a majority of the shares entitled to vote are represented. Suppose that 5,001 shares are voted in favor of the amendment. The amendment passes. In this example, just over 25 percent of the shares of the corporation bind the other shareholders to the action taken at the shareholders' meeting.

annual shareholders' meeting
A meeting of the shareholders of a corporation that must be held by the corporation to elect directors and to vote on other matters.

special shareholders' meetings
Meetings of shareholders that may be called to consider and vote on important or emergency issues, such as a proposed merger or amending the articles of incorporation.

proxy (proxy card)
A shareholder's authorization of another person to vote the shareholder's shares at the shareholders' meetings in the event of the shareholder's absence.

quorum
The number of directors necessary to hold a board meeting or transact business of the board.

The articles of incorporation or the bylaws of a corporation can require a greater than majority of the shares to constitute a quorum of the vote of the shareholders [RMBCA Section 7.27]. This is called a **supramajority voting requirement** (or **supermajority voting requirement**). Such votes are often required to approve mergers, consolidation, the sale of substantially all the assets of a corporation, and such.

Straight versus Cumulative Voting

Voting for the election of directors is usually by the **straight voting**, or **noncumulative voting**, method. This voting method is quite simple: Each shareholder votes the number of shares he or she owns on candidates for each of the positions open for election. Thus, a majority shareholder can elect the entire board of directors.

A corporation's articles of incorporation may provide for **cumulative voting** for the election of directors. This means that each shareholder is entitled to multiply the number of shares he or she owns by the number of directors to be elected and cast the *accumulative number* for a single candidate or distribute the product among two or more candidates [RMBCA Section 7.28]. Cumulative voting gives a minority shareholder a better opportunity to elect someone to the board of directors.

Examples A corporation has 10,000 outstanding shares. Erin owns 5,100 shares (51 percent), and Michael owns 4,900 shares (49 percent). Suppose that three directors of the corporation are to be elected from a potential pool of 10 candidates. Under *straight voting*, Erin casts 5,100 votes each for her three chosen candidates; Michael votes 4,900 shares for each of his three chosen candidates, who are different from those favored by Erin. Each of the three candidates Erin voted for wins, with 5,100 votes each. However, under *cumulative voting*, Michael can multiply the number of shares he owns (4,900) by the number of directors to be elected (three), take the resulting number of votes (14,700), and cast them all for one candidate or split them among candidates, as he determines.

Dividends

Profit corporations operate to make a profit. The objective of the shareholders is to share in those profits, either through capital appreciation, the receipt of dividends, or both. **Dividends** are paid at the discretion of the board of directors [RMBCA Section 6.40]. The directors may opt to retain the profits in the corporation to be used for corporate purposes instead of as dividends. Once declared, a cash or property dividend cannot be revoked. Shareholders can sue to recover declared but unpaid dividends.

Piercing the Corporate Veil

Shareholders of a corporation generally have *limited liability* (i.e., they are liable for the debts and obligations of the corporation only to the extent of their capital contribution), and they are not personally liable for the debts and obligations of the corporation. However, if a shareholder or shareholders dominate a corporation and misuse it for improper purposes, a court of equity can *disregard the corporate entity* and hold the shareholders of the corporation personally liable for the corporation's debts and obligations. This doctrine is commonly referred to as **piercing the corporate veil**. It is often resorted to by unpaid creditors who are trying to collect from shareholders a debt owed by the corporation. The piercing the corporate veil doctrine is also called the **alter ego doctrine** because the corporation becomes the *alter ego* of the shareholder.

Courts will pierce the corporate veil if (1) the corporation has been formed without sufficient capital (i.e., *thin capitalization*) or (2) separateness has not been maintained between the corporation and its shareholders (e.g., commingling of personal and corporate assets, failure to hold required shareholders' meetings, failure to maintain corporate records and books). The courts examine this doctrine on a case-by-case basis.

shareholder resolution
A resolution that a shareholder who meets certain ownership requirements may submit to other shareholders for a vote. Many shareholder resolutions concern social issues.

Ethics

Shareholder Resolutions

At times, shareholders may wish to submit issues for a vote of other shareholders. The Securities Exchange Act of 1934 and Securities and Exchange Commission (SEC) rules permit a shareholder to submit a resolution to be considered by other shareholders if (1) the shareholder has owned at least $2,000 worth of shares of the company's stock or 1 percent of all shares of the company (2) for at least one year prior to submitting the proposal. The resolution cannot exceed five hundred words. Such **shareholder resolutions** are usually made when the corporation is soliciting proxies from its shareholders.

If management does not oppose a resolution, it may be included in the proxy materials issued by the corporation. Even if management is not in favor of a resolution, a shareholder has a right to have the shareholder resolution included in the corporation's proxy materials if it (1) relates to the corporation's business, (2) concerns a *policy issue* (and not the day-to-day operations of the corporation), and (3) does not concern the payment of dividends. The SEC rules on whether a resolution can be submitted to shareholders.

Examples Shareholder resolutions have been presented concerning reducing global warming; preventing the overcutting of the rain forests in Brazil; prohibiting U.S. corporations from purchasing goods manufactured in developing countries under poor working conditions, including the use of forced and child labor; protecting human rights; and engaging in other socially responsible conduct.

Most shareholder resolutions have a slim chance of being enacted because large-scale investors usually support management. Shareholder resolutions can, however, cause a corporation to change the way it does business. For example, to avoid the adverse publicity such issues can create, some corporations voluntarily adopt the changes contained in shareholder resolutions. Others negotiate settlements with the sponsors of resolutions to get the measures off the agenda before the annual shareholders' meetings.

Ethics Questions Why do companies usually not support shareholder resolutions? Does the threat of shareholder resolutions make companies act more socially responsible?

Board of Directors

The **board of directors** of a corporation is elected by the shareholders of the corporation. The board of directors is responsible for formulating *policy decisions* that affect the management, supervision, control, and operation of the corporation (see **Exhibit 16.4**) [RMBCA Section 8.01]. Such policy decisions include deciding the business or businesses in which the corporation should be engaged, selecting and removing the top officers of the corporation, determining the capital structure of the corporation, and the like.

Boards of directors are typically composed of inside and outside directors. An **inside director** is a person who is also an officer of the corporation. An **outside director** is a person who sits on the board of directors of a corporation but is not an officer of that corporation. Outside directors are often selected for their business knowledge and expertise.

Examples The president of a corporation who also sits as a director of the corporation is an inside director. Outside directors are often officers and directors of other corporations, bankers, lawyers, professors, and others.

board of directors
A panel of persons who are elected by shareholders to make policy decisions concerning the operation of a corporation.

inside director
A member of a board of directors who is also an officer of the corporation.

outside director
A member of a board of directors who is not an officer of the corporation.

Exhibit 16.4 BOARD OF DIRECTORS

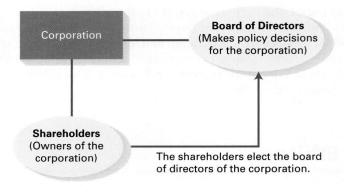

Corporation

Board of Directors
(Makes policy decisions
for the corporation)

Shareholders
(Owners of the
corporation)

The shareholders elect the board
of directors of the corporation.

Meetings of the Board of Directors

Regular meetings of a board of directors are held at the times and places established in the bylaws. A board can call **special meetings of the board of directors** as provided in the bylaws [RMBCA Section 8.20(a)]. Special meetings are usually convened for reasons such as issuing new shares, considering proposals to merge with other corporations, adopting maneuvers to defend against hostile takeover attempts, and the like. The board of directors may act without a meeting if all the directors sign written consents that set forth the actions taken. The RMBCA permits meetings of the board to be held via conference calls [RMBCA Section 8.20(b)].

A simple majority of the number of directors established in the articles of incorporation or bylaws usually constitute a *quorum* for transacting business. However, the articles of incorporation and the bylaws may increase this number. If a quorum is present, the approval or disapproval of a majority of the quorum binds the entire board. The articles of incorporation or the bylaws can require a greater than majority of directors to constitute a quorum of the vote of the board [RMBCA Section 8.24].

The following feature discusses how modern corporation codes authorize electronic communications.

Digital Law

Corporation E-Communications

Most state corporation codes have been amended to permit the use of **corporate electronic communications** (**corporate e-communications**) by corporations to communicate with shareholders and among directors. For example, the Delaware General Corporation Law recognizes the following uses of electronic technology:

- Delivery of notices to shareholders may be made electronically to shareholders who consent to the delivery of notices in this form.
- Proxy solicitation for shareholder votes may be made by electronic transmission.
- The shareholders list of a corporation that must be made available during the ten days prior to a shareholders' meeting may be made available either at

the principal place of business of the corporation or by posting the list on an electronic network.

- Shareholders who are not physically present at a meeting may be deemed present, participate in, and vote at the meeting by electronic communication; a meeting may be held solely by electronic communication, without a physical location.
- An election of directors of the corporation may be held by electronic transmission.
- Directors' actions by unanimous consent may be taken by electronic transmission.

The use of electronic transmissions, electronic networks, and communications by e-mail makes the operation and administration of corporate affairs more efficient.

Corporate Officers

A corporation's board of directors has the authority to appoint the officers of the corporation. The **corporate officers** are elected by the board of directors at such time and by such manner as prescribed in the corporation's bylaws. The directors can delegate certain management authority to the officers of the corporation (see **Exhibit 16.5**).

corporate officers
Employees of a corporation who are appointed by the board of directors to manage the day-to-day operations of the corporation.

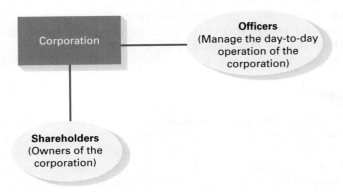

Exhibit 16.5 CORPORATE OFFICERS

At a minimum, most corporations have the following officers: a *president*, one or more *vice presidents*, a *secretary*, and a *treasurer*. The bylaws or the board of directors can authorize duly appointed officers the power to appoint assistant officers. The same individual may simultaneously hold more than one office in the corporation [RMBCA Section 8.40]. The duties of each officer are specified in the bylaws of the corporation.

Officers and agents of a corporation have such authority as may be provided in the bylaws of the corporation or as determined by resolution of the board of directors [RMBCA Section 8.41]. Because they are agents, officers have the express authority granted to them, as well as implied authority and apparent authority, to bind a corporation to contracts.

The law does not permit the stockholders to create a sterilized board of directors.

Justice Collins
Manson v. Curtis (1918)

CONCEPT SUMMARY
MANAGEMENT OF A CORPORATION

Group	Function
Shareholders	Owners of the corporation. They vote on the directors and other major actions to be taken by the corporation.
Board of directors	Elected by the shareholders. Directors are responsible for making policy decisions and employing the major officers for the corporation. The board may initiate certain actions that require shareholders' approval.
Officers	Officers are responsible for the day-to-day operation of the corporation, including acting as agents for the corporation, hiring other officers and employees, and the like.

Fiduciary Duties of Directors and Officers

Directors and officers of a corporation owe **fiduciary duties** of trust and competence to the corporation and its shareholders. These include the (1) *duty of loyalty* and (2) the *duty of care*. These fiduciary duties are discussed in the following paragraphs.

fiduciary duties
The duties of care and loyalty owed by directors and officers to their corporation and its shareholders.

Duty of Loyalty

Directors and officers of a corporation owe a fiduciary duty to act honestly. This duty, called the **duty of loyalty**, requires directors and officers to subordinate their personal interests to those of the corporation and its shareholders. If a director or an officer breaches his or her duty of loyalty and makes a secret profit on a transaction, the corporation can sue the director or officer to recover the secret profit.

Some of the most common breaches of the duty of loyalty are (1) **usurping a corporate opportunity** (taking a corporate opportunity for oneself), (2) undisclosed and unauthorized **competing with the corporation**, (3) undisclosed and unauthorized **self-dealing** (e.g., selling property to the corporation), and (4) making a **secret profit** (e.g., taking a bribe).

Duty of Care

The **duty of care** requires corporate directors and officers to use *care and diligence* when acting on behalf of the corporation. To meet this duty of care, the directors and officers must discharge their duties (1) in good faith, (2) with the care that an *ordinary prudent person* in a like position would use under similar circumstances, and (3) in a manner they reasonably believe to be in the best interests of the corporation [RMBCA Sections 8.30(a), 8.42(a)].

A director or an officer who breaches the duty of care is personally liable to the corporation and its shareholders for any damages caused by the breach. Such breaches, which are normally caused by **negligence**, often involve a director's or an officer's failure to keep adequately informed about corporate affairs.

Business Judgment Rule The determination of whether a corporate director or officer has met his or her duty of care is measured as of the time the decision is made; the benefit of hindsight is not a factor. Therefore, the directors and officers are not liable to the corporation or its shareholders for honest mistakes of judgment. This is called the **business judgment rule**. Were it not for the protection afforded by the business judgment rule, many high-risk but socially desirable endeavors might not be undertaken.

Example After conducting considerable research and investigation, the directors of a major automobile company decide to produce large and expensive sport-utility vehicles (SUVs). Three years later, when the SUVs are introduced to the public for sale, few of them are sold because of the public's interest in buying smaller, less expensive automobiles due to an economic recession and an increase in gasoline prices. Because this was an honest mistake of judgment on the part of corporate management, their judgment is shielded by the business judgment rule.

Sarbanes-Oxley Act

During the late 1990s and early 2000s, the U.S. economy was wracked by a number of business and accounting scandals. Many of the companies involved went bankrupt, causing huge losses to their shareholders, employees, and creditors. Boards of directors were complacent, not keeping a watchful eye over the conduct of their officers and employees.

In response, Congress enacted the federal *Sarbanes-Oxley Act* of 2002. This act establishes far-reaching rules regarding corporate governance. The goals of the Sarbanes-Oxley Act are to improve corporate governance rules, eliminate conflicts of interest, and instill confidence in investors and the public that management will run public companies in the best interests of all constituents. Excerpts from the Sarbanes-Oxley Act are set forth as Appendix C to this book.

The following feature discusses some of the major provisions of the Sarbanes-Oxley Act that regulate corporate governance.

Ethics

Sarbanes-Oxley Act Regulates Corporate Governance

The **Sarbanes-Oxley Act** is a federal statute that has changed the rules of corporate governance in important respects. Several major provisions of the act regarding corporate governance are discussed in the following paragraphs:

- **CEO and CFO certification.** The chief executive officer (CEO) and chief financial officer (CFO) of a public company must file a statement accompanying each annual and quarterly report, certifying that the signing officer has reviewed the report; that, based on the officer's knowledge, the **CEO and CFO certify** that the report does not contain any untrue statement of a material fact or omit to state a material fact that would make the statement misleading; and that the financial statement and disclosures fairly present, in all material aspects, the operation and financial condition of the company. A knowing and willful violation is punishable by up to twenty years in prison and a monetary fine.
- **Reimbursement of bonuses and incentive pay.** If a public company is required to restate its financial statements because of material noncompliance with financial reporting requirements, the CEO and CFO must reimburse the company for any bonuses, incentive

pay, or securities trading profits made because of the noncompliance.
- **Prohibition on personal loans.** The act prohibits public companies from making personal loans to their directors or executive officers.
- **Penalties for tampering with evidence.** The act makes it a crime for any person to knowingly alter, destroy, mutilate, conceal, or create any document to impair, impede, influence, or obstruct any federal investigation. A violation is punishable by up to twenty years in prison and a monetary fine.
- **Bar from acting as an officer or a director.** The Securities and Exchange Commission (SEC), a federal government agency, may issue an order prohibiting any person who has committed securities fraud from acting as an officer or a director of a public company.

Although the Sarbanes-Oxley Act applies only to public companies, private companies and nonprofit organizations are also influenced by the act's accounting and corporate governance rules.

Ethics Questions Will the CEO and CFO certification requirement reduce corporate fraudulent conduct? Will the Sarbanes-Oxley Act promote more ethical behavior among corporate officers and directors?

Mergers and Acquisitions

Corporations sometimes engage in fundamental changes that involve the acquisition of another corporation. The major form of acquisition is by merger.

A **merger** occurs when one corporation is absorbed into another corporation. In a merger, one corporation survives and the other corporation ceases to exist. The corporation that continues to exist is called the **surviving corporation**. The other corporation, which ceases to exist, is called the **merged corporation** [RMBCA Section 11.01]. The surviving corporation gains all the rights, privileges, powers, duties, obligations, and liabilities of the merged corporation. Title to property owned by the merged corporation transfers to the surviving corporation, without formality or deeds. The shareholders of the merged corporation receive stock or securities of the surviving corporation or other consideration, as provided in the plan of merger. The merged company often keeps the name of the surviving corporation but sometimes change the name to reflect the merger.

merger
A situation in which one corporation is absorbed into another corporation and ceases to exist.

surviving corporation
The corporation that continues to exist after a merger.

merged corporation
The corporation that is absorbed in a merger and ceases to exist after the merger.

Example Corporation A and Corporation B merge, and it is agreed that Corporation A will absorb Corporation B. Corporation A is the surviving corporation. Corporation B is the merged corporation. The representation of this merger is A + B = A (see **Exhibit 16.6**).

An ordinary merger or share exchange requires (1) the recommendation of the board of directors of each corporation and (2) an affirmative vote of the majority

Exhibit 16.6 MERGER

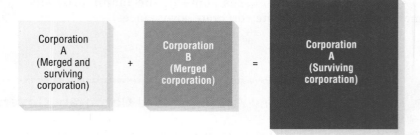

of shares of each corporation that are entitled to vote [RMBCA Section 11.03]. The articles of incorporation or corporate bylaws can require the approval of a supramajority, such 80 percent of the voting shares.

Dissolution of a Corporation

The life of a corporation may be dissolved voluntarily by the owners or involuntarily by the state. The methods for dissolving corporations are as follows:

voluntary dissolution
Dissolution of a corporation that has begun business or issued shares upon recommendation of the board of directors and a majority vote of the shares entitled to vote.

administrative dissolution
Involuntary dissolution of a corporation that is ordered by the secretary of state if a corporation has failed to comply with certain procedures required by law.

- **Voluntary dissolution.**   A corporation can be voluntarily dissolved if the board of directors recommends dissolution and a majority of shares entitled to vote (or a greater number, if required by the articles of incorporation or bylaws) votes for dissolution as well [RMBCA Section 14.02]. For a **voluntary dissolution** to be effective, **articles of dissolution** must be filed with the secretary of state of the state of incorporation. A corporation is dissolved upon the effective date of the articles of dissolution [RMBCA Section 14.03].
- **Administrative dissolution.**   The secretary of state can obtain **administrative dissolution** of a corporation if (1) it failed to file an annual report, (2) it failed for sixty days to maintain a registered agent in the state, (3) it failed for sixty days after a change of its registered agent to file a statement of such change with the secretary of state, (4) it did not pay its franchise fee, or (5) the period of duration stated in the corporation's articles of incorporation has expired [RMBCA Section 14.20]. If the corporation does not cure the default within sixty days of being notified of it, the secretary of state issues a **certificate of dissolution** that dissolves the corporation [RMBCA Section 14.21].

Winding Up, Liquidation, and Termination

winding up and liquidation
The process by which a dissolved corporation's assets are collected, liquidated, and distributed to creditors, preferred shareholders, and common shareholders.

termination
The end of a corporation that occurs after winding up the corporation's affairs, liquidating its assets, and distributing the proceeds and property to the claimants.

A dissolved corporation continues its corporate existence but may not carry on any business except as required to **wind up and liquidate** its business and affairs [RMBCA Section 14.05]. In a voluntary dissolution, the liquidation is usually carried out by the board of directors. If the dissolution is involuntary or the dissolution is voluntary but the directors refuse to carry out the liquidation, a court-appointed receiver carries out the winding up and liquidation of the corporation [RMBCA Section 14.32].

Termination occurs only after the winding up of the corporation's affairs, the liquidation of its assets, and the distribution of the proceeds to the claimants. The liquidated assets are paid to claimants according to the following priority: (1) expenses of liquidation and creditors according to their respective liens and contract rights, (2) preferred shareholders according to their liquidation preferences and contract rights, and (3) common stockholders.

Multinational Corporations

multinational corporation
(transnational corporation)
A corporation that operates in more than one country.

Many of the largest corporations in the world are **multinational corporations**—that is, corporations that operate in many countries. These corporations are also called **transnational corporations**. Multinational corporations operate in other countries through a variety of means, including the use of agents, branch offices, subsidiary corporations, business alliances, strategic partnerships, franchising, and other arrangements.

The following feature discusses a U.S. federal law that applies to bribery in the international environment.

Did you ever expect a corporation to have a conscience, when it has no soul to be damned, and no body to be kicked?

Lord Edward Thurlow, first
Baron Thurlow

International Law

Foreign Corrupt Practices Act

BRIBERY BY U.S. COMPANIES IN FOREIGN COUNTRIES
It is well known that the payment of bribes is pervasive in conducting international business. To prevent U.S. companies from engaging in this type of conduct, the U.S. Congress enacted the **Foreign Corrupt Practices Act (FCPA).**[2] *The FCPA makes it illegal for U.S. companies, or their officers, directors, agents, or employees, to bribe a foreign official, a foreign political party official, or a candidate for foreign political office. A bribe is illegal only where it is meant to influence the awarding of new business or the retention of a continuing business activity.*

Key Terms and Concepts

Administrative
    dissolution (346)
Alien corporation (333)
Annual shareholders'
    meeting (339)
Articles of dissolution
    (346)
Articles of incorporation
    (corporate charter)
    (333)
Authorized shares (337)

Board of directors
    (341)
Bond (337)
Business judgment rule
    (344)
Bylaws (334)
C corporation (335)
CEO and CFO
    certification (345)
Certificate of dissolution
    (346)

Closely held corporation
    (332)
Common stock (336)
Common stock
    certificate (336)
Common stockholder
    (336)
Competing with the
    corporation (344)
Convertible preferred
    stock (336)

Corporate electronic
    communications
    (corporate
    e-communications)
    (342)
Corporate management
    (330)
Corporate officer (343)
Corporation (330)
Corporation code (330)
Court of chancery (338)

Cumulative preferred stock (336)
Cumulative voting (340)
Debenture (337)
Debt securities (fixed income securities) (337)
Delaware General Corporation Law (338)
Dividend preference (336)
Dividends (340)
Domain name (333)
Domestic corporation (333)
Double taxation (335)
Duty of care (344)
Duty of loyalty (344)
Equity securities (stocks) (335)
Fiduciary duties (343)
Fixed dividend (336)
Foreign corporation (333)
Foreign Corrupt Practices Act (FCPA) (347)
Form 2553 (335)
Free transferability of shares (330)

Indenture agreement (indenture) (337)
Inside director (341)
Issued shares (337)
Legal entity (legal person) (330)
Limited liability of shareholders (330)
Liquidation preference (336)
Merged corporation (345)
Merger (345)
Model Business Corporation Act (MBCA) (332)
Multinational corporation (transnational corporation) (346)
Negligence (344)
Note (337)
Organizational meeting (335)
Outside director (341)
Outstanding shares (337)
Participating preferred stock (336)
Perpetual existence (330)

Piercing the corporate veil (alter ego doctrine) (340)
Preferred stock (336)
Preferred stock certificate (336)
Preferred stockholder (336)
Proxy (proxy card) (339)
Publicly held corporation (332)
Quorum (339)
Redeemable preferred stock (callable preferred stock) (336)
Registered agent (333)
Regular meetings of a board of directors (342)
Revised Model Business Corporation Act (RMBCA) (332)
S corporation (335)
Sarbanes-Oxley Act (344)
Secret profit (344)
Self-dealing (344)
Shareholders (338)

Shareholder resolution (341)
Special meetings of the board of directors (342)
Special shareholders' meeting (339)
Straight voting (noncumulative voting) (340)
Subchapter S corporation (335)
Subchapter S Revision Act (335)
Supramajority voting requirement (supermajority voting requirement) (340)
Surviving corporation (345)
Termination (346)
Treasury shares (337)
Unissued shares (337)
Usurping a corporate opportunity (344)
Voluntary dissolution (346)
Winding up and liquidation (346)

Law Case with Answer

Smith v. Van Gorkom

Facts   Trans Union Corporation (Trans Union) was a publicly traded, diversified holding company that was incorporated in Delaware. Its principal earnings were generated by its railcar leasing business. Jerome W. Van Gorkom was a Trans Union officer for more than twenty-four years, its chief executive officer for more than seventeen years, and the chairman of the board of directors for two years. Van Gorkom, a lawyer and certified public accountant, owned 75,000 shares of Trans Union. He was approaching sixty-five years of age and mandatory retirement. Trans Union's board of directors was composed of ten members—five inside directors and five outside directors.

Van Gorkom decided to meet with Jay A. Pritzker, a well-known corporate takeover specialist and a social acquaintance of Van Gorkom's, to discuss the possible sale of Trans Union to Pritzker. Van Gorkom met Pritzker at Pritzker's home on Saturday. He did so without consulting Trans Union's board of directors. At this meeting, Van Gorkom proposed a sale of Trans Union to Pritzker at a price of $55 per share. The stock was trading at about $38 in the market. On Monday, Pritzker notified Van Gorkom that he was interested in

the $55 cash-out merger proposal. Van Gorkom, along with two inside directors, privately met with Pritzker on Tuesday and Wednesday. After meeting with Van Gorkom on Thursday, Pritzker notified his attorney to begin drafting the merger documents.

On Friday, Van Gorkom called a special meeting of Trans Union's board of directors for the following day. The board members were not told the purpose of the meeting. At the meeting, Van Gorkom disclosed the Pritzker offer and described its terms in a twenty-minute presentation. Neither the merger agreement nor a written summary of the terms of agreement was furnished to the directors. No valuation study as to the value of Trans Union was prepared for the meeting. After two hours, the board voted in favor of the cash-out merger with Pritzker's company at $55 per share for Trans Union's stock. The board also voted not to solicit other offers. The merger agreement was executed by Van Gorkom on Saturday evening, at a formal social event he hosted for the opening of the Chicago Lyric Opera's season. Neither he nor any other director read the agreement prior to its signing and delivery to Pritzker.

Trans Union's board of directors recommended the merger be approved by its shareholders and distributed proxy materials to the shareholders stating that the $55 per share price for their stock was fair. In the meantime, Trans Union's board of directors took steps to dissuade two other possible suitors who showed interest in purchasing Trans Union. Subsequently, 69.9 percent of the shares of Trans Union stock were voted in favor of the merger. The merger was consummated. Alden Smith and other Trans Union shareholders sued Van Gorkom and the other directors for damages. The plaintiffs alleged that the defendant directors were negligent in their conduct in selling Trans Union to Pritzker. Did Trans Union's directors breach their duty of care?

Answer Yes, the directors of Trans Union breached their duty of care to the corporation and its shareholders. In the context of a proposed merger, a director has a duty to act in an informed and deliberate manner in determining whether to approve an agreement of merger. Here, (1) the directors did not adequately inform themselves as to Van Gorkom's role in forcing the sale of the company and in establishing the per-share purchase price; (2) they were uninformed as to the intrinsic value of the company; and

(3) given these circumstances, at a minimum, they were grossly negligent in approving the sale of the company upon two hours' consideration, without prior notice, and without the exigency of a crisis or emergency.

Without any documents before them concerning the proposed transaction, the members of the board were required to rely entirely upon Van Gorkom's twenty-minute oral presentation of the proposal. No written summary of the terms of the merger was presented; the directors were given no documentation to support the adequacy of $55 price per share for sale of the company; and the board had before it nothing more than Van Gorkom's statement of his understanding of the substance of an agreement that he admittedly had never read or that any member of the board had ever seen.

Thus, the record compels the conclusion that the board lacked valuation information to reach an informed business judgment as to the fairness of $55 per share for sale of the company. Trans Union's board was grossly negligent in that it failed to act with informed reasonable deliberation in agreeing to the Pritzker merger proposal. *Smith v. Van Gorkom*, 488 A.2d 858, **Web** 1985 Del. Lexis 421 (Supreme Court of Delaware)

Critical Legal Thinking Cases

16.1 Piercing the Corporate Veil Local farmers in Manchester, Iowa, decided to build an ethanol plant. The farmers and other investors invested $3,865,000 and formed Northeast Iowa Ethanol, LLC (Northeast Iowa), to hold the money and develop the project. The project needed another $20 million, for which financing needed to be secured.

Jerry Drizin formed Global Syndicate International, Inc. (GSI), a Nevada corporation, with $250 capital. Drizin formed GSI for the purpose of assisting Northeast Iowa to raise the additional financing for the project. Drizin talked Northeast Iowa into transferring its money to GSI, and the money was placed in a bank in south Florida to serve as security for a possible loan. Drizin commingled those funds with his own personal funds. Through an array of complex transfers by GSI, the funds of Northeast Iowa were stolen. Some funds were invested in a worthless gold mine and other worthless investments.

Plaintiff Northeast Iowa sued Drizin for civil fraud to recover its funds. Drizin defended, arguing that GSI, the corporation, was liable but that he was not personally liable because he was but a shareholder of GSI. The plaintiffs alleged that the doctrine of piercing the corporate veil applied and that Drizin was therefore personally liable for the funds. Who wins? *Northeast Iowa Ethanol, LLC v. Drizin*, **Web** 2006 U.S. Dist. Lexis 4828 (United States District Court for the Northern District of Iowa)

16.2 Limited Liability of Shareholders Joseph M. Billy was an employee of the USM Corporation (USM), a publicly held corporation. Billy was at work when a 4,600-pound ram from a vertical boring mill broke loose and crushed him to death. Billy's widow sued, alleging that the accident was caused by certain defects in the manufacture and design of the vertical boring mill and the two moving parts directly involved in the accident, a metal lifting arm and the 4,600-pound ram. If Mrs. Billy's suit is successful, can the shareholders of USM be held personally liable for any judgment against USM? *Billy v. Consolidated Machine Tool Corp.*, 51 N.Y.2d 152, 412 N.E.2d 934, 432 N.Y.S.2d 879, **Web** 1980 N.Y. Lexis 2638 (Court of Appeals of New York)

16.3 Corporation Leo V. Mysels was the president of Florida Fashions of Interior Design, Inc. (Florida Fashions). Florida Fashions, which was a Pennsylvania corporation, had never registered to do business in the state of Florida. While acting in the capacity of a salesman for the corporation, Mysels took an order for goods from Francis E. Barry. The transaction took place in Florida. Barry paid Florida Fashions for the goods ordered. When Florida Fashions failed to perform its obligations under the sales agreement, Barry brought suit in Florida. What type of corporation is Florida Fashions in regard to the state of Pennsylvania and in regard to the state of Florida? Can Florida Fashions defend itself in a lawsuit? *Mysels v. Barry*, 332 So.2d 38, **Web** 1976 Fla.App. Lexis 14344 (Court of Appeal of Florida)

16.4 Debt Security   United Financial Corporation of California (United Financial) was incorporated in the state of Delaware. United Financial owned the majority of a California savings and loan association as well as three insurance agencies. The next year, the original investors in United Financial decided to capitalize on an increase in investor interest in savings and loans. The first public offering of United Federal stock was made. The stock was sold as a unit, with sixty thousand units being offered. Each unit consisted of two shares of United Financial stock and one $100, 5 percent interest-bearing debenture bond. This initial offering was a success. It provided $7.2 million to the corporation, of which $6.2 million was distributed as a return of capital to the original investors. What is the difference between the stock offered for sale by United Financial and the debenture bonds? *Jones v. H.F. Ahmanson & Company*, 1 Cal. 3d 93, 460 P.2d 464, 81 Cal.Rptr. 592, **Web** 1969 Cal. Lexis 195 (Supreme Court of California)

16.5 Special Shareholders' Meeting   Jack C. Schoenholtz was a shareholder and member of the board of directors of Rye Psychiatric Hospital Center, Inc. (Rye Hospital). Four years after the hospital was incorporated, a split had developed among the board of directors concerning the operation of the facility. Three directors stood on one side of the dispute, and three directors stood on the other side. In an attempt to break the deadlock, Schoenholtz, who owned over 10 percent of the corporation's voting stock, asked the corporation's secretary to call a special meeting of the shareholders. In response, the secretary sent a notice to the shareholders, stating that a special meeting of the shareholders would be held "for the purpose of electing directors." The meeting was held as scheduled. Some shareholders brought suit, claiming that the special shareholders' meeting was not called properly. Who wins? *Rye Psychiatric Hospital Center, Inc. v. Schoenholtz*, 101 A.D.2d 309, 476 N.Y.S.2d 339, **Web** 1984 N.Y.App. Div. Lexis 17818 (Supreme Court of New York)

16.6 Dividends   Gay's Super Markets, Inc. (Super Markets), was a corporation formed under the laws of the state of Maine. Hannaford Bros. Company held 51 percent of the corporation's common stock. Lawrence F. Gay and his brother Carrol were both minority shareholders in Super Markets. Lawrence Gay was also the manager of the corporation's store at Machias, Maine. One day, he was dismissed from his job. At the meeting of Super Markets's board of directors, a decision was made not to declare a stock dividend for the prior year. The directors cited expected losses from increased competition and the expense of opening a new store as reasons for not paying a dividend. Lawrence Gay claims that the reason for not paying a dividend was to force him to sell his shares in Super Markets. Lawrence sued to force the corporation to declare a dividend. Who wins? *Gay v. Gay's Super Markets, Inc.*, 343 A.2d 577, **Web** 1975 Me. Lexis 391 (Supreme Judicial Court of Maine)

16.7 Duty of Loyalty   Edward Hellenbrand ran a comedy club known as the Comedy Cottage in Rosemont, Illinois. The business was incorporated, with Hellenbrand and his wife as the corporation's sole shareholders. The corporation leased the premises in which the club was located. Hellenbrand hired Jay Berk as general manager of the club. Two years later, Berk was made vice president of the corporation and given 10 percent of its stock. Hellenbrand experienced health problems and moved to Nevada, leaving Berk to manage the daily affairs of the business. Four years later, the ownership of the building where the Comedy Cottage was located changed hands. Shortly thereafter, the club's lease on the premises expired. Hellenbrand instructed Berk to negotiate a new lease. Berk arranged a month-to-month lease but had the lease agreement drawn up in his name instead of that of the corporation. When Hellenbrand learned of Berk's move, he fired him. Berk continued to lease the building in his own name and opened his own club, the Comedy Company, Inc., there. Hellenbrand sued Berk for an injunction to prevent Berk from leasing the building. Who wins? *Comedy Cottage, Inc. v. Berk*, 145 Ill.App.3d 355, 495 N.E.2d 1006, **Web** 1986 Ill.App. Lexis 2486 (Appellate Court of Illinois)

16.8 Shareholder Resolution   The Medical Committee for Human Rights (Committee), a nonprofit corporation organized to advance concerns for human life, received a gift of shares of Dow Chemical (Dow) stock. Dow manufactured napalm, a chemical defoliant that was used during the Vietnam Conflict. Committee objected to the sale of napalm by Dow primarily because of its concerns for human life. Committee owned sufficient shares for a long enough time to propose a shareholders' resolution, as long as it met the other requirements to propose such a resolution. Committee proposed that the following resolution be included in the proxy materials circulated by management for the annual shareholders' meeting:

RESOLVED, that the shareholders of the Dow Chemical company request that the Board of Directors, in accordance with the law, consider the advisability of adopting a resolution setting forth an amendment to the composite certificate of incorporation of the Dow Chemical Company that the company shall not make napalm.

Dow's management refused to include the requested resolution in its proxy materials. Committee sued, alleging that its resolution met the requirements to be included in the proxy materials. Who wins? *Medical Committee for Human Rights v. Securities and Exchange Commission*, 139 U.S. App. D.C. 226, 432 F.2d 659, **Web** 1970 U.S. App. Lexis 8284 (United States Court of Appeals for the District of Columbia Circuit)

Ethics Cases

16.9 Ethics   Lawrence Gaffney was the president and general manager of Ideal Tape Company (Ideal). Ideal, which was a subsidiary of Chelsea Industries, Inc. (Chelsea), was engaged in the business of manufacturing pressure-sensitive tape. Gaffney recruited three other Ideal executives to join him in starting a tape manufacturing business. The four men remained at Ideal for the two years it took them to plan the new enterprise. During this time, they used their positions at Ideal to travel around the country to gather business ideas, recruit potential customers, and purchase equipment for their business. At no time did they reveal to Chelsea their intention to open a competing business. The new business was incorporated as Action Manufacturing Company (Action). When executives at Chelsea discovered the existence of the new venture, Gaffney and the others resigned from Chelsea. Chelsea sued Gaffney and the others to recover damages. *Chelsea Industries, Inc. v. Gaffney*, 389 Mass. 1, 449 N.E.2d 320, **Web** 1983 Mass. Lexis 1413 (Supreme Judicial Court of Massachusetts)

1. What is the fiduciary duty of loyalty?
2. Did Gaffney act ethically in this case?
3. Did Gaffney and his partners breach their fiduciary duty of loyalty?

16.10 Ethics   M.R. Watters was the majority shareholder of several closely held corporations, including Wildhorn Ranch, Inc. (Wildhorn). All these businesses were run out of Watters's home in Rocky Ford, Colorado. Wildhorn operated a resort called the Wildhorn Ranch Resort in Teller County, Colorado. Although Watters claimed that the ranch was owned by the corporation, the deed for the property listed Watters as the owner. Watters paid little attention to corporate formalities, holding corporate meetings at his house, never taking minutes of those meetings, and paying the debts of one corporation with the assets of another. During a vacation visit, two guests of Wildhorn Ranch Resort drowned while operating a paddleboat at the ranch. The family of the deceased guests sued Watters to recover from Watters. *Geringer v. Wildhorn Ranch, Inc.*, 706 F.Supp. 1442, **Web** 1988 U.S. Dist. Lexis 15701 (United States District Court for the District of Colorado)

1. What does the doctrine of piercing the corporate veil provide?
2. Did Watters act ethically in denying liability on the contract?
3. Is Watters personally liable in this case?

Internet Exercises

1. Select a name you would like to use as a corporate name. Go to the website of the U.S. Patent and Trademark Office, at **www.uspto.gov**. Click on "Trademarks" and then "Search Marks" and check to see if the name you have chosen has been trademarked.

2. Visit the website of Network Solutions, at **www.networksolutions.com**. Pick out a name that you would like to get as a domain name. Check the availability of that domain name.

3. Go to **www.harley-davidson.com/en_US/media/downloads/Foundation/Articles_of_Incorporation.pdf** to view the articles of incorporation of Harley-Davidson, Inc.

4. Go to **http://investor.harley-davidson.com/CorporateGovernance.cfm?locale=en_US&bmLocale=en_US** to view the bylaws of Harley-Davidson, Inc.

5. Go to the website of the Delaware Division of Corporations, at **http://corp.delaware.gov/faqs.shtml**. Read about incorporating a corporation on Delaware.

Endnotes

1. Public Law 107-204 (2002).
2. 26 U.S.C. Section 6242 et seq.

CHAPTER

17 Investor Protection, E-Securities, and Wall Street Reform

NEW YORK STOCK EXCHANGE
This is the home of the New York Stock Exchange (NYSE) in New York City. The NYSE, nicknamed the Big Board, is the premier stock exchange in the world. It lists the stocks and securities of approximately 3,000 of the world's largest companies for trading. The origin of the NYSE dates to 1792, when several stockbrokers met under a buttonwood tree on Wall Street. The NYSE is located at 11 Wall Street, which has been designated a National Historic Landmark. The NYSE is now operated by NYSE Euronext, which was formed when the NYSE merged with the fully electronic stock exchange Euronext.

Learning Objectives

After studying this chapter, you should be able to:

1. Describe the procedure for going public and how securities are registered with the Securities and Exchange Commission.
2. Describe the requirements for qualifying for private placement, intrastate, and small offering exemptions from registration.
3. Describe insider trading that violates Section 10(b) of the Securities Exchange Act of 1934.
4. Describe e-securities transactions.
5. Describe how provisions of the Sarbanes-Oxley Act and the Dodd-Frank Wall Street Reform and Consumer Protection Act increase investor protection.

Chapter Outline

Introduction to Investor Protection, E-Securities, and Wall Street Reform

Securities Law
 LANDMARK LAW • *Federal Securities Laws*

Securities and Exchange Commission (SEC)

Definition of *Security*

Initial Public Offering

E-Securities Transactions

Securities Exempt from Registration

Transactions Exempt from Registration

Sarbanes-Oxley Act
 ETHICS • *Sarbanes-Oxley Act Erects Wall Between Investment Bankers and Securities Analysts*

Trading in Securities
 CASE 17.1 • *United States v. Bhagat*

Short-Swing Profits

Chapter Outline *(continued)*

Dodd-Frank Wall Street Reform and Consumer Protection Act
   CONTEMPORARY ENVIRONMENT • *Dodd-Frank Wall Street Reform and Consumer Protection*
   Act Regulates Hedge Funds and Derivatives
State "Blue-Sky" Laws

" *When there is blood on the street, I am buying.* "

—Nathaniel Mayer Victor Rothschild, third Baron Rothschild

Introduction to Investor Protection, E-Securities, and Wall Street Reform

Prior to the 1920s and 1930s, the securities markets in this country were not regulated by the federal government. Securities were issued and sold to investors with little, if any, disclosure. Fraud in these transactions was common. Unregulated securities markets and trading have been blamed as one of the causes of the Great Depression that the country suffered during the 1930s. To respond to this lack of regulation, in the early 1930s Congress enacted federal securities statutes to regulate the securities markets. The federal securities statutes were designed to require disclosure of information to investors, provide for the regulation of securities issues and trading, and prevent fraud. Today, many securities are issued over the Internet. These e-securities transactions are subject to federal regulation.

Congress enacted the *Sarbanes-Oxley Act*[1] of 2002 to bring more transparency to securities markets and to eliminate conflicts of interests that previously existed in the securities industry. In 2010, Congress enacted the *Dodd-Frank Wall Street Reform and Consumer Protection Act*[2] to regulate hedge funds, derivatives, and abusive practices in the securities industry.

This chapter discusses federal securities laws, e-securities transactions, investor protection, and securities reform.

The insiders here were not trading on an equal footing with the outside investors.

Judge Waterman
Securities and Exchange Commission v. Texas Gulf Sulphur Company (1968)

Securities Law

The federal and state governments have enacted statutes that regulate the issuance and trading of securities. The primary purpose of these acts is to promote full disclosure to investors and to prevent fraud in the issuance and trading of securities. These federal and state statutes are enforced by federal and state regulatory authorities, respectively. The following feature discusses major federal securities statutes.

Landmark Law

Federal Securities Laws

Following the stock market crash of 1929, Congress enacted a series of statutes designed to regulate securities markets. These federal securities statutes are designed to require disclosure to investors and prevent securities fraud. The two primary securities statutes enacted by the federal government, both of which were enacted during the

(continued)

Great Depression years, are the *Securities Act of 1933* and the *Securities Exchange Act of 1934*.

The Securities Act of 1933 is a federal statute that primarily regulates the issue of securities by companies and other businesses. This act applies to original issue of securities, both initial public offerings (IPOs) by new public companies and sales of new securities by established companies. The primary purpose of this act is to require full and honest disclosure of information to investors at the time of the issuance of the securities. The act also prohibits fraud during the sale of issued securities. Securities are now issued online, and the 1933 act regulates the issue of securities online.

The Securities Exchange Act of 1934 is a federal statute primarily designed to prevent fraud in the subsequent trading of securities. This act has been applied to prohibit insider trading and other frauds in the purchase and sale of securities in the after markets, such as trading on securities exchanges and other purchases and sales of securities. The act also requires continuous reporting—annual reports, quarterly reports, and other reports—to investors and the Securities and Exchange Commission (SEC). Securities are now sold online and on electronic stock exchanges. The 1934 act regulates the purchase and sale of securities online.

The SEC is a federal administrative agency that administers federal securities statutes.

WEB EXERCISE
Go to the website of the Securities and Exchange Commission at **www.sec.gov**. Click on "What We Do" and read the introduction.

Securities and Exchange Commission (SEC)
The federal administrative agency that is empowered to administer federal securities laws. The SEC can adopt rules and regulations to interpret and implement federal securities laws.

security
(1) An interest or instrument that is common stock, preferred stock, a bond, a debenture, or a warrant; (2) an interest or instrument that is expressly mentioned in securities acts; or (3) an investment contract.

Anyone who thinks there's safety in numbers hasn't looked at the stock market pages.

Irene Peter

investment contract
A flexible standard for defining a security.

Securities and Exchange Commission (SEC)

The Securities Exchange Act of 1934 created the **Securities and Exchange Commission (SEC)** and empowered it to administer federal securities laws. The SEC is an administrative agency composed of five members who are appointed by the president. The major responsibilities of the SEC are:

- Adopting **rules** (also called **regulations**) that further the purpose of the federal securities statutes. These rules have the force of law.
- Investigating alleged securities violations and bringing enforcement actions against suspected violators. This may include recommendations of criminal prosecution. Criminal prosecutions of violations of federal securities laws are brought by the U.S. Department of Justice.
- The SEC may bring a civil action to recover monetary damages from violators of securities laws. A "whistleblower bounty program" allows a person who provides information that leads to a successful SEC action to recover 10 percent to 30 percent of the monetary sanctions over $1 million recovered by the SEC.
- Regulating the activities of securities brokers and advisors. This includes registering brokers and advisors and taking enforcement action against those who violate securities laws.

Definition of *Security*

Congress has enacted the Securities Act of 1933, the Securities Exchange Act of 1934, and several other securities statutes to regulate the issuance and sale of securities. For these federal statutes to apply, however, a **security** must first be found. Federal securities laws define securities as:

- **Common securities.**   Interests or instruments that are commonly known as securities are **common securities**.

  Examples Common stock, preferred stock, bonds, debentures, and warrants are common securities.

- **Statutorily defined securities.**   Interests or instruments that are expressly mentioned in securities acts are **statutorily defined securities**.

  Examples The securities acts specifically define preorganization subscription agreements; interests in oil, gas, and mineral rights; and deposit receipts for foreign securities as securities.

- **Investment contracts.**   A statutory term that permits courts to define **investment contracts** as securities. The courts apply the *Howey* test[3] in determining whether an arrangement is an investment contract and therefore a security. Under this test, an arrangement is considered an investment contract if there is an investment of money by an investor in a common enterprise and the investor expects to make profits based on the sole or substantial efforts of the promoter or others.

Examples A limited partnership interest is an investment contract because the limited partner expects to make money based on the effort of the general partners. Pyramid sales schemes where persons give money to a promoter who promises them a high rate of return on their investment is an investment contract because the investors expect to make money from the efforts of the promoter.

Example **Mutual funds** sells shares to the public, make investments in stocks and bonds for the long term, and are restricted from investing in risky investments. Because mutual funds sell to the public, they must be registered with the SEC.

Howey **test**
A test which states that an arrangement is an investment contract if there is an investment of money by an investor in a common enterprise and the investor expects to make profits based on the sole or substantial efforts of the promoter or others.

CONCEPT SUMMARY

DEFINITION OF *SECURITY*

Type of Security	Definition
Common securities	Interests or instruments that are commonly known as securities, such as common stock, preferred stock, debentures, and warrants.
Statutorily defined securities	Interests and instruments that are expressly mentioned in securities acts as being securities, such as interests in oil, gas, and mineral rights.
Investment contracts	A flexible standard for defining a security. Under the Howey test, a security exists if an investor invests money in a common enterprise and expects to make a profit from the significant efforts of others.

Initial Public Offering

The **Securities Act of 1933** primarily regulates the issuance of securities by corporations, limited partnerships, and companies.[4] **Section 5 of the Securities Act of 1933** requires securities offered to the *public* through the use of the mails or any facility of interstate commerce to be registered with the SEC by means of a registration statement and an accompanying prospectus.

A business or party selling securities to the public is called an **issuer**. An issuer may be a new company (e.g., Skype) that is selling securities to the public for the first time. This is referred to as **going public**. Or the issuer may be an established company (e.g., General Motors Corporation) that sells a new security to the public. The issuance of securities by an issuer is called an **initial public offering (IPO)**.

Many issuers of securities employ **investment bankers**, which are independent securities companies, to sell their securities to the public. Issuers pay a fee to investment bankers for this service.

Securities Act of 1933
A federal statute that primarily regulates the issuance of securities by corporations, limited partnerships, and associations.

Section 5 of the Securities Act of 1933
A section that requires an issuer to register its securities with the SEC prior to selling them to the public.

initial public offering (IPO)
The sale of securities by an issuer to the public

Registration Statement

A covered issuer must file a written **registration statement** with the SEC. The issuer's lawyer normally prepares this statement with the help of the issuer's management, accountants, and underwriters.

A registration statement must contain descriptions of (1) the securities being offered for sale; (2) the registrant's business; (3) the management of the registrant, including compensation, stock options and benefits, and material transactions with the registrant; (4) pending litigation; (5) how the proceeds from the offering will be used; (6) government regulation; (7) the degree of competition in the industry; and (8) any special risk factors. In addition, a registration

registration statement
A document that an issuer of securities files with the SEC that contains required information about the issuer, the securities to be issued, and other relevant information.

statement must be accompanied by financial statements certified by certified public accountants.

Registration statements usually become effective (the **effective date**) twenty business days after they are filed, unless the SEC requires additional information to be disclosed. A new twenty-day period begins each time a registration statement is amended. At the registrant's request, the SEC may "accelerate the *effective date*" (i.e., not require the registrant to wait twenty days after the last amendment is filed).

The SEC does not pass judgment on the merits of the securities offered. It decides only whether the issuer has met the disclosure requirements.

Prospectus

A **prospectus** is a written disclosure document that must be submitted to the SEC along with the registration statement. A prospectus is used as a selling tool by the issuer. It is provided to prospective investors to enable them to evaluate the financial risk of an investment.

A prospectus must contain the following language in capital letters and boldface (usually red) type:

THESE SECURITIES HAVE NOT BEEN APPROVED OR DISAPPROVED BY THE SECURITIES AND EXCHANGE COMMISSION OR ANY STATE SECURITIES COMMISSION NOR HAS THE SECURITIES AND EXCHANGE COMMISSION OR ANY STATE SECURITIES COMMISSION PASSED UPON THE ACCURACY OR ADEQUACY OF THIS PROSPECTUS. ANY REPRESENTATION TO THE CONTRARY IS A CRIMINAL OFFENSE.

Sale of Unregistered Securities

Sale of securities that should have been registered with the SEC but were not violates the Securities Act of 1933. Investors can rescind their purchase and recover damages. The U.S. government can impose criminal penalties on any person who willfully violates the Securities Act of 1933.

Example A corporation sells shares of its stock to the public but did not register its stock offering with the SEC. Here, because there has been a sale of unregistered securities, the purchasers can rescind their purchase of the stock and get their money back (which is often highly unlikely). If the company willfully did not register the securities, the U.S. government can file a criminal lawsuit to seek criminal penalties against the responsible individuals and the company.

Regulation A Offering

Regulation A
A regulation that permits an issuer to sell securities pursuant to a simplified registration process.

Regulation A permits issuers to sell up to $5 million of securities to the public during a 12-month period, pursuant to a simplified registration process. Such offerings may have an unlimited number of purchasers who do not have to be accredited investors. Issuers with offerings exceeding $100,000 must file an **offering statement** with the SEC. An offering statement requires less disclosure than a registration statement and is less costly to prepare. Investors must be provided with an offering circular prior to the purchase of securities. The issuer can advertise the sale of the security. There are no **resale restrictions** on the securities.

Small Company Offering Registration (SCOR)
A method for small companies to sell up to $1 million of securities to the public by using a question-and-answer disclosure form called Form U-7.

Small Company Offering Registration (SCOR)   Small businesses often need to raise capital and must find public investors to buy company stock. After years of investigation, the SEC amended Regulation A by adopting the **Small Company Offering Registration (SCOR)**. The SCOR form, **Form U-7**, is a question-and-answer disclosure form that small businesses can complete and file with the SEC if they plan on raising $1 million or less from the public issue of securities. An issuer must answer the questions on Form U-7, which then becomes the offering circular that must be given to prospective investors.

Form U-7 questions are so clearly and specifically drawn that they can be answered by the issuer without the help of an expensive securities lawyer. SCOR form questions require the issuer to develop a business plan that states specific company goals and how it intends to reach them. The SCOR form is available only to domestic businesses. A SCOR form offering cannot exceed $1 million, and the offering price of the common stock or its equivalent may not be less than $5 per share.

SCOR form offerings are a welcome addition for entrepreneur-owners who want to raise money through a small public offering. The SCOR Form U-7 has been adopted or accepted in almost all states.

WEB EXERCISE
Go to **http://com.ohio.gov/secu/ docs\U-7.pdf**. Review Form U-7 to determine what information an issuer must provide when completing the form.

Civil Liability Under Section 11 of the Securities Act of 1933

Private parties who have been injured by certain registration statement violations by an issuer or others may bring a **civil action** against the violator under **Section 11 of the Securities Act of 1933**. Plaintiffs may recover monetary damages when a registration statement on its effective date misstates or omits a material fact. Liability under Section 11 is imposed on those who (1) intentionally defraud investors or (2) are negligent in not discovering the fraud. Thus, the issuer, certain corporate officers (e.g., chief executive officer, chief financial officer, chief accounting officer), directors, signers of the registration statement, underwriters, and experts (e.g., accountants who certify financial statements and lawyers who issue legal opinions that are included in a registration statement) may be liable.

All defendants except the issuer may assert a **due diligence defense** against the imposition of Section 11 liability. If this defense is proven, the defendant is not liable. To establish a due diligence defense, the defendant must prove that after reasonable investigation, he or she had reasonable grounds to believe and did believe that, at the time the registration statement became effective, the statements contained therein were true, and there was no omission of material facts.

Section 11 of the Securities Act of 1933
A provision of the Securities Act of 1933 that imposes civil liability on persons who intentionally defraud investors by making misrepresentations or omissions of material facts in the registration statement or who are negligent for not discovering the fraud.

Example In the classic case ***Escott v. BarChris Construction Corporation***,[5] the company was going to issue a new bond to the public. The company prepared financial statements wherein the company overstated current assets, understated current liabilities, overstated sales, overstated gross profits, overstated the backlog of orders, did not disclose loans to officers, did not disclose customer delinquencies in paying for goods, and lied about the use of the proceeds from the offering. The company gave these financial statements to its auditors, Peat, Marwick, Mitchell & Co. (Peat Marwick), who did not discover the lies. Peat Marwick certified the financial statements that became part of the registration statement filed with the SEC. The bonds were sold to the public. One year later, the company filed for bankruptcy. The bondholders sued Russo, the chief executive officer (CEO) of BarChris; Vitolo and Puglies, the founders of the business and the president and vice president, respectively; Trilling, the controller; and Peat Marwick, the auditors. Each defendant pleaded the due diligence defense. The court rejected each of the party's defenses, finding that the CEO, president, vice president, and controller were all in positions to either have created or discovered the misrepresentations. The court also found that the auditor, Peat Marwick, did not do a proper investigation and had not proven its due diligence defense. The court found that the defendants had violated Section 11 of the Securities Act of 1933 by submitting misrepresentations and omissions of material facts in the registration statement filed with the SEC.

Civil Liability Under Section 12 of the Securities Act of 1933

Private parties who have been injured by certain securities violations may bring a *civil action* against the violator under **Section 12 of the Securities Act of 1933**. Section 12 imposes civil liability on any person who violates the provisions of Section 5 of the act. Violations include selling securities pursuant to an unwarranted exemption and making misrepresentations concerning the offer or sale of securities. The purchaser's remedy for a violation of Section 12 is either to rescind the purchase or to sue for damages.

Example Technology Inc., a corporation, issues securities to investors without qualifying for any of the exempt transactions permitted under the Securities Exchange Act. The securities decrease in value. Here, the issuer has issued unregistered securities to the public. The investors can sue the issuer to rescind the purchase agreement and get their money back or to sue and recover monetary damages.

SEC Actions Under the Securities Act of 1933

The SEC may take certain legal actions against parties who violate the Securities Act of 1933. The SEC may (1) issue a **consent decree** whereby a defendant agrees not to violate securities laws in the future but does not admit to having violated securities laws in the past, (2) bring an action in U.S. District Court to obtain an **injunction** to stop challenged conduct, or (3) request the court to grant ancillary relief, such as *disgorgement of profits* by the defendant.

Criminal Liability Under the Securities Act of 1933

Section 24 of the Securities Act of 1933 imposes *criminal liability* on any person who *willfully* violates either the act or the rules and regulations adopted thereunder.[6] A violator may be fined or imprisoned up to 5 years or both. Criminal actions are brought by the Department of Justice.

E-Securities Transactions

The **Internet** has become an important vehicle of the disclosure of information about companies, online trading, and the public issuance of securities. Securities—stocks and bonds—are purchased and sold **online** worldwide by millions of persons and businesses each day. Individuals and businesses can open accounts at online stock brokers, such as Charles Schwab, Ameritrade, and others, and freely trade securities and manage their accounts online. **Electronic securities transactions,** or **e-securities transactions** are becoming commonplace in disseminating information to investors, trading in securities, and issuing stocks and other securities to the public. E-securities transactions will become an even more important medium for offering, selling, and purchasing securities.

E-Securities Exchanges

The **New York Stock Exchange (NYSE)** is operated by **NYSE Euronext**, which was formed when the NYSE merged with the fully electronic stock exchange Euronext. The NYSE lists the stocks and securities of approximately 3,000 of world's largest companies for trading. These companies include Ford Motor Company, IBM Corporation, The Coca-Cola Company, China Mobile Communications Corporation, and others.

The **National Association of Securities Dealers Automated Quotation System (NASDAQ)** is an *electronic stock market*. NASDAQ has the largest trading

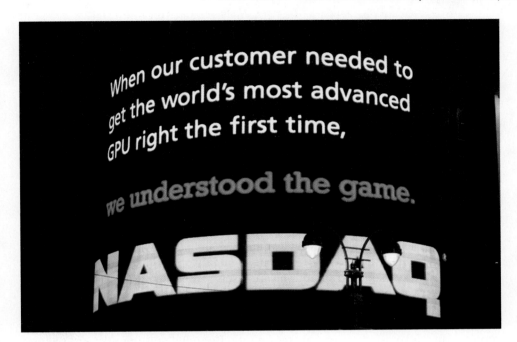

NASDAQ
NASDAQ is the world's largest electronic securities exchange. It lists more than 3,500 U.S. and global companies and corporations.

volume of any securities exchange in the world. More than three thousand companies are traded on NASDAQ, including companies such as Microsoft Corporation, Yahoo! Inc., Starbucks Corporation, Amazon.com, Inc., and eBay Inc., as well as companies from China, India, and other countries from around the world. NASDAQ, which is located in New York City, owns interests in electronic stock exchanges around the world.

EDGAR

Most public company documents—such as annual and quarterly reports—are now available online. The SEC requires both foreign and domestic companies to file registration statements, periodic reports, and other forms on its electronic filing and forms system, **EDGAR**, the SEC electronic data and records system. Anyone can access and download this information for free.

EDGAR
The electronic data and record system of the Securities and Exchange Commission (SEC).

WEB EXERCISE
Visit the website of EDGAR, at **www.sec.gov/edgar.shtml**. Click on "About EDGAR." Read the first two paragraphs of "Important Information About EDGAR."

E-Public Offerings

Companies are now *issuing* shares of stock over the Internet. This includes companies that are making **electronic initial public offerings**, or **e-initial public offerings (e-IPOs)**, by selling stock to the public for the first time. E-securities offerings provide an efficient way to distribute securities to the public. Google Inc. is one of the most famous IPOs to be conducted online.

Securities Exempt from Registration

Certain securities are exempt from registration with the SEC. Once a security is exempt, it is exempt forever. It does not matter how many times the security is transferred. **Exempt securities** include:

exempt securities
Securities that are exempt from registration with the SEC.

- Securities issued by any government in the United States (e.g., municipal bonds issued by city governments).
- Short-term notes and drafts that have a maturity date that does not exceed nine months (e.g., **commercial paper** issued by corporations).

- Securities issued by nonprofit issuers, such as religious institutions, charitable institutions, and colleges and universities.
- Securities of financial institutions (e.g., banks, savings associations) that are regulated by the appropriate banking authorities.
- Insurance and annuity contracts issued by insurance companies.
- Stock dividends and stock splits.
- Securities issued in a corporate reorganization in which one security is exchanged for another security.

Transactions Exempt from Registration

exempt transactions
Transactions in which securities are sold that are exempt from registration with the SEC if certain requirements are met.

Certain transactions where securities are sold are exempt from registration with the SEC if they meet specified requirements. These are called **exempt transactions**. Securities sold pursuant to an exempt transaction do not have to be registered with the SEC. The most widely used exemptions include the *nonissuer exemption, intrastate offering exemption, private placement exemption,* and *small offering exemption*. These exempt transactions are discussed in the paragraphs that follow.

Exempt transactions that do not have to be registered with the SEC are subject to the antifraud provisions of the federal securities laws. Therefore, the issuer must provide investors with adequate information—including annual reports, quarterly reports, proxy statements, financial statements, and so on—even though a registration statement is not required.

Nonissuer Exemption

nonissuer exemption
An exemption from registration which states that securities transactions not made by an issuer, an underwriter, or a dealer do not have to be registered with the SEC (e.g., normal purchases of securities by investors).

Nonissuers, such as average investors, do not have to file a registration statement prior to reselling securities they have purchased. This **nonissuer exemption** exists because the Securities Act of 1933 exempts from registration securities transactions not made by an issuer, an underwriter, or a dealer.

Example An investor who owns shares of IBM can resell those shares to another investor at any time without having to register with the SEC.

Intrastate Offering Exemption

intrastate offering exemption
An exemption from registration that permits local businesses to raise capital from local investors to be used in the local economy without the need to register with the SEC.

The Securities Act of 1933 provides an **intrastate offering exemption** that permits local businesses to obtain from local investors capital to be used in the local economy without the need to register with the SEC.[7] There is no limit on the dollar amount of capital that can be raised pursuant to an intrastate offering exemption. **SEC Rule 147** stipulates that an intrastate offering can be made only in the one state in which all of the following requirements are met[8]:

1. The issuer must be a resident of the state for which the exemption is claimed. A corporation is a resident of the state in which it is incorporated.
2. The issuer must be doing business in that state. This requires that 80 percent of the issuer's assets be located in the state, 80 percent of its gross revenues be derived from the state, its principal office be located in the state, and 80 percent of the proceeds of the offering be used in the state.
3. The purchasers of the securities must all be residents of that state.

The intrastate offering exemption assumes that local investors are sufficiently aware of local conditions to understand the risks associated with their investment, although this rationale has been called into question based on the large size of many states.

Private Placement Exemption

The Securities Act of 1933 provides that an issue of securities that does not involve a public offering is exempt from the registration requirements.[9] **SEC**

Rule 506—known as the **private placement exemption**—allows issuers to raise capital from an unlimited number of *accredited investors* without having to register the offering with the SEC.[10] There is no dollar limit on the securities that can be sold pursuant to this exemption. General selling efforts, such as advertising to the public, are not permitted.

An **accredited investor** is[11]:

- Any natural person who has individual net worth or joint net worth with a spouse that exceeds $1 million, to be calculated by excluding the value of the person's primary residence.
- A natural person with income exceeding $200,000 in each of the two most recent years or joint income with a spouse exceeding $300,000 for those years and a reasonable expectation of the same income level in the current year.
- A charitable organization, a corporation, a partnership, a trust, or an employee benefit plan with assets exceeding $5 million.
- A bank, an insurance company, a registered investment company, a business development company, or a small business investment company.
- Insiders of the issuers, such as directors, executive officers, or general partners of the company selling the securities.
- A business in which all the equity owners are accredited investors.

The rationale underlying the private placement exemption is that accredited investors have the sophistication to understand the risk involved with the investment and also can afford to lose their money if the investment fails. The SEC is empowered to periodically review the definition of accredited investor and make changes to the definition.

The law permits no more than thirty-five **nonaccredited investors** to purchase securities pursuant to a private placement exemption. These nonaccredited investors are usually friends and family members of the insiders. Nonaccredited investors must be sophisticated investors, however, either through their own experience and education or through representatives (e.g., accountants, lawyers, business managers).

More than $500 billion in capital is raised annually in private placement offerings. Many emerging businesses use this exemption to raise capital. In addition, many large established companies use this exemption to sell securities, such as bonds, to a single investor or a very small group of investors such as pension funds and investment companies.

Small Offering Exemption

Securities offerings that do not exceed a certain dollar amount are exempt from registration.[12] **SEC Rule 504** exempts from registration the sale of securities not exceeding $1 million during a 12-month period. The securities may be sold to an unlimited number of accredited and unaccredited investors, but general selling efforts to the public are not permitted. This is called the **small offering exemption**.

Restricted Securities

Securities sold pursuant to the intrastate, private placement, and small offering exemptions are subject to restrictions on resale for a period of time after the securities are issued. Securities sold pursuant to these exemptions are called **restricted securities**. SEC Rule 147 states that securities issued pursuant to an *intrastate offering exemption* cannot be sold to nonresidents for a period of nine months. **SEC Rule 144** states that securities issued pursuant to the *private placement exemption* or the *small offering exemption* cannot be resold for six months if the issuer is an SEC reporting company (e.g., larger firms) or one year if the issuer is not an SEC reporting company (e.g., smaller firms).

SEC Rule 506 (private placement exemption)
An exemption from registration that permits issuers to raise capital from an unlimited number of accredited investors and no more than thirty-five nonaccredited investors without having to register the offering with the SEC.

accredited investor
A person, a corporation, a company, an institution, or an organization that meets the net worth, income, asset, position, and other requirements established by the SEC to qualify as an accredited investor.

SEC Rule 504 (small offering exemption)
An exemption from registration that permits the sale of securities not exceeding $1 million during a twelve-month period.

Sarbanes-Oxley Act

Section 501 of the Sarbanes-Oxley Act
A section of a federal statute that eliminates conflicts of interest by establishing rules for the separation of the investment banking and securities advice functions of securities firms.

Investment banking is a service provided by many securities firms, whereby they assist companies in going public when issuing shares to the public and otherwise selling securities. The securities firms are paid lucrative fees for providing investment banking services in assisting companies to sell their securities and finding customers to purchase these securities. These same securities firms often provide securities analysis—providing investment advice and recommending securities listed on the stock exchanges and other securities to be purchased by the public.

In the late 1990s and early 2000s, many conflicts of interest were uncovered. Investment bankers and securities analysts of the same firm shared information, and the analysts were paid or pressured by the securities firms to write glowing reports of companies from which the investment bankers of the firm were earning fees.

The following feature discusses the **Sarbanes-Oxley Act** of 2002 and how it removes the conflict of interest problem.

Ethics

Sarbanes-Oxley Act Erects Wall Between Investment Bankers and Securities Analysts

Section 501 of the Sarbanes-Oxley Act established rules for separating the investment banking and securities advice functions of securities firms, thus eliminating many conflicts of interest:

- Securities firms must establish structural and institutional "walls" between their investment banking and securities analysis areas. These walls must protect analysts from review, pressure, and oversight by persons employed by the investment banking area of a securities firm.

- Securities analysts must disclose in each research report or public appearance any conflicts of interest that are known or should have been known to exist at the time of publication or public appearance.

Ethics Questions Why did investment bankers of securities firms put pressure on analysts to issue positive reports on certain companies? Will the required "wall" between security analysts and investment bankers make an analyst's information more reliable?

Trading in Securities

Securities Exchange Act of 1934
A federal statute that primarily regulates trading in securities.

Section 10(b) of the Securities Exchange Act of 1934
A provision of the Securities Exchange Act of 1934 that prohibits the use of manipulative and deceptive devices in the purchase or sale of securities in contravention of the rules and regulations prescribed by the SEC.

SEC Rule 10b-5
A rule adopted by the SEC to clarify the reach of Section 10(b) against deceptive and fraudulent activities in the purchase and sale of securities.

Unlike the Securities Act of 1933, which regulates the original issuance of securities, the **Securities Exchange Act of 1934** primarily regulates subsequent trading.[13] It provides for the registration of certain companies with the SEC, the continuous filing of periodic reports by these companies to the SEC, and the regulation of securities exchanges, brokers, and dealers. It also contains provisions that assess civil and criminal liability on violators of the 1934 act and rules and regulations adopted thereunder.

Section 10(b) and Rule 10b-5

Section 10(b) of the Securities Exchange Act of 1934 is one of the most important sections in the entire 1934 act.[14] Section 10(b) prohibits the use of manipulative and deceptive devices in contravention of the rules and regulations prescribed by the SEC. Pursuant to its rule-making authority, the SEC has adopted **SEC Rule 10b-5**,[15] which provides:

It shall be unlawful for any person, directly or indirectly, by use of any means or instrumentality of interstate commerce or of the mails, or of any facility of any national securities exchange,

    a. *to employ any device, scheme, or artifice to defraud,*

    b. *to make any untrue statement of a material fact or to omit to state a material fact necessary in order to make the statements made, in light of the circumstances under which they were made, not misleading, or*

    c. *to engage in any act, practice, or course of business that operates or would operate as a fraud or deceit upon any person, in connection with the purchase or sale of any security.*

Rule 10b-5 is not restricted to purchases and sales of securities of reporting companies.[16] All transfers of securities, whether made on a stock exchange, in the over-the-counter market, in a private sale, or in connection with a merger, are subject to this rule.[17] The U.S. Supreme Court has held that only conduct involving **scienter** (intentional conduct) violates Section 10(b) and Rule 10b-5. Negligent conduct is not a violation.[18]

scienter
Intentional conduct. Scienter is required for there to be a violation of Section 10(b) and Rule 10b-5.

Section 10(b) and Rule 10b-5 require reliance by the injured party on the misstatement. However, many sales and purchases of securities occur in open-market transactions (e.g., over stock exchanges), where there is no direct communication between the buyer and the seller.

Civil Liability Under the Securities Exchange Act of 1934

Although Section 10(b) and Rule 10b-5 do not expressly provide for a private right of action, courts have *implied* such a right. If there is a violation of Section 10(b) and Rule 10b-5, an injured private plaintiff may bring a *civil action* and seek rescission of the securities contract or recover damages (e.g., disgorgements of the illegal profits by the defendants). Private securities fraud claims must be brought within two years after discovery or five years after the violation occurs, whichever is shorter.

SEC Actions Under the Securities Exchange Act of 1934

The SEC may investigate suspected violations of the Securities Exchange Act of 1934 and of the rules and regulations adopted thereunder. The SEC may enter into *consent decrees* with defendants, seek *injunctions* in federal District Court, or seek court orders requiring defendants to *disgorge* illegally gained profits.

In 1984, Congress enacted the **Insider Trading Sanctions Act**,[19] which permits the SEC to obtain a **civil penalty** of up to three times the illegal profits gained or losses avoided on insider trading. The fine is payable to the U.S. Treasury. Under the Sarbanes-Oxley Act, the SEC may issue an order prohibiting any person who has committed securities fraud from acting as an officer or a director of a public company.

Insider Trading Sanctions Act
A federal statute that permits the SEC to obtain a civil penalty of up to three times the illegal benefits received from insider trading.

Criminal Liability Under the Securities Exchange Act of 1934

Section 32 of the Securities Exchange Act of 1934 makes it a criminal offense to willfully violate the provisions of the act or the rules and regulations adopted thereunder.[20] Under the Sarbanes-Oxley Act of 2002, a person who willfully violates the Securities Exchange Act of 1934 can be fined up to $5 million or imprisoned for up to twenty-five years, or both. A corporation or another entity may be fined up to $2.5 million.

There is a six-year statute of limitations for criminal prosecution of violations of the Securities Act of 1933 and the Securities Exchange Act of 1934.

Section 32 of the Securities Exchange Act of 1934
A provision of the Securities Exchange Act of 1934 that imposes criminal liability on any person who willfully violates the 1934 act or the rules or regulations adopted thereunder.

Insider Trading

insider trading
A situation in which an insider makes a profit by personally purchasing shares of the corporation prior to public release of favorable information or by selling shares of the corporation prior to the public disclosure of unfavorable information.

One of the most important purposes of Section 10(b) and Rule 10b-5 is to prevent **insider trading**. Insider trading occurs when a company employee or company advisor uses material nonpublic information to make a profit by trading in the securities of the company. This practice is considered illegal because it allows insiders to take advantage of the investing public.

In the *Matter of Cady, Roberts & Company*[21] the SEC announced that the duty of an insider who possesses material nonpublic information is to either (1) abstain from trading in the securities of the company or (2) disclose the information to the person on the other side of the transaction before the insider purchases the securities from or sells the securities to him or her.

insiders under Section 10(b)
(1) Officers, directors, and employees at all levels of a company; (2) lawyers, accountants, consultants, and agents and representatives who are hired by the company on a temporary and nonemployee basis to provide services or work to the company; and (3) others who owe a fiduciary duty to the company.

For purposes of Section 10(b) and Rule 10b-5, **insiders** are defined as (1) officers, directors, and employees at all levels of a company; (2) lawyers, accountants, consultants, and agents and representatives who are hired by the company on a temporary and nonemployee basis to provide services or work to the company; and (3) others who owe a fiduciary duty to the company.

Example The Widger Corporation has its annual audit done by its outside CPAs, Young & Old, CPAs. Priscilla is one of the CPAs who conduct the audit. The audit discloses that the Widger Corporation's profits have doubled since last year, and Priscilla rightfully discloses this fact to Martha, the chief financial officer (CFO) of Widger Corporation. Both Martha and Priscilla are *insiders*. The earnings information is definitely *material*, and it is *nonpublic* until the corporation publicly announces its earnings in two days. Prior to the earnings information being made public, Priscilla and Martha buy stock in Widger Corporation at $100 per share. After the earnings information is made public, the stock of Widger Corporation increases to $150 per share. Both Priscilla and Martha are liable for insider trading, in violation of Section 10(b) and Rule 10b-5, because they traded in the securities of Widger Corporation while they were insiders in possession of material nonpublic inside information. Martha and Priscilla could be held civilly liable and criminally guilty of insider trading, in violation of Section 10(b) and Rule 10b-5.

Tipper–Tippee Liability

tipper
A person who discloses material nonpublic information to another person.

tippee
A person who receives material nonpublic information from a tipper.

A person who discloses material nonpublic information to another person is called a **tipper**. A person who receives such information is known as a **tippee**. A tippee is liable for acting on material information that he or she knew or should have known was not public. The tipper is liable for the profits made by the tippee. This is called **tipper–tippee liability**. If the tippee tips other persons, both the tippee (who is now a tipper) and the original tipper are liable for the profits made by these remote tippees. The remote tippees are liable for their own trades if they knew or should have known that they possessed material inside information.

Example Nicole is the CFO of Max Steel Corporation. In her position, she receives copies of the audits of the financial statements from the company's auditors—certified public accountants—before they are made public. Nicole receives an audit report which shows that the company's earnings have tripled this year. This is material nonpublic information. Nicole calls her brother Peter and tells him the news. Peter knows Nicole's position at Max Steel. Peter purchases stock in Max Steel before the audit reports are made public and makes a significant profit after the audit reports are made public and the price of Max Steel stock increases. Here there is illegal tipping. Nicole the tipper and Peter the tippee could be held civilly liable and criminally guilty for tipping, in violation of Section 10(b) and Rule 10b-5.

In the following case, the court found an insider criminally liable for insider trading and tipping.

CASE 17.1 *Insider Trading and Tipping*

United States v. Bhagat
436 F.3d 1140, Web 2006 U.S. App. Lexis 3008 (2006)
United States Court of Appeals for the Ninth Circuit

"The fact that this evidence was all circumstantial does not lessen its sufficiency to support a guilty verdict."

—Rawlinson, Circuit Judge

Facts
Atul Bhagat worked for NVIDIA Corporation (Nvidia). Nvidia competed for and won a multi-million-dollar contract to develop a video game console (the Xbox) for Microsoft Corporation. Upon receiving the news, Nvidia's chief executive officer (CEO) sent company-wide e-mails announcing the contract award, advised Nvidia employees that the Xbox information should be kept confidential, and imposed a trading blackout on the purchase of Nvidia stock by employees for several days.

Within roughly twenty minutes after the final e-mail was sent, Bhagat purchased a large quantity of Nvidia stock. Bhagat testified that he read the e-mails roughly forty minutes after he purchased the stock. Less than one-half hour after Bhagat made his purchase, his friend Mamat Gill purchased Nvidia stock. Bhagat denied having told anyone about the Xbox contract before the information was made public.

The United States brought criminal charges against Bhagat, charging him with insider trading and tipping. Bhagat stuck with his story regarding his purchase of Nvidia stock and denied tipping Gill about the Xbox contract. Based on circumstantial evidence, the jury convicted Bhagat of insider trading and tipping. Bhagat appealed.

Issue
Is Bhagat criminally guilty of insider trading and tipping?

Language of the Court
To convict Bhagat of insider trading, the government was required to prove that

he traded stock on the basis of material, nonpublic information. The government offered significant evidence to support the jury's conclusion that Bhagat was aware of the confidential X-Box information before he executed his trades. The X-Box e-mails were sent prior to his purchase. The e-mails were found on his computer. Finally, Bhagat took virtually no action to divest himself of the stock, or to inform his company that he had violated the company's trading blackout.

To convict Bhagat of tipping Gill, the government was required to prove that the tipper, Bhagat, provided the tippee, Gill, with material, inside information, prior to the tippee's purchase of stock. Bhagat and Gill were friends, Gill purchased stock shortly after Bhagat, and Gill's purchase was his largest purchase of the year.

Decision
The U.S. Court of Appeals upheld the U.S. District Court's judgment, finding Bhagat criminally guilty of insider trading and tipping. The U.S. Court of Appeals remanded the case to the U.S. District Court for sentencing of Bhagat.

Case Questions

Critical Legal Thinking
What is insider trading? Explain. What is tipping? Explain.

Ethics
Do you think Bhagat committed the crimes he was convicted of? Why or why not?

Contemporary Business
What percentage of insider trading do you think the government catches?

Misappropriation Theory

As previously discussed, the courts have developed laws that address trading in securities by insiders who possess inside information. But sometimes a person who possesses inside information about a company is not an employee or a temporary insider of that company. Instead, the party may be an *outsider* to the company. The SEC adopted **SEC Rule 10b5-1**, which prohibits outsiders from trading in the security of any issuer on the basis of material nonpublic information that is obtained by a breach of duty of trust or confidence owed to the person who is the source of the information. Thus, an outsider's misappropriation of information in violation of his or her fiduciary duty, and trading on that information, violates Section 10(b) and Rule 10b-5. This rule is called the **misappropriation theory**.

Example iCorporation and eCorporation are in secret merger discussions. iCorporation hires an investment bank to counsel it during merger negotiations. An employee of the investment bank purchases stock in eCorporation. Once the merger is publicly announced, the stock of eCorporation substantially increases in value, and the employee of the investment bank sells the stock and makes a significant profit. Here, because the employee is not an insider to eCorporation, he cannot be held liable under Section 10(b) for traditional insider trading. However, under the misappropriation theory, the employee of the investment bank can be held liable for violating Section 10(b) because he *misappropriated* the secret merger information when he was a temporary insider of iCorporation in order to illegally purchase the stock of eCorporation before the merger was publicly announced.

Aiders and Abettors

Many principal actors in a securities fraud obtain the knowing assistance of other parties to successfully complete the fraud. These other parties are known as **aiders and abettors**. The U.S. Supreme Court has held that aiders and abettors are not civilly liable under Section 10(b)-5 and Rule 10b-5.[22] They can, however, be held criminally liable.

Short-Swing Profits

Section 16(a) of the Securities Exchange Act of 1934 defines any person who is an executive officer, a director, or a 10 percent shareholder of an equity security of a reporting company as a **statutory insider** for Section 16 purposes. Statutory insiders must file reports with the SEC, disclosing their ownership and trading in the company's securities.[23] These reports must be filed with the SEC and made available on the company's website within two days after the trade occurs.

Section 16(b)

Section 16(b) of the Securities Exchange Act of 1934 requires that any profits made by a statutory insider on transactions involving **short-swing profits**—that is, trades involving equity securities occurring within six months of each other— belong to the corporation.[24] The corporation may bring a legal action to recover these profits. Involuntary transactions, such as forced redemption of securities by the corporation or an exchange of securities in a bankruptcy proceeding, are exempt. Section 16(b) is a strict liability provision. Generally, no defenses are recognized. Neither intent nor the possession of inside information need be shown.

Example Rosanne is the president of a corporation and a statutory insider who does not possess any inside information. On February 1, she purchases one thousand shares of her employer's stock, at $10 per share. On June 1, she sells the stock for $14 per share. The corporation can recover the $4,000 profit because the trades occurred within six months of each other.

SEC Section 16 Rules

The SEC has adopted the following rules under Section 16:

- It defines **officer** to include only executive officers who perform *policy-making* functions. Officers who run day-to-day operations but are not responsible for policy decisions are not included.

  Examples Policy-making executives include the CEO, the president, vice presidents in charge of business units or divisions, the CFO, the principal accounting officer, and the like.

- It relieves insiders of liability for transactions that occur within six months before becoming a insider.

  Example If a noninsider buys shares of a company on January 15, is hired by the company and becomes an insider March 15, and sells the shares on May 15, there is no liability.

- It provides that insiders are liable for transactions that occur within six months of the last transaction engaged in while an insider.

  Example If an insider buys shares in his company April 30 and leaves the company May 15, he cannot sell the shares before October 30. If he does, he violates Section 16(b).

> *He will lie sir, with such volubility that you would think truth were a tool.*
>
> William Shakespeare
> *All's Well That Ends Well (1604)*

CONCEPT SUMMARY

SECTION 10(B) AND SECTION 16(B) COMPARED

Element	Section 10(b) and Rule 10b-5	Section 16(b)
Covered securities	All securities.	Securities required to be registered with the SEC under the 1934 act.
Inside information	Defendant made a misrepresentation or traded on inside (or perhaps misappropriated) information.	Short-swing profits recoverable whether or not they are attributable to misappropriation or inside information.
Recovery	Belongs to the injured purchaser or seller.	Belongs to the corporation.

Dodd-Frank Wall Street Reform and Consumer Protection Act

In 2008 and several years thereafter, the United States suffered from a severe financial crisis. Many large financial institutions were on the verge of failure and would have gone bankrupt had the federal government not come to the rescue

Dodd-Frank Wall Street Reform and Consumer Protection Act
A 2010 federal statute that regulates hedge funds and derivatives and provides protection to consumers regarding financial products and services.

with taxpayer bailout funds. Financial institutions near failure included commercial banks, savings banks, insurance companies, investment banks, securities firms, and others. Much of the blame for the severe financial crisis was placed on the failure of complex Wall Street investment vehicles such as hedge funds and derivatives that were unregulated.

In 2010, Congress enacted the *Dodd-Frank Wall Street Reform and Consumer Protection Act*, a federal statute. This act imposes regulation on hedge funds and derivatives and other speculative investment devices. The following feature discusses this statute.

Contemporary Environment

Dodd-Frank Wall Street Reform and Consumer Protection Act Regulates Hedge Funds and Derivatives

A **hedge fund** is a private investment company that has a limited number of wealthy investors. A hedge fund invests in a wide range of risky investments that include stocks, sector investing (e.g., technology stocks), fixed-income securities, distressed securities (companies in bankruptcy), emerging markets (smaller, unproven companies), short-selling (betting that a stock will go down in value), commodities, currency, derivatives, and other risky investments. Hedge funds usually use leverage—that is, they borrow substantial amounts of money from banks, insurance companies, and other institutional lenders to fund their investments. A leverage of 10:1 is not unusual (i.e., the hedge fund borrows $10 for every $1 of invested by investors), and many have much higher leverage ratios. Speculative investments and leverage make hedge funds risky to their investors and to the financial institutions that have loaned the hedge funds money.

A **derivative** is a financial instrument whose value is determined by the price movements of another asset. For example,

a derivative may be based on the interest rate movements of a specified bond, a country's currency, the price of a stock or commodities index, or other underlying asset.

Prior to 2010, hedge funds and over-the-counter derivatives were not regulated. This changed in 2010, with the enactment of the **Dodd-Frank Wall Street Reform and Consumer Protection Act**. The act requires hedge funds to register with the Securities and Exchange Commission (SEC) and to disclose information about their portfolios and trades to the SEC. The act also authorizes the SEC and the Commodity Futures Trading Commission (CFTC), another federal government agency, to regulate derivatives and requires exchange trading of most derivatives and disclosure of such transactions to the SEC and CFTC. The act restricts banks' investments in hedge funds and derivatives.

Many believe that because hedge funds are now subject to federal regulation and public disclosure, they are less likely to cause another major financial crisis.

State "Blue-Sky" Laws

state securities laws ("blue-sky" laws)
State laws that regulate the issuance and trading of securities.

WEB EXERCISE
Visit the website of the Office of the New York State Attorney, at **www.ag.ny.gov**. Click on "Investor Protection" and read the description of what the New York Investor Protection Bureau does.

Most states have enacted securities laws. These laws generally require the registration of certain securities, provide exemptions from registration, and contain broad antifraud provisions. State securities laws are usually applied when smaller companies are issuing securities within that state. The **Uniform Securities Act** has been adopted by many states. This act coordinates **state securities laws** with federal securities laws.

State securities laws are often referred to as **"blue-sky" laws** because they help prevent investors from purchasing a piece of the blue sky. The state that has most actively enforced its securities laws is New York. The office of the New York state attorney has brought many high-profile criminal fraud cases in recent years.

Key Terms and Concepts

Accredited investor (361)

Aiders and abettors (366)

Civil action (357)

Civil penalty (363)

Commercial paper (359)

Common securities (354)

Consent decree (358)

Derivative (368)

Dodd-Frank Wall Street Reform and Consumer Protection Act (368)

Due diligence defense (357)

Effective date (356)

Electronic initial public offering (e-initial public offering, E-IPO) (359)

Electronic securities transaction (e-securities transaction) (358)

EDGAR (359)

Escott v. BarChris Construction Corporation (357)

Exempt securities (359)

Exempt transactions (360)

Form U-7 (356)

Going public (355)

Hedge fund (368)

Howey test (354)

Injunction (358)

Initial public offering (IPO) (355)

Insiders under Section 10(b) (364)

Insider trading (364)

Insider Trading Sanctions Act (363)

Internet (358)

Intrastate offering exemption (360)

Investment banker (355)

Investment contract (354)

Issuer (355)

Matter of Cady, Roberts & Company (364)

Misappropriation theory (366)

Mutual fund (355)

National Association of Securities Dealers Automated Quotation System (NASDAQ) (358)

New York Stock Exchange (NYSE) (358)

Nonaccredited investor (361)

Nonissuer exemption (360)

NYSE Euronext (358)

Offering statement (356)

Officer (367)

Online (358)

Prospectus (356)

Registration statement (355)

Regulation A (356)

Resale restrictions (356)

Restricted securities (361)

Rules (regulations) (354)

Sarbanes-Oxley Act (362)

Scienter (363)

SEC Rule 10b-5 (362)

SEC Rule 10b5-1 (366)

SEC Rule 144 (361)

SEC Rule 147 (360)

SEC Rule 504 (small offering exemption) (361)

SEC Rule 506 (private placement exemption) (361)

Section 501 of the Sarbanes-Oxley Act (362)

Section 5 of the Securities Act of 1933 (355)

Section 11 of the Securities Act of 1933 (357)

Section 12 of the Securities Act of 1933 (358)

Section 24 of the Securities Act of 1933 (358)

Section 10(b) of the Securities Exchange Act of 1934 (362)

Section 16(a) of the Securities Exchange Act of 1934 (366)

Section 16(b) of the Securities Exchange Act of 1934 (366)

Section 32 of the Securities Exchange Act of 1934 (363)

Securities Act of 1933 (355)

Securities and Exchange Commission (SEC) (354)

Securities Exchange Act of 1934 (362)

Security (354)

Short-swing profits (366)

Small Company Offering Registration (SCOR) (356)

State securities laws ("blue-sky" laws) (368)

Statutory insider (366)

Statutorily defined securities (354)

Tippee (364)

Tipper (364)

Tipper–tippee liability (364)

Uniform Securities Act (368)

Law Case with Answer

Securities and Exchange Commission v. Texas Gulf Sulphur Company

Facts Texas Gulf Sulphur Co. (TGS), a mining company, drilled an exploratory hole—Kidd 55—near Timmins, Ontario. Assay reports showed that the core from this drilling proved to be remarkably high in copper, zinc, and silver. TGS kept the discovery secret, camouflaged the drill site, and diverted drilling efforts to another site to allow TGS to acquire land around Kidd 55. TGS stock traded at $18 per share.

Eventually, rumors of a rich mineral strike began circulating. On Saturday, the *New York Times* published an unauthorized report of TGS drilling efforts in Canada and its rich mineral strike. On Sunday, officers of TGS drafted a press release that was issued that afternoon. The press release appeared in morning newspapers of general circulation on Monday. It read, in pertinent part, "The work done to date has not been sufficient to reach definite conclusions and any statement as to size and grade of ore would be premature and possibly misleading."

The rumors persisted. Three days later, at 10:00 A.M., TGS held a press conference for the financial media. At the time of the press conference, TGS stock was trading at $37 per share. At this press conference, which lasted about ten minutes, TGS disclosed the richness of the Timmins mineral strike and that the strike should run to at least 25 million tons in ore.

The following two company executives who had knowledge of the mineral strike at Timmins traded in the stock of TGS:

- **Crawford.** Crawford telephoned orders to his Chicago broker about midnight on the day before the announcement and again at 8:30 in the morning of the day of the announcement, with instructions to buy at the opening of the stock exchange that morning. Crawford purchased the stock he ordered.
- **Coates.** Coates telephoned orders to his stock broker son-in-law to purchase the company's stock shortly before 10:20 A.M. on the day of the announcement, which was just after the announcement had been made. Coates purchased the stock he had ordered.

After the public announcement, TGS stock was selling at $58. The SEC brought an action against Crawford and Coates for insider trading, in violation of Section 10(b) of the Securities Exchange Act of 1934. Are the defendant executives liable for engaging in insider trading?

Answer   Yes, the defendant executives are liable for engaging in insider trading, in violation of Section 10(b) of the Securities Exchange Act of 1934. The insiders here were not trading on an equal footing with the outside investors. They alone were in a position to evaluate the probability and magnitude of what seemed from the outset to be a major ore strike.

Crawford telephoned his orders to his Chicago broker about midnight on the day before the announcement and again at 8:30 in the morning of the day of the announcement, with instructions to buy at the opening of the stock exchange that morning. Crawford sought to, and did, "beat the news." Before insiders may act upon material information, such information must have been effectively disclosed in a manner sufficient to ensure its availability to the investing public. Here, where a formal announcement to the entire financial news media had been promised in a prior official release known to the media, all insider activity must await dissemination of the promised official announcement. Crawford, an insider, traded while in the possession of material nonpublic information and is therefore liable for violating Section 10(b).

Coates's telephone order was placed shortly before 10:20 A.M. on the day of the announcement, which occurred a few minutes after the public announcement. When Coates purchased the stock, the news could not be considered already a matter of public information. Insiders should keep out of the market until the established procedures for public release of the information are carried out instead of hastening to execute transactions in advance of, and in frustration of, the objectives of the release. Assuming that the contents of the official release could instantaneously be acted upon, at a minimum, Coates should have waited until the news could reasonably have been expected to appear over the media of widest circulation rather than hastening to ensure an advantage to himself and his broker son-in-law.

Both Crawford and Coates, insider executives of TGS, engaged in illegal insider trading, in violation of Section 10(b) of the Securities Exchange Act of 1934. *Securities and Exchange Commission v. Texas Gulf Sulphur Company*, 401 F.2d 833, **Web** 1968 U.S. App. Lexis 5797 (United States Court of Appeals for the Second Circuit)

Critical Legal Thinking Cases

17.1 Definition of *Security*   Dare To Be Great, Inc. (Dare), was a Florida corporation that was wholly owned by Glenn W. Turner Enterprises, Inc. Dare offered self-improvement courses aimed at improving self-motivation and sales ability. In return for an investment of money, the purchaser received certain tapes, records, and written materials. In addition, depending on the level of involvement, the purchaser had the opportunity to help sell the Dare courses to others and to receive part of the purchase price as a commission. There were four different levels of involvement.

The task of salespersons was to bring prospective purchasers to "Adventure Meetings." The meetings, which were conducted by Dare people and not the salespersons, were conducted in a preordained format that included great enthusiasm, cheering and charming, exuberant handshaking, standing on chairs, and shouting. The Dare people and the salespersons dressed in modern, expensive clothes, displayed large sums of cash, drove new expensive automobiles, and engaged in "hard-sell" tactics to induce prospects to sign their name and part with their money. In actuality, few Dare purchasers ever attained the wealth promised. The tape recordings and materials distributed by Dare were worthless. Is this sales scheme a "security" that should have been registered with the SEC? *Securities and Exchange Commission v. Glenn W. Turner Enterprises, Inc.*, 474 F.2d 476, **Web** 1973

U.S. App. Lexis 11903 (United States Court of Appeals for the Ninth Circuit)

17.2 Intrastate Offering Exemption   The McDonald Investment Company was a corporation organized and incorporated in the state of Minnesota. The principal and only place of business from which the company conducted operations was Rush City, Minnesota. More than 80 percent of the company's assets were located in Minnesota, and more than 80 percent of its income was derived from Minnesota. McDonald sold securities to Minnesota residents only. The proceeds from the sale were used entirely to make loans and other investments in real estate and other assets located outside the state of Minnesota. The company did not file a registration statement with the SEC. Does this offering qualify for an intrastate offering exemption from registration? *Securities and Exchange Commission v. McDonald Investment Company*, 343 F.Supp. 343, **Web** 1972 U.S. Dist. Lexis 13547 (United States District Court for the District of Minnesota)

17.3 Transaction Exemption   Continental Enterprises, Inc. (Continental), had 2,510,000 shares of stock issued and outstanding. Louis E. Wolfson and members of his immediate family and associates owned in excess of 40 percent of those shares. The balance was in the hands of approximately five thousand outside shareholders. Wolfson was Continental's largest shareholder and the guiding spirit of the corporation, who gave direction to and controlled the company's officers. During the course of five months, without public disclosure, Wolfson and his family and associates sold 55 percent of their stock through six brokerage houses. Wolfson and his family and associates did not file a registration statement with the SEC with respect to these sales. Do the securities sales by Wolfson and his family and associates qualify for an exemption for registration as a sale "not by an issuer, an underwriter, or a dealer"? *United States v. Wolfson*, 405 F.2d 779, **Web** 1968 U.S. App. Lexis 4342 (United States Court of Appeals for the Second Circuit)

17.4 Insider Trading   Chiarella worked as a "markup man" in the New York composing room of Pandick Press, a financial printer. Among the documents that Chiarella handled were five secret announcements of corporate takeovers. The tender offerors had hired Pandick Press to print the offers, which would later be made public, when the tender offers were made to the shareholders of the target corporations. When the documents were delivered to Pandick Press, the identities of the acquiring and target corporations were concealed by blank spaces or false names. The true names would not be sent to Pandick Press until the night of the final printing.

Chiarella was able to deduce the names of the target companies before the final printing. Without disclosing this knowledge, he purchased stock in the target companies and sold the shares immediately after the takeover attempts were made public. Chiarella realized a gain of $30,000 in the course of fourteen months. The federal government indicted Chiarella for criminal violations of Section 10(b) of the Securities Exchange Act of 1934. Is Chiarella guilty? *Chiarella v. United States*, 445 U.S. 222, 100 S.Ct. 1108, 63 L.Ed.2d 348, **Web** 1980 U.S. Lexis 88 (Supreme Court of the United States)

17.5 Section 10(b)   Leslie Neadeau was the president of T.O.N.M. Oil & Gas Exploration Corporation (TONM). Charles Lazzaro was a registered securities broker employed by Bateman Eichler, Hill Richards, Inc. (Bateman Eichler). The stock of TONM was traded in the over-the-counter market. Lazzaro made statements to potential investors that he had "inside information" about TONM, including that (1) vast amounts of gold had been discovered in Surinam and that TONM had options on thousands of acres in the gold-producing regions of Surinam; (2) the discovery was "not publicly known, but would be subsequently announced"; and (3) when this information was made public, TONM stock, which was then selling for $1.50 to $3.00 per share, would increase to $10.00 to $15.00 within a short period of time and might increase to $100.00 per share within a year.

Potential investors contacted Neadeau at TONM, and he confirmed that the information was not public knowledge. In reliance on Lazzaro's and Neadeau's statements, the investors purchased TONM stock. The "inside information" turned out to be false, and the shares declined substantially below the purchase price. The investors sued Lazzaro, Bateman Eichler, Neadeau, and TONM, alleging violations of Section 10(b) of the Securities Exchange Act of 1934. The defendants asserted that the plaintiffs' complaint should be dismissed because they participated in the fraud. Who wins? *Bateman Eichler, Hill Richards, Inc. v. Berner*, 472 U.S. 299, 105 S.Ct. 2622, 86 L.Ed.2d 215, **Web** 1985 U.S. Lexis 95 (Supreme Court of the United States)

17.6 Insider Trading   Donald C. Hoodes was the chief executive officer of the Sullair Corporation. As an officer of the corporation, he was regularly granted stock options to purchase stock of the company at a discount. On July 20, Hoodes sold six thousand shares of Sullair common stock for $38,350. On July 31, Sullair terminated Hoodes as an officer of the corporation. On August 20, Hoodes exercised options to purchase six thousand shares of Sullair stock that cost Hoodes $3.01 per share ($18,060) at a time when they were trading at $4.50 per share ($27,000). Hoodes did not possess material nonpublic information about Sullair when he sold or purchased the securities of the company. The corporation brought suit against Hoodes to recover the profits Hoodes made on these trades. Who wins? *Sullair Corporation v. Hoodes*, 672 F.Supp. 337, **Web** 1987 U.S. Dist. Lexis 10152 (United States District Court for the Northern District of Illinois)

17.7 Transaction Exemption Stephen Murphy owned Intertie, a California company that was involved in financing and managing cable television stations. Murphy was both an officer of the corporation and chairman of the board of directors. Intertie would buy a cable television station, make a small cash down payment, and finance the remainder of the purchase price. It would then create a limited partnership and sell the cable station to the partnership for a cash down payment and a promissory note in favor of Intertie. Finally, Intertie would lease the station back from the partnership. Intertie purchased more than thirty stations and created an equal number of limited partnerships, from which it received more than $7.5 million from approximately four hundred investors.

Evidence showed that most of the limited partnerships were not self-supporting but that this fact was not disclosed to investors. Intertie commingled partnership funds, taking funds generated from the sale of new partnership offerings to meet debt service obligations of previously sold cable systems; Intertie also used funds from limited partnerships that were formed but that never acquired cable systems. Intertie did not keep any records regarding the qualifications of investors to purchase the securities and also refused to make its financial statements available to investors.

Intertie suffered severe financial difficulties and eventually filed for bankruptcy. The limited partners suffered substantial losses. Do each of the limited partnership offerings alone qualify for the private placement exemption from registration? Should the thirty limited partnership offerings be integrated? Has Murphy acted ethically in this case? *Securities and Exchange Commission v. Murphy*, 626 F.2d 633, **Web** 1980 U.S. App. Lexis 15483 (United States Court of Appeals for the Ninth Circuit)

17.8 Definition of *Security* The Farmer's Cooperative of Arkansas and Oklahoma (Co-Op) was an agricultural cooperative that had approximately 23,000 members. To raise money to support its general business operations, Co-Op sold promissory notes to investors that were payable upon demand. Co-Op offered the notes to both members and nonmembers, advertised the notes as an "investment program," and offered an interest rate higher than that available on savings accounts at financial institutions. More than 1,600 people purchased the notes, worth a total of $10 million. Subsequently, Co-Op filed for bankruptcy. A class of holders of the notes filed suit against Ernst & Young, a national firm of certified public accountants that had audited Co-Op's financial statements, alleging that Ernst & Young had violated Section 10(b) of the Securities Exchange Act of 1934. Are the notes issued by Co-Op securities? *Reeves v. Ernst & Young*, 494 U.S. 56, 110 S.Ct. 945, 108 L.Ed.2d 47, **Web** 1990 U.S. Lexis 1051 (Supreme Court of the United States)

Ethics Cases

17.9 Ethics James O'Hagan was a partner in the law firm Dorsey & Whitney in Minneapolis, Minnesota. Grand Metropolitan PLC (Grand Met), a company based in London, England, hired Dorsey & Whitney to represent it in a secret tender offer for the stock of the Pillsbury Company, headquartered in Minneapolis. While this transaction was still secret, O'Hagan began purchasing call options for Pillsbury stock. Each call option gave O'Hagan the right to purchase one hundred shares of Pillsbury stock at a specified price.

O'Hagan continued to purchase call options for two months, and he became the largest holder of call options for Pillsbury stock. O'Hagan also purchased five thousand shares of Pillsbury common stock at $39 per share. These purchases were all made while Grand Met's proposed tender offer for Pillsbury remained secret to the public. When Grand Met publicly announced its tender offer one month later, Pillsbury stock increased to nearly $60 per share. O'Hagan sold his Pillsbury call options and common stock, making a profit of more than $4.3 million.

The U.S. Department of Justice charged O'Hagan with criminally violating Section 10(b) and Rule 10b-5. Because this was not a case of classic insider trading because O'Hagan did not trade in the stock of his law firm's client, Grand Met, the government alleged that O'Hagan was liable under the misappropriation theory for trading in Pillsbury stock by engaging in deceptive conduct by misappropriating the secret information about Grand Met's tender offer from his employer, Dorsey & Whitney, and from its client, Grand Met. *United States v. O'Hagen*, 521 U.S. 642, 117 S.Ct. 2199, 138 L.Ed.2d 724, **Web** 1997 U.S. Lexis 4033 (Supreme Court of the United States)

1. Describe the misappropriation theory.
2. Did O'Hagen act ethically in this case?
3. Did O'Hagen act illegally in this case?

17.10 Ethics   R. Foster Winans, a reporter for the *Wall Street Journal*, was one of the writers of the "Heard on the Street" column, a widely read and influential column in the *Journal*. This column frequently included articles that discussed the prospects of companies listed on national and regional stock exchanges and the over-the-counter market. David Carpenter worked as a news clerk at the *Journal*. The *Journal* had a conflict of interest policy that prohibited employees from using nonpublic information learned on the job for their personal benefit. Winans and Carpenter were aware of this policy.

Kenneth P. Felis and Peter Brant were stockbrokers at the brokerage house Kidder Peabody. Winans agreed to provide Felis and Brant with information that was to appear in the "Heard" column in advance of its publication in the *Journal*. Generally, Winans would provide this information to the brokers the day before a story about a company was to appear in the *Journal*. Carpenter served as a messenger between the parties. Based on this advance information, the brokers bought and sold securities of companies discussed in the "Heard" column before publication of the information. During the course of one year, Felis and Brant's prepublication trades based on twenty-seven "Heard" columns netted

profits of almost $690,000. The parties used telephones to transfer information. The *Wall Street Journal* is distributed by mail to many of its subscribers.

Eventually, Kidder Peabody noticed a correlation between the "Heard" column and trading by the brokers. After an SEC investigation, criminal charges were brought against defendants Winans, Carpenter, and Felis in U.S. District Court. Brant became the government's key witness at the trial, having made a plea bargain with the federal government to testify against his co-conspirators in exchange for a reduced sentence. Winans and Felis were convicted of conspiracy to commit fraud, in violation of Section 10(b) of the Securities Exchange Act of 1934, and wire and mail fraud. Carpenter was convicted of aiding and abetting the commission of securities, mail, and wire fraud. The defendants appealed their convictions. *United States v. Carpenter*, 484 U.S. 19, 108 S.Ct. 316, 98 L.Ed.2d 275, **Web** 1987 U.S. Lexis 4815 (Supreme Court of the United States)

1. What is insider trading? Does Section 10(b) apply to this case?
2. Did Winans act ethically in this case? Did Carpenter act ethically in this case? Did Felis and Brant act ethically in this case? Did Brant act ethically by turning government's witness?
3. Are the defendants Winans and Felis criminally liable for conspiring to violate Section 10(b) of the Securities Exchange Act of 1934?

Internet Exercises

1. Go to the website of NASDAQ, at **www.nasdaq.com**. Click on "Market Activity." Is the NASDAQ Composite Index up or down in price?

2. Go to **http://finance.yahoo.com**. In the "Get Quotes" box, type in the Microsoft's stock trading symbol, MSFT. What is the current price of Microsoft stock? Is it up or down in price?

3. Go to the New York Stock Exchange website, at **www.nyse.com/about/listed/IPO_Index.html**, to view the "IPO Showcase" list of the most recent IPOs. What is the most recent listing? Click on the company's name and read the brief history of the company.

4. Go to **www.nasaa.org/industry___regulatory_resources/corporation_finance/535.cfm** to read information about the Small Corporate Offering Registration (SCOR) and Form U-7.

5. Go to **http://en.wikipedia.org/wiki/Martha_Stewart_insider_trading_charges** and read about the insider trading case against Samuel Waksal and the case against Martha Stewart concerning their sales of ImClone Systems stock.

6. Visit the website of the Shanghai Stock Exchange, at **www.sse.com.cn/sseportal/en_us/ps/home.shtml**. Click on "About SSE" and read the brief introduction.

Endnotes

1. Public Law 107-204 (2002).
2. Public Law 111-203 (2010).
3. *Securities and Exchange Commission v. W. J. Howey Co.*, 328 U.S. 293, 66 S.Ct. 1100, 90 L.Ed. 1244, **Web** 1946 U.S. Lexis 3159 (Supreme Court of the United States).
4. 15 U.S.C. Sections 77a–77aa.
5. 283 F.Supp. 643, **Web** 1968 U.S. Dist. Lexis 3853 (United States District Court for the Southern District of New York).
6. 15 U.S.C. Section 77x.
7. Securities Act of 1933, Section 3(a)(11).

8. SEC Rule 147.

9. Securities Act of 1933, Section 4(2).

10. SEC Rule 506.

11. SEC Rule 501.

12. Securities Act of 1933, Section 3(b).

13. 15 U.S.C. Sections 78a–78mm.

14. 15 U.S.C. Section 78j(b).

15. 17 C.F.R.240.10b-5.

16. Litigation instituted pursuant to Section 10(b) and Rule 10b-5 must be commenced within one year after the discovery of the violation and within three years after such violation. *Lampf, Pleva, Lipkind, Prupis & Petigrow v. Gilbertson*, 501 U.S. 350, 111 S.Ct. 2773, 115 L.Ed.2d 321, **Web** 1991 U.S. Lexis 3629 (Supreme Court of the United States).

17. The U.S. Supreme Court has held that the sale of a business is a sale of securities that is subject to Section 10(b). *See Gould v. Ruefenacht*, 471 U.S. 701, 105 S.Ct. 2308, 85 L.Ed.2d 708, **Web** 1985 U.S. Lexis 21 (Supreme Court of the United States), where 50 percent of a business was sold, and *Landreth Timber Co. v. Landreth*, 471 U.S. 681, 105 S.Ct. 2297, 85 L.Ed.2d 692, **Web** 1985 U.S. Lexis 20 (Supreme Court of the United States), where 100 percent of a business was sold.

18. *Ernst & Ernst v. Hochfelder*, 425 U.S. 185, 96 S.Ct. 1375, 47 L.Ed.2d 668, **Web** 1976 U.S. Lexis 2 (Supreme Court of the United States).

19. 15 U.S.C. Section 78ff.

20. Public Law 98–376.

21. 40 SEC 907 (1961).

22. *Stoneridge Investment Partners, LLC. V. Scientific-Atlanta, Inc.*, 552 U.S. 148, 128 S.Ct. 761, 169 L.Ed.2d 627, **Web** 2008 U.S. Lexis 1091 (Supreme Court of the United States).

23. 15 U.S.C. Section 78l.

24. 15 U.S.C. Section 78p(b).

Agency, Employment, and Labor Law

CHAPTER

18 Agency Law

NEW YORK CITY CABS
Many taxis are owned by one party, and another party—the taxi driver—is hired to drive the taxi. Here a principal–agency relationship has been created. The owner is the principal, and the taxi driver is the agent. The owner of the taxi cab is liable for the negligent conduct of the driver while the driver is acting within the scope of employment.

Learning Objectives

After studying this chapter, you should be able to:

1. Define *agency* and the parties to an agency.
2. Identify and define a principal–independent contractor relationship.
3. List and describe an agent's duties to a principal and a principal's duties to an agent.
4. Describe a principal's and an agent's liability on third-party contracts.
5. Describe a principal's, an agent's and an independent contractor's liability for tortious conduct.

Chapter Outline

Introduction to Agency Law

Agency

Formation of an Agency
  CONTEMPORARY ENVIRONMENT • *Power of Attorney*

Principal's and Agent's Duties
  ETHICS • *Agent's Duty of Loyalty*

Tort Liability to Third Parties
  CASE 18.1 • *Burlarley v. Walmart Stores, Inc.*

Contract Liability to Third Parties

Independent Contractor
  CASE 18.2 • *Lewis v. D. Hays Trucking, Inc.*

Termination of an Agency

> " *Let every eye negotiate for itself, and trust no agent.* "
>
> —William Shakespeare
> *Much Ado About Nothing (1598)*

Introduction to Agency Law

If businesspeople had to personally conduct all their business, the scope of their activities would be severely curtailed. Partnerships would not be able to operate; corporations could not act through managers and employees; and sole proprietorships would not be able to hire employees. The use of *agents* (or *agency*), which allows one person to act on behalf of another, solves this problem. Examples of agency relationships are a salesperson selling goods for a store, an executive working for a corporation, and a partner acting on behalf of a partnership.

Some parties who work for a principal are *independent contractors*. That is, they are outside contractors who are employed by a principal to conducted limited activities for the principal. Examples of independent contractors are an attorney hired to represent a client and a real estate broker employed by an owner to sell the owner's house.

Agency is governed by a large body of common law known as **agency law**. The formation of agencies, the formation of independent contractor relationships, the duties of principals and agents, and the tort liability of principals, agents, and independent contractors are discussed in this chapter.

Agency

Agency relationships are formed through the mutual consent of a principal and an agent. Section 1(1) of the *Restatement (Second) of Agency* defines **agency** as a fiduciary relationship "which results from the manifestation of consent by one person to another that the other shall act in his behalf and subject to his control, and consent by the other so to act." The *Restatement (Second) of Agency* is the reference source for the rules of agency. A party who employs another person to act on his or her behalf is called a **principal**. A party who agrees to act on behalf of another is called an **agent**. The principal–agent relationship is commonly referred to as an *agency*. This relationship is depicted in **Exhibit 18.1**.

Principal–Agent Relationship

A **principal–agent relationship** is formed when an employer hires an employee and gives that employee authority to act and enter into contracts on his or her behalf. The extent of this authority is governed by any express agreement between the parties and implied from the circumstances of the agency.

> *It isn't the people you fire who make your life miserable, it's the people you don't.*
>
> Harvey MacKay

agency law
The large body of common law that governs agency; a mixture of contract law and tort law.

agency
The principal-agent relationship; the fiduciary relationship "which results from the manifestation of consent by one person to another that the other shall act in his behalf and subject to his control, and consent by the other so to act" [*Restatement (Second) of Agency*].

principal
A party who employs another person to act on his or her behalf.

agent
A party who agrees to act on behalf of another.

principal–agent relationship
A relationship formed when an employer hires an employee and gives that employee authority to act and enter into contracts on his or her behalf.

Exhibit 18.1 PRINCIPAL–AGENT RELATIONSHIP

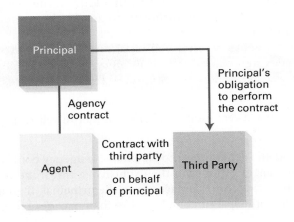

Examples The president of a corporation usually has the authority to enter into major contracts on the corporation's behalf, and a supervisor on the corporation's assembly line may have the authority only to purchase the supplies necessary to keep the line running.

Employer–Employee Relationship

employer–employee relationship
A relationship that results when an employer hires an employee to perform some task or service but the employee has not been authorized to enter into contracts on behalf of the employer.

An **employer–employee relationship** exists when an employer hires an employee to perform some form of physical service.

Example A welder on a General Motors automobile assembly line is employed in an employer–employee relationship because he performs a physical task.

An employee is not an agent unless he or she is specifically empowered to enter into contracts on the principal employer's behalf. Employees may only enter into contracts that are within the scope of their employment.

Example The welder in the previous example is not an agent because he cannot enter into contracts on behalf of General Motors Corporation. If the company empowered him to enter into contracts, he would become an agent.

CONCEPT SUMMARY

KINDS OF EMPLOYMENT RELATIONSHIPS

Type of Relationship	Description
Principal–agent	The agent has authority to act on behalf of the principal, as authorized by the principal and implied from the agency. An employee is often the agent of his employer.
Employer–employee	An employee is hired to perform a task or service. An employee cannot enter into contracts on behalf of the employer.

Formation of an Agency

An agency and the resulting authority of an agent can arise in any of the following four ways: *express agency*, *implied agency*, *agency by ratification*, and *apparent agency*. These types of agencies are discussed in the paragraphs that follow.

Express Agency

express agency
An agency that occurs when a principal and an agent expressly agree to enter into an agency agreement with each other.

Express agency is the most common form of agency. In an express agency, the agent has the authority to contract or otherwise act on the principal's behalf, as expressly stated in the agency agreement. In addition, the agent may also possess certain implied or apparent authority to act on the principal's behalf (as discussed later in this chapter).

Express agency occurs when a principal and an agent expressly agree to enter into an agency agreement with each other. Express agency contracts can be either oral or written, unless the Statute of Frauds stipulates that they must be written.

Example In most states, a real estate broker's contract to sell real estate must be in writing.

exclusive agency contract
A contract a principal and an agent enter into that says the principal cannot employ any agent other than the exclusive agent.

If a principal and an agent enter into an **exclusive agency contract**, the principal cannot employ any agent other than the exclusive agent. If the principal does so, the exclusive agent can recover damages from the principal. If an agency is not an exclusive agency, the principal can employ more than one agent to try to accomplish a stated purpose. When multiple agents are employed, the agencies with all the agents terminate when any one of the agents accomplishes the stated purpose.

The following feature describes the creation of a special form of agency relationship.

power of attorney
An express agency agreement that is often used to give an agent the power to sign legal documents on behalf of the principal.

Contemporary Environment

Power of Attorney

A **power of attorney** is one of the most formal types of express agency agreements. It is often used by a principal to give an agent the power to sign legal documents, such as deeds to real estate, on behalf of the principal. There are two kinds of powers of attorney:

1. **General power of attorney** confers broad powers on the agent to act in any matters on the principal's behalf.

   Example Henry gives a general power of attorney to his twin brother, Gregory, permitting Gregory to make all decisions on his behalf while he is gone. Gregory can make decisions to purchase or sell stocks on Henry's behalf, to sell Henry's real estate if Gregory deems it is in Henry's best interest to do so, to pursue or defend lawsuits on Henry's behalf, and to make all other relevant decisions for Henry.

2. **Special power of attorney** limits the agent to the acts enumerated in the agreement. This is often referred to as a **limited power of attorney**.

   Example Henry lists his house for sale. He then gives his twin brother, Gregory, a special power of attorney to make decisions regarding selling of his house while he is gone. This would include accepting offers to sell the house, making a decision to sell the house to a buyer, signing documents and deeds necessary to sell the house, and taking other actions in connection with the sale of Henry's house.

The agent is called an **attorney-in-fact** even though he or she does not have to be a lawyer. Powers of attorney must be written. Usually, they must also be notarized. Often, a principal makes a power of attorney a **durable power of attorney**. A durable power of attorney remains effective even though the principal is incapacitated.

Implied Agency

In many situations, a principal and an agent do not expressly create an agency. Instead, the agency is implied from the conduct of the parties. This type of agency is referred to as an **implied agency**. The extent of the agent's authority is determined from the facts and circumstances of the particular situation. Implied authority can be conferred by either industry custom, prior dealing between the parties, the agent's position and acts deemed necessary to carry out the agent's duties, and other factors the court deems relevant. Implied authority cannot conflict with express authority or with stated limitations on express authority.

Example A homeowner employs a real estate broker to sell his house. The real estate broker's express powers are to advertise and market the house for sale, show the house to prospective buyers, and accept offers from persons who want to purchase the house. The homeowner goes away on a month-long trip and cannot be contacted. During this time, a water pipe breaks and begins to leak water into the house. The real estate broker has implied authority to hire a plumber to repair the pipe to stop the water leak. The homeowner is responsible for paying for the repairs.

general power of attorney
A power of attorney in which a principal confers broad powers on the agent to act in any matters on the principal's behalf.

special power of attorney (limited power of attorney)
A power of attorney in which a principal confers powers on an agent to act in specified matters on the principal's behalf.

implied agency
An agency that occurs when a principal and an agent do not expressly create an agency, but the agency is inferred from the conduct of the parties.

Agency by Ratification

Agency by ratification occurs when (1) a person misrepresents himself or herself as another's agent when in fact he or she is not and (2) the purported principal ratifies (accepts) the unauthorized act. In such cases, the principal is bound to perform, and the agent is relieved of any liability for misrepresentation.

Example Bill Levine sees a house for sale and thinks his friend Sherry Maxwell would want it. Bill Levine enters into a contract to purchase the house from the seller and

agency by ratification
An agency that occurs when (1) a person misrepresents him- or herself as another's agent when in fact he or she is not and (2) the purported principal ratifies the unauthorized act.

signs the contract "Bill Levine, agent for Sherry Maxwell." Because Bill is not Sherry Maxwell's agent, she is not bound to the contract. However, if Sherry agrees to purchase the house, there is an agency by ratification. The ratification "relates back" to the moment Bill Levine entered into the contract. Upon ratification of the contract, Sherry Maxwell is obligated to purchase the house.

Apparent Agency

apparent agency (agency by estoppel)
Agency that arises when a principal creates the appearance of an agency that in actuality does not exist.

Apparent agency (or **agency by estoppel**) arises when a principal creates the appearance of an agency that in actuality does not exist. Where an apparent agency is established, the principal is *estopped* (stopped) from denying the agency relationship and is bound to contracts entered into by the apparent agent while acting within the scope of the apparent agency. Note that the principal's actions—not the agent's—create an apparent agency.

Example Georgia Pacific, Inc., interviews Albert Iorio for a sales representative position. Mr. Iorio, accompanied by Jane Franklin, the national sales manager, visits retail stores located in the open sales territory. While visiting one store, Jane tells the store manager, "I wish I had more sales reps like Albert." Nevertheless, Albert is not hired. If Albert later enters into contracts with the store on behalf of Georgia Pacific and Jane has not controverted the impression of Albert she left with the store manager, the company will be bound to the contract.

CONCEPT SUMMARY
FORMATION OF AGENCY RELATIONSHIPS

Type of Agency	Formation	Enforcement of the Contract
Express	Authority is expressly given to the agent by the principal.	Principal and third party are bound to the contract.
Implied	Authority is implied from the conduct of the parties, custom and usage of trade, or act incidental to carrying out the agent's duties.	Principal and third party are bound to the contract.
Incidental	Authority that is implied to act beyond express agency powers to take all actions reasonably necessary to protect the principal's property and rights.	Principal and third party are bound to the contract.
Apparent	Authority is created when the principal leads a third party to believe that the agent has authority.	Principal and third party are bound to the contract.
By ratification	Acts of the agent are committed outside the scope of his or her authority.	Principal and third party are not bound to the contract unless the principal ratifies the contract.

Principal's and Agent's Duties

A principal and an agent owe each other certain duties. These duties are discussed in the following paragraphs.

Principal's Duties

A principal owes duties of *compensation*, *reimbursement*, *indemnification*, and *cooperation* to an agent.

Duty to Compensate   A principal owes a **duty to compensate** an agent for services provided. Usually, the agency contract (whether written or oral) specifies the compensation to be paid. The principal must pay this amount either upon the completion of the agency or at some other mutually agreeable time.

If there is no agreement as to the amount of compensation, the law implies a promise that a principal will pay the agent the customary fee paid in the industry. If the compensation cannot be established by custom, the principal owes a duty to pay the reasonable value of the agent's services. There is no duty to compensate a gratuitous agent. However, gratuitous agents who agree to provide their services free of charge may be paid voluntarily.

Certain types of agents traditionally perform their services on a **contingency-fee basis**. Under this type of arrangement, the principal owes a duty to pay the agent the agreed-upon contingency fee only if the agency is completed.

Examples Real estate brokers, finders, lawyers, and salespersons often work on a contingency-fee basis.

duty to compensate
A duty that a principal owes to pay an agreed-upon amount to the agent either upon the completion of the agency or at some other mutually agreeable time.

Duty to Reimburse   In carrying out an agency, an agent may spend his or her own money on the principal's behalf. Unless otherwise agreed, the principal owes a **duty to reimburse** the agent for all such expenses if they were (1) authorized by the principal, (2) within the scope of the agency, and (3) necessary to discharge the agent's duties in carrying out the agency.

Example A principal must reimburse an agent for authorized business trips taken on the principal's behalf.

duty to reimburse
Unless otherwise agreed, a duty a principal owes to reimburse an agent for expenses incurred by the agent if the expenses were (1) authorized by the principal, (2) within the scope of the agency, and (3) necessary to discharge the agent's duties in carrying out the agency.

Duty to Indemnify   A principal owes a **duty to indemnify** the agent for any losses the agent suffers because of the principal's conduct. This duty usually arises where an agent is held liable for the principal's misconduct.

Example An agent enters into an authorized contract with a third party on the principal's behalf, the principal fails to perform on the contract, and the third party recovers a judgment against the agent. The agent can recover indemnification of this amount from the principal.

Duty to Cooperate   Unless otherwise agreed, a principal owes a **duty to cooperate** with and assist an agent in the performance of the agent's duties and the accomplishment of the agency.

Example Unless otherwise agreed, a principal who employs a real estate agent to sell her house owes a duty to allow the agent to show the house to prospective purchasers during reasonable hours.

duty to cooperate
Unless otherwise agreed, a principal's duty to cooperate with and assist an agent in the performance of the agent's duties and the accomplishment of the agency.

Agent's Duties

An agent owes duties of *performance*, *notification*, and *accountability* to a principal.

Duty to Perform   An agent who enters into a contract with a principal has two distinct obligations: (1) to perform the lawful duties expressed in the contract and (2) to meet the standards of reasonable care, skill, and diligence implicit in all contracts. Collectively, these duties are referred to as the agent's **duty to perform**.

Normally, an agent is required to render the same standard of care, skill, and diligence that a fictitious reasonable agent in the same occupation would render in the same locality and under the same circumstances.

Examples A general medical practitioner in a rural area would be held to the standard of a reasonable general practitioner in rural areas. The standard might be different for

duty to perform
An agent's duty to a principal that includes (1) performing the lawful duties expressed in the contract and (2) meeting the standards of reasonable care, skill, and diligence implicit in all contracts.

a general medical practitioner in a big city. In some professions, such as accounting, a national standard of performance (e.g., generally accepted accounting principles) is imposed. If an agent holds himself or herself as possessing higher-than-customary skills, the agent will be held to that higher standard of performance. For example, a lawyer who claims to be a specialist in securities law will be held to a reasonable specialist-in-securities-law standard.

An agent who does not perform his or her express duties or who fails to use the standard degree of care, skill, or diligence is liable to the principal for breach of contract. An agent who negligently or intentionally fails to perform properly is also liable in tort.

duty to notify
An agent's duty to notify the principal of important information concerning the agency.

Duty to Notify   In the course of an agency, the agent usually learns information that is important to the principal. This information may come from third parties or other sources. An agent owes a duty to notify the principal of important information he or she learns concerning the agency. The agent's duty to notify the principal of such information is called the **duty to notify**. The agent is liable to the principal for any injuries resulting from a breach of this duty.

imputed knowledge
Information that is learned by an agent that is attributed to the principal.

Most information learned by an agent in the course of an agency is *imputed* to the principal. The legal rule of **imputed knowledge** means that the principal is assumed to know what the agent knows. This is so even if the agent does not tell the principal certain relevant information.

Example Sonia owns a piece of vacant real estate through which a small river runs. Sonia hires Matthew, a licensed real estate broker, to list the property for sale and try to sell the property. While inquiring in the neighborhood, Leonard, the owner of property that is adjacent to Sonia's property, tells Matthew that a chemical plant upstream has polluted his property and that Matthew should have environmental engineers test the soil on Sonia's property. Matthew does not tell Sonia this information. Sonia sells the property to Macy. It is later discovered that the property Macy bought from Sonia is also polluted. Here, the information that Matthew was told about the possible pollution of the property is imputed to Sonia. Sonia will be held liable to Macy.

duty to account (duty of accountability)
A duty that an agent owes to maintain an accurate accounting of all transactions undertaken on the principal's behalf.

Duty to Account   Unless otherwise agreed, an agent owes a duty to maintain an accurate accounting of all transactions undertaken on the principal's behalf. This **duty to account** (sometimes called the **duty of accountability**) includes keeping records of all property and money received and expended during the course of the agency. A principal has a right to demand an accounting from the agent at any time, and the agent owes a legal duty to make the accounting. This duty also requires the agent to (1) maintain a separate account for the principal and (2) use the principal's property in an authorized manner.

Any property, money, or other benefit received by the agent in the course of an agency belongs to the principal.

Example All secret profits received by an agent are the property of the principal.

If an agent breaches the agency contract, the principal can sue the agent to recover damages caused by breach. The court can impose a **constructive trust** on any secret profits made by the agent or property purchased with the secret profits. The constructive trust is for the benefit of the principal and gives the principal ownership rights to the property of the trust.

duty of loyalty
A fiduciary duty owed by an agent not to act adversely to the interests of the principal.

Example An employee of an employer is paid bribes for steering contracts to a certain supplier. The employee purchases real estate with the money. Here, the employer can obtain a constructive trust over the real property and be awarded the property at the conclusion of a successful trial.

The following feature discusses an agent's duty of loyalty to the principal.

Ethics

Agent's Duty of Loyalty

Because the agency relationship is based on trust and confidence, an agent owes the principal a **duty of loyalty** in all agency-related matters. Thus, an agent owes a **fiduciary duty** not to act adversely to the interests of the principal. If this duty is breached, the agent is liable to the principal. The most common types of breaches of loyalty by an agent are discussed in the following paragraphs:

- **Self-dealing.**   Agents are generally prohibited from undisclosed **self-dealing** with the principal. If there has been undisclosed self-dealing by an agent, the principal can rescind the purchase and recover the money paid to the agent. As an alternative, the principal can ratify the purchase.

  Example A real estate agent who is employed to purchase real estate for a principal cannot secretly sell her own property to the principal. However, the deal is lawful if the principal agrees to buy the property after the agent discloses her ownership of the property.

- **Usurping an opportunity.**   Sometimes an agent is offered a business opportunity or some other opportunity that is meant for the principal. An agent cannot personally **usurp an opportunity** that belongs to the principal. If the agent does so, the principal can recover the opportunity from the agent. The agent can appropriate the opportunity for himself or herself if the principal rejects it after due consideration.

  Example An agent works for a principal that is in the business of real estate development. The principal is looking for vacant land to purchase and develop. A third party who owns and wants to sell his vacant land tells an agent of the principal of the availability of the land. The agent, without informing the principal, purchases the land for his own use. This is a violation of the agent's duty of loyalty.

- **Competing with the principal.**   Agents are prohibited from **competing with the principal** during the course of an agency unless the principal agrees. The reason for this rule is that an agent cannot meet his or her duty of loyalty when his or her personal interests conflict with the principal's interests. The principal may recover the profits made by the agent as well as damages caused by the agent's conduct, such as lost sales. An agent is free to compete with the principal when the agency has ended unless the parties have entered into an enforceable covenant not to compete.

  Example An agent works as a salesperson for a principal who owns an automotive parts business. The agent's job is to sell the principal's automotive parts to auto repair shops and other purchasers. While doing so, the agent also works as a salesperson for a competing seller of automotive parts. Here there is a conflict of interest, and the agent has violated his duty of loyalty.

- **Misuse of confidential information.**   In the course of an agency, the agent often acquires **confidential information** about the principal's affairs (e.g., business plans, technological innovations, customer lists, trade secrets). The agent is under a legal duty not to disclose or **misuse confidential information** either during or after the course of the agency. If the agent violates this duty, the principal can recover damages, lost profits, and any remuneration the agent received from another party to obtain the confidential information. The principal can also obtain an injunction ordering a third party to return the confidential information and to not use such information. There is no prohibition against using general information, knowledge, or experience acquired during the course of an agency in later employment.

  Example An agent works for a principal who owns and operates a bank that specializes in serving wealthy clients. Over many years, the bank has carefully developed a unique and selective list of wealthy individuals that the bank serves or is courting to serve. The agent quits his job at the bank and is hired by another bank. The agent takes the list of wealthy clients developed by his previous employer and discloses the list to his new employer. This is a violation of the agent's duty of loyalty.

- **Dual agency.**   An agent cannot meet a duty of loyalty to two parties with conflicting interests. **Dual agency** occurs when an agent acts for two or more different principals in the same transaction. This practice is generally prohibited unless all the parties involved in the transaction agree to it. If an agent acts as an undisclosed dual agent, he or she must forfeit all compensation received in the transaction. Some agents, such as middlemen and finders, are not considered dual agents. This is because they only bring interested parties together; they do not take part in any negotiations.

  Example A homeowner hires a real estate broker to sell his house. The real estate broker is approached by a person interested in purchasing the house. The real estate broker agrees to accept compensation from the proposed purchaser if the agent can get the seller to agree to a lower price than the asking price. The real estate owner accomplishes this and recovers fees from both the seller and buyer of the house. The agent has violated her duty of loyalty by acting as a double agent.

Tort Liability to Third Parties

A principal and an agent are each personally liable for their own **tortious conduct**. The principal is liable for the tortious conduct of an agent who is acting within the scope of his or her authority. The agent, however, is liable for the tortious conduct of the principal only if he or she directly or indirectly participates in or aids and abets the principal's conduct.

The courts have applied a broad and flexible standard in interpreting scope of authority in the context of employment. Although other factors may also be considered, the courts rely on the following factors to determine whether an agent's conduct occurred within the scope of his or her employment:

- Was the act specifically requested or authorized by the principal?
- Was it the kind of act that the agent was employed to perform?
- Did the act occur substantially within the time period of employment authorized by the principal?
- Did the act occur substantially within the location of employment authorized by the employer?
- Was the agent advancing the principal's purpose when the act occurred?

Where liability is found, tort remedies are available to the injured party. These remedies include recovery for medical expenses, lost wages, pain and suffering, emotional distress, and, in some cases, punitive damages. As discussed in the following paragraphs, the three main sources of **tort liability** for principals and agents are *negligence*, *intentional torts*, and *misrepresentation*.

Negligence

Principals are liable for the negligent conduct of agents acting within the **scope of their employment**. This liability is based on the common law doctrine of **respondeat superior** ("let the master answer"), which, in turn, is based on the legal theory of **vicarious liability** (liability without fault). In other words, the principal is liable because of his or her employment contract with the negligent agent, not because the principal was personally at fault.

respondeat superior
A rule that says an employer is liable for the tortious conduct of its employees or agents while they are acting within the scope of the employer's authority.

The doctrine of **negligence** rests on the principle that if someone (i.e., the principal) expects to derive certain benefits from acting through others (i.e., an agent), that person should also bear the liability for injuries caused to third persons by the negligent conduct of an agent who is acting within their scope of employment.

vicarious liability
Liability without fault that occurs where a principal is liable for an agent's tortious conduct because of the employment contract between the principal and agent, not because the principal was personally at fault.

Example Business Unlimited Corporation employs Harriet as its marketing manager. Harriet is driving her automobile to attend a meeting with a client on behalf of her employer. On her way to the meeting, Harriet is involved in an automobile accident that is caused by her negligence. Several people are seriously injured because of Harriet's negligence. Here, Harriet is personally liable to the injured parties. In addition, Business Unlimited Corporation is also liable as the principal because Harriet was acting within the scope of her employment when she caused the accident.

Frolic and Detour

Agents sometimes do things during the course of their employment to further their own interests rather than the principal's interests. An agent might take a detour to run a personal errand while on assignment for the principal. This is commonly referred to as **frolic and detour**. Negligence actions stemming from frolic and detour are examined on a case-by-case basis. Agents are always personally liable for their tortious conduct in such situations. Principals are generally relieved of liability if the agent's frolic and detour is substantial. However, if

frolic and detour
A situation in which an agent does something during the course of his or her employment to further his or her own interests rather than the principal's.

the deviation is minor, the principal is liable for the injuries caused by the agent's tortious conduct.

Example A salesperson stops home for lunch while on an assignment for his principal. While leaving his home, the agent hits and injures a pedestrian with his automobile. The principal would be liable if the agent's home were not too far out of the way from the agent's assignment. However, the principal would not be liable if an agent who is on an assignment for his employer in Cleveland, Ohio, deviates from his assignment and drives to a nearby city to meet a friend and is involved in an accident. The facts and circumstances of each case determine its outcome.

Coming and Going Rule

Under the common law, a principal is generally not liable for injuries caused by its agents and employees while they are on their way to or from work. This so-called **coming and going rule**, which is sometimes referred to as the **going and coming rule**, applies even if the principal supplies the agent's automobile or other transportation or pays for gasoline, repairs, and other automobile operating expenses. This rule is quite logical: Because principals do not control where their agents and employees live, they should not be held liable for tortious conduct of agents on their way to and from work. This rule applies even if the employer pays for the vehicle or vehicle expenses for the employee.

coming and going rule (going and coming rule)
A rule that says a principal is generally not liable for injuries caused by its agents and employees while they are on their way to or from work.

Example Sarah works as a professor at a university. Her home is 20 miles from the campus. One morning Sarah leaves her home and is driving to work when her negligence causes an automobile accident in which several pedestrians are injured. Here, Sarah is personally liable for her negligence, but the university is not liable because of the coming and going rule.

Dual-Purpose Mission

Sometimes, principals request that agents run errands or conduct other acts on their behalf while the agent or employee is on personal business. In this case, the agent is on a **dual-purpose mission**. That is, he or she is acting partly for himself or herself and partly for the principal. Most jurisdictions hold both the principal and the agent liable if the agent injures someone while on such a mission.

dual-purpose mission
A situation that occurs when a principal requests an employee or agent to run an errand or do another act for the principal while the agent is on his or her own personal business.

Example Suppose a principal asks an employee to drop off a package at a client's office on the employee's way home. If the employee negligently injures a pedestrian while on this dual-purpose mission, the principal is liable to the pedestrian.

Intentional Tort

Intentional torts include acts such as assault, battery, false imprisonment, and other intentional conduct that causes injury to another person. A principal is not liable for the intentional torts of agents and employees that are committed outside the principal's scope of business.

Example If an employee attends a sporting event after working hours and gets into a fight with another spectator at the event, the employer is not liable. This is because the fight was a personal affair and outside the employee's business responsibilities.

However, a principal is liable under the doctrine of vicarious liability for intentional torts of agents and employees committed within the agent's scope of employment. The courts generally apply one of the following tests in determining whether an agent's intentional torts were committed within the agent's scope of employment:

motivation test
A test that determines whether an agent's motivation in committing an intentional tort is to promote the principal's business; if so, the principal is liable for any injury caused by the tort.

- **Motivation test.** Under the **motivation test**, if the agent's motivation in committing an intentional tort is to promote the principal's business, the principal is liable for any injury caused by the tort. However, if an agent's motivation in committing the intentional tort is personal, the principal is not liable, even if the tort takes place during business hours or on business premises.

Example Under the motivation test, an employer—the principal—is not liable if his employee, who is motivated by jealousy, injures someone on the job who dated her boyfriend. Here, the motivation of the employee was personal and not work related.

work-related test

A test that determines whether an agent committed an intentional tort within a work-related time or space; if so, the principal is liable for any injury caused by the agent's intentional tort.

- **Work-related test.** Some jurisdictions have rejected the motivation test as being too narrow. These jurisdictions apply the **work-related test** instead. Under this test, if an agent commits an intentional tort within a work-related time or space—for example, during working hours or on the principal's premises—the principal is liable for any injuries caused by the agent's intentional torts. Under this test, the agent's motivation is immaterial.

Example Under the work-related test, an employer—the principal—is liable if his employee, who was motivated by jealousy, injures someone on the work premises and during work hours who dated her boyfriend. Here, the motivation of the employee is not relevant. What is relevant is that the intentional tort was committed on work premises and during the employee's work hours.

In the following case, the court was called upon to determine whether an employer was liable for an employee's intentional tort.

CASE 18.1   *Intentional Tort*

Burlarley v. Walmart Stores, Inc.

904 N.Y.S.2d 826, Web 2010 N.Y.App. Div. Lexis 6278 (2010)
Appellate Division of the Supreme Court of New York

"In our view, Supreme Court properly concluded that throwing a full bag of heavy items at an unsuspecting customer's face as a 'joke' is not commonly done by a cashier and, indeed, substantially departs from a cashier's normal methods of performance."

—Mercure, Judge

Facts

After an hour of shopping at a Walmart store, Michael Burlarley and his wife proceeded to the checkout at the store. The cashier, joking with the couple in an effort to make her work shift "go a little faster," pretended to ring up items for vastly more than their price and threw various items at Michael. Michael, not amused, told her to stop, and the cashier initially complied. When Michael turned away, however, the cashier threw a bag containing a pair of shoes and shampoo at him. Michael was struck in the face. Michael sued Walmart Stores, Inc., to recover damages. Walmart filed a motion for summary judgment, alleging that the cashier's actions were personally motivated and that Walmart was not liable under the motivation test. The trial court granted summary judgment to Walmart. Michael appealed.

Issue

Is Walmart vicariously liable for the personally motivated acts of its cashier?

Language of the Court

In our view, the court properly concluded that throwing a full bag of heavy items at an unsuspecting customer's face as a "joke" is not commonly done by a cashier and, indeed, substantially departs from a cashier's normal methods of performance. Moreover, the cashier's actions arose not from any work-related motivation, but rather her desire to pass the time and relieve mounting frustration with her job. Accordingly, inasmuch as the cashier acted for purely personal reasons and not in the furtherance of any duty owed to Walmart, the court appropriately determined that the doctrine of respondeat superior was inapplicable.

Decision

Applying the motivation test, the appellate court held that Walmart was not vicariously liable for the intentional tort of its cashier, which was solely motivated by personal reasons and not in the furtherance of Walmart's business. The appellate court affirmed the trial court's grant of summary judgment in favor of Walmart.

Case Questions

Critical Legal Thinking
If the court applied the work-related test, would the outcome of the case be different?

Ethics
Was it ethical for Walmart to deny liability for its employee's actions in this case?

Contemporary Business
Do employers prefer the use of the motivation test or the work-related test when assessing liability for the intentional torts of their employees?

Misrepresentation

Intentional misrepresentations are also known as **fraud** or **deceit**. They occur when an agent makes statements that he or she knows are not true. An **innocent misrepresentation** occurs when an agent negligently makes a misrepresentation to a third party. A principal is liable for the intentional and innocent misrepresentations made by an agent acting within the scope of employment. The third party can either (1) rescind the contract with the principal and recover any consideration paid or (2) affirm the contract and recover damages.

Example Assume that a car salesperson is employed to sell the principal's car, and the principal tells the agent that the car was repaired after it was involved in a major accident. If the agent intentionally tells the buyer that the car was never involved in an accident, the agent has made an intentional misrepresentation. Both the principal and the agent are liable for this misrepresentation.

> **intentional misrepresentation (fraud or deceit)**
> A deceit in which an agent makes an untrue statement that he or she knows is not true.

CONCEPT SUMMARY

TORT LIABILITY OF PRINCIPALS AND AGENTS TO THIRD PARTIES

Agent's Conduct	Agent Liable	Principal Liable
Negligence	Yes	The principal is liable under the doctrine of *respondeat superior* if the agent's negligent act was committed within his or her scope of employment.
Intentional tort	Yes	*Motivation test:* The principal is liable if the agent's motivation in committing the intentional tort was to promote the principal's business.
	Yes	*Work-related test:* The principal is liable if the agent committed the intentional tort within work-related time and space.
Misrepresentation	Yes	The principal is liable for the intentional and innocent misrepresentations made by an agent acting within the scope of his or her authority.

Contract Liability to Third Parties

Agency law imposes **contract liability** on principals and agents, depending on the circumstances. A principal who authorizes an agent to enter into a contract with a third party is liable on the contract. Thus, the third party can enforce the contract against the principal and recover damages from the principal if the principal fails to perform it.

The agent can also be held liable on the contract in certain circumstances. Imposition of such liability depends on whether the agency is classified as *fully disclosed*, *partially disclosed*, or *undisclosed*.

> *The crowning fortune of a man is to be born to some pursuit which finds him employment and happiness, whether it be to make baskets, or broad swords, or canals, or statues, or songs.*
>
> Ralph Waldo Emerson

Fully Disclosed Agency

fully disclosed agency
An agency in which a contracting third party knows (1) that the agent is acting for a principal and (2) the identity of the principal.

A **fully disclosed agency** results if a third party entering into a contract knows (1) that the agent is acting as an agent for a principal and (2) the actual identity of the principal.[1] The third party has the requisite knowledge if the principal's identity is disclosed to the third party by either the agent or some other source.

In a fully disclosed agency, the contract is between the principal and the third party. Thus, the principal, who is called a **fully disclosed principal**, is liable on the contract. The agent, however, is not liable on the contract because the third party relied on the principal's credit and reputation when the contract was made. An agent is liable on the contract if he or she guarantees that the principal will perform the contract.

The *agent's signature* on a contract entered into on the principal's behalf is important. It can establish the agent's status and, therefore, his or her liability. For instance, in a fully disclosed agency, the agent's signature must clearly indicate that he or she is acting as an agent for a specifically identified principal.

Examples Proper agent's signatures include "Allison Adams, agent for Peter Perceival," "Peter Perceival, by Allison Adams, agent," and "Peter Perceival, by Allison Adams."

Example Poran Kawamara decides to sell her house and hires Mark Robbins, a real estate broker, to list and sell the house for a price of $1 million. They agree that Mark will disclose the existence of the agency and the identity of the principal to interested third parties. This is a fully disclosed agency. Mark shows the house to Heather, a prospective buyer, and discloses to Heather that he is acting as an agent for Poran. Heather makes an offer for the house at the $1 million asking price. Mark signs the contract with Heather on behalf of Poran by signing "Mark Robbins, agent for Poran Kawamara." Poran is liable on the contract with Heather, but Mark is not liable on the contract with Heather.

Partially Disclosed Agency

partially disclosed agency
An agency in which a contracting third party knows that the agent is acting for a principal but does not know the identity of the principal.

A **partially disclosed agency** occurs if an agent discloses his or her agency status but does not reveal the principal's identity and the third party does not know the principal's identity from another source. The nondisclosure may be because (1) the principal instructs the agent not to disclose his or her identity to the third party or (2) the agent forgets to tell the third party the principal's identity. In this kind of agency, the principal is called a **partially disclosed principal**.

In a partially disclosed agency, both the principal and the agent are liable on third-party contracts.[2] This is because the third party must rely on the agent's reputation, integrity, and credit because the principal is unidentified. If the agent is made to pay the contract, the agent can sue the principal for indemnification. The third party and the agent can agree to relieve the agent's liability. A partially disclosed agency can be created either expressly or by mistake.

Example A principal and an agent agree that the agent will represent the principal to purchase a business and that the agent will disclose the existence of the agency and the identity of the principal to third parties; this is a fully disclosed agency. Suppose the agent finds a suitable business for the principal and contracts to purchase the business on behalf of the principal, but the agent mistakenly signs the contract with the third party "Allison Adams, agent." This is a partially disclosed agency that occurs because of mistake. The principal is liable on the contract with the third party, and the agent is also liable.

Undisclosed Agency

undisclosed agency
An agency in which a contracting third party does not know of either the existence of the agency or the principal's identity.

An **undisclosed agency** occurs when a third party is unaware of he existence of an agency. The principal is called an **undisclosed principal**. Undisclosed agencies are lawful. They are often used when the principal feels that the terms of the contract would be changed if his or her identity were known. For example, a wealthy party may use an undisclosed agency to purchase property if he thinks that the seller would raise the price of the property if her identity were revealed.

In an undisclosed agency, both the principal and the agent are liable on the contract with the third party. This is because the agent, by not divulging that he or she is acting as an agent, becomes a principal to the contract. The third party relies on the reputation and credit of the agent in entering into the contract. If the principal fails to perform the contract, the third party can recover against the principal or the agent. If the agent is made to pay the contract, he or she can recover indemnification from the principal. An undisclosed agency can be created either expressly or by mistake.

Example The Walt Disney Company wants to open a new theme park in Chicago but needs to first acquire land for the park. Disney employs an agent to work on its behalf to acquire the needed property, with an express agreement that the agent will not disclose the existence of the agency to a third-party seller. If a seller agrees to sell the needed land and the agent signs her name "Allison Adams," without disclosing the existence of the agency, it is an undisclosed agency. Disney is liable on the contract with the third-party seller, and so is the agent.

Agent Exceeding the Scope of Authority

An agent who enters into a contract on behalf of another party impliedly warrants that he has the authority to do so. This is called the agent's **implied warranty of authority**. If the agent exceeds the scope of his or her authority, the principal is not liable on the contract. The agent, however, is liable to the third party for breaching the implied warranty of authority. To recover, the third party must show (1) reliance on the agent's representation and (2) ignorance of the agent's lack of status. A principal is bound on the contract only if she *ratifies* the contract—that is, accepts it as his own. This is called **ratification of a contract**.

Example Henry hires April, a real estate broker, to find him a house in a specified area for $1 million or less. Henry specifies that the house must be at least four thousand square feet and must be a two-story house, with four bedrooms and four bathrooms. Henry, the principal, gives April, the agent, authority to sign a contract on his behalf to purchase such a home. April finds a house she thinks Henry would want to own that is six thousand square feet and costs $1.5 million. April signs a contract with the seller as the disclosed agent of Henry. Here, April has exceeded her authority, and Henry is not bound to purchase the house. April, on the other hand, is bound to the contract to purchase the house. If, however, Henry likes the $1.5 million house, he can ratify the contract with the seller. If Henry does so, he is bound to the contract with the seller.

implied warranty of authority
A warranty of an agent who enters into a contract on behalf of another party that he or she has the authority to do so.

ratification of a contract
A situation in which a principal accepts an agent's unauthorized contract.

CONCEPT SUMMARY
CONTRACT LIABILITY OF PRINCIPALS AND AGENTS TO THIRD PARTIES

Type of Agency	Principal Liable	Agent Liable
Fully disclosed	Yes	No, unless the agent (1) acts as a principal or (2) guarantees the performance of the contract
Partially disclosed	Yes	Yes, unless the third party relieves the agent's liability
Undisclosed	Yes	Yes
Nonexistent	No, unless the principal ratifies the contract	Yes, the agent is liable for breaching the implied warranty of authority.

independent contractor
"A person who contracts with another to do something for him who is not controlled by the other nor subject to the other's right to control with respect to his physical conduct in the performance of the undertaking" [*Restatement (Second) of Agency*].

principal–independent contractor relationship
A relationship between a principal and an independent contractor who is not an employee of the principal but has been employed by the principal to perform a certain task on behalf of the principal.

Exhibit 18.2 PRINCIPAL–INDEPENDENT CONTRACTOR RELATIONSHIP

Independent Contractor

Principals often employ outsiders—that is, persons and businesses that are not employees—to perform certain tasks on their behalf. These persons and businesses are called **independent contractors**. An independent contractor operates his or her own business or profession. The arrangement creates a **principal–independent contractor relationship**. The party that employs an independent contractor is called a *principal*.

Examples Lawyers, doctors, dentists, consultants, stockbrokers, architects, certified public accountants, real estate brokers, and plumbers are examples of those in professions and trades who commonly act as independent contractors.

Example Jamie is a lawyer who specializes in business law. Ace Corporation hires Jamie to represent it in a business transaction. Ace Corporation is the principal, and Jamie is the independent contractor.

A principal–independent contractor relationship is depicted in **Exhibit 18.2**.

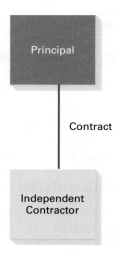

Principal

Contract

Independent Contractor

Factors for Determining Independent Contractor Status

Section 2 of the *Restatement (Second) of Agency* defines *independent contractor* as "a person who contracts with another to do something for him who is not controlled by the other nor subject to the other's right to control with respect to his physical conduct in the performance of the undertaking." Independent contractors usually work for a number of clients, have their own offices, hire employees, and control the performance of their work.

The crucial factor in determining whether someone is an independent contractor or an employee is the **degree of control** that the principal has over that party. Critical factors in determining independent contractor status include:

- Whether the worker is engaged in a distinct occupation or an independently established business
- The length of time the agent has been employed by the principal
- The amount of time that the agent works for the principal
- Whether the principal supplies the tools and equipment used in the work
- The method of payment, whether by time or by the job
- The degree of skill necessary to complete the task

- Whether the worker hires employees to assist him or her
- Whether the employer has the **right to control** the manner and means of accomplishing the desired result

If an examination of these factors shows that the principal asserts little control, the person is an independent contractor. Substantial control indicates an employer–employee relationship. Labeling someone an independent contractor is only one factor in determining whether independent contractor status exists.

Liability for an Independent Contractor's Torts

Generally, a principal is not liable for the torts of its independent contractors. Independent contractors are personally liable for their own torts. The rationale behind this rule is that principals do not control the means by which the results are accomplished.

Example Qixia hires Harold, a lawyer and an independent contractor, to represent her in a court case. While driving to the courthouse to represent Qixia at trial, Harold negligently causes an automobile accident in which Mildred is severely injured. Harold is liable to Mildred because he caused the accident. Qixia is not liable to Mildred because Harold was an independent contractor when he caused the accident.

Principals cannot avoid liability for **inherently dangerous activities** that they assign to independent contractors. For example, the use of explosives, clearing of land by fire, crop dusting, and other inherently dangerous activities involve special risks. In these cases, a principal is liable for the negligence of the independent contractor the principal hired to perform the dangerous task.

In the following case, the court had to determine whether a party was an independent contractor.

> *Nature seems to have taken a particular care to disseminate her blessings among the different regions of the world, with an eye to their mutual intercourse and traffic among mankind, that the nations of the several parts of the globe might have a kind of dependence upon one another and be united together by their common interest.*
>
> Joseph Addison

CASE 18.2   *Independent Contractor*

Lewis v. D. Hays Trucking, Inc.

701 F.Supp.2d 1300, Web 2010 U.S. Dist. Lexis 28035 (2010)
United States District Court for the Northern District of Georgia

"**Therefore no reasonable jury could determine that Hays is an employee and not an independent contractor.**"

—Forrester, District Judge

Facts

Hercules, Inc., is a large chemical corporation. Its operations in Brunswick, Georgia, extracts resins from tree stumps, processes the resins into chemical compounds, and sells them to other manufacturers. Hercules purchases tree stumps from various parties, including D. Hays Trucking, Inc. (Hays). Hercules and Hays entered into a harvesting contract and a freight contract. Among other terms, these contracts specified the price Hercules would pay per ton for tree stumps. These contracts stated:

> *It is understood that the Contractor is an independent contractor and that the Contractor will perform all work and furnish all labor, equipment, machinery, and do everything necessary for the harvesting and delivery of whatever wood the Contractor sells to Hercules. This includes, but is not limited to, compliance with the worker's compensation laws and all laws and regulations relating to hiring, wages, hours, and taxes as may be applicable to the Contractor's operation. Contractor, its employees and agents will*

(continued)

in no way be regarded, nor shall they act as agents or employees of Hercules.

Hays owned its own equipment and delivery vehicles, hired its own truckers and other employees, paid for its employees' workers' compensation coverage and the company's liability insurance, and withheld federal and state taxes from employees' paychecks. Hercules employees often marked tree stumps for Hays to pull out of the ground, but Hays was free to choose the stumps to be pulled and often ignored the suggested tree stumps marked by Hercules. Hays directed the work of its employees who pulled the stumps from the ground and the truckers who delivered the stumps to Hercules. On several occasions, Hays borrowed money from Hercules to pay for operational costs, and it gave Hercules a security interest in its tractors and other equipment as collateral for the repayment of the loans. During the twelve months preceding the accident at issue in this case, Hays delivered 84 loads of stumps to Hercules. Mr. Floyd Dexter Hays, the owner of D. Hays Trucking, Inc., delivered only one truckload of stumps to Hercules prior to the accident involved in this lawsuit.

One night, Mr. Hays was driving a trailer tracker loaded with pine stumps from Alabama to the Hercules plant in Georgia. Just prior to midnight, when he was ten miles from the Hercules plant, Mr. Hays crashed the tractor trailer into the car of Phyllis Lewis, killing her. Mr. Hays was driving the tractor trailer approximately 10 to 15 miles per hour over the 65-miles-per-hour speed limit. The tractor trailer was carrying more than eighty thousand pounds of tree stumps. According to accident reconstruction experts, there were no skid marks from the tractor trailer prior to the collision. Preston Lewis, the executor of the estate of Phyllis Lewis, brought suit in U.S. District Court against Mr. Hays, D. Hays Trucking, Inc., and Hercules, Inc. to recover damages for negligence and *respondeat superior*. Hercules made a motion for summary judgment, alleging that D. Hays Trucking, Inc. was an independent contractor and therefore Hercules could not be held liable for its negligence.

Issue

Is D. Hays Trucking, Inc., an independent contractor or an employee of Hercules?

Language of the Court

Here, the terms of the Harvesting Contract and Freight Contract between Hays and Hercules clearly denominate Hays as an independent contractor. Nothing about those contracts purports to subject Hays to any rules or policies of Hercules. Thus, the presumption arises that Hays is an independent contractor. In the end, it is Hays who determined the time, manner, and method of his work. It was Hays who decided whether he would work a particular tract to "push" the stumps and Hays who hired other individuals to haul the harvested stumps to Hercules. Therefore no reasonable jury could determine that Hays is an employee and not an independent contractor.

Decision

The U.S. District Court held that Hays was an independent contractor, and not an employee, of Hercules. The Court granted Hercules's motion for summary judgment.

Case Questions

Critical Legal Thinking
What factors should be considered in determining whether a party is an employee or independent contractor?

Ethics
Was this a difficult case for the District Court to decide?

Contemporary Business
What is the public policy for relieving liability of parties for the negligence committed by independent contractors they hire?

Liability for an Independent Contractor's Contracts

A principal can authorize an independent contractor to enter into contracts. Principals are bound by the authorized contracts of their independent contractors.

Example Suppose a client hires a lawyer as an independent contractor to represent her in a civil lawsuit against a defendant to recover monetary damages. If the client authorizes the lawyer to settle a case within a certain dollar amount and the lawyer does so, the settlement agreement is binding.

If an independent contractor enters into a contract with a third party on behalf of the principal without express or implied authority from the principal to do so, the principal is not liable on the contract.

Termination of an Agency

An agency contract can be terminated by an *act of the parties*, an *unusual change in circumstances*, *impossibility of performance*, and *operation of law*.

Termination by an Act of the Parties

An agency contract is similar to other contracts in that it can be **terminated by an act of the parties**. An agency can be terminated by the following acts:

1. The mutual assent of the parties

   Example A principal hires a lawyer to represent her in a lawsuit until the lawsuit is resolved. If prior to the resolution of the case by trial or settlement the principal and the lawyer voluntarily agree to terminate the relationship, the agency is terminated.

2. The passage of a stated time

   Example If an agency agreement states "This agency agreement will terminate on August 1, 2015," the agency terminates when that date arrives.

3. The achievement of a specified purpose

   Example If a homeowner hires a real estate broker to sell the owner's house within six months and the house sells after three months, the agency terminates upon the sale of the house.

4. The occurrence of a stated event

   Example If a principal employs an agent to take care of her dog until she returns from a trip, the agency terminates when the principal returns from the trip.

Notice of Termination

The termination of an agency extinguishes an agent's actual authority to act on the principal's behalf. However, if the principal fails to give the proper **notice of termination** to a third party, the agent still has *apparent authority* to bind the principal to contracts with these third parties. To avoid this liability, the principal needs to provide the following notices:

- **Direct notice** of termination to all persons with whom the agent dealt. The notice may be oral or written unless required to be in writing.
- **Constructive notice** of termination to any third party who has knowledge of the agency but with whom the agent has not dealt.

  Example Notice of the termination of an agency that is printed in a newspaper that serves the vicinity of the parties is constructive notice.

  Generally, a principal is not obliged to give notice of termination to strangers who have no knowledge of the agency. Constructive notice is valid against strangers who assert claims of apparent agency.

Termination by an Unusual Change in Circumstances

An agency terminates when there is an **unusual change in circumstances** that would lead the agent to believe that the principal's original instructions should no longer be valid.

The way to wealth is as plain as the way to market. It depends chiefly on two words, industry and frugality: that is, waste neither time nor money, but make the best use of both. Without industry and frugality nothing will do, and with them everything.

Benjamin Franklin

*Shortly his fortune shall be lifted higher;
True industry doth kindle honour's fire.*

William Shakespeare

Most are engaged in business the greater part of their lives, because the soul abhors a vacuum and they have not discovered any continuous employment for man's nobler faculties.

Henry David Thoreau

Example An owner of a farm employs a real estate agent to sell the farm for $1 million. The agent thereafter learns that oil has been discovered on the property, making the property worth $5 million. The agency terminates because of this change in circumstances.

Termination by Impossibility of Performance

An agency relationship terminates if a situation arises that makes its fulfillment impossible. The following circumstances can lead to **termination by impossibility of performance**:

- The loss or destruction of the subject matter of the agency

  Example A principal employs an agent to sell his horse, but the horse dies before it is sold. The agency relationship terminates at the moment the horse dies.

- The loss of a required qualification

  Example A principal employs a licensed real estate agent to sell her house, and the real estate agent's license is revoked before he can sell the principal's house. The agency relationship terminates when the agent loses his license.

- A change in the law

  Example A principal employs an agent to trap alligators. If a law is passed that makes trapping alligators illegal, the agency contract terminates when the law becomes effective.

Termination by Operation of Law

Agency contracts can be **terminated by operation of law**. An agency contract is terminated by operation of law in the following circumstances:

- The death of either the principal or the agent
- The insanity of either the principal or the agent
- The bankruptcy of the principal
- The outbreak of a war between the principal's country and the agent's country

If an agency terminates by operation of law, there is no duty to notify third parties about the termination.

Wrongful Termination

The termination of an agency extinguishes the power of the agent to act on behalf of the principal. If the principal's or agent's termination of an agency contract breaches the contract, the other party can sue to recover damages for **wrongful termination**.

wrongful termination
The termination of an agency contract in violation of the terms of the agency contract. In such a situation, the nonbreaching party may recover damages from the breaching party.

Example A principal employs a licensed real estate agent to sell his house. The agency contract gives the agent an exclusive listing for four months. After one month, the principal unilaterally terminates the agency. The agent can no longer act on behalf of the principal. However, because the principal did not have the right to terminate the contract, the agent can sue him and recover damages (i.e., lost commission) for wrongful termination.

Key Terms and Concepts

Agency (377)
Agency by ratification (379)
Agency law (377)

Agent (377)
Apparent agency (agency by estoppel) (380)

Attorney-in-fact (379)
Coming and going rule (going and coming rule) (385)

Competing with the principal (383)
Confidential information (383)

Law Case with Answer

Desert Cab, Inc. v. Marino

Facts Maria Marino, a cab driver with Yellow-Checkered Cab Company (Yellow Cab), and James Edwards, a cab driver with Desert Cab Inc. (Desert Cab), parked their cabs at the taxicab stand at the Sundance Hotel and Casino in Las Vegas to await fares. Marino's cab occupied the first position in the line, and Edwards's cab occupied the third. As Marino stood alongside her cab, conversing with the driver of another taxi, Edwards began verbally harassing her from inside his cab. When Marino approached Edwards to inquire as to the reason for the harassment, a verbal argument ensued. Edwards jumped from his cab, grabbed Marino by her neck and shoulders, began choking her, and threw her in front of his taxicab. A bystander pulled Edwards off Marino and escorted her back to her cab. Marino sustained injuries that rendered her unable to work for a time. Edwards was convicted of misdemeanor assault and battery. Marino brought a personal injury action against Desert Cab. Is Desert Cab liable for the intentional tort of its employee Edwards?

Answer Yes, Desert Cab is liable for the intentional tort of its employee Edwards. Edwards's misdemeanor assault and battery conviction conclusively prove Edwards's civil liability to Marino. Edwards's wrongful act of attacking Marino is a prerequisite to imposing liability upon his employer Desert Cab. In order to find Desert Cab liable, Marino still had to establish that Desert Cab was responsible for Edwards's conduct. Under the work-related test, if an agent commits an intentional tort within a work-related time or space—during working hours or on the principal's premises—the principal is liable for any injuries caused by the agent's intentional torts. Here, when the attack occurred, Edwards, who was working as a taxicab driver, was waiting in line with Marino to pick up passengers. Edwards's attack on Marino was work related and arose out of the course and scope of Edwards's employment. Whether Edwards had any personal motive for the attack is immaterial. Under the work-related test, the principal Desert Cab is liable for the intentional tort committed by its agent Edwards. Marino can recover damages for her injuries from Desert Cab. *Desert Cab Inc. v. Marino*, 823 P.2d 898, **Web** 1992 Nev. Lexis 6 (Supreme Court of Nevada)

Critical Legal Thinking Cases

18.1 Agency Brendan Bosse and Michael Griffin were part of a group of four teenagers eating a meal at a Chili's restaurant in Dedham, Massachusetts. Chili's is owned by Brinker Restaurant Corporation (collectively "Chili's"). The cost of the meal was $56. The teenagers decided not to pay. They went out of the building, got in their car, and drove away, heading northward up Route 1.

A patron of the restaurant saw the teenagers leave without payment. He followed them in his white sport-utility vehicle (SUV). The teenagers saw him following them. A high-speed chase ensued through Dedham side streets. The patron used his cell phone to call the Chili's manager. The manager called 911 and reported the incident and the location of the car chase. The teenagers' car collided with a cement wall, and Bosse and Griffin were seriously injured. The Chili's patron drove past the crash scene and was never identified.

Bosse and Griffin sued Chili's for compensatory damages for their injuries. The plaintiffs argued that the patron was an agent of Chili's, and therefore Chili's was liable to the plaintiffs, based on the doctrine of *respondeat superior*, which holds a principal liable for the acts of its agents. Chili's filed a motion for summary judgment, arguing that the patron was not its agent. Is the restaurant patron who engaged in the high-speed car chase an agent of Chili's? *Bosse v. Brinker Restaurant Corporation, d.b.a. Chili's Grill and Bar*, **Web** 2005 Mass.Super. Lexis 372 (Superior Court of Massachusetts)

18.2 Scope of Employment Lapp Roofing and Sheet Metal Company, Inc., is an Ohio corporation headquartered in Dayton, Ohio. The company provides construction services in several states. Lapp Roofing sent James Goldick and other Lapp Roofing employees to work on a roofing project in Wilmington, Delaware. Lapp Roofing entrusted Goldick, as job foreman, with a white Ford van to transport the workers to the job site and to provide transportation to meals and other necessities. Lapp Roofing's company policy prohibited employees from driving company vehicles for personal purposes.

While in Wilmington, Goldick and another Lapp Roofing employee, James McNees, went to Gators Bar and Restaurant. Goldick, after eating and drinking for several hours, was ejected from the bar. Shortly thereafter, Goldick drove the company van onto the curb in front of the bar, striking two people in the parking lot and seven individuals on the curb outside the bar. Subsequently, the police stopped the van and apprehended Goldick. Goldick was arrested and pleaded guilty to criminal assault charges. Christopher M. Keating and the other injured individuals filed a personal injury lawsuit against Goldick and Lapp Roofing. Lapp Roofing defended, alleging that it was not liable because Goldick's negligent conduct was committed outside the scope of his employment. Is Goldick's negligent conduct committed within the scope of his employment for Lapp Roofing, thus making Lapp Roofing liable? *Keating v. Goldick and Lapp Roofing and Sheet Metal Company, Inc.*, **Web** 2004 Del.Super. Lexis 102 (Superior Court of Delaware)

18.3 Frolic and Detour Jesse Spires was employed as a welder by Johnson Welded Products, Inc. Johnson Welded Products provides a lunchroom equipped with a microwave, refrigerator, and vending machine for sandwiches, snacks, and drinks. Spires worked a shift that ran from 3:15 P.M. until 12:15 A.M. One day at work, Spires was on his way to a friend's house for lunch during his lunch break, driving his own pickup truck, when he collided with Donald Siegenthaler, who was riding a motorcycle. The collision, which was the result of Spires's negligence, caused injury to Siegenthaler. Siegenthaler sued Johnson Welded Products, alleging that Spires was an agent of Johnson Welded Products at the time of the accident and that Johnson Welded Products was vicariously liable under the doctrine of *respondeat superior*. Johnson Welded Products argued that Spires was on personal business and a frolic and detour when he caused the accident. Is Spires an agent of Johnson Welded Products, acting within the scope of his employment, at the time of the accident that injured Siegenthaler? *Siegenthaler v. Johnson Welded Products, Inc.*, **Web** 2006 OhioApp. Lexis 5616 (Court of Appeals of Ohio)

18.4 Agent Marc Brandon worked for Warner Bros. Entertainment, Inc. (Warner), as vice-president of antipiracy Internet operations. Brandon drove his car from his home in southern California to the Burbank Airport, where he parked his car in an airport parking lot. Brandon then flew to a three-day conference he attended in Sunnyvale, California, that was sponsored by one of Warner's antipiracy venders. Warner approved Brandon's trip and paid for his airfare, hotel, and airport parking. When Brandon left the conference, he flew back to the Burbank Airport, where he retrieved his car from the parking lot. On his way home from the airport, his route took him past his Warner office location. He continued on toward his house, using his normal route from the office to his home. Brandon did not stop at his Warner office. Approximately 2 or 3 miles past the office, he was involved in an automobile collision with Jared Southard. One or both cars struck and injured pedestrians Chuenchomporn Jeewarat, Tipphawan Tantisriyanurak, and Kanhathai Vutthicharoen.

Vutthicharoen died as a result of her injuries. Jeewarat, Tantisriyanurak, and Vutthicharoen's heirs sued Brandon, Southard, and Warner to recover damages for negligence and *respondeat superior*. Warner filed a motion for summary judgment, alleging that because Brandon was taking his normal route home, Warner was protected from liability by the coming and going rule. Does the coming and going rule protect Warner from liability? *Jeewarat v. Warner Bros. Entertainment, Inc.*, 177 Cal.App.4th 427, 98 Cal.Rptr.3d 837, **Web** 2009 Cal.App. Lexis 1478 (Court of Appeal of California)

18.5 Intentional Tort Kenya Massey and Raymond Rodriquez entered a Starbucks coffee shop in Manhattan, New York City. The couple ordered two beverages from a Starbucks employee and paid for the drinks. When Massey and Rodriquez moved toward the seating area while waiting for their drinks to be prepared, Karen Morales, the shift supervisor at the store, told Massey and Rodriquez that they could not sit down because the store was closing. Massey informed Morales that when she received her drinks, she and Rodriquez intended to sit and enjoy them at Starbucks.

Morales instructed a Starbucks employee to cancel Massey's beverage order and refund Massey's money. Massey asked to speak with a manager. Morales identified herself as the manager and told Massey to "get a life." At that point, Starbucks employee Melissa Polanco told Massey, "I get off at ten o'clock, and we can go outside." Massey and Rodriquez exited and walked away from the store while Massey and the employees yelled profanities at each other. As Massey continued to walk away, Polanco ran after and caught her and punched Massey in the face. Morales then jumped on Massey's back, and a physical altercation ensued. A pedestrian passerby finally separated the parties. Massey's face was bleeding when she got up.

The Starbucks employees who were involved in the altercation were terminated by Starbucks. Massey sued Starbucks for damages for the injuries she suffered. Starbucks moved for summary judgment, alleging that the employees were not acting within the scope of their employment when they assaulted Massey. Are the Starbucks employees acting within their scope of employment when they assault Massey? *Massey v. Starbucks Corporation*, **Web** 2004 U.S. Dist. Lexis 12993 (United States District Court for the Southern District of New York)

18.6 Duty of Loyalty Peter Shields was the president and a member of the board of directors of Production Finishing Corporation for seven years. The company provided steel-polishing services. It did most, if not all, of the polishing work in the Detroit area, except for that of the Ford Motor Company. (Ford did its own polishing.) On a number of occasions, Shields discussed with Ford, on behalf of Production Finishing, the possibility of providing Ford's steel-polishing services. When Shields learned that Ford was discontinuing its polishing operation, he incorporated Flat Rock Metal and submitted a confidential proposal to Ford which provided that he would buy Ford's equipment and provide polishing services to Ford. It was not until he resigned from Production Finishing that he informed the board of directors that he was pursuing the Ford business himself. Production Finishing sued Shields. Has Shields breached his fiduciary duty of loyalty to Production Finishing? Who wins? *Production Finishing Corporation v. Shields*, 158 Mich.App. 479, 405 N.W.2d 171, **Web** 1987 Mich. App. Lexis 2379 (Court of Appeals of Michigan)

18.7 Independent Contractor Yvonne Sanchez borrowed money from MBank to purchase an automobile. She gave MBank a security interest in the vehicle as collateral to secure the loan. When Sanchez defaulted on the loan, MBank hired El Paso Recovery Service, an independent contractor, to repossess the automobile. The two men from El Paso who were dispatched to Sanchez's house found the car parked in the driveway and hooked it to a tow truck. Sanchez approached them and demanded that they cease their efforts and leave the premises, but the men nonetheless continued with the repossession. Before the men could tow the automobile into the street, Sanchez jumped into the car, locked the doors, and refused to leave. The men towed the car at a high rate of speed to the repossession yard. They parked the car in the fenced repossession yard, with Sanchez inside, and padlocked the gate. Sanchez was left in the repossession lot with a Doberman Pinscher guard dog loose in the yard. Later, she was rescued by the police. Sanchez filed suit against MBank, alleging that it was liable for the tortious conduct of El Paso. MBank challenged it was not liable because El Paso was an independent contractor. Who wins? *MBank El Paso, N.A. v. Sanchez*, 836 S.W.2d 151, **Web** 1992 Tex. Lexis 97 (Supreme Court of Texas)

Ethics Cases

18.8 Ethics National Biscuit Company (Nabisco) is a corporation that produces and distributes cookies and other food products to grocery stores and other outlets across the nation. Nabisco hired Ronnell Lynch as a cookie salesperson-trainee, and eventually assigned Lynch to his own sales territory. Lynch's duties involved making sales calls, taking orders, and making sure the shelves of stores in his territory were stocked with Nabisco products. During the first two months, Nabisco received numerous complaints from store owners in Lynch's territory that Lynch was overly aggressive and was taking shelf space for Nabisco products that was reserved for competing brands.

One day, after being in his territory for two months, Lynch visited a grocery store that was managed by Jerome Lange. Lynch was there to place previously delivered merchandise on the store's shelves. An argument developed between Lynch and Lange. Lynch became very angry and started swearing. Lange told Lynch to stop swearing or leave the store because children were present. Lynch became uncontrollably angry and went behind the counter and dared Lange to fight. When Lange refused to fight, Lynch proceeded to viciously assault and batter Lange, causing severe injuries. When Lange sued Nabisco, Nabisco denied liability. *Lange v. National Biscuit Company*, 297 Minn. 399, 211 N.W.2d 783, **Web** 1973 Minn. Lexis 1106 (Supreme Court of Minnesota)

1. What are the rules for determining the liability of a principal for the intentional torts of an agent? Explain.
2. Was it ethical for Nabisco to deny liability in this case? Do you think the prior complaints against Lynch would have had any effect on the decision in this case?
3. Is Nabisco liable for the intentional tort (assault and battery) of its employee Ronnell Lynch?

18.9 Ethics   The Hagues, husband and wife, owned a 160-acre tract that they decided to sell. They entered into a listing agreement with Harvey C. Hilgendorf, a licensed real estate broker, which gave Hilgendorf the exclusive right to sell the property for a period of twelve months. The Hagues agreed to pay Hilgendorf a commission of 6 percent of the accepted sale price if a bona fide buyer was found during the listing period. By letter five months later, the Hagues terminated the listing agreement with Hilgendorf. Hilgendorf did not acquiesce to the Hagues' termination, however. One month later, Hilgendorf presented an offer to the Hagues from a buyer willing to purchase the property at the full listing price. The Hagues ignored the offer and sold the property to another buyer. Hilgendorf sued the Hagues for breach of the agency agreement. *Hilgendorf v. Hague*, 293 N.W.2d 272, **Web** 1980 IowaSup. Lexis 882 (Supreme Court of Iowa)

1. Does a principal have the power to terminate an agency? Does a principal have a right to terminate an agency? Explain.
2. Did the Hagues act ethically in this case?
3. Who wins the lawsuit and why?

Internet Exercises

1. Go to http://findarticles.com/p/articles/mi_qa3898/is_199812/ai_n8825591 and read the article "Bar patron hit by truck in parking lot."

2. Go to www.sband.org/Pattern_Jury_Instructions/viewarticle.asp?ID=441&parent_category=civil and read the pattern jury instruction "Negligence Action—Disputed Liability."

3. Go to http://en.wikipedia.org/wiki/Walt_Disney_World. Read the information about how the Walt Disney Company used dummy corporations to acquire much of the land in central Florida for its Walt Disney World Resort.

Endnotes

1. *Restatement (Second) of Agency*, Section 4.
2. *Restatement (Second) of Agency*, Section 321.

19 Equal Opportunity in Employment

PHYSICALLY CHALLENGED PERSON'S PARKING SPOT

The federal Americans with Disabilities Act (ADA) protects persons with disabilities from discrimination in many facets of life. Title I of the ADA requires employers to make reasonable accommodations for individuals with disabilities that do not cause undue hardship to the employer. Title II requires public agencies and public transportation to be accessible to persons with disabilities. Title III requires public accommodations and commercial facilities—such as lodging and hotels, recreation, transportation, education, dining, and stores—to reasonably accommodate persons with disabilities. And Title VI requires telecommunications companies to provide functionally equivalent services to persons who are deaf or hard of hearing and persons with speech impairments.

Learning Objectives

After studying this chapter, you should be able to:

1. Describe the scope of coverage of Title VII of the Civil Rights Act of 1964.
2. Identify race, color, and national origin discrimination that violate Title VII.
3. Identify and describe gender discrimination, sexual harassment, and genetic information discrimination.
4. Describe the scope of coverage of the Age Discrimination in Employment Act.
5. Describe the protections afforded by the Americans with Disabilities Act.

Chapter Outline

Introduction to Equal Opportunity in Employment

Equal Employment Opportunity Commission (EEOC)

Title VII of the Civil Rights Act of 1964
   LANDMARK LAW • *Title VII of the Civil Rights Act of 1964*

Race, Color, and National Origin Discrimination
   CONTEMPORARY ENVIRONMENT • *English-Only Requirement in the Workplace*
   LANDMARK LAW • *Civil Rights Act of 1866*

Gender Discrimination
   DIGITAL LAW • *Offensive E-Mails Constitute Sexual Harassment*

Religious Discrimination

Defenses to a Title VII Action

Equal Pay Act

Age Discrimination

Chapter Outline *(continued)*

> " *What people have always sought is equality of rights before the law. For rights that were not open to all equally would not be rights.*"
>
> —Cicero
> *De Officilis, Book II, Chapter XII*

Introduction to Equal Opportunity in Employment

We hold these truths to be self-evident, that all men and women are created equal.

Elizabeth Cady Stanton (1848)

Under common law, employers could terminate an employee at any time and for any reason. In this same vein, employers were free to hire and promote anyone they chose, without violating the law. This often created unreasonable hardship on employees and erected employment barriers to certain minority classes.

Starting in the 1960s, Congress began enacting a comprehensive set of federal laws that eliminated major forms of **employment discrimination**. These laws, which were passed to guarantee **equal opportunity in employment** to all employees and job applicants, have been broadly interpreted by the federal courts, particularly the U.S. Supreme Court. States have also enacted antidiscrimination laws. Many state and local governments have adopted laws that prevent discrimination in employment.

This chapter discusses equal opportunity in employment laws.

equal opportunity in employment

The rights of all employees and job applicants (1) to be treated without discrimination and (2) to be able to sue employers if they are discriminated against.

Equal Employment Opportunity Commission (EEOC)

Equal Employment Opportunity Commission (EEOC)

The federal administrative agency that is responsible for enforcing most federal antidiscrimination laws.

The **Equal Employment Opportunity Commission (EEOC)** is the federal agency responsible for enforcing most federal antidiscrimination laws. The members of the EEOC are appointed by the U.S. president. The EEOC is empowered to conduct investigations, interpret the statutes, encourage conciliation between employees and employers, and bring suits to enforce the law. The EEOC can also seek injunctive relief.

The EEOC has jurisdiction to investigate charges of **discrimination** based on race, color, national origin, gender, religion, age, disability, and genetic information.

WEB EXERCISE

Go to **www.eeoc.gov/field/index .cfm**. Find the location and address of the EEOC field office that serves your area.

Complaint Process

If a person believes that he or she has been discriminated against in the workplace, he or she cannot immediately file a lawsuit against the employer. The complainant must first file a complaint with the EEOC. The EEOC often requests that the parties try to resolve their dispute through mediation. If mediation does not work, the EEOC will investigate the charge. If the EEOC finds a violation, it will decide whether to sue the employer. If the EEOC sues the employer, the complainant cannot sue the employer. In this case, the EEOC represents the complainant. If the EEOC finds a violation and chooses not to bring suit, or does not find a violation, the EEOC will issue a **right to sue letter** to the complainant. This gives the complainant the right to sue his or her employer.

If a state has a **Fair Employment Practices Agency (FEPA)**, the complainant may file his or her claim with the FEPA instead of the EEOC. Often a complainant will file a complaint with an FEPA if state law provides protection from discrimination not covered by federal laws or if the FEPA's procedure permits a filing date that is longer than that of the EEOC. The FEPA complaint process is similar to that of the EEOC.

right to sue letter
A letter that is issued by the EEOC if it chooses not to bring an action against an employer that authorizes a complainant to sue the employer for employment discrimination.

Lilly Ledbetter Fair Pay Act of 2009

The Civil Rights Act provided that a rejected applicant for a job or an employee who suffers pay discrimination must file a discrimination lawsuit within 180 days of the employer's act that causes the discrimination. In *Ledbetter v. Goodyear Tire & Rubber Co., Inc.*,[1] the U.S. Supreme Court held that the 180-day statute of limitations began to run on the date the pay was agreed upon, not when the most recent paycheck violation occurred. Thus, a victim who had been subject to pay discrimination for more than 180 days and had failed to report the claim within 180 days of the first violation was denied his or her claim.

Congress responded by enacting the **Lilly Ledbetter Fair Pay Act of 2009**,[2] which overruled the U.S. Supreme Court's decision. The act provides that each discriminatory pay decision restarts the statutory 180-day clock. Thus, a plaintiff can file a claim against an employer within 180 days of the most recent paycheck violation. The act provides that a court can award back pay for up to two years preceding the filing of the claim if similar violations occurred during the prior two-year time period.

Example A female is hired by an employer as an employee. During a thirty-six-month period the employer engages in pay act violations and underpays the female employee each pay period during the three-year period. Here, the female employee has 180 days from date of the last paycheck violation to file her claim. If she files the claim and the employer is found to have violated the law during the three-year period, the female employee can recover back pay for the two years preceding the date of the last paycheck violation.

Lilly Ledbetter Fair Pay Act of 2009
A federal statute that permits a complainant to file an employment discrimination claim against an employer within 180 days of the most recent paycheck violation and to recover back pay for up to two years preceding the filing of the claim if similar violations occurred during the two-year period.

Title VII of the Civil Rights Act of 1964

Prior to the passage of major federal antidiscrimination laws in the 1960s, much discrimination in employment existed in this country. In the 1960s, Congress enacted several major federal statutes that outlawed employment discrimination

CIVIL RIGHTS ACT OF 1964
This is a photograph of President Lyndon Baines Johnson signing the Civil Rights Act of 1964[3] on July 2, 1964. Dr. Martin Luther King, Jr. is standing directly behind the President. Dr. King was an influential civil rights leader who worked to end racial segregation and racial discrimination.

WEB EXERCISE
To read a biography of Dr. Martin Luther King, Jr., go to **www. thekingcenter.org/history/ about-dr-king/**.

Title VII of the Civil Rights Act of 1964 (Fair Employment Practices Act)
A title of a federal statute enacted to eliminate job discrimination based on five protected classes: *race, color, religion, sex,* and *national origin.*

against members of certain classes. These federal laws were instrumental in providing equal opportunity in employment in this country. One of the main statutes is *Title VII of the Civil Rights Act of 1964.*[3] This statute is discussed in the following feature.

Landmark Law

Title VII of the Civil Rights Act of 1964

After substantial debate, Congress enacted the **Civil Rights Act of 1964**. **Title VII of the Civil Rights Act** (also called the **Fair Employment Practices Act**) was intended to eliminate job discrimination based on the following *protected classes: race, color, national origin, sex,* and *religion.*

As amended by the **Equal Employment Opportunity Act of 1972**, Section 703(a)(2) of Title VII provides, in pertinent part, that:

It shall be an unlawful employment practice for an employer
    (1) to fail or refuse to hire or to discharge any individual, or otherwise to discriminate against any

individual with respect to his compensation, terms, conditions, or privileges of employment, because of such individual's race, color, religion, sex, or national origin; or
    (2) to limit, segregate, or classify his employees or applicants for employment in any way which would deprive or tend to deprive any individual of employment opportunities or otherwise adversely affect his status as an employee, because of such individual's race, color, religion, sex, or national origin.

Rights matter most when they are claimed by unpopular minorities.

J. Michael Kirby
Sydney Morning Herald,
November 30, 1985

Scope of Coverage of Title VII

Title VII of the Civil Rights Act of 1964 applies to (1) employers with fifteen or more employees, (2) all employment agencies, (3) labor unions with fifteen or more members, (4) state and local governments and their agencies, and (5) most federal government employment. Native American tribes and tax-exempt private clubs are expressly excluded from coverage. Other portions of the Civil Rights Act of 1964 prohibit discrimination in housing, education, and other facets of life.

Title VII prohibits discrimination in hiring, decisions regarding promotion or demotion, payment of compensation and fringe benefits, availability of job training and apprenticeship opportunities, referral systems for employment, decisions regarding dismissal, work rules, and any other "term, condition, or privilege" of employment. Any employee of a covered employer, including undocumented aliens,[4] may bring actions for employment discrimination under Title VII.

U.S. citizens employed by U.S.-controlled companies in foreign countries are covered by Title VII. Foreign nationals employed in foreign countries by U.S.-controlled companies are not covered by Title VII.

Title VII prohibits two major forms of employment discrimination: *disparate-treatment discrimination* and *disparate-impact discrimination*. These are discussed in the following paragraphs.

Disparate-Treatment Discrimination

Disparate-treatment discrimination occurs when an employer treats a specific *individual* less favorably than others because of that person's race, color, national origin, sex, or religion. In such situations, the complainant must prove that (1) he or she belongs to a Title VII protected class, (2) he or she applied for and was qualified for the employment position, (3) he or she was rejected despite this, and (4) the employer kept the position open and sought applications from persons with the complainant's qualifications.[5]

Example A member of a minority race applies for a promotion to a position advertised as available at his company. The minority applicant, who is qualified for the position, is rejected by the company, which hires a nonminority applicant for the position. The minority applicant sues under Title VII. He has a *prima facie* case of illegal discrimination. The burden of proof shifts to the employer to prove a nondiscriminatory reason for its decision. If the employer offers a reason, such as saying that the minority applicant lacked sufficient experience, the burden shifts back to the minority applicant to prove that this was just a *pretext* (i.e., not the real reason) for the employer's decision.

> **disparate-treatment discrimination**
> A form of discrimination that occurs when an employer discriminates against a specific individual because of his or her race, color, national origin, sex, or religion.

Disparate-Impact Discrimination

Disparate-impact discrimination occurs when an employer discriminates against an entire protected *class*. Many disparate-impact cases are brought as class action lawsuits. Often, this type of discrimination is proven through statistical data about an employer's employment practices. The plaintiff must demonstrate a *causal link* between the challenged practice and the statistical imbalance. Showing a statistical disparity between the percentages of protected class employees and the percentage of the population that the protected class makes within the surrounding community is not enough, by itself, to prove discrimination. Disparate-impact discrimination can occur when an employer adopts a work rule that is neutral on its face but is shown to cause an adverse impact on a protected class.

> **disparate-impact discrimination**
> A form of discrimination that occurs when an employer discriminates against an entire protected class. An example is discrimination in which a racially neutral employment practice or rule causes an adverse impact on a protected class.

Example If an employer has a rule that all applicants for an executive position must be at least 5 feet 8 inches tall, this looks like a neutral rule because it applies to both males and females. However, because this rule is unrelated to the performance of an executive position and eliminates many more females than males from being hired or promoted to an executive position, it is disparate-impact sex discrimination in violation of Title VII.

Remedies for Violations of Title VII

A successful plaintiff in a Title VII action can recover back pay and reasonable attorneys' fees. The courts also have broad authority to grant equitable remedies. For instance, the courts can order reinstatement, grant fictional seniority, and issue injunctions to compel the hiring or promotion of protected minorities.

A court can award **punitive damages** against an employer in a case involving an employer's malice or reckless indifference to federally protected rights. The sum of compensatory and punitive damages is capped at different amounts of money, depending on the size of the employer.

Race, Color, and National Origin Discrimination

Title VII of the Civil Rights Act of 1964 was primarily enacted to prohibit employment discrimination based on *race*, *color*, and *national origin*.

Race Discrimination

race discrimination
Employment discrimination against a person because of his or her race.

Race discrimination in employment violates Title VII. *Race* refers to following categories:

Racial Group	Description
African American	A person having origins in any of the black racial groups of Africa.
Asian	A person having origins in any of the original peoples of the Far East, Southeast Asia, or the Indian subcontinent.
Caucasian	A person having origins in any of the original peoples of Europe, the Middle East, and North Africa.
Native American	A person having origins in any of the original peoples of North, South, or Central America.
Pacific Islander	A person having origins in any of the original people of Hawaii and the Pacific Islands.

Example National Corporation has a job opening for its chief executive officer (CEO) position. The employer receives applications for this position from many persons, including Joe Thomas, who is an African American. Mr. Thomas is the best-qualified applicant for the job. If National Corporation does not hire Mr. Thomas because of his race, the company has engaged in race discrimination, in violation of Title VII. This would be disparate-treatment racial discrimination.

Example If an employer refuses to hire or promote all persons of a racial class, then the company has engaged in employment discrimination, in violation of Title VII. This would be disparate impact discrimination.

National Origin Discrimination

national origin discrimination
Employment discrimination against a person because of his or her heritage, cultural characteristics, or the country of the person's ancestors.

National origin refers to the place of origin of a person's ancestors, physical, linguistic, or cultural characteristics, or heritage. **National origin discrimination** would include discrimination against persons of a particular nationality (e.g., persons of Irish descent), against persons who come from a certain place (e.g., Iran), against persons of a certain culture (e.g., Hispanics), or against persons because of their accents. Discrimination by an employer based on a person's national origin or heritage violates Title VII.

Example National Corporation has a chief operations officer (COO) position open. Several persons from within the company apply for a promotion to this position. Naseem al-Gharsi, whose national origin is Yemen, is one of the applicants. Naseem has a Ph.D. in information sciences, ten years' work experience, and has been with the company for five years, in the capacity of operations manager. Although Naseem is the best-qualified person for the position, Naseem is not promoted because of his Arabic heritage, and a less-qualified person is promoted. National Corporation has engaged in national origin discrimination in violation of Title VII.

The following feature discusses the lawfulness of English-only rules in the workplace.

Contemporary Environment

English-Only Requirement in the Workplace

In today's multicultural society, many persons can speak two languages, usually English and another language. Often, these persons will speak their native language in the workplace. In response, many employers have adopted "English-only" rules for the workplace. The issue is whether English-only rules are lawful or whether they create national origin discrimination, in violation of Title VII. Title VII permits employers to adopt English-only rules under certain circumstances. The Equal Employment Opportunity Commission (EEOC) states that an English-only rule that is justified by "business necessity" is lawful. As with any other workplace policy, an English-only rule must be adopted for nondiscriminatory reasons.

An employer English-only rule that prohibits the use of a non-English language in the entire work premises at all times usually is presumed to be national origin discrimination in violation of Title VII. Consider the following case. Premier Operating Services, Inc. adopted an English-only rule that provided "All conversations on these premises are to be in English. Other languages may be spoken to customers who cannot speak English." A large number of employees were Hispanic and spoke Spanish as well as English. The employer's rule prohibited these workers from not only speaking Spanish while on the job, but also during breaks, lunchtime, and even while on the premises coming to or leaving work. The Hispanic

workers filed a claim with the EEOC. The U.S. District Court held that the blanket English-only rule constituted national origin discrimination in violation of Title VII.[6]

However, an English-only rule that is limited to the work area is usually lawful. Consider the following case. A hospital adopted an English-only rule which required that employees speak only English in the course of performing their duties, and wherever patients could hear workers speaking. The employees were free to speak a language other than English during breaks, lunchtime, and before and after work while still on the premises. A Hispanic employee challenged the English-only rule as constituting national origin discrimination. A court declared that the limited English-only rule did not violate Title VII.[7]

On the other hand, an employer's rule which requires that employees be bilingual to qualify for a job does not violate Title VII as long as there is justification for the rule. Consider the following case. A school district that served a Hispanic neighborhood required that its teachers be bilingual in English and Spanish. A job applicant who was fluent in English but did not speak Spanish applied for a job. Although otherwise qualified for the job, he was not hired. He brought a Title VII charge of a violation of Title VII. The court held that the bilingual requirement was justified and therefore did not violate Title VII.[8]

Color Discrimination

Color refers to the color or complexion of a person's skin. Discrimination by an employer based on color violates Title VII. **Color discrimination** cases are not brought as often as cases involving other forms of discrimination.

Example If a light-skinned member of a race refuses to hire a dark-skinned member of the same race, this constitutes color discrimination in violation of Title VII.

The following feature discusses the Civil Rights Act of 1866.

color discrimination
Employment discrimination against a person because of his or her color, for example, where a light-skinned person of a race discriminates against dark-skinned person of the same race.

Landmark Law

Civil Rights Act of 1866

The **Civil Rights Act of 1866** was enacted after the Civil War. **Section 1981** of this act states that all persons "have the same right ... to make and enforce contracts ... as is enjoyed by white persons."[9] This law was enacted to give African Americans, just freed from slavery, the same right to contract as whites. Section 1981 expressly prohibits racial discrimination; it has also been held to forbid discrimination based on national origin.

Employment decisions are covered by Section 1981 because the employment relationship is contractual. Although most racial and national origin employment discrimination cases are brought under Title VII, a complainant might bring an action under Section 1981 for two reasons: (1) A private plaintiff can bring an action without going through the procedural requirements of Title VII, and (2) there is no cap on the recovery of compensatory or punitive damages under Section 1981.

Civil Rights Act of 1866
A federal statute enacted after the Civil War that says all persons "have the same right ... to make and enforce contracts ... as is enjoyed by white persons." This act prohibits racial and national origin employment discrimination.

Gender Discrimination

Title VII of the Civil Rights Act of 1964 prohibits job discrimination based on gender. The act, as amended, the EEOC's rules, and court decisions prohibit employment discrimination based on *gender, pregnancy,* and *sexual orientation.* In addition, *sexual harassment* is also prohibited.

Gender Discrimination

gender discrimination (sex discrimination)
Discrimination against a person because of his or her gender.

Title VII prohibits employment discrimination based on gender. Although the prohibition against **gender discrimination**, also known as **sex discrimination**, applies equally to men and women, the overwhelming majority of Title VII sex discrimination cases are brought by women. Sex discrimination cases are brought where there is direct sex discrimination.

Example If an employer refuses to promote a qualified female to a management position because of her gender, this would be direct sex discrimination in violation of Title VII.

Title VII also prohibits any form of gender discrimination where sexual favors are requested in order to obtain a job or be promoted. This is called **quid pro quo sex discrimination**.

Example If a manager refuses to promote a female unless she engages in sexual activities with the manager, this is quid pro quo sex discrimination that violates Title VII.

Pregnancy Discrimination

Pregnancy Discrimination Act
A federal act that forbids employment discrimination because of pregnancy, childbirth, or related medical conditions.

In 1978, the **Pregnancy Discrimination Act** was enacted as an amendment to Title VII.[10] This amendment forbids employment discrimination because of "pregnancy, childbirth, or related medical conditions."

Example Susan, a 30-year-old college graduate, goes on a job interview for an open position at a company. During a job interview, the interviewer asks Susan if she plans on having children, if that would affect her ability to come to work every day or to perform her duties, and if it would affect her ability to travel on company business. The company refuses to hire Susan because she is a female of an age who might have children. This is a violation of the Pregnancy Discrimination Act.

Sex-Plus Discrimination

Courts have recently been called upon to address claims of **sex-plus discrimination**. In this form of discrimination, an employer does not discriminate against a class as a whole but treats a subset of the class differently. Primary examples of such discrimination are an employer not discriminating against females in general but discriminating against married women or women with children. The discriminated against subset of females may assert sex discrimination in violation of Title VII.

Sexual Harassment

Sometimes managers and co-workers engage in conduct that is offensive because it is sexually charged. Such conduct is often referred to as **sexual harassment**. This includes lewd remarks, offensive or sexually oriented jokes; name-calling, slurs, intimidation, ridicule, mockery, and insults or put-downs; offensive or sexually explicit objects, pictures, cartoons, posters, and screen savers; physical threats; touching; and other verbal or physical conduct of a sexual nature.

The U.S. Supreme Court has held that sexual harassment that creates a **hostile work environment** violates Title VII.[11] To determine what conduct creates a hostile work environment, the U.S. Supreme Court has stated:

> We can say that whether an environment is "hostile" or "abusive" can be determined only by looking at all the circumstances. These may include the frequency of the discriminatory conduct; its severity; whether it is physically threatening or humiliating, or a mere offensive utterance; and whether it unreasonably interferes with an employee's work performance.[12]

sexual harassment
Lewd remarks, touching, intimidation, posting of indecent materials, and other verbal or physical conduct of a sexual nature that occurs on the job.

Employer's Defense to a Charge of Sexual Harassment

Employers are not strictly liable for the sexual harassment of their employees. An employer may raise an **affirmative defense** against liability by proving two elements:[13]

1. The employer exercised reasonable care to prevent, and promptly correct, any sexual harassing behavior.
2. The plaintiff-employee unreasonably failed to take advantage of any preventive or corrective opportunities provided by the employer or to otherwise avoid harm.

The defendant-employer has the burden of proving this affirmative defense. In determining whether the defense has been proven, a court must consider (1) whether the employer has an antiharassment policy, (2) whether the employer had a complaint mechanism in place, (3) whether employees were informed of the antiharassment policy and complaint procedure, and (4) other factors that the court deems relevant.

An employee who believes that he or she is being sexually harassed has a duty to report the harassment to his or her employer, usually to the human resources manager of the employer. An employer can be found liable for sexual harassment of its employees if it has not adopted an antiharassment policy or has not established a complaint policy, or if an employer has been informed of sexual harassment but does not take steps to investigate the charge or to remedy the situation if harassment has been found.

The following feature discusses sexual harassment caused by sending offensive e-mails.

WEB EXERCISE
Go to **www.eeoc.gov/eeoc/ newsroom**. Under the term "Press Releases" replace "Search all releases" with "sexual harassment" and click on the "Search" button. Read an EEOC press release of a case involving sexual harassment.

Digital Law

Offensive E-Mails Constitute Sexual Harassment

The use of e-mail in business has dramatically increased efficiency and information sharing among employees. Managers and workers can communicate with each other, send documents, and keep each other appraised of business developments. In many organizations, e-mail has replaced the telephone as the most-used method of communication, and it has eliminated the need for many meetings. This is a boon for business. But the downside is that e-mail has increased the exposure of businesses to sexual and racial harassment lawsuits.

E-mail often sets the social tone of an office and has been permitted to be slightly ribald. At some point, however, e-mail conduct becomes impermissible and crosses the line to actionable sexual or racial harassment. The standard of whether e-mail creates an illegal hostile work environment is the same as that for measuring harassment in any other context: The offensive conduct must be severe and cannot consist of isolated or trivial remarks and incidents.

E-mail harassment differs from many other incidents of harassment because it is subtle and insidious. E-mail has increased sexual or racial harassment on the job, and it has also become a smoking gun that undermines a company's attempt to defend such cases. Therefore, employers must adopt policies pertaining to the use of e-mail by their employees and make their employees aware that certain e-mail messages constitute sexual or racial harassment and violate the law. Employers should make periodic inspections and audits of stored e-mail to ensure that employees are complying with company antiharassment policies.

Same-Sex Harassment

In *Oncale v. Sundowner Offshore Services, Incorporated*,[14] the U.S. Supreme Court held that **same-sex harassment** violates Title VII. In *Oncale*, a male who worked on an eight-man crew on an oil rig sued because he was subjected to repeated sex-related humiliating actions against him by his male coworkers. The Supreme Court held that an employee who has been harassed by members of his or her own sex can sue for sexual harassment. Many state and local antidiscrimination laws outlaw same-sex discrimination and harassment in the workplace.

Other Forms of Harassment

In addition to gender, a hostile work environment can also be found if harassment is based on a person's race, color, national origin, religion, age, disability, genetic information, and other factors.

Religious Discrimination

religious discrimination
Discrimination against a person because of his or her religion or religious practices.

reasonable accommodation for religion
Under Title VII, an employer's duty to *reasonably accommodate* the religious observances, practices, or beliefs of its employees if doing so does not cause an *undue hardship* on the employer.

Title VII prohibits employment discrimination based on a person's religion. *Religions* include traditional religions, other religions that recognize a supreme being, and religions based on ethical or spiritual tenets. Many **religious discrimination** cases involve a conflict between an employer's work rule and an employee's religious beliefs (e.g., an employee being required to work on his or her religious holiday).

The right of an employee to practice his or her religion is not absolute. Under Title VII, an employer is under a duty to **reasonably accommodate** the religious observances, practices, or beliefs of its employees if doing so does not cause an **undue hardship** on the employer. The courts must apply these general standards to specific fact situations. In making their decisions, the courts must consider factors such as the size of the employer, the importance of the employee's position, and the availability of alternative workers.

Example An employer with five hundred employees could most likely make a reasonable accommodation for a Jewish employee to not work on the holy day of Yum

Kippur. With so many employees, it would likely not cause an undue hardship on the employer to require another worker to cover for one day.

Title VII expressly permits religious organizations to give preference in employment to individuals of a particular religion. For example, if a person applies for a job with a religious organization but does not subscribe to its religious tenets, the organization may refuse to hire that person.

Defenses to a Title VII Action

Title VII and case law recognize several defenses to a charge of discrimination under Title VII. Employers can select or promote employees based on *merit*. Merit decisions are often based on work, educational experience, and professionally developed ability tests. To be lawful under Title VII, such a requirement must be job related.

Many employers maintain *seniority* systems that reward long-term employees. Higher wages, fringe benefits, and other preferential treatment (e.g., choice of working hours, choice of vacation schedule) are examples of such rewards. Seniority systems provide an incentive for employees to stay with the company. Such systems are lawful if they are not the result of intentional discrimination.

Bona Fide Occupational Qualification (BFOQ)

Discrimination based on protected classes other than race or color is permitted if it is shown to be a **bona fide occupational qualification (BFOQ)**. Thus, an employer can justify discrimination based on gender in some circumstances. To be legal, a BFOQ must be both *job related* and a *business necessity*.

Examples Allowing only women to be locker room attendants in a women's gym is a valid BFOQ. Prohibiting males from being managers or instructors at the same gym would not be a BFOQ.

bona fide occupational qualification (BFOQ)
A true job qualification. Employment discrimination based on a protected class other than race or color is lawful if it is *job related* and a *business necessity*. This exception is narrowly interpreted by the courts.

CONCEPT SUMMARY

TITLE VII OF THE CIVIL RIGHTS ACT

Covered employers and employment decisions	1. **Employers.** Employers with 15 or more employees for 20 weeks in the current or preceding year, all employment agencies, labor unions with 15 or more members, state and local governments and their agencies, and most federal government employment.
	2. **Employment decisions.** Decisions regarding hiring; promotion; demotion; payment of salaries, wages, and fringe benefits; dismissal; job training and apprenticeships; work rules; or any other term, condition, or privilege of employment. Decisions to admit partners to a partnership are also covered.
Protected classes	1. **Race.** A broad class of individuals with common characteristics (e.g., African American, Caucasian, Asian, Native American).
	2. **Color.** The color of a person's skin (e.g., light-skinned person, dark-skinned person).
	3. **National origin.** A person's country of origin or national heritage (e.g., Italian, Hispanic).
	4. **Sex.** A person's sex, whether male or female. Includes sexual harassment and discrimination against females who are pregnant.
	5. **Religion.** A person's religious beliefs. An employer has a duty to reasonably accommodate an employee's religious beliefs if doing so does not cause an undue hardship on the employer.

(continued)

Types of discrimination	1. **Disparate-treatment discrimination.** Discrimination against a specific individual because that person belongs to a protected class.
	2. **Disparate-impact discrimination.** Discrimination in which an employer discriminates against a protected class. A neutral-looking employment rule that causes discrimination against a protected class is disparate-impact discrimination.
Defenses	1. **Merit.** Job-related experience, education, or unbiased ability test.
	2. **Seniority.** Length of time an employee has been employed by the employer. Intentional discrimination based on seniority is unlawful.
	3. **Bona fide occupational qualification (BFOQ).** Discrimination based on sex, religion, or national origin is permitted if it is a valid BFOQ for the position. Qualification based on race or color is not a permissible BFOQ.
Remedies	1. **Equitable remedy.** The court may order the payment of back pay, issue an injunction awarding reinstatement, grant fictional seniority, or order some other equitable remedy.
	2. **Damages.** The court can award compensatory damages in cases of intentional discrimination. The court can award punitive damages in cases involving an employer's malice or reckless indifference to federally protected rights.

Equal Pay Act

Equal Pay Act
A federal statute that protects both sexes from pay discrimination based on sex. It extends to jobs that require equal skill, equal effort, equal responsibility, and similar working conditions.

Discrimination often takes the form of different pay scales for men and women performing the same job. The **Equal Pay Act** of 1963 protects both sexes from pay discrimination based on sex.[15] This act covers all levels of private-sector employees and state and local government employees. Federal workers are not covered, however.

The act prohibits disparity in pay for jobs that require *equal skill* (i.e., equal experience), *equal effort* (i.e., mental and physical exertion), *equal responsibility* (i.e., equal supervision and accountability), or *similar working conditions* (e.g., dangers of injury, exposure to the elements). To make this determination, the courts examine the actual requirements of jobs to determine whether they are equal and similar. If two jobs are determined to be equal and similar, an employer cannot pay disparate wages to members of different sexes.

Legislation to apply the principle of equal pay for equal work without discrimination because of sex is a matter of simple justice.

Dwight D. Eisenhower

Employees can bring a private cause of action against an employer for violating the Equal Pay Act. Back pay and liquidated damages are recoverable. In addition, the employer must increase the wages of the discriminated-against employee to eliminate the unlawful disparity of wages. The wages of other employees may not be lowered.

Criteria That Justify a Differential in Wages

The Equal Pay Act expressly provides four criteria that justify a differential in wages. These defenses include payment systems that are based on:

- Seniority
- Merit (as long as there is some identifiable measurement standard)
- Quantity or quality of product (i.e., commission, piecework, or quality-control–based payment systems are permitted)
- "Any factor other than sex" (including shift differentials, such as night versus day shifts)

The employer bears the burden of proving these defenses.

Example Mary and Peter both meet the educational requirements for a particular entry-level job and are both hired as staff accountants by a company to perform exactly the same duties at their job. If the company pays Peter a salary that is 20 percent higher than Mary's salary, this would be a violation of the Equal Pay Act.

Example Peter, a college graduate, has been working for a company for five years as a staff accountant. Mary, a new college graduate with no experience, is hired by the company as a staff accountant, with the same job duties and responsibilities as Peter. Peter is paid a 20 percent higher salary than Mary. This differential is justified based on seniority and therefore does not violate the Equal Pay Act.

Age Discrimination

Some employers have discriminated against employees and prospective employees based on their age. Primarily, employers have often refused to hire older workers. The **Age Discrimination in Employment Act (ADEA)**, which prohibits certain **age discrimination** practices, was enacted in 1967.[16]

The ADEA protects employees who are 40 and older from job discrimination based on their age. The ADEA prohibits age discrimination in all employment decisions, including hiring, promotions, payment of compensation, and other terms and conditions of employment. Employers cannot use employment advertisements that discriminate against applicants covered by the ADEA. The **Older Workers Benefit Protection Act (OWBPA)** amended the ADEA to prohibit age discrimination with regard to employee benefits.[17]

Example Wayne, who is 50 years old, applies for an open position as manager at Big Box Retail Stores, Inc. Wayne meets the job requirements of having a college degree and prior experience as a store manager and is otherwise qualified for the job. The employer refuses to hire Wayne because of his age and hires someone who is 30 for the job. This would be age discrimination in violation of ADEA.

Because persons under 40 are not protected by the ADEA, an employer can maintain an employment policy of hiring only workers who are 40 years of age or older without violating the ADEA. However, some state laws protect persons under 40 from being discriminated against. Under ADEA, an employer can maintain an employment practice whereby it gives preferential treatment to older workers over younger workers when they are both within the 40 years and older category.[18]

Example An employer can legally prefer to hire persons 50 years of age and older over persons aged 40 to 49.

The ADEA permits age discrimination where a bona fide occupational qualification is shown. The BFOQ may be asserted as a necessary qualification of the job or for public safety.

Example Hiring a young person to play a young character in a movie or play is a lawful BFOQ. Setting an age limit for pilots would be a lawful BFOQ for public safety reasons.

The ADEA is administered by the EEOC. Private plaintiffs can also sue under the ADEA. A successful plaintiff in an ADEA action can recover back wages, attorneys' fees, and equitable relief, including hiring, reinstatement, and promotion. Where a violation of the ADEA is found, the employer must raise the wages of the discriminated-against employee. It cannot lower the wages of other employees.

Physically Challenged Person Discrimination

The **Americans with Disabilities Act (ADA)**,[19] which was signed into law July 26, 1990, is the most comprehensive piece of civil rights legislation since the Civil Rights Act of 1964. The ADA imposes obligations on employers and providers of public transportation, telecommunications, and public accommodations to accommodate individuals with disabilities.

Age Discrimination in Employment Act (ADEA)
A federal statute that prohibits age discrimination practices against employees who are 40 years and older.

Older Workers Benefit Protection Act (OWBPA)
A federal statute that prohibits age discrimination regarding employee benefits.

Americans with Disabilities Act (ADA)
A federal statute that imposes obligations on employers and providers of public transportation, telecommunications, and public accommodations to accommodate individuals with disabilities.

The following feature discusses Title I of the ADA that prohibits employment discrimination against persons with covered disabilities.

Landmark Law

Title I of Americans with Disabilities Act

Title I of the ADA[20] prohibits employment discrimination against qualified individuals with disabilities in regard to job application procedures, hiring, compensation, training, promotion, and termination. Title I covers employers with fifteen or more employees. The United States and corporations wholly owned by the United States are exempt from Title I coverage.

Title I of the ADA is administered by the EEOC. An aggrieved individual must first file a charge with the EEOC, which may take action against the employer or permit the individual to pursue a private cause of action. If a disability discrimination lawsuit is successful, the court can issue an injunction against the employer, order the hiring or reinstatement (with back pay) of the discriminated-against individual, award attorneys' fees, and order the employer to pay compensatory and punitive damages to the discriminated-against individual; the

dollar amounts are subject to the same caps as Title VII damages.

Americans with Disabilities Act Amendments Act of 2008

Congress passed the **Americans with Disabilities Act Amendments Act (ADAAA) of 2008**[21] which amended the ADA. The primary purposes of the ADAAA were to reverse narrow interpretations of the ADA made by the U.S. Supreme Court[22] and other courts and regulations of the EEOC, expand the definition of disability, require that the definition of disability be broadly construed, and require common-sense assessments in applying certain provisions of the ADA.

The ADA, as amended by the ADAAA, provides expansive protections for disabled individuals in the workplace. The following discussion is based on the cumulative provisions of the ADA and the ADAAA.

Title I of the ADA
A title of a federal statute that prohibits employment discrimination against qualified individuals with disabilities in regard to job application procedures, hiring, compensation, training, promotion, and termination.

Americans with Disabilities Act Amendments Act (ADAAA) of 2008
A federal act that amends the ADA by expanding the definition of disability, requiring that the definition of disability be broadly construed, and requiring commonsense assessments in applying certain provisions of the ADA.

qualified individual with a disability
A person who has a physical or mental impairment that substantially limits a major life activity who, with or without reasonable accommodation, can perform the essential functions of the job that person desires or holds.

Qualified Individual with a Disability

A **qualified individual with a disability** is a person who has a physiological or psychological impairment that substantially limits a major life activity who, with or without reasonable accommodation, can perform the essential functions of the job that person desires or holds. A disabled person is someone who (1) has a physical or mental impairment that substantially limits one or more of his or her major life activities, (2) has a record of such impairment, or (3) is regarded as having such impairment. The ADAA's mandate is to construe the term "disability" broadly.

A **physiological impairment** includes any physical disorder or condition, cosmetic disfigurement, or anatomical loss affecting one or more of the following body systems: neurological, musculoskeletal, special sense organs, respiratory, cardiovascular, reproductive, digestive, genitourinary, hemic and lymphatic, skin, and endocrine.

Examples Examples of physiological impairments include deafness, blindness, speech impediments, partially or completely missing limbs, mobility impairments requiring the use of a wheelchair, autism, cancer, cerebral palsy, diabetes, epilepsy, HIV/AIDS, multiple sclerosis, and muscular dystrophy.

Impairment also includes **mental or psychological disorders**, such as intellectual disability (e.g., mental retardation), organic brain syndrome, emotional or mental illness, and specific learning disabilities.

Examples Examples of mental or psychological impairments include major depression, bipolar disorder, posttraumatic stress disorder, obsessive-compulsive disorder, and schizophrenia.

In addition to defining a disabled person as having an existing impairment, as discussed above, the ADA also defines a disabled person as someone who has a *record* of a physical or mental impairment that substantially limits a major life activity. An individual meets the "record of" definition of disability when in the past, although not currently, he or she had such an impairment. If an employer discriminates against that individual because of such a record, the employer violates the ADA.

Limits on Employer Questions

Title I of the ADA limits an employer's ability to inquire into or test for an applicant's disabilities. Title I forbids an employer from asking a job applicant about the existence, nature, and severity of a disability. An employer may, however, inquire about the applicant's ability to perform job-related functions. Preemployment medical examinations before a job offer are forbidden. Once a job offer has been made, an employer may require a medical examination and may condition the offer on the examination results, as long as all entering employees are subject to such an examination. The information obtained must be kept confidential.

Reasonable Accommodation

Under Title I, an employer is under the obligation to make a **reasonable accommodation** to accommodate an individual's disability as long as such accommodation does not cause an *undue hardship* on the employer.

If an employer makes a reasonable accommodation to accommodate an individual's disability, there is no violation of the ADA. However, if an employer does not make a reasonable accommodation that could be made without causing an undue hardship on the employer, the employer has violated the ADA.

Examples Reasonable accommodations may include making facilities readily accessible to individuals with disabilities, providing part-time or modified work schedules, acquiring equipment or devices, modifying examination and training materials, and providing qualified readers or interpreters.

reasonable accommodation for disability
Under Title I of the ADA, an employer's duty to *reasonably accommodate* an individual's disability if doing so does not cause an *undue hardship* on the employer.

Undue Hardship

Employers are not obligated to provide accommodations that would impose an undue hardship—that is, actions that would require significant difficulty or expense. The EEOC and the courts consider factors such as the nature and cost of accommodation, the overall financial resources of the employer, and the employer's type of operation. Obviously, what may be a significant difficulty or expense for a small employer may not be an undue hardship for a large employer. If the needed accommodation would cause an undue hardship on the employer, there is no violation of the ADA if the emploer does not make the accomodation.

Uncovered Conditions

The ADA does not consider some impairments or illnesses or certain conditions disabilities. In fact, the act expressly states that certain impairments are not covered by the ADA. Temporary or nonchronic impairments of short duration with little or no residual effects usually are not considered disabilities.

Examples Temporary or nonchronic impairments that are not considered disabilities include common colds, seasonal or common influenzas, sprained joints, minor or nonchronic gastrointestinal disorders, broken bones that are expected to heal completely, and seasonal allergies that do not substantially limit a person's major life activities. Pregnancy is not considered an impairment and, therefore, is not considered a disability under the ADA.

Genetic Information Nondiscrimination Act (GINA)
A federal statute that makes it illegal for an employer to discriminate against job applicants and employees based on genetic information.

A current user of illegal drugs or an alcoholic who uses alcohol or is under the influence of alcohol at the workplace is not covered by the ADA. However, former users of illegal drugs and recovering alcoholics could meet the definition of disability if they have successfully completed a supervised rehabilitation program or are participating in a supervised rehabilitation program (e.g., Narcotics Anonymous, Alcoholics Anonymous).

The following feature discusses genetic information discrimination.

Contemporary Environment

Genetic Information Nondiscrimination Act (GINA)

There have been and will continue to be tremendous advances in developing genetic tests that identify a person's DNA and other genetic information. With *genetic information*, it is possible to determine a person's propensity to be stricken by many diseases, such as diabetes, heart disease, Huntington's disease, Lou Gehrig's disease, Alzheimer's disease, multiple sclerosis, certain types of cancers, and other diseases. With genetic information, preventive steps can be instituted, including medical, pharmaceutical, dietary, and exercise.

However, genetic information can be misused, possibly by employers if they have access to or knowledge of an applicant's or an employee's genetic information or his or her family's genetic information. Such misuse is called **genetic information discrimination**.

Example An employer might discriminate against an applicant or employee if it had information that the person's family members have been stricken by a debilitating or a fatal disease and, because of genetics,

the applicant or employee is at increased risk of suffering from the same disease.

To address this concern, Congress enacted the **Genetic Information Nondiscrimination Act (GINA)** in 2008.[23] **Title II of GINA** makes it illegal for an employer to discriminate against job applicants and employees based on genetic information. Thus, an employer may not use genetic information in making employment decisions, including decisions to hire, promote, provide benefits, or terminate, or other employment decisions. GINA is administered by the EEOC and other federal government agencies. Remedies for violations include corrective action and monetary fines. Individuals have a right to pursue private lawsuits to seek hiring, reinstatement, back pay, and compensatory and punitive damages.

Inadvertent discovery of genetic information (the "water cooler" exemption) and voluntary submission of genetic information to an employer (e.g., as part of a wellness program) do not violate the act. The misuse of such information does violate the act.

genetic information discrimination
Discrimination based on information from which it is possible to determine a person's propensity to be stricken by diseases.

retaliation
Unlawful act taken by an employer against an employee for filing a charge of discrimination or participating in a discrimination proceeding.

Retaliation

Federal antidiscrimination laws prohibit employers from engaging in **retaliation** against an employee for filing a charge of discrimination or participating in a discrimination proceeding concerning race, color, national origin, gender, religion, age, disability, genetic information, and other forms of discrimination. Acts of retaliation include dismissing, demoting, harassing, or other methods of reprisal.

Example Mary filed a gender discrimination claim with the EEOC which states that her employer has engaged in sex discrimination in violation of Title VII. The employer may not retaliate against Mary for filing this claim.

In the following case, the U.S. Supreme Court decided an important issue regarding employer retaliation.

Thompson v. North American Stainless, LP

131 S.Ct. 863, 178 L.Ed.2d 694, Web 2011 U.S. Lexis 913 (2011)
Supreme Court of the United States

"We think it obvious that a reasonable worker might be dissuaded from engaging in protected activity if she knew that her fiancé would be fired."

—Scalia, Justice

Facts

Miriam Regalado and Eric Thompson, who were engaged to be married, both worked at North American Stainless, LP (NAS). Regalado filed a charge with the Equal Employment Opportunity Commission (EEOC), alleging sex discrimination by NAS, in violation of Title VII of the Civil Rights Act. Three weeks later NAS fired Thompson. Thompson filed a charge with the EEOC, claiming that NAS fired him to retaliate against Regalado for filing her charge against NAS. After conciliation efforts proved unsuccessful, Thompson sued NAS, alleging third-party retaliation, in violation of Title VII. The U.S. District Court granted summary judgment to NAS, concluding that Title VII does not permit third-party retaliation claims. An en banc hearing of the U.S. Court of Appeals upheld this decision. The Court of Appeals reasoned that Thompson, as a third party, was not included in the class of persons who could bring a retaliation case under Title VII. Thompson appealed to the U.S. Supreme Court.

Issue

Does Title VII permit third-party retaliation claims against an employer?

Language of the U.S. Supreme Court

Title VII's antiretaliation provision prohibits any employer action that well might have dissuaded a reasonable worker from making or supporting a charge of discrimination. We think it obvious that a reasonable worker might be dissuaded from engaging in protected activity if she knew that her fiancé would be fired.

The more difficult question in this case is whether Thompson may sue NAS for its alleged violation of Title VII. We conclude that Thompson falls within the zone of interests protected by Title VII. Thompson was an employee of NAS, and the purpose of Title VII is to protect employees from their employers' unlawful actions. Moreover, accepting the facts as alleged, Thompson is not an accidental victim of the retaliation—collateral damage, so to speak, of the employer's unlawful act. To the contrary, injuring him was the employer's intended means of harming Regalado. Hurting him was the unlawful act by which the employer punished her. In those circumstances, we think Thompson well within the zone of interests sought to be protected by Title VII. He is a person aggrieved with standing to sue.

Decision of the U.S. Supreme Court

The U.S. Supreme Court held that Title VII grants a third party the right to file a claim against his or her employer for retaliation. Thus, Thompson may proceed with his claim of retaliation against NAS for firing him to retaliate against his fiancée Regalado. The Supreme Court remanded the case for further proceedings.

Note

An employee against whom an employer retaliates for filing a Title VII charge of discrimination may rightfully file a claim of retaliation against the employer. Thus, Regalado could file a charge of retaliation against NAS for retaliating against her by firing her fiancé Thompson.

Case Questions

Critical Legal Thinking
Why does Title VII permit retaliation claims? What would be the consequences if Title VII did not permit retaliation claims against an employer?

Ethics
Did North American Stainless act ethically by firing Thompson?

Contemporary Business
Does this case increase the possibility that employers could face other retaliation claims, such as for firing an employee's boyfriend, girlfriend, relative, friend, or coworker?

Affirmative Action

Title VII of the Civil Rights Act of 1964 outlawed discrimination in employment based on race, color, national origin, sex, and religion. The law clearly prohibited any further discrimination based on these protected classes. However, did the federal statute intend to grant a favorable status to the classes of persons who had been previously discriminated against? In a series of cases, the U.S. Supreme Court upheld the use of **affirmative action** to make up for egregious past discrimination, particularly based on race.

affirmative action
A policy which provides that certain job preferences will be given to minority or other protected-class applicants when an employer makes an employment decision.

Affirmative Action Plan

Employers often adopt an **affirmative action plan**, which provides that certain job preferences will be given to members of minority racial and ethnic groups, females, and other protected-class applicants when making employment decisions. Such plans can be voluntarily adopted by employers, undertaken to settle a discrimination action, or ordered by the courts.

To be lawful, an affirmative action plan must be *narrowly tailored* to achieve some *compelling interest*. Employment quotas based on a specified number or percentage of minority applicants or employees are unlawful. If a person's minority status is only one factor of many factors considered in an employment decision, that decision will usually be considered lawful.

Reverse Discrimination

Title VII applies to members of minority groups and also protects members of majority classes from discrimination. Lawful affirmative action plans have an effect on members of majority classes. The courts have held that if an affirmative action plan is based on preestablished numbers or percentage quotas for hiring or promoting minority applicants, then it causes illegal **reverse discrimination**. In this case, the members of the majority class may sue under Title VII and recover damages and other remedies for reverse discrimination. Some reverse discrimination cases are successful.

reverse discrimination
Discrimination against a group that is usually thought of as a majority.

Key Terms and Concepts

Affirmative action (416)
Affirmative action plan (416)
Affirmative defense (407)
Age discrimination (411)
Age Discrimination in Employment Act (ADEA) (411)
Americans with Disabilities Act (ADA) (411)
Americans with Disabilities Act Amendments Act (ADAAA) of 2008 (412)

Bona fide occupational qualification (BFOQ) (409)
Civil Rights Act of 1866 (406)
Civil Rights Act of 1964 (402)
Color discrimination (405)
Discrimination (400)
Disparate-impact discrimination (403)
Disparate-treatment discrimination (403)

Employment discrimination (400)
Equal Employment Opportunity Act of 1972 (402)
Equal Employment Opportunity Commission (EEOC) (400)
Equal opportunity in employment (400)
Equal Pay Act (410)
Fair Employment Practices Agency (FEPA) (401)

Gender discrimination (sex discrimination) (406)
Genetic information discrimination (414)
Genetic Information Nondiscrimination Act (GINA) (414)
Hostile work environment (407)
Lilly Ledbetter Fair Pay Act of 2009 (401)
Mental or psychological disorders (412)
National origin discrimination (404)

Law Case with Answer

National Association for the Advancement of Colored People, Newark Branch v. Town of Harrison, New Jersey

Facts   The town of Harrison, New Jersey adopted Ordinance 747, which stipulated that "all officers and employees of the Town shall, as a condition of employment, be bona fide residents of the Town." Because of the implementation of this ordinance for years, none of the fifty-one police officers, fifty-five firefighters, or eighty nonuniformed employees of the town were African Americans. Although the town of Harrison is a small, primarily white community, located in Hudson County, New Jersey, it is clearly aligned with Essex County to the west and is considered an extension of the city of Newark, which it abuts. Newark's population is approximately 60 percent African American. Essex County's civilian labor force totals 391,612, of which 130,397 (or 33.3 percent) are African American. In addition, two other counties—Bergen and Union counties—are within an easy commute of the town of Harrison. The four counties have a total civilian labor force of 1,353,555, of which 214,747 are African American. Only 0.2 percent of Harrison's population is African American. Several African Americans who were members of the National Association for the Advancement of Colored People, Newark Branch (NAACP) applied for employment with the town of Harrison but were rejected because they did not meet the residency requirement. The NAACP sued Harrison for race discrimination, in violation of Title VII. Does the residency requirement of the town of Harrison constitute race discrimination, in violation of Title VII of the Civil Rights Act of 1964?

Answer   Yes, the residency requirement of the town of Harrison constitutes race discrimination, in violation of Title VII of the Civil Rights Act of 1964. Evidence shows that the town of Hudson is part of a larger, more diverse cosmopolitan area. The town of Hudson is within Hudson County, New Jersey, and abuts the city of Newark. By reason of the geographical location and the flow of transportation facilities, the town of Harrison could reasonably be viewed as a component of the city of Newark and a part of Essex County. The city of Newark's population is approximately 60 percent African American. Essex County's civilian labor force totals 391,612, of which 130,397 (or 33.3 percent) are African American. The town of Harrison could draw employees from its own county of Hudson as well as Bergen, Essex, and Union counties. These four counties have a total civilian labor force of 1,353,555, of which 214,747 are African American. Thus, the town of Harrison could easily draw employees from a four-county area. It would be hard to conclude that among the very substantial number of African Americans in the four-county labor market there are not large numbers of persons qualified to serve as managers, police officers, firefighters, clerks, and laborers.

For all practical purposes, Harrison has no African American residents. Thus, to limit employment to residents effectively excludes African Americans from employment by the town of Harrison. If the residency requirement were removed, qualified African Americans would seek positions with the town of Harrison's municipal government. Thus, the town of Harrison's residency requirement is a facially neutral policy that has a disproportionate discriminatory impact on African Americans. Because of this discriminatory effect, the town of Harrison's residency ordinance constitutes disparate-impact race discrimination, in violation of Title VII of the Civil Rights Act of 1964. An injunction against the enforcement of the residency requirement should be issued. *National Association for the Advancement of Colored People, Newark Branch v. Town of Harrison, New Jersey*, 907 F.2d 1408, **Web** 1990 U.S. App. Lexis 11793 (United States Court of Appeals for the Third Circuit)

Critical Legal Thinking Cases

19.1 Hostile Work Environment   The Pennsylvania State Police (PSP) hired Nancy Drew Suders as a police communications operator for the McConnellsburg barracks. Suders's supervisors were Sergeant Eric D. Easton, station commander at the McConnellsburg barracks, Patrol Corporal William D. Baker, and Corporal Eric B. Prendergast. Those three supervisors subjected Suders to a continuous barrage of sexual harassment that ceased only when she resigned from the force. Easton would bring up the subject of people having sex with animals each time Suders entered his office. He told Prendergast, in front of Suders, that young girls should be given instruction in how to gratify men with oral sex. Easton also would sit down near Suders, wearing Spandex shorts, and spread his legs apart. Baker repeatedly made obscene gestures in Suders's presence and shouted out vulgar comments inviting sex. Baker made these gestures as many as five to ten times per night throughout Suders's employment at the barracks. Further, Baker would rub his rear end in front of her and remark "I have a nice ass, don't I?"

Five months after being hired, Suders contacted Virginia Smith-Elliot, PSP's equal opportunity officer, and stated that she was being harassed at work and was afraid. Smith-Elliot's response appeared to Suders to be insensitive and unhelpful. Two days later, Suders resigned from the force. Suders sued PSP, alleging that she had been subject to sexual harassment and constructively discharged and forced to resign. Can an employer be held liable when the sexual harassment conduct of its employees is so severe that the victim of the harassment resigns? *Pennsylvania State Police v. Suders*, 542 U.S. 129, 124 S.Ct. 2342, 159 L.Ed.2d 204, **Web** 2004 U.S. Lexis 4176 (Supreme Court of the United States)

19.2 Religious Discrimination   Trans World Airlines (TWA), an airline, operated a large maintenance and overhaul base for its airplanes in Kansas City, Missouri. Because of its essential role, the stores department at the base operated 24 hours per day, 365 days per year. The employees at the base were represented by the International Association of Machinists and Aerospace Workers (Union). TWA and Union entered into a collective bargaining agreement that included a seniority system for the assignment of jobs and shifts.

TWA hired Larry Hardison to work as a clerk in the stores department. Soon after beginning work, Hardison joined the Worldwide Church of God, which does not allow its members to work from sunset on Friday until sunset on Saturday and on certain religious holidays. Hardison, who had the second-lowest seniority within the stores department, did not have enough seniority to observe his Sabbath regularly. When Hardison asked for special consideration, TWA offered to allow him to take his Sabbath off if he could switch shifts with another employee-union member. None of the other employees would do so. TWA refused Hardison's request for a four-day workweek because it would have had to hire and train a part-time worker to work on Saturdays or incur the cost of paying overtime to an existing full-time worker on Saturdays. Hardison sued TWA for religious discrimination, in violation of Title VII of the Civil Rights Act. Do TWA's actions violate Title VII? Who wins? *Trans World Airlines v. Hardison*, 432 U.S. 63, 97 S.Ct. 2264, 53 L.Ed.2d 113, **Web** 1977 U.S. Lexis 115 (Supreme Court of the United States)

19.3 National Origin Discrimination   Irma Rivera is a Hispanic woman who was born in Puerto Rico. She began working for Baccarat, Inc. (Baccarat), a distributor of fine crystal, as a sales representative in its retail store in Manhattan. Eight years later, Rivera was the top sales representative at the Baccarat store. Jean Luc Negre became the new president of Baccarat, with ultimate authority for personnel decisions. Subsequently, Negre angrily told Rivera that he did not like her attitude and that he did not want her to speak Spanish on the job. Ms. Rivera testified that during her one face-to-face meeting with Mr. Negre, he specifically stated that he did not like her accent. Six months later, Dennis Russell, the chief financial officer of Baccarat, notified Rivera that Negre had made a decision to terminate her. Rivera pressed Russell to tell her why she was being fired. According to Rivera, he replied, "Irma, he doesn't want Hispanics." Negre also terminated Ivette Brigantty, another Hispanic sales representative. Evidence showed that Rivera and Brigantty were terminated because of their accent when speaking English. The store retained its non-Hispanic salesperson. Rivera sued Baccarat for national origin discrimination, in violation of Title VII of the Civil Rights Act. Has Baccarat engaged in unlawful national origin discrimination? *Rivera v. Baccarat, Inc.*, 10 F.Supp.2d 318, **Web** 1998 U.S. Dist. Lexis 9099 (United States District Court for the Southern District of New York)

19.4 Sexual Harassment   Teresa Harris worked as a manager at Forklift Systems Incorporated (Forklift), an equipment rental company, for two and one-half years. Charles Hardy was Forklift's president. Throughout Harris's time at Forklift, Hardy often insulted her because of her sex and made her the target of unwanted sexual innuendos. Hardy told Harris on several occasions, in the presence of other employees, "You're a woman, what do you know?" and "We need a man as the rental manager"; at least once, he told her she was "a dumb ass woman." Again in front of others, he suggested that the two of them "go to the Holiday Inn to negotiate Harris's raise." He made sexual innuendos about Harris's and other women's clothing.

Six weeks before Harris quit her job, Harris complained to Hardy about his conduct. Hardy said he was surprised that Harris was offended, claimed he was only joking, and apologized. He also promised he would stop, and based on this assurance, Harris stayed on the job. But two weeks later, Hardy began anew. While Harris was arranging a deal with one of Forklift's customers, he asked her, again in front of other employees, "What did you do, promise the guy some sex Saturday night?" One month later, Harris collected her paycheck and quit.

Harris then sued Forklift, claiming that Hardy's conduct was sexual harassment that created a hostile work environment for her because of her gender. Who wins? *Harris v. Forklift Systems Incorporated*, 510 U.S. 17, 114 S.Ct. 367, 126 L.Ed.2d 295, **Web** 1993 U.S. Lexis 7155 (Supreme Court of the United States)

19.5 Bona Fide Occupational Qualification (BFOQ) Johnson Controls, Inc. (Johnson Controls), manufactures batteries. Lead is the primary ingredient in the manufacturing process. Exposure to lead entails health risks, including risk of harm to a fetus carried by a female employee. To protect unborn children from such risk, Johnson Controls adopted an employment rule that prevented pregnant women and women of childbearing age from working at jobs involving lead exposure. Only women who were sterilized or could prove they could not have children were not affected by the rule. Consequently, most female employees were relegated to lower-paying clerical jobs at the company. Several female employees filed a class action suit, challenging Johnson Controls's fetal-protection policy as sex discrimination, in violation of Title VII of the Civil Rights Act. Johnson Controls defended, asserting that its fetal-protection policy was justified as a bona fide occupational qualification (BFOQ). Is Johnson Controls's fetal-protection policy a BFOQ, or does it constitute sex discrimination, in violation of Title VII? *International Union, United Automobile, Aerospace*

and Agricultural Implement Workers of America, UAW v. Johnson Controls, Inc., 499 U.S. 187, 111 S.Ct. 1196, 113 L.Ed.2d 158, **Web** 1991 U.S. Lexis 1715 (Supreme Court of the United States)

19.6 Sex Discrimination The Los Angeles Department of Water and Power maintains a pension plan for its employees that is funded by both employer and employee contributions. The plan pays men and women retirees' pensions with the same monthly benefits. However, because statistically women live, on average, several years longer than men, female employees are required to make monthly contributions to the pension fund that are 14.84 percent higher than the contributions required of male employees. Because employee contributions are withheld from paychecks, a female employee takes home less pay than a male employee earning the same salary. Does this practice violate Title VII? *City of Los Angeles Department of Water and Power v. Manhart*, 435 U.S. 702, 98 S.Ct. 1370, 55 L.Ed.2d 657, **Web** 1978 U.S. Lexis 23 (Supreme Court of the United States)

19.7 Sex Discrimination The position of director of the Madison County Veterans Service Agency became vacant. The Madison County Board of Supervisors (Board) appointed a committee of five men to hold interviews. Maureen E. Barbano applied for the position and was interviewed by the committee. Upon entering the interview, Barbano heard someone say, "Oh, another woman." When the interview began, Donald Greene, a committee member, said he would not consider "some woman" for the position. He then asked Barbano personal questions about her plans on having a family and whether her husband would object to her transporting male veterans. No committee member asked Barbano any substantive questions. Ultimately, Board acted on the committee's recommendation and hired a male candidate. Barbano sued Madison County for sex discrimination, in violation of Title VII of the Civil Rights Act. Has the Madison County Board of Supervisors engaged in sex discrimination, in violation of Title VII? *Barbano v. Madison County, New York*, 922 F.2d 139, **Web** 1990 U.S. App. Lexis 22494 (United States Court of Appeals for the Second Circuit)

Ethics Cases

19.8 Ethics Dianne Rawlinson, 22 years old, was a college graduate whose major course of study was correctional psychology. After graduation, she applied for a position as a correctional

counselor (prison guard) with the Alabama Board of Corrections. Her application was rejected because she failed to meet the minimum 120-pound weight requirement of an Alabama statute that also established a height minimum of 5 feet 2 inches. In addition, the Alabama Board of Corrections adopted Administrative Regulation 204, which established gender criteria for assigning correctional counselors to maximum-security prisons for "contact positions." These are correctional counselor positions that require continual close physical proximity to inmates. Under this no-contact with the other gender rule, Rawlinson did not qualify for contact positions with male prisoners in Alabama maximum-security prisons. Rawlinson brought a class action lawsuit against Dothard, who was the director of the Department of Public Safety of Alabama. Alabama alleged that the height–weight requirement and the no-contact position rule constitute bona fide occupational qualifications (BFOQs) that justify the sexual discrimination in this case. *Dothard, Director, Department of Public Safety of Alabama v. Rawlinson*, 433 U.S. 321, 97 S.Ct. 2720, 53 L.Ed.2d 786, **Web** 1977 U.S. Lexis 143 (Supreme Court of the United States)

1. What is a BFOQ?
2. Does the neutral height–weight requirement or the no-contact rule have a discriminatory effect? Explain.
3. Is the height–weight requirement a BFOQ? Is the no-contact rule a BFOQ?

19.9 Ethics   The PGA Tour, Inc., is a nonprofit entity that sponsors professional golf tournaments. The PGA has adopted a set of rules that apply to its golf tour. One rule requires golfers to walk the golf course during PGA-sponsored tournaments. Casey Martin is a talented amateur golfer who won many high school and university golf championships. Martin has been afflicted with Klippel-Trenaunay-Weber Syndrome, a degenerative circulatory disorder that obstructs the flow of blood from his right leg to his heart. The disease is progressive and has atrophied his right leg. Walking causes Martin pain, fatigue, and anxiety, with significant risk of hemorrhaging.

When Martin turned professional, he qualified for the PGA Tour. He made a request to use a golf cart while playing in PGA tournaments. When the PGA denied his request, Martin sued the PGA for violation of the Americans with Disabilities Act (ADA) for not making reasonable accommodations for his disability. *PGA Tour v. Martin*, 532 U.S. 661, 212 S.Ct. 1879, 149 L.Ed.2d 904, **Web** 2001 U.S. Lexis 4115 (Supreme Court of the United States)

1. Was Casey Martin protected by the Americans with Disabilities Act (ADA)?
2. Was it ethical for the PGA Tour to deny Martin's request to use a golf cart?
3. Who wins this case, and why?

Internet Exercise

1. Go to www.eeoc.gov/press/12-10-07a.html and read the EEOC press release "Target Corp. to Pay $510,000 for Race Discrimination."

Endnotes

1. 550 U.S. 618, 127 S.Ct. 2162, 167 L.Ed.2d 982, **Web** 2007 U.S. Lexis 6298 (Supreme Court of the United States).
2. Public Law No 111-2, 123 Stat. 5 (2009).
3. 42 U.S.C. Sections 2000(d) et seq.
4. *Equal Employment Opportunity Commission v. Tortilleria "La Mejor,"* 758 F.Supp. 585, **Web** 1991 U.S. Dist. Lexis 5754 (United States District Court for the Eastern District of California).
5. *McDonnell Douglas v. Green*, 411 U.S. 792, 93 S.Ct. 1817, 36 L.Ed.2d 668, **Web** 1973 U.S. Lexis154 (Supreme Court of the United States).
6. *Equal Employment Opportunity Commission v. Premier Operator Services, Inc.*, 113 F.Supp.2d 1066 (United States District Court for the Western District of Texas).
7. *Pacheco v. New York Presbyterian Hospital*, 593 F.Supp.2d 599 (United States District Court for the Southern District of New York).
8. *Chhim v. Spring Branch Independent School District*, H-09-3032 (United States District Court for the Southern District of Texas).
9. 42 U.S.C. Section 1981.
10. 42 U.S.C. Section 2000(e)(K).
11. *Meritor Savings Bank v. Vinson*, 477 U.S. 57, 106 S.Ct. 2399, 91 L.Ed.2d 49, **Web** 1986 U.S. Lexis 108 (Supreme Court of the United States).
12. *Harris v. Forklift Systems, Inc.*, 510 U.S. 17, 114 S.Ct. 367, 126 L.Ed.2d 295, **Web** 1993 U.S. Lexis 7155 (Supreme Court of the United States).
13. *Faragher v. City of Boca Raton*, 524 U.S. 775, 118 S.Ct. 2275, 141 L.Ed.2d 662, **Web** 1998 U.S. Lexis 4216 (Supreme Court of the United States) and *Burlington Industries, Inc. v. Ellerth*, 524 U.S. 742, 118 S.Ct. 2257, 141 L.Ed.2d 633, **Web** 1998 U.S. Lexis 4217 (Supreme Court of the United States).

14. 523 U.S. 75, 118 S.Ct. 998, 140 L.Ed.2d 201, **Web** 1998 U.S. Lexis 1599 (Supreme Court of the United States).
15. 29 U.S.C. Section 206(d).
16. 29 U.S.C. Sections 621–634.
17. Public Law 101-433.
18. *Dynamics Land Systems, Inc. v. Cline*, 540 U.S. 581, 124 S.Ct. 1236 (Supreme Court of the United States).
19. 42 U.S.C. Sections 12101 et seq.
20. 42 U.S.C. Sections 12111–12117.
21. Public Law 110-325, 122 Stat. 3553 (2008).
22. *Toyota Motors Manufacturing, Kentucky v. Williams*, 543 U.S. 134 (Supreme Court of the United States).
23. Public Law 110-233, 122 Stat. 881.

CHAPTER

20 Employment Law and Worker Protection

WASHINGTON, D.C.
*Federal and state laws provide workers'
compensation and occupational safety laws
to protect workers in this country.*

Learning Objectives

After studying this chapter, you should be able to:

1. Explain how state workers' compensation programs work and describe the benefits available.
2. Describe employers' duty to provide safe working conditions under the Occupational Safety and Health Act.
3. Describe the minimum wage and overtime pay rules of the Fair Labor Standards Act.
4. Describe the protections afforded by the Family and Medical Leave Act.
5. Describe unemployment insurance and Social Security.

Chapter Outline

Introduction to Employment Law and Worker Protection

Workers' Compensation
  CASE 20.1 • *Kelley v. Coca-Cola Enterprises, Inc.*

Occupational Safety
  CASE 20.2 • *R. Williams Construction Company v. Occupational Safety and Health Review Commission*

Fair Labor Standards Act
  CASE 20.3 • **U.S. SUPREME COURT** • *IBP, Inc. v. Alvarez*

Family and Medical Leave Act

Cobra and Erisa

Government Programs

> " *It is difficult to imagine any grounds, other than our own personal economic predilections, for saying that the contract of employment is any the less an appropriate subject of legislation than are scores of others, in dealing with which this Court has held that legislatures may curtail individual freedom in the public interest."*
>
> —Stone, Justice
> *Dissenting opinion, Morehead v. New York (1936)*

Introduction to Employment Law and Worker Protection

Before the Industrial Revolution, the doctrine of laissez-faire governed the employment relationship in this country. Generally, this meant that employment was subject to the common law of contracts and agency law. In most instances, employees and employers had somewhat equal bargaining power.

This changed dramatically when the country became industrialized in the late 1800s. For one thing, large corporate employers had much more bargaining power than their employees. For another, the issues of child labor, unsafe working conditions, long hours, and low pay caused concern. Both federal and state legislation were enacted to protect workers' rights.

This chapter discusses employment law, workers' compensation, occupational safety, pay, government programs, and other laws affecting employment.

Poorly paid labor is inefficient labor, the world over.

Henry George

Workers' Compensation

Many types of employment are dangerous, and each year, many workers are injured on the job. Under common law, employees who were injured on the job could sue their employers for negligence. This time-consuming process placed the employee at odds with his or her employer. In addition, there was no guarantee that the employee would win the case. Ultimately, many injured workers—or the heirs of deceased workers—were left uncompensated. States enacted **workers' compensation acts** in response to the unfairness of that result. These acts create an administrative procedure for workers to receive **workers' compensation** for injuries that occur on the job.

Under workers' compensation, an injured worker files a claim with the appropriate state government agency (often called the workers' compensation board or commission). Next, that entity determines the legitimacy of the claim. If the worker disagrees with the agency's findings, he or she may appeal the decision through the state court system. Workers' compensation benefits are paid according to preset limits established by statute or regulation. The amounts that are recoverable vary from state to state.

workers' compensation
Compensation paid to workers and their families when workers are injured in connection with their jobs.

Workers' Compensation Insurance

States usually require employers to purchase **workers' compensation insurance** from private insurance companies or state funds to cover workers' compensation claims. Some states permit employers to self-insure if they demonstrate that they have the ability to pay workers' compensation claims. Many large companies self-insure.

workers' compensation insurance
Insurance that employers obtain and pay for from private insurance companies or from government-sponsored programs. Some states permit employers to self-insure.

Employment-Related Injury

For an injury to be compensable under workers' compensation, the claimant must prove that he or she was harmed by an **employment-related injury**. Thus, injuries that arise out of and in the course of employment are compensable.

Examples If an employee is injured in an automobile accident when she is driving to a business lunch for her employer, the injury is covered by workers' compensation. However, if an employee is injured in an automobile accident while she is driving to an off-premises restaurant during her personal lunch hour, the injury is not covered by workers' compensation.

In addition to covering physical injuries, workers' compensation insurance covers stress and mental illness that are employment related.

Exclusive Remedy

Workers' compensation is an **exclusive remedy**. Thus, workers cannot both receive workers' compensation and sue their employers in court for damages. Workers' compensation laws make a trade-off: An injured worker qualifies for workers' compensation benefits and does not have to spend time and money to sue his employer, with a possible risk of not winning. The employer has to pay for workers' compensation insurance but does not have to incur the expense and risk of a lawsuit.

Example A professor is covered by her university's workers' compensation insurance. While teaching her class, the professor is injured when she trips over a power cord that was lying on the floor in the classroom. In this case, the professor's sole remedy is to recover workers' compensation. The worker cannot sue the university to recover damages.

Workers' compensation acts do not bar injured workers from suing responsible third parties to recover damages.

Example A worker, who is covered by workers' compensation insurance, is operating a machine while performing his job. The worker is injured when the machine breaks. The worker can recover workers' compensation benefits but cannot sue his employer. If it is proven that a defect in the machine has caused the injury, the worker can sue the manufacturer to recover damages caused by the defective machine.

Workers can sue an employer in court to recover damages for employment-related injuries if the employer does not carry workers' compensation insurance or does not self-insure if permitted to do so. If an employer intentionally injures a worker, the worker can collect workers' compensation benefits and can also sue the employer.

The following case involves a workers' compensation claim.

CASE 20.1 *Workers' Compensation*

Kelley v. Coca-Cola Enterprises, Inc.

Web 2010 Ohio App. Lexis 1269 (2010)
Court of Appeals of Ohio

"Despite Coca-Cola's assertion, an exception to the general rule prohibiting one from participating in workers' compensation benefits applies where the employee is injured by horseplay commonly carried on by the employees with the knowledge and consent or acquiescence of the employer."

—Powell, Judge

Facts

Chad Kelley, an account manager with Coca-Cola Enterprises, Inc., attended a mandatory corporate kick-off event celebrating the release of a new Coca-Cola product. As part of a team-building event, all the employees in attendance, including Kelley, were encouraged to canoe down a 3-mile stretch of a river.

Kelley and a coworker paddled on the river without incident. Thereafter, Kelley walked up an embankment to the parking lot and waited for a bus to arrive to take him back to his vehicle. However, while Kelley waited for the bus, a number of employees, including Whitaker, who was in charge of the entire event, were seen splashing, tipping canoes, and getting everyone wet. A short time later, Whitaker, who was soaking wet, and Hall, a Coca-Cola distribution manager, grabbed Kelley and tried to pull him down the embankment and into the river. When their efforts failed, Hall grabbed Kelley and slammed him to the ground, causing Kelley to injure his neck. As a result of the incident, Kelley was treated for a herniated disc and a cervical dorsal strain.

Kelley filed a claim for workers' compensation. Coca-Cola opposed the claim, asserting that because Kelley was involved in employee horseplay, he was not entitled to workers' compensation benefits. The trial court returned a verdict in favor of Kelley, entitling him to participate in workers' compensation benefits. Coca-Cola appealed.

Issue

Is Kelley entitled to workers' compensation benefits?

Language of the Court

Coca-Cola argues that the trial court erred by instructing the jury that even if it found *Kelley instigated or participated in horseplay that proximately caused his injury, he was, nonetheless, still entitled to participate in workers' compensation benefits so long as Coca-Cola acquiesced or consented to that horseplay. Despite Coca-Cola's assertion, an exception to the general rule prohibiting one from participating in workers' compensation benefits applies where the employee is injured by horseplay commonly carried on by the employees with the knowledge and consent or acquiescence of the employer.*

Decision

The court of appeals affirmed the trial court's judgment, holding that Kelley was entitled to participate in workers' compensation benefits.

Case Questions

Critical Legal Thinking
What are the benefits and detriments to workers under the workers' compensation system?

Ethics
Did Coca-Cola act ethically in denying Kelley's workers' compensation claim?

Contemporary Business
Are there any benefits to businesses for being required to pay for workers' compensation insurance?

Occupational Safety

In 1970, Congress enacted the **Occupational Safety and Health Act**[1] to promote safety in the workplace. Virtually all private employers are within the scope of the act, but federal, state, and local governments are exempt. Industries regulated by other federal safety legislation are also exempt.[2] The act also established the **Occupational Safety and Health Administration (OSHA)**, a federal administrative agency within the Department of Labor that is empowered to enforce the act. The act imposes record-keeping and reporting requirements on employers and requires them to post notices in the workplace, informing employees of their rights under the act.

OSHA is empowered to adopt rules and regulations to interpret and enforce the Occupational Safety and Health Act. OSHA has adopted thousands of regulations to enforce the safety standards established by the act.

Occupational Safety and Health Act
A federal act enacted in 1970 that promotes safety in the workplace.

Occupational Safety and Health Administration (OSHA)
A federal administrative agency that is empowered to enforce the Occupational Safety and Health Act.

Specific Duty Standards

specific duty standards
OSHA standards that set safety rules for specific equipment, procedures, types of work, unique work conditions, and the like.

Many of the OSHA standards are **specific duty standards**. That is, these rules are developed and apply to specific equipment, procedures, work, individual industry, unique work conditions, and the like.

Examples OSHA standards establish safety requirements for safety guards on saws, set maximum exposure levels for hazardous chemicals, and regulate the location of machinery in the workplace.

General Duty Standard

general duty standard
An OSHA standard that requires an employer to provide a work environment free from recognized hazards that are causing or are likely to cause death or serious physical harm to employees.

The Occupational Safety and Health Act contains a **general duty standard** that imposes on an employer a duty to provide employment and a work environment that is free from recognized hazards that are causing or are likely to cause death or serious physical harm to its employees. This general duty standard is a catchall provision that applies even if no specific workplace safety regulation addresses the situation.

Example A worker in a factory reports for work and is walking toward his work station when he trips over some boxes stored on the floor. This would be a violation of the OSHA general duty requirement to provide safe working conditions.

OSHA is empowered to inspect places of employment for health hazards and safety violations. If a violation is found, OSHA can issue a *written citation* that requires the employer to abate or correct the situation. Contested citations are reviewed by the Occupational Safety and Health Review Commission. Its decision is appealable to the Court of Appeals for the Federal Circuit. Employers who violate the act, OSHA rules and regulations, or OSHA citations are subject to both civil and criminal penalties.

In the following case, the court addressed the law of occupational safety.

CASE 20.2   *Occupational Safety*

R. Williams Construction Company v. Occupational Safety and Health Review Commission

464 F.3d 1060 (2006)
United States Court of Appeals for the Ninth Circuit

"The Company also violated 29 C.F.R. Section 1926.652(a)(1) for failing to protect employees from cave-ins."

—Fletcher, Circuit Judge

Facts

R. Williams Construction Company (Williams) was constructing a sewer project at a building site. Williams had constructed a trench that was 10 to 12 feet deep, 13 feet wide at the top, and 45 feet long. An earthen slope at one end of the trench provided the only access to and egress from the bottom of the trench. Ground water seeped into the soil continuously. Williams used a number of submersible pumps to remove the ground water that seeped into the trench. Two Williams employees, Jose Aguiniga and Adam Palomar, were responsible for cleaning the pumps and did so throughout each working day, as needed.

On the day before the accident, a shoring system that supported the walls of the trench, had been removed. On the day of the accident, Aguiniga and Palomar entered the unshored trench to clean the pumps and remained there for about fifteen minutes. As the two men were exiting the trench, the north end wall collapsed, burying Aguiniga completely and Palomar almost completely. Aguiniga died and Palomar was severely injured. The Occupational Safety and Health Administration (OSHA), a federal agency that regulates safety in the workplace, conducted an investigation and cited Williams for violating the following OSHA trench safety standards:

- Failing to instruct its employees in the recognition and avoidance of unsafe conditions and in the regulations applicable to their work environment, as required by 29 C.F.R. Section 1926.21(b)(2)
- Failing to ensure that no worker would have to travel more than 25 feet to reach a safe point of egress, as required by 29 C.F.R. Section 1926.651(c)(2)
- Failing to ensure that a "competent person" (i.e., one with specific training in soil analysis and protective systems and capable of identifying dangerous conditions) performed daily inspections of excavations for evidence of hazardous conditions, as required by 29 C.F.R. Sections 1926.651(k)(1)
- Failing to ensure that the walls of the excavation were either sloped or supported, as required by 29 C.F.R. Section 1926.652(a)(1)

The administrative law judge (ALJ) conducted a hearing and heard testimony from Palomar, other employees at the jobsite, and the supervisor at the job site. The ALJ found that Williams had violated the four OSHA trench safety standards, issued citations against Williams, and imposed penalties of $22,000 on Williams. Williams appealed.

Issue
Has Williams violated the OSHA trench safety standards?

Language of the Court

The ALJ's findings, based upon the witnesses' testimony regarding Williams' lack of attention to safety standards, is supported by substantial evidence. Williams violated 29 C.F.R. Section 1926.21(b)(2) for failing to instruct each employee in the recognition and avoidance of unsafe conditions and for failing to eliminate other hazards: Williams provided no training in trenching hazards to at least the two employees working in the trench; moreover, no Williams supervisor was familiar with OSHA regulations. Williams also violated 29 C.F.R. Section 1926.651(c)(2) by providing only one safe means of egress at the east end of the 45-foot trench.

In addition, Williams violated 29 C.F.R. Section 1926.651(k)(1) for failing to designate a "competent person" with sufficient training and knowledge to identify and correct existing and predictable hazards. No supervisor at the Company was familiar with the basic standards applicable to the worksite or otherwise capable of identifying and correcting existing and predictable hazards in their surroundings. The Company also violated 29 C.F.R. Section 1926.652(a)(1) for failing to protect employees from cave-ins: Williams had reason to know that its employees would enter the trench on the day of the cave-in and had actual knowledge that two of its employees entered the trench prior to the cave-in.

Decision
The U.S. Court of Appeals held that Williams had violated the OSHA trench safety standards, and upheld the citations issued against Williams and the imposition of the $22,000 penalty.

Note
The OSHA proceeding imposed government fines on the company for violating OSHA safety standards. Mr. Palomar could recover workers' compensation benefits for his injuries, and the heirs of Mr. Aguiniga could recover workers' compensation death benefits, assuming that Williams carried workers' compensation coverage.

Case Questions

Critical Legal Thinking
What is the purpose of OSHA safety standards? Do you think that businesses would take substantial safety precautions without the imposition of such standards?

Ethics
Did Williams act unethically in this case?

Contemporary Business
Does compliance with OSHA safety standards increase the cost of doing business in the United States?

Fair Labor Standards Act

In 1938, Congress enacted the **Fair Labor Standards Act (FLSA)** to protect workers.[3] The FLSA applies to private employers and employees engaged in the production of goods for interstate commerce. The **U.S. Department of Labor** is empowered to enforce the FLSA. Private civil actions are also permitted under the FLSA.

Fair Labor Standards Act (FLSA)
A federal act enacted in 1938 to protect workers. It prohibits child labor and spells out minimum wage and overtime pay requirements.

Child Labor

The FLSA forbids the use of oppressive **child labor** and makes it unlawful to ship goods produced by businesses that use oppressive child labor. The Department of Labor has adopted the following regulations that define lawful child labor: (1) Children under the age of 14 cannot work except as newspaper deliverers; (2) children ages 14 and 15 may work limited hours in nonhazardous jobs approved by the Department of Labor (e.g., restaurants, gasoline stations); and (3) children ages 16 and 17 may work unlimited hours in nonhazardous jobs. The Department of Labor determines which occupations are hazardous (e.g., mining, roofing, working with explosives). Children who work in agricultural employment and child actors and performers are exempt from these restrictions. Persons age 18 and older may work at any job, whether it is hazardous or not.

Minimum Wage

The FLSA establishes minimum wage and overtime pay requirements for workers. Managerial, administrative, and professional employees are exempt from the act's wage and hour provisions. The FLSA requires that most employees in the United States be paid at least the federal minimum wage for all hours worked. The federal **minimum wage** is set by Congress and can be changed. As of 2010, it was set at $7.25 per hour. The Department of Labor permits employers to pay less than the minimum wage to students and apprentices. An employer may reduce the minimum wage by an amount equal to the reasonable cost of food and lodging provided to employees.

There is a special minimum wage rule for tipped employees. An employee who earns tips can be paid $2.13 an hour by an employer if that amount plus the tips received equals at least the minimum wage. If an employee's tips and direct employer payment does not equal the minimum wage, the employer must make up the difference.

Over half of the states have enacted minimum wage laws that set minimum wages at a rate higher than the federal rate. Some cities have enacted minimum wage requirements, usually called **living wage laws**, which also set higher minimum wage rates than the federal level.

Overtime Pay

Under the FLSA, an employer cannot require nonexempt employees to work more than 40 hours per week unless they are paid **overtime pay** of one-and-a-half times their regular pay for each hour worked in excess of 40 hours that week. Each week is treated separately.

Example If an employee works 50 hours one week and 30 hours the next, the employer owes the employee 10 hours of overtime pay for the first week.

In the following case, the U.S. Supreme Court was called upon to interpret the FLSA.

CASE 20.3 *U.S. SUPREME COURT Fair Labor Standards Act*

IBP, Inc. v. Alvarez

546 U.S. 21, 126 S.Ct. 514, 163 L.Ed.2d 288, Web 2005 U.S. Lexis 8373 (2005)
Supreme Court of the United States

"The relevant text describes the workday as roughly the period from 'whistle to whistle.'"
—Stevens, Justice

Facts

IBP, Inc., produces fresh beef, pork, and related meat products. At its plant in Pasco, Washington, it employed approximately 178 workers in its slaughter division and 800 line workers. All workers must wear gear such as outer garments, hardhats, earplugs, gloves, aprons, leggings, and boots. Those who use knives must wear additional protective equipment. IBP requires employees to store their equipment and tools in company locker rooms, where the workers don and doff their equipment and protective gear.

The pay of production workers is based on time spent cutting and bagging meat. Pay begins with the first piece of meat and ends with the last piece of meat. IBP pays for four minutes of clothing-changing time. IBP employees filed a class action lawsuit against IBP to recover compensation for pre-production and postproduction work, including time spent donning and doffing protective gear and time walking between the locker room and the production floor before and after their assigned shifts. The employees alleged that IBP was in violation of the Fair Labor Standards Act (FLSA).

The U.S. District Court held that the donning and doffing of protective gear and the walking time between the locker room and the production floor were compensable time and awarded $3 million damages. The U.S. Court of Appeals agreed with the District Court's ultimate conclusions. IBP appealed. On appeal, IBP did not challenge the District Court's holding regarding payment for donning and doffing of protective gear, but it did challenge the District Court's decision to require payment of compensation to workers for the time spent walking between the locker room and the production area. The U.S. Supreme Court granted a writ of certiorari to hear the appeal.

Issue

Is the time spent by employees walking between the locker room and production area compensable under the Fair Labor Standards Act?

Language of the U.S. Supreme Court

The Department of Labor has adopted the continuous workday rule, which means that the "workday" is generally defined as the period between the commencement and completion on the same workday of an employee's principal activity or activities. The relevant text describes the workday as roughly the period from "whistle to whistle." We hold that any activity that is integral and indispensable to a principal activity is itself a principal activity. Moreover, during a continuous workday, any walking time that occurs after the beginning of the employee's first principal activity and before the end of the employee's last principal activity is covered by the FLSA.

Decision

The U.S. Supreme Court held that the time spent by employees walking between the locker room and the production areas of the plant was compensable under the Fair Labor Standards Act.

Case Questions

Critical Legal Thinking
Was this the type of situation that the FLSA was meant to address?

Ethics
Did IBP, Inc., act ethically in this case?

Contemporary Business
Why do you think IBP, Inc., fought so hard against the workers' demands?

Exemptions from Minimum Wage and Overtime Pay Requirements

The FLSA establishes the following categories of exemptions from federal minimum wage and overtime pay requirements:

- **Executive exemption.**   The **executive exemption** applies to executives who are compensated on a salary basis, who engage in management, who have authority to hire employees, and who regularly direct two or more employees.
- **Administrative employee exemption.**   The **administrative employee exemption** applies to employees who are compensated on a salary or fee basis, whose primary duty is the performance of office or nonmanual work, and whose work includes the exercise of discretion and independent judgment with respect to matters of significance.

- **Learned professional exemption.** The **learned professional exemption** applies to employees compensated on a salary or fee basis that perform work that is predominantly intellectual in character, who possess advanced knowledge in a field of science or learning, and whose advanced knowledge was acquired through a prolonged course of specialized intellectual instruction.
- **Highly compensated employee exemption.** The **highly compensated employee exemption** applies to employees who are paid total annual compensation of $100,000 or more, perform office or nonmanual work, and regularly perform at least one of the duties of an exempt executive, administrative, or professional employee.
- **Computer employee exemption.** The **computer employee exemption** applies to employees who are compensated either on a salary or fee basis; are employed as computer systems analysts, computer programmers, software engineers or other similarly skilled workers in the computer field; and are engaged in the design, development, documentation, analysis, creation, testing, or modification of computer systems or programs.
- **Outside sales representative exemption.** The **outside sales representative exemption** applies to employees who will be paid by the client or customer, whose primary duty is making sales or obtaining orders or contracts for services, and who are customarily and regularly engaged away from the employer's place of business.

Sometimes employers give employees the title of "manager" to avoid the minimum wage and overtime pay requirements of the FLSA.

Example A large big-box store labels lower-level workers who actually stock shelves with goods as "managers" in order to avoid paying them overtime pay.

Family and Medical Leave Act

Family and Medical Leave Act (FMLA)
A federal act that guarantees workers up to twelve weeks of unpaid leave in a twelve-month period to attend to family and medical emergencies and other specified situations.

In February 1993, Congress enacted the **Family and Medical Leave Act (FMLA)**.[4] This act guarantees workers unpaid time off from work for family and medical emergencies and other specified situations. The act, which applies to companies with 50 or more workers as well as federal, state, and local governments, covers about half of the nation's workforce. To be covered by the act, an employee must have worked for the employer for at least one year and must have performed more than 1,250 hours of service during the previous twelve-month period.

Covered employers are required to provide up to twelve weeks of unpaid leave during any twelve-month period due to:

1. The birth of and care for a child
2. The placement of a child with an employee for adoption or foster care
3. A serious health condition that makes the employee unable to perform his or her duties
4. Care for a spouse, child, or parent with a serious health problem

Leave because of the birth of a child or the placement of a child for adoption or foster care cannot be taken intermittently unless the employer agrees to such arrangement. Other leaves may be taken on an intermittent basis. The employer may require medical proof of claimed serious health conditions.

An eligible employee who takes leave must, upon returning to work, be restored to either the same or an equivalent position with equivalent employment benefits and pay. The restored employee is not entitled to the accrual of seniority during the leave period, however. A covered employer may deny restoration to a salaried employee who is among the highest-paid 10 percent of that employer's employees if the denial is necessary to prevent "substantial and grievous economic injury" to the employer's operations.

Cobra and Erisa

In addition to the statutes already discussed in this chapter, the federal government has enacted many other statutes that regulate employment relationships. Two important federal statutes are the Consolidated Omnibus Budget Reconciliation Act (COBRA) and Employee Retirement Income Security Act (ERISA). These statutes are discussed in the following paragraphs.

Consolidated Omnibus Budget Reconciliation Act (COBRA)

The **Consolidated Omnibus Budget Reconciliation Act (COBRA)** of 1985[5] provides that an employee of a private employer or the employee's beneficiaries must be offered the opportunity to continue his or her group health insurance after the voluntary or involuntary termination of a worker's employment or the loss of coverage due to certain qualifying events defined in the law. The employer must notify covered employees and their beneficiaries of their rights under COBRA. To continue coverage, a person must pay the required group rate premium. Government employees are subject to parallel provisions found in the Public Health Service Act.

Consolidated Omnibus Budget Reconciliation Act (COBRA)
A federal law that permits employees and their beneficiaries to continue their group health insurance after an employee's employment has ended.

Employee Retirement Income Security Act (ERISA)

Employers are not required to establish pension plans for their employees. If they do, however, they are subject to the record-keeping, disclosure, and other requirements of the **Employee Retirement Income Security Act (ERISA)**.[6] ERISA is a complex act designed to prevent fraud and other abuses associated with private pension funds. Federal, state, and local government pension funds are exempt from its coverage. ERISA is administered by the Department of Labor.

Employee Retirement Income Security Act (ERISA)
A federal act designed to prevent fraud and other abuses associated with private pension funds.

Among other things, ERISA requires pension plans to be in writing and to name a pension fund manager. The plan manager owes a fiduciary duty to act as a "prudent person" in managing the fund and investing its assets. No more than 10 percent of a pension fund's assets can be invested in the securities of the sponsoring employer.

Vesting occurs when an employee has a nonforfeitable right to receive pension benefits. First, ERISA provides for immediate vesting of each employee's own contributions to the plan. Second, it requires employers' contributions to be either (1) totally vested after five years (*cliff vesting*) or (2) gradually vested over a seven-year period and completely vested after that time.

Government Programs

The U.S. government has established several programs that provide benefits to workers and their dependents. Two of these programs, *unemployment compensation* and *Social Security*, are discussed in the following paragraphs.

Unemployment Compensation

In 1935, Congress established an **unemployment compensation** program to assist workers who are temporarily unemployed. Under the **Federal Unemployment Tax Act (FUTA)**[7] and state laws enacted to implement the program, employers are required to pay unemployment contributions (taxes). The tax rate and unemployment wage level are subject to change. Employees do not pay unemployment taxes.

unemployment compensation
Compensation that is paid to workers who are temporarily unemployed.

State governments administer unemployment compensation programs under general guidelines set by the federal government. Each state establishes its own eligibility requirements and the amount and duration of the benefits. To collect benefits, applicants must be able to work and available for work and seeking employment. Workers who have been let go because of bad conduct (e.g., illegal activity, drug use on the job) or who voluntarily quit work without just cause are not eligible to receive unemployment benefits.

Social Security

Social Security
A federal system that provides limited retirement and death benefits to covered employees and their dependents.

In 1935, Congress established the federal **Social Security** system to provide limited retirement and death benefits to certain employees and their dependents. The Social Security system is administered by the **Social Security Administration**. Today, Social Security benefits include (1) retirement benefits, (2) survivors' benefits to family members of deceased workers, (3) disability benefits, and (4) medical and hospitalization benefits (Medicare).

Under the **Federal Insurance Contributions Act (FICA)**,[8] employees must make contributions (i.e., pay taxes) into the Social Security fund. An employee's employer must pay a matching amount. Social Security does not operate like a savings account. Instead, current contributions are used to fund current claims. The employer is responsible for deducting employees' portions from their wages and remitting the entire payment to the IRS.

Under the **Self-Employment Contributions Act**,[9] self-employed individuals must pay Social Security contributions, too. The amount of tax self-employed individuals must pay is equal to the combined employer–employee amount.

Failure to submit Social Security taxes subjects the violator to interest payments, penalties, and possible criminal liability. Social Security taxes may be changed by act of Congress.

Key Terms and Concepts

Administrative employee exemption (429)
Child labor (428)
Computer employee exemption (430)
Consolidated Omnibus Budget Reconciliation Act (COBRA) (431)
Employee Retirement Income Security Act (ERISA) (431)
Employment-related injury (423)
Exclusive remedy (424)
Executive exemption (429)

Fair Labor Standards Act (FLSA) (427)
Family and Medical Leave Act (FMLA) (430)
Federal Insurance Contributions Act (FICA) (432)
Federal Unemployment Tax Act (FUTA) (431)
General duty standard (426)
Highly compensated employee exemption (430)

Learned professional exemption (430)
Living wage law (428)
Minimum wage (428)
Occupational Safety and Health Act (425)
Occupational Safety and Health Administration (OSHA) (425)
Outside sales representative exemption (430)
Overtime pay (428)
Self-Employment Contributions Act (432)
Social Security (432)

Social Security Administration (432)
Specific duty standards (426)
Unemployment compensation (431)
U.S. Department of Labor (427)
Vesting (431)
Workers' compensation (423)
Workers' compensation acts (423)
Workers' compensation insurance (423)

Law Case with Answer
Smith v. Workers' Compensation Appeals Board

Facts Ronald Wayne Smith was employed by Modesto High School as a temporary math instructor. In addition, he coached the girls' baseball and basketball teams. The contract under which he was employed stated that he "may be required to devote a reasonable amount of time to other duties" in addition to instructional duties. The teachers in the school system were evaluated once

a year regarding both instructional duties and non-instructional duties, including "sponsorship or the supervision of out-of-classroom student activities."

The high school's math club held an annual end-of-year outing. A picnic was scheduled at the Modesto Reservoir. The students invited their math teachers, including Smith, to attend. The food was paid for by the math club member's dues. Smith attended the picnic with his wife and three children. One of the students brought along a windsurfer. Smith watched the students as they used it before and after the picnic. When Smith tried it, he fell and was seriously injured. He died shortly thereafter. Mrs. Smith filed a claim for workers' compensation benefits, to which the employer objected. When the accident occurred, was Smith engaged in employment-related activities that would permit his surviving wife and family to recover workers' compensation benefits?

Answer Yes, when the accident occurred, Smith was engaged in employment-related activities that would permit his surviving wife and family to recover workers' compensation benefits. Decedent was a temporary instructor at Modesto High. As such, he was especially vulnerable to pressure or suggestion that he participate in extracurricular activities to better his chances of being rehired. The math club was an official school club. The food for the event was paid for out of the math club funds. The school was more than minimally involved in the picnic. Teachers were encouraged to involve themselves in extracurricular activities of the school, thus conferring the benefit of better teacher–student relationships. More importantly, teachers were evaluated on whether they shared equally in the sponsorship or the supervision of out-of-classroom student activities, and decedent had been commended for his participation in this area. In addition, the court rejected the employer's argument which alleged that if Smith's attendance at the picnic was required by his employment, then his activities in using the windsurfer were outside the course and scope of his employment. Because attendance at the picnic was an implied requirement of decedent's employment, his accident that resulted from his engaging in the recreational activities that were part and parcel of the picnic's entertainment is causally connected to his employment. Therefore, the decedent's accident was causally connected to his employment for purposes of awarding workers' compensation benefits to his heirs. *Smith v. Workers' Compensation Appeals Board*, 191 Cal.App.3d 127, 236 Cal.Rptr.248, **Web** 1987 Cal.App. Lexis 1587 (Court of Appeal of California)

Critical Legal Thinking Cases

20.1 Workers' Compensation Immar Medrano was employed as a journeyman electrician by Marshall Electrical Contracting, Inc. (MEC), in Marshall, Missouri. Medrano attended an electrician apprenticeship night class at a community college in Sedalia, Missouri. MEC paid Medrano's tuition and book fees. Attendance at the course required Medrano to drive 70 miles round-trip. One night, when Medrano was driving home from the class, a drunk driver crossed the centerline of U.S. Highway 65 and collided head-on with Medrano's automobile. Medrano died in the accident. His wife and two children filed a workers' compensation claim for death benefits against MEC. Are Medrano's actions at the time of the automobile accident within the course and scope of his employment, thus entitling him to workers' compensation benefits? *Medrano v. Marshall Electrical Contracting Inc.*, 173 S.W.3d 333, **Web** 2005 Mo.App. Lexis 1088 (Court of Appeals of Missouri)

20.2 Occupational Safety Getty Oil Company (Getty) operates a separation facility where it gathers gas and oil from wells and transmits them to an outgoing pipeline under high pressure. Getty engineers designed and produced a pressure vessel, called a fluid booster, which was to be installed to increase pressure in the system. Robinson, a Getty engineer, was instructed to install the vessel. Robinson picked up the vessel from the welding shop without having it tested. After he completed the installation, the pressure valve was put into operation. When the pressure increased from 300 to 930 pounds per square inch, an explosion occurred. Robinson died from the explosion, and another Getty employee was seriously injured. The secretary of labor issued a citation against Getty for violating the general duty provision for worker safety contained in the Occupational Safety and Health Act. Getty challenged the citation. Who wins? *Getty Oil Company v. Occupational Safety and Health Review Commission*, 530 F.2d 1143, **Web** 1976 U.S. App. Lexis 11640 (United States Court of Appeals for the Fifth Circuit)

20.3 Occupational Safety Corbesco, Inc. (Corbesco), an industrial roofing and siding installation company, was hired to put metal roofing and siding over the skeletal structure of five aircraft hangars at Chennault Air Base in Louisiana. Corbesco assigned three of its employees to work on the partially completed flat roof of Hangar B, a large single-story building measuring 60 feet high, 374 feet wide, and 574 feet long. Soon after starting work, one of the workers, Roger Matthew, who was on his knees installing insulation on the roof, lost his balance and fell 60 feet to the concrete below. He was killed by the fall.

The next day, an Occupational Safety and Health Administration (OSHA) compliance officer cited Corbesco for failing to install a safety net under the work site. The officer cited an OSHA safety standard that requires that safety nets be provided when workers are more than 25 feet above the ground. Corbesco argued that the flat roof on which the employees were working served as a "temporary floor," and therefore it was not required to install a safety net. Has Corbesco violated the OSHA safety standard? *Corbesco, Inc. v. Dole, Secretary of Labor*, 926 F.2d 422, 1991 U.S. App. 3369 (United States Court of Appeals for the Fifth Circuit)

20.4 ERISA   United Artists was a Maryland corporation doing business in the state of Texas. United Pension Fund (Plan) was a defined-contribution employee pension benefit plan sponsored by United Artists for its employees. Each employee had his or her own individual pension account, but Plan's assets were pooled for investment purposes. Plan was administered by a board of trustees. During a period of nine years, seven of the trustees used Plan to make a series of loans to themselves. The trustees did not (1) require the borrowers to submit written applications for the subject loans, (2) assess the prospective borrowers' ability to repay the loans, (3) specify a period in which the loans were to be repaid, or (4) call in the loans when they remained unpaid. The trustees also charged less than fair market value interest rates for the loans. The secretary of labor sued the trustees, alleging that they had breached their fiduciary duty, in violation of ERISA. Who wins? *McLaughlin v. Rowley*, 698 F.Supp. 1333, **Web** 1988 U.S. Dist. Lexis 12674 (United States District Court for the Northern District of Texas)

20.5 Unemployment Benefits   Devon Overstreet, who worked as a bus driver for the Chicago Transit Authority (CTA) for more than six years, took sick leave for six weeks. Because she had been on sick leave for more than seven days, CTA required her to take a medical examination. The blood and urine analysis indicated the presence of cocaine. A second test confirmed this finding. The CTA suspended Overstreet and placed her in the employee assistance program for substance abuse for not less than thirty days, with a chance of reassignment to a nonoperating job if she successfully completed the program. The program is an alternative to discharge and is available at the election of the employee. Overstreet filed for unemployment compensation benefits. CTA contested her claim. Who wins? *Overstreet v. Illinois Department of Employment Security*, 168 Ill.App.3d 24, 522 N.E.2d 185, **Web** 1988 Ill.App. Lexis 269 (Appellate Court of Illinois)

20.6 Workers' Compensation   John B. Wilson was employed by the city of Modesto, California, as a police officer. He was a member of the special emergency reaction team (SERT), a tactical unit of the city's police department that is trained and equipped to handle highly dangerous criminal situations. Membership in SERT is voluntary for police officers. No additional pay or benefits are involved. To be a member of SERT, each officer is required to pass physical tests four times a year. One such test requires members to run 2 miles in seventeen minutes. Other tests call for minimum numbers of push-ups, pull-ups, and sit-ups. Officers who do not belong to SERT are not required to undergo these physical tests. One day, Wilson completed his patrol shift, changed clothes, and drove to the Modesto Junior College track. While running there, he injured his left ankle. Wilson filed a claim for workers' compensation benefits, which was contested by his employer. Who wins? *Wilson v. Workers' Compensation Appeals Board*, 196 Cal.App.3d 902, 239 Cal.Rptr. 719, **Web** 1987 Cal.App. Lexis 2382 (Court of Appeal of California)

Ethics Cases

20.7 Ethics   Jeffrey Glockzin was an employee of Nordyne, Inc. (Nordyne), which manufactured air-conditioning units. Sometimes Glockzin worked as an assembly line tester. The job consisted of using bare metal alligator-type clips to attach one of two wire leads from the testing equipment to each side of the air-conditioning unit. When the tester turned on a toggle switch, the air-conditioning unit was energized. Once a determination was made that the air-conditioning unit was working properly, the toggle switch would be turned off and the wire leads removed.

One day, while testing an air-conditioning unit, Glockzin grabbed both alligator clips at the same time. He had failed to turn off the toggle switch, however. Glockzin received a 240-volt electric shock, causing

his death. Glockzin's heirs sued Nordyne for wrongful death and sought to recover damages for an intentional tort. Nordyne made a motion for summary judgment, alleging that workers' compensation benefits were the exclusive remedy for Glockzin's death. Glockzin's heirs argued that the "intentional tort" exception to the rule that workers' compensation is the exclusive remedy for a worker's injury applied in this case. *Glockzin v. Nordyne, Inc.*, 815 F.Supp. 1050, **Web** 1992 U.S. Dist. Lexis 8059 (United States District Court for the Western District of Michigan)

1. What is the exclusive remedy rule of workers' compensation? What is the intentional tort exception to this rule?

2. Did Nordyne's management violate its ethical duty by not providing safer testing equipment?

3. Who wins, and why?

20.8 Ethics   Whirlpool Corporation (Whirlpool) operated a manufacturing plant in Marion, Ohio, for the production of household appliances. Overhead conveyors transported appliance components throughout the plant. To protect employees from objects that occasionally fell from the conveyors, Whirlpool installed a horizontal wire-mesh guard screen approximately 20 feet above the plant floor. The mesh screen was welded to angle-iron frames suspended from the building's structural steel skeleton.

Maintenance employees spent several hours each week removing objects from the screen, replacing paper spread on the screen to catch grease drippings from the materials on the conveyors, and performing occasional maintenance work on the conveyors. To perform these duties, maintenance employees were usually able to stand on the iron frames, but sometimes they found it necessary to step onto the wire-mesh screen itself. Several employees had fallen partly through the screen. One day, a maintenance employee fell to his death through the guard screen.

The next month, two maintenance employees, Virgil Deemer and Thomas Cornwell, met with the plant supervisor to voice their concern about the safety of the screen. Unsatisfied with the supervisor's response, two days later, they met with the plant safety director and voiced similar concerns. When they asked him for the name, address, and telephone number of the local OSHA office, he told them they "had better stop and think about" what they were doing. The safety director then furnished them with the requested information, and later that day, one of the men contacted the regional OSHA office and discussed the guard screen.

The next day, Deemer and Cornwell reported for the night shift at 10:45 P.M. Their foreman directed the two men to perform their usual maintenance duties on a section of the screen. Claiming that the screen was unsafe, they refused to carry out the directive. The foreman sent them to the personnel office, where they were ordered to punch out without working or being paid for the remaining six hours of the shift. The two men subsequently received written reprimands, which were placed in their employment files.

The U.S. Secretary of Labor filed suit, alleging that Whirlpool's actions constituted discrimination against the two men in violation of the Occupational Safety and Health Act. *Whirlpool Corporation v. Marshall, Secretary of Labor*, 445 U.S. 1, 100 S.Ct. 883, 63 L.Ed.2d 154, **Web** 1980 U.S. Lexis 81 (Supreme Court of the United States)

1. Under OSHA regulations, can employees engage in self-help in certain circumstances?
2. Did Whirlpool act ethically in this case?
3. Does the U.S. Secretary of Labor win this case? Why or why not?

Internet Exercises

1. Go to www.dir.ca.gov/dwc/WCFaqIW.html#1 to learn more about workers' compensation. Read the first four questions and answers.

2. Go to www.ohiobwc.com/basics/guidedtour/generalinfo/empgeneralinfo22.asp. Read the section "Spotting injured worker claim fraud."

3. Go to www.osha.gov/dep/oia/whistleblower/index.html and read OSHA's article "The Whistleblower Protection Program."

4. Use www.google.com to determine the current amount of the federal minimum wage. Go to the website www.dol.gov/esa/minwage/america.htm. What is the minimum wage for your state?

5. Visit the website of the Social Security Administration, at www.ssa.gov. Go to www.ssa.gov/online and find the SS-5 form. What is this form used for?

Endnotes

1. 29 U.S.C. Sections 553, 651–678.
2. For example, the Railway Safety Act and the Coal Mine Safety Act regulate workplace safety of railway workers and coal miners, respectively.
3. 29 U.S.C. Sections 201–206.
4. 29 U.S.C. Sections 2601, 2611–2619, 2651–2654.
5. 26 U.S.C. Sections 1161–1169.
6. 29 U.S.C. Sections 1001 et seq.
7. 26 U.S.C. Sections 3301–3310.
8. 26 U.S.C. Sections 3101–3125.
9. 26 U.S.C. Sections 1401–1403.

CHAPTER
21
Labor Law and Immigration Law

LABOR UNION

Many workers in America belong to labor unions. Today, approximately 12 percent of wage and salary workers in the United States belong to labor unions. Less than 8 percent of private sector employees belonged to unions, with the largest unionized occupations being in transportation, construction, and utilities. The fastest growing union sector is service employees such as janitors, restaurant workers, hotel workers, and such. More than 37 percent of public-sector employees belong to unions, including such heavily unionized occupations as teachers, police officers, and firefighters.

Learning Objectives

After studying this chapter, you should be able to:

1. Describe how a union is organized.
2. Explain the consequences of an employer's illegal interference with a union election.
3. Describe the process of collective bargaining.
4. Describe employees' rights to strike and picket.
5. Describe immigration laws and foreign guest worker visas.

Chapter Outline

Introduction to Labor Law and Immigration Law

Labor Law

Organizing a Union
   CASE 21.1 • U.S. SUPREME COURT • *Lechmere, Inc. v. National Labor Relations Board*

Collective Bargaining
   CONTEMPORARY ENVIRONMENT • *State Right-to-Work Laws*

Strikes

Picketing
   ETHICS • *Mock Funeral by Striking Workers Is Lawful*

Internal Union Affairs
   ETHICS • *Plant Closing Act*

Immigration Law

> " *Strong responsible unions are essential to industrial fair play.*
> *Without them the labor bargain is wholly one-sided."*
>
> —Louis D. Brandeis (1935)
> *U.S. Supreme Court Justice*

Introduction to Labor Law and Immigration Law

A truly American sentiment recognizes the dignity of labor and the fact that honor lies in honest toil.

S. Grover Cleveland
Letter accepting the nomination for president

Prior to the Industrial Revolution, employees and employers had somewhat equal bargaining power. Once the country became industrialized in the late 1800s, large corporate employers had much more bargaining power than their employees. In response, beginning in the 1930s, federal legislation was enacted that gave employees the right to form and join labor unions.

Through collective bargaining with employers, labor unions obtained better working conditions, higher wages, and greater benefits for their members. Labor unions have the right to strike and to engage in picketing in support of their positions. However, there are some limits on these activities.

Labor unions were instrumental in forming political parties in many countries. The Labour Party of the United Kingdom and the Labour Party of Canada are examples. However, labor unions in the United States have not formed their own political party.

Today, many high-technology and other businesses rely on employees who are foreign nationals. U.S. immigration laws provide that visas may be issued by the federal government for a specified number of foreign nationals to work in the United States.

This chapter discusses labor law, organization of unions, collective bargaining, strikes and picketing, labor's bill of rights, and immigration law.

Labor Law

Once permitted to do so, workers organized and joined unions in an attempt to gain bargaining strength with employers. In the early 1900s, employers used violent tactics against workers who were trying to organize into unions. At that time, courts often sided with employers in such disputes.

The **American Federation of Labor (AFL)** was formed in 1886, under the leadership of Samuel Gompers. Only skilled craft workers such as silversmiths and artisans were allowed to belong. In 1935, John L. Lewis formed the **Congress of Industrial Organizations (CIO)**. The CIO permitted semiskilled and unskilled workers to become members. In 1955, the AFL and CIO combined to form the **AFL-CIO**. Individual unions (e.g., United Auto Workers, United Steel Workers) may choose to belong to the AFL-CIO, but not all unions opt to join.

In the early 1900s, members of the labor movement lobbied Congress to pass laws to protect the right to organize and bargain with management. During the Great Depression of the 1930s, several statutes that were enacted gave workers certain rights and protections. Other statutes have been added since then.

The major federal statutes that regulate the labor-management relationship are as follows:

National Labor Relations Act (NLRA) (Wagner Act)
A federal statute enacted in 1935 that establishes the right of employees to form and join labor organizations.

- **Norris-LaGuardia Act.** Enacted in 1932, the **Norris-LaGuardia Act** stipulates that it is legal for employees to organize.[1]
- **National Labor Relations Act (NLRA).** The **National Labor Relations Act (NLRA)**, also known as the **Wagner Act**, was enacted in 1935.[2] The NLRA establishes the right of employees to form and join labor organizations, to bargain collectively with employers, and to engage in concerted activity to promote these rights.
- **Labor Management Relations Act.** In 1947, Congress enacted the **Labor Management Relations Act**, also known as the **Taft-Hartley Act**.[3] This act (1) expands the activities that labor unions can engage in, (2) gives employers the right to engage in free-speech efforts against unions prior to a union election,

and (3) gives the president of the United States the right to seek an injunction (for up to 80 days) against a strike that would create a national emergency.

- **Labor Management Reporting and Disclosure Act.**   In 1959, Congress enacted the **Labor Management Reporting and Disclosure Act**, also known as the **Landrum-Griffin Act**.[4] This act regulates internal union affairs and establishes the rights of union members.

- **Railway Labor Act.**   The **Railway Labor Act** of 1926, as amended in 1934, covers employees of railroad and airline carriers.[5]

These statutes, rules and regulations adopted pursuant to these statutes, and court decisions interpreting and applying the statutes and rules and regulations are collectively referred to as **labor law**.

National Labor Relations Board (NLRB)

The National Labor Relations Act created the **National Labor Relations Board (NLRB)**. The NLRB is an administrative body composed of five members appointed by the president and approved by the Senate. The NLRB oversees union elections, prevents employers and unions from engaging in illegal and unfair labor practices, and enforces and interprets certain federal labor laws. The decisions of the NLRB are enforceable in court.

Organizing a Union

Section 7 of the NLRA gives employees the right to join together to form a union. Section 7 provides that employees shall have the right to self-organize; to form, join, or assist labor organizations; to bargain collectively through representatives of their own choosing; and to engage in other concerted activities for the purpose of collective bargaining or other mutual aid protection.

The group that a union is seeking to represent—which is called the **appropriate bargaining unit**, or **bargaining unit**—must be defined before the union can petition for an election. This group can be the employees of a single company or plant, a group within a single company (e.g., maintenance workers at all of a company's plants), or an entire industry (e.g., nurses at all hospitals in the country). Managers and professional employees may not belong to unions formed by employees whom they manage.

Types of Union Elections

If it can be shown that at least 30 percent of the employees in a bargaining unit are interested in joining or forming a union, the NLRB can be petitioned to investigate and set an election date. The following types of elections are possible:

- **Contested election.**   Most union elections are contested by the employer. The NLRB is required to supervise all **contested elections**. A simple majority vote (more than 50 percent) wins the election.

    Example If 51 of 100 employees vote for the union, the union is certified as the bargaining agent for all 100 employees.

- **Consent election.**   If management does not contest an election, a **consent election** may be held without NLRB supervision.

- **Decertification election.**   If employees no longer want to be represented by a union, a **decertification election** will be held. Decertification elections must be supervised by the NLRB.

National Labor Relations Board (NLRB)
A federal administrative agency that oversees union elections, prevents employers and unions from engaging in illegal and unfair labor practices, and enforces and interprets certain federal labor laws.

Section 7 of the NLRA
A federal law that gives employees the right to form, join, and assist labor unions; to bargain collectively with employers; and to engage in concerted activity to promote these rights.

appropriate bargaining unit (bargaining unit)
A group of employees that a union is seeking to represent.

Labor is discovered to be the grand conqueror, enriching and building up nations more surely than the proudest battles.

William Ellery Channing
War

contested election
An election for a union that an employer's management contests. The NLRB must supervise this type of election.

Union Solicitation on Company Property

If union solicitation is being conducted by employees, an employer may restrict solicitation activities to the employees' free time (e.g., coffee breaks, lunch breaks, before and after work). The activities may also be limited to nonworking areas, such as the cafeteria, rest room, or parking lot. Off-duty employees may be barred from union solicitation on company premises, and nonemployees (e.g., union management) may be prohibited from soliciting on behalf of the union anywhere on company property. Employers may dismiss employees who violate these rules.

An exception to this rule applies if the location of the business and the living quarters of the employees place the employees beyond the reach of reasonable union efforts to communicate with them. This exception, called the **inaccessibility exception**, applies to logging camps, mining towns, company towns, and the like.

In the following case, the U.S. Supreme Court addressed the issue of whether an employer had to allow nonemployee union organizers on its property.

inaccessibility exception
A rule that permits employees and union officials to engage in union solicitation on company property if the employees are beyond reach of reasonable union efforts to communicate with them.

CASE 21.1   *U.S. SUPREME COURT Organizing a Labor Union*

Lechmere, Inc. v. National Labor Relations Board

502 U.S. 527, 112 S.Ct. 841, 117 L.Ed.2d 79, Web 1992 U.S. Lexis 555
Supreme Court of the United States

"In practice, nonemployee organizational trespassing had generally been prohibited except where 'unique obstacles' prevented nontresspassory methods of communication with the employees."

—Thomas, Justice

Facts

Lechmere, Inc. (Lechmere), owned and operated a retail store in the Lechmere Shopping Plaza in Newington, Connecticut. Thirteen smaller stores were located between the Lechmere store and the parking lot, which was owned by Lechmere. The United Food and Commercial Workers Union, AFL-CIO (Union), attempted to organize Lechmere's 200 employees, none of whom belonged to a union. After a full-page advertisement in a local newspaper drew little response, nonemployee Union organizers entered Lechmere's parking lot and began placing handbills on windshields of cars parked in the employee section of the parking lot. Lechmere's manager informed the organizers that Lechmere prohibited solicitation and handbill distribution of any kind on the property and asked them to leave. They did so, and Lechmere personnel removed the handbills. Union organizers renewed their handbill effort in the parking lot on several subsequent occasions, but each time, they were asked to leave,

and the handbills were removed. Union filed a grievance with the NLRB. The NLRB ruled in favor of Union and ordered Lechmere to allow handbill distribution in the parking lot. The Court of Appeals affirmed this decision. Lechmere appealed to the U.S. Supreme Court.

Issue

May a storeowner prohibit nonemployee union organizers from distributing leaflets in a shopping mall parking lot owned by the store?

Language of the U.S. Supreme Court

In practice, nonemployee organizational trespassing had generally been prohibited except where "unique obstacles" prevented nontresspassory methods of communication with the employees. The inaccessibility exception is a narrow one. Although the employees live in a large metropolitan area (Greater Hartford), that fact does not in itself render them "inaccessible." Their accessibility is suggested by the union's success in contacting a substantial percentage of them directly, via mailings, phone calls, and home visits. In this case, other alternative means of communication were readily available. Thus, signs (displayed,

(continued)

for example, from the public grassy strip adjoining Lechmere's parking lot) would have informed the employees about the union's organizational efforts. Access to employees, not success in winning them over, is the critical issue.

Decision

The U.S. Supreme Court held that under the facts of this case, Lechmere could prohibit nonemployee union organizers from distributing leaflets to employees in the store's parking lot. The Supreme Court reversed the decision of the Court of Appeals.

Case Questions

Critical Legal Thinking
Should property rights take precedence over a union's right to organize employees? Explain.

Ethics
Is it ethical for an employer to deny union organizers access to company property to conduct their organizational efforts? Is it ethical for union organizers to demand this as a right?

Contemporary Business
What implication does this case have for business? Was the decision in this case a pro- or anti-business decision?

Illegal Interference with an Election

Section 8(a) of the NLRA
A law that makes it an unfair labor practice for an employer to interfere with, coerce, or restrain employees from exercising their statutory right to form and join unions.

Section 8(a) of the NLRA makes it an **unfair labor practice** for an employer to interfere with, coerce, or restrain employees from exercising their statutory right to form and join unions. Threats of loss of benefits for joining the union, statements such as "I'll close this plant if a union comes in here," and the like are unfair labor practices. Also, an employer may not form a company union. **Section 8(b) of the NLRA** prohibits unions from engaging in unfair labor practices that interfere with a union election. Coercion, physical threats, and such are unfair labor practices.

Where an unfair labor practice has been found, the NLRB or the courts may issue a cease-and-desist order or an injunction to restrain unfair labor practices and may set aside an election and order a new election.

Collective Bargaining

collective bargaining
The act of negotiating contract terms between an employer and the members of a union.

collective bargaining agreement
A contract formed during a collective bargaining procedure.

compulsory subjects of collective bargaining
Wages, hours, and other terms and conditions of employment.

Once a union has been elected, the employer and the union discuss the terms of employment of union members and try to negotiate a contract that embodies these terms. The act of negotiating is called **collective bargaining**, and the resulting contract is called a **collective bargaining agreement**. The employer and the union must negotiate with each other in good faith. Among other things, this prohibits making take-it-or-leave-it proposals.

The subjects of collective bargaining are classified as follows:

- **Compulsory subjects.** Wages, hours, and other terms and conditions of employment are **compulsory subjects of collective bargaining**.

  Examples In addition to wages and hours, other compulsory subjects of collective bargaining include fringe benefits, health benefits, retirement plans, work assignments, safety rules, and the like.

- **Permissive subjects.** Subjects that are not compulsory or illegal are **permissive subjects of collective bargaining**. These subjects may be bargained for if the company and union agree to do so.

  Examples Permissive subjects of collective bargaining include such issues as the size and composition of the supervisory force, location of plants, corporate reorganizations, and the like.

- **Illegal subjects.** Certain topics are **illegal subjects of collective bargaining** and therefore cannot be subjects of negotiation or agreement.

Examples Subjects such as discrimination and closed shops are illegal subjects of collective bargaining.

Union Security Agreements

To obtain the greatest power possible, elected unions sometimes try to install a **union security agreement**. There are several types of security agreements:

- **Closed shop.**   Under a **closed shop** agreement, an employer agrees to hire only employees who are already members of a union. The employer cannot hire employees who are not members of a union. Closed shops are illegal in the United States.

- **Union shop.**   Under a **union shop** agreement, an employer may hire anyone whether he belongs to a union or not. However, an employee must join the union within a certain time period (e.g., thirty days) after being hired. Union shops are lawful.

- **Agency shop.**   Under an **agency shop** agreement, an employer may hire anyone whether she belongs to a union or not. After an employee has been hired, she does not have to join the union, but if she does not join the union, he must pay an agency fee to the union. This fee will include an amount to help pay for the costs of collective bargaining. A nonunion employee cannot be assessed fees for noncollective bargaining union activities, such as political campaigning and such. The agency fee prevents the "free rider" problem that would occur if an employee did not have to pay union dues or their equivalent but was the recipient of union collective bargaining activities. Agency shops are lawful.

Upon proper notification by the union, union and agency shop employers are required to deduct union dues and agency fees from employees' wages and forward these dues to the union. This is called **dues checkoff**.

The following feature discusses state right-to-work laws.

union shop
A workplace in which an employee must join the union within a certain number of days after being hired.

agency shop
A workplace in which an employee does not have to join the union but must pay an agency fee to the union.

Contemporary Environment

State Right-to-Work Laws

In 1947, Congress amended the Taft-Hartley Act by enacting Section 14(b), which provides: "Nothing in this Act shall be construed as authorizing the execution or application of agreements requiring membership in a labor organization as a condition of employment in any State or Territory in which such execution or application is prohibited by State or Territorial Law." In other words, states can enact **right-to-work laws** —either by constitutional amendment or statute—that outlaw union and agency shops.

If a state enacts a right-to-work law, individual employees cannot be forced to join a union or pay union dues and fees, even though a labor union has been elected by other employees.

Right-to-work laws are often enacted by states to attract new businesses to a nonunion and low-wage environment. Unions vehemently oppose the enactment of right-to-work

laws because they substantially erode union power. The remedies for violation of right-to-work laws vary from state to state but usually include damages to persons injured by the violation, injunctive relief, and criminal penalties. Today, the following twenty-two states have enacted right-to-work laws:

Alabama	Nevada
Arizona	North Carolina
Arkansas	North Dakota
Florida	Oklahoma
Georgia	South Carolina
Idaho	South Dakota
Iowa	Tennessee
Kansas	Texas
Louisiana	Utah
Mississippi	Virginia
Nebraska	Wyoming

Strikes

The NLRA gives union management the right to recommend that a union call a **strike** if a collective bargaining agreement cannot be reached. In a strike, union members refuse to work. Strikes are permitted by federal labor law. Before there can be a strike, though, a majority of the union's members must vote in favor of the action.

Cooling-Off Period

Before a strike, a union must give sixty days' notice to the employer that the union intends to strike. It is illegal for a strike to begin during the mandatory sixty-day **cooling-off period**. The sixty-day time period is designed to give the employer and the union enough time to negotiate a settlement of the union grievances and avoid a strike. Any strike without a proper sixty-day notice is illegal, and the employer may dismiss the striking workers.

Illegal Strikes

The majority of strikes are lawful strikes. However, several types of strikes have been held to be illegal and are not protected by federal labor law. The following are **illegal strikes**:

- **Violent strikes.** In **violent strikes**, striking employees cause substantial damage to property of the employer or a third party. Courts usually tolerate a certain amount of isolated violence before finding that an entire strike is illegal.
- **Sit-down strikes.** In **sit-down strikes**, striking employees continue to occupy the employer's premises. Such strikes are illegal because they deny the employer's statutory right to continue its operations during the strike.
- **Partial or intermittent strikes.** In **partial strikes**, or **intermittent strikes**, employees strike part of the day or workweek and work the other part. This type of strike is illegal because it interferes with the employer's right to operate its facilities at full operation.
- **Wildcat strikes.** In **wildcat strikes**, individual union members go on strike without proper authorization from the union. The courts have recognized that a wildcat strike becomes lawful if it is quickly ratified by the union.

An employer can discharge illegal strikers, who then have no rights to reinstatement.

No-Strike Clause

An employer and a union can agree in a collective bargaining agreement that the union will not strike during a particular period of time. The employer gives economic benefits to the union and, in exchange, the union agrees that no strike will be called for the set time. It is illegal for a strike to take place in violation of a negotiated **no-strike clause**. An employer may dismiss union members who strike in violation of a no-strike clause.

Crossover and Replacement Workers

Individual members of a union do not have to honor a strike. They may (1) choose not to strike or (2) return to work after joining the strikers for a time. Employees who choose either of these options are known as **crossover workers**.

Once a strike begins, the employer may continue operations by using management personnel and hiring **replacement workers** to take the place of the striking employees. Replacement workers can be hired on either a temporary or permanent basis. If replacement workers are given permanent status, they do not have to be dismissed when the strike is over.

Employer Lockout

If an employer reasonably anticipates a strike by some of its employees, it may prevent those employees from entering the plant or premises. This is called an **employer lockout**.

Example The National Hockey League (NHL) is a professional hockey league with teams located in Canada and the United States. The National Hockey League Players' Association, a labor union, represents the players. The NHL and the players' association negotiate and enter into collective bargaining agreements that establish working conditions and financial matters. On several occasions, the players' association has gone on strike. Therefore, in 2004, when it looked as if the players might go on strike, the NHL locked the players out before they could strike. The team owners and the union could not reach an agreement, and the 2004–2005 season was canceled.

employer lockout
An act of an employer to prevent employees from entering the work premises when the employer reasonably anticipates a strike.

Picketing

Striking union members often engage in **picketing** in support of their strike. Picketing usually takes the form of the striking employees and union representatives walking in front of the employer's premises, carrying signs announcing their strike. Picketing is used to put pressure on an employer to settle a strike. The right to picket is implied from the NLRA.

picketing
The action of strikers walking in front of an employer's premises, carrying signs announcing their strike.

Example Union members of a large grocery chain engage in a union-sanctioned strike over issues of pay and benefits. The union members can picket the employer. This may consist of carrying signs bearing messages announcing the strike, identifying the issues, and criticizing the employer.

Picketing is lawful unless it (1) is accompanied by violence, (2) obstructs customers from entering the employer's place of business, (3) prevents nonstriking employees from entering the employer's premises, or (4) prevents pickups and deliveries at the employer's place of business. An employer may seek an injunction against unlawful picketing.

Example If union members picketing a large grocery store chain block customers from entering the store, this is illegal picketing.

Secondary Boycott Picketing

Unions sometimes try to bring pressure against an employer by picketing the employer's suppliers or customers. Such **secondary boycott picketing** is lawful only if it is product picketing (i.e., if the picketing is against the primary employer's product). The picketing is illegal if it is directed against the neutral employer instead of the struck employer's product.

secondary boycott picketing
A type of picketing in which a union tries to bring pressure against an employer by picketing the employer's suppliers or customers.

Example Union members go on strike against their employer, a toy manufacturer. The union members picket retail stores that sell the manufacturer's toy products. They carry signs announcing their strike and request that consumers not buy toy products manufacturer by their employer. This is lawful secondary boycott picketing.

Example Union members go on strike against their employer, a toy manufacturer. The union members picket retail stores that sell the manufacturer's toy products. They carry signs requesting that consumers not shop at the retail stores. This is unlawful secondary boycott picketing.

The following feature discusses the lawfulness of picketing activities by a labor union.

Ethics

Mock Funeral by Striking Workers Is Lawful

"Their message may have been unsettling or even offensive to someone visiting a dying relative, but unsettling and even offensive speech is not without the protection of the First Amendment."

—Ginsburg, Circuit Judge

The Sheet Metal Workers' International Association Local 15, AFL-CIO, had a labor dispute with Massey Metals, Inc. (Massey) and also with Workers Temporary Staffing (WTS), which supplied nonunion labor employees to Massey, whom Massey used on its various construction projects. The Brandon Regional Medical Center, a hospital, employed Massey as the metal fabricator and installation contractor for a construction project at the hospital.

One day, the union staged a mock funeral procession in front of the hospital. The procession consisted of four union representatives acting as pallbearers and carrying a large coffin back and forth on the sidewalk near the entrance to the hospital. Another union representative accompanied the procession dressed as the "Grim Reaper." The funeral procession took place about 100 feet from the hospital. Union members broadcast somber funeral music over loudspeakers mounted on a flatbed trailer that was positioned nearby. Four other union representatives, who did not impede ingress or egress to the hospital, distributed to persons entering and leaving the hospital handbills that stated "Going to Brandon Regional Hospital Should Not be a Grave Decision." The procession lasted approximately two hours.

The regional director of the National Labor Relations Board (NLRB) immediately filed a petition for a temporary injunction against the union's mock funeral. The NLRB alleged that the union's mock funeral procession at the hospital constituted illegal secondary boycott picketing. The U.S. District Court agreed and issued an injunction against the union, prohibiting such mock funeral processions at the hospital. The union appealed.

On appeal, the U.S. Court of Appeals reversed, finding that the mock funeral was not coercive, threatening, restraining, or intimidating and therefore was not illegal secondary boycott picketing. The Court of Appeals stated, "Their message may have been unsettling or even offensive to someone visiting a dying relative, but unsettling and even offensive speech is not without the protection of the First Amendment." The Court of Appeals remanded the case to the NLRB for proceedings consistent with the Court's opinion. *Sheet Metal Workers' International Association, Local 15, AFL-CIO v. National Labor Relations Board*, 491 F.3d 429, **Web** 2007 U.S. App. Lexis 14361 (United States Court of Appeals for the District of Columbia Circuit, 2007)

Ethics Questions   What is secondary boycott picketing? For what purpose did the union hold a mock funeral procession at the hospital? Do you think that the union's conduct was ethical in this case?

Internal Union Affairs

Title I of the Landrum-Griffin Act
Labor's "bill of rights," which gives each union member equal rights and privileges to nominate candidates for union office, vote in elections, and participate in membership meetings.

A union may adopt **internal union rules** to regulate the operation of the union, acquire and maintain union membership, and the like. The undemocratic manner in which many unions were formulating these rules prompted Congress in 1959 to enact **Title I of the Landrum-Griffin Act**. Title I, which is often referred to as **labor's "bill of rights,"** gives each union member equal rights and privileges to nominate candidates for union office, vote in elections, and participate in membership meetings. It further guarantees union members the rights of free speech and assembly, provides for due process (notice and hearing), and permits union members to initiate judicial or administrative action.

A union may discipline members for participating in certain activities, including (1) walking off the job in a nonsanctioned strike, (2) working for wages below union scale, (3) spying for an employer, and (4) any other unauthorized activity that has an adverse economic impact on the union. A union may not punish a union member for participating in a civic duty, such as testifying in court against the union.

The following feature discusses a federal act that regulates the closing of plants by employers.

Ethics

Plant Closing Act

In the past, companies often chose to close plants without giving their employees prior notice of the closing. To remedy this situation, in 1988, Congress enacted the **Worker Adjustment and Retraining Notification (WARN) Act**, also called the **Plant Closing Act**.[6] The act requires employers with one hundred or more employees to give their employees sixty days' notice before engaging in certain plant closings or layoffs.

If employees are represented by a union, the notice must be given to the union; if they are not, the notice must be given to the employees individually. The act covers the following actions:

- **Plant closings.** A **plant closing** is a permanent or temporary shutdown of a single site that results in a loss of employment for fifty or more employees during any thirty-day period.
- **Mass layoffs.** A **mass layoff** is a reduction of 33 percent of the employees or at least fifty employees during any thirty-day period.

An employer is exempted from having to give such notice if:

- The closing or layoff is caused by business circumstances that were not reasonably foreseeable at the time that the notice would have been required.
- The business was actively seeking capital or business that, if obtained, would have avoided or postponed the shutdown and the employer in good faith believed that giving notice would have precluded it from obtaining the needed capital or business.

Ethics Questions   What does the WARN Act provide? Why was the WARN Act enacted? Does it curtail unethical behavior of business?

Immigration Law

The United States of America was colonized by immigrants, originally those from Western Europe. Many sought wealth and prosperity; some sought religious freedom, and others were running from their debts. But no matter the reason, during the 16th, 17th, and 18th centuries, the immigrants kept coming, and they moved increasingly further inland from the Atlantic Ocean. In doing so, however, they tragically displaced the Native Americans who occupied the land prior to the arrival of the immigrants.

Many immigrants involuntarily came from the continent of Africa, most forcibly to become slaves. In the 20th and 21st centuries, many immigrants have come from Mexico, Central and South America, China and other Asian countries, India, and other areas of the world.

In 1921, the United States enacted its first immigration quota law, setting a limit on the number of immigrants that could be admitted to the United States from each foreign country each year. During different times, the quotas for each foreign country have been raised or lowered, depending on the world situation. For example, after World War II, the United States increased the quotas dramatically to accept many persons who had been displaced by the war. A quota system is in effect today.

Currently, the immigration laws of this country are administered by the **U.S. Citizenship and Immigration Services (USCIS)**, which is part of the U.S. Department of Homeland Security. The USCIS processes immigrant visa and naturalization petitions.

Worker Adjustment and Retraining Notification (WARN) Act (Plant Closing Act)
A federal act that requires employers with one hundred or more employees to give their employees sixty days' notice before engaging in certain plant closings or layoffs.

U.S. Citizenship and Immigration Services (USCIS)
A federal agency empowered to enforce U.S. immigration laws.

Foreign nationals who qualify and have met the requirements to do so may become citizens of the United States. During their swearing-in ceremony, they must swear the Oath of Citizenship.

H-1B Foreign Guest Worker Visa

H-1B visa
A visa that allows U.S. employers to employ in the United States foreign nationals who are skilled in specialty occupations. These workers are called *foreign guest workers*.

An **H-1B visa** is a visa that allows U.S. employers to employ in the United States foreign nationals who are skilled in specialty occupations.[7] A foreign guest worker under an H-1B visa must have a bachelor's degree or higher and have a "specialty occupation," such as engineering, mathematics, computer science, physical sciences, or medicine. A **foreign guest worker** must be sponsored by a U.S. employer. Employers, and not individual applicants, apply for H-1B visas for proposed foreign guest workers. The USCIS determines H-1B eligibility.

The number of H-1B visas is limited, usually to fewer than one hundred thousand per year, so the competition is fierce to obtain such visas. H-1B visa holders are allowed to bring their immediate family members (i.e., spouse and children under 21) to the United States under the **H4 visa** category as dependents. An H4 visa holder may remain in the United States as long as he or she remains in legal status. An H4 visa holder is not eligible to work in the United States.

The duration of stay for a worker on an H-1B visa is three years, and this can be extended another three years. During this time, an employer may sponsor an H-1B holder for a green card, which if issued permits the foreign national to eventually obtain U.S. citizenship. If the employer does not apply for a green card for the foreign national or if the foreign national is denied a green card, he or she must leave the country after six years from the time of employment.

EB-1 Extraordinary Ability Visa

EB-1 visa
A visa that allows U.S. employers to employ in the United States foreign nationals who possess exceptional qualifications for certain types of employment.

An **EB-1 visa** is a visa that allows U.S. employers to employ in the United States foreign nationals who possess extraordinary ability for certain types of employment. The three categories of workers who can qualify for an EB-1 visa are (1) persons who can demonstrate extraordinary ability in the sciences, arts, education, business, or athletics through sustained national or international acclaim; (2) outstanding professors and researchers who can demonstrate international recognition for outstanding achievements in a particular academic field; and (3) multinational managers or executives employed by a firm outside the United States who seek to continue to work for that firm in the United States. Employers must file for the visa for workers in categories (2) and (3), while applicants in category (1) can file for the visa themselves. Fewer than fifty thousand EB-1 visas are granted each year. The USCIS determines EB-1 eligibility. Persons who are granted an EB-1 visa may become U.S. citizens, usually in five years.

Undocumented Workers

For many people like myself, it can be called the Ellis Island of the 20th century.

Theodore H. M. Prudon
Describing Kennedy Airport

Many persons enter the United States without permission, and once in the country, many of these persons seek employment in the United States. The **Immigration Reform and Control Act (IRCA)** of 1986,[8] which is administered by the USCIS, requires employers to verify whether prospective employees are either U.S. citizens or otherwise authorized to work in the country (e.g., have proper work visas).

Employers are required to have prospective employees complete **Form I-9, "Employment Eligibility Verification."** Employers must obtain a completed Form I-9 for every employee, regardless of citizenship or national origin. Employers must examine evidence of prospective employees' identity and employment eligibility. A state-issued driver's license is not sufficient. Employers must review other documents to establish eligibility, such as Social Security cards, birth certificates, and such.

Employers must maintain records and post in the workplace notices of the contents of the law. The IRCA imposes criminal and financial penalties on employers who knowingly hire undocumented workers.

Key Terms and Concepts

AFL-CIO (437)

Agency shop (441)

American Federation of Labor (AFL) (437)

Appropriate bargaining unit (bargaining unit) (438)

Closed shop (441)

Collective bargaining (440)

Collective bargaining agreement (440)

Compulsory subject of collective bargaining (440)

Congress of Industrial Organizations (CIO) (437)

Consent election (438)

Contested election (438)

Cooling-off period (442)

Crossover worker (442)

Decertification election (438)

Dues checkoff (441)

EB-1 visa (446)

Employer lockout (443)

Foreign guest worker (446)

Form I-9, "Employment Eligibility Verification" (446)

H-1B visa (446)

H4 visa (446)

Illegal strike (442)

Illegal subjects of collective bargaining (440)

Inaccessibility exception (439)

Immigration Reform and Control Act of 1986 (IRCA) (446)

Internal union rules (444)

Labor law (438)

Labor Management Relations Act (Taft-Hartley Act) (437)

Labor Management Reporting and Disclosure Act (Landrum-Griffin Act) (438)

Mass layoff (445)

National Labor Relations Act (NLRA) (Wagner Act) (437)

National Labor Relations Board (NLRB) (438)

Norris-LaGuardia Act (437)

No-strike clause (442)

Partial strike (intermittent strike) (442)

Permissive subjects of collective bargaining (440)

Picketing (443)

Plant closing (445)

Railway Labor Act (438)

Replacement worker (442)

Right-to-work laws (441)

Secondary boycott picketing (443)

Section 7 of the NLRA (438)

Section 8(a) of the NLRA (440)

Section 8(b) of the NLRA (440)

Secondary boycott picketing (443)

Sit-down strike (442)

Strike (442)

Title I of the Landrum-Griffin Act (labor's "bill of rights") (444)

Unfair labor practice (440)

Union security agreement (441)

Union shop (441)

U.S. Citizenship and Immigration Services (USCIS) (445)

Violent strike (442)

Wildcat strike (442)

Worker Adjustment and Retraining Notification (WARN) Act (Plant Closing Act) (445)

Law Case with Answer
Marquez v. Screen Actors Guild, Inc.

Facts The Screen Actors Guild (SAG) is a labor union that represents performers in the entertainment industry. Lakeside Productions, an entertainment production company, signed a collective bargaining agreement with SAG, making SAG the exclusive union for performers that Lakeside hired for its productions. The collective bargaining agreement contained a standard "union security clause" which provided that any performer who worked for Lakeside must be a member of SAG. Naomi Marquez, a part-time actress, auditioned for a one-line role in a TV episode to be filmed by Lakeside and won the part. When Marquez did not pay the $500 membership fee to SAG, Lakeside hired another actress for the part. Marquez sued SAG and Lakeside, alleging that the union security clause was unlawful. Does the union security clause negotiated between Lakeside Productions and SAG violate federal labor law?

Answer No, the union security clause negotiated between Lakeside Productions and SAG does not violate federal labor law. Section 8(a)(3) of the National Labor Relations

Act (NLRA) permits unions and employers to negotiate an agreement that requires union membership as a condition of employment for all employees. Although Section 8(a)(3) states that unions may negotiate a clause requiring membership in the union, an employee can satisfy the membership condition merely by paying to the union an amount equal to the union's initiation fees and dues. In other words, the membership that may be required as a condition of employment is whittled down to its financial core.

Section 8(a)(3) does not permit unions to exact dues or fees from employees for activities that are not germane to collective bargaining, grievance adjustment, or contract administration. Section 8(a)(3) permits unions and employers to require only that employees pay the fees and dues necessary to support the union's activities as the employees' exclusive bargaining representative. The union security clause negotiated between Lakeside Productions and SAG is lawful under federal labor law. *Marquez v. Screen Actors Guild, Inc.*, 525 U.S. 33, 119 S.Ct. 292, 142 L.Ed.2d 242, **Web** 1998 U.S. Lexis 7110 (Supreme Court of the United States)

Critical Legal Thinking Cases

21.1 Unfair Labor Practice The Teamsters Union (Teamsters) began a campaign to organize the employees at a Sinclair Company (Sinclair) plant. When the president of Sinclair learned of the Teamsters' drive, he talked with all of his employees and emphasized the results of a long strike thirteen years earlier that he claimed "almost put our company out of business," and he expressed worry that the employees were forgetting the "lessons of the past." He emphasized that Sinclair was on "thin ice" financially, that the Teamsters' "only weapon is to strike," and that a strike "could lead to the closing of the plant" because Sinclair had manufacturing facilities elsewhere. He also noted that because of the employees' ages and the limited usefulness of their skills, they might not be able to find reemployment if they lost their jobs. Finally, he sent literature to the employees stating that "the Teamsters Union is a strike happy outfit" and that they were under "hoodlum control," and included a cartoon showing the preparation of a grave for Sinclair and other headstones containing the names of other plants allegedly victimized by unions. The Teamsters lost the election 7 to 6 and then filed an unfair labor practice charge with the National Labor Relations Board (NLRB). Has Sinclair violated labor law? Who wins? *N.L.R.B. v. Gissel Packing Co.*, 395 U.S. 575, 89 S.Ct. 1918, 23 L.Ed.2d 547, **Web** 1969 U.S. Lexis 3172 (Supreme Court of the United States)

21.2 Right-to-Work Law Mobil Oil Corporation (Mobil) had its headquarters in Beaumont, Texas. It operated a fleet of eight oceangoing tankers that transported its petroleum products from Texas to ports on the East Coast. A typical trip on a tanker from Beaumont to New York took about five days. No more than 10 to 20 percent of the seamen's work time was spent in Texas. The three hundred or so seamen who were employed to work on the tankers belonged to the Oil, Chemical & Atomic Workers International Union, AFL-CIO (Union), which had an agency shop agreement with Mobil. The state of Texas enacted a right-to-work law. Mobil sued Union, claiming that the agency shop agreement was unenforceable because it violated the Texas right-to-work law. Who wins? *Oil, Chemical & Atomic Workers International Union, AFL-CIO v. Mobil Oil Corp.*, 426 U.S. 407, 96 S.Ct. 2140, 48 L.Ed.2d 736, **Web** 1976 U.S. Lexis 106 (Supreme Court of the United States)

21.3 Plant Closing Arrow Automotive Industries, Inc. (Arrow), was engaged in the remanufacture and distribution of automobile and truck parts. All its operating plants produced identical product lines. Arrow was planning to open a new facility in Santa Maria, California. The employees at the Arrow plant in Hudson, Massachusetts, were represented by the United Automobile, Aerospace, and Agricultural Implement Workers of America (Union). The Hudson plant had a history of unprofitable operations. Union called a strike when the existing collective bargaining agreement expired and a new agreement could not be reached. After several months, the board of directors of Arrow voted to close the striking plant. The closing gave Arrow a 24 percent increase in gross profits and freed capital and equipment for the new Santa Maria plant. In addition, the existing customers of the Hudson plant could be serviced by the Spartanburg plant, which was being underutilized. Union filed an unfair labor practice claim with the National Labor Relations Board (NLRB). Does Arrow have to bargain with Union over the decision to close a plant? What must be done if the Plant Closing Act applies to this situation? *Arrow Automotive Industries, Inc. v. N.L.R.B.*, 853 F.2d 223, **Web** 1988 U.S. App. Lexis 10091 (United States Court of Appeals for the Fourth Circuit)

21.4 Unfair Labor Practice The Frouge Corporation (Frouge) was the general contractor on a housing project in Philadelphia. The carpenter employees of Frouge were represented by the Carpenters' International Union (Union). Traditional jobs of carpenters included taking blank wooden doors and mortising them for doorknobs, routing them for hinges, and beveling them to fit between the doorjambs. Union had entered into a collective bargaining agreement with Frouge that provided that no member of Union would handle any doors that had been fitted prior to being furnished to the job site. The housing project called for 3,600 doors. Frouge contracted for the purchase of premachined doors that were already mortised, routed, and beveled. When Union ordered its members not to hang the prefabricated doors, the National Woodwork Manufacturers Association filed an unfair labor practice charge against Union with the National Labor Relations Board (NLRB). Is Union's refusal to hang prefabricated doors lawful? *National Woodwork Manufacturers Association v. N.L.R.B.*, 386 U.S. 612, 87 S.Ct. 1250, **Web** 1967 U.S. Lexis 2858 (Supreme Court of the United States)

21.5 Replacement Workers The union (Union) member-employees of the Erie Resistor Company (Company) struck Company over the terms of a new collective bargaining agreement that was being negotiated between Company and Union. Company continued production operations during the strike by hiring new hires and crossover union members who were persuaded to abandon the strike and come back to work. Company promised all replacement workers super seniority. This would take the form of adding twenty years to the length of a worker's actual service for the purpose of future layoffs and recalls. Many union members accepted the offer. Union filed an unfair labor practice charge with the National Labor Relations Board (NLRB). Is Company's offer of the super seniority lawful? *N.L.R.B. v. Erie Resistor Co.*, 373 U.S. 221, 83 S.Ct. 1139, 10 L.Ed.2d 308, **Web** 1963 U.S. Lexis 2492 (Supreme Court of the United States)

21.6 Secondary Boycott Safeco Title Insurance Company (Safeco) was a major insurance company that underwrote title insurance for real estate in the state of Washington. Five local title companies acted as insurance brokers that exclusively sold Safeco insurance. Local 1001 of the Retail Store Employees Union, AFL-CIO (Union), was elected as the bargaining agent for certain Safeco employees. When negotiations between Safeco and Union reached an impasse, the employees

went on strike. Union did not confine its picketing to Safeco's office in Seattle but also picketed each of the five local title companies. The picketers carried signs declaring that Safeco had no contract with Union and distributed handbills, asking consumers to support the strike by canceling their Safeco insurance policies. The local title companies filed a complaint with the National Labor Relations Board (NLRB). Is the picketing of the neutral title insurance companies lawful? *N.L.R.B. v. Retail Store Employees Union, Local 1001, Retail Clerks International Association, AFL-CIO*, 447 U.S. 607, 100 S.Ct. 2372, 65 L.Ed.2d 377, **Web** 1980 U.S. Lexis 133 (Supreme Court of the United States)

21.7 Ethics The American Ship Building Company (American) operated a shipyard in Chicago, Illinois, where it repaired Great Lakes ships during the winter months, when freezing on the Great Lakes rendered shipping impossible. The workers at the shipyard were represented by several labor unions. The unions notified American of their intention to seek modification of the current collective bargaining agreement when it expired three months later. On five previous occasions, agreements had been preceded by strikes (including illegal strikes) that were called just after the ships had arrived in the shipyard for repairs so that the unions increased their leverage in negotiations with the company.

Based on this history, American displayed anxiety as to the unions' strike plans and possible work stoppage. On the day that the collective bargaining agreement expired, after extensive negotiations, American and the unions reached an impasse in their collective bargaining. American decided to lay off most of the workers at the shipyard. It sent them the following notice: "Because of the labor dispute which has been unresolved, you are laid off until further notice." The unions filed unfair labor practice charges with the National Labor Relations Board (NLRB). Did American act ethically in locking out the employees? Are American's actions legal? *American Ship Building Company v. N.L.R.B.*, 380 U.S. 300, 85 S.Ct. 955, 13 L.Ed.2d 855, **Web** 1965 U.S. Lexis 2310 (Supreme Court of the United States)

Ethics Cases

21.8 Ethics The International Association of Machinists and Aerospace Workers, AFL-CIO (Union), began soliciting the employees of Whitcraft Houseboat Division, North American Rockwell Corp. (Whitcraft), to organize a union. For three days, Whitcraft management dispersed congregating groups of employees. During these three days,

production was down almost 50 percent. On the third day, Whitcraft adopted the following no-solicitation rule and mailed a copy to each employee and posted it around the workplace:

As you well know working time is for work. No one will be allowed to solicit or distribute literature during our working time, that is, when he or she should be working. Anyone doing so and neglecting his work or interfering with the work of another employee will be subject to discharge.

Two days later, a manager of Whitcraft found that two employees of the company were engaged in union solicitation during working hours in a working area. Whitcraft discharged them for violating the no-solicitation rule. *Whitcraft Houseboat Division, North American Rockwell Corporation v. International Association of Machinists and Aerospace Workers*, AFL-CIO, 195 N.L.R.B. 1046 (N.L.R.B.), **Web 1972** NLRB Lexis 1117 (National Labor Relations Board)

1. When can an employee lawfully solicit members for a union?
2. Did the employees act ethically by using work hours to solicit other employees to join a union? Did Whitcraft act ethically in discharging the employees?
3. Is the discharge of the employees by Whitcraft lawful?

21.9 Ethics The employees of the Shop Rite Foods, Inc. (Shop Rite), warehouse in Lubbock, Texas, elected the United Packinghouse, Food and Allied Workers (Union), as its bargaining agent. Negotiations for a collective bargaining agreement began. Three months later, when an agreement had not yet been reached, Shop Rite found excessive amounts of damage to merchandise in its warehouse and concluded that it was being intentionally caused by dissident employees, as a pressure tactic to secure concessions from Shop Rite. Shop Rite notified Union representative that employees caught doing such acts would be terminated; Union representative in turn notified the employees.

A Shop Rite manager observed an employee in the flour section—where he had no business being—making quick motions with his hands. The manager found several bags of flour that had been cut. The employee was immediately fired. Another employee (a fellow Union member) led about thirty other employees in an immediate walkout. The company discharged these employees and refused to rehire them. The employees filed a grievance with the National Labor Relations Board (NLRB). *N.L.R.B. v. Shop Rite Foods, Inc.*, 430 F.2d 786, **Web 1970** U.S. App. Lexis 7613 (United States Court of Appeals for the Fifth Circuit)

1. What is an illegal strike?
2. Did the fired employees act ethically in this case? Did Shop Rite act ethically in firing the employees?
3. Can the fired employees get their old jobs back? Why or why not?

Internet Exercises

1. Visit the website of the AFL-CIO, at **www.aflcio.org**. Find a recent political issue that the AFL-CIO has taken a position on.

2. Go to the website of the National Labor Relations Board (NLRB), at **www.nlrb.gov**. What is the stated purpose of the NLRB?

3. Go to the website of the United Food and Commercial Workers International Union, AFL-CIO, at **www.ufcw.org**. What are some of the types of employees who are members of this union?

4. Go to the website of the International Brotherhood of Boilermakers, at **www.boilermakers.org/resources/what_is_a_boilermaker**. Who is a "boilermaker"?

5. Visit the website of the International Brotherhood of Teamsters, at **www.teamster.org**. What types of workers belong to this union?

6. Visit the website of the U.S. Immigration and Customs Enforcement (ICE), at **www.ice.gov**.

Endnotes

1. 29 U.S.C. Sections 101–110, 113–115.
2. 29 U.S.C. Sections 151–169.
3. 29 U.S.C. Sections 141 et seq.
4. 29 U.S.C. Sections 401 et seq.
5. 45 U.S.C. Sections 151–162, 181–188.

6. 29 U.S.C. Section 2102.
7. Immigration and Nationality Act, 8 U.S.C. Section 101(a)(15)(H).
8. 29 U.S.C. Section 1802.

PART

VI

Government Regulation

22 Antitrust Law and Unfair Trade Practices

BASEBALL PARK
In 1922, the U.S. Supreme Court held that professional baseball was exempt from antitrust laws because baseball was not engaged in interstate commerce.[1] The merits of this exemption have been debated ever since then.

Learning Objectives

After studying this chapter, you should be able to:

1. Describe the enforcement of federal antitrust laws.
2. Describe the horizontal and vertical restraints of trade that violate Section 1 of the Sherman Act.
3. Identify acts of monopolization that violate Section 2 of the Sherman Act.
4. Explain how the lawfulness of mergers is examined under Section 7 of the Clayton Act.
5. Apply Section 5 of the Federal Trade Commission Act to antitrust cases.

Chapter Outline

Chapter Outline *(continued)*

Federal Trade Commission Act

Exemptions from Antitrust Laws

State Antitrust Laws
> **INTERNATIONAL LAW** • *European Union Strictly Enforces Antitrust Law*

" *While competition cannot be created by statutory enactment, it can in large measure be revived by changing the laws and forbidding the practices that killed it, and by enacting laws that will give it heart and occasion again. We can arrest and prevent monopoly."*

—Woodrow Wilson
Speech, August 7, 1912

Introduction to Antitrust Law and Unfair Trade Practices

The U.S. economic system was built on the theory of freedom of competition. After the Civil War, however, the U.S. economy changed from a rural and agricultural economy to an industrialized and urban one. Many large industrial trusts were formed during this period. These arrangements resulted in a series of monopolies in basic industries such as oil and gas, sugar, cotton, and whiskey.

Because the common law could not deal effectively with these monopolies, Congress enacted a comprehensive system of **antitrust laws** to limit anticompetitive behavior. Almost all industries, businesses, and professions operating in the United States were affected. Although many states have also enacted antitrust laws, most actions in this area are brought under federal law.

This chapter discusses antitrust laws and laws against unfair trade practice.

People of the same trade seldom meet together, even for merriment and diversion, but that the conversation ends in a conspiracy against the public, or in some contrivance to raise prices.

Adam Smith
The Wealth of Nations (1776)

antitrust laws
A series of laws enacted to limit anticompetitive behavior in almost all industries, businesses, and professions operating in the United States.

Federal Antitrust Law

Federal antitrust law comprises several major statutes that prohibit certain anticompetitive and monopolistic practices. The federal antitrust statutes are broadly drafted to reflect the government's enforcement policy and to allow it to respond to economic, business, and technological changes. Federal antitrust laws provide for both government and private lawsuits.

Each administration that occupies the White House adopts a policy for the enforcement of antitrust laws. These policies differ from one administration to another. From the 1940s through the 1970s, antitrust enforcement was quite stringent. From the 1980s into the second decade of the 2000s, government enforcement of antitrust laws has been more relaxed. It will be interesting to see how future administrations will enforce antitrust law.

The following feature discusses the major federal antitrust statutes.

The notion that a business is clothed with a public interest and has been devoted to the public use is little more than a fiction intended to beautify what is disagreeable to the sufferers.

Justice Holmes
Tyson & Bro-United Theatre Ticket Offices v. Banton (1927)

Landmark Law

Federal Antitrust Statutes

After the Civil War, the United States became a leader of the Industrial Revolution. Behemoth companies and trusts were established. The most powerful of these were John D. Rockefeller's Standard Oil Company, Andrew Carnegie's Carnegie Steel, Cornelius Vanderbilt's New York Central Railroad System, and J.P. Morgan's banking house. These corporations dominated their respective industries, many obtaining monopoly power. For example, the Rockefeller oil trust controlled 90 percent of the country's oil refining capacity. Mergers and monopolization of industries were rampant.

During the late 1800s and early 1900s, Congress enacted a series of antitrust laws aimed at curbing abusive and monopoly practices by business. During this time, Congress enacted the following federal statutes:

- The **Sherman Act**[2] is a federal statute, enacted in 1890, that makes certain restraints of trade and monopolistic acts illegal.
- The **Clayton Act**[3] is a federal statute, enacted in 1914, that regulates mergers and prohibits certain exclusive dealing arrangements.
- The **Federal Trade Commission Act (FTC Act)**[4] is a federal statute, enacted in 1914, that prohibits unfair methods of competition.
- The **Robinson-Patman Act**[5] is a federal statute, enacted in 1930, that prohibits price discrimination.

Each of these important statutes is discussed in this chapter.

Government Actions

The federal government is authorized to bring actions to enforce federal antitrust laws. Government enforcement of federal antitrust laws is divided between the Antitrust Division of the Department of Justice and the Bureau of Competition of the FTC. The Sherman Act is the only major antitrust act that includes criminal sanctions. Intent is the prerequisite for criminal liability under this act. Penalties for individuals include fines and prison terms; corporations may be fined.[6]

The government may seek **civil damages**, including *treble damages*, for violations of antitrust laws.[7] Broad remedial powers allow the courts to order a number of civil remedies, including orders for divestiture of assets, cancellation of contracts, liquidation of businesses, licensing of patents, and such. Private parties cannot intervene in public antitrust actions brought by the government.

Private Actions

Section 4 of the Clayton Act permits any person who suffers antitrust injury in his or her "business or property" to bring a **private civil action** against the offenders.[8] Consumers who have to pay higher prices because of an antitrust violation have recourse under this provision.[9] To recover damages, plaintiffs must prove that they suffered **antitrust injuries** caused by the prohibited act. The courts have required that consumers must have dealt *directly* with the alleged violators to have standing to sue; indirect injury resulting from higher prices being "passed on" is insufficient.

Successful plaintiffs may recover **treble damages** (i.e., triple the amount of the actual damages), plus reasonable costs and attorneys' fees. Damages may be calculated as lost profits, an increase in the cost of doing business, or a decrease in the value of tangible or intangible property caused by the antitrust violation. This rule applies to all violations of the Sherman Act, the Clayton Act, and the Robinson-Patman Act. Only actual damages—not treble damages—may be recovered for violations of the FTC Act. A private plaintiff has four years from the date on which an antitrust injury occurred to bring a private civil treble-damages action. Only damages incurred during this four-year period are recoverable. This statute is *tolled* (i.e., does not run) during a suit by the government.

Section 4 of the Clayton Act
A section which provides that anyone injured in his or her business or property by the defendant's violation of any federal antitrust law (except the Federal Trade Commission Act) may bring a private civil action and recover from the defendant treble damages plus reasonable costs and attorneys' fees.

treble damages
Damages that may be awarded in a successful civil antitrust lawsuit, in an amount that is triple the amount of actual damages.

Effect of a Government Judgment

A **government judgment** obtained against a defendant for an antitrust violation may be used as *prima facie* evidence of liability in a private civil treble-damages action. Antitrust defendants often opt to settle government-brought antitrust actions by entering a plea of **nolo contendere** in a criminal action or a **consent decree** in a government civil action. These pleas usually subject the defendant to penalty without an admission of guilt or liability.

Section 16 of the Clayton Act permits the government or a private plaintiff to obtain an injunction against anticompetitive behavior that violates antitrust laws.[10] Only the FTC can obtain an injunction under the FTC Act.

government judgment
A judgment obtained by the government against a defendant for an antitrust violation that may be used as *prima facie* evidence of liability in a private civil treble-damages action.

Restraints of Trade: Section 1 of the Sherman Act

In 1890, Congress enacted the *Sherman Act* in order to outlaw anticompetitive behavior. The Sherman Act has been called the "Magna Carta of free enterprise."[11] **Section 1 of the Sherman Act** is intended to prohibit certain concerted anticompetitive activities. It provides:

> *Every contract, combination in the form of trust or otherwise, or conspiracy, in restraint of trade or commerce among the several states, or with foreign nations, is hereby declared to be illegal. Every person who shall make any contract or engage in any combination or conspiracy hereby declared to be illegal shall be deemed guilty of a felony.*[12]

In other words, Section 1 outlaws *contracts*, *combinations*, and *conspiracies* in restraint of trade. Thus, it applies to unlawful conduct by two or more parties. The agreement may be written, oral, or inferred from the conduct of the parties. The two tests the U.S. Supreme Court has developed for determining the lawfulness of a restraint—the *rule of reason* and the *per se rule*—are discussed in the following paragraphs.

The following feature discusses tests used by courts for determining the lawfulness of a challenged restraint.

Section 1 of the Sherman Act
A section that prohibits contracts, combinations, and conspiracies in restraint of trade.

rule of reason
A rule which holds that only unreasonable restraints of trade violate Section 1 of the Sherman Act. The court must examine the pro- and anticompetitive effects of a challenged restraint.

per se rule
A rule that is applicable to restraints of trade considered inherently anticompetitive. Once this determination is made about a restraint of trade, the court will not permit any defenses or justifications to save it.

Contemporary Environment

Rule of Reason and *Per Se* Rule

The U.S. Supreme Court has developed two different tests for determining the lawfulness of a restraint. These two tests—the *rule of reason* and the *per se rule*—are discussed in the following paragraphs.

Rule of Reason
If Section 1 of the Sherman Act were read literally, it would prohibit almost all contracts. In the landmark case *Standard Oil Company of New Jersey v. United States*,[13] the Supreme Court adopted the **rule of reason** standard for analyzing Section 1 cases. This rule holds that only *unreasonable restraints of trade* violate Section 1 of the Sherman Act. Reasonable restraints are lawful. The courts examine the following factors in applying the rule of reason to a particular case:

- The pro- and anticompetitive effects of the challenged restraint

- The competitive structure of the industry
- The firm's market share and power
- The history and duration of the restraint
- Other relevant factors

Per Se Rule
The Supreme Court adopted the **per se rule**, which is applicable to restraints of trade that are considered inherently anticompetitive. No balancing of pro- and anticompetitive effects is necessary in such cases: Such a restraint is automatically in violation of Section 1 of the Sherman Act. When a restraint is characterized as a *per se* violation, no defenses or justifications for the restraint will save it, and no further evidence need be considered. Restraints that are not characterized as *per se* violations are examined using the rule of reason.

CONCEPT SUMMARY

RESTRAINTS OF TRADE: SECTION 1 OF THE SHERMAN ACT

Rule	Description
Rule of reason	Requires a balancing of pro- and anticompetitive effects of the challenged restraint. Restraints that are found to be unreasonable are unlawful and violate Section 1 of the Sherman Act. Restraints that are found to be reasonable are lawful and do not violate Section 1 of the Sherman Act.
Per se rule	Applies to restraints that are inherently anticompetitive. No justification for the restraint is permitted. Such restraints automatically violate Section 1 of the Sherman Act.

Horizontal Restraints of Trade

horizontal restraint of trade
A restraint of trade that occurs when two or more competitors at the same *level of distribution* enter into a contract, combination, or conspiracy to restrain trade.

A **horizontal restraint of trade** occurs when two or more competitors at the *same level of distribution* enter into a contract, combination, or conspiracy to restrain trade (see **Exhibit 22.1**). Many horizontal restraints fall under the *per se* rule; others are examined under the rule of reason. The most common forms of horizontal restraint are discussed in the following paragraphs.

Exhibit 22.1 HORIZONTAL RESTRAINT OF TRADE

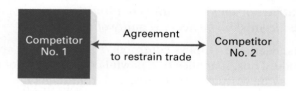

Price Fixing

price fixing
A restraint of trade that occurs when competitors in the same line of business agree to set the price of the goods or services they sell, raising, depressing, fixing, pegging, or stabilizing the price of a commodity or service.

Horizontal **price fixing** occurs when competitors in the same line of business agree to set the price of goods or services they sell. Price fixing is defined as raising, depressing, fixing, pegging, or stabilizing the price of a commodity or service. Illegal price fixing includes setting minimum or maximum prices or fixing the quantity of a product or service to be produced or provided. Although most price fixing agreements occur between sellers, an agreement among buyers to set the price they will pay for goods or services is also price fixing. The plaintiff bears the burden of proving a price fixing agreement.

Price fixing is a *per se* violation of Section 1 of the Sherman Act. No defenses or justifications of any kind—such as "the price fixing helps consumers or protects competitors from ruinous competition"—can prevent the *per se* rule from applying.

Example If the three largest automobile manufacturers agreed among themselves what prices to charge automobile dealers for this year's models, this would be sellers' illegal *per se* price fixing.

Example If the three largest automobile manufacturers agreed among themselves what price they would pay to purchase tires from tire manufactures, this would be buyers' illegal *per se* price fixing.

Division of Markets

division of markets (market sharing)
A restraint of trade in which competitors agree that each will serve only a designated portion of the market.

Competitors who agree that each will serve only a designated portion of the market are engaging in a **division of markets** (or **market sharing**), which is a *per se* violation of Section 1 of the Sherman Act. Each market segment is considered a small monopoly served only by its designated "owner." Horizontal market-sharing arrangements include division by geographical territories, customers, and products.

Example Suppose that three national breweries agree among themselves that each one will be assigned one-third of the country as its geographical "territory," and each agrees not to sell beer in the other two companies' territories. This would be a *per se* illegal geographical division of markets.

Example Suppose that the three largest sellers of media software agree that each can sell media software only to one designated media software purchaser and not to any other media software purchasers. This would be a *per se* illegal product division of markets.

Group Boycotts

A **group boycott** (or **refusal to deal**) occurs when two or more competitors at one level of distribution agree not to deal with others at a different level of distribution.

Examples If a group of sellers agreed not to sell their products to a certain buyer, this would be a group boycott by sellers. If a group of purchasers agreed not to purchase a product from a certain seller, this would be a group boycott by purchasers.

Example A group of high-fashion clothes designers and sellers agree not to sell their clothes to a certain discount retailer, such as Walmart. This is a group boycott by sellers (see **Exhibit 22.2**).

group boycott (refusal to deal)
A restraint of trade in which two or more competitors at one level of distribution agree not to deal with others at another level of distribution.

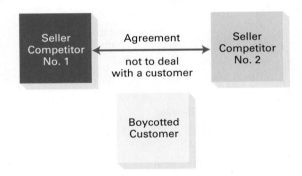

Exhibit 22.2 GROUP BOYCOTT BY SELLERS

Example A group of rental car companies agree not to purchase Chrysler automobiles for their fleets. This is a group boycott by purchasers (see **Exhibit 22.3**).

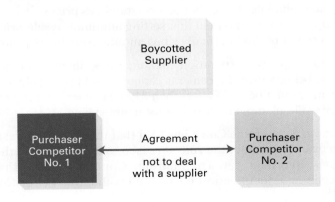

Exhibit 22.3 GROUP BOYCOTT BY PURCHASERS

In the past, the U.S. Supreme Court held that all group boycotts were *per se* illegal. However, the Supreme Court changed this rule and now holds that only certain group boycotts are *per se* illegal; others are to be examined under the rule of reason. Nevertheless, most group boycotts are still found to be illegal.

Other Horizontal Agreements

Some horizontal agreements entered into by competitors at the same level of distribution—including trade association activities and rules, exchange of non-price information, participation in joint ventures, and the like—are examined using the rule of reason. Reasonable restraints are lawful; unreasonable restraints violate Section 1 of the Sherman Act.

Vertical Restraints of Trade

vertical restraint of trade
A restraint of trade that occurs when two or more parties on *different levels of distribution* enter into a contract, combination, or conspiracy to restrain trade.

A **vertical restraint of trade** occurs when two or more parties on *different levels of distribution* enter into a contact, combination, or conspiracy to restrain trade (see **Exhibit 22.4**). The Supreme Court has applied both the *per se* rule and the rule of reason in determining the legality of vertical restraints of trade under Section 1 of the Sherman Act. The most common forms of vertical restraint are discussed in the following paragraphs.

Exhibit 22.4 VERTICAL RESTRAINT OF TRADE

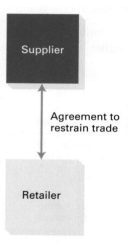

Resale Price Maintenance

resale price maintenance (vertical price fixing)
A *per se* violation of Section 1 of the Sherman Act that occurs when a party at one level of distribution enters into an agreement with a party at another level to adhere to a price schedule that either sets or stabilizes prices.

Resale price maintenance (or **vertical price fixing**) occurs when a party at one level of distribution enters into an agreement with a party at another level to adhere to a price schedule that either sets or stabilizes prices.

The U.S. Supreme Court has held that setting **minimum resale prices** is a *per se* violation of Section 1 of the Sherman Act as an unreasonable restraint of trade.[14]

Example Integral Camera Corporation manufactures digital cameras and sets a *minimum* price below which the cameras cannot be sold by retailers to consumers (e.g., the cameras cannot be sold for less than $1,000 to consumers by retailers). This constitutes *per se* illegal minimum resale price maintenance.

However, the U.S. Supreme Court has held that the setting of **maximum resale prices** will be examined under the rule of reason to determine whether it violates Section 1 of the Sherman Act. The Supreme Court concluded that there was insufficient economic justification for *per se* invalidation of vertical maximum price fixing.[15]

Example Virtual Corporation manufactures the e-television and sets a *maximum price* above which the e-television cannot be sold by retailers to consumers. Here, the court will apply a rule of reason to determine whether the anticompetitive effects outweigh the procompetitive effects for setting the maximum resale price.

Nonprice Vertical Restraints

The legality of **nonprice vertical restraints** of trade under Section 1 of the Sherman Act is examined by using the rule of reason.[16] Nonprice restraints are unlawful under this analysis if their anticompetitive effects outweigh their procompetitive effects. Nonprice vertical restraints include situations in which a manufacturer assigns exclusive territories to retail dealers or limits the number of dealers that may be located in a certain territory.

The following U.S. Supreme Court case involves the issue of defining concerted action for Sherman Act Section 1 purposes.

nonprice vertical restraints
Restraints of trade that are unlawful under Section 1 of the Sherman Act if their anticompetitive effects outweigh their procompetitive effects.

CASE 22.1   *U.S. SUPREME COURT Contract, Combination, or Conspiracy*

American Needle, Inc. v. National Football League

130 S.Ct. 2201, 76 L.Ed.2d 947, Web 2010 U.S. Lexis 4166 (2010)
Supreme Court of the United States

"Section 1 applies only to concerted action that restrains trade."

—Stevens, Justice

Facts

The National Football League (NFL) is an unincorporated association that includes thirty-two separately owned professional football teams. Each team has its own name, colors, logo, trademarks, and other intellectual property. Rather than sell their sports memorabilia individually, the teams formed National Football League Properties (NFLP) to market caps, jerseys, and other sports memorabilia for all of the teams. Until 2000, NFLP granted nonexclusive licenses to a number of vendors, including American Needle, Inc. In December 2000, the teams voted to authorize NFLP to grant exclusive licenses. NFLP granted Reebok International Ltd. an exclusive ten-year license to manufacture and sell trademarked caps and other memorabilia for all thirty-two NFL teams.

American Needle sued the NFL, the teams, and NFLP, alleging that the defendants engaged in an illegal contract, combination, or conspiracy, in violation of Section 1 of the Sherman Act. The defendants argued that they were a single economic enterprise and therefore incapable of the alleged conduct. The U.S. District Court held that the defendants were a single entity and granted summary judgment for the defendants. The U.S. Court of Appeals affirmed the judgment. The case was appealed to the U.S. Supreme Court

Issue

Are the NFL, the NFL teams, and the NFLP separate legal entities, capable of engaging in a contract, combination, or conspiracy, as defined by Section 1 of the Sherman Act?

Language of the U.S. Supreme Court

Section 1 applies only to concerted action that restrains trade. The teams compete with one another, not only on the playing field, but to attract fans, for gate receipts and for contracts with managerial and playing personnel. Directly relevant to this case, the teams compete in the market for intellectual property. To a firm making hats, the Saints and the Colts are two potentially competing suppliers of valuable trademarks. Decisions by NFL teams to license their separately owned trademarks collectively and to only one vendor are decisions that deprive the marketplace of independent centers of decision making, and therefore of actual or potential competition. Joint ventures have no immunity from antitrust laws. For that reason, decisions by the NFLP regarding the teams' separately owned intellectual property constitute concerted action.

Decision

The U.S. Supreme Court held that the NFL, the individual teams, and the NFLP were separate entities capable of engaging in concerted activity, in violation of Section 1 of the Sherman

(continued)

Act. The Supreme Court remanded the case for a determination as to whether this concerted activity was an unreasonable restraint of trade that violated Section 1 of the Sherman Act.

Case Questions

Critical Legal Thinking

Do firms that enter into a joint venture avoid the reach of Section 1 of the Sherman Act?

Ethics

Do you think there was any unethical conduct in this case?

Contemporary Business

Does the decision in this case have any consequences in determining whether entities have engaged in a contract, combination, or conspiracy that violates Section 1 of the Sherman Act?

---

unilateral refusal to deal
A unilateral choice by one party not to deal with another party. This does not violate Section 1 of the Sherman Act because there is not concerted action.

Unilateral Refusal to Deal

The U.S. Supreme Court has held that a firm can unilaterally choose not to deal with another party without being liable under Section 1 of the Sherman Act. A **unilateral refusal to deal** is not a violation of Section 1 because there is no concerted action with others. This rule was announced in *United States v. Colgate & Co.*[17] and is therefore often referred to as the **Colgate doctrine**.

Example If Louis Vuitton, a maker of expensive women's clothing, shoes, handbags, and accessories, refuses to sell its merchandise to Walmart stores, this is a lawful unilateral refusal to deal.

The following feature discusses a defense to a charge of an illegal restraint of trade.

conscious parallelism
A doctrine which states that if two or more firms act the same but no concerted action is shown, there is no violation of Section 1 of the Sherman Act.

Contemporary Environment

Conscious Parallelism

Sometimes two or more firms act the same, but they have done so individually. If two or more firms act the same but no concerted action is shown, there is no violation of Section 1 of the Sherman Act. This doctrine is often referred to as **conscious parallelism**. Thus, if two competing manufacturers of a similar product both separately reach an independent decision not to deal with a retailer, there is no violation of Section 1 of the Sherman Act. The key is that each of the manufacturers acted on its own.

Example If Louis Vuitton, Gucci, and Chanel, makers of expensive women's clothing, shoes, handbags, and accessories, each independently make a decision not to sell their products to Walmart, this is lawful conscious parallelism. There is no violation of Section 1 of the Sherman Act because the parties did not agree with one another in making their decisions.

Noerr doctrine
A doctrine which says that two or more persons can petition the executive, legislative, or judicial branch of the government or administrative agencies to enact laws or take other action without violating antitrust laws.

Noerr Doctrine

The *Noerr* **doctrine** holds that two or more persons may petition the executive, legislative, or judicial branch of the government or administrative agencies to enact laws or to take other action without violating antitrust laws. The rationale behind this doctrine is that the right to petition the government has precedence because it is guaranteed by the Bill of Rights.[18]

Example General Motors and Ford collectively petition Congress to pass a law that would limit the import of foreign automobiles into this country. This is lawful activity under the *Noerr* doctrine.

There is an exception to this doctrine. Under the *"sham" exception*, petitioners are not protected if their petition or lawsuit is baseless—that is, if a reasonable petitioner or litigant could not realistically expect to succeed on the merits of the petition or lawsuit. If the protection of the *Noerr* doctrine is lost, an antitrust action may be maintained against the parties who asserted its protection.

Monopolization: Section 2 of the Sherman Act

By definition, monopolies have the ability to affect the prices of goods and services. **Section 2 of the Sherman Act** was enacted in response to widespread concern about the power generated by this type of anticompetitive activity. Section 2 of the Sherman Act prohibits the act of monopolization. It provides:

> *Every person who shall monopolize, or attempt to monopolize, or combine or conspire with any other person or persons, to monopolize any part of the trade or commerce among the several States, or with foreign nations, shall be deemed guilty of a felony.*[19]

Proving that a defendant is in violation of Section 2 means proving that the defendant (1) possesses *monopoly power* (2) in the *relevant market* and (3) has engaged in a *willful act of monopolization* to acquire or maintain that power. Each of these elements is discussed in the following paragraphs.

Section 2 of the Sherman Act
A section that prohibits monopolization and attempts or conspiracies to monopolize trade.

Defining the Relevant Market

Identifying the **relevant market** for a Section 2 action requires defining the relevant product or service market and geographical market. The definition of the relevant market often determines whether the defendant has monopoly power. Consequently, this determination is often litigated.

The **relevant product or service market** generally includes substitute products or services that are reasonably interchangeable with the defendant's products or services. Defendants often try to make their market share seem smaller by arguing for a broad definition of the product or service market. Plaintiffs, on the other hand, usually argue for a narrow definition.

Example If the government sued the Anheuser-Busch Corporation InBev, which is the largest beer producer in the United States, for violating Section 2 of the Sherman Act, the government would argue that the relevant product market is beer sales. Anheuser-Busch, on the other hand, would argue that the relevant product market is sales of all alcoholic beverages, or even of all drinkable beverages.

relevant product or service market
A relevant market that includes substitute products or services that are reasonably interchangeable with the defendant's products or services.

The **relevant geographical market** is usually defined as the area in which the defendant and its competitors sell the product or service. This may be a national, regional, state, or local area, depending on the circumstances.

Examples If the government sued the Coca-Cola Company for violating Section 2 of the Sherman Act, the relevant geographical market would be the nation. If the largest owner of automobile dealerships in south Florida were sued for violating Section 2, the geographical market would be the counties of south Florida.

relevant geographical market
A relevant market that is defined as the area in which the defendant and its competitors sell the product or service.

Monopoly Power

For an antitrust action to be sustained, the defendant must possess **monopoly power** in the relevant market. Monopoly power is defined by the courts as the power to control prices or exclude competition. The courts generally apply the following guidelines: Market share above 70 percent is monopoly power; market share under 20 percent is not monopoly power. Otherwise, the courts generally prefer to examine the facts and circumstances of each case before making a determination about monopoly power.

monopoly power
The power to control prices or exclude competition, measured by the market share the defendant possesses in the relevant market.

Willful Act of Monopolizing

act of monopolizing
An act that is required to find a violation of Section 2 of the Sherman Act. Possession of monopoly power without such act does not violate Section 2.

Section 2 of the Sherman Act outlaws the **act of monopolizing**, not monopolies. Any act that otherwise violates any other antitrust law (e.g., illegal restraints of trade, in violation of Section 1 of the Sherman Act) is an act of monopolizing that violates Section 2. When coupled with monopoly power, certain otherwise lawful acts have been held to constitute acts of monopolizing. **Predatory pricing**—that is, pricing below average or marginal cost—that is intended to drive out competition has been held to violate Section 2.[20]

CONCEPT SUMMARY

MONOPOLIZATION: SECTION 2 OF THE SHERMAN ACT

Element	Description
Relevant product or service market	The market that includes substitute products or services that are reasonably interchangeable with the defendant's products or services.
Relevant geographic market	The geographic area in which the defendant and its competitors sell the product or service.
Monopoly power	The power to control prices or exclude competition. If the defendant does not possess monopoly power, it cannot be held liable for monopolization. If the defendant possesses monopoly power, the court will determine whether the monopolist has engaged in an act of monopolizing.
Act of monopolizing	The defendant's engagement in a willful act of monopolizing trade or commerce in the relevant market

---

A monopoly granted either to an individual or to a trading company has the same effect as a secret in trade or manufacture. The monopolists, by keeping the market constantly understocked, by never fully supplying the effectual demand, sell their commodities much above the natural price, and raise their emoluments greatly above their natural rate.

Adam Smith
Wealth of Nations (1776)

Attempts and Conspiracies to Monopolize

Firms that *attempt* or *conspire* to monopolize a relevant market may be found liable under Section 2 of the Sherman Act. A single firm may be found liable for monopolizing or attempting to monopolize. Two or more firms may be found liable for conspiring to monopolize.

Defenses to Monopolization

Only two narrow defenses to a charge of monopolizing have been recognized: (1) **innocent acquisition** (e.g., acquisition because of superior business acumen, skill, foresight, or industry) and (2) **natural monopoly** (e.g., a small market that can support only one competitor, such as a small-town newspaper). If a monopoly that fits into one of these categories exercises its power in a predatory or exclusionary way, the defense is lost.

CONCEPT SUMMARY

THE SHERMAN ACT

Section	Description
1	Prohibits contracts, combinations, and conspiracies in restraint of trade. To violate Section 1, the restraint must be found to be unreasonable under either of two tests: (1) rule of reason or (2) *per se* rule. A violation requires the concerted action of two or more parties.
2	Prohibits the act of monopolizing and attempts or conspiracies to monopolize. This act can be violated by the conduct of one firm.

Mergers: Section 7 of the Clayton Act

In the late 1800s and early 1900s, *mergers* led to increased concentration of wealth in the hands of a few wealthy individuals and large corporations. In response, in 1914, Congress enacted **Section 7 of the Clayton Act**, which gave the federal government the power to prevent anticompetitive mergers. Originally, Section 7 of the Clayton Act applied only to stock mergers. The **Celler-Kefauver Act**, which was enacted in 1950, widened the scope of Section 7 to include asset acquisitions.

Today, Section 7 applies to all methods of external expansion, including technical mergers, consolidations, purchases of assets, subsidiary operations, joint ventures, and other combinations.

Section 7 of the Clayton Act provides that it is unlawful for a person or business to acquire stock or assets of another "where in any line of commerce or in any activity affecting commerce in any section of the country, the effect of such acquisition may be substantially to lessen competition, or to tend to create a monopoly."[21]

In deciding whether a merger is lawful under Section 7 of the Clayton Act, the courts must define the relevant *line of commerce* and *section of the country* involved and then determine whether the merger or acquisition creates a reasonable *probability of the substantial lessening of competition* or is *likely to create a monopoly* in that market. These elements are discussed in the following paragraphs.

Section 7 of the Clayton Act
A section which provides that it is unlawful for a person or business to acquire the stock or assets of another "where in any line of commerce or in any activity affecting commerce in any section of the country, the effect of such acquisition may be substantially to lessen competition, or to tend to create a monopoly."

Line of Commerce

Determining the **line of commerce** that will be affected by a merger involves defining the relevant *product or service market*. Traditionally, the courts have done this by applying the functional interchangeability test. Under this test, the relevant line of commerce includes products or services that consumers use as substitutes. If two products are substitutes for each other, they are considered part of the same line of commerce.

Example Suppose a price increase for regular coffee causes consumers to switch to tea. The two products are part of the same line of commerce because they are considered interchangeable.

line of commerce
The products or services that will be affected by a merger, including those that consumers use as substitutes. If an increase in the price of one product or service leads consumers to purchase another product or service, the two products are substitutes for each other.

Section of the Country

Defining the relevant **section of the country** consists of determining the relevant *geographical market*. The courts traditionally identify this market as the geographical area that will feel the direct and immediate effects of the merger. It may be a local, state, or regional market; the entire country; or some other geographical area.

Example Anheuser-Busch InBev and Miller Brewing Company, two brewers, sell beer nationally. If Anheuser-Busch and Miller Brewing Company plan to merge, the relevant section of the country is the nation.

Example Anheuser-Busch InBev is a brewer that sells beer nationally. Upper Brewery is a local brewery that sells beer only in the state of Michigan. If Anheuser-Busch intends to acquire Upper Brewery, the relevant section of the country is the state of Michigan.

section of the country
A division of the country that is based on the relevant geographical market; the geographical area that will feel the direct and immediate effects of a merger.

Probability of a Substantial Lessening of Competition or Likely to Create a Monopoly

After the relevant product or service and geographical market have been defined, the court must determine whether a merger or an acquisition creates a reasonable **probability of a substantial lessening of competition** or is likely to **create**

probability of a substantial lessening of competition
The probability that a merger will substantially lessen competition or create a monopoly, in which case the court may prevent the merger under Section 7 of the Clayton Act.

a monopoly. If the court feels that a merger is likely to do either, it may prevent the merger. Section 7 tries to prevent potentially anticompetitive mergers before they occur. It deals in probabilities; actual proof of the lessening of competition is not required.

CONCEPT SUMMARY

MERGER: SECTION 7 OF THE CLAYTON ACT

Element	Description
Line of commerce	The market that will be affected by a merger. It includes products or services that consumers use as substitutes for those produced or sold by the merging firms.
Section of the country	The geographic market that will be affected by a merger.
Probability of a substantial lessening of competition	A probability of a substantial lessening of competition after a merger, in which case the merger may be prohibited. The statute deals with probabilities; actual proof of the lessening of competition is not required.

In applying Section 7, mergers are generally classified as one of the following: *horizontal merger*, *vertical merger*, *market extension merger*, or *conglomerate merger*. These are discussed in the paragraphs that follow.

Horizontal Merger

horizontal merger
A merger between two or more companies that compete in the same business and geographical market.

A **horizontal merger** is a merger between two or more companies that compete in the same business and geographical market. The merger of two grocery store chains that serve the same geographical market fits this definition. Such mergers are subjected to strict review under Section 7 because they clearly result in an increase in concentration in the relevant market.

Example General Motors Corporation and Ford Motor Company are two of the largest automobile, SUV, and truck manufacturers. If General Motors Corporation and Ford Motor Company tried to merge, this would be a horizontal merger. This merger would most likely violate Section 7.

Vertical Merger

vertical merger
A merger that integrates the operations of a supplier and a customer.

A **vertical merger** is a merger that integrates the operations of a supplier and a customer. In examining the legality of vertical mergers, the courts usually consider such factors as the history of the firms, the trend toward concentration in the industries involved, the barriers to entry, the economic efficiencies of the merger, and the elimination of potential competition caused by the merger.

backward vertical merger
A vertical merger in which a customer acquires a supplier.

forward vertical merger
A vertical merger in which a supplier acquires a customer.

Example If the book publisher Simon & Schuster acquires a paper mill, this would be a **backward vertical merger**. If the book publisher Simon & Schuster acquires the retail bookstore chain such as Barnes & Noble, this would be a **forward vertical merger**.

Vertical mergers do not create an increase in market share because the merging firms serve different markets. They may, however, cause anticompetitive effects such as **foreclosing competition**—that is, foreclosing competitors from either selling goods or services to or buying them from the merged firm.

Example A furniture manufacturer wants to acquire a chain of retail furniture stores. The merger is unlawful if it is likely that the merged firm will not buy furniture from other manufacturers or sell furniture to other retailers.

Market Extension Merger

A **market extension merger** is a merger between two companies in similar fields whose sales do not overlap. The merger may expand the acquiring firm's geographical or product market. The legality of market extension mergers is examined under Section 7 of the Clayton Act.

Example A merger between two regional brewers that do not sell beer in the same geographical area is called a **geographical market extension merger**.

Example A merger between sellers of similar products, such as a soft drink manufacturer and an orange juice producer, is called a **product market extension merger**.

market extension merger
A merger between two companies in similar fields whose sales do not overlap.

Conglomerate Merger

Conglomerate mergers are mergers that do not fit into any other category. That is, they are mergers between firms in unrelated businesses.

Example If the large oil company ExxonMobil merged with Neiman-Marcus, a company that owns and operates retail clothing stores, the result would be a conglomerate merger.

The **unfair advantage theory** holds that a conglomerate merger may not give the acquiring firm an unfair advantage over its competitors in finance, marketing, or expertise. This rule is intended to prevent wealthy companies from overwhelming the competition in a given market.

Example Walmart Stores, Inc., a giant discount warehouse store and one of the largest and wealthiest companies in the world, may be prevented from acquiring Almost Death Row Records, a small recording studio, under the unfair advantage theory. The court would be concerned that Walmart could bring its wealth to support and grow Almost Death Row Records into an extremely large and monopolistic recording label.

conglomerate merger
A merger that does not fit into any other category; a merger between firms in totally unrelated businesses.

Defenses to Section 7 Actions

There are two primary defenses to Section 7 actions. These defenses can be raised even if the merger would otherwise violate Section 7. The defenses are:

1. **The failing company doctrine.** According to the **failing company doctrine**, a competitor may merge with a failing company if (1) there is no other reasonable alternative for the failing company, (2) no other purchaser is available, and (3) the assets of the failing company would completely disappear from the market if the anticompetitive merger were not allowed to go through.
2. **The small company doctrine.** The courts have permitted two or more small companies to merge without liability under Section 7 if the merger allows them to compete more effectively with a large company. This is called the **small company doctrine**.

Premerger Notification

The **Hart-Scott-Rodino Antitrust Improvement Act (HSR Act)**[22] requires certain larger firms to notify the Federal Trade Commission (FTC) and the U.S. Department of Justice of any proposed merger and to provide information about the parties and the proposed transaction. Upon the filing, a thirty-day waiting period begins (fifteen days for all-cash tender offers), during which time the government agencies may investigate the transaction. If the government agencies believe that the acquisition would have anticompetitive effects, they may extend the waiting period and request additional information from the parties. If within the waiting period the government sues, the suit is entitled to expedited treatment in the courts. If the government does not challenge a proposed merger within thirty

Hart-Scott-Rodino Antitrust Improvement Act (HSR Act)
An act that requires certain firms to notify the Federal Trade Commission and the Justice Department in advance of a proposed merger. Unless the government challenges a proposed merger within thirty days, the merger may proceed.

days, the merger may proceed. The parties may request that the waiting period be terminated early if the government agencies do not find anticompetitive effects.

The sizes of the firms that are subject to the HSR Act are determined by complex rules concerning the size of the parties and the value of the transaction. Generally, the premerger notification rules apply if (1) one party has assets or sales that exceed approximately $130 million and the other party has assets or sales that exceed approximately $13 million and the value of the assets or securities being acquired exceed approximately $65 million or (2) the total value of the transaction exceeds approximately $260 million. These thresholds are adjusted on an annual basis.

Tying Arrangements: Section 3 of the Clayton Act

Section 3 of the Clayton Act
An act that prohibits tying arrangements involving sales and leases of goods.

tying arrangement
A restraint of trade in which a seller refuses to sell one product to a customer unless the customer agrees to purchase a second product from the seller.

Section 3 of the Clayton Act prohibits tying arrangements that involve sales and leases of goods (tangible personal property).[23] **Tying arrangements** are vertical trade restraints that involve the seller's refusal to sell a product (the *tying item*) to a customer unless the customer purchases a second product (the *tied item*). Section 1 of the Sherman Act (restraints of trade) forbids tying arrangements involving goods, services, intangible property, and real property. The defendant must be shown to have had sufficient economic power in the tying product market to restrain competition in the tied product market.

Example A manufacturer makes one patented product and one unpatented product. An illegal tying arrangement occurs if the manufacturer refuses to sell the patented product to a buyer unless the buyer also purchases the unpatented product. The patented product is the tying product, and the unpatented product is the tied product. Here, the patented product and the unpatented product can be sold separately.

A tying arrangement is lawful if there is some justifiable reason for it.

Example The protection of quality control coupled with a trade secret may make a tying arrangement lawful.

Price Discrimination: Section 2 of the Clayton Act

Section 2 of the Clayton Act (Robinson-Patman Act)
A federal statute that prohibits price discrimination in the sale of goods if certain requirements are met.

Section 2(a) of the Robinson-Patman Act
A section that prohibits direct and indirect price discrimination by sellers of a commodity of a like grade and quality, where the effect of such discrimination may be to substantially lessen competition or to tend to create a monopoly in any line of commerce.

Businesses in the U.S. economy survive by selling their goods at prices that allow them to make a profit. Sellers often offer favorable terms to their preferred customers. **Price discrimination** occurs if a seller does this without just cause. **Section 2 of the Clayton Act**, which is commonly referred to as the **Robinson-Patman Act**, prohibits price discrimination in the sale of goods if certain requirements are met. **Section 2(a) of the Robinson-Patman Act** contains the following basic prohibition against price discrimination in the sale of goods:

It shall be unlawful for any person engaged in commerce, either directly or indirectly, to discriminate in price between different purchases of commodities of like grade and quality, where either or any of the purchases involved in such discrimination are in commerce, where the effect of such discrimination may be substantially to lessen competition or tend to create a monopoly in any line of commerce, or to injure, destroy, or prevent competition with any person who either grants or knowingly receives the benefit of such discrimination, or with customers of either of them.[24]

Section 2 does not apply to the sale of services, real estate, intangible property, securities, leases, consignments, or gifts. Mixed sales (i.e., sales involving both services and commodities) are controlled based on the dominant nature of the transaction.

Direct Price Discrimination

To prove a violation of Section 2(a) of the Robinson-Patman Act, the following elements of **direct price discrimination** must be shown:

- **Commodities of like grade and quality.** A Section 2(a) violation must involve goods of "like grade and quality." To avoid this rule, sellers sometimes try to differentiate identical or similar products by using brand names. Nevertheless, as one court stated, "Four roses under any other name would still swill the same."[25]
- **Sales to two or more purchasers.** To violate Section 2(a), the price discrimination must involve sales to at least two different purchasers at approximately the same time. It is legal to make two or more sales of the same product to the same purchaser at different prices. The Robinson-Patman Act requires that the discrimination occur "in commerce."
- **Injury.** To recover damages, the plaintiff must have suffered actual injury because of the price discrimination. The injured party may be the purchaser who did not receive the favored price (*primary line injury*), that party's customers to whom the lower price could not be passed along (*secondary line injury*), and so on down the line.

A plaintiff who has not suffered injury because of a price discrimination cannot recover.

Example A wholesaler sells the same type of Michelin tires to one automobile repair and tire shop at a lower price than to another similar-size repair and tire shop. If the second tire shop cannot purchase the same type of Michelin tires at this or a lower price, it has a good case of price discrimination against the wholesaler. If the second tire shop could have purchased comparable Michelin tires elsewhere at the lower price, it cannot recover for price discrimination.

Indirect Price Discrimination

Because direct forms of price discrimination are readily apparent, sellers of goods have devised sophisticated ways to provide discriminatory prices to favored customers. Favorable credit terms, freight charges, and such are examples of **indirect price discrimination** that violate the Robinson-Patman Act.

Defenses to Price Discrimination

The Robinson-Patman Act establishes the following three statutory defenses to Section 2(a) liability:

1. **Cost justification.** Section 2(a) provides that a seller's price discrimination is not unlawful if the price differential is due to "differences in the cost of manufacture, sale, or delivery" of the product. This is called the **cost justification defense.** For example, quantity or volume discounts are lawful to the extent that they are supported by cost savings. Sellers may classify buyers into various broad groups and compute an average cost of selling to the group. The seller may then charge members of different groups different prices without being liable for price discrimination. The seller bears the burden of proving this defense.

   Example If Procter & Gamble can prove that bulk shipping rates make it less costly to deliver ten thousand bottles of Tide than lesser quantities, it may charge purchasers accordingly. However, Procter & Gamble cannot simply lower its price per box because the buyer is a good customer.

2. **Changing conditions.** Price discrimination is not unlawful, under Section 2(a), if it is in response to "changing conditions in the market for or the marketability of the goods." This is called the **changing conditions defense.**

direct price discrimination
Price discrimination in which (1) the defendant sold commodities of like grade and quality, (2) to two or more purchasers at different prices at approximately the same time, and (3) the plaintiff suffered injury because of the price discrimination.

indirect price discrimination
A form of price discrimination (e.g., favorable credit terms) that is less readily apparent than direct forms of price discrimination.

cost justification defense
A defense in a Section 2(a) action which provides that a seller's price discrimination is not unlawful if the price differential is due to "differences in the cost of manufacture, sale, or delivery" of the product.

changing conditions defense
A price discrimination defense that claims prices were lowered in response to changing conditions in the market for or the marketability of the goods.

Examples The price of goods can be lowered to subsequent purchasers to reflect the deterioration of perishable goods (e.g., fish), obsolescence of seasonable goods (e.g., winter coats sold in the spring), a distress sale pursuant to court order, or discontinuance of a business.

3. **Meeting the competition.**   The **meeting the competition defense** to price discrimination is stipulated in **Section 2(b) of the Robinson-Patman Act**[26] This defense holds that a seller may lawfully engage in price discrimination to meet a competitor's price.

Example Rockport sells its Pro Walker shoe nationally at $100 per pair, while the Great Lakes Shoe Co. (Great Lakes), which produces and sells a comparable walking shoe, sells its product only in Michigan and Wisconsin. If Great Lake sells its walking shoes at $75 per pair, Rockport can do the same in Michigan and Wisconsin. Rockport does not have to reduce the price of the shoe in the other 48 states. The seller can only meet, not beat, the competitor's price, however.

Federal Trade Commission Act

In 1914, Congress enacted the *Federal Trade Commission Act (FTC Act)* and created the **Federal Trade Commission (FTC)**. **Section 5 of the FTC Act** prohibits "**unfair methods of competition** and unfair or deceptive acts or practices" in or affecting commerce.[27]

Section 5, which is broader than the other antitrust laws, covers conduct that (1) violates any provision of the Sherman Act or the Clayton Act, (2) violates the "spirit" of those acts, (3) fills the gaps of those acts, and (4) offends public policy; is immoral, oppressive, unscrupulous, or unethical; or causes substantial injury to competitors or consumers.

The FTC is exclusively empowered to enforce the FTC Act. It can issue interpretive rules, general statements of policy, trade regulation rules, and guidelines that define unfair or deceptive practices, and it can conduct investigations of suspected antitrust violations. It can also issue cease-and-desist orders against violators. These orders are appealable to federal court. The FTC Act provides for a private civil cause of action for injured parties. Treble damages are not available.

Exemptions from Antitrust Laws

Certain industries and businesses are exempt from federal antitrust laws. The three categories of exemptions are *statutory exemptions*, *implied exemptions*, and the *state action exemption*. These are discussed in the following paragraphs.

Statutory Exemptions

Certain statutes expressly exempt some forms of business and other activities from the reach of antitrust laws. **Statutory exemptions** include labor unions,[28] agricultural cooperatives,[29] export activities of American companies,[30] and insurance business that is regulated by a state.[31] Other federal statutes exempt railroad, utility, shipping, and securities industries from most antitrust laws.

Implied Exemptions

The federal courts have implied several exemptions from antitrust laws. Examples of **implied exemptions** include professional baseball (but not other professional sports) and airlines.[32] The airline exemption was granted on the ground that railroads and other forms of transportation were expressly exempt. The Supreme Court has held that professionals such as lawyers do not qualify for an implied

meeting the competition defense
A defense provided in Section 2(b) of the Robinson-Patman Act that says a seller may lawfully engage in price discrimination to meet a competitor's price.

Federal Trade Commission
A federal government administrative agency that is empowered to enforce the Federal Trade Commission Act.

Section 5 of the FTC Act
A section that prohibits unfair methods of competition and unfair or deceptive acts or practices in or affecting commerce.

statutory exemptions
Exemptions from antitrust laws that are expressly provided in statutes enacted by Congress.

implied exemptions
Exemptions from antitrust laws that are implied by the federal courts.

exemption from antitrust laws.[33] The Supreme Court strictly construes implied exemptions from antitrust laws.

State Action Exemption

The U.S. Supreme Court has held that economic regulations mandated by state law are exempt from federal antitrust laws. The **state action exemption** extends to businesses that must comply with these regulations.

Example States may set the rates that public utilities (e.g., gas, electric, and cable television companies) may charge their customers. The states that set these rates and the companies that must abide by them are not liable for price fixing, in violation of federal antitrust law.

state action exemption
Business activities that are mandated by state law and are therefore exempt from federal antitrust laws.

State Antitrust Laws

Most states have enacted antitrust statutes. These statutes are usually patterned after federal antitrust statutes. They often contain the same language as well. State antitrust laws are used to attack anticompetitive activity that occurs in intrastate commerce. When federal antitrust laws are laxly applied, plaintiffs often bring lawsuits under state antitrust laws.

WEB EXERCISE
Visit the website of the European Union Commission at **http://ec. europa.eu/comm/competition/ index_en.html.** Find information about a recent EU Commission enforcement action. Read it.

International Law

European Union Strictly Enforces Antitrust Law

PARIS, FRANCE
France is a member of the European Union (EU), a regional organization of more than 25 countries located in western and eastern Europe. The EU's commission on competition enforces EU antitrust laws. In recent decades, EU enforcement of antitrust laws has been more stringent than the enforcement of antitrust laws in the United States. For example, the EU antitrust authorities have blocked mergers of multinational corporations that the U.S. antitrust authorities did not challenge. The EU fined Microsoft about $600 million for anticompetitive conduct and ordered Microsoft to change its operating system. Thus, multinational corporations must take into account EU antitrust laws when proposing mergers or engaging in business.

Key Terms and Concepts

Act of monopolizing (462)

Antitrust injury (454)

Antitrust laws (453)

Backward vertical merger (464)

Celler-Kefauver Act (463)

Changing conditions defense (467)

Civil damages (454)

Clayton Act (454)

Colgate doctrine (460)

Conglomerate merger (465)

Conscious parallelism (460)

Consent decree (455)

Cost justification defense (467)

Creation of a monopoly (463)

Direct price discrimination (467)

Division of markets (market sharing) (456)

Failing company doctrine (465)

Federal Trade Commission (FTC) (468)

Federal Trade Commission Act (FTC Act) (454)

Foreclosing competition (464)

Forward vertical merger (464)

Geographical market extension merger (465)

Government judgment (455)

Group boycott (refusal to deal) (457)

Hart-Scott-Rodino Antitrust Improvement Act (HRS Act) (465)

Horizontal merger (464)

Horizontal restraint of trade (456)

Implied exemptions (468)

Indirect price discrimination (467)

Innocent acquisition (462)

Line of commerce (463)

Market extension merger (465)

Maximum resale price (458)

Meeting the competition defense (468)

Minimum resale price (458)

Monopoly power (461)

Natural monopoly (462)

Noerr doctrine (460)

Nolo contendere (455)

Nonprice vertical restraint (459)

Per se rule (455)

Predatory pricing (462)

Price discrimination (466)

Price fixing (456)

Private civil action (454)

Probability of a substantial lessening of competition (463)

Product market extension merger (465)

Relevant geographical market (461)

Relevant market (461)

Relevant product or service market (461)

Resale price maintenance (vertical price fixing) (458)

Robinson-Patman Act (454)

Rule of reason (455)

Section of the country (463)

Section 1 of the Sherman Act (455)

Section 2 of the Clayton Act (Robinson-Patman Act) (466)

Section 2 of the Sherman Act (461)

Section 2(a) of the Robinson-Patman Act (466)

Section 2(b) of the Robinson-Patman Act (468)

Section 3 of the Clayton Act (466)

Section 4 of the Clayton Act (454)

Section 5 of the FTC Act (468)

Section 7 of the Clayton Act (463)

Section 16 of the Clayton Act (455)

Sherman Act (454)

Small company doctrine (465)

Standard Oil Company of New Jersey v. United States (455)

State action exemption (469)

Statutory exemptions (468)

Treble damages (454)

Tying arrangement (466)

Unfair advantage theory (465)

Unfair methods of competition (468)

Unilateral refusal to deal (460)

Vertical merger (464)

Vertical restraint of trade (458)

Law Case with Answer
Palmer v. BRG of Georgia, Inc.

Facts   Law school students, after they graduate from law school, must take and pass a bar exam before they can become a lawyer in a state. Most law students take a preparatory bar exam course before they sit to take the bar exam. Harcourt Brace Jovanovich Legal (HBJ) was the nation's largest provider of bar review materials and preparatory services. HBJ began offering a Georgia bar review course in direct competition with BRG of Georgia, Inc. (BRG), which was the only other main provider of a bar review preparatory course in the state of Georgia. Subsequently, HBJ and BRG entered into an agreement whereby BRG was granted an exclusive license to market HBJ bar review materials in Georgia in exchange for paying HBJ $100 per student enrolled by BRG in the course. Thus, HBJ agreed not to compete with BRG in Georgia, and BRG agreed not to compete with HBJ outside Georgia. Immediately after the agreement was struck, the price of BRG's course in the state of Georgia was increased from $150 to $400. Jay Palmer and other law school graduates who took the BRG bar review course in preparation for the Georgia bar exam sued BRG and HBJ, alleging a geographical division of markets, in violation of Section 1 of the Sherman Act. Does the BRG–HBJ agreement constitute a division of markets and a *per se* violation of Section 1 of the Sherman Act?

Answer Yes, the BRG–HBJ agreement constitutes a division of markets and is therefore a *per se* violation of Section 1 of the Sherman Act. The revenue-sharing formula in the agreement between BRG and HBJ, coupled with the price increase that took place immediately after the parties agreed to cease competing with each other, indicates that this agreement was formed for the purpose and with the effect of raising the price of the bar review course. Here, HBJ and BRG had previously competed in the Georgia market; under their allocation agreement, BRG received the Georgia market, while HBJ received the remainder of the United States. Each agreed not to compete in the other's territories. Such agreements are *per se* anticompetitive. Thus, the agreement between HBJ and BRG is unlawful on its face. The agreement between BRG and HBJ is a division of markets and as such is a *per se* violation of Section 1 of the Sherman Act. *Palmer v. BRG of Georgia, Inc.*, 498 U.S. 46, 111 S.Ct. 401, 112 L.Ed.2d 349, **Web** 1990 U.S. Lexis 5901 (Supreme Court of the United States)

Critical Legal Thinking Cases

22.1 Price Fixing The Maricopa County Medical Society (Society) is a professional association that represents doctors of medicine, osteopathy, and podiatry in Maricopa County, Arizona. The society formed the Maricopa Foundation for Medical Care (Foundation), a nonprofit Arizona corporation. Approximately 1,750 doctors, who represent 70 percent of the practitioners in the country, belong to Foundation. Foundation acts as an insurance administrator between its member doctors and insurance companies that pay patients' medical bills.

Foundation established a maximum fee schedule for various medical services. The member doctors agreed to abide by this fee schedule when providing services to patients. The state of Arizona brought this action against Society and Foundation and its members, alleging price fixing, in violation of Section 1 of the Sherman Act. Who wins? *Arizona v. Maricopa County Medical Society*, 457 U.S. 332, 102 S.Ct. 2466, 73 L.Ed.2d 48, **Web** 1982 U.S. Lexis 5 (Supreme Court of the United States)

22.2 Division of Market Topco Associates, Inc. (Topco), was founded in the 1940s by a group of small, local grocery store chains to act as a buying cooperative for the member stores. In this capacity, Topco procured for and distributed to its members more than one thousand different food and related items. Topco did not itself own any manufacturing or processing facilities, and the items it procured were shipped directly from the manufacturer or packer to Topco members. Topco members agreed to sell only Topco brand products within an exclusive territory. The United States sued Topco and its members, alleging a violation of Section 1 of the Sherman Act. Who wins? *United States v. Topco Associates, Inc.*, 405 U.S. 596, 92 S.Ct. 1126, 31 L.Ed.2d 515, **Web** 1972 U.S. Lexis 167 (Supreme Court of the United States)

22.3 Tying Arrangement Mercedes-Benz of North America (MBNA) was the exclusive franchiser of Mercedes-Benz dealerships in the United States. MBNA's franchise agreements required each dealer to establish a customer service department for the repair of Mercedes-Benz automobiles and required dealers to purchase Mercedes-Benz replacement parts from MBNA. At least eight independent wholesale distributors, including Metrix Warehouse, Inc. (Metrix), sold replacement parts for Mercedes-Benz automobiles. Because they were precluded from selling parts to Mercedes-Benz dealers, these parts distributors sold their replacement parts to independent garages that specialized in the repair of Mercedes-Benz automobiles. Evidence showed that Metrix sold replacement parts for Mercedes-Benz automobiles of equal quality and at a lower price than those sold by MBNA. Metrix sued MBNA, alleging a tying arrangement, in violation of Section 1 of the Sherman Act. Who wins? *Metrix Warehouse, Inc. v. Mercedes-Benz of North America, Inc.*, 828 F.2d 1033, **Web** 1987 U.S. App. Lexis 12341 (United States Court of Appeals for the Fourth Circuit)

22.4 Resale Price Maintenance The Union Oil Company (Union Oil) was a major oil company that operated a nationwide network of franchised service station dealers that sold Union Oil gasoline and other products throughout the United States. The franchise dealers leased their stations from Union Oil; they also signed a franchise agreement to purchase gasoline and other products on assignment from Union Oil. Both the lease and the franchise agreement were one-year contracts that Union Oil could cancel if a dealer did not adhere to the contract. The franchise agreement provided that all dealers must adhere to the retail price of gasoline as set by Union Oil. The retail price fixed by Union Oil for gasoline during the period in question was 29.9 cents per gallon. Simpson, a franchised dealer, violated this provision in the franchise agreement and sold gasoline at 27.9 cents per gallon to meet competitive prices. Because of this, Union Oil canceled Simpson's lease and franchise agreement. Simpson sued Union Oil, alleging a violation of Section 1 of the Sherman Act. Who wins? *Simpson v. Union Oil Company*, 377 U.S. 13, 84 S.Ct. 1051, 12 L.Ed.2d 98, **Web** 1964 U.S. Lexis 2378 (Supreme Court of the United States)

22.5 Monopolization The International Business Machines Corporation (IBM) manufactured entire computer systems, including mainframes and peripherals, and provided software and support services to customers. IBM both sold and leased computers. Greyhound Computer Corporation, Inc. (Greyhound), was a computer leasing company that bought older computers from IBM and then leased them to businesses. Thus, Greyhound was both a customer and a competitor of IBM. Prior to 1963, IBM sold its older equipment at a 10 percent discount per year, up to a maximum of 75 percent. Thus, equipment on the market for several years could be purchased at a substantial discount from its original cost.

IBM's market share of this leasing market was 82.5 percent. The portion of the leasing market not controlled by IBM was dispersed among many other companies, including Greyhound. IBM officials became concerned that the balance between sales and leases was turned too heavily toward sales and that the rapid increase in leasing companies occurred because of their ability to purchase second-generation computers from IBM at a substantial discount. In 1963, IBM reduced the annual discount to 5 percent per year, with a maximum of 35 percent. In 1964, the discount was changed to 12 percent after the first year, with no further discounts. Greyhound sued IBM, alleging that IBM engaged in monopolization, in violation of Section 2 of the Sherman Act. Who wins? *Greyhound Computer Corporation v. International Business Machine Corporation*, 559 F.2d 488, **Web** 1977 U.S. App. Lexis 11957 (United States Court of Appeals for the Ninth Circuit)

22.6 Merger The Lipton Tea Co. (Lipton) was the second-largest U.S. producer of herbal teas, controlling 32 percent of the national market. Lipton announced that it would acquire Celestial Seasonings, the largest U.S. producer of herbal teas, which controlled 52 percent of the national market. R.C. Bigelow, Inc., the third-largest producer of herbal teas, with 13 percent of the national market, brought an action, alleging that the merger would violate Section 7 of the Clayton Act, and sought an injunction against the merger. What type of merger is proposed in this case? What is the relevant market? Should the merger be enjoined? *R. C. Bigelow, Inc., v. Unilever, N.V.*, 867 F.2d 102,

Web 1989 U.S. App. Lexis 574 (United States Court of Appeals for the Second Circuit)

22.7 Antitrust Injury The Brunswick Corporation was the second-largest manufacturer of bowling equipment in the United States. In the late 1950s, the bowling industry expanded rapidly. Brunswick's sales of lanes, automatic pinsetters, and ancillary equipment to bowling alley operators rose accordingly. Because the equipment required a major capital expenditure by bowling center operators, Brunswick required a cash down payment and extended credit for the rest of the purchase price. It took a security interest in the equipment.

Brunswick's sales dropped in the early 1960s, when the bowling industry went into a sharp decline. In addition, many of the bowling center operators defaulted on their loans. By the end of 1964, Brunswick was in financial difficulty. It met with limited success when it foreclosed on its security interests and attempted to lease or sell the repossessed equipment and bowling centers. To avoid complete loss, Brunswick started running the centers that would provide a positive cash flow. This made Brunswick the largest operator of bowling centers in the country, with more than five times as many bowling centers as its next largest competitor. Because the bowling industry was so deconcentrated, however, Brunswick controlled fewer than 2 percent of the bowling centers in the country.

Pueblo Bowl-O-Mat, Inc., operated three bowling centers in markets where Brunswick had repossessed bowling centers and begun operating them. Pueblo Bowl sued Brunswick, alleging that Brunswick had violated Section 7 of the Clayton Act. Pueblo Bowl alleged that it had suffered injury in the form of lost profits that it would have made had Brunswick allowed the bowling centers to go bankrupt, and it requested treble damages. Is Brunswick liable? *Brunswick Corporation v. Pueblo Bowl-O-Mat, Inc.*, 429 U.S. 477, 97 S.Ct. 690, 50 L.Ed.2d 701, **Web** 1977 U.S. Lexis 37 (Supreme Court of the United States)

22.8 Price Discrimination Corn Products Refining Company (Corn Products) manufactured corn syrup, or glucose (a principal ingredient of low-priced candy), at two plants, one located in Chicago, Illinois, and the other in Kansas City, Missouri. Corn Products sold glucose at the same retail price to all purchasers but charged separately for freight charges. Instead of charging actual freight charges, Corn Products charged every purchaser the price it would have cost for the glucose to be shipped from Chicago, even if the glucose was shipped from its Kansas City plant. This "base point pricing" system created a favored price zone for Chicago-based purchasers and put them in a better position to compete for business. The Federal Trade Commission sued Corn Products, alleging that it was engaging in price discrimination, in violation of Section 2(a) of the Robinson-Patman Act. Has Corn Products acted ethically in adopting its base point pricing system? Why would the company adopt such a pricing system? Who wins? *Corn Products Refining Company v. Federal Trade Commission*, 324 U.S. 726, 65 S.Ct. 961, 89 L.Ed. 1320, **Web** 1945 U.S. Lexis 2749 (Supreme Court of the United States)

Ethics Cases

22.9 Ethics E. I. du Pont de Nemours & Co. (Du Pont) is a manufacturer of chemicals, paints, finishes, fabrics, and other products. General Motors Corporation is a major manufacturer of automobiles. During the period 1917–1919, Du Pont purchased 23 percent of the stock of General Motors. Du Pont became a major supplier of finishes and fabrics to General Motors.

Du Pont's commanding position as a General Motors supplier was not achieved until shortly after its purchase of a sizable block of General Motors stock in 1917. The company's interest in buying into General Motors was stimulated by John J. Raskob, Du Pont's treasurer, and Pierre S. du Pont, Du Pont's president, who acquired personal holdings of General Motors stock in 1914. General Motors had been organized six years earlier by William C. Durant to acquire the previously independent automobile manufacturing companies Buick, Cadillac, Oakland, and Oldsmobile. Durant later brought in Chevrolet, organized by Durant when he was temporarily out of power, during 1910–1915, and a bankers' group controlled General Motors. In 1915, when Durant and the bankers deadlocked on the choice of a board of directors, they resolved the deadlock by an agreement under which Pierre S. du Pont was named chairman of the General Motors board, and Pierre S. du Pont, Raskob, and two nominees of Mr. du Pont were named neutral directors. By 1916, Durant settled his differences with the bankers and resumed the presidency and his controlling position in General Motors. He prevailed upon Pierre S. du Pont and Raskob to continue their interest in General Motors's affairs, which both did as members of the finance committee, working closely with Durant in matters of finances and operations and plans for future expansion.

Raskob foresaw the success of the automobile industry and the opportunity for great profit in a substantial purchase of General Motors stock. On December 19, 1917, Raskob submitted a treasurer's report to the Du Pont finance committee, recommending a purchase of General Motors stock in the amount of $25 million. The report made it clear that more than just a profitable investment was contemplated. A major consideration was that an expanding General Motors would provide a substantial market needed by the burgeoning Du Pont organization. Raskob's summary of reasons in support of the purchase included this statement: "Our interest in the General Motors Company will undoubtedly secure for us the entire Fabrikoid, Pyralin (celluloid), paint and varnish business of those companies, which is a substantial factor."

General Motors was the colossus of the giant automobile industry. It accounted annually for upward of two-fifths of the total sales of automotive vehicles in the nation. Expressed in percentages, Du Pont supplied 67 percent of General Motors's requirements for finishes in 1946 and 68 percent in 1947. In fabrics, Du Pont supplied 52.3 percent of requirements in 1946 and 38.5 percent in 1947. Because General Motors accounted for almost one-half of the automobile industry's annual sales, its requirements for automotive finishes and fabrics must have represented approximately one-half of the relevant market for these materials.

In 1949, the United States brought an antitrust action against Du Pont, alleging violation of Section 7 of the Clayton Act and seeking the divestiture of Du Pont's ownership of stock in General Motors. The United States argued that Du Pont's ownership of 23 percent of the stock of General Motors constituted a vertical merger that gave Du Pont illegal preferences over competitors in the sale of finishes and fabrics to General Motors and therefore violated Section 7 of the Clayton Act. *United States v. E. I. du Pont de Nemours & Co.*, 353 U.S. 586, 77 S.Ct. 872, 1 L.Ed.2d 1057, **Web** 1957 U.S. Lexis 1755 (Supreme Court of the United States)

1. What is a vertical merger? What requirements must be proven to find a vertical merger illegal?
2. Did the du Ponts act ethically in this case?
3. Did Du Pont's ownership of 23 percent of the stock of General Motors constitute a vertical merger that gave Du Pont illegal preferences over competitors in the sale of finishes and fabrics to General Motors and therefore violate Section 7 of the Clayton Act?

22.10 Ethics Falls City Industries, Inc. (Falls City), was a regional brewer located in Nebraska. It sold its Falls City brand beer in thirteen states, including Indiana and Kentucky. In Indiana, Falls City sold its beer to Vanco Beverage, Inc., a beer wholesaler located in Vanderburgh County. In Kentucky, Falls City sold its beer to wholesalers located in Henderson County. The two counties are directly across from each other and are separated only by the Indiana–Kentucky state line. A four-lane interstate highway connects the two counties. When other brewers raised their wholesale prices in Indiana, Falls City also raised its prices. Falls City also raised its wholesale prices in Kentucky, but less than it raised its prices in Indiana. Vanco brought a treble-damages action against Falls City, alleging that Falls City had engaged in price discrimination, in violation of Section 2(a) of the Robinson-Patman Act by raising prices less in Kentucky than in Indiana. Falls City argued that the meeting the competition defense protected it from liability for price discrimination. *Falls City Industries, Inc. v. Vanco Beverage, Inc.*, 460 U.S. 428, 103 S.Ct. 1282, 75 L.Ed.2d 174, **Web** 1983 U.S. Lexis 148 (Supreme Court of the United States)

1. What elements must be proven to find price discrimination? What is the meeting the competition defense?
2. Did Falls City act unethically in this case?
3. Does the meeting the competition defense protect Falls City Industries from liability for price discrimination?

Internet Exercises

1. Visit the website of the U.S. Department of Justice, at **www.usdoj.gov** and read the U.S. Justice Department's overview of the Antitrust Division.

2. Visit the website of the European Union Commission, at **http://ec.europa.eu/competition/index_en.html**. Find information about a recent EU Commission enforcement action. Read it.

3. Visit the website of the Federal Trade Commission (FTC), at **www.ftc.gov**. Click the "Competition" tab. What does the FTC's Bureau of Competition do?

Endnotes

1. *Federal Baseball Club v. National League*, 259 U.S. 200 (1922) (Supreme Court of the United States).
2. 26 Stat. 209, 15 U.S.C. Sections 1–7.
3. 38 Stat. 730, 15 U.S.C. Sections 12–27, 29 U.S.C. Sections 52–53.
4. 15 U.S.C. Sections 41–58.
5. 49 Stat. 1526, 15 Section 13.
6. Antitrust Amendments Act of 1990, P.L. 101-588.
7. Antitrust Amendments Act of 1990, P.L. 101-588.
8. 15 U.S.C. Section 15.
9. *Reiter v. Sonotone Corporation*, 442 U.S. 330, 99 S.Ct. 2326, 60 L.Ed.2d 931, **Web** 1979 U.S. Lexis 108 (Supreme Court of the United States).
10. 15 U.S.C. Section 26.
11. Justice Marshall, *United States v. Topco Associates, Inc.*, 405 U.S. 596, 92 S.Ct. 1126, 31 L.Ed.2d 515, **Web** 1972 U.S. Lexis 167 (Supreme Court of the United States).
12. 15 U.S.C. Section 1.
13. 221 U.S. 1, 31 S.Ct. 502, 55 L.Ed. 619, **Web** 1911 U.S. Lexis 1725 (Supreme Court of the United States). The Court found that Rockefeller's oil trust violated the Sherman Act and ordered the trust broken up into thirty separate companies.
14. *Dr. Miles Medical Co. v. John D. Park & Sons, Co.*, 220 U.S. 373, 31 S.Ct. 376, 55 L.Ed. 502, **Web** 1911 U.S. Lexis 1685 (Supreme Court of the United States).
15. *State Oil Company v. Khan*, 522 U.S. 3, 118 S.Ct. 275, 139 L.Ed.2d 199, **Web** 1997 U.S. Lexis 6705 (Supreme Court of the United States).
16. *Continental T.V., Inc. v. GTE Sylvania, Inc.*, 433 U.S. 36, 97 S.Ct. 2549, 53 L.Ed.2d 568, **Web** 1977 U.S. Lexis 134 (Supreme Court of the United States), reversing *United States v. Arnold Schwinn & Co.*, 388 U.S. 365, 87 S.Ct. 1856, 18 L.Ed.2d 1249, **Web** 1967 U.S. Lexis 2965 (Supreme Court of the United States).
17. 250 U.S. 300, 39 S.Ct. 465, 63 L.Ed. 992, **Web** 1919 U.S. Lexis 1748 (Supreme Court of the United States).
18. This doctrine is a result of two U.S. Supreme Court decisions: *Eastern R.R. President's Conference v. Noerr Motor Freight, Inc.*, 365 U.S. 127, 81 S.Ct. 523, 5 L.Ed.2d 464, **Web** 1961 U.S. Lexis 2128 (Supreme Court of the United States) and *United Mine Workers v. Pennington*, 381 U.S. 657, 85 S.Ct. 1585, 14 L.Ed.2d 626, **Web** 1965 U.S. Lexis 2207 (Supreme Court of the United States).
19. 15 U.S.C. Section 2.
20. *William Inglis & Sons Baking Company v. ITT Continental Baking Company, Inc.*, 668 F.2d 1014, **Web** 1982 U.S. App. Lexis 21926 (United States Court of Appeals for the Ninth Circuit).
21. 15 U.S.C. Section 18.
22. 15 U.S.C. Section 18(a).
23. 15 U.S.C. Section 14.

24. 15 U.S.C. Section 13(a).

25. *Hartley & Parker, Inc. v. Florida Beverage Corp.*, 307 F.2d 916, 923, **Web** 1962 U.S. App. Lexis 4196 (United States Court of Appeals for the Fifth Circuit).

26. 15 U.S.C. Section 13(b).

27. 15 U.S.C. Section 45.

28. Section 6 of the Clayton Act, 15 U.S.C. Section 17; the Norris-LaGuardia Act of 1932, 29 U.S.C. Sections 101–155; and the National Labor Relations Act of 1935, 29 U.S.C. Sections 141 et seq. Labor unions that conspire or combine with nonlabor groups to accomplish a goal prohibited by federal antitrust law lose their exemption.

29. Capper-Volstrand Act of 1922, 7 U.S.C. Section 291; and Cooperative Marketing Act of 1926, 15 U.S.C. Section 521.

30. Webb-Pomerene Act, 15 U.S.C. Sections 61–65.

31. McCarran-Ferguson Act of 1945, 15 U.S.C. Sections 1011–1015.

32. *Community Communications Co., Inc. v. City of Boulder*, 455 U.S. 40, 102 S.Ct. 835, 70 L.Ed.2d 810, **Web** 1982 U.S. Lexis 65 (Supreme Court of the United States).

33. *Goldfarb v. Virginia State Bar*, 421 U.S. 773, 95 S.Ct. 2004, 44 L.Ed.2d 572, **Web** 1975 U.S. Lexis 13 (Supreme Court of the United States).

CHAPTER

23 Consumer Protection

RESTAURANT
*The federal and state governments have
enacted many statutes to protect consumers
from unsafe food items.*

Learning Objectives

After studying this chapter, you should be able to:

1. Describe government regulation of food and food additives.
2. Describe government regulation of drugs, cosmetics, medicinal devices, and products.
3. Identify and describe unfair and deceptive business practices.
4. Describe the United Nations Biosafety Protocol concerning genetically altered foods.
5. Describe the functions of the Consumer Financial Protection Bureau and the provisions of the Consumer Financial Protection Act of 2010.

Chapter Outline

Introduction to Consumer Protection

Meat and Related Products Safety

Food, Drugs, and Cosmetics Safety
  ETHICS • *Restaurants Required to Disclose Calories of Food Items*
  INTERNATIONAL LAW • *United Nations Biosafety Protocol for Genetically Altered Foods*
  ETHICS • *Ethics of Using Animal Testing in the Development of Cosmetics*

Product and Automobile Safety
  CONTEMPORARY ENVIRONMENT • *Warnings on Cigarette Packages and Advertisements*

Medical and Health Care Protection
  LANDMARK LAW • *Health Care Reform Act of 2010*

Unfair and Deceptive Practices
  CONTEMPORARY ENVIRONMENT • *Do-Not-Call Registry Protects Against Unwanted Telemarketing Phone Calls*

Chapter Outline *(continued)*

Consumer Financial Protection
    CONTEMPORARY ENVIRONMENT • *Bureau of Consumer Financial Protection*
    CONTEMPORARY ENVIRONMENT • *Credit CARD Act of 2009*

> *I should regret to find that the law was powerless to enforce the most elementary principles of commercial morality."*
>
> —Lord Herschell
>   *Reddaway v. Banham (1896)*

Introduction to Consumer Protection

Originally, sales transactions in this country were guided by the principle of **caveat emptor** ("let the buyer beware"). This led to abusive practices by businesses that sold adulterated food products and other unsafe products. In response, federal and state governments have enacted a variety of statutes that regulate the safety of food and other products. These laws, collectively referred to as **consumer protection laws**, are the subject of this chapter.

    This chapter covers these and other consumer protections laws.

 United States Department of Agriculture

Meat and Related Products Safety

The safety of food is an important concern in the United States and worldwide. In the United States, the **U.S. Department of Agriculture (USDA)** is the federal administrative agency that is primarily responsible for regulating meat, poultry, and other food products. The USDA conducts inspections of food processing and storage facilities. The USDA can initiate legal proceedings against violators.

Food, Drugs, and Cosmetics Safety

The **Food, Drug, and Cosmetic Act (FDCA or FDC Act)**[1] was enacted in 1938. This federal statute, as amended, regulates the testing, manufacture, distribution, and sale of foods, drugs, cosmetics, and medicinal devices in the United States. The **Food and Drug Administration (FDA)** is the federal administrative agency empowered to enforce the FDCA.

  U.S. Food and Drug Administration   *U.S. Department of Health and Human Services*

    Before certain food additives, drugs, cosmetics, and medicinal devices can be sold to the public, they must receive FDA approval. An applicant must submit to the FDA an application that contains relevant information about the safety and

---

consumer protection laws
Federal and state statutes and regulations that promote product safety and prohibit abusive, unfair, and deceptive business practices.

You can fool some of the people all of the time, and all of the people some of the time, but you cannot fool all of the people all of the time.

        P.T. Barnum

U.S. Department of Agriculture
A federal administrative agency that is responsible for regulating the safety of meat, poultry, and other food products.

Food, Drug, and Cosmetic Act (FDCA or FDC Act)
A federal statute that provides the basis for the regulation of much of the testing, manufacture, distribution, and sale of foods, drugs, cosmetics, and medicinal products.

Food and Drug Administration (FDA)
The federal administrative agency that administers and enforces the federal Food, Drug, and Cosmetic Act and other federal consumer protection laws.

uses of the product. The FDA, after considering the evidence, will either approve or deny the application.

The FDA can seek search warrants and conduct inspections; obtain orders for the seizure, recall, and condemnation of products; seek injunctions; and turn over suspected criminal violations to the U.S. Department of Justice for prosecution.

Regulation of Food

The FDCA prohibits the shipment, distribution, or sale of **adulterated food**. Food is deemed adulterated if it consists in whole or in part of any "filthy, putrid, or decomposed substance" or if it is otherwise "unfit for food." Note that food does not have to be entirely pure to be distributed or sold; it only has to be unadulterated.

The FDCA also prohibits **false and misleading labeling** of food products. In addition, it mandates affirmative disclosure of information on food labels, including the name of the food, the name and place of the manufacturer, a statement of ingredients, and nutrition content. A manufacturer may be held liable for deceptive labeling or packaging.

Food Labeling

Nutrition Labeling and Education Act (NLEA)
A federal statute that requires food manufacturers to disclose on food labels nutritional information about the food.

In 1990, Congress passed a sweeping truth-in-labeling law called the **Nutrition Labeling and Education Act (NLEA)**.[2] This statute requires food manufacturers and processors to provide nutrition information on many foods and prohibits them from making scientifically unsubstantiated health claims.

The NLEA applies to packaged foods and other foods regulated by the Food and Drug Administration. The law requires food labels to disclose the number of calories derived from fat and the amount of dietary fiber, saturated fat, trans fat, cholesterol, and a variety of other substances contained in the food. The law also requires the disclosure of uniform information about serving sizes and nutrients, and it establishes standard definitions for *light* (or *lite*), *low fat, fat free, cholesterol free*, *lean*, *natural*, *organic*, and other terms routinely bandied about by food processors.

The Department of Agriculture adopted consistent labeling requirements for the meat and poultry products it regulates. Nutrition labeling for raw fruits and vegetables and raw seafood is voluntary. Many sellers of these products provide point-of-purchase nutrition information.

The following feature discusses food labeling at restaurants.

Ethics

Restaurants Required to Disclose Calories of Food Items

Did you know that a Big Mac contains 540 calories, a Domino's medium pepperoni pizza 1,660 calories, a hot fudge with Snickers sundae from Baskin-Robbins 1,000 calories, a blueberry muffin from Starbucks 450 calories, and a medium-size bucket of buttered popcorn at the movie theater approximately 1,000 calories? Well, you will now.

Section 4205 of the Patient Protection and Affordable Health Care Act of 2010 requires restaurants and retail food establishments with twenty or more locations to disclose calorie counts of their food items and supply information on how many calories a healthy person should eat in a day. The disclosures are required to be made on menus and menu

boards, including drive-through menu boards. The law also applies to vending machine operators with twenty or more vending machines. The law is administered by the U.S. Food and Drug Administration, a federal government agency that is empowered to adopt rules and regulations to enforce the law.

Calorie disclosure rules had been fought by the National Restaurant Association for years, but the trade group eventually supported the passage of the federal law partially to add uniformity to disclosure rules rather than face the many different state and local laws that were being enacted to require such disclosures. Proponents of the law assert that with such disclosures people will make better food choices and reduce the most preventable American health care crisis, obesity. Critics argue the disclosures will not change peoples' eating habits and just adds another layer of federal bureaucracy.

Ethics Questions   Should restaurants have provided visible calorie information before being required to do so by law? Do you think that the new disclosures will change many people's eating habits?

The following feature discusses an important issue regarding food processing and safety.

International Law

United Nations Biosafety Protocol for Genetically Altered Foods

In many countries, the food is not genetically altered. However, many food processors in the United States and elsewhere around the world genetically modify some foods by adding genes from other organisms to help crops grow faster or ward off pests. Although the companies insist that genetically altered foods are safe, consumers and many countries began to demand that such foods be clearly labeled so that buyers could decide for themselves.

In 2000, more than 150 countries, including the United States, agreed to the United Nations–sponsored *Biosafety Protocol* for genetically altered foods. The **United Nations Biosafety Protocol for Genetically Altered Foods** requires that all genetically engineered foods be clearly labeled with the phrase "May contain living modified organisms." This allows consumers to decide on their own whether to purchase such altered food products.

United Nations Biosafety Protocol for Genetically Altered Foods
A United Nations-sponsored protocol that requires signatory countries to place the label "May contain living modified organisms" on all genetically engineered foods.

Drug Amendment to the FDCA
A federal law that gives the FDA broad powers to license new drugs in the United States.

Justice is the end of government. It is the end of civil society. It ever has been, and ever will be pursued, until it be obtained, or until liberty be lost in the pursuit.

James Madison
The Federalist No. 51 (1788)

Regulation of Drugs

The FDCA gives the FDA the authority to regulate the testing, manufacture, distribution, and sale of drugs. The **Drug Amendment to the FDCA**,[3] enacted in 1962, gives the FDA broad powers to license new drugs in the United States. After a new drug application is filed, the FDA holds a hearing and investigates the merits of the application. This process can take many years. The FDA may withdraw approval of any previously licensed drug.

This law requires all users of prescription and nonprescription drugs to receive proper directions for use (including the method and duration of use) and adequate warnings about any related side effects. The manufacture, distribution, or sale of adulterated or misbranded drugs is prohibited.

Regulation of Cosmetics

The FDA's definition of cosmetics includes substances and preparations for cleansing, altering the appearance of, and promoting the attractiveness of a person. Eye shadow and other facial makeup products are examples of cosmetics subject to FDA regulation. Ordinary household soap is expressly exempted from this definition.

The FDA has issued regulations that require cosmetics to be labeled, to disclose ingredients, and to contain warnings if they are carcinogenic (i.e., cancer causing) or otherwise dangerous to a person's health. The manufacture, distribution, or sale of adulterated or misbranded cosmetics is prohibited. The FDA may remove from commerce any cosmetics that contain unsubstantiated claims of preserving youth, increasing virility, growing hair, and such.

The following feature discusses the ethics of using animal testing in creating cosmetics.

Ethics

Ethics of Using Animal Testing in the Development of Cosmetics

Under the law, cosmetics must be safe for human use. Potential cosmetics are often tested on animals in order to determine whether they can be safely used on humans. Obviously such testing often causes injury, and sometimes death, to the animals. The cosmetics industry has been criticized for the use of animal testing. However, there is no law in the United States against animal testing for cosmetics.

The Food and Drug Administration (FDA), which is responsible for ensuring that cosmetics are safe, does not specifically require that animals be used to test the safety of cosmetics. However, the agency advises cosmetics manufacturers to employ whatever testing is appropriate and effective for substantiating the safety of their products, which may include animal testing. The FDA's position is that companies may determine that animal testing is necessary to ensure the safety of a product or ingredient.

Some cosmetics companies promote their products with claims such as "CRUELTY-FREE" or "NOT TESTED ON ANIMALS" in their labeling or advertising. However, the unrestricted use of these phrases by cosmetics companies is possible because there are no legal definitions for these terms. Some cosmetics companies apply such claims to their finished cosmetic products when in fact these companies rely on raw material suppliers or contract laboratories to perform animal testing necessary to substantiate product or ingredient safety.

The use of animal testing for determining the safety of cosmetics will remain a contested issue.

Ethics Questions   Is the use of animals for testing the safety of cosmetics ethical? Should animal testing be permitted if there is no other way to determine the safety of cosmetics? Should animal testing be prohibited by law?

Regulation of Medicinal Devices

In 1976, Congress enacted the **Medicinal Device Amendment to the FDCA.**[4] This amendment gives the FDA authority to regulate medicinal devices, such as heart pacemakers, kidney dialysis machines, defibrillators, surgical equipment, and other diagnostic, therapeutic, and health devices. The mislabeling of such devices is prohibited. The FDA is empowered to remove "quack" devices from the market.

Product and Automobile Safety

Consumer Product Safety Act (CPSA)
A federal statute that regulates potentially dangerous consumer products and that created the Consumer Product Safety Commission.

Consumer Product Safety Commission (CPSC)
A federal administrative agency empowered to adopt rules and regulations to interpret and enforce the Consumer Product Safety Act.

In 1972, Congress enacted the **Consumer Product Safety Act (CPSA)**[5] and created the **Consumer Product Safety Commission (CPSC).** The CPSC is an independent federal administrative agency empowered to (1) adopt rules and regulations to interpret and enforce the CPSA, (2) conduct research on the safety of consumer products, and (3) collect data regarding injuries caused by consumer products.

Because the CPSC regulates potentially dangerous consumer products, it issues **product safety standards** for consumer products that pose unreasonable risk of injury. If a consumer product is found to be imminently hazardous—that is, if its use causes an unreasonable risk of death or serious injury or illness—the manufacturer can be required to recall, repair, or replace the product or take other corrective action. Alternatively, the CPSC can seek injunctions, bring actions to seize hazardous consumer products, seek civil penalties for knowing violations of the act or of CPSC rules, and seek criminal penalties for knowing and willful violations of the act or of CPSC rules. A private party can sue for an injunction to prevent violations of the act or of CPSC rules and regulations.

Certain consumer products, including motor vehicles, boats, aircraft, and firearms, are regulated by other government agencies.

The following feature describes a law requiring graphic warnings about the risks of cigarette smoking.

Contemporary Environment

Warnings on Cigarette Packages and Advertisements

The United States was one of the first countries of the world to require health warnings on cigarette packages. However, these warning appeared somewhat inconspicuously on the sides of cigarette packages. After use for more than twenty-five years, these warnings became some of the smallest in the world.

In 2009, the U.S. Congress enacted the **Family Smoking Prevention and Tobacco Control Act**.[6] This act requires nine new larger and noticeable warnings to be placed on cigarette packages. The warnings include nine new textual statements (e.g., "Warning: Tobacco Smoke Can Harm Your Children") to be placed over color graphic images that depict the negative consequences of smoking. A warning must appear on the top 50 percent of both the front and back of each cigarette package. The warnings that depict the physical results of smoking are bold. Each warning must also contain the telephone number "1-QUIT-NOW," where a smoker can call to get help to quit smoking. The law also requires that the warnings appear on the left 50 percent of the front and back panels of cigarette cartons. The nine different warnings must be rotated an equal number of times during each twelve-month period in the area of the country in which the product is sold. The act specified that use of the warnings became mandatory September 2012.

In addition, the law requires that the health warnings occupy at least 20 percent of cigarette advertisements and appear in the upper-left portion of an advertisement. The rule applies to all forms of advertisings, including billboards, posters, magazines and newspapers, direct mailers, coupons, brochures, retail point-of-sale displays, Internet advertising (e.g., webpages, banner ads), and other forms of advertising.

The federal Food and Drug Administration (FDA), a federal government agency, is authorized to enforce the act and adopt rules to implement the provisions of the act. Penalties for violating the act may lead to FDA actions, including the assessment of civil monetary fines, injunctions, seizure of goods, or no-tobacco-sales orders.

The new law was enacted with the goals of conveying the health risks of smoking, encouraging smokers to quit smoking, preventing youths and adults from starting to smoke, reducing medical costs associated with smoking, and promoting the health of people in the United States.

Medical and Health Care Protection

Many employees and their dependents are covered by health insurance that is provided by their employers. This makes up a large proportion of the persons who are covered by health insurance. Under these insurance programs, the employer may pay all of the health insurance premiums or part of the insurance premiums. If the employer pays part of the insurance premium, the employee pays the remainder. This insurance covers medical bills, hospital costs, doctors' fees, the cost of medicine, and other medical costs. Many insurance programs require copays—that is, the employee must pay a certain percentage (e.g., 5 percent) of

WEB EXERCISE
To view the nine new cigarette health warnings, go to **www.fda .gov/TobaccoProducts/ Labeling/CigaretteWarning Labels/ucm259214.htm** and click on the warnings on the left side of the page.

Health Care Reform Act
A 2010 federal statute that increases the number of persons who have health care insurance in the United States and provides new protections for insured persons from abusive practices of insurance companies.

the cost of an office or hospital visit. Many insurance programs contain a deductible clause. For example, the employee must pay for the first $500 of coverage during a year before the medical insurance provides coverage.

However, many small employers do not provide health care insurance for their employees. Several government programs provide health care coverage. For example, Social Security provides retirement, disability, survivorship, and death benefits. Medicare provides medical coverage to persons aged 65 years and older. And Medicaid provides health care coverage for low-income people and families with dependent children. These government programs are funded by taxes. However, in 2010, that still left more than fifty-five million people in the United States without health insurance.

The following feature discusses the landmark Health Care Reform Act, a federal statute that was enacted by the U.S. Congress and signed by the president in 2010.

Landmark Law

Health Care Reform Act of 2010

After much public debate, in 2010, Congress enacted the **Patient Protection and Affordable Care Act (PPACA)**.[7] This act was immediately amended by the **Health Care and Education Reconciliation Act**.[8] The amended act is commonly referred to as the **Health Care Reform Act** of 2010. The goal of this act was to increase the number of persons who have health care insurance in this country.

The 2010 Health Care Reform Act mandates that most U.S. citizens and legal residents purchase "minimal essential" health care insurance coverage. This can be done through an employer if a person is employed. However, if an employer does not offer health insurance, or if a person does not work, then the person can purchase health insurance from new insurance marketplaces that are called "exchanges." Persons who do not obtain coverage will be required to pay a tax penalty to the federal government.

Pursuant to the act, the federal government will subsidize health care premiums for individuals with income up to 400% of the poverty line. The act also creates a tax credit for small business employers for contributions made to purchase health insurance for employees. These combined subsidies are a crucial element of the act, allowing people who could not otherwise afford to purchase health insurance to be subsidized by the federal government to do so. The act also increases the funding for the government's Medicaid program.

The new health care program will be funded through a number of taxes, assessment of fees, and cuts in government spending for existing health care programs. An increased Medicare tax and a new tax on investment income are levied against single persons who make $200,000 and couples who make $250,000 in income

per year. Excise taxes are imposed on pharmaceutical and health insurance companies, and a sales tax is assessed on medical device manufacturers. "Cadillac" health insurance programs—those that provide health care benefits that cost above a certain level—are assessed a special tax. Some existing Medicare benefits are reduced by the act.

In addition to requiring and helping fund health care coverage, the Health Care Reform Act provides a number of new protections for insured persons. These protections do the following:

- Prevent insurance companies from denying health care insurance to individuals with preexisting health conditions
- Prohibit health insurance companies from terminating health insurance coverage when a person gets sick
- Prohibit insurers from establishing an annual spending cap for benefit payments
- Prohibit insurers from imposing lifetime limits on benefit payments
- Require health plans that provide dependent coverage to continue coverage for a dependent child until the child turns 26 years of age

The Health Care Reform Act was meant to cover more than 32 million people who were not previously covered by health insurance. However, even after the act was signed into law in 2010, more than 20 million people in this country were not covered by health insurance. These included illegal immigrants who were not eligible for health insurance subsidies and persons who did not qualify for coverage or choose not to be covered.

Federal Trade Commission (FTC)
A federal administrative agency empowered to enforce the Federal Trade Commission Act and other federal consumer protection statutes.

Unfair and Deceptive Practices

The **Federal Trade Commission Act (FTC Act)** was enacted in 1914.[9] The **Federal Trade Commission (FTC)** was created the following year to enforce the FTC Act as well as other federal consumer protection statutes.

Section 5 of the FTC Act, as amended, prohibits **unfair and deceptive practices**. It has been used extensively to regulate business conduct. This section gives the FTC the authority to bring an administrative proceeding to attack a deceptive or unfair practice. If, after a public administrative hearing, the FTC finds a violation of Section 5, it may issue a cease-and-desist order, an affirmative disclosure to consumers, corrective advertising, or the like. The FTC may sue in state or federal court to obtain compensation on behalf of consumers. A decision of the FTC may be appealed to federal court.

Section 5 of the FTC Act
A provision in the FTC Act that prohibits unfair and deceptive practices.

False and Deceptive Advertising

Advertising is **false and deceptive advertising** under Section 5 of the FTC Act if it (1) contains misinformation or omits important information that is likely to mislead a "reasonable consumer" or (2) makes an unsubstantiated claim (e.g., "This product is 33 percent better than our competitor's"). Proof of actual deception is not required. Statements of opinion and "sales talk" (e.g., "This is a great car") do not constitute false and deceptive advertising.

Example Kentucky Fried Chicken entered into an agreement with the FTC whereby KFC withdrew television commercials in which it claimed that its "fried chicken can, in fact, be part of a healthy diet."

Bait and Switch

Bait and switch is a type of deceptive advertising under Section 5 of the FTC Act. It occurs when a seller advertises the availability of a low-cost discounted item (the "bait") to attract customers to its store. Once the customers are in the store, however, the seller pressures them to purchase more expensive merchandise (the "switch"). The FTC states that a bait and switch occurs if the seller refuses to show consumers the advertised merchandise, discourages employees from selling the advertised merchandise, or fails to have adequate quantities of the advertised merchandise available.

Door-to-Door Sales

Some salespersons sell merchandise and services door to door. In some **door-to-door sales** situations, these salespersons use aggressive sales tactics to overcome a consumer's resistance to the sale. To protect consumers from ill-advised decisions, many states have enacted laws that give the consumer a certain number of days to rescind (i.e., cancel) a door-to-door sales contract. The usual period is three days. The consumer must send a required notice of cancellation to the seller. An FTC regulation requires the salesperson to permit cancellation of the contract within the stipulated time.

The following feature discusses an important law that was passed to protect consumers from unwanted telemarketing phone calls.

Do-Not-Call Registry
A registry created by federal law on which consumers can place their names and free themselves from most unsolicited commercial telephone calls.

Contemporary Environment

Do-Not-Call Registry Protects Against Unwanted Telemarketing Phone Calls

The **Federal Communications Commission (FCC)** is a federal administrative agency that regulates communications by radio, television, cable, wire, and satellite. In 2003, two federal administrative agencies—the Federal Trade Commission (FTC) and the FCC—promulgated administrative rules that created the **Do-Not-Call Registry**, on which

(continued)

consumers can place their names and free themselves from most unsolicited commercial telephone calls. The FTC and FCC were given authority to adopt their coordinated do-not-call rules in several federal statutes. Both wire-connected phones and wireless phones can be registered.

Telemarketers have three months from the date on which a consumer signs up for the registry to remove the customer's phone number from their sales call list. Customer registration remains valid for five years and can be renewed. Charitable and political organizations are exempt from the registry. Also, an "established business relationship" exception allows businesses to call a customer for ten months after they sell or lease goods or services to that person or conduct a financial transaction with that person. The Do-Not-Call Registry allows consumers to designate specific companies not to call them, including those that otherwise qualify for the established business relationship exemption.

**NATIONAL
DO NOT CALL
REGISTRY**

Telemarketers sued the U.S. government, arguing that the Do-Not-Call Registry violated their free speech rights under the First Amendment to the U.S. Constitution. However, the U.S. Supreme Court upheld the registry, finding that it is a valid restriction on commercial speech. The Supreme Court stated, "The Do-Not-Call Registry lets consumers avoid unwanted sales pitches that invade the home via telephone." *Mainstream Marketing Services, Inc. v. Federal Trade Commission*, 358 F.3d 1228, **Web** 2004 U.S. App. Lexis 2564 (United States Court of Appeals for the Tenth Circuit)

WEB EXERCISE
Go to **www.donotcall.gov/register/ reg.aspx** to see how to register your telephone number on the Do-Not-Call Registry.

Consumer Financial Protection

Consumers borrow money for many purposes, such as for purchasing a home; buying an automobile, furniture, and appliances; and making credit card purchases. In most consumer credit transactions, the lender has greater leverage than the borrower. Creditors have been known to engage in various abusive, deceptive, and unfair practices when dealing with consumer-debtors. To protect consumer-debtors from such practices, the federal government has enacted a comprehensive scheme of **consumer financial protection** laws concerning the extension and collection of credit.

Dodd-Frank Wall Street Reform and Consumer Protection Act
A federal statute that regulates the financial industry and provides protection to consumers regarding financial products and services.

Dodd-Frank Wall Street Reform and Consumer Protection Act

Prior to 2010, the economy suffered a major recession and financial and housing crises. The result was that a large number of consumers lost their homes to foreclosure. Easy credit terms, loans made without sufficient verification of the income and assets of the borrower, and abusive credit practices by lenders were partially to blame for the recession and financial crisis.

In 2010, Congress enacted the **Dodd-Frank Wall Street Reform and Consumer Protection Act**.[10] This act is the most sweeping financial reform law enacted since the Great Depression of the 1930s. Major goals of the act are to regulate consumer credit and mortgage lending.

The following feature discusses the Consumer Financial Protection Bureau.

Consumer Financial Protection Bureau (CFPB)
A federal administrative agency that is responsible for enforcing federal consumer financial protection statutes.

Contemporary Environment

Consumer Financial Protection Bureau

The Dodd-Frank Wall Street Reform and Consumer Protection Act created a new federal government agency called the **Consumer Financial Protection Bureau (CFPB)**. The CFPB has authority to supervise all participants in the consumer finance and mortgage area, including depository institutions such as commercial and savings banks and nondepository parties such as insurance companies, mortgage brokers, credit counseling firms, debt collectors, and debt buyers. The CFPB provides uniform model forms that covered parties can use to make such disclosures.

The CFPB has authority to prohibit unfair, deceptive, or abusive acts or practices regarding consumer financial products and services. The CFPB has investigative and subpoena powers, and it may refer matters to the U.S. Attorney General for criminal prosecution. The CFPB acts as a watchdog over credit cards, debit cards, mortgages, payday loans, and other consumer financial products and services. The CFPB does not have authority to regulate nonfinancial goods and services. The automobile industry is exempt from CFPB supervision and is instead subject to oversight by the Federal Trade Commission (FTC).

The CFPB is charged with regulating credit extended to older persons, members of the armed services, and persons who are unlikely to understand the complexities of credit. The CFPB is also charged with making credit available on fair terms to members of minority groups. Federal law permits state consumer laws to provide greater protection than federal law unless the state law interferes with the normal operation of a bank or financial institution.

The CFPB has authority to enforce the Consumer Financial Protection Act of 2010 and the Mortgage Reform and Anti-Predatory Lending Act of 2010. In addition, enforcement of the consumer protection responsibilities of many existing federal laws, such as the Truth in Lending Act (TILA), Equal Credit Opportunity Act, Fair Credit Reporting Act, Fair Debt Collection Practices Act, Home Mortgage Disclosure Act, Electronic Funds Transfer Act, and Truth in Savings Act, were transferred from other government agencies to the CFPB. The CFPB is authorized to adopt rules to interpret and enforce the provisions of the acts it administers.

The consumer financial protection laws that the CFPB has authority to enforce are discussed in the following paragraphs.

Consumer Financial Protection Act of 2010

Title X of the Dodd-Frank Wall Street Reform and Consumer Protection Act is the called the **Consumer Financial Protection Act of 2010**. The act is designed to increase relevant disclosure regarding consumer financial products and services and to eliminate deceptive and abusive loan practices. The act is also designed to prevent hidden fees and charges.

The law requires disclosure of relevant information to consumers in plain language that permits consumers to understand the costs, benefits, and risks associated with consumer financial products and services. The act requires that credit card companies provide calculators that give the payoff terms under different scenarios, such as if only minimum payments are made or the payments that are needed to pay the balance off in one year and such. Other provisions limit fees for using debit cards to be reasonable and proportional to the cost incurred in processing the payment.

Consumer Financial Protection Act of 2010
A federal statute that requires increased disclosure of credit information and terms to consumers and regulates consumer credit providers and others.

Mortgage Reform and Anti-Predatory Lending Act of 2010

Title XIV of the Dodd-Frank Act, called the **Mortgage Reform and Anti-Predatory Lending Act**, is designed to eliminate many abusive loan practices and mandates new duties and disclosure requirements for mortgage lenders. The act requires mortgage originators and lenders to verify the assets and income of prospective borrowers, their credit history, employment status, debt-to-income ratio, and other relevant factors when making a decision to extend credit.

The act is particularly designed to regulate the subprime mortgage market—that is, the home loan market where lenders make loans to unqualified borrowers. The act puts the burden on lenders to verify that a borrower can afford to repay the loan for which they have applied. The act provides civil remedies for borrowers to sue lenders for engaging in deceptive and predatory practices and for violating the provisions of the act.

Mortgage Reform and Anti-Predatory Lending Act
A federal statute that eliminates many abusive mortgage loan practices and mandates new duties and disclosure requirements on mortgage lenders and others.

Truth-in-Lending Act

The **Truth-in-Lending Act (TILA)**[11] is one of the first federal consumer protection statutes enacted by Congress. The TILA, as amended, requires creditors to make certain disclosures to debtors in consumer transactions (e.g., retail installment sales, automobile loans) and real estate loans on the debtor's principal dwelling. The TILA covers only creditors that regularly (1) extend credit for goods or

Truth-in-Lending Act (TILA)
A federal statute that requires creditors to make certain disclosures to debtors in consumer transactions and real estate loans on the debtor's principal dwelling.

services to consumers or (2) arrange such credit in the ordinary course of their business. Consumer credit is defined as credit extended to natural persons for personal, family, or household purposes.

Regulation Z   Regulation Z,[12] an administrative agency regulation, sets forth detailed rules for compliance with the TILA. The TILA and Regulation Z require the creditor to disclose the following information to the consumer-debtor:

- Cash price of the product or service
- Down payment and trade-in allowance
- Unpaid cash price
- Finance charge, including interest, points, and other fees paid for the extension of credit
- **Annual percentage rate (APR)** of the finance charges
- Charges not included in the finance charge (e.g., appraisal fees)
- Total dollar amount financed
- Date the finance charge begins to accrue
- Number, amounts, and due dates of payments
- Description of any security interest
- Penalties to be assessed for delinquent payments and late charges
- Prepayment penalties
- Comparative costs of credit (optional)

The uniform disclosures required by the TILA and Regulation Z are intended to help consumers shop for the best credit terms.

Consumer Leasing Act

Consumers often opt to lease consumer products, such as automobiles, rather than purchase them. The **Consumer Leasing Act (CLA)**[13] is a federal statute that extends the TILA's coverage to lease terms in consumer leases. The CLA applies to lessors who engage in leasing or arranging leases for consumer goods in the ordinary course of their business. Casual leases (e.g., leases between consumers) are not subject to the CLA. Creditors that violate the CLA are subject to the civil and criminal penalties provided in the TILA.

Fair Credit Billing Act

The **Fair Credit Billing Act (FCBA)**[14] is a federal statute that regulates billing errors involving consumer credit. The act requires that creditors promptly acknowledge in writing consumer billing complaints and investigate billing errors. The act prohibits creditors from taking actions that adversely affect a consumer's credit standing until an investigation is completed. The act affords other protections during disputes. The act, as amended, requires creditors to promptly post payments to the consumer's account and either refund overpayments or credit them to the consumer's account.

Fair Credit Reporting Act

The **Fair Credit Reporting Act (FCRA)**[15] is a federal statute that regulates credit reporting companies. This act protects a consumer who is the subject of a **credit report** by setting rules for consumer reporting agencies—that is, credit bureaus that compile and sell credit reports for a fee. A consumer may request the following information at any time: (1) the nature and substance of all the information in his or her credit file, (2) the sources of this information, and (3) the names of recipients of his or her credit report.

If a consumer challenges the accuracy of pertinent information contained in a credit file, the agency may be compelled to reinvestigate. If the agency cannot find an error, despite the consumer's complaint, the consumer may file a brief

---

Regulation Z
A regulation that sets forth detailed rules for compliance with the Truth-in-Lending Act (TILA).

Consumer Leasing Act (CLA)
A federal statute that extends the coverage of the Truth-in-Lending Act (TILA) to lease terms in consumer leases.

Fair Credit Billing Act (FCBA)
A federal statute which requires that creditors promptly acknowledge in writing consumer billing complaints and investigate billing errors and which affords consumer-debtors other protection during billing disputes.

Fair Credit Reporting Act (FCRA)
A federal statute that protects a consumer who is the subject of a credit report by setting rules for credit bureaus to follow and permitting consumer to obtain information from credit reporting businesses.

credit report
Information about a person's credit history that can be secured from a credit bureau reporting company.

written statement of his or her version of the disputed information. If a consumer reporting agency or user violates the FCRA, the injured consumer may bring a civil action against the violator and recover actual damages. The FCRA also provides for criminal penalties.

The **Fair and Accurate Credit Transactions Act**[16] of 2003 gives consumers the right to obtain one free credit report each year from the credit reporting agencies, and consumers may purchase for a reasonable fee a credit score and how the credit score is calculated. The act permits consumers to place fraud alerts in their credit files.

Fair Debt Collection Practices Act

The **Fair Debt Collection Practices Act (FDCPA)**[17] is a federal statute that protects consumer-debtors from abusive, deceptive, and unfair practices used by **debt collectors**. The FDCPA expressly prohibits debt collectors from using certain practices: (1) harassing, abusive, or intimidating tactics (e.g., threats of violence, obscene or abusive language), (2) false or misleading misrepresentations (e.g., posing as a police officer or an attorney), and (3) unfair or unconscionable practices (e.g., threatening the debtor with imprisonment).

A debt collector is not allowed to contact a debtor in some circumstances, including the following:

1. At any inconvenient time. The FDCPA provides that convenient hours are between 8:00 A.M. and 9:00 P.M., unless this time is otherwise inconvenient for the debtor (e.g., the debtor works a night shift and sleeps during the day).
2. At inconvenient places, such as at a place of worship or social events.
3. At the debtor's place of employment, if the employer objects to such contact.
4. If the debtor is represented by an attorney.
5. If the debtor gives a written notice to the debt collector that he or she refuses to pay the debt or does not want the debt collector to contact him or her again.

The FDCPA limits the contact that a debt collector may have with third persons other than the debtor's spouse or parents. Such contact is strictly limited. Unless the court has given its approval, third parties can be consulted only for the purpose of locating a debtor, and a third party can be contacted only once. A debt collector may not inform a third person that a consumer owes a debt that is in the process of collection. A debtor may bring a civil action against a debt collector for intentionally violating the FDCPA.

Equal Credit Opportunity Act

The **Equal Credit Opportunity Act (ECOA)**[18] is a federal statute that prohibits discrimination in the extension of credit based on sex, marital status, race, color, national origin, religion, age, or receipt of income from public assistance programs. The ECOA applies to all creditors that extend or arrange credit in the ordinary course of their business, including banks, savings and loan associations, automobile dealers, real estate brokers, credit card issuers, and the like.

A creditor must notify an applicant within thirty days regarding an action taken on a credit application. If the creditor takes an *adverse action* (i.e., denies, revokes, or changes the credit terms), the creditor must provide the applicant with a statement containing the specific reasons for the action. If a creditor violates the ECOA, the consumer may bring a civil action against the creditor and recover actual damages (including emotional distress and embarrassment).

Fair Credit and Charge Card Disclosure Act

The **Fair Credit and Charge Card Disclosure Act**[19] is a federal statute that requires disclosure of credit terms on credit card and charge card solicitations and applications. The regulations adopted under the act require that any direct written

Fair Debt Collection Practices Act (FDCPA)
A federal act that protects consumer-debtors from abusive, deceptive, and unfair practices used by debt collectors.

Credit is a system whereby a person who can't pay gets another person who can't pay to guarantee that he can pay.

Charles Dickens

Equal Credit Opportunity Act (ECOA)
A federal statute that prohibits discrimination in the extension of credit based on sex, marital status, race, color, national origin, religion, age, or receipt of income from public assistance programs.

Fair Credit and Charge Card Disclosure Act
An amendment to the Truth-in-Lending Act (TILA) that requires disclosure of certain credit terms on credit card and charge card solicitations and applications.

Credit Card Accountability Responsibility and Disclosure Act of 2009 (Credit CARD Act)
A federal statute that requires disclosures to consumers concerning credit card terms, adds transparency to the creditor–debtor relationship, and eliminates many of the abusive practices of credit card issuers.

solicitation to a consumer display, in tabular form, the following information: (1) the APR, (2) any annual membership fee, (3) any minimum or fixed finance charge, (4) any transaction charge for use of the card for purchases, and (5) a statement that charges are due when the periodic statement is received by the debtor.

The following feature discusses the Credit CARD Act of 2009.

Contemporary Environment

Credit CARD Act of 2009

Currently, there are approximately 600 million credit cards in circulation in the United States, accounting for more than $900 billion of debt. These include credit cards issued by Visa, MasterCard, American Express, Discover, banks, department stores, gas stations, and others. The default rate on credit cards is more than 11 percent.

For many years, credit card companies, including banks and other issuers of credit cards, engaged in unfair, abusive, deceptive, and unethical practices that took advantage of consumer-debtors. Most of the practices did not, however, violate the law. This changed when Congress enacted the **Credit Card Accountability Responsibility and Disclosure Act of 2009**, commonly referred to as the **Credit CARD Act.**[20] This federal statute requires disclosures to consumers, adds transparency to the creditor–debtor relationship, and eliminates many of the abusive practices of credit card issuers.

Some of the main provisions of the Credit CARD Act are:

- Requires that the terms of the credit card agreement must be written in plain English and in no less than twelve-point font (thus avoiding "legalese" and fine-print agreements).
- Credit cards cannot be issued to anyone under the age of 21 (thus raising the minimum age from 18) unless they have a cosigner (e.g., parent) or they can prove they have the means to pay credit card expenses.
- Prohibits banks from giving promotional items (e.g., free pizza) to entice persons (e.g., college students) to sign up for a credit card.
- Provides that the interest rate and other terms of a credit card agreement must be stable during the first year of the card (unless there is a default where interest rates can be increased but that is subject to other restrictions of the act).
- Requires that payments above the minimum payment be applied to pay higher-interest balances first (whereas previously issuers applied payments to lower-interest balances first). The minimum payment can be applied to pay off lowest-interest-rate balances first.
- Prevents card companies from retroactively increasing interest rates on existing balances.
- Provides that if a card company intends to raise the interest rate, the card holder has the right to cancel the credit card.
- Provides that a card holder has the right to cancel a card without extra fees (e.g., no prepayment fees).
- Provides that if a card holder cancels a card, he or she has the right to pay off existing balances at the existing interest rate and on the existing payment schedule (e.g., current minimum monthly payment).
- Provides that for card holders who have been subject to an interest rate increase because of default but then pay on time for six months, the card issuer must return the interest rate to the rate prior to the rate increase.
- Prohibits the application of the "universal default" rule from being applied retroactively to existing balances that the card holder has on his or her credit cards. The universal default rule (which was used extensively by credit card companies prior to the act) allowed *all* credit card companies with whom a card holder had a credit card to raise the interest rate on their card, including on the existing balances, if the card holder was late in making a payment to *any* credit card company. The act does not eliminate the universal default rule but only permits credit card companies to apply the rule to future balances (subject to the notice and timing rules that allow a card holder to reject a card where the interest rate is being increased).
- Permits card holders to set fixed dollar limits on a credit card that cannot be exceeded, and if exceeded, prohibits card companies from charging an over-the-limit fee.
- Requires credit card companies to place their credit card agreements and amendments thereto online on a website so that card holders, potential card holders, government agencies, consumer protection organizations, and others can monitor the terms and changes in the terms of credit card agreements.
- Requires card companies to place a notice on each billing statement that notifies the card holder how long it would take to pay off the existing balance plus interest if the card holder were to make minimum payments on the card.
- Requires card companies to place a notice on each billing statement that notifies the card holder what monthly payment would be necessary for the cardholder to pay off the balance plus interest in 36 months.

The Credit CARD Act does not put an upper limit on the interest rate that can be charged on a credit card. Many credit card companies raised the interest rates on their cards before the Credit CARD Act became effective. The act does not apply to commercial or business credit cards. The Credit CARD Act imposes fines up to $5,000 per incident for violations of the act. Violations of the act are subject to criminal prosecution and civil lawsuits.

Key Terms and Concepts

Adulterated food (478)

Annual percentage rate (APR) (486)

Bait and switch (483)

Caveat emptor (477)

Consumer financial protection (484)

Consumer Financial Protection Act of 2010 (485)

Consumer Financial Protection Bureau (CFPB) (484)

Consumer Leasing Act (CLA) (486)

Consumer Product Safety Act (CPSA) (480)

Consumer Product Safety Commission (CPSC) (480)

Consumer protection laws (477)

Credit report (486)

Credit Card Accountability Responsibility and Disclosure Act of 2009

(Credit CARD Act) (488)

Debt collector (487)

Do-Not-Call Registry (483)

Dodd-Frank Wall Street Reform and Consumer Protection Act (484)

Door-to-door sales (483)

Drug Amendment to the FDCA (479)

Equal Credit Opportunity Act (ECOA) (487)

Fair and Accurate Credit Transactions Act (487)

Fair Credit and Charge Card Disclosure Act (487)

Fair Credit Billing Act (FCBA) (486)

Fair Credit Reporting Act (FCRA) (486)

Fair Debt Collection Practices Act (FDCPA) (487)

False and deceptive advertising (483)

False and misleading labeling (478)

Family Smoking Prevention and Tobacco Control Act (481)

Federal Communications Commission (FCC) (483)

Federal Trade Commission (FTC) (482)

Federal Trade Commission Act (FTC Act) (482)

Food and Drug Administration (FDA) (477)

Food, Drug, and Cosmetic Act (FDCA or FDC Act) (477)

Health Care and Education Reconciliation Act (482)

Health Care Reform Act (482)

Medicinal Device Amendment to the FDCA (480)

Mortgage Reform and Anti-Predatory Lending Act (485)

Nutrition Labeling and Education Act (NLEA) (478)

Patient Protection and Affordable Care Act (PPACA) (482)

Product safety standards (480)

Regulation Z (486)

Section 4205 of the Patient Protection and Affordable Care Act (478)

Section 5 of the FTC Act (483)

Truth-in-Lending Act (TILA) (485)

Unfair and deceptive practices (483)

United Nations Biosafety Protocol for Genetically Altered Foods (479)

U.S. Department of Agriculture (USDA) (477)

Law Case with Answer

United States v. Capital City Foods, Inc.

Facts   Capital City Foods, Inc., manufactured and distributed butter. The federal Food and Drug Administration (FDA) checked 9.1 pounds of butter produced by Capital City and found twenty-eight minuscule particles of insect parts, including twelve particles of fly hair, eleven unidentified insect fragments, two moth scales, two feather barbules, and one particle of rabbit hair. The overall ration was three particles of insect fragments per pound of butter. Evidence showed that some of these particles were visible to the naked eye, and some, such as the fly hair, would require a 30x microscope to see. The insect fragments were cooked and distributed in the finished butter. The federal Food, Drug, and Cosmetic Act, as interpreted by the FDA, provides that food is adulterated if it consists in whole or in part of any filthy substance or if is otherwise unfit for food. The U.S. government brought criminal charges against Capital City, based on alleged violations of the federal Food, Drug, and Cosmetic Act. Was the butter adulterated, in violation of the federal Food, Drug, and Cosmetic Act?

Answer   No, the butter was not adulterated and therefore did not violate the federal Food, Drug, and Cosmetic Act. The federal Food, Drug, and Cosmetic Act, as interpreted by the FDA, provides that food is adulterated if it consists in whole or in part of any filthy substance or if is otherwise unfit for food. Insect fragments in other than infinitesimal quantity are filth. However, few fresh foods contain no natural or unavoidable defects. Even with modern technology, all defects in foods cannot be eliminated. Foreign material cannot be wholly processed out of foods, and many contaminants introduced into foods through the environment can be reduced only by reducing their occurrence in the environment. If the FDA required food to be entirely pure and free of foreign material, then almost every food manufactured in the United States could be criminally prosecuted. This would obviously be an undesirable result. Therefore, the presence of a miniscule amount of filth in a food is insufficient for its condemnation. The contamination of the butter in this case is trifle and does not warrant banning the product. Capital City Foods is not criminally liable. *United States v. Capital City Foods, Inc.*, 345 F.Supp. 277, **Web** 1972 U.S. Dist. Lexis 12796 (United States District Court for North Dakota)

Critical Legal Thinking Cases

23.1 Food Regulation Barry Engel owned and operated the Gel Spice Co., Inc. (Gel Spice), which specialized in the importation and packaging of various food spices for resale. All the spices Gel Spice imported were unloaded at a pier in New York City and taken to a warehouse on McDonald Avenue. Storage and repackaging of the spices took place in the warehouse. During three years, the McDonald Avenue warehouse was inspected four times by investigators from the Food and Drug Administration (FDA). The investigators found live rats in bags of basil leaves, rodent droppings in boxes of chili peppers, and mammalian urine in bags of sesame seeds. The investigators produced additional evidence which showed that spices packaged and sold from the warehouse contained insects, rodent excreta pellets, rodent hair, and rodent urine. The FDA brought criminal charges against Engel and Gel Spice. Are they guilty? *United States v. Gel Spice Co., Inc.*, 601 F.Supp. 1205, **Web** 1984 U.S. Dist. Lexis 21041 (United States District Court for the Eastern District of New York)

23.2 Regulation of Drugs Dey Laboratories, Inc. (Dey), was a drug manufacturer operating in the state of Texas. Dey scientists created an inhalant known as ASI. The only active ingredient in ASI was atropine sulfate. The inhalant was sold to physicians, who then prescribed the medication for patients suffering from asthma, bronchitis, and other pulmonary diseases. Dey filed a new drug application with the Food and Drug Administration (FDA). Four months later, Dey was advised that its application would not be approved. Despite the lack of FDA approval, Dey began marketing ASI. The United States filed a complaint for forfeiture of all ASI manufactured by Dey. The inhalant was seized, and Dey sued to have the FDA's seizure declared illegal. Who wins? *United States v. Atropine Sulfate 1.0 Mg. (Article of Drug)*, 843 F.2d 860, **Web** 1988 U.S. App. Lexis 5817 (United States Court of Appeals for the Fifth Circuit)

23.3 Cosmetics Regulation FBNH Enterprises, Inc. (FBNH), was a distributor of a product known as French Bronze Tablets. The purpose of the tablets was to allow a person to achieve an even tan without exposure to the sun. When ingested, the tablets imparted color to the skin through the use of various ingredients, one of which is canthaxanthin, a coloring agent. The Food and Drug Administration (FDA) had not approved the use of canthaxanthin as a coloring additive. The FDA became aware that FBNH was marketing the tablets and that each contained 30 milligrams of canthaxanthin. The FDA filed a lawsuit, seeking the forfeiture and condemnation of eight cases of the tablets in the possession of FBNH. FBNH challenged the government's right to seize the tablets. Who wins? *United States v. Eight Unlabeled Cases of an Article of Cosmetic*, 888 F.2d 945, **Web** 1989 U.S. App. Lexis 15589 (United States Court of Appeals for the Second Circuit)

23.4 Drug Regulation Joseph Wahba had a prescription filled at Zuckerman's Pharmacy (Zuckerman's) in Brooklyn, New York. The prescription was for Lomotil, a drug used to counteract stomach disorders. The pharmacy dispensed thirty tablets in a small plastic container unequipped with a "childproof" cap. Joseph took the medicine home, where it was discovered by Wahba's 2-year-old son, Mark. Mark opened the container and ingested approximately twenty pills before Mark's mother saw him and stopped him. She rushed him to a hospital but, despite the efforts of the doctors, Mark lapsed into a coma and died. The Wahbas sued H&N Prescription Center, Inc., the company that owns Zuckerman's, for damages. Who wins? *Wahba v. H&N Prescription Center, Inc.*, 539 F.Supp. 352, **Web** 1982 U.S. Dist. Lexis 12327 (United States District Court for the Eastern District of New York)

23.5 Federal Trade Commission Act The Colgate-Palmolive Co. (Colgate) manufactured and sold a shaving cream called Rapid Shave. Colgate hired Ted Bates & Company (Bates), an advertising agency, to prepare television commercials designed to show that Rapid Shave could shave the toughest beards. With Colgate's consent, Bates prepared a television commercial that included the sandpaper test. The announcer informed the audience, "To prove Rapid Shave's super-moisturizing power, we put it right from the can onto this tough, dry sandpaper. And off in a stroke."

While the announcer was speaking, Rapid Shave was applied to a substance that appeared to be sandpaper, and immediately a razor was shown shaving the substance clean. Evidence showed that the substance resembling sandpaper was in fact a simulated prop, or "mock-up," made of Plexiglas to which sand had been glued. The Federal Trade Commission (FTC) issued a complaint against Colgate and Bates, alleging a violation of Section 5 of the Federal Trade Commission Act. Did the defendants act ethically in this case? Have the defendants acted ethically in this case? Have the defendants engaged in false and deceptive advertising, in violation of Section 5 of the FTC Act? *Federal Trade Commission v. Colgate-Palmolive Company*, 380 U.S. 374, 85 S.Ct. 1035, 13 L.Ed.2d 904, **Web** 1965 U.S. Lexis 2300 (Supreme Court of the United States)

23.6 Fair Credit Billing Oscar S. Gray had been an American Express cardholder. Gray used his card to purchase airline tickets costing $9,312. American Express agreed that Gray could pay for the tickets in twelve equal monthly installments. In January and February, Gray made substantial prepayments of $3,500 and $1,156, respectively. When his March bill arrived, Gray was surprised because American Express had converted the deferred payment plan to a currently due charge, making the entire amount for the tickets due and payable. Gray paid the normal monthly charge under the deferred payment plan and in April informed American Express in writing of its error. In the letter, Gray identified himself, his card number, and the nature of the error. Gray did not learn of any adverse action by American Express until almost one year later, on the night of his and his wife's anniversary. When he offered his American Express card to pay for their wedding anniversary dinner, the restaurant informed Gray that American Express had canceled his account and had instructed the restaurant to destroy the card. Gray sued American Express. Has American Express violated the Fair Credit Billing Act? Who wins? *Gray v. American Express Company*, 743 F.2d 10, **Web** 1984 U.S. App. Lexis 19033 (United States Court of Appeals for the Washington, DC, Circuit)

23.7 Fair Debt Collection Stanley M. Juras was a student at Montana State University (MSU). During his four years at MSU, Juras took out several student loans from the school, under the National Direct Student Loan program. By the time Juras left MSU, he owed the school over $5,000. Juras defaulted on these loans, and MSU assigned the debt to Aman Collection Services, Inc. (Aman), for purposes of collection. Aman obtained a judgment against Juras in a Montana state court for $5,015 on the debt and $1,920 in interest and attorneys' fees. Juras, who at the time lived in California, still refused to pay these amounts. Subsequently, a vice president of Aman, Mr. Gloss, telephoned Juras twice in California before 8:00 A.M. Pacific Standard Time. Gloss told Juras that if he did not pay the debt, he would not receive a college transcript. Juras sued Aman, claiming that the telephone calls violated the Fair Debt Collection Practices Act. Gloss testified at trial that he made the calls before 8:00 A.M. because he had forgotten the difference in time zones between California and Aman's offices in South Dakota. Who wins? *Juras v. Aman Collection Services, Inc.*, 829 F.2d 739, **Web** 1987 U.S. App. Lexis 12888 (United States Court of Appeals for the Ninth Circuit)

Ethics Cases

23.8 Ethics Charles of the Ritz Distributing Corporation (Ritz) was a New York corporation that engaged in the sale and distribution of a product called "Rejuvenescence Cream." The extensive advertising campaign that accompanied the sale of the cream placed emphasis upon the supposed rejuvenating powers of the products. The ads claimed that the cream would bring to the user's skin "quickly the clear radiance" and "the petal-like quality and texture of youth." Another advertisement claimed that the product would "restore natural moisture necessary for a live, healthy skin" with the result that "Your face need not know drought years." The Federal Trade Commission (FTC) learned of the ads and asked several experts to investigate the claimed benefits of Rejuvenescence Cream. The experts reported to the FTC that it is impossible for an external application of cosmetics to overcome skin conditions that result from physiological changes occurring with the passage of time. The FTC issued a cease-and-desist order with regard to the advertising. Ritz appealed the FTC's decision to a federal court. *Charles of the Ritz Distributing Corp. v. FTC*, 143 F.2d 676, **Web** 1944 U.S. App. Lexis 3172 (United States Court of Appeals for the Second Circuit)

1. Was does Section 5 of the Federal Trade Commission Act provide?
2. Did Ritz act ethically in making its advertising claims?
3. Who wins, and why?

23.9 Ethics Leon A. Tashof operated a store known as the New York Jewelry Company. The store was located in an area that served low-income consumers, many of whom had low-paying jobs and had no bank or charge accounts. About 85 percent of the store's sales were made on credit. The store advertised eyeglasses "from $7.50 complete," including "lenses, frames and case." Tashof advertised this sale extensively on radio and in newspapers. Evidence showed that of the 1,400 pairs of eyeglasses sold by the store, fewer than 10 were sold for $7.50; the rest were more expensive glasses. The Federal Trade Commission sued Tashof for engaging in bait-and-switch marketing, in violation of Section 5 of the Federal Trade Commission Act. *Tashof v. Federal Trade Commission*, 141 U.S. App. D.C. 274, 437 F.2d 707, **Web** 1970 U.S. App. Lexis 5809 (United States Court of Appeals for the District of Columbia Circuit)

1. What is "bait and switch"?
2. Was Tashof's conduct in this case ethical?
3. Who wins, and why?

Internet Exercises

1. Go to the website of the U.S. Department of Agriculture, at **www.usda.gov**. Read one of the articles currently listed on the website.

2. Visit the website of the Food and Drug Administration, at **www.fda.gov**. In the "Search" column type in the word "Vioxx" and then click "Go." What information do you find about this drug? Read it.

3. Visit the website of the Food and Drug Administration, at **www.fda.gov**. Click on "Cosmetics." Then click on "Quiz Yourself: How Smart Are You About Cosmetics." Take the quiz.

5. Visit the website of the Consumer Product Safety Commission (CPSC) at **www.cpsc.gov**. Find information about a product that the CPSC has recently recalled. What is the product, and why was it recalled?

6. Visit the website of the Federal Trade Commission, at **www.ftc.gov**. Click on "Consumer Protection." What is "Today's Tip"?

7. Go to **http://news.bbc.co.uk/1/hi/business/4391731.stm** and read the article "KFC burger advertisement banned."

8. Go to the website for consumer affairs of the European Union (EU), at **http://ec.europa.eu/consumers/safety/news/index_en.htm**. Choose one of the articles under "Latest safety news" and read it.

Endnotes

1. 21 U.S.C. Section 301.
2. Public Law 101-535.
3. 21 U.S.C. Section 321.
4. 21 U.S.C. Sections 360(c) et seq.
5. 15 U.S.C. Section 2051.
6. Public Law 111-31 (2009).
7. Public Law Sections 111–148.
8. Public Law Sections 111–152.
9. 15 U.S.C. Sections 41–51.
10. Public Law 111-203 (2010).
11. 15 U.S.C. Sections 1601–1667.
12. 12 C.F.R. 226.
13. 15 U.S.C. Sections 1667–1667f.
14. 15 U.S.C. Sections 1666–1666j.
15. 15 U.S.C. Sections 1681–1681u.
16. 15 U.S.C. Sections 1681–1681x.
17. 15 U.S.C. Sections 1692–1692f.
18. 15 U.S.C. Sections 1691–1691f.
19. 15 U.S.C. Sections 1637c–g.
20. Public Law 24, 123 Stat. 1734–1766.

24 Environmental Protection

SUN VALLEY, IDAHO
The federal and state governments have enacted many statutes to protect water, air, and the environment from pollution.

Learning Objectives

After studying this chapter, you should be able to:

1. Describe an environmental impact statement and identify when one is needed.
2. Describe the Clean Air Act and national ambient air quality standards.
3. Describe the Clean Water Act and effluent water standards.
4. Explain how environmental laws regulate the use of toxic substances and the disposal of hazardous wastes.
5. Describe how the Endangered Species Act protects endangered and threatened species and their habitats.

Chapter Outline

> *"All animals are equal but some animals are more equal than others."*
>
> —George Orwell
> *Animal Farm (1945)*

Introduction to Environmental Protection

We won't have a society if we destroy the environment.

Margaret Mead

Businesses and consumers generate air pollution, water pollution, and hazardous and toxic wastes that cause harm to the environment and human health. Pollution has reached alarming rates in this country and the rest of the world. Pollution causes injury and death to various forms of wildlife, pollutes drinking water, pollutes the air we breathe, and harms human health and the environment.

Federal and state governments have enacted environmental protection laws to contain the levels of pollution and to clean up hazardous waste sites in this country. Many laws provide both civil and criminal penalties. This chapter covers the major federal and state laws that protect the environment from pollution.

Environmental Protection

In the 1970s, the federal government began enacting statutes to protect our nation's air and water from pollution, to regulate hazardous wastes, and to protect wildlife. In many instances, states have enacted their own environmental laws that now coexist with federal law. These laws provide both civil and criminal penalties. **Environmental protection** is one of the most important, and costly, issues facing business and society today.

Environmental Protection Agency

Environmental Protection Agency (EPA)
A federal administrative agency created by Congress to coordinate the implementation and enforcement of the federal environmental protection laws.

In 1970, Congress created the **Environmental Protection Agency (EPA)** to coordinate the enforcement of the federal **environmental protection laws**. The EPA has broad rule-making powers to adopt regulations to advance the laws that it is empowered to administer. The agency also has adjudicative powers to hold hearings, make decisions, and order remedies for violations of federal environmental laws. In addition, the EPA can initiate judicial proceedings in court against suspected violators of federal environmental laws.

Environmental Impact Statement

National Environmental Policy Act (NEPA)
A federal statute which mandates that the federal government consider the adverse impact a federal government action would have on the environment before the action is implemented.

environmental impact statement (EIS)
A document that must be prepared for any proposed legislation or major federal action that significantly affects the quality of the human environment.

The **National Environmental Policy Act (NEPA)** became effective January 1, 1970.[1] The NEPA mandates that the federal government consider the "adverse impact" of proposed legislation, rule making, or other federal government action on the environment before the action is implemented. The EPA administers the NEPA and has the authority to adopt regulations for the enforcement of the act.

The NEPA and EPA regulations require that an **environmental impact statement (EIS)** be prepared by the federal government for any proposed legislation or major federal action that significantly affects the quality of the natural and human environment.

Examples The federal government must prepare an EIS for a proposed construction project involving highways, bridges, waterways, nuclear power plants, and such.

The purpose of an EIS is to provide enough information about the environment to enable the federal government to determine the feasibility of the project. An EIS must (1) describe the affected environment, (2) describe the impact of the proposed federal action on the environment, (3) identify and discuss alternatives to the proposed action, (4) list the resources that will be committed to the action, and (5) contain a cost–benefit analysis of the proposed action and alternative actions. Expert professionals, such as engineers, geologists, and accountants, may be consulted during the preparation of an EIS.

Once an EIS is prepared and published, interested parties can submit comments to the EPA. After the comments have been received and reviewed, the EPA will issue an order that states whether the proposed federal action may proceed. An EIS can be challenged in court by environmentalists and other interested parties. Many projects have been blocked or altered because of such challenges.

Most states and many local governments have enacted laws that require an EIS to be prepared regarding proposed state and local government action as well as private development. State and local laws often require private parties who want to build resorts, housing projects, or other major developments to file an EIS or equivalent document. These projects can be challenged in state court. Where a private action is challenged, the parties often settle the dispute.

Example A real estate developer proposes to build a one thousand-house project on private land. Environmentalists challenge the development, arguing that it will destroy a wildlife habitat. The developer and environmentalists may settle the case in a number of ways. For example, the developer might agree to build fewer houses or to give part of the property to the government for a wildlife preserve.

Air Pollution

One of the major problems facing the United States is **air pollution**. The **Clean Air Act**[2] was enacted in 1963 to assist states in dealing with air pollution. The act was amended in 1970 and 1977 and, most recently, by the **Clean Air Act Amendments** of 1990.[3] The Clean Air Act, as amended, provides comprehensive regulation of air quality in this country.

Sources of Air Pollution

Substantial amounts of air pollution are emitted by **stationary sources of air pollution** (e.g., industrial plants, oil refineries, public utilities). The Clean Air Act requires states to identify major stationary sources and develop plans to reduce air pollution from these sources.

Automobile and other vehicle emissions are a major source of air pollution in this country. In an effort to control emissions from these **mobile sources of air pollution**, the Clean Air Act requires air pollution controls to be installed on motor vehicles. Emission standards have been set for automobiles, trucks, buses, motorcycles, and airplanes. In addition, the Clean Air Act authorizes the EPA to regulate air pollution caused by fuel and fuel additives.

National Ambient Air Quality Standards

The Clean Air Act directs the EPA to establish **national ambient air quality standards (NAAQS)** for certain pollutants. These standards are set at two different levels: primary (to protect human beings) and secondary (to protect vegetation, matter, climate, visibility, and economic values). Specific standards have been established for carbon monoxide, nitrogen oxide, sulfur oxide, ozone, lead, and particulate matter.

Although the EPA establishes air quality standards, the states are responsible for their enforcement. The federal government has the right to enforce these air pollution standards if the states fail to do so. Each state is required to prepare a **state implementation plan (SIP)** that sets out how the state plans to meet the federal standards. The EPA has divided each state into **air quality control regions (AQCRs)**. Each region is monitored to ensure compliance.

air pollution
Pollution caused by factories, homes, vehicles, and the like that affects the air.

Clean Air Act
A federal statute that provides comprehensive regulation of air quality in the United States.

national ambient air quality standards (NAAQS)
Standards for certain pollutants set by the EPA that protect (1) human beings (primary level) and (2) vegetation, matter, climate, visibility, and economic values (secondary level).

Nonattainment Areas

nonattainment area
A geographical area that does not meet established air quality standards.

Regions that do not meet air quality standards are designated **nonattainment areas**. A nonattainment area is classified into one of five categories—*marginal, moderate, serious, severe,* or *extreme*—based on the degree to which it exceeds the ozone standard. Deadlines are established for areas to meet the attainment level.

States must submit compliance plans that (1) identify major sources of air pollution and require them to install pollution-control equipment, (2) institute permit systems for new stationary sources, and (3) implement inspection programs to monitor mobile sources. States that fail to develop or implement approved plans are subject to the following sanctions: loss of federal highway funds and limitations on new sources of emissions (e.g., the EPA can prohibit the construction of a new pollution-causing industrial plant in a nonattainment area).

The following feature discusses a modern source of air pollution.

Contemporary Environment

Indoor Air Pollution Causes Health Risks

According to officials at the Environmental Protection Agency (EPA), the air inside some buildings may be one hundred times more polluted than outside air. Doctors increasingly attribute a wide range of symptoms to **indoor air pollution**, or **sick building syndrome**. Indoor air pollution has two primary causes. In an effort to reduce dependence on foreign oil, many recently constructed office buildings have been overly insulated and built with sealed windows and no outside air ducts. As a result, no fresh air enters many workplaces. This lack of fresh air can cause headaches, fatigue, and dizziness among workers.

The other chief cause of sick building syndrome, which is believed to affect up to one-third of U.S. office buildings, is hazardous chemicals and construction materials. In the office, these include everything from asbestos to noxious fumes omitted from copy machines, carbonless paper, and cleaning fluids. In the home, radon, an odorless gas that is emitted from the natural breakdown of uranium in soil, poses a particularly widespread danger. Radon gas damages and may destroy lung tissue. The costs of eliminating these conditions can be colossal.

Sick building syndrome is likely to spawn a flood of litigation, with a wide range of parties being sued. Manufacturers, employers, home sellers, builders, engineers, and architects will increasingly be forced to defend themselves against tort and breach of contract actions filed by homeowners, employees, and others affected by indoor air pollution. Insurance companies will undoubtedly be drawn into costly lawsuits stemming from indoor air pollution.

Water Pollution

water pollution
Pollution of lakes, rivers, oceans, and other bodies of water.

Water pollution affects human health, recreation, agriculture, and business. Pollution of waterways by industry and humans has caused severe ecological and environmental problems, including making water sources unsafe for human consumption, fish, birds, and animals. The federal government has enacted a comprehensive scheme of statutes and regulations to prevent and control water pollution.

In 1948, Congress enacted the **Federal Water Pollution Control Act (FWPCA)**[4] to regulate water pollution. This act has been amended several times. As amended, it is simply referred to as the **Clean Water Act**.[5] This act is administered by the EPA.

Clean Water Act
A federal statute that establishes water quality standards and regulates water pollution.

Pursuant to the Clean Water Act, the EPA has established water quality standards that define which bodies of water can be used for public drinking water, recreation (e.g., swimming), propagation of fish and wildlife, and agricultural and industrial uses. States are primarily responsible for enforcing the provisions of the Clean Water Act and EPA regulations adopted thereunder. If a state fails to do so, the federal government may enforce the act.

Point Sources of Water Pollution

The Clean Water Act authorizes the EPA to establish water pollution control standards for **point sources of water pollution**. Point sources are sources of pollution that are fixed and stationary. Point source dischargers of pollutants are required to maintain monitoring equipment, keep samples of discharges, and keep records.

Examples Mines, manufacturing plants, paper mills, electric utility plants, and municipal sewage plants are examples of stationary sources of water pollution.

In the following case, the U.S. Supreme Court decided an important water pollution issue.

CASE 24.1 *U.S. SUPREME COURT Water Pollution*

Entergy Corporation v. Riverkeeper, Inc.

129 S.Ct. 1498, 173 L.Ed.2d 369, Web 2009 U.S. Lexis 2498 (2009)
Supreme Court of the United States

"In the requirements challenged here the EPA sought only to avoid extreme disparities between costs and benefits."

—Scalia, Justice

Facts

Entergy Corporation operates large power plants that generate electrical power. In the course of generating power, these plants also generate large amounts of heat. To cool its facilities, Entergy uses cooling water intake structures that extract water from nearby water sources. These structures pose various risks to the environment, particularly to aquatic organisms that live in the affected water, by squashing them against intake screens (called "impingement") or suctioning them into the cooling system (called "entrainment").

The Clean Water Act mandates that a point source of pollution, such as a power plant, install the "best technology" available for minimizing adverse environmental impact.[6] The Environmental Protection Agency (EPA) adopted a rule that requires new power plants to install the "most effective technology" to reduce impingement and entrainment mortality by up to 98 percent.

The EPA conducted a cost–benefit analysis and adopted a different rule for existing power plants. This EPA rule allows existing plants to deploy a mix of less expensive technology that is "commercially available and practicable." This technology would reduce impingement and entrainment by more than 80 percent. Thus, the EPA chose not to require existing plants to deploy the more expensive but most effective technology that it requires for new power plants.

Riverkeeper, Inc., and other environmental groups (Riverkeeper) challenged the EPA rule for existing power plants, alleging that the EPA was not empowered to use cost–benefit analysis when setting performance standards for power plants. Riverkeeper asserted that the Clean Water Act's "best technology" language requires existing power plants to deploy the most effective technology equal to that required of new power plants. The U.S. Court of Appeals held that the EPA's use of cost–benefit analysis was impermissible and set aside the EPA's rule for existing power plants. Entergy appealed to the U.S. Supreme Court.

Issue

Is the EPA permitted to use cost–benefit analysis in promulgating rules for technology to be deployed by existing point sources of water pollution under the Clean Water Act?

Language of the U.S. Supreme Court

In the requirements challenged here the EPA sought only to avoid extreme disparities between costs and benefits. It surely tends to show that the EPA's current practice is a reasonable and hence legitimate exercise of its discretion to weigh benefits against costs. Even respondents ultimately recognize that some form of cost–benefit analysis is permissible. They acknowledge that the statute's language is "plainly not so constricted as to require EPA to require industry petitioners to spend billions to save one more fish or plankton."[7]

(continued)

Decision

The U.S. Supreme Court held that the EPA is permitted to use cost–benefit analysis in setting performance standards for point sources of water pollution.

Case Questions

Critical Legal Thinking

Do you think that the EPA should be able to use a cost–benefit analysis in setting rules to enforce the Clean Water Act?

Ethics

Do companies such as Entergy owe a duty of social responsibility to voluntarily adopt the most effective technology available to reduce water pollution?

Contemporary Business

What would have been the consequences if the U.S. Supreme Court had not allowed the EPA to use cost–benefit analysis, and existing power plants would have had to adopt the most effective technology for reducing water pollution?

Thermal Pollution

thermal pollution
Heated water or material discharged into waterways that upsets the ecological balance and decreases the oxygen content.

The Clean Water Act expressly forbids **thermal pollution** because the discharge of heated water or materials into the nation's waterways can upset the ecological balance; decrease the oxygen content of water; and harm fish, birds, and other animals that use the waterways.[8] Sources of thermal pollution (e.g., electric utility companies, manufacturing plants) are subject to the provisions of the Clean Water Act and regulations adopted by the EPA.

Examples Electric utility plants and manufacturing plants often cause thermal pollution by discharging heated water or materials into the water. This heated water or material could harm fish in the water as well as birds and other animals that use the water.

Wetlands

wetlands
Areas that are inundated or saturated by surface water or ground water that support vegetation typically adapted for life in such conditions.

Wetlands are defined as areas that are inundated or saturated by surface water or ground water that support vegetation typically adapted for life in saturated soil conditions. Wetlands include swamps, marshes, bogs, and similar areas that support birds, animals, and vegetative life. The federal Clean Water Act regulates the discharge of dredged or fill material into navigable water and wetlands that have a significant nexus to navigable waters. The **U.S. Army Corps of Engineers (USACE)** is authorized to enforce this statute and to issue permits for discharge of dredged or fill material into navigable waters and qualified wetlands in the United States. The Clean Water Act forbids the filling or dredging of navigable waters and qualified wetlands unless a permit has been obtained from the Army Corps of Engineers.

Example Thomas owns 40 acres of beachfront property in a rural area that fronts an inland lake. On Thomas's property, there is high ground upon which houses can be built and there are ponds and wetland areas that cannot support buildings. The ponds and wetlands are a result of the lake flowing into the ponds and wetlands on the property. The ponds are therefore considered navigable waters under the Clean Water Act. Swans and other birds and animals use the wetlands as their habitat. Thomas secretly fills in the ponds and wetlands to create more hard ground upon which additional houses can be built. The Army Corps of Engineers is empowered to bring proceedings against Thomas to correct his illegal act and to report Thomas for criminal proceedings.

Safe Drinking Water Act

Safe Drinking Water Act
A federal statute that authorizes the EPA to establish national primary drinking water standards.

The **Safe Drinking Water Act**,[9] enacted in 1974 and amended in 1986, authorizes the EPA to establish national primary drinking water standards (setting the minimum quality of water for human consumption). The act prohibits the dumping of wastes into wells used for drinking water. The states are primarily responsible for enforcing the act. If a state fails to do so, the federal government can enforce the act.

Ocean Pollution

The **Marine Protection, Research, and Sanctuaries Act**,[10] enacted in 1972, extends environmental protection to the oceans. It (1) requires a permit for dumping wastes and other foreign materials into ocean waters and (2) establishes marine sanctuaries in ocean waters as far seaward as the edge of the continental shelf and in the Great Lakes and their connecting waters. The Clean Water Act authorizes the U.S. government to clean up oil spills and spills of other hazardous substances in ocean waters within 12 miles of the shore and on the continental shelf and to recover the cleanup costs from responsible parties.

There have been several major oil spills from oil tankers and oil drilling facilities in ocean waters off the coast of the United States. These oil spills have caused significant damage to plant, animal, and human life, as well as to their habitats. In response, in 1990, Congress enacted the federal **Oil Pollution Act**,[11] which is administered by the U.S. Coast Guard. This act requires the oil industry to adopt procedures and contingency plans to readily respond to and clean up oil spills. A tanker owner-operator must prove that it is fully insured to cover any liability that may occur from an oil spill. The act also requires oil tankers to have double hulls by 2015.

The following feature discusses the BP oil spill in the Gulf of Mexico.

Marine Protection, Research, and Sanctuaries Act
A federal statute that extends limited environmental protection to the oceans.

Oil Pollution Act
A federal statute that requires the oil industry to take measures to prevent oil spills and to readily respond to and clean up oil spills.

Ethics

BP Oil Spill

In 2010, the *Deepwater Horizon* oil spill—commonly referred to as the *BP oil spill*—occurred in the Gulf of Mexico. This oil spill was caused by a leak in a mobile off-shore oil drilling rig called Deepwater Horizon. This rig was drilling on a platform owned by BP p.l.c. (formerly British Petroleum), a global oil and gas company headquartered in London. An exploratory well was being drilled at a depth of approximately 5,000 feet when an explosion occurred, killing eleven workers and injuring many others. This explosion caused a sea-floor oil gusher that began spilling oil into the ocean waters that continued for more than three months. The spill gushed more than five million barrels of oil over a 5,000 mile area of the Gulf of Mexico before the leak was finally capped.

The oil spill caused extensive damage to hundreds of miles of coastline, particularly in Louisiana, Florida, Mississippi, and other southern states. Thousands of marine animals were killed, including sea turtles, dolphins, and other mammals. Tens of thousands of birds perished as well. Hundreds of species of marine animals and birds specific to the area are at risk of possible extinction. The projected three-year loss to tourism in the affected communities from the spill is more than $25 billion. The extent of the damage to the marine environment and the ecosystem

of the Gulf Coast and the affected states will not be known for years.

The BP oil spill was the largest in U.S. history; in fact, it was more than twenty times larger than the previously largest oil spill, the *Exxon-Valdez* oil spill in the waters off the coast of Alaska. That spill was caused when the oil tanker *Exxon-Valdez* struck a reef in Prince Edward Sound and began leaking oil into the waters off Alaska. The oil spill severely damaged the coastline of Alaska, ruined fishing grounds, and caused the deaths of thousands of marine and fish species. The litigation in that case went on for over twenty years, with Exxon-Mobil Corporation, the primary defendant, paying over $1 billion to settle some of the cases against it. In one case that went to trial, a jury awarded $287 million in compensatory damages and assessed punitive damages of $5 billion. The case went to the U.S. Supreme Court, which ruled that the amount of punitive damages that could be awarded in a maritime case can be no more than equal to the amount of compensatory damages, a 1:1 ratio.[12] This limit will be applied if punitive damages are assessed against BP and the other defendants in BP oil spill cases.

The BP oil spill is one of the greatest environmental disasters in U.S. history. The damage caused to the

(continued)

coastline and to the ecosystem will take decades to restore, and some of the damage will never be repaired. A class action lawsuit involving more than sixty thousand claims has been filed against the defendants, and thousands of other individual claims have also been filed. BP has sued the other defendants, who have in turn countersued against BP and each other. Insurance companies will end up paying a substantial portion of the damages, although they too will fight among themselves about which company's insured is responsible.

The civil lawsuits against BP and the other parties could go on for several decades before they are resolved, either through settlements of court decisions.

Ethics Questions How many individuals' lives were severely affected by the BP oil spill? Do you think that all of them will be fully compensated? Are the damages difficult to assess? Should punitive damages in marine cases be limited to no more than compensatory damages?

Toxic Substances and Hazardous Wastes

toxic substances
Chemicals used by agriculture, industry, business, mining, and households that cause injury to humans, birds, animals, fish, and vegetation.

Many chemicals used by agriculture, industry, business, mining, and households contain **toxic substances** that cause cancer, birth defects, and other health-related problems in human beings, as well as injury or death to birds, fish, other animals, and vegetation. Many chemical compounds that are used in the manufacture of products are toxic (e.g., PCBs, asbestos). Each year, hundreds of chemicals and chemical compounds are found to be possibly toxic.

Agriculture, mining, industry, other businesses, and households generate wastes that often contain hazardous substances that can harm the environment or pose danger to human health. The mishandling and disposal of *hazardous wastes* can cause air, water, and land pollution.

Examples Hazardous wastes consist of garbage, sewage, industrial discharges, old equipment, and such that are discharged or placed in the environment.

Toxic Substances Control

Toxic Substances Control Act
A federal statute that authorizes the EPA to regulate toxic substances.

In 1976, Congress enacted the **Toxic Substances Control Act**[13] and gave the EPA authority to administer the act. The act requires the EPA to identify **toxic air pollutants** that present a substantial risk of injury to human health or the environment. So far, more than two hundred chemicals have been listed as toxic, including asbestos, mercury, vinyl chloride, benzene, beryllium, and radionuclides.

The act requires the EPA to establish standards for toxic chemicals and requires stationary sources to install equipment and technology to control emissions of toxic substances. EPA standards for toxic substances are set without regard to economic or technological feasibility. The act requires manufacturers and processors to test new chemicals to determine their effects on human health and the environment and to report the results to the EPA before the chemicals are marketed.

The EPA may limit or prohibit the manufacture and sale of toxic substances, and it can remove them from commerce if it finds that they pose an imminent hazard or an unreasonable risk of injury to human health or the environment. The EPA also requires special labeling of toxic substances.

Insecticides, Fungicides, and Rodenticides

Insecticide, Fungicide, and Rodenticide Act
A federal statute that requires pesticides, herbicides, fungicides, and rodenticides to be registered with the EPA; the EPA may deny, suspend, or cancel registration.

land pollution
Pollution of the land that is generally caused by hazardous waste being disposed of in an improper manner.

Resource Conservation and Recovery Act (RCRA)
A federal statute that authorizes the EPA to regulate facilities that generate, treat, store, transport, and dispose of hazardous wastes.

Farmers and ranchers use chemical pesticides, herbicides, fungicides, and rodenticides to kill insects, weeds, and pests. Evidence shows that the use of some of these chemicals on food and their residual accumulation in soil pose health hazards. In 1947, Congress enacted the **Insecticide, Fungicide, and Rodenticide Act**, which gave the federal government authority to regulate pesticides and related chemicals. This act, which was substantially amended in 1972,[14] is administered by the EPA. Under the act, pesticides must be registered with the EPA before they can be sold. The EPA may suspend the registration of a registered pesticide that it finds poses an imminent danger or emergency.

Hazardous Waste

The disposal of hazardous wastes sometimes causes **land pollution**. In 1976, Congress enacted the **Resource Conservation and Recovery Act (RCRA)**,[15] which regulates the disposal of new hazardous wastes. This act, which has been amended several times, authorizes the EPA to regulate facilities that generate, treat, store, transport, and dispose of hazardous wastes. States have primary responsibility for implementing the standards established by the act and EPA regulations.

The act defines **hazardous waste** as a solid waste that may cause or significantly contribute to an increase in mortality or serious illness or pose a hazard to human health or the environment if improperly managed. The EPA has designated substances that are toxic, radioactive, or corrosive or ignitable as hazardous and can add to the list of hazardous wastes as needed.

The EPA also establishes standards and procedures for the safe treatment, storage, disposal, and transportation of hazardous wastes. Under the act, the EPA is authorized to regulate underground storage facilities, such as underground gasoline tanks.

The following feature discusses an important environmental law.

hazardous waste
Hazardous waste that may cause or significantly contribute to an increase in mortality or serious illness or pose a hazard to human health or the environment if improperly managed.

Comprehensive Environmental Response, Compensation, and Liability Act (CERCLA or Superfund)
A federal statute that authorizes the federal government to deal with hazardous wastes. The act creates a monetary fund to finance the cleanup of hazardous waste sites.

Landmark Law

Superfund

In 1980, Congress enacted the **Comprehensive Environmental Response, Compensation, and Liability Act (CERCLA)**, which is commonly called the **Superfund**.[16] The act is administered by the EPA. The act gives the federal government a mandate to deal with hazardous wastes that have been spilled, stored, or abandoned. The act provides for the creation of a government fund to finance the cleanup of hazardous waste sites (hence the name *Superfund*). The fund is financed through taxes on chemicals, feedstock, motor fuels, and other products that contain hazardous substances.

The Superfund requires the EPA to (1) identify sites in the United States where hazardous wastes have been disposed of, stored, abandoned, or spilled and (2) rank these sites regarding the severity of the risk. The hazardous waste sites with the highest ranking receive first consideration for cleanup.

The EPA can order a responsible party to clean up a hazardous waste site. If that party fails to do so, the EPA can spend Superfund money and clean up the site and recover the cost of the cleanup from responsible parties. The Superfund imposes **strict liability**—that is, liability without fault. The EPA can recover the cost of the cleanup from (1) the generator who deposited the wastes, (2) the transporter of the wastes to the site, (3) the owner of the site at the time of the disposal, and (4) the current owner and operator of the site.

The Superfund permits states and private parties who clean up hazardous waste sites to seek reimbursement from the fund. The EPA has the authority to clean up hazardous sites quickly to prevent fire, explosion, contamination of drinking water, and other imminent danger.

WEB EXERCISE
Go to **www.epa.gov/superfund/** and find out the closest EPA Superfund site to your hometown. How far away is the polluted site from your hometown? Why is it listed as a Superfund site?

Nuclear Waste

Nuclear-powered fuel plants create radioactive wastes that maintain a high level of *radioactivity*. Radioactivity can cause injury and death to humans and other life and can also cause severe damage to the environment. Accidents, human error, faulty construction, and such can all be causes of **radiation pollution**.

The **Nuclear Regulatory Commission (NRC)**, which was created by Congress in 1977, licenses the construction and opening of commercial nuclear power plants. It continually monitors the operation of nuclear power plants and may close a plant if safety violations are found. The EPA is empowered to set standards for radioactivity in the environment and to regulate the disposal of radioactive waste. The EPA

radiation pollution
Emissions from radioactive wastes that can cause injury and death to humans and other life and can cause severe damage to the environment.

Nuclear Regulatory Commission (NRC)
A federal agency that licenses the construction and opening of commercial nuclear power plants.

Endangered Species Act
A federal statute that protects endangered and threatened species of wildlife.

also regulates thermal pollution from nuclear power plants and emissions from uranium mines and mills. The **Nuclear Waste Policy Act** of 1982[17] mandates that the federal government select a permanent site for the disposal of **nuclear wastes**.

Endangered Species

Many species of birds, fish, reptiles, and animals are endangered or threatened with extinction. The reduction of certain species of wildlife may be caused by environmental pollution, real estate development, or hunting. The **Endangered Species Act** was enacted in 1973.[18] The act, as amended, protects *endangered* and *threatened* species of wildlife. The secretary of the interior is empowered to declare a form of wildlife as endangered or threatened.

The act requires the EPA and the Department of Commerce to designate *critical habitats* for each endangered and threatened species. Real estate and other development in these areas is prohibited or severely limited. The secretary of commerce is empowered to enforce the provisions of the act as to marine species. In addition, the Endangered Species Act, which applies to both government and private persons, prohibits the taking of any endangered species. *Taking* is defined as an act intended to "harass, harm, pursue, hunt, shoot, wound, kill, trap, capture, or collect" an endangered animal.

Numerous other federal laws protect wildlife. These include (1) the Migratory Bird Treaty Act, (2) the Bald Eagle Protection Act, (3) the Wild Free-Roaming Horses and Burros Act, (4) the Marine Mammal Protection Act, (5) the Migratory Bird Conservation Act, (6) the Fishery Conservation and Management Act, (7) the Fish and Wildlife Coordination Act, and (8) the National Wildlife Refuge System. Many states have enacted statutes that protect and preserve wildlife.

The following is a classic case of the application of the Endangered Species Act.

Landmark Law

Endangered Species: Snail Darter Saved from Extinction

"It may seem curious to some that the survival of a relatively small number of 3-inch fish among all the countless millions of species extant would require the permanent halting of a virtually completed dam for which Congress has expended more than $100 million."

—Burger, Chief Justice

The Tennessee Valley Authority (TVA) is a wholly owned public corporation of the United States. It operates a series of dams, reservoirs, and water projects that provide electric power, irrigation, and flood control to areas in several southern states. With appropriations from Congress, the TVA began construction of the Tellico Dam on the Little Tennessee River. When completed, the dam would impound water covering 16,500 acres, thereby converting the river's shallow, fast-flowing waters into a deep reservoir over 30 miles long.

Seven years after construction began, a previously unknown species of perch called the *Percina tanasi*—or "snail darter"—was found in the Little Tennessee River. After further investigation, it was determined that approximately 10,000 to 15,000 of these 3-inch fish existed in the river's waters that would be flooded by the operation of the Tellico Dam. The snail darter is not found anywhere else in the world. It feeds exclusively on snails and requires substan-

tial oxygen, both supplied by the fast-moving waters of the Little Tennessee River. The impounding of the water behind the Tellico Dam would destroy the snail darter's food and oxygen supplies, thus causing its extinction.

Congress continued to appropriate funds for the construction of the dam, which was completed at a cost of more than $100 million. A regional association of biological scientists, a Tennessee conservation group, filed an action seeking to enjoin the TVA from closing the gates of the dam and impounding the water in the reservoir on the grounds that those actions would violate the Endangered Species Act by causing the extinction of the snail darter. The District Court held in favor of the TVA. The Court of Appeals reversed and issued a permanent injunction halting the operation of the Tellico Dam. The TVA appealed to the U.S. Supreme Court.

The U.S. Supreme Court held that the Endangered Species Act prohibited the impoundment of the Little Tennessee River by the Tellico Dam. The Supreme Court affirmed the injunction against the operation of the dam. The Court stated:

It may seem curious to some that the survival of a relatively small number of 3-inch fish among all the countless millions of species extant would require the permanent halting of a virtually completed dam for which Congress has expended more than $100 million.

We conclude, however, that the explicit provisions of the Endangered Species Act required precisely this result.

Eventually, after substantial research and investigation, it was determined that the snail darter could live in another habitat that was found for it. After the snail darter was

removed to this new location, the TVA was permitted to close the gates of the Tellico Dam and begin its operation. *Tennessee Valley Authority v. Hill, Secretary of the Interior*, 437 U.S. 153, 98 S.Ct. 2279, 57 L.Ed.2d 117, **Web** 1978 U.S. Lexis 33 (Supreme Court of the United States)

State Environmental Protection Laws

Many state and local governments have enacted statutes and ordinances to protect the environment. Most states require that an EIS or a report be prepared for any proposed state action. In addition, under their police power to protect the "health, safety, and welfare" of their residents, many states require private industry to prepare EISs for proposed developments. Some states have enacted special environmental statutes to protect unique areas within their boundaries.

Examples Florida has enacted laws to protect the Everglades subtropical landscape, California has enacted laws to protect its Pacific Ocean coastline, Washington has enacted laws to protect the water ecosystem of Puget Sound, and Alaska has enacted laws to protect its wilderness areas.

International Law

Global Warming

MONGOLIA
*Even places like the rural country of Mongolia feel the effects of pollution caused by the industrialized countries of the world. For decades, some scientists and others have been concerned that **greenhouse gases** that are released into the air—particularly from carbon dioxide created by burning coal, oil, and gas, as well as deforestation—are causing an increase in atmospheric temperature. This is referred to as **global warming**. Global warming is blamed for sea levels rising worldwide, primarily due to the melting of glaciers and ice caps. Rising global temperature are predicted to increase the occurrence and intensity of extreme weather events, changes in agricultural yields, increases in diseases, and the extinction of species.*

Key Terms and Concepts

Air pollution (495)
Air quality control regions (AQCRs) (495)
Clean Air Act (495)
Clean Air Act Amendments (495)
Clean Water Act (496)
Comprehensive Environmental Response, Compensation, and Liability Act (CERCLA or Superfund) (501)
Endangered Species Act (502)
Environmental impact statement (EIS) (494)
Environmental Protection Agency (EPA) (494)

Environmental protection (494)
Environmental protection laws (494)
Federal Water Pollution Control Act (FWPCA) (496)
Global warming (503)
Greenhouse gases (503)
Hazardous wastes (501)
Indoor air pollution (sick building syndrome) (496)
Insecticide, Fungicide, and Rodenticide Act (500)
Land pollution (501)
Marine Protection, Research, and Sanctuaries Act (499)

Mobile sources of air pollution (495)
National ambient air quality standards (NAAQS) (495)
National Environmental Policy Act (NEPA) (494)
Nonattainment areas (496)
Nuclear Regulatory Commission (NRC) (501)
Nuclear Waste Policy Act (502)
Nuclear wastes (502)
Oil Pollution Act (499)
Point sources of water pollution (497)
Radiation pollution (501)

Resource Conservation and Recovery Act (RCRA) (501)
Safe Drinking Water Act (498)
State implementation plan (SIP) (495)
Stationary sources of air pollution (495)
Strict liability (501)
Thermal pollution (498)
Toxic air pollutants (500)
Toxic substances (500)
Toxic Substances Control Act (500)
U.S. Army Corps of Engineers (USACE) (498)
Water pollution (496)
Wetlands (498)

Law Case with Answer
Solid Waste Agency of North Cook County v. United States Army Corps of Engineers

Facts   Section 404 of the federal Clean Water Act (CWA) regulates the discharge of dredged or fill material into *navigable waters*. The U.S. Army Corps of Engineers (Corps) is authorized to enforce this statute and to issue permits for discharge of dredged or fill material into navigable waters in the United States. Section 404 defines navigable waters as "the waters of the United States, including the territorial seas." The Solid Waste Agency of Northern Cook County, Illinois (Agency), a consortium of twenty-three suburban Chicago cities and villages, located a 533-acre parcel of real property that was a closed sand and gravel pit mining operation as a proposed disposal site for placing baled nonhazardous solid waste. Long since abandoned, the old mining site had permanent and seasonal water ponds of varying sizes and depths that served several species of migrating birds. The ponds were not connected to any water tributary but were filled by rain water and melting snow. Corps refused to issue the requested permit. Agency sued Corps, arguing that Corps had no jurisdiction over the site because it did not contain any *navigable waters*. Does the gravel and sand pit contain navigable waters that give the Army Corps of Engineers jurisdiction over the site?

Answer   No. The gravel and sand pit does not contain navigable waters, and thus the Army Corps of Engineers has no jurisdiction over the site. Corps could therefore not block Agency's use of the abandoned sand and gravel pit as the dumping site for its solid wastes. Congress enacted the Clean Water Act for the purpose of restoring and maintaining the chemical, physical, and biological integrity of the nation's water. Section 404 authorizes the U.S. Army Corps of Engineers to regulate the discharge of fill material into "navigable waters," which the statute defines as "the waters of the United States, including the territorial seas." Corps interpreted these words to cover the abandoned gravel pit at issue here because it is used as habitat for migratory birds. However, isolated ponds, some only seasonal, wholly located within Illinois, do not fall under Section 404's definition of "navigable waters" merely because they serve as habitat for migratory birds. The ponds located on the sand and gravel pit are not navigable waters, as defined by Section 404 of the Clean Water Act. Therefore, the U.S. Army Corps of Engineers does not have authority or jurisdiction over these ponds. *Solid Waste Agency of Northern Cook County v. United States Army Corps of Engineers*, 531 U.S. 159, 121 S.Ct. 675, 148 L.Ed.2d 576, **Web** 2001 U.S. Lexis 640 (Supreme Court of the United States)

Critical Legal Thinking Cases

24.1 Environmental Impact Statement The U.S. Forest Service is responsible for managing the country's national forests for recreational and other purposes. This includes issuing special-use permits to private companies to operate ski areas on federal lands. Sandy Butte is a 6,000-foot mountain located in the Okanogan National Forest in Okanogan County, Washington. Sandy Butte, like the Methow Valley it overlooks, is a pristine, unspoiled, sparsely populated area located within the North Cascades National Park. Large populations of mule deer and other animals exist in the park.

Methow Recreation, Inc. (MRI), applied to the Forest Service for a special-use permit to develop and operate its proposed Early Winters Ski Resort on Sandy Butte and a 1,165-acre parcel of private land it had acquired adjacent to the national forest. The proposed development would make use of approximately 3,900 acres of Sandy Butte to provide up to 16 ski lifts capable of accommodating 10,500 skiers at one time. Is an environmental impact statement required? *Robertson v. Methow Valley Citizens Council*, 490 U.S. 332, 109 S.Ct. 1835, 104 L.Ed.2d 351, **Web** 1989 U.S. Lexis 2160 (Supreme Court of the United States)

24.2 Clean Air Act Pilot Petroleum Associates, Inc., and various affiliated companies distributed gasoline to retail gasoline stations in the state of New York. Pilot owned some of these stations and leased them to individual operators who were under contract to purchase gasoline from Pilot. The EPA took samples of gasoline from five different service stations to which Pilot had sold unleaded gasoline. These samples showed that Pilot had delivered "unleaded gasoline that contained amounts of lead in excess of that permitted by the Clean Air Act and EPA regulations." The United States brought criminal charges against Pilot for violating the act and EPA regulations and sought fines from Pilot. Who wins? *United States v. Pilot Petroleum Associates, Inc.*, 712 F.Supp. 1077, **Web** 1989 U.S. Dist. Lexis 6119 (United States District Court for the Eastern District of New York)

24.3 Wetlands Leslie Salt Company owned a 153-acre tract of undeveloped land south of San Francisco. The property abutted the San Francisco National Wildlife Refuge and was approximately one-quarter mile from Newark Slough, a tidal arm of San Francisco Bay. Originally, the property was pastureland. The first change occurred in the early 1900s, when Leslie's predecessors constructed facilities to manufacture salt on the property. They excavated pits and created large, shallow, watertight basins on the property. Salt production on the property was stopped in 1959. The construction of a sewer line and public roads on and around the property created ditches and culverts on the property. Newark Slough is connected to the property by these culverts, and tidewaters reach the property. Water accumulates in the ponds, ditches, and culverts, providing wetland vegetation to wildlife and migratory birds. Fish live in the ponds on the property. More than twenty-five years later, Leslie started to dig a ditch to drain the property and began construction to block the culvert that connected the property to the Newark Slough. The Army Corps of Engineers issued a cease-and-desist order against Leslie. Leslie challenged the order. Who wins? *Leslie Salt Co. v. United States*, 896 F.2d 354, **Web** 1990 U.S. App. Lexis 1524 (United States Court of Appeals for the Ninth Circuit)

24.4 Clean Water Act The Reserve Mining Company (Reserve) owned and operated a mine in Minnesota that was located on the shores of Lake Superior and produced hazardous waste. Reserve obtained a permit from the state of Minnesota to dump its wastes into Lake Superior. The permits prohibited discharges that would "result in any clouding or discoloration of the water outside the specific discharge zone" or "result in any material adverse affects on public water supplies." Reserve discharged its wastes into Lake Superior for years. Evidence showed that the discharges caused discoloration of surface waters outside the zone of discharge and contained carcinogens that adversely affected public water supplies. The United States sued Reserve for engaging in unlawful water pollution. Who wins? *United States v. Reserve Mining Company*, 543 F.2d 1210, **Web** 1976 U.S. App. Lexis 6503 (United States Court of Appeals for the Eighth Circuit)

24.5 Hazardous Waste Douglas Hoflin was the director of the Public Works Department for Ocean Shores, Washington. During a period of seven years, the department purchased 3,500 gallons of paint for road maintenance. As painting jobs were finished, the 55-gallon drums that had contained the paint were returned to the department's yard. Paint contains hazardous substances such as lead. When fourteen of the drums were discovered to still contain unused paint, Hoflin instructed employees to haul the paint drums to the city's sewage treatment plant and bury them. The employees dug a hole on the grounds of the treatment plant and dumped in the drums. Some of the drums were rusted and leaking. The hole was not deep enough, so the employees crushed the drums with a front-end loader to make them fit. The refuse was then covered with sand. Almost two years later, one of the city's employees reported the incident to state authorities, who referred the matter to the EPA. Investigation showed that the paint had contaminated the soil. The United States brought criminal charges against Hoflin for aiding and abetting the illegal dumping of hazardous waste. Who wins? *United States v. Hoflin*, 880 F.2d 1033, **Web** 1989 U.S. App. Lexis 10169 (United States Court of Appeals for the Ninth Circuit)

24.6 Nuclear Waste   Metropolitan Edison Company owned and operated two nuclear-fueled power plants at Three Mile Island near Harrisburg, Pennsylvania. Both power plants were licensed by the NRC after extensive proceedings and investigations, including the preparation of the required environmental impact statements. When one of the power plants was shut down for refueling, the other plant suffered a serious accident that damaged the reactor. The governor of Pennsylvania recommended an evacuation of all pregnant women and small children, and many area residents did leave their homes for several days. As it turned out, no dangerous radiation was released.

People Against Nuclear Energy (PANE), an association of area residents who opposed further operation of the nuclear power plants at Three Mile Island, sued to enjoin the plants from reopening. They argued that the reopening of the plants would cause severe psychological health damage to persons living in the vicinity and serious damage to the stability and cohesiveness of the community. Are these reasons sufficient to prevent the reopening of the nuclear power plants?

Metropolitan Edison Company v. People Against Nuclear Energy, 460 U.S. 766, 103 S.Ct. 1556, 75 L.Ed.2d 534, **Web** 1983 U.S. Lexis 21 (Supreme Court of the United States)

24.7 Endangered Species   The red-cockaded woodpecker is a small bird that lives almost exclusively in old pine forests throughout the southern United States. Its survival depends on a very specialized habitat of pine trees that are at least thirty, if not sixty, years old, in which they build nests and forage for insects. The population of this bird decreased substantially as pine forests were destroyed by clear-cutting. The U.S. secretary of the interior has named the red-cockaded woodpecker an endangered species.

The U.S. Forest Service manages federal forests and is charged with duties to provide recreation, protect wildlife, and provide timber. To accomplish the charge of providing timber, the Forest Service often leases national forest lands to private companies for lumbering. When the Forest Service proposed to lease several national forests in Texas, where the red-cockaded woodpecker lives, to private companies for lumbering, the Sierra Club, an environmental organization, sued. The Sierra Club sought to enjoin the Forest Service from leasing these national forests for lumbering. Who wins? *Sierra Club v. Lyng, Secretary of Agriculture*, 694 F.Supp. 1260, **Web** 1988 U.S. Dist. Lexis 9203 (United States District Court for the Eastern District of Texas)

Ethics Cases

24.8 Ethics   The state of Michigan owns approximately 57,000 acres of land that comprise the Pigeon River County State Forest in southwestern Michigan. Shell Oil Company applied to the Michigan Department of Natural Resources (DNR) for a permit to drill ten exploratory oil wells in the forest. Roads had to be constructed to reach the proposed drill sites. Evidence showed that the only sizable elk herd east of the Mississippi River annually used the forest as its habitat and returned to this range every year to breed. Experts testified that elk avoid roads, even when there is no traffic, and that the construction of the roads and wells would destroy the elk's habitat. Michigan law prohibits activities that adversely affect natural resources. The West Michigan Environmental Action Council sued the DNR, seeking to enjoin the DNR from granting the drilling permits to Shell. *West Michigan Environmental Action Council, Inc.*

v. Natural Resources Commission, 405 Mich. 741, 275 N.W.2d 538, **Web** 1979 Mich. Lexis 347 (Supreme Court of Michigan)

1. What did the state of Michigan law provide?
2. Did Shell Oil Company act socially responsibly in this case?
3. Who wins, and why?

24.9 Ethics   Riverside Bayview Homes, Inc. (Riverside), owned 80 acres of low-lying marshland—wetlands—near the shores of Lake St. Clair in Macomb County, Michigan. Riverside began to fill in the wetlands with hard materials as part of its preparations for construction of a housing development. Riverside did not notify the Army Corps of Engineers (Corps) nor obtain permit to fill in the wetlands. Upon discovery of Riverside's activities, the Corps sued, seeking to enjoin Riverside from discharging a pollutant (fill) onto wetlands. *United States v. Riverside Bayview Homes, Inc.*, 474 U.S. 121, 106 S.Ct. 455, 88 L.Ed.2d 419, **Web** 1985 U.S. Lexis 145 (Supreme Court of the United States)

1. What are wetlands?
2. Did Riverside Bayview Homes act ethically in this case?
3. Is the property in this case subject to the Army Corps of Engineers permit system?

Internet Exercises

1. Visit the website of the U.S. Environmental Protection Agency, at **www.epa.gov**.

2. Go to **www.epa.gov/air/criteria.html** and read information about national ambient air quality standards (NAAQS).

3. Visit the website of the Army Corps of Engineers, at **www.usace.army.mil**. What is the Army Corps of Engineers, and what is its mission?

4. The website of the Nuclear Regulatory Commission (NRC) is **www.nrc.gov**. Go to this website and read what this agency does.

5. Go to the website **www.fws.gov/endangered/**. Has any new species recently been added to the endangered species list? Has any species been removed from the endangered species list?

6. Go to the website of the U.S. Environmental Protection Agency, at **www.epa.gov**. Click on "Newsroom." Click "Regional Newsrooms" and then select your state. Read a current news release.

Endnotes

1. 42 U.S.C. Sections 4321–4370d
2. Public Law 88-206.
3. 42 U.S.C. Sections 7401–7671q.
4. 33 U.S.C. Sections 1251–1376, 62 Stat. 1155.
5. 33 U.S.C. Sections 1251–1367.
6. 33 U.S.C. Section 1326(b).
7. Brief for Respondents Riverkeeper, Inc. 29.
8. 33 U.S.C. Section 1254(t).
9. 21 U.S.C. Sections 349 and 300f–300j-25.
10. 16 U.S.C. Sections 1431 et seq.; 33 U.S.C. Sections 1401–1445.
11. 33 U.S.C. Sections 2701–2761.
12. *Exxon Shipping Company v. Baker*, 554 U.S. 471 (Supreme Court of the United States).
13. 15 U.S.C. Sections 2601–2692.
14. 7 U.S.C. Sections 135 et seq.
15. 42 U.S.C. Sections 6901–6986.
16. 42 U.S.C. Sections 9601–9675.
17. 42 U.S.C. Sections 10101–10270.
18. 16 U.S.C. Sections 1531–1544

CHAPTER

25 Land Use Regulation and Real Property

COTTAGE, MACKINAC ISLAND, MICHIGAN
A person's house is often his most valuable asset.

Learning Objectives

After studying this chapter, you should be able to:

1. List and describe the different types of real property.
2. Describe the different types of freehold estates and future interests in real property.
3. Identify the different types of joint tenancy and concurrent ownership of real property.
4. Describe the rights of landlords and tenants.
5. Describe civil rights acts, eminent domain, zoning, and government regulation of property.

Chapter Outline

Introduction to Land Use Regulation and Real Property

Real Property
  CONTEMPORARY ENVIRONMENT • *Air Rights*

Estates in Land

Concurrent Ownership
  CASE 25.1 • *Cunningham v. Hastings*

Future Interests

Transfer of Ownership of Real Property

Adverse Possession

Nonpossessory Interests

Landlord–Tenant Relationship
  CONTEMPORARY ENVIRONMENT • *Rent Control*

Civil Rights Laws

Zoning

Eminent Domain and "Taking"
  CONTEMPORARY ENVIRONMENT • *The* Kelo *Takings Case*

> " *Without that sense of security which property gives, the land would still be uncultivated.*"
>
> —Francois Quesnay
> *Maximes, IV*

Introduction to Land Use Regulation and Real Property

Property and ownership rights in *real property* play an important part in the society and economy of the United States. Individuals and families own houses, farmers and ranchers own farmland and ranches, and businesses own commercial and office buildings. The concept of real property is concerned with the legal rights to the property. Individuals and families rent houses and apartments, professionals and businesses lease office space, small businesses rent stores, and businesses lease commercial and manufacturing facilities. In these situations, a *landlord–tenant relationship* is created.

The ownership and possession of real estate in the United States is commonly a private affair. However, the ownership and leasing of real property is not free from government regulation. Federal, state, and local governments have enacted many laws to regulate the ownership, possession, lease, and use of real property. These laws include antidiscrimination laws, zoning laws, and the like. The government may also take private property for public use under its power of *eminent domain*, assuming that certain requirements are met and just compensation is paid to the owner. This is referred to as *land use regulation*.

This chapter covers the law concerning the ownership and transfer of real property, laws concerning landlord–tenant relationships, and the government regulation of real estate.

> Property and law are born and must die together.
>
> Jeremy Bentham
> *Principles of the Civil Code, I Works 309*

> Only a ghost can exist without material property.
>
> Ayn Rand
> *Atlas Shrugged (1957)*

Real Property

Property is usually classified as either real or personal property. **Real property** is immovable or attached to immovable land or buildings, whereas personal property is movable. The various types of real property are described in the following paragraphs.

real property
The land itself as well as buildings, trees, soil, minerals, timber, plants, and other things permanently affixed to the land.

Land and Buildings

Land is the most common form of real property. A landowner usually purchases the **surface rights** to the land—that is, the right to occupy the land. The owner may use, enjoy, and develop the property as he or she sees fit, subject to any applicable government regulation.

Buildings constructed on land are real property. Houses, apartment buildings, manufacturing plants, and office buildings constructed on land are real property. Such things as radio towers and bridges are usually considered real property as well.

Subsurface Rights

The owner of land possesses **subsurface rights**, or **mineral rights**, to the earth located beneath the surface of the land. These rights can be very valuable. Gold, uranium, oil, or natural gas may lie beneath the surface of the land. Theoretically, mineral rights extend to the center of the earth. In reality, mines and oil wells usually extend only several miles into the earth. Subsurface rights may be sold separately from surface rights.

subsurface rights (mineral rights)
Rights to the earth located beneath the surface of the land.

Plant Life and Vegetation

plant life and vegetation
Plants growing on the surface of land that are considered real property.

Plant life and vegetation growing on the surface of land are considered real property. Such vegetation includes both natural plant life (e.g., trees) and cultivated plant life (e.g., crops). When land is sold, any plant life growing on the land is included, unless the parties agree otherwise. Plant life that is severed from the land is considered personal property.

Fixtures

fixtures
Goods that are affixed to real estate so as to become part thereof.

Certain personal property is so closely associated with real property that it becomes part of the realty. Such items are called **fixtures**.

air rights
Rights to air space parcels above their land that the owners of land may sell or lease.

Example Kitchen cabinets, carpet, and doorknobs are fixtures, but throw rugs and furniture are personal property. Unless otherwise provided, if a building is sold, the fixtures are included in the sale. If the sale agreement is silent as to whether an item is a fixture, the courts make their determination on the basis of whether the item can be removed without causing substantial damage to the realty.

The following feature discusses air rights.

Contemporary Environment

Air Rights

Common law provided that the owners of real property owned that property from the center of the earth to the heavens. This rule has been eroded by modern legal restrictions such as land use regulation laws, environmental protection laws, and air navigation requirements. Even today, however, the owners of land may sell or lease air space parcels above their land; this is referred to as **air rights**.

An **air space parcel** is the air space above the surface of the earth of an owner's real property. Air space parcels are valuable property rights, particularly in densely populated metropolitan areas, where building property is scarce.

Examples Railroads have made money by leasing or selling air rights over their railroad tracks. For example, the Grand Central Terminal in New York City sold air rights over its railroad property for the construction of the PanAm

Building (now MetLife Building) next to Grand Central Terminal. Many other developments have been built in air space parcels in New York City.

Owners of highways—including states and cities—often sell or lease air rights over the highways. Fast-food restaurants and gasoline stations are often located on air rights over freeways.

In addition, air rights are often developed so that **historic buildings** can be preserved. This is often accomplished by a city permitting a developer to purchase air rights above the historic building in exchange for preserving the historic building.

Owners of air rights and parties who want to build on those air rights will continue to come up with unique solutions to meet building needs.

Estates in Land

estate in land (estate)
Ownership rights in real property; the bundle of legal rights that an owner has to possess, use, and enjoy the property.

A person's ownership right in real property is called an **estate in land** (or **estate**). An estate is defined as the bundle of *legal rights* that the owner has to possess, use, and enjoy the property. The type of estate that an owner possesses is determined from the deed, will, lease, or other document that transferred the ownership rights to him or her.

Freehold Estate

freehold estate
An estate in which the owner has a present possessory interest in the real property.

A **freehold estate** is an estate in which the owner has a **present possessory interest** in the real property; that is, the owner may use and enjoy the property as he or she sees fit, subject to any applicable government regulation or private restraint. There are three types of freehold estates: *fee simple absolute* (or *fee simple*), *fee simple defeasible* (or *qualified fee*), and *life estate*. These are discussed in the following paragraphs.

Fee Simple Absolute (or Fee Simple)

A **fee simple absolute** (or **fee simple**) is an estate in fee that is the highest form of ownership of real property because it grants the owner the fullest bundle of legal rights that a person can hold in real property. It is the type of ownership most people connect with "owning" real property. A fee simple owner has the right to exclusively possess and use his or her property to the extent that the owner has not transferred any interest in the property (e.g., by lease).

If a person owns real property in fee simple, his or her ownership (1) is infinite in duration (fee), (2) has no limitation on inheritability (simple), and (3) does not end upon the happening of any event (absolute).

Example Mary owns a fee simple absolute in a piece of real property. This means that there are no limitations on her ownership rights. Mary owns this property while she is alive, with no conditions on her ownership rights, and she can transfer the property by will to a named beneficiary or beneficiaries when she dies.

fee simple absolute (fee simple)
A type of ownership of real property that grants the owner the fullest bundle of legal rights that a person can hold in real property.

Fee Simple Defeasible (or Qualified Fee)

A **fee simple defeasible** (or **qualified fee**) grants the owner all the incidents of a fee simple absolute except that ownership may be taken away if a specified *condition* occurs or does not occur.

Example A conveyance of property to a church "as long as the land is used as a church or for church purposes" creates a qualified fee. The church has all the rights of a fee simple absolute owner except that its ownership rights are terminated if the property is no longer used for church purposes.

fee simple defeasible (qualified fee)
A type of ownership of real property that grants the owner all the incidents of a fee simple absolute except that it may be taken away if a specified condition occurs or does not occur.

Life Estate

A **life estate** is an interest in real property that lasts for the life of a specified person, usually the grantee. The person who is given a life estate is called the **life tenant**. For example, an owner of real estate who makes a conveyance of real property "to Anna for her life" creates a life estate. A life estate may also be measured by the life of a third party, which is called **estate pour autre vie** (e.g., "To Anna for the life of Benjamin"). A life estate may be defeasible (e.g., "To John for his life but only if he continues to occupy this residence").

A life tenant is treated as the owner of the property throughout the duration of the life estate. He or she has the right to possess and use the property except to the extent that it would cause permanent *waste* of the property. Upon the death of the life tenant, the life estate terminates, and the property reverts to the grantor or the grantor's estate or another designated person.

life estate
An interest in real property for a person's lifetime; upon that person's death, the interest is transferred to another party.

estate pour autre vie
A life estate that is measured by the life of a third party.

The right of property has not made poverty, but it has powerfully contributed to make wealth.

J.R. McCulloch
Principles of Political Economy (1825)

CONCEPT SUMMARY
FREEHOLD ESTATES

Estate	Description
Fee simple absolute	Is the highest form of ownership of real property. Ownership (1) is infinite in duration, (2) has no limitation on inheritability, and (3) does not end upon the occurrence or nonoccurrence of an event.
Fee simple defeasible	Grants the owner all the incidents of a fee simple absolute except that it may be taken away if a specified condition occurs or does not occur.
Life estate	Is an interest in property that lasts for the life of a specified person. A life estate terminates upon the death of the named person and reverts back to the grantor or his or her estate or other designated person.

Concurrent Ownership

Two or more persons may own a piece of real property. This is called **concurrent ownership**, or **co-ownership**. The following forms of co-ownership of real property are recognized: *joint tenancy, tenancy in common, tenancy by the entirety, community property, condominiums,* and *cooperatives.*

Joint Tenancy

Two or more parties can own real estate as **joint tenants**. To create a **joint tenancy**, words that clearly show a person's intent to create a joint tenancy must be used. Language such as "Marsha Leest and James Leest, as joint tenants" is usually sufficient.

The distinguishing feature of a joint tenancy is the co-owners' **right of survivorship**. This means that upon the death of one of the co-owners (or joint tenants), the deceased person's interest in the property automatically passes to the surviving joint tenant or joint tenants. Any contrary provision in the deceased's will is ineffective.

Example ZiYi, Heathcliff, Manuel, and Mohammad own a large commercial building as joint tenants. They are joint tenants with the right to survivorship. Heathcliff executes a will that leaves all of his property to his alma mater university. Heathcliff dies. The surviving joint tenants—ZiYi, Manuel, and Mohammad—and not the university—acquire Heathcliff's ownership interest in the building. ZiYi, Manuel, and Mohammad are now joint tenants with a one-third interest in the building.

Each joint tenant has a right to sell or transfer his or her interest in the property, but such conveyance terminates the joint tenancy. The parties then become tenants in common.

Example ZiYi, Heathcliff, Manuel, and Mohammad own a large commercial building as joint tenants. They are joint tenants with the right to survivorship. ZiYi sells her one-quarter interest in the building to Wolfgang. At that time, the joint tenancy is broken, and the four owners—Wolfgang, Heathcliff, Manuel, and Mohammad—become tenants in common, with no right of survivorship. Wolfgang executes a will that leaves all of his property to his alma mater university. Wolfgang dies. Because the owners are not joint tenants, but are instead tenants in common, Wolfgang's quarter interest in the building goes to the university. The university is now a tenant in common with Heathcliff, Manuel, and Mohammad.

Tenancy in Common

In a **tenancy in common**, the interests of a surviving tenant in common pass to the deceased tenant's estate and not to the co-tenants. The parties to a tenancy in common are called **tenants in common**. A tenancy in common may be created by express words (e.g., "Ian Cespedes and Joy Park, as tenants in common"). Unless otherwise agreed, a tenant in common can sell, give, devise, or otherwise transfer his or her interest in the property without the consent of the other co-owners.

Example Lopez, who is one of four tenants in common who own a piece of property, has a will that leaves all his property to his granddaughter. When Lopez dies, the granddaughter receives his interest in the tenancy in common, and the granddaughter becomes a tenant in common with the other three owners.

In the following case, the court had to decide how to split the proceeds from the sale of real property owned by two co-owners.

CASE 25.1 *Concurrent Ownership of Real Property*

Cunningham v. Hastings

556 N.E.2d 12, Web 1990 Ind.App. Lexis 764
Court of Appeals of Indiana

"Once a joint tenancy relationship is found to exist between two people in a partition action, it is axiomatic that each person owns a one-half interest."

—Baker, Judge

Facts

Warren R. Hastings and Joan L. Cunningham, who were unmarried, purchased a house together. Hastings paid a $45,000 down payment toward the purchase price, out of his own funds. The deed referred to Hastings and Cunningham as "joint tenants with the right of survivorship." Hastings and Cunningham occupied the property jointly. After their relationship ended, Hastings took sole possession of the property. Cunningham filed a complaint, seeking partition of the real estate. Based on its determination that the property could not be split, the trial court ordered it to be sold. The trial court further ordered that the sale proceeds be paid to Hastings to reimburse him for his down payment and that the remainder of the proceeds be divided equally between Hastings and Cunningham. Cunningham appealed, alleging that Hastings should not have been given credit for the down payment.

Issue

Is Cunningham entitled to an equal share of the proceeds of the sale of the real estate?

Language of the Court

> The parties do not dispute that the unequivocal language of the deed created a joint tenancy in the real estate. The determination of the parties' interests in the present case is simple. There are only two parties involved in the joint tenancy. Once a joint tenancy relationship is found to exist between two people in a partition action, it is axiomatic that each person owns a one-half interest. Based

> on this reasoning, we find that the trial court erred in allowing Hastings a $45,000 credit for the purchase price he paid. Regardless of who provided the money to purchase the land, the creation of a joint tenancy relationship entitles each party to an equal share of the proceeds of the sale upon partition. Equitable adjustments to cotenants' equal shares are allowed when the cotenants hold the property as tenants in common, not when they hold as joint tenants. The deed in the case before us unequivocally states that the parties held the property as joint tenants, not as tenants in common.

Decision

The court of appeals held that Cunningham was entitled to an equal share of the proceeds of the sale because she and Hastings owned the property as joint tenants. The court of appeals reversed the trial court's judgment and remanded the case to the trial court, with instructions to order the entire proceeds of the sale to be divided equally between Cunningham and Hastings.

Case Questions

Critical Legal Thinking
Do you think most people understand the legal consequences of taking title in the various forms?

Ethics
Did Cunningham act ethically in demanding one-half the value of the down payment even though she did not contribute to it?

Contemporary Business
Could Hastings have protected the $45,000 he paid for the down payment? If so, how could he have done it?

Tenancy by the Entirety

Tenancy by the entirety is a form of co-ownership of real property that can be used only by married couples. This type of tenancy must be created by express words (e.g., "Harold Jones and Maude Jones, husband and wife, as tenants by the entirety"). A surviving spouse has the right of survivorship. Tenancy by the

tenancy by the entirety
A form of co-ownership of real property that can be used only by married couples.

entirety is distinguished from joint tenancy in that neither spouse may sell or transfer his or her interest in the property without the other spouse's consent. Only about half of the states recognize tenancy by the entirety.

Community Property

community property
A form of ownership in which each spouse owns an equal one-half share of the income of both spouses and the assets acquired during the marriage.

Nine states—Arizona, California, Idaho, Louisiana, Nevada, New Mexico, Texas, Washington, and Wisconsin—recognize a form of co-ownership known as **community property**. This method of co-ownership applies only to married couples. It is based on the notion that a husband and wife should share equally in the fruits of the marital partnership. Under these laws, each spouse owns an equal one-half share of the *income* both spouses earned during the marriage and one-half of the *assets acquired by this income during the marriage*, regardless of who earns the income. Property that is acquired through gift or inheritance either before or during marriage remains **separate property**. Interest payments, dividends, and appreciation of separate property received or accrued during marriage is also separate property.

When a spouse dies, the surviving spouse automatically receives one-half of the community property. The other half passes to the heirs of the deceased spouse, as directed by will or by state intestate statute if there is no will. During the marriage, neither spouse can sell, transfer, or gift community property without the consent of the other spouse. Upon a divorce, each spouse has a right to one-half of the community property.

The location of the real property determines whether community property law applies. If a married couple who lives in a noncommunity property state purchases real property located in a community property state, community property laws apply to that property.

Example Elma is a successful brain surgeon who makes $500,000 income per year. She meets and marries Brad, a struggling actor who makes $10,000 per year. When Elma gets married, she owns $1 million of real estate and $2 million in securities, which she retains as her separate property. Brad has no separate property when he and Elma are married. After three years, Elma and Brad get a divorce. Assume that Elma has made $500,000 and Brad has made $10,000 each of the three years of their marriage, their living expenses were $110,000 per year, and they have $1.2 million of earned income saved in a bank account. During the marriage, Elma's real estate has increased in value to $1.5 million, and her securities have increased in value to $3 million. Upon divorce, Elma receives her $1.5 million in real estate and $3 million in securities as her separate property. If they live in a state that recognizes community property, Elma and Brad each receive $600,000 from the community property bank account.

CONCEPT SUMMARY
CONCURRENT OWNERSHIP

Form of Ownership	Right of Survivorship	Tenant May Unilaterally Transfer His or Her Interest
Joint tenancy	Yes, deceased tenant's interest automatically passes to co-tenants.	Yes, tenant may transfer his or her interest without the consent of co-tenants. Transfer severs joint tenancy.
Tenancy in common	No, deceased tenant's interest passes to his or her estate.	Yes, tenant may transfer his or her interest without the consent of co-tenants. Transfer does not sever tenancy in common.

Form of Ownership	Right of Survivorship	Tenant May Unilaterally Transfer His or Her Interest
Tenancy by the entirety	Yes, deceased tenant's interest automatically passes to his or her spouse.	No, neither spouse may transfer his or her interest without the other spouse's consent.
Community property	Yes, when a spouse dies, the surviving spouse automatically receives one-half of the community property. The other half passes to the heirs of the deceased spouse, as directed by a valid will or by state intestate statute if there is no will.	No, neither spouse may transfer his or her interest without the other spouse's consent.

Condominium

Condominiums are a common form of ownership in multiple-dwelling buildings. Purchasers of a condominium (1) have title to their individual units and (2) own the common areas (e.g., hallways, elevators, parking areas, recreational facilities) as tenants in common with the other owners. Owners may sell or mortgage their units without the permission of the other owners. Owners are assessed monthly fees for the maintenance of common areas. In addition to being used for dwelling units, the condominium form of ownership is often used for office buildings, boat docks, and such.

condominium
A common form of ownership in a multiple-dwelling building where the purchaser has title to the individual unit and owns the common areas as a tenant in common with the other condominium owners.

Cooperative

A **cooperative** is a form of co-ownership of a multiple-dwelling building in which a corporation owns the building, and the residents own shares in the corporation. Each cooperative owner leases a unit in the building from the corporation under a renewable, long-term, proprietary lease. Individual residents may not secure loans for the units they occupy. The corporation can borrow money on a blanket mortgage, and each shareholder is jointly and severally liable on the loan. Usually, cooperative owners may not sell their shares or sublease their units without the approval of the other owners.

cooperative
A form of co-ownership of a multiple-dwelling building in which a corporation owns the building and the residents own shares in the corporation.

Future Interests

A person may be given the right to possess property in the *future* rather than in the present. This right is called a **future interest**. The two forms of future interests are *reversion* and *remainder*.

future interest
The interest that a grantor retains for himself or herself or a third party.

Reversion

A **reversion** is a right of possession that returns to the grantor after the expiration of a limited or contingent estate. Reversions do not have to be expressly stated because they arise automatically by law.

reversion
A right of possession that returns to a grantor after the expiration of a limited or contingent estate.

Example Edgar, an owner of real property, conveys his property "to Harriet Lawson for life." The grantor, Edgar, has retained a reversion in the property. That is, when Harriet dies, the property reverts to Edgar or, if he is not living, to his estate.

Remainder

If the right of possession returns to a *third party* upon the expiration of a limited or contingent estate, it is called a **remainder**. The person who is entitled to the future interest is called a **remainder beneficiary**.

remainder
A right of possession that returns to a third party upon the expiration of a limited or contingent estate. A person who possesses this right is called a *remainder beneficiary.*

Example Janice, an owner of real property, conveys her property "to Joe Jackson for life, remainder to Meredith Smith." This creates a vested remainder, with Meredith being the remainder beneficiary. The only contingency to Meredith's possessory interest is Joe's death. When Joe dies, Meredith obtains ownership to the property, or if she is not living, it goes to her estate.

CONCEPT SUMMARY
FUTURE INTERESTS

Future Interest	Description
Reversion	Right to possession of real property returns to the grantor after the expiration of a limited or contingent estate.
Remainder	Right to possession of real property goes to a third person upon the expiration of a limited or contingent estate.

Transfer of Ownership of Real Property

Ownership of real property can be transferred from one person to another. Title to real property can be transferred by sale; tax sale; gift, will, or inheritance; and adverse possession. The different methods of transfer provide different degrees of protection to the transferee.

Sale of Real Estate

sale (conveyance)
The passing of title from a seller to a buyer for a price.

A **sale**, or **conveyance**, is the most common method for transferring ownership rights in real property. An owner may offer his or her real estate for sale either by himself or herself or by using a real estate broker. When a buyer has been located and the parties have negotiated the terms of the sale, a **real estate sales contract** is executed by the parties. The Statute of Frauds in most states requires this contract to be in writing.

The seller delivers a deed to the buyer, and the buyer pays the purchase price at the **closing**, or **settlement**. Unless otherwise agreed, it is implied that the seller is conveying fee simple absolute title to the buyer. If either party fails to perform, the other party may sue for breach of contract and obtain either monetary damages or specific performance.

Deeds

deed
An instrument that describes a person's ownership interest in a piece of real property.

grantor
A party who transfers an ownership interest in real property.

grantee
A party to whom an interest in real property is transferred.

general warranty deed (grant deed)
A deed that protects a grantee of real property from defects in title caused by the grantor and prior owners of the property.

Deeds are used to convey real property by sale or gift. The seller or donor is called the **grantor**. The buyer or recipient is called the **grantee**. A deed may be used to transfer a fee simple absolute interest in real property or any lesser estate (e.g., life estate). State laws recognize different types of deeds that provide different degrees of protection to grantees. These types of deeds are as follows.

- **General warranty deed.** A **general warranty deed** (or **grant deed**) contains the greatest number of warranties and provides the highest level of protection to a grantee. A general warranty deed is usually used as a deed from a seller to a buyer of real property. In a general warranty deed, the seller warrants that he owns the property and has the legal right to sell it; that the property is not subject to encumbrances (e.g., mortgages), leases, or easements other than those that are disclosed; that his title is superior to any other claim of title to the property; that he will defend the grantee's title against all other claims; and that he will compensate the grantee for any losses suffered if title proves faulty. The guarantee is not limited to the time that the grantor owned the property but extends back to the property's origins.

Although the grantor is legally bound to compensate the grantee for losses caused by a breach of warranty, this guarantee is not helpful if the grantor is dead when the breach of warranty is discovered or if the grantor is financially unable to cover the losses. Often, a buyer of real estate will purchase title insurance to cover this risk.

Example A buyer purchases a house from a seller who signs a warranty deed transferring the title to the house to the buyer. If it is subsequently discovered that another party had an interest in the property and challenges the grantee's ownership of the property, the warranty has been breached, and the buyer may recover losses from the grantor.

- **Special warranty deed.** A **special warranty deed** (or **limited warranty deed**) only protects a buyer from defects in title that were caused by the seller. Thus, under this type of deed, the seller is not liable for defects in title that existed before the seller obtained the property or for encumbrances that were present when the seller obtained the property.

- **Quitclaim deed.** A **quitclaim deed** is a deed in which the grantor transfers only whatever interest she has in the real property. In a quitclaim deed, the grantor does not guarantee that she owns the property. A quitclaim deed provides the least amount of protection to a grantee because only the grantor's interest in the property is conveyed. A quitclaim deed is not usually used as a deed from a seller to a buyer. Quitclaim deeds are most often used when property is transferred between relatives by gift or otherwise.

Example A husband and wife own a house. In their divorce settlement, the wife is to receive the house. Here, the husband signs a quitclaim deed to the wife that eliminates his interest in the property.

special warranty deed (limited warranty deed)
A deed that protects a grantee of real property from defects in title caused by a grantor.

quitclaim deed
A deed in which a grantor of real property transfers whatever interest he or she has in the property to a grantee.

Recording Statute

Every state has a **recording statute** which provides that copies of deeds and other documents concerning interests in real property (e.g., mortgages, liens, easements) may be filed in a government office, where they become public records open to viewing by the public. Recording statutes are intended to prevent fraud and to establish certainty in the ownership and transfer of property. Instruments are usually filed in the **county recorder's office** of the county in which the property is located. A fee is charged to record an instrument.

Persons interested in purchasing property or lending on property should check these records to determine whether the grantor or borrower actually owns the property in question and whether any other parties (e.g., lienholders, mortgagees, easement holders) have an interest in the property. The recordation of a deed is not required to pass title from the grantor to the grantee. Recording the deed gives **constructive notice** to the world of the owner's interest in the property.

recording statute
A state statute that requires a mortgage or deed of trust to be recorded in the county recorder's office of the county in which the real property is located.

Example City Bank makes a loan to Mary Smith to purchase a house, and the bank takes back a mortgage, making the house security for the repayment of the loan. At the time of making the loan, City Bank fails to record the mortgage in the proper county recorder's office. When Mary tries to borrow more money on the house from Country Bank, Country Bank checks the county recorder's office and finds no recorded mortgage. Country Bank makes the loan to Mary, takes back a mortgage on the house, and records the mortgage in the proper county recorder's office. If Mary defaults on these two loans, Country Bank has priority in foreclosing on the property to recover payment for its loan because it recorded its loan.

Quiet Title Action

quiet title action
An action brought by a party, seeking an order of the court declaring who has title to disputed property. The court "quiets title" by its decision.

A party who is concerned about his or her ownership rights in a parcel of real property can bring a **quiet title action**, which is a lawsuit to have a court determine the extent of those rights. Public notice of the hearing must be given so that anyone claiming an interest in the property can appear and be heard. After the hearing, the judge declares who has title to the property; that is, the court "quiets title" by its decision.

Adverse Possession

adverse possession
A situation in which a person who wrongfully possesses someone else's real property obtains title to that property if certain statutory requirements are met.

In most states, a person who wrongfully possesses someone else's real property obtains title to that property if certain statutory requirements are met. This is called **adverse possession**. Property owned by federal and state governments is not subject to adverse possession.

Under the doctrine of adverse possession, the transfer of the property is involuntary and does not require the delivery of a deed. To obtain title under adverse possession, most states require that the wrongful possession be:

- **For a statutorily prescribed period of time.** In most states, this period is between ten and twenty years.
- **Open, visible, and notorious.** The adverse possessor must occupy the property so as to put the owner on notice of the possession.
- **Actual and exclusive.** The adverse possessor must physically occupy the premises. The planting of crops, grazing of animals, or building of a structure on the land constitutes physical occupancy.
- **Continuous and peaceful.** The occupancy must be continuous and uninterrupted for the required statutory period. Any break in normal occupancy terminates the adverse possession. This means that the adverse possessor may leave the property to go to work, to the store, on a vacation, and such. The adverse possessor cannot take the property by force from an owner.
- **Hostile and adverse.** The possessor must occupy the property without the express or implied permission of the owner. Thus, a lessee cannot claim title to property under adverse possession.

The disseisor must unfurl his flag on the land, and keep it flying, so that the owner may see, if he will, that an enemy has invaded his domains, and planted the standard of conquest.

Judge Ellington
Johnson v. Asfaw and Tanus (2005)

If the elements of adverse possession are met, the adverse possessor acquires clear title to the land. However, title is acquired only as to the property actually possessed and occupied during the statutory period, and not the entire tract.

Example An adverse possessor who occupies 1 acre of a 200,000-acre ranch for the statutory period of time acquires title only to the 1 acre.

Nonpossessory Interests

nonpossessory interest
A situation in which a person holds an interest in another person's property without actually owning any part of the property.

easement
A given or required right to make limited use of someone else's land without owning or leasing it.

A person may own a **nonpossessory interest** in another's real estate, such as an easement. An **easement** is an interest in land that gives the holder the right to make limited use of another's property without taking anything from it.

Examples Typical easements are common driveways, party walls, and rights-of-way.

The following types of easements may be created:

- **Easement by grant.** Easements may be expressly created by grant.

  Example An owner gives another party an easement across his or her property.

- **Easement by reservation.** An easement may be expressly created by reservation.

Example An owner sells land that he or she owns but reserves an easement on the land.

- **Easement by implication.**   An easement can be created by implication.

    Example An owner subdivides a piece of property with a well, path, road, or another beneficial appurtenant that serves the entire parcel.

- **Easement by necessity.**   An easement may be created by necessity.

    Example "Landlocked" property has an implied easement across surrounding property to enter and exit the landlocked property.

- **Easement by adverse possession.**   Easements can be created by *prescription*— that is, adverse possession.

    Example A property owner uses a road across an adjoining property for the specified time for adverse possession to occur.

Laws are always useful to persons of property, and hurtful to those who have none.
Jean-Jacques Rousseau
Du Contrat Social (1761)

Landlord–Tenant Relationship

Landlord–tenant relationships are very common in the United States. Approximately two-thirds of the population rent their homes. Many businesses lease office space, stores, manufacturing facilities, and other commercial property. The parties to the relationship have certain legal rights and duties that are governed by a mixture of real estate and contract law. The landlord–tenant relationship is subject to different forms of government regulation.

A **landlord–tenant relationship** is created when the owner of a freehold estate in real estate (i.e., an estate in fee or a life estate) transfers a right to exclusively and temporarily possess the owner's property. The tenant receives a **nonfreehold estate** in the real property; that is, the tenant has a right to possession of the property but not title to the property.

The tenant's interest in the real property is called a **leasehold estate**, or **leasehold**. The owner who transfers the leasehold estate is called the **lessor**, or **landlord**. The party to whom the leasehold estate is transferred is called the **lessee**, or **tenant**. A landlord–tenant relationship is illustrated in **Exhibit 25.1**.

leasehold
A tenant's interest in property.

lessor (landlord)
An owner who transfers a leasehold.

lessee (tenant)
A party to whom a leasehold is transferred.

APARTMENT BUILDING, NEW YORK CITY
Individuals often rent apartments. Businesses often rent office and commercial space.

Exhibit 25.1 LANDLORD–TENANT RELATIONSHIP

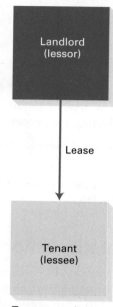

Owner-landlord owns title
to the real property

Landlord
(lessor)

Lease

Tenant
(lessee)

Tenant acquires a
nonfreehold estate in the
real property that gives
the tenant a right to
possession of the property

*Good fences make good
neighbors.*

Robert Frost
"Mending Wall" (1914)

tenancy for years
A tenancy created when a landlord and a tenant agree on a specific duration for a lease.

periodic tenancy
A tenancy created when a lease specifies intervals at which payments are due but does not specify the duration of the lease.

tenancy at will
A tenancy created by a lease that may be terminated at any time by either party.

There are four types of *tenancies*: *tenancy for years*, *periodic tenancy*, *tenancy at will*, and *tenancy at sufferance*. They are described in the following paragraphs.

Tenancy for Years

A **tenancy for years** is created when a landlord and a tenant agree on a specific duration for the lease. Any lease for a stated period—no matter how long or short—is called a tenancy for years. A tenancy for years terminates automatically, without notice, upon the expiration of the stated term.

Examples A business leases an office in a high-rise office building on a ten-year lease. This lease terminates after ten years. A family leases a cabin for the month of July in the summer. This lease expires on July 31.

Periodic Tenancy

A **periodic tenancy** is created when a lease specifies intervals at which payments are due but does not specify the duration of the lease. A periodic tenancy may be terminated by either party at the end of any payment interval, but adequate notice of the termination must be given. Under common law, the notice period equaled the length of the payment period. That is, a *month-to-month tenancy* required a one-month notice of termination.

Example A lease that states "Rent is due on the first day of the month" establishes a periodic tenancy. Many such leases are created by implication.

Tenancy at Will

A lease that may be terminated at any time by either party creates a **tenancy at will**. A tenancy at will may be created expressly (e.g., "to tenant as long as landlord wishes") but is more likely to be created by implication. Most states have enacted statutes requiring minimum advance notice for the termination of a tenancy at will. The death of either party terminates a tenancy at will.

Example A lessee and landlord agree to a lease that can be canceled at any time by either party. This is a tenancy at will.

Tenancy at Sufferance

A **tenancy at sufferance** is created when a tenant retains possession of property after the expiration of a tenancy or a life estate without the owner's consent. That is, the owner suffers the **wrongful possession** of his or her property by the holdover tenant. This is not a true tenancy but merely the possession of property without right. Technically, a tenant at sufferance is a trespasser. A tenant at sufferance is liable for the payment of rent during the period of sufferance. Most states require an owner to go through certain legal proceedings, called an **eviction proceeding**, or **unlawful detainer action**, to evict a holdover tenant. A few states allow owners to use self-help to evict a holdover tenant, as long as force is not used.

Example A landlord enters into a lease whereby he rents an apartment to a tenant for a one-year period, which expires on September 1, 2014. If the tenant remains longer than this date, it is a tenancy at sufferance.

tenancy at sufferance
A tenancy created when a tenant retains possession of property after the expiration of another tenancy or a life estate without the owner's consent.

CONCEPT SUMMARY
TYPES OF TENANCIES

Types of Tenancy	Description
Tenancy for years	Continues for the duration of the lease and terminates automatically upon expiration of the stated term without requiring notice. It does not terminate upon the death of either party.
Periodic tenancy	Continues from payment interval to payment interval. It may be terminated by either party with adequate notice. It does not terminate upon the death of either party.
Tenancy at will	Continues at the will of the parties and may be terminated by either party at any time with adequate notice. It terminates upon the death of either party.
Tenancy at sufferance	Arises when a tenant wrongfully occupies real property after the expiration of another tenancy or life estate. It continues until the owner either evicts the tenant or holds him or her over for another term. It terminates upon the death of the tenant.

Implied Warranty of Habitability

The courts of many jurisdictions hold that an **implied warranty of habitability** applies to residential leases for their duration. This warranty provides that the leased premises must be fit, safe, and suitable for ordinary residential use.

Examples Unchecked rodent infestation, leaking roofs, unworkable bathroom facilities, and the like have been held to breach the implied warranty of habitability. On the other hand, a small crack in a wall or some paint peeling from a door does not breach this warranty.

State statutes and judicial decisions provide various remedies that can be used if a landlord's failure to maintain or repair leased premises affects the tenant's use or enjoyment of the premises. Generally, the tenant may (1) withhold from his or her rent the amount by which the defect reduced the value of the premises to him or her, (2) repair the defect and deduct the cost of repairs from the rent due for the leased premises, (3) cancel the lease if the failure to repair constitutes constructive eviction, or (4) sue for damages in the amount by which the landlord's failure to repair the defect reduced the value of the leasehold.

implied warranty of habitability
A warranty which provides that leased premises must be fit, safe, and suitable for ordinary residential use.

The right of property enables an industrious man to reap where he has sown.

Anonymous

Contemporary Environment

Rent Control

Many local communities across the country have enacted **rent control ordinances** that stipulate an amount of rent a landlord can charge for residential housing. Most of these ordinances fix the rent at a specific amount and provide for minor annual increases. Although many communities have adopted rent control ordinances, New York City is the most famous one.

Landlords, of course, oppose rent control, arguing that rent control ordinances are merely a "regulatory tax" that transfers wealth from landowners to tenants. Tenants and proponents of rent control say that it is necessary to create affordable housing, particularly in high-rent urban areas. The U.S. Supreme Court has upheld rent control.[1]

rent control ordinances
Local laws that stipulate the amount of rent a landlord can charge for residential housing.

Civil Rights Laws

Federal and state governments have enacted statutes that prohibit discrimination in the sale and rental of real property. Important federal statutes that prohibit discrimination in housing are the *Civil Rights Act of 1866*, the *Fair Housing Act of 1968*, and the *Americans with Disabilities Act of 1990*. These statutes are discussed in the following paragraphs.

Civil Rights Act of 1866

Civil Rights Act of 1866
A federal statute that prohibits discrimination in the selling and renting of property based on race or color.

The **Civil Rights Act of 1866**[2] was passed at the end of the Civil War. This federal statute prohibits discrimination in the selling and renting of property based on race or color. It was designed to eliminate historically prevalent discrimination in housing. The law applies to all rentals of public and private property, property owners renting separate units within a dwelling in which they live, and persons renting out space in their own homes.

Fair Housing Act

Fair Housing Act of 1968
A federal statute that makes it unlawful for a party to refuse to sell, rent, finance, or advertise housing to any person because of his or her race, color, national origin, sex, religion, disability, or familial status (e.g., pregnant women, a family with children under 18 years of age).

The **Fair Housing Act of 1968**,[3] as amended, is a federal statute that makes it unlawful for a party to refuse to sell, rent, finance, or advertise housing to any person because of his or her race, color, national origin, sex, religion, disability, or family status (e.g., pregnant women, a family with children under 18 years of age). These are called *protected classes*. The act applies to sellers, landlords, real estate brokers, banks and mortgage lenders, advertisers, and others involved in the housing market.

Examples Violations include refusing to rent or sell housing, setting different terms and conditions for the sale or rental of housing, falsely denying that housing is available for inspection, persuading owners to rent or sell only to persons who are not members of a protected class (i.e., blockbusting), refusing to make a mortgage loan, refusing to provide information regarding loans, imposing different terms or conditions on a loan (e.g., different interest rates or fees), discriminating in appraising property, discriminating against persons with a physical or mental disability, and threatening or intimidating anyone from exercising a fair housing right because of his or her protected class status.

The law does not apply to the following: (1) a person who owns a building of four or fewer units and occupies one of the units and leases the others and (2) a person who leases a single-family dwelling and does not own more than three single-family dwellings. To qualify for either exemption, the lessor cannot use a real estate broker or advertise in a discriminating manner.

The Fair Housing Act is administered by the **U.S. Department of Housing and Urban Development (HUD)**, a federal administrative agency. Complaints may be filed with HUD, which then conducts an investigation. If HUD determines that there is reasonable cause to believe that a discriminatory housing practice has occurred, it will hold an administrative hearing. However, either party has the right to elect to have the matter heard in federal court. The law provides for civil and criminal penalties.

Americans with Disabilities Act of 1990

The **Americans with Disabilities Act of 1990 (ADA)**,[4] as amended by the **Americans with Disabilities Act Amendments Act of 2008 (ADAAA)**,[5] is a federal statute that prohibits discrimination against disabled individuals in employment, public services, public accommodations and services, and telecommunications. **Title III of the ADA** prohibits discrimination on the basis of a physical or mental disability in **places of public accommodation** operated by private entities.

Title III of the ADA applies to public accommodations and commercial facilities such as motels, hotels, restaurants, theaters, colleges and universities, department stores, retail stores, shopping malls, office buildings, doctor and lawyer offices, banks, recreation facilities, licensing centers, sports stadiums, convention centers, and transportation depots.

Title III requires covered facilities to be designed, constructed, and altered in compliance with specific accessibility requirements established by regulations issued pursuant to the ADA. This includes constructing ramps to accommodate wheelchairs, installing railings next to steps, placing signs written in Braille in elevators and at elevator call buttons, and so on.

New construction must be built in such a manner as to be readily accessible to and usable by disabled individuals. Any alterations made to existing buildings must be made so that the altered portions of the building are readily accessible to disabled individuals to the maximum extent feasible. With respect to existing buildings, architectural barriers must be removed if such removal is readily achievable. In determining when an action is readily achievable, the factors to be considered include the nature and cost of the action, the financial resources of the facility, and the type of operations of the facility.

The ADA provides for both private right of action and enforcement by the attorney general. Individuals may seek injunctive relief and monetary damages, and the attorney general may seek equitable relief and civil fines for any violation. Complaints are filed with the **U.S. Department of Justice (DOJ)**. The DOJ will bring a lawsuit if it finds a pattern or practice of discrimination in violation of Title III or where an act of discrimination raises an issue of general public importance. Parties may also bring private lawsuits.

Title III of the ADA
A section of a federal statute that prohibits discrimination on the basis of physical or mental disability in places of public accommodation operated by private entities.

State and Local Fair Housing Laws

State and local governments may provide fair housing laws that prohibit discrimination in housing. State and local laws that are stricter than federal laws are permitted.

Zoning

Most counties and municipalities have enacted **zoning ordinances** to regulate land use. **Zoning** generally (1) establish land use districts within the municipality (i.e., areas are generally designated residential, commercial, or industrial); (2) restrict the height, size, and location of buildings on a building site; and (3) establish *aesthetic requirements* or limitations for the exterior of buildings.

Example If a zoning ordinance designates an area zoned for only single-family houses, no apartment buildings, commercial buildings, or other nonconforming structures can

zoning ordinances
Local laws that are adopted by municipalities and local governments to regulate land use within their boundaries.

be built in this zoned area. If a zoning ordinance states that only apartment buildings four stories high can be built in a certain multifamily zoned area, buildings taller than four stories cannot be built in this area.

Example A landowner in an area zoned for traditional-style homes applies to build a geodesic dome house made out of glass and steel in this area. The zoning commission can rightfully turn down a building permit for this proposed house because it does not meet the aesthetic requirements of the area.

A **zoning commission** usually formulates zoning ordinances, conducts public hearings, and makes recommendations to the city council, which must vote to enact an ordinance. Once a zoning ordinance is enacted, the zoning commission enforces it. If landowners believe that a zoning ordinance is illegal or that it has been unlawfully applied to them or their property, they may institute a court proceeding, seeking judicial review of the ordinance or its application.

An owner who wants to use his or her property for a use different from that permitted under a current zoning ordinance may seek relief from the ordinance by obtaining a **variance**. To obtain a variance, the landowner must prove that the ordinance causes an undue hardship by preventing him or her from making a reasonable return on the land as zoned. Variances are usually difficult to obtain.

Zoning laws act prospectively; that is, uses and buildings that already exist in the zoned area are permitted to continue even if they do not fit within new zoning ordinances. Such uses are called **nonconforming uses**.

Example If a new zoning ordinance is enacted, making an area a residential zone that was previously not zoned for residential housing, an existing funeral parlor is a nonconforming use that would usually be permitted to stay.

Eminent Domain and "Taking"

The **Due Process Clause** of the Fifth Amendment to the U.S. Constitution (and state constitutions, where applicable) allows the government to take private property for *public use*. This is done by the government exercising its power of **eminent domain**. The government must allow the owner of the property to make a case for keeping the property.

The **Just Compensation Clause** of the Fifth Amendment to the U.S. Constitution requires the government to compensate the property owner (and possibly others, such as lessees) when it exercises the power of eminent domain. Anyone who is not satisfied with the compensation offered by the government can bring an action to have the court determine the compensation to be paid. States and local governments are also required to pay just compensation for property they take under the power of eminent domain.

Example Henry owns a large piece of vacant beachfront property and intends to build his retirement home on the property at some future time. The city in which the property is located wants to build a new public boat dock on the property. The city can use its power of eminent domain to acquire the property for this public use. There has been a **taking**, and the government must pay Henry just compensation.

Government regulation usually does not constitute a taking.

Example A corporation owns a large piece of property with the intent of erecting a ten-story commercial building at some future time. Suppose the government enacts a zoning law that restricts buildings in the area to five stories. Although the corporation would suffer a substantial economic loss because of the zoning law, nevertheless this would not constitute a taking that required the payment of compensation.

The following is an important U.S. Supreme Court case that involves the government's power of eminent domain.

variance
An exception that permits a type of building or use in an area that would not otherwise be allowed by a zoning ordinance.

nonconforming uses
Uses for real estate and buildings that already exist in a zoned area that are permitted to continue even though they do not fit within a new zoning use established for the area.

Due Process Clause
A clause of the U.S. Constitution that allows the government to take property for "public use."

eminent domain
The government's power to take private property for public use, provided that just compensation is paid to the private property holder.

Just Compensation Clause
A clause of the U.S. Constitution that requires the government to compensate the property owner, and possibly others, when the government takes property under its power of eminent domain.

Contemporary Environment

The *Kelo* Takings Case

"The concept of the public welfare is broad and exclusive. The values it represents are spiritual as well as physical, aesthetic as well as monetary."

—Stevens, Justice

The city of New London is located in southeastern Connecticut, at the junction of the Thames River and Long Island Sound. The city suffered decades of economic decline, including the closing of the federal military base in the Fort Trumbull area of the city. The city's unemployment rate was nearly double the state's unemployment rate, and the city's population of 24,000 was the lowest since 1920.

To try to remedy the situation, state and local officials targeted the city of New London for economic revitalization. The government created the New London Development Corporation (NLDC) to assist the city in planning economic redevelopment. The NLDC finalized an integrated redevelopment plan for 90 acres in the Fort Trumbull area of the city. The redevelopment plan included a waterfront conference hotel, restaurants, stores, a marina, eighty new residences, and office buildings. Importantly, these projects were to be constructed and owned by private developers and parties selected by the city. The stated purposes were to make the city more attractive, create jobs, and increase tax revenue.

The city purchased most of the land needed for the redevelopment from private owners. However, Susette Kelo and several other homeowners in the redevelopment district (collectively Kelo) refused to sell their properties. Their properties were well kept and were not blighted.

A Connecticut state statute authorized the use of eminent domain to take property to promote economic development. Thus, the NLDC initiated eminent domain actions to take the properties. Kelo defended, arguing that the taking violated the "public use" requirement of the Fifth Amendment to the U.S. Constitution because the properties were being taken from one private party—Kelo and the other holdout homeowners—and were being transferred to other private owners—the developers. The state trial court held for Kelo. However, the Connecticut Supreme Court held that the taking of private property by the NLDC was valid. Kelo appealed to the U.S. Supreme Court.

The issue for the U.S. Supreme Court to decide was whether the city of New London's decision to take Kelo's property by eminent domain for the purpose of economic development satisfies the "public use" requirement of the Fifth Amendment.

The U.S. Supreme Court, in a five-to-four decision, held that the general benefit a community enjoys from economic growth qualifies as a permissible "public use" to support the taking of private property for redevelopment plans under the Takings Clause of the Fifth Amendment.

The U.S. Supreme Court upheld the statute of the state of Connecticut that permitted the taking of private property for the purposes of economic development. Thus, Kelo's property could be taken by the redevelopment agency and transferred to another private party—the developers—who in turn would build and own commercial property where Kelo's house had once stood.

The Supreme Court's decision was widely criticized by members of the public who believed the decision violated private property rights. State politicians were quick to respond, with over half of the states enacting state laws that make it more difficult for state and local governments to acquire private property by eminent domain than the standard permitted in the *Kelo* ruling. *Kelo v. City of New London, Connecticut*, 545 U.S. 469, 125 S.Ct. 2655, 162 L.Ed.2d 439, **Web** 2005 U.S. Lexis 5011 (Supreme Court of the United States).

Key Terms and Concepts

Actual and exclusive (518)
Adverse possession (518)
Air rights (510)
Air space parcel (510)
Americans with Disabilities Act Amendments Act (ADAAA) of 2008 (523)
Americans with Disabilities Act (ADA) of 1990 (523)

Buildings (509)
Civil Rights Act of 1866 (522)
Closing (settlement) (516)
Community property (514)
Concurrent ownership (co-ownership) (512)
Condominium (515)
Constructive notice (517)

Continuous and peaceful (518)
Cooperative (515)
County recorder's office (517)
Deed (516)
Due Process Clause (524)
Easement (518)
Easement by adverse possession (519)
Easement by grant (518)

Easement by implication (519)
Easement by necessity (519)
Easement by reservation (518)
Eminent domain (524)
Estate in land (estate) (510)
Estate pour autre vie (511)

Law Case with Answer
Solow v. Wellner

Facts The defendants were approximately eighty tenants of a three hundred-unit luxury apartment building on the Upper East Side of Manhattan. The monthly rents in the all-glass-enclosed building, which had won several architectural awards, were very high. The landlord brought a summary proceeding against the tenants to recover rent when they engaged in a rent strike, in protest against what they viewed as deteriorating conditions and services. Among other things, the evidence showed that during the period in question, the elevator system made tenants and their guests wait interminable lengths of time; the elevators skipped floors and opened on the wrong floors; a stench emanated from garbage stored near the garage, and mice appeared in that area; fixtures were missing in public areas; water seeped into mailboxes; the air conditioning in the lobby was inoperative; and air conditioners in individual units leaked. The defendant-tenants sought abatement of rent for breach of the implied warranty of habitability. Has the landlord breached the implied warranty of habitability?

Answer Yes, the landlord has breached the implied warranty of habitability. In determining whether the implied warranty of habitability has been breached, the law implies a "reasonable expectation" test. This means that the premises are to be maintained in accordance with the reasonable expectations of the tenant. Certain amenities not necessarily life threatening, but consistent with the nature of the bargain—air conditioning, for example—fall under the protection of this branch of the warranty. Predictability and reliability of services is another factor.

Tenants have obvious expectations of a uniquely designed all-glass-enclosed building on Manhattan's fashionable Upper East Side. Add to this the comparatively high rents exacted for these apartments, and one can assume that the expectations of the tenants encompassed more than the minimal amenities. The warranty certainly entitled them to freedom from conditions threatening their life, health, and safety, and their high rents justified increased expectations of a well-run, impeccably clean building with consistent and reliable services. The reality fell far short of their expectations. As to the public areas, the landlord has breached the implied warranty of habitability. The tenants' rent should be abated by 80 percent until the landlord corrects the problems. *Solow v. Wellner*, 150 Misc.2d 642, 569 N.Y.S.2d 882, **Web** 1991 N.Y. Misc. Lexis 169 (Civil Court of the City of New York)

Critical Legal Thinking Cases

25.1 Adverse Possession Edward and Mary Shaughnessey purchased a 16-acre tract in St. Louis County, Missouri. Subsequently, they subdivided 12 acres into eighteen lots offered for sale and retained possession of the remaining 4-acre tract. Thirteen years later, Charles and Elaine Witt purchased lot 12, which is adjacent to the 4-acre tract. The Witts constructed and moved into a house on their lot. The next year, they cleared an area of land that ran the length of their property and extended 40 feet onto the 4-acre tract. The Witts constructed a pool and a deck, planted a garden, made a playground for their children, set up a dog run, and built a fence along the edge of the property line, which included the now-disputed property. Neither the Witts nor the Shaughnesseys realized that the Witts had encroached on the Shaughnesseys' property.

Twenty years later, the Shaughnesseys sold the 4-acre tract to Thomas and Rosanne Miller. When a survey showed the Witts' encroachment, the Millers demanded that the Witts remove the pool and cease using the property. When the Witts refused to do so, the Millers sued to quiet title. The Witts defended, arguing that they had obtained title to the disputed property through adverse possession. Have the Witts established the necessary requirements to acquire the disputed property by adverse possession? *Witt v. Miller*, 845 S.W.2d 665, **Web** 1993 Mo.App. Lexis 20 (Court of Appeals of Missouri)

25.2 Americans with Disabilities Act Title III of the Americans with Disabilities Act (ADA) requires that public accommodations must be "readily accessible to and usable by individuals with disabilities." The U.S. Department of Justice (DOJ) is empowered to adopt regulations to enforce the ADA. The DOJ adopted Standard 4.33.3 for movie theaters, which provides:

Wheelchair areas shall be an integral part of any fixed seating plan and shall be provided so as to provide people with physical disabilities a choice of admission prices and lines of sight comparable to those for members of the general public. They shall adjoin an accessible route that also serves as a means of egress in case of emergency. At least one companion fixed seat shall be provided next to each wheelchair seating area. When the seating capacity exceeds 300, wheelchair spaces shall be provided in more than one location. Readily removable seats may be installed in wheelchair spaces when the spaces are not required to accommodate wheelchair users.

Cinemark USA, Inc., owns and operates movie theaters throughout the United States. Cinemark has constructed "stadium-style" movie theaters. The theaters have stadium-style seating configuration, with the rows of seats rising at a relatively steep grade to provide better "sight lines" for movie patrons. The stadium-style seating is inaccessible for wheelchair-using patrons. For wheelchair-using patrons, the theaters provide a flat area in front of the screen where these patrons do not have the same sight line to the screen as non-wheelchair-using patrons. The United States sued Cinemark, alleging that the seating arrangement in Cinemark stadium-style theaters violated Standard 4.33.3 and Title III of the ADA. Does Cinemark's wheelchair seating arrangement in its stadium-style theaters violate Standard 4.33.3 and Title III of the ADA? *United States of America v. Cinemark USA, Inc.*, 348 F.3d 569, **Web** 2003 U.S. App. Lexis 22757 (United States Court of Appeals for the Sixth Circuit)

25.3 Life Estate and Remainder Baudilio Bowles died testate. His will devised to his sister, Julianita B. Vigil, "one-half of any income, rents, or profits from any real property located in Bull Creek or Colonias, New Mexico." The will contained another clause that left to his children "my interest in any real property owned by me at the time of my death, located in Bull Creek and/or Colonias, San Miguel County." The property referred to in both devises is the same property. Julianita died before the will was probated. Her heirs claim a one-half ownership interest in the real property. Bowles's children asserted that they owned all his property. Who wins? *In the Matter of the Estate of Bowles*, 107 N.M. 739, 764 P.2d 510, **Web** 1988 N.M.App. Lexis 93 (Court of Appeals of New Mexico)

25.4 Reversion W.E. and Jennie Hutton conveyed land they owned to the trustees of schools of District Number One of the Town of Allison, Illinois (School District), by warranty deed "to be used for school purpose only; otherwise to revert to Grantor." School District built a school on the site, commonly known as Hutton School. The Huttons conveyed the adjoining farmland and their reversionary interest in the school site to the Jacqmains, who in turn conveyed their interest to Herbert and Betty Mahrenholz (Mahrenholz). The 1.5-acre site sits in the middle of Mahrenhoz's farmland. Over thirty years after School District built the school, School District discontinued holding regular classes at Hutton School. Instead, it used the school building to warehouse and store miscellaneous school equipment, supplies, unused desks, and the like. Mahrenholz filed suit to quiet title to the school property to them. Who wins? *Mahrenholz v. County Board of School Trustees of Lawrence Country*, 188 Ill.App.3d 260, 544 N.E.2d 128, **Web** 1989 Ill.App. Lexis 1445 (Appellate Court of Illinois)

25.5 Adverse Possession Joseph and Helen Naab purchased a tract of land in a subdivision of Williamstown, West Virginia. At the time of purchase, there were both a house and a small concrete garage on the property. Evidence showed that the garage had been erected sometime prior to twenty years earlier by one of the Naabs' predecessors in title. Two years after the Naabs bought their property, Roger and Cynthia Nolan purchased a lot contiguous to that owned by the Naabs. The following year, the Nolans had their property surveyed. The survey indicated that one corner of the Naabs' garage encroached 1.22 feet onto the Nolans' property and the other corner encroached 0.91 feet over the property line. The Nolans requested that the Naabs remove the garage from their property. When the Naabs refused, a lawsuit ensued. Who wins? *Naab v. Nolan*, 174 W.Va. 390, 327 S.E.2d 151, **Web** 1985 W.Va. Lexis 476 (Supreme Court of Appeals of West Virginia)

25.6 Zoning The city of Ladue is one of the wealthy suburban residential areas of metropolitan St. Louis. The homes in the city are considerably more expensive than those in surrounding areas and consist of homes of traditional design such as colonial, French provincial, and English. The city set up an architectural board to approve plans for buildings that "conform to certain minimum architectural standards of appearance and conformity with surrounding structures, and that unsightly, grotesque, and unsuitable structures, detrimental to the stability of value and the welfare of surrounding property, structures, and residents, and to the general welfare and happiness of the community, be avoided." The owner of a lot in the city submitted a plan to build a house of ultramodern design. It was pyramid-shaped, with a flat top and triangular-shaped windows and doors. Although the house plans met other city zoning ordinances and building codes, the architectural board rejected the owner's petition for a building permit, based on aesthetic reasons. The owner sued the city. Who wins? *State of Missouri v. Berkeley*, 458 S.W.2d 305, **Web** 1970 Mo. Lexis 902 (Supreme Court of Missouri)

25.7 Implied Warranty of Habitability Sharon Love entered into a written lease agreement with Monarch Apartments for apartment 4 at 441 Winfield in Topeka, Kansas. Shortly after moving in, she experienced serious problems with termites. Her walls swelled, clouds of dirt came out, and when she checked on her children one night, she saw termites flying around the room. She complained to Monarch, which arranged for the apartment to be fumigated. When the termite problem persisted, Monarch moved Love and her children to apartment 2. Upon moving in, Love noticed that roaches crawled over the walls, ceilings, and floors of the apartment. She complained, and Monarch called an exterminator, who sprayed the apartment. When the roach problem persisted, Love vacated the premises. Has Love lawfully terminated the lease? *Love v. Monarch Apartments*, 13 Kan.App.2d 341, 771 P.2d 79, **Web** 1989 Kan.App. Lexis 219 (Court of Appeals of Kansas)

25.8 Lease Susan Nylen, Elizabeth Lewis, and Julie Reed, students at Indiana University, signed a rental agreement as cosigners to lease an apartment from Park Doral Apartments. The rental term was from August 26 until August 19 of the following year. The lessees agreed to pay a monthly rent for the apartment. The tenants paid a security deposit, constituting prepayment of rent for the last month of the lease term. At the end of the fall semester, Reed moved out of the apartment and refused to pay any further rent. Nylen and Lewis remained in possession of the apartment, paying only two-thirds of the total rent due for the month for several months. Nylen and Lewis made a full payment of the rent for March and then vacated the apartment. The landlord, who was unable to re-lease the apartment during the lease term, sued Reed, Nylen, and Lewis for the unpaid rent. Who wins? *Nylen v. Park Doral Apartments*, 535 N.E.2d 178, **Web** 1989 Ind.App. Lexis 185 (Court of Appeals of Indiana)

Ethics Cases

25.9 Ethics Victor and Phyllis Garber acquired a piece of real property by warranty deed. The deed was recorded. The property consisted of 80 acres enclosed by a fence that had been in place for over fifty years. The enclosed area was used to graze cattle and produce hay. Ten years later, William and Herbert Doenz acquired a piece of real property adjacent to the Garbers' and employed a surveyor to locate their land's boundaries. As a result of the survey, it was discovered that the shared fence was 20 to 30 feet inside the deed line on the Doenz property. The amount of property between the old fence and the deed line was 3.01 acres. The Doenzes removed the old fence and constructed a new fence along the deed line. The Garbers brought suit to quiet title. *Doenz v. Garber*, 665 P.2d 932, **Web** 1983 Wyo. Lexis 339 (Supreme Court of Wyoming)

1. What are the requirements of adverse possession?
2. Did the Doenzes act ethically in removing the fence? Did the Garbers act ethically in claiming

title to property that originally belonged with the adjacent property?

3. Did the Garbers acquire title to the property between the fence and the deed through adverse possession?

25.10 Ethics Moe and Joe Rappaport (tenants) leased space in a shopping mall owned by Bermuda Avenue Shopping Center Associates, L.P. (landlord), to use as an indoor golf arcade. The lease was signed, and the tenants were given possession of the leased premises. The tenants were not told by the landlord of the extensive renovations planned for the mall. For one month, the golf arcade was busy and earned a net profit. However, at the end of the month, renovation of the mall began in front of the arcade. According to the tenants, their store sign was taken down, there was debris and dust in front of the store, the sidewalks and parking spaces in front of the store were taken away, and their business "died." The tenants closed their arcade approximately one month later and sued the landlord for damages. The landlord counterclaimed, seeking to recover lost rental income. *Bermuda Avenue Shopping Center Associates v. Rappaport*, 565 So.2d 805, **Web** 1990 Fla.App. Lexis 5354 (Court of Appeal of Florida)

1. Did the landlord act ethically in not explaining the planned renovations to the tenants?
2. Did the tenants act ethically in terminating the lease?
3. Who wins, and why?

Internet Exercises

1. Use an Internet search engine, such as **www.google.com**, to find the time requirement for adverse possession in your state.

2. Go to **www.dca.ca.gov/publications/landlordbook/ problems.shtml** and read "Dealing with Problems," from the California Department of Consumer Affairs

3. Go to **www.cnn.com/2005/LAW/04/06/jagger/index .html** and read the article about mold in an apartment.

4. Go to **www.housingnyc.com/html/about/about.html** and read the mission statement of the New York City Rent Guidelines Board.

5. Visit the website of Cinemark Theaters, at **www .cinemark.com**. Can you find Cinemark's corporate policy regarding accessibility of its theaters by physically disabled patrons?

Endnotes

1. *Yee v. City of Escondido, California*, 503 U.S. 519, 112 S.Ct. 1522, 118 L.Ed.2d 153, **Web** 1992 U.S. Lexis 2115 (Supreme Court of the United States)
2. 42 U.S.C. Section 1981.
3. 42 U.S.C. Sections 360 et seq.
4. 42 U.C.C. Sections 1201 et seq.
5. Public Law 110-325, 122 Stat. 3553 (2008).

26 International and World Trade Law

PYONGYANG, NORTH KOREA
This is a presentation at the mass games of the Ari-rang Festival in Pyongyang, North Korea. The mass games involve up to 100,000 participants. The North Korean words shown here are made of cards held by participants in Pyongyang's 150,000-seat stadium. Countries around the world have various political systems—democracy, communist, dictatorship, socialist, and variations of these. North Korea—officially the Democratic People's Republic of Korea (DPRK)—is a socialist dictatorship. In the past 50 years, the country has been ruled by the late Kim Il-sung and then by his son Kim Jong-il. Because of its isolationist policy, North Korea is often referred to as the "Hermit Kingdom."

Learning Objectives

After studying this chapter, you should be able to:

1. Describe the U.S. government's power under the Foreign Commerce Clause and Treaty Clause of the U.S. Constitution.
2. Describe a nation's court jurisdiction over international disputes.
3. Describe the functions and governance of the United Nations.
4. Describe the North American Free Trade Agreement (NAFTA) and other regional economic organizations.
5. Describe the World Trade Organization (WTO) and explain how its dispute resolution procedure works.

Chapter Outline

Introduction to International and World Trade Law

The United States and Foreign Affairs

United Nations (UN)
  INTERNATIONAL LAW • *International Monetary Fund (IMF)*
  INTERNATIONAL LAW • *World Bank*
  INTERNATIONAL LAW • *UNICEF*

European Union (EU)

North American Free Trade Agreement (NAFTA)

Other Regional Trade Organizations

World Trade Organization (WTO)

National Courts and International Dispute Resolution
  CASE 26.1 • *Glen v. Club Mediterranee, S.A.*

International Religious Laws
  INTERNATIONAL LAW • *Jewish Law and the Torah*

Chapter Outline *(continued)*

> *International law, or the law that governs between nations, has at times, been like the common law within states, a twilight existence during which it is hardly distinguishable from morality or justice, till at length the imprimatur of a court attests its jural quality."*
>
> —Cardozo, Justice
> *New Jersey v. Delaware (1934)*

Introduction to International and World Trade Law

International law, important to both nations and businesses, has many unique features. First, there is no single legislative source of international law. All countries of the world and numerous international organizations are responsible for enacting international law. Second, there is no single world court that is responsible for interpreting international law. There are, however, several courts and tribunals that hear and decide international legal disputes of parties that agree to appear before them. Third, there is no world executive branch that can enforce international law. Thus, nations do not have to obey international law enacted by other countries or international organizations. Because of these uncertainties, some commentators question whether international law is really law.

As technology and transportation bring nations closer together and as American and foreign firms increase their global activities, international law will become even more important to governments and businesses. This chapter introduces the main concepts of international law and discusses the sources of international law and the organizations responsible for its administration.

international law
Law that governs affairs between nations and that regulates transactions between individuals and businesses of different countries.

Only when the world is civilized enough to keep promises will we get any kind of international law.

Julius Henry Cohen

The United States and Foreign Affairs

The U.S. Constitution divides the power to regulate the internal affairs of this country between the federal and state governments. On the international level, however, the Constitution gives most of the power to the federal government. Two constitutional provisions establish this authority: the *Foreign Commerce Clause* and the *Treaty Clause*.

Foreign Commerce Clause

Article I, Section 8, Clause 3 of the U.S. Constitution—the **Foreign Commerce Clause**—vests Congress with the power "to regulate commerce with foreign nations." The Constitution does not vest exclusive power over foreign affairs

Foreign Commerce Clause
A clause of the U.S. Constitution that vests Congress with the power "to regulate commerce with foreign nations."

in the federal government, but any state or local law that unduly burdens foreign commerce is unconstitutional, in violation of the Foreign Commerce Clause.

Example General Motors Corporation and Ford Motor Company, two of America's automobile manufactures, are headquartered in the state of Michigan. The state of Michigan, in order to reduce the sales of foreign-made automobiles in the state, enacts a state law that imposes a 50 percent tax on foreign-made automobiles sold in the state but does not imposes this tax on American-made automobiles sold in the state. This tax violates the Foreign Commerce Clause because it unduly burdens foreign commerce.

Example General Motors Corporation and Ford Motor Company, two of America's automobile manufactures, are headquartered in the state of Michigan. The state of Michigan, in order to protect the Great Lakes and the environment from pollution, enacts a state tax that places a 10 percent tax on all automobile sales made in the state. This tax does not violate the Foreign Commerce because it does not treat foreign commerce any differently than domestic commerce.

Treaty Clause

Article II, Section 2, Clause 2 of the U.S. Constitution—the **Treaty Clause**—states that the president "shall have power, by and with the advice and consent of the Senate, to make treaties, provided two-thirds of the senators present concur."

Under the Treaty Clause, only the federal government can enter into treaties with foreign nations. Under the Supremacy Clause of the Constitution, treaties become part of the "law of the land," and conflicting state or local law is void. The president is the agent of the United States in dealing with foreign countries.

Treaties and *conventions* are the equivalents of legislation at the international level. A **treaty** is an agreement or a contract between two or more nations that is formally signed by an authorized representative and ratified by the supreme power of each nation. **Bilateral treaties** are between two nations; **multilateral treaties** involve more than two nations. **Conventions** are treaties that are sponsored by international organizations, such as the United Nations. Conventions normally have many signatories. Treaties and conventions address such matters as human rights, foreign aid, navigation, commerce, and the settlement of disputes. Most treaties are registered with and published by the United Nations.

Examples The federal government of the United States can enter into a treaty with the country of China whereby the two countries agree to reduce trade barriers between the two countries. However, the state of California cannot enter into a treaty with the country of China that reduces trade barriers between the state of California and China.

Treaty Clause
A clause of the U.S. Constitution which states that the president "shall have the power ... to make treaties, provided two-thirds of the senators present concur."

treaty
An agreement between two or more nations that is formally signed by an authorized representative of each nation and ratified by each nation.

bilateral treaty
A treaty between two nations.

multilateral treaty
A treaty involving more than two nations.

convention
A treaty that is sponsored by an international organization.

United Nations (UN)

One of the most important international organizations is the **United Nations (UN)**, which was created by a multilateral treaty on October 24, 1945.[1] Most countries of the world are members of the UN. The goals of the UN, which is headquartered in New York City, are to maintain peace and security in the world, promote economic and social cooperation, and protect human rights.

The UN is governed by the *General Assembly*, the *Security Council*, and the *Secretariat*, which are discussed in the following paragraphs.

General Assembly

The **General Assembly** is composed of all UN member nations. As the legislative body of the UN, it adopts resolutions concerning human rights, trade, finance and economics, as well as other matters within the scope of the UN Charter. Although resolutions have limited force, they are often enforced through persuasion and the use of economic and other sanctions.

Security Council

The UN **Security Council** is composed of fifteen member nations, five of which are permanent members (China, France, Russia, the United Kingdom, and the United States), and ten other countries selected by the members of the General Assembly to serve two-year terms. The council is primarily responsible for maintaining international peace and security and has authority to use armed force.

Secretariat

The **Secretariat** administers the day-to-day operations of the UN. It is headed by the **secretary-general**, who is elected by the General Assembly. The secretary-general may refer matters that threaten international peace and security to the Security Council and use his or her office to help solve international disputes.

United Nations Agencies

The UN is composed of various autonomous agencies that deal with a wide range of economic and social problems. These include the **United Nations Educational, Scientific, and Cultural Organization (UNESCO)**, the **International Fund for Agricultural Development (IFAD)**, the *International Monetary Fund (IMF)*, the *World Bank*, and the *United Nations Children's Fund (UNICEF)*.

The first feature that follows discusses the work of the *International Monetary Fund*. The second feature that follows discusses the *World Bank*. The third feature discusses *UNICEF*.

United Nations (UN)
An international organization created by a multilateral treaty in 1945 to promote social and economic cooperation among nations and to protect human rights.

General Assembly
The legislative body of the United Nations that is composed of all UN member nations.

Security Council
A council composed of fifteen member nations, five of which are permanent members and ten other countries chosen by the members of the General Assembly, that is responsible for maintaining international peace and security.

WEB EXERCISE
Visit the website of the Security Council of the United Nations, at **www.un.org**. What countries make up the Security Council?

Secretariat
A staff of persons that administers the day-to-day operations of the UN. It is headed by the *secretary-general*.

WEB EXERCISE
Go to **www.imf.org/external/ np/exr/facts/poor.htm**. Click on the link "Key Issues: Low-income countries." Read the featured article.

International Monetary Fund (IMF)
An agency of the United Nations whose primary function is to promote sound monetary, fiscal, and macroeconomic policies worldwide by providing assistance to needy countries.

International Law

International Monetary Fund (IMF)

The **International Monetary Fund (IMF)**, an agency of the United Nations, was established by treaty in 1945 to help promote the world economy following the Great Depression of the 1930s and following the end of World War II in 1945. The IMF comprises more than 180 countries that are each represented on the board of directors, which makes the policy decisions of the IMF. The IMF is funded by monetary contributions of member nations, assessed based on the size of each nation's economy. The IMF's headquarters is located in Washington, DC.

The primary function of the IMF is to promote sound monetary, fiscal, and macroeconomic policies worldwide by providing assistance to needy countries. The IMF responds to financial crises around the globe. It does

(continued)

so by providing short-term loans to member countries to help them weather problems caused by unstable currencies, to balance payment problems, and to recover from the economic policies of past governments. The IMF examines a country's economy as a whole and its currency accounts, inflation, balance of payments with other countries, employment, consumer and business spending, and other factors to determine whether the country needs assistance. In return for the financial assistance, a country must agree to meet certain monetary, fiscal, employment, inflation, and other goals established by the IMF.

International Law

World Bank

The **World Bank** is a United Nations agency that comprises more than 180 member nations. The World Bank is financed by contributions from developed countries, with the United States, the United Kingdom, Japan, Germany, and France being its main contributors. The World Bank has employees located in its headquarters in Washington, DC, and regional offices elsewhere throughout the world.

The World Bank provides money to developing countries to fund projects for humanitarian purposes and to relieve poverty. The World Bank provides funds to build roads, construct dams, and build other water projects, establish hospitals and provide medical assistance, develop agriculture, and provide humanitarian aid. The World Bank provides outright grants of funds to developing countries for such projects, and it makes long-term low-interest-rate loans to those countries. The bank routinely grants debt relief for these loans.

WEB EXERCISE
Go to **www.worldbank.org**. Read one of the featured articles.

International Court of Justice (ICJ) (World Court)
The judicial branch of the United Nations, located in The Hague, the Netherlands.

The International Court of Justice

The **International Court of Justice (ICJ)**, also called the **World Court**, is located in The Hague, the Netherlands. It is the judicial branch of the UN. Only nations, not individuals or businesses, can have cases decided by this court. The ICJ hears cases that nations refer to it as well as cases involving treaties and the UN Charter. A nation may seek redress on behalf of an individual or a business that has a claim against another country. The ICJ is composed of fifteen judges who serve nine-year terms.

UNITED NATIONS, NEW YORK CITY
This is the United Nations headquarters located in New York City. Almost all of the countries of the world are members of the United Nations.

MALI, WEST AFRICA
This is a photograph of the mud Mosque of Djenne, Mali. The country of Mali in West Africa is one of the world's poorest countries. Mali signed agreements with the World Bank to reorganize its economy and with the International Monetary Fund (IMF) to receive monetary assistance to build projects to provide fresh water and medical care, develop agriculture, improve education, and provide humanitarian aid to its citizens.

European Union (EU)

There are several significant regional organizations whose members have agreed to work together to promote peace and security as well as economic, social, and cultural development.

World Bank

An agency of the United Nations whose primary function is to provide money to developing countries to fund projects for humanitarian purposes and to relieve poverty.

WEB EXERCISE
Go to **www.unicef.org**. Read one of the featured articles or view one of the featured videos.

International Law

UNICEF

UNICEF
The United Nations Children's Fund (UNICEF) is an agency of the United Nations. UNICEF's goal is to provide humanitarian aid and assistance to children and mothers of children, primarily in developing countries. UNICEF provides vaccines, medicines, nutritional supplements, emergency shelter, educational supplies, and other assistance promote the health and well-being of children. UNICEF operates in more than 190 countries and territories around the world. UNICEF is funded by government and private donations.

United Nations Children's Fund (UNICEF)
An agency of the United Nations whose primary function is to provide aid to improve the lives of the world's children.

European Union (EU)
A regional international organization that comprises many countries of Western and Eastern Europe and was created to promote peace and security as well as economic, social, and cultural development.

WEB EXERCISE
Go to **http://europa.eu/about-eu/countries/index_en.htm** and review the map of the European Union. What are the current candidate countries for membership in the EU?

euro
A single monetary unit that has been adopted by many countries of the EU that comprise the *eurozone*.

North American Free Trade Agreement (NAFTA)
A treaty that has removed or reduced tariffs, duties, quotas, and other trade barriers between the United States, Canada, and Mexico.

One of the most important international regional organizations is the **European Union (EU)**, formerly called the *European Community*, or *Common Market*. The EU, which was created in 1957, is composed of many countries of Western and Eastern Europe. Member nations are Austria, Belgium, Bulgaria, Cyprus (the Greek part), Czech Republic, Denmark, Estonia, Finland, France, Germany, Greece, Hungary, Ireland, Italy, Latvia, Lithuania, Luxembourg, Malta, the Netherlands, Poland, Portugal, Romania, Slovakia, Slovenia, Spain, Sweden, and the United Kingdom of Great Britain and Northern Ireland. The EU represents more than 500 million people and a gross community product that exceeds that of the United States, Canada, and Mexico combined.

EU Administration

The EU's **Council of Ministers** is composed of representatives from each member country who meet periodically to coordinate efforts to fulfill the objectives of the treaty. The council votes on significant issues and changes to the treaty. Some matters require unanimity, whereas others require only a majority vote. The member nations have surrendered substantial sovereignty to the EU. The **European Union Commission**, which is independent of its member nations, is charged to act in the best interests of the union. The member nations have delegated substantial powers to the commission, including authority to enact legislation and to take enforcement actions to ensure member compliance with the treaty.

The EU treaty creates open borders for trade by providing for the free flow of capital, labor, goods, and services among member nations. Under the EU, customs duties have been eliminated among member nations. Common customs tariffs have been established for EU trade with the rest of the world.

Euro

A single monetary unit, the **euro**, has been introduced. Many, but not all, EU countries have voted to use the euro. The countries that have voted to use the euro comprise the **eurozone**. The euro can be used in all countries of the eurozone. An EU central bank, equivalent to the U.S. Federal Reserve Board, has been established to set common monetary policy.

A unanimous vote of existing EU members is needed to admit a new member. Other nonmember European countries are expected to apply for and be admitted as members of the EU.

A map of EU member countries is shown in **Exhibit 26.1**.

North American Free Trade Agreement (NAFTA)

In 1990, Mexico asked the United States to set up a two-country trade pact. Negotiations between the two countries began. Canada joined the negotiations, and on August 12, 1992, the **North American Free Trade Agreement (NAFTA)** was signed by the leaders of the three countries. The treaty creates a free trade zone stretching from the Yukon to the Yucatan, bringing together more than 400 million people in the three countries.

NAFTA has eliminated or reduced most of the duties, tariffs, quotas, and other trade barriers between Mexico, the United States, and Canada. Agriculture, automobiles, computers, electronics, energy and petrochemicals, financial services, insurance, telecommunications, and many other industries are affected. The treaty contains a safety valve: A country can reimpose tariffs if

Exhibit 26.1 MAP OF THE EUROPEAN UNION (EU) MEMBER COUNTRIES

an import surge from one of the other nations hurts its economy or workers. Like other regional trading agreements, NAFTA allows the bloc to discriminate against outsiders and to cut deals among its members. NAFTA also includes special protection for favored industries that have a lot of lobby muscle. Thus, many economists assert that NAFTA is not a "free trade" pact but a *managed trade* agreement.

NAFTA forms a supranational trading region that more effectively competes with Japan and the EU. Consumers in all three countries began to pay lower prices on a wide variety of goods and services as trade barriers fell and competition increased. Critics contend that NAFTA shifted U.S. jobs—particularly blue-collar jobs—south of the border, where Mexican wage rates are about one-tenth those in the United States. Environmentalists criticize the pact for not doing enough to prevent and clean up pollution in Mexico.

A map of NAFTA member countries is shown in **Exhibit 26.2**.

WEB EXERCISE
Go to **www.worldtradelaw.net/ nafta/preamble.pdf** and read the Preamble to the North American Free Trade Agreement (NAFTA).

Exhibit 26.2 MAP OF THE NORTH AMERICAN FREE TRADE AGREEMENT (NAFTA) MEMBER COUNTRIES

Other Regional Trade Organizations

In addition to the EU and NAFTA, many other regional organizations have been established in different parts of the world. Some of these regional organizations are discussed in the following paragraphs.

Association of Southeast Asian Nations (ASEAN)

Association of Southeast Asian Nations (ASEAN)
An association of many countries of Southeast Asia that provides for economic and other coordination among member nations.

In 1967, the **Association of Southeast Asian Nations (ASEAN)** was created. The countries that belong to ASEAN are Brunei Darussalam, Cambodia, Indonesia, Laos, Malaysia, Myanmar, Philippines, Singapore, Thailand, and Vietnam. This is a cooperative association of diverse nations.

Two of the world's largest countries, Japan and China, do not belong to any significant economic community. South Korea also does not belong to ASEAN. Although not a member of ASEAN, Japan has been instrumental in providing financing for the countries that make up that organization. China also works closely with the countries of ASEAN and is a potential member of ASEAN.

A current association called **ASEAN Plus Three**—the three being China, Japan, and South Korea—has informal relations to discuss regional issues. There is a possibility that many Asian countries could establish the Asian Economic Community, patterned after the European Union.

SAUDI ARABIA
The Kingdom of Saudi Arabia, which is a member of OPEC, is the largest producer of oil in the world and has the largest known oil reserve of any country.

Organization of the Petroleum Exporting Countries (OPEC)

One of the most well-known economic organizations is the **Organization of the Petroleum Exporting Countries (OPEC)**. OPEC consists of oil-producing and exporting countries from Africa, Asia, the Middle East, and South America. The member nations are Algeria, Angola, Ecuador, Iran, Iraq, Kuwait, Libya, Nigeria, Qatar, Saudi Arabia, United Arab Emirates (UAE), and Venezuela. OPEC sets quotas on the output of oil production by member nations.

Organization of the Petroleum Exporting Countries (OPEC)
An association comprising many of the oil-producing countries of the world.

Dominican Republic–Central America Free Trade Agreement (DR-CAFTA)

After years of negotiations, the United States and several Central American countries formed the **Central America Free Trade Agreement (CAFTA)**. The agreement originally encompassed the United States and the Central American countries of Costa Rica, El Salvador, Guatemala, Honduras, and Nicaragua. The Dominican Republic subsequently joined CAFTA, which is now commonly called **Dominican Republic–Central America Free Trade Agreement (DR-CAFTA)**. This agreement lowered tariffs and reduced trade restrictions among the member nations. The United States has bilateral trade agreements with several other Central American countries that are not members of DR-CAFTA.

The formation of DR-CAFTA is seen as a stepping stone toward the creation of the **Free Trade Area of the Americas (FTAA)**, which would be an ambitious free trade agreement that would encompass most of the countries of Central America, North America, and South America. The negotiation of the FTAA is difficult because of the different interests of the countries that would be members.

Dominican Republic–Central America Free Trade Agreement (DR-CAFTA)
An association of several Central American countries and the United States designed to reduce tariffs and trade barriers among member nations.

Other Regional Economic Organizations

Countries of Latin America and the Caribbean have established several regional organizations to promote economic development and cooperation. Mexico, the largest industrialized country in Latin America and the Caribbean, has entered into a free trade agreement with all the countries of Central America, as well as Chile, Colombia, and Venezuela. Other regional economic organizations include countries of Central America and South America. Several regional economic communities have been formed in Africa as well.

World Trade Organization (WTO)

WORLD TRADE ORGANIZATION

World Trade Organization (WTO)
An international organization of 153 member nations created to promote and enforce trade agreements among member countries and customs territories.

General Agreement on Tariffs and Trade (GATT)
A multilateral treaty that establishes trade agreements and limits tariffs and trade restrictions among its member nations.

My nationalism is intense internationalism. I am sick of the strife between nations or religions.

Mahatma Gandhi

WTO panel
A body of three WTO judges that hears trade disputes between member nations and issues panel reports.

WTO dispute settlement body
A board composed of one representative from each WTO member nation that reviews panel reports.

WTO appellate body
A panel of seven judges selected from WTO member nations that hears and decides appeals from decisions of the dispute-settlement body.

national courts
The courts of individual nations.

In 1995, the **World Trade Organization (WTO)** was created as a successor to the **General Agreement on Tariffs and Trade (GATT)**.

The WTO is an international organization whose headquarters is located in Geneva, Switzerland. Its main function is to ensure that trade flows as smoothly, predictably, and freely as possible. WTO members have entered into many trade agreements among themselves, covering goods, provision of services, and intellectual property.

Through rounds of negotiations among its membership, the WTO aims to achieve major reform of the international trading system through the introduction of lower trade barriers and revised trade rules. The Doha Round is the latest round of trade negotiations among the WTO membership. The Round is also known semi-officially as the Doha Development Agenda as a fundamental objective is to improve the trading prospects of developing countries.

The WTO has jurisdiction to enforce the most important and comprehensive trade agreements in the world among its 153 member nations and customs territories. Many believe the WTO is a much-needed world court that can peaceably solve trade disputes among nations.

WTO Dispute Resolution

One of the primary functions of the WTO is to hear and decide trade disputes between member nations.

A member nation which believes that another member nation has breached one of the trade agreements can initiate a proceeding to have the WTO hear and decide the dispute. The dispute is first heard by a three-member **WTO panel**, which issues a panel report. The members of the panel are professional judges from member nations. The report, which is the decision of the panel, contains the panel's findings of fact and law, and it orders a remedy if a violation has been found. The report is then referred to the **WTO dispute settlement body**. This body is required to adopt the panel report unless the body, by consensus, agrees not to adopt it.

There is a **WTO appellate body** to which a party can appeal a decision of the dispute-settlement body. This appeals court is composed of seven professional justices selected from member nations. Appeals are limited to issues of law, not fact.

If a violation of a trade agreement is found, the panel report and appellate decision can order the offending nation to cease engaging in the violating practice and to pay damages to the other party. If the offending nation refuses to abide by the order, the WTO can order retaliatory trade sanctions (e.g., tariffs) by other member nations against the noncomplying nation.

National Courts and International Dispute Resolution

The majority of cases involving international law disputes are heard by **national courts** of individual nations. This is primarily the case for commercial disputes between private litigants that do not qualify to be heard by international courts. Some countries have specialized courts that hear international commercial disputes. Other countries permit such disputes to proceed through their regular court systems. In the United States, commercial disputes between U.S. companies and foreign governments or parties may be brought in U.S. District Court.

Judicial Procedure

A party seeking judicial resolution of an international dispute faces several problems, including which nation's courts will hear the case and what law should be applied to the case. Jurisdiction is often a highly contested issue. Absent an agreement providing otherwise, a case involving an international dispute will be brought in the national court of the plaintiff's home country.

Many international contracts contain a **choice of forum clause** (or **forum-selection clause**) that designates which nation's court has jurisdiction to hear a case arising out of a contract. In addition, many contracts also include a **choice of law clause** that designates which nation's laws will be applied in deciding such a case. Absent these two clauses, and without the parties agreeing to these matters, an international dispute may never be resolved.

choice of forum clause (forum-selection clause)
A clause in an international contract that designates which nation's court has jurisdiction to hear a case arising out of the contract.

choice of law clause
A clause in an international contract that designates which nation's laws will be applied in deciding a dispute arising out of the contract.

CONCEPT SUMMARY
INTERNATIONAL CONTRACT CLAUSES

Clause	Description
Forum-selection	A clause that designates the judicial or arbitral forum that will hear and decide a case.
Choice of law	A clause that designates the law to be applied by the court or arbitrator in deciding a case.

Act of State Doctrine

A general principle of international law is that a country has absolute authority over what transpires *within* its own territory. In furtherance of this principle, the **act of state doctrine** states that judges of one country cannot question the validity of an act committed by another country within that other country's own borders. In *United States v. Belmont*,[2] the U.S. Supreme Court declared, "Every sovereign state must recognize the independence of every other sovereign state; and the courts of one will not sit in judgment upon the acts of the government of another, done within its own territory." This restraint on the jurisdiction is justified under the doctrine of separation of powers and permits the executive branch of the federal government to arrange affairs with foreign governments.

act of state doctrine
A doctrine which states that judges of one country cannot question the validity of an act committed by another country within that other country's borders. It is based on the principle that a country has absolute authority over what transpires within its own territory.

Example Suppose the country of North Korea outlaws the practice of all religions in that country. Paul, a Christian who is a citizen of, and living in, the United States, disagrees with North Korea's law. Paul brings a lawsuit against North Korea in a U.S. District Court located in the state of Idaho, arguing to the Court that the North Korean law should be declared illegal. The U.S. District Court will apply the act of state doctrine and dismiss Paul's lawsuit again North Korea. The U.S. District Court will rule that North Korea's law is an act of that state (country) and that a U.S. court does not have authority to hear and decide Paul's case.

In the following case, the Court was called upon to apply the act of state doctrine.

CASE 26.1   *Act of State Doctrine*

Glen v. Club Mediterranee, S.A.

450 F.3d 1251, Web 2006 U.S. App. Lexis 13400 (2006)
United States Court of Appeals for the Eleventh District

"The act of state doctrine is a judicially-created rule of decision that precludes the courts of this country from inquiring into the validity of the public acts a recognized foreign sovereign power committed within its own territory."

—Cox, Circuit Judge

Facts

Prior to the Communist revolution in Cuba, Elvira de la Vega Glen and her sister, Ana Maria de la Vega Glen, were Cuban citizens and residents who jointly owned beachfront property on the Peninsula de Hicacos in Varadero, Cuba. On or about January 1, 1959, in conjunction with Fidel Castro's Communist revolution, the Cuban government expropriated the property without paying the Glens. Also in 1959, the sisters fled Cuba. Ana Maria de la Vega Glen died and passed any interest she had in the Varadero beach property to her nephew, Robert M. Glen.

Approximately forty years after the property was taken by Cuba, Club Mediterranee, S.A., and Club Mediterranee Group (Club Med) entered into a joint venture with the Cuban government to develop the property. Club Med constructed and operated a five-star luxury hotel on the property that the Glens had owned. The Glens sued Club Med in a U.S. District Court located in the state of Florida. The Glens alleged that the original expropriation of their property by the Cuban government was illegal and that Club Med had trespassed on their property and had been unduly enriched by its joint venture with the Cuban government to operate a hotel on their expropriated property. The Glens sought to recover the millions of dollars in profits earned by Club Med from its alleged wrongful occupation and use of the Glens' expropriated property. The U.S. District Court held that the act of state doctrine barred recovery by the Glens and dismissed the Glens' claims against Club Med. The Glens appealed.

Issue

Does the act of state doctrine bar recovery by the Glens?

Language of the Court

The doctrine prevents any court in the United States from declaring that an official act of a foreign sovereign performed within its own territory is invalid. It requires that the acts of foreign sovereigns taken within their own jurisdictions shall be deemed valid. The validity of the Cuban government's act of expropriation is directly at issue in this litigation. The act of state doctrine is properly applied to claims, like the Glens', that necessarily require U.S. courts to pass on the legality of the Cuban government's expropriation of property within Cuba from then-Cuban citizens. Because the act of state doctrine requires the courts deem valid the Cuban government's expropriation of the real property at issue in this case, the Glens cannot maintain their claims for trespass and unjust enrichment against Club Med.

Decision

The U.S. Court of Appeals applied the act of state doctrine and affirmed the judgment of the U.S. District Court that dismissed the Glens' claim against Club Med.

Case Questions

Critical Legal Thinking
What does the act of state doctrine provide? Explain.

Ethics
Did the Cuban government act ethically when it expropriated the Glens' property? Did Club Med act ethically when it entered into a joint venture with the Cuban government to develop the property that had been expropriated from the Glens?

Contemporary Business
What is the expropriation of property by a government?

Doctrine of Sovereign Immunity

One of the oldest principles of international law is the **doctrine of sovereign immunity**. Under this doctrine, *countries* are granted immunity from suits in courts in other countries. For example, if a U.S. citizen wanted to sue the government of China in a U.S. court, he or she could not (subject to certain exceptions).

Originally, the United States granted absolute immunity to foreign governments from suits in U.S. courts. In 1952, the United States switched to the principle of **qualified immunity**, or **restricted immunity**, which was eventually codified in the **Foreign Sovereign Immunities Act (FSIA)** of 1976.[3] This act now exclusively governs suits against foreign nations in the United States, whether in federal court or state court. Most Western nations have adopted the principle of restricted immunity. Other countries still follow the doctrine of absolute immunity.

Exceptions to the FSIA

The FSIA provides that a foreign country is not immune to lawsuits in U.S. courts in the following situations:

- If the foreign country has waived its immunity, either explicitly or by implication.
- If the action is based on a commercial activity carried on in the United States by the foreign country or carried on outside the United States but causing a direct effect in the United States. This is called the **commercial activity exception**.

What constitutes "commercial activity" is the most litigated aspect of the FSIA. With commercial activity, the foreign sovereign is subject to suit in the United States; without it, the foreign sovereign is immune to suit in this country.

Example The country of Cuba has state-owned enterprises. The government of Cuba wants to raise capital for these state-owned enterprises. To do so, the Cuban government sells twenty-year bonds in these companies to investors in the United States. The bondholders are to be paid 10 percent interest annually. By selling bonds to investors in the United States, the government of Cuba is involved in commercial activity in the United States. If Cuba defaults and does not pay the U.S. investors the 10 percent interest on the bonds or the principal when due, the bondholders can sue Cuba in U.S. court, under the commercial activity exception to the doctrine of sovereign immunity to recover the unpaid interest.

doctrine of sovereign immunity
A doctrine which states that countries are granted immunity from suits in courts of other countries.

Foreign Sovereign Immunities Act (FSIA)
An act that exclusively governs suits against foreign nations that are brought in federal or state courts in the United States. It codifies the principle of *qualified*, or *restricted, immunity*.

commercial activity exception
An exception which states that a foreign country is subject to lawsuit in the United States if it engages in commercial activity in the United States or if it carries on such activity outside the United States but causes a direct effect in the United States.

When Kansas and Colorado have a quarrel over the water in the Arkansas River they don't call out the National Guard in each state and go to war over it. They bring a suit in the Supreme Court of the United States and abide by the decision. There isn't a reason in the world why we cannot do that internationally.

Harry S. Truman
Speech (1945)

CONCEPT SUMMARY

ACT OF STATE AND SOVEREIGN IMMUNITY DOCTRINES COMPARED

Doctrine	Description
Act of state	A doctrine that states that an act of a government in its *own country* is not subject to suit in a foreign country's courts.
Sovereign Immunity	A doctrine that states that an act of a government in a *foreign country* is not subject to suit in the foreign country. Some countries provide absolute immunity, and other countries (such as the United States) provide limited immunity.

International Religious Laws

Religious law governs or at least affects the laws of many nations. The following features discuss *Jewish law*, *Islamic law*, *Christian and Canon law*, and *Hindu law*.

International Law

Jewish Law and the Torah

Jewish law, which has existed for centuries, is a complex legal system based on the ideology and theology of the *Torah*. The Torah prescribes comprehensive and integrated rules of religious, political, and legal life that together form Jewish thought. Jewish law is decided by rabbis who are scholars of the Torah and other Jewish scriptures. Rabbinic jurisprudence, known as *Halakhah*, is administered by rabbi-judges sitting as the *Beis Din*, Hebrew for the "house of judgment." As a court, the *Beis Din* has roots that go back three thousand years.

Today, Jews are citizens of countries worldwide. As such, they are subject to the criminal and civil laws of their host countries. But Jews, no matter where they live, abide by the principles of the Torah in many legal matters, such as marriage, divorce, inheritance, and other family matters. Thus, the legal principles embedded in the Torah coexist with the secular laws of Jews' home countries.

Rabbinical judges tend to be actively involved in cases. True to its roots, the *Beis Din* is more a search for the truth than it is an adversarial process.

International Law

Islamic Law and the Qur'an

Approximately 20 percent of the world's population is Muslim. Islam is the principal religion of Afghanistan, Algeria, Bangladesh, Egypt, Indonesia, Iran, Iraq, Jordan, Kuwait, Libya, Malaysia, Mali, Mauritania, Morocco, Niger, North Yemen, Oman, Pakistan, Qatar, Saudi Arabia, Somalia, South Yemen, Sudan, Syria, Tunisia, Turkey, and the United Arab Emirates. **Islamic law** (or **Shari'a**) is the only law in Saudi Arabia. In other Islamic countries, the *Shari'a* forms the basis of family law but coexists with other laws.

The Islamic law system is derived from the *Qur'an*, the *Sunnah* (decisions and sayings of the prophet Muhammad), and reasonings by Islamic scholars. By the 10th century CE, Islamic scholars had decided that no further improvement of the divine law could be made, closed the door of *ijtihad* (independent reasoning), and froze the evolution of Islamic law at that point. Islamic law prohibits *riba*, or the making of unearned or unjustified profit. Making a profit from the sale of goods or the provision of services is permitted. The most notable consequence of *riba* is that the payment of interest on loans is forbidden. To circumvent this result, the party with the money is permitted to purchase the item and resell it to the other party at a profit or to advance the money and become a trading partner who shares in the profits of the enterprise.

Today, Islamic law is primarily used in the areas of marriage, divorce, and inheritance and, to a limited degree, criminal law. To resolve the tension between *Shari'a* and the practice of modern commercial law, the *Shari'a* is often not applied to commercial transactions.

International Law

Christian and Canon Law

Canon law consists of laws and regulations that have been adopted by Catholic and other Christian ecclesiastical authorities that relates to internal laws that govern the church and its members. Christians are followers of Jesus Christ. Throughout Christianity, divine and natural laws have been issued in the form of *canons*. Canons established the structure of the church, definition of faith, rules of conduct, laws of marriage, and laws of inheritance.

The Roman Catholic Church, with more than one billion adherents worldwide, is headed by the Pope, who is located in Vatican City, a landlocked city-state in Rome, Italy. The Catholic Church's legal system predates European common law and civil law systems. In the early 20th century, the Roman Catholic Church ordered that its diverse canons be reduced to a single code. In 1917, the Code of Canon Law was produced. It was again revised with the publication of the *Code of Canon Law of 1983*. This Code of Canon Law regulates the conduct of the Church and individual Catholics.

The Orthodox Church, commonly referred to as the Eastern Orthodox Church, developed in the eastern part of the Roman Empire. The Orthodox Church is Catholic, but not Roman Catholic. It is also not Protestant. The Orthodox Church traces its roots to its formation by Christ's apostles. Its recognized leader is the Patriarch of Constantinople. Eastern Orthodox Churches include the Greek Orthodox Church, the Russian Orthodox Church, the Serbian Orthodox Church, and other Orthodox churches of Eastern Europe and other countries. Worldwide membership approaches 250 million adherents. The Orthodox churches have their own canon law. The Orthodox churches treat their canons more as guidelines than as laws.

Many Christian congregations broke off from the Catholic Church, primarily because of their nonrecognition of the authority of the Pope. They are commonly called Protestants. The Church of England, which broke with the Catholic Church, developed its own ecclesiastical courts

and canons. Other Anglican churches, such as the Episcopal Church in the United States and the Anglican Church of Canada, function under their own systems of canon law. In addition, many Protestant churches have their own canon laws. For example, the Lutheran Church has its Book of Concord, and the Methodist Church has its Book of Discipline. Some Christians are not affiliated with Protestant churches. There are an estimated 900 million Protestants, evangelicals, and independent Christians worldwide.

The canons of Christian faiths provide rules for believers to follow in living their lives and professing their faith. However, the Christian canons are usually separate from the secular laws that govern the conduct of persons.

International Law

Hindu Law—*Dharmasastra*

More than 20 percent of the world's population is Hindu. Most Hindus live in India, where they make up 80 percent of the population. Others live in Burma, Kenya, Malaysia, Pakistan, Singapore, Tanzania, and Uganda. **Hindu law** is a religious law. As such, individual Hindus apply this law to themselves, regardless of their nationality or place of domicile.

Classical Hindu law rests neither on civil codes nor on court decisions but on the works of private scholars that were passed along for centuries by oral tradition and eventually were recorded in the *smitris* ("law books"). Hindu law—called *dharmasastra* in Sanskrit ("the doctrine of proper behavior")—is linked to the divine revelation of Veda (the holy collection of Indian religious songs, prayers,

(continued)

hymns, and sayings written between 2000 and 1000 BCE). Most Hindu law is concerned with family matters and the law of succession.

After India became a British colony, British judges applied a combination of Hindu law and common law in solving cases. This Anglo-Hindu law, as it was called, was ousted when India gained its independence. In the mid-1950s, India codified Hindu law by enacting the Hindu Marriage Act, the Hindu Minority and Guardianship Act, the Hindu Succession Act, and the Hindu Adoptions and Maintenance Act. Outside India, Anglo-Hindu law applies in most other countries populated by Hindus.

Key Terms and Concepts

Act of state doctrine (543)
ASEAN Plus Three (540)
Association of Southeast Asian Nations (ASEAN) (540)
Bilateral treaty (534)
Canon law (547)
Central America Free Trade Agreement (CAFTA) (541)
Choice of forum clause (forum-selection clause) (543)
Choice of law clause (543)
Commercial activity exception (545)
Convention (534)
Council of Ministers (538)
Doctrine of sovereign immunity (545)

Dominican Republic–Central America Free Trade Agreement (DR-CAFTA) (541)
Euro (538)
European Union (EU) (538)
European Union Commission (538)
Eurozone (538)
Foreign Commerce Clause (533)
Foreign Sovereign Immunities Act (FSIA) (545)
Free Trade Area of the Americas (FTAA) (541)
General Agreement on Tariffs and Trade (GATT) (542)
General Assembly (535)
Hindu law (547)

International Court of Justice (ICJ) (World Court) (536)
International Fund for Agricultural Development (IFAD) (535)
International law (533)
International Monetary Fund (IMF) (535)
Islamic law (*Shari'a*) (546)
Jewish law (546)
Multilateral treaty (534)
National courts (542)
North American Free Trade Agreement (NAFTA) (538)
Organization of the Petroleum Exporting Countries (OPEC) (541)
Qualified immunity (restricted immunity) (545)

Secretariat (535)
Secretary-general (535)
Security Council (535)
Treaty (534)
Treaty Clause (534)
United Nations (UN) (535)
United Nations Children's Fund (UNICEF) (537)
United Nations Educational, Scientific, and Cultural Organization (UNESCO) (535)
World Bank (536)
World Trade Organization (WTO) (542)
WTO appellate body (542)
WTO dispute settlement body (542)
WTO panel (542)

Law Case with Answer
Republic of Argentina v. Weltover, Inc.

Facts In an attempt to stabilize its currency, Argentina and its central bank, Banco Central (collectively Argentina), issued bonds called "Bonods." The bonds, which were sold to investors worldwide, provided for repayment in U.S. dollars through transfers on the London, Frankfurt, Zurich, and New York markets at the bondholder's election. Argentina lacked sufficient foreign exchange to pay the bonds when they matured. Argentina unilaterally extended the time for payment and offered bondholders substitute instruments as a means of rescheduling the debts. Two Panamanian corporations and a Swiss bank refused the rescheduling and insisted that full payment be made in New York. When Argentina did not pay, the Panamanian corporations brought a breach of contract action against Argentina in U.S. District Court in New York. Argentina moved to dismiss, alleging that it was not subject to suit in U.S. courts, under the federal Foreign Sovereign Immunities Act (FSIA). The plaintiffs asserted that the commercial activity exception to the FSIA applied that subjected Argentina to lawsuit in U.S. court. Does the commercial activity exception to the Foreign Sovereign Immunities Act permit the plaintiffs to sue Argentina in a U.S. court?

Answer Yes, the commercial activity exception to the Foreign Sovereign Immunities Act permits the plaintiffs to sue Argentina in a U.S. court. When a foreign government acts as a private player in a financial market, the foreign sovereign's actions are "commercial," within the meaning of the FSIA. The commercial character of the Bonods is confirmed by the fact that they are in almost all respects garden-variety debt instruments: They may be held by private parties, they are negotiable and may be traded on the international market, and they promise a future stream of cash income. Argentina's issuance of the Bonods was a "commercial activity" under the FSIA. Argentina's issuance of the bonds, and its unilateral rescheduling of the maturity dates on the Bonods, was a commercial activity that had a direct effect in the United States. Therefore, the commercial activity exception to the Sovereign Immunities Act applies, which means the plaintiffs can sue Argentina in a U.S. court. *Republic of Argentina v. Weltover, Inc.*, 504 U.S. 607, 112 S.Ct. 2160, 119 L.Ed.2d 394, **Web** 1992 U.S. Lexis 3542 (Supreme Court of the United States)

Critical Legal Thinking Cases

26.1 Act of State Doctrine Prior to 1918, the Petrograd Metal Works, a Russian corporation, deposited a large sum of money with August Belmont, a private banker doing business in New York City under the name August Belmont & Co. (Belmont). In 1918, the Soviet government nationalized the corporation and appropriated all its property and assets wherever situated, including the deposit account with Belmont. As a result, the deposit became the property of the Soviet government. In 1933, the Soviet government and the United States entered into an agreement to settle claims and counterclaims between them. As part of the settlement, it was agreed that the Soviet government would take no steps to enforce claims against American nationals (including Belmont) and assigned all such claims to the United States. The United States brought an action against the executors of Belmont's estate to recover the money originally deposited with Belmont by Petrograd Metal Works. Who owns the money? *United States v. Belmont*, 301 U.S. 324, 57 S.Ct. 758, 81 L.Ed. 1134, **Web** 1937 U.S. Lexis 293 (Supreme Court of the United States)

26.2 Act of State Doctrine Banco Nacional de Costa Rica is a bank wholly owned by the government of Costa Rica. It is subject to the rules and regulations adopted by the minister of finance and the central bank of Costa Rica. The bank borrowed $40 million from a consortium of private banks located in the United Kingdom and the United States. The bank signed promissory notes, agreeing to repay the principal plus interest on the loan in four equal installments, due on July 30, August 30, September 30, and October 30 of the following year. The money was to be used to provide export financing of sugar and sugar products from Costa Rica. The loan agreements and promissory notes were signed in New York City, and the loan proceeds were tendered to the bank there.

The bank paid the first installment on the loan. The bank did not, however, make the other three installment payments and defaulted on the loan. The lending banks sued the bank in U.S. District Court in New York to recover the unpaid principal and interest. The bank alleged in defense that the minister of finance and the central bank of Costa Rica had issued a decree forbidding the repayment of loans by the bank to private lenders, including the lending banks in this case. The action was taken because Costa Rica was having trouble servicing debts to foreign creditors. The bank alleged that the act of state doctrine prevented the plaintiffs from recovering on their loans to the bank. Who wins? *Libra Bank Limited v. Banco Nacional de Costa Rica*, 570 F.Supp. 870, **Web** 1983 U.S. Dist. Lexis 14677 (United States District Court for the Southern District of New York)

26.3 Forum-Selection Clause Zapata Off-Shore Company (Zapata) was a Houston, Texas–based American corporation that engaged in drilling oil wells throughout the world. Unterweser Reederei, GMBH (Unterweser), was a German corporation that provided ocean shipping and towing services. Zapata requested bids from companies to tow its self-elevating drilling rig *Chaparral* from Louisiana to a point off Ravenna, Italy, in the Adriatic Sea, where Zapata had agreed to drill certain wells. Unterweser submitted the lowest bid and was requested to submit a proposed contract to Zapata,

which it did. The contract submitted by Unterweser contained the following provision: "Any dispute arising must be treated before the London Court of Justice." Zapata executed the contract without deleting or modifying this provision.

Unterweser's deep sea tug *Bremen* departed Venice, Louisiana, with the *Chaparral* in tow, bound for Italy. While the flotilla was in international waters in the middle of the Gulf of Mexico, a severe storm arose. The sharp roll of the *Chaparral* in Gulf waters caused portions of it to break off and fall into the sea, seriously damaging the *Chaparral*. Zapata instructed the *Bremen* to tow the *Chaparral* to Tampa, Florida, the nearest port of refuge, which it did. Zapata filed suit against Unterweser and the *Bremen* in U.S. District Court in Florida, alleging negligent towing and breach of contract. The defendants asserted that suit could be brought only in the London Court of Justice. Who is correct? *M/S Bremen and Unterweser Reederei, GMBH v. Zapata Off-Shore Company*, 407 U.S. 1, 92 S.Ct. 1907, 32 L.Ed.2d 513, **Web** 1972 U.S. Lexis 114 (Supreme Court of the United States)

Ethics Cases

26.4 Ethics Bank of Jamaica is wholly owned by the government of Jamaica. Chisholm & Co. was a Florida corporation owned by James Henry Chisholm, a Florida resident. The U.S. Export–Import Bank (Ex-Im Bank) provides financial services and credit insurance to export and import companies. Bank of Jamaica and Chisholm & Co. agreed that Chisholm & Co. would arrange lines of credit from various banks and procure $50 million of credit insurance from Ex-Im Bank to be available to aid Jamaican importers. Chisholm & Co. was to be paid commissions for its services.

Chisholm & Co. negotiated and arranged for $50 million of credit insurance from Ex-Im Bank and lines of credit from Florida National Bank, Bankers Trust Company, and Irving Trust Company. Chisholm also arranged meetings between Bank of Jamaica and the U.S. banks. Unbeknownst to Chisholm & Co., Bank of Jamaica went directly to Ex-Im Bank to exclude Chisholm & Co. from the Jamaica program and requested that the credit insurance be issued solely in the name of the Bank of Jamaica. As a result, Chisholm & Co.'s Ex-Im Bank insurance application was not considered. Bank of Jamaica also obtained lines of credit from other companies and paid commissions to them. Chisholm & Co. sued Bank of Jamaica in U.S. District Court in Miami, Florida, alleging breach of contract and seeking damages. Bank of Jamaica filed a motion

to dismiss the complaint, alleging that its actions were protected by sovereign immunity. *Chisholm & Co. v. Bank of Jamaica*, 643 F.Supp. 1393, **Web** 1986 U.S. Dist. Lexis 20789 (United States District Court for the Southern District of Florida)

1. What does the doctrine of sovereign immunity provide?
2. Did Bank of Jamaica act ethically in trying to avoid its contract obligations owed to Chisholm & Co.?
3. Who wins, and why?

26.5 Ethics Nigeria, an African nation, while in the midst of a boom period due to oil exports, entered into $1 billion of contracts with companies in various countries to purchase huge quantities of Portland cement. Nigeria was going to use the cement to build and improve the country's infrastructure. Several of the contracts were with American companies, including Texas Trading & Milling Corporation (Texas Trading). Nigeria substantially overbought cement, and the country's docks and harbors became clogged with ships waiting to unload. Unable to accept delivery of the cement it had bought, Nigeria repudiated many of its contracts, including the one with Texas Trading. When Texas Trading sued Nigeria in U.S. District Court to recover damages for breach of contract, Nigeria asserted in defense that the doctrine of sovereign immunity protected it from liability. *Texas Trading & Milling Corp. v. Federal*

Republic of Nigeria, 647 F.2d 300, **Web** 1981 U.S. App. Lexis 14231 (United States Court of Appeals for the Second Circuit)

1. What does the commercial activity exception to the doctrine of sovereign immunity provide?

2. Did Nigeria act ethically in trying to avoid the contract obligations it owed to Texas Trading & Milling Corporation?

3. Does the doctrine of sovereign immunity protect Nigeria from liability? Why or why not?

Internet Exercises

1. Go to **www.un.org/en/members/** to see a list of the member states of the United Nations. How many countries are currently members of the United Nations?

2. Visit the website of UNESCO, at **www.unesco.org**. What purposes does this agency serve?

3. Go to the website of the International Monetary Fund (IMF), at **www.imf.org**, and find the description of the functions of the IMF. Read it.

4. Visit the website of the World Bank, at **www.worldbank.org**, and find the description of the functions of the World Bank. Read it.

5. Visit the website of the International Court of Justice, at **www.icj-cij.org/homepage/index.php**. Click on "The Court." Read this page.

6. Use **http://finance.yahoo.com** and find the current exchange rate of the euro to the U.S. dollar.

7. Go to the map of the European Union (EU), at **http://europa.eu/about-eu/countries/index_en.htm**. Are there any countries in the EU that you might not have expected to be in the EU?

8. Visit the website of ASEAN, at **www.aseansec.org/64.htm**, and read about the establishment of ASEAN.

9. Visit the website of OPEC, at **www.opec.org**, and click "About Us." Then click "Brief History of OPEC" and read this page.

Endnotes

1. The Charter of the United Nations was entered into force October 24, 1945, and it was adopted by the United States October 24, 1945 (59 Stat. 1031, T.S. 993, 3 Bevans 1153, 1976 Y.B.U.N. 1043).

2. 301 U.S. 324, 57 S.Ct. 758, 81 L.Ed. 1134, **Web** 1937 U.S. Lexis 293 (Supreme Court of the United States).

3. 28 U.S.C. Sections 1602–1611.

APPENDIX A   The Constitution of the United States of America

We the People of the United States, in Order to form a more perfect Union, establish Justice, insure domestic Tranquility, provide for the common defense, promote the general Welfare, and secure the Blessings of Liberty to ourselves and our Posterity, do ordain and establish this Constitution for the United States of America.

Article I

Section 1. All legislative Powers herein granted shall be vested in a Congress of the United States, which shall consist of a Senate and House of Representatives.

Section 2. The House of Representatives shall be composed of Members chosen every second Year by the People of the several states, and the Electors in each State shall have the Qualifications requisite for Electors of the most numerous Branch of the State Legislature.

No Person shall be a Representative who shall not have attained to the Age of twenty five Years, and been seven Years a Citizen of the United States, and who shall not, when elected, be an Inhabitant of that State in which he shall be chosen.

Representatives and direct Taxes shall be apportioned among the several states which may be included within this Union, according to their respective Numbers, which shall be determined by adding to the whole Number of free Persons, including those bound to Service for a Term of Years, and excluding Indians not taxed, three fifths of all other Persons. The actual Enumeration shall be made within three Years after the first Meeting of the Congress of the United States, and within every subsequent Term of ten Years, in such Manner as they shall by Law direct. The number of Representatives shall not exceed one for every thirty Thousand, but each State shall have at Least one Representative; and until such enumeration shall be made, the State of New Hamp-shire shall be entitled to chuse three, Massachusetts eight, Rhode Island and Providence Plantations one, Connecticut five, New York six, New Jersey four, Pennsylvania eight, Delaware one, Maryland six, Virginia ten, North Carolina five, South Carolina five, and Georgia three.

When vacancies happen in the Representation from any State, the Executive Authority thereof shall issue Writs of Election to fill such vacancies.

The House of Representatives shall chuse their Speaker and other Officers; and shall have the sole Power of Impeachment.

Section 3. The Senate of the United States shall be composed of two Senators from each State, chosen by the Legislature thereof, for six Years; and each Senator shall have one Vote.

Immediately after they shall be assembled in Consequence of the first Election, they shall be divided as equally as may be into three Classes. The Seats of the Senators of the first Class shall be vacated at the Expiration of the second Year, of the second Class at the Expiration of the fourth Year, and the third Class at the Expiration of the sixth Year, so that one third may be chosen every second Year; and if Vacancies happen by Resignation, or otherwise, during the Recess of the Legislature of any State, the Executive thereof may make temporary Appointments until the next meeting of the Legislature, which shall then fill such Vacancies.

No person shall be a Senator who shall not have attained to the Age of thirty Years, and been nine Years a Citizen of the United States, and who shall not, when elected, be an Inhabitant of that State for which he shall be chosen.

The Vice President of the United States shall be President of the Senate, but shall have no Vote, unless they be equally divided.

The Senate shall chuse their other Officers, and also a President pro tempore, in the Absence of the Vice President, or when he shall exercise the Office of President of the United States.

The Senate shall have the sole power to try all Impeachments. When sitting for that Purpose, they shall be an Oath or Affirmation. When the President of the United States is tried, the Chief Justice shall preside: And no Person shall be convicted without the Concurrence of two thirds of the Members present.

Judgment in Cases of Impeachment shall not extend further than to removal from Office, and disqualification to hold and enjoy any Office of honor, Trust or Profit under the United States: but the Party convicted shall nevertheless be liable and subject to Indictment, Trial, Judgment and Punishment, according to Law.

Section 4. The Times, Places and Manner of holding Elections for Senators and Representatives, shall be prescribed in each State by the Legislature thereof: but the Congress may at any time by Law make or alter such Regulations, except as to the Places of choosing Senators.

The Congress shall assemble at least once in every Year, and such Meeting shall be on the first Monday in December, unless they shall by Law appoint a different day.

Section 5. Each House shall be the Judge of the Elections, Returns and Qualifications of its own Members, and a Majority of each shall constitute a Quorum to do Business; but a smaller Number may adjourn from day to day, and may be authorized to compel the Attendance of absent Members, in such Manner, and under such Penalties as each House may provide.

Each House may determine the Rules of its Proceedings, punish its Members for disorderly Behaviour, and, with the Concurrence of two thirds, expel a Member.

Each House shall keep a Journal of its Proceedings, and from time to time publish the same, excepting such Parts as may in their Judgment require Secrecy; and the Yeas and Nays of the Members of either House on any question shall, at the Desire of one fifth of those Present, be entered on the Journal.

Neither House, during the Session of Congress, shall, without the Consent of the other, adjourn for more than three days, nor to any other Place than that in which the two Houses shall be sitting.

Section 6. The Senators and Representatives shall receive a Compensation for their Services, to be ascertained by Law, and paid out of the Treasury of the United States. They shall in all Cases, except Treason, Felony and Breach of the Peace, be privileged from Arrest during their Attendance at the Session of their respective Houses, and in going to and returning from the same; and for any Speech or Debate in either House, they shall not be questioned in any other Place.

No Senator or Representative shall, during the Time for which he was elected, be appointed to any civil Office under the Authority of the United States, which shall have been created, or the Emoluments whereof shall have been encreased during such time; and no Person holding any Office under the United States, shall be a Member of either House during his Continuance in Office.

Section 7. All Bills for raising Revenue shall originate in the House of Representatives; but the Senate may propose or concur with Amendments as on other Bills.

Every Bill which shall have passed the House of Representatives and the Senate, shall, before it become a Law, be presented to the President of the United States; If he approve he shall sign it, but if not he shall return it, with his Objections to that House in which it shall have originated, who shall enter the Objections at large on their Journal, and proceed to reconsider it. If after such Reconsideration two thirds of that House shall agree to pass the Bill, it shall be sent, together with the Objections, to the other House, by which it shall likewise be reconsidered, and if approved by two thirds of that House, it shall become a Law. But in all such Cases the Votes of both Houses shall be determined by Yeas and Nays, and the Names of the Persons voting for and against the Bill shall be entered on the Journal of each House respectively. If any Bill shall not be returned by the President within ten Days (Sundays excepted) after it shall have been presented to him, the Same shall be a Law, in like Manner as if he had signed it, unless the Congress by their Adjournment prevent its Return, in which Case it shall not be a Law.

Every Order, Resolution, or Vote to which the Concurrence of the Senate and House of Representatives may be necessary (except on a question of Adjournment) shall be presented to the President of the United States; and before the Same shall take Effect, shall be approved by him, or being disapproved by him, shall be repassed by two thirds of the Senate and House of Representatives, according to the Rules and Limitations prescribed in the Case of a Bill.

Section 8. The Congress shall have Power to lay and collect Taxes, Duties, Imposts and Excises, to pay the Debts and provide for the common Defence and general Welfare of the United States; but all Duties, Imposts and Excises shall be uniform throughout the United States;

To borrow Money on the credit of the United States;

To regulate Commerce with foreign Nations, and among the several States, and with the Indian Tribes;

To establish an uniform Rule of Naturalization, and uniform Laws on the subject of Bankruptcies throughout the United States;

To coin Money, regulate the Value thereof, and of foreign Coin, and fix the Standard of Weights and Measures;

To provide for the Punishment of counterfeiting the Securities and current Coin of the United States;

To establish Post Offices and post Roads;

To promote the Progress of Science and useful Arts, by securing for limited Times to Authors and Inventors the exclusive Right to their respective Writings and Discoveries;

To constitute Tribunals inferior to the supreme Court;

To define and punish Piracies and Felonies committed on the high Seas, and Offenses against the Law of Nations;

To declare War, grant Letters of Marque and Reprisal, and make Rules concerning Captures on Land and Water;

To raise and support Armies, but no Appropriation of Money to that Use shall be for a longer Term than two Years;

To provide and maintain a Navy;

To make Rules for the Government and Regulation of the land and naval Forces;

To provide for calling forth the Militia to execute the Laws of the Union, suppress Insurrections and repel Invasions;

To provide for organizing, arming, and disciplining, the Militia, and for governing such Part of them as may be employed in the Service of the United States, reserving to the States respectively, the Appointment of the Officers, and the Authority of training the Militia according to the discipline prescribed by Congress;

To exercise exclusive Legislation in all Cases whatsoever, over such District (not exceeding ten Miles square) as may, by Cession of particular States, and the Acceptance of Congress, become the Seat of the Government of the United States, and to exercise like Authority over all Places purchased by the Consent of the Legislature of the State in which the Same shall be, for the Erection of Forts, Magazines, Arsenals, dock-Yards, and other needful Buildings;—And

To make all Laws which shall be necessary and proper for carrying into Execution the foregoing Powers, and all other Powers vested by this Constitution in the Government of the United States, or in any Department or Officer thereof.

Section 9. The Migration or Importation of such Persons as any of the States now existing shall think proper to admit, shall not be prohibited by the Congress prior to the Year one thousand eight hundred and eight, but a Tax or Duty may be imposed on such Importation, not exceeding ten dollars for each Person.

The Privilege of the Writ of Habeas Corpus shall not be suspended, unless when in Cases of Rebellion or Invasion the public Safety may require it.

No Bill of Attainder or ex post facto Law shall be passed.

No Capitation, or other direct, Tax shall be laid, unless in Proportion to the Census or Enumeration herein before directed to be taken.

No Tax or Duty shall be laid on Articles exported from any State.

No Preference shall be given by any Regulation of Commerce or Revenue to the Ports of one State over those of another; nor shall Vessels bound to, or from, one State, be obliged to enter, clear, or pay Duties in another.

No Money shall be drawn from the Treasury, but in Consequence of Appropriations made by Laws; and a regular Statement and Account of the Receipts and Expenditures of all public Money shall be published from time to time.

No Title of Nobility shall be granted by the United States: And no Person holding any Office of Profit or Trust under them, shall, without the Consent of the Congress, accept of any present, Emolument, Office, or Title, of any kind whatever, from any King, Prince, or foreign State.

Section 10. No State shall enter into any Treaty, Alliance, or Confederation; grant Letters of Marque and Reprisal; coin Money; emit Bills of Credit; make any Thing but gold and silver Coin a Tender in Payment of Debts; pass any Bill of Attainder, ex post facto Law, or Law impairing the Obligation of Contracts, or grant any Title of Nobility.

No State shall, without the Consent of the Congress, lay any Imposts or Duties on Imports or Exports, except what may be absolutely necessary for executing its inspection Laws: and the net Produce of all Duties and Imposts, laid by any State on Imports or Exports, shall be for the Use of the Treasury of the United States; and all such Laws shall be subject to the Revision and Control of the Congress.

No State shall, without the Consent of Congress, lay any Duty of Tonnage, keep Troops, or Ships of War in time of Peace, enter into any Agreement or Compact with another State, or with a foreign Power, or engage in War, unless actually invaded, or in such imminent Danger as will not admit of delay.

Article II

Section 1. The executive Power shall be vested in a President of the United States of America. He shall hold his Office during the Term of four Years, and, together with the Vice President, chosen for the same Term, be elected, as follows:

Each State shall appoint, in such Manner as the Legislature thereof may direct, a Number of Electors, equal to the whole Number of Senators and Representatives to which the State may be entitled in the Congress: but no Senator or Representative, or Person holding an Office of Trust or Profit under the United States, shall be appointed an Elector.

The Electors shall meet in their respective States, and vote by Ballot for two Persons, of whom one at least shall not be an Inhabitant of the same State with themselves. And they shall make a list of all the Persons voted for, and of the Number of Votes for each; which List they shall sign and certify, and transmit sealed to the Seat of the Government of the United States, directed to the President of the Senate. The

President of the Senate shall, in the presence of the Senate and House of Representatives, open all the Certificates, and the Votes shall be counted. The Person having the greatest Number of Votes shall be the President, if such Number be a Majority of the whole Number of Electors appointed; and if there be more than one who have such Majority, and have an equal Number of Votes, then the House of Representatives shall immediately choose by Ballot one of them for President; and if no Person have a Majority, then from the five highest on the List the said House shall in like Manner choose the President. But in chusing the President, the Votes shall be taken by States, the Representation from each State having one Vote; A quorum for this Purpose shall consist of a Member or Members from two thirds of the States, and a Majority of all the States shall be necessary to a Choice. In every Case, after the Choice of the President, the Person having the greatest Number of Votes of the Electors shall be the Vice President. But if there should remain two or more who have equal Votes, the Senate shall chuse from them by Ballot the Vice President.

The Congress may determine the Time of Chusing the Electors, and the Day on which they shall give their Votes; which Day shall be the same throughout the United States.

No Person except a natural born Citizen, or a Citizen of the United States, at the time of the Adoption of this Constitution, shall be eligible to the Office of President; neither shall any Person be eligible to that Office who shall not have attained to the Age of thirty five Years, and been fourteen Years a Resident within the United States.

In Case of the Removal of the President from Office, or of his Death, Resignation, or Inability to discharge the Powers and Duties of the said Office, the Same shall devolve on the Vice President, and the Congress may by Law provide for the Case of Removal, Death, Resignation or Inability, both of the President and Vice President, declaring what Officer shall then act as President, and such Officer shall act accordingly, until the Disability be removed, or a President shall be elected.

The President shall, at stated Times, receive for his Services, a Compensation, which shall neither be encreased nor diminished during the Period for which he shall have been elected, and he shall not receive within that Period any other Emolument from the United States, or any of them.

Before he enter on the Execution of his Office, he shall take the following Oath or Affirmation:—"I do solemnly swear (or affirm) that I will faithfully execute the Office of President of the United States, and will to the best of my Ability, preserve, protect and defend the Constitution of the United States."

Section 2. The President shall be Commander in Chief of the Army and Navy of the United States, and of the Militia of the several States, when called into the actual Service of the United States; he may require the Opinion, in writing, of the principal Officer in each of the executive Departments, upon any Subject relating to the Duties of their respective Offices, and he shall have Power to grant Reprieves and Pardons for Offences against the United States, except in Cases of Impeachment.

He shall have Power, by and with the Advice and Consent of the Senate, to make Treaties, provided two thirds of the Senators present concur; and he shall nominate, and by and with the Advice and Consent of the Senate, shall appoint Ambassadors, other public Ministers and Consuls, Judges of the supreme Court, and all other Officers of the United States, whose Appointments are not herein otherwise provided for, and which shall be established by Law: but the Congress may by Law vest the Appointment of such inferior Officers, as they think proper, in the President alone, in the Courts of Law, or in the Heads of Departments.

The President shall have Power to fill up all Vacancies that may happen during the Recess of the Senate, by granting Commissions which shall expire at the End of their next Session.

Section 3. He shall from time to time give to the Congress Information of the State of the Union, and recommend to their Consideration such Measures as he shall judge necessary and expedient; he may, on extraordinary Occasions, convene both Houses, or either of them, and in Case of Disagreement between them, with Respect to the Time of Adjournment, he may adjourn them to such Time as he shall think proper; he shall receive Ambassadors and other public Ministers; he shall take Care that the Laws be faithfully executed, and shall Commission all the Officers of the United States.

Section 4. The President, Vice President and all civil Officers of the United States, shall be removed from Office on Impeachment for, and Conviction of, Treason, Bribery, or other high Crimes and Misdemeanors.

Article III

Section 1. The judicial Power of the United States, shall be vested in one supreme Court, and in such inferior Courts as the Congress may from time to time ordain and establish. The Judges, both of the supreme and inferior Courts, shall hold their Offices during good Behaviour, and shall, at Times, receive for their Services, a Compensation, which shall not be diminished during their Continuance in Office.

Section 2. The judicial Power shall extend to all Cases, in Law and Equity, arising under this Constitution, the Laws of the United States, and Treaties made, or which shall be made, under their Authority;—to all Cases affecting Ambassadors, other public Ministers and Consuls;—to all Cases of admiralty and maritime Jurisdiction;—to Controversies to which the United States shall be a Party;—to controversies between two or more States;—between a State and Citizens of another State;—between Citizens of different States;—between Citizens of the same State claiming Lands under Grants of different States, and between a State, or the Citizens thereof, and foreign States, Citizens or Subjects.

In all Cases affecting Ambassadors, other public Ministers and Consuls, and those in which a State shall be Party, the supreme Court shall have original Jurisdiction. In all the other Cases before mentioned, the supreme Court shall have appellate Jurisdiction, both as to Law and Fact, with such Exceptions, and under such Regulations as the Congress shall make.

The Trial of all Crimes, except in Cases of Impeachment, shall be by Jury; and such Trial shall be held in the State where the said Crimes shall have been committed; but when not committed within any State, the Trial shall be at such Place or Places as the Congress may by Law have directed.

Section 3. Treason against the United States, shall consist only in levying War against them, or in adhering to their Enemies, giving them Aid and Comfort. No Person shall be convicted of Treason unless on the Testimony of two Witnesses to the same overt Act, or on Confession in open Court.

The Congress shall have Power to declare the Punishment of Treason, but no Attainder of Treason shall work Corruption of Blood, or Forfeiture except during the Life of the Person attainted.

Article IV

Section 1. Full Faith and Credit shall be given in each State to the public Acts, Records, and judicial Proceedings of every other State. And the Congress may by general Laws prescribe the Manner in which such Arts, Records, and Proceedings shall be proved, and the Effect thereof.

Section 2. The Citizens of each State shall be entitled to all Privileges and Immunities of Citizens in the several States.

A person charged in any State with Treason, Felony, or other Crime, who shall flee from Justice, and be found in another State, shall on Demand of the executive Authority of the State from which he fled, be delivered up, to be removed to the State having Jurisdiction of the Crime.

No Person held to Service or Labour in one State, under the Laws thereof, escaping into another, shall, in Consequence of any Law or Regulation therein, be discharged from such Service or Labour, but shall be delivered up on Claim of the Party to whom such Service or Labour may be due.

Section 3. New States may be admitted by the Congress into this Union; but no new state shall be formed or erected within the Jurisdiction of any other State; nor any State be formed by the Junction of two or more States, or Parts of States, without the Consent of the Legislatures of the States concerned as well as of the Congress.

The Congress shall have Power to dispose of and make all needful Rules and Regulations respecting the Territory or other Property belonging to the United States; and nothing in this Constitution shall be so construed as to Prejudice any Claims of the United States, or of any particular State.

Section 4. The United States shall guarantee to every State in this Union a Republican Form of Government, and shall protect each of them against Invasion; and on Application of the Legislature, or of the Executive (when the Legislature cannot be convened) against domestic Violence.

Article V

The Congress, whenever two thirds of both Houses shall deem it necessary, shall propose Amendments to this Constitution, or, on the Application of the Legislatures of two thirds of the several States, shall call a Convention for proposing Amendments, which, in either Case, shall be valid to all Intents and Purposes, as Part of this Constitution, when ratified by the Legislatures of three fourths of the several States, or by Conventions in three fourths thereof, as the one or the other Mode of Ratification may be proposed by the Congress; Provided that no Amendment which may be made prior to the Year One thousand eight hundred and eight shall in any Manner affect the first and fourth Clauses in the Ninth Section of the first Article; and that no State, without its Consent, shall be deprived of its equal Suffrage in the Senate.

Article VI

All Debts contracted and Engagements entered into, before the Adoption of this Constitution, shall be as valid against the United States under this Constitution, as under the Confederation.

This Constitution, and the Laws of the United States which shall be made in Pursuance thereof; and all Treaties made, or which shall be made, under the

Authority of the United States, shall be the supreme Law of the Land; and the Judges in every State shall be bound thereby, any Thing in the Constitution or Laws of any State to the Contrary notwithstanding.

The Senators and Representatives before mentioned, and the Members of the several State Legislatures, and all executive and judicial Officers, both of the United States and of the Several States, shall be bound by Oath or Affirmation, to support this Constitution; but no religious Test shall ever be required as a Qualification to any Office or public Trust under the United States.

Article VII

The Ratification of the Conventions of nine States, shall be sufficient for the Establishment of this Constitution between the States so ratifying the Same.

Amendment I [1791]

Congress shall make no law respecting an establishment of religion, or prohibiting the free exercise thereof; or abridging the freedom of speech, or the press; or the right of the people peaceably to assemble, and to petition the Government for a redress of grievances.

Amendment II [1791]

A well regulated Militia, being necessary to the security for a free State, the right of the people to keep and bear Arms, shall not be infringed.

Amendment III [1791]

No Soldier shall, in time of peace be quartered in any house, without the consent of the Owner, nor in time of war, but in a manner to be prescribed by law.

Amendment IV [1791]

The right of the people to be secure in their persons, houses, papers, and effects, against unreasonable searches and seizures, shall not be violated, and no Warrants shall issue, but upon probable cause, supported by Oath or Affirmation, and particularly describing the place to be searched, and the persons or things to be seized.

Amendment V [1791]

No person shall be held to answer for a capital, or otherwise infamous crime, unless on a presentment or indictment of a Grand Jury, except in cases arising in the land or naval forces, or in the Militia, when in actual service in time of War or public danger; nor shall any person be subject for the same offense to be twice put in jeopardy of life or limb; nor shall be compelled in any criminal case to be a witness against himself, nor be deprived of life, liberty, or property, without due process of law; nor shall private property be taken for public use, without just compensation.

Amendment VI [1791]

In all criminal prosecutions, the accused shall enjoy the right to a speedy and public trial, by an impartial jury of the State and district wherein the crime shall have been committed, which district shall have been previously ascertained by law, and to be informed of the nature and cause of the accusation; to be confronted with the Witnesses against him; to have compulsory process for obtaining witnesses in his favor, and to have the Assistance of counsel for his defence.

Amendment VII [1791]

In suits at common law, where the value in controversy shall exceed twenty dollars, the right of trial by jury shall be preserved, and no fact tried by a jury, shall be otherwise reexamined in any Court of the United States, than according to the rules of the common law.

Amendment VIII [1791]

Excessive bail shall not be required, nor excessive fines imposed, nor cruel and unusual punishments inflicted.

Amendment IX [1791]

The enumeration in the Constitution, of certain rights, shall not be construed to deny or disparage others retained by the people.

Amendment X [1791]

The powers not delegated to the United States by the Constitution, nor prohibited by it to the States, are reserved to the States respectively, or to the people.

Amendment XI [1798]

The judicial power of the United States shall not be construed to extend to any suit in law or equity, commenced or prosecuted against one of the United States by Citizens of another State, or by Citizens or Subjects of any Foreign State.

Amendment XII [1804]

The Electors shall meet in their respective states and vote by ballot for President and Vice-President, one of whom, at least, shall not be an inhabitant of the same state with themselves; they shall name in their ballots the person voted for as President, and in distinct ballots the person voted for as Vice-President, and they shall make distinct lists of all persons voted for as President, and of all persons voted for as Vice-President, and of the number of votes for each, which lists they shall sign and certify, and transmit sealed to the seat of the government of the United States, directed to the President of the Senate;—The President of the Senate shall, in the presence of the Senate and House of Representatives, open all the certificates and the votes shall then be counted;—The person having the greatest number of votes for President, shall be the President, if such number be a majority of the whole number of Electors appointed; and if no person have such majority, then from the persons having the highest numbers not exceeding three on the list of those voted for as President, the House of Representatives shall choose immediately, by ballot, the President. But in choosing the President, the votes shall be taken by states, the representation from each state having one vote; a quorum for this purpose shall consist of a member or members from two-thirds of the states, and a majority of all the states shall be necessary to a choice. And if the House of Representatives shall not choose a President whenever the right of choice shall devolve upon them, before the fourth day of March next following, then the Vice-President shall act as President, as in the case of the death or other constitutional disability of the President. The person having the greatest number of votes as Vice-President, shall be the Vice-President, if such number be a majority of the whole number of Electors appointed, and if no person have a majority, then from the two highest numbers on the list, the Senate shall choose the Vice-President; a quorum for the purpose shall consist of two-thirds of the whole number of Senators, and a majority of the whole number shall be necessary to a choice. But no person constitutionally ineligible to the office of President shall be eligible to that of the Vice-President of the United States.

Amendment XIII [1865]

Section 1. Neither slavery nor involuntary servitude, except as a punishment for crime whereof the party shall have been duly convicted, shall exist within the United States, or any place subject to their jurisdiction.

Section 2. Congress shall have power to enforce this article by appropriate legislation.

Amendment XIV [1868]

Section 1. All persons born or naturalized in the United States, and subject to the jurisdiction thereof, are citizens of the United States and of the State wherein they reside. No State shall make or enforce any law which shall abridge the privileges or immunities of citizens of the United States; nor shall any State deprive any person of life, liberty, or property, without due process of law; nor deny to any person within its jurisdiction the equal protection of the laws.

Section 2. Representatives shall be appointed among the several States according to their respective numbers, counting the whole number of persons in each State, excluding Indians not taxed. But when the right to vote at any election for the choice of electors for President and Vice President of the United States, Representatives in Congress, the Executive and Judicial officers of a State, or the members of the Legislature thereof, is denied to any of the male inhabitants of such State, being twenty-one years of age, and citizens of the United States, or in any way abridged, except for participation in rebellion, or other crime, the basis of representation therein shall be reduced in the proportion which the number of such male citizens shall bear to the whole number of male citizens twenty-one years of age in such State.

Section 3. No person shall be a Senator or Representative in Congress, or elector of President and Vice President, or hold any office, civil or military, under the United States, or under any State, who, having previously taken an oath, as a member of Congress, or as an officer of the United States, or as a member of any State legislature, or as an executive or judicial officer of any State, to support the Constitution of the United States, shall have engaged in insurrection or rebellion against the same, or given aid or comfort to the enemies thereof. But Congress may by a vote of two-thirds of each House, remove such disability.

Section 4. The validity of the public debt of the United States, authorized by law, including debts incurred for payment of pensions and bounties for services in suppressing insurrection or rebellion, shall not be questioned. But neither the United States nor any State shall assume or pay any debt or obligation incurred in aid of insurrection of rebellion against the United States, or any claim for the loss or emancipation of any slave; but all such debts, obligations and claims shall be held illegal and void.

Section 5. The Congress shall have power to enforce, by appropriate legislation, the provisions of this article.

Amendment XV [1870]

Section 1. The right of citizens of the United States to vote shall not be denied or abridged by the United States or by any State on account of race, color, or previous condition of servitude.

Section 2. The Congress shall have power to enforce this article by appropriate legislation.

Amendment XVI [1913]

The Congress shall have power to lay and collect taxes on incomes, from whatever source derived, without apportionment among the several States, and without regard to any census or enumeration.

Amendment XVII [1913]

The Senate of the United States shall be composed of two Senators from each State, elected by the people thereof, for six years; and each Senator shall have one vote. The electors in each State shall have the qualifications requisite for electors of the most numerous branch of the State legislatures.

When vacancies happen in the representation of any State in the Senate, the executive authority of each State shall issue writs of election to fill such vacancies; *Provided,* That the legislature of any State may empower the executive thereof to make temporary appointments until the people fill the vacancies by election as the legislature may direct. This amendment shall not be so construed as to affect the election or term of any Senator chosen before it becomes valid as part of the Constitution.

Amendment XVIII [1919]

Section 1. After one year from the ratification of this article the manufacture, sale, or transportation of intoxicating liquors within, the importation thereof into, or the exportation thereof from the United States and all territory subject to the jurisdiction thereof for beverage purposes is hereby prohibited.

Section 2. The Congress and the several States shall have concurrent power to enforce this article by appropriate legislation.

Section 3. This article shall be inoperative unless it shall have been ratified as an amendment to the Constitution by the legislatures of the several States, as provided in the Constitution, within seven years from the date of the submission hereof to the States by the Congress.

Amendment XIX [1920]

The right of citizens of the United States to vote shall not be denied or abridged by the United States or by any State on account of sex.

Congress shall have power to enforce this article by appropriate legislation.

Amendment XX [1933]

Section 1. The terms of the President and Vice President shall end at noon on the 20th day of January, and the terms of Senators and Representatives at noon on the 3rd day of January, of the years in which such terms would have ended if this article had not been ratified; and the terms of their successors shall then begin.

Section 2. The Congress shall assemble at least once in every year, and such meeting shall begin at noon on the 3rd day of January, unless they shall by law appoint a different day.

Section 3. If, at the time fixed for the beginning of the term of the President, the President elect shall have died, the Vice President elect shall become President. If a President shall not have been chosen before the time fixed for the beginning of his term, or if the President elect shall have failed to qualify, then the Vice President elect shall act as President until a President shall have qualified; and the Congress may by law provide for the case wherein neither a President elect nor a Vice President elect shall have qualified, declaring who shall then act as President, or the manner in which one who is to act shall be selected, and such person shall act accordingly until a President or Vice President shall have qualified.

Section 4. The Congress may by law provide for the case of the death of any of the persons from whom the House of Representatives may choose a President whenever the right of choice shall have devolved upon them, and for the case of the death of any of the persons from whom the Senate may choose a Vice President whenever the right of choice shall have devolved upon them.

Section 5. Sections 1 and 2 shall take effect on the 15th day of October following the ratification of this article.

Section 6. This article shall be inoperative unless it shall have been ratified as an amendment to the Constitution by the legislatures of three-fourths of the several States within seven years from the date of its submission.

Amendment XXI [1933]

Section 1. The eighteenth article of amendment to the Constitution of the United States is hereby repealed.

Section 2. The transportation or importation into any State, Territory, or possession of the United States for delivery or use therein of intoxicating liquors, in violation of the laws thereof, is hereby prohibited.

Section 3. This article shall be inoperative unless it shall have been ratified as an amendment to the Constitution by conventions in the several States, as provided in the Constitution, within seven years from the date of the submission hereof to the States by the Congress.

Amendment XXII [1951]

Section 1. No person shall be elected to the office of the President more than twice, and no person who has held the office of President, or acted as President, for more than two years of a term to which some other person was elected President shall be elected to the office of the President more than once. But this Article shall not apply to any person holding the office of President when this article was proposed by the Congress, and shall not prevent any person who may be holding the office of President, or acting as President, during the term within which this Article becomes operative from holding the office of President, or acting as President during the remainder of such term.

Section 2. This article shall be inoperative unless it shall have been ratified as an amendment to the Constitution by the legislatures of three-fourths of the several States within seven years from the date of its submission to the States by the Congress.

Amendment XXIII [1961]

Section 1. The District constituting the seat of government of the United States shall appoint in such manner as the Congress may direct:

A number of electors of President and Vice President equal to the whole number of Senators and Representatives in Congress to which the District would be entitled if it were a State, but in no event more than the least populous State; they shall be in addition to those appointed by the States, but they shall be considered, for the purposes of the election of President and Vice President, to be electors appointed by a State; and they shall meet in the District and perform such duties as provided by the twelfth article of amendment.

Section 2. The Congress shall have power to enforce this article by appropriate legislation.

Amendment XXIV [1964]

Section 1. The right of citizens of the United States to vote in any primary or other election for President or Vice President, for electors for President or Vice President, or for Senator or Representative in Congress, shall not be denied or abridged by the United States or any State by reason of failure to pay any poll tax or other tax.

Section 2. The Congress shall have power to enforce this article by appropriate legislation.

Amendment XXV [1967]

Section 1. In case of the removal of the President from office or of his death or resignation, the Vice President shall become President.

Section 2. Whenever there is a vacancy in the office of the Vice President, the President shall nominate a Vice President who shall take office upon confirmation by a majority vote of both Houses of Congress.

Section 3. Whenever the President transmits to the President pro tempore of the Senate and the Speaker of the House of Representatives his written declaration that he is unable to discharge the powers and duties of his office, and until he transmits to them a written declaration to the contrary, such powers and duties shall be discharged by the Vice President as Acting President.

Section 4. Whenever the Vice President and a majority of either the principal officers of the executive departments or of such other body as Congress may by law provide, transmit to the President pro tempore of the Senate and the Speaker of the House of Representatives their written declaration that the President is unable to discharge the powers and duties of his office, the Vice President shall immediately assume the powers and duties of the office as Acting President.

Thereafter, when the President transmits to the President pro tempore of the Senate and the Speaker of the House of Representatives his written declaration that no inability exists, he shall resume the powers and duties of his office unless the Vice President and a majority of either the principal officers of the executive department or of such other body as Congress may by law provide, transmit within four days to the President pro tempore of the Senate and the Speaker of the House of Representatives their written declaration that the President is unable to discharge the powers and duties of his office. Thereupon Congress shall decide the issue, assembling within forty-eight hours for that purpose if not in session. If the

Congress, within twenty-one days after receipt of the latter written declaration, or, if Congress is not in session, within twenty-one days after Congress is required to assemble, determines by two-thirds vote of both Houses that the President shall continue to discharge the same as Acting President; otherwise, the President shall resume the powers and duties of his office.

Amendment XXVI [1971]

Section 1. The right of citizens of the United States, who are 18 years of age or older, to vote, shall not be denied or abridged by the United States or any State on account of age.

Section 2. The Congress shall have the power to enforce this article by appropriate legislation.

Amendment XXVII [1992]

No law, varying the compensation for the services of the Senators and Representatives, shall take effect, until an election of Representatives shall have intervened.

APPENDIX B Sarbanes-Oxley Act of 2002 (Excerpts)

Title I—Public Company Accounting Oversight Board

Sec. 101 Establishment; Administrative Provisions.

(a) Establishment of Board.—There is established the Public Company Accounting Oversight Board, to oversee the audit of public companies that are subject to the securities laws, and related matters, in order to protect the interests of investors and further the public interest in the preparation of informative, accurate, and independent audit reports for companies the securities of which are sold to, and held by and for, public investors. The Board shall be a body corporate, operate as a nonprofit corporation, and have succession until dissolved by an Act of Congress.

Sec. 102 Registration with the Board.

(a) Mandatory Registration.—It shall be unlawful for any person that is not a registered public accounting firm to prepare or issue, or to participate in the preparation or issuance of, any audit report with respect to any issuer.

(b) Application for Registration.—

(1) Form of application.—A public accounting firm shall use such form as the Board may prescribe, by rule, to apply for registration under this section.

Sec. 104 Inspections of Registered Public Accounting Firms.

(a) In General.—The Board shall conduct a continuing program of inspections to assess the degree of compliance of each registered public accounting firm and associated persons of that firm with this Act, the rules of the Board, the rules of the Commission, or professional standards, in connection with its performance of audits, issuance of audit reports, and related matters involving issuers.

(b) Inspection Frequency.—

(1) In general.—Subject to paragraph (2), inspections required by this section shall be conducted—

(A) annually with respect to each registered public accounting firm that regularly provides audit reports for more than 100 issuers; and

(B) not less frequently than once every 3 years with respect to each registered public accounting firm that regularly provides audit reports for 100 or fewer issuers.

Sec. 105 Investigations and Disciplinary Proceedings.

(a) In General.—The Board shall establish, by rule, subject to the requirements of this section, fair procedures for the investigation and disciplining of registered public accounting firms and associated persons of such firms.

(c) Disciplinary Procedures.—

(4) Sanctions.—If the Board finds, based on all of the facts and circumstances, that a registered public accounting firm or associated person thereof has engaged in any act or practice, or omitted to act, in violation of this Act, the rules of the Board, the provisions of the securities laws relating to the preparation and issuance of audit reports and the obligations and liabilities of accountants with respect thereto, including the rules of the Commission issued under this Act, or professional standards, the Board may impose such disciplinary or remedial sanctions as it determines appropriate, subject to applicable limitations under paragraph (5), including—

(A) temporary suspension or permanent revocation of registration under this title;

(B) temporary or permanent suspension or bar of a person from further association with any registered public accounting firm;

(C) temporary or permanent limitation on the activities, functions, or operations of such firm or person (other than in connection with required additional professional education or training);

   (D) a civil money penalty for each such violation, in an amount equal to—

      (i) not more than $100,000 for a natural person or $2,000,000 for any other person; and

      (ii) in any case to which paragraph (5) applies, not more than $750,000 for a natural person or $15,000,000 for any other person;

   (E) censure;

   (F) required additional professional education or training; or

   (G) any other appropriate sanction provided for in the rules of the Board.

(5) Intentional or other knowing conduct.— The sanctions and penalties described in subparagraphs (A) through (C) and (D) (ii) of paragraph (4) shall only apply to—

   (A) intentional or knowing conduct, including reckless conduct, that results in violation of the applicable statutory, regulatory, or professional standard; or

   (B) repeated instances of negligent conduct, each resulting in a violation of the applicable statutory, regulatory, or professional standard.

Title II—Auditor Independence

Sec. 201 Services Outside the Scope of Practice of Auditors.

(a) Prohibited Activities.—Section 10A of the Securities Exchange Act of 1934 (15 U.S.C. 78j–1) is amended by adding at the end of the following:

"(g) Prohibited Activities.—Except as provided in subsection (h), it shall be unlawful for a registered public accounting firm (and any associated person of that firm, to the extent determined appropriate by the Commission) that performs for any issuer any audit required by this title or the rules of the Commission under this title or, beginning 180 days after the date of commencement of the operations of the Public Company Accounting Oversight Board established under section 101 of the Sarbanes-Oxley Act of 2002 (in this section referred to as the 'Board'), the rules of the Board, to provide to that issuer, contemporaneously with the audit, any non-audit service, including—

"(1) bookkeeping or other services related to the accounting records or financial statements of the audit client;

"(2) financial information systems design and implementation;

"(3) appraisal or valuation services, fairness opinions, or contribution-in-kind reports;

"(4) actuarial services;

"(5) internal audit outsourcing services;

"(6) management functions or human resources;

"(7) broker or dealer, investment adviser, or investment banking services;

"(8) legal services and expert services unrelated to the audit; and

"(9) any other service that the Board determines, by regulation, is impermissible.

"(h) Preapproval Required for Non-Audit Services.— A registered public accounting firm may engage in any non-audit service, including tax services, that is not described in any of paragraphs (1) through (9) of subsection (g) for an audit client, only if the activity is approved in advance by the audit committee of the issuer, in accordance with subsection (i)."

Sec. 206 Conflicts of Interest.

Section 10A of the Securities Exchange Act of 1934 (15 U.S.C. 78j–1), as amended by this Act, is amended by adding at the end the following:

"(l) Conflicts of Interest.—It shall be unlawful for a registered public accounting firm to perform for an issuer any audit service required by this title, if a chief executive officer, controller, chief financial officer, chief accounting officer, or any person serving in an equivalent position for the issuer, was employed by that registered independent public accounting firm and participated in any capacity in the audit of that issuer during the 1-year period preceding the date of the initiation of the audit."

Title III—Corporate Responsibility

Sec. 301 Public Company Audit Committees.

Section 10A of the Securities Exchange Act of 1934 (15 U.S.C. 78f) is amended by adding at the end the following:

"(m) Standards Relating to Audit Committees.—

"(2) Responsibilities relating to registered public accounting firms.—The audit committee of each issuer, in its capacity as a committee of the board of directors, shall be directly responsible for the appointment, compensation, and oversight of the work of any registered public accounting firm employed by that issuer (including resolution of disagreements between management and the auditor regarding financial reporting) for the purpose of preparing or issuing an audit report or related work, and each such registered public accounting firm shall report directly to the audit committee.

"(3) Independence.—

"(A) In general.—Each member of the audit committee of the issuer shall be a member of the board of directors of the issuer, and shall otherwise be independent.

"(B) Criteria.—In order to be considered to be independent for purposes of this paragraph, a member of an audit committee of an issuer may not, other than in his or her capacity as a member of the audit committee, the board of directors, or any other board committee—

"(i) accept any consulting, advisory, or other compensatory fee from the issuer; or

"(ii) be an affiliated person of the issuer or any subsidiary thereof.

Sec. 302 Corporate Responsibility for Financial Reports.

(a) Regulations Required.—The Commission shall, by rule, require, for each company filing periodic reports under section 13(a) or 15(d) of the Securities Exchange Act of 1934 (15 U.S.C. 78m, 78o(d)), that the principal executive officer or officers and the principal financial officer or officers, or persons performing similar functions, certify in each annual or quarterly report filed or submitted under either such section of such Act that—

(1) the signing officer has reviewed the report;

(2) based on the officer's knowledge, the report does not contain any untrue statement of a material fact or omit to state a material fact necessary in order to make the statements made, in light of the circumstances under which such statements were made, not misleading;

(3) based on such officer's knowledge, the financial statements, and other financial information included in the report fairly present in all material respects the financial condition and results of operations of the issuer as of, and for, the periods presented in the report;

(4) the signing officers—

(A) are responsible for establishing and maintaining internal controls;

(B) have designed such internal controls to ensure that material information relating to the issuer and its consolidated subsidiaries is made known to such officers by others within those entities, particularly during the period in which the periodic reports are being prepared;

(C) have evaluated the effectiveness of the issuer's internal controls as of a date within 90 days prior to the report; and

(D) have presented in the report their conclusions about the effectiveness of their internal controls based on their evaluation as of that date;

(5) the signing officers have disclosed to the issuer's auditors and the audit committee of the board of directors (or persons fulfilling the equivalent function)—

(A) all significant deficiencies in the design or operation of internal controls which could adversely affect the issuer's ability to record, process, summarize, and report financial data and have identified for the issuer's auditors any material weaknesses in internal controls; and

(B) any fraud, whether or not material, that involves management or other employees who have a significant role in the issuer's internal controls; and

(6) the signing officers have indicated in the report whether or not there were significant changes in internal controls or in other factors that could significantly affect internal controls subsequent to the date of their evaluation, including any corrective actions with regard to significant deficiencies and material weaknesses.

Sec. 303 Improper Influence on Conduct of Audits.

(a) Rules to Prohibit.—It shall be unlawful, in contravention of such rules or regulations as the Commission shall prescribe as necessary and appropriate in the public interest or for the protection of investors, for any officer or director of an issuer, or any other person acting under the direction thereof, to take any action to fraudulently influence, coerce, manipulate, or mislead any independent public or certified accountant engaged in the performance of an audit of the financial statements of that issuer for the purpose of rendering such financial statements materially misleading.

Title IV—Enhanced Financial Disclosures

Sec. 401 Disclosures in Periodic Reports.

(a) Disclosures Required.—Section 13 of the Securities Exchange Act of 1934 (15 U.S.C. 78m) is amended by adding at the end the following:

"(i) Accuracy of Financial Reports.—Each financial report that contains financial statements, and that is required to be prepared in accordance with (or reconciled to) generally accepted accounting principles under this title and filed with the Commission shall reflect all material correcting adjustments that have been identified by a registered public accounting firm in accordance with generally accepted accounting principles and the rules and regulations of the Commission.

"(j) Off–Balance Sheet Transactions.—Not later than 180 days after the date of enactment of the Sarbanes-Oxley Act of 2002, the Commission shall issue final rules providing that each annual and quarterly financial report required to be filed with the Commission shall disclose all material off-balance sheet transactions, arrangements, obligations (including contingent obligations), and other relationships of the issuer with unconsolidated entities or other persons, that may have a material current or future effect on financial condition, changes in financial condition, results of operations, liquidity, capital expenditures, capital resources, or significant components of revenues or expenses."

(b) Commission Rules on Pro Forma Figures.— Not later than 180 days after the date of enactment of the Sarbanes-Oxley Act of 2002, the Commission shall issue final rules providing that pro forma financial information included in any periodic or other report filed with the Commission pursuant to the securities laws, or in any public disclosure or press or other release, shall be presented in a manner that—

(1) does not contain an untrue statement of a material fact or omit to state a material fact necessary in order to make the pro forma financial information, in light of the circumstances under which it is presented, not misleading; and

(2) reconciles it with the financial condition and results of operations of the issuer under generally accepted accounting principles.

Sec. 402 Enhanced Conflict of Interest Provisions.

(a) Prohibition on Personal Loans to Executives.—Section 13 of the Securities Exchange Act of 1934 (15 U.S.C. 78m), as amended by this Act, is amended by adding at the end the following:

"(k) Prohibition on Personal Loans to Executives.—

"(1) In general.—It shall be unlawful for any issuer (as defined in section 2 of the Sarbanes-Oxley Act of 2002), directly or indirectly, including through any subsidiary, to extend or maintain credit, to arrange for the extension of credit, or to renew an extension of credit, in the form of a personal loan to or for any director or executive officer (or equivalent thereof) of that issuer. An extension of credit maintained by the issuer on the date of enactment of this subsection shall not be subject to the provisions of this subsection, provided that there is no material modification to any term of any such extension of credit or any renewal of any such extension of credit on or after that date of enactment.

Sec. 406 Code of Ethics for Senior Financial Officers.

(a) Code of Ethics Disclosure.—The Commission shall issue rules to require each issuer, together with periodic reports required pursuant to section 13(a) or 15(d) of the Securities Exchange Act of 1934, to disclose whether or not, and if not, the reason therefor, such issuer has adopted a code of ethics for senior financial officers, applicable to its principal financial officer and comptroller or principal accounting officer, or persons performing similar functions.

(b) Changes in Codes of Ethics.—The Commission shall revise its regulations concerning matters requiring prompt disclosure on Form 8-K (or any successor thereto) to require the immediate disclosure by means of the filing of such form, dissemination by the Internet or by other electronic means, by any issuer of any change in or waiver of the code of ethics for senior financial officers.

(c) Definition.—In this section, the term "code of ethics" means such standards as are reasonably necessary to promote—

(1) honest and ethical conduct, including the ethical handling of actual or apparent conflicts of interest between personal and professional relationships;

(2) full, fair, accurate, timely, and understandable disclosure in the periodic reports required to be filed by the issuer; and

(3) compliance with applicable governmental rules and regulations.

Title V—Analyst Conflicts of Interest

Sec. 501 Treatment of Securities Analysts by Registered Securities Associations and National Securities Exchanges.

(a) Rules Regarding Securities Analysts.—The Securities Exchange Act of 1934 (15 U.S.C. 78a et seq.) is amended by inserting after section 15C the following new section:

"Sec. 15D. Securities Analysts and Research Reports

"(a) Analyst Protections.—The Commission, or upon the authorization and direction of the Commission, a registered securities association or national securities exchange, shall have adopted, not later than 1 year after the date of enactment of this section, rules reasonably designed to address conflicts of interest that can arise when securities analysts recommend equity securities in research reports and public appearances, in order to improve the objectivity of research and provide investors with more useful and reliable information, including rules designed—

"(1) to foster greater public confidence in securities research, and to protect the objectivity and independence of securities analysts, by—

"(A) restricting the prepublication clearance or approval of research reports by persons employed by the broker or dealer who are engaged in investment banking activities, or persons not directly responsible for investment research, other than legal or compliance staff;

"(B) limiting the supervision and compensatory evaluation of securities analysts to officials employed by the broker or dealer who are not engaged in investment banking activities; and

"(C) requiring that a broker or dealer and persons employed by a broker or dealer who are involved with investment banking activities may not, directly or indirectly, retaliate against or threaten to retaliate against any securities analyst employed by that broker or dealer or its affiliates as a result of an adverse, negative, or otherwise unfavorable research report that may adversely affect the present or prospective investment banking relationship of the broker or dealer with the issuer that is the subject of the research report, except that such rules may not limit the authority of a broker or dealer to discipline a securities analyst for causes other than such research report in accordance with the policies and procedures of the firm;

"(2) to define periods during which brokers or dealers who have participated, or are to participate, in a public offering of securities as underwriters or dealers should not publish or otherwise distribute research reports relating to such securities or to the issuer of such securities;

"(3) to establish structural and institutional safeguards within registered brokers or dealers to assure that securities analysts are separated by appropriate informational partitions within the firm from the review, pressure, or oversight of those whose involvement in investment banking activities might potentially bias their judgment or supervision; and

"(4) to address such other issues as the Commission, or such association or exchange, determines appropriate.

"(b) Disclosure.—The Commission, or upon the authorization and direction of the Commission, a registered securities association or national securities exchange, shall have adopted, not later than 1 year after the date of enactment of this section, rules reasonably designed to require each securities analyst to disclose in public appearances, and each registered broker or dealer to disclose in each research report, as applicable, conflicts of interest that are known or should have been known by the securities analyst or the broker or dealer, to exist at the time of the appearance or the date of distribution of the report, including—

"(1) the extent to which the securities analyst has debt or equity investments in the issuer that is the subject of the appearance or research report;

"(2) whether any compensation has been received by the registered broker or dealer, or any affiliate thereof, including the securities analyst, from the issuer that is the subject of the appearance or research report, subject to such exemptions as the Commission may determine appropriate and necessary to prevent disclosure by virtue of this paragraph of material non-public information regarding specific potential future investment banking transactions of such issuer, as is appropriate in the public interest and consistent with the protection of investors;

"(3) whether an issuer, the securities of which are recommended in the appearance or research report, currently is, or during the 1-year period preceding the date of the appearance or date of distribution of the report has been, a client of the registered broker or dealer, and if so, stating the types of services provided to the issuer;

"(4) whether the securities analyst received compensation with respect to a research report, based upon (among any other factors) the investment banking revenues (either generally or specifically earned from the issuer being analyzed) of the registered broker or dealer; and

"(5) such other disclosures of conflicts of interest that are material to investors, research analysts, or the broker or dealer as the Commission, or such association or exchange, determines appropriate.

"(c) Definitions.—In this section—

"(1) the term 'securities analyst' means any associated person of a registered broker or dealer that is principally responsible for, and any associated person who reports directly or indirectly to a securities analyst in connection with, the preparation of the substance of a research report, whether or not any such person has the job title of 'securities analyst'; and

"(2) the term 'research report' means a written or electronic communication that includes an analysis of equity securities of individual companies or industries, and that provides information reasonably sufficient upon which to base an investment decision."

(b) Enforcement.—Section 21B(a) of the Securities Exchange Act of 1934 (15 U.S.C. 78u–2(a)) is amended by inserting "15D," before "15B".

(c) Commission Authority.—The Commission may promulgate and amend its regulations, or direct a registered securities association or national securities exchange to promulgate and amend its rules, to carry out section 15D of the Securities Exchange Act of 1934, as added by this section, as is necessary for the protection of investors and in the public interest.

Title VI—Commission Resources and Authority

Sec. 602 Appearance and Practice Before the Commission.

The Securities Exchange Act of 1934 (15 U.S.C. 78a et seq.) is amended by inserting after section 4B the following:

"Sec 4C. Appearance and Practice Before the Commission

"(a) Authority to Censure.—The Commission may censure any person, or deny, temporarily or permanently, to any person the privilege of appearing or practicing before the Commission in any way, if that person is found by the Commission, after notice and opportunity for hearing in the matter—

"(1) not to possess the requisite qualifications to represent others;

"(2) to be lacking in character or integrity, or to have engaged in unethical or improper professional conduct; or

"(3) to have willfully violated or willfully aided and abetted the violation of, any provision of the securities laws or the rules and regulations issued thereunder.

Title VII—Studies and Reports

Sec. 705 Study of Investment Banks.

(a) GAO Study.—The Comptroller General of the United States shall conduct a study on whether investment banks and financial advisers assisted public companies in manipulating their earnings and obfuscating their true financial condition. The study should address the rule of investment banks and financial advisers—

(1) in the collapse of the Enron Corporation, including with respect to the design and implementation of derivatives transactions, transactions involving special purpose vehicles, and other financial arrangements that may have had the effect of altering the company's reported financial statements in ways that obscured the true financial picture of the company;

(2) in the failure of Global Crossing, including with respect to transactions involving swaps of fiberoptic cable capacity, in the designing transactions that may have had the effect of altering the company's reported financial statements in ways that obscured the true financial picture of the company; and

(3) generally, in creating and marketing transactions which may have been designed solely to enable companies to manipulate revenue streams, obtain loans, or move liabilities off balance sheets without altering the economic and business risks faced by the companies or any other mechanism to obscure a company's financial picture.

Title VIII—Corporate and Criminal Fraud Accountability

Sec. 801 Short Title.

This title may be cited as the "Corporate and Criminal Fraud Accountability Act of 2002".

Sec. 802 Criminal Penalties for Altering Documents.

(a) In General.—Chapter 73 of title 18, United States Code, is amended by adding at the end the following:

§1519. Destruction, alteration, or falsification of records in Federal investigations and bankruptcy

"Whoever knowingly alters, destroys, mutilates, conceals, covers up, falsifies, or makes a false entry in any record, document, or tangible object with the intent to impede, obstruct, or influence the investigation or proper administration of any matter within the jurisdiction of any department or agency of the United States or any case filed under Title 11, or in relation to or contemplation of any such matter or case, shall be fined under this title, imprisoned not more than 20 years, or both.

§1520. Destruction of corporate audit records

"(a) (1) Any accountant who conducts an audit of an issuer of securities to which section 10A(a) of the Securities Exchange Act of 1934 (15 U.S.C. 78j–l(a)) applies, shall maintain all audit or review workpapers for a period of 5 years from the end of the fiscal period in which the audit or review was concluded.

Sec. 807 Criminal Penalties for Defrauding Shareholders of Publicly Traded Companies.

(a) In General.—Chapter 63 of title 18, United States Code, is amended by adding at the end the following:

§1348. Securities fraud

"Whoever knowingly executes, or attempts to execute, a scheme or artifice—

"(1) to defraud any person in connection with any security of an issuer with a class of securities registered under section 12 of the Securities Exchange Act of 1934 (15 U.S.C. 78l) or that is required to file reports under section 15(d) of the Securities Exchange Act of 1934 (15 U.S.C. 78o(d)); or

"(2) to obtain, by means of false or fraudulent pretenses, representations, or promises, any money or property in connection with the purchase or sale of any security of an issuer with a class of securities registered under section 12 of the Securities Exchange Act of 1934 (15 U.S.C. 78l) or that is required to file reports under section 15(d) of the Securities Exchange Act of 1934 (15 U.S.C. 78o(d));

shall be fined under this title, or imprisoned not more than 25 years, or both."

Title IX—White-Collar Crime Penalty Enhancements

Sec. 901 Short Title.

This title may be cited as the "White-Collar Crime Penalty Enhancement Act of 2002".

Sec. 906 Corporate Responsibility for Financial Reports.

(a) In General.—Chapter 63 of title 18, United States Code, is amended by inserting after section 1349, as created by this Act, the following:

§1350. Failure of corporate officers to certify financial reports

(a) Certification of Periodic Financial Reports.—Each periodic report containing financial statements filed by an issuer with the Securities Exchange Commission pursuant to section 13(a) or 15(d) of the Securities Exchange Act of 1934 (15 U.S.C. 78m(a) or 78o(d)) shall be accompanied by a written statement by the chief executive officer and chief financial officer (or equivalent thereof) of the issuer.

"(b) Content.—The statement required under subsection (a) shall certify that the periodic report containing the financial statements fully complies with the requirements of section 13(a) or 15(d) of the Securities Exchange Act of 1934 (15 U.S.C. 78m or 78o(d)) and that information contained in the periodic report fairly presents, in all material respects, the financial condition and results of operations of the issuer.

"(c) Criminal Penalties.—Whoever—

"(1) certifies any statement as set forth in subsections (a) and (b) of this section knowing that the periodic report accompanying the statement does not comport with all the requirements set forth in this section shall be fined not more than $1,000,000 or imprisoned not more than 10 years, or both; or

"(2) willfully certifies any statement as set forth in subsections (a) and (b) of this section knowing that the periodic report accompanying the statement does not comport with all the requirements set forth in this section shall be fined not more than $5,000,000, or imprisoned not more than 20 years, or both."

(b) Clerical Amendment.—The table of sections at the beginning of chapter 63 of title 18, United States Code, is amended by adding at the end the following:
"1350". Failure of corporate officers to certify financial reports."

Title X—Corporate Tax Returns

Sec. 1001 Sense of the Senate Regarding the Signing of Corporate Tax Returns by Chief Executive Officers.

It is the sense of the Senate that the Federal income tax return of a corporation should be signed by the chief executive officer of such corporation.

Title XI—Corporate Fraud Accountability

Sec. 1101 Short Title.

This title may be cited as the "Corporate Fraud Accountability Act of 2002".

Sec. 1102 Tampering with a Record or Otherwise Impeding an Official Proceeding.

Section 1512 of title 18, United States Code, is amended—

(1) by redesignating subsections (c) through (i) as subsections (d) through (j), respectively; and

(2) by inserting after subsection (b) the following new subsection:

"(c) Whoever corruptly—

"(1) alters, destroys, mutilates, or conceals a record, document, or other object, or attempts to do so, with the intent to impair the object's integrity or availability for use in an official proceeding; or

"(2) otherwise obstructs, influences, or impedes any official proceeding, or attempts to do so,

shall be fined under this title or imprisoned not more than 20 years, or both."

Sec. 1105 Authority of the Commission to Prohibit Persons from Serving as Officers or Directors.

(a) Securities Exchange Act of 1934.—Section 21C of the Securities Exchange Act of 1934 (15 U.S.C. 78u–3) is amended by adding at the end the following:

"(f) Authority of the Commission to Prohibit Persons from Serving as Officers or Directors.—In any cease-and-desist proceeding under subsection (a), the Commission may issue an order to prohibit, conditionally or unconditionally, and permanently or for such period of time as it shall determine, any person who has violated section 10(b) or the rules or regulations thereunder, from acting as an officer or director of any issuer that has a class of securities registered pursuant to section 12, or that is required to file reports pursuant to section 15(d), if the conduct of that person demonstrates unfitness to serve as an officer or director of any such issuer."

(b) Securities Act of 1933.—Section 8A of the Securities Act of 1933 (15 U.S.C. 77h–1) is amended by adding at the end of the following:

"(f) Authority of the Commission to Prohibit Persons from Serving as Officers or Directors.—In any cease-and-desist proceeding under subsection (a), the Commission may issue an order to prohibit, conditionally or unconditionally, and permanently or for such period of time as it shall determine, any person who has violated section 17(a)(1) or the rules or regulations thereunder, from acting as an officer or director of any issuer that has a class of securities registered pursuant to section 12 of the Securities Exchange Act of 1934, or that is required to file reports pursuant to section 15(d) of that Act, if the conduct of that person demonstrates unfitness to serve as an officer or director of any such issuer."

GLOSSARY

© A symbol that provides notification that the work to which it is attached is copyrighted. The symbol should be accompanied by the author's name and the year of publication.

® A symbol that designates marks that have been registered with the U.S. Patent and Trademark Office.

abnormal misuse A defense that relieves a seller of product liability if the user *abnormally* misused the product.

abnormally dangerous activities Dangerous activities for which strict liability is imposed.

abusive filing A Chapter 7 filing that is found to be an abuse of Chapter 7 liquidation bankruptcy. In such a case, the court can dismiss the case or convert the case to a Chapter 13 or Chapter 11 proceeding, with the debtor's consent.

abusive homestead exemption A bankruptcy rule that stipulates that a debtor may not exempt more that a specified dollar amount as a homestead exemption.

acceptance A manifestation of assent by the offeree to the terms of the offer in a manner invited or required by the offer as measured by the objective theory of contracts.

acceptance method A method whereby the court confirms a plan of reorganization if the creditors accept the plan and if other requirements are met.

acceptance-upon-dispatch rule A rule that states that an acceptance is effective when it is dispatched, even if it is lost in transmission; also known as the *mailbox rule*.

accommodation A shipment of goods that is offered to a buyer as a replacement for the original shipment when the original shipment cannot be filled.

accommodation party (co-signer) A party who signs an instrument and lends his or her name (and credit) to another party to the instrument.

accord An agreement whereby the parties agree to accept something different in satisfaction of the original contract.

accord and satisfaction The settlement of a contract dispute. Also called *compromise.*

accountant–client privilege A state law that provides that an accountant cannot be called as a witness against a client in a court action. Federal courts do not recognize this privilege.

accredited investor A person, a corporation, a company, an institution, or an organization that meets the net worth, income, asset, position, and other requirements established by the Securities and Exchange Commission (SEC) to qualify as an *accredited investor.*

act of monopolizing An act that is required for there to be a violation of Section 2 of the Sherman Act. Possession of monopoly power without such act does not violate Section 2.

act of state doctrine A doctrine that states that judges of one country cannot question the validity of an act committed by another country within that other country's borders. It is based on the principle that a country has absolute authority over what transpires within its own territory.

action for an accounting A formal judicial proceeding in which the court is authorized to (1) review the partnership and the partners' transactions and (2) award each partner his or her share of the partnership assets.

actual and exclusive A requirement that must be proven by a person to obtain real property by adverse possession. It requires that the adverse possessor has physically occupied the premises.

actual cause The actual cause of negligence. A person who commits a negligent act is not liable unless actual cause can be proven; also called *causation in fact.*

actual contract A contract that is either *express* or *implied-in-fact.*

actual fraud An intentional misrepresentation or omission of a material fact that is relied on by a person and causes that person damage.

actual notice Giving an express notice verbally or in writing.

actus reus "Guilty act"—the actual performance of a criminal act.

additional terms Terms in a sales contract that the UCC permits in an acceptance rather than creating a counteroffer.

adequate assurance of performance Adequate assurance of performance from the other party if there is an indication that a contract will be breached by that party.

adjudged insane Declared legally insane by a proper court or administrative agency. A contract entered into by a person adjudged insane is *void.*

administrative agencies Agencies that the legislative and executive branches of federal and state governments establish.

administrative dissolution Involuntary dissolution of a corporation that is ordered by the secretary of state if a corporation has failed to comply with certain procedures required by law.

administrative employee exemption An exemption from federal minimum wage and overtime pay requirements that applies to employees who are compensated on a salary or fee basis, whose primary duty is the performance of office or nonmanual work, and whose work includes the exercise of discretion and independent judgment with respect to matters of significance.

administrative law Substantive and procedural law that governs the operation of administrative agencies.

administrative law judge (ALJ) A judge who presides over administrative proceedings and decides questions of law and fact concerning a case.

administrative order A decision made by an administrative law judge.

Administrative Procedure Act (APA) A federal statute that establishes certain administrative procedures that federal administrative agencies must follow in conducting their affairs.

administrative rules and regulations Directives issued by federal and state administrative agencies that interpret the statutes that the agency is authorized to enforce.

administrative subpoena A subpoena issued to an administrative agency to conduct a search of business or other premises.

adulterated food Food that consists in whole or in part of any filthy, putrid, or decomposed substance or is otherwise unfit for food.

adverse possession A situation in which a person who wrongfully possesses someone else's real property obtains title to that property if certain statutory requirements are met.

affirmative action A policy that provides that certain job preferences will be given to minority or other protected-class applicants when an employer makes an employment decision.

affirmative action plan A plan adopted by an employer that provides that certain job preferences will be given to members of minority racial and ethnic groups, females, and other protected-class applicants when an employer makes an employment decision.

affirmative defense (1) A defense that an employer may raise against a charge of sexual, racial, or other harassment. (2) A defense asserted in a defendant's answer to allegations contained in a plaintiff's complaint.

AFL-CIO A labor organization formed in 1955 by the combination of the American Federation of Labor (AFL) and the Congress of Industrial Organizations (CIO).

after-acquired property Property that a debtor acquires after a security agreement is executed.

age discrimination Discrimination in employment based on a person's age. Federal law prohibits age discrimination against employees who are 40 and older. State and local laws can establish younger ages for protection against age discrimination.

Age Discrimination in Employment Act (ADEA)   A federal statute that prohibits age discrimination practices against employees who are 40 and older.

age of majority   The legal age, as set by state law, for a person to have the capacity to enter into a contract. The most prevalent age of majority is 18 years for both males and females.

agency   A fiduciary relationship that results from the manifestation of consent by one person to act on behalf of another person, with that person's consent.

agency by ratification   An agency that occurs when (1) a person misrepresents himself or herself as another's agent when in fact he or she is not and (2) the purported principal ratifies the unauthorized act.

agency law   The large body of common law that governs agency; a mixture of contract law and tort law.

agency shop   A workplace where an employer may hire anyone whether he belongs to a union or not. After an employee has been hired, he does not have to join an existing labor union, but if he does not join the union, he must pay an agency fee to the union.

agent   A party who agrees to act on behalf of another.

agents' contracts   Real estate agents' contracts to sell real property for another party that are covered by the Statute of Frauds and must be in writing to be enforceable.

agreement   The manifestation by two or more persons of the substance of a contract.

aiders and abettors   Parties who knowingly assist principal actors in the commission of securities fraud.

air pollution   Pollution caused by factories, homes, vehicles, and the like that affects the air.

air quality control regions (AQCRs)   Regions of each state that the Environmental Protection Agency (EPA) has designated to measure compliance with air quality standards.

air rights   The owners of land own air rights above the real property they own.

air space parcel   Property rights owned by the owner of real property above the land they own. The owners of air space parcels often sell or lease them to other parties.

alien corporation   A corporation that is incorporated in another country.

alter ego doctrine   A doctrine that says if a shareholder dominates a corporation and uses it for improper purposes, a court of equity can disregard the corporate entity and hold the shareholder personally liable for the corporation's debts and

obligations; also called *piercing the corporate veil*.

alternative dispute resolution (ADR)   Methods of resolving disputes other than litigation.

amendments to the U.S. Constitution   Amendments that have been added to the U.S. Constitution.

American Federation of Labor (AFL)   A labor organization that was formed in 1886 to which only skilled craft workers such as silversmiths and artisans were allowed to belong.

American Inventors Protection Act   A federal statute that permits an inventor to file a provisional application with the U.S. Patent and Trademark Office three months before the filing of a final patent application, among other provisions.

Americans with Disabilities Act Amendments Act (ADAAA) of 2008   A federal statute that amends the Americans with Disabilities Act of 1990 (ADA) by expanding the definition of disability, requiring that the definition of disability be broadly construed, and requiring common-sense assessments in applying certain provisions of the ADA.

Americans with Disabilities Act of 1990 (ADA)   A federal statute that imposes obligations on employers and providers of public transportation, telecommunications, and public accommodations to accommodate individuals with disabilities.

analytical school of jurisprudence   A school of thought which maintains that law is shaped by logic.

annual percentage rate (APR)   The annual interest rate that a debtor will pay on a debt, which includes in its calculation many of the fees charged by the lender.

annual shareholders' meeting   A meeting of the shareholders of a corporation that must be held by the corporation to elect directors and to vote on other matters.

answer   The defendant's written response to a plaintiff's complaint that is filed with the court and served on the plaintiff.

antecedent debt   Existing debt of a partnership when an new partner joins the partnership.

Anticybersquatting Consumer Protection Act (ACPA)   A federal statute that permits trademark owners and famous persons to recover domain names that use their names where the domain name has been registered by another person or business in bad faith.

antideficiency statute   A statute that prohibits deficiency judgments regarding certain types of mortgages, such as those on residential property.

antitakeover statutes   Statutes enacted by a state legislature that protect against the hostile takeover of corporations incorporated in or doing business in the state.

antitrust injuries   Injuries suffered by a person or business to his or her "business or property" caused by an antitrust violation.

antitrust laws   A series of laws enacted to limit anticompetitive behavior in almost all industries, businesses, and professions operating in the United States.

apparent agency   Agency that arises when a principal creates the appearance of an agency that in actuality does not exist. Also known as *agency by estoppels*.

appeal   The act of asking an appellate court to overturn a decision after the trial court's final judgment has been entered.

appellant (petitioner)   The appealing party in an appeal.

appellee (respondent)   The responding party in an appeal.

appropriate bargaining unit   A group of employees that a union seeks to represent; also referred to as a *bargaining unit*.

arbitration   A form of alternative dispute resolution in which the parties choose an impartial third party to hear and decide their dispute.

arbitrator   A neutral third party who hears and decides a dispute in arbitration.

area franchise   A business that a franchisor authorizes a franchisee to run on its behalf in designated areas. The area franchisee is called a *subfranchisor*.

arraignment   A hearing during which the accused is brought before a court and is (1) informed of the charges against him or her and (2) asked to enter a plea.

arrearages   The amount of unpaid cumulative dividends.

arrest   A situation in which a person is taken into custody for the alleged commission of a crime.

arrest warrant   A document for a person's detainment based on a showing of probable cause that the person committed a crime.

arson   The willful or malicious burning of a building.

Article I of the U.S. Constitution   Part of the Constitution that establishes the legislative branch of the federal government.

Article I, section 8, clause 4 of the U.S. Constitution   Part of the Constitution that provides that "The Congress shall have the power . . . to establish . . . uniform laws on the subject of bankruptcies throughout the United States."

Article II of the U.S. Constitution   Part of the Constitution that establishes the executive branch of the federal government.

Article 2 (Sales) of the Uniform Commercial Code   An article of the Uniform Commercial Code (UCC) that governs sale of goods.

Article 2A (Leases) of the Uniform Commercial Code   An article of the Uniform Commercial Code (UCC) that governs leases of goods.

Article III of the U.S. Constitution   Part of the Constitution that establishes the judicial branch of the federal government.

Article 3 (Commercial Paper) of the Uniform Commercial Code A model act promulgated in 1952 that established rules for the creation of, transfer of, enforcement of, and liability on negotiable instruments.

Article 4 (Bank Deposits and Collections) of the Uniform Commercial Code An article of the Uniform Commercial Code (UCC) that establishes the rules and principles that regulate bank deposits and collection procedures.

Article 4A (Funds Transfers) of the Uniform Commercial Code An article of the Uniform Commercial Code (UCC) that establishes rules regulating the creation and collection of and liability for commercial wire transfers.

Article 5 (Letters of Credit) of the Uniform Commercial Code An article of the Uniform Commercial Code (UCC) that governs letters of credit.

Article 9 (Secured Transactions) of the Uniform Commercial Code An article of the Uniform Commercial Code (UCC) that governs secured transactions in personal property.

Articles of Confederation A document adopted in 1778 that created a federal Congress composed of representatives of the thirteen new states.

articles of dissolution A document that must be filed with the secretary of state that makes the voluntary dissolution of a corporation effective.

articles of incorporation The basic governing documents of a corporation. It must be filed with the secretary of state of the state of incorporation; also known as a *corporate charter*.

articles of limited liability partnership The formal documents that must be filed at the secretary of state's office of the state of organization of a limited liability partnership (LLP) to form the LLP.

articles of organization A document that must be filed at the secretary of state's office of the state of organization of an LLC to form the LLC.

artisan's lien A statutory lien given to workers on personal property to which they furnish services or materials in the ordinary course of business which usually prevails over all other security interests in the goods. Also called a *super-priority lien*.

"as is" disclaimer A term that makes it clear to the buyer of a good that no implied warranties attach to the sale of the good.

ASEAN Plus Three Member nations of the Association of Southeast Asian Nations (ASEAN) plus China, Japan, and South Korea, which have informal relations to discuss regional issues.

assault (1) The threat of immediate harm or offensive contact. (2) Any action that arouses reasonable apprehension of imminent harm. Actual physical contact is unnecessary.

assignee A party to whom a right to receive performance under a contract has been transferred.

assignment The transfer of rights under a contract; also called *assignment of a right*.

assignor A party who transfers the right to receive performance under a contract.

Associate Justices of the U.S. Supreme Court Justices of the U.S. Supreme Court other than the Chief Justice.

Association of Southeast Asian Nations (ASEAN) An association of many countries of Southeast Asia that provides for economic and other coordination among member nations.

assumption of the risk A defense a defendant can use against a plaintiff who knowingly and voluntarily enters into or participates in a risky activity that results in injury.

attachment A prejudgment court order that permits the seizure of a debtor's property while the lawsuit is pending.

attachment in a secured transaction A prejudgment court order that indicates that the creditor has an enforceable security interest against the debtor and can satisfy the debt out of the designated collateral.

attorney–client privilege A rule that says a client can tell his or her lawyer anything about the case without fear that the attorney will be called as a witness against the client.

attorney-in-fact The agent named in a power of attorney. This agent does not have to be a lawyer.

auction A sale in which a seller of goods offers goods for sale through an auctioneer.

auction with reserve An auction in which the seller retains the right to refuse the highest bid and withdraw the goods from sale. Unless expressly stated otherwise, an auction is an auction with reserve.

auction without reserve An auction in which the seller expressly gives up his or her right to withdraw the goods from sale and must accept the highest bid.

authorized means of communication An acceptable format for communicating an offer, as expressly specified in the offer, or if there is no such requirement, then by any means customary in similar transactions, usage of trade, or prior dealings between the parties.

authorized shares The number of shares provided for in a corporation's the articles of incorporation.

automatic stay The suspension of certain legal actions by creditors against a debtor or the debtor's property.

backward vertical merger A vertical merger in which the customer acquires the supplier.

bad faith An element that must be proven in order to find a violation of the Anticybersquatting Consumer Protection Act (ACPA).

bait and switch A type of deceptive advertising that occurs when a seller advertises the availability of a low cost discounted item but then pressures the buyer into purchasing more expensive merchandise.

Bankruptcy Abuse Prevention and Consumer Protection Act of 2005 A federal statute that substantially amended federal bankruptcy law. This act makes it more difficult for debtors to file for bankruptcy and have their unpaid debts discharged.

Bankruptcy Code The name given to federal bankruptcy law, as amended.

bankruptcy courts Special federal courts that hear and decide bankruptcy cases.

bankruptcy estate The debtor's property and earnings that comprise the estate in a bankruptcy proceeding.

bankruptcy law Federal law that establishes procedures for filing for bankruptcy, resolving creditors' claims, and protecting debtors' rights.

Bankruptcy Reform Act of 1978 A federal statute that substantially changed federal bankruptcy law. The act made it easier for debtors to file for bankruptcy and have their unpaid debts discharged. This act was considered debtor friendly.

bankruptcy trustee The legal representative of a debtor's estate that is appointed in a Chapter 7 (liquidation), Chapter 12 (family farmer or family fisherman), or Chapter 13 (adjustment of debts) bankruptcy case. May be appointed in a Chapter 11 (reorganization) case upon a showing of cause.

bargained-for exchange Exchange that parties engage in that leads to an enforceable contract.

battery Unauthorized and harmful or offensive direct or indirect physical contact with another person that causes injury.

battle of the forms A UCC rule that states that if both parties are merchants, then additional terms contained in the acceptance become part of the sales contract *unless* (1) the offer expressly limits the acceptance to the terms of the offer, (2) the additional terms materially alter the original contract, or (3) the offeror notifies the offeree that he or she objects to the additional terms within a reasonable time after receiving the offeree's modified acceptance. There is no contract if the additional terms so materially alter the terms of the original offer that the parties cannot agree on the contract.

Berne Convention An international copyright treaty.

beyond a reasonable doubt A doctrine that requires that the government prove that the accused is guilty beyond a reasonable doubt in order to be found guilty of a crime.

bicameral Being composed of two chambers, as the legislative branch of the government is composed of the house and the senate.

bilateral contract   A contract entered into by way of exchange of promises of the parties; "a promise for a promise."

bilateral treaty   A treaty between two nations.

bill   A document introduced in the U.S. Congress that begins the process whereby a bill can become a statute.

Bill of Rights   The first ten amendments to the U.S. Constitution that were added in 1791.

binding arbitration   An agreement between the parties to a dispute whereby they agree that the decision and award of the arbitrator cannot be appealed to the courts.

blue-sky laws   State laws that regulate the issuance and trading of securities.

blurring   A situation that occurs when a party uses another party's famous mark to designate a product or service in another market so that the unique significance of the famous mark is weakened.

board of directors   A panel of persons who are elected by the shareholders that makes policy decisions concerning the operation of a corporation.

bona fide occupational qualification (BFOQ)   A true job qualification. Employment discrimination based on a protected class (other than race or color) is lawful if it is *job related* and a *business necessity*. This exception is narrowly interpreted by the courts.

bond   A long-term debt security that is secured by some form of collateral (e.g., real estate, personal property).

booking   An administrative procedure that occurs at a police station after a person is arrested whereby the arrest is recorded, the suspect is fingerprinted, and a photograph is taken of the suspect.

borrower   A party who borrows money or other asset; the *debtor* in a credit transaction.

breach of contract   A contracting party's failure to perform an absolute duty owed under a contract.

breach of the duty of care   A failure to exercise care or to act as a reasonable person would act.

bribery   A crime in which one person gives another person money, property, favors, or anything else of value for a favor in return. A bribe is often referred to as a *payoff* or *kickback*.

Brown v. Board of Education   A U.S. Supreme Court case decided in 1954 that held that the "separate but equal" doctrine for schools that was established by an earlier U.S. Supreme Court decision violated the Equal Protection Clause of the Fourteenth Amendment to the Constitution and was unconstitutional.

building   A structure constructed on land.

burden of proof   A burden a plaintiff bears to persuade the trier of fact of the merits of his or her case.

burden of proof in a criminal trial   A concept that provides that the government bears the burden to prove that the accused is guilty of the crime charged.

Bureau of Consumer Financial Protection   A federal regulatory agency that has broad authority to regulate consumer financial products and services.

burglary   The taking of personal property from another's home, office, or commercial or other type of building.

business judgment rule   A rule that protects the decisions of a board of directors of a corporation where the board has acted on an informed basis, in good faith, and in the honest belief that the action taken was in the best interests of the corporation and its shareholders.

buyer in the ordinary course of business   A person who in good faith and without knowledge of another's ownership or security interest in goods buys the goods in the ordinary course of business from a person in the business of selling goods of that kind.

buyer's or lessee's cancellation   A right of a buyer or lessee to cancel a sales or lease contract if the seller or lessor fails to deliver conforming goods or repudiates the contract or if the buyer or lessee rightfully rejects the goods or justifiably revokes acceptance of the goods.

bylaws   A detailed set of rules adopted by the board of directors after a corporation is incorporated that contains provisions for managing the business and the affairs of the corporation.

C corporation   A corporation that does not qualify for or has not elected to be taxed as an S corporation. Where there is a C corporation, there is double taxation—that is, a C corporation pays taxes at the corporate level, and shareholders pay taxes on dividends paid by the corporation.

C.&F. (cost and freight)   A pricing term that means the price of goods includes the cost of the goods and the cost of freight.

cabinet-level federal departments   Highest-level federal departments that advise the president and are responsible for enforcing specific laws enacted by Congress.

cancellation of a licensing agreement   A cancellation by a licensee or licensor of software programs and digital applications that can occur if there has been a material breach of the licensing agreement by the other party.

canon law   Laws and regulations that have been adopted by Catholic and other Christian ecclesiastical authorities that relates to internal laws that govern the church and its members, definition of faith, rules of conduct, laws of marriage, and laws of inheritance.

caveat emptor   "Let the buyer beware," the traditional guideline of sales transactions.

Celler-Kefauver Act   A federal statute, enacted in 1950, that widened Section 7 of the Clayton Act's scope to include asset acquisitions (previously only applied to stock mergers).

Central America Free Trade Agreement (CAFTA)   An association composed of the United States and the Central American countries of Costa Rica, El Salvador, Guatemala, Honduras, and Nicaragua.

CEO and CFO certification   A certification that the Sarbanes-Oxley Act requires that the chief executive officer (CEO) and chief financial officer (CFO) of a public company file with each annual and quarterly report of the company.

certificate of cancellation   A certificate that must be filed with the secretary of state upon the dissolution and the commencement of the winding up of a limited partnership.

certificate of dissolution   A document issued by the secretary of state that dissolves a corporation.

certificate of interest   A document that evidences a member's ownership interest in a limited liability company (LLC).

certificate of limited partnership   A document that two or more persons must execute and sign that makes a limited partnership legal and binding and that must be filed with the secretary of state of the state organization.

certification mark   A mark that certifies that a seller of a product or service has met certain geographical location requirements, quality standards, material standards, or mode of manufacturing standards established by the owner of the mark.

chain of distribution   The chain of manufacturers, distributors, wholesalers, retailers, lessors, subcomponent manufacturers, and others who distribute a defective product.

chain-style franchise   A situation in which a franchisor licenses a franchisee to make and sell its products or distribute its services to the public from a retail outlet serving an exclusive territory.

chamber   A portion of the legislative branch; refers to either the U.S. House of Representatives of the U.S. Senate.

change of venue   Movement of a trial to a venue where a more impartial jury can be found in cases where pretrial publicity or other reason may prejudice jurors located in the proper venue.

changing conditions defense   A defense to a Robinson-Patman Act Section 2(a) price discrimination action in which prices were lowered in response to changing conditions in the market for the goods.

Chapter 7 discharge   The termination of the legal duty of an individual debtor to pay unsecured debts that remain unpaid upon the completion of a Chapter 7 proceeding.

Chapter 7—Liquidation A form of bankruptcy in which the debtor's nonexempt property is sold for cash, the cash is distributed to the creditors, and any unpaid debts are discharged; also referred to as *straight bankruptcy*.

Chapter 11 plan of reorganization A plan that sets forth a proposed new capital structure for a debtor to assume when it emerges from Chapter 11 reorganization bankruptcy.

Chapter 11—Reorganization A bankruptcy method that allows the reorganization of the debtor's financial affairs under the supervision of the bankruptcy court.

Chapter 12—Adjustment of Debts of a Family Farmer or Fisherman with Regular Income A special form of bankruptcy that provides for the reorganization bankruptcy of family farmers and fisherman.

Chapter 13—Adjustment of Debts of an Individual with Regular Income A rehabilitation form of bankruptcy that permits bankruptcy courts to supervise the debtor's plan for the payment of unpaid debts in installments over the plan period.

Chapter 13 discharge A discharge in a Chapter 13 case that is granted to the debtor after the debtor's plan of payment is completed (which could be up to three or up to five years).

Chapter 13 plan of payment A plan set forth by a debtor in a Chapter 13—Adjustment of Debts of an Individual with Regular Income bankruptcy proceeding that lays out the debtor's plan for paying his or her disposable income to prepetition creditors during the plan period.

checks and balances A system built into the U.S. Constitution to prevent any one of the three branches of the government from becoming too powerful.

Chief Justice of the U.S. Supreme Court The justice who is responsible for the administration of the Supreme Court.

child labor The use of children to work is restricted and regulated by the Fair Labor Standards Act (FLSA).

choice of forum clause A clause in an international contract that designates which nation's court has jurisdiction to hear a case arising out of the contract; also known as a *forum-selection clause.*

choice-of-law clause A contract provision that designates a certain state's law or country's law that will be applied in any dispute concerning nonperformance of the contract.

C.I.F. (cost, insurance, and freight) A pricing term that means the price of goods includes the cost of the goods and the costs of insurance and freight.

circuit The geographical area served by a U.S. Circuit Court of Appeals.

civil action A lawsuit brought by a party to recover monetary damages or other remedies from a defendant.

civil damages Damages awarded for violations of antitrust laws, including *treble damages.*

civil law Law based on codes or statutes. In civil law, the adjudication of a case is based on the application of the code or statutes to a particular set of facts.

civil lawsuit A lawsuit brought by a plaintiff against a defendant that seeks monetary compensation, an equitable remedy, or other form of redress.

civil penalty A penalty that the Securities and Exchange Commission (SEC) can obtain against a defendant of up to three times (*treble damages*) the illegal profits gained or losses avoided on insider trading.

civil RICO A federal statute that permits a civil lawsuit to be brought by persons injured by a pattern of racketeering to recover treble damages from the racketeer for injury cause to the plaintiff's business or property.

Civil Rights Act of 1866 A federal statute enacted after the Civil War that says all persons "have the same right . . . to make and enforce contracts . . . as is enjoyed by white persons." It prohibits racial and color discrimination.

Civil Rights Act of 1964 A federal statute that makes it illegal to discriminate in employment, housing, transportation, and public accommodations based on race, national origin, color, gender, or religion.

class action A situation in which a group of plaintiffs collectively bring a lawsuit against a defendant.

Clayton Act A federal statute, enacted in 1914, that regulates mergers and prohibits certain exclusive dealing arrangements.

Clean Air Act A federal statute that provides comprehensive regulation of air quality in the United States.

Clean Air Act Amendments Amendments to the Clean Air Act that increase the protection of air quality.

Clean Water Act A federal statute that establishes water quality standards and regulates water pollution.

close corporation A small corporation that has met specified requirements and may choose this distinction under state law. As such, the corporation may dispense with some corporate formalities and operate without a board of directors, without bylaws, and without keeping minutes of meetings.

closed shop A business where an employer hires only employees who are already members of a labor union and cannot hire employees who are not members of a union. Closed shops are illegal in the United States.

closely held corporation A corporation owned by one or a few shareholders.

closing (settlement) The finalization of a real estate sales transaction that passes title to the property from the seller to the buyer.

closing arguments Statements made by each party's attorney to the jury at the close of a trial.

code books Books that contain statutes enacted by the U.S. Congress and state legislatures and ordinances enacted by municipalities.

code of ethics A code adopted by a company wherein the company sets forth rules of ethics for the company's managers and employees to follow when dealing with customers, employees, suppliers, and others.

codified law Statutes enacted by the federal Congress and state legislatures and ordinances passed by municipalities and local government bodies.

Colgate doctrine A rule announced in the U.S. Supreme Court case *United States v. Colgate & Co.* that states that a unilateral choice by one party not to deal with another party does not violate Section 1 of the Sherman Act because there is not concerted action.

collateral Security against repayment of the debt that lenders sometimes require; can be a car, a house, or other property. The property that is subject to the security interest.

collective bargaining The process of negotiating contract terms between an employer and the members of a union.

collective bargaining agreement The contract that results from a collective bargaining procedure.

collective membership mark A mark that indicates that a person has met the standards set by an organization and is a member of that organization.

color discrimination Employment discrimination against a person because of his or her color, for example, where a light-skinned person of a race discriminates against a dark-skinned person of the same race.

coming and going rule A rule that says a principal is generally not liable for injuries caused by its agents and employees while they are on their way to or from work. Also known as the *going and coming rule.*

Command School of jurisprudence A school of thought that postulates that law is a set of rules developed, communicated, and enforced by the ruling party.

Commerce Clause A clause of the U.S. Constitution that grants Congress the power "to regulate commerce with foreign nations, and among the several states, and with Indian tribes."

commercial activity exception An exception that states that a foreign country is subject to lawsuit in the United States if it engages in commercial activity in the United States or if it carries on such activity outside the United States but causes a direct effect in the United States.

commercial paper Short-term notes issued by corporations that do not exceed nine months.

commercial reasonableness A term used in the Uniform Commercial Code that applies to merchants in the performance of their duties under sales and lease contracts.

commercial speech Speech used by businesses such as advertising. It is subject to time, place, and manner restrictions.

committee A special group composed of members of the U.S. House of Representatives or U.S. Senate.

common carrier A company that offers transportation services to the public, such as an airline, a railroad, or a trucking firm; the *bailee* in a bailment situation.

common crimes Ordinary crimes that are committed against persons and property.

common law of contracts Contract law developed primarily by state courts.

common securities Interests or instruments that are commonly known as securities, such as common stock, preferred stock, bonds, debentures, and warrants.

common stock A type of equity security that represents the *residual* value of a corporation.

common stock certificate A document that represents a common shareholder's investment in the corporation.

common stockholder A person who owns common stock.

Communications Decency Act A federal statute that states that Internet service providers (ISPs) are not liable for the content transmitted over their networks by e-mail users and websites.

community property A form of ownership in which each spouse owns an equal one-half share of the income of both spouses and the assets acquired during the marriage.

comparative negligence (comparative fault) A doctrine under which damages are apportioned according to fault.

compensatory damages An award of money intended to compensate a non-breaching party for the loss of a bargain. Compensatory damages place the non-breaching party in the same position as if the contract had been fully performed by restoring the "benefit of the bargain."

competing with a corporation A situation that occurs when an officer or director of a corporation engages in a business that is in competition with the corporation that he or she is an officer or director of.

competing with the principal A situation that occurs when an agent, a general partner, a director or officer of a corporation, a partner in a limited liability partnership (LLP), certain members of a limited liability company (LLC), and anyone else who owes a fiduciary duty to a principal engages in undisclosed and unauthorized competition with their principal.

complaint A document a plaintiff files with the court and serves on the defendant to initiate a lawsuit.

complete integration A concept that a written contract is a complete and final statement of the parties' agreement.

complete performance A situation in which a party to a contract renders performance exactly as required by the contract. Complete performance discharges that party's obligations under the contract; also known as *strict performance*.

composition An agreement that provides for the reduction of a debtor's debts.

Comprehensive Environmental Response, Compensation, and Liability Act (CERCLA or Superfund) A federal statute that authorizes the federal government to deal with hazardous wastes. The act creates a monetary fund to finance the cleanup of hazardous waste sites.

compulsory subjects of collective bargaining Subjects of collective bargaining that must be negotiated by an employer with a labor union, such as issues concerning wages, hours, and other terms and conditions of employment.

Computer Decency Act A federal statute that makes it a felony to knowingly make "indecent" or "patently offensive" materials available on computer systems, including the Internet, to persons less than 18 years of age.

computer employee exemption An exemption from federal minimum wage and overtime pay requirements that applies to employees compensated either on a salary or fee basis; are employed as computer systems analysts, computer programmers, software engineers or other similarly skilled workers in the computer field; and are engaged in the design, development, documentation, analysis, creation, testing, or modification of computer systems or programs.

concurrent condition A condition that exists when the parties to a contract must render performance simultaneously; each party's absolute duty to perform is conditioned on the other party's absolute duty to perform.

concurrent jurisdiction Jurisdiction shared by two or more courts.

concurrent ownership A situation in which two or more persons own a piece of real property; also called *co-ownership*. The following forms of co-ownership of real property are recognized: joint tenancy, tenancy in common, tenancy by the entirety, community property, condominiums, and cooperatives.

concurring opinion An opinion written by a justice who agrees with the outcome of a case reached by other justices but not the reason proffered by them, wherein the justice sets forth his or her reasons for deciding the case.

condition A qualification of a promise that becomes a covenant if it is met. There are three types of conditions: conditions precedent, conditions subsequent, and concurrent conditions.

condition precedent A condition that requires the occurrence of an event before a party is obligated to perform a duty under a contract.

condition subsequent A condition whose occurrence or nonoccurrence of a specific event automatically excuses the performance of an existing contractual duty to perform.

conditional promise A situation in which a promisor's duty to perform or not perform a contract arises only if a condition does or does not occur; also known as a *qualified promise*.

condominium A common form of ownership in a multiple-dwelling building where the purchaser has title to the individual unit and owns the common areas as a tenant in common with the other condominium owners.

conference committee A special group composed of members of both the U.S. House of Representatives and the U.S. Senate whose task is to try to reconcile the differences in bills passed by each chamber.

confidential information Information about a principal's affairs (e.g., business plans, technological innovations, customer lists, trade secrets).

confirmation of a Chapter 11 plan of reorganization The bankruptcy court's approval of a plan of reorganization.

conflicts of interest In securities law, situations that occur when investment bankers and securities analysts of the same firm share information.

conglomerate merger A merger that does not fit into any other category; a merger between firms in totally unrelated businesses.

Congress of Industrial Organizations (CIO) A labor organization formed in 1935 that permitted semiskilled and unskilled workers to become members.

conscious parallelism A situation in which two or more firms act the same but no concerted action is shown, there is no violation of Section 1 of the Sherman Act.

consent decree A plea entered by a civil defendant who has been sued by the government whereby the accused agrees to the imposition of a penalty but does not admit liability.

consent election An election to establish a labor union that is not contested by the employer and may be held without National Labor Relations Board (NLRB) supervision.

consequential damages Foreseeable damages that arise from circumstances outside a contract. To be liable for these damages, the breaching party must know or have reason to know that the breach will cause special damages to the other party; also known as *special damages*.

consideration Something of legal value given in exchange for a promise.

Consolidated Omnibus Budget Reconciliation Act (COBRA) A federal statute that permits employees and their beneficiaries to continue their group health insurance after an employee's employment has ended.

consolidation The act of a court to combine two or more separate lawsuits into one lawsuit.

conspicuous disclaimer A written disclaimer of an implied warranty associated with the sale of goods that must be noticeable to a reasonable person.

Constitution of the United States of America The fundamental law of the United States of America. It was ratified by the states in 1788 and is the supreme law of the United States.

Constitutional Convention A meeting convened by delegates of many states in 1787 with the primary purpose of strengthening the federal government.

constitutions of states State constitutions that are often patterned after the U.S. Constitution, although many are more detailed.

constructive notice Notice given by publishing the information in a newspaper of general circulation.

constructive notice by recoding Recording of a deed, mortgage, lien, or other document pertaining to an interest in real property gives constructive notice to the world of the owner's or other recorder's interest in the real property.

constructive trust An equitable trust that is implied by law to avoid fraud, unjust enrichment, and injustice.

consumer debt For bankruptcy purposes, debts incurred by an individual for personal, family, or household purposes.

consumer goods Goods that are purchased by consumers, such as furniture, television sets, home appliances, and other goods used primarily for personal, family, or household purposes.

consumer financial protection A set of government laws that protect consumer-debtors in credit transactions.

Consumer Financial Protection Act of 2010 A federal statute that requires increased disclosure of credit information and terms to consumers and regulates consumer credit providers and others.

Consumer Financial Protection Bureau (CFPB) A federal government agency that has authority to supervise all participants in the consumer finance and mortgage area and to prohibit unfair, deceptive, or abusive acts or practices regarding consumer financial products and services.

Consumer Leasing Act (CLA) An amendment to the Truth-in-Lending Act (TILA) that extends the TILA's coverage to lease terms in consumer leases.

Consumer Product Safety Act (CPSA) A federal statute that regulates potentially dangerous consumer products and that created the Consumer Product Safety Commission.

Consumer Product Safety Commission (CPSC) A federal administrative agency empowered to adopt rules and regulations to interpret and enforce the Consumer Product Safety Act.

consumer products Products that are sold to consumers.

consumer protection laws Federal and state statutes and regulations that promote product safety and prohibit abusive, unfair, and deceptive business practices.

contested election An election to establish a labor union that is opposed and contested by the employer and must be supervised by the National Labor Relations Board (NLRB).

contingency-fee A fee arrangement between a lawyer and client whereby the lawyer is paid a percentage of damages won through trial judgment or by settlement.

continuation agreement An agreement among the surviving or remaining general partners of a partnership to continue a partnership after its dissolution.

continuation statement A document that can be filed by a creditor up to six months prior to the expiration of a financing statement's term to continue the creditor's perfected interest in the collateral designated in the financing statement.

continuous and peaceful A requirement that must be proven by a person to obtain real property by adverse possession. It requires that the adverse possessor has occupied the property continuously and uninterrupted for the required statutory period. Any break in normal occupancy terminates the adverse possession.

contract An agreement that is enforceable by a court of law or equity. "A contract is a promise or a set of promises for the breach of which the law gives a remedy or the performance of which the law in some way recognizes a duty" (*Restatement (Second) of Contracts*).

contract contrary to public policy A contract to perform activities that have a negative impact on society or interferes with the public's safety and welfare that constitutes an illegal contract.

contract contrary to statutes A contract to perform activities that are prohibited by government statute (e.g., statute against gambling) that constitutes an illegal contract.

contract liability Liability of principals and agents for contracts entered into with third parties.

contract of adhesion A preprinted contract prepared by a provider of goods or services where the contract terms are set and the consumer or other party cannot negotiate the contract terms and must accept the terms of the contract in order to obtain the product or service.

contract under seal A contract where a seal (usually a wax seal) is attached to the contract.

contractual capacity The necessary capacity of parties to enter into the contract.

contributory negligence A doctrine that says a plaintiff who is partially at fault for his or her own injury cannot recover against the negligent defendant.

control rule A rule that provides that a limited partner who takes part in the management of the affairs of the limited partnership, and who has not been expressly elected to office to do so, loses their limited liability shield and become general partners and are personally liable for the debts and obligations of the limited partnership.

Controlling the Assault of Non-Solicited Pornography and Marketing Act (CAN-SPAM Act) A federal statute that places certain restrictions on persons and businesses that send unsolicited commercial advertising (spam) to e-mail accounts, prohibits falsified headers, prohibits deceptive subject lines, and requires spammers to label sexually oriented e-mail as such.

convention A treaty that is sponsored by an international organization.

convertible preferred stock Stock that permits the preferred stockholders to convert their shares into common stock.

cooling-off period A mandatory sixty days' notice before a strike can commence.

cooperative A form of co-ownership of a multiple-dwelling building in which a corporation owns the building and the residents own shares in the corporation.

copyright A legal right that gives the author of qualifying subject matter, and who meets other requirements established by copyright law, the exclusive right to publish, produce, sell, license, and distribute the work.

copyright infringement An infringement that occurs when a party copies a substantial and material part of a plaintiff's copyrighted work without permission. A copyright holder may recover damages and other remedies against the infringer.

copyright registration certificate A certificate that is issued to a copyright holder who has properly registered his or her copyright with the U.S. Copyright Office.

Copyright Revision Act A federal statute that (1) establishes the requirements for obtaining a copyright and (2) protects copyrighted works from infringement.

corporate citizenship A theory of responsibility that says a business has a responsibility to do good.

corporate criminal liability Criminal liability of corporations for actions of their officers, employees, or agents.

corporate electronic communications (corporate e-communications) The use of electronic communications (e-communication) by a corporation to communicate with shareholders and among directors.

corporate management   Together, the directors and the officers of a corporation.

corporate officers   Employees of a corporation who are appointed by the board of directors to manage the day-to-day operations of the corporation.

corporation   A fictitious legal entity that is created according to statutory requirements.

corporation codes   State statutes that regulate the formation, operation, and dissolution of corporations.

cost–benefit analysis   The examination of relevant factors to determine whether to bring or settle a lawsuit.

cost justification defense   A defense to a Robinson-Patman Act Section 2(a) price discrimination action that provides that a seller's price discrimination is not unlawful if the price differential is due to "differences in the cost of manufacture, sale, or delivery" of the product.

Council of Ministers   A council of the European Union (EU) that is composed of representatives from each member country who meet periodically to coordinate efforts to fulfill the objectives of the European Union.

counteroffer   A response by an offeree that contains terms and conditions different from or in addition to those of the offer. A counteroffer terminates an offer.

county recorder's office   An office where deeds, mortgages, and other documents pertaining to real property located in the county are recorded.

course of dealing   The conduct of contracting parties in prior transactions and contracts.

course of performance   Previous conduct of contracting parties concerning the contract in question.

Court of Appeals for the Federal Circuit   A court of appeals located in Washington, DC, that has special appellate jurisdiction to review the decisions of the U.S. Court of Federal Claims, the U.S. Patent and Trademark Office, and the U.S. Court of International Trade.

court of chancery (equity court)   Court that granted relief based on fairness; also called *equity court*.

covenant   An unconditional promise to perform.

covenant of quiet enjoyment   An implied covenant that says a landlord may not interfere with the tenant's quiet and peaceful possession, use, and enjoyment of the leased premises.

crashworthiness doctrine   A doctrine that says automobile manufacturers are under a duty to design automobiles so they take into account the possibility of harm from a person's body striking something inside the automobile in the case of a car accident.

credit   A situation in which one party makes a loan to another party.

Credit Card Accountability Responsibility and Disclosure Act of 2009 (Credit CARD Act)   A federal statute that requires disclosures to consumers, adds transparency to the creditor–debtor relationship, and eliminates many of the abusive practices of credit card issuers.

credit report   Information about a person's credit history that can be secured from a credit bureau.

creditor   The lender in a credit transaction.

crime   A violation of a statute for which the government imposes a punishment.

criminal act   The performance of a criminal act prohibited by law. Also called *actus reus* ("guilty act").

criminal conspiracy   A crime in which two or more persons enter into an agreement to commit a crime, and an overt act is taken to further the crime.

criminal fraud   A crime that involves obtaining title to property through deception or trickery; also known as *false pretenses* or *deceit*.

criminal intent   The requisite state of mind when an act was performed for an accused to be found guilty of an intent crime. Also called *mens rea* ("evil intent").

criminal laws   Laws that prohibit certain conduct and provide an incentive for persons to act reasonably in society and imposes penalties on persons who violate them.

criminal RICO   A federal statute that makes it a crime to acquire or maintain an interest in, use income from, or conduct or participate in the affairs of an enterprise through a pattern of racketeering activity.

Critical Legal Studies School of jurisprudence   A school of thought that maintains that legal rules are unnecessary and that legal disputes should be solved by applying arbitrary rules based on fairness.

cross-complainant   A defendant who files a cross-complaint against a plaintiff.

cross-complaint   A document filed by a defendant against a plaintiff to seek damages or some other remedy.

cross-defendant   A plaintiff against whom a cross-complaint is filed by the defendant.

cross-examination   Examination of the plaintiff's witness by the defendant and examination of the defendant's witnesses by the plaintiff.

crossover workers   Individual members of a labor union that is on strike who choose not to strike and remain working or who return to work after joining the strikers for a time.

cruel and unusual punishment   A clause of the Eighth Amendment to the U.S. Constitution that protects criminal defendants from torture and other cruel and abusive punishment.

cumulative preferred stock   Stock for which any missed dividend payments must be paid in the future to the preferred shareholders before the common shareholders can receive any dividends.

cumulative voting   A system of shareholder voting for the board of directors of a corporation whereby each shareholder can *accumulate* all of his or her votes (determined by the number of directors to be elected multiplied by the number of shares the shareholder owns) and vote them all for a single candidate or split them among several candidates.

cure   The legal right of a seller or lessor who has delivered defective or nonconforming goods to repair or replace the defective or nonconforming goods if the time for performance has not expired and the seller or lessor notifies the buyer or lessee of his or her intention to make a conforming delivery within the contract time.

cyber crimes   Crimes that are committed using computers, e-mail, the Internet, and other electronic means.

cybersquatting   A situation that occurs when a party registers a domain name that is the same as another party's trademarked name or a famous person's name.

d.b.a. (doing business as)   A designation for a business that is operating under a trade name.

damages   Money a buyer or lessee recovers from a seller or lessor who fails to deliver the goods or repudiates the contract. Damages are measured as the difference between the contract price (or original rent) and the market price (or rent) at the time the buyer or lessee learned of the breach.

debenture   A long-term (often thirty years or more) unsecured debt instrument that is based on a corporation's general credit standing.

debt collectors   An agent who collects debts for other parties.

debt securities   Securities that establish a debtor–creditor relationship in which the corporation borrows money from the investor to whom a debt security is issued; also known as *fixed income securities*.

debtor   The borrower in a credit transaction.

decertification election   An election to decertify a labor union that is held if some employees no longer want to be represented by a union. Decertification elections must be supervised by the National Labor Relations Board (NLRB).

Declaration of Independence   A document that declared the independence of the American colonies from England.

deed   A document that describes a person's ownership interest in a piece of real property.

deed of trust   An instrument that gives a creditor a security interest in the debtor's property that is pledged as collateral.

defamation of character False statement(s) made by one person about another. In court, the plaintiff must prove that (1) the defendant made an untrue statement of fact about the plaintiff and (2) the statement was intentionally or accidentally published to a third party.

default A situation that occurs when a debtor does not make the required payments when due.

default judgment A judgment that is entered against a defendant if he does not answer a plaintiff's complaint.

defect The condition of goods that an injured party must show in order to recover damages under the doctrine of strict liability. Common types of defects are (1) *defect in manufacture*, (2) *defect in design*, (3) *failure to warn*, and (4) *defect in packaging*.

defect in design A defect that occurs when a product is improperly designed.

defect in manufacture A defect that occurs when a manufacturer fails to (1) properly assemble a product, (2) properly test a product, or (3) adequately check the quality of the product.

defect in packaging A defect that occurs when a product has been placed in packaging that is insufficiently tamperproof.

defective formation A situation that occurs when a certificate of limited partnership of a limited partnership, articles of organization of a limited liability company (LLC), articles of limited liability partnership of a limited liability partnership (LLP), or articles of incorporation of a corporation is not properly filed with the secretary of state or other required government agency, or there are defects in the document that is filed, or some other statutory requirement for the creation of the entity is not met.

defendant A party who is being sued.

defendant's case The part of a train that occurs after the plaintiff has put on his case, when the defendant calls and examines witnesses and introduces evidence supporting his or her case.

defense attorney The lawyer who represents the accused defendant in a criminal trial.

deficiency judgment A judgment of a court that permits a secured lender to recover other property or income from a defaulting debtor if the collateral is insufficient to repay the unpaid loan.

degree of control A crucial factor in determining whether someone is an independent contractor or an employee is the *degree of control* that the principal has over that party.

Delaware antitakeover statute An antitakeover statute enacted by the state of Delaware.

Delaware Court of Chancery A Delaware state court that hears and decides cases involving business and corporate matters.

Delaware General Corporation Law A state statute that was enacted by the legislature of the state of Delaware that governs the formation, operation, and dissolution of corporations incorporated in the state of Delaware.

delegated Occurred when the states ratified the Constitution and granted certain powers to the federal government. These powers are called *enumerated powers*.

deponent A party who gives his or her deposition.

deposition Oral testimony given by a party or witness prior to trial. The testimony is given under oath and is transcribed.

derivative A financial instrument in which the value is determined by the price movements of another asset.

derivative lawsuit A lawsuit a shareholder brings against an offending party on behalf of a corporation when the corporation fails to bring the lawsuit; also called a *derivative action*.

design patent A patent that may be obtained for the ornamental nonfunctional design of an item.

destination contract A contract that requires the seller to deliver the goods either to the buyer's place of business or to another destination specified in the sales contract.

Digital Millennium Copyright Act (DMCA) A federal statute that prohibits unauthorized access to copyrighted digital works by circumventing encryption technology or the manufacture and distribution of technologies designed for the purpose of circumventing encryption protection of digital works.

digital signature An electronic method for identifying an individual.

dilution The lessening of the capacity of a famous mark to identify and distinguish its holder's goods and services. The two most common forms of dilution are *blurring* and *tarnishment*.

direct examination Examination of the plaintiff's witness by the plaintiff.

direct notice Express notice of the termination of an agency that needs to be given to all persons with whom the agent dealt.

direct price discrimination Price discrimination in which (1) the defendant sold commodities of like grade and quality, (2) to two or more purchasers at different prices at approximately the same time, and (3) the plaintiff suffered injury because of the price discrimination.

disability Includes physiological impairments such as a physical disorder or condition, cosmetic disfigurement, or anatomical loss affecting one or more of the following body systems: neurological, musculoskeletal, special sense organs, respiratory, cardiovascular, reproductive, digestive, genitourinary, hemic and lymphatic, skin, and endocrine; and mental or psychological disorders such as intellectual disability (i.e., mental retardation), organic brain syndrome, emotional or mental illness, and specific learning disabilities.

disaffirm a contract The act of a minor that rescinds a contract under the infancy doctrine.

disaffirmance The act of a minor to rescind a contract under the infancy doctrine. Disaffirmance may be accomplished orally, in writing, or by the minor's conduct.

discharge Discharge from liability on negotiable instruments.

discharge by agreement Discharge of contractual duties under a contract by mutual assent of the parties.

discharge in bankruptcy A bankruptcy court order that relieves a debtor of the legal liability to pay his or her unpaid debts that were not required to be paid and remain unpaid in the bankruptcy proceeding.

discovery A legal process during which each party engages in various activities to discover facts of the case from the other party and witnesses prior to trial.

discrimination Acts by employers, universities, public accommodations, and others that treats a person or a class of persons differently because of their race, color, national origin, gender, religion, age, disability, or other classes protected by law.

disparagement False statements about a competitor's products, services, property, or business reputation. Also known as *trade libel*, *product disparagement*, and *slander of title*.

disparate-impact discrimination A form of discrimination that occurs when an employer discriminates against an entire protected class. An example would be discrimination in which a racially neutral employment practice or rule causes an adverse impact on a protected class.

disparate-treatment discrimination A form of discrimination that occurs when an employer discriminates against a specific individual because of his or her race, color, national origin, sex, or religion.

disposable income For bankruptcy purposes, income that is determined by taking the debtor's actual income and subtracting expenses for a typical family the same size as the debtor's family, as determined by government tables.

disposition of collateral A secured creditor's repossession of collateral upon a debtor's default and selling, leasing, or otherwise disposing of it in a commercially reasonable manner.

dissenting opinion An opinion written by a justice who does not agree with a decision of the majority of the justices wherein the justice sets forth the reasons for his or her dissent.

dissolution of a corporation The process of ending a corporation's existence.

dissolution of a partnership The change in the relationship of partners caused by any partner ceasing to be associated in the carrying on of the business.

distinctive A word or design being unique and therefore qualifying for a trademark.

distribution of assets of a limited partnership A rule that sets forth the priority for the distribution of assets upon the dissolution of a limited partnership, which is first to creditors (including partners who are creditors), and then to partners with respect to unpaid distributions, capital contributions, and the remainder of the proceeds.

distributional interest A member's ownership interest in a limited liability company (LLC) that entitles the member to receive distributions of money and property from the LLC.

distributorship franchise A business in which a franchisor manufactures a product and licenses a franchisee to distribute the product to the public.

district The area served by a U.S. District Court.

District of Columbia circuit A federal intermediate appellate court located in Washington, DC.

diversity of citizenship A means for bringing a lawsuit in federal court that involves a nonfederal question but where the parties are (1) citizens of different states or (2) a citizen of a state and a citizen or subject of a foreign country.

dividend A distribution of profits of a corporation to shareholders.

dividend preference The right to receive a fixed dividend at stipulated periods during the year (e.g., quarterly).

division of markets A restraint of trade in which competitors agree that each will serve only a designated portion of the market; also known as *market sharing*. This is a *per se* violation of Section 1 of the Sherman Act as an unreasonable restraint of trade.

doctrine of sovereign immunity A doctrine that states that countries are granted immunity from suits in courts of other countries.

doctrine of *stare decisis* A doctrine that involves adhering to precedent. *Stare decisis* is Latin for "to stand by the decision."

Dodd-Frank Wall Street Reform and Consumer Protection Act A federal statute that reorganizes the federal government's supervision of the banking system, correct abuses in the banking system, regulates previous unregulated financial products and institutions, ends abusive practices in the securities industry, establishes new federal consumer-debtor financial protection laws, and adds a new federal consumer protection agency to protect consumers from abusive lending practices.

Doha Development Agenda A round of trade negotiations among World Trade Organization (WTO) members to improve the trading prospects of developing countries.

domain name A unique name that identifies an individual's or company's website.

domestic corporation A corporation in the state in which it is organized.

domestic limited liability company (domestic LLC) A limited liability company (LLC) in the state in which it is organized.

domestic limited liability partnership (domestic LLP) A limited liability partnership (LLP) in the state in which it is organized.

dominant estate The land that benefits from an easement.

dominant party A person who has a dominant position over another person who takes advantage of the other person's mental, emotional, or physical weakness and unduly influences that person to enter into a contract.

Dominican Republic–Central America Free Trade Agreement (DR-CAFTA) An association of the Dominican Republic, several Central American countries, and the United States designed to reduce tariffs and trade barriers among member nations.

Do-Not-Call Registry A federal registry on which consumers can place their names to free themselves from most unsolicited commercial telephone calls.

door-to-door sales A situation that occurs when a salesperson personally contacts people at their homes to try to sell them goods or services.

Dormant Commerce Clause A clause by which the federal government has chosen not to regulate an area of interstate commerce that it has the power to regulate under its Commerce Clause powers.

Double Jeopardy Clause A clause of the Fifth Amendment to the U.S. Constitution that protects persons from being tried twice for the same crime.

double taxation Taxation that occurs where there is a C corporation because one tax is paid at the corporate level and another tax is paid on dividends received by shareholders on their personal income tax forms.

Drug Amendment An amendment to the Food, Drug, and Cosmetic Act (FDCA) that gives the Food and Drug Administration (FDA) broad powers to license new drugs in the United States.

dual agency A situation that occurs when an agent acts for two or more different principals in the same transaction. This practice is generally prohibited unless all the parties involved in the transaction agree to it.

dual-purpose mission An errand or another act that a principal requests of an agent while the agent is on his or her own personal business.

due diligence defense A defense that accountants, lawyers, directors, managers, and others can assert, which, if proven, avoids liability under Section 11(a) of the Securities Act of 1933.

Due Process Clause A clause that provides that no person shall be deprived of "life, liberty, or property" without due process of the law.

dues checkoff A situation in which, upon proper notification by a labor union, employers are required to deduct union dues or agency fees from labor union employees' wages and forward these dues to the union.

durable power of attorney A power of attorney that remains effective even though the principal becomes incapacitated.

duress A situation in which one party threatens to do a wrongful act unless the other party enters into a contract.

duty of care of corporate officers and directors A duty of corporate directors and officers to use care and diligence when acting on behalf of the corporation.

duty of care of general partners The obligation partners owe to use the same level of care and skill that a reasonable person in the same position would use in the same circumstances. A breach of the duty of care is *negligence*.

duty of care of individuals The obligation people owe each other not to cause any unreasonable harm or risk of harm.

duty of care of members of a limited liability company (LLC) A duty owed by a member of a member-managed limited liability company (LLC) and a manager of a manager-managed LLC not to engage in (1) a known violation of law, (2) intentional conduct, (3) reckless conduct, or (4) grossly negligent conduct that injures the LLC.

duty of loyalty of agents A fiduciary duty owed by an agent not to act adversely to the interests of the principal.

duty of loyalty of corporate officers and directors A duty that directors and officers of a corporation owe not to act adversely to the interests of the corporation and to subordinate their personal interests to those of the corporation and its shareholders.

duty of loyalty of general partners A duty that a general partner owes not to act adversely to the interests of the partnership.

duty of loyalty of members of a limited liability company (LLC) A duty owed by a member of a member-managed LLC and a manager of a manager-managed LLC to be honest in his or her dealings with the LLC and not act adversely to the interests of the LLC.

duty of restitution A duty of an adult when a minor has disaffirmed a contract to return any money, property, or other valuables received from the minor, or if the consideration has been sold or has depreciated in value, then to pay the minor the cash equivalent; a minor owes a duty of restitution if the minor's intentional, reckless, or grossly negligent conduct caused the loss of value to the adult's property or if the minor misrepresented his or her age when entering into a contract.

duty of restoration A duty of a minor who has disaffirmed a contract to return the goods or property he or she has received from the other party in the condition it is in at the time of disaffirmance.

duty to account A duty that an agent owes to maintain an accurate accounting of all transactions undertaken on the principal's behalf; also known as the *duty of accountability.*

duty to compensate A duty that a principal owes to pay an agreed-upon amount to the agent either upon the completion of the agency or at some other mutually agreeable time.

duty to cooperate Unless otherwise agreed, the duty of a principal to cooperate with and assist the agent in the performance of the agent's duties and the accomplishment of the agency.

duty to deliver possession A duty a landlord owes to deliver possession of the leased premises to the lessee.

duty to indemnify A duty of a principal to indemnify the agent for any losses the agent suffers because of the principal's conduct.

duty to maintain the leased premises A duty of a landlord to maintain the leased premises as provided in the lease, by express law, and as implied by law.

duty to notify A duty of an agent to notify the principal of important information concerning the agency.

duty to pay rent A duty of a commercial or residential tenant to pay the agreed-upon amount of rent for the leased premises to the landlord at the agreed-upon time and place.

duty to perform An agent's duty to a principal that includes (1) performing the lawful duties expressed in the contract and (2) meeting the standards of reasonable care, skill, and diligence implicit in all contracts.

duty to reimburse Unless otherwise agreed, the duty of a principal to reimburse the agent for expenses incurred by the agent if the expenses were (1) authorized by the principal, (2) within the scope of the agency, and (3) necessary to discharge the agent's duties in carrying out the agency.

easement A given or required right to make limited use of someone else's land without owning or leasing it.

easement by grant An easements that is expressly created, for example when an owner gives another party an easement across his or her property.

easement by implication An easement that is implied from the facts and circumstances, for example when an owner subdivides a piece of property with a well,

path, road, or another beneficial appurtenant that serves the entire parcel.

easement by necessity An easement that is created by necessity, for example a "landlocked" property has an easement across surrounding property to enter and exit the landlocked property.

easement by reservation An easement that is expressly created by reservation, for example when an owner sells land that he or she owns but reserves an easement on the land.

EB-1 visa A visa issued by the U.S. government that allows U.S. employers to employ foreign nationals in the United States who possess extraordinary ability for certain types of employment such as having extraordinary ability in the sciences, arts, education, business, or athletics, outstanding professors and researchers, and multinational managers or executives employed by a firm outside the United States and who seeks to continue to work for that firm in the United States.

Economic Espionage Act (EEA) A federal statute that makes it a crime for any person to convert a trade secret for his or her own or another's benefit, knowing or intending to cause injury to the owners of the trade secret.

economic injury Injury caused to an innocent party because of another person's fraud.

EDGAR The electronic data and record system of the Securities and Exchange Commission (SEC).

effect of illegality A doctrine that states that the courts will refuse to enforce or rescind an illegal contract and will leave the parties where it finds them.

effective date The date on which a registration of securities filed with the Securities and Exchange Commission (SEC) becomes effective.

effects on interstate commerce test A test developed by the U.S. Supreme Court to determine whether commerce is interstate commerce that can be regulated by the federal government.

Eighth Amendment to the U.S. Constitution An amendment to the U.S. Constitution that protects criminal defendants from *cruel and unusual punishment.*

Electoral College A group of persons composed of representatives appointed by state delegations to vote for a presidential candidate.

electronic Relating to technology having electrical, digital, magnetic, wireless, optical, electromagnetic, or similar capabilities.

electronic acknowledgment An electronic communication that establishes that an electronic communication was received but, in itself, does not establish that the content sent corresponds to the content received.

electronic agent A computer program or an electronic or other automated means

used independently to initiate an action or respond to electronic records or performances in whole or in part, without review or action by an individual.

electronic arbitration (e-arbitration) The arbitration of a dispute using online arbitration services.

electronic commerce (e-commerce) The sale of goods and services or the licensing of intellectual property by computer over the Internet.

electronic communication A form of communication that is sent electronically.

Electronic Communications Privacy Act (ECPA) A federal statute that makes it a crime, without the victim's consent, to intercept an electronic communication at the point of transmission, while in transit, when stored by a router or server or after receipt by the intended recipient. There are some exceptions to this law.

electronic contract (e-contract) A contract that is formed electronically.

electronic court (e-court or virtual court) A court that either mandates or permits the electronic filing of pleadings, briefs, and other documents related to a lawsuit; also called a *virtual courthouse.*

electronic dispute resolution (e-dispute resolution) Use of online alternative dispute resolution services to resolve a dispute.

electronic filing (e-filing) The electronic filing of pleadings, briefs, and other documents related to a lawsuit.

electronic financing statement (e-financing statement) A financing statement in personal property that is electronic.

electronic initial public offering (e-public offering or E-IPOs) The process of an issuer selling shares of stock to the public over the Internet.

electronic lease contract (e-lease contract) A contract for the lease of goods that is entered into electronically.

electronic license (e-license) A contract whereby the owner of software or a digital application grants limited rights to the owner of a computer or digital device to use the software or digital application for a limited period and under specified conditions.

electronic licensee (e-licensee) The owner of a computer or digital device to whom an electronic license (e-license) is granted to use another's software program or digital application.

electronic licensor (e-licensor) The owner of software program or digital application that grants a license to someone to use the software program or digital application.

electronic mail (e-mail) Electronic written communication between individuals and businesses using computers connected to the Internet.

electronic mail contracts (e-mail contracts) Contracts that are formed using e-mail.

electronic mediation (e-mediation) The mediation of a dispute using online mediation services.

electronic record A record that is created, generated, sent, communicated, received, or stored by electronic means.

electronic sales contract (e-sales contract) A contract for the sale of goods that is entered into electronically.

electronic secured transaction (e-secured transaction) A secured transaction that is created electronically.

electronic securities transactions (e-securities transactions) The issuing of securities, trading in securities, disseminating information to investors, managing securities accounts online, and other securities activities are being conducted electronically.

electronic signature (e-signature or digital signature) A signature that is inscribed using an electronic means.

Electronic Signatures in Global and National Commerce Act (E-Sign Act) A federal statute that (1) recognizes electronic contracts as meeting the writing requirement of the Statute of Frauds and (2) recognizes and gives electronic signatures—e-signatures—the same force and effect as pen inscribed signatures on paper.

embezzlement The fraudulent conversion of property by a person to whom that property was entrusted.

eminent domain The government's power to take private property for public use, provided that just compensation is paid to the private property holder.

Employee Retirement Income Security Act (ERISA) A federal statute designed to prevent fraud and other abuses associated with private pension funds.

employer–employee relationship A relationship that results when an employer hires an employee to perform some task or service but the employee has not been authorized to enter into contracts on behalf of his employer.

employer lockout An act of an employer to prevent employees from entering the work premises when the employer reasonably anticipates a strike.

employment discrimination Discrimination by an employer against a prospective employee or employee based on race, national origin, color, gender, religion, age, disability, veteran's status, and other protected classes.

employment-related injury A requirement that employees who are awarded workers' compensation benefits have suffered from injuries that have arisen out of and in the course of their employment.

***en banc* review** The review of a decision of a three-judge panel by the all of the justices of a U.S. courts of appeals.

encryption technology Technology and software that protect copyrighted works from unauthorized access.

Endangered Species Act A federal statute that protects endangered and threatened species of wildlife.

English common law Law developed by judges who issued their opinions when deciding a case. The principles announced in these cases became precedent for deciding similar cases in the future.

entrepreneur A person who forms and operates a new business either by himself or herself or with others.

entrustment rule A rule that states that if the owner of goods entrusts the possession of these goods to a merchant who deals in goods of that kind (e.g., for repair or consignment), the merchant has the power to transfer all rights (including title) in the goods to a buyer in the ordinary course of business. The real owner cannot reclaim the goods from this buyer.

enumerated powers Certain powers delegated to the federal government.

environmental impact statement (EIS) A document that must be prepared for any proposed legislation or major federal action that significantly affects the quality of the human environment.

environmental protection Actions and laws that protect the nation's and world's air and water from pollution, reduce the harm from hazardous wastes, and protect wildlife.

Environmental Protection Agency (EPA) A federal administrative agency created by Congress to coordinate the implementation and enforcement of the federal environmental protection laws.

environmental protection laws Laws enacted by federal and state governments to protect air and water from pollution, reduce the harm from hazardous wastes, and protect wildlife.

Equal Credit Opportunity Act (ECOA) A federal statute that prohibits discrimination in the extension of credit based on sex, marital status, race, color, national origin, religion, age, or receipt of income from public assistance programs.

equal dignity rule A rule that says that real estate agents' contracts to sell the real property of another are covered by the Statute of Frauds and must be in writing to be enforceable.

Equal Employment Opportunity Act of 1972 A federal statute that provides that "It shall be an unlawful employment practice for an employer to fail or refuse to hire or to discharge any individual, or otherwise to discriminate against any individual with respect to his compensation, terms, conditions, or privileges of employment, because of such individual's race, color, religion, sex, or national origin."

Equal Employment Opportunity Commission (EEOC) A federal administrative agency that is responsible for enforcing most federal antidiscrimination laws.

equal opportunity in employment The right of all employees and job applicants (1) to be treated without discrimination and (2) to be able to sue employers if they are discriminated against.

Equal Pay Act A federal statute that protects both sexes from pay discrimination based on sex. It extends to jobs that require equal skill, equal effort, equal responsibility, and similar working conditions.

Equal Protection Clause A clause that provides that a state cannot "deny to any person within its jurisdiction the equal protection of the laws."

equitable remedy A remedy that is available if there has been a breach of contract that cannot be adequately compensated through a legal remedy or to prevent unjust enrichment.

equity A doctrine that permits judges to make decisions based on fairness, equality, moral rights, and natural law.

equity securities Representation of ownership rights to a corporation; also called *stocks*.

equivocal response An offeree's response to an offer that is not clear, unambiguous, or has more than one possible meaning. An offeree's equivocal response to an offer does not create a contract.

error of law Error regarding law decisions made by a court during a trial.

Escott v. BarChris Construction Corporation A decision of a court that found certain defendants liable for material misrepresentations and omissions made by an issuer of securities in a registration statement that was filed with the Securities and Exchange Commission (SEC); the court rejected many of the defendants proffered *due diligence defenses*.

Establishment Clause A clause of the First Amendment to the U.S. Constitution that prohibits the government from either establishing a state religion or promoting one religion over another.

estate Ownership rights in real property; the bundle of legal rights that the owner has to possess, use, and enjoy the property; also known as *estate in land*.

estate *pour autre vie* A life estate that is measured by the life of a third party.

ethical fundamentalism A theory of ethics that says a person looks to an outside source for ethical rules or commands.

ethical relativism A moral theory that holds that individuals must decide what is ethical, based on their own feelings about what is right and wrong.

ethics A set of moral principles or values that governs the conduct of an individual or a group.

ethics and the law The relationship between ethics and the law. Sometimes the rule of law and the rule of ethics demand the same response by a person confronted with a problem, while in some situations the law may permit an act that is ethically wrong.

euro A single monetary unit that has been adopted by many countries of the EU that comprise the *eurozone*.

European Union (EU) A regional international organization that comprises many countries of Western and Eastern Europe and was created to promote peace and security as well as economic, social, and cultural development.

European Union Commission A commission that is independent of its member nations, that has been delegated substantial powers, including authority to enact legislation and to take enforcement actions to ensure member nations' compliance with the European Union treaty.

eurozone Countries of the European Union that use the euro as their currency.

eviction proceeding A legal process that a landlord must complete to *evict* a holdover tenant. Also known as an *unlawful detainer action.*

exclusionary rule A rule that says evidence obtained from an unreasonable search and seizure can generally be prohibited from introduction at a trial or an administrative proceeding against the person searched.

exclusive agency contract A contract a principal and agent enter into that says the principal cannot employ any agent other than the exclusive agent.

exclusive jurisdiction Sole jurisdiction of a federal court to hear and decide cases involving specified subject matters.

exclusive license A license in which for the specified duration of the license, the licensor will not grant to any other person rights in the same information.

exclusive possession A lessee's exclusive right to leased premises for the term of the lease or until the tenant defaults on the obligations under the lease.

exclusive remedy A sole remedy for employees who are covered by workers' compensation and have been injured on the job. Thus, workers have given up their right to sue their employer for damages. There are several exceptions to this rule.

exculpatory clause A contractual provision that relieves one (or both) of the parties to a contract from tort liability for ordinary negligence; also known as a *release of liability clause.*

executed contract A contract that has been fully performed on both sides; a completed contract.

executive branch (president) The part of the government that consists of the president and vice president.

executive exemption An exemption from federal minimum wage and overtime pay requirements that applies to executives who are compensated on a salary basis, who engage in management, have authority to hire employees, and regularly direct two or more employees.

executive order An order issued by a member of the executive branch of the government.

executive power The power of an administrative agency to investigate and prosecute possible violations of statutes, administrative rules, and administrative orders.

executory contract A contract that has not been fully performed by either or both sides.

executory contract In bankruptcy law, a contract that has not been fully performed. With the bankruptcy court's approval, a debtor may reject executory contracts in bankruptcy.

exempt property Property that may be retained by a debtor pursuant to federal or state law that does not become part of the bankruptcy estate.

exempt securities Securities that are exempt from registration with the Securities and Exchange Commission (SEC).

exempt transactions Transactions in which securities are issued but are exempt from registration with the Securities and Exchange Commission (SEC) because they meet specified requirements. The most widely used exempt transactions include the *non-issuer exemption*, *intrastate offering exemption*, *private placement exemption*, and *small offering exemption*.

express agency An agency that occurs when a principal and an agent expressly agree to enter into an agency agreement with each other.

express authorization A means of communication for accepting an offer to enter into a contract that is specified in the offer (e.g, registered mail).

express contract An agreement that is expressed in written or oral words.

express terms Terms in offers and contracts that expressly identify the parties, the subject matter of the offer or contract, the consideration to be paid by the parties, and the time of performance, as well as other terms of the offer and contract.

express trust A trust created voluntarily by the settlor.

express warranty A warranty that is created when a seller or lessor makes an affirmation that the goods he or she is selling or leasing meet certain standards of quality, description, performance, or condition.

ex-ship (from the carrying vessel) A shipping term that requires the seller to bear the expense and risk of loss until the goods are unloaded from the ship at its port of destination.

extension A provision that allows a debtor a longer period of time to pay his or her debts.

extortion A threat to expose something about another person unless that other person gives money or property; often referred to as *blackmail.*

extortion under color of official right Extortion of a public official.

fact-finding A form of alternative dispute resolution in which the parties employ a fact-finder to investigate the dispute, gather evidence, and prepare reports of his or her findings.

failing company doctrine A doctrine that permits a competitor to merge with another competitor that is failing company if there is no other reasonable alternative for the failing company.

failure to warn A defect that occurs when a manufacturer does not place a warning on the packaging of products that could cause injury if the danger is unknown.

Fair and Accurate Credit Transactions Act of 2003 A federal statute that gives consumers the right to obtain one free credit report each year from the credit reporting agencies, permits consumers to purchase their credit score, and allows consumers to place fraud alerts in their credit files.

Fair Credit and Charge Card Disclosure Act An amendment to the Truth-in-Lending Act (TILA) that requires disclosure of certain credit terms on credit- and charge-card solicitations and applications.

Fair Credit Billing Act (FCBA) A federal statute that regulates billing errors involving consumer credit and requires that creditors promptly acknowledge in writing consumer billing complaints and investigate billing errors.

Fair Credit Reporting Act (FCRA) An amendment to the Truth-in-Lending Act (TILA) that protects customers who are subjects of a credit report by setting out guidelines for credit bureaus.

Fair Debt Collection Practices Act (FDCPA) A federal statute that protects consumer debtors from abusive, deceptive, and unfair practices used by debt collectors.

Fair Employment Practice Agency (FEPA) A state agency that some states have where a complainant may file his or her employment discrimination claim instead of with the federal Equal Employment Opportunity Commission (EEOC).

Fair Housing Act A federal statute that makes it unlawful for a party to refuse to rent or sell a dwelling to any person because of his or her race, color, national origin, sex, or religion.

Fair Labor Standards Act (FLSA) A federal statute enacted to protect workers. It prohibits child labor and sets minimum wage and overtime pay requirements.

fair use doctrine A doctrine that permits certain limited use of a copyright by someone other than the copyright holder without the permission of the copyright holder.

false and deceptive advertising Advertising that contains misinformation or omits important information that is likely to mislead a reasonable consumer or that makes unsubstantiated claims.

false and misleading labeling Labeling that contains misinformation or omits important information that is likely to mislead a reasonable consumer or that makes unsubstantiated claims. The Food,

Drug, and Cosmetic Act (FDCA) prohibits false and misleading labeling of food products.

False Claims Act (Whistleblower Statute) A federal statute that permits private parties to sue companies for fraud on behalf of the government and share in any monetary recovery.

false imprisonment The intentional confinement or restraint of another person without authority or justification and without that person's consent.

false pretenses A crime that involves obtaining title to property through deception or trickery; also known as *criminal fraud* or *deceit*.

Family and Medical Leave Act (FMLA) A federal statute that guarantees workers up to twelve weeks of unpaid leave in a twelve-month period to attend to family and medical emergencies and other specified situations.

F.A.S. (free alongside ship) *port of shipment* or **F.A.S. (vessel)** *port of shipment* A shipping term that requires the seller to deliver and tender the goods alongside the named vessel or on the dock designated and provided by the buyer.

federal administrative agencies Administrative agencies that are created by the executive or legislative branch of federal government.

Federal Arbitration Act (FAA) A federal statute that provides for the enforcement of most arbitration agreements.

Federal Communications Commission (FCC) A federal administrative agency that regulates communications by radio, television, cable, wire, and satellite.

federal government The government of the United States of America.

Federal Insurance Contributions Act (FICA) A federal statute that requires certain employees to make contributions (pay taxes) into the Social Security fund.

Federal Patent Statute A federal statute that establishes the requirements for obtaining a patent and protects patented inventions from infringement.

federal question case A means for bringing a lawsuit in federal court because it arises under the U.S. Constitution, treaties, federal statutes, federal regulations, or executive orders.

federal statutes Statutes enacted by the U.S. Congress.

Federal Trade Commission (FTC) A federal administrative agency empowered to enforce the Federal Trade Commission Act (FTC Act) and other federal consumer protection statutes.

Federal Trade Commission Act (FTC Act) A federal statute, enacted in 1914, that creates certain consumer protections, regulates business conduct, prohibits unfair and deceptive practices, and grants certain antitrust powers to the Federal Trade Commission (FTC).

Federal Trademark Dilution Act (FTDA) A federal statute that protects famous marks from dilution, erosion, blurring, or tarnishing.

Federal Unemployment Tax Act (FUTA) A federal statute that requires employers to pay unemployment taxes; unemployment compensation is paid to workers who are temporarily unemployed.

Federal Water Pollution Control Act (FWPCA) A federal statute that regulates water pollution.

federalism The U.S. form of government in which the federal government and the 50 state governments share powers.

fee simple absolute A type of ownership of real property that grants the owner the full bundle of legal rights that a person can hold in real property; also known as *fee simple*.

fee simple defeasible A type of ownership of real property that grants the owner all the incidents of a fee simple absolute except that it may be taken away if a specified condition occurs or does not occur; also known as *qualified fee*.

felony The most serious type of crime; inherently evil crime. Most crimes against persons and some business-related crimes are felonies.

felony murder rule A rule that stipulates that if a murder is committed during the commission of another crime, even though the perpetrator did not originally intend to commit murder, the perpetrator is liable for the crime of murder.

fictitious business name statement A document that is filed with the state that designates a trade name of the business, the name and address of the applicant, and the address of the business; also known as *certificate of trade name*.

fiduciary duties of agents Agents' fiduciary duties of loyalty and care when acting on behalf of their principals.

fiduciary duties of directors and officers Duties of loyalty, honesty, integrity, trust, and confidence owed by directors and officers to their corporate employers. The duties the directors and officers of a corporation owe to act carefully when acting on behalf of the corporation.

fiduciary relationship A relationship that exists among general partners where they owe each other a duty of loyalty.

Fifth Amendment to the U.S. Constitution An amendment to the U.S. Constitution that provides that no person "shall be compelled in any criminal case to be a witness against himself." Thus, a person cannot be compelled to give testimony against himself. The right is referred to as the *privilege against self incrimination*. The Fifth Amendment also contains the *Double Jeopardy Clause* that protects persons from being tried twice for the same crime.

final judgment Judgment of a trial court entered after all posttrial motions are decided.

financing statement A document filed by a secured creditor with the appropriate government office that constructively notifies the world of his or her security interest in personal property.

finding of fact A decision regarding the facts of a case made by a jury, or if there is no jury then by the judge.

firm offer rule A UCC rule that says that a merchant who (1) makes an offer to buy, sell, or lease goods and (2) assures the other party in a separate writing that the offer will be held open cannot revoke the offer for the time stated or, if no time is stated, for a reasonable time.

First Amendment to the U.S. Constitution An amendment to the U.S. Constitution that guarantees freedom of speech, freedom to assemble, freedom of the press, and freedom of religion.

first purchase money mortgage A mortgage (or deed of trust and note) taken out to purchase a house.

first-to-invent rule A rule that stipulates that the first person to invent an item or a process is given patent protection over a later inventor who was first to file a patent application.

fixed dividend A preferred dividend that is paid a set periods during the year (e.g., quarterly).

fixture Personal property that is permanently affixed to land or buildings.

floating lien A security interest in property that was not in the possession of the debtor when the security agreement was executed.

flow-through taxation A tax rule that provides that the income and losses of a sole proprietorship, general partnership, limited partnership, limited liability company, limited liability partnership, and S corporation are reported on the owner's personal income tax return.

F.O.B. (free on board) place of destination A shipping term that requires the seller to bear the expense and risk of loss of goods until the goods are tendered to the buyer at the place of destination.

F.O.B. (free on board) point of shipment A shipping term that requires the seller to arrange to ship the goods and put the goods in the carrier's possession.

Food and Drug Administration (FDA) A federal administrative agency that administers and enforces the federal Food, Drug, and Cosmetic Act and other federal consumer protection laws.

Food, Drug, and Cosmetic Act (FDCA) A federal statute that provides the basis for the regulation of much of the testing, manufacture, distribution, and sale of food, drugs, cosmetics, and medicinal products.

force majeure **clause** A clause in a contract in which the parties specify certain events that will excuse nonperformance.

foreclosing competition Competition that occurs in a vertical merger if competitors of the merged firms are prevented (foreclosed) from either selling goods or services to, or buying goods or services from, the merged firm.

foreign commerce Commerce with foreign nations.

Foreign Commerce Clause A clause of the U.S. Constitution that vests Congress with the power "to regulate commerce with foreign nations."

foreign corporation A corporation in any state other than the one in which it is organized.

Foreign Corrupt Practices Act A federal statute that makes it a crime for U.S. companies, or their officers, directors, agents, or employees, to bribe a foreign official, a foreign political party official, or a candidate for foreign political office, where the bribe is paid to influence the awarding of new business or for the retention of a continuing business activity.

foreign guest worker A person from a foreign country who is permitted to work in the United States pursuant to a visa issued by the U.S. government.

foreign limited liability company (foreign LLC) A limited liability company (LLC) in any state other than the one in which it is organized.

foreign limited liability partnership (foreign LLP) A limited liability partnership (LLP) in any state other than the one in which it is organized.

Foreign Sovereign Immunities Act (FSIA) A federal statute that exclusively governs suits against foreign nations that are brought in federal or state courts in the United States. It codifies the principle of *qualified, or restricted, immunity*.

forgery The fraudulent making or alteration of a written document that affects the legal liability of another person.

form contract A contract in which a seller or lessor offers goods to buyers or lessees on a take-it-or-leave-it basis and a consumer or other party has no ability to negotiate the terms of the contract.

Form 1040 U.S. Individual Income Tax Return A personal income tax form that is filed by a sole proprietor with the federal government that reports his or her personal income.

Form 2553 A form that is filed with the Internal Revenue Service (IRS) to elect Subchapter S federal income tax status for a qualifying corporation.

Form I-9 Employment Eligibility Verification A form that employers must obtain from every prospective employee, regardless of citizenship or national origin, with supporting documents, that demonstrates whether the prospective employee is either U.S. citizens or otherwise authorized to work in the country (e.g., have proper work visas).

Form U-7 A question-and-answer disclosure form that small businesses can complete and file with the Securities and Exchange Commission (SEC) if they plan on raising $1 million or less from a public issue of securities.

Form UCC-1 A uniform financing statement form that is used in all states to perfect a security interest in personal property.

formal contract A contract that requires a special form, words, or method of creation.

formal rulemaking Rulemaking by an administrative agency that involves conducting a trial-like hearing at which parties may present evidence, engage in cross-examination, present rebuttal evidence, and such before the agency decides whether to adopt the proposed rule.

forum-selection clause A clause in a contract that designates that a certain court has jurisdiction to hear and decide a case arising out of the contract. Also called a *choice of forum clause*.

forum shopping A party's looking for a favorable court in which to bring a lawsuit without a valid reason for being in that court.

forward vertical merger A vertical merger in which the supplier acquires the customer.

Fourteenth Amendment to the U.S. Constitution An 1868 amendment added to the U.S. Constitution that contains the Due Process, Equal Protection, and Privileges and Immunities clauses.

Fourth Amendment to the U.S. Constitution An amendment to the U.S. Constitution that protects the rights of the people from *unreasonable search and seizure* by the government.

franchise An arrangement that is established when one party (the *franchisor*) licenses another party (the *franchisee*) to use the franchisor's trade name, trademarks, commercial symbols, patents, copyrights, and other property in the distribution and selling of goods and services.

franchise agreement An agreement that a franchisor and franchisee enter into that sets forth the terms and conditions of a franchise.

franchise application An application filed by a prospective franchisee to obtain a franchise from a franchisor. The application includes detailed financial and other information about the applicant.

franchisee A party who is granted a franchise and license by a franchisor in a franchise arrangement; also the *licensee*.

franchisor A party who grants a franchise and license to a franchisee in a franchise arrangement; also the *licensor*.

fraudulent misrepresentation An event that occurs when one person consciously decides to induce another person to rely and act on a misrepresentation; also called *fraud*.

fraudulent transfer A transfer of a debtor's property or an obligation incurred by a debtor within two years of the filing of a petition, where (1) the debtor had actual intent to hinder, delay, or defraud

a creditor or (2) the debtor received less than a reasonable equivalent in value.

Free Exercise Clause A clause of the First Amendment to the U.S. Constitution that prohibits the government from interfering with the free exercise of religion in the United States.

Free Trade Area of the Americas (FTAA) A proposed free trade agreement that would encompass most of the countries of Central America, North America, and South America.

free transferability of shares A characteristic of corporations where the shares of the corporation may be transferred by a shareholder by sale, assignment, pledge, or gift unless they are issued pursuant to certain exemptions from securities registration.

freedom of religion A right established in the First Amendment to the U.S. Constitution.

freedom of speech The right to engage in oral, written, and symbolic speech that is protected by the First Amendment.

freehold estate An estate in which the owner has a present possessory interest in the real property. There are three types of freehold estates: *fee simple absolute* (or *fee simple*), *fee simple defeasible* (or *qualified fee*), and *life estate*.

French Civil Code of 1804 (Napoleonic Code) A civil law based on a code of laws.

fresh start The goal of federal bankruptcy law to grant a debtor relief from some of his or her burdensome debts while protecting creditors by requiring the debtor to pay more of his or her debts than would otherwise have been required prior to the 2005 act.

frolic and detour A situation in which an agent does something during the course of his or her employment to further his or her own interests rather than the principal's.

full express warranty An express warranty made by a seller or lessor of goods that guarantees free repair or replacement of a defective product.

Full Faith and Credit Clause A clause in the U.S. Constitution (Article IV, Section 1) that states that a judgment of a court of one state must be given "full faith and credit" by the courts of another state.

Full Warranty An express warranty made by a seller or lessor of goods that guarantees free repair or replacement of a defective product.

fully disclosed agency An agency in which a contracting third party knows (1) that the agent is acting for a principal and (2) the identity of the principal.

fully disclosed principal The principal in a fully disclosed agency.

fully protected speech Speech that the government cannot prohibit or regulate.

future advances Funds advanced to a debtor from a line of credit secured by collateral. Future advances are future withdrawals from a line of credit.

future goods Goods not yet in existence (e.g., ungrown crops, unborn stock animals).

future interest The interest in real property that a grantor retains for himself or herself or a third party. Two forms of future interests are *reversion* and *remainder*.

gambling statutes Statutes that make certain forms of gambling illegal.

gap-filling rule A rule that says an open term can be "read into" a sales or lease contract.

gender discrimination Discrimination against a person because of his or her gender; also known as *sex discrimination*.

General Agreement on Tariffs and Trade (GATT) A multilateral treaty that establishes trade agreements and limits tariffs and trade restrictions among its member nations.

General Assembly The legislative body of the United Nations that is composed of all member nations.

general corporation statutes State statutes that permit corporations to be formed without the separate approval of the legislature.

general duty standard An Occupational Safety and Health Administration (OSHA) standard that require an employer to provide a work environment free from recognized hazards that are causing or are likely to cause death or serious physical harm to employees.

general intent crime A crime that requires that the perpetrator either knew or should have known that his or her actions would lead to harmful results.

general-jurisdiction trial courts (courts of record) Courts that hear cases of a general nature that are not within the jurisdiction of limited-jurisdiction trial courts.

general partners of a general partnership Partners of a general partnership who invest capital, manage the business, and are personally liable for the partnership's debts; also known simply as *partners*.

general partners of a limited partnership Partners in a limited partnership who invest capital, manage the business, and are personally liable for partnership debts.

general partnership An association of two or more persons to carry on as co-owners of a business for profit; also known as an *ordinary partnership*.

general partnership agreement A written agreement that partners sign; also called *articles of general partnership*.

general power of attorney A power of attorney where a principal confers broad powers on the agent to act in any matters on the principal's behalf.

general warranty deed (grant deed) A deed to real property that contains the greatest number of warranties and provides the highest level of protection to a grantee. The seller warrants that he owns the property, has the legal right to sell it, and that the property is not subject to encumbrances other than those that are disclosed.

generally known danger A defense that acknowledges that certain products are inherently dangerous and are known to the general population to be so.

generic name A term for a mark that has become a common term for a product line or type of service and therefore has lost its trademark protection.

genetic information Information from which it is possible to determine a person's propensity to be stricken by many diseases.

genetic information discrimination Employment discrimination based on a person's propensity to be stricken diseases.

Genetic Information Nondiscrimination Act (GINA) An act that makes it illegal for an employer to discriminate against job applicants and employees based on genetic information.

genuineness of assent The requirement that a party's assent to a contract be genuine.

geographical market extension merger A market extension merger between two firms that sell the same products or services but do not sell their products or services in the same geographical areas.

German Civil Code of 1896 A civil law based on a code of laws.

gift promise A promise that is unenforceable because it lacks consideration; also known as a *gratuitous promise*.

global warming A condition that occurs when the temperatures of the earth and waters increase, which is often attributable to air and other forms of pollution.

going public A situation that occurs where a company sells securities to the public for the first time.

good faith in the Uniform Commercial Code An obligation of good faith that every contract or duty within the UCC imposes in its performance or enforcement.

good faith purchaser for value A person to whom good title can be transferred from a person with voidable title. The real owner cannot reclaim goods from a good faith purchaser for value.

good faith subsequent lessee A person to whom a lease interest can be transferred from a person with voidable title. The real owner cannot reclaim the goods from the subsequent lessee until the lease expires.

Good Samaritan law A statute that relieves medical professionals from liability for ordinary negligence when they stop and render aid to victims in emergency situations.

goods Tangible things that are movable at the time of their identification to a contract.

government contractor defense A defense that says a contractor who was provided specifications by the government is not liable for any defect in the product that occurs as a result of those specifications.

government judgment A government judgment obtained against a defendant for an antitrust violation may be used as *prima facie* evidence of liability in a private, civil treble-damages action.

government-owned corporations Corporations that are formed by government entities to meet specific government or political purposes; also known as *public corporations*.

grand jury A special jury that hears evidence of serious crimes (e.g., murder) against an accused person, evaluates the evidence presented, and determines whether there is sufficient evidence to hold the accused for trial. The grand jury does not determine guilt. If the grand jury issues an *indictment*, the accused will be held for later trial.

grand jury indictment The charge of having committed a crime (usually a felony), based on the judgment of a grand jury.

grantee The party to whom an interest in real property is transferred.

grantor The party who transfers an ownership interest in real property.

group boycott A restraint of trade in which two or more competitors at one level of distribution agree not to deal with others at another level of distribution; also known as *refusal to deal*.

guarantor A person who agrees to pay a debt if the primary debtor does not; a third person who agrees to be liable in a guaranty arrangement. The guarantor is *secondarily liable* on the debt.

guaranty arrangement An arrangement in which a third party promises to be *secondarily liable* for the payment of another's debt.

guaranty contract A promise in which one person agrees to answer for the debts or duties of another person. It is a contract between the guarantor and the original creditor.

guilty A plea that may be entered by an accused at his or her arraignment whereby the accused states that he or she committed the crime that he or she is charged with.

H-1B visa A visa issued by the U.S. government that allows U.S. employers to employ foreign nationals in the United States who are skilled in specialty occupations.

H4 visa A visa issued by the U.S. government that allows immediate family members (i.e., spouse and children under 21) into the United States as dependants of workers issued H-1B work visas.

Hart-Scott-Rodino Antitrust Improvement Act (HSR Act) A federal statute that requires certain firms to notify the Federal Trade Commission (FTC) and the U.S. Department of Justice in advance of a proposed merger. Unless the government challenges a proposed merger within thirty days, the merger may proceed.

hazardous waste   Waste that may cause or significantly contribute to an increase in mortality or serious illness or pose a hazard to human health or the environment if improperly managed.

Health Care and Education Reconciliation Act   A federal statute that amended the Patient Protection and Affordable Care Act (PPACA) and created the Health Care Reform Act.

Health Care Reform Act of 2010   A federal statute composed of the Patient Protection and Affordable Care Act (PPACA), as amended by the Health Care and Education Reconciliation Act, that mandates that most U.S. citizens and legal residents purchase "minimal essential" health care insurance coverage, provides methods for accomplishing this goal, and provides new protection for insured persons from abusive practices of insurance companies.

Heart of Atlanta Motel v. United States   A U.S. Supreme Court decision that upheld the Civil Rights Act of 1964, a federal statute, as constitutionally regulating interstate commerce.

hedge fund   A private investment company that has a limited number of wealthy investors that invests in a wide range of risky investments.

highest state court (state supreme court)   The highest court in a state court system, which hears appeals from intermediate appellate state courts and certain trial courts.

highly compensated employee exemption   An exemption from federal minimum wage and overtime pay requirements that applies to employees who are paid total annual compensation of $100,000 or more, perform office or nonmanual work, and regularly perform at least one of the duties of an exempt executive, administrative, or professional employee.

Hindu law   Called *dharmasastra* in Sanskrit ("the doctrine of proper behavior"), law that is linked to the divine revelation of Veda (the holy collection of Indian religious songs, prayers, hymns, and sayings written between 2000 and 1000 BCE). Most Hindu law is concerned with family matters and the law of succession.

historic buildings   Buildings that have an historical value.

Historical School of jurisprudence   A school of thought which postulates that law is an aggregate of social traditions and customs.

homestead exemption   Equity in a debtor's home that the debtor is permitted to retain in bankruptcy.

horizontal merger   A merger between two or more companies that compete in the same business and geographical market.

horizontal restraint of trade   A restraint of trade that occurs when two or more competitors at the same *level of distribution* enter into a contract, combination, or conspiracy to restrain trade.

hostile and adverse   A requirement that must be proven by a person to obtain real property by adverse possession. It requires that the adverse possessor has occupied the property without the express or implied permission of the owner.

hostile work environment   A work environment that involves sexual or racial harassment or harassment against other protected classes that creates a physically threatening or humiliating workplace, a workplace that negatively impacts an employee's ability to go to work, or unreasonably interferes with an employee's work performance.

***Howey* test**   A test that states that an arrangement is an investment contract if there is an investment of money by an investor in a common enterprise and the investor expects to make profits based on the sole or substantial efforts of the promoter or others.

hung jury   A jury that cannot come to a unanimous decision about the defendant's guilt. In the case of a hung jury, the government may choose to retry the case.

identification of goods   Under a contract for the sale or lease of goods, the distinguishing of the goods named in a sales or lease contract from the seller's or lessor's other goods.

identity theft   A theft in which someone steals information about another person and poses as that person and take the innocent person's money or property or to purchase goods and services using the victim's credit information. Identity theft is a crime. Also called *ID theft*.

Identity Theft and Assumption Deterrence Act   A federal statute that makes it a federal crime to knowingly transfer or use, without authority, the identity of another person with the intent to commit any unlawful activity as defined by federal law and state and local felony laws.

illegal consideration   A promise to refrain from doing an illegal act. Such a promise will not support a contract.

illegal contract   A contract that has an illegal object. Such contracts are *void*.

illegal strikes   Strikes by employees that are illegal and not protected by federal labor law.

illegal subjects of collective bargaining   Subjects that are illegal for a company and a labor union to bargain over during collective bargaining (e.g., engaging in discrimination).

illusory promise   A contract into which both parties enter but one or both of the parties can choose not to perform their contractual obligations. Thus, the contract lacks consideration; also known as an *illusory contract*.

Immigration Reform and Control Act of 1986 (IRCA)   A federal statute that makes it unlawful for employers to hire illegal immigrants.

immunity from prosecution   The government's agreement with a person not to use any evidence given by that person against that person.

impaneled   The act of being sworn in to hear a case.

implied agency   An agency that occurs when a principal and an agent do not expressly create an agency but is inferred from the conduct of the parties.

implied authorization   A means of communication for accepting an offer to enter into a contract that is inferred from what is customary in similar transactions, usage of trade, or prior dealings between the parties.

implied exemptions   Exemptions from antitrust laws that are implied by the federal courts.

implied term   A missing term that is not expressly stated in an offer or a contract that can reasonably be supplied by the courts if a reasonable term can be implied from other sources.

implied warranty of authority   A warranty of an agent who enters into a contract on behalf of another party that he or she has the authority to do so.

implied warranty of fitness for a particular purpose   A warranty that arises where a seller or lessor warrants that the goods will meet the buyer's or lessee's expressed needs.

implied warranty of fitness for human consumption   A warranty that applies to food or drink consumed on or off the premises of restaurants, grocery stores, fast food outlets, and vending machines.

implied warranty of habitability   A implied warranty that provides that leased premises must be fit, safe, and suitable for ordinary residential use.

implied warranty of merchantability   Unless properly disclosed, a warranty that is implied that sold or leased goods are fit for the ordinary purpose for which they are sold or leased, as well as other assurances.

implied-in-fact contract   A contract in which agreement between parties has been inferred from their conduct.

implied-in-law contract   An equitable doctrine whereby a court may award monetary damages to a plaintiff for providing work or services to a defendant even though no actual contract existed. The doctrine is intended to prevent unjust enrichment and unjust detriment. Also called *quasi-contract*.

impossibility of performance Nonperformance that is excused if a contract becomes impossible to perform. It must be objective impossibility, not subjective. Also called *objective impossibility*.

imputed knowledge Information that is learned by an agent that is attributed to the principal.

in personam **jurisdiction (personal jurisdiction)** A court's jurisdiction over a party to a lawsuit.

in rem **jurisdiction** Jurisdiction of a court to hear and decide a case because the property of the lawsuit is located in that state.

inaccessibility exception A rule that permits employees and union officials to engage in union solicitation on company property if the employees are beyond reach of reasonable union efforts to communicate with them.

incidental beneficiary A third party who is unintentionally benefited by other people's contracts.

incoming partner A person who becomes a partner in an existing partnership.

incorporation doctrine A doctrine applied by the U.S. Supreme Court that holds that most of the fundamental guarantees contained in the Bill of Rights are not only applicable to federal government action but are also applicable to state and local government action.

indenture agreement A contract between a corporation and a holder that contains the terms of a debt security; also known as an *indenture*.

independent contractor A person who contracts with another to do something for him who is not controlled by the other nor subject to the other's right to control with respect to his physical conduct in the performance of the undertaking.

Indian Gaming Regulatory Act A federal statute that sets the requirements for establishing casino gambling and other gaming activities on tribal land.

indictment The charge of having committed a crime (usually a felony), based on the judgment of a grand jury.

indirect price discrimination A form of price discrimination (e.g., favorable credit terms) that is less readily apparent than direct forms of price discrimination.

individual with regular income An individual whose income is sufficiently stable and regular to enable the individual to make payments under a Chapter 13 plan.

indoor air pollution Air pollution that occurs inside some buildings; also known as *sick building syndrome*.

infancy doctrine A doctrine that allows minors to disaffirm (cancel) most contracts they have entered into with adults.

inferior performance A situation in which a party fails to perform express or implied contractual obligations and impairs or destroys the essence of a contract; there is a *material breach*.

informal contract A contract that is not formal. Valid informal contracts are fully enforceable and may be sued upon if breached. Also called a *simple contract*.

information The charge of having committed a crime (usually a misdemeanor), based on the judgment of a judge (magistrate).

Information Infrastructure Protection Act (IIP Act) A federal statute that makes it a federal crime for anyone to intentionally access and acquires information from a protected computer without authorization.

information statement The charge of having committed a crime (usually a misdemeanor), based on the judgment of a judge (magistrate).

inherently dangerous activities Activities (e.g., use of explosives, clearing of land by fire) for which a principal is liable for the negligence of an independent contractor whom the principal has hired.

initial public offering (IPO) A situation in which a company or other issuer sells securities to the public for the first time.

injunction A court order that prohibits a person from doing a certain act.

injury A plaintiff's personal injury or damage to his or her property that enables him or her to recover monetary damages for the defendant's negligence.

injury to the innocent party An element of fraud. The measure of damages caused to the innocent victim of fraud is the difference between the value of the property as represented and the actual value of the property.

innocent acquisition The acquisition of a monopoly through innocent means, such as by superior business acumen, skill, foresight, or industry. This is a defense to a charge of committing an act of monopolization.

innocent misrepresentation Fraud that occurs when a person makes a statement of fact that he or she honestly and reasonably believes to be true even though it is not.

insane but not adjudged insane Being insane but not having been adjudged insane by a court or an administrative agency. A contract entered into by such person is generally *voidable*. Some states hold that such a contract is void.

Insecticide, Fungicide, and Rodenticide Act A federal statute that requires pesticides, herbicides, fungicides, and rodenticides to be registered with the EPA; the EPA may deny, suspend, or cancel registration.

inside director A member of the board of directors of a corporation who is also an officer of the corporation.

insider trading A situation in which an insider makes a profit by personally purchasing shares of the corporation prior to public release of favorable information or by selling shares of the corporation prior to the public disclosure of unfavorable information.

Insider Trading Sanctions Act A federal statute that permits the Securities and Exchange Commission (SEC) to obtain a civil penalty of up to three times (*treble damages*) the illegal benefits received from insider trading.

insiders under Section 10(b) Parties that include (1) officers, directors, and employees at all levels of a company; (2) lawyers, accountants, consultants, and agents and representatives who are hired by the company on a temporary and nonemployee basis to provide services or work to the company; and (3) others who owe a fiduciary duty to the company.

intangible personal property Property that includes securities, patents, trademarks, and copyrights.

integration clause A clause in a contract that stipulates that it is a complete integration and the exclusive expression of the parties' agreement; also known as a *merger clause*.

intellectual property Patents, copyrights, trademarks, and trade secrets. Federal and state laws protect intellectual property rights from misappropriation and infringement.

intended third-party beneficiary A third party who is not in privity of contract but who has rights under the contract and can enforce the contract against the promisor.

intent crime A crime that requires the defendant to be found guilty of committing a criminal act (*actus reus*) with criminal intent (*mens rea*).

intent to deceive An element of fraud that occurs when a person makes a misrepresentation of a material fact with knowledge that the representation is false or makes it without sufficient knowledge of the truth. This is called *scienter* ("guilty mind").

intentional infliction of emotional distress A tort that says a person whose extreme and outrageous conduct intentionally or recklessly causes severe emotional distress to another person is liable for that emotional distress; also known as the *tort of outrage*.

intentional misrepresentation The intentional defrauding of a person out of money, property, or something else of value; also known as *fraud* or *deceit*.

intentional tort A category of torts that requires that the defendant possessed the intent to do the act that caused the plaintiff's injuries. Occurs when a person has intentionally committed a wrong against (1) another person or his or her character, or (2) another person's property.

intermediate appellate court (appellate court or court of appeal) A court that hears appeals from trial courts.

intermediate scrutiny test A test that is applied to determine the constitutionality of classifications by the government based on protected classes other than race (e.g., gender).

internal union rules Rules adopted by a labor union that regulate the operation of the union.

International Court of Justice (ICJ) The judicial branch of the United Nations that is located in The Hague, the Netherlands; also called the *World Court*.

International Fund for Agricultural Development (IFAD) An autonomous agency of the United Nations that deals with a wide range of agricultural issues.

international law Law that governs affairs between nations and that regulates transactions between individuals and businesses of different countries.

International Monetary Fund (IMF) An agency of the United Nations whose primary function is to promote sound monetary, fiscal, and macroeconomic policies worldwide by providing assistance to needy countries.

International Shoe Company v. State of Washington A U.S. Supreme Court decision that established the "minimum contacts" and "traditional notions of fair play and substantial justice" tests to determine whether a defendant is subject to the jurisdiction of a court.

Internet A collection of millions of computers that provide a network of electronic connections between computers.

Internet Corporation for Assigned Names and Numbers (ICANN) The organization that oversees the registration and regulation of domain names.

Internet service provider (ISP) A company that operates servers on which websites and web pages are stored.

interrogatories Written questions submitted by one party to another party. The questions must be answered in writing within a stipulated time.

interstate commerce Commerce that moves between states or that affects commerce between states.

intervention The act of others to join as parties to an existing lawsuit.

intoxicated person A person who is under contractual incapacity because of ingestion of alcohol or drugs to the point of incompetence.

intrastate commerce Commerce within a state.

intrastate offering exemption An exemption from registration that permits local businesses to raise capital from local investors to be used in the local economy without the need to register with the Securities and Exchange Commission (SEC).

invasion of the right to privacy The unwarranted and undesired publicity of a private fact about a person. The fact does not have to be untrue.

investment bankers Independent securities companies that to sell issuer's securities to the public and perform other securities-related functions.

investment contract A flexible standard for defining a *security*. An arrangement where there is an investment of money by an investor in a common enterprise in which the investor expects to make profits based on the sole or substantial efforts of the promoter or others.

involuntary manslaughter A nonintent crime that occurs when the death of a person results from the reckless or grossly negligent conduct of another person.

involuntary petition A petition filed by creditors of a debtor to begin an involuntary bankruptcy proceeding against the debtor.

Islamic law (*Shari'a*) A law system that is derived from the *Qur'an*, the *Sunnah* (decisions and sayings of the prophet Muhammad), and reasonings by Islamic scholars, and is the law of some countries, while in other countries it forms the basis of religious and family law.

issued shares Authorized shares that have been sold by a corporation.

issuer A business or party selling securities to the public.

issuing shares The process of an issuer selling shares of stock.

Jewish law Complex law based on the ideology and theology of the *Torah*, which prescribes comprehensive and integrated rules of religious, political, and legal life that together form Jewish thought.

joint and several liability (1) A rule that holds that where there are multiple defendants who have been found liable for the same action, each defendant is personally liable for the entire judgment. The plaintiff can sue one, any, or all of the defendants to recover damages. (2) In a partnership situation, a rule that holds that partners are jointly and severally liable for tort liability of the partnership. This means that the plaintiff can sue one or more of the partners separately. If successful, the plaintiff can recover the entire amount of the judgment from any or all of the defendant-partners.

joint liability Liability of partners for contracts and debts of the partnership. A plaintiff must name the partnership and all of the partners as defendants in a lawsuit.

joint tenancy A form of co-ownership of real property that includes the *right of survivorship*.

joint tenants Parties who co-own real property in a joint tenancy arrangement.

judgment The decision of the judge in a trial usually based on the verdict of the jury; the judge may enter a judgment if there is no jury.

judgment notwithstanding the verdict (judgment n.o.v., j.n.o.v.) A judgment issued by a judge that overturns the verdict of the jury if the judge finds jury bias or misconduct.

judgment proof A situation in which a defendant does not have the money to pay a civil judgment.

judicial authority The power of an administrative agency to adjudicate cases through an administrative proceeding often conducted by an administrative law judge (ALJ).

judicial branch (courts) The branch of state and federal governments that is composed of courts of the relevant jurisdiction.

judicial decision A decision in a lawsuit made by a federal or state court.

judicial referee A person appointed by a court to conduct a private trial and render a judgment of a dispute if the parties agree the appointment.

judicial review The review of decisions of administrative law judges by courts.

jurisprudence The philosophy or science of law.

jury deliberation A process whereby a jury retires to the jury room to consider the evidence.

jury instructions (charges) Instructions given by a judge to the jury to inform them of the law to be applied in the case.

jury trial A lawsuit decided by a jury. The parties to a civil lawsuit have a right to a jury trial.

Just Compensation Clause A clause of the U.S. Constitution that requires the government to compensate the property owner, and possibly others, when the government takes property under its power of eminent domain.

Kantian ethics (duty ethics) A moral theory that says that people owe moral duties that are based on universal rules, such as the categorical imperative "Do unto others as you would have them do unto you."

labor law The statutes, rules, and regulations adopted by administrative agencies and court decisions interpreting and applying the statutes and rules and regulations.

Labor Management Relations Act (Taft-Hartley Act) A federal statute enacted in 1947 that expanded the activities that labor unions could engage in.

Labor Management Reporting and Disclosure Act (Landrum-Griffin Act) A federal statute enacted in 1959 that regulates internal union affairs and establishes the rights of union members.

labor's "bill of rights" A section in Title I of the Landrum-Griffin Act that gives each union member equal rights and privileges to nominate candidates for union office, vote in elections, and participate in membership meetings.

laissez-faire Freedom of contract without government regulation.

land The most common form of real property; includes the land and buildings and other structures permanently attached to the land.

land pollution Pollution of the land that is generally caused by hazardous waste being disposed of in an improper manner.

landlord An owner of real property who transfers a leasehold. Also known as a *lessor*.

landlord–tenant relationship A relationship that is created when the owner of a freehold estate transfers to another person the right to exclusively and temporarily possess the owner's real property.

Lanham (Trademark) Act (Lanham Act) A federal statute that (1) establishes the requirements for obtaining a federal mark and (2) protects marks from infringement.

lapse of time A stated time period after which an offer terminates. If no time is stated, an offer terminates after a reasonable time.

larceny The taking of another's personal property other than from his or her person or building.

law That which must be obeyed and followed by citizens, subject to sanctions or legal consequences; a body of rules of action or conduct prescribed by controlling authority and having binding legal force.

Law and Economics School of jurisprudence A school of thought that postulates that promoting market efficiency should be the central concern of legal decision making.

law court A court that developed and administered a uniform set of laws decreed by the kings and queens after William the Conqueror; legal procedure was emphasized over merits at this time.

Law Merchant Rules developed in England to solve commercial disputes that were based on common trade practices and usage.

lawful contract A contract whose object is lawful.

lawful object An element of a contract that is met where the object of a contract is not illegal.

learned professional exemption An exemption from federal minimum wage and overtime pay requirements that applies to employees compensated on a salary or fee basis that perform work that is predominantly intellectual in character, who possess advanced knowledge in a field of science or learning, and whose advanced knowledge was acquired through a prolonged course of specialized intellectual instruction.

lease A term that is used to indicate a contract for the lease of goods and a contract for the rental of real property.

lease contract A contract for the lease of goods that is subject to Article 2A (Leases) of the Uniform Commercial Code (UCC).

lease of goods A transfer of the right to the possession and use of named goods for a set term in return for certain consideration.

lease of real property The transfer of the right to use real property for a specified period of time. The rental agreement between a landlord and a tenant is called a *lease*.

leasehold estate A tenant's interest in property; also known as a *leasehold*.

legal entity (legal person) A corporation, limited liability company (LLC), general partnership, limited partnership, and limited liability partnership (LLP) is a separate legal entity—an artificial person—that can own property, sue and be sued, enter into and enforce contracts, and such.

legal value A requirement for finding consideration for a contract that is met if (1) the promisee suffers a *legal detriment* or (2) the promisor receives a *legal benefit*.

legally enforceable contract A contract in which if one party fails to perform as promised, the other party can use the court system to enforce the contract and recover damages or other remedy.

legislative branch (Congress) The branch of the federal government that consists of the U.S. Congress (the U.S. Senate and the U.S. House of Representatives). The U.S. Congress enacts federal statutes.

lender A party who lends money or another asset. The *creditor* in a credit transaction.

lessee of goods A person who acquires the right to possession and use of goods under a lease of goods.

lessor of goods A person who transfers the right of possession and use of goods under a lease of goods.

letter of credit A document that is issued by a bank on behalf of a buyer who purchases goods on credit from a seller that guarantees that if the buyer does not pay for the goods, then the bank will pay the seller.

liability without fault (strict liability) Liability that is imposed on a party even though he or she has exercised all possible care and has not been at fault for the injuries suffered by the plaintiff.

libel A false statement that appears in a letter, newspaper, magazine, book, photograph, movie, video, and so on.

license A grant issued by an administrative agency that permits a person to enter certain types of industry (e.g., banks, television and radio stations) or profession (e.g., doctors, lawyers, contractors).

license In a licensing arrangement, a grant that permits one party (the *licensee*) to use the trademarks, service marks, trade names, and other intellectual property of another party (*licensor*) in the distribution of goods and services.

license of intellectual property A contract that transfers limited rights in intellectual property and informational rights.

licensee The party to whom a license is granted.

licensing A business arrangement that occurs when the owner of intellectual property (the *licensor*) contracts to permit another party (the *licensee*) to use the intellectual property.

licensing agreement A detailed and comprehensive written agreement between a licensor and a licensee that sets forth the express terms of their agreement.

licensing statute A statute that requires a person or business to obtain a license from the government prior to engaging in a specified occupation or activity.

licensor The party who grants a license.

lien release A written document signed by a contractor, subcontractor, laborer, or material person, waiving his or her statutory lien against real property; also known as *release of lien*.

life estate An interest in real property for a person's lifetime; upon that person's death, the interest will be transferred to another party.

life tenant A person who is given a life estate.

Lilly Ledbetter Fair Pay Act of 2009 A federal statute that permits a complainant to file an employment discrimination claim against an employer within 180 days of the most recent paycheck violation and to recover back pay for up to two years preceding the filing of the claim if similar violations had occurred during the two-year period.

limitation of remedies A clause that may be used in a licensing agreement that restricts remedies to the return of copies of the licensed software programs or digital applications and repayment of the licensing fee, or limits remedies to the repair or replacement of the nonconforming copies.

limited-jurisdiction trial court (inferior trial court) A court that hears matters of a specialized or limited nature.

limited liability company (LLC) An unincorporated business entity that combines the most favorable attributes of general partnerships, limited partnerships, and corporations.

limited liability company code State statutes that regulate the formation, operation, and dissolution of limited liability companies (LLCs).

limited liability of limited partners The liability of limited partners of a limited partnership is limited to their capital contributions to the limited partnership; limited partners are not personally liable for the debts and obligations of the limited partnership.

limited liability of members of LLCs The liability of the members of a limited liability company (LLC) for the LLC's debts, obligations, and liabilities is limited to the extent of their capital contributions. Members of LLCs are not personally liable for the LLC's debts, obligations, and liabilities.

limited liability of partners of LLPs The liability of partners of a limited liability partnership (LLP) for the LLP's debts, obligations, and liabilities is limited only to the extent of their capital contributions. Partners of an LLP are not personally liable for the LLP's debts, obligations, and liabilities.

limited liability of shareholders A general rule of corporate law that provides that generally shareholders are liable only to the extent of their capital contributions for the debts and obligations of their corporation and are not personally liable for the debts and obligations of the corporation.

limited liability partnership (LLP) A special form of partnership in which all partners are limited partners and there are no general partners.

limited liability partnership code State statutes that regulates the formation, operation, and dissolution of limited liability partnerships (LLPs).

limited partners of a limited partnership Partners in a limited partnership who invest capital but do not participate in management and are not personally liable for partnership debts beyond their capital contributions.

limited partners of an LLP Partners in a limited liability partnership (LLP) who invest capital, participate in management, and who are not personally liable for partnership debts beyond their capital contributions; also referred to as *partners*.

limited partnership A type of partnership that has two types of partners: (1) general partners and (2) limited partners; also known as *special partnerships*.

limited partnership agreement A document that sets forth the rights and duties of general and limited partners; the terms and conditions regarding the operation, termination, and dissolution of a partnership, and so on; also known as *articles of limited partnership*.

limited protected speech Speech that is subject to time, place, and manner restrictions.

limited warranty An express warranty made by a seller or lessor of goods that restricts or limits the remedy for the sale or lease of a defective product.

line of commerce The products or services that will be affected by a merger, including those that consumers use as substitutes. If an increase in the price of one product or service leads consumers to purchase another product or service, the two products are substitutes for each other.

liquidated damages Damages that parties to a contract agree in advance should be paid if the contract is breached.

liquidation preference The right to be paid a stated dollar amount if a corporation is dissolved and liquidated.

litigation The process of bringing, maintaining, and defending a lawsuit.

living wage laws Local laws that set higher minimum wage rates than the federal level.

local administrative agencies Administrative agencies created by cities, municipalities, and counties to administer local regulatory laws.

long-arm statute A statute that extends a state's jurisdiction to nonresidents who were not served a summons within the state.

magistrate A judge who hears evidence of lesser crimes against an accused person, evaluates the evidence presented, and determines whether there is sufficient evidence to hold the accused for trial. The magistrate does not determine guilt. If the magistrate issues an *information statement*, the accused will be held for later trial.

magistrate's information statement The charge of having committed a crime (usually a misdemeanor), based on the judgment of a judge (magistrate).

Magnuson-Moss Warranty Act A federal statute that regulates written warranties on consumer products.

mail fraud The use of mail to defraud another person.

mailbox rule A rule that states that an acceptance is effective when it is dispatched, even if it is lost in transmission; also known as the *acceptance-upon-dispatch rule*.

majority decision A decision in which a majority of the justices agree as to the outcome and reasoning used to decide a case. The decision becomes precedent.

mala in se Crimes that are inherently evil.

mala prohibita Crimes that are not inherently evil but are prohibited by society.

malicious prosecution A lawsuit in which the original defendant sues the original plaintiff. In the second lawsuit, the defendant becomes the plaintiff and vice versa.

manager-managed LLC A limited liability company (LLC) that has designated in its articles of organization that it is a manager-managed LLC; the nonmanager members give their management rights over to designated managers. The managers have authority to bind the LLC to contracts, but nonmanager members cannot bind the LLC to contracts. Managers of a manager-managed LLC owe a duty of loyalty to the LLC; nonmanager members of a manager-managed LLC do not owe a duty of loyalty to the LLC. A manager of a manager-managed LLC owes a duty of care not to engage in intentional, reckless, or grossly negligent conduct that injures the LLC.

managers of LLCs Members or nonmembers of a manager-managed limited liability company (LLC) that have been designated as managers of the LLC.

Marine Protection, Research, and Sanctuaries Act A federal statute that

extends limited environmental protection to the oceans.

mark Any trade name, symbol, word, logo, design, or device used to identify and distinguish goods of a manufacturer or seller or services of a provider from those of other manufacturers, sellers, or providers. Collectively refers to trademarks, service marks, certification marks, and collective marks.

market extension merger A merger between two companies in similar fields whose sales do not overlap.

mass layoff As defined in the Worker Adjustment and Retraining Notification (WARN) Act, it is the reduction of 33 percent of the employees or at least fifty employees during any thirty-day period.

material breach A breach that occurs when a party renders inferior performance of his or her contractual duties.

material fact A fact that is important to the subject matter of a contract.

Matter of Cady, Roberts & Company A decision wherein the Securities and Exchange Commission (SEC) announced the duty of an insider who possesses material nonpublic information to abstain from trading in the securities of the company or disclose the information to the person on the other side of the transaction.

maximum resale price A manufacturer's requirement that a retailer not sell a good it produces for more than a designated price. This arrangement is examined under the *rule of reason* to determine if it violates of Section 1 of the Sherman Act as an unreasonable restraint of trade.

maximize profits A theory of social responsibility that says a corporation owes a duty to take actions that maximize profits for shareholders.

means test A bankruptcy rule that applies to a debtor who has a median family income that exceeds the state's median family income for families the same size as the debtor's family. A debtor in this category qualifies for Chapter 7 bankruptcy if he has disposable income below an amount determined by bankruptcy law, but does not qualify for Chapter 7 bankruptcy if he has disposable income above an amount determined by bankruptcy law.

mechanic's lien A contractor's, laborer's, and material person's statutory lien that makes the real property to which services or materials have been provided security for the payment of the services and materials.

median income test A bankruptcy rule that states that if a debtor's median family income is at or below the state's median family income for a family the same size as the debtor's family, the debtor can receive Chapter 7 relief.

mediation A form of alternative dispute resolution in which the parties use a mediator to assist to possibly reach a settlement of their dispute.

mediator A neutral third party that presides at a mediation proceeding.

medical payment coverage Insurance that covers medical expenses incurred by insured, other authorized drivers of the car, and passengers in the car who are injured in an automobile accident.

Medicinal Device Amendment An amendment to the Food, Drug, and Cosmetic Act (FDCA) that gives the Food and Drug Administration (FDA) authority to regulate medicinal devices and equipment (e.g., heart pacemakers, surgical equipment).

meeting of the creditors A meeting of the creditors in a bankruptcy case that must occur within a reasonable time after an order for relief. The debtor must appear at this meeting. Also referred to as the *first meeting of the creditors*.

meeting the competition defense A defense to a Robinson-Patman Act Section 2(a) price discrimination action that provides that a seller's price discrimination is not unlawful if a seller lawfully engaged in the price discrimination to meet a competitor's price.

member An owner of a limited liability company (LLC).

member-managed LLC A limited liability company (LLC) that has not designated that it is a manager-managed LLC in its articles of organization and is managed by its members. All members have agency authority to bind the LLC to contracts. A member of a member-managed LLC owes a duty of loyalty to the LLC. A member of a member-managed LLC owes a duty of care to the LLC not to engage in an intentional, reckless, or grossly negligent conduct that injures the LLC.

mens rea "Evil intent"—the possession of the requisite state of mind to commit a prohibited act.

mental or psychological disorders Under the Americans with Disabilities Act, as amended, a disability, such as intellectual disability (i.e., mental retardation), organic brain syndrome, emotional or mental illness, and specific learning disabilities.

merchant A person who (1) deals in the goods of the kind involved in a transaction or (2) by his or her occupation holds himself or herself out as having knowledge or skill peculiar to the goods involved in the transaction.

Merchant Court A court in England that solved commercial disputes by applying common trade practices and usage.

merchant protection statutes Statutes that allow merchants to stop, detain, and investigate suspected shoplifters without being held liable for false imprisonment if (1) there are reasonable grounds for the suspicion, (2) suspects are detained for only a reasonable time, and (3) investigations are conducted in a reasonable

manner. Also known as the *shopkeeper's privilege*.

merged corporation The corporation that is absorbed in a merger and ceases to exist after the merger.

merger A situation in which one corporation is absorbed into another corporation and ceases to exist.

merger clause A clause in a contract that stipulates that it is a complete integration and the exclusive expression of the parties' agreement; also known as an *integration clause*.

Miller v. California A U.S. Supreme Court decision that set forth the elements for determining when speech is obscene speech.

minimum contact An amount of contact that a defendant must have with a state in order for that state's courts to have jurisdiction over that person or business.

minimum resale price A manufacturer's requirement that a retailer not sell a good it produces for less than a designated price. This is a *per se* violation of Section 1 of the Sherman Act as an unreasonable restraint of trade.

minimum wage A requirement of the Fair Labor Standards Act (FLSA), a federal statute, that workers be paid a minimum wage. The federal minimum wage is set by Congress and can be changed. States and local governments may set minimum wages that are higher than the federal minimum wage.

mini-trial A voluntary private proceeding in which lawyers for each side present a shortened version of their case to the representatives of both sides. The representatives of each side who attend the mini-trial have the authority to settle the dispute.

minor A person who has not reached the age of majority.

minor breach A breach that occurs when a party renders substantial performance of his or her contractual duties.

Miranda rights Rights that a suspect must be informed of before being interrogated so that the suspect will not unwittingly give up his or her Fifth Amendment rights.

mirror image rule A rule that states that for an acceptance to exist, the offeree must accept the terms as stated in the offer.

misappropriation of a trade secret The unlawful misappropriation of another's trade secret.

misappropriation of the right to publicity An attempt by person to appropriate another living person's name or identity for commercial purposes. Also known as the *tort of appropriation*.

misappropriation theory A rule that imposes liability under Section 10(b) of the Securities Exchange Act of 1934 and SEC Rule 10b-5 on an *outsider* who misappropriates information about a company in violation of his or her fiduciary

duty and then trades in the securities of that company.

misdemeanor A less-serious crime; not inherently evil but prohibited by society. Many crimes against property are misdemeanors.

misrepresentation of a material fact An element of fraud that occurs when a wrongdoer makes a false representation of material fact to another person.

mistake An event that occurs where one or both of the parties to a contract have an erroneous belief about the subject matter, value, or some other aspect of the contract.

misuse of confidential information A duty of agents, general partners, officers, directors and employees of corporations, employees of businesses, and others not to disclose or misuse confidential information (e.g., trade secrets, formulas, customer lists) of the principal either during or after the course of the agency.

misuse of property A duty of agents, general partners, officers, directors and employees of corporations, employees of businesses, and others not to misuse the property of their principal for their own personal use.

mitigate The duty of a nonbreaching party to make reasonable efforts to avoid or reduce damages caused by another party's breach of the contract.

mitigation of damages A nonbreaching party's legal duty to avoid or reduce damages caused by a breach of contract.

mixed sale A sale that involves the provision of a service and a good in the same transaction.

mobile sources of air pollution Sources of air pollution such as automobiles, trucks, buses, motorcycles, and airplanes.

model act A uniform set of proposed legal rules for an area of the law promulgated by different professional and scholarly groups; model acts do not become law until a state enacts it as a state statute.

Model Business Corporation Act (MBCA) A model act, drafted in 1950, that was intended to provide a uniform law for the formation, operation, and termination of corporations.

monetary damages An award of money; also known as *dollar damages*.

money A medium of exchange authorized or adopted by a domestic or foreign government as part of its currency.

money laundering The crime of running illegally obtained money through legitimate businesses to "wash" the money and make it look as though it was earned legitimately.

Money Laundering Control Act A federal statute that makes it a crime to (1) knowingly engage in a money transaction through a financial institution involving property from an unlawful activity worth more than $10,000 and (2) knowingly engage in a financial transaction involving the proceeds of an unlawful activity.

monopoly power The power to control prices or exclude competition, measured by the market share the defendant possesses in the relevant market.

month-to-month tenancy A periodic tenancy of real property where length of the tenancy is one month.

moral minimum A theory of social responsibility that says a corporation's duty is to make a profit while avoiding causing harm to others.

moral theory of law A school of thought that emphasizes that law should be based on morality and ethics.

mortgage An interest in real property given to a lender as security for the repayment of a loan.

Mortgage Reform and Anti-Predatory Lending Act A federal statute that is designed to eliminate many abusive mortgage loan practices and mandates new duties and disclosure requirements on mortgage lenders and others.

mortgagee The creditor in a mortgage transaction.

mortgagor The owner-debtor in a mortgage transaction.

motion for judgment on the pleadings A motion that alleges that if all the facts presented in the pleadings are taken as true, the party making the motion would win the lawsuit when the proper law is applied to these asserted facts.

motion for summary judgment A motion that asserts that there are no factual disputes to be decided by the jury and that the judge can apply the proper law to the undisputed facts and decide the case without a jury. These motions are supported by affidavits, documents, and deposition testimony.

motivation test A test that determines whether an agent's motivation in committing an intentional tort is to promote the principal's business; if so, the principal is liable for any injury caused by the tort.

multilateral treaty A treaty involving more than two nations.

multinational corporation A corporation that operates in more than one country; also called a *transnational corporation*.

murder The unlawful killing of a human being by another with *malice aforethought*—the element of *mens rea (guilty mind)*.

mutual assent An assent by the parties—a "meeting of the minds"—to perform current or future contractual duties.

mutual fund An investment fund that sells shares to the public and invests in stocks and bonds for the long-term and is restricted from investing in risky investments.

mutual mistake of a material fact A mistake made by both parties concerning a material fact that is important to the subject matter of a contract.

mutual mistake of value A mistake that occurs if both parties know the object of the contract but are mistaken as to its value.

mutual rescission Mutual termination of a contract that occurs when the parties to a contract enter into a second contract that expressly terminates the first one.

national ambient air quality standards (NAAQS) Standards for certain pollutants set by the EPA that protect (1) human beings (primary level) and (2) vegetation, climate, visibility, and economic values (secondary level).

national courts The courts of individual nations.

National Association of Securities Dealers Automated Quotation System (NASDAQ) An electronic stock market where more than three thousand companies are traded.

National Environmental Policy Act (NEPA) A federal statute that mandates that the federal government consider the adverse impact a federal government action would have on the environment before the action is implemented.

National Labor Relations Act (NLRA) (Wagner Act) A federal statute enacted in 1935 that established the right of employees to form and join labor organizations, to bargain collectively with employers, and to engage in concerted activity to promote these rights.

National Labor Relations Board (NLRB) A federal administrative agency that oversees union elections, prevents employers and unions from engaging in illegal and unfair labor practices, and enforces and interprets certain federal labor laws.

national origin discrimination Employment discrimination against a person because of his or her heritage, cultural characteristics, or country of the person's ancestors.

Natural Law School of jurisprudence A school of thought which postulates that law is based on what is "correct." It emphasizes a moral theory of law—that is, law should be based on morality and ethics.

natural law school of jurisprudence A school of thought that postulates that law is based on what is "correct." It emphasizes a moral theory of law—that is, law should be based on morality and ethics. Also known as the *moral theory of law*.

natural monopoly A monopoly that exists because of the nature of the market (e.g., a small market that can support only one competitor, such as a small-town newspaper). This is a defense to a charge of committing an act of monopolization.

necessaries of life Food, clothing, shelter, medical care, and other items considered necessary to the maintenance of life. Minors must pay the reasonable value of necessaries of life for which they contract.

negligence The failure to do something that a reasonable person would do, or doing something that a reasonable

person would not do, in like or similar circumstances.

negligence *per se* A tort in which the violation of a statute or an ordinance constitutes the breach of the duty of care.

negligent infliction of emotional distress A tort that permits a person to recover for emotional distress caused by the defendant's negligent conduct.

negotiable instrument A special form of contract that satisfies the requirements established by Article 3 of the UCC; also called *commercial paper* or *instrument*.

negotiation A procedure whereby the parties to a dispute engage in discussions and bargaining to try to reach a voluntary settlement of their dispute.

New York Stock Exchange (NYSE) A primary stock exchange that lists the stocks and securities of approximately three thousand of the world's largest companies for trading.

New York Times Co. v. Sullivan U.S. Supreme Court decision that held that *public officials* cannot recover for defamation unless they can prove that the defendant acted with "actual malice."

no-arrival, no-sale contract A shipping term that requires the seller of goods to bear the expense and risk of loss of the goods during transportation.

No Electronic Theft Act (NET Act) A federal statute that makes it a crime for a person to willfully infringe on a copyright.

Noerr doctrine A doctrine that says that two or more persons can petition the executive, legislative, or judicial branch of the government or administrative agencies to enact laws or take other action without violating antitrust laws.

no-strike clause A clause in a collective bargaining agreement between an employer and a labor union whereby the union agrees not strike during a particular period of time.

nolo contendere A plea entered by a criminal defendant who has been sued by the government whereby the accused agrees to the imposition of a penalty but does not admit guilt.

nonaccredited investors An investor who does not meet the net worth, income, asset, position, and other requirements established by the Securities and Exchange Commission (SEC) to qualify as an *accredited investor*.

nonattainment area A geographical area that does not meet government-established air quality standards.

nonbinding arbitration An agreement between the parties to a dispute whereby they agree that the decision and award of the arbitrator can be appealed to the courts.

nonconforming uses Uses and buildings that already exist in a zoned area that are permitted to continue even though they do not fit within new zoning ordinances.

noncumulative voting A system of shareholder voting for the board of directors of a corporation whereby each shareholder votes the number of shares he or she owns for his or her choices from the candidates running for the board of director positions that must be filed; also called *straight voting*.

nonexempt property Property of a debtor that is not exempt from the bankruptcy estate that is distributed to the debtor's secured and unsecured creditors pursuant to statutory priority established by the Bankruptcy Code.

nonfreehold estate An estate where the tenant has a right to possess the real property but does not own title to the property.

nonintent crime A crime that imposes criminal liability without a finding of *mens rea* (intent).

nonissuer exemption An exemption which says that securities transactions not performed by an issuer, an underwriter, or a dealer do not have to be registered with the Securities and Exchange Commission (SEC) (e.g., normal purchases of securities by investors).

nonobvious A patent requirement that an invention nonobvious; if it is obvious, then it does not qualify for a patent.

nonparticipating preferred stock Preferred stock that does not give a preferred stockholder a right to participate in the profits of the corporation beyond the fixed dividend rate of the preferred stock.

nonpossessory interest A situation in which a person holds an interest in another person's property without actually owning any part of the property. Three types of nonpossessory interests are *easements*, *licenses*, and *profits*.

nonprice vertical restraints Restraints of trade that are unlawful under Section 1 of the Sherman Act if their anticompetitive effects outweigh their precompetitive effects.

nonrecordation of a mortgage A situation that occurs if a mortgage or deed of trust is not recorded in the county recorder's office in the county in which the real property is located.

nonredeemable preferred stock Preferred stock that does not permit a corporation to buy back the preferred stock at some future date.

Norris-LaGuardia Act A federal statute enacted in 1932 that made it lawful for employees to organize labor unions.

North American Free Trade Agreement (NAFTA) A treaty that has removed or reduced tariffs, duties, quotas, and other trade barriers between the United States, Canada, and Mexico.

not guilty A plea that may be entered by an accused at his or her arraignment whereby the accused states that he or she did not commit the crime that he or she is charged with.

note (1) A debt security with a maturity of five years or less. Notes can be either *unsecured* or *secured*. (2) An instrument that evidences a borrower's debt to a lender where a deed of trust and note is used for the purchase of real property on credit.

not-for-profit corporation A corporation formed to operate charitable institutions, colleges, universities, and other not-for-profit entities. These corporations have no shareholders. Also known as *nonprofit corporations*.

notice of a shareholders' meeting Written notice required to be given to shareholders of a corporation of the place, day, and time of annual and special shareholders' meetings, and the purpose of the meeting.

notice of appeal A document filed by a party within a prescribed time after judgment is entered to appeal the decision of a court.

notice of lien Notice filed by a lienholder with the county recorder's office in the county in which real property is located stating that a mechanic's lien has been filed against the property.

notice of termination of an agency A notice that must be given by a principal that notifies third parties that person is no longer his or her agent. Failure to give such notice may make the principal liable for the prior agent's acts under the doctrine of apparent agency.

novation agreement An agreement that substitutes a new party for one of the original contracting parties and relieves the exiting party of liability on the contract; also simply known as a *novation*.

novel A patent requirement that an invention is new and has not been invented and used in the past.

Nuclear Regulatory Commission (NRC) A federal administrative agency that licenses the construction and opening of commercial nuclear power plants.

Nuclear Waste Policy Act A federal statute that mandates that the federal government select permanent sites for the disposal of *nuclear wastes*.

nuclear wastes Consists of pollution from nuclear power plants and emissions from uranium mines and mills.

Nutrition Labeling and Education Act (NLEA) A federal statute that requires food manufacturers to place on food labels that disclose nutritional information about the food.

NYSE Euronext The organization that operates the New York Stock Exchange (NYSE) and Euronext electronic stock exchange.

objective theory of contracts A theory that says the intent to contract is judged by the reasonable person standard and not by the subjective intent of the parties.

obligee The party who is owed a right under a contract.

obligor The party who owes a duty of performance under a contract.

obscene speech Speech that (1) appeals to the prurient interest, (2) depicts sexual conduct in a patently offensive way, and (3) lacks serious literary, artistic, political, or scientific value.

Occupational Safety and Health Act A federal statute that promotes safety in the workplace.

Occupational Safety and Health Administration (OSHA) A federal administrative agency that is empowered to enforce the Occupational Safety and Health Act.

offensive speech Speech that is offensive to many members of society. It is subject to time, place, and manner restrictions.

offer The manifestation of willingness to enter into a bargain, so made as to justify another person in understanding that his assent to that bargain is invited and will conclude it.

offeree The party to whom an offer to enter into a contract is made.

offeror The party who makes an offer to enter into a contract.

offering statement A document that must be filed by an issuer with the Securities and Exchange Commission (SEC) prior to selling most securities pursuant to Regulation A.

officers Employees of a corporation who are appointed by the board of directors to manage the day-to-day operations of the corporation.

Oil Pollution Act A federal statute that requires the oil industry to take measures to prevent oil spills and to readily respond to and clean up oil spills.

Older Workers Benefit Protection Act (OWBPA) A federal statute that prohibits age discrimination in regard to employee benefits.

one-year "on sale" doctrine A doctrine that says a patent may not be granted if the invention was used by the public for more than one year prior to the filing of the patent application; also called the *public use doctrine*.

one-year rule A rule which states that an executory contract that cannot be performed by its own terms within one year of its formation must be in writing.

online Conducting transactions electronically using the internet and other electronic means.

open assortment term A term in a contract that says that if the assortment of goods to a sales contract is left open, the buyer is given the option of choosing those goods but must make the selection in good faith and within limits set by commercial reasonableness.

open delivery term A term in a contract that says that if the parties to a sales contract do not agree to the time, place, and manner of delivery of the goods, the place for delivery is the seller's place of business. If the seller does not have a place of business, delivery is to be made at the seller's residence.

open payment term   A term in a contract that says that if the parties to a sales contract do not agree as to the time and place of payment, then payment is due at the time and place at which the buyer is to receive the goods.

open price term   A term in a contract that says that if a sales contract does not contain a specific price then a "reasonable price" is implied at the time of delivery.

open terms   Terms left open in a sales or lease contract that are permitted to be "read into" the sales or lease contract.

open time term   A term in a contract that says that if the parties to a sales contract do not set a specific time of performance for any obligation under the contract, the contract must be performed within a reasonable time.

open, visible, and notorious   A requirement that must be proven by a person to obtain real property by adverse possession. It requires that the adverse possessor has occupied the property so as to put the owner on notice of the possession.

opening brief   A written document prepared by an appellant and filed with an appellate court that sets forth legal research and other information that supports the appellant's contentions on appeal.

opening statements   Statements made by each party's attorney to the jury at the beginning of a trial.

operating agreement   An agreement entered into among members that governs the affairs and business of the limited liability company (LLC) and the relations among members, managers, and the LLC.

option contract   A contract that is created when an offeree pays an offeror compensation to keep an offer open for an agreed-upon period of time. An option contract prevents the offeror from revoking his or her offer during the option period.

ordinance   Law enacted by local government bodies, such as cities and municipalities, counties, school districts, and water districts.

ordinary lease   Under the Uniform Commercial Code (UCC), a lease of goods by a lessor to a lessee.

Organization of the Petroleum Exporting Countries (OPEC)   An association composed of many of the oil-producing countries of the world.

organizational meeting   A meeting that must be held by the initial directors of a corporation after the articles of incorporation are filed.

original contract   In a guarantee situation, the contract between the debtor and the creditor which the guarantor has guaranteed to pay; also known as the *primary contract*.

outgoing partner   A partner who leaves a partnership.

outside director   A member of a board of directors of a corporation who is not an officer of the corporation.

outside sales representative exemption   An exemption from federal minimum wage and overtime pay requirements that applies to employees who will be paid by the client or customer, whose primary duty is making sales or obtaining orders or contracts for services, and who are customarily and regularly engaged away from the employer's place of business.

outstanding shares   Shares that are in shareholder hands, whether originally issued shares or reissued treasury shares. Only outstanding shares have the right to vote.

overtime pay   A requirement of the Fair Labor Standards Act (FLSA), a federal statute, that workers be paid overtime pay of one-and-a-half times their regular pay for each hour worked in excess of forty hours per week with each week being treated separately.

Palsgraf v. The Long Island Railroad Company   A landmark case that established the doctrine of proximate cause.

parol evidence   Any oral or written words outside the four corners of a written contract.

parent–child privilege   A privilege granted to an accused through the Fifth Amendment to the U.S. Constitution to keep his or her child or his or her parent from testifying against him or her; a child or parent may testify against his or her parent or child where the accused is charged with harming his or her child or parent.

parol evidence rule   A rule that says if a written contract is a complete and final statement of the parties' agreement, any prior or contemporaneous oral or written statements that alter, contradict, or are in addition to the terms of the written contract are inadmissible in court regarding a dispute over the contract. There are several exceptions to this rule.

part performance   An equitable doctrine that allows the court to order an oral contract for the sale of land or transfer of another interest in real property to be specifically performed if it has been partially performed and performance is necessary to avoid injustice.

partial comparative negligence   A rule that provides that a plaintiff must be less than 50 percent responsible for causing his or her own injuries to recover under comparative negligence; otherwise, contributory negligence applies.

partial strike   A labor strike where the striking employees strike part of the day or workweek and work the other part. Such strikes are illegal because they deny the employer's statutory right to continue its operations during a strike; also known as *intermittent strike*.

partially disclosed agency   An agency in which a contracting third party knows that the agent is acting for a principal but does not know the identity of the principal.

partially disclosed principal   The principal in a partially disclosed agency.

participating preferred stock   Stock that allows the preferred stockholder to participate in the profits of the corporation along with the common stockholders.

partnership at will   A partnership with no fixed duration.

partnership for a term   A partnership with a fixed duration.

passage of title in sales contracts   Precise rules in Article 2 of the Uniform Commercial Code (UCC) for determining how title passes in sales contracts.

past consideration   A prior act or performance. Past consideration (e.g., prior acts) will not support a new contract. New consideration must be given.

patent   A grant by the federal government upon the inventor of an invention for the exclusive right to use, sell, or license the patent for a limited amount of time.

patent application   An application that is filed with the U.S. Patent and Trademark Office (PTO) that must contain a written description of the invention sought to be patented.

patent infringement   Unauthorized use of another's patent. A patent holder may recover damages and other remedies against a patent infringer.

patent number   A number that is assigned to a patent if a patent is granted.

patent pending   A designation that an applicant can use on an article if a patent application has been filed but a patent has not yet been issued.

Patient Protection and Affordable Care Act (PPACA)   A federal statute, as amended by the Health Care and Education Reconciliation Act, that is referred to as the Health Care Reform Act. These combined acts mandate that most U.S. citizens and legal residents purchase "minimal essential" health care insurance coverage and provides methods for accomplishing this goal.

penal code   A collection of criminal statutes.

penalty   A fine that is imposed if liquidated damages are excessive or unconscionable or if actual damages are clearly determinable in advance and makes the liquidated damage clause unenforceable.

per se **rule**   A rule that is applicable to restraints of trade considered inherently anticompetitive (e.g., price fixing). Once this determination is made about a restraint of trade, the court will not permit any defenses or justifications to save it.

perfect tender rule   A rule that says if the goods or tender of a delivery fail in any respect to conform to the contract, the buyer may opt either (1) to reject the whole shipment, (2) to accept the whole shipment, or (3) to reject part and accept part of the shipment.

perfection by attachment (automatic perfection rule)   A rule that stipulates that a creditor who extends credit to a consumer to purchase a consumer good under a written security agreement has an automatically perfected security interest in the goods at the time of the sale without having to file a financing statement.

perfection by a purchase money security interest in consumer goods   A creditor who extends credit to a consumer to purchase a consumer good under a written security agreement obtains a security interest in the consumer good that automatically perfects the creditor's security interest at the time of the sale. Also known as *perfection by attachment* or the *automatic perfection rule*.

perfection by filing a financing statement   In a secured transaction, perfecting a creditor's security interest in collateral by filing a financing statement in the appropriate government office.

perfection by possession of collateral   A rule that says if a secured creditor has physical possession of the collateral, no financing statement has to be filed; the creditor's possession is sufficient to put other potential creditors on notice of the creditor's secured interest in the property.

perfection of a security interest   A process that establishes the right of a secured creditor against other creditors who claim an interest in the collateral.

period of minority   The period below the statutory age of majority, as set by state law for a person to have the capacity to enter into contracts.

periodic tenancy   A tenancy of real property created when a lease specifies intervals at which payments are due but does not specify how long the lease is for.

permissive subjects of collective bargaining   Subjects of collective bargaining that are not compulsory subjects of bargaining but are employment issues that the company and union agree bargain over.

perpetual existence   A characteristic of a corporation where a corporation has unlimited duration until the shareholders agree to terminate the corporation or a legal proceeding terminates the corporation.

personal guarantee   A guarantee given by a limited partner of a limited partnership, a partner of a limited liability partnership, a member of a limited liability company, a shareholder of a corporation, and others whereby they guaranty that if the business does not repay a loan or debt or obligation then they will pay the unpaid amount.

personal property   Tangible property such as equipment, vehicles, furniture, and jewelry, as well as intangible property

such as securities, patents, trademarks, and copyrights.

petition   A document that is filed with the bankruptcy court to commence a bankruptcy proceeding.

petition for bankruptcy   A document filed with a bankruptcy court that starts a bankruptcy proceeding.

petition for certiorari   A petition asking the Supreme Court to hear a case.

physical or mental examination   A court-ordered examination of a party to a lawsuit before trial to determine the extent of the alleged injuries.

physiological impairment   Under the Americans with Disabilities Act, as amended, a disability such as a physical disorder or condition, cosmetic disfigurement, or anatomical loss affecting one or more of the following body systems: neurological, musculoskeletal, special sense organs, respiratory, cardiovascular, reproductive, digestive, genitourinary, hemic and lymphatic, skin, and endocrine.

picketing   The action of strikers walking in front of an employer's premises, carrying signs announcing their strike.

piercing the corporate veil   A doctrine that says if a shareholder dominates a corporation and uses it for improper purposes, a court of equity can disregard the corporate entity and hold the shareholder personally liable for the corporation's debts and obligations; also called the *alter ego doctrine*.

place of delivery   The place where goods subject to a sales or lease contract are to be delivered to the buyer or lessee.

places of public accommodation   Places of public accommodation such as motels, hotels, restaurants, movie theaters, and such.

plaintiff   The party who files a complaint that initiates a lawsuit.

plaintiff's case   The case of the plaintiff, who bears the burden of proof and therefore proceeds before the defendant in calling and examining witnesses and introducing evidence supporting his or her case.

plan of payment   A plan submitted in a Chapter 13 bankruptcy proceeding wherein the debtor commits to pay his or her disposable income during the plan period to pay prepetition creditors.

plan of reorganization   A plan that sets forth a proposed new capital structure for a debtor to assume when it emerges from Chapter 11 reorganization bankruptcy.

plant closing   As defined in the Worker Adjustment and Retraining Notification (WARN) Act, it is the permanent or temporary shutdown of a single site that results in a loss of employment of fifty or more employees during any thirty-day period.

plant life and vegetation   Real property that is growing on the surface of land.

plea   An accused's claim of being *guilty* or *not guilty* at his or her arraignment.

plea bargain   Negotiations between an accused and the government with the intent of reaching an agreement between the parties to avoid a trial.

plea bargain agreement   An agreement in which the accused admits to a lesser crime than charged. In return, the government agrees to impose a lesser sentence than might have been obtained had the case gone to trial.

pleadings   The paperwork that is filed with the court to initiate and respond to a lawsuit.

plurality decision   A decision in which a majority of the appellate or supreme court justices agree to the outcome of a case but not as to the reasoning for reaching the outcome. A plurality decision settles the case but is not precedent for later cases.

point sources of water pollution   Sources of water pollution such as paper mills, manufacturing plants, electric utility plants, and sewage plants.

police power   Power that permits states and local governments to enact laws to protect or promote the public health, safety, morals, and general welfare.

power of attorney   An express agency agreement that is often used to give an agent the power to sign legal documents on behalf of the principal.

precedent   A rule of law established in a court decision. Lower courts must follow the precedent established by higher courts.

predatory pricing   Pricing of a product or service below average or marginal cost that is intended to drive out competition.

preemption doctrine   A doctrine that provides that federal law takes precedence over state or local law.

preemptive rights   Rights that give existing shareholders of a corporation the option to purchase new shares issued by the corporation in proportion to their current ownership interests.

preexisting duty   Something a person is already under an obligation to do. A promise lacks consideration if a person promises to perform a preexisting duty.

preferred stock   A type of equity security that is given certain preferences and rights over common stock.

preferred stock certificate   A document that represents a preferred shareholder's investment in the corporation.

preferred stockholder   A person who owns preferred stock.

Pregnancy Discrimination Act   A federal statute that forbids employment discrimination because of pregnancy, childbirth, or related medical conditions.

present possessory interest   A principle that states that an owner of real property may use and enjoy the property as he or she sees fit, subject to any applicable government regulation or private restraint.

presumed innocent until proven guilty A legal rule that provides that a person charged with a crime in the United States is presumed innocent until proven guilty.

pretrial motion A motion a party can make to try to dispose of all or part of a lawsuit prior to trial.

price discrimination Discrimination that occurs when a seller sells goods of like grade and quality to different buyers at different prices contemporaneously in time. There are several exceptions to this rule.

price fixing A restraint of trade that occurs when competitors in the same line of business agree to set the price of the goods or services they sell, raising, depressing, fixing, pegging, or stabilizing the price of a commodity or service. This is a *per se* violation of Section 1 of the Sherman Act as an unreasonable restraint of trade.

priest/rabbi/minister/imam–penitent privilege A privilege granted to an accused through the Fifth Amendment to the U.S. Constitution to keep his or her psychiatrist or psychologist from testifying against him or her. There are exceptions to this privilege.

primarily liable The liability of the surety (co-debtor) in a surety arrangement where the surety is liable for the payment of another person's debt.

principal A party who employs another person to act on his or her behalf.

principal–agent relationship A relationship formed when an employer hires an employee and gives that employee authority to act and enter into contracts on his or her behalf.

principal–independent contractor relationship The relationship between a principal and an independent contractor who is not an employee of the principal but has been employed by the principal to perform a certain task on behalf of the principal.

priority of claims The order in which conflicting claims of creditors in the same collateral are solved.

private civil action A lawsuit that any person who suffers antitrust injury in his or her "business or property" may bring against offenders to recover monetary damages caused by the violation, including *treble damages*.

private placement exemption An exemption from registration that permits issuers to raise capital from an unlimited number of accredited investors and no more thirty-five nonaccredited investors without having to register the offering with the Securities and Exchange Commission (SEC).

Private Securities Litigation Reform Act of 1995 A federal statute that limits a defendant's liability to its proportionate degree of fault.

privilege against self-incrimination A provision of the Fifth Amendment that a person need not be a witness against himself or herself in any criminal case. This is called the *privilege against self incrimination*.

Privileges and Immunities Clause A clause in the U.S. Constitution that prohibits states from enacting laws that unduly discriminate in favor of their residents.

privity of contract The state of two specified parties being in a contract.

probability of a substantial lessening of competition A test that is used to determine whether a merger would violate federal antitrust law. A merger violates antitrust law if it would create a reasonable probability of a substantial lessening of competition or is likely to create a monopoly.

probable cause Evidence of the substantial likelihood that a person either committed or is about to commit a crime.

procedural administrative law Law that establishes the procedures that must be followed by administrative agencies while enforcing substantive laws.

procedural due process A category of due process that requires that the government give a person proper notice and hearing of the legal action before that person is deprived of his or her life, liberty, or property.

processing plant franchise A business in which a franchisor provides a secret formula or process to a franchisee, and the franchisee manufactures the product and distributes it to retail dealers.

product defect Something wrong, inadequate, or improper in the manufacture, design, packaging, warning, or instructions about a product.

product liability The liability of manufacturers, sellers, and others for the injuries caused by defective products.

product market extension merger A market extension merger between two firms that sell similar but not the same products in the same geographical area (e.g., a soft drink manufacturer and an orange juice producer).

product safety standards Safety standards issued by the Consumer Product Safety Commission (CPSC) for consumer products that pose unreasonable risk of injury.

production of documents A request by one party to another party to produce all documents relevant to the case prior to the trial.

professional malpractice The liability of a professional who breaches his or her duty of ordinary care.

profit corporation A corporation created to conduct a business for profit that can distribute profits to shareholders in the form of dividends.

proof of claim A document required to be filed by a creditor that states the amount of his or her claim against the debtor.

proof of interest A document required to be filed by an equity security holder that states the amount of his or her interest against the debtor.

proportionate liability A rule that limits a defendant's liability to its proportionate degree of fault.

proposed additions Additions to a sales contract proposed by an offeree where one or both parties are nonmerchants. If the offeree's proposed additions are accepted by the offeror they become part of the contract; If they are not accepted, the sales contract is formed on the basis of the terms of the original offer.

prosecutor The lawyer who represents the government in a criminal trial. Also called *prosecuting attorney*.

prospectus A written disclosure document that must be submitted to the Securities and Exchange Commission (SEC) along with the registration statement and be provided to prospective purchasers of securities.

provisional application An application that an inventor may file with the PTO that gives the inventor three months to prepare a final patent application.

proximate cause A point along a chain of events caused by a negligent party after which that party is no longer legally responsible for the consequences of his or her actions; also called *legal cause*.

proxy A written document signed by a shareholder that authorizes another person to vote the shareholder's shares; also called a *proxy card*.

psychiatrist/psychologist–patient privilege A privilege granted to an accused through the Fifth Amendment to the U.S. Constitution to keep his or her psychiatrist or psychologist from testifying against him or her. There are exceptions to this privilege.

public defender A government or government-paid attorney who represents the accused defendant in a criminal trial if the accused cannot afford a private defense lawyer.

public domain The point in time when anyone can produce and sell the prior patented invention, copyrighted material, or trademark, which includes after a patent period or copyright period runs out, or trademark is not renewed, or the patent, copyright, or trademark is abandoned.

public figure Plaintiffs such as movie stars, sports personalities, and other celebrities who cannot recover for defamation unless they can prove that the defendant acted with "actual malice."

publicly held corporation A corporation that has many shareholders and whose securities are often traded on national stock exchanges.

punitive damages Damages that are awarded to punish the defendant, to deter the defendant from similar conduct in the future, and to set an example for others.

purchase money security interest An interest a creditor automatically obtains when he or she extends credit to a consumer to purchase consumer goods.

pyramid scheme (Ponzi scheme) An arrangement in which a person steals money or property from others through a fraudulent scheme.

qualified immunity A doctrine that states that foreign governments have qualified immunity from suits in U.S. courts, and are therefore subject to prosecution in U.S. courts under certain circumstances; also known as *restricted immunity*.

qualified individual with a disability A person who has a physical or mental impairment that substantially limits a major life activity who, with or without reasonable accommodation, can perform the essential functions of the job he or she desires or holds.

***quasi in rem* jurisdiction (attachment jurisdiction)** Jurisdiction that allows a plaintiff who obtains a judgment in one state to try to collect the judgment by attaching property of the defendant located in another state.

quasi-contract An equitable doctrine whereby a court may award monetary damages to a plaintiff for providing work or services to a defendant even though no actual contract existed. The doctrine is intended to prevent unjust enrichment and unjust detriment. Also called *implied-in-law contract*.

***qui tam* lawsuit** A lawsuit that is brought under the federal False Claims Act—also known as the Whistleblower Statute—which permits private parties to sue companies for fraud on behalf of the government and share in any monetary recovery.

quid pro quo sex discrimination Gender discrimination in employment that occurs where sexual favors are requested in order to obtain a job or be promoted. This violates Title VII of the Civil Rights Act.

quiet title action An action brought by a party, seeking an order of the court declaring who has title to disputed property. The court "quiets title" by its decision.

quitclaim deed A deed that provides the least amount of protection to the grantee because the grantor transfers only the interest he or she has in the property.

quorum of the board of directors The number of directors necessary to hold a board meeting or transact business of the board.

quorum of the shareholders A rule that requires that a majority of shares entitled to vote are represented at a shareholder's meeting in person or by proxy before a shareholder's meeting can be held; the articles of incorporation may require a greater number of shares than majority to constitute quorum.

quorum to hold a meeting of the shareholders The required number of shares that must be represented in person or by proxy to hold a shareholders' meeting. Many corporation codes and corporate documents establish a majority of outstanding shares as the quorum.

race discrimination Employment discrimination against a person because of his or her race, which include African Americans, Asians, Caucasians, Native Americans, and Pacific Islanders.

Racketeer Influenced and Corrupt Organizations Act (RICO) A federal act that provides for both criminal and civil penalties for racketeering.

radiation pollution Emissions from radioactive wastes that can cause injury and death to humans and other life and can cause severe damage to the environment.

Railway Labor Act A federal statute enacted in 1926 and amended in 1934 that regulates labor organizing by employees of railroads and airlines.

ratification The act of a person after he or she has reached the age of majority by which he or she accepts a contract entered into when he or she was a minor.

ratification of a contract A situation in which a principal accepts an agent's unauthorized contract.

rational basis test A test that is applied to determine the constitutionality of classifications by the government based on classifications not involving suspect or protected class such as race, sex, or age.

Rawls's social justice theory A moral theory that asserts that fairness is the essence of justice. The theory proffers that each person is presumed to have entered into a social contract with all others in society to obey moral rules that are necessary for people to live in peace and harmony.

real estate sales contract A contract for the sale of real property.

real property The land itself, as well as buildings, trees, soil, minerals, timber, plants, crops, fixtures, and other things permanently affixed to the land or buildings.

reasonable accommodation for a disability Under Title I of the Americans with Disabilities Act, assistance an employer is under an obligation to give to accommodate an individual's disability if doing so does not cause an undue hardship to the employer.

reasonable accommodation for religion Under Title VII of the Civil Rights Act of 1964, assistance an employer is under an obligation to give for the religious observances, practices, or beliefs of its employees if doing so does not cause an undue hardship to the employer.

reasonable person standard How an objective, careful, and conscientious person would have acted in the same circumstances. In a negligence action, the defendant's conduct is measured against that standard.

reasonable professional standard How an objective, careful, and conscientious equivalent professional would have acted in the same circumstances. In a negligence action, the defendant professional's conduct is measured against that standard.

reasonable search and seizure Searches and seizures that are based on *probable cause* and do not violate the Fourth Amendment to the U.S. Constitution.

reasonableness in the Uniform Commercial Code A word used throughout the UCC to establish the duties of performance by the parties to sales and lease contracts.

rebuttal A process whereby after the defendant's attorney has finished calling witnesses, the plaintiff's attorney can call additional witnesses and put forth evidence to rebut the defendant's case.

receiving stolen property To (1) knowingly receive stolen property and (2) intend to deprive the rightful owner of that property.

recognizance A formal contract in which a party acknowledges in court that he or she will pay a specified sum of money if a certain event occurs.

record (1) As defined by the Uniform Commercial Code, information that is inscribed on a tangible medium or that is stored in an electronic or other medium and is retrievable in perceivable form. (2) Information about a trial such as the trial transcript, evidence introduced at trial, and the court's written memorandum.

recording statute A state statute that requires a mortgage or deed of trust to be recorded in the county recorder's office of the county in which the real property is located.

redeemable preferred stock Preferred stock that permits a corporation to buy back the preferred stock at some future date; also known as *callable preferred stock*.

re-direct examination Examination of the plaintiff's witness by the plaintiff after the defendant has examined the plaintiff's witnesses on cross-examination.

reformation An equitable doctrine that permits the court to rewrite a contract to express the parties' true intentions.

registered agent A person or corporation that is empowered to accept service of process on behalf of a corporation.

registration of a copyright The permissive and voluntary registration of a copyright of a published and unpublished work with the U.S. Copyright Office in Washington, DC.

registration statement A document that an issuer of securities files with the Securities and Exchange Commission (SEC) that contains required information about the issuer, the securities to be issued, and other relevant information.

regular meeting of a board of directors A meeting held by the board of directors at the time and place established in the bylaws.

Regulation A A regulation that permits the issuer to sell securities pursuant to a simplified registration process.

Regulation Z A regulation that sets forth detailed rules for compliance with the TILA.

regulations Rule adopted by administrative agencies to enforce and interpret statutes.

regulatory statutes Statutes such as environmental laws, securities laws, and antitrust laws that provide for criminal violations and penalties.

rejection of an offer Express words or conduct by the offeree that rejects an offer. Rejection terminates the offer.

rejoinder A process whereby a defendant's attorney can call additional witnesses and introduce other evidence to counter the plaintiff's rebuttal.

release of liability clause A contractual provision that relieves one (or both) of the parties to a contract from tort liability for ordinary negligence; also known as an *exculpatory clause*.

release of lien A written document signed by a contractor, subcontractor, laborer, or material person, waiving his or her statutory lien against real property; also known as *lien release*.

relevant geographical market A relevant market that is defined as the area in which the defendant and its competitors sell the product or service.

relevant market The market required to be defined for a Sherman Act Section 2 charge of monopolization; includes defining the relevant product or service market and geographical market.

relevant product or service market A relevant market that includes substitute products or services that are reasonably interchangeable with the defendant's products or services.

reliance on a misrepresentation An element of fraud that occurs when the innocent party to whom a misrepresentation of a material fact has been made justifiably relies on the misrepresentation and acts on it.

religious discrimination Discrimination against a person solely because of his or her religion or religious practices.

remainder A right of possession to real property that returns to a third party upon the expiration of a limited or contingent estate (e.g., life estate).

remainder beneficiary A person who possesses the right of remainder to real property upon the expiration of a limited or contingent estate (e.g., life estate).

remittitur An action of a judge that reduces the amount of monetary damages awarded by the jury where the judge finds that the jury was biased, emotional, or inflamed in awarding damages.

rent control ordinances Local laws that stipulate the amount of rent a landlord can charge for residential housing.

reorganization bankruptcy A form of bankruptcy in which a debtor reorganize its capital structure, receives a partial discharge of unpaid debts, and takes other actions to emerge from bankruptcy as a viable concern.

replacement workers Workers who are hired by a company to take the place of the striking employees. Replacement workers do not have to be dismissed when the strike is over.

reply A document filed by the original plaintiff to answer the defendant's cross complaint.

repossession A right granted to a secured creditor to take possession of the collateral upon default by the debtor.

res ipsa loquitur A tort in which the presumption of negligence arises because (1) the defendant was in exclusive control of the situation and (2) the plaintiff would not have suffered injury but for someone's negligence. The burden switches to the defendant to prove that he or she was not negligent.

resale price maintenance A *per se* violation of Section 1 of the Sherman Act that occurs when a party at one level of distribution enters into an agreement with a party at another level to adhere to a price schedule that either sets or stabilizes prices; also called *vertical price-fixing*.

rescind The act of a nonbreaching party to undo a contract where the other party to the contract has caused a material breach of the contract.

rescission An action to *rescind* (undo) a contract. Rescission is available if there has been a material breach of contract, fraud, duress, undue influence, or mistake.

reserved powers Powers that are not specifically delegated to the federal government in the U.S. Constitution are reserved to the state governments.

resolutions Actions taken by the board of directors of a corporation usually at a board meeting (e.g., authorize the corporation to enter into contracts or mergers, employ corporate officers). Corporate resolutions are recorded in minutes of the board of directors' meetings and specify the decisions that were made by the board during their meetings.

Resource Conservation and Recovery Act (RCRA) A federal statute that authorizes the EPA to regulate facilities that generate, treat, store, transport, and dispose of hazardous wastes.

respondeat superior A rule that says an employer or a principal is liable for the tortious conduct of its employees or agents while they are acting within the scope of its authority.

responding brief A written document prepared by an appellee and filed with an appellate court that sets forth legal research and other information that supports the appellee's position on appeal.

Restatement (Second) of Contracts The second edition of the *Restatement of the Law of Contracts*. The *Restatement* is not law.

restitution The return of goods or property received from the other party to rescind a contract. If the actual goods or property are not available, a cash equivalent must be made.

restricted securities Securities that are sold pursuant to the intrastate, private placement, and small offering exemptions that are subject to restrictions on resale for a period of time after the securities are issued.

retaliation An action taken by an employer against an employee for filing a charge of discrimination or participating in a discrimination proceeding against the employer (e.g., dismissal or demotion). Retaliation violates antidiscrimination laws.

reverse discrimination Discrimination against a group that is usually thought of as a majority.

reverse engineering Taking apart and examining a rival's product or re-creating a secret recipe.

reversion The right of possession that returns to the grantor of real property after the expiration of a limited or contingent estate (e.g., life estate).

Revised Article 2 (Sales) of the Uniform Commercial Code A revision of UCC Article 2 (Sales) that includes provisions that recognize changes in the commercial environment and the importance of electronic sales contracts.

Revised Article 2A (Leases) of the Uniform Commercial Code A revision of UCC Article 2A (Leases) that includes provisions that recognize changes in the commercial environment and the importance of electronic lease contracts.

Revised Article 3 (Negotiable Instruments) of the Uniform Commercial Code A comprehensive revision of the Uniform Commercial Code law of negotiable instruments that reflects modern commercial practices for the creation of, transfer of, enforcement of, and liability on negotiable instruments.

Revised Article 9 (Secured Transactions) of the Uniform Commercial Code An article of the Uniform Commercial Code that governs secured transactions in personal property.

Revised Model Business Corporation Act (RMBCA) A revision of the Model Business Corporation Act (MBCA) that arranges the provisions of the act more logically, revises the language to be more consistent, and makes substantial changes in the provisions. A model act that is intended to provide a uniform law for the formation, operation, and termination of corporations.

Revised Uniform Limited Liability Company Act (RULLCA) A revision of the Uniform Limited Liability Company

Act (ULLCA) that provides a more modern, comprehensive law for the formation, operation, and dissolution of limited liability companies.

Revised Uniform Limited Partnership Act (RULPA) A revision of the Uniform Limited Partnership Act (ULPA) that provides a more modern, comprehensive law for the formation, operation, and dissolution of limited partnerships.

Revised Uniform Partnership Act (RUPA) A revision of the Uniform Partnership Act (UPA) that provides a more modern, comprehensive law for the formation, operation, and dissolution of general partnerships.

revocation of acceptance Reversal of acceptance.

revocation of an offer Withdrawal of an offer by the offeror that terminates the offer.

right of first refusal An agreement among shareholders of a corporation that requires a selling shareholder who is a signatory to the agreement to offer his or her shares for sale to the other parties to the agreement before selling them to anyone else.

right of survivorship A right that provides that upon the death of a general partner the deceased partner's right in specific partnership property vests in the remaining partner or partners; it does not pass to his or her heirs or next of kin. The *value* of the deceased general partner's interest in the partnership passes to his or her beneficiaries or heirs upon his or her death, however.

right of survivorship of general partners A rule that provides that upon the death of a general partner, the deceased partner's right in specific partnership property vests in the remaining partner or partners; the value of the deceased general partner's interest in the partnership passes to his or her beneficiaries or heirs.

right of survivorship of joint tenants A legal rule that provides upon the death of one joint tenant, the deceased person's interest in the real property automatically passes to the surviving joint tenant or joint tenants.

right to a public jury trial A right contained in the Sixth Amendment to the U.S. Constitution that guarantees a criminal defendant the right to a public jury trial.

right to cancel a contract by the buyer or lessee The right of a buyer or lessee of goods if a seller or lessor fails to deliver conforming goods or repudiates the contract.

right to cancel a contract by the seller or lessor The right of a seller or lessor of goods if the buyer or lessee breaches the contract by rejecting or revoking acceptance of the goods, failing to pay for the goods, or repudiating all or any part of the contract.

right to cover The right of a buyer or lessee to purchase or lease substitute goods if a seller or lessor fails to make delivery of the goods or repudiates the contract or if the buyer or lessee rightfully rejects the goods or justifiably revokes their acceptance.

right to cure The right of a seller or lessor who delivers nonconforming goods to repair or replace defective or nonconforming goods if the time for performance has not expired and the seller or lessor notifies the buyer or lessee of his or her intention to make a conforming delivery within the contract period.

right to dispose of goods The right to dispose of goods in a good faith and commercially reasonable manner. A seller or lessor who is in possession of goods at the time the buyer or lessee breaches or repudiates a contract may in good faith resell, release, or otherwise dispose of the goods in a commercially reasonable manner and recover damages, including incidental damages, from the buyer or lessee.

right to inspect goods The right of a buyer or lessee of goods to inspect goods that are tendered, delivered, or identified in a sales or lease contract prior to accepting or paying for them.

right to obtain specific performance The right of a buyer or lessee of goods to obtain the goods from a seller or lessor if the goods are unique.

right to participate in management A situation in which, unless otherwise agreed, each general partner of a general or limited partnership and each partner of a limited liability partnership has a right to participate in the management of a partnership and has an equal vote on partnership matters.

right to reclaim goods The right of a seller or lessor to demand the return of goods from the buyer or lessee under specified situations.

right to recover damages for accepted nonconforming goods The right of a buyer or lessee of goods who has accepted nonconforming goods to recover damages from the breaching seller or lessor.

right to recover damages for breach of contract A seller's or lessor's right to recover damages measured as the difference between the contract price (or rent) and the market price (or rent) at the time and place the goods were to be delivered, plus incidental damages, from a buyer or lessee who repudiates the contract or wrongfully rejects tendered goods.

right to recover damages for nondelivery or repudiation The right of the buyer or lessee of goods to recover damages if a seller or lessor fails to deliver the goods or repudiates the sales or lease contract.

right to recover the goods from the insolvent seller or lessor The right of a buyer or lessee who has wholly or partially paid for goods before they are received to recover the goods from a seller or lessor who becomes insolvent within ten days after receiving the first payment; the buyer or lessee must tender

the remaining purchase price or rent due under the contract.

right to recover the purchase price or rent A seller's or lessor's right to recover the contracted-for purchase price or rent from the buyer or lessee (1) if the buyer or lessee fails to pay for accepted goods, (2) if the buyer or lessee breaches the contract and the seller or lessor cannot dispose of the goods, or (3) if the goods are damaged or lost after the risk of loss passes to the buyer or lessee.

right to reject nonconforming goods or improperly tendered goods A situation in which a buyer or lessee rejects goods that do not conform to the contract. If the goods or the seller's or lessor's tender of delivery fails to conform to the contract, the buyer or lessee may (1) reject the whole, (2) accept the whole, or (3) accept any commercial unit and reject the rest.

right to replevy (recover) goods The right of a buyer or lessee to recover goods from a seller or lessor who is wrongfully withholding the goods.

right to share in the profits A situation in which, unless otherwise agreed, each partner has a right to an equal share in the partnership's profits; losses are treated similarly.

right to stop delivery of goods in transit The right of a seller or lessor to stop delivery of goods in transit if he or she learns of the buyer's or lessee's insolvency or if the buyer or lessee repudiates the contract, fails to make payment when due, or gives the seller or lessor some other right to withhold the goods.

right to sue letter A letter that is issued by EEOC if it chooses not to bring an action against an employer that authorizes a complainant to sue the employer for employment discrimination.

right to withhold delivery A seller's or lessor's right to refuse to deliver goods to a buyer or lessee upon breach of a sales or lease contract by the buyer or lessee or the insolvency of the buyer or lessee.

right-to-work laws Laws enacted by some states that provide that an individual employee cannot be forced to join a union or pay union dues and fees even though a labor union has been elected by other employees.

risk of loss A rule that identifies which party to a contract will bear cost if the goods subject to the contract are lost or destroyed.

risk of loss: common law Under the common law of contracts, a risk placed on the party who holds title to the goods.

risk of loss: destination contract A situation in which the seller bears the risk of loss during transportation.

risk of loss: shipment contract A situation in which the buyer bears the risk of loss during transportation.

risk of loss: Uniform Commercial Code (UCC) The UCC's detailed rules as to who bears the risk of loss in destination and shipment contracts.

risk–utility analysis A method for determining whether a product's design is defective that requires a court to consider the gravity of the danger posed by the design, the likelihood that injury will occur, the availability and cost of producing a safer alternative design, the social utility of the product, and other factors.

robbery The taking of personal property from another person by the use of fear or force.

Robinson-Patman Act A federal statute, enacted in 1930, that prohibits price discrimination in the sale of goods if certain requirements are met.

Romano-Germanic civil law system A civil law system based on a code of laws, which dates to 450 BCE, when Rome adopted the Twelve Tables, a code of laws applicable to the Romans.

rule making A process whereby administrative agencies adopt rules and regulations.

rule of four A rule that requires the votes of four justices to grant an appeal and schedule an oral argument before the U.S. Supreme Court.

rule of reason A rule that holds that only unreasonable restraints of trade violate Section 1 of the Sherman Act. The court must examine the pro- and anticompetitive effects of a challenged restraint.

rules and regulations Laws adopted by administrative agencies to enforce and interpret statutes.

S corporation A corporation that has met certain requirements and has elected to be taxed as an S corporation for federal income tax purposes. An S corporation pays no federal income tax at the corporate level. The S corporation's income or loss flows to the shareholders and must be reported on the shareholders' individual income tax returns.

Safe Drinking Water Act A federal statute that authorizes the EPA to establish national primary drinking water standards.

sale The passing of title of goods from a seller to a buyer for a price.

sale of goods The passing of title to goods from a seller to a buyer for a price; also called a *conveyance*.

sale of real property The passing of title to real property from a seller to a buyer; also called a *conveyance*.

sale proceeds The resulting assets from the sale, exchange, or disposal of collateral subject to a security agreement.

sales contract A contract for the sales of goods that is subject to Article 2 (Sales) of the Uniform Commercial Code (UCC).

same-sex harassment Harassment in the workplace against an employee by another employee of the same sex that constitutes actionable sexual harassment.

Sarbanes-Oxley Act of 2002 A federal statute enacted by Congress to improve corporate governance, bring more transparency to securities markets, eliminate conflicts of interests that previously existed in the securities industry, promote business ethics, and impose civil and criminal penalties for violations of the act.

Schedule C (Profit or Loss from Business) A federal income tax form that is attached to a sole proprietor's federal personal income tax form that shows the income or loss from his or her sole proprietorship.

schedules Documents filed by a debtor upon filing a voluntary petition for bankruptcy that name secured and unsecured creditors and that describe property owned by the debtor, the debtor's income, and other financial information.

scienter ("guilty mind") Knowledge that a representation is false or that it was made without sufficient knowledge of the truth. Intent to deceive.

scope of employment The scope of an agent's or employee's duties while conducting work for their principal or employer.

search warrant A warrant issued by a court that authorizes the police to search a designated place for specified contraband, articles, items, or documents. A search warrant must be based on probable cause.

SEC Rule 10b-5 A rule of the Securities and Exchange Commission (SEC) that helps define the prohibitions of Section 10(b) of the Securities and Exchange Act of 1934 against deceptive and fraudulent activities in the purchase and sale of securities.

SEC Rule 10b5-1 A rule of the Securities and Exchange Commission (SEC) that prohibits outsiders from trading in the security of any issuer on the basis of material nonpublic information that is obtained by a breach of duty of trust or confidence owed to the person who is the source of the information.

SEC Rule 144 A rule of the Securities and Exchange Commission (SEC) that stipulates that securities issued pursuant to the private placement exemption or the small offering exemption are *restricted securities* that cannot be resold for six months if the issuer is an SEC reporting company (e.g., larger firms) or one year if the issuer is not an SEC reporting company (e.g., smaller firms).

SEC Rule 147 A rule of the Securities and Exchange Commission (SEC) that provides that an *intrastate* offering of securities can be made without registration with the Securities and Exchange Commission (SEC) in the one state if certain requirements are met. The rule also states that securities sold pursuant to an intrastate offering exemption cannot be sold to nonresidents for a period of nine months.

SEC Rule 504 A rule of the Securities and Exchange Commission (SEC) that exempts from registration the sale of securities not exceeding $1 million during a twelve-month period.

SEC Rule 506 A rule of the Securities and Exchange Commission (SEC) that provides that an offering of securities can be made without registration with the Securities and Exchange Commission (SEC) in a *private placement* to an unlimited number of *accredited investors* if certain requirements are met.

secondarily liable The liability of the guarantor in a guaranty arrangement where the guarantor is liable for the payment of another person's debt.

secondary boycott picketing A type of picketing in which a union tries to bring pressure against an employer by picketing the employer's suppliers or customers.

secondary meaning A mark where ordinary words or symbols have taken on a secondary meaning.

secret profits Profits that occur where an agent, a general partner, a director or an officer of a corporation, a partner in a limited liability partnership (LLP), certain members of a limited liability company (LLC), or someone else who owes a fiduciary duty to a principal makes a secret profit during the course of their employment by their principal.

Secretariat A staff of persons that administers the day-to-day operations of the United Nations. It is headed by the *secretary-general*.

secretary of state An office of state governments where many legal documents are filed.

secretary-general The person who heads the Secretariat of the United Nations. The secretary-general is elected by the General Assembly of the United Nations.

Section 1 of the Sherman Act A section of a federal statute that prohibits contracts, combinations, and conspiracies in restraint of trade.

Section 2 of the Clayton Act (Robinson-Patman Act) A section of a federal statute that prohibits price discrimination in the sale of goods if certain requirements are met.

Section 2 of the Sherman Act A section of a federal statute that prohibits monopolization and attempts or conspiracies to monopolize trade.

Section 2(a) of the Robinson-Patman Act A section of a federal statute that prohibits price discrimination in the sale of commodities of like grade and quality in sales to two or more purchasers contemporaneously in time that causes actual injury to the plaintiff.

Section 2(b) of the Robinson-Patman Act A section of a federal statute that establishes the meeting the competition defense to price discrimination.

Section 2-201(1) of the Uniform Commercial Code (UCC) A section of the Uniform Commercial Code (UCC) that states that sales contracts for the sale of goods costing $500 or more must be in writing. Revised Article 2 raises this amount to $5,000.

Section 2A-201(1) of the Uniform Commercial Code (UCC)   A section of the Uniform Commercial Code (UCC) that states that lease contracts involving payments of $1,000 or more must be in writing. Revised Article 2A raises this amount to $20,000.

Section 3 of the Clayton Act   A section of a federal statute that prohibits tying arrangements involving sales and leases of goods.

Section 4 of the Clayton Act   A section of a federal statute that provides that anyone injured in his or her business or property by the defendant's violation of any federal antitrust law (except the Federal Trade Commission Act) may bring a private civil action and recover from the defendant treble damages plus reasonable costs and attorneys' fees.

Section 5 of the Federal Trade Commission Act (FTC Act)   A section of a federal statute that prohibits unfair methods of competition and unfair or deceptive acts or practices in or affecting commerce.

Section 5 of the Securities Act of 1933   A section of a federal statute that requires an issuer to register its securities with the Securities and Exchange Commission (SEC) prior to selling them to the public.

Section 7 of the Clayton Act   A section of a federal statute that provides that it is unlawful for a person or business to acquire the stock or assets of another "where in any line of commerce or in any activity affecting commerce in any section of the country, the effect of such acquisition may be substantially to lessen competition, or to tend to create a monopoly."

Section 7 of the National Labor Relations Act (NLRA)   A section of a federal statute that provides that employees shall have the right to self-organize, to form, join, or assist labor organizations, to bargain collectively with employers through representatives of their own choosing, and to engage in other concerted activities in support of union organization and collective bargaining.

Section 8(a) of the National Labor Relations Act (NLRA)   A section of a federal statute that makes it an unfair labor practice for an employer to interfere with, coerce, or restrain employees from exercising their statutory right to form and join unions.

Section 8(b) of the National Labor Relations Act (NLRA)   A section of a federal statute that makes it an unfair labor practice for a labor union to interfere with, coerce, or restrain employees from exercising their statutory right to form and join unions.

Section 10(b) of the Securities Exchange Act of 1934   A section of a federal statute that prohibits any manipulative or deceptive practice in connection with the purchase or sale of a security.

Section 10(b) insider   (1) Officers, directors, and employees at all levels of a company; (2) lawyers, accountants, consultants, and agents and representatives who are hired by the company on a temporary and nonemployee basis to provide services or work to the company; and (3) others who owe a fiduciary duty to the company.

Section 11 of the Securities Act of 1933   A section of a federal statute that imposes civil liability on persons who intentionally defraud investors by making misrepresentations or omissions of material facts in the registration statement or who are negligent for not discovering the fraud.

Section 12 of the Securities Act of 1933   A section of a federal statute that imposes civil liability on any person who violates the provisions of Section 5 of the act.

Section 16 of the Clayton Act   A section of a federal statute that permits the government or a private plaintiff to obtain an injunction against anticompetitive behavior that violates antitrust laws.

Section 16 statutory insider   Any person who is an executive officer, a director, or a 10 percent shareholder of an equity security of a reporting company.

Section 16(a) of the Securities Exchange Act of 1934   A section of a federal statute that defines any person who is an executive officer, a director, or a 10 percent shareholder of an equity security of a reporting company as a statutory insider for Section 16 purposes.

Section 16(b) of the Securities Exchange Act of 1934   A section of a federal statute that requires that any profits made by a statutory insider on transactions involving *short-swing profits* belong to the corporation.

Section 24 of the Securities Act of 1933   A section of a federal statute that imposes criminal liability on any person who willfully violates the Securities Act of 1933 act or the rules or regulations adopted thereunder.

Section 32 of the Securities Exchange Act of 1934   A section of a federal statute that imposes criminal liability on any person who willfully violates the Securities Exchange Act of 1934 or the rules or regulations adopted thereunder.

Section 303 of the Revised Uniform Limited Partnership Act (RULPA)   A 2001 amendment to the Revised Uniform Limited Partnership Act (RULPA) that permits limited partners to participate in the management of a limited partnership without losing their limited liability shield.

Section 406 of the Sarbanes-Oxley Act   A section of a federal statute that requires a public company to disclose whether it has adopted a *code of ethics* for senior financial officers, including its principal financial officer and principal accounting officer.

Section 501 of the Sarbanes-Oxley Act   A section of a federal statute that establishes rules for separating the investment banking and securities advice functions of securities firms to eliminate conflicts of interest.

Section 1981 of the Civil Rights Act of 1866   A section of a federal statute enacted after the Civil War that says all persons "have the same right . . . to make and enforce contracts . . . as is enjoyed by white persons." It prohibits racial and color discrimination.

Section 4205 of the Patient Protection and Affordable Care Act   A section of a federal statute that requires restaurants and retail food establishments and vending machine operators with twenty or more locations to disclose calorie counts of the food items they serve on menus, menu boards, and drive-through menu boards.

section of the country   A division of the country that is based on the relevant geographical market; the geographical area that will feel the direct and immediate effects of the merger.

secured credit   Credit that requires security (collateral) to secure payment of the loan.

secured creditor   A creditor who has a security interest in collateral. Also called a *secured party*.

secured party in a secured transaction   The seller, lender, or other party in whose favor there is a security interest.

secured transaction   A transaction that is created when a creditor makes a loan to a debtor in exchange for the debtor's pledge of personal property as security.

Securities Act of 1933   A federal statute that primarily regulates the issuance of securities by corporations, limited partnerships, and associations.

Securities and Exchange Commission (SEC)   A federal administrative agency that is empowered to administer federal securities laws. The Securities and Exchange Commission (SEC) can adopt rules and regulations to interpret and implement federal securities laws.

Securities Exchange Act of 1934   A federal statute that primarily regulates the trading in securities.

security   (1) An interest or instrument that is common stock, preferred stock, a bond, a debenture, or a warrant; (2) an interest or instrument that is expressly mentioned in securities acts; and (3) an investment contract.

security agreement   A written document signed by a debtor that creates a security interest in personal property.

Security Council   A council of the United Nations that is composed of fifteen member nations, five of which are permanent members and ten other countries are chosen by the members of the General Assembly, that is responsible for maintaining international peace and security.

security interest in personal property An interest that is created when a party borrows money from a lender and pledges personal property as security for repayment of the loan.

security interest in real property An interest that is created when a party borrows money from a lender and pledges real estate as security for repayment of the loan.

self-dealing A situation that occurs when an agent, a general partner, a director or an officer of a corporation, a partner in a limited liability partnership (LLP), certain members of a limited liability company (LLC), or anyone else who owes a fiduciary duty to a principal engages in undisclosed self-dealing with their principal, such as undisclosed purchasing, selling, or leasing of property with their principal.

Self-Employment Contributions Act A federal statute that requires certain self-employed persons to contribute (pay taxes) to the Social Security fund.

self-incrimination A provision of the Fifth Amendment that no person shall be compelled in any criminal case to be a witness against himself or herself.

separate property Property owned by a spouse prior to marriage, as well as inheritances and gifts received by a spouse during the marriage.

sequestered A process in which jurors are separate from family and others during jury deliberation.

service mark A mark that distinguishes the services of the holder from those of its competitors.

service of process The process of serving a summons on a defendant to obtain personal jurisdiction over him or her.

servient estate The land over which an easement is granted.

servient party A person who is subject to the influence of dominate person who takes advantage of the servient person's mental, emotional, or physical weakness and unduly influences the servient person to enter into a contract.

settlement agreement In a divorce proceeding, a written document signed by divorcing parties that evidences their agreement settling property rights and other issues of their divorce.

settlement conference (pretrial hearing) A hearing before a trial in order to facilitate the settlement of a case.

sex discrimination Discrimination against a person because of his or her gender; also known as *gender discrimination*.

sex-plus discrimination A form of gender discrimination in which an employer does not discriminate against a class as a whole but treats a subset of the class differently (e.g., does not discriminate

against females in general, but does discriminate against married women or women with children)

sexual harassment Lewd remarks, touching, intimidation, posting of indecent materials, or other verbal or physical conduct of a sexual nature that occurs on the job that creates a hostile work environment.

shareholder resolution A resolution that a shareholder who meets certain ownership requirements may submit to other shareholders for a vote. Many shareholder resolutions concern social issues.

shareholder voting agreement An agreement between two or more shareholders of a corporation that stipulates how they will vote their shares for the election of directors or other matters that require a shareholder vote.

shareholders Owners of a corporation who elect the board of directors and vote on fundamental changes in the corporation.

Sherman Act A federal statute, enacted in 1890, that makes certain restraints of trade and monopolistic acts illegal.

shipment contract A contract that requires a seller to ship the goods to the buyer via a common carrier.

shipping terms Terms in sales contracts that establish duties and assesses risk of loss when goods are shipped by a common carrier such as a trucking company, a ship, or a railroad.

short-swing profits Profits that are made by statutory insiders on trades involving equity securities of their corporation that occur within six months of each other.

sit-down strike A labor strike in which the striking employees continue to occupy the employer's premises. Such strikes are illegal because they deny the employer's statutory right to continue its operations during a strike.

Sixth Amendment to the U.S. Constitution An amendment to the U.S. Constitution that guarantees that a criminal defendant has the right to a public jury trial, to have a speedy trail, to examine witnesses, and other trial related rights.

slander Oral defamation of character.

SM A symbol that designates an owner's legal claim to an unregistered mark that is associated with a service.

small business bankruptcy A bankruptcy proceeding that provides an efficient and cost-saving method for small businesses to reorganize under Chapter 11 reorganization bankruptcy.

small claims court A court that hears civil cases involving small dollar amounts.

small company doctrine A doctrine that permits two or more small competing companies to merge without violating antitrust law if the merger would allow the merged firm to compete more effectively with a large company.

Small Company Offering Registration (SCOR) A method for small companies to sell up to $1 million of securities to the public by using a question-and-answer disclosure Form U-7.

small offering exemption An exemption from registration that permits the sale of securities not exceeding $1 million during a twelve-month period.

social responsibility A requirement that corporations and businesses act with awareness of the consequences and impact that their decisions will have on others.

Social Security A federal system that provides government benefits to covered persons and their dependents, including (1) retirement benefits, (2) survivors' benefits to family members of deceased workers, (3) disability benefits, and (4) medical and hospitalization benefits.

Social Security Administration A federal agency that administers the Social Security system.

Sociological School of jurisprudence A school of thought that asserts that law is a means of achieving and advancing certain sociological goals.

sole proprietor The owner of a sole proprietorship.

sole proprietorship A form of business in which the owner is actually the business; the business is not a separate legal entity.

Sonny Bono Copyright Term Extension Act A federal statute that established the time periods for copyright protection.

spam Unsolicited commercial e-mail.

special federal courts Federal courts that hear matters of specialized or limited jurisdiction.

special meeting of a board of directors A meeting convened by a board of directors to consider important topics such as the issuance of new shares, merger proposals, hostile takeover attempts, and so forth.

special power of attorney A power of attorney in which a principal confers powers on an agent to act in specified matters on the principal's behalf.

special shareholders' meetings Meetings of shareholders that may be called to consider and vote on important or emergency issues, such as a proposed merger or amending the articles of incorporation.

special warranty deed (limited warranty deed) A deed to real property that protects a buyer from defects in title that were caused by the seller. The seller is not liable for defects in title or for encumbrances that existed before the seller obtained the property.

specially manufactured goods Goods that buyers and lessees order that are to be manufactured to the buyer's or lessee's unique specifications.

specific duty standards Occupational Safety and Health Administration (OSHA) standards that address safety problems of a specific nature (e.g., a requirement for a safety guard on a particular type of equipment).

specific intent crime A crime that requires that the perpetrator intended to achieve a specific result from his illegal act.

specific performance A remedy that orders the breaching party to perform the acts promised in the contract. Specific performance is usually awarded in cases in which the subject matter is unique, such as in contracts involving land, heirlooms, and paintings.

spouse–spouse privilege A privilege granted to an accused through the Fifth Amendment to the U.S. Constitution to keep his or her spouse from testifying against him or her; a spouse may testify against his or her spouse where the accused spouse is charged with harming his or her spouse.

stakeholder interest A theory of social responsibility that says a corporation must consider the effects its actions have on persons other than its stockholders.

Standard Oil Company of New Jersey v. United States A U.S. Supreme Court decision that found Standard Oil Company guilty of monopolizing the petroleum industry through abusive and anticompetitive practices and as a remedy broke up Standard Oil into thirty competing firms. The court adopted the *rule of reason* standard for analyzing Section 1 of the Sherman Act antitrust cases.

standing to sue A requirement that a plaintiff have some stake in the outcome of a lawsuit in order to bring a lawsuit.

stare decisis Latin for "to stand by the decision." Adherence to precedent.

state action exemption Business activities that are mandated by state law and are therefore exempt from federal antitrust laws.

state administrative agencies Administrative agencies that states create to enforce and interpret state law.

state constitution Constitutions that are adopted by states. State constitutions that are often patterned after the U.S. Constitution, although many are more detailed.

state courts Courts established by states.

state implementation plan (SIP) A plan that must be submitted by each state that sets forth how the state plans to meet federal ambient air quality standards.

state median income For a family of any size, income for which half of the state's families of this size have incomes above this figure and half of the state's families of this size have incomes less than this figure.

state securities laws State laws that regulate the issuance and trading of securities; often referred to as *blue-sky laws*.

state statutes Statutes enacted by state legislatures.

statement of opinion A commendation of goods, made by a seller or lessor, that does not create an express warranty; also known as *puffing*.

stationary sources of air pollution Sources of air pollution such as industrial plants, oil refineries, and public utilities.

statute Written law enacted by the legislative branch of the federal and state governments that establishes certain courses of conduct that must be adhered to by covered parties.

Statute of Frauds A state statute that requires certain types of contracts to be in writing.

statute of limitations A statute that establishes the period during which a plaintiff must bring a lawsuit against a defendant.

statute of repose A statute that limits the seller's liability to a certain number of years from the date the product was first sold.

statutorily defined securities Interests or instruments that are expressly defined as *securities*, including interests in oil, gas, and mineral rights; preorganization subscription agreements; and deposit receipts for foreign securities.

statutorily prescribed period of time The required statutory period during which an adverse possessor must have occupied another's real property to acquire it through adverse possession.

statutory exemptions Exemptions from antitrust laws that are expressly provided in statutes enacted by Congress.

statutory insider Any person who is an executive officer, a director, or a 10 percent shareholder of an equity security of a reporting company is a statutory insider for purposes of Section 16 of the Securities Exchange Act of 1934.

straight voting A system of shareholder voting for the board of directors of a corporation whereby each shareholder votes the number of shares he or she owns for his or her choices from the candidates running for the board of director positions that must be filed; also called *noncumulative voting*.

strict liability Liability without fault.

strict scrutiny test A test that is applied to determine the constitutionality of classifications by the government based on race, national origin, citizenship, or voting rights.

strike A cessation of work by union members in order to obtain economic benefits or to correct an unfair labor practice.

student loans Under bankruptcy law, educational loans made by or guaranteed by governmental units or nongovernmental commercial institutions such as banks, as well as funds for scholarships, benefits, or stipends granted by educational institutions.

Subchapter S Revision Act A federal statute that allows shareholders of qualifying corporations to avoid double taxation by electing S corporation status.

subcommittee A special group composed of members of a committee of the U.S. House of Representatives or U.S. Senate.

subfranchisor An area franchisee who has been granted for an area franchise for a designated geographical area and who has the authority to negotiate and sell franchises on behalf of the franchisor in that area.

submission agreement An agreement entered into by parties to a dispute where there is no arbitration agreement to have their dispute arbitrated.

subsequent assignee A party to whom an assignee has transferred a right to receive performance under a contract; also known as *subassignee*.

substantial performance Performance by a contracting party that deviates only slightly from complete performance; there is a *minor breach*.

substantive administrative law Law that administrative agencies enforce.

substantive due process A category of due process that requires that government statutes, ordinances, regulations, or other laws be clear on their face and not overly broad in scope.

substantive rule Government regulation that has the force of law and must be adhered to by covered persons and businesses.

subsurface rights Rights to the earth located beneath the surface of the land; also known as *mineral rights*.

summons A court order directing the defendant to appear in court and answer the complaint.

Superfund A federal statute that authorizes the federal government to deal with hazardous wastes. The act creates a monetary fund to finance the cleanup of hazardous waste sites. Common name for the *Comprehensive Environmental Response, Compensation, and Liability Act (CERCLA)*.

super-priority lien A statutory lien given to workers on personal property to which they furnish services or materials in the ordinary course of business which usually prevails over all other security interests in the goods. Also called an *artisan's lien*.

supervening event An alteration or a modification of a product by a party in the chain of distribution that absolves all prior sellers from strict liability.

supramajority voting requirement A rule established by a corporation that stipulates that a greater than majority of the number of shares (the percent as set by corporation code or corporate document) are needed to constitutes a quorum for a vote of the shareholders; also known as *supermajority voting requirement*.

Supremacy Clause A clause of the U.S. Constitution that establishes that the U.S. Constitution and federal treaties, laws, and regulations are the supreme law of the land.

Supreme Court of the United States The highest court of the federal court system. It hears appeals from the U.S. Courts of Appeals and, in some instances, from special federal courts, U.S. District Courts, and the highest state courts. Also called the *U.S. Supreme Court*.

surety (co-debtor) The third person who agrees to be liable in a surety arrangement; also known as the *co-signer* or *accommodation party*. The surety is *primarily liable* on the debt.

surety arrangement An arrangement in which a third party promises to be *primarily liable* with the borrower for the payment of the borrower's debt.

surface rights The right to occupy the land. The owner may use, enjoy, and develop the property as he or she sees fit, subject to any applicable government laws and regulations.

surviving corporation The corporation that continues to exist after a merger.

taking The taking of private property by the government for public use. The government must pay the private owner the reasonable value of the real property taken.

taking possession of the collateral A situation that occurs when a creditor takes possession of collateral when a secured loan is in default.

tangible personal property Property such as goods, equipment, vehicles, furniture, computers, clothing, and jewelry.

tangible writing Writings that can be physically seen that are subject to copyright registration and protection.

target corporation A corporation that is proposed to be acquired in a tender offer situation.

tarnishment A situation that occurs when a famous mark is linked to products of inferior quality or is portrayed in an unflattering, immoral, or reprehensible context likely to evoke negative beliefs about the mark's owner.

tenancy at sufferance A tenancy created when a tenant retains possession of property after the expiration of another tenancy or a life estate without the owner's consent.

tenancy at will A tenancy created by a lease of real property that may be terminated at any time by either party.

tenancy by the entirety A form of co-ownership of real property that can be used only by married couples.

tenancy for years A tenancy for real property created when a landlord and a tenant agree on a specific duration for a lease.

tenancy in common A form of co-ownership in which the interest of a surviving tenant in common passes to the deceased tenant's estate and not to the co-tenants.

tenant The party to whom a leasehold is transferred. Also known as a *lessee*.

tenant in common Parties who co-own real property in a tenancy in common arrangement.

tenant in partnership A legal rule that provides that general partners are co-owners with the other general partners of the specific property owned by the partnership.

tender of delivery The obligation of a seller to transfer and deliver goods to the buyer or lessee in accordance with a sales or lease contract.

tender of performance An unconditional and absolute offer by a contracting party to perform his or her obligations under a contract; also known as *tender*.

termination of a corporation An act that occurs after the winding up of the corporation's affairs, the liquidation of its assets, and the distribution of the proceeds to the claimants.

termination of an agency by an act of the parties The termination of an agency that occurs because of the mutual assent of the parties, the passage of a stated time, the achievement of a specified purpose, or the occurrence of a stated event.

termination of an agency by impossibility of performance The termination of an agency that occurs because of the loss or destruction of the subject matter of the agency, the loss of a required qualification, or a change in the law.

termination of an agency by operation of law The termination of an agency that occurs because of the death of either the principal or the agent, the insanity of either the principal or the agent, the bankruptcy of the principal, or the outbreak of a war between the principal's country and the agent's country.

termination of an offer by act of the parties The termination of an offer when one party takes an action that indicates that he is not interested in forming a contract under the terms of the offer, including (1) rejection of an offer by the offeree, (2) counteroffer by the offeree, and (3) revocation of an offer by the offeror.

termination of an offer by operation of law The termination of an offer by the operation of law, including (1) the destruction of the subject matter, (2) the death of incompetency of the offeror or the offeree, (3) a supervening illegality, and (4) lapse of time of the offer.

theft A crime that does not distinguish among and includes the crimes of robbery, burglary, and larceny.

thermal pollution Heated water or material discharged into waterways that upsets the ecological balance and decreases the oxygen content.

third-party beneficiary A third party who benefits by the performance by others of the others' contracts.

three-party secured transaction A transaction that occurs when a seller sells goods to a buyer who has obtained financing from a third-party lender who takes a security interest in the goods sold.

tie decision A decision in which the appellate or supreme court justices reach a tie (equal) vote. The lower court's decision stands. The decision is not precedent.

tippee A person who receives material nonpublic information from a tipper.

tipper A person who discloses material nonpublic information to another person.

tipper-tippee liability Liability that occurs when a tipper discloses material nonpublic information to a tippee that the tippee knows or has reason to know is inside information, and the tippee trades securities based on this information.

title to goods Legal, tangible evidence of ownership of goods.

Title I of the Americans with Disabilities Act A title of a federal statute that prohibits employment discrimination against qualified individuals with disabilities in regard to job application procedures, hiring, compensation, training, promotion, and termination.

Title I of the Landrum-Griffin Act Labor's "bill of rights," which gives each union member equal rights and privileges to nominate candidates for union office, vote in elections, and participate in membership meetings.

Title II of the Genetic Information Nondiscrimination Act (GINA) A title of a federal statute that makes it illegal for an employer to discriminate against job applicants and employees based on genetic information (e.g., propensity to be stricken by diseases).

Title III of the Americans with Disabilities Act (ADA) A title of a federal statute that prohibits discrimination on the basis of disability in places of public accommodation operated by private entities.

Title VII of the Civil Rights Act of 1964 A title of a federal statute enacted to eliminate job discrimination based on five protected classes: *race, color, religion, sex,* and *national origin.* Also known as the *Fair Employment Practices Act.*

TM A symbol that designates an owner's legal claim to an unregistered mark that is associated with a product.

top-level domain name (TLD) The most commonly used extensions for domain names (e.g., .com, .org, .edu).

tort A wrong. There are three categories of torts: (1) intentional torts, (2) unintentional torts (negligence), and (3) strict liability.

tort liability Liability of a person that arises by the violation of the legal doctrines of intentional tort, negligence, or strict liability.

tortfeasor A person who intentionally or unintentionally (negligently) causes injury or death to another person. A person liable to persons he or she injures and to the heirs of persons who die because of his or her conduct.

tortious conduct An act that is a tort (wrong).

toxic air pollutants Toxic chemicals such asbestos, mercury, vinyl chloride, benzene, beryllium, and radionuclides.

toxic substances Chemicals used by agriculture, industry, business, mining, and households that cause injury to humans, birds, animals, fish, and vegetation.

Toxic Substances Control Act A federal statute that authorizes the Environmental Protection Agency to regulate toxic substances.

trade dress The protection of the "look and feel" of a product, a product's packaging, or a service establishment.

trade name A name under which a sole proprietor, partnership, or corporation may operate a business.

trade secret A product formula, pattern, design, compilation of data, customer list, or other business secret.

trademark A distinctive mark, symbol, name, word, motto, or device that identifies the goods of a particular business.

Trademark Dilution Revision Act of 2006 A federal statute that provides that a dilution plaintiff does not need to show that it has suffered actual harm to prevail in its dilution lawsuit, but instead only show that there would be the *likelihood of dilution*.

Trademark Electronic Application System (TEAS) A system that permits the electronic filing of trademark applications with the U.S. Patent and Trademark Office (PTO).

trademark infringement Unauthorized use of another's mark. The holder may recover damages and other remedies from the infringer.

transnational corporation A corporation that operates in more than one country; also called a *multinational corporation*.

treasury shares Issued shares that have been repurchased by the corporation. Treasury shares may not be voted by the corporation. Treasury shares may be resold by the corporation.

treaty An agreement between two or more nations that is formally signed by an authorized representative of each nation and ratified by each nation.

Treaty Clause A clause of the U.S. Constitution that states that the president "shall have the power . . . to make treaties, provided two-thirds of the senators present concur."

treble damages Damages that may be awarded in a successful civil antitrust lawsuit that is an amount that is triple the amount of actual damages.

trial brief Documents submitted by the parties' attorneys to the judge that contain legal support for their side of the case.

trier of fact The jury in a jury trial; the judge where there is no jury trial.

Truth-in-Lending Act (TILA) A federal statute that requires creditors to make certain disclosures to debtors in consumer transactions and real estate loans on the debtor's principal dwelling.

two-party secured transaction A transaction that occurs when a seller sells goods to a buyer on credit and retains a security interest in the goods.

tying arrangement A restraint of trade in which a seller refuses to sell one product to a customer unless the customer agrees to purchase a second product from the seller. Types of sales where the seller entrusts possession of goods to a buyer on a trial basis.

U.S. Army Corps of Engineers (USACE) A federal agency that is authorized to issue permits for discharge of dredged or fill material into navigable waters and qualified wetlands in the United States.

U.S. Bankruptcy Courts Federal courts that decide cases that involve federal bankruptcy laws.

U.S. Citizenship and Immigration Services (USCIS) A federal agency which is part of the U.S. Department of Homeland Security that processes immigrant visa and naturalization petitions and has other duties involving immigration.

U.S. Congress (Congress) The name of the U.S. Senate and the U.S. House of Representatives jointly.

U.S. Constitution The fundamental law of the United States of America. It was ratified by the states in 1788. The supreme law of the United States.

U.S. Copyright Office A federal government agency with which copyrights for published and unpublished works may be registered.

U.S. Court of Appeals for the Armed Forces A federal court that decides cases involving members of the armed forces.

U.S. Court of Appeals for the Federal Circuit A court of appeals located in Washington, DC, that has special appellate jurisdiction to review the decisions of the U.S. Court of Federal Claims, the U.S. Patent and Trademark Office, and the U.S. Court of International Trade.

U.S. Court of Appeals for Veterans Claims A federal court that decides cases involving veterans of the armed forces.

U.S. Court of Federal Claims A federal court that decides cases brought against the United States.

U.S. Court of International Trade A federal court that decides cases involving tariffs and international trade disputes.

U.S. courts of appeal Federal intermediate appellate courts that decide appeals from U.S. District Courts, several other federal courts, and some federal administrative agencies.

U.S. Department of Agriculture (USDA) A federal cabinet-level department that is primarily responsible for regulating meat, poultry, and other food products.

U.S. Department of Housing and Urban Development (HUD) A federal cabinet-level department that enforces the Fair Housing Act and other federal statutes and provides other government housing services.

U.S. Department of Justice (Justice Department or DOJ) A federal cabinet-level department that is responsible for the enforcement of federal laws.

U.S. Department of Labor A federal cabinet-level department that is empowered to enforce specific federal employment laws.

U.S. district courts Federal trial courts of general jurisdiction that decide cases not within the jurisdiction of specialized federal courts.

U.S. District of Columbia Circuit A federal intermediate appellate court located in Washington, DC.

U.S. House of Representatives One of the two legislative bodies that make up the bicameral legislative system of the U.S. government. The number of representatives in the U.S. House of Representatives is determined according to the population of each state.

U.S. Patent and Trademark Office (PTO) A federal government agency where applications for patents and trademarks are filed and decisions regarding these applications are made.

U.S. Senate One of the two legislative bodies that make up the bicameral legislative system of the U.S. government. The U.S. Senate is composed of two U.S. senators from each state.

U.S. Supreme Court The highest court of the federal court system. It hears appeals from the U.S. Courts of Appeals and, in some instances, from special federal courts, U.S. District Courts, and the highest state courts. Also known as the *Supreme Court of the United States*.

U.S. Tax Court A federal court that decides cases that involve federal tax laws.

U.S. Trustee A federal government official who is responsible for handling and supervising many of the administrative tasks of a bankruptcy case.

UCC Financing Statement (Form UCC-1) A uniform financing statement form that is used in all states to perfect a security interest in personal property.

UCC Statute of Frauds A rule that requires all contracts for the sale of goods costing $500 or more and lease contracts involving payments of $1,000 or more to be in writing.

UCC Statute of Frauds Section 2- 201(1) A section of the Uniform Commercial

Code (UCC) that states that sales contracts for the sale of goods costing $500 or more must be in writing. Revised Article 2 raises this amount to $5,000.

UCC Statute of Frauds Section 2A-201(1) A section of the Uniform Commercial Code (UCC) that states that lease contracts involving payments of $1,000 or more must be in writing. "Revised Article 2A raises this amount to $20,000."

UCC statute of limitations A rule that provides that an action for breach of any written or oral sales or lease contract must commence within four years after the cause of action accrues. The parties may agree to reduce the limitations period to one year.

unanimous decision A decision in which all of the justices agree as to the outcome and reasoning used to decide the case. The decision becomes precedent.

unanimous decision at a criminal trial A decision in a criminal trial in which the jury members unanimously find the defendant guilty or not guilty.

unconscionable contract A contract that courts refuse to enforce in part or at all because it is oppressive or manifestly unfair as to be unjust.

undersecured creditor A secured creditor in a bankruptcy proceeding where the value of the collateral securing the secured loan is less than the creditor's secured interest.

undisclosed agency An agency in which a contracting third party does not know of either the existence of the agency or the principal's identity.

undisclosed principal The principal in an undisclosed agency.

undue hardship A bankruptcy test that stipulates that student loans cannot be discharged in any form of bankruptcy unless their nondischarge would cause an undue hardship to the debtor and his or her dependants. Whether undue hardship exists is construed strictly.

undue hardship (1) Under Title I of the Americans with Disabilities Act, a problem that is great enough to prevent an employer from accommodating an individual's disability. (2) Under Title VII of the Civil Rights Act of 1964, a problem that is great enough to prevent an employer from accommodating the religious observances, practices, or beliefs of its employees.

undue influence A situation in which one person takes advantage of another person's mental, emotional, or physical weakness and unduly persuades that person to enter into a contract or make a will; the persuasion by the wrongdoer must overcome the free will of the innocent party.

unduly burden interstate commerce A concept that says states may enact laws that protect or promote the public health, safety, morals, and general welfare, as long as the laws do not unduly burden interstate commerce.

unemployment compensation Compensation that is paid by the government to workers who are temporarily unemployed.

unenforceable contract A contract in which the essential elements to create a valid contract are met but there is some legal defense to the enforcement of the contract.

unequivocal acceptance An offeree's acceptance of an offer that is clear, unambiguous, and has only one possible meaning.

unexpired lease (1) A lease that has not been fully performed. (2) In bankruptcy law, a lease that has not been fully performed. With the bankruptcy court's approval, a debtor may reject unexpired leases in bankruptcy.

unfair advantage theory A theory that holds that a merger may not give the acquiring firm an unfair advantage over its competitors in finance, marketing, or expertise.

unfair labor practice A practice that occurs when an employer or a labor union interferes with, coerces, or restrains employees from exercising their statutory right to form and join labor unions.

unfair methods of competition and unfair or deceptive acts or practices Conduct such as false and deceptive advertising, bait-and-switch operations, overly aggressive sales tactics, and such. Unfair and deceptive practices are prohibited by Section 5 of the Federal Trade Commission Act (FTC Act).

Uniform Arbitration Act A uniform law that many states have adopted that promotes the arbitration of disputes at the state level.

Uniform Commercial Code (UCC) A comprehensive statutory scheme that includes laws that cover aspects of commercial transactions.

Uniform Computer Information Transactions Act (UCITA) A model act that establishes uniform legal rules for the formation and enforcement of electronic contracts and licenses.

Uniform Limited Liability Company Act (ULLCA) A model act that provides comprehensive and uniform laws for the formation, operation, and dissolution of LLCs.

Uniform Limited Partnership Act (ULPA) A model act that provides comprehensive and uniform laws for the formation, operation, and dissolution of limited partnerships.

Uniform Partnership Act (UPA) A model act that codifies partnership law. Most states have adopted the UPA in whole or in part.

Uniform Sales Act A uniform law that was promulgated in the United States in 1906 to govern the sales of goods.

Uniform Securities Act An act that was drafted to coordinate state securities laws with federal securities laws; it has been adopted by many states.

Uniform Trade Secrets Act A uniform law that many states have adopted that gives statutory protection to trade secrets.

unilateral contract A contract in which the offeror's offer can be accepted only by the performance of an act by the offeree; a "promise for an act."

unilateral mistake A mistake in which only one party is mistaken about a material fact regarding the subject matter of a contract.

unilateral refusal to deal A unilateral choice by one party not to deal with another party. This does not violate Section 1 of the Sherman Act because there is not concerted action. Also known as the *Colgate doctrine*.

unintentional tort A doctrine that says a person is liable for harm that is the foreseeable consequence of his or her actions; also known as *negligence*.

union security agreement An agreement between an employer and a union that provides some form of security for union workers, such as a union shop or an agency shop agreement.

union shop A workplace where an employee must join the union within a certain number of days after being hired.

unissued shares Authorized shares that have not been sold by the corporation.

units Shares of master limited partnerships whose interests are traded on organized securities exchanges.

United Nations (UN) An international organization created by a multilateral treaty in 1945 to promote social and economic cooperation among nations and to protect human rights.

United Nations Biosafety Protocol for Genetically Altered Foods A United Nations–sponsored agreement that more than 150 countries have agreed to that requires all genetically engineered foods be clearly labeled with the phrase "May contain living modified organisms."

United Nations Children's Fund (UNICEF) An agency of the United Nations whose goal is to provide humanitarian aid and assistance to children and mothers of children, primarily in developing countries.

United Nations Commission on International Trade Law (UNCITRAL) A model code for the cooperation of courts and parties in different countries in cross-border bankruptcies.

United Nations Convention on Contracts for the International Sale of Goods (CISG) A model act promulgated by the United Nations that provides legal rules that govern the formation, performance, and enforcement of international sales contracts.

United Nations Educational, Scientific, and Cultural Organization

(UNESCO) An autonomous agency of the United Nations that deals with a wide range social and cultural issues.

unlawful detainer action A legal process that a landlord must complete to *evict* a holdover tenant; also known as an *eviction proceeding*.

unlimited personal liability of a general partner The personal liability of general partners of a general partnership or a limited partnership for the debts and obligations of the partnership.

unlimited personal liability of a sole proprietor The personal liability of a sole proprietor for the debts and obligations of the sole proprietorship.

unprotected speech Speech that is not protected by the First Amendment and may be forbidden by the government.

unreasonable search and seizure Protection granted to people and businesses by the Fourth Amendment to the U.S. Constitution against unreasonable search and seizure by the government.

unsecured credit Credit that does not require any security (collateral) to protect the payment of the debt.

unsecured creditor The creditor in a credit transaction where the debtor does give security (collateral) to protect the payment of the debt.

usage of trade Any practice or method of dealing that is regularly observed or adhered to in a place, a vocation, a trade, a profession, or an industry.

useful A patent requirement that an invention has some practical purpose.

usurping an opportunity A situation that occurs when an agent, a general partner, a director or an officer of a corporation, a partner in a limited liability partnership (LLP), certain members of a limited liability company (LLC), and anyone else who owes a fiduciary duty to a principal personally takes (usurps) an opportunity that belongs to their principal.

utilitarianism A moral theory that dictates that people must choose the action or follow the rule that provides the greatest good to society.

utility patent A patent that protects the functionality of the invention.

valid contract A contract that meets all the essential elements to establish a contract; a contract that is enforceable by at least one of the parties.

variance An exception to a zoning ordinance that permits a type of building or use in an area that would not otherwise be allowed in the area by a zoning ordinance.

venue A concept that requires lawsuits to be heard by the court within the proper jurisdiction that is nearest to the location in which the incident occurred or where the parties reside.

verdict A decision reached by a jury.

vertical merger A merger that integrates the operations of a supplier and a customer.

vertical restraint of trade A restraint of trade that occurs when two or more parties on *different levels of distribution* enter into a contract, combination, or conspiracy to restrain trade.

vesting A situation that occurs when an employee has a nonforfeitable right to receive pension benefits.

vicarious liability Liability without fault that occurs when a principal is liable for an agent's tortious conduct because of the employment contract between the principal and agent, not because the principal was personally at fault.

violation A crime that is neither a felony nor a misdemeanor that is usually punishable by a fine.

violent strike A labor strike where the striking employees cause substantial damage to property of the employer or a third party. Violent strikes are illegal.

void contract A contract that has no legal effect; a nullity.

void leasehold interest An invalid leasehold interest. In a case in which a lessee leases goods from a thief who has stolen them, the lessee does not acquire any leasehold interest in the goods. The lessee has a void leasehold interest, and the real owner can reclaim the goods from lessee.

void title An invalid title. In a case in which a buyer purchases goods from a thief who has stolen them, the purchaser does not acquire title to the goods. The buyer has *void title* and the real owner can reclaim the goods from the purchaser.

voidable contract A contract in which one or both parties have the option to void their contractual obligations. If a contract is voided, both parties are released from their contractual obligations.

voidable leasehold interest An interest in goods that a lessee acquires if he leases the goods through fraud, a check that is later dishonored, or impersonation of another person. A person with a voidable leasehold interest in goods can transfer a valid leasehold interest to a *good faith subsequent lessee*.

voidable title A title to goods that a purchaser acquires if he acquires the goods through fraud, a check that is later dishonored, or impersonation of another person. A person with voidable title to goods can transfer good title to a *good faith purchaser for value*.

voir dire A process whereby prospective jurors are asked questions by the judge and attorneys to determine whether they would be biased in their decisions.

voluntary dissolution Dissolution of a corporation that has begun business or

issued shares, upon recommendation of the board of directors and a majority vote of the shares entitled to vote.

voluntary petition A petition voluntarily filed by a debtor to begin a bankruptcy proceeding.

warrantless arrest An arrest that is made without an arrest warrant. The arrest must be based on probable cause and have viable proof that it was not feasible to obtain an arrest warrant prior to the arrest.

warrantless search A search that is made without a search warrant. Warrantless searches are constitutional if they are based on *probable cause* and are made (1) incident to arrest, (2) where evidence is in "plain view," or (3) where it is likely that evidence will be destroyed.

warranty A seller's or lessor's express or implied assurance to a buyer or lessee that the goods sold or leased meet certain quality standards.

warranty disclaimer A statement that negates implied warranties and sometimes express warranties if certain requirements are met.

water pollution Pollution of lakes, rivers, oceans, and other bodies of water.

web contract Contracts entered into with Internet sellers, lessors, and licensors who use web addresses to sell and lease goods and services and license software and other intellectual property over the Internet.

website Internet address used by persons and businesses to sell and lease goods, license software, or otherwise communicate information.

wetlands Areas that are inundated or saturated by surface water or ground water that support vegetation typically adapted for life in such conditions.

white-collar crime Crimes that are prone to being committed by businesspersons.

Wickard, Secretary of Agriculture v. Filburn U.S. Supreme Court decision that upheld a federal government statute as constitutionally regulating interstate commerce.

wildcat strike A labor strike where the striking employee union members go on strike without proper authorization from the union. Such a strike is illegal but becomes lawful if it is quickly ratified by the union.

winding up and liquidation The process of liquidating the assets of a business and distributing the proceeds to satisfy claims against the business.

wire fraud The use of telephone or telegraph to defraud another person.

Worker Adjustment and Retraining Notification Act (WARN Act) (Plant Closing Act) A federal statute that requires employers with one hundred or more employees to give their employees sixty days' notice before engaging in certain plant closings and layoffs.

workers' compensation Compensation paid to workers and their families when workers are injured in connection with their jobs.

workers' compensation acts Acts that compensate workers and their families if workers are injured in connection with their jobs.

workers' compensation insurance Insurance that compensates employees for work-related injuries.

work-related test A test that determines whether an agent committed an intentional tort within a work-related time or space; if so, the principal is liable for any injury caused by the agent's intentional tort.

World Bank An agency of the United Nations whose primary function is to provide money to developing countries to fund projects for humanitarian purposes and to relieve poverty.

World Trade Organization (WTO) An international organization of 153 member nations created to promote and enforce trade agreements among member countries and customs territories.

World Wide Web An electronic connection of millions of computers that support a standard set of rules for the exchange of information; also known as the *Web*.

writ of certiorari An official notice that the Supreme Court will review a case.

writing and form Contract law that requires that certain contracts must be in *writing* or in a certain form to be enforceable

written confirmation rule A UCC rule that provides that if both parties to an oral sales or lease contract are merchants, the Statute of Frauds writing requirement can be satisfied if (1) one of the parties to an oral agreement sends a written confirmation of the sale or lease within a reasonable time after contracting and (2) the other merchant does not give written notice of an objection to the contract within ten days after receiving the confirmation.

written memorandum A memorandum issued by a trial court that sets forth the reasons for the judgment.

wrongful dissolution A situation in which a partner withdraws from a partnership without having the right to do so at that time.

wrongful eviction (unlawful eviction) A situation that occurs when a landlord, or anyone acting with the landlord's consent, interferes with the tenant's use and enjoyment of the property. A violation of the covenant of quiet enjoyment; also called *unlawful eviction*.

wrongful possession A situation that occurs when a tenant retains possession of property after the expiration of a tenancy or a life estate without the owner's consent.

wrongful termination The termination of an agency contract, in violation of the terms of the agency contract. In this situation, the nonbreaching party may recover damages from the breaching party.

wrongful termination of a franchise A situation that occurs if a franchisor terminates a franchise agreement without just cause. The franchisee may recover damages from the franchisor.

WTO appellate body A panel of seven judges selected from World Trade Organization member nations that hears and decides appeals from decisions of the dispute-settlement body.

WTO dispute settlement body A board composed of one representative from each World Trade Organization member nation that reviews panel reports.

WTO panel A body of three World Trade Organization judges that hears trade disputes between member nations and issues a panel report.

Zippo Manufacturing Company v. Zippo Dot Com, Inc. A seminal case that establishes rules for determining the jurisdiction of courts over parties that sell goods over the Internet.

zoning Government regulation that establishes land use districts (i.e., areas are generally designated residential, commercial, or industrial), restricts the height, size, and location of buildings, and establishes aesthetic requirements or other limitations for the exterior of buildings.

zoning commission A local administrative body that formulates zoning ordinances, conducts public hearings, and makes recommendations to the city council.

zoning ordinances Local laws that are adopted by municipalities and local governments to regulate land use within their boundaries.

CASE INDEX

Cases cited or discussed are in roman type.
Principle cases are in **bold** type.

SUBJECT INDEX